SOURCES AND METHODS
LABOUR STATISTICS
VOLUME 5
TOTAL AND ECONOMICALLY ACTIVE
POPULATION, EMPLOYMENT AND
UNEMPLOYMENT (POPULATION CENSUSES)

SECOND EDITION

SOURCES ET MÉTHODES
STATISTIQUES DU TRAVAIL
VOLUME 5
POPULATION TOTALE ET POPULATION
ACTIVE, EMPLOI ET CHÔMAGE
(RECENSEMENTS DE POPULATION)

DEUXIÈME ÉDITION

FUENTES Y METODOS
ESTADISTICAS DEL TRABAJO
VOLUMEN 5
POBLACION TOTAL Y POBLACION
ECONOMICAMENTE ACTIVA, EMPLEO
Y DESEMPLEO (CENSOS DE POBLACION)

SEGUNDA EDICION

SOURCES
AND METHODS
LABOUR STATISTICS
VOLUME 5
TOTAL AND ECONOMICALLY ACTIVE POPULATION, EMPLOYMENT AND UNEMPLOYMENT (POPULATION CENSUSES)

Companion to the *Yearbook of Labour Statistics*

SECOND EDITION

SOURCES
ET MÉTHODES
STATISTIQUES DU TRAVAIL
VOLUME 5
POPULATION TOTALE ET POPULATION ACTIVE, EMPLOI ET CHÔMAGE (RECENSEMENTS DE POPULATION)

Complément de l'*Annuaire des statistiques du travail*

DEUXIÈME ÉDITION

FUENTES
Y METODOS
ESTADISTICAS DEL TRABAJO
VOLUMEN 5
POBLACION TOTAL Y POBLACION ECONOMICAMENTE ACTIVA, EMPLEO Y DESEMPLEO (CENSOS DE POBLACION)

Complemento del *Anuario de Estadísticas del Trabajo*

SEGUNDA EDICION

INTERNATIONAL LABOUR OFFICE   GENEVA
BUREAU INTERNATIONAL DU TRAVAIL   GENÈVE
OFICINA INTERNACIONAL DEL TRABAJO   GINEBRA

Important

● In order to enhance the usefulness of the *Yearbook of Labour Statistics,* each issue is now accompanied by a methodological volume of the series *Sources and Methods: Labour Statistics* (formerly entitled *Statistical Sources and Methods*).

● This series provides methodological descriptions of the data published in the *Yearbook* and *Bulletin of Labour Statistics.* Each volume covers different subjects according to the source of the data ; gradually, all the subjects in the *Yearbook* will be covered by a volume in this series.

● The methodological descriptions include information on the method of data collection, coverage, concepts and definitions, classifications, historical changes, technical references, etc. In each volume the information is presented by country under standard headings.

Important

● Afin de mettre en valeur l'utilité de l'*Annuaire des statistiques du travail,* chaque édition est maintenant accompagnée d'un volume méthodologique de la série *Sources et méthodes: statistiques du travail* (intitulée précédemment *Sources et méthodes statistiques*).

● Cette série fournit des descriptions méthodologiques des données publiées dans l'*Annuaire* et dans le *Bulletin des statistiques du travail.* Chaque volume traite de sujets différents suivant la source des données; progessivement, tous les sujets traités dans l'*Annuaire* seront couverts.

● Les descriptions méthodologiques contiennent des informations sur la méthode de collecte des données, la portée, les concepts et définitions, les classifications, les modifications apportées aux séries, les références techniques, etc. Dans chaque volume, les informations sont présentées par pays sous des rubriques standardisées.

Importante

● Con el fin de mejorar la utilidad del *Anuario de Estadísticas del Trabajo,* ahora cada edición va acompañada de un volumen metodológico de la serie *Fuentes y Métodos: Estadísticas del Trabajo* (titulada anteriormente *Fuentes y Métodos Estadísticos*).

● Esta serie proporciona las descripciones metodológicas de los datos que se publican en el *Anuario* y el *Boletín de Estadísticas del Trabajo.* Cada volumen abarca diferentes temas del *Anuario* de acuerdo con la fuente de los datos.

● Las descripciones metodológicas incluyen informaciones acerca del método de recolección de datos, el alcance, los conceptos y definiciones, las clasificaciones, los cambios históricos, las referencias técnicas, etc. En cada volumen, la información se presenta por país de acuerdo a encabezamientos estándar.

PREFACE

This is a revised version of *Sources and Methods: Labour statistics* (formerly *Statistical Sources and Methods*), *Volume 5: Total and economically active population, employment and unemployment (population censuses)*, first published in 1990. The other published volumes of the series are:

Volume 1, Consumer price indices (Geneva, 1992, third edition).

Volume 2, Employment, wages, hours of work and labour cost (establishment surveys) (Geneva, 1995, second edition).

Volume 3, Economically active population, employment, unemployment and hours of work (household surveys) (Geneva, 1990, second edition).

Volume 4, Employment, unemployment, wages and hours of work (administrative records and related sources) (Geneva, 1989).

Volume 6, Household income and expenditure surveys (Geneva, 1994).

Volume 7, Strikes and lockouts (Geneva, 1993).

Further topics to be covered by the series include occupational injuries and diseases, occupational wages and hours of work and retail food prices (ILO *October Inquiry*).

The purpose of these volumes is to document national practices used in the collection of various types of labour statistics, in order to assist the users of these statistics in evaluating their quality and comparability, and their suitability for particular needs. *Sources and Methods: Labour statistics* are companion volumes to the ILO *Yearbook of Labour Statistics* and *Bulletin of Labour Statistics*.

The methodological descriptions presented in this volume relate to population censuses carried out during the period 1989-94. They cover 115 countries.

The information has been collected from the respective national statistical organizations responsible for conducting the censuses.

With this issue, the trilingual translation of the Sources and Methods series has been carried out for the first time using a computer-assisted translation software.

This volume was produced by the ILO Bureau of Statistics. The descriptions were prepared by Ms B. du Jeu and Mr. R. Doss.

Its computerized production was designed and supervised by Mr. P. Cornu.

AVANT-PROPOS

Cet ouvrage constitue la deuxième édition de *Sources et méthodes: statistiques du travail* (prédédemment *Sources et méthodes statistiques*), *Volume 5: Population totale et population active, emploi et chômage (recensements de population)* dont la première édition a été publiée en 1990. Les autres volumes publiés dans cette série sont les suivants:

Volume 1: Indices des prix à la consommation (troisième édition, Genève, 1992).

Volume 2: Emploi, salaires, durée du travail et coût de la main-d'oeuvre (enquêtes auprès des établissements) (deuxième édition, Genève, 1995).

Volume 3: Population active, emploi, chômage et durée du travail (enquêtes auprès des ménages) (deuxième édition, Genève, 1991, publiée sous forme de Document de travail).

Volume 4: Emploi, chômage, salaires et durée du travail (documents administratifs et sources assimilées) (Genève, 1989, publié sous forme de Document de travail).

Volume 6: Enquêtes sur le revenu et les dépenses des ménages, (Genève, 1994).

Volume 7: Grèves et lock-out (Genève, 1993).

Les sujets qui seront traités dans d'autres volumes comprennent les lésions et les maladies professionnelles, les salaires et la durée du travail par profession et les prix des articles alimentaires (*Enquête d'octobre* du BIT).

Ces volumes ont pour but de renseigner sur les pratiques nationales appliquées pour établir différentes statistiques du travail, et d'aider ainsi les utilisateurs de ces statistiques à en apprécier la qualité, la comparabilité, et la valeur pour des besoins différents. Les volumes de *Sources et méthodes statistiques* sont des compléments de l'*Annuaire des statistiques du travail* et du *Bulletin des statistiques du travail* du BIT.

Les descriptions méthodologiques présentées dans ce volume se réfèrent aux recensements de la population effectués au cours de la période 1989-1994. Elles couvrent 115 pays.

Les informations contenues dans le présent volume ont été obtenues auprès des organismes statistiques nationaux chargés de la conduite des recensements.

Pour la première fois, un logiciel de traduction assistée par ordinateur a été utilisé pour la traduction trilingue de la série Sources et Méthodes.

Ce volume a été réalisé par le Bureau de statistique du BIT. Les descriptions ont été préparées par Mme B. du Jeu et M. R. Doss.

Sa réalisation informatique a été conçue et supervisée par M. P. Cornu.

PREFACIO

Se presenta aquí una actualización de *Fuentes y Métodos: Estadísticas del Trabajo* (anteriormente *Fuentes y Métodos Estadísticos*), *volumen 5: Población total y población económicamente activa, empleo y desempleo (censos de población)*, cuya primera versión se publicó en 1990. Los otros volúmenes de esta serie son:

Volumen 1, Indices de los precios del consumo (tercera edición, Ginebra, 1992).

Volumen 2, Empleo, salarios, horas de trabajo y costo de la mano de obra (encuestas de establecimientos) (segunda edición, Ginebra, 1995).

Volumen 3, Población económicamente activa, empleo, desempleo y horas de trabajo (encuesta de hogares) (segunda edición, Ginebra 1992, publicada como Documento de trabajo).

Volumen 4, Empleo, desempleo, salarios y horas de trabajo (registros administrativos y fuentes conexas) (Ginebra, 1989, publicado como Documento de trabajo).

Volumen 6, Encuestas de ingresos y gastos de los hogares (Ginebra, 1994).

Volumen 7, Huelgas y cierres patronales (Ginebra, 1993).

Otros volúmenes abarcarán lesiones y enfermedades profesionales, salarios y horas de trabajo por ocupación, y precios de artículos alimenticios (*Encuesta de octubre de la OIT*).

Estas publicaciones tienen por objetivo documentar las prácticas nacionales seguidas en materia de recopilación de las distintas clases de estadísticas del trabajo, a efectos de ayudar a los usuarios a evaluar su calidad y comparabilidad, así como su adaptabilidad a distintas necesidades. Las *Fuentes y Métodos: Estadísticas del trabajo* son volúmenes complementarios del *Anuario de Estadísticas del Trabajo* y del *Boletín de Estadísticas del Trabajo* de la OIT.

Las descripciones metodológicas que se presentan en este volumen se refieren a los censos de población llevados a cabo durante el período 1989-1994, y abarcan 115 países.

La información se ha recabado de los respectivos organismos nacionales de estadística encargados de la realización de los censos.

Esta es la primera vez que la traducción trilingüe de un volumen de la serie Fuentes y Métodos se lleva a cabo utilizando un programa de traducción asistida por computadora.

La producción de este volumen estuvo a cargo de la Oficina de Estadísticas de la OIT. Prepararon las descripciones la señora B. du Jeu y el señor R. Doss.

La realización informática fue concebida y supervisada por el señor P. Cornu.

Synoptic table   Tableau synoptique   Cuadro sinóptico

Country, area or territory	Census year	Age limits	Ref. per.	Armed forces included		Students included		Data on time worked		Classification used						Stat. in Emp.
										Industry			Occupation			
				Regular	Conscr.	With a part time job	Seeking work	Last week or month	Last year	Number of groups	Links to ISIC	Number of digits	Number of groups	Links to ISCO	Number of digits	Number of groups
Albania	1989	15+	no	yes	yes	yes	no	no	.	...	no	.	...	no	.	3
American Samoa	1990	16+	w/y	yes	yes	yes	yes	ah	ww	231	Rev.2	...	13	no	.	7
Anguilla	1992	12+	m	yes	.	yes	yes	no	.	...	Rev.3	1	...	88	1	3
Antigua and Barbuda	1991	15-64	w/y	no	no	yes	yes	ah	mw	157	Rev.3	3	136	88	...	6
Argentina	1991	14+	w/m	yes	yes	yes	yes	no	.	...	Rev.3	3	9	88	1	7
Aruba	1991	14+	w	yes	yes	yes	no	uh	.	...	Rev.2	4	...	88	4	6
Australia	1991	15+	w/m	yes		yes	no	ah	.	615	Rev.2	4	337	no	.	4
Austria	1991	15+	d/4w	yes	yes	yes	no	uh	.	117	Rev.3	2	175	88	2	8
Bahamas	1990	15+	w/y	yes	yes	yes	yes	no	ww	9	Rev.2	1	9	88	1	5
Bahrain	1991	12+	w	yes	yes	yes	yes	no	.	17	Rev.3	1	...	no	.	4
Barbados	1990	15+	w/y	yes	yes	yes	yes	ah	mw	17	Rev.3	1	9	88	1	7
Belgium	1991	14+	d	yes	yes	yes	no	uh/ah	.	809	Rev.2	4	1700	88	3	9
Belize	1991	15+	w/y	yes pr.	yes pr.	yes	no	ah	mw	...	Rev.3	4	...	88	4	6
Benin	1992	10+	3m	yes	yes	no	no	no	.	9	Rev.2	1	9	68	1	8
Bermuda	1991	16+	w/y	yes	yes	yes	yes	uh	mw	18	Rev.2	1	...	68	...	7
Bolivia	1992	7+	w	yes	no	yes	yes	no	.	...	Rev.3	4	...	88	3	7
Botswana	1991	12+	m	yes	yes	yes	no	no	.	9	Rev.2	1	10	88	1	2
Brazil	1991	10+	y	yes	yes	yes	yes	.	uh	26	Rev.2	1	10	68	1	11
Brunei Darussalam	1991	15+	w	yes	yes	no	no	ah	.	10	Rev.3	1	10	88	1	4
Bulgaria	1992	10-90	d	yes	yes	yes	no	no	.	184	Rev.3	2	642	88	3	.
Burundi	1990	10+	6m	yes pr.	yes pr.	no	no	no	.	10	Rev.2	1	10	88	1	6
Canada	1991	15+	w	yes	yes	yes	yes	ah	.	296	no	.	514	no	.	4
Cape Verde	1990	10+	w	yes	yes	yes	yes	no	.	10	Rev.2	1	9	68	1	7
Cayman Islands	1989	15+	w	yes	.	yes	yes	uh	.	65	Rev.3	2	94	88	3	4
Central African Rep.	1988	6+	w	yes	no	no	yes	no	.	9	Rev.2	1	99	68	3	5
Chad	1993	6-98	w/y	yes	yes	no	no	no	no	60	Rev.3	2	...	88	2	6
Chile	1992	14+	w	yes	no	yes	yes	no	.	...	Rev.3	3	...	88	4	5
China	1990	see (a)	d/m	yes	yes	no	no	no	.	13	Rev.2	1	8	68	1	.
Comoros	1991	12+	m	no	no	no	yes	no	.	...	no	.	8	no	.	7
Cook Islands	1991	15+	m	.	.	yes	...	uh	.	162	Rev.2	4	390	88	4	6
Cyprus	1992	15+	w	yes	yes	yes	no	uh	.	61	Rev.3	2	30	88	2	6
Czech Republic	1991	see (b)	d	yes	yes	no	yes	.	.	47	Rev.3	2	91	68&88	1	9
Dominican Republic	1993	10+	w	yes	yes	yes	no	no	.	10	Rev.2	1	10	68	1	5
Ecuador	1990	8+	w	yes	yes	yes	no	uh/ah	.	72	Rev.2	3	284	68	3	7
El Salvador	1992	10+	w	yes	no	yes	yes	uh	.	...	Rev.3	4	...	88	4	8
Equatorial Guinea	1994	6+	w	no	no	no	no	no	.	...	Rev.3	...	10	88	1	.
Finland	1990	15-74	w/y	yes	no	yes	no	no	no	460	R.2&3	4	400	68	3	2
France	1990	15+	no	yes	yes	yes	no	no	.	600	Rev.2	2	455	68	2	4
French Guiana	1990	14+	w	yes pr.	yes pr.	yes	yes	no	.	100	no	.	42	no	.	5
Gabon	1993	10+	w/6m	yes	yes	no	no	no	.	40	no	.	350	88	3	6
Gambia	1993	10+	m	yes	no	no	no	days	.	...	Rev.3	1	...	88	1	5
Gibraltar	1991	15+	d	no	no	no	no	no	.	23	Rev.3	1	125	no	.	3
Greece	1991	10+	w/y	yes	no	yes	yes	ah	no	159	Rev.3	3	284	68	3	4
Grenada	1991	15+	w	yes	.	yes	yes	ah	.	...	Rev.3	...	...	88	4	6
Guadeloupe	1990	14+	w	yes pr.	yes pr.	yes	yes	no	.	100	no	.	42	no	.	5
Guam	1990	15+	w/y	yes	.	yes	yes	ah	ww	231	no	.	503	no	.	7
Guatemala	1994	7+	w	yes	no	yes	yes	no	.	...	Rev.3	4	...	88	4	6
Hong Kong	1991	15+	w/m	yes	.	yes	yes	no	.	87	Rev.3	3	116	88	3	4
Hungary	1990	no	w	yes	yes	no	no	no	.	294	no	.	808	no	.	8
India	1991	no	y	yes	yes	yes	yes	.	no	462	Rev.3	3	512	68	2	4
Indonesia	1990	10+	w/y	yes	yes	yes	yes	uh/ah	.	47	Rev.2	2	334	68	3	5
Iran, Islamic Rep. of	1991	10+	w	yes	yes	yes	yes	no	.	292	Rev.3	4	284	68	3	5

Country, area or territory	Census year	Age limits	Ref. per.	Armed forces included		Students included		Data on time worked		Classification used						Stat. in Emp.
										Industry			Occupation			
				Regular	Conscr.	With a part time job	Seeking work	Last week or month	Last year	Number of groups	Links to ISIC	Number of digits	Number of groups	Links to ISCO	Number of digits	Number of groups
Ireland	1991	15+	d	yes	.	no	yes	no	.	263	R.2&3	2	210	68&88	2	4
Isle of Man	1991	16+	w/5m	yes	.	no	no	ah	ww	21	no	.	371	88	3	3
Italy	1991	14+	w	yes	no	no	no	ah	.	60	Rev.3	2	35	88	1	14
Jamaica	1991	14+	w/y	yes	yes	no	no	ah	mw	...	Rev.3	2	...	88	2	7
Japan	1990	15+	w	yes	.	yes	no	no	.	213	Rev.2	3	294	68	1	6
Kenya	1989	10+	w	...	...	no	no	no	.	no	.	.	8	88	1	4
Korea, Republic of	1990	15+	y	yes pr.	no	yes	no	.	no	90	Rev.2	3	286	68	2	4
Luxembourg	1991	no	no	yes	...	yes	no	uh	.	500	no	.	390	88	4	9
Macau	1991	14+	w/m	yes	yes	yes	yes	no	.	10	Rev.3	1	10	88	1	.
Macedonia	1994	15+	d	yes	yes	no	no	no	.	14	no	.	10	no	.	5
Madagascar	1993	10+	w	yes	yes	no	no	no	.	159	Rev.3	3	10	88	1	7
Malaysia	1991	10+	w	yes	yes	yes	yes	ah	.	...	Rev.2	...	...	68	...	4
Maldives	1990	12+	w/3m	no	no	yes	no	uh/ah	.	292	Rev.3	4	390	88	4	4
Martinique	1990	14+	w	yes pr.	yes pr.	yes	yes	no	.	100	no	.	42	no	.	5
Mauritius	1990	12+	w/y	.	.	yes	yes	ah	ww	263	Rev.2	4	390	88	4	8
Mexico	1990	12+	w	yes	yes	yes	yes	ah	.	220	Rev.2	2	508	88	4	5
Mongolia	1989	see (c)	d	no	no	no	no	no	.	12	no	.	982	no	.	5
Morocco	1994	see (d)	d	yes	yes	no	no	no	.	215	Rev.3	4	65	88	...	7
Namibia	1991	10+	w	no	no	yes	no	no	.	307	Rev.3	4	396	88	4	8
Nauru	1992	10+	w	.	.	yes	no	uh/ah	.	5	no	.	...	88	1	7
Nepal	1991	10+	y	yes	...	yes	.	.	mw	9	Rev.2	1	7	68	1	4
Netherlands Antilles	1992	15-99	w/y	yes	yes	yes	yes	uh	ww	17	Rev.3	1	10	88	1	9
New Caledonia	1989	14+	w	yes	yes	no	no	uh	.	14	no	.	33	no	.	9
New Zealand	1991	15+	d/m	yes	.	yes	yes	uh/ah	.	...	Rev.2	4	...	88	4	4
Northern Mariana Islands	1990	15+	w/y	no	no	yes	yes	ah	ww/uh	...	no	.	...	no	.	7
Norway	1990	16+	w/y	yes	yes	yes	no	uh/ah	mw	...	Rev.2	4	84	68	1	3
Panama	1990	10+	w	yes	yes	yes	yes	no	.	18	Rev.3	1	10	68	1	5
Papua New Guinea	1990	10+	w/y	yes	yes	no	no	no	.	no	.	.	9	88	1	.
Paraguay	1992	10+	w	yes	no	no	no	no	.	9	Rev.2	1	9	88	1	6
Peru	1993	6+	w	yes	no	yes	yes	no	.	292	Rev.3	4	116	88	3	6
Philippines	1990	10+	w/y	yes pr.	no	yes	yes	no	.	...	Rev.2	3	...	88	4	.
Portugal	1991	12+	w	yes	yes	yes	yes	ah	.	292	Rev.3	4	390	88	4	7
Puerto Rico	1990	16+	w/m/y	yes	yes	no	no	uh	ww	231	no	.	503	no	.	8
Réunion	1990	14+	w	yes pr.	yes pr.	yes	yes	no	.	100	no	.	42	no	.	5
Romania	1992	see (e)	y	yes	yes	yes	no	.	no	99	Rev.3	3	437	88	3	6
St. Lucia	1991	15+	w/y	no	no	no	no	ah	mw	17	Rev.3	1	9	88	1	6
St.Vincent and the Grenadines	1991	15+	w/y	no	.	no	no	ah	mw	17	Rev.3	1	10	88	1	6
Samoa	1991	10+	w	no	no	yes	yes	no	.	...	Rev.2	...	...	88	3	4
Sao Tome and Principe	1991	10+	w/y	yes	yes	yes	no	uh/ah	mw	9	Rev.2	1	116	88	3	5
Saudi Arabia	1992	12+	w	yes	yes	no	no	no	.	60	Rev.3	2	284	68	3	4
Singapore	1990	no	w	yes	yes	no	no	no	.	317	Rev.3	1	314	88	1	5
Slovakia	1991	see (b)	d	yes	yes	no	yes	.	.	47	Rev.3	2	91	68&88	1	9
Slovenia	1991	15+	d/y	yes	yes	no	no	no	no	700	no	.	...	no	.	5
South Africa	1991	no	d	yes	yes	no	no	no	.	40	Rev.2	2	165	68	...	2
Spain	1991	16+	w	yes	no	yes	yes	no	.	...	R.2&3	2	...	68&88	2	7
Sudan	1993	10+	w	no	no	no	no	no	.	72	Rev.2	3	390	88	4	5
Sweden	1990	16+	m	yes	yes	yes	.	uh	.	340	Rev.2	4	321	68	1	4
Switzerland	1990	15+	d	yes	yes	yes	yes	uh	.	210	Rev.2	2	404	88	.	7
Syrian Arab Republic	1994	10+	w/y	yes	yes	no	no	uh/ah	mw	...	Rev.3	4	...	88	2	5
Thailand	1990	13+	w/y	yes	yes	yes	no	no	no	13	Rev.2	1	83	68	2	6
Trinidad and Tobago	1990	15+	w/y	yes	yes	yes	no	uh	no	9	Rev.2	1	116	88	3	9
Turkey	1990	12+	w	yes	no	no	no	no	.	10	Rev.2	1	7	68	1	4
Uganda	1991	10+	w	yes pr.	yes pr.	yes	yes	no	.	no	.	.	161	88	3	3
United Kingdom	1991	16+	w	yes	.	yes	yes	uh	.	320	Rev.3	2	371	88	...	5
United States	1990	16+	w/y	yes	.	yes	yes	ah	ww/uh	236	no	.	501	no	.	8
Vanuatu	1989	10+	w	.	.	no	...	no	.	9	Rev.2	1	284	68	3	4

Country, area or territory	Census year	Age limits	Ref. per.	Armed forces included		Students included		Data on time worked		Classification used						Stat. in Emp.
										Industry			Occupation			
				Regular	Conscr.	With a part time job	Seeking work	Last week or month	Last year	Number of groups	Links to ISIC	Number of digits	Number of groups	Links to ISCO	Number of digits	Number of groups
Venezuela	1990	12+	d	yes	yes	yes	yes	no	.	9	Rev.2	1	...	68	1	7
Viet Nam	1994	see (f)	w	no	no	yes	yes	ah	.	20	no	.	33	68	1	2
Virgin Islands (British)	1991	15+	w/y	yes	.	no	yes	ah	mw	292	Rev.3	4	390	88	4	5
Virgin Islands (US)	1990	16+	w/y	yes	yes	no	no	uh/ah	ah/mw	7	no	.	39	no	.	7
Yemen	1994	10+	w	yes	yes	yes	no	no	.	...	Rev.3	...	390	88	4	5
Zambia	1990	12+	w/y	yes	yes	yes	yes	no	mw (see g)	9	Rev.2	1	91	68	1	4
Zimbabwe	1992	10+	y	yes	yes	no	no	.	no	no	.	.	109	88	3	4

Signs and symbols used

	not applicable
...	not available
d	day
w	week
ww	weeks worked
m	month
mw	months worked
y	year
uh	usual hours
ah	actual hours
pr.	if residing in private households
ISIC	International Standard Industrial Classification of all economic activities
Rev.2	ISIC (1968 Edition)
Rev.3	ISIC (1989 Edition)
ISCO	International Standard Classification of Occupations
68	ISCO (1968 Edition)
88	ISCO (1988 Edition)

(a) employment: 15 years and over; unemployment: 15 to 50 years for men and 15 to 45 years for women (China).

(b) employment: 15 years and over; unemployment: 15 to 59 years for men and 15 to 56 years for women (Czech Republic and Slovakia).

(c) 16 to 59 years for men, and 16 to 54 years for women (Mongolia).

(d) 7 years and over for employment, 15 years and over for unemployment (Morocco).

(e) employment: 14 to 80 years; unemployment: 14 to 64 years for men and 14 to 59 years for women (Romania).

(f) 15 to 60 years for men, and 15 to 55 years for women (Viet Nam).

(g) only multiple job holders were asked this question (Zambia).

Signes et symboles utilisés

	ne s'applique pas
...	non disponible
d	jour
w	semaine
ww	semaines travaillées
m	mois
mw	mois travaillés
y	année
uh	heures habituelles
ah	heures effectuées
pr.	s'ils résident dans des ménages privés
CITI	Classification internationale type, par industrie de toutes les branches d'activité économique
Rev.2	CITI (version 1968)
Rev.3	CITI (version 1989)
CITP	Classification Internationale Type des Professions
68	CITP (version 1968)
88	CITP (version 1988)

(a) emploi: 15 ans et plus; chômage: 15 à 50 ans pour les hommes et 15 à 45 ans pour les femmes (Chine).

(b) emploi: 15 ans et plus; chômage: 15 à 59 ans pour les hommes et 15 à 56 ans pour les femmes (République tchèque et Slovakie).

(c) 16 à 59 ans pour les hommes, et 16 à 54 ans pour les femmes (Mongolie).

(d) 7 ans et plus pour l'emploi, 15 ans et plus pour le chômage (Maroc).

(e) emploi: 14 à 80 ans; chômage: 14 à 64 ans pour les hommes et 14 à 59 ans pour les femmes (Roumanie).

(f) 15 à 60 ans pour les hommes, et 15 à 55 ans pour les femmes (Viet Nam).

(g) la question n'a été posée qu'aux détenteurs de plusieurs emplois (Zambie).

Signos y símbolos utilizados

	no aplicable
...	no disponible
d	día
w	semana
ww	semanas trabajadas
m	mes
mw	meses trabajados
y	año
uh	horas habituales
ah	horas efectuadas
pr.	si viven en viviendas privadas
CIIU	Clasificación Industrial Internacional Uniforme de todas las actividades económicas
Rev.2	CIIU (Edición de 1968)
Rev.3	CIIU (Edición de 1989)
CIUO	Clasificación Internacional Uniforme de Ocupaciones
68	CIUO (Edición de 1968)
88	CIUO (Edición de 1988)

(a) empleo: 15 años y más; desempleo: 15 a 50 años para los hombres y 15 a 45 años para las mujeres (China).

(b) empleo: 15 años y más; desempleo: 15 a 59 años para los hombres y 15 a 56 años para las mujeres (República Checa y Eslovaquia).

(c) 16 a 59 años para los hombres, y 16 a 54 años para las mujeres (Mongolia).

(d) 7 años y mas para el empleo, 15 años y mas para el desempleo (Marruecos).

(e) empleo: 14 a 80 años; desempleo: 14 a 64 años para los hombres y 14 a 59 años para las mujeres (Rumania).

(f) 15 a 60 años para los hombres, y 15 a 55 años para las mujeres (Viet Nam).

(g) se preguntó solamente a los trabajadores con más de un empleo (Zambia).

CONTENTS

xiv

TABLE DES MATIERES

INDICE

INTRODUCTION

This volume of "Sources and Methods: Labour statistics" presents methodological descriptions of population censuses carried out during the period 1989-94. It has two main purposes:

- to provide basic information on national practices in the collection of statistics on total and economically active population, employment and unemployment derived from population censuses;
- to illustrate the comparability of the statistics provided by countries.

A synoptic table presents the essential features of the censuses described.

The descriptions presented in this volume cover 115 countries. They were prepared on the basis of information provided by national statistical organizations responsible for conducting the censuses. In some cases, the information was collected from national publications. Each description was submitted to the country concerned for comments, which were taken into account if received within the limits of the publication programme.

In order to facilitate comparisons, the descriptions are structured and presented using standard sections and headings, as shown below. Whenever possible, the questions used in the census to obtain the information are given.

1. Name and address of the organization responsible for the census:
The name and address of the organization responsible are given in the original language or in the language used in official correspondence between the country and the ILO.

2. Population censuses conducted since 1945 (years):
This indicates the years in which population censuses have been conducted since 1945.

3. Coverage of the census:
(a) Geographical scope: This indicates whether the census covered the whole country or territory or, in cases where the coverage was limited, the areas or regions that were excluded.

(b) Persons covered: The population covered by the census, and any groups that are specifically excluded, such as foreign residents, persons usually resident elsewhere.

4. Reference period:
The period of time (e.g. a specific day, week or year) for which the data on economic characteristics were collected.

5. Main topics:
The main economic activity topics on which information was collected in the census, in terms of a standard list:
(a) Total population, by sex and age: ...
Economically active population by:
(b) Sex and age group: ...
(c) Industry: ...
(d) Occupation: ...
(e) Status in employment: ...
(f) Highest educational level: ...
(g) Hours of work: ...
(h) Other characteristics: ...
Details concerning the different topics are provided such as how the age is defined, the concept used for hours of work (actually worked, usually worked, etc.), and the different types of additional information collected about the person's economic activity (income, full-time or part-time work, etc.).

6. Concepts and definitions:
(a) Economically active population: The composition of the economically active population given in the "Resolution concerning Statistics of the Economically Active Population, Employment, Unemployment and Underemployment" (adopted by the Thirteenth International Conference of Labour Statisticians, 1982) is used as the standard against which the national definition used in the census is described. The inclusion or exclusion of certain groups (retired persons, home-makers, etc.) is indicated in relation to the resolution (the relevant extracts of which are given in Annex).

The following are mentioned under this heading:
- Age limits for inclusion in the economically active population;
- Inclusion or exclusion of members of the armed forces.

(b) Employment: The national definition used in the census is given, along with the different categories that are included and, where relevant, can be identified separately.

Multiple-job holders are given in the list only if they can be identified separately.

(c) Unemployment: The national definition used in the census is given.

7. Classifications used:
(a) Industry: Whenever possible, the questions asked to determine the group of industry and the number of groups used to code the data have been given under this heading. It is also indicated whether the national classification is linked to the International Standard Industrial Classification of all economic activities (ISIC), Revision 2 (1968) or Revision 3 (1990).

(b) Occupation: Whenever possible, the questions asked to determine the group of occupation and the number of groups used to code the data have been given under this heading. It is also indicated whether the national classification is linked to the International Standard Classification of Occupations (ISCO-68 or ISCO-88).

(c) Status in employment: This indicates the number of groups used to code the data and, whenever possible, the titles of the groups.

8. Main differences compared with the previous census:
Any changes that were introduced in the coverage, concepts and definitions, etc. since the previous census are given under this heading.

9. Publication of the census results:
This section provides the title of the national publication in which the final census results were released, the organization responsible for the publication, and whether the results are available in other forms (diskettes, magnetic tapes, CD-ROM, etc).

ALBANIA

1. Name and address of the organization responsible for the census:
Commission du Plan d'Etat, Direction de la Statistique, Tirana.

2. Population censuses conducted since 1945 (years):
1960, 1989. The present description relates to the 1989 population census (held from 1 to 7 April).

3. Coverage of the census:
(a) Geographical scope: Whole territory.

(b) Persons covered: All persons of all ages.

4. Reference period:
A reference period has not been specified.

5. Main topics:
(a) Total population, by sex and age: yes
Economically active population by:
(b) Sex and age group: yes
(c) Industry: yes
(d) Occupation: yes
(e) Status in employment: yes
(f) Highest educational level: yes
(g) Hours of work: no
(h) Other characteristics: yes
Re (a): The age is defined in terms of year and month of birth.

Re (h): The census also collected information on annual income over the course of the previous year, and on the total number of years during which the person worked in state employment or in a cooperative. Persons were also asked to indicate the year in which they would retire.

6. Concepts and definitions:
(a) Economically active population: It comprises all persons aged 15 years and over who were either employed or unemployed, according to the definitions given below. Members of the armed forces are included in the definition.

(b) Employment: Employment is determined on the basis of the question: "Do you work? (1) yes; (2) no." Persons who replied no were asked if they were: (1) retired or past working age; (2) retired owing to disability; (3) inactive; (4) student; (5) seeking work; (6) not seeking work; or (7) other.

It is reported that the following categories are included:

i) persons doing unpaid work in family firm or business;
ii) persons engaged in the production of primary products for own consumption;
iii) employed persons, temporarily absent from work;
iv) working students with a part time job;
v) seasonal or occasional workers;
vi) conscripts for military/civilian service;
vii) apprentices and trainees.

None of these categories can be identified separately.

(c) Unemployment: Considered as "unemployed" are all persons who stated that they were without work and seeking work. Students seeking work are excluded from the definition.

7. Classifications used:
Only employed persons are classified by industry, by occupation and by status in employment.

(a) Industry: Based on the question: "Economic activity?." For coding industry, the national classification was used. Links to the ISIC have not been established.

(b) Occupation: Based on the question: "Occupation or function performed?." The national classification was used for coding occupation. Links to the ISCO have not been established.

(c) Status in employment: Based on the question: "Status in employment? (1) wage earner; (2) employer; (3) member of a cooperative." These three groups were used for coding this variable.

8. Main differences compared with the previous census:
No major difference.

9. Publication of the census results:
The title of the publication containing the final census results is: "Recensement de la population et de l'habitat, 1989," published in 1991.

The organization responsible for the publication is Institut de la Statistique, Rr Lek Dukagjini n 5, Tirana.

The census results are not available in other forms.

AMERICAN SAMOA

1. Name and address of the organization responsible for the census:
Economic Development and Planning Office, American Samoa Government, Pago Pago, A.S. 96799, in conjunction with the US Bureau of the Census.

2. Population censuses conducted since 1945 (years):
1945, 1950, 1956, 1960, 1970, 1974, 1980 and 1990. The present description relates to the 1990 census (held on 1st April).

3. Coverage of the census:
(a) Geographical scope: Whole area.

(b) Persons covered: The 1990 census counted every person at his or her "usual residence"; this means the place where the person lives and sleeps most of the time. The census excluded: persons who usually live somewhere else; college students who live somewhere else while attending college; persons in the armed forces who live somewhere else, and persons who stay somewhere else most of the week while working.

4. Reference period:
The week prior to the census and the year preceding the census year.

5. Main topics:
(a) Total population, by sex and age:	yes

Economically active population by:
(b) Sex and age group:	yes
(c) Industry:	yes
(d) Occupation:	yes
(e) Status in employment:	yes
(f) Highest educational level:	yes
(g) Hours of work:	yes
(h) Other characteristics:	yes

Re (a): The age is defined both in terms of year of birth and of age at last birthday.

Re (g): For both short and long reference periods, employed persons were asked to specify, respectively, the number of hours worked last week and the total period worked in 1989 (expressed in number of weeks).

Re (h): The census also collected information on total income and on means of transport to travel to workplace.

6. Concepts and definitions:

(a) Economically active population: It comprises all persons aged 16 years and over (except those engaged in subsistence farming) who, during the reference periods, were either employed or unemployed, according to the definitions given below. The definition includes members of the armed forces.

(b) Employment: The questions used to determine if a person is to be counted as employed are "Did X work at any time last week, either full time or part time?" (work includes part-time work such as delivering papers, or helping without pay in a family business or farm; it also includes active duty in the Armed Forces; it does not include own homework, school work, or volunteer work), and "How many hours did X work last week at all jobs, excluding subsistence activity?."

It is reported that the following categories are included:
i) persons doing unpaid work in family firm or business;
ii) employed persons temporarily absent from work;
iii) working students with a part time job;
iv) seasonal or occasional workers;
v) conscripts for military/civilian service;
vi) apprentices and trainees.

None of the above categories can be identified separately.

(c) Unemployment: Considered as "unemployed" are all persons who, during the reference week, were without work and seeking work. To determine if a person is to be counted as unemployed, the questions used are: "Were you temporarily absent or on lay-off from job or business last week?," "Has X been looking for work to earn money during the last 4 weeks?" and "Could X have taken a job last week if one had been offered?."

7. Classifications used:
Both employed persons and unemployed persons previously employed are classified by industry, by occupation and by status in employment.

(a) Industry: Based on the questions: "For whom did X last work?," "What kind of business or industry was this?" and "Is this mainly manufacturing, wholesale trade, retail trade, or something else (agriculture, construction, service, government, etc.)?." For coding industry, 231 categories classified into 13 major industry groups of the Standard Industrial Classification Manual (SIC) were used. Links to the ISIC-rev.2 have been established to the level of United States 1972 and 1977 Supplement.

(b) Occupation: Based on the questions: "What kind of work was X doing (for example registered nurse, industrial machinery mechanic, cake icer)?" and "What were X's most important activities or duties (for example patient care, repair machines in factory, icing cakes)?." For coding occupation, 13 major occupation groups of the Standard Occupational Classification Manual (SOC) were used. Links to the ISCO have not been established.

(c) Status in employment: Based on the question: "Was X: employee of a private for profit company or business or of an individual, for wages, salary or commissions; employee of a private not-for-profit, tax-exempt, or charitable organization; local or territorial government employee (territorial/commonwealth, etc.); federal government employee; self-employed in own not incorporated business, professional practice, or farm; self-employed in own-incorporated business, professional practice, or farm; working without pay in family business or farm?." For coding status in employment, the seven groups above were used.

8. Main differences compared with the previous census:
No major difference.

9. Publication of the census results:
The title of the publication containing the final census results is "1990 CPH-6-AS," issued in 1992.

The organizations responsible for this publication are either the U.S. Department of Commerce, U.S. Bureau of the Census, Washington, D.C. 20233, or the Superintendent of Documents, U.S. Government Printing Office, Washington, D.C. 20402.

The census results are also available in the form of STF files 1 and 3, diskettes and tapes.

ANGUILLA

1. Name and address of the organization responsible for the census:
Government of Anguilla, Statistical Unit, Ministry of Finance, The Secretariat, Valley.

2. Population censuses conducted since 1945 (years):
1960, 1974, 1984 and 1992. The present description relates to the 1992 population census (held on 14 April).

3. Coverage of the census:
(a) Geographical scope: Whole country.

(b) Persons covered: All persons of all ages.

4. Reference period:
The month preceding the census day.

5. Main topics:
(a) Total population, by sex and age: yes
Economically active population by:
(b) Sex and age group: yes
(c) Industry: yes
(d) Occupation: yes
(e) Status in employment: yes
(f) Highest educational level: yes
(g) Hours of work: no
(h) Other characteristics: no

Re (a): The age is defined in terms of age at last birthday.

6. Concepts and definitions:
(a) Economically active population: It comprises all persons aged 12 years and over who, during the reference period, were either employed or unemployed, according to the definitions given below. The definition also includes members of the police force.

(b) Employment: Employment is determined on the basis of the questions: "What is the person's occupation?," and "If the person does not work, what is the reason?."

It is reported that the following categories are included:
i) employed persons, temporarily absent from work;
ii) working students with a part time job;
iii) seasonal or occasional workers;
iv) conscripts for military/civilian service;
v) apprentices and trainees.

None of these categories can be identified separately.

(c) Unemployment: Considered as "unemployed" are all persons who where without work and wanted to work. The definition includes those who actively looked for work as well as those who did nothing about finding a job because they knew none were available.

7. Classifications used:
Only employed persons are classified by industry, by occupation and by status in employment.

(a) Industry: Based on the questions: "Who does this person work for?" and "Where does this person work?" e.g. "Cable and Wireless," "Mariners Hotel." For coding industry, the ISIC-rev.3 has been used to the tabulation category (1-digit) level.

(b) Occupation: Based on the question: "What is the person's occupation? e.g. foreman carpenter, diesel mechanic, primary teacher." For coding occupation, 39 groups were used. Links to the ISCO-88 have been established to the major group (1-digit) level.

(c) Status in employment: For coding this variable, three groups were used, namely: Public sector; Private sector; and Self-employed.

8. Main differences compared with the previous census:
No major difference.

9. Publication of the census results:
The title of the publication containing the census results is "Anguilla Census of Population," issued in September 1992.

The organization responsible for the publication is the Government of Anguilla, The Secretariat, Statistical Unit, Ministry of Finance, Valley.

Possibilities also exist for obtaining census data on diskettes.

ANTIGUA AND BARBUDA

1. Name and address of the organization responsible for the census:
Census Office, Statistics Division, Upper Redcliffe Street, St. John's, Antigua.

2. Population censuses conducted since 1945 (years):
1945, 1960, 1970 and 1991. The present description relates to the 1991 population census (held on 28 May).

3. Coverage of the census:
(a) Geographical scope: Whole area.

(b) Persons covered: All persons of all ages.

4. Reference period:
The week and the year preceding the census.

5. Main topics:
(a) Total population, by sex and age: yes
Economically active population by:
(b) Sex and age group: yes
(c) Industry: yes
(d) Occupation: yes
(e) Status in employment: yes
(f) Highest educational level: yes
(g) Hours of work: yes
(h) Other characteristics: yes

Re (a): The age is defined in terms of age at last birthday.

Re (g): Hours of work relate to the actual hours of work during the reference week and to the number of months worked during the reference year.

Re (h): The census also collected information on: (i) means of transports to travel to work; (ii) engagement on informal trade; (iii) last pay/income period; and (iv) gross pay/income during the last pay period.

6. Concepts and definitions:
(a) Economically active population: It comprises all persons aged 15 to 64 years who, during the reference periods, were either employed or unemployed, according to the definitions given below. Members of the armed forces are excluded from the definition.

(b) Employment: The questions asked to determine if a person is to be counted as employed are: "What did you do most during the past 12 months?" and "What did you do most during the past week?." For both questions, the possible answers were: (1) worked; (2) had a job but did not work; (3) looked for work; (4) wanted work and available; (5) home duties; (6) attended school; (7) retired; (8) disabled, unable to work; (9) other; (10) not stated. Those who classified themselves under 1 or 2 were counted as "employed."

It is reported that the following categories are included:
i) persons doing unpaid work in family firm or business;
ii) persons engaged in the production of primary products for own consumption;
iii) employed persons, temporarily absent from work;
iv) working students with a part time job;
v) seasonal or occasional workers;

Only persons belonging to categories (i), (iii) and (iv) can be identified separately.

(c) Unemployment: The questions used to determine if a person is to be counted as unemployed, in addition to that one indicated under 6 (b) above, are: "Did you do any work at all in the past 12 months? include work at home" and "Have you ever worked or had a job?."

7. Classifications used:
Both employed persons and unemployed persons previously employed are classified by industry, by occupation and by status in employment.

(a) Industry: Based on the questions: "What kind of industry or business is/was carried on at your workplace?" and "What is the name and address of your present workplace?." For coding industry, 157 groups of the National Classification were used. Links to the ISIC-rev.3 have been established to the group (3-digit) level.

(b) *Occupation*: Based on the question: "What sort of work did you/do you do in your main occupation?." For coding occupation, 136 groups of the National classification were used. Links have been established to the ISCO-88.

(c) *Status in employment*: Based on the question: "Did you carry on your own business, work for a wage or salary or as an unpaid worker in a family business?." For coding this variable, six groups were used, namely: (1) paid employee - government; (2) paid employee - private; (3) unpaid worker; (4) own business with paid help (employer); (5) own business without paid help (own account); and (6) don't know/not stated.

8. Main differences compared with the previous census:
No major difference.

9. Publication of the census results:
The title of the publication containing the census results is: "1991 Population and Housing Census, Summary Report, Volume II, (Pard. 1)," issued in December 1994.

The organization responsible for this publication is the Statistics Division, Ministry of Finance & Social Security.

The census results are also available in the form of unpublished tables and diskettes.

ARGENTINA

1. Name and address of the organization responsible for the census:
Instituto Nacional de Estadística y Censos (INDEC), Diagonal Presidente Julio A. Roca 609, Código Postal 1067, Buenos Aires, Capital Federal.

2. Population censuses conducted since 1945 (years):
1947, 1960, 1970, 1980 and 1991. The present description relates to the 1991 population census (held on 15 May).

3. Coverage of the census:

(a) *Geographical scope*: Whole country, except the Falkland Islands and the South Atlantic Islands.

(b) *Persons covered*: All persons of all ages residing in the national territory on the date of the census, except Argentina nationals residing abroad and foreign nationals residing in embassies in Argentina.

4. Reference period:
The week preceding the census date, as regards employment, and the four weeks preceding the census date, as regards unemployment.

5. Main topics:

(a) Total population, by sex and age:	yes
Economically active population by:	
(b) Sex and age group:	yes
(c) Industry:	yes
(d) Occupation:	yes
(e) Status in employment:	yes
(f) Highest educational level:	yes
(g) Hours of work:	no
(h) Other characteristics:	no

Re (a): The age is defined in terms of age at last birthday.

6. Concepts and definitions:

(a) *Economically active population*: It comprises all persons aged 14 years and over who, during the reference periods, were either employed or unemployed, according to the definitions given below. The questions on economic activity were put to a sampling which ranged from 10 per cent in cities with a population of 500,000 or more, to 20 per cent in cities with a population of 100,000 to 499,999. All members of the armed forces are included in the definition.

(b) *Employment*: Considered as "employed" are all persons who worked in a paid or unpaid occupation during the reference week. The questions used to determine whether the person worked are "Did you work last week, even if only a few hours?," "Did you work at home for someone else, or did you help someone in their trade, farm or job?," and "Were you away from work owing to illness, vacation, etc.?."

It is reported that the following categories are included:

i) persons doing unpaid work in family firm or business;

ii) employed persons, temporarily absent from work owing to: illness or accident, labour dispute, vacation or other leave, interruption of work due to poor weather or equipment failure;

iii) working students with a part-time job;

iv) seasonal or occasional workers;

v) conscripts for military/civilian service.

Persons falling in categories (i), (ii), (iii) and (v) can be identified separately by means of their replies to specific questions.

(c) *Unemployment*: Considered as "unemployed" are all persons who, during the four-week reference period, were seeking work because they had lost their job, or were seeking work for the first time. The question used to determine if the person was unemployed is "Did you look for work during the past four weeks?."

7. Classifications used:
Only employed persons in the samplings were classified by industry, by occupation and by status in employment.

(a) *Industry*: The question used to determine industry group is "What is the line of business or product of the establishment where you work?." For coding industry, the ISIC-rev.3 has been be used to the 3-digit level.

(b) *Occupation*: The question used to determine occupation group is "What tasks do you perform in your job?." For coding occupation, 9 groups of the 1990 national classification were used. Links to the ISCO-88 have been established.

(c) *Status in employment*: The question used to determine this variable is "In your main job, in other words in the job in which you work the most hours, are you: employer, private sector worker or employee, public sector worker or employee, household employee, self-employed, unpaid family worker, other?." For coding status in employment, these seven groups were used.

8. Main differences compared with the previous census:
There were certain minor differences with respect to the 1980 census in the phrasing of the questions used to determine:

- industry group: "Is the establishment or place where you work primarily: agricultural, industrial, commercial or other?," "What is the line of business or product of this establishment?," and "How many persons are employed in the establishment where you work: five or less, more than five?."

- occupation group: "What is your occupation, function or kind of work?."

- status in employment: "What is your status in that occupation (public sector worker or employee; private sector worker or employee; household employee; self-employed with no employees; proprietor or partner with employees; unpaid family worker; other?."

9. Publication of the census results:
No information available.

ARUBA

1. Name and address of the organization responsible for the census:
Central Bureau of Statistics, L.G. Smith Boulevard no. 160.

2. Population censuses conducted since 1945 (years):
1981 and 1991. The present description relates to the 1991 population census (held on 6 October).

3. Coverage of the census:

(a) *Geographical scope*: Whole country.

(b) *Persons covered*: All persons of all ages.

4. Reference period:
The week preceding the census day.

5. Main topics:

(a) Total population, by sex and age:	yes
Economically active population by:	
(b) Sex and age group:	yes
(c) Industry:	yes
(d) Occupation:	yes
(e) Status in employment:	yes
(f) Highest educational level:	...
(g) Hours of work:	yes
(h) Other characteristics:	yes

Re (a): The age is defined in terms of age at last birthday.

Re (g): Employed persons were asked to specify their usual hours of work.

Re (h): The census also collected information on means of transport to travel to workplace, duration of employment, reason why the person is out of work, on how many months unemployed person has worked in previous job, on income and source of income.

6. Concepts and definitions:

(a) Economically active population: It comprises all persons aged 14 years and over who, during the reference week, were either employed or unemployed, according to the definitions given below. The definition includes members of the armed forces.

(b) Employment: Considered as "employed" are all persons who gave an affirmative reply to the question: "Do you have a job for which you worked four hours or more in the past week (or would have worked if you had not been away due to vacation, illness, pregnancy, or a labour dispute, etc)?."

It is reported that the following categories are included:

i) persons doing unpaid work in family firm or business;
ii) employed persons, temporarily absent from work;
iii) working students with a part time job;
iv) conscripts for military/civilian service;
v) apprentices and trainees.

Only persons belonging to categories (i), (iii) and (iv) can be identified separately.

(c) Unemployment: Considered as "unemployed" are all persons who, during the reference period, did not work for at least four hours, and gave an affirmative reply to the two following questions: "Have you been actively looking for work in the past month or were you busy with preparations for starting your own business?" and "If you find a job or start your own business would you be able to start working within two weeks?." Students seeking work are excluded from the definition.

7. Classifications used:

Both employed and unemployed persons are classified by industry and by occupation. Status in employment is ascertained for employed persons and only for a sample of unemployed persons.

(a) Industry: Based on the question: "Where do you (did you) work? work address; name of company/organization; type of activity engaged by the company (employer)." For coding industry, the ISIC-rev.2 was used to the group (4-digit) level.

(b) Occupation: Based on the question: "What type of work do you or did you mainly perform? name of profession or job; job description." For coding occupation, the ISCO-88 was used to the unit group (4-digit) level.

(c) Status in employment: Six groups were used for coding this variable, namely: employer (3 or more employees); own small business (0 to 3 employees); wage or salary earner or permanent or temporary staff; wage or salary earner for standby work, odd jobs; unpaid working relative (in family business); other (volunteer, member in cooperative, etc).

8. Main differences compared with the previous census:
No major difference.

9. Publication of the census results:
The final census data were issued in October 1992 in a publication entitled "Selected Tables - Third Population and Housing Census, Aruba - October 6, 1991."

The organization responsible for the publication is the Central Bureau of Statistics, L.G. Smith Boulevard no. 160.

The census results are also available in the form of diskettes. Unpublished tables are available on request.

AUSTRALIA

1. Name and address of the organization responsible for the census:
Australian Bureau of Statistics, P.O. Box 10, Belconnen ACT 2616.

2. Population censuses conducted since 1945 (years):
1947, 1954, 1961, 1966, 1971, 1976, 1981, 1986 and 1991. The present description relates to the 1991 census (held on 6 August).

3. Coverage of the census:

(a) Geographical scope: Whole country.

(b) Persons covered: All persons of all ages, except foreign diplomats and their families.

4. Reference period:
The week prior to the census for full- and part-time workers, and the four weeks preceding the census day for jobseekers.

5. Main topics:

(a) Total population, by sex and age:	yes
Economically active population by:	
(b) Sex and age group:	yes
(c) Industry:	yes
(d) Occupation:	yes
(e) Status in employment:	yes
(f) Highest educational level:	yes
(g) Hours of work:	yes
(h) Other characteristics:	yes

Re (a): The age is defined in terms of age at last birthday.

Re (g): Employed persons, at work, were asked to specify their actual hours of work during the reference period in the main job held.

Re (h): The census also collected information on gross income and means of transport used to travel to workplace.

6. Concepts and definitions:

(a) Economically active population: It comprises all persons aged 15 years and over who, during the reference period, were either employed or unemployed, according to the definitions given below. Excluded are persons who did not have a job and did not look for work in the 4 week period immediately prior to the census day; these persons were considered as inactive. Members of the armed forces are included in the definition.

(b) Employment: Considered as "employed" are all persons who, during the reference period, performed any full or part time work for payment or profit, or any unpaid work in a family business. Home duties are excluded unless payment was received for work in other households. The question used to determine if a person is to be counted as employed was: "Last week, did the person have a full-time or part-time job of any kind?."

It is reported that the following categories are included:

i) persons doing unpaid work in family firm or business;
ii) employed persons, temporarily absent from work;
iii) working students with a part time job;
iv) seasonal or occasional workers;
v) apprentices and trainees.

Only persons belonging to categories (i) and (ii) can be identified separately according to status in employment and by cross-classification with data on hours worked.

(c) Unemployment: Considered as "unemployed" are all persons who were without work and seeking work. To determine if a person is to be counted as unemployed, the question used was "Did the person actively look for work at any time in the last four weeks?." Actively looking for work means being registered with the Commonwealth Employment Service; writing, telephoning or applying in person to an employer for work, or advertising for work. Students seeking work are excluded from the definition.

7. Classifications used:
Only employed persons are classified by industry, by occupation and by status in employment.

(a) Industry: Based on the questions: "For the main job held last week, what was the employers' trading name and workplace address?" and "What kind of industry, business or service is carried out by the employer at that address?." The answers provided information for industry coding. The industry classification is based on the Australian Standard Industrial Classification (ASIC) and the Industry and Destination Zone Index which is a listing of all establishments in Australia known to carry out economic activity. For coding industry, 615 classes were used. Links to the ISIC-rev.2 have been established to the group (4-digit) level.

(b) Occupation: Based on the questions: "In the main job held last week, what was the person's occupation? (give full title; for example: accounts clerk, civil engineering draftsman, fast foods cook, floor tiler, extruding machine operator; for public servants, state official designation as well as occupation; for armed services personnel, state rank as well as occupation)" and

"What are the main tasks or duties that the person himself/herself usually performs in that occupation? (describe as fully as possible; for example: recording accounts, preparing drawings for dam construction, cooking hamburgers and chips, fixing cork tiles, operating plastic extruding machine)." Occupation was classified in terms of the Australian Standard Classification of Occupations (ASCO) and coded to the unit group level of the classification. For coding occupation 337 group codes were used which comprised 282 unit groups, 52 minor groups, eight major groups and three additional codes to process responses which were inadequately described. Links to the ISCO have not been established.

(c) Status in employment: Based on the question: "In the main job held last week, was the person: a wage or salary earner; conducting own business but not employing others; conducting own business and employing others; a helper not receiving wages or salary?." For coding status in employment, the four following categories were used: wage or salary earner; self employed; employer; unpaid helper.

8. Main differences compared with the previous census:
No major difference.

9. Publication of the census results:
Final census data on the economically active population and its components (employment and unemployment) were available on a state by state basis beginning September 1992.

Preliminary results from the 1991 Census were released in a publication series "First Counts for Statistical Local Areas" (Cat. no. 2701.1-8) on a state by state basis from February to April 1992.

The ABS released final census results on a state by state basis in a publication series "Census Counts for Small Areas." Detailed data are available on demand from ABS Information Services.

The 1991 census results are also available in other forms, such as thematic reports, social atlases, matrixes and maps. Media include hard copy, floppy disk, magnetic tape, microfiche, cartridge and CD-ROM. For further information see "1991 Census: A Guide to Products and Services" (Cat. no. 2910.0) or contact Census Marketing, Australian Bureau of Statistics, P.O. Box 10 Belconnen ACT 2616, phone 61 6 252 7879, fax 61 6 253 1809.

AUSTRIA

1. Name and address of the organization responsible for the census:
Oesterreichisches Statistisches Zentralamt, Hintere Zollamtsstrasse 2B, A-1033 Vienna.

2. Population censuses conducted since 1945 (years):
1951, 1961, 1971, 1981 and 1991. The present description relates to the 1991 population census (held on 15 May).

3. Coverage of the census:
(a) Geographical scope: Whole country.

(b) Persons covered: Resident population of all ages, including aliens living permanently in Austria and nationals working temporarily abroad; excluding exterritorial persons and nationals permanently living abroad.

4. Reference period:
The last weeks preceding the census day; in case of doubt, the person's situation on the census day (15 May) is taken into account.

5. Main topics:
(a) Total population, by sex and age: yes
Economically active population by:
(b) Sex and age group: yes
(c) Industry: yes
(d) Occupation: yes
(e) Status in employment: yes
(f) Highest educational level: yes
(g) Hours of work: yes
(h) Other characteristics: yes

Re (a): The age is defined in terms of exact birth date, i.e. day, month and year.

Re (g): Hours of work relate to usual hours of work of both full time and part time employed persons.

Re (h): The census also covers information on other topics, such as: frequency of travel to work (daily, non-daily); place of work; time used for the daily travel to work; usual means of transports for the longest distance; type of employer (public or private, 12 categories).

6. Concepts and definitions:
(a) Economically active population: It comprises all persons aged 15 years and over who, during the reference period, were either employed or unemployed, according to the definitions given below. The definition covers all members of the armed forces.

(b) Employment: Considered as "employed" are all persons who had full time activity (i.e. 33 hours and more per week) or part time activity (i.e. 12 to 32 hours per week). Persons on maternity or unpaid parental leave are counted as employed.

It is reported that the following categories are included:
i) persons doing unpaid work in family firm or business;
ii) persons engaged in the production of primary products for own consumption;
iii) employed persons, temporarily absent from work;
iv) working students with a part time job;
v) seasonal or occasional workers;
vi) conscripts for military/civilian service;
vii) apprentices and trainees.

Persons belonging to categories (i), (vi) and (vii) above can be identified separately. Other groups of persons in vocational training (e.g. student nurses, trainees, volunteers) are also regarded as employed, but cannot be identified separately.

(c) Unemployment: Considered as "unemployed" are all persons who were without work and seeking work. The definition excludes students seeking work.

7. Classifications used:
Both employed persons and unemployed persons previously employed are classified by industry, by occupation and by status in employment.

(a) Industry: Specific questions were asked, i.e. name of company (workplace or employer) and branch of economic activity of the company or office (e.g.: weaving mill, underwear factory, fabric wholesaler); self-employed were requested to reply "own business." For coding industry, 117 groups of the national classification of industries were used. Links to the ISIC-rev.3 have been established to the division (2-digit) level.

(b) Occupation: Specific questions were asked, i.e. exact title of present or last occupation and main task performed (e.g.: bookkeeper, shoe salesman, mounting of video machines on assembly line, contractual employee in social welfare service, home carpenter, street cleaner). For coding occupation, 175 groups of the national classification of occupations were used. Links to the ISCO-88 have been established to the sub-major group level (2-digit).

(c) Status in employment: Specific questions were asked of employed and unemployed persons previously employed to determine their present or previous status in employment, i.e.: self-employed with employees (employer); self-employed without employees (own-account worker); unpaid family worker; employee/civil servant; skilled worker; semi-skilled worker; unskilled worker; in an apprenticeship. For coding status in employment, these eight groups were used.

8. Main differences compared with the previous census:
The main differences relate to the classifications used in 1991. For industry, additional codes were introduced for better links to ISIC-89, and for occupation, a compressed range of codes was adopted.

9. Publication of the census results:
A variety of publications relating to the census results were issued in 1993 in the series "Beiträge zur österreichischen Statistik." The title of the volume containing the census data for the whole country is "Hauptergebnisse II - Oesterreich," Reference 1030/20. More detailed data are available by ISIS - Statistical Data Base, Tailor-made cross-classifications.

The organization responsible for these publications is Oesterreichisches Statistisches Zentralamt, in Vienna.

All census data are also available on request on printed booklets, paper, diskettes and magnetic tapes.

BAHAMAS

1. Name and address of the organization responsible for the census:
Department of Statistics, Ministry of Finance, P.O. Box N-3904, Nassau.

2. Population censuses conducted since 1945 (years):
1953, 1963, 1970, 1980 and 1990. The present description relates to the 1990 population census (held on 1st May).

3. Coverage of the census:
(a) Geographical scope: Whole area.

(b) Persons covered: All persons of all ages, except foreign diplomatic personnel residing in the Bahamas. A record, by sex, of visitors to the country during the census period was made; however, visitors were not interviewed and are therefore not included in the census count.

4. Reference period:
The week ending 28 April 1990 and the 12 months prior to the census.

5. Main topics:
(a) Total population, by sex and age:	yes
Economically active population by:	
(b) Sex and age group:	yes
(c) Industry:	yes
(d) Occupation:	yes
(e) Status in employment:	yes
(f) Highest educational level:	yes
(g) Hours of work:	yes
(h) Other characteristics:	yes

Re (a): The age is defined both in terms of year of birth and of age at last birthday.

Re (g): Hours of work relate to the total period (expressed in number of weeks) worked by employed persons during the long reference period.

Re (h): The census also collected information on: (i) when did the person last work at a regular job for at least two weeks since 1979; and (ii) person's total income during the 12 months preceding the date of the census.

6. Concepts and definitions:
(a) Economically active population: It comprises all persons aged 15 years and over who, during the reference periods, were either employed or unemployed, according to the definitions given below. The definition also includes armed forces.

(b) Employment: The questions asked to determine if a person is to be counted as employed are "What was your main employment situation during the week ending April 28, 1990?" and "What was your main employment situation during the past 12 months?." Persons answering "worked" and "with job but not at work" are considered employed.

It is reported that the following categories are included:
i) persons doing unpaid work in family firm or business;
ii) persons engaged in the production of primary products for own consumption;
iii) employed persons, temporarily absent from work;
iv) working students with a part time job;
v) seasonal or occasional workers;
vi) conscripts for military/civilian service;
vii) apprentices and trainees.

Only persons belonging to categories (i) and (iii) can be identified separately through the replies to the questions on employment and status in employment.

(c) Unemployment: Considered as "unemployed" are all persons who did not have a job and were seeking work. A person is counted as unemployed if the reply to the questions asked under 6 (b) above is "Seeking first job," "Seeking job (other than first)," or "Seeking work for the past four weeks."

7. Classifications used:
Both employed persons and unemployed persons previously employed are classified by industry, by occupation and by status in employment.

(a) Industry: Based on the question: "What kind of industry or business was this? (Describe the kind of business, e.g. retail store, primary school, law firm, bank, brewery, etc.)." For coding industry, nine groups were used. Links to the ISIC-rev.2 have been established to the major division (1-digit) level.

(b) Occupation: Based on the question: "What kind of work did you do? (Describe your job as accurately as possible, e.g. sales clerk, typist, doctor, auto mechanic, civil engineer, taxi driver, housemaid, etc.)." For coding occupation, nine groups were used. Links to the ISCO-88 have been established to the major group (1-digit) level.

(c) Status in employment: Based on the question: "What was your employment status when you last worked?." For coding status in employment, five groups were used: employee (private business); employee (government corporation); unpaid family worker; operated own business with paid help; and operated own business without paid help.

8. Main differences compared with the previous census:
In the 1980 census only a short reference period (i.e., the week prior to the census) was used (although tabulations were only produced for persons who worked sometime during the 12 months preceding the census).

Moreover, in the 1990 census the question dealing with the short reference period (a week) also asked persons whether they were seeking work during the past four weeks (cf. para. 6 (c)).

9. Publication of the census results:
The title of the publication containing the census results is: "Commonwealth of the Bahamas - Report of the 1990 Census of Population: Economic Activity and Income," issued in 1992.

The organization responsible for this publication is the Department of Statistics, Ministry of Finance, P.O. Box N-3904, Nassau, Bahamas.

The census results are also available in the form of unpublished tables and diskettes.

BAHRAIN

1. Name and address of the organization responsible for the census:
Central Statistics Organization, Directorate of Statistics, Cabinet Affairs, P.O. Box 5835, Manama.

2. Population censuses conducted since 1945 (years):
1950, 1959, 1965, 1971, 1981 and 1991. The present description relates to the 1991 population census (held on 16 November).

3. Coverage of the census:
(a) Geographical scope: Whole country.

(b) Persons covered: All persons of all ages.

4. Reference period:
The week prior to the census day.

5. Main topics:
(a) Total population, by sex and age:	yes
Economically active population by:	
(b) Sex and age group:	yes
(c) Industry:	yes
(d) Occupation:	yes
(e) Status in employment:	yes
(f) Highest educational level:	yes
(g) Hours of work:	no
(h) Other characteristics:	yes

Re (a): The age is defined in terms of age at last birthday.

Re (h): The census also collected information on duration of unemployment.

6. Concepts and definitions:
(a) Economically active population: It comprises all persons aged 12 years and over who, during the reference week, were either employed or unemployed, according to the definitions given below. Members of the armed forces are included in the definition.

(b) Employment: Considered as "employed" are all persons who, during the reference week, performed any work of an economic value out of home. The question used to determine if a person is to be counted as employed is "What is your employment status? 1) employer; 2) self-employed; 3) paid employee; 4) unpaid employee; 5) unemployed and worked before; 6) unemployed and never worked before; 7) student; 8) home-

maker; 9) income recipient; 10) unable to work; 11) no desire to work; 12) not applicable."

It is reported that the following categories are included:

i)   persons doing unpaid work in family firm or business;
ii)   persons engaged in the production of primary products for own consumption;
iii) employed persons, temporarily absent from work;
iv)   working students with a part time job;
v)   seasonal or occasional workers;
vi)   conscripts for military/civilian service.

Only persons doing unpaid work in family firm or business can be identified separately.

(c) Unemployment: Considered as "unemployed" are all persons who, during the reference week, were without work, able and desire to work. The unemployed were registered as "Unemployed and worked before" or "Unemployed and never worked before."

7. Classifications used:
Only employed persons were classified by industry and by status in employment. Both employed persons and unemployed persons previously employed were classified by occupation.

(a) Industry: Based on the question: "What is the main activity of your establishment?." For coding industry, 17 groups of the national classification were used. Links to the ISIC-rev.3 have been established to the tabulation category (1-digit) level.

(b) Occupation: Based on the question: "What kind of work did you do?." For coding occupation, the Standard Arab Gulf Directory for Occupational Classification was used to the one digit level. No links to the ISCO have been established.

(c) Status in employment: The same question as for employment was used to determine this variable. For coding status in employment the four following groups were used: employer; self-employed; paid employee; unpaid employee.

8. Main differences compared with the previous census:
The minimum age limit used for inclusion in the economically active population was 15 years in the 1981 census.

9. Publication of the census results:
The final data have been published in October 1993 in the following publications: "The population, Housing, Buildings and Establishments Census - 1991. I - Summary results. II - Demographic and social characteristics. III - Economic characteristics. IV - Characteristics of Housing, Buildings and Establishments."

The organization responsible for this publication is the Directorate of Statistics, Central Statistics Organization, P.O. Box 5835, Manama.

The final results are also available in other forms: unpublished tables, diskettes, magnetic tapes.

BARBADOS

1. Name and address of the organization responsible for the census:
Barbados Statistical Service, 3rd Floor, National Insurance Building, Fairchild Street, Bridgetown.

2. Population censuses conducted since 1945 (years):
1946, 1960, 1970, 1980 and 1990. The present description relates to the 1990 population census (held on 1st May).

3. Coverage of the census:
(a) Geographical scope: Whole country.

(b) Persons covered: All persons of all ages.

4. Reference period:
The week and the 12 months prior to the census.

5. Main topics:
(a) Total population, by sex and age:	yes

Economically active population by:

(b) Sex and age group:	yes
(c) Industry:	yes
(d) Occupation:	yes
(e) Status in employment:	yes
(f) Highest educational level:	yes
(g) Hours of work:	yes
(h) Other characteristics:	no

Re (a): The age is defined in terms of age at last birthday.

Re (g): Hours of work relate to the total number of hours worked during the week ending 28th April and to the total number of months worked during the 12 months ending 30th April.

6. Concepts and definitions:
(a) Economically active population: It comprises all persons aged 15 years and over who, during the reference periods, were either mainly employed or mainly looking for work, according to the definitions given below. The definition also includes all members of the armed forces.

(b) Employment: The specific questions used to determine whether or not a person was to be counted as employed are "What was your main activity during the 12 months ending 30th April?" and "What was your main activity during the week ending 28th April?." The possible answers were: 1) worked; 2) with job not working; 3) looked for work; 4) home duties; 5) student; 6) retired; 7) incapacitated; 8) other; 9) not stated.

It is reported that the following categories are included:

i)   persons doing unpaid work in family firm or business;
ii)   employed persons, temporarily absent from work;
iii) working students with a part time job;
iv)   seasonal or occasional workers;
v)   conscripts for military/civilian service;
vi)   apprentices and trainees.

Only categories (i), (ii) and (iii) can be identified separately.

(c) Unemployment: Among persons aged 15 years and over, a category of persons who were mainly looking for work during the reference periods can be identified.

7. Classifications used:
Both employed persons and unemployed persons previously employed are classified by industry, by occupation and by status in employment.

(a) Industry: Based on the question: "In which industry or type of business did you work during the past 12 months?." For coding industry, the ISIC-rev.3 has been used to the tabulation category (1-digit) level.

(b) Occupation: Based on the question: "What was your main type of job or occupation during the past 12 months?." For coding occupation, the ISCO-88 has been used to the major group (1-digit) level.

(c) Status in employment: Based on the question: "During the 12 months ending 30th April, did you work for an employer or for yourself?" ("Worked for employer" includes: government; private enterprises; private households; unpaid family workers. "Worked for self" includes: for self, with paid help and for self, without paid help). For coding status in employment, the six groups above were used. A seventh group ("not stated") was also used.

8. Main differences compared with the previous census:
No major difference.

9. Publication of the census results:
The final census data on the economically active population and its components was issued in 1995 in a publication entitled "1990 Population Census of Barbados."

The organization responsible for the publication is the Barbados Statistical Service, Fairchild Street, Bridgetown.

Possibilities also exist for obtaining census data on diskettes and tapes.

BELGIUM

1. Name and address of the organization responsible for the census:
Institut national de Statistique (INS), 44 rue de Louvain, 1000 Brussels.

2. Population censuses conducted since 1945 (years):
1947, 1961, 1970, 1981 and 1991. The present description relates to the 1991 population and housing census (held on 1st March).

3. Coverage of the census:
(a) Geographical scope: Whole territory.

(b) Persons covered: All persons of all ages usually resident in Belgium, i.e. including foreigners resident in Belgium and nationals temporarily resident abroad, but excluding persons in

transit through the country and persons who have not obtained the authorization for definitive registration (temporary residence permit).

4. Reference period:
The day of the census, but reference was also made to the usual situation of the surveyed person.

5. Main topics:
(a) Total population, by sex and age:	yes
Economically active population by:	
(b) Sex and age group:	yes
(c) Industry:	yes
(d) Occupation:	yes
(e) Status in employment:	yes
(f) Highest educational level:	yes
(g) Hours of work:	yes
(h) Other characteristics:	yes

Re (a): The age is defined either in terms of year of birth or in terms of age at last birthday; however, most of the available tables are based on the latter approach.

Re (g): Hours of work relate to the normal hours of work (as regards employed persons) and to actual hours worked (for employed persons at work), during the reference period.

Re (h): The census also covers information on the means of travel and travel time to and from the workplace.

6. Concepts and definitions:
(a) Economically active population: It comprises all persons aged 14 years and over who, at the time of the census, were either employed or unemployed, according to the definitions given below. The definition also covers professional members of the armed forces and conscripts; the latter are classified as part of the non-employed economically active population.

(b) Employment: Considered as "employed" are all persons who answered yes to the question "Do you have an occupation, function or any economic activity? (Answer yes if this is a temporary occupation, function or activity, or if it does not represent your primary source of income; family workers should also answer yes; answer yes even if you are not actually engaged in the occupation at the time of the census owing to sickness, leave, short hours, labour dispute, etc.)"

It is reported that the following categories are included:
i) persons doing unpaid work in family firm or business;
ii) persons engaged in the production of primary products for own consumption;
iii) working students with a part-time job;
iv) seasonal or occasional workers who were working on the date of the census;
v) conscripts for military/civilian service;
vi) multiple-job holders;
vii) apprentices and trainees.

Only persons falling in categories (i), (iii), (v), (vi) and (vii) can be identified separately by means of their responses to specific questions. Apprentices and trainees, however, can be identified separately only if they are bound by a contract.

(c) Unemployment: Considered as "unemployed" are all persons who, at the time of the census, were without work and seeking work, including first-time jobseekers. Students seeking work are excluded from the definition.

7. Classifications used:
Only employed persons are classified by industry, by occupation and by status in employment.

(a) Industry: Surveyed persons were asked to provide the name of the establishment, institution or administration where they work or which they manage; and the nature of its activities (special instructions are given to avoid confusion with the person's occupation).

For coding industry, 809 groups matching the General Nomenclature of Economic Activities in the European Communities (NEAE, rev.1) were used. Links to the ISIC-rev.2 have been established at the most detailed level possible. The establishment of links to the ISIC-rev.3 was under consideration.

(b) Occupation: Based on the questions: "Describe your occupation or function in such a way as to permit a determination of the nature of your work"; "Indicate your current grade, describe your current function or specify the skill mentioned on any appointment order, employment contract or similar document"; "Identify the service or branch where you work, within the firm, institution or administration where you are employed

(reception; purchasing and procurement; production and manufacturing; sales and shipping; bookkeeping and finance, etc."

For coding occupation, some 1,700 groups of the National Classification of Occupations were used. Links to the ISCO-88 have been established to the minor group (3-digit) level.

(c) Status in employment: Based on the question: "Which category describes your status in employment?: self-employed, head of establishment or business, not bound by labour contract; head of establishment or business bound by labour contract; assistant (to a self-employed person); public sector employee; public sector worker; private sector employee; private sector worker; apprentice bound by an apprenticeship contract; domestic or service staff?." For coding status in employment, the nine groups above were used. Self-employed persons and heads of establishment or business not bound by labour contract, were asked: "Do you employ paid staff? If so, how many persons?." All others were asked: "Do you manage or supervise other persons? If so, how many?."

8. Main differences compared with the previous census:
The only change concerned the procedure for collecting data. In earlier censuses, census agents handed out questionnaires and collected them during a subsequent visit. In 1991, personalized forms generated on the basis of information contained in the National Register were mailed to surveyed persons. Census agents, who had lists of all forms mailed out in their district, then visited the corresponding households and:
– collected the completed forms;
– if necessary, distributed new forms to persons who had not received or had lost the personalized forms, whether or not the names of such persons were included on their list of residents.

The personalized forms were processed with an optical scanner, which helped to speed up their examination.

9. Publication of the census results:
The title of the publication containing the final results on the economically active population is "Recensement général de la population du 1.3.1991 - Population active" (1994).

The organization responsible for the publication is Institut national de Statistique, Brussels.

The results of the 1991 census are also available in the form of tables, microfiche, diskettes, CD-ROM and magnetic tapes.

BELIZE

1. Name and address of the organization responsible for the census:
Central Statistical Office, Ministry of Finance, Belmopan.

2. Population censuses conducted since 1945 (years):
1946, 1960, 1970, 1980 and 1991. The present description relates to the 1991 population census (held on 12 May).

3. Coverage of the census:
(a) Geographical scope: Whole area.

(b) Persons covered: All persons of all ages.

4. Reference period:
The week and the 12 months preceding the census day.

5. Main topics:
(a) Total population, by sex and age:	yes
Economically active population by:	
(b) Sex and age group:	yes
(c) Industry:	yes
(d) Occupation:	yes
(e) Status in employment:	yes
(f) Highest educational level:	yes
(g) Hours of work:	yes
(h) Other characteristics:	yes

Re (a): The age is defined in terms of age at last birthday.

Re (g): The census collected information on the number of months worked by employed persons during the long reference period, and on the number of hours worked by employed persons during the short reference period.

Re (h): The census collected information on income and on means of transport used to travel to work (walk, bicycle, private car or vehicle, public transport, hired transport, etc.).

6. Concepts and definitions:

(a) Economically active population: It comprises all persons aged 15 years and over who, during the 12-month reference period, were either employed or unemployed according to the definitions below. Armed forces residing in private households are included, whereas members of the armed forces residing in Army Camps are excluded.

(b) Employment: Considered as "employed" are all persons who most worked during the reference periods. The questions used to determine if a person is to be counted as employed are: "What did you do most during the past 12 months?" and "What did you do most during the past week?." The possible answers are: 1) worked; 2) had a job but did not work; 3) looked for work; 4) wanted work and available; 5) home duties; 6) attended school; 7) retired; 8) disabled, unable to work; 9) other; 10) not stated.

It is reported that the following categories are included:
i)   persons doing unpaid work in family firm or business;
ii)   persons engaged in the production of primary products for own consumption;
iii) employed persons, temporarily absent from work;
iv)   working students with a part-time job, if their work takes precedence over their studies;
v)   seasonal or occasional workers;
vi)   conscripts for military/civilian service.

Categories (i), (iii), (iv) and (v) can be identified separately, in combination with other questions.

(c) Unemployment: Considered as "unemployed" are all persons who, during the reference periods, most wanted work, were available and looking for work. The definition excludes students seeking work.

7. Classifications used:
Employed persons and unemployed persons previously employed were classified by industry and by occupation. Only employed persons were classified by status in employment.

(a) Industry: Based on the question: "What type of business is/was carried on at your workplace?." For coding industry, the national classification was used. Links to the ISIC-rev.3 have been established to the classes (4-digit) level.

(b) Occupation: Based on the question: "What sort of work do/did you do in your main occupation?." For coding occupation, the national classification was used. Links to the ISCO-88 have been established to the unit group (4-digit) level.

(c) Status in employment: Based on the question: "Did you carry on your own business, work for a wage or salary or work as an unpaid worker in a family business?." Six groups were used for coding status in employment, namely: paid employee (Government); paid employee (private); unpaid worker; own business with paid help (employer); own business without paid help (own account); not stated.

8. Main differences compared with the previous census:
In the 1980 census, only a long reference period (12 months) was used.

9. Publication of the census results:
The final data were issued in 1992 in the publication entitled "Major Findings - 1991 Population and Housing Census."

The organization responsible for the publication is the Central Statistical Office in Belmopan, Ministry of Finance.

Unpublished tables and data on diskettes are also available from the Central Statistical Office.

BENIN

1. Name and address of the organization responsible for the census:
Institut National de la Statistique et de l'Analyse Economique, Bureau central du recensement, B.P. 323, Cotonou.

2. Population censuses conducted since 1945 (years):
1979 and 1992. The present description relates to the 1992 census (held from 15 to 29 February).

3. Coverage of the census:

(a) Geographical scope: Whole territory.

(b) Persons covered: All persons of all ages, except members of the diplomatic corps and nationals residing abroad.

4. Reference period:
The three-month period preceding the day of the interview.

5. Main topics:
(a) Total population, by sex and age:	yes
Economically active population by:	
(b) Sex and age group:	yes
(c) Industry:	yes
(d) Occupation:	yes
(e) Status in employment:	yes
(f) Highest educational level:	yes
(g) Hours of work:	no
(h) Other characteristics:	no

Re (a): The age is defined in terms of age at last birthday.

6. Concepts and definitions:

(a) Economically active population: It comprises all persons aged 10 years and over who, during the reference period, were either employed or unemployed, according to the definitions given below. However, published data relating to the economically active population, employment and unemployment refer only to persons aged from 10 to 65 years. The definition covers all members of the armed forces. Working students with a part-time job and students seeking work are excluded from the definition.

(b) Employment: Considered as "employed" are all persons who worked at least one week during the reference period (the previous three months). Also considered as employed are women who, in addition to household work, also worked on their own account or in a family business (salesperson, seamstress, farmer, potter). The question used is: "Occupation: Employed; first-time jobseeker; unemployed; homemaker; pupil or student; self-sufficient."

It is reported that the following categories are included:
i)   persons doing unpaid work in family firm or business;
ii)   persons engaged in the production of primary products for own consumption;
iii) employed persons, temporarily absent from work;
iv)   seasonal or occasional workers;
v)   conscripts for military/civilian service;
vi)   apprentices and trainees.

Only persons belonging to categories (i) and (vi) can be identified separately.

(c) Unemployment: Considered as "unemployed" are all persons who had been previously employed but who, during the reference period, were without work and seeking work. First-time jobseekers are identified separately.

7. Classifications used:
Both employed persons and unemployed persons previously employed are classified by industry, by occupation and by status in employment.

(a) Industry: Based on the question: "What is the primary activity of the worker's enterprise or employer?" In respect of unemployed persons, the industry is determined by reference to their last employment. For coding industry, nine groups were used. Links to the ISIC-rev.2 have been established to the division (1-digit) level.

(b) Occupation: Census agents were asked to put the question according to the instruction manual, which refers to the primary occupation or major activity of the person in question during the reference period. For unemployed persons, the question concerned the last occupation prior to the reference period. Respondents were asked to avoid vague replies such as: merchant, official, etc..., but to specify, for example: seller of cloth, seller of fritters, police inspector, tax inspector, etc... For coding occupation, nine groups were used. Links to the ISCO-68 have been established to the major group (1-digit) level.

(c) Status in employment: Based on the question: "What was the employed person's status in employment during the reference period?." For coding this variable, eight groups were used, namely: self-employed; employer; permanent employee; temporary employee; member of a cooperative; apprentice; family helper; other.

8. Main differences compared with the previous census:
The 1979 census had used the month preceding the census date as the reference period.

9. Publication of the census results:

The final data were published in December 1993 in the following publication: "Deuxième recensement général de la population et de l'habitation, février 1992," Volume I, résultats définitifs.

The organization responsible for this publication is Institut National de la Statistique et de l'analyse économique, Bureau central du recensement (BCR), B.P. 323, Cotonou.

The census data is also available in the form of Bernoulli cartridges.

BERMUDA

1. Name and address of the organization responsible for the census:

Bermuda Government Statistical Department, P.O. Box HM 177, Hamilton HM AX.

2. Population censuses conducted since 1945 (years):

1950, 1960, 1970, 1980 and 1991. The present description relates to the 1991 census (held on 20 May).

3. Coverage of the census:

(a) Geographical scope: Whole country.

(b) Persons covered: All persons of all ages.

4. Reference period:

The week and the 12-months period preceding the census day.

5. Main topics:

(a) Total population, by sex and age:	yes
Economically active population by:	
(b) Sex and age group:	yes
(c) Industry:	yes
(d) Occupation:	yes
(e) Status in employment:	yes
(f) Highest educational level:	yes
(g) Hours of work:	yes
(h) Other characteristics:	yes

Re (a): The age is defined in terms of the number of years on the day of the census.

Re (g): Persons aged 16 years and over are asked to specify how many months, if any, did they work for pay during the past 12 months, either for an employer or in their own business. Employed persons are asked how many hours they normally work in a typical week, including overtime whether they are paid for it or not.

Re (h): The census also collected information on means of transport used to travel to workplace, time to start work and income range.

6. Concepts and definitions:

(a) Economically active population: It comprises all persons aged 16 years and over who, during the short reference period, were either employed or unemployed, according to the definitions given below. Members of the armed forces are included in the definition.

(b) Employment: Considered as "employed" are all persons who, during the reference week, performed any work of an economical value, either for an employer or in their own business. The question used to determine whether or not a person was to be counted as employed was: "Last week, what were you doing most, for example, were you working for pay, looking for another job, attending school, keeping house, or carrying on some other activity?." The possible answers were: 1) working for pay; 2) with job but not at work; 3) looking for work; 4) engaged in home duties; 5) voluntary work without pay; 6) full-time student; 7) unable to work; 8) retired; 9) other; 10) not stated.

It is reported that the following categories are included:

i) persons doing unpaid work in family firm or business;
ii) persons engaged in the production of primary products for own consumption;
iii) employed persons, temporarily absent from work;
iv) working students with a part time job;
v) seasonal or occasional workers;
vi) conscripts for military/civilian service;
vii) multiple-job holders;
viii) apprentices and trainees.

Only persons belonging to categories i), iii) and vii) can be identified separately.

(c) Unemployment: Considered as "unemployed" are all persons who, during the reference week, did not work but were seeking a job for the first time, or trying to get another job, having discontinued a previous job for any reason.

7. Classifications used:

Only employed persons are classified by industry, by occupation and by status in employment.

(a) Industry: Based on the question: "What kind of business or activity is mainly carried on at your (main) place of work? e.g. bank, primary school, lawyers offices, retail clothing store, restaurant, etc." For coding Industry, 18 groups of the national classification were used. Links to the ISIC-rev.2 have been established to the major-division (1-digit) level.

(b) Occupation: Based on the question: "What kind of work do you do in your (main) job? e.g. sales clerk, civil engineer, printing shop supervisor, auto mechanic, etc." National classification has been used for coding occupation. Links to the ISCO-68 have been established.

(c) Status in employment: Based on the question: "Were you self-employed or working for someone else in your (main) job last week?." Seven groups were used for coding status in employment: Self-employed: with paid help (employer), without paid help; Worked for someone else: as Bermuda Government employee, as employee of a foreign government, as employee of a private company/ person, as unpaid worker in family business or farm, and not stated.

8. Main differences compared with the previous census:

Most of the data items included on the census questionnaire tend to be carried over from one census to the next in order to establish whether significant changes have occured. Bermuda's questionnaire provides for this but it also seeks to establish new data in a few areas: (a) journey to work and work location; (b) physical and mental health conditions as they constrain the activities of daily life for some persons; and (c) personal income.

9. Publication of the census results:

The final data were issued in the publication entitled "The 1991 Census of Population and Housing" in March 1993, and the "1991 Map Supplement" in November 1993.

The organization responsible for these publications is the Bermuda Government Statistics Department, P.O. Box HM 177, Hamilton HM AX.

Unpublished tables on the census results are available upon request from the Bermuda Government Statistics Department.

BOLIVIA

1. Name and address of the organization responsible for the census:

Instituto Nacional de Estadística (INE), Plaza Mario Guzman Aspiazu No. 1, Casilla 6129, La Paz.

2. Population censuses conducted since 1945 (years):

1950, 1976 and 1992. The present description relates to the 1992 population census (held on 3 June).

3. Coverage of the census:

(a) Geographical scope: Whole country.

(b) Persons covered: All persons of all ages, except nationals residing abroad.

4. Reference period:

The week preceding the census date.

5. Main topics:

(a) Total population, by sex and age:	yes
Economically active population by:	
(b) Sex and age group:	yes
(c) Industry:	yes
(d) Occupation:	yes
(e) Status in employment:	yes
(f) Highest educational level:	...
(g) Hours of work:	no
(h) Other characteristics:	no

Re (a): The age is defined in terms of age at last birthday.

6. Concepts and definitions:

(a) Economically active population: It comprises all persons aged 7 years and over who, during the reference week, were either employed or unemployed, according to the definitions given below. The definition excludes conscripts in military or civilian service, but includes professional members of the armed forces.

(b) Employment: Considered as "employed" are all persons aged 7 years and over who reported that they had worked during the reference week.

It is reported that the following categories are included:

i)   persons doing unpaid work in family firm or business;
ii)   persons engaged in the production of primary products for own consumption;
iii) employed persons temporarily absent from work;
iv)   working students with a part-time job;
v)   seasonal or occasional workers;
vi)   multiple job holders;
vii) apprentices and trainees.

Only persons falling in categories (i), (iii) and (vi) can be identified separately by means of their responses to specific questions.

(c) Unemployment: Considered as "unemployed" are all persons who, during the reference week, were without work and seeking work. The questions used to determine if the person was unemployed are "Were you seeking work and have you been previously employed?" and "Were you seeking work for the first time?."

7. Classifications used:

Only employed persons were classified by industry, by occupation and by status in employment.

(a) Industry: Based on the question: "What does the establishment where you work (or last worked) produce, or what is its activity?." To determine industry group, employed persons were asked to give the name, address and economic sector of the enterprise, establishment or administration in which they were employed or which they managed. For coding industry, the ISIC-rev.3 was used to the 4-digit level.

(b) Occupation: Based on the question: "What was your primary occupation last week (or your most recent occupation, if then unemployed)?." To determine occupation group, employed persons were asked to identify as accurately as possible their occupation or activity at that time. For coding occupation, the ISCO-88 was used to the minor group (3-digit) level.

(c) Status in employment: The following seven categories were used to determine status in employment: employee, worker, self-employed, proprietor or employer, member of a cooperative, self-employed professional, family worker.

8. Main differences compared with the previous census:
No major differences.

9. Publication of the census results:
The final census data were published in May 1993.

The title of the publication containing the final census results is "Censo Nacional de Población y Vivienda 1992: Resultados finales."

The organization responsible for this publication is Instituto Nacional de Estadística, Plaza Mario Guzman Aspiazu No. 1, Casilla 6129, La Paz.

The census data are also available in other formats: archives (working papers); published detailed results (sociodemographic indicators of regional capitals, broken down by census zones, and of provinces); and data base on diskettes.

BOTSWANA

1. Name and address of the organization responsible for the census:
Central Statistics Office, Private Bag 0024, Gaborone.

2. Population censuses conducted since 1945 (years):
1946, 1956, 1964, 1971, 1981 and 1991. The present description relates to the 1991 population census (held during the period 14-28 August).

3. Coverage of the census:

(a) Geographical scope: Whole country.

(b) Persons covered: All persons of all ages.

4. Reference period:
The month prior to the day of interview.

5. Main topics:

(a) Total population, by sex and age:	yes
Economically active population by:	
(b) Sex and age group:	yes
(c) Industry:	yes
(d) Occupation:	yes
(e) Status in employment:	yes
(f) Highest educational level:	yes
(g) Hours of work:	no
(h) Other characteristics:	no

Re (a): The age is defined in terms of age at last birthday.

6. Concepts and definitions:

(a) Economically active population: It comprises all persons aged 12 years and over who, during the reference month, were either employed or unemployed, according to the definitions given below. The definition includes members of the armed forces.

(b) Employment: Considered as "employed" are all persons who, during the reference month, performed any work for cash, either for themselves or for someone else. The definition also includes those persons working at the family lands or at the cattleposts.

It is reported that the following categories are included:

i)   persons doing unpaid work in family firm or business;
ii)   persons engaged in the production of primary products for own consumption;
iii) employed persons, temporarily absent from work;
iv)   working students with a part time job;
v)   seasonal or occasional workers.

Only persons belonging to the categories (i) and (ii) can be identified separately.

(c) Unemployment: Considered as "unemployed" are all persons who, during the reference month, were without work and actively seeking work. Students seeking work are excluded from the definition.

7. Classifications used:
Only employed persons are classified by industry, by occupation and by status in employment.

(a) Industry: Based on the question: "What was the main product, service or activity of X's place of work?." For coding industry, nine groups of the national classification were used. Links to the ISIC-rev.2 have been established to the major division (1-digit) level.

(b) Occupation: Based on the question: "What type of work did X do?." For coding occupation, 10 groups of the national classification were used. Links to the ISCO-88 have been established to the major group (1-digit) level.

(c) Status in employment: Employed persons were asked to specify their status in employment. For coding status in employment, the two main following groups were used: employees (i.e. persons who have worked for somebody else for wages, salaries, fees, commission and the like) and self-employed (i.e. those who are in business for themselves, for example: farmers who farm with specific intention of selling their products, store owners, hawkers and people such as those who repair shoes or cut hair under a tree, etc.).

8. Main differences compared with the previous census:
1991 information included occupation of people who were reported working in family business and at lands/farm/cattlepost.

9. Publication of the census results:
The final data have been issued in 1994 in a publication entitled "1991 Population and Housing Census Administrative/Technical Report and National Statistical Tables."

The organization responsible for this publication is the Central Statistics Office, Private Bag 0024, Gaborone.

The census data is also available in other forms, such as diskettes and unpublished tables.

BRAZIL

1. Name and address of the organization responsible for the census:
Instituto Brasileiro de Geografía e Estatística (IBGE/DPE/DEPOP), Rua Visconde de Niterói, 1246/Bloco B - 8o andar, Rio de Janeiro, RJ.

2. Population censuses conducted since 1945 (years):
1950, 1960, 1970, 1980 and 1991. The present description relates to the 1991 population census (held on 1st September).

3. Coverage of the census:
(a) Geographical scope: Whole country.

(b) Persons covered: All persons of all ages, except aborigines.

4. Reference period:
One year (from 1st September 1990 to 31 August 1991).

5. Main topics:
(a) Total population, by sex and age: yes
Economically active population by:
(b) Sex and age group: yes
(c) Industry: yes
(d) Occupation: yes
(e) Status in employment: yes
(f) Highest educational level: yes
(g) Hours of work: yes
(h) Other characteristics: yes

Re (a): The age is defined in terms of month and year of birth or, if the latter is not known, in terms of assumed age.
Re (g): Relates to the usual weekly hours worked by employed persons, both in the main job and in other jobs held.
Re (h): Relates to income from the main job and other jobs held.

6. Concepts and definitions:
(a) Economically active population: It comprises all persons aged 10 years and over who, during the reference year, were either employed or unemployed, according to the definitions given below. All members of the armed forces are included in the definition. Questions regarding employment and unemployment refer only to a 20 per cent sampling of households in municipalities with a population of 15,000 or less, and to a 10 per cent sampling in municipalities with a population in excess of 15,000.

(b) Employment: Considered as "employed" are all persons who, during the reference year, worked for pay, profit or grant, etc., and unpaid family workers who worked for a minimum of 15 hours per week, helping a family member with whom they live, and who replied yes to the question "Did you work during part or all of the past 12 months (from 1/9/1990 to 31/8/1991)?."

It is reported that the following categories are included:
i) persons doing unpaid work in family firm or business;
ii) employed persons, temporarily absent from work;
iii) working students with a part-time job;
iv) seasonal or occasional workers;
v) conscripts for military/civilian service;
vi) multiple job holders;
vii) apprentices and trainees.

Only persons falling in categories (i), (iii) and (vi) can be identified separately by means of their replies to specific questions.

(c) Unemployment: Considered as "unemployed" are all persons who did not work but looked for work during the reference year, whether or not previously employed, and who replied no to the question used to define employment.

7. Classifications used:
Only employed persons were classified by industry, by occupation and by status in employment.

(a) Industry: To determine industry group, employed persons were asked to give the name of the firm, organization, institution, etc. where they are engaged in their primary occupation. For coding this variable, 26 groups of the national classification of economic activities were used, which are compatible with the ISIC-rev.2 to the major division (1-digit) level.

(b) Occupation: To determine occupation group, employed persons were asked to specify the occupation, job, function, etc., they usually carried on during the reference year. In case

the person had definitively changed his/her occupation during that period, reference is made to the current, rather than usual, occupation. For coding this variable, 10 major groups of the national classification of occupations were used, which are comparable with ISCO-68 at the major group (1-digit) level.

(c) Status in employment: To determine this variable, employed persons were asked to indicate their position in the firm, organization or institution in which they work. Coding was based on 11 categories (temporary agricultural worker; household worker (employed or self-employed); sharecropper (employed or self-employed); public sector employee (public service or state-owned enterprise); private sector employee; self-employed worker; employer; unpaid worker).

8. Main differences compared with the previous census:
The 1980 census used two reference periods, namely, a long period (one year) to define the economically active population, employment and unemployment, and a short period (the week preceding the census) to measure the characteristics of the population.

9. Publication of the census results:
The final census results were published in 1993.

The organization responsible for publishing the census results is Instituto Brasileiro de Geografia e Estatistica, Av. Franklin Roosevelt 166, 10o. andar Centro, Rio de Janeiro, RJ.

The census results are also available in the forms of unpublished tables, diskettes, magnetic tapes and microfiches.

BRUNEI DARUSSALAM

1. Name and address of the organization responsible for the census:
Economic Planning Unit, Ministry of Finance, Bandar Seri Begawan 2012, Brunei Darussalam.

2. Population censuses conducted since 1945 (years):
1971, 1981 and 1991. The present description relates to the 1991 population census (held on 6 August).

3. Coverage of the census:
(a) Geographical scope: Whole country.

(b) Persons covered: All persons of all ages.

4. Reference period:
The week preceding the enumeration.

5. Main topics:
(a) Total population, by sex and age: yes
Economically active population by:
(b) Sex and age group: yes
(c) Industry: yes
(d) Occupation: yes
(e) Status in employment: yes
(f) Highest educational level: yes
(g) Hours of work: yes
(h) Other characteristics: yes

Re (a): The age is defined in terms of date of birth.
Re (g): Employed persons were asked to specify their actual hours of work during the reference period.
Re (h): The census also collected information on gross monthly income from work and on bonus received in the last 12 months.

6. Concepts and definitions:
(a) Economically active population: It comprises all persons aged 15 years and over who, during the reference week, were either employed or unemployed, according to the definitions given below. The definition covers all members of the armed forces but excludes working students with a part time job and students seeking work.

(b) Employment: Considered as "employed" are all persons who stated that they were working during the reference period. The question used to determine if a person is to be counted as employed was "Economic activity: working; seeking for job; other."

It is reported that the following categories are included:
i) persons doing unpaid work in family firm or business;
ii) persons engaged in the production of primary products for own consumption;
iii) employed persons, temporarily absent from work.
iv) seasonal or occasional workers;

v) conscripts for military/civilian service;
vi) apprentices and trainees.

None of the above categories can be identified separately.

(c) Unemployment: Considered as "unemployed" are all persons who stated that they were seeking for job during the reference period. To determine if a person is to be counted as unemployed, the question used was the same as that indicated under 6 (b) above.

7. Classifications used:
Only employed persons are classified by industry, by occupation and by status in employment.

(a) Industry: Employed persons were asked to specify the name and address of their employer/company, and to state in detail the industry of their employer/company. For coding industry, 10 groups from the national classification were used. Links to the ISIC-rev.3 have been established to the tabulation category (1-digit) level.

(b) Occupation: Employed persons were asked to state in detail their occupation. For coding occupation, 10 groups of the national classification were used. Links to the ISCO-88 have been established to the major group (1-digit) level.

(c) Status in employment: Employed persons were asked to specify their status in employment. For coding this variable, four groups were used: employer; employee; own account worker; family worker.

8. Main differences compared with the previous census:
No major difference.

9. Publication of the census results:
The final data have been published in 1993 in publications entitled "Report on the 1991 Population Census - June 1993" and "Summary Tables of the 1991 Population Census - January 1993."

The Organization responsible for these publications is the Economic Planning Unit, Ministry of Finance, B.S.B. 2012, Brunei Darussalam.

Other tables from the 1991 census which are not included in the publications are available on request, in hard copy only.

BULGARIA

1. Name and address of the organization responsible for the census:
Institut national de statistique, Division "Recensement de la population" 2, rue P. Volov, Sofia.

2. Population censuses conducted since 1945 (years):
1946, 1956, 1965, 1975, 1985 and 1992. The present description relates to the 1992 population census (held on 4 December).

3. Coverage of the census:

(a) Geographical scope: Whole territory.

(b) Persons covered: All persons of all ages.

4. Reference period:
The day of the census.

5. Main topics:
(a) Total population, by sex and age:	yes
Economically active population by:	
(b) Sex and age group:	yes
(c) Industry:	yes
(d) Occupation:	yes
(e) Status in employment:	no
(f) Highest educational level:	yes
(g) Hours of work:	no
(h) Other characteristics:	no

Re (a): The age is defined in terms of year of birth.

6. Concepts and definitions:

(a) Economically active population: It comprises all persons between the ages of 10 and 90 years who, on the census day, were either employed or unemployed, according to the definitions given below. Members of the armed forces are included in the definition.

(b) Employment: Considered as "employed" are all persons who replied yes to the question "Was the person working on 4.12.1992?."

It is reported that the following categories are included:

i) persons doing unpaid work in family firm or business;
ii) persons engaged in the production of primary products for own consumption;
iii) employed persons, temporarily absent from work;
iv) working students with a part time job;
v) seasonal or occasional workers;
vi) conscripts for military/civilian service;
vii) apprentices and trainees.

Only categories (ii) and (iv) can be identified separately.

(c) Unemployment: Considered as "unemployed" are all persons who stated that they were not working on the date of the census, and that they were without work and seeking work. Students seeking work are excluded from the definition.

7. Classifications used:
All persons, except unemployed persons, are classified by industry. Both employed persons and unemployed persons previously employed are classified by occupation.

(a) Industry: The question used concerns the workplace: name, main activity and address. For coding industry, 40 groups and 184 minor groups of the national classification were used. Links to the ISIC-rev.3 have been established to the division (2-digit) level.

(b) Occupation: Based on the question: "What is your occupation or function?." For coding occupation, 46 major groups and 642 minor groups were used. Links to the ISCO-88 have been established to the minor group (3-digit) level.

(c) Status in employment: There was no classification for this variable.

8. Main differences compared with the previous census:
The 1992 census was the first to identify unemployed persons.

Also, in 1985 a long reference period was used for the questions on economic activity (the three months preceding the date of the census); moreover, the lower age limit for inclusion in the economically active population was 16 years.

9. Publication of the census results:
The census results were published between 1993 and 1995 in a considerable number of publications, including "Demographic Characteristics (Volume I)" and "Socio-Economic Characteristics of the Population (Volume II)."

The organization responsible for these publications is l'Institut National de Statistique, Division "Recensement de la population," 2. rue P. Volov, Sofia.

The 1992 census results are also available in the form of unpublished tables and diskettes.

BURUNDI

1. Name and address of the organization responsible for the census:
Département de la Population, Bureau Central de Recensement, Pavillon administratif No. 3, B.P. 174, Gitega.

2. Population censuses conducted since 1945 (years):
1979 and 1990. The present description relates to the 1990 census (which refers to the night of 15 to 16 August).

3. Coverage of the census:

(a) Geographical scope: Whole territory.

(b) Persons covered: All persons of all ages.

4. Reference period:
The six months preceding the date of the census (in other words, 15 February to 15 August 1990). Persons who did not work at all during this period were asked if they had worked before.

5. Main topics:
(a) Total population, by sex and age:	yes
Economically active population by:	
(b) Sex and age group:	yes
(c) Industry:	yes
(d) Occupation:	yes
(e) Status in employment:	yes
(f) Highest educational level:	yes
(g) Hours of work:	no
(h) Other characteristics:	yes

Re (a): The age is defined in terms of age at last birthday.

Re (h): Information was also collected regarding the trade learned by employed persons and by unemployed persons.

6. Concepts and definitions:

(a) Economically active population: It comprises all persons aged 10 years and over who, during the reference period, were most either employed or unemployed, according to the definitions given below. The definition also includes members of the armed forces living in ordinary households (an "ordinary household" is generally defined as a group of persons, whether related or not, who share the same dwelling and who, in general, meet their food and other basic needs together. A household may be composed of one or more persons).

(b) Employment: Considered as "employed" are all persons who, during the reference period, most had an occupation, function or any economic activity. Farmers, livestock breeders and women who, in addition to household work, also engage regularly in field or other work for pay or income, are also covered by the definition. The question asked was: "During most of the six months preceding 15 August, was X: (1) employed; (2) unemployed; (3) student; (4) homemaker; (5) retired; (6) other." Working students with a part-time job are excluded from the definition.

It is reported that the following categories are included:

i) persons engaged in the production of primary products for own consumption;
ii) employed persons, temporarily absent from work;
iii) seasonal or occasional workers;
iv) conscripts (military or civilian service) living in ordinary households;
v) apprentices and trainees.

Only persons belonging to category (i) can be identified separately. Students who can work part time or occasionally (for example during the holidays), as well as persons doing unpaid work in family firm or business, although not part of the economically active population, may nevertheless be identified separately.

(c) Unemployment: Considered as "unemployed" are all persons who, during the reference period, had done no work and were looking either for their first job or for a new job. The definition also covers persons who, though wishing to work, were not actively seeking work because they considered that they had no chance of finding a job, as well as persons who were expecting to take up paid employment within the next 30 days.

7. Classifications used:

Only employed persons are classified by industry, by occupation and by status in employment.

(a) Industry: Based on the questions: "In what industry or branch of economic activity does Mr. or Mrs. X work?" and "What is the activity of the production unit (modern or traditional) in which Mr. or Mrs. X works?." The industry corresponds to the economic sector in which a person who reported a primary activity during the reference period was employed. For coding industry, 10 groups were used. Links to the ISIC-rev.2 have been established to the major division (1-digit) level.

(b) Occupation: Based on the question: "What was X's occupation during the six months preceding 15 August 1990?." The occupation corresponds to the type of work performed by an employed person; it is related, not to the rank, grade, function or trade of the person, but only to the nature of the work actually performed during the reference period. For coding occupation, 10 major groups were used. Links to the ISCO-88 have been established to the major group (1-digit) level.

(c) Status in employment: Based on the question: "As regards the occupation in question, was Mr. or Mrs. X: employer, employee, self-employed, apprentice, family helper or pieceworker?." For coding status in employment, the above six categories were used. Additional questions were asked to determine whether self-employed persons worked on their own account or employed other workers.

8. Main differences compared with the previous census:

In the 1979 census:

(a) The reference period used when asking questions on the economically active population, employment and unemployment was the week preceding the day of the census.

(b) The question on skills was not asked.

(c) The questions concerning industry, occupation and status in employment were asked of both employed persons and unemployed persons.

9. Publication of the census results:

The publication containing the final census results was to have come out in 1992.

The organization responsible for this publication is the Département de la Population, Bureau Central de Recensement, B.P. 174, Gitega.

The results of the 1990 census are also available in the form of unpublished tables containing raw data and diskettes.

CANADA

1. Name and address of the organization responsible for the census:

Statistics Canada, Jean-Talon Building, Section A-2, 5th floor, Tunney's Pasture, Ottawa.

2. Population censuses conducted since 1945 (years):

1951, 1961, 1971, 1976, 1981, 1986 and 1991. The present description relates to the 1991 population census (held on 4 June).

3. Coverage of the census:

(a) Geographical scope: Whole country.

(b) Persons covered: All persons of all ages, except foreign residents. The labour questions are asked of non-institutional residents 15 years of age and over.

4. Reference period:

The week prior to the census day. If the respondent did not work in the previous week, industry and occupation were to be reported for the job of longest duration since 1st January 1990.

5. Main topics:

(a) Total population, by sex and age:	yes

Economically active population by:

(b) Sex and age group:	yes
(c) Industry:	yes
(d) Occupation:	yes
(e) Status in employment:	yes
(f) Highest educational level:	yes
(g) Hours of work:	yes
(h) Other characteristics:	yes

Re (a): The age is defined either in terms of year of birth or of exact date of birth (day, month and year).

Re (g): Hours of work relate to hours actually worked by employed persons, at work.

Re (h): The census also covers information on other topics, namely: the incorporation status of businesses of self-employed persons; the number of weeks worked in the previous calendar year, whether these were mostly full time or part time weeks (not including housework, maintenance or repairs for own home); the sources of income, including earnings from employment.

6. Concepts and definitions:

(a) Economically active population: It comprises all persons aged 15 years and over who, during the reference week, were either employed or unemployed, according to the definitions given below. Questions on economic activity were asked of a 20 per cent sample. The definition covers all members of the armed forces.

(b) Employment: Considered as "employed" are all persons in the sample who, during the reference week, had a job and either worked hours or were temporarily absent from work (i.e. on temporary lay-off from a job to which they expected to return, or on vacation, strike or lock-out, on sick-leave or for other reasons). The questions used were: "Last week, how many hours did you work (not including volunteer work, housework, maintenance, or repairs for your own home)?," and "Last week, were you absent from your job or business?."

It is reported that the following categories are included:

i) persons doing unpaid work in family firm or business;
ii) some persons engaged in the production of primary products for own consumption;
iii) working students with a part-time job (post-secondary students only, and must have been available to start work during the reference week);

iv) seasonal or occasional workers;
v) conscripts for military/civilian service;
vi) apprentices and trainees.

Persons belonging to categories (i) and (iii), as well as employed persons, temporarily absent from work, can be identified separately by means of specific questions. The identification of working students may be misleading: respondents are asked if they attended school in the past nine months, i.e., since the previous September; this does not necessarily mean that they are still attending school in the reference week or at the same time as they are doing the job reported for industry and occupation (part-time, full-time work etc.).

(c) Unemployment: Considered as "unemployed" are all persons in the sample who, during the reference week, were without work or on lay-off and expected to return to their job, or had actively looked for work in the past four weeks and were available for work. Also included are persons who had definitive arrangements to start a new job in four weeks or less. The questions used were: "Last week, were you on temporary lay-off or absent from your job or business?"; "Last week, did you have definite arrangements to start a new job within the next four weeks?"; "Did you look for work during the past four weeks?"; and "Could you have started work last week had a job been available?."

7. Classifications used:
Both employed persons and unemployed persons previously employed in the sample are classified by industry, by occupation and by status in employment. Questions were asked of these persons concerning, respectively, their job or business during the reference week or their job of longest duration since 1st January 1990. Multiple job holders during the reference week were asked for the job at which they worked the most hours.

(a) Industry: Based on the questions: "For whom did you work? (name of firm, government agency, etc.; department, branch, division, section or plant)"; "What kind of business, industry or service was this? (for example, wheat farm, trapping, road maintenance, retail shoe store, secondary school, municipal police)"; and "At what address did you work?." For coding industry, 286 unit groups of the 1970 Standard Industrial Classification and 296 unit groups of the 1980 Standard Industrial Classification were used. Links to the ISIC have not been established; however, an approximation was done for providing data to ILO and other Agencies of the United Nations System at the major division (1-digit) level of ISIC-rev.2.

(b) Occupation: Based on the questions: "What kind of work were you doing? (for example, medical lab technician, accounting clerk, manager of civil engineering department, secondary school teacher, supervisor of data entry unit, food processing labourer, fishing guide; if in the armed forces: rank only)," and "In this work, what were your most important duties or activities? (for example, analysing blood samples, verifying invoices, co-ordinating civil engineering projects, teaching mathematics, organizing work schedules and monitoring data entry systems, cleaning vegetables, guiding fishing parties)." In addition, questions were asked on the address of usual workplace. For coding occupation, 496 unit groups of the 1971 Occupational Classification, 514 unit groups of the 1980 Standard Occupational Classification and 505 unit groups of the new National Occupational Classification were used. Links to the ISCO have not been established; however, an approximation was done for providing data to ILO and other Agencies of the UN System at the major group (1-digit) level of ISCO-68.

(c) Status in employment: Based on the questions: "In this job were you mainly: working for wages, salary, tips or commission; working without pay for your spouse or another relative in a family farm or business; self-employed without paid help (alone or in partnership); self-employed with paid help (alone or in partnership)?," and, for self-employed: "Was your farm or business incorporated?." For coding status in employment, the four groups above were used.

8. Main differences compared with the previous census:
Coverage of the population was expanded in 1991 to include refugee claimants, those having student or employment authorization, and those holding Minister's permits.

9. Publication of the census results:
The Nation Series publications containing the census results are: "Labour Force Activity" (cat. 93-324); "Labour Force Activity of Women by Presence of Children" (cat. 93-325);

"Industry and Class of Worker" (cat. 93-326), and "Occupation" (cat. 93-327), issued in 1993.

The organization responsible for these publications is Statistics Canada, Ottawa.

The census results are also available in the form of diskettes, magnetic tapes and CD-ROM.

CAPE VERDE

1. Name and address of the organization responsible for the census:
Ministério do Plano e das Finanças, Direcçao Geral de Estatística, Divisao de Censos e Inquéritos, C.P. 116, Praia.

2. Population censuses conducted since 1945 (years):
1960, 1970, 1980 and 1990. The present description relates to the 1990 census (held from 16 to 30 June).

3. Coverage of the census:
(a) Geographical scope: Whole territory.

(b) Persons covered: All persons of all ages, except national residents abroad.

4. Reference period:
The week preceding the date of the census.

5. Main topics:
(a) Total population, by sex and age:	yes
Economically active population by:	
(b) Sex and age group:	yes
(c) Industry:	yes
(d) Occupation:	yes
(e) Status in employment:	yes
(f) Highest educational level:	yes
(g) Hours of work:	no
(h) Other characteristics:	yes

Re (a): The age is defined in terms of year of birth.

Re (h): Non-working persons were also asked other questions concerning their primary means of subsistence.

6. Concepts and definitions:
(a) Economically active population: It comprises all persons aged 10 years and over who, during the reference week, were either employed or unemployed, according to the definitions given below. The definition also covers all members of the armed forces (career military staff and conscripts).

(b) Employment: Considered as "employed" are all persons who, during the reference week, had an occupation, function or any economic activity, whether paid or unpaid. The question asked was: "What is your situation as regards work: (1) employed; (2) unemployed and worked before; (3) unemployed and first-time jobseeker; (4) student; (5) homemaker; (6) retired or pensioner; (7) invalid or infirm; and (8) other."

It is reported that the following categories are included:
i) persons doing unpaid work in family firm or business;
ii) persons engaged in the production of primary products for own consumption;
iii) employed persons, temporarily absent from work;
iv) working students with a part time job;
v) seasonal or occasional workers;
vi) conscripts for military/civilian service;
vii) apprentices and trainees.

Only persons falling in categories (i), (vi) and (vii) can be identified separately by means of their responses to specific questions.

(c) Unemployment: Considered as "unemployed" are all persons who, during the reference week, were without work and were looking either for their first job or for a new job. The definition also covers persons who, though wishing to work, were not looking for work because they did not think they had any chance of finding a job.

7. Classifications used:
Both employed persons and unemployed persons previously employed are classified by industry, by occupation and by status in employment.

(a) Industry: Based on the question: "Indicate the activity of the firm where the person works or last worked." For coding industry, 10 groups of the national classification were used. Links to the ISIC-rev.2 have been established to the division (1-digit) level.

(b) Occupation: Based on the question: "Indicate the person's current or most recent primary occupation." For coding occupation, nine groups of the national classification were used. Links to the ISCO-68 have been established to the major group (1-digit) level.

(c) Status in employment: A specific question was asked of both employed persons and unemployed persons previously employed to determine their current or most recent status in employment. For coding status in employment seven groups were used: self-employed; employer; official or employee; day labourer; apprentice; member of a producers' co-operative; other unpaid worker.

8. Main differences compared with the previous census:
In the 1980 census, the questions concerning economic circumstances had been put to persons aged 7 years and over; nevertheless, published data on the economically active population and its component groups (employed and unemployed persons) was confined to persons aged 14 years and over.

9. Publication of the census results:
The title of the publication containing the census results is: "IIo recenseamento da Populaçao e Habitaçao - 1990," published in 1992.

The organization responsible for this publication is Direcçao Geral de Estatística, Ministério das Finanças e do Plano, Praia.

The results of the 1990 census are also available in the form of unpublished tables, diskettes and magnetic tapes.

CAYMAN ISLANDS

1. Name and address of the organization responsible for the census:
Statistics Office, Cayman Islands Government, Government Administration Building, George Town, Grand Cayman, B.W.I.

2. Population censuses conducted since 1945 (years):
1960, 1970, 1979 and 1989. The present description relates to the 1989 population census (held on 15 October).

3. Coverage of the census:

(a) Geographical scope: Whole country.

(b) Persons covered: All persons of all ages.

4. Reference period:
The week preceding the census day.

5. Main topics:
(a) Total population, by sex and age:	yes
Economically active population by:	
(b) Sex and age group:	yes
(c) Industry:	yes
(d) Occupation:	yes
(e) Status in employment:	yes
(f) Highest educational level:	yes
(g) Hours of work:	yes
(h) Other characteristics:	yes

Re (a): The age is defined in terms of age at last birthday.

Re (g): Employed persons were asked to specify the number of hours usually worked each week in their main job.

Re (h): The census also collected information on weekly income from the main job and on means of transport used to travel to workplace.

6. Concepts and definitions:

(a) Economically active population: It comprises all persons aged 15 years and over who, during the reference week, were either employed or unemployed, according to the definitions given below. The definition also includes all members of the armed forces.

(b) Employment: Considered as "employed" are all persons who, during the reference week, worked at least one hour. The specific question used to determine whether or not a person was to be counted as employed was "Did the person have a job at any time during the last week?."

It is reported that the following categories are included:

i) persons doing unpaid work in family firm or business;
ii) employed persons, temporarily absent from work;
iii) working students with a part time job;
iv) seasonal or occasional workers;
v) multiple job holders;

vi) apprentices and trainees.

Only persons belonging to the categories (i), (iii) and (v) can be identified separately.

(c) Unemployment: Considered as "unemployed" are all persons who, during the reference week, were without work, seeking and available for work.

7. Classifications used:
Both employed persons and unemployed persons previously employed are classified by industry, by occupation and by status in employment.

(a) Industry: Based on the question: "Please state the person's main employer (or last full time employer) and describe clearly what the employer makes or does, e.g. finance, hotels, retail, construction, etc." For coding industry, 65 groups of the national classification were used. Links to the ISIC-rev.3 have been established to the division (2-digit) level.

(b) Occupation: Based on the question: "What is the person's occupation (That is the job they usually spend the most time on - or last full time job)? e.g. lawyers, bankers, civil servants, electricians, plumbers, etc." For coding occupation, 94 groups of the national classification were used. Links to the ISCO-88 have been established to the minor group (3-digit) level.

(c) Status in employment: For coding this variable, four groups were used: self employed not employing others; self employed employing others; employed in a full time or part time job; unpaid work in a family business.

8. Main differences compared with the previous census:
No major difference.

9. Publication of the census results:
The final census data were issued in September 1990 in a publication entitled "Cayman Islands 1989 Census - Commentary and tabulations of results, volume I."

The organization responsible for the publication is the Economics and Statistics Office, Government Administration Building, George Town, Grand Cayman, B.W.I.

The census results are also available in the form of unpublished tables.

CENTRAL AFRICAN REP.

The description of the 1988 census in the Central African Republic is presented in this volume because it was not available when the first edition was published.

1. Name and address of the organization responsible for the census:
Ministère de l'Economie, du Plan, des Statistiques et de la Coopération internationale, Bureau Central du Recensement (BCR), B.P. 696, Bangui.

2. Population censuses conducted since 1945 (years):
1975 and 1988. The present description relates to the 1988 census, which was held from 8 to 22 December (reference date 15 December).

3. Coverage of the census:

(a) Geographical scope: Whole territory.

(b) Persons covered: All persons of all ages.

4. Reference period:
The seven days preceding the census day.

5. Main topics:
(a) Total population, by sex and age:	yes
Economically active population by:	
(b) Sex and age group:	yes
(c) Industry:	yes
(d) Occupation:	yes
(e) Status in employment:	yes
(f) Highest educational level:	yes
(g) Hours of work:	no
(h) Other characteristics:	no

Re (a): The age is defined in terms of age at last birthday for persons whose day, month and year of birth are known, and in terms of year of birth for all others.

6. Concepts and definitions:

(a) Economically active population: It comprises all persons aged 6 years and over who, during the reference period, were either employed or unemployed, according to the definitions

given below. The definition includes career members of the armed forces, but excludes conscripts.

(b) Employment: Considered as "employed" are all persons who reported having had an occupation, function or any economic activity during the reference period, for pay or otherwise, at home or elsewhere. Women who, in addition to household work, also engage regularly in field or other work, are also covered by the definition. Working students with a part-time job are excluded from the definition.

It is reported that the following categories are included:

i)   persons doing unpaid work in family firm or business (provided they work full-time);
ii)   persons engaged in the production of primary products for own consumption;
iii) employed persons, temporarily absent from work;
iv)   seasonal or occasional workers;
v)   apprentices and trainees.

Only persons falling in categories (i) and (v) can be identified separately by means of their responses to specific questions.

(c) Unemployment: Considered as "unemployed" are all persons who reported not having worked at all during the reference period. The definition covers both unemployed persons who had previously been employed, and first-time jobseekers.

It should be noted that the 1988 census had underestimated the extent of unemployment by around 6 per cent, owing to a short reference period (one week) and to insufficient information on hours of work. At the same time, the inclusion of temporary and informal sector workers had led to overstating the number of employed persons.

7. Classifications used:
Both employed persons and unemployed persons previously employed are classified by industry, by occupation and by status in employment.

(a) Industry: To determine industry group, the question asked concerned the activity of the establishment in which the person was (or had last been) employed. For coding industry, the ISIC-rev.2 has been used to the major division (1-digit) level.

(b) Occupation: Both employed persons and unemployed persons previously employed were asked a specific question to determine their current or most recent occupation group. For coding occupation, the ISCO-68 was used to the unit group (3-digit) level.

(c) Status in employment: A specific question was asked of both employed persons and unemployed persons previously employed to determine their current or most recent status. For coding status in employment, the following five categories were used: self-employed; employer; employee; family worker; unpaid apprentice.

8. Main differences compared with the previous census:
Essentially, the same questions and reference period had been used in the 1975 census to determine and describe the economically active population and its component groups (employed and unemployed).

As noted under 6 (c), the short one-week reference period, on the one hand, and the inclusion of temporary and informal sector workers, on the other, led respectively to underestimating the volume of unemployment and to overstating of the number of employed persons. It has therefore been proposed to review definitions and the reference period for the next census, which is planned for 1998.

9. Publication of the census results:
The results were to have been published in 1992 in the following volumes: "Tableaux statistiques," containing data on the economically active population and its component groups, and "Rapports d'analyse" (12 volumes devoted to 12 distinct topics).

The Bureau Central du Recensement (BCR), Division des Statistiques et des Etudes Economiques, in Bangui, is responsible for these publications.

All data concerning the 1988 census are stored on hard disk and can be copied to floppy diskettes.

CHAD

1. Name and address of the organization responsible for the census:
Bureau central du Recensement (B.C.R.), B.P. 453, Ndjamena.

2. Population censuses conducted since 1945 (years):
The present description relates to the 1993 population census (held from 1 to 15 April.

3. Coverage of the census:
(a) Geographical scope: Whole country, excluding six cantons in the eastern Logone prefecture (Béboto, Bodo, Békan, Kaba Roangar, Goré rural and Yamodo) and five villages in the Signar canton (Ouaddoï prefecture): Andjaména, Ardéba, Fosso, Hiné Hésseina and Hille Koukon, the Aouzou strip and several lake islands (owing to unsafe conditions).

(b) Persons covered: All persons of all ages, except members of the diplomatic and consular corps.

4. Reference period:
The week preceding the day of the interview, and for farmers the preceding year (the last rainy season).

5. Main topics:
(a) Total population, by sex and age:	yes
Economically active population by:	
(b) Sex and age group:	yes
(c) Industry:	yes
(d) Occupation:	yes
(e) Status in employment:	yes
(f) Highest educational level:	yes
(g) Hours of work:	no
(h) Other characteristics:	no

Re (a): The age is defined in terms of age at last birthday.

6. Concepts and definitions:
(a) Economically active population: It comprises all persons aged from 6 to 98 years who, during the reference period, were either employed or unemployed, according to the definitions given below. Working students with a part-time job and students seeking work are excluded from the definition, but members of the armed forces are included.

(b) Employment: Considered as "employed" are all persons who worked during the reference week, or during the last season, in the case of farmers. Women who, in addition to housework, are also engagee in fieldwork or trade, are considered as employed. The question used is: "Occupational situation: (1) employed; (2) unemployed; (3) first-time jobseeker; (4) homemaker; (5) retired/independent means; (6) student; and (7) other."

It is reported that the following categories are included:

i)   persons doing unpaid work in family firm or business;
ii)   persons engaged in the production of primary products for own consumption;
iii) employed persons, temporarily absent from work;
iv)   seasonal or occasional workers;
v)   apprentices and trainees.

Only persons belonging to categories (i) and (ii) can be identified separately.

(c) Unemployment: Considered as "unemployed" are all persons who had been previously employed but who, during the reference period, were without work and seeking work. First-time jobseekers are identified separately.

7. Classifications used:
Both employed persons and unemployed persons previously employed are classified by industry, by occupation and by status in employment.

(a) Industry: Based on the question: "Indicate the nature of the activity of the firm or business. If unable to do so, indicate the full name of the establishment." For coding industry group, the ISIC-rev.3 was used to the 2-digit level (60 divisions), with some modifications as regards recovery activities, an important component of the informal sector in Chad.

(b) Occupation: Occupation group is based on the current occupation of employed persons, on the most recent occupation of unemployed persons, and on the occupation which takes up the largest share of time, in respect of multiple job holders. Respondents were asked to give detailed replies, such as: cotton farmer, millet farmer, street vendor, vendor (oil, fish, vegetables, peanuts, rice, etc.), stall vendor (shoes, sugar, tea, etc.). For coding occupation, the ISCO-88 has been used to the sub-major group (2-digit) level.

(c) Status in employment: For coding this variable, six groups were used, namely: employee; self-employed; employer; family helper; unpaid apprentice; and other.

8. Main differences compared with the previous census:
Not applicable.

9. Publication of the census results:
The final data were published in April 1995 in the following publications: "Rapport de séminaire-atelier," "Rapport de synthèse" and "Rapport d'analyse de 10 thèmes."

The organization responsible for these publications is Bureau central du recensement, B.P. 453, Ndjamena.

The 1993 census results are also available in the form of tables containing raw data. A data base exists, but the data is not available on either diskettes or magnetic tapes.

CHILE

1. Name and address of the organization responsible for the census:
Instituto Nacional de Estadísticas (INE), Avda. Bulnes 418, Santiago, Chile.

2. Population censuses conducted since 1945 (years):
1952, 1960, 1970, 1982 and 1992. The present description relates to the 1992 population census (held on 22 April).

3. Coverage of the census:
(a) Geographical scope: Whole country.

(b) Persons covered: All persons of all ages.

4. Reference period:
The week prior to the census day.

5. Main topics:
(a) Total population, by sex and age:	yes
Economically active population by:	
(b) Sex and age group:	yes
(c) Industry:	yes
(d) Occupation:	yes
(e) Status in employment:	yes
(f) Highest educational level:	...
(g) Hours of work:	no
(h) Other characteristics:	no

Re (a): The age is defined in terms of age at last birthday.

6. Concepts and definitions:
(a) Economically active population: It comprises all persons aged 14 years and over who, during the reference week, were either employed or unemployed, according to the definitions given below. The definition also includes professional members of the armed forces, but excludes conscripts in compulsory military service.

(b) Employment: Considered as "employed" are all persons who, during the reference week, worked in a paid occupation. The question used is "Which of the following characterizes your situation last week? (1) Working for pay; (2) Not at work, but employed; (3) Doing unpaid work for a family member; (4) Previously employed and seeking work; (5) Seeking a first job; (6) Homemaker; (7) Student without a job; (8) Retired or pensioner and not working; (9) Permanently disabled; (10) Other."

It is reported that the following categories are included:
i) persons doing unpaid work in family firm or business;
ii) persons engaged in the production of primary products for own consumption;
iii) employed persons temporarily absent from work;
iv) working students with a part-time job;
v) seasonal or occasional workers, provided they were employed during the reference week;
vi) apprentices and trainees.

Only persons belonging to categories (i) and (iii) can be identified separately.

(c) Unemployment: Considered as "unemployed" are all persons who had no work during the reference week but had previously worked, or who had not previously worked and were actively looking for work during the reference week (first-time jobseekers).

7. Classifications used:
Both employed persons and unemployed persons previously employed are classified by industry, by occupation and by status in employment.

(a) Industry: To determine industry group, the question used is "What is the main activity of the establishment, enterprise, shop, factory, etc., where you work (or last worked, if now unemployed)? Examples: shirt factory, hospital, ministry, ranch, bank, supermarket, radio and TV repair, general goods store, etc.." For coding this variable, the ISIC-rev.3 was used to the group (3-digit) level.

(b) Occupation: To determine occupation group, the question used is "What is (was) your occupation, or what type of work do (did) you perform? Examples: construction worker, paediatrician, tailor, automobile mechanic, textile machine operator, hawker, etc.." For coding this variable, the ISCO-88 was used to the unit group (4-digit) level.

(c) Status in employment: To determine this variable, coded in five groups, the question used is "In this occupation, are (were) you proprietor or employer, self-employed, domestic employee, wage-earner (employee, labourer, day labourer), unpaid family worker?."

8. Main differences compared with the previous census:
No major difference.

9. Publication of the census results:
The final results were published in September 1993.

The title of the publication containing the final census data is "Resultados Generales - XVI Censo Nacional y V de Vivienda 1992."

The organization responsible for this publication is Instituto Nacional de Estadísticas, Avda. Bulnes 418, Santiago.

The census results are also available in the form of diskettes.

CHINA

1. Name and address of the organization responsible for the census:
State Statistical Bureau, 38 Yuetan Nanjie, Sanlihe, Beijing 100826.

2. Population censuses conducted since 1945 (years):
1953, 1964, 1982 and 1990. The present description relates to the 1990 population census (held on 1st July).

3. Coverage of the census:
(a) Geographical scope: Whole country.

(b) Persons covered: All persons of all ages.

4. Reference period:
The day and the month preceding the census day.

5. Main topics:
(a) Total population, by sex and age:	yes
Economically active population by:	
(b) Sex and age group:	yes
(c) Industry:	yes
(d) Occupation:	yes
(e) Status in employment:	no
(f) Highest educational level:	yes
(g) Hours of work:	no
(h) Other characteristics:	no

Re (a): The age is defined in terms of age at last birthday.

6. Concepts and definitions:
(a) Economically active population: It comprises all persons aged 15 years and over who, during the reference month, were either employed or unemployed, according to the definitions given below. The definition includes all members of the armed forces but excludes working students with a part time job and students seeking work.

(b) Employment: Considered as "employed" are all persons who receive remuneration for work or receive an income from a business. The definition includes those who hold a regular job at the census reference time and those who do not have a regular job but have a temporary job on June 30th 1990 and have participated in social labour for an accumulative period of over 16 days in June.

It is reported that the following categories are included:
i) employed persons, temporarily absent from work;
ii) seasonal or occasional workers;
iii) conscripts for military/civilian service;
iv) apprentices and trainees.

Only conscripts for military/civilian service can be enumerated separately.

(c) Unemployment: Considered as "unemployed" are all persons at working ages (15 to 50 for males and 15 to 45 for females), who are able to work, currently seeking jobs and who have registered at local government agencies as unemployed.

7. Classifications used:
Only employed are classified by industry and by occupation. No classification by status in employment was made.

(a) Industry: To determine industry group, employed persons were asked to state the name and specific activity of the establishment in which they worked or last worked. The name entered is an independant accounting unit of state ownership, collective ownership or jointownership, or of private entreprise. In case of large complex or large scale factory/ mine (e.g. a corporation, a large plant, etc.), the name of the subordinate unit is clearly identified. For instance, ironworks of iron and steel company, poultry/eggs department, etc. For coding industry, 13 groups of the national classification were used. Links to the ISIC-rev.2 have been established to the major division (1-digit) level.

(b) Occupation: Questions were asked of employed persons to determine the specific work performed or the work they had been engaged in. For example, industrial workers are registered as fitter, typesetter, driver, etc. Office workers may be classified as planner, statistician, secretary, etc. Persons with multiple jobs were asked to report the occupation that employed them most of the year. For coding occupation, eight groups from the national classification were used. Links to the ISCO-68 have been established to the major group (1-digit) level.

(c) Status in employment: No classification was made.

8. Main differences compared with the previous census:
Persons waiting for a job assignment were reported in the 1990 census as economically active whereas they were reported as economically inactive in the 1982 census.

Moreover, there was item on migration including residence place five years ago in the 1990 census.

9. Publication of the census results:
The final results of the population census were issued in August 1993 in the publication entitled "Tabulation on the 1990 Population Census of the People's Republic of China."

The organization responsible for the publication is the State Statistical Bureau, Sanlihe, Beijing.

COMOROS

1. Name and address of the organization responsible for the census:
Direction générale du Plan, Direction de la Statistique, B.P. 131, Moroni.

2. Population censuses conducted since 1945 (years):
1958, 1966, 1980 and 1991. The present description relates to the 1991 general population and housing census (held on 15 September).

3. Coverage of the census:
(a) Geographical scope: Whole area, excluding the Island of Mayotte (administered by France).

(b) Persons covered: All persons of all ages, except members of the diplomatic corps and their families.

4. Reference period:
One month (August 1991).

5. Main topics:
(a) Total population, by sex and age:	yes
Economically active population by:	
(b) Sex and age group:	yes
(c) Industry:	yes
(d) Occupation:	yes
(e) Status in employment:	yes
(f) Highest educational level:	yes
(g) Hours of work:	no
(h) Other characteristics:	yes

Re (a): The age is defined in terms of age at last birthday.

Re (h): Information was also collected on the monthly remuneration of employees.

6. Concepts and definitions:
(a) Economically active population: It comprises all persons aged 12 years and over who, during the reference period, were either employed or unemployed, according to the definitions given below. Members of the armed forces are excluded from the definition.

(b) Employment: Employment is determined on the basis of the question: "During the month of August, was X: permanent employee; temporary employee; unemployed; first-time jobseeker; homemaker; pupil or student; retired or of independent means; other non-working person." Considered as "permanently employed" are employed persons permanently engaged in an economic activity who worked at least three weeks during the reference month (unless not at work owing to illness, leave or vacation). Working students with a part-time job are excluded from the definition.

It is reported that the following categories are included:
i) persons doing unpaid work in family firm or business;
ii) persons engaged in the production of primary products for own consumption;
iii) employed persons, temporarily absent from work;
iv) seasonal or occasional workers;
v) apprentices and trainees.

Only persons belonging to categories (i), (iv) and (v) can be identified separately.

(c) Unemployment: Considered as "unemployed" are all persons who had been previously employed but who, during the reference period, were without work and seeking work. First-time jobseekers are identified separately.

7. Classifications used:
Both employed persons and unemployed persons are classified by industry. Only employed persons are classified by occupation and by status in employment.

(a) Industry: Based on the question: "What is the activity of the firm or establishment in which X works (or last worked, if now unemployed)?." Links to the ISIC have not been established.

(b) Occupation: Based on the question: "During the month of August 1991, what was X's primary occupation?." For coding occupation, eight groups were used. Links to the ISCO have not been established.

(c) Status in employment: Based on the question: "In his occupation, is X an employer; self-employed; public-sector employee; private-sector employee; unpaid apprentice; pieceworker; family worker." For coding this variable, these seven groups were used.

8. Main differences compared with the previous census:
No major difference.

9. Publication of the census results:
The title of the publication containing the final census results is: "Résultats du recensement général de la population et de l'habitat, 1991"; it was expected to come out in summer 1996.

The organization responsible for this publication is Direction Nationale du recensement, B.P. 131, Moroni.

The census data are to be available also in the form of diskettes.

COOK ISLANDS

1. Name and address of the organization responsible for the census:
Statistics Office, P.O. Box 125, Rarotonga.

2. Population censuses conducted since 1945 (years):
1945, 1956, 1961, 1966, 1971, 1976, 1981, 1986 and 1991. The present description relates to the 1991 population census (held on 1st December).

3. Coverage of the census:
(a) Geographical scope: Whole area.

(b) Persons covered: All persons of all ages.

4. Reference period:
The month prior to the census.

5. Main topics:
(a) Total population, by sex and age:	yes
Economically active population by:	

(b) Sex and age group: yes
(c) Industry: yes
(d) Occupation: yes
(e) Status in employment: yes
(f) Highest educational level: yes
(g) Hours of work: yes
(h) Other characteristics: no

Re (a): The age is defined in terms of age at last birthday.

Re (g): Hours of work relate to the total number of hours usually worked by employed persons during the week prior to the census (if not available, then to the number of hours usually worked in a week).

6. Concepts and definitions:

(a) Economically active population: It comprises all persons aged 15 years and over who, during the reference month, were either employed or unemployed, according to the definitions given below. The definition also includes temporary contract workers of other ethnic origin. There are no armed forces in Cook Islands.

(b) Employment: Employment is determined on the basis of the question: "Activity status: (1) Employer, own business/plantation; (2) Own Account business/self employed and no employees; (3) Working full time for wages/salary; (4) Working part time for wage or on casual basis; (5) Unemployed and looking for work; (6) Family worker in plantation/store or other for own use or household consumption and not receiving wages; (7) Retired; (8) Full time student and not working for wage/salary; (9) Disabled; (10) Home duties." Those who classified themselves under 1, 2, 3, 4 or 6 were counted as "employed."

It is reported that the following categories are included:
i) persons doing unpaid work in family firm or business;
ii) persons engaged in the production of primary products for own consumption;
iii) employed persons, temporarily absent from work;
iv) working students with a part time job;
v) seasonal or occasional workers;
vi) apprentices and trainees.

Only persons belonging to categories (i) and (ii) can be identified separately on the basis of their activity status.

(c) Unemployment: Considered as "unemployed" are all persons who, during the reference period, were without work and seeking work. The definition includes both unemployed persons with previous job experience and those who never worked before.

7. Classifications used:

Only employed persons are classified by industry, by occupation and by status in employment.

(a) Industry: The specific questions asked of employed persons both for principal occupation and secondary occupation to determine industry group relate to the name of employer, company, government, store or person worked for, as well as to the type of business or activity employed in, e.g. agriculture, fishing, retail store and to number of hours worked last week, or if not worked, to number of hours usually worked. For coding industry, the ISIC-rev.2 has been used to the group (4-digit) level, but the data will only be published to the major division (1-digit) level.

(b) Occupation: The specific question asked of employed persons both for principal occupation and secondary occupation relates to the work done by the person in the place of work during the reference period, e.g. citrus grower, wharf labourer, accounts clerk, etc. For coding occupation, the ISCO-88 has been used to the unit-group (4-digit) level, but the data will only be published to the major group (1-digit) level.

(c) Status in employment: Based on the same question as that indicated under 6 (b) above. For coding status in employment, six groups were used: employer, own business or plantation; own account business, self employed and no employees; working full time for wages or salary; working part time for wage or on casual basis; family worker in plantation or store or other for own use or household consumption and not receiving wages ("home duties" is extended to cover production of fishing and agriculture); other.

8. Main differences compared with the previous census:

No major difference.

9. Publication of the census results:

As for the 1986 census, various reports containing the 1991 census results were issued between 1992 and 1993 under the general title "Cook Islands Census of population and dwellings 1991." They can be ordered from the Statistics Office in Rarotonga.

The organization responsible for the publication of the census results is the Statistics Office, P.O. Box 125, Rarotonga.

The census data are not available in other forms.

CYPRUS

1. Name and address of the organization responsible for the census:

Department of Statistics and Research, 13 Lord Byron Avenue, P.C. 1444, Nicosia.

2. Population censuses conducted since 1945 (years):

1946, 1960, 1973, 1976, 1982 and 1992. The present description relates to the 1992 census (held on 1 October). The 1976 census was the last census prior to the 1992 census that collected information on the economically active population.

3. Coverage of the census:

(a) Geographical scope: The census only covered the Government controlled area of the country.

(b) Persons covered: All persons of all ages.

4. Reference period:

The week prior to the interview day.

5. Main topics:

(a) Total population, by sex and age: yes
Economically active population by:
(b) Sex and age group: yes
(c) Industry: yes
(d) Occupation: yes
(e) Status in employment: yes
(f) Highest educational level: yes
(g) Hours of work: yes
(h) Other characteristics: yes

Re (a): The age is defined in terms of date of birth, i.e. day, month and year of birth, and will be classified by age at last birthday.

Re (g): Employed persons were asked to specify whether they worked full time (30+ hours per week) or part time (less than 30 hours per week).

Re (h): Duration of unemployment measured in months was collected.

6. Concepts and definitions:

(a) Economically active population: It comprises all persons aged 15 years and over who, during the reference week, were either employed or unemployed according to the definitions given below. Members of the armed forces are included in the definition.

(b) Employment: Considered as "employed" are all persons who gave an affirmative reply to the questions "Do you usually work?" or "Did you work last week, even for one hour?."

It is reported that the following categories are included:
i) persons doing unpaid work in family firm or business;
ii) employed persons, temporarily absent from work;
iii) working students with a part time job;
iv) seasonal or occasional workers;
v) conscripts for military/civilian service;
vi) apprentices and trainees.

Seasonal or occasional workers are included in the definition if they worked during the reference week. Only categories (i), (ii), (v) and (vi) can be identified separately.

(c) Unemployment: Considered as "unemployed" are all persons who gave a negative reply to the questions "Do you usually work?" and "Did you work last week, even for one hour?" and indicated that they were unemployed or looking for work when asked what they did during the reference week. Students seeking work are excluded from the definition.

7. Classifications used:

Employed persons and unemployed persons previously employed are classified by industry, by occupation and by status in employment.

(a) Industry: Based on the question: "In what kind of business or industry are/were you working?." For coding industry, 61 groups of the national classification were used. Links to the ISIC-rev.3 have been established to the division (2-digit) level.

(b) Occupation: Based on the question: "What kind of work did you do last week/would you have done last week?." For coding occupation, 30 groups of the national classification were used. Links to the ISCO-88 have been established to the major (1-digit) and sub-major group (2-digit) level.

(c) Status in employment: Based on the question: "In your job, are you: self-employed (with employees); self-employed (without employees); employee; unpaid family worker; apprentice; other?." Status in employment was coded into these six groups.

8. Main differences compared with the previous census:
The 1992 census set a minimum age of 15 years and over for the collection of data on the economically active population, whereas the 1976 census set no minimum age.

The 1992 census classified both employed persons and unemployed persons previously employed by industry, by occupation and by status in employment, whereas the 1976 census classified only employed persons by industry, employed persons and unemployed persons previously employed by occupation, and made no classification by status in employment.

9. Publication of the census results:
The final data on total and economically active population have been published in 1995 in the following publications:
- Volume I: "General and Demographic Characteristics of the Population" (June 1994).
- Volume III: "Labour Force" (1995).

The organization responsible for these publications is the Department of Statistics and Research, 13 Lord Byron Avenue, P.C. 162, Nicosia.

Some of the census results are also available in the form of unpublished tables and diskettes.

CZECH REPUBLIC

1. Name and address of the organization responsible for the census:
Statistical Office, Sokolovská 142, 18613 Prague 8 Karlin.

2. Population censuses conducted since 1945 (years):
1950, 1961, 1970, 1980 and 1991. The present description relates to the 1991 population census (which took place at midnight between the 2nd and the 3rd of March).

3. Coverage of the census:

(a) Geographical scope: Whole country.

(b) Persons covered: All persons of all ages who reside permanently in the country and nationals living permanently abroad; excluding are members of the diplomatic corps and those of the Soviet army and their related persons.

4. Reference period:
At midnight between the 2nd and 3rd of March.

5. Main topics:
(a) Total population, by sex and age:	yes

Economically active population by:
(b) Sex and age group:	yes
(c) Industry:	yes
(d) Occupation:	yes
(e) Status in employment:	yes
(f) Highest educational level:	yes
(g) Hours of work:	no
(h) Other characteristics:	yes

Re (a): The age is defined in terms of year of birth.

Re (h): The census also collected information on the place of work (address), frequency of travel to work (daily, other) and time used to travel one-way "from the door to the door" (minutes).

6. Concepts and definitions:

(a) Economically active population: The economic activity is based on the current activity concept. Thus, the economically active population comprises all persons aged 15 years and over who, at the time of the census, were either employed or unemployed, according to the definitions given below. The definition also covers members of the armed forces as well as prisoners,

on the basis of the civilian equivalent of their present or last work.

(b) Employment: Considered as "employed" are all persons who stated that they were employed as: employers, own-account workers, employees and members of agricultural and production co-operatives (including working pensioners, women on paid maternity leave and unpaid family workers). Working students with a part-time job are excluded from the definition.

It is reported that the following categories are included:
- i) persons doing unpaid work in family firm or business;
- ii) employed persons, temporarily absent from work;
- iii) seasonal or occasional workers;
- iv) conscripts for military/civilian service.

Only persons belonging to category (i) can be identified separately. Apprentices and trainees, although not covered by the definition of the economically active population, can also be identified separately.

(c) Unemployment: Considered as "unemployed" are all persons aged 15 to 59 years (for men) and 15 to 56 years (for women), who stated that, at the time of the census, they were seeking work.

7. Classifications used:
Both employed and unemployed persons previously employed are classified by industry, by occupation and by status in employment.

(a) Industry: Based on the question: "Indicate the name of the establishment, co-operative, office, organization or school." The coding of branches of economic activity or school attendance was carried out according to special lists of organizations with branch codes based on prevailing activities. For the processing of the 1991 census results, a national classification of 47 groups was used (i.e., branches and subbranches of the national classification). The national industrial classification provides a full comparability with the ISIC-rev.3. A conversion table between the national classification and ISIC-rev.3 was established to the division (2-digit) level.

(b) Occupation: Respondents were asked to indicate as precisely as possible their executed work or function. Non-working pensioners, women on maternity leave, conscripts for military service, persons in prison and those seeking employment were asked to indicate their last job. For coding occupation, 91 groups of the national classification were used. Links to the ISCO (both ISCO-68 and ISCO-88) have been established to the major group (1-digit) level.

(c) Status in employment: Respondents were asked to indicate their social group, e.g. manual worker, employee, member of agricultural co-operative, member of producing co-operative, employer (with one or more employees), private farmer, own-account tradesman, freelancer, unpaid family worker, etc.. Manual workers and employees were requested to specify the sector of the national economy (state, private, co-operative, mixed sector). For coding status in employment, the following nine groups were used: manual workers and employees in private sector; other manual workers and employees; members of agricultural co-operatives; members of other co-operatives; employers; private farmers; own-account workers; freelancers; unpaid family workers.

8. Main differences compared with the previous census:
In 1991, the definition of the economically active population has been extended by the inclusion of unemployed persons seeking employment, but no distinction was made for those seeking their first job. Working pensioners, persons receiving old or disability pension and wages have also been included in the definition.

In the 1961, 1970 and 1980 censuses, unpaid family workers were counted as dependent persons, i.e., not economically active, and persons who declared themselves as unemployed were considered as employed on the basis of their last work.

In the 1991 census, the classification by status in employment has been extended by the inclusion of employers, and unpaid family workers have been identified as a special group.

Finally, the question on travel to work has been extended in 1991 by the inclusion of a question on the time used to travel one-way "from the door to the door."

9. Publication of the census results:
The title of the publication containing the final census results is: "1991 Population and Housing Census," issued in 1992.

The organization responsible for this publication is the Statistical Office, Sokolovská 142, 18613 Prague 8 Karlin.

The 1991 final census data are also available on diskettes and magnetic tapes.

DOMINICAN REPUBLIC

1. Name and address of the organization responsible for the census:
Oficina Nacional de Estadística (ONE), Ave. México, Esquina Leopoldo Navarro, Edificio Gubernamental Juan Pablo Duarte (El Huacal) 9no. Piso., Santo Domingo.

2. Population censuses conducted since 1945 (years):
1950, 1960, 1970, 1981 and 1993. The present description relates to the 1993 population census (held on 24 and 25 September).

3. Coverage of the census:
(a) Geographical scope: Whole country.

(b) Persons covered: All persons of all ages.

4. Reference period:
The week prior to the census day.

5. Main topics:
(a) Total population, by sex and age: yes

Economically active population by:
(b) Sex and age group: yes
(c) Industry: yes
(d) Occupation: yes
(e) Status in employment: yes
(f) Highest educational level: no
(g) Hours of work: no
(h) Other characteristics: no

Re (a): The age is defined in terms of age at last birthday, and in terms of year of birth.

6. Concepts and definitions:
(a) Economically active population: It comprises all persons aged 10 years and over who, during the reference week, were either employed or unemployed, according to the definitions given below. All members of the armed forces are included in the definition.

(b) Employment: Considered as "employed" are all persons who, during the reference week, performed some work or had a job, received pay for work done that week, or did unpaid work at home or in a family firm or business. The question used is: "Which of the following best describes your situation last week?

i) in paid employment;
ii) not at work, but have a job;
iii) doing unpaid work for a family member;
iv) previously employed and seeking work;
v) retired, no longer working;
vi) homemaker;
vii) non-working student;
viii) first-time jobseeker;
ix) unable to work owing to permanent disability;
x) not interested in working;
xi) not seeking work, but would accept work if it were offered;
xii) independent means."

It is reported that the following categories are included:
i) persons doing unpaid work in family firm or business;
ii) persons engaged in the production of primary products for own consumption;
iii) employed persons, temporarily absent from work;
iv) working students with a part-time job;
v) conscripts for military/civilian service.

All categories can be identified separately.

(c) Unemployment: Considered as "unemployed" are all persons who, during the reference week, did not work, or who had not worked previously but were seeking work. Both previously employed persons and first-time jobseekers are included. Students looking for work are excluded from the definition.

7. Classifications used:
Both employed persons and unemployed persons previously employed are classified by industry, by occupation and by status in employment.

(a) Industry: To determine industry group, persons were asked to indicate the activity of the organization, business, firm or office in which they work or last worked. For coding this variable, 10 groups of the national classification were used. Links to the ISIC-rev.2 have been established to the major division (1-digit) level.

(b) Occupation: To determine occupation group, persons were asked to indicate their function or job in their current or most recent place of work. For coding this variable, 10 groups of the national classification were used. Links to the ISCO-68 have been established to the major group (1-digit) level.

(c) Status in employment: To determine this variable, persons were asked to indicate which of the following five categories applied to them: proprietor or employer, self-employed worker, household employee, wage earner (employee, worker, day labourer), and unpaid family worker.

8. Main differences compared with the previous census:
The 1981 census was carried out "de jure" and "de facto," while the 1993 census was only "de facto."

The 1981 census used 14 questions to determine the employment situation, which made it possible to go deeper into economic characteristics. The questions which were not included in the 1993 census were:

"If you did not work, how did you spend most of your time last week?

How long have you been without work?

How many hours did you work last week in all your jobs?

Who was your main employer last week, or in your most recent job?"

The 1981 census measured annual or monthly earned income. The 1993 census, on the other hand, measured weekly earned income. The time-frame for the 1981 census was one year or one month.

9. Publication of the census results:
The title of the publication containing the final census results is "Censo Nacional de Población y Vivienda 24 y 25 de septiembre de 1993; Resultados definitivos Region Sur-Oeste Vol. I, Junio de 1996."

The organization responsible for this publication is Oficina nacional de estadística, ave. Mexico, Esquina Leopoldo Navarro, edificio gubernamental Juan Pablo Duarte (El Huacal), 9no. Piso.

The census results are also available in the form of diskettes and unpublished tables.

ECUADOR

1. Name and address of the organization responsible for the census:
Instituto Nacional de Estadísticas y Censos (INEC), Av. 10 de Agosto 229 y Pasaje Carlos Ibarra, Quito.

2. Population censuses conducted since 1945 (years):
1950, 1962, 1974, 1982 and 1990. The present description relates to the 1990 census (held on 25 November).

3. Coverage of the census:
(a) Geographical scope: Whole country, except areas experiencing temporary problems with the indigenous population.

(b) Persons covered: All persons of all ages, except persons living in the areas mentioned above.

4. Reference period:
The week prior to the census day.

5. Main topics:
(a) Total population, by sex and age: yes

Economically active population by:
(b) Sex and age group: yes
(c) Industry: yes
(d) Occupation: yes
(e) Status in employment: yes
(f) Highest educational level: ...
(g) Hours of work: yes
(h) Other characteristics: yes

Re (a): The age is defined in terms of age at last birthday.

Re (g): Relates both to the usual hours of work and the hours actually worked by employed persons at work during the reference period. The question asked was "How many hours did you work last week in your stated occupation?."

6. Concepts and definitions:

(a) Economically active population: It comprises all persons aged 8 years and over who, during the reference week, were either employed or unemployed, according to the definitions given below. All members of the armed forces are also included in the definition.

(b) Employment: Considered as "employed" are all persons who worked in employment or self-employment during the reference week. The questions used to determine if a person was employed are "What did you do last week?" and "Did you undertake or engage in any activity last week, even without remuneration?."

It is reported that the following categories are included:

i) persons doing unpaid work in family firm or business;
ii) employed persons, temporarily absent from work;
iii) working students with a part-time job;
iv) seasonal or occasional workers;
v) conscripts for military/civilian service;
vi) apprentices and trainees.

None of these categories can be identified separately.

(c) Unemployment: Considered as "unemployed" are all persons who replied no to the questions mentioned in (b) above, and who, during the reference week, looked for work, whether or not previously employed. Students looking for work are excluded from the definition.

7. Classifications used:

Both employed persons and unemployed persons previously employed are classified by industry, by occupation and by status in employment.

(a) Industry: Based on the question: "What is the principle activity of the establishment or firm in which you worked?." The ISIC-rev.2 was used to the 3-digit level for coding industry, and to the 1-digit level for the publication of data.

(b) Occupation: Based on the question: "What was your main occupation or work during the past week, or in your last job, if then unemployed?." For coding occupation, the ISCO-68 was used to the major group and unit group level.

(c) Status in employment: Based on the question: "What was your position or category in your occupation?." The following seven categories were used to code status in employment: employer or active partner; self-employed worker; employee or wage-earner in: municipal or provincial government; state employment; private sector; unpaid family worker; other.

8. Main differences compared with the previous census:

In 1982 the lower age limit for inclusion in the economically active polulation and its component groups (employment and unemployment) was 12 years; in 1990 this age limit was lowered to 8 years.

The question used in 1982 to identify employed persons was "What activity accounted for most of your time between 7 and 13 November?"; in the 1990 census the question was "What did you do last week?."

The 1990 census includes the questions "Did you undertake or engage in any activity last week, even without remuneration?" and "How many hours did you work last week in your stated occupation?."

The 1990 census includes the category "unable to work" under the heading of activity.

In 1990 the "employed or wage-earner" category was broken down into the following groups: municipal or provincial government; state employment; private sector.

Lastly, the 1990 census did not include questions on social security.

9. Publication of the census results:

The title of the publication containing the final census data is "V Censo de Población y IV de Vivienda 1990 - Resultados Definitivos, Resumen Nacional," November 1991.

The organization responsible for this publication is Instituto Nacional de Estadísticas y Censos - INEC, Quito.

Data from the 1990 census are also available in various other forms, upon request.

EL SALVADOR

1. Name and address of the organization responsible for the census:

Dirección General de Estadística y Censos, 1a. Calle Poniente y 43 Avenida Norte, San Salvador, El Salvador.

2. Population censuses conducted since 1945 (years):

1950, 1961, 1971 and 1992. The present description relates to the 1992 population census (held on 27 September).

3. Coverage of the census:

(a) Geographical scope: Whole country.

(b) Persons covered: All persons of all ages.

4. Reference period:

The week preceding the census date.

5. Main topics:

(a) Total population, by sex and age:	yes
Economically active population by:	
(b) Sex and age group:	yes
(c) Industry:	yes
(d) Occupation:	yes
(e) Status in employment:	yes
(f) Highest educational level:	yes
(g) Hours of work:	yes
(h) Other characteristics:	no

Re (a): The age is defined in terms of age at last birthday.

Re (g): Relates to the usual hours of work of employed persons at work during the reference period.

6. Concepts and definitions:

(a) Economically active population: It comprises all persons aged 10 years and over who, during the reference week, were either employed or unemployed, according to the definitions given below. Members of the armed forces are included in the definition.

(b) Employment: Considered as "employed" are all persons who worked during the reference week. The question used is: "The week prior to the census day, did you: Work for remuneration in cash or in kind? Work for someone else without remuneration? Not work, but have a job or your own firm or farm? Seek work, having previously been employed? Seek work for the first time (not previously employed)? Not seek work because you did not think you could find any? Engage exclusively in homemaking? Study exclusively? Are you retired, or do you have a pension or your own means of support? Were you confined? Do you have a permanent disability which prevents you from working? Other?."

It is reported that the following categories are included:

i) persons doing unpaid work in family firm or business;
ii) employed persons temporarily absent from work;
iii) working students with a part-time job;
iv) seasonal or occasional workers;
v) apprentices and trainees.

Persons falling in categories (i), (ii), (iii) and (iv) can be identified separately by means of their responses to specific questions.

(c) Unemployment: Considered as "unemployed" are all persons who, during the reference week, were without work and seeking work. Included in the definition are persons who had made arrangements to begin working after the reference week, persons who were temporarily or permanently laid off and not receiving remuneration, and persons who did not think that they could find work.

7. Classifications used:

Both employed persons and unemployed persons are classified by industry, by occupation and by status in employment.

(a) Industry: The questions used to determine industry group are "Where do you work or did you last work (on a farm, in a factory, in a machine shop, in a private or public office, on the street, etc.)?" and "What do you do or produce, or what is the line of business and product of the establishment where you work or last worked?." For coding industry, the ISIC-rev.3 was used to the 4-digit level.

(b) Occupation: The question used to determine occupation group is "What is your occupation, job or function in your current or most recent job?" For coding occupation, the ISCO-88 was used to the unit group level.

(c) Status in employment: The question used to determine status in employment is "In this job are you, or were you: public sector employee or worker, private sector employee or worker, proprietor or employer, unpaid family worker, self-employed, household employee, member of a producers' cooperative, other?." For coding this variable, these eight groups were used.

8. Main differences compared with the previous census:
No major difference.

9. Publication of the census results:
The final census results were published in December 1995.

The title of the publication containing the final census results is "V Censos nacionales de población."

The organization responsible for this publication is Dirección General de Estadística y Censos, 1a. Calle Poniente y 43 Avenida Norte, San Salvador, El Salvador.

The census results are also available in the form of unpublished tables.

EQUATORIAL GUINEA

1. Name and address of the organization responsible for the census:
Dirección General de Estadística, Ministerio de Economía y Hacienda, Malabo.

2. Population censuses conducted since 1945 (years):
1981 and 1994. The present description relates to the 1994 population census (held on 11 September).

3. Coverage of the census:

(a) Geographical scope: Whole country.

(b) Persons covered: All persons of all ages, excluding foreign diplomats residing in Equatorial Guinea.

4. Reference period:
The week preceding the census date.

5. Main topics:
(a) Total population, by sex and age:	yes
Economically active population by:	
(b) Sex and age group:	yes
(c) Industry:	yes
(d) Occupation:	yes
(e) Status in employment:	no
(f) Highest educational level:	...
(g) Hours of work:	no
(h) Other characteristics:	no

Re (a): The age is defined in terms of year of birth.

6. Concepts and definitions:

(a) Economically active population: It comprises all persons aged 6 years and over who, during the reference week, were either employed or unemployed, according to the definitions given below. Questions on economic activity were asked of a 15.3 per cent sampling of the population. The data on the economically active population and its components (employment and unemployment) were tabulated only in respect of persons aged between 6 and 64 years. Members of the armed forces are excluded from the definition. Also excluded are working students with a part-time job and students seeking work.

(b) Employment: Considered as "employed" are all persons who worked during the reference week. For this purpose, persons were asked what they did during the week preceding the census day.

It is reported that the following categories are included:
i)   employed persons who are temporarily absent from work;
ii) seasonal or occasional workers.

Neither of these categories can be identified separately.

(c) Unemployment: Considered as "unemployed" are all persons who, during the reference week, were without work and seeking work. The questions used to determine if the person was unemployed are "Were you seeking work and have you been previously employed?" and "Were you seeking work for the first time?."

7. Classifications used:
Both employed persons and unemployed persons previously employed are classified by industry and by occupation.

(a) Industry: Based on the question: "What is the line of business of the firm or enterprise where you worked?." For coding industry, the ISIC-rev.3 was used.

(b) Occupation: To determine occupation group, the questions are "What is your occupation?" and "What is your occupational category?." For coding occupation group, 10 groups of the national classification were used. Links to the ISCO-88 have been established to the major group (1-digit) level.

(c) Status in employment: No classification was made by status in employment.

8. Main differences compared with the previous census:
No major difference.

9. Publication of the census results:
The final results were published in January 1995.

The title of the publication containing the final census data is "Características de la Población y de las Viviendas."

The organization responsible for this publication is Dirección General de Estadística, Ministerio de Economía y Hacienda, Malabo.

The census data are also available on magnetic media.

FINLAND

1. Name and address of the organization responsible for the census:
Central Statistical Office of Finland (CSO), P.B. 504, 00101 Helsinki.

2. Population censuses conducted since 1945 (years):
1950, 1960, 1970, 1975, 1980, 1985 and 1990. The present description relates to the 1990 census (held on 31 December).

Under a decision taken in 1979 in Finland, the Population and Housing Census of 1980 was to be the last one based directly on data collected by form. The Population and Housing Census of 1990 was intended to be carried out entirely with the help of registers and administrative records. Preparations for register-based censuses started therefore in 1981 and a National Register of Buildings and Dwellings based on the buildings and dwellings data of the 1980 Population and Housing Census has been established in Finland.

As this was the first time a full-scale census was carried out as a register-based census, entirely without questionnaires, a sufficiently large sample-based parallel study will be needed for analyzing the break in the time series resulting from the change in the data collection method. To determine the quality of the basic registers to be used in the census, it will be necessary to carry out a control and quality study of the register-based system at regular intervals (e.g. every five years) independent of the administrative systems.

3. Coverage of the census:

(a) Geographical scope: Whole country.

(b) Persons covered: All persons of all ages.

4. Reference period:
The census week (25-31 December 1990) for current activity, and the whole year 1990 for usual activity.

5. Main topics:
(a) Total population, by sex and age:	yes
Economically active population by:	
(b) Sex and age group:	yes
(c) Industry:	yes
(d) Occupation:	yes
(e) Status in employment:	yes
(f) Highest educational level:	yes
(g) Hours of work:	no
(h) Other characteristics:	yes

Re (a): The age is defined in terms of date of birth, which is obtained directly from the central population register.

Re (h): The census also collected information on: location of the place of work; legal form of the employer (private business, central Government, local Government); duration of employment and of unemployment; earnings; socio-economic status.

6. Concepts and definitions:

(a) Economically active population: It comprises all persons aged 15 to 74 years who, during the census week, were either employed or unemployed, according to the definitions given below. Excluded are conscripts in barracks and institutional populations.

(b) Employment: Considered as "employed" are all persons who, according to Employment Pension Insurance Registers, worked at least one day during the census week (current activity concept) or at least six months during the reference year (usual activity concept), at home or out of home, and had taxable incomes according to Taxation Registers.

It is reported that the following categories are included:

i)   persons doing unpaid work in family firm or business: only part of these persons are included, i.e., those who have an entrepreneurial pension insurance (which is not compulsory for unpaid family workers);
ii) employed persons, temporarily absent from work;
iii) working students with a part time job;
iv) seasonal or occasional workers;
v)   multiple job holders;
vi) apprentices and trainees.

Only persons belonging to category (v) can be identified separately on the basis of information from the Employment Pension Insurance Registers. The data relating to conscripts for military/civilian service can be obtained from the special Ministry of Defence register, although these persons are excluded from the definition of the economically active population.

(c) Unemployment: Considered as "unemployed" are all persons who, according to the Register of Unemployed Job-seekers of the Ministry of Labour, were without work on the 29th of December 1990, but were seeking employment and available for work. Students seeking work are excluded from the definition.

7. Classifications used:

Both employed and unemployed persons previously employed are classified by industry and by occupation. Only employed persons are classified by status in employment.

(a) Industry: The industry (as well as some other information) is obtained from the Register of Enterprises and Establishments of the Central Statistical Office (CSO) which uses the same identifiers as the Taxation Registers. The Register of Enterprises and Establishments contains the same code which can be used to transfer all information to employed persons. The procedure varies somewhat, depending whether the enterprise has one or several establishments. For some entrepreneurs, the industry is deduced from Pension Insurance data and from the type of income. For coding industry, about 460 groups of the standard industrial classification of the CSO were used. Links to the ISIC (both ISIC-rev.2 and ISIC-rev.3) have been established to the 4-digit level.

(b) Occupation: The information used to determine occupation group is obtained from the Wage and Salary Registers of Central and Local Governments, from the Taxation Registers and from the Job-seekers Register of the Ministry of Labour. The occupational titles obtained from Registers are coded using the automatic coding system developed by the CSO. For coding occupation, about 400 groups were used. Links to the ISCO-68 have been established to the unit group (3-digit) level. Links to the ISCO-88 are planned, but have not yet been established.

(c) Status in employment: The status in employment is defined using information about the kind of pension insurance (employment or entrepreneurial pension) and source of income (wage or salary income or entrepreneurial income). For coding status in employment, two main groups were used: (i) wage and salary earners, and (ii) entrepreneurs (which includes own-account workers, employers and unpaid family workers).

8. Main differences compared with the previous census:

The 1990 census was carried out on a register-based census and the data collection method was totally different from that of the 1985 census. All the data used in determining the economically active population were obtained from administrative records and no questionnaire was used. Though the data collection method was different, the definitions concerning the economically active population and its components did not differ significantly. The most important difference in the data content was that information on part-time work was not included.

Registers generally describe official data, i.e., they give information on the work on which tax is paid and which falls in the sphere of occupational insurance systems. The aim of the register-based census is to produce essentially the same information as in censuses carried out by questionnaire. However, in the 1990 census, data on weekly working time and on way of travelling to work were not obtained at all.

The benefits of the registered-based census relate mainly to data on persons. The 1990 census will therefore provide information on all employment of those who were employed in the course of 1990, including information on the number of successive jobs and secondary jobs. In addition, it will be possible to monitor shifts of population groups away from, e.g., studying, unemployment or household work to the labour force by, e.g., persons retiring, becoming unemployed or taking up household work. The registers also record short-term employment, which will make it possible to find out how generally and for how many months a year students, for example, are in gainful employment.

9. Publication of the census results:

The title of the publication containing the final census results is "Economic activity of the population," 1993.

The organization responsible for this publication is the Central Statistical Office of Finland, P.B. 504, 00101 Helsinki.

The census results are also available in the form of unpublished tables, table packages, diskettes and magnetic tapes.

FRANCE

1. Name and address of the organization responsible for the census:

Institut national de la statistique et des études économiques (INSEE), 18 boulevard Adolphe Pinard, Paris Cedex 14.

2. Population censuses conducted since 1945 (years):

1954, 1962, 1968, 1975, 1982 and 1990. The present description relates to the 1990 census (held on 5 March).

3. Coverage of the census:

(a) Geographical scope: Whole country (Metropolitan France). Separate censuses of the Overseas Departments made at the same time are not used in connection with the census for Metropolitan France.

(b) Persons covered: All persons residing in France for at least six months, excluding foreign members of the diplomatic corps and foreign personnel of embassies living in a building having extra-territorial status.

4. Reference period:

A reference period has not been established. Persons surveyed were asked to indicate whether or not they were economically active on the reference date of the census, namely on 5 March at midnight.

5. Main topics:

(a) Total population, by sex and age:	yes

Economically active population by:

(b) Sex and age group:	yes
(c) Industry:	yes
(d) Occupation:	yes
(e) Status in employment:	yes
(f) Highest educational level:	yes
(g) Hours of work:	no
(h) Other characteristics:	yes

Re (a): The age is generally defined in terms of year of birth.

Re (h): Persons surveyed were also asked if they worked full time or part time.

6. Concepts and definitions:

(a) Economically active population: It comprises all persons aged 15 years and over who, at the time of the census, were either employed or unemployed, according to the definitions given below. The questions relating to economic activity were put to all persons, but answers were processed only for a sample of 1/4. The definition also covers professional members of the armed forces and conscripts.

(b) Employment: Considered as "employed" are all persons who, at the date of the census, have a full-time or part-time occupation, whether self-employed (farmer, craftsman, shopkeeper, industrialist, member of a liberal profession, etc.), or employed (worker or employee), or as an unpaid family helper

(spouse, child or any other family member of a farmer or shop-keeper, etc.). Self-employed workers must indicate whether they have employees and, if so, how many (excluding apprentices, household staff and, in agriculture, non-permanent employees).

The definition also covers persons engaged in paid community work provided to the unemployed, persons with an adaptation or training contract, as well as persons who have been placed by a temporary employment agency and persons holding a fixed-term employment contract. It also includes employed persons who are looking for another job, retired persons who have taken up a new occupation, retired farmers who still keep up small-scale farming activities, as well as members of the clergy.

It is reported that the following categories are included:

i)   persons engaged in the production of primary products for own consumption;
ii) employed persons, temporarily absent from work;
iii) working students with a part-time job;
iv) conscripts for military/civilian service;
v)   seasonal or occasional workers, if they are employed on the date of the census;
vi) paid trainees who work in an enterprise.

Persons belonging to categories (i) and (vi) can be identified separately by means of questions used for this purpose. The same is true for conscripts who, for the first time, are included in the definition of the economically active population as the third component, after employed and unemployed persons.

(c) Unemployment: Considered as "unemployed" are all persons who, on the date of the census, were without work and seeking work. The question asked to determine whether a person is to be counted as unemployed is "Are you looking for work?." In the event of an affirmative reply, the person must specify whether he/she has been looking for work for "less than three months," "three months to less than one year," "one year to less than two years," "two years or more." Students seeking work are excluded from the definition.

7. Classifications used:

Only employed persons in the sample are classified by industry, by occupation and by status in employment. Unemployed persons previously employed are classified only by their last occupation.

(a) Industry: Specific questions are asked to employed persons in the sample, concerning the address, name and activity of the establishment where they work or which they manage (for example: wholesale wine distributor, manufacture of metal framework, road passenger transport, etc.) to facilitate searches in the SIRENE database (directory of enterprises). For coding industry, 600 groups of the Nomenclature of Activities and Products (NAP) were used. Links to the ISIC-rev.2 have been established to the division (2-digit) level.

(b) Occupation: Specific questions are asked concerning the current or most recent occupation or trade (for example: electrical maintenance worker, lorry driver, household appliance salesperson, chemical engineer, self-service cashier, etc.). For coding occupation, 455 groups of the Nomenclature of Occupations and Socio-occupational Categories (PCS) were used. Links to the ISCO-68 have been established to the minor group (2-digit) level.

(c) Status in employment: Persons other than employees were asked whether they were engaged in their occupation (i) as employers or on a self-employed basis and, if so, whether they had employees (one or two, three to nine, ten or more), or (ii) as helpers to a member of their family in his or her work (farming, crafts, trade, liberal profession, etc.). Employees were asked if they were engaged in their occupation as such (in agriculture, only permanent employees are included). For coding status in employment, four major groups were used: employee, employer, self-employed worker without employees, and family helper.

8. Main differences compared with the previous census:

Conscripts, who had previously been excluded from the definition of the economically active population, were included in the definition in the 1990 census.

9. Publication of the census results:

The final census results were published in 1992.

The title of the publication containing the summary results is: Série "Logement-Population-Emploi"; that of the publication containing the 1/4 sample is: Série "Population-Activité-Ménages."

The Institut national de la statistique et des études économiques (INSEE), 18 boulevard Adolphe Pinard, 75675 Paris Cedex 14, is responsible for these publications.

The 1990 final census data are also available on diskettes, magnetic tapes and other formats on request.

FRENCH GUIANA

1. Name and address of the organization responsible for the census:

Institut national de la statistique et des études économiques (INSEE), Service régional de la Guyane, 1 rue Maillard Dumesle, B.P. 6017, 97306 Cayenne Cedex.

2. Population censuses conducted since 1945 (years):

1954, 1961, 1967, 1974, 1982 and 1990. The present description relates to the 1990 census (held on 15 March).

3. Coverage of the census:

(a) Geographical scope: Whole territory.

(b) Persons covered: All persons of all ages.

4. Reference period:

The week preceding the census day.

5. Main topics:

(a) Total population, by sex and age:	yes
Economically active population by:	
(b) Sex and age group:	yes
(c) Industry:	yes
(d) Occupation:	yes
(e) Status in employment:	yes
(f) Highest educational level:	yes
(g) Hours of work:	no
(h) Other characteristics:	yes

Re (a): The age is defined in terms of year of birth.

Re (h): The census also covered information on other topics, such as: full-time and part-time work, primary activity, the number of workers employed by self-employed persons, the length of time spent looking for work, etc.

6. Concepts and definitions:

(a) Economically active population: It comprises all persons aged 14 years and over who, during the reference week, were either employed or unemployed, according to the definitions given below. The definition also covers all members of the armed forces (career military staff and conscripts). Questions concerning economic activity were asked only of a sample of persons, which excluded military staff living in barracks and prisonners.

(b) Employment: Considered as "employed" are all persons who, during the reference week, had an occupation, function or any economic activity, whether paid or unpaid. Specific questions used to determine if a person is to be counted as employed are: "Do you work (full time or part time)?"; "Are you: employed or self-employed (farmer, craftsman, merchant, industrialist, professional, unpaid family worker, etc.)?," and "If you are self-employed: how many workers do you employ? (do not count apprentices or domestic staff; in agriculture, count only permanent employees)." The definition also covers persons engaged in paid community work provided to the unemployed, persons who have been placed by a temporary employment agency, persons holding a fixed-term employment contract, and persons with a retraining contract.

It is reported that the following categories are included:

i)   persons doing unpaid work in family firm or business;
ii)   persons engaged in the production of primary products for own consumption;
iii) employed persons, temporarily absent from work;
iv)   working students with a part time job;
v)   seasonal or occasional workers who were working at the time of the census;
vi)   conscripts for military/civilian service;
vii) apprentices (bound by a contract) and trainees (mainly in enterprises or training centres).

Only persons belonging to categories (i), (vi) and (vii) can be identified separately.

(c) Unemployment: Considered as "unemployed" are all persons who, on their own initiative, stated that they were without work, and who were seeking work. The questions used to determine if a person should be considered as unemployed

are "Are you unemployed (whether registered or not with the National Employment Agency)?," "Have you previously worked? (if so, what was your primary occupation?," and "Are you seeking work (for: less than three months; three months to less than one year; one year to less than two years; two years or more)?."

7. Classifications used:
Both employed persons and unemployed persons previously employed included in the sample are classified by occupation. Only employed persons in the sample are classified by industry and by status in employment.

(a) Industry: Surveyed persons were asked to give the address and name of the establishment where they work or which they manage, and to identify its activity as accurately as possible (for example: wholesale wine dealers, manufacture of metal scaffolding, road passenger transport, etc.). For coding industry, 100 groups of the Nomenclature of Activities and Products (NAP) were used. Links to the ISIC have not been established.

(b) Occupation: Surveyed persons were asked to identify their current or most recent occupation as accurately as possible (for example: electrical maintenance worker, lorry driver, household appliance salesperson, chemical engineer, self-service cashier, etc.) to permit the determination of their occupational group. The question, however, was left open-ended, so that surveyed persons could reply in their own words. The classification in a specific group takes place when the data is processed. For coding occupation, a direct coding system entailing 42 groups was used. Links to the ISCO have not been established.

(c) Status in employment: For coding this variable, five categories were used, namely: self-employed person; employer; employee; unpaid family worker; other.

8. Main differences compared with the previous census:
The minimum age limit used for inclusion in the economically active population was 15 years in the 1982 census.

Moreover, both employed persons and unemployed persons previously employed had been classified by industry and by status in employment in the 1982 census.

9. Publication of the census results:
The title of the publication containing the final census results is: "Population, Emploi, Logements; Evolution 1975-1982-1990 (Série jaune)," 1992.

The Institut national de la statistique et des études économiques (INSEE), 18 boulevard Adolphe Pinard, 75675 Paris Cedex 14, is responsible for this publication.

The 1990 final census data will also be available on diskettes, magnetic tapes and other formats on request.

GABON

1. Name and address of the organization responsible for the census:
Bureau central du recensement, Direction générale de la statistique et des études économiques, B.P. 2119, Libreville.

2. Population censuses conducted since 1945 (years):
1981 and 1993. The present description relates to the 1993 census (held on 31 July).

3. Coverage of the census:
(a) Geographical scope: Whole territory.

(b) Persons covered: All persons of all ages, except members of the diplomatic corps and nationals residing abroad.

4. Reference period:
The week and the six months prior to the census day.

5. Main topics:
(a) Total population, by sex and age:	yes
Economically active population by:	
(b) Sex and age group:	yes
(c) Industry:	yes
(d) Occupation:	yes
(e) Status in employment:	yes
(f) Highest educational level:	yes
(g) Hours of work:	no
(h) Other characteristics:	no

Re (a): The age is defined in terms of age at last birthday.

6. Concepts and definitions:
(a) Economically active population: It comprises all persons aged 10 years and over who, during the long reference period, were either employed or unemployed, according to the definitions given below. The definition includes all members of the armed forces but excludes working students with a part time job and students seeking work.

(b) Employment: Considered as "employed" are all persons who stated that they worked at least one week during the long reference period. The questions used were: "Have you worked since January 1993?" and "How long did you work?."

It is reported that the following categories are included:

i) persons doing unpaid work in family firm or business;
ii) persons engaged in the production of primary products for own consumption;
iii) employed persons, temporarily absent from work;
iv) seasonal or occasional workers;
v) conscripts for military/civilian service;
vi) apprentices and trainees.

Only persons belonging to categories (i), (iii) and (iv) can be identified separately.

(c) Unemployment: Considered as "unemployed" are all persons who stated that they worked less than one week during the long reference period. The questions used are the same as those reproduced in paragraph 6 (b) above.

7. Classifications used:
Both employed persons and unemployed persons previously employed are classified by industry, by occupation and by status in employment.

(a) Industry: The question asked refers to the main occupation and the economic sector of the enterprise in which the person is or was employed. For coding industry, 40 groups of the national classification were used. Links to the ISIC have not been established.

(b) Occupation: Based on the question: "What is your occupation?." For coding occupation, 100 one-digit groups and 350 four-digit groups were used. Links to the ISCO-88 have been established to the minor group (3-digit) level.

(c) Status in employment: Based on the question: "Are you self-employed? (a) if so, do you employ staff? (b) if not, are you paid for your work? if not, do you work for a family member or as an apprentice?." For coding this variable, six groups were used, namely: self-employed; employee; proprietor; family helper; apprentice; other.

8. Main differences compared with the previous census:
The lower age limit in the 1993 census was 10 years, compared to 6 years in the 1980 census.

The 1993 census did not include a specific question on vocational training, but did cover sector of economic activity and migration.

9. Publication of the census results:
The census results were to have been published in the second half of 1995 in the following publications: "Résultats bruts, Volume II" and "Analyse des résultats, Volume III."

The organization responsible for these publications is Bureau central du recensement, Direction générale de la statistique, B.P. 2119, Libreville.

The 1993 census results are also available in the form of diskettes.

GAMBIA

1. Name and address of the organization responsible for the census:
Central Statistics Department, Central Bank Building, Buckle Street, Banjul.

2. Population censuses conducted since 1945 (years):
1963, 1973, 1983 and 1993. The present description relates to the 1993 population census (held on 15 April).

3. Coverage of the census:
(a) Geographical scope: Whole country.

(b) Persons covered: All persons of all ages.

4. Reference period:
The month prior to the census day.

5. Main topics:

(a) Total population, by sex and age:	yes
Economically active population by:	
(b) Sex and age group:	yes
(c) Industry:	yes
(d) Occupation:	yes
(e) Status in employment:	yes
(f) Highest educational level:	yes
(g) Hours of work:	yes
(h) Other characteristics:	no

Re (a): The age is defined in terms of age at last birthday.

Re (g): Hours of work relate to the number of days worked by employed persons, at work, during the reference period.

6. Concepts and definitions:

(a) Economically active population: It comprises all persons aged 10 years and over who, during the reference month, were either employed or unemployed, according to the definitions given below. The definition includes members of the armed forces, but excludes conscripts. Working students with a part time job and students seeking work also are excluded from the definition.

(b) Employment: The questions used to determine if a person is to be counted as employed are "What were you doing most of the time (during the past 30 days)? 1) working; 2) had a job, but not at work; 3) did not work and did not have job; 4) home making; 5) student; 6) something else.," and if answer is 4) or 6): "Did you work at all for pay or profit? (includes work for family farm or business, including pay in kind)."

It is reported that the following categories are included:

i)   persons doing unpaid work in family firm or business;
ii) persons engaged in the production of primary products for own consumption;
iii) employed persons, temporarily absent from work;
iv) seasonal or occasional workers;
v)   apprentices and trainees.

Only persons belonging to categories (i) and (iii) can be identified separately.

(c) Unemployment: Considered as "unemployed" are all persons who, during the reference month, were without work and looking for work.

7. Classifications used:

Both employed persons and unemployed persons previously employed are classified by industry, by occupation and by status in employment.

(a) Industry: Based on the questions: "What is the name of the establishment where you work (for unemployed: last establishment)?" and "What is the main product or service of this establishment?." For coding industry, ten groups of the national classification were used. Links to the ISIC-rev.3 have been established to the tabulation category (1-digit) level.

(b) Occupation: Based on the question: "What is your main job/work (for unemployed: last kind of work)?." For coding occupation, the ISCO-88 has been used to the major group (1-digit) level.

(c) Status in employment: Based on the question: "What is/was your employment status in this establishment?." For coding status in employment, five groups were used, namely: employee for pay or wages; self-employed without employees; employer; unpaid family worker; other.

8. Main differences compared with the previous census:

No major difference.

9. Publication of the census results:

The final results of the population census were expected to be issued in December 1995 in a publication entitled "Population and Housing Census 1993, Economic Characteristics."

The organization responsible for the publication of the results is the Central Statistics Department, Central Bank Building, Buckle Street, Banjul.

The census results are also available in the form of unpublished tables.

GIBRALTAR

1. Name and address of the organization responsible for the census:

Statistics Office, 6 Convent Place, Gibraltar.

2. Population censuses conducted since 1945 (years):

1951, 1961, 1970, 1981 and 1991. The present description relates to the 1991 population census (held 14 October).

3. Coverage of the census:

(a) Geographical scope: Whole area.

(b) Persons covered: All persons of all ages. Members of the armed forces stationed in the area are excluded from the census count; their wives and family members are included.

4. Reference period:

The census day.

5. Main topics:

(a) Total population, by sex and age:	yes
Economically active population by:	
(b) Sex and age group:	yes
(c) Industry:	yes
(d) Occupation:	yes
(e) Status in employment:	yes
(f) Highest educational level:	no
(g) Hours of work:	no
(h) Other characteristics:	yes

Re (a): The age is defined in terms of age at last birthday.

Re (h): The census also collected information on the means of transport used to go to the workplace (by foot, bus, bicycle, motor cycle or moped, car or van).

6. Concepts and definitions:

(a) Economically active population: It comprises all persons aged 15 years and over who, on the census day, were either employed or unemployed, according to the definitions given below. All members of the armed forces, students working part-time and those seeking work are excluded from the definition.

(b) Employment: Considered as "employed" are all persons who, on the census day, had a full-time or part-time job. Persons in employment were requested to indicate their present occupation and whether their job was full-time or part-time. Those persons waiting to take up a job already accepted and housewives with a full-time or part-time job are included.

It is reported that the following categories are included:

i) persons doing unpaid work in family firm or business;
ii) employed persons, temporarily absent from work.

None of these categories can be identified separately.

(c) Unemployment: Considered as "unemployed" are all persons who, on the census day, were without work and seeking work.

7. Classifications used:

Only employed persons are classified by industry, by occupation and by status in employment.

(a) Industry: A specific question is asked of employed persons to determine industry group. The question asked is "If you work for a private firm (or are self-employed) state what the employer does or makes; e.g. retail shop, printers, hotel, bank, hairdresser,etc. If you work for the Government state the Department and Section." Persons are asked to provide the name of the employer or place of work and address. For coding industry, 23 groups of the national classification were used. Links to the ISIC-rev.3 have been established to the tabulation category (1-digit) level.

(b) Occupation: To determine occupation group, employed persons were asked to state their occupation using as precise name as possible (e.g. garage mechanic, radio-mechanic, civil engineer, chartered accountant, economist, etc., and for public sector employees in the administrative service, head of department, executive officer, administrative officer or assistant, personal secretary or typist). For coding occupation, 125 groups of the national classification were used. Links to the ISCO have not been established.

(c) Status in employment: To determine status in employment, employed persons were asked to indicate whether they were an employee, self-employed or an employer. Family workers were to be included under employees.

8. Main differences compared with the previous census:
The reference period for the 1981 census was one week. Moreover, both employed persons and unemployed persons previously employed were classified by industry, by occupation and by status in employment.

9. Publication of the census results:
The final data were published in November 1992 in the publication entitled "Census of Gibraltar 1991."

The organization responsible for the publication is the Statistics Office in Gibraltar.

Copies of the publication are available from the Government Publications Office, 6 Convent Place, Gibraltar. Data on diskette or magnetic tape are not available.

GREECE

1. Name and address of the organization responsible for the census:
Office national de statistique de Grèce (ONSG), Direction des Recensements, 43-45 Agissilaou, 10166 Athens.

2. Population censuses conducted since 1945 (years):
1951, 1961, 1971, 1981 and 1991. The present description relates to the 1991 census (held on 17 March).

3. Coverage of the census:
(a) Geographical scope: Whole territory.
(b) Persons covered: All persons of all ages.

4. Reference period:
The week preceding the date of the census and the 12 months preceding the census (March 1990 to February 1991).

5. Main topics:

(a) Total population, by sex and age:	yes

Economically active population by:

(b) Sex and age group:	yes
(c) Industry:	yes
(d) Occupation:	yes
(e) Status in employment:	yes
(f) Highest educational level:	yes
(g) Hours of work:	yes
(h) Other characteristics:	yes

Re (a): The age is defined in terms of year of birth.

Re (g): Hours of work are expressed in terms of actual hours worked by employed persons, at work, during the short reference period.

Re (h): The census also collected information on the means of travel and travel time to the workplace.

6. Concepts and definitions:

(a) Economically active population: It comprises all persons aged 10 years and over who, during the reference periods, were usually either employed or unemployed, according to the definitions given below. Conscripts in compulsory military service are excluded from the definition.

(b) Employment: Considered as "employed" are all persons who, during the reference periods, had an occupation, function or any economic activity. To determine whether a person should be considered as employed, the questions asked were "Did X work during the period from March 1990 to February 1991?" and "How was X employed during the week preceding the census (10-16 March 1991)?."

It is reported that the following categories are included:

i) persons doing unpaid work in family firm or business;
ii) persons engaged in the production of primary products for own consumption;
iii) employed persons, temporarily absent from work;
iv) working students with a part time job;
v) seasonal or occasional workers (provided they were working at the time of the census);
vi) apprentices and trainees.

Only persons falling in category (i) can be identified separately by means of their responses to the question on status in employment.

(c) Unemployment: Considered as "unemployed" are all persons who, during the reference week, were without work, seeking work and immediately available for work. Young persons and first-time jobseekers are also included in the definition. On the other hand, employed persons looking for a new job are not covered by this definition and are considered as employed.

7. Classifications used:
Both employed persons and unemployed persons previously employed are classified by industry, by occupation and by status in employment.

(a) Industry: The question asked concerns the type of activity of the firm, business, establishment or service in which the person currently works or last worked. For coding industry, the ISIC-rev.3 was used to the group (3-digit) level.

(b) Occupation: The question asked concerns the exact nature of the person's current or most recent occupation. For coding occupation, the ISCO-68 was used to the unit group (3-digit) level.

(c) Status in employment: Based on the question: "What is (was) X's status in employment?." For coding status in employment, four categories were used, namely: employer (employing one or more persons); self employed; wage earner or day labourer; family helper (in a family firm or agricultural undertaking).

8. Main differences compared with the previous census:
The 1991 census differed from the previous census in the following respects:

- The data will be fully processed.
- In addition to a short reference period (the week preceding the census date), a long reference period was also used (the year preceding the census).
- As regards the short reference period, persons who worked at least one hour were considered as employed and therefore included in the definition of employment.
- For the first time, the census collected information on the means and time of travel to the workplace.

9. Publication of the census results:
The title of the publication containing the census results is "Results of the 17 March 1991 population and housing census."

The organization responsible for this publication is Office National de Statistique de Grèce, Direction de l'Information Statistique et des Publications, 14-16 Lycourgou, 10166 Athens.

The results of the 1991 census are also available in the form of unpublished tables, diskettes and magnetic tapes.

GRENADA

1. Name and address of the organization responsible for the census:
Central Statistical Office, Ministry of Finance, Financial Complex, The Carenage, St. George's, Grenada.

2. Population censuses conducted since 1945 (years):
1960, 1970 and 1991. The present description relates to the 1991 population census (held on 12 May).

3. Coverage of the census:
(a) Geographical scope: Whole country.
(b) Persons covered: All persons of all ages.

4. Reference period:
The week prior to the census day.

5. Main topics:

(a) Total population, by sex and age:	yes

Economically active population by:

(b) Sex and age group:	yes
(c) Industry:	yes
(d) Occupation:	yes
(e) Status in employment:	yes
(f) Highest educational level:	yes
(g) Hours of work:	yes
(h) Other characteristics:	yes

Re (a): The age is defined in terms of age at last birthday.

Re (g): Hours of work relate to the actual number of hours of employed persons.

Re (h): The census also collected information on means of transport to travel to work.

6. Concepts and definitions:

(a) Economically active population: It comprises all persons aged 15 years and over who, during the reference week, were either employed or unemployed according to the definitions given below. Members of the armed forces are included in the definition.

(b) Employment: Employment is determined on the basis of the questions: "What did you do most during the past week? For example did you work, look for a job, keep house or carry on some other activity?" and "Did you do any work at all last week for any length of time, including helping in a family business/farm, street vending or work at home?."

It is reported that the following categories are included:

i)   persons doing unpaid work in family firm or business;
ii) employed persons, temporarily absent from work;
iii) working students with a part time job.

All persons belonging to these categories can be identified separately.

(c) Unemployment: The question used to determine unemployment was the same as indicated under 6 (b) above. Considered as unemployed were the persons who, during the reference week, were without work and looked for a job.

7. Classifications used:

Both employed persons and unemployed persons previously employed are classified by industry and by occupation. Only employed persons are classified by status in employment.

(a) Industry: Based on the questions: "What kind of business is/was carried on at your workplace?" and "What is the name & address of your present workplace?." For coding industry, the ISIC-rev.3 was used.

(b) Occupation: Based on the question: "What sort of work do you do/did you do in your main occupation?." For coding occupation, the ISCO-88 was used to the unit-group (4-digit) level.

(c) Status in employment: Based on the question: "Do you work for a wage, carry on your own business or as an unpaid?." For coding status in employment, six groups were used, namely: work in a family business; paid employee (Government); paid employee (private); unpaid worker; own business with paid help (employer); own business without paid help (own account).

8. Main differences compared with the previous census:
No major difference.

9. Publication of the census results:
The final results will be issued in December 1996.

The organization responsible for the publication of the results is the Central Statistical Office, Financial Complex, The Carenage, St. George's.

Results will also available on diskette or unpublished tables.

GUADELOUPE

1. Name and address of the organization responsible for the census:
Institut national de la statistique et des études économiques (INSEE), Service régional de la Guadeloupe, Avenue Paul Lacave, B.P. 96, 97102 Basse-Terre, Guadeloupe.

2. Population censuses conducted since 1945 (years):
1954, 1961, 1967, 1974, 1982 and 1990. The present description relates to the 1990 census (held on 15 March).

3. Coverage of the census:
(a) Geographical scope: Whole territory.

(b) Persons covered: All persons of all ages.

4. Reference period:
The week preceding the census day.

5. Main topics:

(a) Total population, by sex and age:	yes

Economically active population by:

(b) Sex and age group:	yes
(c) Industry:	yes
(d) Occupation:	yes
(e) Status in employment:	yes
(f) Highest educational level:	yes
(g) Hours of work:	no
(h) Other characteristics:	yes

Re (a): The age is defined in terms of year of birth.

Re (h): The census also covered information on other topics, such as: full-time and part-time work, primary activity, the number of workers employed by self-employed persons, the length of time spent looking for work, etc.

6. Concepts and definitions:

(a) Economically active population: It comprises all persons aged 14 years and over who, during the reference week, were either employed or unemployed, according to the definitions given below. The definition also covers all members of the armed forces (career military staff and conscripts). Questions concerning economic activity were asked only of a sample of persons, which excluded military staff living in barracks and prisonners.

(b) Employment: Considered as "employed" are all persons who, during the reference week, had an occupation, function or any economic activity, whether paid or unpaid. Specific questions used to determine if a person is to be counted as employed are: "Do you work (full time or part time)?"; "Are you: employed or self-employed (farmer, craftsman, merchant, industrialist, professional, unpaid family worker, etc.)?," and "If you are self-employed: how many workers do you employ? (do not count apprentices or domestic staff; in agriculture, count only permanent employees)." The definition also covers persons engaged in paid community work provided to the unemployed, persons who have been placed by a temporary employment agency, persons holding a fixed-term employment contract, and persons with a retraining contract.

It is reported that the following categories are included:

i)   persons doing unpaid work in family firm or business;
ii)   persons engaged in the production of primary products for own consumption;
iii) employed persons, temporarily absent from work;
iv)   working students with a part time job;
v)   seasonal or occasional workers who were working at the time of the census;
vi)   conscripts for military/civilian service;
vii) apprentices (bound by a contract) and trainees (mainly in enterprises or training centres).

Only persons belonging to categories (i), (vi) and (vii) can be identified separately.

(c) Unemployment: Considered as "unemployed" are all persons who, on their own initiative, stated that they were without work, and who were seeking work. The questions used to determine if a person should be considered as unemployed are "Are you unemployed (whether registered or not with the National Employment Agency)?," "Have you previously worked? (if so, what was your primary occupation?," and "Are you seeking work (for: less than three months; three months to less than one year; one year to less than two years; two years or more)?."

7. Classifications used:
Both employed persons and unemployed persons previously employed included in the sample are classified by occupation. Only employed persons in the sample are classified by industry and by status in employment.

(a) Industry: Surveyed persons were asked to give the address and name of the establishment where they work or which they manage, and to identify its activity as accurately as possible (for example: wholesale wine dealers, manufacture of metal scaffolding, road passenger transport, etc.). For coding industry, 100 groups of the Nomenclature of Activities and Products (NAP) were used. Links to the ISIC have not been established.

(b) Occupation: Surveyed persons were asked to identify their current or most recent occupation as accurately as possible (for example: electrical maintenance worker, lorry driver, household appliance salesperson, chemical engineer, self-service cashier, etc.) to permit the determination of their occupational group. The question, however, was left open-ended, so that surveyed persons could reply in their own words. The classification in a specific group takes place when the data is processed. For coding occupation, a direct coding system entailing 42 groups was used. Links to the ISCO have not been established.

(c) Status in employment: For coding this variable, five categories were used, namely: self-employed person; employer; employee; unpaid family worker; other.

8. Main differences compared with the previous census:
The minimum age limit used for inclusion in the economically active population was 15 years in the 1982 census.

Moreover, both employed persons and unemployed persons previously employed had been classified by industry and by status in employment in the 1982 census.

9. Publication of the census results:
The title of the publication containing the final census results is: "Evolution 1975-1982-1990 (Série jaune)," 1992.

The Institut national de la statistique et des études économiques (INSEE), 18 boulevard Adolphe Pinard, 75675 Paris Cedex 14, is responsible for this publication.

The 1990 final census data will also be available on diskettes, magnetic tapes and other formats on request.

GUAM

1. Name and address of the organization responsible for the census:
Guam Department of Commerce, Suite 601, ITC Bldg, 590 S. Marine Drive, Tamuning 96911.

2. Population censuses conducted since 1945 (years):
1950, 1960, 1970, 1980 and 1990. The present description relates to the 1990 population census (held on 1st April).

3. Coverage of the census:
(a) Geographical scope: Whole area.
(b) Persons covered: All persons of all ages.

4. Reference period:
The week prior to the census date and the year prior to the census year.

5. Main topics:
(a) Total population, by sex and age:	yes

Economically active population by:
(b) Sex and age group:	yes
(c) Industry:	yes
(d) Occupation:	yes
(e) Status in employment:	yes
(f) Highest educational level:	yes
(g) Hours of work:	yes
(h) Other characteristics:	yes

Re (a): The age is defined both in terms of year of birth and of age at last birthday.

Re (g): Hours of work relate both to actual hours worked by employed persons, at work, during the reference week and to the total period (expressed in number of hours or weeks) worked by employed persons during the year 1989.

Re (h): The census also collected other information, such as: location of work; type of transport to work; how many people rode together to work (for private vehicles only); time used to travel to work; income from wages, salaries, tips and commissions; income from own farm or non-farm business, proprietorship or partnership.

6. Concepts and definitions:
(a) Economically active population: It comprises all persons aged 15 years and over who, during the reference periods, were either employed or unemployed, according to the definitions given below. However, the census results will only be published for persons aged 16 years and over. Members of the armed forces are included in the definition.

(b) Employment: The questions used to determine if a person is to be counted as employed are "Did you work at any time last week, either full time or part time?" and "Last year (1989) did you work, even for a few days, at a paid job or in a business or farm, excluding subsistence activity?."

It is reported that the following categories are included:
i) persons doing unpaid work in family firm or business;
ii) persons engaged in the production of primary products for own consumption;
iii) employed persons, temporarily absent from work;
iv) working students with a part time job;
v) seasonal or occasional workers;

vi) apprentices and trainees.
Only persons belonging to categories (i) and (ii) can be identified separately through specific questions.

(c) Unemployment: Considered as "unemployed" are all persons who, during the reference week, were without work and seeking work. To determine if a person is to be counted as unemployed, the following questions were used: "Were you on lay-off from a job or business last week?"; "Have you been looking for work to earn money during the last four weeks?"; "Could you have taken a job last week if one had been offered?"; and "When did you last work at a job, business or farm, even for a few days?."

7. Classifications used:
Both employed persons and unemployed persons who had worked any time in the year before the census year (1989) are classified by industry, by occupation and by status in employment.

(a) Industry: Based on the questions: "For whom did you work?;" "What kind of business or industry was this?"; and "Is this mainly manufacturing, wholesale trade, retail trade, construction, or something else?." For coding industry, 13 major groups and 231 categories of the U.S. Standard Industrial Classification (1972 and 1977 supplement) were used. No links to the ISIC have been established.

(b) Occupation: Based on the questions: "What kind of work were you doing?" and "What were your most important activities or duties?." For coding occupation, 13 major groups and 503 categories of the U.S. Standard Occupational Classification were used. No links to the ISCO have been established.

(c) Status in employment: Based on the question: "Were you: (1) Employee of a private for profit company or business or of an individual, for wages, salary, or commissions; (2) Employee of a private not-for-profit, tax-exempt, or charitable organization; (3) Local or territorial Government employee (territorial/commonwealth, etc.); (4) Federal Government employee; (5) Self-employed in own not-incorporated business, professional practice, or farm; (6) Self-employed in own incorporated business, professional practice, or farm; (7) Working without pay in family business or farm." For coding status in employment, the above seven groups were used.

8. Main differences compared with the previous census:
The only difference between the 1980 and 1990 censuses is the inclusion of armed forces personnel in the questions on industry, occupation and status in employment.

9. Publication of the census results:
Several summary tables of information from the 1990 census were released in August 1991. The completed document was available in 1992.

The organization responsible for this publication is: Puerto Rico and Outlying Areas Branch, Decennial Planning Division, U.S. Bureau of the Census, Washington, D.C. 20233.

The census results are also available in the form of diskettes, CD-ROM and unpublished tables.

GUATEMALA

1. Name and address of the organization responsible for the census:
Instituto Nacional de Estadística, 8a calle 9-55, Zona 1, Ciudad Guatemala, Guatemala 010001.

2. Population censuses conducted since 1945 (years):
1950, 1964, 1973, 1981 and 1994. The present description relates to the 1994 population census (held on 17 April).

3. Coverage of the census:
(a) Geographical scope: Whole country.
(b) Persons covered: All persons of all ages.

4. Reference period:
The week preceding the census date.

5. Main topics:
(a) Total population, by sex and age:	yes

Economically active population by:
(b) Sex and age group:	yes
(c) Industry:	yes
(d) Occupation:	yes
(e) Status in employment:	yes

(f) Highest educational level: yes
(g) Hours of work: no
(h) Other characteristics: no

Re (a): The age is defined in terms of age at last birthday, and in terms of year of birth.

6. Concepts and definitions:

(a) Economically active population: It comprises all persons aged 7 years and over who, during the reference week, were either employed or unemployed, according to the definitions given below. The definition includes professional members of the armed forces, but excludes conscripts in military or civilian service.

(b) Employment: Considered as "employed" are all persons who replied that they worked or did not work but had a job, when asked: "What did you do the week before the date of the census?." The choices were: Worked; Did not work but had a job; Looked for work, having been employed previously; Looked for a first job; Lived off savings or pension and did not work; Studied and did not work; Kept a home and did not work; Other.

It is reported that the following categories are included:

i)   persons doing unpaid work in family firm or business;
ii) employed persons, temporarily absent from work;
iii) working students with a part-time job.

All categories can be identified separately.

(c) Unemployment: Considered as "unemployed" are all persons who, when asked "What did you do the week before the date of the census?" replied that they had looked for work, whether or not previously employed.

7. Classifications used:

Both employed persons and unemployed persons (excluding first-time jobseekers) are classified by industry, by occupation and by status in employment.

(a) Industry: To determine industry group, persons were asked to indicate the activity of the factory, shop, office, farm, establishment, etc. where they were engaged in their stated occupation. Links to the ISIC-rev.3 have been established to the 4-digit level.

(b) Occupation: To determine occupation group, persons were asked to identify the occupation, type of work or function performed during the reference week or in their last job. Links to the ISCO-88 have been established to the unit group (4-digit) level.

(c) Status in employment: To determine this variable, persons were asked to indicate the category of their primary occupation, which was coded in six categories (employer, self-employed with own business premises, self-employed without own business premises, public sector employee, private sector employee, unpaid family worker).

8. Main differences compared with the previous census:

The only difference concerns the age limit, inasmuch as the 1994 census studied the economic characteristics of persons as from 7 years of age (compared to 10 years and over in the 1981 census).

9. Publication of the census results:

The title of the publication containing the final census data is "Características Generales de Habitación y Población," October 1995.

The organization responsible for this publication is Instituto Nacional de Estadística, - INE - 8va. Calle 9-55 Zona 1.

The census results are also available in the form of diskettes.

HONG KONG

1. Name and address of the organization responsible for the census:

Census and Statistics Department, 21/F., Wanchai Tower I, 12 Harbour Road, Wanchai, Hong Kong.

2. Population censuses conducted since 1945 (years):

Full censuses: 1961, 1971, 1981 and 1991; sample By-Censuses: 1966, 1976 and 1986. The present description relates to the 1991 census (which took place from 15 to 24 March).

3. Coverage of the census:

(a) Geographical scope: Whole territory.

(b) Persons covered: All persons of all ages.

4. Reference period:

The seven days prior to enumeration. However, for determining whether a person was seeking work, a period of 30 days prior to the census reference date was used.

5. Main topics:

(a) Total population, by sex and age: yes
Economically active population by:
(b) Sex and age group: yes
(c) Industry: yes
(d) Occupation: yes
(e) Status in employment: yes
(f) Highest educational level: yes
(g) Hours of work: no
(h) Other characteristics: no

Re (a): The age is defined in terms of age at last birthday.

6. Concepts and definitions:

(a) Economically active population: It comprises all persons aged 15 years and over in the sample who, during the reference periods were either employed or unemployed, according to the definitions given below. The definition also includes armed forces. Questions on economic activity were asked of a one-in-seven sample and only the residents present in Hong Kong on the census reference date were asked.

(b) Employment: Considered as "employed" are all persons in the sample who replied affirmatively to either one of the following three questions: "Did you work in the past seven days for wage or profit, including private tuition and work for hourly wage?," "Did you have a job in the past seven days?" and "Did you work without pay in your family's business in the past seven days?."

The employed persons may belong to the following categories:

i)   persons doing unpaid work in family firm or business;
ii) employed persons, temporarily absent from work;
iii) working students with a part time job;
iv) seasonal or occasional workers;
v)   multiple job holders;
vi) apprentices and trainees.

Only persons belonging to categories (i) and (v), can be identified separately by means of specific questions. For example: persons in category (i) can be identified through the reply to the question "Did you work without pay in your family's business in the past seven days?"; those in category (v) can be identified through the reply to the question "Did you have a secondary employment during the past 30 days?."

(c) Unemployment: Considered as "unemployed" are all persons in the sample who replied "no" to all three questions under 6 (b) above. They are further asked to answer the following questions: "Were you seeking work during the past 30 days?," "Why were you not seeking work?," "Were you available for work in the past seven days?" and "Why were you not available for work?." Based on their answers, they are then classified as "unemployed" or "economically inactive."

7. Classifications used:

Only employed persons in the sample are classified by industry, by occupation and by status in employment.

(a) Industry: Two types of questions were asked of employed persons in the sample. The question asked of employees was: "What kind of industry, business or service was carried out by your establishment at the location where you worked?." The question asked of employers, self-employed and family workers was: "What kind of industry, business or service was carried out by you/your family?." For coding industry, 87 codes of the national classification were used. Links to the ISIC-rev.3 have been established to the group (3-digit) level.

(b) Occupation: Based on the questions: "What was your occupation?," "What are the main tasks or duties you have to perform in that occupation?" and "What educational or professional qualifications are required by that job?." For coding occupation, 116 codes of the national classification of occupations were used. Links to the ISCO-88 have been established to the minor-group (3-digit) level.

(c) Status in employment: Based on the question: "Were you an employer, self-employed or an employee?." Unpaid family workers are identified in determining employed persons and

this question is skipped for them. For coding status in employment, the following four groups were used: self-employed; employers; employees (including out-workers); unpaid family workers.

8. Main differences compared with the previous census:
No major difference.

9. Publication of the census results:
The title of the publication containing the census results is "Hong Kong 1991 Population Census Summary Results," issued in October 1991, which is the first report within the series of summary publications.

The organization responsible for this publication is the Census Planning Section, Census and Statistics Department, Koway Court, 2/F, 111 Chai Wan Road.

The census results are also available in the form of unpublished tables, diskettes, magnetic tapes and CD-ROM.

HUNGARY

1. Name and address of the organization responsible for the census:
Office Central de Statistique de Hongrie, Division des Recensements, (KSH-Népszámlálás), Budafoki út 59, H-1111 Budapest.

2. Population censuses conducted since 1945 (years):
1949, 1960, 1970, 1980 and 1990. The present description relates to the 1990 census (held on 1 January).

3. Coverage of the census:
(a) Geographical scope: Whole territory.

(b) Persons covered: All persons of all ages, except: diplomats and foreign workers in the missions of foreign countries; members of foreign military contingents stationed in Hungary under the Warsaw Pact, and members of their families; foreign tourists who do not have a residence permit.

4. Reference period:
The reference period for all questions asked of employees, members of cooperatives, self-employed workers and unpaid workers working in a non-agricultural family business, is a short period, namely the last week of 1989; for unpaid family workers in agriculture the reference period is a longer period, i.e. at least 90 working days of ten hours during the year 1989.

5. Main topics:
(a) Total population, by sex and age:	yes

Economically active population by:
(b) Sex and age group:	yes
(c) Industry:	yes
(d) Occupation:	yes
(e) Status in employment:	yes
(f) Highest educational level:	yes
(g) Hours of work:	no
(h) Other characteristics:	yes

Re (a): The age is defined in terms of year of birth.

Re (g): Nevertheless, within the framework of the "representative programme" (affecting a sample of 20 per cent of the population), persons were asked if they worked full time or part time. As part of the same programme, retired persons who were still economically active were asked how many hours they had worked.

Re (h): Other questions on persons' economic activity were asked, in particular on: skill levels; the name and address of the workplace; the means of transport used and the time needed to commute to and from work; position in workforce; the date of initial entry into paid employment; any secondary economic activities in 1989 and their duration; etc. Some of these questions were asked of the whole of the economically active population, while other questions were put only to persons in the 20 per cent sample.

6. Concepts and definitions:
(a) Economically active population: It comprises all persons who, during the reference periods, were either employed or unemployed, according to the definitions given below. The definition also includes members of the armed forces. Students with a part-time job, students seeking job and pensioners in employment are excluded from this definition. No minimum or maximum age limit was set for the collection of information on the economically active population and its component groups; however, the published results will be confined to persons aged from 14 to 85 years. All persons were asked "Do you work, do you have a job?." Those replying no were asked to explain why they were not working.

Within the "basic programme" (affecting 80 per cent of the population), none of the questions on economic activity were asked of the following categories: retired persons, persons of independent means and other persons whose income was not linked to a current economic activity; unemployed persons looking for work; dependants. On the other hand, persons on leave from work under the child-rearing entitlement, although not considered economically active, were required to reply to all the questions concerning their situation prior to exercising their entitlement to such leave.

In the "representative programme" (a sample of 20 per cent of the whole of the population), employed persons were asked to reply to all the questions concerning employment and occupation. Retired persons as well as unemployed persons looking for work were asked to reply only to questions concerning their most recent economic activity, while retired persons who still worked either full time or part time were asked to provide some additional information in this connection. Dependants, for their part, were asked questions concerning those who provided for their support.

(b) Employment: Considered as "employed" are all persons who, during the reference periods, had an occupation, function or any economic activity. To determine if a person is to be counted as employed, the question used is the same as that asked of all persons, as indicated under 6 (a) above. If the answer is yes, the person was asked to give details of his/her activity, irrespective of whether it is pursued at home or outside the home and whether it is paid or unpaid.

It is reported that the following categories are included:
i) persons doing unpaid work in family firm or business;
ii) persons engaged in the production of products for own consumption;
iii) employed persons temporarily absent from work because on paid or unpaid leave or participating in training related to their occupation;
iv) conscripts (military or civilian service);
v) seasonal or occasional workers;
vi) multiple-job holders.

Persons belonging to these categories can be identified separately either on the basis of their reply to the question concerning status in employment (employee; member of co-operative; self-employed person; member of a liberal profession; family helper), or by reference to a special code. Multiple-job holders can be identified separately in the framework of the "representative programme," on the basis of their reply to the question "Did you, in addition to your primary occupation, have a secondary paid activity in 1989?."

(c) Unemployment: Considered as unemployed are all persons who answered no to the question asked under 6 (a) above, and who stated that they were looking for work or were first-time jobseekers. Persons who gave other reasons (such as: entitlement to leave for child-rearing; entitlement to a personal pension; receipt of a disability pension or any other personal annuity; entitlement to survivors' benefit or widow/widower's pension; enrolment in a day-care centre, preschool, primary or secondary school, college or university), as well as other dependant persons, are excluded from the definition of unemployment.

7. Classifications used:
Both employed persons and unemployed persons in the sample who were previously employed are classified by industry, by occupation and by status in employment.

(a) Industry: The questions asked to determine industry group concern the name of the employer and the address of the place of work. The person is required to identify the nature of the workplace accurately (for example: factory, company headquarters, store, school, health care institution, etc.). For coding industry, 38 main groups, 104 major divisions and 294 individual branches (to the 4-digit level) of the Hungarian nomenclature were used.

Links to the ISIC have not been established. Nevertheless, a new national classification system of branches of economic activity has recently been established; under this new system, which is consistent with the ISIC-rev.3, a recoding of at least a representative sample of questionnaires will permit comparisons at the international level.

(b) Occupation: Questions asked to determine occupation group refer to the nature of the occupation of the person surveyed and to his/her position in the hierarchy. For coding occupation, 16 major groups, 144 occupation groups and 808 individual occupations (to the 4-digit level) of the Hungarian nomenclature were used.

Links to the ISCO have not been established. Nevertheless, a new national classification system for occupations is to be prepared; under this new system, which will be consistent with ISCO-88 to the ten major group and sub-major-group level, the recoding of at least a representative sample of the questionnaires will permit comparisons at the international level.

(c) Status in employment: Specific questions were asked in both the "basic programme" and the "representative programme" to determine status in employment. For coding this variable, eight groups were used, namely: salaried employee; member of a cooperative; self-employed person in manual labour; self-employed person in non-manual labour; unpaid family member working for a member of an agricultural cooperative; unpaid family member working in a supplementary agricultural activity; unpaid family member working for a self-employed farmer; unpaid family member working for a self-employed person outside agriculture.

8. Main differences compared with the previous census:
The major difference between the 1990 census and 1980 census concerns the inclusion of unemployment as a new and significant component of economically active population.

In addition, the "representative programme" (affecting a sample of 20 per cent of the population) includes a number of new questions aimed at defining and describing the economically active population and its component groups, and at better determining status in employment. Other questions permit the identification of the primary occupation and secondary activities, full-time work and part-time work, educational and training levels, skill levels, etc.

9. Publication of the census results:
The titles of the some of the publications containing the census data are: "1.Preliminary data" August 1990, "Socio-occupational composition of active earners, households and families" 1992, "Place of work and place of residence of active earners" 1994, and "Detailed data of the 20% representative sample survey," 1995.

The organization responsible for these publications is Office Central de Statistique de Hongrie, Division des Recensements (KSH-Népszámlálás), H-1111 Budapest.

The 1990 census results are also available on diskette, CD-ROM and on-line.

INDIA

1. Name and address of the organization responsible for the census:
Office of the Registrar General and Census Commissioner, 2-A, Man Singh Road, New Delhi-110 011.

2. Population censuses conducted since 1945 (years):
1951, 1961, 1971, 1981 and 1991. The present description relates to the 1991 population census (held on 1st March).

3. Coverage of the census:
(a) Geographical scope: Whole country, except Jammu and Kashmir.

(b) Persons covered: All persons of all ages, except foreign diplomats and their families and nationals residing abroad. The staff of Indian Missions abroad and their families were covered by the census.

4. Reference period:
The year preceding the census day.

5. Main topics:
(a) Total population, by sex and age:	yes
Economically active population by:	
(b) Sex and age group:	yes
(c) Industry:	yes
(d) Occupation:	yes
(e) Status in employment:	yes
(f) Highest educational level:	yes
(g) Hours of work:	no
(h) Other characteristics:	no

Re (a): The age is defined in terms of age at last birthday.

6. Concepts and definitions:
(a) Economically active population: It comprises all persons who, during the reference year, were usually either employed or unemployed, according to the definitions given below. No age limit was fixed for inclusion in the economically active population; however, for employed persons, the published results relate to persons aged 5 years and over (except in the primary census abstract where age-wise data were not presented). Members of the armed forces are included in the definition.

The economic activity data were processed in two stages. In stage-1, tables were based on a 10 per cent sample of individuals in bigger states with a population of ten million and above, and on a 100 per cent basis in other smaller states and union territories. In stage-2, the data relating to "main workers" other than cultivators and agricultural workers, "marginal workers" and "non-workers" seeking/available for work, were entered on the computer on a 100 per cent basis to generate more detailed and reliable tabulations for lower administrative units.

(b) Employment: Employment is determined on the basis of the questions: "Did you work any time at all last year?" and "If yes, did you work for major part of last year?."

Work may be defined as participation in any economically productive activity. Such participation may be physical or mental in nature. Work involves not only actual work but also effective supervision and direction of work.

Main worker is a person who has worked a major part of the year, i.e. for 183 days or more or, in other words, for 6 months or more. Marginal worker is a person who might have done some work any time during the previous year, but not for the major part of the year. The data on secondary work done by main workers are also collected.

It is reported that the following categories are included:
i) persons doing unpaid work in family firm or business;
ii) employed persons, temporarily absent from work;
iii) working students with a part time job;
iv) seasonal or occasional workers;
v) conscripts for military/civilian service;
vi) apprentices and trainees.

Persons doing unpaid work in family firm or business can be identified separately from the census tabulation on family workers (except in cultivation).

Persons engaged in cultivation of land for own consumption are included in the economically active population but cannot be separately identified. Persons engaged in other production for own consumption are excluded from the economically active population. In the census, cultivation includes growing of cereal crops, pulses fibre crops, oil seeds and sugar-cane but not roots, vegetables, fruits, fodder crops, horticulture, etc.

Working students, who are marginal workers, can be identified separately through specific questions. However, the term "marginal worker" used in the census is not necessarily same as part-time worker.

(c) Unemployment: Considered as "unemployed" are all persons who, during the reference year, did not work at all and were therefore treated as non-workers. All non-workers were asked whether they were seeking work or available for work.

Students seeking work and persons seeking/available for work who had ever worked before can be identified separately through specific questions.

7. Classifications used:
Only employed persons other than cultivators and agricultural labourers are classified by industry, by occupation and by status in employment.

(a) Industry: Respondents are asked questions on the nature of industry, trade or service where they work to determine industry group. For coding industry, 462 groups of the National Industrial Classification of 1987 were used. Links to the ISIC-rev.3 have been established to the group (3-digit) level.

(b) Occupation: Respondents are asked to describe their work; both main workers and marginal workers are requested to reply this question to determine occupation group. For coding occupation, 512 occupational families of the National Classification of Occupations of 1968 were used. Links to the ISCO-68 have been established to the minor group (2-digit) level.

(c) Status in employment: Respondents are asked to specify their class of worker to determine their status in employment. For coding this variable, three groups (in case of household industry) and four groups (in case of others) were used, namely: employer; employee; single worker; family worker. There is no "employer" in the household industry according to the definition of household industry.

8. Main differences compared with the previous census:
The only difference in the data collection is that the question on seeking/available for work was canvassed only from non-workers in the 1991 census, whereas in the 1981 census it was canvassed both from non-workers and marginal workers. In case of persons seeking/available for work, a question whether they had ever worked before was asked for the first time in 1991, in order to know the fresh entrants in the labour force.

9. Publication of the census results:
The tables relating to the 1991 census were scheduled to be published in three stages: around 1993, by end 1994 and by end 1995. The final population totals, based on manual compilation, were to be released by end 1992.

The organization responsible for the publication of the census results is the Office of the Registrar General and Census Commissioner for India, 2-A, Man Singh Road, New Delhi.

The final results are also available in the form of diskettes, magnetic tapes, etc. on certain terms and conditions.

INDONESIA

1. Name and address of the organization responsible for the census:
Central Bureau of Statistics, J1. Dr. Sutomo Nr. 8, P.O. Box 1003, Jakarta 10010.

2. Population censuses conducted since 1945 (years):
1961, 1971, 1980 and 1990. The present description relates to the 1990 census (held on 31 October).

3. Coverage of the census:
(a) Geographical scope: Whole country.

(b) Persons covered: All persons of all ages. The sample census excluded those who are living outside the enumeration area, i.e., those living in forests (primitives), shipmen sailing for more than six months and undwellers.

4. Reference period:
The week preceding the census day. Persons in the sample were also asked to specify whether they worked or not during the previous year.

5. Main topics:

(a) Total population, by sex and age:	yes
Economically active population by:	
(b) Sex and age group:	yes
(c) Industry:	yes
(d) Occupation:	yes
(e) Status in employment:	yes
(f) Highest educational level:	yes
(g) Hours of work:	yes
(h) Other characteristics:	yes

Re (a): The age is defined in terms of age at last birthday.

Re (g): Hours of work relate both to usual hours of work of all employed persons and to actual hours of work of employed persons, at work.

Re (h): The census also collected information on: total number of hours worked in all jobs (i.e., main and additional); type of industry of the second job during the reference week; type of industry during the previous year; reason for not seeking work.

6. Concepts and definitions:

(a) Economically active population: It comprises all persons aged 10 years and over in the sample who, during the reference week, were either employed or unemployed, according to the definitions given below. However, questions concerning economic activity were asked of a 5 per cent sample through multistage random sampling, households being the ultimate sample unit. Members of the armed forces are included in the definition.

(b) Employment: Considered as "employed" are all persons in the sample who, during the reference week, performed any work of an economic value, at home or out of home, for at least one hour. The questions used to determine if a person is to be counted as employed are "Primary activity in the previous week: (1) Employed; (2) Attending school; (3) Housekeeping; (4) Other." and "In addition to 2, 3 and 4, also worked for at least one hour during the previous week?."

It is reported that the following categories are included:
i) persons doing unpaid work in family firm or business;
ii) persons engaged in the production of primary products for own consumption;
iii) employed persons, temporarily absent from work;
iv) working students with a part time job;
v) seasonal or occasional workers;
vi) conscripts for military/civilian service;
vii) multiple job holders;
viii) apprentices and trainees.

Only persons belonging to categories (i), (iii), (iv) and (vii) can be identified separately.

(c) Unemployment: Considered as "unemployed" are all persons in the sample who, during the reference week, were without work and looking for work. The questions asked to respondents who hadn't worked for at least one hour during the previous week are "Have you ever worked?" and "Did you look for work during the previous week?."

7. Classifications used:
Only employed persons in the sample are classified by industry, by occupation and by status in employment.

(a) Industry: Based on the question: "Please specify the type of industry in the primary activity during the previous week." For coding industry, 47 groups of the national classification were used. Links to the ISIC-rev.2 have been established to the division (2-digit) level.

(b) Occupation: Based on the question: "Please specify your occupation in the primary activity during the previous week." For coding occupation, 334 groups of the national classification were used. Links to the ISCO-68 have been established to the unit group (3-digit) level.

(c) Status in employment: Based on the question: "Please specify employment status in the primary activity during the previous week." For coding status in employment five groups were used: self-employed; self-employed assisted by family member or temporary help; employer; employee; unpaid family worker.

8. Main differences compared with the previous census:
No major difference.

9. Publication of the census results:
Advanced or provisional results were published in October 1991.

The title of the publication containing the final census results is "The Results of the 1990 Population Census."

The organization responsible for this publication is the Central Bureau of Statistics, P.O. Box 1003, Jakarta 10010.

Raw census results are also available in the form of magnetic tapes or diskettes.

IRAN, ISLAMIC REP. OF

1. Name and address of the organization responsible for the census:
Statistical Centre of Iran, Dr. Fatemi Avenue, Tehran 14144.

2. Population censuses conducted since 1945 (years):
1956, 1966, 1976, 1986 and 1991. The present description relates to the 1991 population census (held on 11 September).

3. Coverage of the census:
(a) Geographical scope: Whole country.

(b) Persons covered: All persons of all ages.

4. Reference period:
The seven days preceding the census day.

5. Main topics:

(a) Total population, by sex and age:	yes
Economically active population by:	
(b) Sex and age group:	yes
(c) Industry:	yes
(d) Occupation:	yes
(e) Status in employment:	yes

(f) Highest educational level: yes
(g) Hours of work: no
(h) Other characteristics: yes

Re (a): The age is defined both in terms of year of birth and age at last birthday.

Re (h): The census also registered the duration of unemployment in months.

6. Concepts and definitions:

(a) Economically active population: It comprises all persons aged 10 years and over who, during the reference period, were either employed or unemployed according to the definitions given below. The census is combined with a household survey based on a 10 per cent sample; all persons aged 10 years and over in the sample were asked questions on economic activity. Members of the armed forces are included in the definition.

(b) Employment: Considered as "employed" are all persons in the sample who, during the reference week, performed any work for wages, profit or family gain, at home or out of home. Persons without permanent job who worked at least two days during the reference period are included in the definition.

It is reported that the following categories are included:
i) persons doing unpaid work in family firm or business;
ii) employed persons, temporarily absent from work;
iii) working students with a part time job;
iv) seasonal or occasional workers, provided they were not seeking work;
v) conscripts for military/civil service;
vi) apprentices and trainees.

Categories (i) and (iii) can be identified separately by means of specific answers to questions on their employment and educational status.

(c) Unemployment: Considered as "unemployed" are all persons in the sample who, during the reference week, were without work and seeking work.

7. Classifications used:
Only employed persons in the sample were classified by industry, by occupation and by status in employment.

(a) Industry: Employed persons were asked to indicate the location and major activity of their work place in order to determine industry group. For coding industry, the ISIC-rev.3 was used to the class (4-digit) level.

(b) Occupation: Respondents were asked to indicate their occupation accurately. For coding occupation, the ISCO-68 was used to the unit group (3-digit) level.

(c) Status in employment: Employed persons were registered under one of the five codes: employer; own-account worker; wage and salary earner (public sector); wage and salary earner (private sector); and unpaid family worker.

8. Main differences compared with the previous census:
The 1986 census was a complete census of all households in which questions relating to the economically active population and its components were asked of all persons aged 6 years and over. No questions were asked in the 1986 census on the duration of unemployment.

9. Publication of the census results:
The final results of the population census have been published in 1992 in the publication entitled "National Results of the 1991 Multi-Round Population Census."

The organization responsible for the publication is the Statistical Centre of Iran, Dr. Fatemi Ave., Tehran 14144.

Data is available as a printed form and also on diskette or magnetic tape.

IRELAND

1. Name and address of the organization responsible for the census:
Central Statistics Office, Ardee Road, Rathmines, Dublin 6, Ireland.

2. Population censuses conducted since 1945 (years):
1946, 1951, 1956, 1961, 1966, 1971, 1979, 1981, 1986 and 1991; the 1979 census was conducted for the purpose of revising the boundaries of electoral constituencies. The present description relates to the 1991 population census (held on 21st April).

3. Coverage of the census:
(a) Geographical scope: Whole country.

(b) Persons covered: All persons of all ages (on the "de facto" basis).

4. Reference period:
The day of the census. The person's present principal status was taken into account on the basis of subjective selection by the respondent.

5. Main topics:
(a) Total population, by sex and age: yes
Economically active population by:
(b) Sex and age group: yes
(c) Industry: yes
(d) Occupation: yes
(e) Status in employment: yes
(f) Highest educational level: yes
(g) Hours of work: no
(h) Other characteristics: no

Re (a): Most tabulations are based on age at last birthday, but some tables based on year of birth are also prepared.

6. Concepts and definitions:

(a) Economically active population: It comprises all persons aged 15 years and over who, at the date of the census, were either employed or unemployed, according to the definitions given below. The definition also covers professional members of the armed forces.

(b) Employment: Considered as "employed" are all persons who, subjectively considered themselves as being in employment on the day of the census. Included in principle are persons who, at the census date, performed any work of an economic value, at home or out of home. Working students with a part-time job are excluded from the definition.

It is reported that the following categories are included:
i) persons doing unpaid work in family firm or business;
ii) persons engaged in the production of primary products for own consumption;
iii) employed persons, temporarily absent from work;
iv) seasonal or occasional workers;
v) apprentices and trainees.

Only persons belonging to category (i) can be identified separately. The incorporation of working students with a part time job depends on how they described their present status.

(c) Unemployment: Considered as "unemployed" are all persons who, at the census date, subjectively classified themselves as such.

7. Classifications used:
Both employed persons and unemployed persons previously employed are classified by industry, by occupation and by status in employment.

(a) Industry: Based on the questions: "a) Employer and employer's business (For persons at work: if an employee, state name of employer and nature of business carried on by employer; if self-employed, state the nature of business carried on. For unemployed, state the name and nature of the business of last employer); b) Address of place of work (Give full and exact address at which actually working: if working from a fixed centre or depot give that address; if working at home, e.g. farmer, shopkeeper living on premises, write 'At home.' For persons with no fixed place of work, e.g. commercial traveller, write 'None')."

Where the information on the employer and address of place of work is sufficient, the census record is linked to a business register from which activity and place of work codes are derived. Otherwise, activity and place of work are coded directly rather than via the business register.

Links to the ISIC (both ISIC-rev.2 and ISIC-rev.3) have been established to the division (2-digit) level.

(b) Occupation: Based on the questions: "If at work, state the usual principal occupation, giving a full description."; "If unemployed or retired, describe the principal occupation previously held."; "Persons described as farmers or farm workers should also state the area of the land currently/previously farmed."

For coding occupation, a national coding system with 8,700 job titles within 210 group-coding was used to the exact job title. Links to the ISCO (both ISCO-68 and ISCO-88) have been established, respectively to the minor and unit group levels.

(c) *Status in employment*: Respondents were asked to specify their current/previous status in employment. For coding status in employment, four groups were used, namely: self-employed, with paid employees; self-employed, without paid employees; employee; assisting relative (not receiving a fixed wage or salary).

8. Main differences compared with the previous census:
The principal differences in coding practice are:
- "industry" will be coded by linking to a business Register, where possible also enabling place of work to be coded;
- "occupation" will be coded to a much more detailed level than previously, allowing results to be presented according to the UK's SOC classification and according to ISCO-88, as well as the existing national classification.

9. Publication of the census results:
Data on the total and economically active population have been issued in 1994 in various publications, such as "Local Population Reports (second series)," as well as in detailed subject-matter census volumes.

The organization responsible for these publications is the Central Statistics Office, Dublin.

The 1991 census results are also available in the form of ad-hoc tables (on request). Small Area Population Statistics are available on paper, tape and diskette.

ISLE OF MAN

1. Name and address of the organization responsible for the census:
Economic Affairs Division, Isle of Man Government, Illiam Dhone House, 2 Circular Road, Douglas, Isle of Man IMI IPQ, British Isles.

2. Population censuses conducted since 1945 (years):
1951, 1961, 1966, 1971, 1976, 1981, 1986 and 1991. The present description relates to the 1991 population census (held on 14 April).

3. Coverage of the census:
(a) *Geographical scope*: Whole country.

(b) *Persons covered*: All persons of all ages.

4. Reference period:
The week preceding the census day, and five months of the previous year (1st May - 30 September 1990) for seasonal work only.

5. Main topics:
(a) Total population, by sex and age:	yes

Economically active population by:
(b) Sex and age group:	yes
(c) Industry:	yes
(d) Occupation:	yes
(e) Status in employment:	yes
(f) Highest educational level:	no
(g) Hours of work:	yes
(h) Other characteristics:	yes

Re (a): The age is defined in terms of age at last birthday.

Re (g): Employed persons are asked to specify their actual hours of work. Seasonal workers are asked to specify the number of weeks and the number of hours per week worked during the long reference period.

Re (h): The census also collected information on work permits ("does the persons hold a current work permit?") and on means of transport used to travel to workplace.

6. Concepts and definitions:
(a) *Economically active population*: It comprises all persons aged 16 years and over who, during the reference period, were either employed or unemployed, according to the definitions given below. The definition excludes working students with a part time job and students seeking work. However, all members of the armed forces are included in the definition. There are no conscripts in the Isle of Man.

(b) *Employment*: Considered as "employed" are all persons who stated that during the reference week they worked either full time (more than 30 hours) or part-time (30 hours or less), for an employer or being self employed. Teachers working 25 hours or more are counted as full-time.

It is reported that the following categories are included:

i) employed persons, temporarily absent from work;
ii) seasonal or occasional workers;
iii) multiple job holders;
iv) apprentices and trainees.

Only persons belonging to categories (ii) and (iii) can be identified separately.

(c) *Unemployment*: Considered as "unemployed" are all persons who stated that during the reference week they were without job and looking for a job.

7. Classifications used:
Only employed persons are classified by industry, by occupation and by status in employment.

(a) *Industry*: Based on the question: "Name and business of Employer or self-employed person's business? e.g. provides office cleaning services; manufactures animal foodstuffs; installs central heating systems; provides professional legal services." For coding industry, 21 groups of the national classification were used. No links to the ISIC have been established.

(b) *Occupation*: Based on the question: "What is the person's occupation? e.g. gas fitter; accounts clerk; banking supervisor; or clerk." Persons were asked to give a description of the work done, e.g. audio-typing; managing accounts for private clients; repairing agricultural machinery; delivering goods to customers. For coding occupation, 371 groups of the SOC (United Kingdom's Standard Occupational Classification) were used. Links to the ISCO-88 have been established to the minor group (3-digit) level.

(c) *Status in employment*: Three groups were used for coding this variable, namely: employee; self-employed employing others; self-employed not employing others.

8. Main differences compared with the previous census:
The 1986 census did not collect data on economic activity.

The minimum age limit was 15 in 1981 (in 1981, the school leaving age was 15. This had been increased to 16 by 1991 and was the reason for the change in coverage in the census).

9. Publication of the census results:
The final census data on the economically active population and its components were issued in a publication entitled "Isle of Man Census Report 1991." Volume I was published in March 1991 and Volume II appeared in February 1992. Additional data is published in "Isle of Man Labour Statistics 1995."

The organization responsible for the publication is the Economic Affairs Division, Illiam Dhone House, 2 Circular Road, Douglas, Isle of Man IMI IPQ, British Isles.

Subject to confidentiality additional information is available, either in the form of unpublished tables or diskettes.

ITALY

1. Name and address of the organization responsible for the census:
Istituto Nazionale di Statistica (ISTAT), Via Adolfo Ravà 150, 00142 Rome.

2. Population censuses conducted since 1945 (years):
1951, 1961, 1971, 1981 and 1991. The present description relates to the 1991 census (held on 20 October).

3. Coverage of the census:
(a) *Geographical scope*: Whole territory.

(b) *Persons covered*: All persons of all ages, except national residents abroad, foreigners holding a diplomatic passport and NATO military staff.

4. Reference period:
The week preceding the census day.

5. Main topics:
(a) Total population, by sex and age:	yes

Economically active population by:
(b) Sex and age group:	yes
(c) Industry:	yes
(d) Occupation:	yes
(e) Status in employment:	yes
(f) Highest educational level:	yes
(g) Hours of work:	yes
(h) Other characteristics:	yes

Re (a): The age is defined in terms of age at last birthday.

Re (g): Hours of work relate to actual hours worked by employed persons, at work.

Re (h): Other information was also collected on: occupational or non-occupational status, workplace, means of transport used to reach workplace and time spent for this purpose.

6. Concepts and definitions:

(a) Economically active population: It comprises all persons aged 14 years and over who, during the reference week, were either employed or unemployed, according to the definitions given below. The definition includes career members of the armed forces, but excludes conscripts; the latter can nevertheless be identified separately. Working students with a part time job and students seeking work are excluded from the definition.

(b) Employment: Considered as "employed" are all persons who, during the reference week, had an occupation, function or any economic activity, whether paid or unpaid.

It is reported that the following categories are included:

i) persons doing unpaid work in family firm or business;
ii) employed persons, temporarily absent from work;
iii) seasonal or occasional workers;
iv) apprentices.

Only categories (i) and (iv) can be identified separately. Conscripts, although not included in the economically active population, can also be identified separately.

(c) Unemployment: Considered as "unemployed" are all persons who, during the reference week, were without work and seeking work. First-time jobseekers are excluded from the definition.

7. Classifications used:

Both employed persons and unemployed persons previously employed are classified by industry, by occupation and by status in employment.

(a) Industry: The questions asked concern the exact location and the main or sole activity of the establishment, farm, shop or store, enterprise, etc, where the person works or last worked. For coding industry, 60 divisions of the national classification of industries were used. Links to the ISIC-rev.3 have been established to the division (2-digit) level.

(b) Occupation: The two questions asked relate, on the one hand, to the type of work performed (for example: middle-school teacher, farmer, electronic technician, architect, computer programmer, secretary, automotive electrician, etc.), avoiding such general terms as employee or worker; and, on the other hand, to the main tasks performed within the framework of the persons's current or most recent activity (for example: teaching of mathematics, viticulture, radar control, computer programming, secretarial work, repair of electrical circuitry in automobiles, etc.). For coding occupation, 35 groups of the national classification of occupations were used. Links to the ISCO-88 have been established to the major group (1-digit) level.

(c) Status in employment: The specific question refers to the person's status in employment. For coding this variable, the following 14 groups were used: company director; senior manager; employee; intermediate category staff; foreman, worker (specialized, skilled or unskilled); other wage earner; apprentice; homeworker for an enterprise; professional member of the armed forces or similar; employer; self-employed person; member of a liberal profession; member of a producers' or service cooperative; family helper (for example: a wife who helps her husband keep shop, a son who helps his father farm, etc.).

8. Main differences compared with the previous census:

During the 1981 census only one question had been asked to determine occupational group, namely: "Indicate your occupation, craft or trade"; the 1991 census entailed two questions for this purpose.

9. Publication of the census results:

The title of the publication containing the data on the economically active population is "Popolazione e abitazioni" (95 provincial sections, 20 regional sections and one national section).

The organization responsible for publishing the census results is Istituto Nazionale di Statistica (ISTAT), Rome.

The 1991 final census data are also available on diskettes and magnetic tapes.

JAMAICA

1. Name and address of the organization responsible for the census:

Statistical Institute of Jamaica, 97B Church Street, Kingston.

2. Population censuses conducted since 1945 (years):

1960, 1970, 1982 and 1991. The present description relates to the 1991 population census (held on 8 April).

3. Coverage of the census:

(a) Geographical scope: Whole country.

(b) Persons covered: All persons of all ages.

4. Reference period:

One week and one year prior to the day of census respectively.

5. Main topics:

(a) Total population, by sex and age:	yes

Economically active population by:

(b) Sex and age group:	yes
(c) Industry:	yes
(d) Occupation:	yes
(e) Status in employment:	yes
(f) Highest educational level:	yes
(g) Hours of work:	yes
(h) Other characteristics:	yes

Re (a): The age is defined in terms of age at last birthday.

Re (g): Hours of work relate to the number of hours worked by employed persons during the short reference period and to the number of months they worked during the long reference period.

Re (h): Employed persons were asked how much did they earn from their job.

6. Concepts and definitions:

(a) Economically active population: It comprises all persons aged 14 years and over who, during the reference week, were either employed or unemployed according to the definitions given below. Members of the armed forces are included in the definition. Excluded are students working part-time and students seeking work.

(b) Employment: Employment is determined on the basis of the question: "What did you do most during the week preceding the census day? For example did you work, look for work, keep house or what?." The possible responses were: Worked; With job not working; Seeking first job; Other, seeking work; Did not seek work but wanted work and available; Student; Home duties; Retired; Disabled, unable to work; Other; Not stated.

It is reported that the following categories are included:

i) persons doing unpaid work in family firm or business;
ii) persons engaged in the production of primary products for own consumption;
iii) seasonal or occasional workers;
iv) conscripts for military/civilian service;
v) apprentices and trainees.

Only persons belonging to first category can be identified separately.

(c) Unemployment: The question used to determine unemployment was the same as indicated under 6 (b) above. Considered as unemployed were the persons who, during the reference week, were without work, wanted to work and were available for work.

7. Classifications used:

Both employed persons and unemployed persons previously employed are classified by industry, by occupation and by status in employment.

(a) Industry: Based on the question: "What kind of business is/was carried on at the work place?." For coding industry the national classification was used. Links to the ISIC-rev.3 have been established to the division (2-digit) level.

(b) Occupation: Based on the question: "What kind of work do you do/did you last do?." For coding occupation the national classification was used. Links to the ISCO-88 have been established to the sub-major group (2-digit) level.

(c) Status in employment: Based on the question: "Do you work for a wage, carry on your own business or what?." For coding status in employment, seven groups were used, namely:

paid employee (Government); paid employee (private enterprise); paid employee (private home); unpaid worker; own business with paid employees; own business without paid employees; not stated.

8. Main differences compared with the previous census:
No major difference.

9. Publication of the census results:
The final results of the population census were published by 1995 in several different publications.

The organization responsible for the publication of the results is the Statistical Institute of Jamaica, 97 B Church Street, Kingston.

Results are also available on diskette, magnetic tape or compact disc.

JAPAN

1. Name and address of the organization responsible for the census:
Population Census Division, Statistics Bureau, Management and Coordination Agency, 19-1 Wakamatsu-cho, Shinjuku-ku, Tokyo 162.

2. Population censuses conducted since 1945 (years):
1947, 1950, 1955, 1960, 1965, 1970, 1975, 1980, 1985 and 1990. The present description relates to the 1990 population census (held on 1st October).

3. Coverage of the census:

(a) Geographical scope: Whole country, except following islands: (1) Habomai-gunto, Shikotan-to, Kunashiri-to and Etorofu-to; and (2) Takeshima in Goka-mura, Shimane-ken.

(b) Persons covered: All persons of all ages, except: foreign diplomatic corps, their suite and their dependents; foreign military personnel including both military corps and civilians, and their dependents; residents abroad (among Japanese who are staying in foreign countries, those who are expected to be absent from respective home for 3 months or more around the date of the census).

4. Reference period:
The week preceding the day of the census (24-30 September 1990).

5. Main topics:
(a) Total population, by sex and age:	yes
Economically active population by:	
(b) Sex and age group:	yes
(c) Industry:	yes
(d) Occupation:	yes
(e) Status in employment:	yes
(f) Highest educational level:	yes
(g) Hours of work:	no
(h) Other characteristics:	yes

Re (a): The age is defined in terms of age at last birthday.
Re (h): The census also collected information concerning the means of transport and time used to travel to work.

6. Concepts and definitions:

(a) Economically active population: It comprises all persons aged 15 years and over who, during the reference week, were either employed or unemployed, according to the definitions given below. The definition also includes self-defence forces, which are classified as government workers.

(b) Employment: The question used to determine if a person is to be counted as employed is "Did the person work at any time during the week from 24th to 30th of September? (1) mostly worked; (2) worked besides doing homework; (3) worked besides attending school; (4) had a job, but temporarily absent from work; (5) looked for a job; (6) did housework; (7) attended school; (8) other." Those who classified themselves under 1, 2, 3 or 4 were counted as "employed."

It is reported that the following categories are included:

i) persons doing unpaid work in a family firm or business;
ii) employed persons, temporarily absent from work;
iii) working students with a part time job;
iv) seasonal or occasional workers;
v) apprentices and trainees: when persons' status and salaries or wages are guaranteed by the company for which they work while receiving education, they are considered

as "employed persons" and included in the economically active population.

Only persons belonging to categories (ii) and (iii) can be identified separately. Working students with a part time job can be identified with "worked besides attending school"; however, concerning the job of the students, it cannot be distinguished whether it is a part time job or a full time job.

(c) Unemployment: Considered as "unemployed" are all persons who, during the reference period, were without work and seeking work. To determine if a person is to be counted as unemployed, the question used is the same as that indicated under 6 (b) above. Students seeking work are excluded from the definition.

7. Classifications used:
Only employed persons are classified by industry, by occupation and by status in employment.

(a) Industry: Specific questions were asked of employed persons on the name of establishment and kind of business, as well as the kind of products or goods. For coding industry, 14 major groups, 75 medium groups and 213 minor groups were used. Links to the ISIC-rev.2 have been established to the major group (3-digit) level.

(b) Occupation: Specific questions were asked of employed persons on the occupation and kind of work. For coding occupation, 10 major groups, 61 medium groups and 294 minor groups were used. Links to the ISCO-68 have been established to the major group (1-digit) level.

(c) Status in employment: Specific questions were asked of employed persons to determine status in employment. For coding status in employment, six groups were used, namely: employee (includes office workers, factory workers, public servants, officers of a corporation, employees in a private retail shop, domestic servants, daily or temporary workers, etc.); director of a firm or corporation; self-employed, employing others; self-employed, not employing others (proprietors of unincorporated shops and factories, farmers, medical practitioners, lawyers, writers, domestic helpers on own account, peddlers, etc., should be classified into "Self-employed, employing others" or "Self-employed, not employing other" according to whether or not they employed persons for their business); family worker; doing home handicraft.

8. Main differences compared with the previous census:
No major difference.

9. Publication of the census results:
The title of the publication containing the census results is "1990 Population Census of Japan," 1994.

The organization responsible for this publication is the Population Census Division, Statistics Bureau, Management and Coordination Agency, 19-1 Wakamatsu-cho, Shinjuku-ku, Tokyo 162.

The census results are also available in other forms, i.e., unpublished tables and magnetic tapes.

KENYA

1. Name and address of the organization responsible for the census:
Central Bureau of Statistics in the Office of the Vice-President and Ministry of Planning and National Development, P.O. Box 30266, Nairobi.

2. Population censuses conducted since 1945 (years):
1948, 1962, 1969, 1979 and 1989. The present description relates to the 1989 population census (held on 24 August).

3. Coverage of the census:

(a) Geographical scope: Whole country.

(b) Persons covered: All persons of all ages.

4. Reference period:
The week preceding the census day.

5. Main topics:
(a) Total population, by sex and age:	yes
Economically active population by:	
(b) Sex and age group:	yes
(c) Industry:	no
(d) Occupation:	yes
(e) Status in employment:	yes

(f) Highest educational level: yes
(g) Hours of work: no
(h) Other characteristics: no

Re (a): The age is defined in terms of age at last birthday.

6. Concepts and definitions:

(a) Economically active population: It comprises all persons aged 10 years and over who, during the reference week, were either employed or unemployed, according to the definitions given below. Working students with a part time job and students seeking work are excluded from the definition.

(b) Employment: Considered as "employed" are all persons who, during the reference period, worked most of the time for wages, salary, commission, tips, contract and those paid in kind. The question used to determine if a person is to be counted as employed is "What was X mainly doing during the last seven days preceeding the census night? 1) worked for pay or profit; 2) on leave/sick leave; 3) working on family holding; 4) no work; 5) seeking work; 6) student; 7) retired; 8) disabled; 9) home makers; 10) other."

It is reported that the following categories are included:

i) persons doing unpaid work in family firm or business;
ii) persons engaged in the production of primary products for own consumption;
iii) employed persons, temporarily absent from work;
iv) seasonal or occasional workers;
v) apprentices and trainees.

Only persons belonging to category (iii) can be identified separately.

(c) Unemployment: Considered as "unemployed" are all persons who, during the reference week, were without work, available for work and seeking work. Persons not actively seeking work were considered as unemployed but categorised separately from those actively looking for work.

7. Classifications used:

Only employed persons are classified by occupation and by status in employment.

(a) Industry: No classification by industry was made.

(b) Occupation: Based on the question: "What was X's main occupation? e.g. clerical, motor mechanic, primary school teacher, etc." For coding occupation, eight major broad groups of the national classification were used. Links to the ISCO-88 have been established to the major group (1-digit) level.

(c) Status in employment: Based on the question: "What was X working as?" For coding status in employment, four groups were used, namely: employer; self-employed; employee; family worker.

8. Main differences compared with the previous census:

The 1989 census was the first census undertaking to elicit information on the Labour Force.

9. Publication of the census results:

The final results of the population census were issued in July 1995 in a publication entitled "The Kenya Population Census 1989, Volume IX: The Labour Force."

The organization responsible for the publication of the results is the Central Bureau of Statistics, P.O. Box 30266, Nairobi.

KOREA, REPUBLIC OF

1. Name and address of the organization responsible for the census:

National Statistical Office, Statistical Survey Bureau, Population Statistics Division, 90 Kyeongun-Dong, Jongro-Gu, Seoul 110-310.

2. Population censuses conducted since 1945 (years):

1949, 1955, 1960, 1966, 1970, 1975, 1980, 1985 and 1990. The present description relates to the 1990 population census (held on 1st November).

3. Coverage of the census:

(a) Geographical scope: Whole country.

(b) Persons covered: All persons of all ages, except: workers and students living abroad; foreigners working in diplomatic and consular offices and their dependents; foreign military personnel; foreign government employees and their dependents.

4. Reference period:

The reference period used when asking questions on the "gainfully worked" and "not-gainfully worked" is a long period, i.e., the twelve months between 1st November 1989 and 31 October 1990.

5. Main topics:

(a) Total population, by sex and age: yes
Economically active population by:
(b) Sex and age group: yes
(c) Industry: yes
(d) Occupation: yes
(e) Status in employment: yes
(f) Highest educational level: yes
(g) Hours of work: no
(h) Other characteristics: no

Re (a): The age is defined in terms of age at last birthday.

6. Concepts and definitions:

(a) Economically active population: Questions concerning economic activity were asked of a 10 per cent sample of persons aged 15 years and over. Members of the armed forces living in barracks and conscripts are excluded from the definition.

(b) Employment: Considered as "gainfully worked" are all persons aged 15 years and over who, during the reference period (i.e. between 1st November 1989 and 31 October 1990), worked for more than 30 days for pay and intended to continue to work for pay, at home or out of home. The question used to determine if a person is to be counted as "gainfully worked" is "Did the person under survey usually work for pay?." However, a person who started to work for pay immediately before the census date with working duration of less than 30 days but intended to continue to work for pay should be counted as gainfully worked. On the contrary, a person who retired before the census date and did not intend to work for pay further should be excluded from the definition.

It is reported that the following categories are included:

i) persons doing unpaid work in family firm or business;
ii) employed persons, temporarily absent from work;
iii) working students with a part time job;
iv) seasonal or occasional workers;
v) apprentices and trainees.

Only persons belonging to categories (i), (ii) and (iii) can be identified separately through replies such as "Worked besides doing homework," "Had a job but temporarily absent from work," "Worked besides attending school," etc.

(c) Unemployment: The "not-gainfully worked" are all persons who, at the date of the census, were "looking for a job," "doing homework," "attending school," "doing nothing," "old" or "ill" To determine if a person is to be counted as not-gainfully worked, the question used is the same as that indicated under 6 (b) above. Students seeking work are excluded from the definition.

7. Classifications used:

Only the gainfully worked in the sample are classified by industry, by occupation and by status in employment.

(a) Industry: Based on the questions: "What is the type of major product which is produced or the type of main activity which is being done by the company/office where the person is working" and "Please give the name of the company/office." For coding industry, 90 codes based on the Korean Standard Industrial Classification to the 3-digit level, which links to the ISIC-rev.2, were used.

(b) Occupation: Based on the questions: "What is the kind of work in which the person is engaged?" and "Please give the person's position in the company/office." For coding occupation, 286 codes based on the Korean Standard Classification of Occupations were used. Links to the ISCO-68 have been established to the minor (2-digit) group level.

(c) Status in employment: Based on the question: "In which status is the person engaged in the work for pay?." For coding status in employment, four groups were used: employer, self-employed, unpaid family worker, employee.

8. Main differences compared with the previous census:

While in 1980 a "labour force" approach with a short reference period (i.e. one week before the day of the census) was used when asking questions on the economically active population, employment and unemployment, both in the 1985 and 1990 censuses a "gainful worker" approach with a long reference period was used when asking such questions as the gainful worker, the not-gainful worker, etc.

Moreover, in 1980 and 1985 the minimum age limit used for the collection of data on the economically active population and its components was 14 years.

9. Publication of the census results:

The title of the publication containing the census results is "1990 Population and Housing Census Report, Vol. 2, 10 Percent Sample, 3-1, Economic Activity."

The organization responsible for this publication is the National Statistical Office, Statistical Survey Bureau, Population Statistics Division, 90 Kyeongun-Dong, Jongro-Gu, Seoul 110-310.

The census results are also available in other forms, i.e. unpublished tables and magnetic tapes.

LUXEMBOURG

1. Name and address of the organization responsible for the census:

Service central de la statistique et des études économiques (STATEC), B.P. 304, Luxembourg.

2. Population censuses conducted since 1945 (years):

1947, 1960, 1966, 1970, 1981 and 1991. The present description relates to the 1991 population census (held on 1st March).

3. Coverage of the census:

(a) Geographical scope: Whole territory.

(b) Persons covered: All persons of all ages.

4. Reference period:

A reference period has not been established. The questions asked concern the person's "current" situation.

5. Main topics:

(a) Total population, by sex and age:	yes
Economically active population by:	
(b) Sex and age group:	yes
(c) Industry:	yes
(d) Occupation:	yes
(e) Status in employment:	yes
(f) Highest educational level:	yes
(g) Hours of work:	yes
(h) Other characteristics:	yes

Re (a): The age is defined in terms of year of birth, in terms of age at last birthday, and in terms of exact age on the date of the census.

Re (g): The normal hours of work of employed persons.

Re (h): The census also collected information on the means of travel and travel time to and from the workplace.

6. Concepts and definitions:

(a) Economically active population: It comprises all persons who, at the time of the census, were either employed or unemployed, according to the definitions given below. An age limit was not been established; however, published data relating to the economically active population, employment and unemployment refer only to persons aged 15 years and over. Members of the armed forces are included in the definition.

(b) Employment: Considered as "employed" are all persons who answered yes to the question "Have you an occupation at present?" when it was put to them at the time of the census. Persons who answered no to this question were asked to describe their current situation.

It is reported that the following categories are included:

i) persons doing unpaid work in family firm or business;
ii) employed persons, temporarily absent from work;
iii) working students with a part-time job;
iv) seasonal or occasional workers;
v) apprentices and trainees.

Only persons falling in categories (i) and (v) can be identified separately by means of their responses to the question on status in employment.

(c) Unemployment: Considered as "unemployed" are all persons who, at the time of the census, replied no to the question "Have you an occupation at present?" and were without work and seeking work during the reference period. Students seeking work are excluded from the definition.

7. Classifications used:

Only employed persons are classified by industry, by occupation and by status in employment.

(a) Industry: Specific questions are asked of employed persons, i.e.: the name, address and branch of activity of the firm, establishment or service which they manage or which employs them. For coding industry, about 500 groups of the 4-digit General Nomenclature of Economic Activities in the European Communities (NEAE) were used. Links to the ISIC have not been established.

(b) Occupation: The following specific question is asked to employed persons: "Indicate your current occupation or trade, even if you are an apprentice or if you merely help a member of your household in his/her occupation." For coding occupation, the ISCO-88 was used to the unit group (4-digit) level.

(c) Status in employment: Based on the question: "What is your status in employment?." For coding status in employment, nine categories were used: farmers, self-employed professional workers, other self-emptoyed workers, workers, private employees, civil servants, international civil servants, apprentices, unpaid family workers.

8. Main differences compared with the previous census:

No major difference.

9. Publication of the census results:

The title of the publication containing the final census results is: Série spéciale "Recensement de la population" (1992/1993).

The organization responsible for this publication is Service central de la statistique et des études économiques (STATEC), B.P. 304, Luxembourg.

The results of the 1991 census are also available in the form of unpublished tables, diskettes and magnetic tapes.

MACAU

1. Name and address of the organization responsible for the census:

The Census and Statistics Department of Macau, Rua Inácio Baptista no. 4-6 "D," Macau.

2. Population censuses conducted since 1945 (years):

1960, 1981 and 1991. The present description relates to the 1991 census (held on 30 August).

3. Coverage of the census:

(a) Geographical scope: Whole territory.

Enumeration was complete on the Island of Coloane, with a 20 per cent sample of the Macau Peninsula, and a 40 per cent sample of the Taipa Island.

(b) Persons covered: All persons of all ages.

4. Reference period:

The seven days prior to enumeration. A period of 30 days prior to the census date was also used as the reference period to determine whether a person was seeking work.

5. Main topics:

(a) Total population, by sex and age:	yes
Economically active population by:	
(b) Sex and age group:	yes
(c) Industry:	yes
(d) Occupation:	yes
(e) Status in employment:	yes
(f) Highest educational level:	yes
(g) Hours of work:	no
(h) Other characteristics:	no

Re (a): The age is defined in terms of year of birth and age at last birthday.

6. Concepts and definitions:

(a) Economically active population: It comprises all persons aged 14 years and over who, during the reference periods, were either employed or unemployed, according to the definitions given below. The definition also includes armed forces.

(b) Employment: Considered as "employed" are all persons interviewed in the respective surveys who replied "working" to the question "During the last seven days, what was your activity? Working; Unemployed; Student; Own housework; Other," or gave an affirmative reply to the following questions: "During the last 7 days, did you do any work for money?" and

"Did you do any work in kind or as family worker, e.g. making toys or flowers, child care sewing or making financial investments?"

It is reported that the following categories are included:

i) persons doing unpaid work in family firm or business;
ii) employed persons, temporarily absent from work;
iii) working students with a part time job;
iv) seasonal or occasional workers;
v) conscripts for military/civilian service;
vi) apprentices and trainees.

Categories (ii) and (iii) can be identified separately by means of their responses to specific questions.

(c) Unemployment: Considered as "unemployed" are all persons interviewed in the respective surveys who replied "unemployed" to the question "During the last seven days, what was your activity?," and gave an affirmative reply to the following questions: "During the last 30 days, did you make any effort to find a job?" and "During the last 7 days, if a suitable job had been offered, would you have accepted it?."

7. Classifications used:
Only employed persons in the respective surveys were classified by industry and by occupation. No questions were asked of either employed or unemployed persons to determine status in employment.

(a) Industry: Based on the question: "What is the product or service provided at the place where you work?." For coding industry, 10 groups of the national classification were used. Links to the ISIC-rev.3 have been established to the tabulation category (1-digit) level.

(b) Occupation: Based on the questions: "What is the title of your position? if manager or administrator, how many office staff do you have?," "What are the major duties that you usually perform?" and "Do you use any tools in your work? If yes, specify.." For coding occupation, 10 groups of the national classification were used. Links to the ISCO-88 have been established to the major-group (1-digit) level.

(c) Status in employment: No classification was made.

8. Main differences compared with the previous census:
In 1981, the age was measured in terms of year of birth only, the minimum age limit for the economically active population was 10 years, and the enumeration was complete.

9. Publication of the census results:
The results were issued in the publication entitled "XIII Population Census & III Housing Census - Global Results," June 1993.

The organization responsible for this publication is The Census and Statistics Department of Macau, Rua Inácio Baptista No. 4-6 "D," Macau.

The census results are also available in the form of unpublished tables and diskettes.

MACEDONIA

1. Name and address of the organization responsible for the census:
Statistical Office of Macedonia, Dame Gruev 4, 91000 Skopje, Republic of Macedonia.

2. Population censuses conducted since 1945 (years):
1948, 1953, 1961, 1971, 1981 and 1994. The present description relates to the 1994 population census (with reference date on 20 June).

3. Coverage of the census:
(a) Geographical scope: Whole country.
(b) Persons covered: All persons of all ages.

4. Reference period:
The day of the census.

5. Main topics:
(a) Total population, by sex and age:	yes
Economically active population by:	
(b) Sex and age group:	yes
(c) Industry:	yes
(d) Occupation:	yes
(e) Status in employment:	yes
(f) Highest educational level:	yes

(g) Hours of work:	no
(h) Other characteristics:	no

Re (a): The age is defined in terms of age at last birthday.

6. Concepts and definitions:
(a) Economically active population: It comprises all persons aged 15 years and over who, at the time of the census, were either employed or unemployed, according to the definitions given below. By way of exception are included children aged 10-14 if they are not attending school and if they are performing some agricultural activities such as shepherd, cowherd and similar. Members of the armed forces are included in the definition. Working students with a part time job and students seeking work are excluded from the definition.

(b) Employment: Considered as "employed" are all persons who, at the time of the census, were performing an occupation as employee or independently (on personal or family agricultural estate, in a workshop or other) with the purpose of obtaining means of livelihood.

It is reported that the following categories are included:

i) persons doing unpaid work in family firm or business;
ii) persons engaged in the production of primary products for own consumption;
iii) employed persons, temporarily absent from work;
iv) seasonal or occasional workers;
v) conscripts for military/civilian service.

Only persons belonging to categories (i) and (ii) can be identified separately.

(c) Unemployment: Considered as "unemployed" are all persons who, at the time of the census, were without work and seeking work. Distinction is made between first job seekers and persons who had a previous job. Among the latter, those whose firm bankrupted can be identified separately.

7. Classifications used:
Both employed persons and unemployed persons previously employed are classified by occupation. Only employed persons are classified by industry and by status in employment. Unemployed persons are asked to specify the industry and status in employment of their supporter.

(a) Industry: Respondents were asked to indicate where they are working (workshop, catering or other shop), and the name of the activity they are performing (agriculture, production of artisan articles of wood and similar). For coding this variable, 14 main branches of the national classification were used. Each branch is divided in groups, and each group in subgroups. No links have been established to the ISIC, it will be done in future.

(b) Occupation: Respondents were asked to write the title of their occupation. Instructions emphasized that it was to reflect the work actually performed during the greatest time. For coding this variable, 10 main groups of the national classification were used. Each main group is divided in types, and each type in subtype. No links have been established to ISCO, it will be done in future.

(c) Status in employment: For coding this variable, five groups were used, namely: worker; owner-joint owner in an enterprise; owner-joint owner in a private shop with employed workers; person performing an activity independently or with the help of family members; helping family member.

8. Main differences compared with the previous census:
In previous censuses, were counted as "total population" all persons with permanent place of residence in the Republic of Macedonia regardless of whether at the time of the census they were absent and how long they were absent abroad.

In the 1994 census, in accordance with the Census Act, the total population include:

1. Persons who have an official (legal) place of residence in the Republic of Macedonia, regardless of whether at the time of the census they are present in their official (legal) place of residence or elsewhere in the Republic of Macedonia;

2. Persons who have a residence permit in the Republic of Macedonia and have been temporarily present in the Republic of Macedonia for at least one year, but have an official (legal) place of residence outside the Republic of Macedonia, with the exception of refugees and persons under humanitarian care;

3. Persons who have an official (legal) place of residence in the Republic of Macedonia, and members of their families, who, at the time of the census and for a maximum of one year prior to its conduct, are temporarily working abroad; and

4. Persons who have an official (legal) place of residence in the Republic of Macedonia and who, at the time of the census, are working in diplomatic and consular representative offices of the Republic of Macedonia, in the UN and its organizations, representative offices or representatives of the Chamber of Commerce abroad, business offices abroad, military personnel of the Republic of Macedonia abroad and also citizens engaged in international, technical and other kinds of cooperation and education and members of households who are staying temporarily abroad with the aforesaid persons.

9. Publication of the census results:
The final data will be published in 1996 in serial publications. Title of each publication depends of data contain.

The organization responsible for these publications is the Statistical Office of Macedonia, Dame Gruev 4, 91000 Skopje.

MADAGASCAR

1. Name and address of the organization responsible for the census:
Direction du Recensement Général de la Population et de l'Habitat, (DRGPH), B.P. 485, Antananarivo.

2. Population censuses conducted since 1945 (years):
1975 and 1993. The present description relates to the 1993 population census (held from 1 to 19 August).

3. Coverage of the census:
(a) Geographical scope: Whole territory.

(b) Persons covered: All persons of all ages, except nationals residing abroad.

4. Reference period:
The week preceding the day of the interview.

5. Main topics:
(a) Total population, by sex and age:	yes
Economically active population by:	
(b) Sex and age group:	yes
(c) Industry:	yes
(d) Occupation:	yes
(e) Status in employment:	yes
(f) Highest educational level:	yes
(g) Hours of work:	no
(h) Other characteristics:	no

Re (a): The age is defined in terms of year of birth, or estimated in years when the date of birth is not known.

6. Concepts and definitions:
(a) Economically active population: It comprises all persons aged 10 years and over who, at the time of the census, were either employed or unemployed, according to the definitions given below. Members of the armed forces are included in the definition. Working students with a part-time job and students seeking work are excluded from the definition.

(b) Employment: Considered as "employed" are all persons who stated that they were "employed" during the reference week, meaning that they had received, would receive or hoped to receive remuneration in cash or in kind for a regular activity to which they had devoted most of their time. The question used to determine if a person should be counted as employed was "Employment situation: employed; unemployed; first-time jobseeker; homemaker; student; retired; unable to work owing to disability; other."

It is reported that the following categories are included:

i) persons doing unpaid work in family firm or business;
ii) persons engaged in the production of primary products for own consumption;
iii) employed persons, temporarily absent from work;
iv) seasonal or occasional workers;
v) conscripts for military/civilian service;
vi) apprentices and trainees.

Except for category (ii), all other categories can be identified separately by means of the responses to questions concerning economic activity, occupation and status in employment.

(c) Unemployment: Considered as "unemployed" are all persons who have been perviously employed but who have been without work for a given period of time and whose primary activity during the reference week was the search for a new job. First-time jobseekers are not covered by this defi-

nition, but are identified separately. The question used is the same one as that mentioned in paragraph 6 (b) above.

7. Classifications used:
Both employed persons and unemployed persons previously employed are classified by industry, by occupation and by status in employment.

(a) Industry: Based on the question: "What is (was) the main activity of your firm or employer? for example: cultivation of rice, transport of goods, oil-works, teaching...." For coding industry, the ISIC-rev.3 was used to the group (3-digit) level.

(b) Occupation: Based on the question: "During the week preceding ... 1993, what was the employed person's primary occupation? For unemployed persons, record the most recent occupation. For example: retailer or wholesaler, chauffeur, rice farmer, tailor, shepherd." For persons with several occupations, the primary occupation is the one from which he/she derives the largest income. For coding occupation, the ISCO-88 was used to the major group (1-digit) level.

(c) Status in employment: Based on the question: "What is or was your situation in your occupation?." For coding status in employment seven groups were used: self-employed; employer; permanent employee; temporary employee; apprentice; family worker; other.

8. Main differences compared with the previous census:
The 1975 census was divided in three parts (26-27 January: the major urban centres (excluding the capital); 6-7 April: the capital and other urban centres; 17-18 August: rural areas), while the 1993 census was carried out simultaneously throughout the national territory.

The 1975 census had used a long reference period (one month).

Lastly, nationals residing abroad had been surveyed in 1975, but were excluded in 1993.

9. Publication of the census results:
The final census results are to be published in two stages: publication of statistical tables (one volume per province) in April 1966, and publication of the volume containing the analysis of the 1993 census data in June 1996.

The organization responsible for the publication is Institut National de la Statistique, B.P. 485, Antananarivo.

The census data will also be available in the form of diskettes.

MALAYSIA

1. Name and address of the organization responsible for the census:
Department of Statistics, Malaysia, Jalan Cenderasari, 50514 Kuala Lumpur, Malaysia.

2. Population censuses conducted since 1945 (years):
1947 and 1957 (Peninsular Malaysia), 1960 (Sabah and Sarawak), 1970, 1980, and 1991 (whole Malaysia). The present description relates to the 1991 population census (held on 14 August).

3. Coverage of the census:
(a) Geographical scope: Whole country.

(b) Persons covered: All persons of all ages.

4. Reference period:
The week prior to the enumeration date. Enumeration was carried out between 14 - 30 August 1991.

5. Main topics:
(a) Total population, by sex and age:	yes
Economically active population by:	
(b) Sex and age group:	yes
(c) Industry:	yes
(d) Occupation:	yes
(e) Status in employment:	yes
(f) Highest educational level:	yes
(g) Hours of work:	yes
(h) Other characteristics:	no

Re (a): The age is defined in terms of year of birth.

Re (g): Employed persons were asked how many hours they had worked during the seven days preceding the date of interview.

6. Concepts and definitions:

(a) Economically active population: It comprises all persons aged 10 years and over who, during the reference period, were either employed or unemployed, according to the definitions given below. However, the published results on occupation and industry only relate to persons aged 15 to 64 years, while labour force population results are shown for ages 10 years and over. Members of the armed forces are included in the definition.

(b) Employment: Considered as "employed" are all persons who, during the reference period, worked at least one hour. The questions asked to determine if a person was employed were "Did you work during the last seven days?" and "Did you work at least one hour during the last seven days?." For employed persons not at work, the question "Do you have any work to return to?" was asked.

It is reported that the following categories are included:

i)   persons doing unpaid work in family firm or business;
ii)   employed persons, temporarily absent from work;
iii) working students with a part time job;
iv)   seasonal or occasional workers;
v)   conscripts for military/civilian service;
vi)   apprentices and trainees.

Categories (i) and (ii) can be identified separately. Seasonal or occasional workers are included only if they are working during the reference period.

(c) Unemployment: Considered as "unemployed" are all persons who, during the reference period, were without work and seeking work. The questions asked to determine whether a person is to be considered unemployed were "Did you look for work during the last seven days?" and "What is the main reason for not seeking work? 1) believe no suitable job available; 2) bad weather; 3) sick/confinement; 4) will start new job; 5) waiting for answers to job applications/have looked for work prior to last seven days; 6) no qualification; 7) still schooling; 8) housewife; 9) going for further studies; 10) handicapped/disabled; 11) not interested; 12) retired/too old; 13) too young; 14) others."

7. Classifications used:

Only employed persons were classified by industry, by occupation and by status in employment.

(a) Industry: Based on the questions: "What are the activities, services, product of your place of work?" and "What is the name and address of your employer?." For coding industry, a 5-digit classification was used, based on the ISIC-rev.2.

(b) Occupation: Based on the questions: "What is your occupation?" and "What are your duties/nature of your work?." For coding occupation, a 3-digit classification was used, based on the ISCO-68.

(c) Status in employment: Based on the question: "What is your employment status?." Four groups were used for coding status in employment, namely: (i) Employer; (ii) Employee; (iii) Self-employed; and (iv) Unpaid family worker.

8. Main differences compared with the previous census:

The 1991 census classified only employed persons by industry and by occupation whereas the 1980 census classified both employed and unemployed persons previously employed by industry and by occupation.

9. Publication of the census results:

Four preliminary reports covering various geographical areas (e.g. Malaysia, State, Administrative Districts; Mukins; Local Authority Areas and Urban/Rural areas) were published over the period 1991-1992. An Advance Report was made available on a restricted basis to selected government agencies in mid-1993. The final reports for various geographical levels were expected to be released in 1995.

The organization responsible for the publication is the Department of Statistics, Kuala Lumpur.

The census results are also available in unpublished tables, sample tape and optical disks.

MALDIVES

1. Name and address of the organization responsible for the census:

Ministry of Planning, Human resources and Environment, Ghazee Building, Male' 20-05.

2. Population censuses conducted since 1945 (years):

1946, 1953, 1957, 1958, 1960, 1961, 1962, 1963, 1964, 1965, 1966, 1967, 1969, 1970, 1971, 1972, 1974, 1977, 1985 and 1990. The present description relates to the 1990 population census (held on 25 March).

3. Coverage of the census:

(a) Geographical scope: Whole country.

(b) Persons covered: All persons of all ages.

4. Reference period:

The week and the three months preceding the census day.

5. Main topics:

(a) Total population, by sex and age:	yes

Economically active population by:

(b) Sex and age group:	yes
(c) Industry:	yes
(d) Occupation:	yes
(e) Status in employment:	yes
(f) Highest educational level:	yes
(g) Hours of work:	yes
(h) Other characteristics:	no

Re (a): The age is defined in terms of age at last birthday.

Re (g): For both short and long reference periods, employed persons were asked to specify respectively their usual hours of work and the total number of hours worked.

6. Concepts and definitions:

(a) Economically active population: It comprises all persons aged 12 years and over who, during the short reference period, were either employed or unemployed, according to the definitions given below. The definition excludes members of the armed forces.

(b) Employment: Considered as "employed" are all persons including family workers who worked during the short reference period or who had a job in which they had already worked but from which they were temporarily absent because of illness or injury, industrial dispute, vacation or other leave of absence, absence without leave or temporary disorganization of work due to such reason as bad weather or mechanical break down.

It is reported that the following categories are included:

i)   persons doing unpaid work in family firm or business;
ii)   employed persons, temporarily absent from work;
iii) working students with a part time job;
iv)   seasonal or occasional workers;
v)   apprentices and trainees.

None of these categories can be identified separately.

(c) Unemployment: Considered as "unemployed" are all persons who, during the short reference period, were without work and seeking work for pay or profit, including those who never worked before. Students seeking work are excluded from the definition.

7. Classifications used:

Both employed persons and unemployed persons previously employed are classified by industry, by occupation and by status in employment.

(a) Industry: Based on the question: "During the reference week (or in your current job), which industry did you worked for most of your time?." For coding industry, the ISIC-rev.3 has been used to the class (4-digit) level.

(b) Occupation: Based on the question: "Describe the specific type of work or designation of this work." For coding occupation, the ISCO-88 has been used to the unit group (4-digit) level.

(c) Status in employment: Based on the question: "What was the category of employment?." For coding this variable, four groups were used, namely: employer; employee; own-account worker; and family worker (without pay).

8. Main differences compared with the previous census:

No major difference.

9. Publication of the census results:
The final census data on the economically active population and its components were issued in a publication entitled "Population and Housing Census of the Maldives 1990."

The organization responsible for the publication is the Ministry of Planning, Human Resources and Environment, Ghazee Building, Male' 20-05.

The census results are also available in the forms of diskettes, unpublished tables and CD-ROM.

MARTINIQUE

1. Name and address of the organization responsible for the census:
Institut national de la statistique et des études économiques (INSEE), Service régional de la Martinique, B.P. 7212, 97233 Schoelcher Cedex, Martinique.

2. Population censuses conducted since 1945 (years):
1954, 1961, 1967, 1974, 1982 and 1990. The present description relates to the 1990 census (held on 15 March).

3. Coverage of the census:

(a) Geographical scope: Whole territory.

(b) Persons covered: All persons of all ages.

4. Reference period:
The week preceding the census day.

5. Main topics:

(a) Total population, by sex and age:	yes
Economically active population by:	
(b) Sex and age group:	yes
(c) Industry:	yes
(d) Occupation:	yes
(e) Status in employment:	yes
(f) Highest educational level:	yes
(g) Hours of work:	no
(h) Other characteristics:	yes

Re (a): The age is defined in terms of year of birth.

Re (h): The census also covered information on other topics, such as: full-time and part-time work, primary activity, the number of workers employed by self-employed persons, the length of time spent looking for work, etc.

6. Concepts and definitions:

(a) Economically active population: It comprises all persons aged 14 years and over who, during the reference week, were either employed or unemployed, according to the definitions given below. The definition also covers all members of the armed forces (career military staff and conscripts). Questions concerning economic activity were asked only of a sample of persons, which excluded military staff living in barracks and prisoners.

(b) Employment: Considered as "employed" are all persons who, during the reference week, had an occupation, function or any economic activity, whether paid or unpaid. Specific questions used to determine if a person is to be counted as employed are: "Do you work (full time or part time)?"; "Are you: employed or self-employed (farmer, craftsman, merchant, industrialist, professional, unpaid family worker, etc.)?," and "If you are self-employed: how many workers do you employ? (do not count apprentices or domestic staff; in agriculture, count only permanent employees)." The definition also covers persons engaged in paid community work provided to the unemployed, persons who have been placed by a temporary employment agency, persons holding a fixed-term employment contract, and persons with an adaptation or training contract.

It is reported that the following categories are included:

i)   persons doing unpaid work in family firm or business;
ii) persons engaged in the production of primary products for own consumption;
iii) employed persons, temporarily absent from work;
iv) working students with a part time job;
v)   seasonal or occasional workers who were working at the time of the census;
vi) conscripts for military/civilian service;
vii) apprentices (bound by a contract) and trainees (mainly in enterprises or training centres).

Only persons belonging to categories (i), (vi) and (vii) can be identified separately.

(c) Unemployment: Considered as "unemployed" are all persons who, on their own initiative, stated that they were without work, and who were seeking work. The questions used to determine if a person should be considered as unemployed are "Are you unemployed (whether registered or not with the National Employment Agency)?," "Have you previously worked? (if so, what was your primary occupation?," and "Are you seeking work (for: less than three months; three months to less than one year; one year to less than two years; two years or more)?."

7. Classifications used:
Both employed persons and unemployed persons previously employed included in the sample are classified by occupation. Only employed persons in the sample are classified by industry and by status in employment.

(a) Industry: Surveyed persons were asked to give the address and name of the establishment where they work or which they manage, and to identify its activity as accurately as possible (for example: wholesale wine dealers, manufacture of metal scaffolding, road passenger transport, etc.). For coding industry, 100 groups of the Nomenclature of Activities and Products (NAP) were used. Links to the ISIC have not been established.

(b) Occupation: Surveyed persons were asked to identify their current or most recent occupation as accurately as possible (for example: electrical maintenance worker, lorry driver, household appliance salesperson, chemical engineer, self-service cashier, etc.) to permit the determination of their occupational group. The question, however, was left open-ended, so that surveyed persons could reply in their own words. The classification in a specific group takes place when the data is processed. For coding occupation, a direct coding system entailing 42 groups was used. Links to the ISCO have not been established.

(c) Status in employment: For coding this variable, five categories were used, namely: self-employed person; employer; employee; unpaid family worker; other.

8. Main differences compared with the previous census:
The minimum age limit used for inclusion in the economically active population was 15 years in the 1982 census.

Moreover, both employed persons and unemployed persons previously employed had been classified by industry and by status in employment in the 1982 census.

9. Publication of the census results:
The title of the publication containing the final census results is: "Evolution 1975-1982-1990 (Série jaune)," 1992.

The Institut national de la statistique et des études économiques (INSEE), 18 boulevard Adolphe Pinard, 75675 Paris Cedex 14, is responsible for this publication.

The 1990 final census data are also available on diskettes, magnetic tapes and other formats on request.

MAURITIUS

1. Name and address of the organization responsible for the census:
Central Statistical Office, Toorawa Centre, Sir S. Ramgoolam St., Port Louis.

2. Population censuses conducted since 1945 (years):
1952, 1962, 1972, 1983 and 1990. The present description relates to the 1990 census (held on 1st July).

3. Coverage of the census:

(a) Geographical scope: Whole country.

(b) Persons covered: All persons of all ages.

4. Reference period:
The week preceding the day of the census, for current activity, and the previous year (i.e., 1989) for usual activity.

5. Main topics:

(a) Total population, by sex and age:	yes
Economically active population by:	
(b) Sex and age group:	yes
(c) Industry:	yes
(d) Occupation:	yes

(e) Status in employment: yes
(f) Highest educational level: yes
(g) Hours of work: yes
(h) Other characteristics: yes

Re (a): The age is defined in terms of age at last birthday.

Re (g): When using the short reference period, employed persons, at work, were asked to specify their actual hours of work. When using the long reference period, employed persons were asked to specify the total period worked, expressed in number of weeks.

Re (h): The census also collected information on: (i) type of establishment; (ii) place of work, and (iii) length of service with present or most recent employer. In addition, persons who stated that they were not available for work during the past week were asked to give the reason (household duties, studies, illness, injury or disability, full retirement, other).

6. Concepts and definitions:

(a) Economically active population: It comprises all persons aged 12 years and over who, during the reference periods, were currently or usually either employed or unemployed, according to the definitions given below. Questions on economic activity were not asked of Non-Mauritians usually residing outside Mauritius. There is no conscription in Mauritius.

(b) Employment: Considered as "employed" are all persons who, during the short reference period, currently performed any work of an economic value, at home or out of home. The following questions were used to determine the current activity of a person: "How many hours in all did the person work for pay, profit or family gain during the past week from Monday 25 June to Sunday 1st July 1990?" and "Was there a job, business, family enterprise or agricultural holding or farm, at which the person did not work because of illness, injury, holiday, industrial dispute, off-season inactivity, temporary disorganisation, etc.?." A person was considered currently employed if the answer to the first question was "one hour or more," or if the answer to the same question was "0 hour" but the answer to the second question was "yes."

It is reported that the following categories are included:

i) persons doing unpaid work in family firm or business;
ii) persons engaged in the production of primary products for own consumption;
iii) employed persons, temporarily absent from work;
iv) working students with a part time job;
v) seasonal or occasional workers;
vi) apprentices and trainees.

Only persons belonging to categories (i), (iii), (iv) and (vi) can be identified separately through questions on employment status and status in employment.

(c) Unemployment: Considered as "unemployed" are all persons who, during the reference periods, were without work and seeking work. A person was counted as "currently" unemployed if the reply was "0 hour" and "no," respectively, to the questions asked under 6 (b) above, and "yes" to the following two questions "Did the person take any active step to look for work anytime during the past eight weeks?" and "Was the person available for work during the past week?" (see also para. 5., Re. (h)).

7. Classifications used:
Both employed persons and unemployed persons previously employed are classified by industry, by occupation and by status in employment.

(a) Industry: Based on the question: "Describe fully the kind of business, industry or service activities carried on at the person's (present or last) place of work. Do not use vague terms (such as agriculture, repairs, factory, school, shop, etc.), but use precise terms (such as sugar cane cultivation, car repairing, pullover knitting mill, primary school, household furniture and appliances shop, etc.). In case of more than one activity, describe the main industry, business or service in which the person's activity was performed." For coding industry, 263 groups of the national classification of industries were used. A one-to-one correspondence was established between the 3-digit national classification and the ISIC-rev.2 to the group (4-digit) level.

(b) Occupation: Based on the question: "Describe clearly the work which the person was doing (or did at last). Do not use vague terms (such as clerk, driver, factory worker, teacher, etc.), but use precise terms (such as accounts clerk, bus driver,

cabinet maker, primary school teacher, etc.). In case of more than one occupation, describe the one at which the person worked most." For coding occupation, the ISCO-88 was used to the unit group (4-digit) level.

(c) Status in employment: For coding this variable, eight groups were used, namely: self-employed, with employees; self-employed, without employees; working without pay for spouse or other relative in his/her farm or business; apprentice with or without pay; employee paid monthly; employee paid by day, week, fortnight, or by job; member of producers' co-operatives; other.

8. Main differences compared with the previous census:
The following main differences should be mentioned:

The 1983 census only included persons present on census night, whereas the 1990 census also included usual members of households who were absent at that time.

Only a short reference period, i.e., one week was used in the 1983 census.

To determine person's activity status (i.e., employed, unemployed or inactive), the following two questions were asked in 1983:

(1) "Did the person work for pay or profit (including self-employment and own farm work), help without pay a member of the same household in his farm or business, or work as unpaid apprentice on any day from Monday 27th June to Saturday 2nd July this year? If 'yes' state the number of days worked, including the number of days on paid leave." A person was considered employed if the answer to the question was "yes."

(2) "If 'no' indicate if the person: (a) had a job but was sick or on leave; or was: (b) a student; (c) a housewife or a relative helping in housework; (d) an inmate of institution; (e) permanently disabled; (f) rentier; (g) wholly retired; (h) a child aged 12 years and over but less than 15 years, not at school and not looking for work; (i) not working and actively looking for work; (j) other." A person was considered unemployed if the answer to question (1) was "no" and the answer to question (2) was "not working and actively looking for work."

In 1983, questions were asked on the number of days worked during the reference week (including the number of days on paid leave). Members of producers' co-operatives did not appear as a separate group. Industry and occupation were asked for all employed and unemployed persons previously employed and coded, respectively, at the 4-digit level of ISIC-rev.2 and the 3-digit level of ISCO-68.

9. Publication of the census results:
The title of the publication containing the final census results is "1990 Housing and Population Census of Mauritius - Economic Characteristics," 1991.

The organization responsible for this publication is the Central Statistical Office, Port Louis.

In addition, some tables are available on diskettes; unpublished tables may be made available on request.

MEXICO

1. Name and address of the organization responsible for the census:
Instituto Nacional de Estadística, Geografía e Informtica (INEGI), Prolongación Héroe de Nacozari No. 2301 Sur, C.P. 20290, Aguascalientes, AGS., México, D.F.

2. Population censuses conducted since 1945 (years):
1950, 1960, 1970, 1980 and 1990. The present description relates to the 1990 population census (held from 12 to 16 March).

3. Coverage of the census:
(a) Geographical scope: Whole country.
(b) Persons covered: All persons of all ages.

4. Reference period:
The week preceding the census, in other words, from 5 to 11 March.

5. Main topics:
(a) Total population, by sex and age: yes
Economically active population by:
(b) Sex and age group: yes
(c) Industry: yes

(d) Occupation: yes
(e) Status in employment: yes
(f) Highest educational level: ...
(g) Hours of work: yes
(h) Other characteristics: yes

Re (a): The age is defined in terms of age at last birthday.

Re (g): Relates to hours actually worked by employed persons at work during the reference period.

Re (h): Total earned income (by week, fortnight, month and year) was studied.

6. Concepts and definitions:

(a) Economically active population: It comprises all persons aged 12 years and over who, during the reference week, were either employed or unemployed, according to the definitions given below. All members of the armed forces are included in the definition.

(b) Employment: Considered as "employed" are all persons aged 12 years and over who replied yes to the question "Last week, did this person: Work? Have a job but did not work?."

It is reported that the following categories are included:

i) persons doing unpaid work in family firm or business;
ii) persons engaged in the production of primary products for own consumption;
iii) employed persons, temporarily absent from work;
iv) working students with a part-time job;
v) seasonal or occasional workers;
vi) conscripts for military/civilian service;
vii) apprentices and trainees.

Only persons belonging to categories (i) and (v) can be identified separately. Persons in category (i) are identified by means of their reply ("unpaid worker in family firm or business") to the question concerning their employment situation. There is no specific question for identifying persons belonging to category (v); their number can be estimated only by means of replies to the question concerning the number of hours worked during the reference week.

(c) Unemployment: Considered as "unemployed" are all persons who answered no to the questions used to define employment, and who replied yes to the question "Did this person seek work?."

7. Classifications used:

Only employed persons were classified by industry, by occupation and by status in employment.

(a) Industry: To determine industry group, the questions used are "What is the main activity of the shop, farm, firm, institution or place where the person worked?" and "Where does the person work (for example: in the field, in a factory, in a machine shop)?." For coding this variable, 14 sectors, 57 subsectors and 220 branches, comparable with the ISIC-rev.2 major divisions and divisions, were used.

(b) Occupation: To determine occupation group, the questions used are "What is the kind of work or post held in the person's main job?" and "What are the person's tasks or functions?." For coding this variable, 18 major groups, 129 groups, 508 unit groups and 9600 individual occupations were used, consistent with ISCO-88 major groups, groups, subgroups and primary groups.

(c) Status in employment: To determine this variable, surveyed persons were asked to classify their primary employment in one of five groups (employee or labourer; day labourer; self-employed; proprietor or employer; unpaid worker in a family firm or business).

8. Main differences compared with the previous census:

The economically active population and the economically inactive population were measured in essentially the same manner as in the 1980 census; however, since the use of the week preceding the census as a reference period significantly limits the identification of jobseekers, it was decided for the 1990 census to forego the distinction made in the previous census between unemployed workers previously employed and first-time jobseekers.

As regards the classification of inactive persons, the census did not provide a separate category for persons of independent means, who were simply assimilated into the category of "other inactive persons."

Unlike the previous census, the 1990 census collected information on economic characteristics (industry, primary occupation, status in employment, hours of work, earned income) only in respect of employed persons, rather than for the economically active population as a whole, which made it possible to simplify the phrasing of the corresponding questions.

The 1990 census included two open-ended questions to collect information on economic activity, unlike the previous census, in which the corresponding question was: "What does the establishment where the person works (or last worked) cultivate, produce, sell, transport, extract, or what service does it provide?."

To determine the primary occupation, the 1990 census included two open-ended questions; the previous census had only asked: "What was your occupation in your primary job last week, or in your last job, if then unemployed?."

The question on status in employment in the 1990 census differed from the corresponding question in the previous census in the following respects: (i) The option "Member of a producers' cooperative" was suppressed; (ii) The option "Worker for a salary or wage or day wage in cash or in kind" was broken down into two options: "Employee or labourer" and "Day labourer"; (iii) The option "Worker not receiving salary, wages, day wage or any other form of payment in cash or in kind" in the previous census was restricted to unpaid family workers, to exclude other unpaid workers.

Concerning "income," the 1980 census collected information on the total income of all persons aged 12 years and over, while the 1990 census confined itself to the earned income of employed persons.

9. Publication of the census results:

The national results were published in March 1992, as were the results of each of the country's 32 federated entities.

The title of the publication containing the national results is "Estados Unidos Mexicanos; Resumen General; XI Censo General de Población y Vivienda, 1990."

The organization responsible for this publication is Instituto Nacional de Estadística, Geografía e Informtica (INEGI), Prolongación Héroe de Nacozari No. 2301 Sur, Aguascalientes, AGS.

The national census results, as well as those of the federated entities, are also available on diskettes.

MONGOLIA

1. Name and address of the organization responsible for the census:

Bureau of Population Census, State Statistical Office, Ulaan Baatar.

2. Population censuses conducted since 1945 (years):

1979 and 1989. The present description relates to the 1989 population census (held on 5 January).

3. Coverage of the census:

(a) Geographical scope: Whole country.

(b) Persons covered: All persons of all ages.

4. Reference period:

The day of the census.

5. Main topics:

(a) Total population, by sex and age: yes
Economically active population by:
(b) Sex and age group: yes
(c) Industry: yes
(d) Occupation: yes
(e) Status in employment: yes
(f) Highest educational level: yes
(g) Hours of work: no
(h) Other characteristics: no

Re (a): The age is defined in terms of age at last birthday.

6. Concepts and definitions:

(a) Economically active population: It comprises all persons aged 16 to 59 for men, and 16 to 54 for women, who were either employed or unemployed, according to the definitions given below. The definition excludes members of the armed forces. Working students with a part time job and students seeking work are also excluded from the definition.

(b) Employment: Considered as "employed" are all persons aged 16 to 59 for men, and 16 to 54 for women, who are on the Employment List of any enterprise at the moment of the census.

It is reported that the following categories are included:

i) persons doing unpaid work in family firm or business;
ii) persons engaged in the production of primary products for own consumption;
iii) employed persons, temporarily absent from work;
iv) seasonal or occasional workers;
v) apprentices and trainees.

None of these categories can be identified separately.

(c) Unemployment: Considered as "unemployed" are all persons aged 16 to 59 for men, and 16 to 54 for women, who are not on the Employment List of any enterprise at the moment of the census.

7. Classifications used:
Both employed persons and unemployed persons previously employed are classified by occupation. Only employed persons are classified by industry and by status in employment.

(a) Industry: 12 groups of the national classification were used to determine this variable: Industry; Agriculture; Construction; Transport; Communication; Trade and Procurement; Housing and domestic services; Sciences; Public health, physical culture; Insurance; Culture, education, art; other. No links to the ISIC have been established.

(b) Occupation: 982 groups of the national classification were used for coding this variable. No links to the ISCO have been established.

(c) Status in employment: For coding this variable, five groups were used, namely: Government and administrative agencies (ministeries, boards); public sector agencies; Aimag's (province) administrative agencies; district's administrative agencies; enterprises.

8. Main differences compared with the previous census:
No major difference.

9. Publication of the census results:
The final census data on the economically active population and its components were issued in March 1990 in a publication entitled "Population Census of Mongolia, 1989."

The organization responsible for the publication is the State Statistical Office, Ulaan Baatar.

The census results are not available in other forms.

MOROCCO

1. Name and address of the organization responsible for the census:
Direction de la Statistique, B.P. 178, Rabat.

2. Population censuses conducted since 1945 (years):
1960, 1971, 1982 and 1994. The present description relates to the 1994 census (held from 2 to 20 September).

3. Coverage of the census:
(a) Geographical scope: Whole territory.

(b) Persons covered: All persons of all ages, except national residents abroad.

4. Reference period:
The day of the interview.

5. Main topics:
(a) Total population, by sex and age:	yes
Economically active population by:	
(b) Sex and age group:	yes
(c) Industry:	yes
(d) Occupation:	yes
(e) Status in employment:	yes
(f) Highest educational level:	yes
(g) Hours of work:	no
(h) Other characteristics:	no

Re (a): The age is defined in terms of age at last birthday.

6. Concepts and definitions:
(a) Economically active population: It comprises all employed persons aged 7 years and over, and all unemployed persons aged 15 years and over who, on the date of the census, were either employed or unemployed, according to the definitions given below. The definition includes members of the armed forces, but excludes working students with a part-time job or seeking work.

(b) Employment: Considered as "employed" (working persons) are all persons aged 7 years and over who, at the date of census, had a "job" or an economic activity. The question asked to determine whether a person is to be counted as employed is "Did you have a job on the census date?."

It is reported that the following categories are included:

i) persons doing unpaid work in family firm or business;
ii) persons engaged in the production of primary products for own consumption;
iii) employed persons, temporarily absent from work;
iv) seasonal or occasional workers, especially in agriculture;
v) conscripts for military/civilian service;
vi) apprentices and trainees.

Only categories (i) (v) and (vi) can be identified separately.

(c) Unemployment: Considered as "unemployed" are all persons aged 15 years and over who, at the date of census, were without work and seeking work. The definition covers both unemployed persons previously employed and first-time jobseekers.

7. Classifications used:
Both employed persons and unemployed persons previously employed are classified by industry, by occupation and by status in employment.

(a) Industry: The question asked concerns the main activity of the firm or workplace in which the person works or last worked. For coding industry, 215 groups of the national classification were used. Links to the ISIC-rev.3 have been established to the class (4-digit) level.

(b) Occupation: The question asked concerns the exact nature of the person's current or most recent occupation. For coding occupation, more than 65 groups of the national nomenclature were used. Links to the ISCO-88 have been established.

(c) Status in employment: The question asked concerns the status in employment in the current (or most recent) occupation. For coding status in employment the following seven groups were used: employer; self-employed, with own business premises; self-employed working at home; self-employed with no premises; employee; family helper; apprentice.

8. Main differences compared with the previous census:
The main difference concerns the updating of the nomenclatures of occupations and economic activities.

9. Publication of the census results:
The final census data are to be published in 1995 in the following publications: "Population légale du Royaume" and "Caractéristiques socio-économiques (niveau national et niveau provincial de 65 provinces)."

The organization responsible for this publication is Direction de la Statistique, B.P. 178, Rabat.

The results of the 1994 census are also to be available in the form of unpublished tables, diskettes and magnetic tapes.

NAMIBIA

1. Name and address of the organization responsible for the census:
Central Statistics Office, National Planning Commission, Private Bag 13356, Windhoek.

2. Population censuses conducted since 1945 (years):
1960, 1981 and 1991. The present description relates to the 1991 population census (held on 20 October).

3. Coverage of the census:
(a) Geographical scope: Whole country.

(b) Persons covered: All persons of all ages.

4. Reference period:
The week prior to the census day.

5. Main topics:
(a) Total population, by sex and age:	yes
Economically active population by:	
(b) Sex and age group:	yes
(c) Industry:	yes
(d) Occupation:	yes
(e) Status in employment:	yes
(f) Highest educational level:	yes

(g) Hours of work: no
(h) Other characteristics: no

Re (a): The age is defined in terms of age at last birthday.

6. Concepts and definitions:

(a) Economically active population: It comprises all persons aged 10 years and over who, during the reference week, were either employed or unemployed, according to the definitions given below. Armed forces are excluded from the definition.

(b) Employment: Considered as "employed" are all persons who, to the question: "During the seven days preceding the census day, did you work for pay, profit or family gain?," replied either "Yes" or "No, but had job or business."

It is reported that the following categories are included:

i) persons doing unpaid work in family firm or business;
ii) persons engaged in the production of primary products for own consumption;
iii) employed persons, temporarily absent from work;
iv) working students with a part time job;
v) seasonal or occasional workers;
vi) apprentices and trainees.

Only persons belonging to categories (i), (iii) and (iv) can be identified separately.

(c) Unemployment: Considered as "unemployed" are all persons who, to the question asked under 6 (b) above, replied either "Unemployed (worked before)" or "Unemployed (first time job seeker)." Students seeking work are excluded from the definition.

7. Classifications used:

Both employed persons and unemployed persons previously employed were classified by industry, by occupation and by status in employment.

(a) Industry: Based on the questions: "What kind of activity is carried out at your workplace?" and "What are the main products produced or service offered at your workplace?." For coding industry, 307 groups of the national classification were used. Links to the ISIC-rev.3 have been established to the class (4-digit) level.

(b) Occupation: Based on the questions: "What kind of work did you do?" and "What are the main duties at this job?." For coding occupation, 396 groups of the national classification were used. Links to the ISCO-88 have been established to the unit group (4-digit) level.

(c) Status in employment: Based on the question: "In this job, did you work as: employer (with paid employees); own-account worker (without paid employees); employee, Government; employee, private; unpaid family worker; employee, foreign government; employee, international organisation; other?." For coding status in employment, the eight groups above were used.

8. Main differences compared with the previous census:

The age limits used in the 1981 census were 16 to 65 for men, and 16 to 60 for women.

In 1981, the definition used for persons looking for work was persons within the age limits who did not report any form of economic activity, who were actively seeking employment and who were able to start working within a week.

9. Publication of the census results:

The final data have been published in August 1993 in the publication entitled: "Republic of Namibia, 1991 Population and Housing Census, Report A, Statistical tables (based on old districts)."

The data were also presented in more recent publications, such as: "Republic of Namibia, 1991 Population and Housing Census, Report B, Volume I-III, Statistical tables (based on new regions)" April 1994; "Republic of Namibia, 1991 Population and Housing Census, Report C, Statistics on enumeration areas" April 1994; "Administrative and Methodological Report" August 1994; and "Republic of Namibia, 1991 Population and Housing Census, Basic analysis with Highlights" 1995.

The organization responsible for these publications is the Central Statistics Office, National Planning Commission, Private Bag 13356, Windhoek.

The final results are also available in the form of diskettes.

NAURU

1. Name and address of the organization responsible for the census:

Department of Island Development and Industry, or Bureau of Statistics, Government Office, Yaren District, Rep. of Nauru.

2. Population censuses conducted since 1945 (years):

1947, 1952, 1957, 1962, 1967, 1977, 1983 and 1992. The present description relates to the 1992 population census (held on 17 April).

3. Coverage of the census:

(a) Geographical scope: Whole country.

(b) Persons covered: All persons of all ages.

4. Reference period:

The week preceding the census day.

5. Main topics:

(a) Total population, by sex and age: yes
Economically active population by:
(b) Sex and age group: yes
(c) Industry: yes
(d) Occupation: yes
(e) Status in employment: yes
(f) Highest educational level: yes
(g) Hours of work: yes
(h) Other characteristics: yes

Re (a): The age is defined in terms of year of birth.

Re (g): Employed persons were asked to specify their usual and actual hours of work during the reference period.

Re (h): The census also collected information on secondary employment, on principal and secondary income, on reason for unemployment and on type and hours spent on traditional work (fishing, diving, crafts, etc).

6. Concepts and definitions:

(a) Economically active population: It comprises all persons who, during the reference week, were either employed or unemployed, according to the definitions given below. The minimum age limit used for inclusion in the economically active population was 10 years. However, in the published results, the minimum 10 years age limit was applied to the general tables on "Employment status" and "Type of employer," while a minimum 15 years age limit was used in specific tables on "Occupational classification," etc. There are no armed forces in Nauru, except for the local police.

(b) Employment: Considered as "employed" are all persons who worked for at least one hour during the reference week.

It is reported that the following categories are included:

i) persons doing unpaid work in family firm or business;
ii) persons engaged in the production of primary products for own consumption;
iii) employed persons, temporarily absent from work;
iv) working students with a part time job;
v) multiple-job holders;
vi) apprentices and trainees.

Except category iv), all above categories can be identified separately.

(c) Unemployment: Considered as "unemployed" are all persons who, during the reference week, were without work, eligible for work but unable to find at least one hour of work within the last seven days. Students seeking work are excluded from the definition.

7. Classifications used:

Only employed persons are classified by industry, by occupation and by status in employment.

(a) Industry: Five "Broad Industry Groups" (all subdivised into "Departments," "Sections," "Type of business," etc) were used for coding industry, namely: Government; Local Council; Nauru Phosphate Corporation; Business; Other. No links have been established to the ISIC.

(b) Occupation: Employed persons were asked to describe their occupation in at least two words. For coding occupation, the national classification was used. Links to the ISCO-88 have been established to the major group (1-digit) level.

(c) Status in employment: Based on the question: "For whom do you work?." Status in employment is given by a combination of "place of employment" and of "occupation." For coding this variable, seven groups were used, namely: employee of Government; employee of local council; employee of Nauru Phosphate Corporation (NPC); sale trader/own-account worker/employer; business partner (employee/employer); Business co-operative (employee/employer); other.

8. Main differences compared with the previous census:
Data on economic activity were not collected in previous censuses.

9. Publication of the census results:
The final census data on the economically active population and its components were issued in December 1993 in a publication entitled "1992 National Census of Nauru: Main Report."

The organization responsible for the publication is the Bureau of Statistics, Government Offices, Yaren District.

The census results are also available in the form of unpublished tables, but with Cabinet approval.

NEPAL

1. Name and address of the organization responsible for the census:
Central Bureau of Statistics, National Planning Commission Secretariat, Ramshah Path, Thapathali, Kathmandu.

2. Population censuses conducted since 1945 (years):
1952/54, 1961, 1971, 1981 and 1991. The present description relates to the 1991 population census (held on 22 June).

3. Coverage of the census:
(a) Geographical scope: Whole country.
(b) Persons covered: All persons of all ages.

4. Reference period:
The 12 month period preceding the day of the census.

5. Main topics:
(a) Total population, by sex and age:	yes
Economically active population by:	
(b) Sex and age group:	yes
(c) Industry:	yes
(d) Occupation:	yes
(e) Status in employment:	yes
(f) Highest educational level:	yes
(g) Hours of work:	yes
(h) Other characteristics:	no

Re (a): The age is defined in terms of age at last birthday.
Re (g): Employed persons are asked to specify the total number of months worked during the last 12 months.

6. Concepts and definitions:
(a) Economically active population: The census only measures employment.

(b) Employment: It comprises all persons aged 10 years and over who, during the reference period, performed any work of an economic value, at home or out of home. The question asked to determine if a person is employed was "What work did you do during the last 12 months? agriculture, salary/wage, household owned business or no gainful work done." Members of the armed forces are included in the definition.

It is reported that the following categories are included:
i) persons doing unpaid work in family firm or business;
ii) persons engaged in the production of primary products for own consumption;
iii) employed persons, temporarily absent from work;
iv) working students with a part time job;
v) seasonal or occasional workers;
vi) apprentices and trainees.

None of the above categories can be identified separately.

(c) Unemployment: Not applicable.

7. Classifications used:
All employed persons were classified by industry, by occupation and by status in employment.

(a) Industry: Based on the question: "Where did you work during the last 12 months?." For coding industry, nine groups of the national classification were used. Links to the ISIC-rev.2 have been established to the major division (1-digit) level.

(b) Occupation: Based on the question: "What work did you do during the last 12 months?." For coding occupation, seven groups of the national classification were used. Links to the ISCO-68 have been established the major group (1-digit) level.

(c) Status in employment: Based on the question: "What was your working status?." Responses were registered in one of four groups, namely: employer, employee, own-account worker; and unpaid family worker.

8. Main differences compared with the previous census:
Both a short (one week) and a long (one year) reference periods were used in the 1981 census. In 1991, only a one year reference period was used, with additional questions such as duration of work, etc.

9. Publication of the census results:
The final data were published in November 1993 in the publication entitled "Population Census - 1991": Vol. I, Part I to XV; Vol. II (Household Tables); Vol. III (Urban Tables); and Vol. IV (Geographical Tables).

The organization responsible for the publication is the Central Bureau of Statistics, Thapathali, Kathmandu.

Data are also available on diskettes and magnetic tapes.

NETHERLANDS ANTILLES

1. Name and address of the organization responsible for the census:
Central Bureau of Statistics, Fort Amsterdam, Curaçao.

2. Population censuses conducted since 1945 (years):
1960, 1972, 1981 and 1992. The present description relates to the 1992 population census (held on 27 January).

3. Coverage of the census:
(a) Geographical scope: Whole country.
(b) Persons covered: All persons of all ages.

4. Reference period:
The week, the year and the five years preceding the census day.

5. Main topics:
(a) Total population, by sex and age:	yes
Economically active population by:	
(b) Sex and age group:	yes
(c) Industry:	yes
(d) Occupation:	yes
(e) Status in employment:	yes
(f) Highest educational level:	yes
(g) Hours of work:	yes
(h) Other characteristics:	yes

Re (a): The age is defined both in terms of year of birth and of age at last birthday.
Re (g): For both week and year reference periods, persons were asked to specify, respectively, their usual hours of work and the total period worked during the past 12 months (expressed in number of weeks). Unemployed persons were asked to specify how long did they work full-time during the past five years.
Re (h): The census also collected information on means of transport used to travel to workplace, on main source of income and on total gross income for the month of January 1992. Unemployed persons were asked to specify in what way did they look for work during the past month.

6. Concepts and definitions:
(a) Economically active population: It comprises all persons aged 15 to 99 years who, during the reference week, were either employed or unemployed, according to the definitions given below. The definition includes all members of the armed forces.

(b) Employment: Considered as "employed" are all persons who, during the reference week, worked or performed casual labour for four hours or more. The question used is: "Did you work or perform casual labour for four hours or more last week?."

It is reported that the following categories are included:
i) persons doing unpaid work in family firm or business;
ii) employed persons, temporarily absent from work;
iii) working students with a part time job;

iv) seasonal or occasional workers;
v) conscripts for military/civilian service;
vi) apprentices and trainees.

Persons belonging to categories (i), (ii), (iii), (iv) and (v) can be identified separately.

(c) Unemployment Considered as "unemployed" are all persons who, during the reference week, were without work, looking for work or wanting to start to work for themselves, and who could start to work within two weeks in the event that they find a job.

7. Classifications used:
Both employed persons and unemployed persons previously employed are classified by industry, by occupation and by status in employment.

(a) Industry: Based on the questions: "At which firm/company do you work? (name and address)" and "What kind of firm is it?." For coding industry, the national classification was used, based on the ISIC-rev.3, with 17 categories.

(b) Occupation: Based on the questions: "What is your profession? (title of profession and a precise description of activity)." For coding occupation, the national classification was used, based on the ISCO-88, with 10 major groups.

(c) Status in employment: Based on the questions: "What is/was your economic position?." For coding this variable, nine groups were used: employer; self employed on small scale (less than 3 employees); employee in permanent service; employee in temporary service; casual service or casual jobs; family worker (unpaid); contract for less than six months; contract for six months or longer; other and unknown.

8. Main differences compared with the previous census:
In 1981, the age limit was 14 years and over. Moreover, the definition of employment was including occasional workers and the reference period was the last two months. Were considered as unemployed persons who were "looking for work."

9. Publication of the census results:
The final census results have been published in January 1993 in a publication entitled "Third Population and Housing Census, Netherlands Antilles 1992" (Three Volumes).

The organization responsible for the publication is the Central Bureau of Statistics, Fort Amsterdam, Curaçao.

Possibilities also exist for obtaining unpublished tables (on request) and diskettes (planned).

NEW CALEDONIA

1. Name and address of the organization responsible for the census:
INSEE (Institut national de la statistique et des études économiques), 18 boulevard Adolphe Pinard, 75675 Paris, Cedex 14.

2. Population censuses conducted since 1945 (years):
1963, 1969, 1976, 1983 and 1989. The present description relates to the 1989 census (held on 4 April).

3. Coverage of the census:
(a) Geographical scope: Whole territory.

(b) Persons covered: All persons of all ages.

4. Reference period:
The week preceding the census day.

5. Main topics:
(a) Total population, by sex and age:	yes
Economically active population by:	
(b) Sex and age group:	yes
(c) Industry:	yes
(d) Occupation:	yes
(e) Status in employment:	yes
(f) Highest educational level:	yes
(g) Hours of work:	yes
(h) Other characteristics:	yes

Re (a): The age is defined in terms of year of birth.

Re (g): Hours of work refer to the normal hours of work of employed persons and the characteristics of the occupation (continuous, seasonal, intermittent or exceptional).

Re (h): The census also gathered detailed information on the duration of unemployment (less than three months, three months to less than one year, one year to less than two years; two years and over).

6. Concepts and definitions:
(a) Economically active population: It comprises all persons aged 14 years and over who, during the reference period, were either employed or unemployed, according to the definitions given below. The definition includes professional members of the armed forces and conscripts, but excludes working students with a part time job or students seeking work.

(b) Employment: Considered as "employed" are all persons who, during the reference period, were working or were temporarily absent from work (leave, sickness, maternity).

It is reported that the following categories are included:
i) persons doing unpaid work in family firm or business;
ii) persons engaged in the production of primary products for own consumption;
iii) employed persons, temporarily absent from work;
iv) seasonal or occasional workers;
v) conscripts (military or civilian service);
vi) apprentices under contract and trainees.

The above categories can be identified separately.

(c) Unemployment: Considered as "unemployed" are all persons who, on their own initiative, reported that they were unemployed during the reference period.

7. Classifications used:
Only employed persons have been classified by industry, by occupation and by status in employment.

(a) Industry: Specific questions were asked to employed persons regarding the address, name and activity of the establishment which employs them or which they manage. For coding industry, 14 groups of the national classification of industries were used. Links to the ISIC have not been established.

(b) Occupation: Employed persons were asked to indicate their occupation very precisely (for example: electrical maintenance worker, lorry driver, household appliance salesperson, chemical engineer, self-service cashier, etc.). For coding occupation, 33 detailed groups were used, and subsequently regrouped in six major groups. Links to the ISCO have not been established.

(c) Status in employment: To determine their status in employment, employed persons were asked to indicate their occupational status. Nine groups were used: farmer and/or stockbreeder, hunter, fisherman; family helper; member of a liberal profession; craftsman, shopkeeper, industrialist; other employer or self-employed worker; homeworker for an enterprise; apprentice under contract; paid employee in the private sector; paid employee in the public sector.

8. Main differences compared with the previous census:
In 1983 only persons receiving unemployment benefit were considered as unemployed.

9. Publication of the census results:
The final census results were published in 1991.

The titles of the publications containing the final census data are:

- Images de la population de Nouvelle-Calédonie 1989 (INSEE).
- Recensement de la population de Nouvelle-Calédonie 1989: inventaire communal.
- L'activité en Nouvelle-Calédonie en 1989, 3 volumes of tables. T1: Constructions logements; T2: Les ménages; T3: Activité individus.
- Inventaire tribal 1989, 3 volumes; Province Iles Loyauté, Province Nord, Province Sud.

The ITSEE (Institut territorial de la statistique et des études économiques, 5 rue du Général Galliéni, B.P. 823, Nouméa, New Caledonia) is responsible for these publications.

The census results are also available in the form of unpublished tables.

NEW ZEALAND

1. Name and address of the organization responsible for the census:
Department of Statistics, 64 Kilmore Street, Christchurch 1.

2. Population censuses conducted since 1945 (years):
1945, 1951, 1956, 1961, 1966, 1971, 1976, 1981, 1986 and 1991. The present description relates to the 1991 census (held on 5 March).

3. Coverage of the census:
(a) Geographical scope: Whole country.

(b) Persons covered: All persons of all ages.

4. Reference period:
The census day was used as reference period to determine employed persons and the last four weeks to determine the unemployed.

5. Main topics:
(a) Total population, by sex and age: yes
Economically active population by:
(b) Sex and age group: yes
(c) Industry: yes
(d) Occupation: yes
(e) Status in employment: yes
(f) Highest educational level: yes
(g) Hours of work: yes
(h) Other characteristics: yes

Re (a): The age is defined in terms of age at last birthday.

Re (g): Hours of work relate to actual hours worked by employed persons, at work. Employed persons temporarily absent from work were asked to state their usual hours of work.

Re (h): Questions were also asked on main means of travel to work on census day and on total income for the year ended 31 March 1991.

6. Concepts and definitions:
(a) Economically active population: It comprises all persons aged 15 years and over who, during the reference periods, were either employed or unemployed, according to the definitions given below. Overseas visitors, who were not working in New Zealand, are excluded from the definition. However, members of the armed forces are included in the definition.

(b) Employment: Considered as "employed" are all persons who, at the time of the census, performed for payment or without payment in a family business, any work of an economic value, at home or out of home. The question used to determine whether or not a person was to be counted as employed was "Do you work in a job, business, farm or profession?."

It is reported that the following categories are included:
i) persons doing unpaid work in family firm or business;
ii) employed persons, temporarily absent from work;
iii) working students with a part time job;
iv) seasonal or occasional workers;
v) multiple-job holders;
vi) apprentices and trainees.

Only persons belonging to categories (i), (iii) and (v) can be identified separately through specific questions.

(c) Unemployment: Considered as "unemployed" are all persons who, during the four weeks prior to the census, were actively seeking and available for full or part time work and were not working in a job, business, farm or profession on census day. To determine if a person was to be counted as unemployed, the questions used were "Did you look for paid work in the last four weeks?," "What methods did you use to look for paid work?" and "If a job had been available, would you have started last week?."

7. Classifications used:
Only employed persons are classified by industry, by occupation and by status in employment.

(a) Industry: Based on the questions: "Who do you work for?," "Where do you work?" and "What is the main activity at your place of work (sheep farming, maternity hospital, poultry processing, management consulting, etc.)?." Main activity refers to employer's predominant business, industry or service. Coding of individual industry was undertaken to the 5-digit level of the New Zealand Standard Industrial Classification (NZSIC). Links to the ISIC-rev.2 have been established to the group (4-digit) level.

(b) Occupation: Based on the questions: "What is your occupation?" and "What tasks or duties do you spend the most time on?." For coding occupation, all groups of the New Zealand Standard Classification of Occupations (NZSCO) were used.

Links to the ISCO-88 have been established to the unit group (4-digit) level.

(c) Status in employment: The question asked to determine status in employment was "In your work, are you: (i) working for wages or salary; (ii) self-employed and not employing others; (iii) employer of others in own business; (iv) working without pay in a family business?." For coding status in employment, the four groups above were used.

8. Main differences compared with the previous census:
The 1991 census included two additional questions relating to job search methods (see 6 (c) above).

9. Publication of the census results:
The title of the publication containing the census results is "National Population Summary," 1992.

The organization responsible for this publication is the Department of Statistics, 64 Kilmore Street, Christchurch 1.

The census results are also available in the form of unpublished tables, diskettes, magnetic tapes and compact disks.

NORTHERN MARIANA ISLANDS

1. Name and address of the organization responsible for the census:
Central Statistics Division, Capitol Hill, Saipan, MP 96950, in conjunction with the US Bureau of the Census.

2. Population censuses conducted since 1945 (years):
1958, 1967, 1973, 1980 and 1990. The present description relates to the 1990 census (held on 1st April).

3. Coverage of the census:
(a) Geographical scope: Whole area.

(b) Persons covered: The 1990 census counted every person at his or her "usual residence"; this means the place where the person lives and sleeps most of the time.

4. Reference period:
The week prior to the census and the year preceding the census year.

5. Main topics:
(a) Total population, by sex and age: yes
Economically active population by:
(b) Sex and age group: yes
(c) Industry: yes
(d) Occupation: yes
(e) Status in employment: yes
(f) Highest educational level: yes
(g) Hours of work: yes
(h) Other characteristics: yes

Re (a): The age is defined both in terms of year of birth and age at last birthday.

Re (g): Employed persons were asked to specify the number of hours worked during the reference week and, for 1989, respectively the number of weeks and the usual number of hours worked.

Re (h): The census also collected information on means of transport and time used to travel to workplace, as well as on total income received in 1989.

6. Concepts and definitions:
(a) Economically active population: It comprises all persons aged 15 years and over who, during the reference periods, were either employed or unemployed, according to the definitions given below. Members of the armed forces are excluded from the definition.

(b) Employment: Considered as "employed" are all persons who, during the reference week, worked for pay as employees for someone else, or worked for profit or pay in their own business, or worked with or without pay in a business or profit-oriented farm operated by a relative, or worked part-time, such as an hour or two. The question used to determine if a person is to be counted as employed is "Did you work at any time last week, either full time or part time?."

It is reported that the following categories are included:
i) persons doing unpaid work in family firm or business;
ii) persons engaged in the production of primary products for own consumption;
iii) employed persons temporarily absent from work;

iv)   working students with a part time job;
v)   seasonal or occasional workers;
vi)   apprentices and trainees.

All these categories can be identified separately.

(c) Unemployment: Considered as "unemployed" are all persons who gave an affirmative reply to both of the following questions: "Have you been looking for work to earn money during the last four weeks?" and "Could you have taken a job last week if one had been offered?."

7. Classifications used:
Both employed persons and unemployed persons previously employed are classified by industry, by occupation and by status in employment.

(a) Industry: Based on the questions: "For whom did you work?," "What kind of business or industry was this? e.g. hospital, fish cannery, retail bakery, etc" and "Is this mainly manufacturing, wholesale trade, retail trade, or something else (agriculture, construction, service, government, etc)?." For coding industry, the 1987 U.S. Standard Industrial Classification (SIC) was used. Links to the ISIC have not been established.

(b) Occupation: Based on the questions: "What kind of work were you doing?" (e.g. registered nurse, industrial machinery, mechanic, cake icer.) and "What were your most important activities or duties? (e.g. patient care, repair machines in factory, icing cakes, etc)?." For coding occupation, the U.S. Standard Occupational Classification Manual (SOC) was used. Coding for the 1990 Census was done by the U.S. Bureau of Census using SOC, 1980. Links to the ISCO have not been established. No adaptation was done for the 1990 U.S. occupational classification.

(c) Status in employment: Based on the question: "Were you: employee of a private for profit company or business or of an individual, for wages, salary or commissions; employee of a private not-for-profit, tax-exempt, or charitable organization; local or territorial government employee (territorial/commonwealth, etc.); federal government employee; self-employed in own not incorporated business, professional practice, or farm; self-employed in own incorporated business, professional practice, or farm; working without pay in family business or farm?." For coding status in employment, the seven groups above were used.

8. Main differences compared with the previous census:
No major difference.

9. Publication of the census results:
The final results have been published in March 1992 in a publication entitled "1990 Census of Population and Housing: Social, Economic, and Housing Characteristics, Commonwealth of the Mariana Islands."

The organizations responsible for this publication are either the U.S. Department of Commerce, U.S. Bureau of the Census, Washington, D.C. 20233, or the Superintendent of Documents, U.S. Government Printing Office, Washington, D.C. 20402.

The census results are also available in the form of diskettes and tapes.

NORWAY

1. Name and address of the organization responsible for the census:
Statistisk Sentralbyrä (Statistics Norway), Population Census Division, Postuttak, N-2201 Kongsvinger.

2. Population censuses conducted since 1945 (years):
1946, 1950, 1960, 1970, 1980 and 1990. The present description relates to the 1990 population census (held on 3 November).

3. Coverage of the census:

(a) Geographical scope: Whole country. As in previous censuses, residents of Norway staying on Svalbard and Jan Mayen are registered as residents of a municipality of the mainland, and not separately identified in census results. Nor are foreign nationals residing there.

(b) Persons covered: All persons of all ages. The census covers all persons registered as residents of Norway on 3 November 1990. Questions describing persons' economic activity were asked as follows: on a complete enumeration basis in municipalities with less than 6,000 inhabitants; else, on

a sampling fraction basis (20.0, 14.3, 10.0 or 8.3 per cent, depending on population size).

4. Reference period:
The week prior to the census day (from 27 October to 2 November) and the year starting on 3 November 1989 and ending on 2 November 1990.

5. Main topics:
(a) Total population, by sex and age:	yes
Economically active population by:	
(b) Sex and age group:	yes
(c) Industry:	yes
(d) Occupation:	yes
(e) Status in employment:	yes
(f) Highest educational level:	yes
(g) Hours of work:	yes
(h) Other characteristics:	yes

Re (a): The age is defined in terms of year of birth (main definition). It is also defined, if possible, in terms of age as per 3 November 1990.

Re (g): When using the short reference period: hours of work relate both to usual hours of work of employed persons and to actual hours of work of employed persons, at work, during the reference week. When using the long reference period: hours of work relate to the total period worked by employed persons (expressed in terms of months in full or part-time employment).

Re (h): The census also covered information on other work related topics, such as: place of work, frequency and duration of travel to workplace (one way) and means of transportation used for this purpose during the week preceding the census day (i.e., the week from 27 October to 2 November).

Variables taken from registers were: demographic information (from the Central Population Register); information on education (from CBS's register of highest completed level of education); information on registered unemployment (from the Directorate of Labour); information on income, etc... (from tax assessment registers, the National Insurance Administration and others).

6. Concepts and definitions:

(a) Economically active population: It comprises all persons aged 16 years and over in the sample who, during the reference periods, were either employed or unemployed, according to the definitions given below. Members of the armed forces are included in the definition.

(b) Employment: The specific questions used to determined if a person was to be counted as employed are "Were you gainfully employed for at least 100 hours in the year from 3 November 1989 to 2 November 1990?" and "Were you gainfully employed in the week 27 October - 2 November 1990?."

It is reported that the following categories are included:
i)   persons doing unpaid work in family firm or business;
ii)   persons engaged in the production of primary products for own consumption;
iii) employed persons, temporarily absent from work;
iv)   working students with a part time job;
v)   seasonal or occasional workers;
vi)   conscripts for military/civilian service;
vii) apprentices and trainees.

Only persons belonging to categories (iii), (iv) and (vi) can be identified separately by means of specific questions. For example, persons in category (iv) can be identified through the question "How many hours were you gainfully employed in the week 27 October - 2 November 1990?" and from the education register. Conscripts can be identified on the basis of data from the armed forces.

(c) Unemployment: Considered as "unemployed" are all persons who were registered as unemployed on the day of the census. Students seeking work are excluded from the definition.

7. Classifications used:
Only employed persons in the sample according to the above definition of employment are classified by industry, by occupation and by status in employment.

(a) Industry: Based on the questions: "State the name and address of the place of work (business) where you were gainfully employed for the longest period in the year from 3 November 1989 to 2 November 1990 (if no firm name is used, state the name of the owner/employer; if you work in your own business without a special firm name, state your own name and address)" and "Describe as accurately as you can the business

of that employer (write for instance: furniture manufacture, car sales, bookshop, farming, leasing of machinery, architecture, etc.)." For 78 per cent of persons, industry was coded by linking to the Business Register, giving all five digits. For manual coding, three digits were used. Links to the ISIC-rev.2 have been established to the group (4-digit) level. Links to ISIC-rev.3 will be established later.

(b) Occupation: Based on the question: "What was your occupation (title) at that place of employment? (do not use a collective term such as industrial worker, councellor, fitter, etc., but a title which describes your duties such as welder, advertising consultant, telephone fitter, home help, plumber, hairdresser, nurse, cleaner, cook, sheet metal worker, salesman, nursery school teacher, etc.)." For coding occupation, 84 groups corresponding to 3-digit codes of the Nordic Standard Classification of Occupations were used. Links to the ISCO-68 have been established to the major group (1-digit) level.

(c) Status in employment: The specific questions asked of employed persons in the sample to determine their status in employment related to their connection with the place of employment. For coding status in employment, three groups were used, namely: permanent or temporary paid employment; self-employed (owner if confirmed by business register); family member employed in family business with no fixed pay.

8. Main differences compared with the previous census:
In 1980, questions on total working hours in the long reference period related to the number of hours while in the 1990 census they related to the number of months (full time, part time). Moreover, in the 1980 census no question was asked on normal/agreed number of working hours in connection with the short reference period.

The "unknown" variable does not occur as a value of file variables of the 1990 data (except for municipality of employment), as missing data have been replaced by estimates based on (i) other variable values given by the person and (ii) answers from other ("corresponding") persons.

9. Publication of the census results:
Final results for the whole country (for all major variables) have been made available on tape since February 1992, but were not published. Provisional figures based on the tabulation of a sample of 10,000 census returns were published in April 1991.

The title of the publication (in Norwegian only) containing the final census results is "Folke-og Boligtelling 1990 Landssammendrag."

A publication entitled "Population and Housing Census. Main results" was issued in 1992 (both in Norwegian and English).

The organization responsible for the publications is the Central Bureau of Statistics, Population Census Division, Postuttak, N-2201 Kongsvinger.

The 1990 final census results are also available in the form of unpublished tables, diskettes, magnetic tapes, on line-data bases, user service (payed).

PANAMA

1. Name and address of the organization responsible for the census:
Dirección de Estadística y Censo, Contraloría General de la República, Apartado 5213, Zona 5, Panamá, República de Panamá.

2. Population censuses conducted since 1945 (years):
1950, 1960, 1970, 1980 and 1990. The present description relates to the 1990 population census (held on 13 May).

3. Coverage of the census:
(a) Geographical scope: Whole country.

(b) Persons covered: All persons of all ages, except nationals residing abroad and United States military personnel in Panama at the time of the census.

4. Reference period:
The week preceding the census date.

5. Main topics:
(a) Total population, by sex and age:	yes

Economically active population by:
(b) Sex and age group:	yes
(c) Industry:	yes
(d) Occupation:	yes
(e) Status in employment:	yes
(f) Highest educational level:	yes
(g) Hours of work:	no
(h) Other characteristics:	yes

Re (a): The age is defined in terms of age at last birthday.

Re (h): The census also collected information on permanent and occasional employment, and on total income during the month preceding the census.

6. Concepts and definitions:
(a) Economically active population: It comprises all persons aged 10 years and over who, during the reference week, were either employed or unemployed, according to the definitions given below. All members of the armed forces are included in the definition.

(b) Employment: Considered as "employed" are all persons who replied yes to the following question: "Did you work last week, or do you have a job from which you were temporarily absent last week?."

It is reported that the following categories are included:
i) persons doing unpaid work in family firm or business;
ii) persons engaged in the production of primary products for own consumption;
iii) employed persons, temporarily absent from work;
iv) working students with a part-time job;
v) seasonal or occasional workers;
vi) conscripts for military or civilian service;
vii) apprentices and trainees.

Only persons falling in categories (i) and (v) can be identified separately by means of their replies to specific questions.

(c) Unemployment: Considered as "unemployed" are all persons who, during the reference week, did not have an occupation or job and who indicated that they were seeking work or that it was impossible to find work.

7. Classifications used:
Both employed persons and unemployed persons previously employed are classified by industry, by occupation and by status in employment.

(a) Industry: The following questions were used to determine industry group: "Where do you work or where did you last work?" and "What is the line of business of the shop, establishment, firm or institution where you work or last worked?." For coding this variable, 18 groups of the national classification of economic activities were used. These groups are compatible with all groups of the ISIC-rev.3.

(b) Occupation: The following question was asked to determine occupation group: "What was your occupation, post or kind of work last week or in your last job?." 10 groups of the national classification of occupations were used. These groups are compatible with the ISCO-68 to the major group (1-digit) level.

(c) Status in employment: This variable was determined by asking whether the person works or last worked as: employee; self-employed or own account; unpaid family worker; employer; member of producers' co-operative or settlement. For coding status in employment, the five above-mentioned groups were used.

8. Main differences compared with the previous census:
No major difference.

9. Publication of the census results:
The title of the publication containing the final census results will be "Resultados finales básicos" (with three publications per district: Panamá, Colón y San Miguelito) supplemented by provincial publications (February 1991).

The organization responsible for these publications is Dirección de Estadística y Censo.

The census results will also be available in the forms of magnetic tapes and unpublished tables.

PAPUA NEW GUINEA

1. Name and address of the organization responsible for the census:
National Statistical Office, P.O. Box 337, Waigani, NCD, Papua New Guinea.

2. Population censuses conducted since 1945 (years):

1966, 1971, 1980 and 1990. The present description relates to the 1990 population census (held during the period 9-13 July).

3. Coverage of the census:

(a) Geographical scope: The North Solomon Province was completely omitted from census count because of a political crisis.

(b) Persons covered: All persons of all ages, except foreign diplomatics workers and their families.

4. Reference period:

The week and the 12 months preceding the census enumeration.

5. Main topics:

(a) Total population, by sex and age:	yes
Economically active population by:	
(b) Sex and age group:	yes
(c) Industry:	no
(d) Occupation:	yes
(e) Status in employment:	no
(f) Highest educational level:	yes
(g) Hours of work:	no
(h) Other characteristics:	no

Re (a): The age is defined in terms of age at last birthday.

6. Concepts and definitions:

(a) Economically active population: It comprises all persons aged 10 years and over who, during the reference periods, were either employed or unemployed, according to the definitions given below. A short reference period (one week) was used to collect information on current activity in the urban sector, whereas a long reference period (12 months) was used to collect information on usual activity in the rural sector. The definition includes members of the armed forces. However, working students with a part time job and students seeking work are excluded from the definition.

(b) Employment: The question used to determine if a person is to be counted as "employed" was "During the last seven days, what did you do most of the time? worked at a wage job; business with paid help; self employed including unpaid helper; farming and fishing for food and money; farming and fishing for subsistence only."

It is reported that the following categories are included:

i) persons doing unpaid work in family firm or business;
ii) persons engaged in the production of primary products for own consumption;
iii) employed persons, temporarily absent from work;
iv) seasonal or occasional workers;
v) conscripts for military/civilian service;
vi) apprentices and trainees.

Only persons belonging to category (ii) can be identified separately.

(c) Unemployment: Considered as "unemployed" are all persons who, during the reference periods (cf. para. 6 (a)), were without work and looking for work, or available for work. This includes a person who is staying at home doing nothing, not even seeking employment because he/she feels there is no hope of finding a job but may say that he/she could take any job if given the chance.

7. Classifications used:

Only employed persons in urban areas are classified by occupation.

(a) Industry: No classification was made.

(b) Occupation: Employed persons were asked to describe their principal activity, i.e. the economic activity which took most of the person's time: e.g. shop assistant, nurse, taxi driver, etc, in at least two words. For coding occupation, nine groups of the national classification were used. Links to the ISCO-88 have been established to the major group (1-digit) level.

(c) Status in employment: No classification was made.

8. Main differences compared with the previous census:

The definition of unemployment was relaxed in 1990 to include persons available for work.

In asking questions on economic activity in the rural areas, a long reference period (12 months) was used in 1990, whereas a short one (last week) was used in 1980.

9. Publication of the census results:

The final census data on the economically active population and its components were issued in August 1994 in a publication entitled "Report on the 1990 National Population and Housing Census in Papua New Guinea."

The organization responsible for the publication is the National Statistics Office (NSO), P.O. Box 337, Waigani, NCD.

The census results are not available in other forms.

PARAGUAY

1. Name and address of the organization responsible for the census:

Dirección General de Estadística, Encuestas y Censos, Luis Aberto de Herrera 1010, c/ Estados Unidos, Casilla de Correo No. 1118, Asunción.

2. Population censuses conducted since 1945 (years):

1950, 1962, 1972, 1982 and 1992. The present description relates to the 1992 population census (held on 26 August).

3. Coverage of the census:

(a) Geographical scope: Whole country.

(b) Persons covered: All persons of all ages.

4. Reference period:

The week prior to the census day.

5. Main topics:

(a) Total population, by sex and age:	yes
Economically active population by:	
(b) Sex and age group:	yes
(c) Industry:	yes
(d) Occupation:	yes
(e) Status in employment:	yes
(f) Highest educational level:	yes
(g) Hours of work:	no
(h) Other characteristics:	no

Re (a): The age is defined in terms of age at last birthday.

6. Concepts and definitions:

(a) Economically active population: It comprises all persons aged 10 years and over who, during the reference week, were either employed or unemployed, according to the definitions given below. The definition excludes conscripts, but includes professional members of the armed forces. It also excludes working students with a part-time job and students seeking work.

(b) Employment: Considered as "employed" are all persons who worked during most of the reference week. The question used is: "Did you work during most of the past week? (1) Worked; (2) Not at work, but employed; (3) Previously employed and seeking work; (4) Seeking a first job; (5) Engaged in homemaking; (6) Student; (7) Self-supporting; (8) Retired or pensioner; (9) Compulsory military service; (10) Other."

It is reported that the following categories are included:

i) persons doing unpaid work in family firm or business;
ii) employed persons temporarily absent from work.

Both the above-mentioned categories can be identified separately.

(c) Unemployment: Considered as "unemployed" are all persons who, during the reference week, looked for work, including both previously employed persons and first-time jobseekers.

7. Classifications used:

Both employed persons and unemployed persons are classified by industry, by occupation and by status in employment.

(a) Industry: Based on the question: "What is the main activity of the firm, business or institution where you work (or last worked)? examples: cultivation of cotton, of vegetables, construction, primary education, health care, manufacture of clothing, trade, etc.." For coding industry group, nine groups of the national classification were used. Links to the ISIC-rev.2 have been established to the division (1-digit) level.

(b) Occupation: Based on the question: "What is (was) your main occupation at work? examples: dressmaker, secretary, chauffeur, shoemaker, sales clerk, farmer, construction worker, electrician, physician, etc.." For coding occupation, the ISCO-88 was used to the major group (1-digit) level.

(c) *Status in employment:* Based on the question: "In that occupation, are you (were you) employee, labourer or day labourer, proprietor or employer, self-employed or own-account worker, unpaid family worker, domestic employee?." For coding this variable, the six groups above were used.

8. Main differences compared with the previous census:
The lower age limit for questions on economic activity in the 1982 census was 12 years (but 10 years in the 1992 census).

9. Publication of the census results:
The final census results for Asunción were published in August 1993, for the Departamento Central in October 1993, and for the Departamento Alto Paran in March 1994. Census results at the national level were published in July 1994.

The title of the publication containing the national results is "Paraguay: Censo Nacional de Población y Viviendas."

The organization responsible for this publication is Dirección General de Estadística, Encuestas y Censos, Luis Alberto de Herrera 1010, c/ Estados Unidos, Casilla de Correo No. 1118, Asunción.

The census results are also available in the form of diskettes and unpublished tables.

PERU

1. Name and address of the organization responsible for the census:
Instituto Nacional de Estadística e Informtica, Av. 28 de Julio No. 1056, Lima.

2. Population censuses conducted since 1945 (years):
1961, 1972, 1981 and 1993. The present description relates to the 1993 population census (held on 11 July).

3. Coverage of the census:
(a) *Geographical scope:* Whole country.
(b) *Persons covered:* All persons of all ages.

4. Reference period:
The week prior to the census day.

5. Main topics:
(a) Total population, by sex and age: yes
Economically active population by:
(b) Sex and age group: yes
(c) Industry: yes
(d) Occupation: yes
(e) Status in employment: yes
(f) Highest educational level: yes
(g) Hours of work: no
(h) Other characteristics: no

Re (a): The age is defined in terms of age at last birthday for persons aged 1 year and over (and in terms of months for infants under 1 year of age).

6. Concepts and definitions:

(a) *Economically active population:* It comprises all persons aged 6 years and over who, during the reference week, were either employed or unemployed, according to the definitions given below. The definition includes professional members of the armed forces, but excludes conscripts in military or civilian service.

(b) *Employment:* Considered as "employed" are all persons who worked during the reference week. The questions used to determine if a person was employed are "Last week, were you: Working for pay?, Temporarily absent from work? An unpaid helper to a family member?."

It is reported that the following categories are included:
i) persons doing unpaid work in family firm or business;
ii) persons engaged in the production of primary products for own consumption;
iii) employed persons temporarily absent from work;
iv) working students with a part-time job;
v) seasonal or occasional workers.

Only persons falling in categories (i) and (iii) can be identified separately by means of their replies to specific questions. As regards category (i), the question used is: "An unpaid helper to a family member?," and as regards category (iii), the question used is: "Temporarily absent from work?."

(c) *Unemployment:* Considered as "unemployed" are all persons who, during the reference week, were seeking work, including both previously employed persons and first-time jobseekers.

7. Classifications used:
Both employed persons and unemployed persons previously employed are classified by industry, by occupation and by status in employment.

(a) *Industry:* To determine industry group, persons were asked to indicate the activity of the business, organization or firm in which they work or last worked. For coding this variable, the ISCO-rev.3 was used to the class (4-digit) level.

(b) *Occupation:* To determine occupation group, persons were asked to indicate their primary occupation, post or trade in the reference week or in their last job. For coding this variable, the ISCO-88 was used to the minor group (3-digit) level.

(c) *Status in employment:* To determine this variable, persons were asked to indicate their occupational category in the business, organization or firm in which they work. This variable was coded in six groups (labourer, employee, unpaid family worker, homemaker, self-employed or own-account worker, employer or proprietor).

8. Main differences compared with the previous census:
No major difference.

9. Publication of the census results:
The final results were published in November 1994.

The title of the publication is "Resultados definitivos Perú Censos Nacionales 1993: IX de poblacion y IV de vivienda."

The organization responsible for this publication is Instituto Nacional de Estadística e Informtica, av. 28 de Julio, No. 1056, Lima, Perú.

The census results are also available in the form of diskettes.

PHILIPPINES

1. Name and address of the organization responsible for the census:
National Statistics Office, R. Magsaysay Boulevard, Sta Mesa, Manila.

2. Population censuses conducted since 1945 (years):
1948, 1960, 1970, 1975, 1980 and 1990. The present description relates to the 1990 population census (held on 1st May).

3. Coverage of the census:
(a) *Geographical scope:* Whole country.
(b) *Persons covered:* All persons of all ages, except: citizens of foreign countries who expect to reside in the Philippines for less than a year from the date of their arrival; citizens of foreign countries who were attached and residing within the compounds of an embassy, a ministry, a legation, a chancellery or a consulate, irrespective of the length of their stay; foreign military and non military personnel and their families, residing within the military base, irrespective of the duration of their stay; citizens of foreign countries who are Chiefs and officials of international Organizations like the United Nations, the ILO or USAID, who are subject to reassignment to their countries after their tour of duty in the Philippines, and members of their families.

4. Reference period:
The week prior to the census day. However, for usual activity/occupation and usual kind of business/industry, a long reference period was used, i.e., the past twelve months.

5. Main topics:
(a) Total population, by sex and age: yes
Economically active population by:
(b) Sex and age group: yes
(c) Industry: yes
(d) Occupation: yes
(e) Status in employment: no
(f) Highest educational level: yes
(g) Hours of work: no
(h) Other characteristics: yes

Re (a): The age is defined in terms of age at last birthday.
Re (h): The census also collected information on the person's usual occupation and kind of business or industry during the past twelve months.

6. Concepts and definitions:

(a) Economically active population: It comprises all persons aged 10 years and over who, during the reference week, were either employed or unemployed, according to the definitions given below. Military officers and members of their households aged 10 years and over who reside in housing units within military camps or installations are included in the definition. Soldiers and other military personnel residing in military barracks/camps without the other members of their households are enumerated as institutional population; as such, they are not asked questions on economic activity and are therefore excluded from the definition.

Questions concerning economic activity were asked of 10 per cent of persons in municipalities with more than 1,500 households, 20 per cent of persons in municipalities with 500 to 1,500 households and 100 per cent of persons in municipalities with less than 500 households.

The publication of data on the economically active population only relate to persons aged 15 years and over.

(b) Employment: The question used to determine whether or not a person was to be counted as employed is: "Did X have a job or business during the past seven days?."

It is reported that the following categories are included:

i)   persons doing unpaid work in family farm or business;
ii)   employed persons, temporarily absent from work;
iii) working students with a part time job;
iv)   seasonal or occasional workers.

None of the above categories can be identified separately.

(c) Unemployment: Considered as "unemployed" are all persons who, during the reference week, were without work, available and looking for work. To determine whether or not a person was to be counted as unemployed, the question used is the same as that indicated under 6 (b) above. If the answer is "no," the following are asked: "Was X available for work during the past seven days?," "Did X look for work during the past seven days?" and "Why did X not look for work?."

7. Classifications used:

Household members aged 15 years and over in the samples are classified by industry and by occupation. No classification by status in employment was made.

(a) Industry: Based on the question: "In what kind of business or industry did X work during the past seven days?." For coding industry, the 1977 Philippines Standard Industrial Classification, based on the ISIC-rev.2, has been used to the 3-digit level.

(b) Occupation: Based on the question: "What was X's activity/occupation during the past seven days?." For coding occupation, the 1990 Philippines Occupational Classification, based on the ISCO-88, has been used to the unit group (4-digit) level.

(c) Status in employment: No classification was made.

8. Main differences compared with the previous census:

In the 1980 census, the questions relating to the economic activity were asked of a sample of 20 per cent of the persons aged 15 years and over, and no reference period was specified in the census questionnaire.

No specific questions were used to determine whether a person should be considered as "employed" or "unemployed."

Questions were only asked on the individual's usual occupation and the kind of industry in which he usually performed his activity. The questions used were "What is X's usual occupation?" and "In what kind of business or industry?."

Occupation referred to the specific job or kind of work that an individual, who worked most of the year, was usually pursuing, or, if unemployed at the time of enumeration, the kind of work he used to do most of the year. Industry referred to the specific character and nature of business or industry, or the place, where the work is being performed in connection with the job or occupation reported for a person.

In the 1990 census, usual activity/occupation refers to the kind of job or business which an individual was engaged in most of the time during the last 12 months preceding the interview.

9. Publication of the census results:

The title of the publication containing the final census results is "Report No. 3 - 1990 Census of Population and Housing," 1992.

The organization responsible for this publication is the National Statistics Office, R. Magsaysay Boulevard, Sta Mesa, Manila.

The census results are also available in the form of printed volumes by province and highly urbanized cities, unpublished tables, as well as of public use tapes and diskettes.

PORTUGAL

1. Name and address of the organization responsible for the census:

Instituto Nacional de Estatística, Ava. António José de Almeida, P-1078 Lisbonne Codex.

2. Population censuses conducted since 1945 (years):

1950, 1960, 1970, 1981 and 1991. The present description relates to the 1991 census (held on 15 April).

3. Coverage of the census:

(a) Geographical scope: Whole territory.

(b) Persons covered: All persons of all ages, except nationals residing abroad for one year or more.

4. Reference period:

The week preceding the census (i.e. 7 to 13 April 1991).

Nevertheless, as regards unemployment, different intervals were used (less than one month, one month to four months, four to seven months, more than seven months).

5. Main topics:

(a) Total population, by sex and age:	yes
Economically active population by:	
(b) Sex and age group:	yes
(c) Industry:	yes
(d) Occupation:	yes
(e) Status in employment:	yes
(f) Highest educational level:	yes
(g) Hours of work:	yes
(h) Other characteristics:	yes

Re (a): The age is defined in terms of date of birth.

Re (g): Employed persons were asked to specify the number of hours they worked in their primary occupation during the reference week.

Re (h): The census also covered information on other topics, such as: place of work; commuting time and means of travel to and from the workplace; main source of income during the last 12 months; etc.

6. Concepts and definitions:

(a) Economically active population: It comprises all persons aged 12 years and over who, during the reference week, were either employed or unemployed, according to the definitions given below. The definition also covers all members of the armed forces (career military staff and conscripts).

(b) Employment: Considered as "employed" are all persons who, during the reference week, had an occupation, function or any economic activity.

It is reported that the following categories are included:

i)   persons doing unpaid work in family firm or business;
ii)   persons engaged in the production of primary products for own consumption;
iii) employed persons, temporarily absent from work;
iv)   working students with a part-time job;
v)   seasonal or occasional workers who were working at the time of the census;
vi)   conscripts (military or civilian service); however, only persons on compulsory military service are identified separately;
vii) apprentices and trainees.

Only persons belonging to categories (i), (iii) and (vi) can be identified separately.

(c) Unemployment: Considered as "unemployed broadly defined" are all persons who, during the reference week, were without work and wishing to work. Considered as "unemployed strictly defined" all persons who, during the reference week, were without work and seeking work, or who had sought work in the past 30 days, or who were registered with the employment office. Seasonal or occasional workers who were without work at the time of the census are also considered as unemployed.

7. Classifications used:
Both employed persons and unemployed persons previously employed are classified by industry, by occupation and by status in employment.

(a) Industry: Based on the question: "Where are you (were you last) employed in your primary occupation?." For coding industry, the ISIC-rev.3 was used to the class (4-digit) level.

(b) Occupation: The question asked concerns the primary occupation. For coding occupation, the ISCO-88 was used, with certain adaptations which amplified the base group level.

(c) Status in employment: Both employed persons and unemployed persons previously employed were asked a specific question to determine whether they work or last worked as: employers; self-employed workers; workers in the service of an employer (employees); unpaid family workers; active members of a producers' cooperative; conscripts (compulsory military service); other. For coding this variable, the seven above-mentioned groups were used.

8. Main differences compared with the previous census:
The 1991 census entailed two new questions aimed at identifying type of unemployment (strictly defined, broadly defined and according to duration), namely: (i) "Have you previously worked" and, if so, (ii) "Do you wish to work and have you, within the past 30 days, looked for work or been registered with an employment office (for the past one to four months, for the past four to seven months, for seven months or more)?," (iii) "Do you wish to work, but have you not sought work?" and (iv) "Do you not wish to work?."

Persons who stated that they wished to work are considered as unemployed even if they did not seek work. On the other hand, those who stated that they did not wish to work are excluded from the economically active population.

The question concerning the primary means of subsistence, unlike the 1981 census, did not take into account the different types of pensions.

Persons in compulsory military service (conscripts) were assigned to a new group as regards status in employment.

9. Publication of the census results:
The final census data on the economically active population and its component groups were to have been published in 1993.

The organization responsible for the publication is Instituto Nacional de Estatística, Lisboa.

The results of the 1991 census are also available in the form of unpublished tables, diskettes and magnetic tapes.

PUERTO RICO

1. Name and address of the organization responsible for the census:
U.S. Census Bureau, Washington, DC, 20233. The methodological information relating to the last census was provided by the Planning Board Census Office of Puerto Rico, San Juan, P.R.

2. Population censuses conducted since 1945 (years):
1950, 1960, 1970, 1980 and 1990. The present description relates to the 1990 census (held on 1st April).

3. Coverage of the census:

(a) Geographical scope: Whole country.

(b) Persons covered: All persons of all ages.

4. Reference period:
The week preceding the census day for employed persons, the four weeks preceding the census day for unemployed persons, and the last year for other economic characteristics.

5. Main topics:

(a) Total population, by sex and age:	yes

Economically active population by:

(b) Sex and age group:	yes
(c) Industry:	yes
(d) Occupation:	yes
(e) Status in employment:	yes
(f) Highest educational level:	yes
(g) Hours of work:	yes
(h) Other characteristics:	yes

Re (a): The age is defined in terms of age at last birthday.

Re (g): Hours of work relate both to usual hours of work during the short reference period, and to the total period worked by employed persons during the past year (expressed in number of weeks).

Re (h): The census also collected information on other topics, namely: earnings; type of income; means of transport and time used to travel to workplace; layoff the last week; year last worked; vocational training.

6. Concepts and definitions:

(a) Economically active population: It comprises all persons aged 16 years and over who, during the reference periods, were either employed or unemployed, according to the definitions given below. Questions on economic activity were asked of a 17 per cent sample of all housing units (one household out of six). The definition includes members of the armed forces, but the data published only relate to the civilian labour force. Excluded from the definition are: working students with a part time job, students seeking work, seasonal workers enumerated in an off season who were not looking for work and persons doing only incidental unpaid family work.

(b) Employment: The questions used to determine whether or not a person was to be counted as employed were "Did X work any time last week?" and "How many hours did X work last week?."

It is reported that the following categories are included:

i)   persons doing unpaid work in family firm or business;
ii)   persons engaged in the production of primary products for own consumption;
iii) employed persons, temporarily absent from work;
iv)   conscripts for military/civilian service;
v)   apprentices and trainees.

Only persons belonging to category (iv) can be identified separately.

(c) Unemployment: The questions used to determine whether or not a person was to be counted as unemployed were "Has X been looking for work during the last four weeks?" and "Could X have taken a job last week?."

7. Classifications used:
Both employed persons and unemployed persons previously employed in the sample are classified by industry, by occupation and by status in employment.

(a) Industry: Based on the questions: "For whom did X work?" and "What kind of business or industry was this (is this mainly manufacturing, wholesale trade, retail trade or something else)?." The industry classification system consists of 231 categories classified into 13 major industry groups. It has been based on the Standard Industrial Classification Manual (SIC) of 1972, with the supplement of 1977. Links to the ISIC have not been established, but an adaptation was made for international comparison purposes.

(b) Occupation: Based on the questions: "What kind of work was X doing?" and "What were X most important activities or duties?." The occupation system consists of 503 specific occupational categories arranged into 6 summary and 13 major occupation groups. This classification was developed to be consistent with the 1980 Standard Occupational Classification Manual (SOC). Links to the ISCO have not been established, but an adaptation was made for international comparison purposes.

(c) Status in employment: Based on the question: "Was X: private not for profit; Municipal government; Commonwealth government; Federal government; self-employed in own not incorporated; self-employed in own incorporated; working without pay; other?." For coding status in employment, the eight categories above were used.

8. Main differences compared with the previous census:
No major difference.

9. Publication of the census results:
The title of the publication containing the 1990 census results is "Summary Social, Economic and Housing Characteristics," 1993.

The organization responsible for this publication is the U.S. Census Bureau, Washington, DC, 20233.

The census results are also available in the form of magnetic tapes, CD-ROM and microfiches, printed reports and floppy disks.

REUNION

1. Name and address of the organization responsible for the census:
Service régional de l'INSEE à la Réunion, 15 rue de l'école, 97490 Ste Clotilde, La Réunion.

2. Population censuses conducted since 1945 (years):
1954, 1961, 1967, 1974, 1982 and 1990. The present description relates to the 1990 census (held on 15 March).

3. Coverage of the census:
(a) Geographical scope: Whole territory.

(b) Persons covered: All persons of all ages.

4. Reference period:
The week preceding the census day.

5. Main topics:
(a) Total population, by sex and age:	yes
Economically active population by:	
(b) Sex and age group:	yes
(c) Industry:	yes
(d) Occupation:	yes
(e) Status in employment:	yes
(f) Highest educational level:	yes
(g) Hours of work:	no
(h) Other characteristics:	yes

Re (a): The age is defined in terms of year of birth.

Re (h): The census also covered information on other topics, such as: full-time and part-time work, primary activity, the number of workers employed by self-employed persons, the length of time spent looking for work, etc.

6. Concepts and definitions:
(a) Economically active population: It comprises all persons aged 14 years and over who, during the reference week, were either employed or unemployed, according to the definitions given below. The definition also covers all members of the armed forces (career military staff and conscripts). Questions concerning economic activity were asked only of a sample of persons, which excluded military staff living in barracks and prisoners.

(b) Employment: Considered as "employed" are all persons who, during the reference week, had an occupation, function or any economic activity, whether paid or unpaid. Specific questions used to determine if a person is to be counted as employed are: "Do you work (full time or part time)?"; "Are you: employed or self-employed (farmer, craftsman, merchant, industrialist, professional, unpaid family worker, etc.)?," and "If you are self-employed: how many workers do you employ? (do not count apprentices or domestic staff; in agriculture, count only permanent employees)." The definition also covers persons engaged in paid community work provided to the unemployed, persons who have been placed by a temporary employment agency, persons holding a fixed-term employment contract, and persons with a retraining contract.

It is reported that the following categories are included:

i) persons doing unpaid work in family firm or business;
ii) persons engaged in the production of primary products for own consumption;
iii) employed persons, temporarily absent from work;
iv) working students with a part time job;
v) seasonal or occasional workers who were working at the time of the census;
vi) conscripts for military/civilian service;
vii) apprentices (bound by a contract) and trainees (mainly in enterprises or training centres).

Only persons belonging to categories (i), (vi) and (vii) can be identified separately.

(c) Unemployment: Considered as "unemployed" are all persons who, on their own initiative, stated that they were without work, and who were seeking work. The questions used to determine if a person should be considered as unemployed are "Are you unemployed (whether registered or not with the National Employment Agency)?," "Have you previously worked? (if so, what was your primary occupation?," and "Are you seeking work (for: less than three months; three months to less than one year; one year to less than two years; two years or more)?."

7. Classifications used:
Both employed persons and unemployed persons previously employed included in the sample are classified by occupation. Only employed persons in the sample are classified by industry and by status in employment.

(a) Industry: Surveyed persons were asked to give the address and name of the establishment where they work or which they manage, and to identify its activity as accurately as possible (for example: wholesale wine dealers, manufacture of metal scaffolding, road passenger transport, etc.). For coding industry, 100 groups of the Nomenclature of Activities and Products (NAP) were used. Links to the ISIC have not been established.

(b) Occupation: Surveyed persons were asked to identify their current or most recent occupation as accurately as possible (for example: electrical maintenance worker, lorry driver, household appliance salesperson, chemical engineer, self-service cashier, etc.) to permit the determination of their occupational group. The question, however, was left open-ended, so that surveyed persons could reply in their own words. The classification in a specific group takes place when the data is processed. For coding occupation, a direct coding system entailing 42 groups was used. Links to the ISCO have not been established.

(c) Status in employment: For coding this variable, five categories were used, namely: self-employed person; employer; employee; unpaid family worker; other.

8. Main differences compared with the previous census:
The minimum age limit used for inclusion in the economically active population was 15 years in the 1982 census.

Moreover, both employed persons and unemployed persons previously employed had been classified by industry and by status in employment in the 1982 census.

9. Publication of the census results:
The title of the publication containing the final census results is: "Population, Emploi, Logements; Evolution 1975-1982-1990 (Série jaune)," 1992.

The Institut national de la statistique et des études économiques (INSEE), 18 boulevard Adolphe Pinard, 75675 Paris Cedex 14, is responsible for this publication.

The 1990 final census data are also available on diskettes, magnetic tapes and other formats on request.

ROMANIA

1. Name and address of the organization responsible for the census:
Central Committee for the 1992 Population and Housing Census. National Statistics Commission, Bd. Libertatii 16, Sector 5, Bucarest 70542.

2. Population censuses conducted since 1945 (years):
1948, 1956, 1966, 1977 and 1992. The present description relates to the 1992 census (held on 7 January).

3. Coverage of the census:
(a) Geographical scope: Whole territory.

(b) Persons covered: All persons of all ages residing permanently in the country, but excluding stateless persons and foreign nationals (diplomatic, consular and commercial representatives, international organizations, foreign enterprises, press correspondents).

4. Reference period:
One year (1991).

5. Main topics:
(a) Total population, by sex and age:	yes
Economically active population by:	
(b) Sex and age group:	yes
(c) Industry:	yes
(d) Occupation:	yes
(e) Status in employment:	yes
(f) Highest educational level:	yes
(g) Hours of work:	no
(h) Other characteristics:	no

Re (a): The age is defined in terms of year of birth.

6. Concepts and definitions:

(a) Economically active population: It comprises all persons aged 14 years or over who, during the reference period, were available to engage (whether they did so or not) in the production of goods and services in the national economy, according to the definitions given below. Members of the armed forces are included in the definition.

(b) Employment: Considered as "employed" are all persons aged from 14 to 80 years who, during the reference period, engaged in an economic activity for remuneration in cash or in kind, under contract or on their own account.

It is reported that the following categories are included:

i)   persons doing unpaid work in family firm or business;
ii) persons engaged in the production of primary products for own consumption;
iii) employed persons, temporarily absent from work;
iv) working students with a part-time job;
v)   seasonal or occasional workers;
vi) conscripts (military or civilian service);
vii) apprentices and trainees.

Only categories (i), (ii) and (vi) can be identified separately on the basis of replies given to questions concerning status in employment.

Excluded from the definition are persons who reported having retired, home-makers and students seeking work, even if they worked on a temporary or occasional basis during the reference period (especially in agriculture).

(c) Unemployment: Considered as unemployed are all men aged from 14 to 64 years, and all women aged from 14 to 59 years who, at the time of the census, stated that they were out of work, even if they had worked during the long reference period (1991), and that they were available for and seeking work (or their first job). Students seeking work are excluded from the definition.

7. Classifications used:

Both employed persons and unemployed persons (excepting first-time jobseekers) are classified by industry, by occupation and by status in employment.

(a) Industry: Specific questions were asked to employed persons and to unemployed persons previously employed concerning the nature of their present or former occupational activity, and the type of activity of the business or establishment in which they currently work or had previously worked. For coding industry, 99 groups of the national classification were used. Links to the ISIC-rev.3 have been established to the group (3-digit) level.

(b) Occupation: Specific questions were asked both of employed persons and unemployed persons previously employed to determine the industry group to which they belong or belonged. Neither secondary nor seasonal occupations were taken into account, but only the primary occupation, in other words the person's main source of income. For coding occupation, the 437 basic groups of the national classification were used. Links to the ISCO-88 have been established to the minor group (3-digit) level.

(c) Status in employment: Specific questions were asked of employed and unemployed persons previously employed to determine their present or previous status in employment. The following six groups were identified: employer, self-employed person, employee, unpaid family worker, member of a producers' cooperative, others.

8. Main differences compared with the previous census:

In 1992, inclusion in the economically active population and its components was subject to a maximum age limit; the reference period was long (the year 1991); the economically active population was divided into employed workers and unemployed workers; links were established with ISIC-rev.3 and ISCO-88 for industry and occupation classifications, respectively; both employed persons and unemployed persons previously employed were classified by status in employment.

9. Publication of the census results:

The final 1992 census results were published in October 1993.

The titles of the publications containing the final census data are: "Vol. I - Population - Demographic structure," "Vol. II - Population - Socio-economic structure" and "Vol. III - Establishments, housing, households."

The agency responsible for these publications is the National Statistics Commission, Bd. Libertatii 16, Sector 5, Bucarest 70542.

The results are also available on diskettes and magnetic tapes.

ST. LUCIA

1. Name and address of the organization responsible for the census:

Statistics Department, Block A, 3rd floor, N.I.S. Building, The Waterfront, Castries, St. Lucia, West Indies.

2. Population censuses conducted since 1945 (years):

1946, 1960, 1970, 1980 and 1991. The present description relates to the 1991 population census (held on 12 May).

3. Coverage of the census:

(a) Geographical scope: Whole island.

(b) Persons covered: All persons of all ages.

4. Reference period:

The week and the 12 months preceding the census day.

5. Main topics:

(a) Total population, by sex and age:	yes
Economically active population by:	
(b) Sex and age group:	yes
(c) Industry:	yes
(d) Occupation:	yes
(e) Status in employment:	yes
(f) Highest educational level:	yes
(g) Hours of work:	yes
(h) Other characteristics:	yes

Re (a): The age is defined in terms of age at last birthday.

Re (g): Hours of work relate to the number of hours actually worked during the reference week, and the total period worked as the number of months during the 12 months prior to the census day.

Re (h): Information on income and means of travel to work were collected.

6. Concepts and definitions:

(a) Economically active population: It comprises all persons aged 15 years and over who, during the reference periods, were most either employed or unemployed, according to the definitions given below. Working students with a part time job and students seeking work are excluded from the definition, as well as members of the armed forces.

(b) Employment: Considered as "employed" are all persons who most worked during the reference periods. The questions used to determine if a person is to be counted as employed are: "What did you do most during the past 12 months?" and "What did you do most during the past week?." The possible answers were: 1) worked; 2) had a job but did not work; 3) looked for work; 4) wanted work and available; 5) home duties; 6) attended school; 7) retired; 8) disabled, unable to work; 9) other; 10) not stated.

It is reported that the following categories are included:

i) persons doing unpaid work in family firm or business;
ii) employed persons, temporarily absent from work.

Both categories can be identified separately.

(c) Unemployment: Considered as "unemployed" are all persons who, during the reference periods, most were without work, wanted work; were available and looking for work.

7. Classifications used:

Both employed persons and unemployed persons previously employed were classified by industry, by occupation and by status in employment.

(a) Industry: Based on the question: "What type of business is/was carried on at your workplace?." Unemployed persons were also asked the following question: "What sort of work did you look for or want?." For coding industry, 17 groups of the national classification were used. Links to the ISIC-rev.3 have been established to the tabulation category (1-digit) level.

(b) Occupation: Based on the question: "What sort of work do/did you do in your main occupation?." For coding occupation, nine groups of the national classification were used. Links to the ISCO-88 have been established to the major-group (1-digit) level.

(c) Status in employment: Based on the question: "Did you carry on your own business, work for a wage or salary or as an unpaid worker in a family business?." Six groups were used for coding status in employment, namely: paid employee (government); paid employee private; unpaid worker; own business with paid help (employer); own business without paid help (own account); and don't know/not stated.

8. Main differences compared with the previous census:
In the 1991 census, more information on the unemployed seeking work was sought.

9. Publication of the census results:
The final data were issued in 1995 in the publication entitled: "1991 Population & Housing Census Volumes 1-9."

The organization responsible for the publication is the Statistics Department, NIS Building, The Waterfront, Castries.

Unpublished tables are also available from the Department since May 1992.

ST.VINCENT AND THE GRENADINES

1. Name and address of the organization responsible for the census:
Census Office, Statistical Office, Central Planning Division.

2. Population censuses conducted since 1945 (years):
1960, 1970, 1980 and 1991. The present description relates to the 1991 population census (held on 12 May).

3. Coverage of the census:

(a) Geographical scope: Whole country.

(b) Persons covered: All persons of all ages.

4. Reference period:
The week and the year preceding the census day.

5. Main topics:

(a) Total population, by sex and age:	yes
Economically active population by:	
(b) Sex and age group:	yes
(c) Industry:	yes
(d) Occupation:	yes
(e) Status in employment:	yes
(f) Highest educational level:	yes
(g) Hours of work:	yes
(h) Other characteristics:	yes

Re (a): The age is defined in terms of age at last birthday.

Re (g): The census collected information from employed persons on the number of months worked during the year reference, and on the number of hours worked during the week reference.

Re (h): The census also collected information on income and on means of transport used to travel to work.

6. Concepts and definitions:

(a) Economically active population: It comprises all persons aged 15 years and over who, during the reference week, were either employed or unemployed, according to the definitions given below. Professional armed forces, working students with a part time job and students seeking work are excluded from the definition.

(b) Employment: Considered as "employed" are all persons who stated that they most worked during the short reference period. The question used to determine if a person is to be counted as employed is "What did you do most during the past week? for example, did you work, look for a job, keep house or carry on some other activity?."

It is reported that the following categories are included:

i) persons doing unpaid work in family firm or business;
ii) employed persons, temporarily absent from work;
iii) seasonal or occasional workers;
iv) apprentices and trainees.

Only persons belonging to categories (i) and (ii) can be identified separately.

(c) Unemployment: Considered as "unemployed" are all persons who, during the reference week, were without work, wanted to work and were available for work. The definition includes those who actively looked for work as well as those who did nothing about finding a job because they knew none were available.

7. Classifications used:
Employed persons and unemployed persons previously employed are classified by industry, by occupation and by status in employment.

(a) Industry: Based on the question: "What type of business is/was carried on at your workplace?." For coding industry, 17 groups of the national classification were used. Links to the ISIC-rev.3 have been established to the tabulation category (1-digit) level.

(b) Occupation: Based on the question: "What sort of work did you/do you do in your main occupation?." For coding occupation, 10 groups of the national classification were used. Links to the ISCO-88 have been established to the major group (1-digit) level.

(c) Status in employment: Based on the question: "Did you carry on your own business, work for a wage or salary or as an unpaid worker in a family business?." For coding status in employment, six groups were used: paid employee-Government; paid employee-private; unpaid worker; own business with paid help (employer); own business without paid help (own-account); don't know/not stated.

8. Main differences compared with the previous census:
No major difference.

9. Publication of the census results:
The final census data on the economically active population and its components have been issued in the publication entitled "1991 - Population and Housing Census Report, Volume 2."

The organization responsible for the publication is the Statistical Office, Central Planning Division, Ministry of Finance.

The census data is also available in the form of diskettes.

SAMOA

1. Name and address of the organization responsible for the census:
Department of Statistics, P.O. Box 1151, Apia, Western Samoa.

2. Population censuses conducted since 1945 (years):
1951, 1956, 1961, 1966, 1971, 1976, 1981, 1986 and 1991. The present description relates to the 1991 population census (held on 5 November).

3. Coverage of the census:

(a) Geographical scope: Whole country.

(b) Persons covered: All persons of all ages.

4. Reference period:
One week (20-26 October 1991).

5. Main topics:

(a) Total population, by sex and age:	yes
Economically active population by:	
(b) Sex and age group:	yes
(c) Industry:	yes
(d) Occupation:	yes
(e) Status in employment:	yes
(f) Highest educational level:	no
(g) Hours of work:	no
(h) Other characteristics:	no

Re (a): The age is defined both in terms of year of birth and in terms of age at last birthday.

6. Concepts and definitions:

(a) Economically active population: It comprises all persons aged 10 years and over who, during the reference week, were either employed or unemployed, according to the definitions given below. The published results are restricted to persons aged 15 years and over. The definition excludes members of the armed forces.

(b) Employment: Considered as "employed" are all persons who, when asked about their type of activity, stated that they had been working during the reference week.

It is reported that the following categories are included:

i) persons doing unpaid work in family firm or business;
ii) persons engaged in the production of primary products for own consumption;
iii) employed persons, temporarily absent from work;

iv) working students with a part time job;
v) seasonal or occasional workers;
vi) apprentices and trainees.

None of the above categories can be identified separately.

(c) Unemployment: Considered as "unemployed" are all persons who, during the reference period, were without work.

7. Classifications used:
Only employed persons are classified by industry, by occupation and by status in employment.

(a) Industry: Based on the question: "Type of industry, business or service?." For coding industry, the ISIC-rev.2 was used.

(b) Occupation: Based on the question: "What is your principal occupation?." For coding occupation, the ISCO-88 was used to the minor-group (3-digit) level.

(c) Status in employment: Four groups were used for coding this variable, namely: employer; employee; self-employed worker; unpaid worker.

8. Main differences compared with the previous census:
A special set of questions were asked in the 1992 Census to women who describe themselves as housewives which were not asked as on previous censuses.

9. Publication of the census results:
The final census data were issued in January 1993 in a publication entitled "Report of the Census of Population and Housing - 1991."

The organization responsible for the publication is the Department of Statistics, P.O. Box 1151, Apia, Western Samoa.

The census results are not available in other forms.

SAO TOME AND PRINCIPE

1. Name and address of the organization responsible for the census:
Direcçao de Economia e Estatística, C.P. 256, Sao Tomé.

2. Population censuses conducted since 1945 (years):
1950, 1960, 1970, 1981 and 1991. The present description relates to the 1991 census (held on 4 August).

3. Coverage of the census:
(a) Geographical scope: Whole territory.
(b) Persons covered: All persons of all ages.

4. Reference period:
The week preceding the census day. A short period (the week preceding the census) and a long reference period (the 12 months preceding the census) are used in the questions put to employed persons regarding their hours of work.

5. Main topics:
(a) Total population, by sex and age:	yes
Economically active population by:	
(b) Sex and age group:	yes
(c) Industry:	yes
(d) Occupation:	yes
(e) Status in employment:	yes
(f) Highest educational level:	yes
(g) Hours of work:	yes
(h) Other characteristics:	yes

Re (a): The age is defined both in terms of year of birth and in terms of age at last birthday;

Re (g): The hours of work relate to the usual hours of work of employed persons, and to the actual hours worked by employed persons at work during the week preceding the census, and to the total period of work (in months) during the 12 months preceding the census.

Re (h): Active persons were also asked a specific question concerning their income.

6. Concepts and definitions:
(a) Economically active population: It comprises all persons aged 10 years and over who, during the reference period, were either employed or unemployed, according to the definitions given below. Members of the armed forces are included in the definition.

(b) Employment: Considered as "employed" are all persons who, in reply to a question concerning their "employment situation" during the reference week, stated that they were working.

It is reported that the following categories are included:
i) persons doing unpaid work in family firm or business;
ii) persons engaged in the production of primary products for own consumption;
iii) employed persons, temporarily absent from work;
iv) working students with a part time job;
v) seasonal or occasional workers;
vi) conscripts for military/civilian service;
vii) apprentices and trainees.

Only persons falling in categories (i) and (vii) can be identified separately by means of their responses to specific questions.

(c) Unemployment: Considered as "unemployed" are all persons who, in reply to a question concerning their "employment situation" during the reference week, stated that they were seeking either a new job or their first job. Students seeking work are excluded from the definition.

7. Classifications used:
Both employed persons and unemployed persons previously employed are classified by industry, by occupation and by status in employment.

(a) Industry: The question used to determine industry group relates to the nature of the workplace (farm, public or private enterprise, etc.) and the economic sector. For coding industry, the ISIC-rev.2 was used to the division (1-digit) level.

(b) Occupation: The questions used refer to the person's occupation during the reference week (or, in respect of unemployed persons, to their most recent occupation). For coding occupation, the ISCO-88 was used to the minor group (3-digit) level.

(c) Status in employment: For coding this variable, five categories were used, namely: employee; self-employed person; employer; unpaid family worker; other, not specified.

8. Main differences compared with the previous census:
No specific questions were asked in the 1981 census regarding the total working time or the income of employed persons.

9. Publication of the census results:
The title of the publication containing the final census results is: "Principais Resultados do II. Recenseamento Geral da Populaçao e da Habitaçao."

The organization responsible for this publication is Direcçao de Economia e Estatística, C.P. 256, Sao Tomé.

The 1991 census results are also available in other forms, including diskettes.

SAUDI ARABIA

1. Name and address of the organization responsible for the census:
Central Department of Statistics, P.O. Box 3735, Riyadh 11118.

2. Population censuses conducted since 1945 (years):
1974 and 1992. The present description relates to the 1992 population census (held on 27 September).

3. Coverage of the census:
(a) Geographical scope: Whole country.
(b) Persons covered: All persons of all ages.

4. Reference period:
The week preceding the census day.

5. Main topics:
(a) Total population, by sex and age:	yes
Economically active population by:	
(b) Sex and age group:	yes
(c) Industry:	yes
(d) Occupation:	yes
(e) Status in employment:	yes
(f) Highest educational level:	yes
(g) Hours of work:	no
(h) Other characteristics:	no

Re (a): The age is defined in terms of age at last birthday.

6. Concepts and definitions:

(a) Economically active population: It comprises all persons aged 12 years and over, who during the reference period were either employed or unemployed, according to the definitions given below. The definition excludes working students with a part time job and students seeking work, but includes members of the armed forces.

(b) Employment: Considered as "employed" are all persons who, during the reference period, worked 15 hours or more at a job or jobs, or were absent from such a job or jobs due to illness, vacation, etc.

It is reported that the following categories are included:
i)   persons doing unpaid work in family firm or business;
ii)   persons engaged in the production of primary products for own consumption;
iii) employed persons, temporarily absent from work;
iv)   seasonal or occasional workers;
v)   conscripts for military/civilian service;
vi)   apprentices and trainees.

Only persons doing unpaid work in family firm or business can be identified separately.

(c) Unemployment: Considered as "unemployed" are all persons who, during the reference period, were without work, able to work, willing to work and looking for work. The unemployed were registered as "Unemployed but had worked" or "Unemployed but never worked."

7. Classifications used:

Only employed persons are classified by industry and by status in employment. Both employed persons and unemployed persons previously employed are classified by occupation.

(a) Industry: To determine industry group, employed persons were asked to indicate the main economic activity of their employer. For coding industry, the ISIC-rev.3 was used to the division (2-digit) level.

(b) Occupation: To determine occupation group, employed persons and unemployed persons previously employed were asked to indicate their main occupation (type of work the person is/was doing). For coding occupation, the ISCO-68 was used to the unit group (3-digit) level.

(c) Status in employment: To determine this variable employed persons were asked to indicate their employment position. For coding status in employment, four groups were used, namely: employer, self employed, employee and work without pay.

8. Main differences compared with the previous census:
No major difference.

9. Publication of the census results:
A report titled "Preliminary Results of the General Population and Housing Census: 413 A.H." was released in March 1995. Additional reports are planned, but no publication dates have been determined.

The organization responsible for the publication is the Central Department of Statistics, P.O. Box 3735, Riyadh 11118.

The census data are not available in other forms.

SINGAPORE

1. Name and address of the organization responsible for the census:
Department of Statistics, 8 Shenton Way, 10-01, Treasury Building, Singapore 0106.

2. Population censuses conducted since 1945 (years):
1947, 1957, 1970, 1980 and 1990. The present description relates to the 1990 census (held on 30 June).

3. Coverage of the census:
(a) Geographical scope: Whole country.

4. Reference period:
The week preceding the interview.

5. Main topics:
(a) Total population, by sex and age:	yes
Economically active population by:	
(b) Sex and age group:	yes
(c) Industry:	yes
(d) Occupation:	yes
(e) Status in employment:	yes

(f) Highest educational level:	yes
(g) Hours of work:	no
(h) Other characteristics:	yes

Re (a): The age is defined in terms of a person's date of birth (the person's age was computed thus: census date - date of birth; the number of additional months and days were stored as a fraction of one year and expressed in decimal form).

Re (h): The census also collected information on other topics, such as: wages and salaries, bonuses, average monthly earnings or profits (for self-employed persons) and mode of transport to workplace.

6. Concepts and definitions:

(a) Economically active population: It comprises all persons who, during the reference week, were either employed or unemployed, according to the definitions given below. No age limit was fixed for inclusion in the economically active population, but data on economic characteristics were tabulated only for persons aged 15 years and over. Members of the armed forces are included in the definition. However, working students with a part time job and students seeking work are excluded.

(b) Employment: Considered as "employed" are all persons who either (i) worked for pay or profit during the last seven days, or (ii) normally work at least 15 hours a week. These two definitions were used to determine whether or not a person was to be counted as employed.

It is reported that the following categories are included:
i)   persons doing unpaid work in family firm or business;
ii)   persons engaged in the production of primary products for own consumption;
iii) employed persons, temporarily absent from work;
iv)   seasonal or occasional workers;
v)   conscripts for military/civilian service;
vi)   apprentices and trainees.

Only persons belonging to categories (i) and (v) can be identified separately. The question used to identify persons in category (i) was "Have you been assisting in any family business as an unpaid family worker?." The data relating to conscripts for military service (category (v)) were obtained from the Ministry of Defence and pre-printed for verification and confirmation by the persons.

(c) Unemployment: The questions used to determine whether or not a person was to be counted as "unemployed" were "Are you looking for work?" and "If yes, what action have you taken to look for work?: (i) registered with Government Employment Service?; (ii) answered advertisements or wrote direct to firms? (iii) asked friends or relatives? (iv) other? (v) making preparations to start own business?."

7. Classifications used:
Only employed persons are classified by industry, by occupation and by status in employment.

(a) Industry: Based on the questions: "What kind of activity is the firm/organization engaged in?" and "What is the main type of product handled/produced?" or "What kind of service does the firm/organization provide?." For coding industry, 117 minor groups (3-digit), 317 unit groups (4-digit) and 945 items (5-digit codes) of the Singapore Standard Industrial Classification, 1990 (SSIC 90) were used. Links to the ISIC-rev.3 have been established to the tabulation category (1-digit) level.

(b) Occupation: Based on the questions: "What is your occupation?" or "What kind of work do you do?." For coding occupation, 119 minor groups (3-digit), 314 unit groups (4-digit) and 1,116 occupations (5-digit codes) of the Singapore Standard Occupational Classification (SSOC) were used. To assist in the coding of occupation, space was provided in the Enumeration Schedule for the enumerator (or the respondent, in the case of self-enumeration) to enter the description of the main duties/tasks which the respondent performed in relation to the work. Links to the ISCO-88 have been established to the major group (1-digit) level.

(c) Status in employment: Based on the question: "Are you: (i) a self-employed without paid help? (ii) a self-employed with paid help? (iii) working as an employee for wages or salaries? (iv) serving National Service? (v) helping in family business without fixed or regular pay?." For coding status in employment, the above five categories were used.

8. Main differences compared with the previous census:
In the 1980 census the age limit for inclusion in the economically active population was 10 years.

In the 1980 census, conscripts for military service were not identifiable separately.

9. Publication of the census results:
The final data relating to the 1990 census was published in August 1993 in the publication entitled "Census of Population 1990 Statistical Release 4 - Economic Characteristics."

The organization responsible for this publication is the Census of Population Office, Department of Statistics, Singapore.

The census results are not available on diskette or magnetic tape.

SLOVAKIA

1. Name and address of the organization responsible for the census:
Slovenského Statistického Urado, Mileticova 3, 824 67 Bratislava.

2. Population censuses conducted since 1945 (years):
1950, 1961, 1970, 1980 and 1991. The present description relates to the 1991 population census (which took place at midnight between the 2nd and the 3rd of March).

3. Coverage of the census:
(a) Geographical scope: Whole country.

(b) Persons covered: All persons of all ages who reside permanently in the country and nationals living permanently abroad; excluding are members of the diplomatic corps and those of the Soviet army and their related persons.

4. Reference period:
At midnight between the 2nd and 3rd of March.

5. Main topics:
(a) Total population, by sex and age:	yes
Economically active population by:	
(b) Sex and age group:	yes
(c) Industry:	yes
(d) Occupation:	yes
(e) Status in employment:	yes
(f) Highest educational level:	...
(g) Hours of work:	no
(h) Other characteristics:	yes

Re (a): The age is defined in terms of year of birth.

Re (h): The census also collected information on the place of work (address), frequency of travel to work (daily, other) and time used to travel one-way "from the door to the door" (minutes).

6. Concepts and definitions:
(a) Economically active population: The economic activity is based on the current activity concept. Thus, the economically active population comprises all persons aged 15 years and over who, at the time of the census, were either employed or unemployed, according to the definitions given below. The definition also covers members of the armed forces as well as prisoners, on the basis of the civilian equivalent of their present or last work.

(b) Employment: Considered as "employed" are all persons who stated that they were employed as: employers, own-account workers, employees and members of agricultural and production co-operatives (including working pensioners, women on paid maternity leave and unpaid family workers). Working students with a part-time job are excluded from the definition.

It is reported that the following categories are included:
i) persons doing unpaid work in family firm or business;
ii) employed persons, temporarily absent from work;
iii) seasonal or occasional workers;
iv) conscripts for military/civilian service.

Only persons belonging to category (i) can be identified separately. Apprentices and trainees, although not covered by the definition of the economically active population, can also be identified separately.

(c) Unemployment: Considered as "unemployed" are all persons aged 15 to 59 years (for men) and 15 to 56 years (for women), who stated that, at the time of the census, they were seeking work.

7. Classifications used:
Both employed and unemployed persons previously employed are classified by industry, by occupation and by status in employment.

(a) Industry: Based on the question: "Indicate the name of the establishment, co-operative, office, organization or school." The coding of branches of economic activity or school attendance was carried out according to special lists of organizations with branch codes based on prevailing activities.

For the processing of the 1991 census results, a national classification of 47 groups was used (i.e., branches and subbranches of the national classification).

The national industrial classification provides a full comparability with the ISIC-rev.3. A conversion table between the national classification and ISIC-rev.3 was established to the division (2-digit) level.

(b) Occupation: Persons were asked to indicate as precisely as possible their executed work or function. Non-working pensioners, women on maternity leave, conscripts for military service, persons in prison and those seeking employment were asked to indicate their last job. For coding occupation, 91 groups of the national classification were used. Links to the ISCO (both ISCO-68 and ISCO-89) have been established to the major group (1-digit) level.

(c) Status in employment: Persons were asked to indicate their social group, e.g. manual worker, employee, member of agricultural co-operative, member of producing co-operative, employer (with one or more employees), private farmer, own-account tradesman, freelancer, unpaid family worker, etc. Manual workers and employees were requested to specify the sector of the national economy (state, private, co-operative, mixed sector).

For coding status in employment, the following nine groups were used: manual workers and employees in private sector; other manual workers and employees; members of agricultural co-operatives; members of other co-operatives; employers; private farmers; own-account workers; freelancers; unpaid family workers.

8. Main differences compared with the previous census:
In 1991, the definition of the economically active population has been extended by the inclusion of unemployed persons seeking employment, but no distinction was been made for those seeking their first job. Working pensioners, persons receiving old or disability pension and wages have also been included in the definition.

In the 1961, 1970 and 1980 censuses, unpaid family workers were counted as dependent persons, i.e., not economically active, and persons who declared themselves as unemployed were considered as employed on the basis of their last work.

In the 1991 census, the classification by status in employment has been extended by the inclusion of employers, and unpaid family workers have been identified as a special group.

Finally, the question on travel to work has been extended in 1991 by the inclusion of a question on the time used to travel one-way "from the door to the door."

9. Publication of the census results:
The title of the publication containing the final census results is: "1991 Population and Housing Census," issued in 1992.

The organization responsible for this publication is the Slovenského Statistického Urado, Mileticova 3, 824 67, Bratislava.

The 1991 final census data are also available on diskettes and magnetic tapes.

SLOVENIA

1. Name and address of the organization responsible for the census:
Statistical Office of the Republic of Slovenia, Ljubljana, Vozarski pot 12.

2. Population censuses conducted since 1945 (years):
1948, 1953, 1961, 1971, 1981 and 1991. The present description relates to the 1991 population census (held on 31 March).

3. Coverage of the census:
(a) Geographical scope: Whole country.
(b) Persons covered: All persons of all ages.

4. Reference period:
The census day and the year preceding the census day.

5. Main topics:
(a) Total population, by sex and age: yes
Economically active population by:
(b) Sex and age group: yes
(c) Industry: yes
(d) Occupation: yes
(e) Status in employment: yes
(f) Highest educational level: yes
(g) Hours of work: no
(h) Other characteristics: yes

Re (a): The age is defined in terms of year of birth.

Re (h): The census also collected information on person's regular incomes and on frequency, time spent (in minutes), and means of transport used to travel to workplace.

6. Concepts and definitions:
(a) Economically active population: It comprises all persons aged 15 and over who, on the census day, were either employed or unemployed, according to the definitions given below. For specific categories of the population (i.e. house-wives, persons who worked mainly on farms, retired persons, seasonal workers who worked occasionally), the reference period used to determine their activity was the year preceding the census day. The definition includes all members of the armed forces but excludes working students with a part time job and students seeking work.

(b) Employment: Considered as "employed" are all persons who, at the time of the census, performed a profession and received payment in money or in kind for their work. In agricultural households are included those family members who help out and agricultural housewives if they are involved predominantly with agricultural work.

It is reported that the following categories are included:
i) persons doing unpaid work in family firm or business;
ii) persons engaged in the production of primary products for own consumption;
iii) employed persons, temporarily absent from work;
iv) seasonal or occasional workers;
v) conscripts for military/civilian service;
vi) apprentices and trainees.

Only persons belonging to the category (i) can be identified separately.

(c) Unemployment: Considered as "unemployed" are all persons who were registered at employment agencies as first employment or new employment seekers at the time of the census.

7. Classifications used:
Both employed persons and unemployed persons previously employed are classified by occupation. Only employed persons are classified by industry and by status in employment.

(a) Industry: Employed persons were asked to specify the industry (branch of economic activity) in which they worked and the name and address of enterprise/organization or association where they worked. For coding industry, 700 groups of the classification of activities of the central statistical office of the Republic of Slovenia valid at the time of the census were used. This classification is not directly comparable to the ISIC. However, on the basis of a combination of answers and by estimation, links can be established to the ISIC-rev.2 to the major division (1-digit) level.

(b) Occupation: Persons were asked to specify the type of work performed. For coding occupation, the classification of occupation of the Central Statistical Office of the Republic of Slovenia valid at the time of the census was used. This classification is not directly comparable to the ISCO. However, on the basis of various data, links can be established to the ISCO-88 to the major group (1-digit) level.

(c) Status in employment: For coding this variable, five groups were used: employee; owner/co-owner (enterprise); owner/co-owner (craft establishment); own account worker; unpaid family worker.

8. Main differences compared with the previous census:
No major difference.

9. Publication of the census results:
The final census results have been issued in many publications, including: "1991 Census of the population, Households, Housing and Agricultural Holdings in the Republic of Slovenia - Final data: Statistical information No. 173 (July 1992)" and "No. 189 (July 1992): population by activity and sex, Economically active population, by industry." The complete list of the publications can be found in "Results of Surveys - Census of the population, households, housings and agricultural holdings in the Republic of Slovenia in 1991, No. 617 (1994)."

The organization responsible for these publications is the Statistical Office of the Republic of Slovenia, Vozarski pot 12, Ljubljana.

The census results are not available in others forms.

SOUTH AFRICA

1. Name and address of the organization responsible for the census:
Central Statistical Service, Private Bag x 44, Steyn's Arcade, 274 Schoeman Street, Pretoria 0001.

2. Population censuses conducted since 1945 (years):
1946, 1951, 1960, 1970, 1980, 1985 and 1991. The present description relates to the 1991 census (held on 7 March).

3. Coverage of the census:
(a) Geographical scope: Republic of South Africa (Transkei, Bophuthatswana, Venda and Ciskei countries excluded).
(b) Persons covered: All persons of all ages.

4. Reference period:
The census day.

5. Main topics:
(a) Total population, by sex and age: yes
Economically active population by:
(b) Sex and age group: yes
(c) Industry: yes
(d) Occupation: yes
(e) Status in employment: yes
(f) Highest educational level: yes
(g) Hours of work: no
(h) Other characteristics: yes

Re (a): The age is defined both in terms of year of birth and in terms of age at last birthday.

Re (h): The census also collected information on annual income.

6. Concepts and definitions:
(a) Economically active population: It comprises all persons who, on the census day, were either employed or unemployed, according to the definitions given below. No age limits were fixed for inclusion in the economically active population and its components; however the data published refer to persons aged 15 years and over. The definition excludes foreigners employed by foreign governments, persons spending less than three months in the country, students working part time and students seeking work, but includes members of the armed forces.

(b) Employment: Considered as "employed" are all persons who identified their present work status on the census day as either "Employer/Self employed" or "Employee."

It is reported that the following categories are included:
i) persons doing unpaid work in family firm or business;
ii) persons engaged in the production of primary products for own consumption;
iii) employed persons, temporarily absent from work;
iv) seasonal or occasional workers;
v) conscripts for military/civilian service;
vi) apprentices and trainees.

Only artisan-related apprentices and trainees can be identified separately.

(c) Unemployment: Considered as "unemployed" are all persons who identified their present work status on the census day as "Unemployed (looking for work)." Persons not working and not looking for work were not considered as unemployed and were coded separately.

7. Classifications used:

Only employed persons are classified by industry. Both employed persons and unemployed persons previously employed are classified by occupation and by status in employment.

(a) Industry: To determine industry group, employed and self-employed persons were asked to indicate the name and the economic sector of the employer/self-employed (e.g. glass factory, gold mine, building of bridges, stockbrokers, camping site, beauty parlour, etc). For coding industry, 40 groups of the national classification were used. Links to the ISIC-rev.2 have been established to the division (2-digit) level.

(b) Occupation: To determine occupation group, employed persons and unemployed persons previously employed were asked to indicate their main or last occupation. The nature of work done is required, e.g. bricklayer, typist, domestic worker, etc. In the case of public servants the rank/occupational class must be given, e.g. deputy director, brigadier, etc. For coding occupation, 165 groups of the national classification were used. Links to the ISCO-68 have been established, but not systematically at the same level.

(c) Status in employment: To determine this variable, employed persons and unemployed persons previously employed were asked to indicate their status in employment for which two coding groups were used, namely: employer/self-employed (including workers for own account and family workers); and employee.

8. Main differences compared with the previous census:

Concerning the data collection procedures, approximately 20% of the population in 88 areas was enumerated on a sample basis. A representative probability sample of occupied shacks or residential premises was drawn in each of the areas and all persons who usually sleep in the shacks or on the premises were enumerated. The sample was designed with the aid of aerial photographs which were taken during February 1991, as close as possible to census day. Preliminary aerial photography was undertaken in certain areas for the designing of the samples. Aerial photographs of these areas were again taken during February 1991.

9. Publication of the census results:

The final results as enumerated were published in March 1992 and the final results after adjustment for undercount in December 1992. A number of other publications on the census results are available.

The organization responsible for these publications is the Central Statistical Service, Private Bag x44, Pretoria 0001.

Unpublished tables, published reports on magnetic tape and the full census data set on magnetic tape are available from the Central Statistical Service. Special tabulations can also be compiled for a fee which covers the cost of programming and processing.

SPAIN

1. Name and address of the organization responsible for the census:

Instituto Nacional de Estadística, Paseo de la Castellana, 183, 28046 Madrid.

2. Population censuses conducted since 1945 (years):

1950, 1960, 1970, 1981 and 1991. The present description relates to the 1991 census (held on 1st March).

3. Coverage of the census:

(a) Geographical scope: Whole country.

(b) Persons covered: All persons of all ages residing or present in the national territory on the day of the census. Excluded are persons living neither in family dwellings nor in fixed collective dwellings (i.e. vagabonds, homeless persons, etc.).

4. Reference period:

The week preceding the date of the census, i.e. 22 to 28 February 1991.

5. Main topics:

(a) Total population, by sex and age:	yes
Economically active population by:	
(b) Sex and age group:	yes
(c) Industry:	yes
(d) Occupation:	yes
(e) Status in employment:	yes
(f) Highest educational level:	yes
(g) Hours of work:	no
(h) Other characteristics:	yes

Re (a): The age is defined in terms of year of birth.

Re (h): Some autonomous communities have collected information on the workplace and means of travel. These communities are: Murcia, Aldalusia, Canary Islands, Catalonia, Galicia, the Basque country and Navarra.

6. Concepts and definitions:

(a) Economically active population: It comprises all persons aged 16 years and over who, during the reference week, were either employed or unemployed, according to the definitions given below. Data on the economically active population and its components (employment and unemployment) were tabulated only for persons aged 16 years and over. The definition also includes professional members of the armed forces, but excludes conscripts in compulsory military service.

(b) Employment: Considered as "employed" are all persons who worked at least one hour during the reference week. The definition also includes persons who, during the reference week, were temporarily absent from work because of sickness, holidays, etc.

It is reported that the following categories are included:

i)   persons doing unpaid work in family firm or business;
ii)   persons engaged in the production of primary products for own consumption;
iii)   employed persons, temporarily absent from work;
iv)   working students with a part-time job;
v)   seasonal or occasional workers who were employed during the reference week;
vi)   apprentices and trainees, provided they received some form of remuneration.

Only persons falling in categories (i), (iv) and (v) can be identified separately. Seasonal and occasional workers are considered as employed only if they worked at least one hour during the reference week. Conscripts in military or civilian service are excluded from the economically active population, but can be identified separately.

(c) Unemployment: Considered as "unemployed" are all persons who, during the reference week, were simultaneously: (i) out of work, in other words, were neither employed nor self-employed; (ii) seeking work, in other words, had taken specific measures to seek employment or to start up in self-employment (for example: registration with the unemployment office, application for employment, reply to vacancy notices, etc.); (iii) available for work in employment or self-employment. Unemployed persons are further divided among first-time jobseekers and persons previously employed.

7. Classifications used:

Both employed persons and unemployed persons previously employed are classified by industry, occupation and status in employment. These variables relate to the main job of employed persons and the most recent job of unemployed persons.

(a) Industry: Based on the question "What is the main activity of the place in which the person works or last worked (for example: agriculture; toy factory; hotel; etc.)?." For coding this variable, the ISIC (rev.2 and rev.3) was used to between one and two digits.

(b) Occupation: Based on the question: "What is the person's current or most recent occupation, profession or trade (for example: shop clerk; construction foreman; etc.)?." For coding this variable, the ISCO (68 and 88) was used to the minor group level.

(c) Status in employment: To determine this variable, a specific question was asked concerning status in employment. This variable was coded on the basis of seven categories: owner, professional or self-employed person employing staff; owner, professional or self-employed person not employing staff; member of a cooperative who works in the cooperative; person working without regulated pay in the enterprise or business of

a member of his/her family with who he/she lives; person permanently employed for wage, commission, day wage or any other kind of payment; person doing casual or temporary work for wage, commission, day wage or any other kind of payment; other.

8. Main differences compared with the previous census:
The most important novelty in the 1991 census is that all questions will be coded and fully processed, permitting a greater geographical disaggregation, although the same degree of disaggregation will not be possible with respect to employment and activity.

The criteria used to classify the population as working, employed, unemployed, etc., are the same as those used in the Survey of the Working Population.

9. Publication of the census results:
The final census data on the economically active population and its components (employment and unemployment) were published in late 1993.

The title of the publication containing the final census data is "Censos de Población y Viviendas 1991."

The organization responsible for this publication is Instituto Nacional de Estadística, Madrid.

The census results are also available in the forms of diskettes, magnetic tapes and CD-ROM.

SUDAN

1. Name and address of the organization responsible for the census:
Central Bureau of Statistics, P.O. Box 700, Khartoum.

2. Population censuses conducted since 1945 (years):
1955-56, 1973, 1983 and 1993. The present description relates to the 1993 population census (held on 15 April).

3. Coverage of the census:
(a) Geographical scope: The three southern regions were only partially covered due to insurgency.

(b) Persons covered: All persons of all ages.

4. Reference period:
The week preceding the census day.

5. Main topics:

(a) Total population, by sex and age:	yes
Economically active population by:	
(b) Sex and age group:	yes
(c) Industry:	yes
(d) Occupation:	yes
(e) Status in employment:	yes
(f) Highest educational level:	yes
(g) Hours of work:	no
(h) Other characteristics:	no

Re (a): The age is defined in terms of age at last birthday.

6. Concepts and definitions:

(a) Economically active population: It comprises all persons aged 10 years and over who, during the reference week, were either employed or unemployed, according to the definitions given below. Armed forces are excluded from the definition, as well as working students with a part time job and students seeking work.

(b) Employment: Considered as "employed" are all persons who, during the reference week, did any job inside or outside their home for at least two days, with payment or without payment. Persons absent from work due to illness or leave are included in the definition.

It is reported that the persons doing unpaid work in family firm or business are included in the definition.

(c) Unemployment: Considered as "unemployed" are all persons who, during the reference week, did not any work and were looking for work or would have accepted a job if offered.

7. Classifications used:
Both employed persons and unemployed persons previously employed are classified by industry, by occupation and by status in employment. Questions on these topics were asked for all private households in urban areas and for 5% sample of private households in rural areas.

(a) Industry: For coding industry, the ISIC-rev.2 was used to the major group (3-digit) level.

(b) Occupation: For coding occupation, the ISCO-88 was used to the unit group (4-digit) level.

(c) Status in employment: For coding this variable, five groups were used, namely: employee; employer; own account worker; unpaid family worker; unpaid working for others.

8. Main differences compared with the previous census:
No major difference.

9. Publication of the census results:
The final data was issued in June 1995 in a publication entitled "Fourth Population Census of Sudan. Final Tabulation."

The organization responsible for this publication is the Central Bureau of Statistics, P.O. Box 700, Khartoum.

The final results are also available in the form of unpublished tables, diskettes and magnetic tapes.

SWEDEN

1. Name and address of the organization responsible for the census:
Statistics Sweden, I/BEF, S-701 89 Örebro.

2. Population censuses conducted since 1945 (years):
1945, 1950, 1960, 1965, 1970, 1975, 1980, 1985 and 1990. The present description relates to the 1990 population census (held on 1st November).

3. Coverage of the census:
(a) Geographical scope: Whole country.

(b) Persons covered: All persons of all ages, except: foreign diplomatic personnel and their families located in the country; civilian aliens temporarily in the country as seasonal workers; civilian aliens who cross a frontier daily to work in the country; civilian aliens, other than those above, temporarily in the country; transients on ship in harbour at the time of the census.

4. Reference period:
One month (October 1990).

5. Main topics:

(a) Total population, by sex and age:	yes
Economically active population by:	
(b) Sex and age group:	yes
(c) Industry:	yes
(d) Occupation:	yes
(e) Status in employment:	yes
(f) Highest educational level:	yes
(g) Hours of work:	yes
(h) Other characteristics:	yes

Re (a): The age is defined in terms of year of birth.

Re (g): Hours of work relate to the number of hours normally worked per week by employed persons.

Re (h): The census also collected information on earnings (from register) and means of transport used.

6. Concepts and definitions:

(a) Economically active population: The census only measures employment.

(b) Employment: Considered as "employed" are all persons aged 16 years and over who, during the reference month, performed any work of an economic value, at home or out of home. No questions were asked to determine if a person is to be counted as employed, but a register of employment was used. The criteria were as follows: An income of 250 SEK or more during October 1990 or, if the period is unknown, 28,000 SEK or more during the whole year.

It is reported that the following categories are included, provided that the criteria of income are fulfilled:

i) persons engaged in the production of primary products for own consumption;
ii) employed persons, temporarily absent from work;
iii) working students with a part time job;
iv) seasonal or occasional workers;
v) conscripts for military/civilian service;
vi) apprentices and trainees.

None of the above categories can be identified separately.

(c) Unemployment: Not applicable.

7. Classifications used:

Employed persons are classified by industry, by occupation and by status in employment.

(a) Industry: Data on industry were obtained from the SCB Central Register of Enterprises. For coding industry, 340 groups of the Swedish Standard Industrial Classification of all Economic Activities (SNI-1969) were used. Links to the ISIC-rev.2 have been established to the group (4-digit) level.

(b) Occupation: The specific questions are either (i) with pre-printed occupation (from the 1985 census): "Does the pre-printed information correspond with your present occupation or position?" or (ii) without pre-printed occupation "How do you classify your occupation? State your occupation as carefully as possible so that it describes your tasks/duties." For coding occupation, 321 groups of the Nordic Classification of Occupations (NYK-1983) were used. Links to the ISCO-68 have been established to the major group (1-digit) level.

(c) Status in employment: The register information was used to determine the status in employment. For coding status in employment, four groups were used: employee; employer; self-employed in farming/forestry; seaman.

8. Main differences compared with the previous census:

No major difference.

9. Publication of the census results:

The lapse of time between the census date and the publication of the final results is one and a half to two years.

The organization responsible for this publication is Statistics Sweden, I/BEF, S-701 89 Örebro, Sweden.

The census results are also available in other forms, i.e., "Computor tables" and "The Regional Statistical Database (RSDB) of Sweden," by March 1992.

SWITZERLAND

1. Name and address of the organization responsible for the census:

Office fédéral de la statistique, Section de la structure de la population et des ménages, Hallwylstrasse 15, 3003 Bern.

2. Population censuses conducted since 1945 (years):

1950, 1960, 1970, 1980 and 1990. The present description relates to the 1990 census (held on 4 December).

3. Coverage of the census:

(a) Geographical scope: Whole territory.

(b) Persons covered: All persons of all ages usually resident in Switzerland, excluding foreign diplomats and members of their families.

4. Reference period:

A short period: the person's situation at end November, at the beginning of December, or on the day of the census.

5. Main topics:

(a) Total population, by sex and age:	yes

Economically active population by:

(b) Sex and age group:	yes
(c) Industry:	yes
(d) Occupation:	yes
(e) Status in employment:	yes
(f) Highest educational level:	yes
(g) Hours of work:	yes
(h) Other characteristics:	yes

Re (a): The age is defined in terms of complete date of birth (day, month and year).

Re (g): Hours of work relate to normal hours of work of employed persons.

Re (h): Other information has also been collected by the census: employed persons were asked questions concerning the length of commuting time to their place of work or school ("How much time does it normally take you to get to work or school?" and "How many times a day do you make the round-trip journey?"), and the means of travel ("What means of transport do you normally use to get to work or school?. If you use several each day, please list them all"). Persons who are retired, in other words persons who are no longer economically active, were asked questions concerning their occupation prior to retirement and their status in that occupation.

6. Concepts and definitions:

(a) Economically active population: It comprises all persons aged 15 years and over who, at the time of the census, were either employed or unemployed, according to the definitions given below. Persons working less than one hour a week are excluded from the definition. Persons on compulsory military service are classified according to their occupation in civilian life.

(b) Employment: Considered as "employed" are all persons who, at the date of the census, had a full-time or part-time occupation, function or gainful activity. Persons employed on a part-time basis are those whose hours of work do not exceed 80 per cent of the usual hours of work in their establishment or branch; they must, however, work at least one hour per week.

It is reported that the following categories are included:

i) persons doing unpaid work in family firm or business;
ii) employed persons, temporarily absent from work;
iii) working students with a part-time job;
iv) seasonal or occasional workers who were working at the time of the census;
v) conscripts (for military/civilian service) who were employed in civilian life;
vi) multiple-job holders;
vii) apprentices and trainees.

Only categories (iii) and (vi), foreign workers in category (iv) and apprentices bound by an apprenticeship contract can be identified separately. Paid and unpaid family workers can be identified together, but not separately.

(c) Unemployment: Considered as "unemployed" are all persons who, at the time of the census, were without work and seeking work, or who held a contract or hiring pledge for future employment. In making the census, the term used was not "unemployed" but "persons seeking employment," in order to avoid any confusion with the concept of "unemployment," as used in labour market statistics.

7. Classifications used:

Only employed persons are classified by industry. Both employed persons and persons seeking employment who have previously been employed are classified by occupation and by status in employment.

(a) Industry: The specific question is "Where do you work?" and refers to the location and name of the enterprise. The industry is determined by reference to the enterprise's entry in the central register of businesses and establishments (REE) of the Office fédéral de la statistique. For coding industry, 54 classes, 210 groups and 703 types of the 1985 General Nomenclature of Economic Activities were used.

Persons working in firms employing one or more persons will be coded with the aid of a register of businesses and establishments.

The Swiss general nomenclature of economic activities is linked to the ISIC rev.2 at the division (2-digit) level.

(b) Occupation: Based on the questions: "What is your present occupation?" and "What was your most recent occupation?" Persons were asked to identify their occupation as accurately as possible and, if necessary, to provide a brief description; for example: "building locksmith" rather than "locksmith"; "salesperson" or "office worker" rather than "employee"; " mechanical engineer," rather than "engineer"; etc. Persons with two or more occupations were asked to report only the more important one. For coding occupation, 404 groups were used. Coding will be done at the same time as coding of occupations learned and level of training. Links to the ISCO-88 have been established.

(c) Status in employment: Based on the questions: "If you are presently employed, please indicate your status in employment" and "If you are looking for work or if you are no longer economically active, please indicate your last status in employment." For coding status in employment seven groups were used: self-employed (for example: shopkeeper, entrepreneur, professional, etc.); employed in an enterprise belonging to a family member; apprentice with an apprenticeship or accelerated practical training contract; manager, authorized representative, senior official; middle or junior manager (for example: head clerk, section or group chief, branch manager, shop foreman, project foreman, team leader); employee, labourer, trainee; other.

8. Main differences compared with the previous census:
The minimum weekly hours of work for inclusion in the employment definition was reduced from six hours in 1980 to one hour in 1990.

9. Publication of the census results:
The Office fédéral de la statistique, Hallwylstrasse 15, 3003 Bern, is responsible for publishing the final census results.

The results of the 1990 census are also available in the form of unpublished tables, diskettes and magnetic tapes.

SYRIAN ARAB REPUBLIC

1. Name and address of the organization responsible for the census:
The Central Bureau of Statistics, Abou Rummaneh, Abdel Malek Ben Marwan Street, Damascus.

2. Population censuses conducted since 1945 (years):
1960, 1970, 1976, 1981 and 1994. The present description relates to the 1994 population census (held on 3 September).

3. Coverage of the census:
(a) *Geographical scope*: Whole country.

(b) *Persons covered*: All persons of all ages.

4. Reference period:
The week and the year preceding the date of interview.

5. Main topics:
(a) Total population, by sex and age:	yes
Economically active population by:	
(b) Sex and age group:	yes
(c) Industry:	yes
(d) Occupation:	yes
(e) Status in employment:	yes
(f) Highest educational level:	yes
(g) Hours of work:	yes
(h) Other characteristics:	no

Re (a): The age is defined in terms of year of birth.

Re (g): When using the short reference period, employed persons were asked to specify their usual hours of work and actual hours worked. When using the long reference period, employed persons were asked to specify the total period worked, expressed in number of months.

6. Concepts and definitions:
(a) *Economically active population*: It comprises all persons aged 10 years and over who, at the time of the census, were either employed or unemployed according to the definitions given below. Questions on economic activity were asked of a 10 per cent sample. The definition includes all members of the armed forces. Working students with a part time job and students seeking work are excluded from the definition.

(b) *Employment*: Considered as "employed" are all persons who performed any work of an economic value for at least 18 hours during the week which finished with the visit of the numerator.

It is reported that the following categories are included:
i) persons doing unpaid work in family firm or business;
ii) conscripts for military/civilian service;
iii) apprentices and trainees.

All above categories can be identified separately.

(c) *Unemployment*: Considered as "unemployed" are all persons who, during the reference week, were seeking, desiring and capable of work but did not find work.

7. Classifications used:
In the sample, both employed and unemployed persons previously employed are classified by industry, by occupation and by status in employment.

(a) *Industry*: For coding industry, the national classification was used, to the 3-digit level. Links to the ISIC-rev.3 have been established to the level classes (4-digit) level.

(b) *Occupation*: For coding occupation, the national classification was used to a 3-digit level. Links to the ISCO-88 have been established to the sub-major group (2-digit) level.

(c) *Status in employment*: Five groups were used for coding this variable: employer; self-employed; recipient of pay; unpaid family worker; unpaid apprentice.

8. Main differences compared with the previous census:
In 1981, only a short reference period was used (the week preceding the census date).

9. Publication of the census results:
The lapse of time between the census date and the publication of the census results should be approximatively one and half year.

The organization responsible is the Central Bureau of Statistics, Abou Roummaneh, Damascus.

THAILAND

1. Name and address of the organization responsible for the census:
National Statistical Office, Larn Luang Road, Bangkok 10100.

2. Population censuses conducted since 1945 (years):
1950, 1960, 1970, 1980 and 1990. The present description relates to the 1990 census (held on 1st April).

3. Coverage of the census:
(a) *Geographical scope*: Whole country.

(b) *Persons covered*: All persons of all ages, except: Hill-tribes with no permanent place of residence; foreign military and diplomatic personnel and their families stationed in Thailand; civilian nationals of foreign countries who were temporary residents and had been residing in Thailand for less than three months before the census date; and immigrants located in camps provided by the government.

4. Reference period:
Last week occupation (i.e., from 25 to 31 March) was asked on a 20 per cent sampling basis, while last year activity status (i.e. from 1st April 1989 to 31 March 1990) was asked on a complete enumeration basis.

5. Main topics:
(a) Total population, by sex and age:	yes
Economically active population by:	
(b) Sex and age group:	yes
(c) Industry:	yes
(d) Occupation:	yes
(e) Status in employment:	yes
(f) Highest educational level:	yes
(g) Hours of work:	no
(h) Other characteristics:	no

Re (a): The age is defined both in terms of year of birth and of age at last birthday.

6. Concepts and definitions:
(a) *Economically active population*: It comprises all persons aged 13 years and over who, during the reference week, were either employed or unemployed, according to the definitions given below. The definition includes all members of the armed forces.

(b) *Employment*: Considered as "employed" are all persons who, during the reference periods, performed on any day any work of an economic value, at home or out of home. The questions used to determine whether or not a person was to be counted as employed were: "On what job did X spend most of his/her work time last year (1st April 1989 to 31 March 1990)?" and, for persons in the sample, "On what job did X spend most of his/her work time during the week 25 to 31 March 1990?."

It is reported that the following categories are included:
i) persons doing unpaid work in family firm or business;
ii) employed persons, temporarily absent from work;
iii) working students with a part time job;
iv) seasonal or occasional workers;
v) conscripts for military/civilian service.

None of the above categories can be identified separately.

(c) *Unemployment*: Considered as "unemployed" are all persons who did not work but who had been looking for work on any day during the reference week. Persons in the sample who replied "Did not work" to the second question mentioned in para. 6 (b) above were counted as unemployed. Also included in the definition are persons waiting for farm season. Students seeking work are excluded from the definition.

7. Classifications used:
Both employed persons and unemployed persons previously employed are classified by industry and by occupation. Only employed persons are classified by status in employment.

(a) Industry: Based on the question: "Last year, in what kind of industry, business or service did you work most of the time? (record characteristics of good/service; example: farming, aerated water factory, government school)." For coding industry, 13 major groups of the National Classification of Industries were used. Links to the ISIC-rev.2 have been established to the major division (1-digit) level.

(b) Occupation: Based on the question: "Last year, in what kind of job did you spend most of your work time? (record job explicitly; example: rice farming, vegetable farming, statistics, accountance)." For coding occupation, the ISCO-68 has been used to the minor group (2-digit) level.

(c) Status in employment: Based on the question: "What is your work status?." For coding status in employment, six groups were used, namely: employer; own account worker; government employee; government enterprise employee; private employee; unpaid family worker.

8. Main differences compared with the previous census:
In the 1980 census the minimum age limit used for inclusion in the economically active population was 11 years.

9. Publication of the census results:
The title of the publication containing the final census results is "1990 Population and Housing Census," 1993.

The organization responsible for the publication of the census data is the National Statistical Office, Social Statistics Division, Bangkok 10100.

The census results are also available in the form of magnetic tapes.

TRINIDAD AND TOBAGO

1. Name and address of the organization responsible for the census:
Central Statistical Office, P.O. Box 98, Port-of-Spain, Trinidad.

2. Population censuses conducted since 1945 (years):
1946, 1960, 1970, 1980 and 1990. The present description relates to the 1990 population census (held on 15 May).

3. Coverage of the census:
(a) Geographical scope: Whole country.
(b) Persons covered: All persons of all ages.

4. Reference period:
The past week, and the 12 months preceding the date of the enumeration for main activity status.

5. Main topics:

(a) Total population, by sex and age:	yes
Economically active population by:	
(b) Sex and age group:	yes
(c) Industry:	yes
(d) Occupation:	yes
(e) Status in employment:	yes
(f) Highest educational level:	yes
(g) Hours of work:	yes
(h) Other characteristics:	yes

Re (a): The age is defined in terms of year of birth.

Re (g): Hours of work relate to usual hours of work of employed persons.

Re (h): The census also collected information on other topics, such as hours worked during the past week (including overtime), address of place of work, gross income during last pay period (week, fortnight, month, quarter, other).

6. Concepts and definitions:
(a) Economically active population: It comprises all persons aged 15 years and over who, during the reference periods, were either employed or unemployed, according to the definitions given below. The definition also covers all members of the armed forces.

(b) Employment: The question used to determine if a person is to be counted as employed is "What did you do during the past week (a) had a job, worked; (b) had a job, did not work; (c) seeking first job; (d) others seeking work; (e) wanted work and

available past three months; (f) student; (g) home duties; (h) retired; (i) disabled; (j) old age pensioner; (k) did not want work; (l) other; (m) not stated." Those who classified themselves under (a) or (b) were counted as "employed."

It is reported that the following categories are included:
i) persons doing unpaid work in family firm or business;
ii) employed persons, temporarily absent from work;
iii) working students with a part time job;
iv) seasonal or occasional workers;
v) conscripts for military/civilian service;
vi) apprentices and trainees.

Only persons belonging to categories (i), (ii), (v) and (vi) can be identified separately by means of specific questions.

(c) Unemployment: Considered as "unemployed" are all persons who, during the reference week, were without work and seeking work. To determine if a person is to be counted as unemployed, the question used is the same as that indicated under 6 (b) above, but the answers could be (c) seeking first job; (d) other seeking work; and, in both cases, (e) wanted work and available past three months. Students seeking work are excluded from the definition.

7. Classifications used:
Both employed persons and unemployed persons previously employed are classified by industry, by occupation and by status in employment.

(a) Industry: Based on the questions: "What is the name of Government department or Establishment in which N worked/had a job? (e.g. Ministry of Health (St. Ann's Hospital), Pete's Advertising Agency)" and "What kind of business is carried on there? (e.g. Psychiatric Hospital, creative designs or advertisements for media)." Interviewers were asked to classify first job seekers by industry of last application, and unemployed persons previously employed by industry of last place of employment. For coding industry, nine major groups of the national classification of industries were used. Links to ISIC-rev.2 have been established to the major division (1-digit) level.

(b) Occupation: Based on the questions: "What kind of work was N doing (job held) during the past week? (e.g. secondary school teacher, accounts clerk, automobile mechanic)" and "What was N's job title (e.g. teacher II, accounts clerk I, automobile mechanic grade A)?." Interviewers were asked to classify first job seekers by kind of job last applied for, and unemployed persons previously employed by job last held. For coding occupation, the ISCO-88 has been used to the minor group (3-digit) level.

(c) Status in employment: Based on the question: "What type of worker status applies to N?." For coding status in employment, the following nine groups were used: Government, public service; Government, public enterprise; non-Government, unpaid; learner; own-account, no paid help; own-account with paid help; never worked; not stated.

8. Main differences compared with the previous census:
No major difference.

9. Publication of the census results:
The title of the publication containing the census results is "Population and Housing Census 1990," Volume III, Part 2: Economic activity, issued in 1993.

The organization responsible for this publication is the Central Statistical Office, Port of Spain, Trinidad.

The census results are also available in other forms, such as unpublished tables, diskettes and magnetic tapes.

TURKEY

1. Name and address of the organization responsible for the census:
State Institute of Statistics, Prime Ministry, Necatibey Caddesi No. 114, 06100 Ankara.

2. Population censuses conducted since 1945 (years):
1945, 1950, 1955, 1960, 1965, 1970, 1975, 1980, 1985 and 1990. The present description relates to the 1990 population census (held on 21 October).

3. Coverage of the census:

(a) Geographical scope: Whole country.

(b) Persons covered: All persons of all ages, except nationals resident abroad.

4. Reference period:
The week preceding the census day.

5. Main topics:
(a) Total population, by sex and age:	yes

Economically active population by:

(b) Sex and age group:	yes
(c) Industry:	yes
(d) Occupation:	yes
(e) Status in employment:	yes
(f) Highest educational level:	yes
(g) Hours of work:	no
(h) Other characteristics:	no

Re (a): The age is defined in terms of age at last birthday.

6. Concepts and definitions:

(a) Economically active population: It comprises all persons aged 12 years and over who, during the reference week, were either employed or unemployed, according to the definitions given below. Students with a part time job and those seeking work are excluded from the definition whereas members of the armed forces are included.

(b) Employment: Considered as "employed" are all persons who gave an affirmative reply to the question: "Did you work last week in any job for money or for payment in kind? if you didn't, do you continue to hold a job?"

It is reported that the following categories are included:

i) persons doing unpaid work in family firm or business;
ii) persons engaged in the production of primary products for own consumption;
iii) seasonal or occasional workers;
iv) conscripts for military/civilian service;
v) apprentices and trainees.

None of the above categories can be identified separately.

(c) Unemployment: Considered as "unemployed" are all persons who, during the reference week, were without work and gave an affirmative reply to the question "Are you looking for a job?."

7. Classifications used:
Only employed persons are classified by industry and by status in employment. Both employed persons and unemployed persons previously employed are classified by occupation.

(a) Industry: Based on the questions: "What is the kind of work place where you worked in last week or where you continue to hold a job? (e.g. field, Ministry of Justice, grocery, barber shop, etc)" and "What is the nature of work done at the work place where you worked? (e.g. public service, retail trade, manufacture of refrigerators, TV repairs, etc)." For coding industry, 10 groups of the national classification were used. Links to the ISIC-rev.2 have been established to the major division (1-digit) level.

(b) Occupation: Based on the questions: to employed persons "Kind of work you did last week or the job you continue to hold? e.g. farmer, bank manager, typist, construction worker, etc"; and to both employed and unemployed previously employed "What is your main occupation?" (e.g. carpenter, lawyer, brick layer, nurse, etc). For coding occupation, seven groups of the national classification were used. Links to the ISCO-68 have been established to the major-group (1-digit) level.

(c) Status in employment: Based on the question: "What was your employment status in the job you worked last week or where you continue to hold a job?." For coding status in employment, four groups were used: employee, employer, self employed, and unpaid family worker.

8. Main differences compared with the previous census:
The 1990 Census did not identify the branch of economic activity (industry) of the unemployed previously employed.

9. Publication of the census results:
The final data have been published at the end of 1993 in a publication entitled "1990 Census of Population - Social and Economic Characteristics of Population."

The organization responsible for this publication is the State Institute of Statistics, Prime Ministry, Ankara.

Data from the above publication are also available in the form of diskettes.

UGANDA

1. Name and address of the organization responsible for the census:
Ministry of Finance and Economic Planning, Department of Statistics, P.O. Box 13, Entebbe.

2. Population censuses conducted since 1945 (years):
1948, 1959, 1969, 1980 and 1991. The present description relates to the 1991 population census (held on 11 January).

3. Coverage of the census:

(a) Geographical scope: Whole country.

(b) Persons covered: All persons of all ages.

4. Reference period:
The week preceding the census day.

5. Main topics:
(a) Total population, by sex and age:	yes

Economically active population by:

(b) Sex and age group:	yes
(c) Industry:	no
(d) Occupation:	yes
(e) Status in employment:	yes
(f) Highest educational level:	yes
(g) Hours of work:	no
(h) Other characteristics:	no

Re (a): The age is defined in terms of age at last birthday.

6. Concepts and definitions:

(a) Economically active population: It comprises all persons aged 10 years and over who, during the reference period, were either employed or unemployed, according to the definitions given below. Questions on economic activity were asked of all urban population and 10 per cent of the rural population. Members of the armed forces residing in private households are included in the definition.

(b) Employment: Considered as "employed" are all persons who performed any work during the reference week. The question asked was: "Activity status last week: employed, self-employed, unpaid family worker, student, household work, looking for work, disabled, too old, etc."

It is reported that the following categories are included:

i) persons doing unpaid work in family firm or business;
ii) working students with a part time job;
iii) seasonal or occasional workers;
iv) conscripts for military/civilian service;

Only categories (i) and (ii) can be identified separately.

(c) Unemployment: Considered as "unemployed" are all persons who, during the reference week, were without job and looking for work. The question asked was the same as that indicated under 6(b) above.

7. Classifications used:
Only employed persons were classified by occupation and by status in employment.

(a) Industry: No classification by industry was made.

(b) Occupation: Based on the question: "Occupation last week: What kind of work did you do?." For coding occupation, 161 groups of the national classification were used. The ISCO-88 was expanded (utilising empty codes) to incorporate Nationally Common Occupations. Links have been established to the minor group (3-digit) level.

(c) Status in employment: The question asked to determine status in employment was the same as that indicated under 6 (b) above. For coding status in employment, three groups were used, namely: employee; self employed; and unpaid family worker.

8. Main differences compared with the previous census:
The 1969 population census did not collect information on employment.

9. Publication of the census results:
The final results of the population census were issued in the following publications: "The 1991 Population and Housing Census Main Results (pre-Release)" in October 1992, "The 1991 Population and Housing Census National Summary" in April

1994, and "The 1991 Population and Housing Final Results (Main Release)" in January 1995.

The organization responsible for these publications is the Statistics Department, PO Box 13, Entebbe.

Unpublished tables and data in the form of diskettes are also available.

UNITED KINGDOM

1. Name and address of the organization responsible for the census:

For England and Wales: Office of Population, Census Surveys, Room 816, St. Catherine's House, 10 Kingsway, London WC 2B 6JP.

For Scotland: General Register Office (Scotland), Ladywell House, Ladywell Road, Edinburgh EH12 7TF.

For Northern Ireland: Census Office, Castle Buildings, Stormont, Belfast BT4 8SJ.

2. Population censuses conducted since 1945 (years):

1951, 1961, 1966, 1971, 1981 and 1991. The present description relates to the 1991 population census (held on 21 April). It primarily concerns England and Wales, but the answers also apply to Scotland and Northern Ireland so that the description can be taken to represent the position in the United Kingdom.

3. Coverage of the census:

(a) Geographical scope: Whole country (see also para. 2 above).

(b) Persons covered: All persons of all ages.

4. Reference period:

The week preceding the day of the census.

5. Main topics:

(a) Total population, by sex and age: yes
Economically active population by:
(b) Sex and age group: yes
(c) Industry: yes
(d) Occupation: yes
(e) Status in employment: yes
(f) Highest educational level: yes
(g) Hours of work: yes
(h) Other characteristics: yes

Re (a): The age is defined in terms of year of birth (complete date, i.e. day, month and year).

Re (g): Employed persons were asked to specify their usual hours of work.

Re (h): The census also collected information on place of work and means of travel to work.

6. Concepts and definitions:

(a) Economically active population: It comprises all persons aged 16 years and over who, during the reference week, were either employed or unemployed, according to the definitions given below. As for the 1981 census, economic position and status in employment are included in the full processing while industry, occupation and workplace are part of the 10 per cent sample. Seasonal and occasional workers were covered by the definition if they were working or looking for a job during the reference week. The definition also includes professional members of the armed forces. There are no conscripts in the United Kingdom.

(b) Employment: Considered as "employed" are all persons who, during the reference week, were working for an employer (full or part time) or were self employed or were on a government employment or training scheme. This included casual or temporary work, and related to work for pay or profit but not to unpaid work (except in a family business). A person was also included if she or he had a job during the reference week but was off sick, on holiday, temporarily laid off or on strike. A part-time job is a job in which the hours worked (excluding any overtime) are usually 30 hours or less per week.

It is reported that the following categories are included:

i) persons doing unpaid work in family firm or business;
ii) employed persons, temporarily absent from work;
iii) working students with a part time job;
iv) seasonal or occasional workers (if working during the reference week);
v) apprentices and trainees.

Only persons belonging to category (iii) can be identified separately.

(c) Unemployment: Considered as "unemployed" are all persons who, during the reference week, were waiting to start a job he or she had already accepted or were without work and looking for a job, including persons wanting a job but prevented from looking by holiday or temporary sickness.

7. Classifications used:

Both employed persons and unemployed persons previously employed in the sample are classified by industry and by occupation (the coverage for unemployed persons is "those who had a job in the last ten years"). Only employed persons are classified by status in employment (see also para. 6 (a) above). Economically inactive persons, such as the retired, were also asked to give information on hours worked, industry and occupation, if they had had a job in the last ten years.

(a) Industry: Respondents were asked to give the name, address and business of the employer (self employed: name, address and nature of the person's business). For coding industry, 320 groups based on the national classification of industries were used, but only 10 per cent sample processed. Links (best fit) to the ISIC-rev.3 have been established at the division (2-digit) level.

(b) Occupation: Respondents were asked to give the full title of the present or last job and to describe the main things they do or did in the job. Precise terms should be used, for example: packing machinist; poultry processor; jig and tool fitter; supervisor of typists; accounts clerk; rather than general titles like: machinist; process worker; supervisor or clerk. For coding occupation, 371 groups of the national classification of occupations were used, but only 10 per cent sample processed. Links to the ISCO-88 have been established to the mixed group level.

(c) Status in employment: A specific question on the economic position was asked. For coding this variable, the following five groups were used in the tables based on full processing, namely: working for an employer full time; working for an employer part time; self employed employing other people; self employed not employing other people; on a government employment or training scheme.

8. Main differences compared with the previous census:

The main changes consist of:

- the use of a new occupational classification (Standard Occupational Classification - SOC);
- the introduction of a question on hours worked;
- the introduction of a separate category for persons on a government employment or training scheme in the economic position question (which also includes status categories, so that apprentices and trainees are no longer a separate status); and
- the inclusion of working students in the economically active population, as employed.

9. Publication of the census results:

First national results on the economically active population were available in 1992. Detailed information on industry, occupation, workplace etc. were available in 1993.

A variety of publications were issued. Customers requiring further information should contact the Census Customer Services, OPCS, Segensworth Road, Titchfield, Hampshire PO15 5RR.

A variety of media were also used for the dissemination of the census data.

UNITED STATES

1. Name and address of the organization responsible for the census:

United States Bureau of the Census, Washington, DC, 20233.

2. Population censuses conducted since 1945 (years):

1950, 1960, 1970, 1980 and 1990. The present description relates to the 1990 census (held on 1st April).

3. Coverage of the census:

(a) Geographical scope: Whole country. Separate censuses were held for the out lying areas of the United States, (i.e.: American Samoa, Guam, Northern Mariana Islands, Palau, Puerto Rico and Virgin Islands).

(b) Persons covered: All persons of all ages, except national residents abroad.

The basic sampling unit was the housing unit, including all occupants. In group-living quarters, the sampling unit was persons. The sampling fraction varied depending on data collection procedures. When all sampling rates across the United States were taken into account, approximately one out of six housing units in the nation were included in the sample.

4. Reference period:

The week preceding the interview to define the currently active population, and the year 1989 to determine the labour force status during that year.

The present description applies to the currently economically active population.

5. Main topics:

(a) Total population, by sex and age:	yes

Economically active population by:

(b) Sex and age group:	yes
(c) Industry:	yes
(d) Occupation:	yes
(e) Status in employment:	yes
(f) Highest educational level:	yes
(g) Hours of work:	yes
(h) Other characteristics:	yes

Re (a): The age is defined in terms of age at last birthday.

Re (g): Hours of work relate to actual hours worked by employed persons at work during the reference week and to total period worked (in weeks) and usual hours worked in 1989.

Re (h): The census also collected information on: place of work; means of transportation to work; private vehicle occupancy; travel time to work; work experience in 1989; income and earnings in 1989; work disability.

6. Concepts and definitions:

(a) Economically active population: It comprises all persons aged 16 years and over who, during the reference week, were either employed or unemployed, according to the definitions given below. Members of the armed forces are included in the definition.

Questions concerning economic activity were asked only of a sample of units and persons. Members of the armed forces living in barracks or on ship were not asked questions concerning temporary absence from a job or business, job search, or availability to accept a new job.

(b) Employment: The primary questions used to determine if a person is to be counted as employed are: "Did this person work at any time last week?" and "How many hours did this person work last week at all jobs?." Another question was also asked, namely "Was this person temporarily absent or on lay off from a job or or business last week?."

It is reported that the following categories are included:

i)   persons doing unpaid work in family farm or business, only if they worked at least 15 hours in the reference week;

ii) employed persons, temporarily absent from work;

iii) working students with a part time job;

iv) seasonal or occasional workers, only during the appropriate season (an occasional worker is not considered as employed during periods when not at work);

v)   apprentices and trainees.

Only persons belonging to categories (i), (iii) and (iv) can be identified separately (cross the economically active population by status in employment (class of worker category) and the employment status by enrollment status and by hours worked last week). Employment status is a recode that uses information from many items to determine whether persons are employed, unemployed, not in the labour force or in the armed forces.

The United States Armed Forces is an "all-volunteer" force. Members of the armed forces who reside in the United States can be identified separately in the census by using the Employment Status field. There are no conscripted persons, either military or civilian, in the United States.

(c) Unemployment: Considered as "unemployed" are all persons who, during the reference week, were without work, seeking work (either in the reference week or during the three prior weeks) and available for work. Also included as "unemployed" are persons on layoff. To determine if a person is to be counted as unemployed, the primary questions used were "Was this person temporarily absent or on layoff from a job or business last week?," "Has this person been looking for work during the last four weeks?" and "Could this person have taken a job last week if one had been offered?."

7. Classifications used:

Both employed persons and unemployed persons previously employed in the sample are classified by industry, by occupation and by status in employment.

(a) Industry: Based on the questions: "For whom did the person work?," "What kind of business or industry was this?" and "Is this mainly: manufacturing, wholesale trade, retail trade, other (agriculture, construction, service, government, etc.)?."

The classification system is based on the 1987 United States standard and was developed for the population census. Coding of responses was done by using the "Alphabetical Index of Industries and Occupations," and by a list of establishment names obtained from American economic censuses and surveys. The 1990 census used 236 categories. Links to the ISIC have not been established. However, for international comparison purposes, an adaptation of the United States 1970 Census industrial classification to the international (which was still valid generally for the United States 1990 system) was developed as closely as possible to the major division (1-digit) level.

(b) Occupation: Based on the questions: "What kind of work was this person doing?" and "What were this person's most important activities or duties?."

The classification system consists of 501 specific occupation categories arranged into 6 summary and 13 major occupation groups. This classification was developed to be consistent with the 1980 Standard Occupational Classification Manual (SOC). Links to the ISCO have not been established. No adaptation was done for the 1990 United States occupational classification.

(c) Status in employment: Based on the question: "Was this person: employee of private for profit company, business or individual for wages, salary or commissions; employee of a private not-for-profit, tax-exempt, or charitable organization; local government employee (city, county, etc.); state government employee; Federal government employee; self-employed in own not incorporated business, professional practice, or farm; self-employed in own incorporated business, professional practice, or farm; working without pay in family business or farm?."

All groups, except not incorporated self-employed persons, are classified as employees. For coding status in employment, the eight groups above were used.

8. Main differences compared with the previous census:
No major difference.

9. Publication of the census results:
The titles of the main publications containing the final census data are: "1990 CPH-5: Summary Social, Economic and Housing Characteristics" and "1990 CP-2: Social and Economic Characteristics" (Reports presenting sample data), January 1991-December 1993.

The organization responsible for these publications is the US Bureau of the Census, Washington, DC, 20233.

The 1990 census results are also available in the form of magnetic tapes, microfiches, on-line information systems, CD-ROM and flexible disks for microcomputers.

VANUATU

1. Name and address of the organization responsible for the census:
Statistics Office (NPSO), Private Mail Bag 19, Port-Vila.

2. Population censuses conducted since 1945 (years):
1967, 1979 and 1989. Also urban censuses were conducted in 1972 and 1986. The present description relates to the 1989 census (which took place on 16 May).

3. Coverage of the census:
(a) Geographical scope: Whole country.

(b) Persons covered: All persons of all ages, except residents abroad at the time of census.

4. Reference period:
The week preceding the census day.

5. Main topics:
(a) Total population, by sex and age: yes
Economically active population by:
(b) Sex and age group: yes
(c) Industry: yes
(d) Occupation: yes
(e) Status in employment: yes
(f) Highest educational level: yes
(g) Hours of work: no
(h) Other characteristics: no

Re (a): The age is defined in terms of year of birth.

6. Concepts and definitions:

(a) Economically active population: It comprises all persons aged 10 years and over who, at the time of the census, were either employed or unemployed, according to the definitions given below. The data actually published relate to persons aged 15 years and over, since the 10-14 age group was found to contain so many students.

(b) Employment: Considered as "employed" are all persons who had worked for one hour or more during the previous week. Working students with a part-time job are excluded from the definition.

It is reported that the following categories are included:

i)   persons doing unpaid work in family firm or business;
ii)   employed persons, temporarily absent from work;
iii) multiple-job holders;
iv) apprentices and trainees.

Only persons belonging to categories (i), (ii) and (iii) can be identified separately.

(c) Unemployment: Considered as "unemployed" are all persons who were without work but actively seeking a job during the previous week. The question used was "Did he/she actively look for work in the last 7 days?."

7. Classifications used:
Both employed persons and unemployed persons previously employed are classified by industry and by occupation. Only employed persons are classified by status in employment.

(a) Industry: Based on the question: "What kind of industry does he/she work for?." For coding industry, the ISIC-rev.2 has been used to the 1-digit level, but the codes were expanded to 2-digits to meet local needs.

(b) Occupation: Based on the question: "What kind of work did he/she do?." For coding occupation, the ISCO-68 has been used to the unit group (3-digit) level.

(c) Status in employment: Based on the questions: "What was his/her employment status?." or "Who was he/she working for?." For coding status in employment the following four groups were used: self-employed; family business (no pay); employee in private company; working for Government.

8. Main differences compared with the previous census:
In 1979, respondents were asked to describe their occupation during the past year, whereas this was not required in 1989.

9. Publication of the census results:
The publication containing the final census results is "Vanuatu National Population Census - May 1989 - Main Report," July 1991.

The organization responsible for this publication is the Statistics Office, Private Mail Bag 19, Port Vila.

VENEZUELA

1. Name and address of the organization responsible for the census:
Oficina Central de Estadística e Informática, Presidencia de la República, Caracas, Venezuela.

2. Population censuses conducted since 1945 (years):
1950, 1961, 1971, 1981 and 1990. The present description relates to the 1990 population census (held on 21 October).

3. Coverage of the census:

(a) Geographical scope: Whole country.

(b) Persons covered: All people of all ages usually resident in the country. This excludes Venezuelans permanently residing abroad, foreigners who are in the country on vacation or for business or other reasons and who have been in the country

for less than four months, and the unassimilated indigenous population, which will be the subject of a separate study to be conducted in 1992.

4. Reference period:
The day of the census.

5. Main topics:
(a) Total population, by sex and age: yes
Economically active population by:
(b) Sex and age group: yes
(c) Industry: yes
(d) Occupation: yes
(e) Status in employment: yes
(f) Highest educational level: yes
(g) Hours of work: no
(h) Other characteristics: yes

Re (a): The age is defined in terms of year of birth and in terms of age at last birthday.

Re (h): The census also collected information on the duration of unemployment, the number of employees in the enterprise, earned income and other forms of income, and the informal sector.

6. Concepts and definitions:

(a) Economically active population: It comprises all persons aged 12 years and over who, on the census date, were either employed or unemployed, according to the definitions given below. All members of the armed forces are included in the definition.

(b) Employment: Considered as "employed" are all persons who replied yes to one of the following questions: "Working?." or "Not at work, but employed?."

It is reported that the following categories are included:

i)   persons doing unpaid work in family firm or business;
ii)   employed persons, temporarily absent from work;
iii) working students with a part-time job;
iv) seasonal or occasional workers;
v)   conscripts for military/civilian service.

Only persons falling in categories (i) and (ii) can be identified separately by means of their replies to the following questions. (i) "In this work, are you helping a family member?" and (ii) "Which of the following best describes your current situation: ...; and Not at work, but employed?."

(c) Unemployment: Considered as "unemployed" are all persons who were without work and who replied yes to one of the following questions: "Seeking work and previously employed?." or "Seeking work for the first time?."

7. Classifications used:
All employed persons as well as all unemployed persons previously employed in rural areas, but only a sampling of such persons in urban areas (estimated at 20 per cent), are classified by industry, by occupation and by status in employment.

(a) Industry: Based on the question: "What is the main activity of the firm, establishment or business where you work (or last worked)? (e.g.: passenger transport, furniture manufacture, coffee plantation, education, etc.)." For coding industry, the ISIC-rev.2 was used to the major division (1-digit) level. The publications contain information to the 1-digit level, but the data was coded to the 3-digit level.

(b) Occupation: Based on the question: "What is your occupation in the firm, establishment or business where you work (or last worked)? (e.g.: chauffeur, apprentice lathe operator, farmer, teacher, etc.)." For coding occupation, the ISCO-68 was used to the major group (1-digit) level for publications, but the data was coded to the 3-digit level.

(c) Status in employment: Based on the question: "In this work, are (were) you: public sector employee or worker; private sector employee or worker; household employee; member of a co-operative; employer or proprietor; self-employed (without employees or workers); unpaid family worker?." This variable was coded on the basis of these seven categories.

8. Main differences compared with the previous census:
The 1981 census collected information on the economic characteristics of all persons aged 12 years and over. Although the 1990 census covered the labour situation of all persons aged 12 years and over, information on other economic characteristics was only collected in respect of 20 per cent of the urban population and all of the rural population

The 1981 census, unlike the 1990 census, collected information on how persons went about seeking work. It also included questions on hours worked in the past week, but the 1990 census did not.

Regarding the duration of unemployment, although both the 1981 and 1990 census collected information on both men and women, the time-frames differed (1981: up to six months; more than six months to 12 months; more than one year. 1990: up to three months; from four to six months; from seven to 12 months; more than one year).

9. Publication of the census results:
The final results were published in late 1992. The title of the publication is "El Censo 90 en Venezuela, XII Censo General de Población y Vivienda" and "El Censo 90 en (The corresponding Federal unit)."

The organization responsible for this publication is Oficina Central de Estadística e Informática.

The census results are also available in the form of unpublished tables, diskettes, magnetic tapes, diskettes, microfiche and image files. They are also available on Mainframix and Micros: the former uses the Informix driver, and the latter Redatam.

VIET NAM

1. Name and address of the organization responsible for the census:
Département général de statistiques, Ministère du Travail, des Invalides de guerre et des affaires sociales, 2 - Hoang Van Thu, Hanoi.

2. Population censuses conducted since 1945 (years):
1979, 1989 and 1994. The present description relates to the 1994 population census (held on 1st October).

3. Coverage of the census:
(a) Geographical scope: All urban areas.

(b) Persons covered: All persons of all ages.

4. Reference period:
The week preceding the census day.

5. Main topics:
(a) Total population, by sex and age: yes
Economically active population by:
(b) Sex and age group: yes
(c) Industry: yes
(d) Occupation: yes
(e) Status in employment: yes
(f) Highest educational level: ...
(g) Hours of work: yes
(h) Other characteristics: no

Re (a): The age is defined in terms of year of birth.

Re (g): Employed persons were asked to specify the number of hours and days they actually worked during the reference week.

6. Concepts and definitions:
(a) Economically active population: It comprises all women aged from 15 to 55 years and all men aged from 15 to 60 years who, during the reference period, were either employed or unemployed, according to the definitions given below. Questions on economic activity were asked of a 2.5 per cent sample of the urban population. Members of the armed forces are excluded from the definition.

(b) Employment: Employment is determined on the basis of the question: "Did you work for pay or without pay during the past seven days? If so, was this work similar to that of the previous month?."

It is reported that the following categories are included:
i) persons doing unpaid work in family firm or business;
ii) persons engaged in the production of primary products for own consumption;
iii) employed persons, temporarily absent from work;
iv) working students with a part time job;
v) seasonal or occasional workers;
vi) apprentices and trainees.

None of these categories can be identified separately.

(c) Unemployment: Considered as "unemployed" are all persons who reported that they did not work during the reference week and who answered yes to the following questions: "Were you previously employed? Are you capable of working at the present time?" and "Do you need to work?."

7. Classifications used:
Both employed persons and unemployed persons previously employed are classified by industry, by occupation and by status in employment.

(a) Industry: Based on the question: "Name of your agency/organism? Name of the supervising organism? Place of work?." For coding industry, 20 groups of the national classification were used. Links to the ISIC have not been established.

(b) Occupation: Based on the question: "What was your main activity during the past seven days? Name of the activity, code." For coding occupation, 33 groups of the national classification were used. Links to the ISCO-68 have been established to the major group (1-digit) level.

(c) Status in employment: Based on the question: "Are you in paid or unpaid employment?." For coding this variable, two groups were used, namely: paid employment, unpaid employment.

8. Main differences compared with the previous census:
No major difference.

9. Publication of the census results:
Information not available.

VIRGIN ISLANDS (BRITISH)

1. Name and address of the organization responsible for the census:
Development Planning Unit, B.V.Is. Government, Central Administration Complex, Road Town, Tortola.

2. Population censuses conducted since 1945 (years):
1960, 1970, 1980 and 1991. The present description relates to the 1991 population census (held on 12 May).

3. Coverage of the census:
(a) Geographical scope: Whole country.

(b) Persons covered: All persons of all ages.

4. Reference period:
The week and the year prior to the census day.

5. Main topics:
(a) Total population, by sex and age: yes
Economically active population by:
(b) Sex and age group: yes
(c) Industry: yes
(d) Occupation: yes
(e) Status in employment: yes
(f) Highest educational level: ...
(g) Hours of work: yes
(h) Other characteristics: yes

Re (a): The age is defined in terms of year of birth and in terms of age at last birthday.

Re (g): Employed persons were asked to specify the number of hours actually worked during the reference week, and the number of months worked during the reference year.

Re (h): The census also collected information on pay period (weekly, monthly, etc), on income per pay period, on moving businesses (informal trading), and on means of transport used to travel to workplace.

6. Concepts and definitions:
(a) Economically active population: It comprises all persons aged 15 years and over who, during the reference periods, were either employed or unemployed, according to the definitions given below. The definition also includes all members of the armed forces.

(b) Employment: Considered as "employed" are all persons who, during the reference period, worked or had a job but did not work. The question used to determine whether or not a person was to be counted as employed was "Have you worked in the reference period or had a job but did not work?." Working students with a part-time job are excluded from the definition.

It is reported that the following categories are included:

i) persons doing unpaid work in family firm or business;
ii) persons engaged in the production of primary products for own consumption;
iii) employed persons, temporarily absent from work;
iv) seasonal or occasional workers;
v) apprentices and trainees.

None of the above categories can be identified separately.

(c) Unemployment: Considered as "unemployed" are all persons who, during the reference period, stated that they had looked for work or that they wanted work and were available.

7. Classifications used:
Both employed persons and unemployed persons previously employed are classified by industry, by occupation and by status in employment.

(a) Industry: Based on the question: "What type of business is carried on at your workplace?." For coding industry, the ISIC-rev.3 was used to the class (4-digit) level.

(b) Occupation: Based on the question: "What sort of work do/did you do in your main occupation?." For coding occupation, the ISCO-88 has been used to the unit group (4-digit) level.

(c) Status in employment: Based on the question: "Did you carry out your own business, work for a wage or a salary or as an unpaid worker in a family business?." Five groups were used for coding status in employment: paid employee-government; paid employee-private; unpaid worker; own business with paid help (employer); own business without paid help (own account).

8. Main differences compared with the previous census:
No major difference.

9. Publication of the census results:
The final census data were issued in August 1994 in a publication entitled "British Virgin Islands, 1991 Population and Housing Census."

The organization responsible for the publication is the Development Planning Unit, Central Administration Complex, Road Town, Tortola.

The census results are also available in the form of diskettes.

VIRGIN ISLANDS (US)

1. Name and address of the organization responsible for the census:
Eastern Caribbean Center, University of the Virgin Islands, St. Thomas Campus, St. Thomas, U.S. Virgin Islands 00802.

2. Population censuses conducted since 1945 (years):
1950, 1960, 1970, 1980 and 1990. The present description relates to the 1990 census (held on 1st April).

3. Coverage of the census:
(a) Geographical scope: Whole area.

(b) Persons covered: All persons of all ages.

4. Reference period:
The week preceding the day of the census and the year prior to the census year.

5. Main topics:
(a) Total population, by sex and age: yes
Economically active population by:
(b) Sex and age group: yes
(c) Industry: yes
(d) Occupation: yes
(e) Status in employment: yes
(f) Highest educational level: yes
(g) Hours of work: yes
(h) Other characteristics: yes

Re (a): The age classification is based on the age of the person in completed years on the day of the census.

Re (g): When using the short reference period: hours of work relate both to usual hours of work of employed persons and to actual hours worked by employed persons, at work. When using the long reference period: employed persons were asked to specify the total period worked during the whole year 1989, expressed in months, weeks, days and hours.

Re (h): When using the short reference period, the census collected information on means of transport used and time spent to go to work. When using the long reference period, information was asked on persons' total income and sources of income in 1989.

6. Concepts and definitions:
(a) Economically active population: It comprises all persons aged 16 years and over who, during the reference week, were either employed or unemployed, according to the definitions given below. The definition also includes members of the armed forces. However, working students with a part-time job as well as students seeking work are excluded from the definition.

(b) Employment: The main question used to determine if a person is to be counted as employed is: "Did X work at any time last week, either full time or part time?."

It is reported that the following categories are included:
i) persons doing unpaid work in family firm or business;
ii) employed persons, temporarily absent from work;
iii) seasonal or occasional workers;
iv) conscripts for military/civilian service;
v) multiple-job holders.

All above categories can be identified separately through specific questions.

(c) Unemployment: Considered as "unemployed" are all persons who, during the reference week, were without work and seeking work. To determine if a person is to be counted as unemployed, the following questions were used: "Was X on layoff from a job or business last week?," "Has X been looking for work during the last 4 weeks?" and "Could X have taken a job last week if one had been offered?."

7. Classifications used:
Both employed persons and unemployed persons previously employed are classified by industry, by occupation and by status in employment. The questions asked related to the job worked last week (if the person had more than one job, s/he was asked to describe the one where s/he worked the most hours; if the person did not work last week, the questions referred to the most recent job or business since 1985).

(a) Industry: Based on the questions: "For whom did X work and what kind of business or industry was this?" and "Is this mainly: manufacturing; wholesale trade; retail trade; other (agriculture, construction, service, government, etc.?." For coding industry, seven groups of the National Classification were used. Links to the ISIC have not been established.

(b) Occupation: Based on the questions: "What kind of work was X doing?" and "What were X's most important activities or duties?." For coding occupation, 39 groups of the National Classification were used. Links to the ISCO have not been established.

(c) Status in employment: Based on the question: "Was X: Employee of a PRIVATE FOR PROFIT company, business or individual for wages, salary or commissions; Employee of a PRIVATE NOT-FOR-PROFIT, tax exempt, or charitable organization; Local GOVERNMENT employee (territorial, etc.); Federal GOVERNMENT employee; SELF-EMPLOYED in own NOT INCORPORATED business, professional practice or farm; SELF-EMPLOYED in own INCORPORATED business, professional practice or farm; Working WITHOUT PAY in family business or farm?." For coding status in employment, the above seven groups were used.

8. Main differences compared with the previous census:
No major difference.

9. Publication of the census results:
The title of the documents containing the final census results are "STF-3 Summary Tape, File 3" (diskette, magnetic tape and CD-ROM) and "CPH-5-55, Summary Social, Economic and Housing Characteristics" (printed), 1992.

The organization responsible for these documents is the Bureau of the Census, Data User Services Division, Customer Services, Washington, D.C. 20233.

The census results are also available in CD-ROM, magnetic tape, diskette and printed reports.

YEMEN

1. Name and address of the organization responsible for the census:
Central Statistical Organization, Ministry of Planning and Development, P.O. Box 13434, Sana'a.

2. Population censuses conducted since 1945 (years):
Two censuses were conducted in each of the two countries before their unification, and one since the unification.

1973 and 1988 in the Southern and Eastern governorates i.e. former PDRY.

1975 and 1986 in the Northern and Western governorates i.e. former YAR.

The present description relates to the 1994 population census (held on 16 December), which is the first census for the unified country in the Republic of Yemen.

3. Coverage of the census:
(a) Geographical scope: Whole country.

(b) Persons covered: All persons of all ages.

4. Reference period:
The week preceding the census day.

5. Main topics:
(a) Total population, by sex and age:	yes
Economically active population by:	
(b) Sex and age group:	yes
(c) Industry:	yes
(d) Occupation:	yes
(e) Status in employment:	yes
(f) Highest educational level:	yes
(g) Hours of work:	no
(h) Other characteristics:	no

Re (a): The age is defined in terms of age at last birthday.

6. Concepts and definitions:
(a) Economically active population: It comprises all persons aged 10 years and over who, during the reference week, were either employed or unemployed, according to the definitions given below. Members of the armed forces are included in the definition.

(b) Employment: Employment is determined on the basis of the question: "What is your relationship to the labour force during the reference week?." The possible responses were: Working; Housewives and working; Student and working; Unemployed but previously worked; Unemployed but never worked; Housewife; Student; Self-sufficient; and Disabled. If a person stated that s/he worked for two days or more, s/he was counted as employed.

It is reported that the following categories are included:

i) persons doing unpaid work in family firm or business;
ii) persons engaged in the production of primary products for own consumption;
iii) employed persons, temporarily absent from work;
iv) working students with a part time job;
v) seasonal or occasional workers (provided that they were employed during the reference period);
vi) conscripts for military/civilian service;
vii) multiple-job holders;
viii) apprentices and trainees.

Persons belonging to categories (i), (iv), (vii) and (viii) can be identified separately.

(c) Unemployment: Considered as "unemployed" are all persons who, during the reference week, worked for less than two days. The definition includes both first job seekers and unemployed persons previously employed. However, students seeking work are excluded from the definition.

7. Classifications used:
Both employed persons and unemployed persons previously employed are classified by industry, by occupation and by status in employment.

(a) Industry: Based on the questions: "What is your present main occupation?" and "Where do you work?." For coding industry, the ISIC-rev.3 has been used.

(b) Occupation: Based on the question: "What is your exact occupation?." For coding occupation, the ISCO-88 has been used to the unit group (4-digit) level.

(c) Status in employment: Based on the question: "What is your status in employment?." For coding status in employment, five groups were used, namely: paid worker; self-employed; employer; unpaid family worker; unpaid working for others.

8. Main differences compared with the previous census:
No major difference.

9. Publication of the census results:
The final data should be published in 1996 in a publication entitled "The Results of the 1994 Population Housing and Establishments Census, Reports No. 1-3."

The organization responsible for this publication is the Central Statistical Organization (CSO), P.O. Box 13434, Sana'a.

The final results will also be available in the form of unpublished tables (printed as hard copy upon request). As a privilege, results could be available in a magnetic media also upon request.

ZAMBIA

1. Name and address of the organization responsible for the census:
Central Statistics Office, P.O. Box 31908, Lusaka.

2. Population censuses conducted since 1945 (years):
1946, 1951, 1956, 1961, 1963, 1969, 1980 and 1990. The present description relates to the 1990 census (held on 20 August).

3. Coverage of the census:
(a) Geographical scope: Whole country.

(b) Persons covered: All persons of all ages, except nationals living abroad and foreign diplomats.

4. Reference period:
The week and the 12 months prior to the census day.

5. Main topics:
(a) Total population, by sex and age:	yes
Economically active population by:	
(b) Sex and age group:	yes
(c) Industry:	yes
(d) Occupation:	yes
(e) Status in employment:	yes
(f) Highest educational level:	yes
(g) Hours of work:	yes
(h) Other characteristics:	no

Re (a): The age is defined in terms of age at last birthday.

Re (g): Only multiple-job holders were asked to specify the total period worked during the last 12 months (expressed in number of months).

6. Concepts and definitions:
(a) Economically active population: It comprises all persons aged 12 years and over who, during the reference periods, were either employed or unemployed, according to the definitions given below. Members of the armed forces are included in the definition.

(b) Employment: Employment is determined on the basis of the questions: "What was X mainly doing in the last seven days?" (the possible responses were: working for pay or profit; on leave; unpaid work on household holding or business), and "What has X mainly been doing since 1989?" (the possible responses were as indicated for the first question).

It is reported that the following categories are included:

i) persons doing unpaid work in family firm or business;
ii) persons engaged in the production of primary products for own consumption;
iii) employed persons, temporarily absent from work;
iv) working students with a part time job;
v) seasonal or occasional workers;
vi) conscripts for military/civilian service;
vii) multiple-job holders.

Only persons belonging to categories (i), (ii) and (iii) can be identified separately through specific questions and on the basis of their status in employment.

(c) Unemployment: Considered as "unemployed" are all persons who, during the reference periods, were without work and seeking work, or not seeking work but available for work. To determine whether or not a person was to be counted as unemployed, the questions under 6 (b) above were also used.

For the unemployed, the specific possible responses were: "unemployed and seeking work" and "not seeking work but available for work." Persons replying "Full-time housewife/homemaker," "Full-time student" or "Not available for work for other reasons" were classified among the economically inactive population.

7. Classifications used:

Only employed persons are classified by industry, by occupation and by status in employment.

(a) Industry: Based on the question: "What kind of main product or service is produced where X works (or worked)?" For coding industry, the ISIC-rev.2 has been used to the major division (1-digit) level.

(b) Occupation: Based on the question: "What was X's main occupation since 1989?." For coding occupation, 91 groups of the national classification of occupations were used. Links to the ISCO-68 have been established to the major group (1-digit) level.

(c) Status in employment: Based on the question: "Since 1989, has X been mainly: an employer; an employee; a self-employed; an unpaid family worker?." For coding status in employment, the above four categories were used.

8. Main differences compared with the previous census:

While in 1980 questions on persons' economic activity were only asked on a sample basis, in the 1990 census such questions were asked of all persons aged 12 years and over.

9. Publication of the census results:

The title of the publication containing the final census results is "Economic and Social Tables," issued in August 1994.

The organization responsible for this publication is the Central Statistics Office, P.O. Box 31908, Lusaka.

The census results are also available in the form of unpublished tables and on diskettes.

ZIMBABWE

1. Name and address of the organization responsible for the census:

Central Statistical Office, Box CY342, Causeway.

2. Population censuses conducted since 1945 (years):

1947, 1952, 1957, 1962, 1969, 1982 and 1992. The present description relates to the 1992 population census (held on 17 August).

3. Coverage of the census:

(a) Geographical scope: Whole country.

(b) Persons covered: All persons of all ages, present in Zimbabwe on the census night (de facto). Nationals abroad were not included.

4. Reference period:

The 12 months preceding the census day.

5. Main topics:

(a) Total population, by sex and age:	yes
Economically active population by:	
(b) Sex and age group:	yes
(c) Industry:	no
(d) Occupation:	yes
(e) Status in employment:	yes
(f) Highest educational level:	yes
(g) Hours of work:	no
(h) Other characteristics:	no

Re (a): The age is defined in terms of age at last birthday.

6. Concepts and definitions:

(a) Economically active population: It comprises all persons aged 10 years and over who, during the reference period, were either employed or unemployed, according to the definitions given below. However, the census results will be published with minimal information on 10-14 age group. The definition includes all members of the armed forces but excludes working students with a part time job and students seeking work.

(b) Employment: Employment is determined on the basis of the question: "What was your main activity for the last 12 months? Paid employee; Employer; Own account worker; Unpaid family worker; Looking for work/unemployed; Student; Homemaker; Retired/sick/too old; Others."

It is reported that the following categories are included:
i) persons doing unpaid work in family firm or business;
ii) persons engaged in the production of primary products for own consumption;
iii) employed persons, temporarily absent from work;
iv) seasonal or occasional workers;
v) conscripts for military/civilian service.

Only categories (i) and (ii) can be identified separately.

(c) Unemployment: Considered as "unemployed" are all persons who, during the reference period, had done no work, or were looking for work, or were available for work.

7. Classifications used:

Only employed persons were classified by occupation, whereas all persons aged 10 years and over were classified by status in employment.

(a) Industry: No classification by industry was made.

(b) Occupation: Based on the question: "What was your main occupation during the last 12 months?." For coding occupation, 109 groups of the national classification were used. Links to the ISCO-88 have been established to the minor group (3-digit) level.

(c) Status in employment: Based on the question: "What was your main activity for the last 12 months?." For coding status in employment, four groups were used, namely: paid employee; employer; own account worker; and unpaid family worker.

8. Main differences compared with the previous census:

A long reference period (i.e. 12 months) was used in the 1992 census whereas a short period (i.e. one week) was used in the 1982 census.

The question asked of employed persons to determine their occupation group and status in employment was different in the 1992 census from that of the 1982 census.

9. Publication of the census results:

The final results were published in December 1994 in a publication entitled "Census 1992: National Profile - Zimbabwe." All provincial final results have also been published.

The organization responsible for the publication is the Central Statistical Office, Box CY342, Causeway.

Unpublished tables and data in other forms are also available.

ANNEX

Extract from:
Resolution concerning statistics of the economically active population, employment, unemployment and underemployment

Thirteenth International Conference of Labour Statisticians
(Geneva, 18-29 October 1982)

Concepts and definitions

The economically active population

5. The "economically active population" comprises all persons of either sex who furnish the supply of labour for the production of economic goods and services as defined by the United Nations systems of national accounts and balances, during a specified time-reference period. According to these systems, the production of economic goods and services includes all production and processing of primary products, whether for the market, for barter or for own consumption, the production of all other goods and services for the market and, in the case of households which produce such goods and services for the market, the corresponding production for own consumption.

6. Two useful measures of the economically active population are the "usually active population" measured in relation to a long reference period such as a year, and the "currently active population", or, equivalently, the "labour force", measured in relation to a short reference period such as one week or one day.

The usually active population

7. (1) The "usually active population" comprises all persons above a specified age whose main activity status, as determined in terms of number of weeks or days during a long specified period (such as the preceding 12 months or the preceding calendar year) was "employed" or "unemployed" as defined in paragraphs 9 and 10.

(2) Where this concept is considered useful and feasible, the usually active population may be subdivided as employed and unemployed in accordance with the main activity.

The labour force (the currently active population)

8. The "labour force" or "currently active population" comprises all persons who fulfil the requirements for inclusion among the employed or the unemployed as defined in paragraphs 9 and 10 below.

Employment

9. (1) The "employed" comprise all persons above a specified age who during a specified brief period, either one week or one day, were in the following categories:

(a) "paid employment":

(a1) "at work": persons who during the reference period performed some work for wage or salary, in cash or in kind;

(a2) "with a job but not at work": persons who, having already worked in their present job, were temporarily not at work during the reference period and had a formal attachment to their job.

This formal job attachment should be determined in the light of national circumstances, according to one or more of the following criteria:

i) the continued receipt of wage or salary;
ii) an assurance of return to work following the end of the contingency, or an agreement as to the date of return;
iii) the elapsed duration of absence from the job which, wherever relevant, may be that duration for which workers can receive compensation benefits without obligations to accept other jobs.

(b) "self-employment":

(b1) "at work": persons who during the reference period performed some work for profit or family gain, in cash or in kind;

(b2) "with an enterprise but not at work": persons with an enterprise, which may be a business enterprise, a farm or a service undertaking, who were temporarily not at work during the reference period for any specific reason.

(2) For operational purposes, the notion of "some work" may be interpreted as work for at least one hour.

(3) Persons temporarily not at work because of illness or injury, holiday or vacation, strike or lock-out, educational or training leave, maternity or parental leave, reduction in economic activity, temporary disorganisation or suspension of work due to such reasons as bad weather, mechanical or electrical breakdown, or shortage of raw materials or fuels, or other temporary absence with or without leave should be considered as in paid employment provided they had a formal job attachment.

(4) Employers, own-account workers and members of producers' co-operatives should be considered as in self-employment and classified as "at work" or "not at work", as the case may be.

(5) Unpaid family workers at work should be considered as in self-employment irrespective of the number of hours worked during the reference period. Countries which prefer for special reasons to set a minimum time criterion for the inclusion of unpaid family workers among the employed should identify and separately classify those who worked less than the prescribed time.

(6) Persons engaged in the production of economic goods and services for own and household consumption should be considered as in self-employment if such production comprises an important contribution to the total consumption of the household.

(7) Apprentices who received pay in cash or in kind should be considered in paid employment and classified as "at work" or "not at work" on the same basis as other persons in paid employment.

(8) Students, homemakers and others mainly engaged in non-economic activities during the reference period, who at the same time were in paid employment or self-employment as defined in subparagraph (1) above should be considered as employed on the same basis as other categories of employed persons and be identified separately, where possible.

(9) Members of the armed forces should be included among persons in paid employment. The armed forces should include both the regular and the temporary members as specified in the most recent revision of the International Standard Classification of Occupations (ISCO).

Unemployment

10. (1) The "unemployed" comprise all persons above a specified age who during the reference period were:

(a) "without work", i.e. were not in paid employment or self-employment as defined in paragraph 9;

(b) "currently available for work", i.e. were available for paid employment of self-employment during the reference period; and

(c) "seeking work", i.e. had taken specific steps in a specified recent period to seek paid employment of self-employment. The specific steps may include registration at a public or private employment exchange; application to employers; checking at worksites, farms, factory gates, market or other assembly places; placing or answering newspaper advertisements; seeking assistance of friends or relatives; looking for land, building, machinery or equipment to establish own enterprise; arranging for financial resources; applying for permits and licences, etc."

(2) In situations where the conventional means of seeking work are of limited relevance, where the labour market is largely unorganised or of limited scope, where labour absorption is, at the time, inadequate, or where the labour force is largely self-employed, the standard definition of unemployment given in subparagraph (1) above may be applied by relaxing the criterion of seeking work.

(3) In the application of the criterion of current availability for work, especially in situations covered by subparagraph (2) above, appropriate tests should be developed to suit national circumstances. Such tests may be based on notions such as present desire for work and previous work experience, willingness to take up work for wage or salary on locally prevailing terms, or readiness to undertake self-employment activity given the necessary resources and facilities.

(4) Notwithstanding the criterion of seeking work embodied in the standard definition of unemployment, persons without work and currently available for work who had made arrangements to take up paid employment or undertake self-employment activity at a date subsequent to the reference period should be considered as unemployed.

(5) Persons temporarily absent from their jobs with no formal job attachment who were currently available for work and seeking work should be regarded as unemployed in accordance with the standard definition of unemployment. Countries may, however, depending on national circumstances and policies, prefer to relax the seeking work criterion in the case of persons temporarily laid off. In such cases, persons temporarily laid off who were not seeking work but classified as unemployed should be identified as a separate subcategory.

(6) Students, homemakers and others mainly engaged in non-economic activities during the reference period who satisfy the criteria laid down in subparagraphs (1) and (2) above should be regarded as unemployed on the same basis as other categories of unemployed persons and be identified separately, where possible.

INTRODUCTION

Le présent volume de «Sources et méthodes: statistiques du travail» présente les descriptions méthodologiques des recensements effectués au cours de la période 1989-1994. Son but est double:

- fournir des informations de base sur les méthodes suivies dans les différents pays pour établir des statistiques sur la population active, l'emploi et le chômage au travers des recensements;
- illustrer la comparabilité des statistiques produites par les différents pays.

Un tableau synoptique présente les principales caractéristiques des recensements décrits.

Les descriptions présentées ici couvrent 115 pays. Elles ont été préparées sur la base des informations communiquées par les bureaux nationaux de statistique en charge des recensements. Dans quelques cas, les informations ont été recueillies dans les publications nationales. Chaque description a été soumise au pays concerné afin qu'il puisse effectuer des observations, qui ont été prises en compte lorsqu'elles ont été reçues dans les limites du programme prévu pour leur publication.

Les descriptions suivent un même plan et utilisent des sections et rubriques types afin de faciliter les comparaisons. Dans la mesure du possible, les questions utilisées lors du recensement ont été indiquées. Les rubriques et leur contenu sont décrits ci-dessous:

1. Nom et adresse de l'organisme responsable du recensement:
Le nom et l'adresse de l'organisme responsable sont indiqués dans la langue du pays ou dans la langue de correspondance officielle du pays avec le BIT.

2. Recensements de population effectués depuis 1945 (années):
Sont indiquées ici les années pendant lesquelles il a été procédé à un recensement depuis 1945.

3. Champ du recensement:

a) Territoire couvert: On a indiqué sous cette rubrique la couverture géographique du pays ou territoire et, quand elle était limitée, les parties ou régions qui en étaient exclues.

b) Personnes couvertes: On a spécifié ici quelle population était couverte par le recensement, et tout groupe qui en était exclu, tel que par exemple les résidents étrangers ou les nationaux résidant habituellement ailleurs.

4. Période de référence:
A été indiquée ici la période de référence (par exemple un jour, une semaine ou une année) utilisée pour la collecte des caractéristiques économiques.

5. Principaux sujets:
On a dressé ici une liste des principaux sujets touchant l'activité économique des personnes pour lesquelles des informations ont été recueillies lors du recensement.

a) Population totale, selon le sexe et l'âge: ...
Population active par:
b) Sexe et âge: ...
c) Branche d'activité économique (industrie): ...
d) Profession: ...
e) Situation dans la profession: ...
f) Niveau d'instruction le plus élevé: ...
g) Durée du travail: ...
h) Autres caractéristiques: ...

Sur ces différents sujets, on a fourni des renseignements tels que la façon dont l'âge est déterminé, le concept utilisé pour la mesure du temps de travail (habituel ou effectif, etc...), et les différents thèmes pour lesquels ont été recueillies des informations supplémentaires concernant l'activité économique des personnes (montant des revenus, travail à temps partiel ou à plein temps, etc...).

6. Concepts et définitions:

a) Population active: La composition de la population active indiquée dans la «Résolution concernant les statistiques de la population active, de l'emploi, du chômage et du sous-emploi» (adoptée par la treizième Conférence internationale des statisticiens du travail, en 1982) a été considérée comme la définition

standard au regard de laquelle la définition utilisée par le pays considéré lors de ce recensement a été décrite. L'inclusion ou l'exclusion de certains groupes de personnes (retraités, ménagères, etc...) a été indiquée en fonction de cette Résolution (dont on trouvera les extraits en question en annexe).

Sont mentionnés sous cette rubrique:
- les limites d'âges utilisées pour la population active;
- l'inclusion ou l'exclusion des forces armées.

b) Emploi: La définition nationale utilisée dans le recensement a été donnée ici, ainsi qu'une liste de certaines catégories que le pays a indiquées être incluses dans la définition de l'emploi, et pour certaines identifiables séparément.

Les détenteurs de plusieurs emplois ne sont listés ici que dans le cas où ils sont identifiables séparément.

c) Chômage: On a indiqué ici la définition nationale utilisée dans le recensement.

7. Classifications utilisées:

a) Branche d'activité économique (industrie): Sont indiquées ici si possible les questions utilisées lors du recensement pour procéder à cette classification par type d'industrie et le nombre de groupes utilisés pour coder cette variable. On a indiqué ici si des liens avaient ou non été établis entre la classification nationale et la Classification internationale type, par industrie, de toutes les branches d'activité économique (CITI), Révision 2 (1968) ou Révision 3 (1990).

b) Profession: Sont indiquées ici si possible les questions utilisées lors du recensement pour procéder à cette classification par type de profession et le nombre de groupes utilisés pour coder cette variable. On a indiqué ici si des liens avaient ou non été établis entre la classification nationale et la Classification internationale type des professions (CITP-1968 ou CITP-1988).

c) Situation dans la profession: Sont indiqués ici les groupes utilisés pour coder cette variable (et leur nombre).

8. Principales différences par rapport au recensement précédent:
Des informations sont fournies ici sur tout changement intervenu depuis le précédent recensement sur la couverture, les concepts ou les définitions, etc...

9. Publication des résultats du recensement:
Cette rubrique fournit le titre de la ou des publications nationales dans lesquelles les résultats du recensement ont paru, le nom de l'organisme responsable de cette publication, et indique si ces résultats sont disponibles sous d'autres formes (disquettes, bandes magnétiques, CD-ROM, etc...).

AFRIQUE DU SUD

1. Nom et adresse de l'organisme responsable du recensement:
Central Statistical Service, Private Bag x 44, Steyn's Arcade, 274 Schoeman Street, Pretoria 0001.

2. Recensements de population effectués depuis 1945 (années):
1946, 1951, 1960, 1970, 1980, 1985 et 1991. La présente description se réfère au recensement de 1991 (qui a eu lieu le 7 mars).

3. Champ du recensement:

a) Territoire couvert: République d'Afrique du Sud (sauf Transkei, Bophuthatswana, Venda et Ciskei).

b) Personnes couvertes: Ensemble de la population.

4. Période de référence:
Jour du recensement.

5. Principaux sujets:
a) Population totale, selon le sexe et l'âge: oui
Population active par:
b) Sexe et âge: oui
c) Branche d'activité économique (industrie): oui
d) Profession: oui
e) Situation dans la profession: oui
f) Niveau d'instruction le plus élevé: oui
g) Durée du travail: non
h) Autres caractéristiques: oui

Réf. a): L'âge est défini à la fois en termes d'année de naissance et en termes d'années révolues à la date du dernier anniversaire.

Réf. h): Le recensement a aussi rassemblé des informations sur le revenu annuel.

6. Concepts et définitions:

a) *Population active*: Elle comprend toutes les personnes qui, le jour du recensement, étaient soit pourvues d'un emploi, soit au chômage, conformément aux définitions données ci-dessous. Aucun âge limite n'a été fixé pour l'inclusion dans la population active et ses composantes; cependant les données publiées concernent les personnes âgées de 15 ans et plus. La définition exclut les étrangers au service de gouvernements étrangers, les personnes séjournant moins de trois mois dans le pays, les étudiants travaillant à temps partiel et les étudiants en quête d'un emploi mais elle inclut les membres de forces armées.

b) *Emploi*: Sont considérées comme «pourvues d'un emploi» toutes les personnes qui ont identifié la position dans l'emploi actuel le jour du recensement soit comme «employeur ou travailleur indépendant», soit comme «salarié».

Il est indiqué que sont inclus dans cette définition:

i) les personnes travaillant sans rémunération dans une entreprise ou une affaire familiale;
ii) les personnes engagées dans la production de produits de base destinés à l'autoconsommation;
iii) les personnes occupées, temporairement absentes de leur travail;
iv) les travailleurs saisonniers ou occasionnels;
v) les conscrits (service militaire ou civil);
vi) les apprentis et les stagiaires.

Seuls les apprentis et les stagiaires artisans peuvent être identifiés séparément.

c) *Chômage*: Sont considérées comme «chômeurs» toutes les personnes qui, le jour du recensement, ont identifié leur position dans l'emploi comme «chômeur (en quête d'emploi)». Les personnes sans emploi qui ne cherchent pas de travail n'ont pas été considérées comme des chômeurs et ont été codées séparément.

7. Classifications utilisées:

Seules les personnes pourvues d'un emploi sont classifiées par branche d'activité économique. Aussi bien les personnes pourvues d'un emploi que les chômeurs ayant précédemment travaillé sont classifiés par la branche d'activité économique et d'après la situation dans la profession.

a) *Branche d'activité économique (industrie)*: Pour déterminer la branche d'activité économique, on a demandé aux personnes pourvues d'un emploi et aux travailleurs indépendants d'indiquer leur nom et leur secteur d'activité (verrerie, mine d'or, construction de ponts, agent de change, terrain de camping, institut de beauté, etc.). Pour coder la branche d'activité économique, on a utilisé 40 groupes de la classification nationale. Des liens avec la CITI-rév.2 ont été établis au niveau des divisions (2 chiffres).

b) *Profession*: Pour déterminer la profession, on a demandé aux personnes pourvues d'un emploi et aux chômeurs ayant précédemment travaillé d'indiquer leur profession principale ou leur dernière profession. On a posé des questions sur la nature du travail: maçon, dactylographe, travailleur familial, etc. Dans le cas des fonctionnaires, on a défini le rang ou le grade, à savoir directeur adjoint ou brigadier, etc.. Pour coder la profession, on a utilisé 165 groupes de la classification nationale. Des liens avec la CITP-68 ont été établis, mais pas systématiquement au même niveau.

c) *Situation dans la profession*: Pour déterminer cette variable, on a demandé aux personnes pourvues d'un emploi et aux chômeurs ayant précédemment travaillé d'indiquer leur situation dans la profession. Pour coder cette dernière, on a utilisé deux groupes de codes, à savoir: employeurs/travailleurs indépendants, (y compris ceux à leur compte et les travailleurs familiaux) et employés.

8. Principales différences par rapport au recensement précédent:

Pour les procédures de rassemblement des données, l'énumération a porté sur un échantillon d'environ 20% de la population répartie dans 88 zones. Un échantillon probabiliste représentatif des cabanes habitées ou des locaux résidentiels a été sélectionné dans chacune des régions et toutes les personnes qui avaient l'habitude de passer la nuit dans ces cabanes ou ces locaux ont été soumises au recensement. L'échantillon a été déterminé grâce à des photographies aériennes qui ont été prises en février 1991 aussi près que possible du jour du recensement. Des photos avaient été prises préalablement pour la détermination des échantillons dans certaines zones qui furent à nouveau photographiées en février 1991.

9. Publication des résultats du recensement:

Les résultats définitifs tels quels ont été publiés en mars 1992 et après ajustement en décembre 1992. D'autres publications sur les résultats du recensement sont disponibles.

L'organisme responsable de ces publications est le Service central des statistiques, Private Bag 44, Pretoria 0001.

Des tableaux non publiés, des rapports publiés sur bandes magnétiques et l'ensemble des données du recensement sur bandes magnétiques sont disponibles auprès du service central des statistiques. On peut également compiler des tabulations spéciales moyennant un versement couvrant le coût de la programmation et du traitement des données.

ALBANIE

1. Nom et adresse de l'organisme responsable du recensement:

Commission du Plan d'Etat, Direction de la Statistique, Tirana.

2. Recensements de population effectués depuis 1945 (années):

1960 et 1989. La présente description se réfère au recensement de la population de 1989 (qui a eu lieu du 1er au 7 avril).

3. Champ du recensement:

a) *Territoire couvert*: Ensemble du pays.

b) *Personnes couvertes*: Ensemble de la population.

4. Période de référence:

Il n'a pas été spécifié de période de référence.

5. Principaux sujets:

a) Population totale, selon le sexe et l'âge:	oui
Population active par:	
b) Sexe et âge:	oui
c) Branche d'activité économique (industrie):	oui
d) Profession:	oui
e) Situation dans la profession:	oui
f) Niveau d'instruction le plus élevé:	oui
g) Durée du travail:	non
h) Autres caractéristiques:	oui

Réf. a): L'âge est défini en termes d'année et de mois de naissance.

Réf. h): Des informations ont aussi été rassemblées sur les revenus annuels au cours de la dernière année et sur le nombre total d'années pendant lesquelles la personne a travaillé au service de l'état ou d'une coopérative. On a également demandé aux personnes interrogées d'indiquer en quelle année elles partiraient en retraite.

6. Concepts et définitions:

a) *Population active*: Elle comprend toutes les personnes âgées de 15 ans et plus qui étaient soit pourvues d'un emploi, soit au chômage, conformément aux définitions données ci-dessous. Les membres des forces armées sont inclus dans la définition.

b) *Emploi*: L'emploi est déterminé sur la base de la question suivante: «Travaillez-vous? 1) oui; 2) non». Aux personnes ayant répondu non, on a demandé si elles étaient: 1) à la retraite ou hors de l'âge de travailler; 2) retraité invalide; 3) inactif; 4) élève ou étudiant; 5) à la recherche d'un emploi; 6) pas à la recherche d'un emploi; ou 7) autres.

Il est indiqué que sont inclus dans cette définition:

i) les personnes travaillant sans rémunération dans une entreprise ou une exploitation familiale;
ii) les personnes engagées dans la production de produits de base destinés à l'autoconsommation;
iii) les personnes occupées, temporairement absentes du travail;
iv) les étudiants travaillant à temps partiel;
v) les travailleurs saisonniers ou occasionnels;
vi) les conscrits (service militaire ou civil);

vii) les apprentis et les stagiaires.

Aucune des catégories ci-dessus ne peut être identifiée séparément.

c) *Chômage*: Sont considérées comme «chômeurs» toutes les personnes qui se sont déclarées sans emploi et à la recherche d'un emploi. Les étudiants en quête de travail sont exclus de la définition.

7. Classifications utilisées:
Seules les personnes pourvues d'un emploi sont classifiées par industrie, par profession et d'après la situation dans la profession.

a) *Branche d'activité économique (industrie)*: Basée sur la question: «Activité économique?». Pour coder la branche d'industrie, on a utilisé la classification nationale. Il n'a pas été établi de liens avec la CITI.

b) *Profession*: Basée sur la question: «Profession ou devoir exercé?». Pour coder la profession, on a utilisé la classification nationale. Il n'a pas été établi de liens avec la CITP.

c) *Situation dans la profession*: Basée sur la question: «Situation sociale? 1) ouvrier; 2) employeur; 3) coopérativiste.» Pour coder cette variable, on a utilisé ces trois groupes.

8. Principales différences par rapport au recensement précédent:
Pas de différence majeure.

9. Publication des résultats du recensement:
Le titre de la publication contenant les résultats définitifs du recensement est: «Recensement de la population et de l'habitat, 1989», paru en 1991.

L'organisme responsable de cette publication est l'Institut de la Statistique, Rr Lek Dukagjini n 5, Tirana.

Les résultats ne sont pas disponibles sous d'autres formes.

ANGUILLA

1. Nom et adresse de l'organisme responsable du recensement:
Government of Anguilla, Statistical Unit, Ministry of Finance, The Secretariat, Valley.

2. Recensements de population effectués depuis 1945 (années):
1960, 1974, 1984 et 1992. La présente description se réfère au recensement de population de 1992 (qui a eu lieu le 14 avril).

3. Champ du recensement:

a) *Territoire couvert*: Ensemble du pays.

b) *Personnes couvertes*: Ensemble de la population.

4. Période de référence:
Le mois précédant le jour du recensement.

5. Principaux sujets:
a) Population totale, selon le sexe et l'âge: oui
Population active par:
b) Sexe et âge: oui
c) Branche d'activité économique (industrie): oui
d) Profession: oui
e) Situation dans la profession: oui
f) Niveau d'instruction le plus élevé: oui
g) Durée du travail: non
h) Autres caractéristiques: non

Réf. a): L'âge est défini en termes d'années révolues à la date du dernier anniversaire.

6. Concepts et définitions:

a) *Population active*: Elle comprend toutes les personnes âgées de 12 ans et plus qui, pendant la période de référence, étaient soit pourvues d'un emploi, soit au chômage, conformément aux définitions données ci-dessous. La définition inclut également les membres des forces de police.

b) *Emploi*: L'emploi est déterminé sur la base des questions suivantes: «Quelle est l'activité professionnelle exercée par la personne interrogée?» et «Si la personne ne travaille pas, quelle en est la raison?»

Il est indiqué que sont inclus dans cette définition:

i) les personnes occupées, temporairement absentes du travail;

ii) les étudiants travaillant à temps partiel;

iii) les travailleurs saisonniers ou occasionnels;

iv) les conscrits (service militaire ou civil);

v) les apprentis et les stagiaires.

Aucune de ces catégories ne peut être identifiée séparément.

c) *Chômage*: Sont considérées comme «chômeurs» toutes les personnes qui étaient sans emploi et désiraient travailler. La définition inclut aussi bien les personnes qui étaient activement engagées dans la recherche d'un emploi que celles qui ne faisaient rien pour trouver du travail parce qu'elles savaient qu'il n'y en avait pas.

7. Classifications utilisées:
Seules les personnes pourvues d'un emploi ont été classifiées par branche d'activité économique, par profession et d'après la situation dans la profession.

a) *Branche d'activité économique (industrie)*: Basée sur la question: «Pour qui travaille cette personne?» et «Où travaille cette personne?», par exemple «Cable and Wireless» ou «Mariners Hotel». Pour coder la branche d'activité, on a utilisé la CITI-rév.3 au niveau des catégories de classement (1 chiffre).

b) *Profession*: Basée sur la question: «Quelle est la profession de la personne?», par exemple, contremaître en menuiserie, mécanicien diesel, instituteur». Pour coder la profession, on a utilisé 39 groupes. Des liens avec la CITP-88 ont été établis au niveau des grands groupes (1 chiffre).

c) *Situation dans la profession*: Pour coder cette variable, on a utilisé les trois groupes suivants: le secteur public; le secteur privé; et les travailleurs indépendants.

8. Principales différences par rapport au recensement précédent:
Pas de différence majeure.

9. Publication des résultats du recensement:
Le titre de la publication contenant les résultats du recensement est «Anguilla Census of Population», septembre 1992.

L'organisme responsable de cette publication est le secrétariat du département des statistiques du Ministère des finances du gouvernement d'Anguilla à Valley.

Il est possible d'obtenir les données du recensement sur disquettes.

ANTIGUA-ET-BARBUDA

1. Nom et adresse de l'organisme responsable du recensement:
Census Office, Statistics Division, Upper Redcliffe Street, St. John's, Antigua.

2. Recensements de population effectués depuis 1945 (années):
1945, 1960, 1970 et 1991. La présente description se réfère au recensement de population de 1991 (qui a eu lieu le 28 mai).

3. Champ du recensement:

a) *Territoire couvert*: Ensemble du pays.

b) *Personnes couvertes*: Ensemble de la population.

4. Période de référence:
La semaine et l'année précédant le recensement.

5. Principaux sujets:
a) Population totale, selon le sexe et l'âge: oui
Population active par:
b) Sexe et âge: oui
c) Branche d'activité économique (industrie): oui
d) Profession: oui
e) Situation dans la profession: oui
f) Niveau d'instruction le plus élevé: oui
g) Durée du travail: oui
h) Autres caractéristiques: oui

Réf. a): L'âge est défini en termes d'années révolues à la date du dernier anniversaire.

Réf. g): La durée du travail se réfère aux heures réellement effectuées pendant la semaine de référence et au nombre de mois travaillés durant l'année de référence.

Réf. h): Le recensement a aussi rassemblé des informations sur: i) les moyens de transport utilisés pour se rendre au travail; ii) les activités du secteur informel; iii) la dernière période de perception d'un salaire ou d'un revenu; et iv) le salaire ou le revenu brut touché pendant la dernière période de travail rémunéré.

6. Concepts et définitions:

a) Population active: Elle comprend toutes les personnes âgées de 15 à 64 ans qui, pendant les périodes de référence, étaient soit pourvues d'un emploi, soit au chômage, conformément aux définitions données ci-dessous. La définition exclut les membres des forces armées.

b) Emploi: Les questions posées pour déterminer si une personne doit être considérée comme pourvue d'un emploi étaient «Comment avez-vous occupé l'essentiel de votre temps au cours des 12 derniers mois?» et «Comment avez-vous occupé l'essentiel de votre temps au cours de la semaine écoulée?». Pour ces deux questions, les réponses possibles étaient: «1) j'ai travaillé; 2) détenteur d'un emploi mais absent du travail; 3) demandeur d'emploi; 4) je souhaitais travailler et j'étais disponible; 5) tâches ménagères; 6) scolarisé; 7) retraité; 8) handicapé, incapable de travailler; 9) autre; 10) non précisé». Les personnes qui se sont rangées dans les catégories 1) ou 2) ont été considérées comme «pourvues d'un emploi».

Il est indiqué que sont inclus dans cette définition:

i) les personnes travaillant sans rémunération dans une entreprise ou une affaire familiale;

ii) les personnes engagées dans la production de produits de base destinés à l'autoconsommation;

iii) les personnes occupées, temporairement absentes du travail;

iv) les étudiants travaillant à temps partiel;

v) les travailleurs saisonniers ou occasionnels.

Seules les personnes des catégories i), iii) et iv) peuvent être identifiées séparément.

c) Chômage: Les questions utilisées pour déterminer si une personne doit être considérée comme étant au chômage sont celles indiquées sous 6b) et les suivantes: «Avez-vous effectué un quelconque travail, même à domicile, au cours des 12 derniers mois?» et «Avez-vous déjà travaillé ou exercé une activité professionnelle?».

7. Classifications utilisées:

Aussi bien les personnes pourvues d'un emploi que les chômeurs ayant précédemment travaillé sont classifiés par industrie, par profession et d'après la situation dans la profession.

a) Branche d'activité économique (industrie): Basée sur la question: «Quel type d'industrie ou d'activité est ou était pratiqué sur votre lieu de travail?» et «Quel est le nom et l'adresse de votre lieu de travail actuel?». Pour coder la branche d'activité économique, on a utilisé 157 groupes de la classification nationale. Des liens avec la CITI-rév.3 ont été établis au niveau des groupes (3 chiffres).

b) Profession: Basée sur la question: «Quel type de travail effectuez ou effectuiez-vous dans votre principal emploi?». Pour coder la profession, on a utilisé 136 groupes de la classification nationale. Des liens ont été établis avec la CITP-88.

c) Situation dans la profession: Basée sur la question: «Etes-vous installé à votre propre compte, travaillez-vous contre un salaire ou un traitement ou travaillez-vous sans rémunération dans une affaire familiale?». Pour coder cette variable, on a utilisé les six groupes suivants: 1) salarié du gouvernement; 2) salarié du secteur privé; 3) travailleur non rémunéré; 4) travailleur indépendant avec des salariés (employeur); 5) travailleur indépendant sans salariés (à son propre compte); et 6) ne sait pas/n'a rien indiqué.

8. Principales différences par rapport au recensement précédent:

Pas de différence majeure.

9. Publication des résultats du recensement:

Le titre de la publication contenant les résultats du recensement est: «1991 Population and Housing Census, Summary Report, Volume II, (Pard. 1)», décembre 1994.

L'organisme responsable de cette publication est le Département des statistiques du Ministère des finances et de la sécurité sociale.

Les résultats du recensement sont également disponibles sous forme de tableaux non publiés et de disquettes.

ANTILLES NEERLANDAISES

1. Nom et adresse de l'organisme responsable du recensement:

Central Bureau of Statistics, Fort Amsterdam, Curaçao.

2. Recensements de population effectués depuis 1945 (années):

1960, 1972, 1981 et 1992. La présente description se réfère au recensement de la population de 1992 (qui a eu lieu le 27 janvier).

3. Champ du recensement:

a) Territoire couvert: Ensemble du pays.

b) Personnes couvertes: Ensemble de la population.

4. Période de référence:

La semaine, l'année et les cinq ans précédant le jour du recensement.

5. Principaux sujets:

a) Population totale, selon le sexe et l'âge:	oui
Population active par:	
b) Sexe et âge:	oui
c) Branche d'activité économique (industrie):	oui
d) Profession:	oui
e) Situation dans la profession:	oui
f) Niveau d'instruction le plus élevé:	oui
g) Durée du travail:	oui
h) Autres caractéristiques:	oui

Réf. a): L'âge est défini à la fois en termes d'année de naissance et en termes d'années révolues à la date du dernier anniversaire.

Réf. g): Pour les périodes de référence d'une semaine et d'un an, les personnes devaient indiquer, respectivement, le nombre habituel de leurs heures de travail et la période de travail totale au cours des 12 derniers mois (exprimée en nombre de semaines). Les chômeurs devaient préciser pendant combien de temps ils avaient travaillé à plein temps au cours des cinq dernières années.

Réf. h): Le recensement a aussi rassemblé des informations sur les moyens de transport utilisés pour se rendre au travail, sur la principale source de revenu des intéressés et sur leur revenu brut total pour le mois de janvier 1992. Les chômeurs devaient préciser de quelle façon ils avaient recherché du travail au cours du mois précédent.

6. Concepts et définitions:

a) Population active: Elle comprend toutes les personnes âgées de 15 à 99 ans qui, au cours de la semaine de référence, étaient soit pourvues d'un emploi soit au chômage, conformément aux définitions données ci-dessous. La définition inclut tous les membres des forces armées.

b) Emploi: Sont considérées comme «pourvues d'un emploi» toutes les personnes qui, au cours de la semaine de référence, avaient soit travaillé normalement soit travaillé occasionnellement pendant quatre heures ou plus. La question utilisée était: «La semaine dernière, avez-vous travaillé normalement ou exercé une activité professionnelle occasionnelle pendant quatre heures ou plus?».

Il est indiqué que sont inclus dans cette définition:

i) les personnes travaillant sans rémunération dans une entreprise ou une affaire familiale;

ii) les personnes pourvues d'un emploi, temporairement absentes du travail;

iii) les étudiants travaillant à temps partiel;

iv) les travailleurs saisonniers ou occasionnels;

v) les conscrits (service militaire ou civil);

vi) les apprentis et les stagiaires.

Les personnes appartenant aux catégories i), ii), iii), iv) et v) peuvent être identifiées séparément.

c) Chômage: Sont considérées comme «chômeurs» toutes les personnes qui, au cours de la semaine de référence, étaient sans travail, recherchaient un emploi ou souhaitaient se lancer dans une activité professionnelle indépendante, et qui auraient été en mesure de commencer à travailler dans les deux semaines au cas où elles auraient trouvé un emploi.

7. Classifications utilisées:

Aussi bien les personnes pourvues d'un emploi que les chômeurs ayant précédemment travaillé sont classifiés par branche d'activité économique, par profession et d'après la situation dans la profession.

a) Branche d'activité économique (industrie): Basée sur les questions: «Dans quelle entreprise/société travaillez-vous? (nom et adresse)» et «De quel type d'entreprise s'agit-il?». Pour coder la branche d'activité économique, on a utilisé la classification nationale, basée sur la CITI-Rév.3, avec 17 catégories.

b) Profession: Basée sur la question: «Quelle est votre profession? (titre de la profession et description précise de l'activité)». Pour coder la profession, on a utilisé la classification nationale, basée sur la CITP-88, avec 10 grands groupes.

c) Situation dans la profession: Basée sur la question: «Quel est votre statut par rapport à votre activité économique?». Neuf groupes ont été utilisés pour coder cette variable: employeur; travailleur pour son propre compte propriétaire d'une petite entreprise (moins de 3 salariés); salarié avec emploi permanent; salarié avec emploi temporaire; travailleur occasionnel ou travailleur occupant un poste occasionnel; travailleur familial non rémunéré; travailleur au bénéfice d'un contrat de travail de moins de six mois; travailleur au bénéfice d'un contrat de travail de 6 mois ou plus; autres et inconnus.

8. Principales différences par rapport au recensement précédent:

En 1981, la limite d'âge était de 14 ans et plus. Par ailleurs, la définition de ce qu'était une personne pourvue d'un emploi incluait les travailleurs occasionnels et la période de référence était les deux derniers mois précédant le recensement. Etaient considérées comme «chômeurs» les personnes qui étaient «à la recherche d'un emploi».

9. Publication des résultats du recensement:

Les chiffres définitifs du recensement sont parus en janvier 1993 dans une publication intitulée «Troisième recensement de la population et des logements, Antilles néerlandaises, 1992» (trois volumes).

L'organisme responsable de cette publication est le Bureau central des statistiques, Fort Amsterdam, Curaçao.

Il est possible d'obtenir, sur demande, des tableaux non publiés, et, ultérieurement, des disquettes (projet).

ARABIE SAOUDITE

1. Nom et adresse de l'organisme responsable du recensement:

Central Department of Statistics, P.O. Box 3735, Riyadh 11118.

2. Recensements de population effectués depuis 1945 (années):

1974 et 1992. La présente description se réfère au recensement de population de 1992 (qui a eu lieu le 27 septembre).

3. Champ du recensement:

a) Territoire couvert: Ensemble du pays.

b) Personnes couvertes: Ensemble de la population.

4. Période de référence:

La semaine précédant le jour du recensement.

5. Principaux sujets:

a) Population totale, selon le sexe et l'âge:	oui
Population active par:	
b) Sexe et âge:	oui
c) Branche d'activité économique (industrie):	oui
d) Profession:	oui
e) Situation dans la profession:	oui
f) Niveau d'instruction le plus élevé:	oui
g) Durée du travail:	non
h) Autres caractéristiques:	non

Réf. a): L'âge est défini en termes d'années révolues à la date du dernier anniversaire.

6. Concepts et définitions:

a) Population active: Elle comprend toutes les personnes âgées de 12 ans et plus qui, pendant la période de référence étaient soit pourvues d'un emploi, soit au chômage, conformément aux définitions données ci-dessous.

La définition exclut les étudiants travaillant à temps partiel et ceux en quête d'un emploi mais elle inclut les forces armées.

b) Emploi: Sont considérées comme «pourvues d'un emploi» toutes les personnes qui, pendant la période de référence, ont travaillé 15 heures ou plus dans un ou plusieurs emplois ou qui étaient absentes de leur(s) emploi(s) à cause d'une maladie, de vacances, etc.

Il est indiqué que sont inclus dans cette définition:

i) les personnes travaillant sans rémunération dans une entreprise ou une affaire familiale;

ii) les personnes engagées dans la production de produits de base destinés à l'autoconsommation;

iii) les personnes pourvues d'un emploi, temporairement absentes de leur travail;

iv) les travailleurs saisonniers ou occasionnels;

v) les conscrits (service militaire ou civil);

vi) les apprentis et les stagiaires.

Seules les personnes travaillant sans rémunération dans une entreprise ou une affaire familiale peuvent être identifiées séparément.

c) Chômage: Sont considérées comme «chômeurs» toutes les personnes qui, pendant la période de référence, étaient sans emploi, désireuses et capables de travailler et à la recherche d'un emploi. Les chômeurs ont été enregistrés comme «chômeurs ayant déjà travaillé» ou «chômeurs n'ayant jamais travaillé».

7. Classifications utilisées:

Seules les personnes pourvues d'un emploi ont été classifiées par branche d'activité économique et d'après la situation dans la profession. Aussi bien les personnes pourvues d'un emploi que les chômeurs ayant précédemment travaillé sont classifiés par profession.

a) Branche d'activité économique (industrie): Pour déterminer la branche d'activité économique, on a demandé aux personnes pourvues d'un emploi de préciser la principale activité économique de leur employeur. Pour coder la branche d'activité, on a utilisé la CITI-rév.3 au niveau des divisions (2 chiffres).

b) Profession: Pour déterminer la profession, on a demandé aux personnes pourvues d'un emploi et aux chômeurs ayant précédemment travaillé d'indiquer leur profession principale (type de travail effectué actuellement ou précédemment par la personne). Pour coder la profession, on a utilisé la CITP-68 au niveau des groupes de base (3 chiffres).

c) Situation dans la profession: Pour déterminer la situation dans la profession, on a demandé aux personnes pourvues d'un emploi de préciser leur situation professionnelle. Pour coder cette variable, on a utilisé quatre groupes, à savoir: employeur, travailleur indépendant, employé et travailleur non rémunéré.

8. Principales différences par rapport au recensement précédent:

Pas de différence majeure.

9. Publication des résultats du recensement:

Un rapport intitulé «Preliminary Results of the General Population and Housing Census, 413 A.H.» a été publié en mars 1995. Des rapports additionnels devraient être publiés mais aucune date n'a encore été fixée.

L'organisme responsable de la publication est le Département central des statistiques, P.O. Box 3735, Riyadh 11118.

Les données du recensement ne sont pas disponibles sous d'autres formes.

ARGENTINE

1. Nom et adresse de l'organisme responsable du recensement:

Instituto Nacional de Estadística y Censos (INDEC), Diagonal Presidente Julio A. Roca 609, Código Postal 1067, Buenos Aires, Capital Federal.

2. Recensements de population effectués depuis 1945 (années):

1947, 1960, 1970, 1980 et 1991. La présente description se réfère au recensement de population de 1991 (qui a eu lieu le 15 mai).

3. Champ du recensement:

a) Territoire couvert: Ensemble du pays, à l'exception des Iles Malouines et des Iles de l'Atlantique Sud.

b) Personnes couvertes: Le recensement avait pour but de couvrir tous les groupes de population se trouvant sur le territoire national à la date à laquelle il a été effectué, ce qui excluait par conséquent les argentins résidant à l'étranger et les étrangers résidant dans les ambassades situées sur territoire argentin.

4. Période de référence:

La semaine précédant la date du recensement pour déterminer quelles sont les personnes pourvues d'un emploi et les quatre dernières semaines précédant le recensement pour déterminer quels sont les chômeurs.

5. Principaux sujets:

a) Population totale, selon le sexe et l'âge:	oui
Population active par:	
b) Sexe et âge:	oui
c) Branche d'activité économique (industrie):	oui
d) Profession:	oui
e) Situation dans la profession:	oui
f) Niveau d'instruction le plus élevé:	oui
g) Durée du travail:	non
h) Autres caractéristiques:	non

Réf. a): L'âge est défini en termes d'années révolues à la date du dernier anniversaire.

6. Concepts et définitions:

a) Population active: Elle comprend toutes les personnes âgées de 14 ans et plus qui, pendant les périodes de référence, étaient soit pourvues d'un emploi soit au chômage, conformément aux définitions données ci-dessous. Les questions relatives à l'activité économique ont été posées à un échantillon variant entre 10 pour cent de la population dans les localités de 500 000 habitants et plus et 20 pour cent dans celles de 100 000 à 499 999 habitants. La définition inclut l'ensemble des membres des forces armées.

b) Emploi: Sont considérées comme «pourvues d'un emploi» toutes les personnes ayant travaillé, avec ou sans rémunération, pendant la semaine de référence. Les questions utilisées pour déterminer si une personne est «pourvue d'un emploi» sont: «Avez-vous travaillé la semaine passée, ne serait-ce que quelques heures?», «Avez-vous fait quelque chose à votre domicile pour quelqu'un n'appartenant pas à votre foyer ou avez-vous aidé quelqu'un dans un commerce, une exploitation agricole ou un autre type d'activité économique?», et «Etiez-vous en congé pour cause de maladie, vacances, etc.?».

Il est indiqué que sont inclus dans cette définition:

i) les personnes travaillant sans rémunération dans une entreprise ou une affaire familiale;

ii) les personnes occupées, temporairement absentes du travail pour des motifs passagers tels que: maladie ou accident, conflit du travail, vacances ou autre type d'absence autorisée, interruption du travail en raison des conditions climatiques ou d'équipements de production endommagés;

iii) les étudiants travaillant à temps partiel;

iv) les travailleurs saisonniers ou occasionnels;

v) les conscrits (service militaire ou civil).

Les personnes appartenant aux catégories i), ii) iii) et v) peuvent être identifiées séparément au moyen de questions spécifiques.

c) Chômage: Sont considérées comme «chômeurs» les personnes qui se trouvaient à la recherche d'un emploi pendant les quatre semaines de référence, et ce qu'elles aient déjà travaillé auparavant ou qu'elles aient été à la recherche d'un premier emploi. La question posée pour déterminer si une personne est au chômage est: «Avez-vous été à la recherche d'un emploi au cours des quatre dernières semaines?».

7. Classifications utilisées:

Seules les personnes pourvues d'un emploi et appartenant aux échantillons pris en compte ont été classifiées par branche d'activité économique, par profession et d'après la situation dans la profession.

a) Branche d'activité économique (industrie): La question utilisée pour déterminer la branche d'activité économique est: «De quoi s'occupe ou que produit l'entreprise ou l'établissement dans lequel vous travaillez?». Pour coder la branche d'activité économique, on a utilisé la CITI-rév.3, jusqu'au niveau des groupes (3 chiffres).

b) Profession: Pour déterminer la profession, on a posé la question suivante: «Quelles sont vos tâches dans cet emploi?». Pour coder la profession, on a utilisé neuf groupes de la classification nationale de 1980. Des liens ont été établis avec la CITP-88.

c) Situation dans la profession: La question utilisée pour déterminer cette caractéristique est: «Dans votre emploi principal - celui pour lequel vous travaillez le plus grand nombre d'heures -, êtes-vous: patron? ouvrier ou employé du secteur privé? ouvrier ou employé du secteur public? employé de maison? travailleur indépendant? travailleur familial sans rémunération fixe? ne sait pas?». Ce sont également ces sept groupes que l'on a utilisé pour coder la situation dans la profession.

8. Principales différences par rapport au recensement précédent:

Certaines différences mineures par rapport au recensement de 1980 concernent essentiellement la formulation des questions utilisées pour déterminer:

– la branche d'activité économique: «L'entreprise ou l'établissement dans lequel vous travaillez est-il principalement de type agricole, industriel, commercial ou d'un autre type?», «De quoi s'occupe ou que produit principalement cet établissement?», et «L'établissement dans lequel vous travaillez emploie-t-il cinq personnes ou moins? ou plus de cinq personnes?».

– la profession: «Quelle est la profession, la fonction ou le type de travail que vous exercez?».

– la situation dans la profession: «Quelle est votre position dans l'exercice de cette profession (employé ou ouvrier du secteur public; employé ou ouvrier du secteur privé; employé de maison; travailleur indépendant sans employés; patron ou associé, avec employés; travailleur familial sans rémunération fixe; ne sait pas)?».

9. Publication des résultats du recensement:
Information non disponible.

ARUBA

1. Nom et adresse de l'organisme responsable du recensement:
Central Bureau of Statistics, L.G. Smith Boulevard no. 160.

2. Recensements de population effectués depuis 1945 (années):
1981 et 1991. La présente description se réfère au recensement de 1991 (qui a eu lieu le 6 octobre).

3. Champ du recensement:

a) Territoire couvert: Ensemble du pays.

b) Personnes couvertes: Ensemble de la population.

4. Période de référence:
La semaine précédant le jour du recensement.

5. Principaux sujets:

a) Population totale, selon le sexe et l'âge:	oui
Population active par:	
b) Sexe et âge:	oui
c) Branche d'activité économique (industrie):	oui
d) Profession:	oui
e) Situation dans la profession:	oui
f) Niveau d'instruction le plus élevé:	...
g) Durée du travail:	oui
h) Autres caractéristiques:	oui

Réf. a): L'âge est défini en termes d'années révolues à la date du dernier anniversaire.

Réf. g): Les personnes pourvues d'un emploi devaient préciser la durée normale de leur travail.

Réf. h): Le recensement a également rassemblé des informations sur les moyens de transport utilisés pour se rendre au travail, la durée de l'emploi, le motif pour lequel la personne est sans travail, le nombre de mois travaillés par un chômeur au cours de son dernier emploi, le revenu et la source de revenu.

6. Concepts et définitions:

a) Population active: Elle comprend toutes les personnes âgées de 14 ans et plus qui, pendant la semaine de référence étaient, soit pourvues d'un emploi, soit au chômage, conformément aux définitions données ci-dessous. Elle inclut les membres des forces armées.

b) Emploi: Sont considérées comme «pourvues d'un emploi» toutes les personnes ayant répondu positivement à la question: «Avez-vous exercé un emploi pendant quatre heures minimum au cours de la semaine écoulée (ou auriez-vous pu l'exercer si des vacances, une maladie, une grossesse ou un conflit de travail etc. ne vous en avait empêché)?».

Il est indiqué que sont inclus dans cette définition:

i)   les personnes travaillant sans rémunération dans une entreprise ou une affaire familiale;
ii) les personnes occupées, temporairement absentes de leur travail;
iii) les étudiants travaillant à temps partiel;
iv) les conscrits (service militaire ou civil);
v)   les apprentis et les stagiaires.

Seules les personnes appartenant aux catégories i), iii) et iv) peuvent être identifiées séparément.

c) Chômage: Sont considérées comme «chômeurs» toutes les personnes qui, pendant la période de référence, n'ont pas travaillé un minimum de quatre heures et qui ont répondu affirmativement aux deux questions suivantes: «Au cours du mois écoulé, étiez-vous activement à la recherche d'un emploi ou étiez-vous occupé par les démarches en vue de créer votre propre entreprise?» et «Si vous trouvez un emploi ou si vous montez votre propre entreprise, seriez-vous à même de commencer à travailler dans un délai de deux semaines?». Les étudiants en quête d'un emploi sont exclus de la définition.

7. Classifications utilisées:

Aussi bien les personnes pourvues d'un emploi que les chômeurs sont classifiés par branche d'activité économique et par profession. La situation dans la profession est établie pour les personnes pourvues d'un emploi mais elle est restreinte à un échantillon pour les chômeurs.

a) Branche d'activité économique (industrie): Basée sur la question: «Où travaillez-vous (ou avez-vous travaillé)? adresse du lieu de travail; nom de l'entreprise ou de l'organisme; type d'activité exercée par l'entreprise (employeur)». Pour coder la branche d'activité, on a utilisé la CITI-rév.2 au niveau des groupes (4 chiffres).

b) Profession: Basée sur la question: «Quel type de travail effectuez-vous (ou avez-vous effectué) principalement? nom de la profession ou du travail; description du travail». Pour coder la profession, on a utilisé la CITP-88 au niveau des groupes de base (4 chiffres).

c) Situation dans la profession: Six groupes ont été utilisés pour coder cette variable, à savoir: employeur (3 employés ou plus); patron d'une petite entreprise (0 à 3 employés); salarié (ouvrier ou employé) ou personnel permanent ou temporaire; salarié (ouvrier ou employé) travaillant comme personnel de réserve ou homme à tout faire; travailleur familial non rémunéré (dans une affaire familiale); autre (volontaire, membre d'une coopérative, etc.).

8. Principales différences par rapport au recensement précédent:

Pas de différence majeure.

9. Publication des résultats du recensement:

Les résultats définitifs du recensement sont parus en octobre 1992 dans une publication intitulée «Selected Tables - Third Population and Housing Census, Aruba - October 6, 1991».

L'organisme responsable de la publication est le Bureau central des statistiques, L.G. Smith Boulevard no. 160.

Les résultats du recensement sont disponibles sous forme de disquettes. Des tableaux non publiés sont également à disposition sur demande.

AUSTRALIE

1. Nom et adresse de l'organisme responsable du recensement:

Australian Bureau of Statistics, P.O. Box 10, Belconnen ACT 2616.

2. Recensements de population effectués depuis 1945 (années):

1947, 1954, 1961, 1966, 1971, 1976, 1981, 1986 et 1991. La présente description se réfère au recensement de 1991 (qui a eu lieu le 6 août).

3. Champ du recensement:

a) Territoire couvert: Ensemble du pays.

b) Personnes couvertes: Ensemble de la population, à l'exception des diplomates étrangers et de leurs familles.

4. Période de référence:

La semaine précédant le recensement pour les travailleurs à plein temps et les travailleurs à temps partiel, et les quatre semaines précédant le jour du recensement pour les personnes à la recherche d'un emploi (voir également le paragraphe 6 c ci-dessous).

5. Principaux sujets:

a) Population totale, selon le sexe et l'âge:	oui
Population active par:	
b) Sexe et âge:	oui
c) Branche d'activité économique (industrie):	oui
d) Profession:	oui
e) Situation dans la profession:	oui
f) Niveau d'instruction le plus élevé:	oui
g) Durée du travail:	oui
h) Autres caractéristiques:	oui

Réf. a): L'âge est défini en termes d'années révolues à la date du dernier anniversaire.

Réf. g): On a demandé aux personnes pourvues d'un emploi et présentes au travail d'indiquer le nombre d'heures réellement effectuées dans leur principal emploi au cours de la période de référence.

Réf. h): Le recensement a aussi rassemblé des informations sur les revenus bruts et sur les moyens de transport utilisés pour se rendre au travail.

6. Concepts et définitions:

a) Population active: Elle comprend toutes les personnes âgées de 15 ans et plus qui, au cours de la période de référence, étaient soit pourvues d'un emploi soit au chômage, conformément aux définitions données ci-dessous. Elle exclut les personnes qui n'avaient pas d'emploi et n'en avaient pas recherché un au cours de la période de quatre semaines précédant le jour du recensement; ces personnes ont été considérées comme inactives. La définition inclut les membres des forces armées.

b) Emploi: Sont considérées comme «pourvues d'un emploi» toutes les personnes qui travaillaient à plein temps ou à temps partiel, soit contre rémunération soit pour en dégager pour elles-mêmes un bénéfice, ou qui travaillaient sans rémunération dans une affaire familiale. Les tâches ménagères sont exclues à moins qu'elles ne soient effectuées dans d'autres foyers et contre rémunération. La question utilisée pour déterminer si une personne devait ou non être considérée comme pourvue d'un emploi était la suivante: «La semaine dernière, l'intéressé(e) a-t-il(elle) exercé une quelconque activité professionnelle, que ce soit à plein temps ou à temps partiel?».

Il est indiqué que sont inclus dans cette définition:

i)   les personnes travaillant sans rémunération dans une entreprise ou une affaire familiale;
ii) les personnes pourvues d'un emploi, temporairement absentes du travail;
iii) les étudiants travaillant à temps partiel;
iv) les travailleurs saisonniers ou occasionnels;
v)   les apprentis et les stagiaires.

Seules les personnes appartenant aux catégories i) et ii) peuvent être identifiées séparément en fonction de leur situation dans la profession et par classification croisée avec le nombre d'heures de travail.

c) Chômage: Sont considérées comme «chômeurs» toutes les personnes qui étaient sans emploi et en recherchaient un. La question utilisée pour déterminer si quelqu'un devait ou non être compté comme chômeur était la suivante: «L'intéressé(e) a-t-il(elle) activement recherché du travail à un moment ou à un autre au cours des quatre dernières semaines?». Par «rechercher activement du travail», il faut entendre le fait d'être inscrit auprès des Services de l'emploi du Commonwealth; d'écrire, de téléphoner ou de rendre visite à un employeur pour lui demander du travail, ou de passer des annonces de demandes d'emploi. Les étudiants à la recherche d'un emploi sont exclus de cette définition.

7. Classifications utilisées:

Seules les personnes pourvues d'un emploi sont classées par branche d'activité économique, par profession et d'après la situation dans la profession.

a) Branche d'activité économique (industrie): Basée sur les questions: «Pour l'activité professionnelle principale que vous avez exercée la semaine dernière, quel était la raison sociale de votre employeur et l'adresse de votre lieu de travail?» et «Quel est le type d'activité de production, commerciale ou de service de l'employeur à cette adresse?». Les réponses ont fourni des informations permettant le codage de la branche d'activité. La classification des différentes branches est basée sur la Classification australienne type des activités et sur l'Index des branches d'activité et des secteurs de destination, qui est une liste de tous les établissements ayant une activité économique en Australie. Pour coder la branche d'activité économique, on a utilisé 615 classes différentes. Des liens ont été établis avec la CITI-Rév.2 au niveau des groupes (4 chiffres).

b) Profession: Basée sur les questions: «Dans votre principal emploi la semaine dernière, quel était votre profession? (veuillez en indiquer l'intitulé complet: employé comptable, dessinateur de génie civil, cuisinier de restauration rapide, carreleur, opérateur de machine extrudeuse; pour les fonctionnaires, indiquez le titre officiel en même temps que la profession; pour les membres des forces armées, indiquez le grade en même temps que la profession)» et «Quels sont les principales tâches ou fonctions habituellement exécutées par l'intéressé(e) lui(elle)-même dans cet emploi? (donnez un maximum de précisions; par exemple: établissement des livres de comptes, réalisation de dessins industriels en vue de la construction d'un barrage, préparation de hamburgers et de frites, pose de carrelage, travail sur une machine extrudeuse de plastique)». Les professions ont été regroupées en fonction de la Classification australienne type des professions et codées au niveau des groupes de base de cette classification. On a utilisé 337 codes de groupes, comprenant 282 groupes de base, 52 sous-groupes et 8 grands groupes, et trois codes supplémentaires ont été rajoutés pour tenir compte des réponses mal rédigées. Aucun lien n'a été établi avec la CITP.

c) Situation dans la profession: Basée sur la question: «Dans l'emploi principal que vous occupiez la semaine dernière, étiez-vous: salarié ou employé; travailleur indépendant n'employant pas de tierces personnes; travailleur indépendant avec des employés; travailleur non rémunéré?». Pour coder la situation dans la profession, on a utilisé les quatre catégories suivantes: salarié ou employé; travailleur indépendant; employeur; et travailleur non rémunéré.

8. Principales différences par rapport au recensement précédent:

Pas de différence majeure.

9. Publication des résultats du recensement:

Les résultats définitifs du recensement de la population active et de ses différentes composantes (personnes pourvues d'un emploi et chômeurs) sont disponibles Etat par Etat depuis septembre 1992.

Les résultats préliminaires du recensement de 1991 ont été publiés dans la série «Premiers décomptes pour les zones statistiques locales» (Cat. no. 2701.1-8), Etat par Etat, de février à avril 1992.

Le Bureau australien des statistiques (BAS) a publié les résultats définitifs du recensement Etat par Etat, dans la série «Décomptes du recensement pour les petites zones». Des chiffres plus détaillés peuvent être obtenus sur demande auprès des Services d'information du BAS.

Les résultats du recensement de 1991 sont également disponibles sous d'autres formes telles que des rapports thématiques, des atlas sociaux, des matrices et des cartes. Les supports utilisés sont notamment des tirages sur papier, des disquettes, des bandes magnétiques, des microfiches, des cartouches et des CD-ROM. Pour toute information supplémentaire, se référer à la publication intitulée «Recensement 1991: Guide des produits et services» (cat. no. 2910.0) ou contacter le Service commercial du recensement, Bureau australien des statistiques, B.P. 10, Belconnen ACT 2616, téléphone 61 6 252 7879, téléfax 61 6 253 1809.

AUTRICHE

1. Nom et adresse de l'organisme responsable du recensement:

Oesterreichisches Statistisches Zentralamt, Hintere Zollamtsstrasse 2B, A-1033 Vienne.

2. Recensements de population effectués depuis 1945 (années):

1951, 1961, 1971, 1981 et 1991. La présente description se réfère au recensement de population de 1991 (qui a eu lieu le 15 mai).

3. Champ du recensement:

a) Territoire couvert: Ensemble du pays.

b) Personnes couvertes: Population résidente, y compris les étrangers vivant en permanence en Autriche et les ressortissants autrichiens travaillant temporairement à l'étranger, mais à l'exclusion des personnes bénéficiant de l'exterritorialité et des ressortissants autrichiens vivant en permanence à l'étranger.

4. Période de référence:

Les dernières semaines précédant le jour du recensement; en cas de doute, on tient compte de la situation de la personne le jour du recensement, à savoir le 15 mai.

5. Principaux sujets:

a) Population totale, selon le sexe et l'âge:	oui
Population active par:	
b) Sexe et âge:	oui
c) Branche d'activité économique (industrie):	oui
d) Profession:	oui
e) Situation dans la profession:	oui
f) Niveau d'instruction le plus élevé:	oui
g) Durée du travail:	oui
h) Autres caractéristiques:	oui

Réf. a): L'âge est défini en termes de date de naissance exacte (jour, mois, année).

Réf. g): La durée du travail se réfère à la durée normale du travail des personnes qui exercent une activité professionnelle à temps complet ou partiel.

Réf. h): Le recensement rassemble aussi des informations sur d'autres sujets, tels que: la fréquence des déplacements pour se rendre au travail (quotidiens ou non); le lieu de travail; la durée des déplacements quotidiens; les moyens de transport utilisés normalement pour les déplacements plus longs; le type d'employeur (public ou privé, 12 catégories).

6. Concepts et définitions:

a) Population active: Elle comprend toutes les personnes âgées de 15 ans et plus qui, pendant la période de référence, étaient soit pourvues d'un emploi, soit au chômage, conformément aux définitions données ci-dessous. La définition inclut l'ensemble des membres des forces armées.

b) Emploi: Sont considérées comme «pourvues d'un emploi» toutes les personnes qui avaient une activité à temps complet (33 heures ou plus par semaine) ou à temps partiel (12 à 32 heures par semaine). Les personnes en congé de maternité ou en congé parental non payé sont considérées comme pourvues d'un emploi.

Il est indiqué que sont inclus dans cette définition:

i) les personnes travaillant sans rémunération dans une entreprise ou une affaire familiale;
ii) les personnes engagées dans la production de produits de base destinés à l'autoconsommation;
iii) les personnes occupées, temporairement absentes du travail;
iv) les étudiants travaillant à temps partiel;
v) les travailleurs saisonniers ou occasionnels;
vi) les conscrits (service militaire ou civil);
vii) les apprentis et les stagiaires.

Les personnes appartenant aux catégories i), vi) et vii) peuvent être identifiées séparément. D'autres groupes de personnes suivant une formation professionnelle (élèves-infirmières, stagiaires, bénévoles, etc.) sont aussi considérés comme occupés, mais ne peuvent pas être identifiés séparément.

c) Chômage: Sont considérées comme «chômeurs» toutes les personnes qui étaient sans emploi et à la recherche d'un travail. La définition exclut les étudiants à la recherche d'un travail.

7. Classifications utilisées:
Aussi bien les personnes pourvues d'un emploi que les chômeurs ayant précédemment travaillé sont classifiés par branche d'activité économique, par profession et d'après la situation dans la profession.

a) Branche d'activité économique (industrie): Des questions bien spécifiques ont été posées: nom de l'entreprise (service ou employeur) et branche d'activité économique de l'entreprise ou de l'organisation (par ex. atelier de tissage, fabrique de sous-vêtements, vente d'usine); les travailleurs indépendants devaient répondre «à son compte». Pour coder la branche d'activité économique, on a utilisé 117 groupes de la classification nationale des branches d'activité économique. Des liens ont été établis avec la CITI-Rév.3 au niveau des divisions (2 chiffres).

b) Profession: Des questions spécifiques ont été posées: le titre exact de l'emploi actuel ou précédent, la principale tâche exécutée (libraire, vendeur de chaussures, monteur de vidéoscopes sur chaîne d'assemblage, employé contractuel dans un service social, menuisier travaillant dans son propre atelier, employé de voirie, etc.). Pour coder la profession, on a utilisé 175 groupes de la classification nationale des emplois. Des liens avec la CITP-88 ont été établis au niveau des sous-grands-groupes (2 chiffres).

c) Situation dans la profession: Des questions spécifiques ont été posées aux personnes pourvues d'un emploi et aux chômeurs ayant précédemment travaillé pour déterminer leur situation dans la profession (actuelle ou précédente), à savoir: indépendant avec salariés (employeur); indépendant sans salariés; salarié/fonctionnaire; aide familial non rémunéré; travailleur qualifié; travailleur semi-qualifié; travailleur non qualifié; apprenti. Ce sont ces huit groupes qui ont été utilisés pour coder la situation dans la profession.

8. Principales différences par rapport au recensement précédent:
Les principales différences concernent les classifications utilisées en 1991. Pour la branche d'activité économique, des codes supplémentaires ont été rajoutés afin d'améliorer les liens avec la CITI-89, et pour la profession, on a adopté une série de codes plus ramassée.

9. Publication des résultats du recensement:
Différentes publications liées aux résultats du recensement sont parues en 1993 dans la série «Beiträge zur österreichischen Statistik». Le titre du volume qui contient les chiffres du recensement pour l'ensemble du pays est «Hauptergebnisse II - Oesterreich», Référence 1030/20. Des informations plus détaillées sont disponibles dans ISIS-Base de données statistiques, classifications croisées sur mesure.

L'organisme responsable de ces publications est le Oesterreichisches Statistisches Zentralamt, à Vienne.

Toutes les données relatives au recensement peuvent également être obtenues sur demande sous forme de brochures, rapports, disquettes et bandes magnétiques.

BAHAMAS

1. Nom et adresse de l'organisme responsable du recensement:
Department of Statistics, Ministry of Finance, P.O. Box N-3904, Nassau.

2. Recensements de population effectués depuis 1945 (années):
1953, 1963, 1970, 1980 et 1990. La présente description se réfère au recensement de la population de 1990 (qui a eu lieu le 1er mai).

3. Champ du recensement:
a) Territoire couvert: Ensemble du pays.

b) Personnes couvertes: Ensemble de la population, à l'exclusion du personnel diplomatique étranger résidant aux Bahamas. Il a été établi un relevé, par sexe, des personnes de passage dans le pays au cours de la période du recensement, mais ces personnes n'ont pas été interrogées et elles ne sont donc pas incluses dans le décompte du recensement.

4. Période de référence:
La semaine qui a pris fin le 28 avril 1990, et les 12 mois précédant le recensement.

5. Principaux sujets:
a) Population totale, selon le sexe et l'âge:	oui
Population active par:	
b) Sexe et âge:	oui
c) Branche d'activité économique (industrie):	oui
d) Profession:	oui
e) Situation dans la profession:	oui
f) Niveau d'instruction le plus élevé:	oui
g) Durée du travail:	oui
h) Autres caractéristiques:	oui

Réf. a): L'âge est défini en termes d'année de naissance et d'années révolues à la date du dernier anniversaire.

Réf. g): Les heures de travail sont celles de la période de travail totale (exprimée en nombre de semaines) des personnes pourvues d'un emploi pendant la période de référence longue.

Réf. h): Le recensement a aussi rassemblé des informations sur: i) le lieu où la personne a exercé pour la dernière fois un emploi régulier pendant au moins deux semaines depuis 1979; et ii) le revenu total de la personne au cours des 12 mois précédant la date du recensement.

6. Concepts et définitions:
a) Population active: Elle comprend toutes les personnes âgées de 15 ans et plus qui, au cours de la période de référence, étaient soit pourvues d'un emploi soit au chômage, conformément aux définitions données ci-dessous. La définition inclut également les membres des forces armées.

b) Emploi: Les questions posées afin de déterminer si une personne pouvait être considérée comme pourvue d'un emploi étaient les suivantes: «Quelle a été votre principale situation au regard de l'emploi au cours de la semaine qui s'est terminée le 28 avril 1990?» et «Quelle a été votre principale situation au regard de l'emploi au cours des 12 derniers mois?». Les personnes ayant répondu «Présent au travail» ou «Pourvu d'un emploi mais absent du travail» ont été considérées comme pourvues d'un emploi.

Il est indiqué que sont inclus dans cette définition:

i) les personnes travaillant sans rémunération dans une entreprise ou une affaire familiale;
ii) les personnes engagées dans la production de produits de base destinés à l'autoconsommation;
iii) les personnes pourvues d'un emploi, temporairement absentes du travail;
iv) les étudiants travaillant à temps partiel;
v) les travailleurs saisonniers ou occasionnels;
vi) les conscrits (service militaire ou civil);
vii) les apprentis et les stagiaires.

Seules les personnes appartenant aux catégories i) et iii) peuvent être identifiées séparément au moyen de leurs réponses aux questions relatives à l'emploi et à la situation dans la profession.

c) Chômage: Sont considérées comme «chômeurs» toutes les personnes qui n'avaient pas d'emploi et qui en recherchaient un. Une personne est considérée comme étant au chômage si ses réponses aux questions susmentionnées au point 6 b sont «A la recherche d'un premier emploi», «A la recherche d'un emploi (autre que le premier)» ou «A la recherche d'un emploi depuis les quatre dernières semaines».

7. Classifications utilisées:
Aussi bien les personnes pourvues d'un emploi que les chômeurs ayant précédemment travaillé sont classifiés par branche d'activité économique, par profession et d'après la situation dans la profession.

a) Branche d'activité économique (industrie): Basée sur la question: «De quel type d'activité économique ou d'entreprise s'agissait-il? (Décrivez le type d'entreprise ou d'organisme, par exemple magasin de vente au détail, école primaire, cabinet de conseil juridique, banque, brasserie, etc.)». Neuf groupes ont été utilisés pour coder la branche d'activité économique. Des liens ont été établis avec la CITI-Rév.2 au niveau des branches (1 chiffre).

b) Profession: Basée sur la question: «Quel type de travail faisiez-vous? (Décrivez votre emploi de la manière la plus précise possible, par ex. vendeur, dactylographe, médecin, mécanicien automobile, ingénieur du génie civil, chauffeur de taxi, femme de chambre, etc.)». Pour coder la profession, on a utilisé neuf groupes. Des liens ont été établis avec la CITP-88 au niveau des grands groupes (1 chiffre).

c) *Situation dans la profession*: Basée sur la question: «Quelle était votre situation dans la profession lorsque vous avez travaillé pour la dernière fois?». Cinq groupes ont été utilisés pour coder la situation dans la profession: salarié (entreprise privée); salarié (organisme gouvernemental); travailleur familial non rémunéré; travailleur à son propre compte avec employé(s) rémunéré(s); travailleur à son propre compte sans employé(s) rémunéré(s).

8. Principales différences par rapport au recensement précédent:

Pour le recensement de 1980, on avait utilisé uniquement une période de référence courte - la semaine précédant le recensement (mais les classifications n'avaient été effectuées que pour les personnes ayant travaillé à un moment ou à un autre au cours des 12 mois précédant le recensement).

De plus, pour le recensement de 1990, dans la question portant sur la période de référence courte (une semaine), il a également été demandé aux gens s'ils avaient été à la recherche d'un emploi au cours des quatre dernières semaines (voir paragraphe 6 c).

9. Publication des résultats du recensement:

Le titre de la publication contenant les chiffres du recensement est: «Commonwealth des Bahamas - Rapport sur le Recensement de la population de 1990: activité économique et revenu», 1992.

L'organisme responsable de cette publication est le Département des statistiques, Ministère des finances, B.P. N-3904, Nassau, Bahamas.

Les résultats du recensement sont également disponibles sous forme de tableaux non publiés et de disquettes.

BAHREIN

1. Nom et adresse de l'organisme responsable du recensement:

Central Statistics Organization, Directorate of Statistics, Cabinet Affairs, P.O. Box 5835, Manama.

2. Recensements de population effectués depuis 1945 (années):

1950, 1959, 1965, 1971, 1981, et 1991. La présente description se réfère au recensement de 1991 (qui a eu lieu le 16 novembre).

3. Champ du recensement:

a) *Territoire couvert*: Ensemble du pays.

b) *Personnes couvertes*: Ensemble de la population.

4. Période de référence:

La semaine précédant le jour du recensement.

5. Principaux sujets:

a) Population totale, selon le sexe et l'âge: oui
Population active par:
b) Sexe et âge: oui
c) Branche d'activité économique (industrie): oui
d) Profession: oui
e) Situation dans la profession: oui
f) Niveau d'instruction le plus élevé: oui
g) Durée du travail: non
h) Autres caractéristiques: oui

Réf. a): L'âge est défini en termes d'années révolues à la date du dernier anniversaire.

Réf. h): Le recensement a aussi rassemblé des informations sur la durée du chômage.

6. Concepts et définitions:

a) *Population active*: Elle comprend toutes les personnes âgées de 12 ans et plus qui, pendant la semaine de référence, étaient soit pourvues d'un emploi, soit au chômage, conformément aux définitions données ci-dessous. Les forces armées sont incluses dans la définition.

b) *Emploi*: Sont considérées comme «pourvues d'un emploi» toutes les personnes qui, pendant la semaine de référence, ont effectué hors de chez elles un travail ayant une valeur économique. La question utilisée pour déterminer si une personne doit être considérée comme pourvue d'un emploi est «Quelle est votre position dans l'emploi? 1) employeur; 2) travailleur indépendant; 3) salarié; 4) employé non salarié; 5) chômeur ayant précédemment travaillé; 6) chômeur n'ayant jamais travaillé; 7) étudiant; 8) ménagère; 9) personne bénéficiant d'autres sources de revenu; 10) incapable de travailler; 11) ne souhaite pas travailler; 12) non applicable».

Il est indiqué que sont inclus dans cette définition:

i) les personnes travaillant sans rémunération dans une entreprise ou une affaire familiale;

ii) les personnes engagées dans la production de produits de base destinés à l'autoconsommation;

iii) les personnes occupées, temporairement absentes du travail;

iv) les étudiants travaillant à temps partiel;

v) les travailleurs saisonniers ou occasionnels;

vi) les conscrits (service militaire ou civil).

Seules les personnes travaillant sans rémunération dans une entreprise ou une affaire familiale peuvent être identifiées séparément.

c) *Chômage*: Sont considérées comme «chômeurs» toutes les personnes qui, pendant la semaine de référence, étaient sans travail, capables et désireuses de travailler. Les chômeurs ont été enregistrés comme «chômeurs ayant précédemment travaillé» ou comme «chômeurs n'ayant jamais travaillé».

7. Classifications utilisées:

Seules les personnes pourvues d'un emploi ont été classifiées par branche d'activité économique et d'après la situation dans la profession. Aussi bien les personnes pourvues d'un emploi que les chômeurs ayant précédemment travaillé sont classifiés par profession.

a) *Branche d'activité économique (industrie)*: Basée sur la question: «Quelle est la principale activité de votre entreprise?». Pour coder l'industrie, on a utilisé 17 groupes de la classification nationale. Des liens avec la CITI-rév.3 ont été établis au niveau des catégories de classement (1 chiffre).

b) *Profession*: Basée sur la question: «Quel type de travail faisiez-vous?». Pour coder la profession, on a utilisé la classification type des professions du répertoire du golfe Arabique (Standard Arab Gulf Directory for Occupational Classification) au niveau d'un chiffre. Aucun lien n'a été établi avec la CITP.

c) *Situation dans la profession*: Pour déterminer cette variable, on a posé la même question que pour l'emploi. Pour coder la situation dans la profession, on a utilisé les quatre catégories suivantes: employeur; travailleur indépendant; salarié; travailleur non rémunéré.

8. Principales différences par rapport au recensement précédent:

Lors du recensement de 1981, la limite d'âge inférieure retenue pour l'inclusion dans la population active était de 15 ans.

9. Publication des résultats du recensement:

Les résultats définitifs ont été publiés en octobre 1993 dans les publications suivantes: «The population, Housing, Buildings and Establishments Census - 1991. I - Summary results. II - Demographic and social characteristics. III - Economic characteristics. IV - Characteristics of Housing, Buildings and Establishments».

L'organisme responsable de cette publication est le département des statistiques du Bureau central des statistiques, P.O. Box 5835, Manama.

Les résultats définitifs sont également disponibles sous d'autres formes: tableaux non publiés, disquettes, bandes magnétiques.

BARBADE

1. Nom et adresse de l'organisme responsable du recensement:

Barbados Statistical Service, 3rd Floor, National Insurance Building, Fairchild Street, Bridgetown.

2. Recensements de population effectués depuis 1945 (années):

1946, 1960, 1970, 1980 et 1990. La présente description se réfère au recensement de la population de 1990 (qui a eu lieu le 1er mai).

3. Champ du recensement:

a) Territoire couvert: Ensemble du pays.

b) Personnes couvertes: Ensemble de la population.

4. Période de référence:
La semaine et les 12 mois précédant la date du recensement.

5. Principaux sujets:

a) Population totale, selon le sexe et l'âge:	oui
Population active par:	
b) Sexe et âge:	oui
c) Branche d'activité économique (industrie):	oui
d) Profession:	oui
e) Situation dans la profession:	oui
f) Niveau d'instruction le plus élevé:	oui
g) Durée du travail:	oui
h) Autres caractéristiques:	non

Réf. a): L'âge est défini en termes d'années révolues à la date du dernier anniversaire.

Réf. g): La durée du travail se réfère au nombre total d'heures effectuées pendant la semaine se terminant le 28 avril et au nombre total de mois travaillés durant la période de 12 mois se terminant le 30 avril.

6. Concepts et définitions:

a) Population active: Elle comprend toutes les personnes âgées de 15 ans et plus qui, pendant les périodes de référence étaient, essentiellement, soit pourvues d'un emploi, soit en quête d'un emploi, conformément aux définitions données ci-dessous. La définition inclut également tous les membres des forces armées.

b) Emploi: Les questions spécifiques utilisées pour déterminer si une personne doit être considérée comme pourvue d'un emploi sont «Quelle a été votre principale activité au cours des 12 mois se terminant le 30 avril?» et «Quelle a été votre principale activité au cours de la semaine se terminant le 28 avril?». Les réponses possibles étaient: «1) j'ai travaillé; 2) détenteur d'un emploi mais absent du travail; 3) demandeur d'emploi; 4) tâches ménagères; 5) étudiant; 6) retraité; 7) incapable de travailler; 8) autre; 9) sans réponse».

Il est indiqué que sont inclus dans cette définition:

i)   les personnes travaillant sans rémunération dans une entreprise ou une affaire familiale;

ii) les personnes occupées, temporairement absentes du travail;

iii) les étudiants travaillant à temps partiel;

iv) les travailleurs saisonniers ou occasionnels;

v)   les conscrits (service militaire ou civil);

vi) les apprentis et les stagiaires.

Seules les personnes appartenant aux catégories i), ii) et iii) peuvent être identifiées séparément.

c) Chômage: Pour les individus âgés de 15 ans et plus, on a pu identifier une catégorie de personnes qui étaient essentiellement demandeurs d'emploi pendant les périodes de référence.

7. Classifications utilisées:
Aussi bien les personnes pourvues d'un emploi que les chômeurs ayant précédemment travaillé sont classifiés par industrie, par profession et d'après la situation dans la profession.

a) Branche d'activité économique (industrie): Basée sur la question: «Dans quel type d'industrie ou d'activité avez-vous travaillé au cours de 12 derniers mois?». Pour coder l'industrie, on a utilisé la CITI-Rév.3 au niveau des catégories de classement (1 chiffre).

b) Profession: Basée sur la question: «Quel type de travail ou de profession avez-vous essentiellement exercé au cours des 12 derniers mois?». Pour coder la profession, on a utilisé la CITP-88 au niveau des grands groupes (1 chiffre).

c) Situation dans la profession: Basée sur la question: «Au cours des 12 mois se terminant le 30 avril, avez-vous travaillé pour un employeur ou pour vous-même?» («travaillé pour un employeur» inclut: le gouvernement; les entreprises privées; les personnes privées; les travailleurs familiaux non rémunérés. «Travaillé pour vous-même» inclut: les travailleurs indépendants avec salariés et les travailleurs indépendants sans salariés). Pour coder la situation dans la profession, on a utilisé les six groupes mentionnés précédemment. Un septième groupe a également été ajouté («non précisé»).

8. Principales différences par rapport au recensement précédent:
Pas de différence majeure.

9. Publication des résultats du recensement:
Les résultats définitifs du recensement concernant la population active et ses composantes ont été publiés en 1995 dans une publication intitulée «1990 Population Census of Barbados».

L'organisme responsable de la publication est le département des statistiques de la Barbade, Fairchild Street, Bridgetown.

Il est également possible d'obtenir les données du recensement sur disquettes et bandes magnétiques.

BELGIQUE

1. Nom et adresse de l'organisme responsable du recensement:
Institut national de Statistique (INS), 44 rue de Louvain, 1000 Bruxelles.

2. Recensements de population effectués depuis 1945 (années):
1947, 1961, 1970, 1981 et 1991. La présente description se réfère au recensement de la population et des logements de 1991 (qui a eu lieu le 1er mars).

3. Champ du recensement:

a) Territoire couvert: Ensemble du pays.

b) Personnes couvertes: Ensemble de la population ayant sa résidence habituelle dans le pays, c'est-à-dire y compris les étrangers résidant en Belgique et les nationaux résidant temporairement à l'étranger, mais non compris les personnes de passage en Belgique ou ne disposant pas de l'autorisation d'inscription définitive (permis de séjour temporaire).

4. Période de référence:
Le jour du recensement, mais il a également été fait référence à la situation habituelle de la personne recensée.

5. Principaux sujets:

a) Population totale, selon le sexe et l'âge:	oui
Population active par:	
b) Sexe et âge:	oui
c) Branche d'activité économique (industrie):	oui
d) Profession:	oui
e) Situation dans la profession:	oui
f) Niveau d'instruction le plus élevé:	oui
g) Durée du travail:	oui
h) Autres caractéristiques:	oui

Réf. a): L'âge est défini, soit en termes d'année de naissance, soit en termes d'années révolues à la date du dernier anniversaire; toutefois, la plupart des tableaux disponibles sont fondés sur cette dernière approche.

Réf. g): La durée du travail se réfère à la durée normale (pour les personnes pourvues d'un emploi) et aux heures réellement effectuées (pour les personnes pourvues d'emploi, présentes au travail) durant la période de référence.

Réf. h): Des informations ont été également rassemblées sur les moyens de transport utilisés et sur le temps consacré pour se rendre au travail et pour en revenir.

6. Concepts et définitions:

a) Population active: Elle comprend toutes les personnes âgées de 14 ans et plus qui, à la date du recensement étaient, soit pourvues d'un emploi, soit au chômage, conformément aux définitions données ci-dessous. La définition couvre également les militaires de carrière et ceux du contingent (miliciens); ces derniers sont classés dans la population active non occupée.

b) Emploi: Sont considérées comme «pourvues d'emploi» toutes les personnes qui ont répondu affirmativement à la question «Exercez-vous une profession, une fonction, une activité lucrative? (on répondra 'oui' même si cette profession, fonction ou activité lucrative est exercée temporairement et/ou ne constitue pas la principale source des moyens d'existence du recensé; les aidants d'un membre du ménage répondront aussi 'oui'; on répondra également 'oui' même si la profession n'est pas effectivement exercée au moment du recensement pour des raisons de maladie, congé, chômage partiel, conflit de travail, etc.)»

Il est indiqué que sont inclus dans cette définition:

i)   les personnes travaillant sans rémunération dans une entreprise ou une affaire familiale;

ii) les personnes engagées dans la production de produits de base destinés à l'autoconsommation;

iii) les étudiants travaillant à temps partiel;

iv) les travailleurs saisonniers ou occasionnels, pour autant qu'ils soient occupés à la date du recensement;

v) les conscrits (service militaire ou civil);

vi) les détenteurs de plusieurs emplois;

vii) les apprentis et les stagiaires.

Les catégories i), iii), v), vi) et vii) ci-dessus peuvent être identifiées séparément au moyen de questions spécifiques. Toutefois, les apprentis et les stagiaires ne peuvent être identifiés séparément que s'ils sont liés par un contrat.

c) Chômage: Sont considérées comme «chômeurs» toutes les personnes qui, à l'époque du recensement, étaient sans emploi et à la recherche d'un emploi, y compris celles qui cherchaient un premier emploi. Les étudiants en quête de travail sont exclus de la définition.

7. Classifications utilisées:

Seules les personnes occupées sont classifiées par industrie, par profession et d'après la situation dans la profession.

a) Branche d'activité économique (industrie): Il a été demandé aux personnes interrogées d'indiquer le nom et l'adresse de l'établissement, de l'institution ou de l'administration qu'elles dirigent ou qui les emploie; la nature de l'activité de l'entreprise (des instructions spéciales sont données pour éviter toute confusion avec la profession de la personne recensée).

Pour coder la branche d'activité, on a utilisé 809 groupes permettant une correspondance avec la Nomenclature générale des activités économiques dans les Communautés européennes (NACE, rév.1). Des liens avec la CITI-rév.2 ont été établis au niveau le plus détaillé possible. L'établissement de liens avec la CITI-rév.3 était à l'examen.

b) Profession: Basée sur les questions: «Décrivez avec précision la profession ou la fonction que vous exercez, de telle sorte qu'on puisse en déduire la nature du travail effectué»; «Indiquez votre grade actuel, décrivez votre fonction actuelle ou précisez la qualification mentionnée dans un arrêté de nomination, un contrat de travail ou un document équivalent»; «Au sein de l'établissement, de l'institution ou de l'administration qui vous occupe, dans quel service travaillez-vous? (réception, accueil; achats, approvisionnement; production et exploitation; ventes, expédition; comptabilité et finances, etc.».

Pour coder la profession, on a utilisé environ 1 700 groupes de la Classification nationale des professions. Des liens avec la CITP-88 ont été établis au niveau des sous-groupes (3 chiffres).

c) Situation dans la profession: Basée sur la question: «Exercez-vous votre profession comme: indépendant; chef d'établissement ou d'entreprise non lié par un contrat d'emploi; chef d'établissement ou d'entreprise lié par un contrat d'emploi; aidant (d'un indépendant); employé dans le secteur public; ouvrier dans le secteur public; employé dans le secteur privé; ouvrier dans le secteur privé; apprenti lié par un contrat d'apprentissage; personnel domestique ou de service?». Pour coder la situation dans la profession, on a utilisé les neuf groupes ci-dessus. Aux indépendants et chefs d'établissement ou d'entreprise non liés par un contrat d'emploi, on a demandé: «Occupez-vous du personnel rémunéré? Si oui, combien de personnes?». A tous les autres, on a demandé: «Dirigez-vous d'autres personnes? Si oui, combien de personnes?».

8. Principales différences par rapport au recensement précédent:

Seule la procédure de collecte des données a été modifiée. En effet, lors des recensements précédents, les agents recenseurs distribuaient les questionnaires et les reprenaient à l'occasion d'une visite ultérieure. En 1991, les bulletins personnalisés au moyen des informations contenues dans le Registre national ont été expédiés par voie postale aux personnes recensées. Les agents recenseurs, qui disposaient d'un relevé des bulletins expédiés, devaient visiter tous les logements situés dans leur circonscription et:

- reprendre les documents remplis;

- distribuer, le cas échéant, des bulletins aux personnes n'ayant pas reçu ou ayant égaré les bulletins personnalisés, qu'elles figurent ou non sur le relevé des résidents en sa possession.

Par un système de lecture optique approprié, l'identification des bulletins personnalisés permettait un dépouillement accéléré.

9. Publication des résultats du recensement:

Le titre de la publication contenant les chiffres définitifs de la population active est «Recensement général de la population du 1.3.1991 - Population active» (1994).

L'organisme responsable de cette publication est l'Institut national de Statistique, Bruxelles.

Les résultats du recensement de 1991 sont également disponibles sous la forme de listings, microfiches, disquettes, CD-ROM et bandes magnétiques.

BELIZE

1. Nom et adresse de l'organisme responsable du recensement:

Central Statistical Office, Ministry of Finance, Belmopan.

2. Recensements de population effectués depuis 1945 (années):

1946, 1960, 1970, 1980 et 1991. La présente description se réfère au recensement de 1991 (qui a eu lieu le 12 mai).

3. Champ du recensement:

a) Territoire couvert: Ensemble du pays.

b) Personnes couvertes: Ensemble de la population.

4. Période de référence:

La semaine et les 12 mois précédant le jour du recensement.

5. Principaux sujets:

a) Population totale, selon le sexe et l'âge:	oui
Population active par:	
b) Sexe et âge:	oui
c) Branche d'activité économique (industrie):	oui
d) Profession:	oui
e) Situation dans la profession:	oui
f) Niveau d'instruction le plus élevé:	oui
g) Durée du travail:	oui
h) Autres caractéristiques:	oui

Réf. a): L'âge est défini en termes d'années révolues à la date du dernier anniversaire.

Réf. g): Le recensement a rassemblé des informations sur le nombre de mois travaillés par les personnes pourvues d'un emploi au cours de la période de référence longue et le nombre d'heures effectuées par les personnes pourvues d'un emploi pendant la période de référence courte.

Réf. h): Le recensement a également permis de récolter des informations sur les revenus et les moyens de transports utilisés pour se rendre au travail (à pied, à bicyclette, en voiture ou autre véhicule privé, en véhicule de location, par les transports en commun, etc.).

6. Concepts et définitions:

a) Population active: Elle comprend toutes les personnes âgées de 15 ans et plus qui, pendant la période de référence de 12 mois, étaient soit pourvues d'un emploi, soit au chômage, conformément aux définitions données ci-dessous. La définition inclut les membres des forces armées résidant dans des logements privés mais exclut ceux qui sont logés dans des camps militaires.

b) Emploi: Sont considérées comme «pourvues d'un emploi» toutes les personnes qui ont essentiellement travaillé au cours des périodes de référence. Les questions utilisées pour déterminer si une personne devait être considérée comme pourvue d'un emploi sont les suivantes: «A quoi avez-vous employé l'essentiel de votre temps au cours des 12 derniers mois?» et «A quoi avez-vous employé l'essentiel de votre temps la semaine dernière?». Les réponses possibles étaient: 1) j'ai travaillé; 2) détenteur d'un emploi mais absent du travail; 3) demandeur d'emploi; 4) je désirais travailler et j'étais disponible; 5) tâches ménagères; 6) scolarisé; 7) retraité; 8) handicapé, incapable de travailler; 9) autre; 10) sans réponse;

Il est indiqué que sont inclus dans cette définition:

i) les personnes travaillant sans rémunération dans une entreprise ou une affaire familiale;

ii) les personnes engagées dans la production de produits de base destinés à l'autoconsommation;

iii) les personnes occupées, temporairement absentes du travail;

iv) les étudiants travaillant à temps partiel, si le travail prend le pas sur les études;

v) les travailleurs saisonniers ou occasionnels;
vi) les conscrits (service militaire ou civil).

Seules les personnes appartenant aux catégories i), iii), iv) et v) peuvent être identifiées séparément en combinaison avec d'autres questions.

c) *Chômage*: Sont considérées comme «chômeurs» toutes les personnes qui, pendant les périodes de référence, désiraient essentiellement travailler, étaient disponibles et à la recherche d'un emploi. La définition exclut les étudiants en quête d'un travail.

7. Classifications utilisées:

Aussi bien les personnes pourvues d'un emploi que les chômeurs ayant précédemment travaillé sont classifiés par branche d'activité économique et par profession. Mais seules les personnes pourvues d'un emploi sont classées d'après la situation dans la profession.

a) *Branche d'activité économique (industrie)*: Basée sur la question: «Quel type d'activité est ou était exercée sur votre lieu de travail?». Pour coder la branche d'activité économique, on a utilisé la classification nationale. Des liens ont été établis avec la CITI-Rév.3 au niveau des classes (4 chiffres).

b) *Profession*: Basée sur la question: «Quel type de travail exercez ou exerciez-vous dans votre principale profession?». Pour coder la profession, on a utilisé la classification nationale. Des liens avec la CITP-88 ont été établis au niveau des groupes de base (4 chiffres).

c) *Situation dans la profession*: Basée sur la question: «Dirigez-vous votre propre entreprise, travaillez-vous contre un salaire ou un traitement, ou travaillez-vous sans rémunération dans une entreprise ou une affaire familiale?». Six groupes ont été utilisés pour coder la situation dans la profession, à savoir: salarié du gouvernement; salarié du secteur privé; travailleur non rémunéré; travailleur indépendant avec des salariés (employeur); travailleur indépendant sans salariés (à son propre compte); sans réponse.

8. Principales différences par rapport au recensement précédent:

Lors du recensement de 1980, on s'était limité à une période de référence longue (12 mois).

9. Publication des résultats du recensement:

Les résultats définitifs sont parus en 1992 dans une publication intitulée «Major Findings - 1991 Population and Housing Census».

L'organisme responsable de cette publication est le Bureau central des statistiques du Ministère des finances de Belmopan.

Les données et des tableaux non publiés sont également disponibles sur disquettes auprès du Bureau central des statistiques.

BENIN

1. Nom et adresse de l'organisme responsable du recensement:

Institut National de la Statistique et de l'Analyse Economique, Bureau central du recensement, B.P. 323, Cotonou.

2. Recensements de population effectués depuis 1945 (années):

1979 et 1992. La présente description se réfère au recensement de 1992 (qui a eu lieu du 15 au 29 février).

3. Champ du recensement:

a) *Territoire couvert*: Ensemble du pays.

b) *Personnes couvertes*: Ensemble de la population à l'exception des membres du corps diplomatique et des nationaux résidant à l'étranger.

4. Période de référence:

Les trois mois précédant le jour de l'interview.

5. Principaux sujets:

a) Population totale, selon le sexe et l'âge:	oui
Population active par:	
b) Sexe et âge:	oui
c) Branche d'activité économique (industrie):	oui
d) Profession:	oui
e) Situation dans la profession:	oui
f) Niveau d'instruction le plus élevé:	oui
g) Durée du travail:	non
h) Autres caractéristiques:	non

Réf. a): L'âge est défini en termes d'années révolues à la date du dernier anniversaire.

6. Concepts et définitions:

a) *Population active*: Elle comprend toutes les personnes âgées de 10 ans et plus qui, pendant la période de référence, étaient, soit pourvues d'un emploi, soit au chômage, conformément aux définitions ci-dessous. Toutefois, les données de population active, d'emploi et de chômage publiées ne se réfèrent qu'aux personnes âgées de 10 à 65 ans. La définition inclut l'ensemble des membres des forces armées. Les étudiants travaillant à temps partiel ainsi que les étudiants en quête de travail sont exclus de la définition.

b) *Emploi*: Sont considérées comme «occupées» toutes les personnes qui ont travaillé au moins une semaine au cours de la période de référence (trois derniers mois). Les femmes qui en plus des travaux ménagers ont travaillé pour leur propre compte ou le compte de la famille (vendeuse, couturière, cultivatrice, potière) sont considérées comme occupées. La question utilisée est: «occupation: occupé; cherche son premier emploi; chômeur; ménagère; ecoliers, élèves et étudiants; rentier».

Il est indiqué que sont inclus dans cette définition:

i) les personnes travaillant sans rémunération dans une entreprise ou une affaire familiale;
ii) les personnes engagées dans la production de produits de base destinés à l'autoconsommation;
iii) les personnes occupées, temporairement absentes du travail;
iv) les travailleurs saisonniers ou occasionnels;
v) les conscrits (service militaire ou civil);
vi) les apprentis et les stagiaires.

Seules les personnes appartenant aux catégories i) et vi) ci-dessus peuvent être identifiées séparément.

c) *Chômage*: Sont considérées comme «chômeurs» toutes les personnes ayant déjà travaillé mais qui, pendant la période de référence, étaient sans travail et à la recherche d'un emploi. Les personnes à la recherche de leur premier emploi sont identifiées séparément.

7. Classifications utilisées:

Aussi bien les personnes occupées que les chômeurs ayant précédemment travaillé sont classifiés par industrie, par profession et d'après la situation dans la profession.

a) *Branche d'activité économique (industrie)*: Basée sur la question: «Quelle est l'activité principale de l'entreprise ou de l'employeur de la personne occupée?». Dans le cas des chômeurs, on a déterminé la branche d'activité par rapport à leur dernier emploi. Pour coder la branche d'activité économique, neuf groupes ont été utilisés. Des liens avec la CITI-rév.2 ont été établis au niveau des branches (1 chiffre).

b) *Profession*: On a demandé à l'agent recenseur de poser la question selon le manuel d'instructions, qui indique qu'il s'agit de l'occupation principale ou de l'activité qui a le plus occupé la personne considérée pendant la période de référence. Pour un chômeur, il s'agit de la dernière profession exercée pendant la période de référence. Il a été recommandé d'éviter les réponses vagues telles que: commerçant, fonctionnaire, etc..., mais d'inscrire par exemple: vendeuse de pagne, vendeuse de beignets, inspecteur de police, inspecteur des impôts, etc... Pour coder la profession, neuf groupes ont été utilisés. Des liens avec la CITP-68 ont été établis au niveau des grands-groupes (1 chiffre).

c) *Situation dans la profession*: Basée sur la question: «Quel est le statut de la personne active par rapport à sa profession pendant la période de référence?». Pour coder cette variable, on a utilisé les huit catégories suivantes: indépendant; employeur; salarié permanent; salarié temporaire; membre de coopérative; apprenti; aide familial; autre.

8. Principales différences par rapport au recensement précédent:

Pour le recensement de 1979, on avait utilisé comme période de référence le mois précédant le jour du recensement.

9. Publication des résultats du recensement:

Les résultats définitifs sont parus en décembre 1993 dans la publication suivante: «Deuxième recensement général de la population et de l'habitation, février 1992», Volume I, résultats définitifs.

L'organisme responsable de la publication est l'Institut National de la Statistique et de l'analyse économique, Bureau central du recensement (BCR), B.P. 323, Cotonou.

Les résultats du recensement sont également disponibles sous forme de cartouches de Bernoulli.

BERMUDES

1. Nom et adresse de l'organisme responsable du recensement:

Bermuda Government Statistical Department, P.O. Box HM 177, Hamilton HM AX.

2. Recensements de population effectués depuis 1945 (années):

1950, 1960, 1970, 1980 et 1991. La présente description se réfère au recensement de 1991 (qui a eu lieu le 20 mai).

3. Champ du recensement:

a) Territoire couvert: Ensemble du pays.

b) Personnes couvertes: Ensemble de la population.

4. Période de référence:

La semaine et les 12 mois précédant le jour du recensement.

5. Principaux sujets:

a) Population totale, selon le sexe et l'âge:	oui
Population active par:	
b) Sexe et âge:	oui
c) Branche d'activité économique (industrie):	oui
d) Profession:	oui
e) Situation dans la profession:	oui
f) Niveau d'instruction le plus élevé:	oui
g) Durée du travail:	oui
h) Autres caractéristiques:	oui

Réf. a): L'âge est défini en termes d'années révolues le jour du recensement.

Réf. g): On a demandé aux personnes âgées de 16 ans et plus de spécifier le nombre de mois pendant lesquels elles avaient éventuellement travaillé contre rémunération au cours des 12 derniers mois soit pour un employeur, soit pour leur propre compte. On a demandé aux employés le nombre d'heures normalement effectuées dans une semaine type, y compris les heures supplémentaires payées ou non.

Réf. h): Le recensement a aussi rassemblé des informations sur les moyens de transport utilisés pour se rendre au travail, l'heure d'embauche et les échelles salariales.

6. Concepts et définitions:

a) Population active: Elle comprend toutes les personnes âgées de 16 ans et plus qui, au cours de la période de référence courte, étaient soit pourvues d'un emploi, soit au chômage, conformément aux définitions données ci-dessous. La définition inclut les membres des forces armées.

b) Emploi: Sont considérées comme «pourvues d'un emploi» toutes les personnes qui, pendant la semaine de référence, ont effectué un travail ayant une valeur économique, soit pour un employeur, soit pour leur propre compte. La question utilisée pour déterminer si une personne devait ou non être considérée comme pourvue d'un emploi était la suivante: «La semaine dernière que faisiez-vous la plupart du temps: travailliez-vous contre rémunération; étiez-vous à la recherche d'un nouvel emploi, étudiant, ménagère ou autre?». Les réponses possibles étaient: 1) salarié; 2) détenteur d'un emploi mais absent du travail; 3) demandeur d'emploi; 4) femme ou homme au foyer; 5) travailleur bénévole; 6) étudiant à plein temps; 7) incapable de travailler; 8) retraité; 9) autre; 10) sans réponse.

Il est indiqué que sont inclus dans cette définition:

i) les personnes travaillant sans rémunération dans une entreprise ou une affaire familiale;

ii) les personnes engagées dans la production de produits de base destinés à l'autoconsommation;

iii) les personnes occupées, temporairement absentes du travail;

iv) les étudiants travaillant à temps partiel;

v) les travailleurs saisonniers ou occasionnels;

vi) les conscrits (service militaire ou civil);

vii) les détenteurs de plusieurs emplois;

viii) les apprentis et les stagiaires.

Seules les personnes appartenant aux catégories i), iii) et vii) peuvent être identifiées séparément.

c) Chômage: Sont considérées comme «chômeurs» toutes les personnes qui, pendant la semaine de référence, ne travaillaient pas mais étaient à la recherche d'un premier emploi ou d'un nouvel emploi suite à la perte de leur précédent travail.

7. Classifications utilisées:

Seules les personnes pourvues d'un emploi ont été classifiées par branche d'activité économique, par profession et d'après la situation dans la profession.

a) Branche d'activité économique (industrie): Basée sur la question: «Quel type d'affaire ou d'activité est principalement exercé sur votre (principal) lieu de travail?» ex: banque, école primaire, étude de notaire, boutique de vêtements, restaurant. Pour coder l'industrie, on a utilisé 18 groupes de la classification nationale. Des liens ont été établis avec la CITI-Rév.2 au niveau des branches (1 chiffre).

b) Profession: Basée sur la question: «Quel type de travail effectuez-vous dans votre (principal) emploi?, ex: vendeur, ingénieur des travaux publics, responsable d'une imprimerie, mécanicien automobile, etc.». Pour coder la profession, on a utilisé la classification nationale. Des liens ont été établis avec la CITP-68.

c) Situation dans la profession: Basée sur la question: «La semaine dernière avez-vous effectué votre (principal) travail pour votre propre compte ou pour celui d'un employeur?». Pour coder la situation dans la profession on a utilisé sept groupes: travailleur indépendant: avec des salariés (employeur), sans salariés; employé: par le gouvernement des Bermudes, par un gouvernement étranger, par une entreprise ou une personne privée, comme travailleur non rémunéré dans une affaire familiale ou une ferme, et non précisé.

8. Principales différences par rapport au recensement précédent:

Les composantes du questionnaire sont très souvent reprises d'un recensement à l'autre afin de mesurer l'importance des changements intervenus. Le questionnaire sur les Bermudes va dans ce sens mais il cherche également à récolter de nouvelles informations dans certains domaines: le trajet pour se rendre au travail et le lieu de travail; b) l'état de santé physique et mental puisqu'il conditionne les activités quotidiennes de certaines personnes; et c) le revenu personnel.

9. Publication des résultats du recensement:

Les résultats définitifs sont parus dans la publication intitulée: «The 1991 Census of Population and Housing» en mars 1993 et dans «1991 Map Supplement» en novembre 1993.

L'organisme responsable de ces publications est le Département des statistiques du gouvernement des Bermudes, P.O. Box HM 177, Hamilton HM AX.

Des tableaux non publiés sur les résultats du recensement sont disponibles sur demande auprès du Département des statistiques du gouvernement des Bermudes.

BOLIVIE

1. Nom et adresse de l'organisme responsable du recensement:

Instituto Nacional de Estadística (INE), Plaza Mario Guzman Aspiazu No1, Casilla 6129, La Paz.

2. Recensements de population effectués depuis 1945 (années):

1950, 1976 et 1992. La présente description se réfère au recensement de population de 1992 (qui a eu lieu le 3 juin).

3. Champ du recensement:

a) Territoire couvert: Ensemble du pays.

b) Personnes couvertes: Ensemble de la population, à l'exception des nationaux résidant à l'étranger.

4. Période de référence:

La semaine précédant le jour du recensement.

5. Principaux sujets:

a) Population totale, selon le sexe et l'âge:	oui
Population active par:	
b) Sexe et âge:	oui
c) Branche d'activité économique (industrie):	oui
d) Profession:	oui

e) Situation dans la profession: oui
f) Niveau d'instruction le plus élevé: ...
g) Durée du travail: non
h) Autres caractéristiques: non

Réf. a): L'âge est défini en termes d'années révolues à la date du dernier anniversaire.

6. Concepts et définitions:

a) *Population active*: Elle comprend toutes les personnes âgées de 7 ans et plus qui, pendant la semaine de référence, étaient soit pourvues d'un emploi soit au chômage, conformément aux définitions données ci-dessous. La définition exclut les conscrits (service militaire ou civil) mais elle inclut les militaires de carrière.

b) *Emploi*: Sont considérées comme «pourvues d'un emploi» toutes les personnes ayant déclaré avoir travaillé pendant la semaine de référence.

Il est indiqué que sont inclus dans cette définition:

i)   les personnes travaillant sans rémunération dans une entreprise ou une affaire familiale;
ii)   les personnes engagées dans la production de produits de base destinés à l'autoconsommation;
iii) les personnes occupées, temporairement absentes de leur travail;
iv) les étudiants travaillant à temps partiel;
v)   les travailleurs saisonniers ou occasionnels;
vi) les détenteurs de plusieurs emplois;
vii) les apprentis et les stagiaires.

Les personnes appartenant aux catégories i), iii) et vi) peuvent être identifiées séparément au moyen de questions spécifiques.

c) *Chômage*: Sont considérées comme «chômeurs» les personnes qui, pendant la semaine de référence, ne travaillaient pas mais étaient à la recherche d'un emploi. Les questions utilisées pour déterminer si une personne est au chômage sont: «Etes-vous à la recherche d'un emploi en ayant déjà travaillé auparavant?» et «Etes-vous à la recherche d'un premier emploi?».

7. Classifications utilisées:
Seules les personnes pourvues d'un emploi sont classifiées par branche d'activité économique, par profession et d'après la situation dans la profession.

a) *Branche d'activité économique (industrie)*: Basée sur la question: «Que produit l'établissement dans lequel vous travaillez (ou dans lequel vous avez travaillé pour la dernière fois), ou quelle est son activité?». Pour déterminer la branche d'activité économique, on a demandé aux personnes pourvues d'un emploi le nom, l'adresse et le secteur d'activité économique de l'entreprise, de l'établissement ou de l'administration qui les employait ou qu'elles dirigeaient. Pour coder la branche d'activité économique, on a utilisé la CITI-rév.3 au niveau des classes (4 chiffres).

b) *Profession*: Basée sur la question: «Quelle était votre profession principale la semaine passée (ou dans votre dernier emploi si vous êtes au chômage)?». Pour déterminer le groupe de professions, on a demandé aux personnes pourvues d'un emploi d'indiquer avec précision la profession ou les fonctions qu'elles exerçaient pendant la période de référence. Pour coder le groupe de professions, on a utilisé la CITP-88 au niveau des sous-groupes (3 chiffres).

c) *Situation dans la profession*: Pour déterminer la situation dans la profession, on a utilisé les sept groupes suivants: employé, ouvrier, travailleur indépendant, patron ou employeur, membre d'une coopérative, profession libérale, travailleur familial.

8. Principales différences par rapport au recensement précédent:
Pas de différence majeure.

9. Publication des résultats du recensement:
Les résultats définitifs ont été publiés en mai 1993.

Le titre exact de la publication est «Censo Nacional de Población y Vivienda 1992: Resultados finales».

L'organisme responsable de cette publication est l'Institut national des statistiques, Plaza Mario Guzman Aspiazu No1, Casilla 6129, La Paz.

Les résultats du recensement sont également disponibles sous d'autres formes: archives (documents de travail); publication plus détaillée des résultats (indicateurs sociodémographiques

des capitales des départements - par zones de recensement - et des provinces); et base de données (disques magnétiques).

BOTSWANA

1. Nom et adresse de l'organisme responsable du recensement:
Central Statistics Office, Private Bag 0024, Gaborone.

2. Recensements de population effectués depuis 1945 (années):
1946, 1956, 1964, 1971, 1981 et 1991. La présente description se réfère au recensement de population de 1991 (qui a eu lieu du 14 au 28 août).

3. Champ du recensement:
a) *Territoire couvert*: Ensemble du pays.

b) *Personnes couvertes*: Ensemble de la population.

4. Période de référence:
Le mois précédant le jour du recensement.

5. Principaux sujets:
a) Population totale, selon le sexe et l'âge: oui
Population active par:
b) Sexe et âge: oui
c) Branche d'activité économique (industrie):   oui
d) Profession: oui
e) Situation dans la profession: oui
f) Niveau d'instruction le plus élevé: oui
g) Durée du travail: non
h) Autres caractéristiques: non

Réf. a): L'âge est défini en termes d'années révolues à la date du dernier anniversaire.

6. Concepts et définitions:

a) *Population active*: Elle comprend toutes les personnes âgées de 12 ans et plus qui, pendant le mois de référence, étaient soit pourvues d'un emploi, soit au chômage, conformément aux définitions données ci-dessous. La définition inclut les membres des forces armées.

b) *Emploi*: Sont considérées comme «pourvues d'un emploi» toutes les personnes qui, pendant le mois de référence, ont effectué un travail contre de l'argent comptant, soit pour leur propre compte, soit pour le compte d'autrui. La définition inclut également les personnes travaillant sur les terres familiales ou sur les lieux d'élevage du bétail.

Il est indiqué que sont inclus dans cette définition:

i)   les personnes travaillant sans rémunération dans une entreprise ou une affaire familiale;
ii)   les personnes engagées dans la production de produits de base destinés à l'autoconsommation;
iii) les personnes occupées, temporairement absentes de leur travail;
iv) les étudiants travaillant à temps partiel;
v)   les travailleurs saisonniers ou occasionnels.

Seules les personnes appartenant aux catégories i) et ii) peuvent être identifiées séparément.

c) *Chômage*: Sont considérées comme «chômeurs» toutes les personnes qui, pendant le mois de référence, étaient sans emploi et activement à la recherche d'un travail. Les étudiants en quête d'emploi sont exclus de la définition.

7. Classifications utilisées:
Seules les personnes pourvues d'un emploi sont classifiées par branche d'activité économique, par profession et d'après la situation dans la profession.

a) *Branche d'activité économique (industrie)*: Basée sur la question: «Quel était le principal type de produits, de services ou d'activités offert sur votre lieu de travail?». Pour coder la branche d'activité économique, on a utilisé neuf groupes de la classification nationale. Des liens ont été établis avec la CITI-rév.2 au niveau des branches (1 chiffre).

b) *Profession*: Basée sur la question: «Quel genre de travail avez-vous effectué?». Pour coder la profession, on a utilisé 10 groupes de la classification nationale. Des liens avec la CITP-88 ont été établis au niveau des grands groupes (1 chiffre).

c) Situation dans la profession: On a demandé aux personnes pourvues d'un emploi de préciser leur situation dans la profession. Pour coder cette dernière, on a utilisé les deux grands groupes suivants: salariés (personnes ayant travaillé pour autrui moyennant un traitement, un salaire, des honoraires, une commission, etc.) et travailleurs indépendants (travaillant pour leur propre compte, par exemple: agriculteurs cultivant la terre dans l'intention de vendre la récolte, propriétaires d'un magasin, colporteurs et personnes réparant les chaussures ou coupant les cheveux sous un arbre, etc.).

8. Principales différences par rapport au recensement précédent:
En 1991 la définition inclut la profession des personnes travaillant dans une affaire familiale, sur les terres, à la ferme ou sur les lieux d'élevage du bétail.

9. Publication des résultats du recensement:
Les résultats définitifs sont parus en 1994 dans une publication intitulée «1991 Population and Housing Census Administrative/Technical Report and National Statistical Tables».

L'organisme responsable de cette publication est le Bureau central des statistiques, Private Bag 0024, Gaborone.

Les données du recensement sont également disponibles sous forme de disquettes et de tableaux non publiés.

BRESIL

1. Nom et adresse de l'organisme responsable du recensement:
Instituto Brasileiro de Geografía e Eststística (IBGE/DPE/DEPOP), Rua Visconde de Niterói, 1246/Bloco B - 80 andar, Rio de Janeiro, RJ.

2. Recensements de population effectués depuis 1945 (années):
1950, 1960, 1970, 1980 et 1991. La présente description se réfère au recensement de population de 1991 (qui a eu lieu le 1er septembre).

3. Champ du recensement:
a) Territoire couvert: Ensemble du pays.

b) Personnes couvertes: Ensemble de la population (à l'exception des aborigènes).

4. Période de référence:
Un an (du 1er septembre 1990 au 31 août 1991).

5. Principaux sujets:
a) Population totale, selon le sexe et l'âge: oui
Population active par:
b) Sexe et âge: oui
c) Branche d'activité économique (industrie):   oui
d) Profession: oui
e) Situation dans la profession: oui
f) Niveau d'instruction le plus élevé: oui
g) Durée du travail: oui
h) Autres caractéristiques: oui

Réf. a): L'âge est défini en termes de mois et année de naissance; si ceux-ci ne sont pas connus, on se réfère à l'âge supposé.

Réf. g): La durée du travail est exprimée en nombre d'heures de travail hebdomadaires habituelles pour les personnes pourvues d'un emploi, dans leur emploi principal et dans tous ceux qu'elles exercent par ailleurs.

Réf. h): Il s'agit du revenu tiré de l'emploi principal et des autres emplois exercés.

6. Concepts et définitions:
a) Population active: Elle comprend toutes les personnes âgées de 10 ans et plus qui, pendant l'année de référence, étaient soit pourvues d'un emploi soit au chômage, conformément aux définitions données ci-dessous. La définition inclut également les membres des forces armées. Les questions relatives à l'emploi ou au chômage ont porté uniquement sur un échantillon de 20 pour cent des foyers dans les municipalités de 15 000 habitants ou moins, et de 10 pour cent des foyers dans les municipalités de plus de 15 000 habitants.

b) Emploi: Sont considérées comme «pourvues d'un emploi» toutes les personnes qui, pendant l'année de référence, ont travaillé pour un salaire, un bénéfice, une bourse, etc., ou qui ont travaillé sans rémunération pendant 15 heures par semaine ou plus pour aider un parent chez lequel elles résidaient, et qui ont répondu par l'affirmative à la question: «Avez-vous travaillé pendant tout ou partie des douze derniers mois (du 1/9/90 au 31/8/91)?».

Il est indiqué que sont inclus dans cette définition:
i)   les personnes travaillant sans rémunération dans une entreprise ou une affaire familiale;
ii)   les personnes occupées, temporairement absentes du travail;
iii)   les étudiants travaillant à temps partiel;
iv)   les travailleurs saisonniers ou occasionnels;
v)   les conscrits (service militaire ou civil);
vi)   les détenteurs de plusieurs emplois;
vii)   les apprentis et les stagiaires.

Seules les personnes appartenant aux catégories i), iii) et vi) peuvent être identifiées séparément au moyen de questions spécifiques.

c) Chômage: Sont considérées comme «chômeurs» toutes les personnes qui étaient sans travail mais à la recherche d'un emploi pendant l'année de référence, et ce qu'elles aient travaillé auparavant ou non, et qui ont répondu par la négative à la question utilisée pour la définition des personnes pourvues d'un emploi.

7. Classifications utilisées:
Seules les personnes pourvues d'un emploi sont classifiées par branche d'activité économique, par profession et d'après la situation dans la profession.

a) Branche d'activité économique (industrie): Pour déterminer la branche d'activité économique, on a demandé à l'intéressé le nom de l'entreprise, de l'organisation, de l'institution, etc. où il exerçait son emploi principal. Pour coder cette variable, on a utilisé 26 groupes de la classification nationale des activités économiques, laquelle est compatible avec la CITI-rév.2 au niveau des branches (1 chiffre).

b) Profession: Pour déterminer la profession, on a demandé aux intéressés quelles étaient la profession, la charge, les fonctions qu'ils exerçaient habituellement pendant l'année de référence. Si la personne avait définitivement changé de travail pendant cette période, la profession prise en compte était la profession actuelle et non la profession habituelle. Pour coder cette variable, on a utilisé 10 grands groupes de la classification nationale des professions, qui est comparable avec la CITP-68 au niveau des grands groupes (1 chiffre).

c) Situation dans la profession: Pour déterminer cette variable, on a demandé aux intéressés quelle était le poste qu'ils occupaient dans l'établissement, l'entreprise ou l'institution dans lequel ils travaillaient. Le codage a été effectué en utilisant 11 groupes (travailleur agricole saisonnier; travailleur à domicile (employé ou indépendant); métayer (employé ou indépendant); salarié du secteur public (services publics ou entreprise d'Etat); salarié du secteur privé; travailleur indépendant; employeur; travailleur bénévole).

8. Principales différences par rapport au recensement précédent:
Pour le recensement de 1980, deux périodes de référence avaient été utilisées: une période longue (de un an) pour définir la population active, les personnes pourvues d'un emploi et les chômeurs, et une période courte (la semaine précédant le recensement) pour mesurer les caractéristiques de la population.

9. Publication des résultats du recensement:
Les résultats définitifs du recensement ont été publiés en 1993.

L'organisme responsable de la publication des résultats est l'Institut brésilien de géographie et de statistiques, av. Franklin Roosevelt 166, 10o. andar Centro, Rio de Janeiro, RJ.

Les résultats du recensement sont également disponibles sous forme de tableaux non publiés, de disquettes, de bandes magnétiques et de micro-fiches.

BRUNEI DARUSSALAM

1. Nom et adresse de l'organisme responsable du recensement:
Economic Planning Unit, Ministry of Finance, Bandar Seri Begawan 2012, Brunei Darussalam.

2. Recensements de population effectués depuis 1945 (années):
1971, 1981 et 1991. La présente description se réfère au recensement de la population de 1991 (qui a eu lieu le 6 août).

3. Champ du recensement:

a) Territoire couvert: Ensemble du pays.

b) Personnes couvertes: Ensemble de la population.

4. Période de référence:
La semaine précédant l'énumération.

5. Principaux sujets:
a) Population totale, selon le sexe et l'âge: oui
Population active par:
b) Sexe et âge: oui
c) Branche d'activité économique (industrie):   oui
d) Profession: oui
e) Situation dans la profession: oui
f) Niveau d'instruction le plus élevé: oui
g) Durée du travail: oui
h) Autres caractéristiques: oui

Réf. a): L'âge est défini en termes de date de naissance.

Réf. g): Les personnes pourvues d'un emploi devaient indiquer leur nombre d'heures de travail effectives au cours de la période de référence.

Réf. h): Le recensement a aussi rassemblé des informations sur le revenu mensuel brut tiré de l'activité professionnelle rémunérée, et sur les primes perçues au cours des 12 derniers mois.

6. Concepts et définitions:

a) Population active: Elle comprend toutes les personnes âgées de 15 ans et plus qui, au cours de la semaine de référence, étaient soit pourvues d'un emploi soit au chômage, conformément aux définitions données ci-dessous. La définition inclut tous les membres des forces armées mais exclut les étudiants qui travaillent à temps partiel et les étudiants à la recherche d'un emploi.

b) Emploi: Sont considérées comme «pourvues d'un emploi» toutes les personnes ayant déclaré qu'elles travaillaient au cours de la période de référence. La question utilisée pour déterminer si une personne devait ou non être considérée comme pourvue d'un emploi était la suivante: «Activité économique: travaille; est à la recherche d'un emploi; autre».

Il est indiqué que sont inclus dans cette définition:

i) les personnes travaillant sans rémunération dans une entreprise ou une affaire familiale;

ii) les personnes engagées dans la production de produits de base destinés à l'autoconsommation;

iii) les personnes pourvues d'un emploi, temporairement absentes du travail;

iv) les travailleurs saisonniers ou occasionnels;

v) les conscrits (service militaire ou civil);

vi) les apprentis et les stagiaires.

Aucune des catégories susmentionnées ne peut être identifiée séparément.

c) Chômage: Sont considérées comme «chômeurs» toutes les personnes ayant déclaré qu'elles étaient à la recherche d'un emploi au cours de la période de référence. La question utilisée pour déterminer si une personne devait ou non être comptée comme chômeur était la même que celle indiquée au paragraphe 6 b ci-dessus.

7. Classifications utilisées:
Seules les personnes pourvues d'un emploi sont classifiées par branche d'activité, par profession et d'après la situation dans la profession.

a) Branche d'activité économique (industrie): Il a été demandé aux personnes pourvues d'un emploi d'indiquer le nom et l'adresse de leur employeur/entreprise, et de fournir des précisions sur la branche d'activité économique de leur employeur/entreprise. Pour coder la branche d'activité économique, on a utilisé 10 groupes de la classification nationale. Des liens avec la CITI-Rév.3 ont été établis au niveau des catégories de classement (1 chiffre).

b) Profession: Il a été demandé aux personnes pourvues d'un emploi d'indiquer de façon précise quelle était leur profession. Pour coder la profession, on a utilisé 10 groupes de la classification nationale. Des liens ont été établis avec la CITP-88 au niveau des grands groupes (1 chiffre).

c) Situation dans la profession: Il a été demandé aux personnes pourvues d'un emploi de préciser leur situation dans la profession. Pour coder cette variable, quatre groupes ont été utilisés: employeur; salarié; personne travaillant pour son propre compte; travailleur familial.

8. Principales différences par rapport au recensement précédent:
Pas de différence majeure.

9. Publication des résultats du recensement:
Les chiffres définitifs du recensement ont été publiés en 1993 dans deux documents intitulés respectivement «Rapport sur le recensement de la population de 1991 - juin 1993» et «Tableaux récapitulatifs du recensement de la population de 1991 - janvier 1993».

L'organisme responsable de ces publications est le Service de planification économique, Ministère des finances, B.S.B. 2012, Brunei Darussalam.

D'autres tableaux du recensement de 1991 qui ne sont pas inclus dans ces publications peuvent être obtenus sur demande, sous forme de tirages sur papier uniquement.

BULGARIE

1. Nom et adresse de l'organisme responsable du recensement:
Institut national de statistique, Division «Recensement de la population» 2, rue P. Volov, Sofia.

2. Recensements de population effectués depuis 1945 (années):
1946, 1956, 1965, 1975, 1985 et 1992. La présente description se réfère au recensement de la population de 1992 (qui a eu lieu le 4 décembre).

3. Champ du recensement:

a) Territoire couvert: Ensemble du pays.

b) Personnes couvertes: Ensemble de la population.

4. Période de référence:
Le jour du recensement.

5. Principaux sujets:
a) Population totale, selon le sexe et l'âge: oui
Population active par:
b) Sexe et âge: oui
c) Branche d'activité économique (industrie):   oui
d) Profession: oui
e) Situation dans la profession: non
f) Niveau d'instruction le plus élevé: oui
g) Durée du travail: non
h) Autres caractéristiques: non

Réf. a): L'âge est défini en termes d'année de naissance.

6. Concepts et définitions:

a) Population active: Elle comprend toutes les personnes âgées de 10 à 90 ans qui, le jour du recensement, étaient soit pourvues d'un emploi, soit au chômage, conformément aux définitions données ci-dessous. Les membres des forces armées sont inclus dans la définition.

b) Emploi: Sont considérées comme «pourvues d'emploi» toutes les personnes qui ont donné une réponse affirmative à la question «Est-ce que la personne travaille au 4.12.1992?».

Il est indiqué qu'entrent également dans cette définition:

i) les personnes travaillant sans rémunération dans une entreprise ou une affaire familiale;

ii) les personnes engagées dans la production de produits de base destinés à l'autoconsommation;

iii) les personnes occupées, temporairement absentes de leur travail;

iv) les étudiants travaillant à temps partiel;

v) les travailleurs saisonniers ou occasionnels;

vi) les conscrits (service militaire ou civil);

vii) les apprentis et les stagiaires.

Seules les catégories ii) et iv) ci-dessus peuvent être identifiées séparément.

c) Chômage: Sont considérées comme «chômeurs» les personnes qui ont déclaré qu'elles ne travaillaient pas à la date du recensement, qu'elles étaient au chômage et qu'elles cherchaient un emploi. Les étudiants en quête de travail sont exclus de la définition.

7. Classifications utilisées:

Toutes les personnes sauf les chômeurs sont classifiées par industrie. Les personnes occupées et les chômeurs ayant précédemment travaillé sont classifiés par profession.

a) Branche d'activité économique (industrie): La question posée se réfère au lieu de travail: dénomination, activité principale, adresse de l'entreprise. Pour coder la branche d'activité on a utilisé 40 groupes et 184 sous-groupes de la classification nationale. Des liens ont été établis avec la CITI-rév.3 au niveau des divisions (2 chiffres).

b) Profession: Basée sur la question: «Quelle est votre profession ou la fonction excercée?». Pour coder la profession, on a utilisé 46 groupes principaux et 642 sous-groupes. Des liens avec la CITP-88 ont été établis au niveau des sous-groupes (3 chiffres).

c) Situation dans la profession: Il n'y a pas eu de classification selon cette variable.

8. Principales différences par rapport au recensement précédent:

Les chômeurs ont été identifiés pour la première fois lors du recensement de 1992.

Par ailleurs, en 1985, la période de référence utilisée dans les questions posées sur l'activité économique était une longue période, à savoir les trois mois précédant la date du recensement; de plus, la limite d'âge inférieure retenue pour inclusion dans la population active était de 16 ans.

9. Publication des résultats du recensement:

Les résultats du recensement ont été publiés entre 1993 et 1995 dans un grand nombre de publications, dont «Demographic Characteristics (Volume I)» et «Socio-Economic Characteristics of the Population (Volume II)».

L'organisme responsable de ces publications est l'Institut National de Statistique, Division «Recensement de la population», 2. rue P. Volov, Sofia.

Les résultats du recensement de 1992 sont également disponibles sous forme de tableaux non publiés et de disquettes.

BURUNDI

1. Nom et adresse de l'organisme responsable du recensement:

Département de la Population, Bureau Central de Recensement, Pavillon administratif No. 3, B.P. 174, Gitega.

2. Recensements de population effectués depuis 1945 (années):

1979 et 1990. La présente description se réfère au recensement de 1990 (qui s'est référé à la nuit du 15 au 16 août).

3. Champ du recensement:

a) Territoire couvert: Ensemble du pays.

b) Personnes couvertes: Ensemble de la population.

4. Période de référence:

Les six mois précédant la date du recensement (soit du 15 février au 15 août 1990). Aux personnes qui n'ont pas du tout travaillé durant cette période, on a demandé si elles avaient travaillé avant.

5. Principaux sujets:

a) Population totale, selon le sexe et l'âge:	oui

Population active par:

b) Sexe et âge:	oui
c) Branche d'activité économique (industrie):	oui
d) Profession:	oui
e) Situation dans la profession:	oui
f) Niveau d'instruction le plus élevé:	oui
g) Durée du travail:	non
h) Autres caractéristiques:	oui

Réf. a): L'âge est défini en termes d'années révolues à la date du dernier anniversaire.

Réf. h): Des informations ont également été collectées sur le métier appris par les personnes occupées et par les chômeurs.

6. Concepts et définitions:

a) Population active: Elle comprend toutes les personnes âgées de 10 ans et plus qui, pendant la période de référence étaient, la plupart du temps, soit pourvues d'un emploi, soit au chômage, conformément aux définitions ci-dessous. La définition couvre également les membres des forces armées vivant dans les ménages ordinaires (un «ménage ordinaire» est généralement défini comme un groupe de personnes, apparentées ou non, qui vivent dans la même maison et qui, d'une façon générale, satisfont en commun à l'essentiel de leurs besoins alimentaires et autres besoins vitaux. Un ménage peut être composé d'une ou de plusieurs personnes).

b) Emploi: Sont considérées comme «pourvues d'emploi» toutes les personnes qui, pendant la période de référence, exerçaient la plupart du temps une profession, une fonction ou une activité économique. Les agriculteurs, les éleveurs et les femmes qui, en plus des travaux ménagers, s'occupent régulièrement des travaux des champs ou d'autres travaux à but lucratif, sont aussi couverts par la définition. La question posée était: «Au cours des six mois précédant le 15 août, X était la plupart du temps: 1) occupé; 2) chômeur; 3) étudiant; 4) ménagère; 5) retraité; 6) autre». Les étudiants qui travaillent à temps partiel sont exclus de la définition.

Il est indiqué que sont inclus dans cette définition:

i) les personnes engagées dans la production de produits de base destinés à l'autoconsommation;

ii) les personnes occupées, temporairement absentes du travail;

iii) les travailleurs saisonniers ou occasionnels;

iv) les conscrits (service militaire ou civil) vivant dans des ménages ordinaires;

v) les apprentis et les stagiaires.

Seules les personnes appartenant à la catégorie i) ci-dessus peuvent être identifiées séparément. Les étudiants qui travaillent ou qui peuvent travailler à temps partiel ou occasionnellement (par exemple pendant les vacances), ainsi que les personnes travaillant sans rémunération dans une entreprise ou dans une affaire familiale, bien que ne faisant pas partie de la population active, peuvent néanmoins être identifiés séparément.

c) Chômage: Sont considérées comme «chômeurs» toutes les personnes qui, pendant la période de référence, étaient sans travail et recherchaient soit un premier emploi soit un nouvel emploi. La définition couvre également les personnes désireuses de travailler, mais qui ne recherchaient pas activement de travail parce qu'elles estimaient qu'elles n'avaient aucune chance de trouver un emploi, ainsi que celles qui étaient dans l'attente d'un emploi à gages ou salarié devant débuter dans les 30 jours à venir.

7. Classifications utilisées:

Seules les personnes pourvues d'un emploi sont classifiées par industrie, par profession et d'après la situation dans la profession.

a) Branche d'activité économique (industrie): Basée sur les questions: «Dans quelle branche ou dans quel domaine d'activité économique travaille Monsieur ou Madame X?» et «Quelle est l'activité de l'unité de production (moderne ou traditionnelle) dans laquelle travaille Monsieur ou Madame X?». La branche d'activité correspond au secteur économique où travaille une personne ayant déclaré une activité principale au cours de la période de référence. Pour coder la branche d'activité, on a utilisé 10 groupes. Des liens avec la CITI-rév.2 ont été établis au niveau des branches (1 chiffre).

b) Profession: Basée sur la question: «Quelle profession X exerçait-il au cours des six mois précédant le 15 août 1990?». La profession exercée correspond au type de travail effectué par une personne occupée; elle ne relève pas du rang, du grade ou de la fonction, ni toujours du métier de la personne, mais uniquement de la nature du travail réellement accompli au cours de la période de référence. Pour coder la profession, on a utilisé 10 grands groupes. Des liens avec la CITP-88 ont été établis au niveau des grands groupes (1 chiffre).

c) Situation dans la profession: Basée sur la question: «Dans l'activité exercée, Monsieur ou Madame X était-il/était-elle: employeur, salarié, indépendant, apprenti, aide familial(e) ou tâcheron?». Pour coder la situation dans la profession, on a utilisé les six catégories ci-dessus. Des questions filtres ont en outre été posées pour savoir si l'actif occupé travaillait seul pour son propre compte ou s'il employait du personnel.

8. Principales différences par rapport au recensement précédent:

Dans le recensement de 1979:

a) la période de référence considérée lors des questions posées sur la population active, l'emploi et le chômage était la semaine précédant le recensement;

b) la question sur la qualification n'avait pas été posée;

c) les questions sur la branche d'activité économique, la profession et la situation dans la profession avaient été posées aussi bien aux personnes pourvues d'un emploi qu'aux chômeurs.

9. Publication des résultats du recensement:

La publication contenant les résultats définitifs du recensement avait été annoncée pour 1992.

L'organisme responsable de la publication est le Département de la Population, Bureau Central de Recensement, B.P. 174, Gitega.

Les résultats du recensement de 1990 sont également disponibles sous forme de tableaux contenant des résultats bruts non publiés et de disquettes.

CANADA

1. Nom et adresse de l'organisme responsable du recensement:

Statistics Canada; Jean-Talon Bldg, Section A-2, 5th floor, Tunney's Pasture, Ottawa.

2. Recensements de population effectués depuis 1945 (années):

1951, 1961, 1971, 1976, 1981, 1986 et 1991. La présente description se réfère au recensement de 1991 (qui a eu lieu le 4 juin).

3. Champ du recensement:

a) Territoire couvert: Ensemble du pays.

b) Personnes couvertes: Ensemble de la population à l'exception des résidents étrangers. Les questions sur l'emploi ont été posées aux résidents non-institutionnels âgés de 15 ans et plus.

4. Période de référence:

La semaine précédant le jour du recensement. Si la personne interrogée ne travaillait pas pendant la semaine de référence, c'est l'emploi de plus longue durée exercé depuis le 1er janvier 1990 qui a servi pour déterminer la branche d'activité économique et la profession.

5. Principaux sujets:

a) Population totale, selon le sexe et l'âge:	oui
Population active par:	
b) Sexe et âge:	oui
c) Branche d'activité économique (industrie):	oui
d) Profession:	oui
e) Situation dans la profession:	oui
f) Niveau d'instruction le plus élevé:	oui
g) Durée du travail:	oui
h) Autres caractéristiques:	oui

Réf. a): L'âge est défini soit en termes d'année de naissance, soit en termes de date de naissance exacte (jour, mois et année).

Réf. g): La durée du travail est exprimée en heures réellement effectuées par les personnes pourvues d'un emploi, présentes au travail.

Réf. h): Le recensement a également rassemblé des informations sur d'autres sujets, à savoir: l'enregistrement des entreprises appartenant à des travailleurs indépendants, le nombre de semaines de travail à plein temps et à temps partiel effectuées dans l'année civile (non compris les travaux ménagers, les travaux d'entretien ou de réparation réalisés pour le logement personnel) ainsi que les sources de revenu, y compris les salaires.

6. Concepts et définitions:

a) Population active: Elle comprend toutes les personnes âgées de 15 ans et plus qui, pendant la semaine de référence, étaient soit pourvues d'un emploi, soit au chômage, conformément aux définitions données ci-dessous. Les questions sur la population active ont été posées à un échantillon de 20 pour cent de la population. La définition inclut tous les membres des forces armées.

b) Emploi: Sont considérées comme «pourvues d'un emploi» toutes les personnes de l'échantillon qui, pendant la semaine de référence, avaient un emploi et avaient effectué des heures de travail ou étaient temporairement absentes de leur travail (mise à pied temporaire d'un emploi qu'elles pensaient retrouver, ou en vacances, en grève, en lock-out, en congé de maladie etc.). Les questions posées étaient: «La semaine dernière, combien d'heures avez-vous accomplies (non compris le bénévolat, les travaux ménagers, les travaux d'entretien ou de réparation pour votre propre logement)?» et «La semaine dernière, étiez-vous absent de votre emploi ou de votre entreprise?».

Il est indiqué que sont inclus dans cette définition:

i) les personnes travaillant sans rémunération dans une entreprise ou une affaire familiale;

ii) les personnes engagées dans la production de produits de base destinés à l'autoconsommation;

iii) les étudiants travaillant à temps partiel (uniquement ceux engagés dans des études supérieures et qui étaient en mesure de démarrer un emploi pendant la semaine de référence).

iv) les travailleurs saisonniers ou occasionnels;

v) les conscrits (service militaire ou civil);

vi) les apprentis et les stagiaires.

Les personnes appartenant aux catégories i) et iii) ainsi que les personnes pourvues d'un emploi mais temporairement absentes du travail, peuvent être identifiées séparément grâce à des questions spécifiques. L'identification des étudiants qui travaillent peut être hasardeuse: on a demandé aux personnes interrogées de préciser si elles avaient poursuivi des études au cours des neuf derniers mois, à savoir depuis le mois de septembre précédent; ce qui ne signifie pas automatiquement qu'elles étaient toujours étudiantes au moment du recensement ou lorsqu'elles effectuaient le travail annoncé dans la branche d'activité économique et la profession (plein temps, temps partiel, etc.).

c) Chômage: Sont considérées comme «chômeurs» toutes les personnes de l'échantillon qui, pendant la semaine de référence, étaient sans emploi ou mises à pied avec espoir de récupérer leur emploi ou celles qui étaient activement à la recherche d'un travail au cours des quatre dernières semaines et disponibles pour travailler. Entrent aussi dans la définition les personnes qui avaient pris des dispositions fermes pour démarrer un nouveau travail dans un délai de quatre semaines ou moins. Les questions posées étaient: «La semaine dernière, étiez-vous temporairement mis à pied ou absent de votre travail ou de votre entreprise?»; «La semaine dernière, aviez-vous pris des dispositions fermes pour prendre un emploi dans un délai de quatre semaines?»; «Recherchiez-vous un emploi au cours des quatre dernières semaines?» et «Etiez-vous disponible la semaine passée pour démarrer un éventuel travail?».

7. Classifications utilisées:

Aussi bien les personnes pourvues d'un emploi que les chômeurs ayant précédemment travaillé sont classifiés par industrie, par profession et d'après la situation dans la profession. Les questions posées à ces personnes concernaient respectivement leur emploi ou leur entreprise pendant la semaine de référence ou l'emploi le plus long exercé depuis le 1er janvier 1990. Les détenteurs de plusieurs emplois pendant la semaine de référence devaient préciser le travail dont la durée a été la plus longue.

a) Branche d'activité économique (industrie): Basée sur les questions: «Pour qui avez-vous travaillé? (nom de l'entreprise, de l'agence gouvernementale, etc.; département, branche, division, service ou usine)»; «Quel type d'affaire, d'industrie ou de service était-ce? (par exemple: céréaliculture, trappe, entretien des routes, boutique de chaussures, école secondaire, police municipale)» et «A quelle adresse avez-vous travaillé?». Pour coder la branche d'activité, on a utilisé 286 groupes de base de la Classification type par industrie de 1970 et 296 groupes de base de la Classification type par industrie de 1980. Il n'a pas été établi de liens avec la CITI; cependant une approximation a été faite au niveau des branches (1 chiffre) de la CITI-rév.2 afin de fournir des données au BIT et à d'autres institutions spécialisées du système des Nations Unies.

b) Profession: Basée sur les questions: «Quel type de travail faisiez-vous? (par exemple: technicien de laboratoire médical, employé comptable, directeur du département des travaux publics, professeur au secondaire, surveillant à l'unité d'entrée des données, ouvrier dans la transformation des aliments, guide de pêche; si vous êtes dans les forces armées, précisez seulement le grade)» et «Dans ce travail, quelles étaient vos principales activités ou tâches? (par exemple: analyse d'échantillons de sang, vérification des factures, coordination des projets de travaux publics, cours de mathématiques, organisation de programmes de travail, contrôle des systèmes d'entrée des données, nettoyage des légumes, organisation de parties de pêche)». En outre, on a posé des questions sur l'adresse du lieu de travail. Pour coder la profession, on a utilisé 496 groupes de base de la Classification des professions de 1971, 514 groupes de base de la Classification type des professions de 1980 et 505 groupes de base de la nouvelle Classification nationale des professions. Il n'a pas été établi de liens avec la CITP. Cependant une approximation a été faite au niveau des grands groupes (1 chiffre) de la CITP-68 afin de fournir des données au BIT et à d'autres institutions spécialisées du système des Nations Unies.

c) *Situation dans la profession*: Basée sur les questions: «Dans cette activité, avez-vous travaillé: moyennant salaire, traitement, pourboire ou commission; sans rémunération pour votre conjoint ou un autre parent dans une exploitation ou une entreprise familiale; comme travailleur indépendant sans aides rémunérés (seul ou en association); comme travailleur indépendant avec des aides rémunérés (seul ou en association)?» et uniquement pour les travailleurs indépendants: «Votre exploitation ou votre entreprise était-elle enregistrée?». Pour coder la situation dans la profession on a utilisé les quatre groupes ci-dessus.

8. Principales différences par rapport au recensement précédent:
En 1991, on a élargi la couverture du recensement par l'inclusion des demandeurs d'asile et des détenteurs d'un visa étudiant, d'un permis de travail ou d'une autorisation ministérielle.

9. Publication des résultats du recensement:
Les séries de publications nationales contenant les résultats du recensement sont: «Labour Force Activity» (cat. 93-324); «Labour Force Activity of Women by Presence of Children» (cat. 93-325); «Industry and Class of Worker» (cat. 93-326) et «Occupation» (cat. 93-327), parues en 1993.

L'organisme responsable de ces publications est Statistics Canada, Ottawa.

Les résultats du recensement sont également disponibles sous forme de disquettes, de bandes magnétiques et de CD-ROM.

CAP-VERT

1. Nom et adresse de l'organisme responsable du recensement:
Ministério do Plano e das Finanças, Direcçao Geral de Estatística, Divisao de Censos e Inquéritos, C.P. 116, Praia.

2. Recensements de population effectués depuis 1945 (années):
1960, 1970, 1980 et 1990. La présente description se réfère au recensement de 1990 (qui s'est déroulé du 16 au 30 juin).

3. Champ du recensement:
a) *Territoire couvert*: Ensemble du pays.

b) *Personnes couvertes*: Ensemble de la population, à l'exception des nationaux résidant à l'étranger.

4. Période de référence:
La semaine précédant la date du dénombrement.

5. Principaux sujets:
a) Population totale, selon le sexe et l'âge:	oui
Population active par:	
b) Sexe et âge:	oui
c) Branche d'activité économique (industrie):	oui
d) Profession:	oui
e) Situation dans la profession:	oui
f) Niveau d'instruction le plus élevé:	oui
g) Durée du travail:	non
h) Autres caractéristiques:	oui

Réf. a): L'âge est défini en termes d'année de naissance.

Réf. h): Des questions ont aussi été posées aux inactifs sur leur principal moyen d'existence.

6. Concepts et définitions:
a) *Population active*: Elle comprend toutes les personnes âgées de 10 ans et plus qui, pendant la semaine de référence, étaient soit pourvues d'un emploi, soit au chômage, conformément aux définitions ci-dessous. La définition inclut tous les membres des forces armées (militaires de carrière et conscrits).

b) *Emploi*: Sont considérées comme «pourvues d'un emploi» toutes les personnes qui, pendant la semaine de référence, exerçaient une profession, une fonction ou une quelconque activité économique, rémunérée ou non. La question utilisée était: «Condition face au travail: 1) occupé; 2) chômeur ayant déjà travaillé; 3) chômeur à la recherche de son premier emploi; 4) étudiant; 5) ménagère; 6) retraité ou pensionné; 7) invalide ou malade; et 8) autre».

Il est indiqué que sont inclus dans cette définition:

i) les personnes travaillant sans rémunération dans une entreprise ou une affaire familiale;

ii) les personnes engagées dans la production de produits de base destinés à l'autoconsommation;

iii) les personnes occupées, temporairement absentes du travail;

iv) les étudiants travaillant à temps partiel;

v) les travailleurs saisonniers ou occasionnels;

vi) les conscrits (service militaire ou civil);

vii) les apprentis et les stagiaires.

Seules les personnes appartenant aux catégories i), vi) et vii) ci-dessus peuvent être identifiées séparément au moyen de questions spécifiques.

c) *Chômage*: Sont considérées comme «chômeurs» toutes les personnes qui, pendant la semaine de référence, étaient sans travail, désiraient travailler et recherchaient soit un premier emploi soit un nouvel emploi. La définition couvre également les personnes désireuses de travailler, mais qui ne recherchaient pas activement de travail parce qu'elles pensaient n'avoir aucune chance de trouver un emploi.

7. Classifications utilisées:
Aussi bien les personnes occupées que les chômeurs ayant précédemment travaillé sont classifiés par industrie, par profession et d'après la situation dans la profession.

a) *Branche d'activité économique (industrie)*: Basée sur la question: «Indiquez l'activité de l'établissement dans lequel la personne travaille ou a travaillé en dernier lieu». Pour coder l'industrie, on a utilisé 10 groupes de la classification nationale. Des liens avec la CITI-rév.2 ont été établis au niveau des branches (1 chiffre).

b) *Profession*: Basée sur la question: «Indiquez la profession principale que la personne exerce ou a exercée en dernier lieu». Pour coder la profession, on a utilisé neuf groupes de la classification nationale. Des liens avec la CITP-68 ont été établis au niveau des grands groupes (1 chiffre).

c) *Situation dans la profession*: Une question a été posée aux personnes occupées et aux chômeurs ayant précédemment travaillé pour déterminer leur situation dans la profession du moment ou dans leur dernière profession. Pour coder la situation dans la profession, on a utilisé sept catégories: indépendant; employeur; fonctionnaire ou employé; salarié à la journée; apprenti; membre d'une coopérative de producteurs; autre travailleur non rémunéré.

8. Principales différences par rapport au recensement précédent:
Lors du recensement de 1980, les questions relatives aux caractéristiques économiques avaient été posées aux personnes âgées de 7 ans et plus; toutefois, la publication des données sur la population active et ses composantes (emploi et chômage) avait été limitée aux personnes âgées de 14 ans et plus.

9. Publication des résultats du recensement:
Le titre de la publication dans laquelle ont été présentés les résultats de ce recensement est: «IIo Recenseamento da Populaçao e Habitaçao - 1990», 1992.

L'organisme responsable de cette publication est la Direcçao Geral de Estatística, Ministério das Finanças e do Plano, Praia.

Les résultats du recensement de 1990 sont également disponibles sous forme de tableaux non publiés, de disquettes et de bandes magnétiques.

REP. CENTRAFRICAINE

La description du recensement de 1988 de la République centrafricaine est publiée dans ce volume parce qu'elle n'était pas disponible lors de la parution de la première édition.

1. Nom et adresse de l'organisme responsable du recensement:

Ministère de l'Economie, du Plan, des Statistiques et de la Coopération internationale, Bureau Central du Recensement (BCR), B.P. 696, Bangui.

2. Recensements de population effectués depuis 1945 (années):

1975 et 1988. La présente description se réfère au recensement de 1988, qui a eu lieu du 8 au 22 décembre (date de référence le 15 décembre).

3. Champ du recensement:

a) *Territoire couvert*: Ensemble du pays.

b) *Personnes couvertes*: Ensemble de la population.

4. Période de référence:

Les sept jours précédant le jour du recensement.

5. Principaux sujets:

a) Population totale, selon le sexe et l'âge:	oui
Population active par:	
b) Sexe et âge:	oui
c) Branche d'activité économique (industrie):	oui
d) Profession:	oui
e) Situation dans la profession:	oui
f) Niveau d'instruction le plus élevé:	oui
g) Durée du travail:	non
h) Autres caractéristiques:	non

Réf. a): L'âge est défini en termes d'années révolues à la date du dernier anniversaire pour les personnes dont le jour, le mois et l'année de naissance sont connus, et en termes d'année de naissance pour les autres.

6. Concepts et définitions:

a) *Population active*: Elle comprend toutes les personnes âgées de 6 ans et plus qui, pendant la période de référence étaient, soit pourvues d'un emploi, soit au chômage, conformément aux définitions ci-dessous. La définition inclut les militaires de carrière, mais exclut les personnes effectuant leur service militaire obligatoire.

b) *Emploi*: Sont considérées comme «pourvues d'emploi» toutes les personnes qui ont déclaré avoir exercé, pendant la période de référence, une profession, une fonction ou une activité économique quelconque, rémunérée ou non, à domicile ou à l'extérieur. Les femmes qui, en plus des travaux ménagers, s'occupent régulièrement des travaux des champs ou d'autres travaux, sont aussi couvertes par la définition. Les étudiants qui travaillent à temps partiel sont exclus de la définition.

Il est indiqué que sont inclus dans cette définition:

i) les personnes travaillant sans rémunération dans une entreprise ou une affaire familiale (à plein temps seulement);

ii) les personnes engagées dans la production de produits de base destinés à l'autoconsommation;

iii) les personnes occupées, temporairement absentes du travail;

iv) les travailleurs saisonniers ou occasionnels;

v) les apprentis et les stagiaires.

Seules les personnes appartenant aux catégories i) et v) ci-dessus peuvent être identifiées séparément au moyen de questions spécifiques.

c) *Chômage*: Sont considérées comme «chômeurs» toutes les personnes qui ont déclaré n'avoir pas travaillé du tout pendant la période de référence. La définition couvre aussi bien les chômeurs qui avaient précédemment travaillé que les personnes qui étaient à la recherche de leur premier emploi.

Il y a lieu de noter que le recensement de 1988 a sous-estimé le volume du chômage d'environ 6 pour cent, en raison de la période de référence courte (une semaine) et à cause du manque d'informations sur la durée du travail. Parallèlement, les travailleurs temporaires et ceux du secteur informel ont gonflé exagérément le nombre des personnes occupées.

7. Classifications utilisées:

Aussi bien les personnes pourvues d'un emploi que les chômeurs ayant précédemment travaillé sont classifiés par industrie, par profession et d'après la situation dans la profession.

a) *Branche d'activité économique (industrie)*: La question posée pour déterminer le groupe d'industrie a trait à l'activité de l'établissement dans lequel a travaillé la personne (ou a travaillé pour la dernière fois). Pour coder la branche d'activité, on a utilisé la CITI-rév.2 au niveau des branches (1 chiffre).

b) *Profession*: Une question spécifique a été posée aussi bien aux personnes occupées qu'aux chômeurs ayant précédemment travaillé pour déterminer la profession qu'ils exercent ou ont exercée pour la dernière fois. Pour coder la profession, on a utilisé la CITP-68 au niveau des groupes de base (3 chiffres).

c) *Situation dans la profession*: Une question spécifique a été posée aussi bien aux personnes occupées qu'aux chômeurs ayant précédemment travaillé pour déterminer leur situation dans la profession actuelle ou antérieure. Pour coder la situation dans la profession, on a utilisé les cinq catégories suivantes: indépendant; employeur; salarié; aide familiale; apprenti(e) non rémunéré(e).

8. Principales différences par rapport au recensement précédent:

Essentiellement, les mêmes questions et la même période de référence avaient été utilisées au recensement de 1975 pour inclure une personne dans la population active et ses composantes (emploi et chômage).

Comme indiqué sous 6 c), la période de référence courte d'une semaine, d'une part, et les travailleurs temporaires ainsi que ceux du secteur informel, d'autre part, ont eu pour effet respectivement de sous-estimer le volume du chômage et de gonfler le nombre des personnes occupées. Il est donc envisagé de revoir les définitions et la période de référence lors du prochain recensement, prévu pour 1998.

9. Publication des résultats du recensement:

Les résultats devaient être publiés en 1992 dans les volumes suivants: «Tableaux statistiques», contenant des données sur la population active et ses composantes, et «Rapports d'analyse» (12 tomes consacrés à 12 thèmes d'analyse).

L'organisme responsable de ces publications est le Bureau Central du Recensement (BCR), Division des Statistiques et des Etudes Economiques, à Bangui.

Toutes les données relatives au recensement de 1988 sont stockées sur disque dur, avec possibilité de les copier sur disquettes.

CHILI

1. Nom et adresse de l'organisme responsable du recensement:

Instituto Nacional de Estadísticas (INE), Avda. Bulnes 418, Santiago, Chili.

2. Recensements de population effectués depuis 1945 (années):

1952, 1960, 1970, 1982 et 1992. La présente description se réfère au recensement de population de 1992 (qui a eu lieu le 22 avril).

3. Champ du recensement:

a) *Territoire couvert*: Ensemble du pays.

b) *Personnes couvertes*: Ensemble de la population.

4. Période de référence:

La semaine précédant le recensement.

5. Principaux sujets:

a) Population totale, selon le sexe et l'âge:	oui
Population active par:	
b) Sexe et âge:	oui
c) Branche d'activité économique (industrie):	oui
d) Profession:	oui
e) Situation dans la profession:	oui
f) Niveau d'instruction le plus élevé:	...
g) Durée du travail:	non
h) Autres caractéristiques:	non

Réf. a): L'âge est défini en termes d'années révolues à la date du dernier anniversaire.

6. Concepts et définitions:

a) Population active: Elle comprend toutes les personnes âgées de 14 ans et plus qui, pendant la semaine de référence, étaient soit pourvues d'un emploi soit au chômage, conformément aux définitions données ci-dessous. La définition inclut les militaires de carrière mais exclut les conscrits effectuant leur service militaire obligatoire.

b) Emploi: Sont considérées comme «pourvues d'un emploi» les personnes qui, pendant la semaine de référence, exerçaient une activité rémunérée. La question utilisée était: «Dans laquelle des situations suivantes vous trouviez-vous la semaine passée? 1) travailleur rémunéré; 2) ne travaillait pas, mais était pourvu d'un emploi; 3) travaillait sans rémunération pour un membre de sa famille; 4) à la recherche d'un emploi en ayant déjà travaillé auparavant; 5) à la recherche d'un premier emploi; 6) travailleur au foyer; 7) étudiant ne travaillant pas; 8) pensionné ou retraité sans emploi; 9) atteint d'une incapacité de travail permanente; 10) autre situation».

Il est indiqué que sont inclus dans cette définition:

i)   les personnes travaillant sans rémunération dans une entreprise ou une affaire familiale;

ii)   les personnes engagées dans la production de produits de base destinés à l'autoconsommation;

iii)   les personnes occupées, temporairement absentes de leur travail;

iv)   les étudiants travaillant à temps partiel;

v)   les travailleurs saisonniers ou occasionnels, à condition qu'ils aient été pourvus d'un emploi pendant la semaine de référence;

vi)   les apprentis et les stagiaires.

Seules les personnes appartenant aux catégories i) et iii) peuvent être identifiées séparément.

c) Chômage: Sont considérées comme «chômeurs» les personnes qui n'avaient pas d'emploi au cours de la semaine de référence et avaient déjà travaillé auparavant (chômeurs avec expérience professionnelle), ou les personnes qui étaient activement à la recherche d'un emploi pendant la semaine de référence et n'avaient jamais travaillé auparavant (à la recherche d'un premier emploi).

7. Classifications utilisées:

Aussi bien les personnes pourvues d'un emploi que les chômeurs ayant déjà travaillé auparavant ont été classifiés par branche d'activité économique, par profession et d'après la situation dans la profession.

a) Branche d'activité économique (industrie): La question utilisée pour déterminer la branche d'activité économique est: «De quoi s'occupe principalement l'établissement, l'entreprise, le commerce, l'usine, etc. où vous travaillez (ou où vous travailliez si vous êtes actuellement chômeur)? Exemples: usine de fabrication de chemises, hôpital, ministère, centre d'élevage, banque, supermarché, atelier radio-TV, magasin de tissus, etc.». Cette variable a été codée en utilisant la CITI-rév.3 au niveau des groupes (3 chiffres).

b) Profession: La question utilisée pour déterminer la profession est: «Indiquez la profession ou le type de travail que vous exercez (ou exerciez si vous êtes sans activité). Exemples: maçon, pédiatre, tailleur, mécanicien auto, opérateur de machine textile, vendeur ambulant, etc.». Cette variable a été codée en utilisant la CITP-88 au niveau des groupes de base (4 chiffres).

c) Situation dans la profession: La question utilisée pour déterminer cette caractéristique, codée en cinq groupes, est: «Dans votre emploi, êtes-vous (ou étiez-vous) patron ou employeur, travailleur indépendant, travailleur au foyer, travailleur salarié (employé, ouvrier, journalier), travailleur familial sans rémunération?».

8. Principales différences par rapport au recensement précédent:

Pas de différence majeure.

9. Publication des résultats du recensement:

Les résultats définitifs du recensement ont été publiés en septembre 1993.

Le titre exact de la publication dans laquelle sont présentés les résultats est «Resultados Generales - XVI Censo Nacional y V de Vivienda 1992».

L'organisme responsable de cette publication est l'Institut national des statistiques, Avda. Bulnes 418, Santiago.

Les résultats du recensement sont également disponibles sous forme de disquettes.

CHINE

1. Nom et adresse de l'organisme responsable du recensement:

State Statistical Bureau, 38 Yuetan Nanjie, Sanlihe, Beijing 100826.

2. Recensements de population effectués depuis 1945 (années):

1953, 1964, 1982 et 1990. La présente description se réfère au recensement de 1990 (qui a eu lieu le 1er juillet).

3. Champ du recensement:

a) Territoire couvert: Ensemble du pays.

b) Personnes couvertes: Ensemble de la population.

4. Période de référence:

Le jour précédant celui du recensement et le mois antérieur au jour du recensement.

5. Principaux sujets:

a) Population totale, selon le sexe et l'âge:	oui
Population active par:	
b) Sexe et âge:	oui
c) Branche d'activité économique (industrie):	oui
d) Profession:	oui
e) Situation dans la profession:	non
f) Niveau d'instruction le plus élevé:	oui
g) Durée du travail:	non
h) Autres caractéristiques:	non

Réf. a): L'âge est défini en termes d'années révolues à la date du dernier anniversaire.

6. Concepts et définitions:

a) Population active: Elle comprend toutes les personnes âgées de 15 ans et plus qui, pendant le mois de référence, étaient soit pourvues d'un emploi, soit au chômage, conformément aux définitions données ci-dessous.

La définition inclut tous les membres des forces armées mais exclut les étudiants travaillant à temps partiel et les étudiants en quête d'emploi.

b) Emploi: Sont considérées comme «pourvues d'un emploi» toutes les personnes qui ont perçu une rémunération en échange d'un travail ou tiré un revenu d'une affaire. La définition inclut les personnes occupant un emploi régulier au cours de la période de référence et celles qui, sans emploi régulier, exerçaient une activité temporaire le 30 juin 1990 en ayant accumulé une période de travail d'au moins 16 jours pendant le mois de juin.

Il est indiqué que sont inclus dans cette définition:

i)   les personnes occupées, temporairement absentes du travail;

ii)   les travailleurs saisonniers ou occasionnels;

iii)   les conscrits (service militaire ou civil);

iv)   les apprentis et les stagiaires.

Seuls les conscrits (service militaire ou civil) peuvent être identifiés séparément.

c) Chômage: Sont considérées comme «chômeurs» toutes les personnes en âge de travailler (15 à 50 ans pour les hommes et 15 à 45 ans pour les femmes), capables d'occuper un emploi, à la recherche d'un travail et inscrites auprès des agences gouvernementales locales comme chômeurs.

7. Classifications utilisées:

Seules les personnes pourvues d'un emploi ont été classifiées par branche d'activité économique et par profession. Aucune classification n'a été faite d'après la situation dans la profession.

a) Branche d'activité économique (industrie): Pour déterminer le groupe d'industrie, on a demandé aux personnes pourvues d'un emploi d'indiquer le nom et l'activité spécifique de l'établissement les employant actuellement ou précédemment. Le nom indiqué est une unité comptable indépendante identifiant une entreprise étatique, collective ou coopérative ou une entreprise privée. Dans le cas d'un grand complexe industriel, d'une grande usine ou entreprise minière, le nom de l'unité subordonnée est clairement identifié. Par exemple, sidérurgie dans l'industrie métallurgique, département volaille ou oeufs, etc. Pour coder l'industrie, on a utilisé 13 groupes de la classification nationale. Des liens ont été établis avec la CITI-rév.2 au niveau des branches (1 chiffre).

b) Profession: On a posé aux personnes pourvues d'un emploi des questions visant à déterminer le travail spécifique effectué ou le travail dans lequel elles se trouvent impliquées. Par exemple, les travailleurs industriels ont été classifiés comme assembleurs, compositeurs, conducteurs, etc.; les employés de bureau comme planificateurs, statisticiens, secrétaires, etc. Les personnes détenant plusieurs emplois devaient préciser la profession à laquelle elles ont consacré le plus de temps pendant l'année en cours. Pour coder la profession, on a utilisé huit groupes de la classification nationale. Des liens ont été établis avec la CITP-68 au niveau des grands groupes (1 chiffre).

c) Situation dans la profession: Il n'y a pas eu de classification selon cette variable.

8. Principales différences par rapport au recensement précédent:
Lors du recensement de 1990, les personnes en attente d'un travail ont été incluses dans la population active alors que pour celui de 1982 elles en étaient exclues.

De plus, en 1990 on a posé une question sur la migration incluant le lieu de résidence cinq ans en arrière.

9. Publication des résultats du recensement:
Les résultats définitifs du recensement de population ont été publiés en août 1993 dans une publication intitulée «Tabulation on the 1990 Population Census of the People's Republic of China».

L'organisme responsable de la publication est le Bureau national des statistiques, Sanlihe, Beijing.

CHYPRE

1. Nom et adresse de l'organisme responsable du recensement:
Department of Statistics and Research, 13 Lord Byron Avenue, P.C. 1444, Nicosia.

2. Recensements de population effectués depuis 1945 (années):
1946, 1960, 1973, 1976, 1982 et 1992. La présente description se réfère au recensement de 1992 (qui a eu lieu le 1er octobre). Le recensement de 1976 était le dernier à rassembler des informations sur la population active avant celui de 1992.

3. Champ du recensement:
a) Territoire couvert: Le recensement ne couvrait que la partie du pays contrôlée par le gouvernement.

b) Personnes couvertes: Ensemble de la population.

4. Période de référence:
La semaine précédant le jour du recensement.

5. Principaux sujets:
a) Population totale, selon le sexe et l'âge: oui
Population active par:
b) Sexe et âge: oui
c) Branche d'activité économique (industrie):   oui
d) Profession: oui
e) Situation dans la profession: oui
f) Niveau d'instruction le plus élevé: oui
g) Durée du travail: oui
h) Autres caractéristiques: oui

Réf. a): L'âge est défini en termes de date de naissance (jour, mois et année de naissance) et la classification est faite d'après les années révolues à la date du dernier anniversaire.

Réf. g): On a demandé aux personnes pourvues d'un emploi de préciser si elles avaient travaillé à plein temps (minimum de 30 heures par semaine) ou à temps partiel (moins de 30 heures par semaine).

Réf. h): Le recensement a aussi rassemblé des informations sur la durée du chômage exprimée en mois.

6. Concepts et définitions:
a) Population active: Elle comprend toutes les personnes de 15 ans et plus qui, pendant la semaine de référence, étaient soit pourvues d'un emploi, soit au chômage, conformément aux définitions données ci-dessous. La définition inclut les membres des forces armées.

b) Emploi: Sont considérées comme «pourvues d'un emploi» toutes les personnes ayant répondu positivement à la question «Occupez-vous généralement un emploi?» ou à la question «Avez-vous travaillé la semaine dernière, ne serait-ce qu'une heure?».

Il est indiqué que sont inclus dans cette définition:
i)   les personnes travaillant sans rémunération dans une entreprise ou une affaire familiale;
ii)   les personnes occupées, temporairement absentes de leur travail;
iii) les étudiants travaillant à temps partiel;
iv) les travailleurs saisonniers ou occasionnels;
v)   les conscrits (service militaire ou civil);
vi) les apprentis et les stagiaires.

Les travailleurs saisonniers ou occasionnels ne sont inclus dans la définition que s'ils ont travaillé pendant la semaine de référence. Seules les catégories i), ii), v) et vi) peuvent être identifiées séparément.

c) Chômage: Sont considérées comme «chômeurs» toutes les personnes qui ont répondu négativement aux questions «Occupez-vous un emploi?» et «Avez-vous travaillé la semaine dernière, ne serait-ce qu'une heure?», et qui ont répondu qu'elles étaient au chômage ou en quête d'un emploi à la question s'intéressant à leur activité pendant la semaine de référence. Les étudiants en quête d'un emploi sont exclus de la définition.

7. Classifications utilisées:
Aussi bien les personnes pourvues d'un emploi que les chômeurs ayant précédemment travaillé sont classifiés par branche d'activité économique, par profession et d'après la situation dans la profession.

a) Branche d'activité économique (industrie): Basée sur la question: «Dans quel type d'affaire ou d'industrie travaillez-vous ou avez-vous travaillé?». Pour coder l'industrie, on a utilisé 61 groupes de la classification nationale. Des liens ont été établis avec la CITI-Rév.3 au niveau des divisions (2 chiffres).

b) Profession: Basée sur la question: «Quel type de travail avez-vous effectué ou auriez-vous dû effectuer la semaine dernière?». Pour coder la profession, on a utilisé 30 groupes de la classification nationale. Des liens avec la CITP-88 ont été établis au niveau des grands-groupes (1 chiffre) et des sous-grands groupes (2 chiffres).

c) Situation dans la profession: Basée sur la question: «Dans votre travail, êtes-vous: travailleur indépendant (avec des salariés); travailleur indépendant (sans salariés); salarié; travailleur familial non rémunéré; apprenti; autre?». La situation dans la profession a été codée d'après ces six groupes.

8. Principales différences par rapport au recensement précédent:
Le recensement de 1992 a fixé un âge minimal de 15 ans et plus pour la collecte des données sur la population active alors qu'en 1976 il n'y avait aucune limite d'âge.

Le recensement de 1992 a classifié par industrie, par profession et d'après la situation dans la profession, aussi bien les personnes pourvues d'un emploi que les chômeurs ayant précédemment travaillé, alors que le recensement de 1976 n'avait classé par industrie que les personnes pourvues d'un emploi, par profession aussi bien les personnes pourvues d'un emploi et celles au chômage mais ayant précédemment travaillé et qu'aucune classification d'après la situation dans la profession n'avait été réalisée.

9. Publication des résultats du recensement:
Les résultats définitifs concernant l'ensemble de la population et la population active sont parus en 1995 dans les publications suivantes:

Volume I: «General and Demographic Characteristics of the Population (June 1994)».

Volume III: «Labour Force» (1995).

L'organisme responsable de ces publications est le Département des statistiques et de la recherche, 13 Lord Byron Avenue, P.C. 162, Nicosia.

Certains résultats du recensement sont également disponibles sous forme de tableaux non publiés et de disquettes.

COMORES

1. Nom et adresse de l'organisme responsable du recensement:
Direction générale du Plan, Direction de la Statistique, B.P. 131, Moroni.

2. Recensements de population effectués depuis 1945 (années):
1958, 1966, 1980 et 1991. La présente description se réfère au recensement général de la population et de l'habitat de 1991, (qui a eu lieu le 15 septembre).

3. Champ du recensement:

a) Territoire couvert: Ensemble du pays, à l'exception de l'île de Mayotte (administrée par la France).

b) Personnes couvertes: Ensemble de la population, à l'exception des membres étrangers du corps diplomatique et de leurs familles.

4. Période de référence:
Un mois (août 1991).

5. Principaux sujets:
a) Population totale, selon le sexe et l'âge: oui
Population active par:
b) Sexe et âge: oui
c) Branche d'activité économique (industrie): oui
d) Profession: oui
e) Situation dans la profession: oui
f) Niveau d'instruction le plus élevé: oui
g) Durée du travail: non
h) Autres caractéristiques: oui

Réf. a): L'âge est défini en termes d'années révolues à la date du dernier anniversaire.

Réf. h): Des informations ont aussi été rassemblées sur la rémunération mensuelle des salariés.

6. Concepts et définitions:

a) Population active: Elle comprend toutes les personnes âgées de 12 ans et plus qui, pendant la période de référence étaient, soit pourvues d'un emploi, soit au chômage, conformément aux définitions données ci-dessous. Les membres des forces armées sont exclus de la définition.

b) Emploi: L'emploi est déterminé sur la base de la question suivante: «Au cours du mois d'août, ... était-il? employé permanent; employé temporaire; chômeur; en quête d'un premier emploi; ménagère; élève-étudiant; retraité-rentier; autres inactifs». Sont considérées en «emploi permanent» les personnes occupées constamment à une activité économique qui ont travaillé au moins trois semaines pendant le mois de référence (sauf cas de maladie, congé ou vacances). Les étudiants qui travaillent à temps partiel sont exclus de la définition.

Il est indiqué que sont inclus dans cette définition:

i) les personnes travaillant sans rémunération dans une entreprise ou une exploitation familiale;

ii) les personnes engagées dans la production de produits de base destinés à l'autoconsommation;

iii) les personnes occupées, temporairement absentes du travail;

iv) les travailleurs saisonniers ou occasionnels;

v) les apprentis et les stagiaires.

Seules les catégories i), iv) et v) ci-dessus peuvent être identifiées séparément.

c) Chômage: Sont considérées comme «chômeurs» toutes les personnes qui avaient déjà travaillé mais étaient, pendant la période de référence, sans emploi et à la recherche d'un emploi. Les personnes en quête d'un premier emploi sont identifiées séparément.

7. Classifications utilisées:
Aussi bien les personnes occupées que les chômeurs sont classifiés par industrie. Seules les personnes pourvues d'emploi sont classifiées par profession et d'après la situation dans la profession.

a) Branche d'activité économique (industrie): Basée sur la question: «Que fait l'entreprise ou l'établissement dans lequel ... travaille (ou travaillait, si chômeur)?». Il n'a pas été établi de liens avec la CITI.

b) Profession: Basée sur la question: «Au cours du mois d'août 1991, quelle a été l'occupation principale de ...?». Pour coder la profession, on a utilisé huit groupes. Il n'a pas été établi de liens avec CITP.

c) Situation dans la profession: Basée sur la question: «Dans l'activité exercée, ... est-il? employeur; indépendant; salarié public; salarié privé; apprenti non rémunéré; travailleur à la tâche; travailleur familial». Pour coder cette variable, on a utilisé ces sept groupes.

8. Principales différences par rapport au recensement précédent:
Pas de différence majeure.

9. Publication des résultats du recensement:
Le titre de la publication contenant les résultats définitifs du recensement est: «Résultats du recensement général de la population et de l'habitat, 1991», dont la parution était prévue pour l'été 1996.

L'organisme responsable de cette publication est la Direction Nationale du recensement, B.P. 131, Moroni.

Les résultats devraient également être disponibles sous la forme de disquettes.

REPUBLIQUE DE COREE

1. Nom et adresse de l'organisme responsable du recensement:
National Statistical Office, Statistical Survey Bureau, Population Statistics Division, 90 Kyeongun-Dong, Jongro-Gu, Seoul 110-310.

2. Recensements de population effectués depuis 1945 (années):
1949, 1955, 1960, 1966, 1970, 1975, 1980, 1985 et 1990. La présente description se réfère au recensement de population de 1990 (qui a eu lieu le 1er novembre).

3. Champ du recensement:

a) Territoire couvert: Ensemble du pays.

b) Personnes couvertes: Ensemble de la population, excepté: les travailleurs et les étudiants vivant à l'étranger; les étrangers travaillant dans les bureaux diplomatiques et consulaires et les personnes à leur charge; les militaires étrangers; les fonctionnaires étrangers et les personnes à leur charge.

4. Période de référence:
La période de référence retenue dans les questions concernant les «personnes pourvues d'un emploi rémunéré» et «les personnes non pourvues d'un emploi rémunéré» est une période longue, à savoir les douze mois allant du 1er novembre 1989 au 31 octobre 1990.

5. Principaux sujets:
a) Population totale, selon le sexe et l'âge: oui
Population active par:
b) Sexe et âge: oui
c) Branche d'activité économique (industrie): oui
d) Profession: oui
e) Situation dans la profession: oui
f) Niveau d'instruction le plus élevé: oui
g) Durée du travail: non
h) Autres caractéristiques: non

Réf. a): L'âge est défini en termes d'années révolues à la date du dernier anniversaire.

6. Concepts et définitions:

a) Population active: Les questions relatives à l'activité économique ont été posées à un échantillon de 10 pour cent des personnes âgées de 15 ans et plus. Les membres des forces armées vivant dans des casernes et les conscrits sont exclus de la définition.

b) Emploi: Sont considérées comme «pourvues d'un emploi rémunéré» toutes les personnes âgées de 15 ans et plus qui, pendant la période de référence (à savoir du 1er novembre 1989 au 31 octobre 1990) ont effectué, à domicile ou à l'extérieur, un travail moyennant salaire pendant 30 jours minimum et qui ont l'intention de continuer en ce sens. La question utilisée pour déterminer si une personne doit être considérée comme «pourvue d'un emploi rémunéré» est: «La personne recensée a-t-elle coutume d'effectuer un travail contre une rémunération?». Cependant toute personne ayant, juste avant le recensement, démarré un travail rémunéré d'une durée inférieure à 30 jours avec intention de le poursuivre, doit être comptée comme pourvue d'un emploi rémunéré. A l'inverse, toute personne partie en retraite avant la date du recensement sans aucune intention future de travailler contre un salaire, doit être exclue de la définition.

Il est indiqué que sont inclus dans cette définition:

i) les personnes travaillant sans rémunération dans une entreprise ou une affaire familiale;
ii) les personnes occupées, temporairement absentes du travail;
iii) les étudiants travaillant à temps partiel;
iv) les travailleurs saisonniers ou occasionnels;
v) les apprentis et les stagiaires.

Seules les personnes appartenant aux catégories i), ii) et iii) peuvent être identifiées séparément au travers de réponses telles que: «J'ai travaillé tout en assumant les tâches ménagères», «J'avais un travail duquel j'étais temporairement absent», «J'ai travaillé tout en poursuivant ma scolarité», etc.

c) *Chômage*: Sont considérées comme «non pourvues d'un emploi rémunéré» toutes les personnes qui, à la date du recensement, «étaient à la recherche d'un emploi», «effectuaient des tâches ménagères», «poursuivaient des études», «sans activité», «trop âgées» ou «malades». Pour déterminer si une personne doit être comptée comme «non pourvue d'un emploi rémunéré», on a utilisé la même question que celle indiquée sous 6 b) ci-dessus. Les étudiants en quête d'emploi sont exclus de la définition.

7. Classifications utilisées:
Seules les personnes de l'échantillon pourvues d'un emploi sont classifiées par industrie, par profession et d'après la situation dans la profession.

a) *Branche d'activité économique (industrie)*: Basée sur les questions: «Quel est le principal type de produits fabriqués ou d'activités exercées par l'entreprise ou le bureau employant la personne» et «Veuillez indiquer le nom de l'entreprise ou du bureau». Pour coder la branche d'activité, on a utilisé 90 codes de la classification coréenne type des industries au niveau 3 chiffres; des liens ont été établis avec la CITI-rév.2.

b) *Profession*: Basée sur les questions: «Quel type de travail effectue la personne?» et «Veuillez spécifier la position de la personne dans l'entreprise ou le bureau». Pour coder la profession on a utilisé 286 codes basés sur la classification coréenne type des professions. Des liens ont été établis avec la CITP-68 au niveau des sous-groupes (2 chiffres).

c) *Situation dans la profession*: Basée sur la question: «Quelle est la position professionnelle de la personne occupant un emploi rémunéré?». Pour coder la situation dans la profession, on a utilisé quatre groupes, à savoir: employeur, travailleur indépendant, travailleur familial non rémunéré, salarié.

8. Principales différences par rapport au recensement précédent:
En 1980 on avait utilisé pour les questions sur la population active, l'emploi et le chômage, le concept de «main-d'oeuvre» avec une période de référence courte (à savoir la semaine précédant le jour du recensement); lors des recensements de 1985 et 1990, on a adopté l'approche d' «activité rémunérée» avec une période de référence longue pour les questions sur les travailleurs rémunérés, les travailleurs non rémunérés, etc.

De plus, en 1980 et 1985 la limite d'âge minimale retenue pour la collecte des données sur la population active et ses composantes était de 14 ans.

9. Publication des résultats du recensement:
Le titre de la publication contenant les résultats du recensement est «1990 Population and Housing Census Report, Vol. 2, 10 Percent Sample, 3-1, Economic Activity».

L'organisme responsable de cette publication est le Bureau national des statistiques, Statistical Survey Bureau, Population Statistics Division, 90 Kyeongun-Dong, Jongro-Gu, Seoul 110-310.

Les résultats du recensement sont également disponibles sous d'autres formes comme des tableaux non publiés et des bandes magnétiques.

REPUBLIQUE DOMINICAINE

1. Nom et adresse de l'organisme responsable du recensement:
Oficina Nacional de Estadistica (ONE), Ave. Mexico, Esquina Leopoldo Navarro, Edificio Gubernamental Juan Pablo Duarte (El Huacal) 9no. Piso., Santo Domingo.

2. Recensements de population effectués depuis 1945 (années):
1950, 1960, 1970, 1981 et 1993. La présente description se réfère au recensement de population de 1993 (qui a eu lieu les 24 et 25 septembre).

3. Champ du recensement:
a) *Territoire couvert*: Ensemble du pays.

b) *Personnes couvertes*: Ensemble de la population.

4. Période de référence:
La semaine précédant le recensement.

5. Principaux sujets:

a) Population totale, selon le sexe et l'âge:	oui
Population active par:	
b) Sexe et âge:	oui
c) Branche d'activité économique (industrie):	oui
d) Profession:	oui
e) Situation dans la profession:	oui
f) Niveau d'instruction le plus élevé:	non
g) Durée du travail:	non
h) Autres caractéristiques:	non

Réf. a): L'âge est défini en termes d'années révolues à la date du dernier anniversaire et en termes d'année de naissance.

6. Concepts et définitions:
a) *Population active*: Elle comprend toutes les personnes âgées de 10 ans et plus qui, pendant la semaine de référence, étaient soit pourvues d'un emploi soit au chômage, conformément aux définitions données ci-dessous. La définition inclut tous les membres des forces armées.

b) *Emploi*: Sont considérées comme «pourvues d'un emploi» les personnes ayant indiqué que pendant la semaine de référence elles avaient travaillé ou qu'elles étaient pourvues d'un emploi, qu'elles avaient perçu une rémunération pour un travail, ou qu'elles avaient effectué sans rémunération un travail à leur domicile, dans un établissement ou dans un commerce appartenant à leur famille. La question utilisée pour déterminer si une personne est ou non pourvue d'un emploi est: «Dans laquelle des situations suivantes vous trouviez-vous la semaine passée: 1) travaillait avec rémunération; 2) ne travaillait pas, mais avait un emploi; 3) travaillait pour un parent sans rémunération en espèces; 4) était à la recherche d'un emploi en ayant déjà travaillé auparavant; 5) pensionné ou retraité ne travaillant pas; 6) occupé à des tâches ménagères au foyer; 7) étudiant ne travaillant pas; 8) à la recherche d'un premier emploi; 9) incapacité de travail permanente; 10) ne souhaitait pas travailler; 11) n'était pas à la recherche d'un emploi, mais en aurait accepté un si on le lui avait proposé; 12) rentier.».

Il est indiqué que sont inclus dans cette définition:

i) les personnes travaillant sans rémunération dans une entreprise ou une affaire familiale;
ii) les personnes engagées dans la production de produits de base destinés à l'autoconsommation;
iii) les personnes occupées, temporairement absentes de leur travail;
iv) les étudiants travaillant à temps partiel;
v) les conscrits (service militaire ou civil).

Toutes ces catégories peuvent être identifiées séparément.

c) *Chômage*: Sont considérées comme «chômeurs» les personnes qui, pendant la semaine de référence, ne travaillaient pas ou étaient à la recherche d'un emploi sans avoir déjà travaillé auparavant. La définition inclut les travailleurs ayant déjà une expérience professionnelle («chômeurs avec expérience professionnelle») et ceux qui n'avaient jamais travaillé auparavant («nouveaux travailleurs»). Elle exclut les étudiants à la recherche d'un emploi.

7. Classifications utilisées:
Aussi bien les personnes pourvues d'un emploi que les chômeurs ayant déjà travaillé auparavant sont classifiés par bran-

che d'activité économique, par profession et d'après la situation dans la profession.

a) Branche d'activité économique (industrie): Pour déterminer la branche d'activité économique, on a demandé quelle était l'activité de l'organisme, de l'entreprise ou du commerce dans lequel l'intéressé travaillait ou avait travaillé la dernière fois. Pour coder cette variable, on a utilisé 10 groupes de la classification nationale. Des liens ont été établis avec la CITI-rév.2 au niveau des branches (1 chiffre).

b) Profession: Pour déterminer la profession, on a demandé quelle était la fonction ou l'emploi que l'intéressé exerçait (ou avait exercé) là où il travaillait (avait travaillé). Pour coder cette variable, on a utilisé 10 groupes de la classification nationale. Des liens ont été établis avec la CITP-68 au niveau des grands groupes (1 chiffre).

c) Situation dans la profession: Pour déterminer cette caractéristique, on a demandé à l'intéressé quelle était celle des cinq catégories suivantes à laquelle il estimait appartenir dans l'exercice de son activité professionnelle: patron ou employeur, travailleur pour son propre compte, travailleur occupé à des tâches ménagères au foyer, travailleur salarié (employé, ouvrier, journalier) et travailleur familial sans rémunération.

8. Principales différences par rapport au recensement précédent:

Le recensement de 1981 avait été un recensement «de facto» et «de jure», alors que le recensement de 1993 n'a été qu'un recensement «de facto».

En 1981, on avait utilisé 14 questions pour mesurer et caractériser l'activité professionnelle, ce qui avait permis de connaître de manière plus approfondie les caractéristiques économiques de la population. Les questions posées alors et qui ne se sont pas retrouvées dans le recensement de 1993 sont les suivantes:

«Si vous ne travailliez pas, à quoi avez-vous occupé la majeure partie de votre temps la semaine passée?

Depuis combien de temps êtes-vous sans travail?

Combien d'heures avez-vous travaillé la semaine passée dans tous vos emplois ou travaux?

Pour qui avez-vous travaillé la semaine passée (ou pour qui aviez-vous travaillé dans votre dernier emploi ou travail?».

Lors du recensement de 1981, le revenu salarial tiré de l'activité professionnelle était le revenu annuel ou mensuel, alors que lors du recensement de 1993, il s'agissait du revenu salarial hebdomadaire. Le recensement de 1981 avait utilisé l'année ou le mois comme paramètres de temps.

9. Publication des résultats du recensement:

Le titre exact de la publication dans laquelle sont présentés les résultats définitifs est «Censo Nacional de Población y Vivienda 24 y 25 de septiembre de 1993; Resultados definitivos Region Sur-Oeste Vol.I», Juin 1996.

L'organisme responsable de cette publication est l'Office national des statistiques, ave. Mexico, Esquina Leopoldo Navarro, edificio gubernamental Juan Pablo Duarte (El Huacal), 9no. Piso.

Les résultats du recensement sont également disponibles sous forme de disquettes et de tableaux non publiés.

EL SALVADOR

1. Nom et adresse de l'organisme responsable du recensement:

Direccion General de Estadística y Censos, 1a. Calle Poniente y 43 Avenida Norte, San Salvador, El Salvador.

2. Recensements de population effectués depuis 1945 (années):

1950, 1961, 1971 et 1992. La présente description se réfère au recensement de population de 1992 (qui a eu lieu le 27 septembre).

3. Champ du recensement:

a) Territoire couvert: Ensemble du pays.

b) Personnes couvertes: Ensemble de la population.

4. Période de référence:

La semaine précédant le recensement.

5. Principaux sujets:

a) Population totale, selon le sexe et l'âge:	oui

Population active par:

b) Sexe et âge:	oui
c) Branche d'activité économique (industrie):	oui
d) Profession:	oui
e) Situation dans la profession:	oui
f) Niveau d'instruction le plus élevé:	oui
g) Durée du travail:	oui
h) Autres caractéristiques:	non

Réf. a): L'âge est défini en termes d'années révolues à la date du dernier anniversaire.

Réf. g): Les heures de travail se réfèrent aux heures habituellement et effectivement travaillées pendant la période de référence par les personnes pourvues d'un emploi.

6. Concepts et définitions:

a) Population active: Elle comprend toutes les personnes âgées de 10 ans et plus qui, pendant la semaine de référence, étaient soit pourvues d'un emploi soit au chômage, conformément aux définitions données ci-dessous. La définition inclut tous les membres des forces armées.

b) Emploi: Sont considérées comme «pourvues d'un emploi» les personnes ayant travaillé pendant la semaine de référence. La question utilisée est: «Pendant la semaine précédant le début du recensement: Travailliez-vous avec une rémunération en espèces ou en nature? Travailliez-vous pour un tiers sans rémunération? Etiez-vous pourvu d'un emploi, propriétaire d'une entreprise ou propriétaire d'une exploitation mais sans travailler? Etiez-vous à la recherche d'un emploi en ayant déjà travaillé auparavant? Etiez-vous à la recherche d'un premier emploi (en n'ayant donc jamais travaillé auparavant)? Aviez-vous renoncé à rechercher un emploi parce que vous considériez qu'il n'y en avait pas de disponible? Etiez-vous exclusivement femme au foyer? Etiez-vous exclusivement étudiant? Etiez-vous retraité, pensionné ou rentier? Etiez-vous en détention? Etiez-vous en incapacité de travail permanente? Etiez-vous dans une autre situation?».

Il est indiqué que sont inclus dans cette définition:

i) les personnes travaillant sans rémunération dans une entreprise ou une affaire familiale;

ii) les personnes occupées, temporairement absentes de leur travail;

iii) les étudiants travaillant à temps partiel;

iv) les travailleurs saisonniers ou occasionnels;

v) les apprentis et les stagiaires.

Les personnes appartenant aux catégories i), ii), iii) et iv) peuvent être identifiées séparément au moyen de questions spécifiques.

c) Chômage: Sont considérées comme «chômeurs» les personnes qui, pendant la semaine de référence, ne travaillaient pas mais étaient à la recherche d'un emploi. Sont incluses dans cette définition les personnes qui avaient déjà effectué des démarches pour commencer à travailler après la semaine de référence, celles qui se trouvaient en arrêt de travail sans rémunération - temporairement ou pour une durée indéterminée -, et celles qui estimaient qu'il n'y avait pas d'emploi disponible pour elles.

7. Classifications utilisées:

Aussi bien les personnes pourvues d'un emploi que les chômeurs sont classifiés par branche d'activité économique, par profession et d'après la situation dans la profession.

a) Branche d'activité économique (industrie): Les questions utilisées pour déterminer la branche d'activité économique sont: «Où travaillez-vous (travailliez-vous) (dans les champs, dans une usine, dans un atelier de mécanique, dans un bureau privé ou public, dans la rue, etc.)»? et «Que faites-vous ou que produisez-vous (vous-même ou l'établissement dans lequel vous travaillez ou dans lequel vous avez travaillé la dernière fois?». Pour coder la branche d'activité économique, on a utilisé la CITI-rév.3 au niveau des classes (4 chiffres).

b) Profession: La question utilisée pour déterminer le groupe de professions est: «Quelle est la profession, l'emploi ou la fonction que vous exercez (ou exerciez) dans le cadre de votre travail?». Pour coder la profession, on a utilisé la CITP-88 au niveau des groupes de base (4 chiffres).

c) Situation dans la profession: La question utilisée pour déterminer la situation dans la profession est: «Dans votre emploi, êtes-vous ou étiez-vous: employé ou ouvrier du secteur public;

employé ou ouvrier du secteur privé; patron ou employeur; travailleur familial sans rémunération; travailleur indépendant (pour son propre compte); employé de maison; travailleur dans une coopérative de production; ne sait pas?». Pour coder cette variable, ce sont les huit groupes susmentionnés que l'on a utilisé.

8. Principales différences par rapport au recensement précédent:
Pas de différence majeure.

9. Publication des résultats du recensement:
Les résultats définitifs du recensement ont été publiés en décembre 1995.

Le titre exact de la publication dans laquelle sont présentés les résultats définitifs est «V Censos nacionales de población».

L'organisme responsable de cette publication est la Direction générale des statistiques et des recensements, 1a. Calle Poniente y 43 Avenida Norte, San Salvador, El Salvador.

Les résultats du recensement sont également disponibles sous forme de tableaux non publiés.

EQUATEUR

1. Nom et adresse de l'organisme responsable du recensement:
Instituto Nacional de Estadísticas y Censos (INEC), Av. 10 de Agosto 229 y Pasaje Carlos Ibarra, Quito.

2. Recensements de population effectués depuis 1945 (années):
1950, 1962, 1974, 1982 et 1990. La présente description se réfère au recensement de population de 1990 (qui a eu lieu le 25 novembre).

3. Champ du recensement:

a) Territoire couvert: Ensemble du pays, à l'exception des zones où ont lieu des conflits temporaires dûs au problème indigène.

b) Personnes couvertes: Ensemble de la population, à l'exception des personnes vivant dans les zones susmentionnées.

4. Période de référence:
La semaine précédant le jour du recensement.

5. Principaux sujets:
a) Population totale, selon le sexe et l'âge: oui
Population active par:
b) Sexe et âge: oui
c) Branche d'activité économique (industrie):   oui
d) Profession: oui
e) Situation dans la profession: oui
f) Niveau d'instruction le plus élevé: ...
g) Durée du travail: oui
h) Autres caractéristiques: oui
Réf. a): L'âge est défini en termes d'années révolues à la date du dernier anniversaire.

Réf. g): La durée du travail est exprimée aussi bien en nombre d'heures habituellement travaillées qu'en nombre d'heures effectivement travaillées par les personnes ayant exercé une activité professionnelle pendant la période de référence. La question utilisée est: «Combien d'heures avez-vous travaillé la semaine passée dans l'emploi indiqué?».

6. Concepts et définitions:

a) Population active: Elle comprend toutes les personnes âgées de 8 ans et plus qui, pendant la semaine de référence, étaient soit pourvues d'un emploi soit au chômage, conformément aux définitions données ci-dessous. La définition inclut tous les membres des forces armées.

b) Emploi: Sont considérées comme «pourvues d'un emploi» toutes les personnes ayant exercé un travail, indépendant ou non, pendant la semaine de référence. Les questions utilisées pour déterminer si une personne peut être considérée comme pourvue d'un emploi sont: «Qu'avez-vous fait la semaine passée?» et «Avez-vous exercé ou aidé à exercer, pendant la majeure partie de la semaine, une activité quelconque, même sans rémunération?».

Il est indiqué que sont inclus dans cette définition:
i) les personnes travaillant sans rémunération dans une entreprise ou une affaire familiale;

ii) les personnes occupées, temporairement absentes de leur travail;
iii) les étudiants travaillant à temps partiel;
iv) les travailleurs saisonniers ou occasionnels;
v) les conscrits (service militaire ou civil);
vi) les apprentis et les stagiaires.
Aucune de ces catégories ne peut être identifiée séparément.

c) Chômage: Sont considérées comme «chômeurs» les personnes ayant répondu par la négative aux questions mentionnées au paragraphe (b) ci-dessus et qui, pendant la semaine de référence, étaient à la recherche d'un emploi en ayant déjà travaillé auparavant ou étaient à la recherche d'un premier emploi. Sont exclus les étudiants à la recherche d'un emploi.

7. Classifications utilisées:
Aussi bien les personnes pourvues d'un emploi que les chômeurs ayant déjà travaillé auparavant sont classifiés par branche d'activité économique, par profession et d'après la situation dans la profession.

a) Branche d'activité économique (industrie): Basée sur la question: «Quelle est l'activité ou la production principale de l'entreprise, de l'établissement ou du commerce où vous exercez la profession que vous avez indiquée?». Pour coder la branche d'activité économique, on a utilisé la CITI-rév.2 au niveau des grands groupes (3 chiffres), et pour la publication des données la CITI-rév.2 au niveau des branches (1 chiffre).

b) Profession: Basée sur la question: «Quelle était votre profession ou votre fonction principale la semaine passée, ou quel a été votre dernier travail si vous êtes sans activité?». Pour coder cette variable, on a utilisé la CITP-68 au niveau des grands groupes (1 chiffre) et des groupes de base (3 chiffres).

c) Situation dans la profession: Basée sur la question: «Quelle a été votre statut ou votre catégorie dans la profession que vous avez indiquée?». La situation dans la profession a été codée en sept groupes: patron ou associé gérant; travailleur pour son propre compte; employé ou salarié d'une municipalité ou d'un conseil de province; de l'Etat; du secteur privé; travailleur familial sans rémunération; ne sait pas.

8. Principales différences par rapport au recensement précédent:
En 1982, la limite d'âge inférieure utilisée pour déterminer la population active et ses composantes (emploi et chômage) était de 12 ans; elle a été ramenée à 8 ans pour le recensement de 1990.

La question utilisée en 1982 pour déterminer si une personne pouvait être considérée comme pourvue d'un emploi était: «Qu'avez-vous fait pendant la majeure partie des journées comprises entre le 7 et le 13 novembre?»; en 1990, la question a été: «Qu'avez-vous fait la semaine passée?».

Le recensement de 1990 a comporté les questions supplémentaires suivantes: «Avez-vous exercé, ou aidé à exercer, pendant la majeure partie de la semaine passée, une activité quelconque, même sans rémunération?» et «Pendant combien d'heures avez-vous travaillé la semaine passée dans l'emploi indiqué?».

Dans le recensement de 1990, on a ajouté la catégorie «Incapacité de travail» aux catégories de réponse possibles pour l'activité.

En 1990, la catégorie de situation dans la profession «employé ou salarié» a été ventilée en trois groupes: d'une municipalité ou d'un conseil de province; de l'Etat; du secteur privé.

Enfin, le recensement de 1990 n'a comporté aucune demande de renseignements concernant la sécurité sociale.

9. Publication des résultats du recensement:
Le titre exact de la publication dans laquelle sont présentés les résultats définitifs du recensement est «V Censo de Población y IV de Vivienda 1990 - Resultados Definitivos, Resumen Nacional», novembre 1991.

L'organisme responsable de cette publication est l'Institut national des statistiques et des recensements - INEC, Quito.

Les chiffres du recensement de 1990 sont également disponibles sous la forme que souhaite l'usager.

ESPAGNE

1. Nom et adresse de l'organisme responsable du recensement:
Instituto Nacional de Estadística, Paseo de la Castellana, 183, 28046 Madrid.

2. Recensements de population effectués depuis 1945 (années):
1950, 1960, 1970, 1981 et 1991. La présente description se réfère au recensement de population de 1991 (qui a eu lieu le 1er mars).

3. Champ du recensement:
a) Territoire couvert: Ensemble du pays.

b) Personnes couvertes: Toutes les personnes résidant sur le territoire national plus celles qui s'y trouvaient à la date du recensement. Sont exclues les personnes qui ne résident ni dans des habitations familiales ni dans des logements ou habitations collectives permanents (vagabonds, personnes sans domicile fixe, etc.).

4. Période de référence:
La semaine précédant le recensement, c'est-à-dire du 22 au 28 février 1991.

5. Principaux sujets:
a) Population totale, selon le sexe et l'âge: oui
Population active par:
b) Sexe et âge: oui
c) Branche d'activité économique (industrie):   oui
d) Profession: oui
e) Situation dans la profession: oui
f) Niveau d'instruction le plus élevé: oui
g) Durée du travail: non
h) Autres caractéristiques: oui

Réf. a): L'âge est défini en termes d'année de naissance.

Réf. h): Certaines communautés autonomes ont enregistré, lors du recensement, le lieu de travail et le mode de déplacement. Ces communautés sont Murcie, l'Andalousie, les Canaries, la Catalogne, la Galice, le Pays Basque et la Navarre.

6. Concepts et définitions:
a) Population active: Elle comprend toutes les personnes âgées de 16 ans et plus qui, pendant la semaine de référence, étaient soit pourvues d'un emploi soit au chômage, conformément aux définitions données ci-dessous. Les données sur la population active et ses composantes (personnes pourvues d'un emploi et chômeurs) n'ont été retenues que pour les personnes âgées de 16 ans et plus. La définition inclut les militaires de carrière mais exclut les conscrits faisant leur service militaire obligatoire.

b) Emploi: Sont considérées comme «pourvues d'un emploi» toutes les personnes ayant travaillé au moins une heure pendant la semaine de référence. La définition inclut également les personnes qui pendant ladite semaine, étaient temporairement absentes de leur travail pour cause de maladie, vacances, etc.

Il est indiqué que sont inclus dans cette définition:
i) les personnes travaillant sans rémunération dans une entreprise ou une affaire familiale;
ii) les personnes engagées dans la production de produits de base destinés à l'autoconsommation;
iii) les personnes pourvues d'un emploi, temporairement absentes de leur travail:
iv) les étudiants travaillant à temps partiel;
v) les travailleurs saisonniers ou occasionnels qui étaient occupés pendant la semaine de référence;
vi) les apprentis et les stagiaires, à condition qu'ils soient rémunérés d'une façon ou d'une autre.

Seules les personnes appartenant aux catégories i), iv) et v) susmentionnées peuvent être identifiées séparément. Les travailleurs saisonniers ou occasionnels ne sont considérés comme pourvus d'un emploi que s'ils ont travaillé au moins une heure pendant la semaine de référence. Les conscrits (service militaire ou civil) sont exclus de la population active mais ils peuvent être identifiés séparément.

c) Chômage: Sont considérées comme «chômeurs» ou sans emploi toutes les personnes qui, pendant la semaine de référence, étaient simultanément: i) «sans travail», c'est-à-dire ni travailleur indépendant ni employé par un tiers; ii) «à la recher-

che d'un emploi», c'est-à-dire qu'elles avaient pris des mesures concrètes pour rechercher un emploi auprès d'un tiers ou qu'elles avaient pris des initiatives pour s'établir à leur propre compte (par exemple: inscription à l'agence pour l'emploi, contacts avec d'éventuels employeurs, réponses à des annonces dans les journaux, etc.); iii) «disponible pour travailler» pour un tiers ou pour leur propre compte. Les chômeurs sont répartis entre ceux qui recherchent un premier emploi et ceux qui ont déjà travaillé auparavant.

7. Classifications utilisées:
Aussi bien les personnes pourvues d'un emploi que les chômeurs ayant déjà travaillé auparavant sont classifiés par branche d'activité économique, par profession et d'après la situation dans la profession. Ces variables se réfèrent à la profession principale des personnes pourvues d'un emploi, et, pour les chômeurs, à la dernière profession qu'ils ont exercée.

a) Branche d'activité économique (industrie): Basée sur la question: «Quelle est l'activité principale de l'établissement dans lequel vous travaillez (ou dans lequel vous travailliez) (par exemple: production agricole; fabrication de jouets; hôtellerie; etc.)?». Pour coder cette variable, on a utilisé la CITI-rév.2 et rév.3 entre un et deux chiffres.

b) Profession: Basée sur la question: «Quelle est l'emploi, la profession ou la fonction que vous exercez (ou que vous exerciez) (par exemple: employé de commerce; contremaître dans le bâtiment; etc.)?». Pour coder cette variable, on a utilisé la CITP (68 et 88) au niveau des sous-groupes.

c) Situation dans la profession: Pour déterminer cette caractéristique, on a demandé aux intéressés quelle était leur situation dans l'emploi qu'ils exerçaient. Cette variable a été codée en sept groupes: chef d'entreprise, personne exerçant une profession libérale ou travailleur indépendant, employant du personnel; chef d'entreprise, personne exerçant une profession libérale ou travailleur indépendant, n'employant pas de personnel; membre d'une coopérative de travail travaillant en tant qu'associé dans cette coopérative; personne travaillant sans rémunération réglementée dans l'entreprise ou l'affaire d'un parent sous le toit duquel elle vit; personne ayant un emploi fixe, rémunérée sous forme d'appointements, de salaire, de commission, d'allocation journalière ou sous une autre forme; personne travaillant occasionnellement ou temporairement et rémunérée sous forme d'appointements, de salaire, de commission, d'allocation journalière ou sous une autre forme; autre situation.

8. Principales différences par rapport au recensement précédent:
La principale innovation du recensement de 1991 est le fait que toutes les questions soient codées et exploitées à cent pour cent, ce qui permet une meilleure désagrégation géographique, encore que la profession et l'activité ne puissent être obtenues avec le même degré de désagrégation.

En ce qui concerne les critères de classification de la population en personnes actives, inactives, chômeurs, etc., ils ont été les mêmes que pour l'Enquête sur la population active.

9. Publication des résultats du recensement:
Les chiffres définitifs relatifs à la population active et à ses composantes (emploi et chômage) ont été publiés fin 1993.

Le titre exact de la publication dans laquelle sont présentés les résultats définitifs du recensement est «Censos de Población y Viviendas 1991».

L'organisme responsable de cette publication est l'Institut national de statistiques, Madrid.

Les résultats du recensement sont également disponibles sous forme de disquettes, bandes magnétiques et CD-ROM.

ETATS-UNIS

1. Nom et adresse de l'organisme responsable du recensement:
United States Bureau of the Census, Washington, DC, 20233.

2. Recensements de population effectués depuis 1945 (années):
1950, 1960, 1970, 1980 et 1990. La présente description se réfère au recensement de 1990 (qui a eu lieu le 1er avril).

3. Champ du recensement:

a) Territoire couvert: Ensemble du pays. Des recensement séparés ont été effectués pour les régions excentrées des Etats-Unis (Samoa américain, Guam, Iles Mariannes du Nord, Palau, Porto Rico et Iles vierges).

b) Personnes couvertes: Ensemble de la population, à l'exception des nationaux résidant à l'étranger.

L'unité de sondage de base était l'unité de logement, avec tous ses occupants. Dans les immeubles collectifs, l'unité de sondage était la personne. La fraction de sondage variait en fonction des procédures de recouvrement des données. Une fois pris en compte tous les taux de sondage sur l'ensemble du territoire des Etats-Unis, environ une unité de logement sur six dans le pays était incluse dans l'échantillonnage.

4. Période de référence:

La semaine précédant l'entretien pour définir la population active du moment, et l'année 1989 pour déterminer le statut par rapport à l'emploi au cours de cette même année.

La présente description s'applique à la population active du moment.

5. Principaux sujets:

a) Population totale, selon le sexe et l'âge: oui
Population active par:
b) Sexe et âge: oui
c) Branche d'activité économique (industrie):   oui
d) Profession: oui
e) Situation dans la profession: oui
f) Niveau d'instruction le plus élevé: oui
g) Durée du travail: oui
h) Autres caractéristiques: oui

Réf. a): L'âge est défini en termes d'années révolues à la date du dernier anniversaire.

Réf. g): La durée du travail se réfère aux heures de travail effectives des personnes pourvues d'un emploi ayant travaillé au cours de la semaine de référence, ainsi qu'à la période totale de travail (exprimée en semaines) et aux heures de travail habituelles en 1989.

Réf. h): Le recensement a aussi rassemblé des informations sur: le lieu de travail; les moyens de transport pour se rendre au travail; le taux d'occupation des véhicules privés; le temps de trajet pour se rendre au travail; l'activité professionnelle en 1989; les revenus et les gains en 1989; l'incapacité de travail.

6. Concepts et définitions:

a) Population active: Elle comprend toutes les personnes âgées de 16 ans et plus qui, au cours de la semaine de référence, étaient soit pourvues d'un emploi soit au chômage, conformément aux définitions données ci-dessous. La définition inclut les membres des forces armées.

Les questions relatives à l'activité économique n'ont été posées qu'à un échantillon d'unités et de personnes. Quant aux membres des forces armées vivant dans des casernes ou à bord de bâtiments de la marine, les questions relatives à l'absence temporaire du travail, à la recherche d'un emploi ou à la disponibilité par rapport à l'emploi ne leur ont pas été posées.

b) Emploi: Les principales questions utilisées pour déterminer si une personne devait ou non être considérée comme pourvue d'un emploi sont les suivantes: «Cette personne a-t-elle travaillé à un moment ou à un autre la semaine dernière?» et «Combien d'heures cette personne a-t-elle travaillé la semaine dernière, tous emplois confondus?». Une autre question a également été posée: «Cette personne était-elle temporairement absente du travail ou en chômage technique la semaine dernière?».

Il est indiqué que sont inclus dans cette définition:

i) les personnes travaillant sans rémunération dans une entreprise ou une affaire familiale, à condition qu'elles aient travaillé au moins 15 heures au cours de la semaine de référence;

ii) les personnes pourvues d'un emploi, temporairement absentes du travail;

iii) les étudiants travaillant à temps partiel;

iv) les travailleurs saisonniers ou occasionnels, seulement pendant la saison appropriée (un travailleur occasionnel n'est pas considéré comme pourvu d'emploi pendant les périodes où il ne travaille pas);

v) les apprentis et les stagiaires.

Seules les personnes appartenant aux catégories i), iii) et iv) peuvent être identifiées séparément (au travers du croisement de la population active par situation dans la profession (type de travailleur), et statut en fonction du type de contrat de travail et du nombre d'heures de travail effectuées au cours de la semaine précédente). Le statut au regard de l'emploi est un code secondaire qui utilise des données déjà recouvrées à d'autres fins et sert à déterminer si une personne est pourvue d'un emploi, est au chômage, n'appartient pas à la population active ou est membre des forces armées.

Les forces armées des Etats-Unis sont exclusivement composées de volontaires. Ceux qui résident aux Etats-Unis peuvent être identifiés séparément par le recensement sur la base du «Statut au regard de l'emploi». La population active des Etats-Unis ne comprend aucun conscrit (service militaire ou civil).

c) Chômage: Sont considérées comme «chômeurs» toutes les personnes qui, au cours de la semaine de référence, étaient sans emploi, étaient à la recherche d'un emploi (soit au cours de la semaine de référence soit pendant les trois autres semaines précédentes) et étaient disponibles pour travailler. La définition inclut également les personnes en chômage technique. Les principales questions utilisées pour déterminer si une personne devait ou non être comptée comme «chômeur» étaient les suivantes: «Cette personne était-elle temporairement absente du travail ou en chômage technique la semaine dernière?», «A-t-elle recherché un emploi au cours des quatre dernières semaines?» et «Aurait-elle pu accepter un emploi la semaine dernière si on lui en avait offert un?».

7. Classifications utilisées:

Aussi bien les personnes pourvues d'un emploi que les chômeurs ayant précédemment travaillé sont classifiés par branche d'activité, par profession et d'après la situation dans la profession.

a) Branche d'activité économique (industrie): Basée sur les questions: «Pour qui cette personne travaillait-elle?», «De quel type ou branche d'activité économique s'agissait-il?» et «S'agissait-il essentiellement de fabrication industrielle, de commerce de gros, de commerce de détail ou d'une autre activité (agriculture, bâtiment, services, fonction publique, etc.)?».

Le système de classification est basé sur le système de classification type des Etats-Unis de 1987 et il a été mis au point spécialement pour le recensement de la population. Le codage des réponses a été effectué sur la base de l'«Index alphabétique des branches d'activité économique et des professions» et d'une liste des noms d'établissements tirée de recensements et enquêtes économiques réalisés aux Etats-Unis. Le recensement de 1990 a utilisé 236 catégories. Il n'a pas été établi de liens avec la CITI. Cependant, à des fins de comparaison internationale, on a procédé à une adaptation de la classification des branches d'activité économique utilisée pour le recensement de la population des Etats-Unis de 1970 pour la rapprocher le plus possible de la classification internationale en vigueur (laquelle était encore valable, d'une manière générale, pour le recensement de 1990), et cette adaptation a été effectuée au niveau des branches (1 chiffre).

b) Profession: Basée sur les questions: «Quel était le type de travail effectué par cette personne?» et «Quelles étaient les activités ou les tâches les plus importantes de cette personne?».

Le système de classification comprend 501 catégories de professions distinctes, elles-mêmes organisées en six groupes récapitulatifs, et 13 grands groupes de professions. Ce système a été conçu de manière à ce qu'il soit compatible avec le Manuel de classification type des professions de 1980. On n'a établi aucun lien avec la CITP. Aucune adaptation n'a été faite pour la classification 1990 des professions aux Etats-Unis.

c) Situation dans la profession: Basée sur la question: «Cette personne était-elle employée par une entreprise ou une société à but lucratif ou par une personne physique, et rémunérée sous forme de salaire, d'honoraires ou de commissions; employée par une organisation privée à but non lucratif, exemptée d'impôts ou caritative; employée par des pouvoirs publics locaux (ville, comté, etc.); fonctionnaire fédéral; travailleur pour son propre compte, membre d'une profession libérale ou exploitant agricole non constitué en société; travailleur pour son propre compte, membre d'une profession libérale ou exploitant agricole constitué en société; employé sans rémunération dans une entreprise ou une exploitation agricole familiale?».

Tous les groupes, à l'exception des personnes travaillant pour leur propre compte non constituées en société, sont classifiés comme employés. Pour coder la situation dans la profession, on a utilisé les huit groupes susmentionnés.

8. Principales différences par rapport au recensement précédent:
Pas de différence majeure.

9. Publication des résultats du recensement:
Les titres des principales publications contenant les résultats définitifs du recensement sont: «1990 CPH-5: Données récapitulatives en matière sociale, économique et de logement» et «1990 CP-2: Caractéristiques sociales et économiques» (Rapports contenant les données obtenues par sondage), janvier 1991 - décembre 1993.

L'organisme responsable de ces publications est le Bureau du recensement des Etats-Unis, Washington DC, 20233.

Les résultats du recensement de 1990 sont également disponibles sous forme de bandes magnétiques, microfiches, serveurs interactifs, CD-ROM et disquettes pour micro-ordinateurs.

FINLANDE

1. Nom et adresse de l'organisme responsable du recensement:
Central Statistical Office of Finland (CSO), P.B. 504, 00101 Helsinki.

2. Recensements de population effectués depuis 1945 (années):
1950, 1960, 1970, 1975, 1980, 1985 et 1990. La présente description se réfère au recensement de 1990 (qui a eu lieu le 31 décembre).

En application d'une décision prise par la Finlande en 1979, le recensement de la population et des logements de 1980 a été le dernier recensement directement basé sur des données recouvrées par questionnaire. Le recensement de la population et des logements de 1990 a été entièrement réalisé à l'aide des registres et dossiers administratifs. Les préparatifs de ce recensement ont commencé dès 1981, et la Finlande a constitué un Registre national des bâtiments et habitations en se basant sur les données obtenues sur ce sujet lors du recensement de la population et des logements de 1980.

Etant donné qu'il s'agit du premier recensement général réalisé uniquement à l'aide de registres, sans aucun questionnaire, il conviendra d'effectuer une étude parallèle basée sur un échantillon suffisamment large pour pouvoir analyser l'interruption de la série chronologique des recensements due au changement de la méthode de recouvrement des données. Pour déterminer la qualité des registres utilisés lors du recensement, il faudra effectuer à intervalles réguliers un contrôle et une étude de qualité du système des registres (par exemple tous les cinq ans), et ce d'une façon indépendante des systèmes administratifs.

3. Champ du recensement:
a) Territoire couvert: Ensemble du pays.
b) Personnes couvertes: Ensemble de la population.

4. Période de référence:
La semaine du recensement (25-31 décembre 1990) pour l'activité actuelle, et l'ensemble de l'année 1990 pour l'activité habituelle.

5. Principaux sujets:
a) Population totale, selon le sexe et l'âge: oui
Population active par:
b) Sexe et âge: oui
c) Branche d'activité économique (industrie):   oui
d) Profession: oui
e) Situation dans la profession: oui
f) Niveau d'instruction le plus élevé: oui
g) Durée du travail: non
h) Autres caractéristiques: oui

Réf. a): L'âge est défini en termes de date de naissance, que l'on a obtenue directement auprès du registre central de la population.

Réf. h): Le recensement a aussi rassemblé des informations sur le lieu de travail, le statut juridique de l'employeur (entreprise privée, gouvernement central, collectivité locale) la durée de l'emploi et du chômage, les revenus, la situation économique et sociale.

6. Concepts et définitions:
a) Population active: Elle comprend toutes les personnes âgées de 15 à 74 ans qui, au cours de la semaine du recensement, étaient soit pourvues d'un emploi soit au chômage, conformément aux définitions données ci-dessous. Elle exclut les militaires du contingent logés en caserne et les populations institutionnelles.

b) Emploi: Sont considérées comme «pourvues d'un emploi» toutes les personnes qui, selon les registres du régime de pensions des salariés, ont travaillé au moins un jour au cours de la semaine du recensement (population active du moment) ou au moins six mois au cours de l'année de référence (population habituellement active), à domicile ou à l'extérieur, et qui selon les registres de l'administration fiscale ont perçu des revenus imposables.

Il est indiqué que sont inclus dans cette définition:

i) les personnes travaillant sans rémunération dans une entreprise ou une affaire familiale; en fait seules sont incluses celles qui bénéficient d'un régime de retraite professionnel (lequel n'est pas obligatoire pour les personnes travaillant sans rémunération dans une entreprise ou une affaire familiale);
ii) les personnes occupées, temporairement absentes du travail;
iii) les étudiants travaillant à temps partiel;
iv) les travailleurs saisonniers ou occasionnels;
v) les détenteurs de plusieurs emplois;
vi) les apprentis et les stagiaires.

Seules les personnes appartenant à la catégorie v) peuvent être identifiées séparément sur la base des données tirées des registres du régime de pensions des salariés. Les données relatives aux conscrits effectuant un service militaire ou civil peuvent être obtenues auprès du registre spécial du Ministère de la défense, bien que ces personnes soient exclues de la définition de la population active.

c) Chômage: Sont considérées comme «chômeurs» toutes les personnes qui, selon le registre des demandeurs d'emploi non occupés du Ministère du Travail, sont sans emploi depuis le 29 décembre 1990, mais désirent travailler et sont à la recherche d'un emploi. Les étudiants en quête de travail sont exclus de cette définition.

7. Classifications utilisées:
Aussi bien les personnes pourvues d'un emploi que les chômeurs ayant précédemment travaillé sont classifiés par branche d'activité économique et par profession. Mais seules les personnes pourvues d'un emploi sont classées d'après la situation dans la profession.

a) Branche d'activité économique (industrie): La branche d'activité économique (de même qu'un certain nombre d'autres informations) est obtenue à partir du registre des entreprises et établissements de l'Office central des statistiques (Central Statistical Office, CSO), qui utilise les mêmes paramètres d'identification que les registres de l'administration fiscale. Le registre des entreprises et établissements contient le même code que celui qui peut être utilisé pour envoyer des informations aux salariés. La procédure varie cependant quelque peu selon que l'entreprise comporte un ou plusieurs établissements. Pour certains chefs d'entreprise, la branche d'activité économique est déterminée sur la base des données du régime de pensions et en fonction du type de revenus. Pour coder la branche d'activité économique, quelque 460 groupes de la classification type du CSO ont été utilisés. Des liens avec la CITI (rév.2 et rév.3) ont été établis respectivement au niveau des groupes et des classes (4 chiffres).

b) Profession: Les données utilisées pour déterminer le groupe de professions sont tirées des registres des salaires du gouvernement central et des collectivités locales, des registres de l'administration fiscale et du registre des demandeurs d'emploi du Ministère du Travail. Les professions obtenues à partir de ces registres sont codées par le système de codage automatique mis au point par le CSO. Quelque 400 groupes ont été utilisés à cet effet. Des liens avec la CITP-68 ont été établis au niveau des groupes de base (3 chiffres). Il n'a pas encore été établi de liens avec la CITP-88, mais cela est prévu.

c) Situation dans la profession: La situation dans la profession est définie sur la base de données concernant le type d'assurance-vieillesse (régime de pensions des salariés ou régime professionnel) et la source des revenus (honoraires, salaire ou revenu de chef d'entreprise). Pour coder la situation dans la profession, deux grands groupes ont été utilisés: i) salariés, et ii) chefs d'entreprise (ce groupe inclut les travailleurs indépendants, les employeurs et les personnes travaillant sans rémunération dans une entreprise ou une affaire familiale).

8. Principales différences par rapport au recensement précédent:

Le recensement de 1990 a été réalisé sur la base des registres et la méthode utilisée pour le recouvrement des données a été entièrement différente de celle employée pour le recensement de 1985. Toutes les données utilisées pour déterminer la population active ont été tirées des dossiers administratifs et aucun questionnaire n'a été utilisé. Bien que la méthode de recouvrement des données ait été différente, les définitions concernant la population active et ses composantes n'ont été qu'assez peu modifiées. La différence la plus importante dans le contenu des données est le fait qu'elles n'incluent plus d'informations sur le travail à temps partiel.

Les registres contiennent généralement des données officielles, c'est-à-dire qu'ils fournissent des informations sur toute activité professionnelle donnant lieu à des prélèvements fiscaux et tombant dans le champ d'application des régimes d'assurance professionnelle. Le but du recensement basé sur les registres est de fournir à peu près les mêmes informations que les recensements par questionnaire. A noter toutefois que le recensement de 1990 n'a permis d'obtenir aucune information sur le temps de travail hebdomadaire et sur le mode de déplacement entre le domicile et le lieu de travail.

Les avantages du recensement basé sur les registres résident essentiellement dans les données qu'il permet d'obtenir sur les individus. Ainsi, le recensement de 1990 permettra d'obtenir des informations sur tous les emplois exercés par les personnes pourvues d'un emploi en 1990, et notamment sur le nombre d'emplois successifs et les emplois secondaires. On pourra en outre suivre les transferts de population d'un groupe à l'autre, par exemple les personnes qui poursuivaient des études, se trouvaient au chômage ou étaient occupées à des travaux ménagers à domicile et qui se sont engagées dans une activité professionnelle rémunérée, ou au contraire les personnes qui ont quitté la vie active parce qu'elles sont parties à la retraite, se sont retrouvées au chômage ou ont décidé de se consacrer à des tâches ménagères à leur domicile. Les registres permettent également d'obtenir des informations sur le chômage de courte durée; l'on peut ainsi savoir quels sont, d'une manière générale, les emplois rémunérés occupés par des étudiants, et pendant combien de mois par an.

9. Publication des résultats du recensement:

Le titre de la publication contenant les chiffres définitifs du recensement est «Activité économique de la population» (1993).

L'organisme responsable de cette publication est l'Office central des statistiques de la Finlande, P.B. 504, 00101 Helsinki.

Les résultats du recensement sont également disponibles sous forme de tableaux non publiés, de séries de tableaux, de disquettes et de bandes magnétiques.

FRANCE

1. Nom et adresse de l'organisme responsable du recensement:

Institut national de la statistique et des études économiques (INSEE), 18 boulevard Adolphe Pinard, Paris Cedex 14.

2. Recensements de population effectués depuis 1945 (années):

1954, 1962, 1968, 1975, 1982 et 1990. La présente description se réfère au recensement de 1990 (qui a eu lieu le 5 mars).

3. Champ du recensement:

a) Territoire couvert: Ensemble du pays (France métropolitaine). Un recensement a été effectué séparément pour les Départements d'Outre-Mer à la même époque, mais les exploitations en ont été déconnectées de celles concernant la métropole.

b) Personnes couvertes: Tous les résidents en France pour une durée d'au moins six mois, à l'exception des membres étrangers du corps diplomatique et du personnel étranger des ambassades logeant dans un bâtiment qui bénéficie de l'exterritorialité.

4. Période de référence:

Il n'a pas été établi de période de référence. On a demandé aux personnes interrogées d'indiquer si elles exerçaient ou non une activité professionnelle à la date de référence du recencement, à savoir le 5 mars 1990 à zéro heure.

5. Principaux sujets:

a) Population totale, selon le sexe et l'âge:	oui
Population active par:	
b) Sexe et âge:	oui
c) Branche d'activité économique (industrie):	oui
d) Profession:	oui
e) Situation dans la profession:	oui
f) Niveau d'instruction le plus élevé:	oui
g) Durée du travail:	non
h) Autres caractéristiques:	oui

Réf. a): L'âge est généralement défini en termes d'année de naissance.

Réf. h): On a également demandé aux personnes recensées si elles travaillent à temps plein ou à temps partiel.

6. Concepts et définitions:

a) Population active: Elle comprend toutes les personnes âgées de 15 ans et plus qui, à la date du recensement étaient, soit pourvues d'un emploi, soit au chômage, conformément aux définitions données ci-dessous. Les questions relatives à l'activité économique ont été posées à l'ensemble des personnes, mais les réponses n'ont été exploitées que pour un échantillon de 1/4 seulement. La définition inclut aussi bien les militaires de carrière que ceux du contingent.

b) Emploi: Sont considérées comme «pourvues d'un emploi» toutes les personnes qui, à la date du recensement, ont une profession qu'ils exercent, à temps complet ou à temps partiel, soit à leur propre compte (exploitant agricole, artisan, commerçant, industriel, membre d'une profession libérale, etc.), soit comme salarié (ouvrier ou employé), ou encore comme aide familial non salarié (conjoint, enfant ou tout autre membre de la famille d'un agriculteur, d'un commerçant, etc.). Les travailleurs à leur propre compte doivent indiquer s'ils emploient des salariés et en préciser le nombre (à l'exception des apprentis, des gens de maison et, dans l'agriculture, des salariés non permanents).

La définition couvre également les personnes exerçant un travail d'utilité collective (TUC, etc.), celles sous contrat d'adaptation ou de qualification, ainsi que celles placées par une agence d'intérim et celles sous contrat de travail à durée déterminée. Elle inclut, en outre, les personnes qui ont un emploi et qui en cherchent un autre, les retraités ou retirés des affaires qui ont repris une nouvelle activité, les agriculteurs retraités qui ont gardé une petite exploitation, ainsi que les membres du clergé.

Il est indiqué que sont inclus dans cette définition:

i)   les personnes engagées dans la production de produits de base destinés à l'autoconsommation;
ii) les personnes occupées, temporairement absentes du travail;
iii) les étudiants travaillant à temps partiel;
iv) les conscrits (service militaire ou civil);
v)   les travailleurs saisonniers ou occasionnels, s'ils sont occupés le jour du recensement;
vi) les stagiaires rémunérés qui travaillent dans une entreprise.

Les personnes appartenant aux catégories i) et vi) ci-dessus peuvent être identifiées séparément par des questions utilisées à cette fin. Il en va de même pour les militaires du contingent qui, pour la première fois, sont inclus dans la définition de la population active en tant que troisième composante de cette dernière, après les actifs ayant un emploi et les chômeurs.

c) Chômage: Sont considérées comme «chômeurs» toutes les personnes qui, à la date du recensement, étaient sans emploi et à la recherche d'un travail. La question utilisée pour déterminer si une personne doit être considérée comme étant au chômage est «Cherchez-vous un emploi?». En cas de réponse affirmative, la personne doit préciser si elle cherche un emploi depuis «moins de trois mois», «trois mois à moins d'un an», «un an à moins de deux ans», «deux ans ou plus». Les étudiants en quête de travail sont exclus de la définition.

7. Classifications utilisées:

Seules les personnes occupées de l'échantillon sont classifiées par industrie, par profession et d'après la situation dans la profession. Les chômeurs ayant précédemment travaillé sont classifiés uniquement selon leur dernière profession.

a) Branche d'activité économique (industrie): Des questions spécifiques sont posées aux personnes occupées de l'échantillon, notamment sur l'adresse, le nom ou la raison sociale et l'activité sociale de l'établissement qui les emploie ou qu'elles dirigent (par exemple: commerce de vin en gros, fabrication de charpentes métalliques, transport routier de voyageurs, etc.) pour permettre la recherche dans le fichier SIRENE (répertoire des entreprises). Pour coder le secteur d'activité, on a utilisé 600 postes de la Nomenclature des Activités et Produits (NAP). Des liens avec la CITI-rév.2 ont été établis au niveau des catégories (2 chiffres).

b) Profession: Des questions spécifiques sont posées sur la profession ou le métier exercé ou exercé en dernier lieu (par exemple: ouvrier électricien d'entretien, chauffeur de poids lourds, vendeur en électroménager, ingénieur chimiste, caissière de libre-service, etc.). Pour coder la profession, on a utilisé 455 postes de la Nomenclature des Professions et des Catégories Socioprofessionnelles (PCS). Des liens avec la CITP-68 ont été établis au niveau des sous-groupes (2 chiffres).

c) Situation dans la profession: Aux non salariés, on a demandé s'ils exercent leur profession i) comme employeurs ou travailleurs à leur propre compte et, dans l'affirmative, s'ils emploient des salariés (1 ou 2, 3 à 9, 10 ou plus), et ii) comme aides d'un membre de leur famille dans son travail (exploitation agricole ou artisanale, commerce, profession libérale, etc.). Aux salariés, on a demandé s'ils exercent leur profession en tant que tels (dans l'agriculture, seuls sont pris en compte les salariés permanents). Pour coder cette variable, on a utilisé quatre grands groupes: salarié, employeur, indépendant sans salariés, aide familial.

8. Principales différences par rapport au recensement précédent:
Lors du recensement de 1990, les militaires du contingent ont été inclus dans la définition de la population active alors qu'ils en étaient précédemment exclus.

9. Publication des résultats du recensement:
Les résultats définitifs du recensement ont été publiés en 1992.

Le titre de la publication contenant les résultats de l'exploitation légère est: Série «Logement-Population-Emploi»; celui de la publication contenant les résultats de l'exploitation au 1/4 est: Série «Population-Activité-Ménages».

L'organisme responsable de ces publications est l'Institut national de la statistique et des études économiques (INSEE), 18 boulevard Adolphe-Pinard, 75675 Paris Cedex 14.

Les résultats du recensement de 1990 sont également disponibles sous forme de disquettes, de bandes magnétiques et d'exploitations à la demande.

GABON

1. Nom et adresse de l'organisme responsable du recensement:
Bureau central du recensement, Direction générale de la statistique et des études économiques, B.P. 2119, Libreville.

2. Recensements de population effectués depuis 1945 (années):
1981 et 1993. La présente description se réfère au recensement de 1993 (qui a eu lieu le 31 juillet).

3. Champ du recensement:

a) Territoire couvert: Ensemble du pays.

b) Personnes couvertes: Ensemble de la population à l'exception des diplomates et des nationaux résidant à l'étranger.

4. Période de référence:
La semaine et les six mois précédant le jour du recensement.

5. Principaux sujets:
a) Population totale, selon le sexe et l'âge: oui
Population active par:
b) Sexe et âge: oui
c) Branche d'activité économique (industrie): oui
d) Profession: oui
e) Situation dans la profession: oui
f) Niveau d'instruction le plus élevé: oui

g) Durée du travail: non
h) Autres caractéristiques: non
Réf. a): L'âge est défini en termes d'années révolues à la date du dernier anniversaire.

6. Concepts et définitions:

a) Population active: Elle comprend toutes les personnes âgées de 10 ans et plus qui, pendant la longue période de référence, étaient soit pourvues d'un emploi, soit au chômage, conformément aux définitions données ci-dessous. La définition inclut l'ensemble des forces armées cependant que les étudiants travaillant à temps partiel et les étudiants en quête de travail en sont exclus.

b) Emploi: Sont considérées comme «pourvues d'un emploi» toutes les personnes qui ont déclaré avoir eu une occupation pendant au moins une semaine au cours de la longue période de référence. Les questions utilisées étaient: «Avez-vous eu une occupation depuis janvier 1993?» et «Pendant combien de temps?».

Il est indiqué que sont inclus dans cette définition:
i) les personnes travaillant sans rémunération dans une entreprise ou une affaire familiale;
ii) les personnes engagées dans la production de produits de base destinés à l'autoconsommation;
iii) les personnes occupées, temporairement absentes de leur travail;
iv) les travailleurs saisonniers ou occasionnels;
v) les conscrits (service militaire ou civil);
vi) les apprentis et les stagiaires.

Seules les catégories i), iii) et iv) ci-dessus peuvent être identifiées séparément.

c) Chômage: Sont considérées comme «chômeurs» les personnes qui ont déclaré n'avoir eu une occupation que pendant une période inférieure à une semaine au cours de la longue période de référence. Les questions utilisées sont les mêmes que celles indiquées au paragraphe 6 b) ci-dessus.

7. Classifications utilisées:
Aussi bien les personnes occupées que les chômeurs ayant précédemment travaillé sont classifiés par industrie, par profession et d'après la situation dans la profession.

a) Branche d'activité économique (industrie): La question posée se réfère à l'occupation principale et au secteur d'activité de l'entreprise dans laquelle la personne est ou a été occupée. Pour coder la branche d'activité on a utilisé 40 groupes de la classification nationale. Il n'a pas été établi de liens avec la CITI.

b) Profession: Basée sur la question: «Quelle est votre occupation?». Pour coder la profession, on a utilisé 100 groupes à 1 chiffre et 350 groupes à 4 chiffres. Des liens avec la CITP-88 ont été établis au niveau des sous-groupes (3 chiffres).

c) Situation dans la profession: Basée sur la question: «Travaillez-vous pour votre propre compte? a) si oui, employez-vous du personnel? b) si non, êtes-vous rémunéré pour votre travail? ou non, travaillez-vous pour le compte d'un membre de votre famille ou apprenez-vous un métier?». Pour coder cette variable, six groupes ont été utilisés, à savoir: indépendant; salarié; patron; aide familial; apprenti; autres.

8. Principales différences par rapport au recensement précédent:
La limite d'âge était de 10 ans et plus en 1993, et de 6 ans et plus en 1980.

Il n'y a pas eu de question spécifique concernant la formation professionnelle en 1993, mais il y a eu des questions sur le secteur d'activité économique ainsi que sur les migrations.

9. Publication des résultats du recensement:
Les résultats du recensement devaient être publiés au cours du deuxième semestre 1995 dans les publications suivantes: «Résultats bruts, Volume II» et «Analyse des résultats, Volume III».

L'organisme responsable de ces publications est le Bureau central du recensement, Direction générale de la statistique, B.P. 2119, Libreville.

Les résultats du recensement de 1993 sont également disponibles sous forme de disquettes.

GAMBIE

1. Nom et adresse de l'organisme responsable du recensement:
Central Statistics Department, Central Bank Building, Buckle Street, Banjul.

2. Recensements de population effectués depuis 1945 (années):
1963, 1973, 1983 et 1993. La présente description se réfère au recensement de population de 1993 (qui a eu lieu le 15 avril).

3. Champ du recensement:

a) Territoire couvert: Ensemble du pays.

b) Personnes couvertes: Ensemble de la population.

4. Période de référence:
Le mois précédant le jour du recensement.

5. Principaux sujets:
a) Population totale, selon le sexe et l'âge:	oui
Population active par:	
b) Sexe et âge:	oui
c) Branche d'activité économique (industrie):	oui
d) Profession:	oui
e) Situation dans la profession:	oui
f) Niveau d'instruction le plus élevé:	oui
g) Durée du travail:	oui
h) Autres caractéristiques:	non

Réf. a): L'âge est défini en termes d'années révolues à la date du dernier anniversaire.

Réf. g): La durée du travail se réfère au nombre de jours travaillés par les personnes pourvues d'un emploi et présentes au travail pendant la période de référence.

6. Concepts et définitions:

a) Population active: Elle comprend toutes les personnes âgées de 10 ans et plus qui, pendant le mois de référence, étaient soit pourvues d'un emploi, soit au chômage conformément aux définitions données ci-dessous. La définition inclut les membres des forces armées mais exclut les conscrits. Les étudiants travaillant à temps partiel et les étudiants en quête d'emploi sont également exclus de la définition.

b) Emploi: Les questions utilisées pour déterminer si une personne doit être considérée comme pourvue d'un emploi sont: «A quoi avez-vous occupé l'essentiel de votre temps (au cours des 30 derniers jours)? 1) j'ai travaillé; 2) détenteur d'un emploi mais absent du travail; 3) je n'ai pas travaillé et j'étais sans emploi; 4) tâches ménagères; 5) étudiant; 6) autre»; et si la personne a coché la réponse 4) ou 6): «Avez-vous jamais travaillé contre une rémunération ou pour le profit? (y compris dans une ferme ou une affaire familiale et contre paiement en nature)».

Il est indiqué que sont inclus dans cette définition:

i) les personnes travaillant sans rémunération dans une entreprise ou une affaire familiale;

ii) les personnes engagées dans la production de produits de base destinés à l'autoconsommation;

iii) les personnes occupées, temporairement absentes de leur travail;

iv) les travailleurs saisonniers ou occasionnels;

v) les apprentis et les stagiaires.

Seules les personnes appartenant aux catégories i) et iii) peuvent être identifiées séparément.

c) Chômage: Sont considérées comme «chômeurs» toutes les personnes qui, pendant le mois de référence, étaient sans emploi et à la recherche d'un travail.

7. Classifications utilisées:
Aussi bien les personnes pourvues d'un emploi que les chômeurs ayant précédemment travaillé sont classifiés par industrie, par profession et d'après la situation dans la profession.

a) Branche d'activité économique (industrie): Basée sur les questions: «Quel est le nom de l'établissement vous employant (pour les chômeurs: l'ex-établissement)?» et «Quel est le principal produit ou service offert par cet établissement?». Pour coder la branche d'activité économique, on a utilisé dix groupes de la classification nationale. Des liens avec la CITI-Rév.3 ont été établis au niveau des catégories de classement (1 chiffre).

b) Profession: Basée sur la question: «Quel est votre principal travail (pour les chômeurs: le dernier type d'emploi)?». Pour coder la profession, on a utilisé la CITP-88 au niveau des grands groupes (1 chiffre).

c) Situation dans la profession: Basée sur la question: «Quelle est ou était votre position dans l'emploi dans cet établissement?». Pour coder cette variable, cinq groupes ont été utilisés, à savoir: employé contre une rémunération ou un salaire; travailleur indépendant sans salariés; employeur; travailleur familial non rémunéré; autres.

8. Principales différences par rapport au recensement précédent:
Pas de différence majeure.

9. Publication des résultats du recensement:
Les résultats définitifs du recensement de population devaient paraître en décembre 1995 dans une publication intitulée «Population and Housing Census 1993, Economic Characteristics».

L'organisme responsable de la publication des résultats est le Bureau central des statistiques, Central Bank Building, Buckle Street, Banjul.

Les résultats du recensement de 1989 sont également disponibles sous la forme de tableaux non publiés.

GIBRALTAR

1. Nom et adresse de l'organisme responsable du recensement:
Statistics Office, 6 Convent Place, Gibraltar.

2. Recensements de population effectués depuis 1945 (années):
1951, 1961, 1970, 1981 et 1991. La présente description se réfère au recensement de 1991 (qui a eu lieu le 14 octobre).

3. Champ du recensement:

a) Territoire couvert: Ensemble du pays.

b) Personnes couvertes: Ensemble de la population. Les membres des forces armées basées dans la région sont exclus de la définition alors que leurs femmes et les membres de leurs familles y sont inclus.

4. Période de référence:
Le jour du recensement.

5. Principaux sujets:
a) Population totale, selon le sexe et l'âge:	oui
Population active par:	
b) Sexe et âge:	oui
c) Branche d'activité économique (industrie):	oui
d) Profession:	oui
e) Situation dans la profession:	oui
f) Niveau d'instruction le plus élevé:	non
g) Durée du travail:	non
h) Autres caractéristiques:	oui

Réf. a): L'âge est défini en termes d'années révolues à la date du dernier anniversaire.

Réf. h): Le recensement a également rassemblé des informations sur les moyens de transport utilisés pour se rendre au travail (à pied, en bus, en bicyclette, en motocyclette ou en vélomoteur, en voiture ou en camionnette).

6. Concepts et définitions:

a) Population active: Elle comprend toutes les personnes de 15 ans et plus qui, le jour du recensement, étaient soit pourvues d'un emploi, soit au chômage, conformément aux définitions données ci-dessous. Les membres des forces armées, les étudiants travaillant à temps partiel et les étudiants en quête d'un emploi sont exclus de la définition.

b) Emploi: Sont considérées comme «pourvues d'un emploi» toutes les personnes qui, le jour du recensement, avaient un travail à plein temps ou à temps partiel. Ces personnes devaient préciser leur profession du moment et le caractère de leur emploi (plein temps ou temps partiel). Les personnes dans l'attente de démarrer un emploi déjà garanti ainsi que les ménagères exerçant un travail à plein temps ou à temps partiel sont incluses dans la définition.

Il est indiqué que sont inclus dans cette définition:

i) les personnes travaillant sans rémunération dans une entreprise ou une affaire familiale;

ii) les personnes occupées, temporairement absentes du travail.

Aucune des catégories ci-dessus ne peut être identifiée séparément.

c) *Chômage*: Sont considérées comme «chômeurs» toutes les personnes qui, le jour du recensement, étaient sans emploi et à la recherche d'un travail.

7. Classifications utilisées:

Seules les personnes pourvues d'un emploi ont été classifiées par branche d'activité économique, par profession et d'après la situation dans la profession.

a) *Branche d'activité économique (industrie)*: Pour déterminer le groupe d'industrie, on a posé une question spécifique aux personnes pourvues d'un emploi: «Si vous travaillez dans une entreprise privée (ou si vous êtes à votre propre compte), précisez le type d'activité exercé par l'employeur, à savoir: commerce de détail, imprimerie, hôtellerie, banque, coiffure, etc. Si vous travaillez pour le gouvernement, précisez le ministère et le service». On a demandé aux personnes de préciser le nom et l'adresse de l'employeur ou du lieu de travail. Pour coder la branche d'activité économique, on a utilisé 23 groupes de la classification nationale. Des liens ont été établis avec la CITI-rév.3 au niveau des catégories de classement (1 chiffre).

b) *Profession*: Pour déterminer le groupe de profession, on a demandé aux personnes pourvues d'un emploi de noter avec précision le titre de leur profession (par exemple, mécanicien, mécanicien radio, ingénieur du génie civil, expert comptable, économiste, etc., et pour les employés des services administratifs du secteur public: chef de département, directeur général ou adjoint, secrétaire personnel(le) ou dactylo). Pour coder la profession, on a utilisé 125 groupes de la classification nationale. Il n'a pas été établi de liens avec la CITP.

c) *Situation dans la profession*: Pour déterminer la situation dans la profession, on a demandé aux personnes pourvues d'un emploi de préciser si elles étaient: salarié; travailleur indépendant; ou employeur. Les travailleurs familiaux sont inclus dans les salariés.

8. Principales différences par rapport au recensement précédent:

Lors du recensement de 1981, la période de référence était d'une semaine. De plus, aussi bien les personnes pourvues d'un emploi que les chômeurs ayant précédemment travaillé étaient classifiés par branche d'activité économique, par profession et d'après la situation dans la profession.

9. Publication des résultats du recensement:

Les résultats définitifs ont été publiés en novembre 1992 dans une publication intitulée «Census of Gibraltar 1991».

L'organisme responsable de cette publication est le Bureau des statistiques de Gibraltar.

Des copies de la publication sont disponibles auprès du Bureau gouvernemental des publications, 6 Convent Place, Gibraltar. Les données ne sont pas disponibles sur disquettes ou bandes magnétiques.

GRECE

1. Nom et adresse de l'organisme responsable du recensement:

Office national de statistique de Grèce (ONSG), Direction des Recensements, 43-45, rue Agissilaou, 10166 Athènes.

2. Recensements de population effectués depuis 1945 (années):

1951, 1961, 1971, 1981 et 1991. La présente description se réfère au recensement de 1991 (qui a eu lieu le 17 mars).

3. Champ du recensement:

a) *Territoire couvert*: Ensemble du pays.

b) *Personnes couvertes*: Ensemble de la population.

4. Période de référence:

La semaine précédant la date du recensement et les douze mois antérieurs au recensement (mars 1990-février 1991).

5. Principaux sujets:

a) Population totale, selon le sexe et l'âge:	oui
Population active par:	
b) Sexe et âge:	oui
c) Branche d'activité économique (industrie):	oui

d) Profession:	oui
e) Situation dans la profession:	oui
f) Niveau d'instruction le plus élevé:	oui
g) Durée du travail:	oui
h) Autres caractéristiques:	oui

Réf. a): L'âge est défini en termes d'année de naissance.

Réf. g): La durée du travail est exprimée en heures réellement effectuées par les personnes pourvues d'emploi, présentes au travail, pendant la courte période de référence.

Réf. h): Le recensement a également rassemblé des informations sur les moyens de transport utilisés et sur le temps consacré pour se rendre au travail.

6. Concepts et définitions:

a) *Population active*: Elle comprend toutes les personnes âgées de 10 ans et plus qui, pendant les périodes de référence étaient, habituellement, soit pourvues d'un emploi, soit au chômage, conformément aux définitions données ci-dessous. Les personnes effectuant leur service militaire obligatoire sont exclues de la définition.

b) *Emploi*: Sont considérées comme «pourvues d'emploi» toutes les personnes qui, pendant les périodes de référence, ont exercé une profession, une fonction ou une quelconque activité économique. Les questions posées pour déterminer si une personne doit être considérée comme pourvue d'emploi sont «X a-t-il travaillé au cours de la période mars 1990-février 1991?» et «Quel était son emploi durant la semaine précédant le recensement (10-16 mars 1991)?».

Il est indiqué que sont inclus dans cette définition:

i)   les personnes travaillant sans rémunération dans une entreprise ou une affaire familiale;

ii) les personnes engagées dans la production de produits de base destinés à l'autoconsommation;

iii) les personnes occupées, temporairement absentes de leur travail;

iv) les étudiants travaillant à temps partiel;

v)   les travailleurs saisonniers ou occasionnels (s'ils étaient en activité à l'époque du recensement);

vi) les apprentis et les stagiaires.

Seules les personnes appartenant au groupe i) peuvent être identifiées séparément au moyen de la question sur la situation dans la profession.

c) *Chômage*: Sont considérées comme «chômeurs» toutes les personnes qui, pendant la semaine de référence, étaient sans travail, à la recherche d'un emploi et immédiatement disponibles pour travailler. Les jeunes et autres personnes à la recherche de leur premier emploi sont également inclus dans la définition. Par contre, les personnes occupées mais qui recherchent un nouvel emploi n'entrent pas dans cette définition et sont considérées comme pourvues d'emploi.

7. Classifications utilisées:

Aussi bien les personnes occupées que les chômeurs ayant précédemment travaillé sont classifiés par industrie, par profession et d'après la situation dans la profession.

a) *Branche d'activité économique (industrie)*: La question posée concerne le type d'activité de l'entreprise, de l'exploitation, de l'établissement ou du service dans lesquels les personnes travaillent ou ont travaillé en dernier lieu. Pour coder la branche d'activité, on a utilisé la CITI-rév.3 au niveau des groupes (3 chiffres).

b) *Profession*: La question posée concerne la nature exacte de la profession que les personnes exercent ou ont exercée en dernier lieu. Pour coder la profession, on a utilisé la CITP-68 au niveau des groupes de base (3 chiffres).

c) *Situation dans la profession*: Basée sur la question: «Quel est (était) le statut de X dans la profession exercée?». Pour coder la situation dans la profession, on a utilisé quatre catégories, à savoir: employeur (occupant une ou plusieurs personnes); travailleur indépendant; salarié au mois ou à la journée; aide familial (dans l'entreprise ou l'exploitation agricole familiale).

8. Principales différences par rapport au recensement précédent:

Par rapport au recensement précédent, le recensement de 1991 présente les différences suivantes:

- Le traitement des données sera exhaustif.

- En plus d'une courte période de référence (la semaine antérieure au jour du recensement), on a aussi utilisé une longue période de référence (l'année précédant le recensement).

- Concernant la courte période de référence, les personnes ayant travaillé au moins une heure ont été considérées comme occupées et donc incluses dans la définition de l'emploi.

- Pour la première fois aussi, on a rassemblé des informations sur les moyens de transport utilisés et le temps consacré pour se rendre au travail.

9. Publication des résultats du recensement:

Le titre de la publication dans laquelle ont été présentés les résultats de ce recensement est «Résultats du recensement de la population et des habitations effectué le 17 mars 1991».

L'organisme responsable de cette publication est l'Office National de Statistique de Grèce, Direction de l'Information Statistique et des Publications, 14-16 rue Lycourgou, 10166 Athènes.

Les résultats du recensement de 1991 sont également disponibles sous forme de tableaux non publiés, de disquettes et de bandes magnétiques.

GRENADE

1. Nom et adresse de l'organisme responsable du recensement:

Central Statistical Office, Ministry of Finance, Financial Complex, The Carenage, St. George's, Grenada.

2. Recensements de population effectués depuis 1945 (années):

1960, 1970 et 1991. La présente description se réfère au recensement de population de 1991 (qui a eu lieu le 12 mai).

3. Champ du recensement:

a) Territoire couvert: Ensemble du pays.

b) Personnes couvertes: Ensemble de la population.

4. Période de référence:

La semaine précédant le jour du recensement.

5. Principaux sujets:

a) Population totale, selon le sexe et l'âge:	oui
Population active par:	
b) Sexe et âge:	oui
c) Branche d'activité économique (industrie):	oui
d) Profession:	oui
e) Situation dans la profession:	oui
f) Niveau d'instruction le plus élevé:	oui
g) Durée du travail:	oui
h) Autres caractéristiques:	oui

Réf. a): L'âge est défini en termes d'années révolues à la date du dernier anniversaire.

Réf. g): La durée du travail se réfère aux heures réellement effectuées par les personnes pourvues d'un emploi.

Réf. h): Le recensement a également permis de rassembler des informations sur les moyens de transports utilisés pour se rendre au travail.

6. Concepts et définitions:

a) Population active: Elle comprend toutes les personnes de 15 ans et plus qui, pendant la semaine de référence, étaient soit pourvues d'un emploi, soit au chômage, conformément aux définitions données ci-dessous. La définition inclut les membres des forces armées.

b) Emploi: L'emploi est déterminé sur la base des questions suivantes: «A quoi avez-vous occupé l'essentiel de votre temps la semaine dernière? par exemple, avez-vous travaillé, recherché un emploi, tenu la maison ou exercé une autre activité?» et «Avez-vous effectué, pendant un temps indéterminé, un quelconque travail au cours de la semaine passée, y compris comme aide dans une affaire familiale ou une ferme, marchand ambulant ou travailleur à domicile?».

Il est indiqué que sont inclus dans cette définition:

i) les personnes travaillant sans rémunération dans une entreprise ou une affaire familiale;

ii) les personnes occupées, temporairement absentes de leur travail;

iii) les étudiants travaillant à temps partiel.

Toutes les personnes appartenant aux catégories ci-dessus peuvent être identifiées séparément.

c) Chômage: La question posée pour déterminer le chômage était la même que celle indiquée sous 6 b). Sont considérées comme «chômeurs» toutes les personnes qui, pendant la semaine de référence, étaient sans travail et à la recherche d'un emploi.

7. Classifications utilisées:

Aussi bien les personnes pourvues d'un emploi que les chômeurs ayant précédemment travaillé sont classifiés par branche d'activité économique et par profession. Mais seules les personnes pourvues d'un emploi sont classées d'après la situation dans la profession.

a) Branche d'activité économique (industrie): Basée sur les questions: «Quel type d'activité est ou était pratiqué sur votre lieu de travail?» et «Quels sont les nom et adresse de votre lieu de travail actuel?». Pour coder la branche d'activité économique, on a utilisé la CITI-rév.3.

b) Profession: Basée sur la question: «Quel type de travail exercez ou exerciez-vous dans votre principale profession?». Pour coder la profession, on a utilisé la CITP-88 au niveau des groupes de base (4 chiffres).

c) Situation dans la profession: Basée sur la question: «Travaillez-vous contre une rémunération, dirigez-vous votre propre entreprise ou exercez-vous une activité non rémunérée?». Pour coder la situation dans la profession, on a utilisé six groupes, à savoir: travailleur dans une entreprise familiale; salarié du gouvernement; salarié du secteur privé; travailleur non rémunéré; travailleur indépendant avec salariés (employeur); travailleur indépendant sans salariés (à son propre compte).

8. Principales différences par rapport au recensement précédent:

Pas de différence majeure.

9. Publication des résultats du recensement:

Les résultats définitifs seront publiés en décembre 1996.

L'organisme responsable de la publication des résultats est le Bureau central des statistiques, Financial Complex, The Carenage, St. George's.

Les résultats seront également disponibles sous forme de disquettes et de tableaux non publiés.

GUADELOUPE

1. Nom et adresse de l'organisme responsable du recensement:

Institut national de la statistique et des études économiques (INSEE), Service régional de la Guadeloupe, Avenue Paul Lacave, B.P. 96, 97102 Basse-Terre, Guadeloupe.

2. Recensements de population effectués depuis 1945 (années):

1954, 1961, 1967, 1974, 1982 et 1990. La présente description se réfère au recensement de 1990 (qui a eu lieu le 15 mars).

3. Champ du recensement:

a) Territoire couvert: Ensemble du territoire.

b) Personnes couvertes: Ensemble de la population.

4. Période de référence:

La semaine précédant le jour du recensement.

5. Principaux sujets:

a) Population totale, selon le sexe et l'âge:	oui
Population active par:	
b) Sexe et âge:	oui
c) Branche d'activité économique (industrie):	oui
d) Profession:	oui
e) Situation dans la profession:	oui
f) Niveau d'instruction le plus élevé:	oui
g) Durée du travail:	non
h) Autres caractéristiques:	oui

Réf. a): L'âge est défini en termes d'année de naissance.

Réf. h): Le recensement a également rassemblé d'autres informations, telles que: le travail à temps complet et à temps partiel, l'activité principale, le nombre de salariés occupés par les personnes travaillant à leur propre compte, la durée de recherche d'un travail, etc.

6. Concepts et définitions:

a) Population active: Elle comprend toutes les personnes âgées de 14 ans et plus qui, pendant la semaine de référence étaient, soit pourvues d'un emploi, soit au chômage, conformément aux définitions données ci-dessous. La définition inclut les membres des forces armées (militaires de carrière et ceux du contingent). Les questions relatives à l'activité économique n'ont été posées qu'à un échantillon, dont étaient exclus les militaires logés en caserne et les détenus.

b) Emploi: Sont considérées comme «pourvues d'un emploi» toutes les personnes qui, pendant la semaine de référence, ont exercé une profession, une fonction ou une activité économique, rémunérée ou non. Des questions spécifiques permettent de déterminer si une personne doit être considérée comme pourvue d'emploi, notamment: «Travaillez-vous (à temps complet ou à temps partiel)?»; «Etes-vous: salarié ou à votre compte (exploitant agricole, artisan, commerçant, industriel, profession libérale, aide familial non salarié, etc.)?», et «Si vous êtes à votre compte: combien de salariés employez-vous? (ne comptez ni les apprentis ni les gens de maison; dans l'agriculture, comptez seulement les salariés permanents)». La définition inclut aussi les personnes exerçant un travail d'utilité collective (TUC, etc.), celles placées par une agence d'intérim, celles sous contrat de travail à durée déterminée et celles sous contrat d'adaptation ou de qualification.

Il est indiqué que sont inclus dans cette définition:
i) les personnes travaillant sans rémunération dans une entreprise ou une exploitation familiale;
ii) les personnes engagées dans la production de produits de base destinés à l'autoconsommation;
iii) les personnes occupées, temporairement absentes du travail;
iv) les étudiants travaillant à temps partiel;
v) les travailleurs saisonniers ou occasionnels, pour autant qu'ils soient en activité à l'époque du recensement;
vi) les conscrits (service militaire ou civil);
vii) les apprentis (sous contrat) et les stagiaires (principalement en entreprise ou dans un centre de formation).

Seules les personnes appartenant aux catégories i), vi) et vii) peuvent être identifiées séparément.

c) Chômage: Sont considérées comme «chômeurs» toutes les personnes qui se sont déclarées spontanément en chômage et qui étaient à la recherche d'un travail. Les questions utilisées pour déterminer si une personne doit être considérée comme chômeur sont «Etes-vous chômeur (inscrit ou non à l'Agence nationale pour l'emploi)?», «Avez-vous déjà travaillé? (si oui, quelle était votre profession principale)?», et «Cherchez-vous un emploi (depuis: moins de trois mois; trois mois à moins d'un an; un an à moins de deux ans; deux ans ou plus)?».

7. Classifications utilisées:

Aussi bien les personnes occupées que les chômeurs ayant précédemment travaillé de l'échantillon sont classés par profession. Seules les personnes occupées de l'échantillon sont classifiées par industrie et d'après la situation dans la profession.

a) Branche d'activité économique (industrie): Il a été demandé aux personnes interrogées d'indiquer l'adresse, le nom ou la raison sociale de l'établissement qui les emploie ou qu'elles dirigent, ainsi que l'activité exacte de cet établissement (par exemple: commerce de vin en gros, fabrication de charpentes métalliques, transport routier de voyageurs, etc.). Pour coder la branche d'activité, on a utilisé 100 groupes de la Nomenclature d'Activités et Produits (NAP). Il n'a pas établi de liens avec la CITI.

b) Profession: Il a été demandé aux personnes interrogées d'indiquer la profession exercée actuellement ou en dernier, avec une identification aussi claire que possible de cette profession (par exemple: ouvrier électricien d'entretien, chauffeur de poids lourds, vendeur en électroménager, ingénieur chimiste, caissière de libre-service, etc.), en vue de déterminer le groupe de professions. Cependant, la question a été laissée ouverte, en ce sens que la personne interrogée était libre de formuler sa réponse. Le reclassement dans un groupe déterminé est fait lors du traitement informatique. Pour coder la profession, on a utilisé un système de codification directe en 42 groupes. Il n'a pas été établi de liens avec la CITP.

c) Situation dans la profession: Pour coder cette variable, on a utilisé les cinq catégories suivantes: indépendant à son compte; employeur; salarié; aide familial non rémunéré; autre.

8. Principales différences par rapport au recensement précédent:

La limite d'âge inférieure qui avait été retenue en 1982 pour l'inclusion des personnes dans la population active était de 15 ans.

De plus, lors du recensement de 1982, aussi bien les personnes occupées que les chômeurs ayant précédemment travaillé avaient été classifiés par industrie et d'après la situation dans la profession.

9. Publication des résultats du recensement:

Le titre de la publication contenant les résultats définitifs est: «Population, Emploi, Logements; Evolution 1975-1982-1990 (Série jaune)», 1992.

L'organisme responsable de cette publication est l'Institut national de la statistique et des études économiques (INSEE), 18 boulevard Adolphe-Pinard, 75675 Paris Cedex 14.

Les résultats du recensement de 1990 seront également disponibles sous forme de disquettes et de bandes magnétiques, ainsi que d'exploitations à la demande.

GUAM

1. Nom et adresse de l'organisme responsable du recensement:

Guam Department of Commerce, Suite 601, ITC Bldg, 590 S. Marine Drive, Tamuning 96911.

2. Recensements de population effectués depuis 1945 (années):

1950, 1960, 1970, 1980 et 1990. La présente description se réfère au recensement de population de 1990 (qui a eu lieu le 1er avril).

3. Champ du recensement:

a) Territoire couvert: Ensemble du pays.

b) Personnes couvertes: Ensemble de la population.

4. Période de référence:

La semaine précédant la date du recensement et l'année précédant le recensement.

5. Principaux sujets:

a) Population totale, selon le sexe et l'âge:	oui
Population active par:	
b) Sexe et âge:	oui
c) Branche d'activité économique (industrie):	oui
d) Profession:	oui
e) Situation dans la profession:	oui
f) Niveau d'instruction le plus élevé:	oui
g) Durée du travail:	oui
h) Autres caractéristiques:	oui

Réf. a): L'âge est défini à la fois en termes d'année de naissance et en termes d'années révolues à la date du dernier anniversaire.

Réf. g): La durée du travail se réfère à la fois aux heures réellement effectuées par les personnes pourvues d'un emploi et présentes au travail pendant la semaine de référence et à la période totale de travail (exprimé en heures ou en semaines) accompli par les personnes pourvues d'un emploi au cours de 1989.

Réf. h): Le recensement a aussi rassemblé des informations sur: le lieu de travail; les moyens de transport utilisés pour se rendre au travail; le nombre de personnes voyageant ensemble pour aller au travail (occupants de véhicules privés uniquement); la durée des déplacements; le revenu provenant de salaires, de traitements, de pourboires et de commissions; le revenu tiré d'exploitations agricoles ou non; le revenu perçu comme propriétaire ou comme associé.

6. Concepts et définitions:

a) Population active: Elle comprend toutes les personnes âgées de 15 ans et plus qui, pendant les périodes de référence, étaient soit pourvues d'un emploi soit au chômage, conformément aux définitions données ci-dessous. Toutefois, les résultats du recensement ne seront publiés que pour les personnes âgées de 16 ans et plus. Les membres des forces armées sont inclus dans la définition.

b) Emploi: Les questions posées pour déterminer si une personne doit être considérée comme pourvue d'un emploi sont: «Avez-vous travaillé, à plein temps ou à temps partiel, à un moment ou à un autre la semaine dernière?» et: «L'année dernière (1989) avez-vous occupé, ne serait-ce que quelques jours, un emploi rémunéré ou travaillé dans une entreprise ou une exploitation familiale, à l'exclusion des activités de subsistance?».

Il est indiqué que sont inclus dans cette définition:

i) les personnes travaillant sans rémunération dans une entreprise ou une affaire familiale;
ii) les personnes engagées dans la production de produits de base destinés à l'autoconsommation;
iii) les personnes occupées, temporairement absentes de leur travail;
iv) les étudiants travaillant à temps partiel;
v) les travailleurs saisonniers ou occasionnels;
vi) les apprentis et les stagiaires.

Seules les personnes appartenant aux catégories i) et ii) peuvent être identifiées séparément au moyen de questions spécifiques.

c) Chômage: Sont considérées comme «chômeurs» toutes les personnes qui, pendant la semaine de référence, étaient sans travail et à la recherche d'un emploi. Les questions utilisées pour déterminer si une personne doit être considérée comme chômeur sont les suivantes: «La semaine dernière, faisiez-vous l'objet d'une mise à pied de votre travail ou de votre activité?»; «Etiez-vous à la recherche d'un travail rémunéré au cours des quatre dernières semaines?»; «Auriez-vous pu accepter un travail la semaine dernière si on vous en avez proposé un?»; «A quand remonte votre dernier travail à un poste, dans une affaire ou dans une exploitation agricole, ne serait-ce que pour quelques jours?».

7. Classifications utilisées:

Aussi bien les personnes pourvues d'un emploi que les chômeurs ayant travaillé à un moment quelconque de l'année précédant celle du recensement (1989) sont classifiés par branche d'activité, par profession et d'après la situation dans la profession.

a) Branche d'activité économique (industrie): Basée sur les questions: «Pour qui avez-vous travaillé? De quel type ou branche d'activité économique s'agissait-il? S'agissait-il essentiellement de production manufacturière, de commerce de gros, de commerce de détail, de construction ou autres?». Pour coder la branche d'activité, on a utilisé 13 grands groupes et 231 catégories de la classification type, par industrie, des Etats-Unis (1972 et supplément de 1977). Aucun lien n'a été établi avec la CITI.

b) Profession: Basée sur les questions: «Quel type de travail effectuiez-vous?» et «Quelles étaient vos activités ou tâches les plus importantes?». Pour coder la profession, on a utilisé 13 grands groupes et 503 catégories de la classification type des professions des Etats-Unis. Aucun lien n'a été établi avec la CITP.

c) Situation dans la profession: Basée sur la question: «Etiez-vous: 1) employé dans une société ou une entreprise privée à but lucratif ou par un particulier moyennant un salaire, un traitement ou une commission; 2) employé dans une organisation privée à but non lucratif, exemptée d'impôts ou caritative; 3) employé par des pouvoirs publics locaux ou territoriaux (région, confédération, etc.); 4) fonctionnaire fédéral; 5) travailleur indépendant, membre d'une profession libérale ou exploitant agricole non constitué en société; 6) travailleur indépendant, membre d'une profession libérale ou exploitant agricole constitué en société; 7) employé non rémunéré dans une entreprise ou une exploitation agricole familiale». Pour coder la situation dans la profession, on a utilisé les sept groupes mentionnés précédemment.

8. Principales différences par rapport au recensement précédent:

La seule différence existant entre les recensements de 1980 et de 1990 est l'inclusion du personnel des forces armées dans les questions sur la branche d'activité, la profession et la situation dans l'emploi.

9. Publication des résultats du recensement:

Plusieurs tableaux récapitulatifs des données sur le recensement de 1990 ont été publiés en août 1991. Le document complet était disponible en 1992.

L'organisme responsable de la publication est: Puerto Rico and Outlying Areas Branch, Decennial Planning Division, U.S. Bureau of the Census, Washington, D.C. 20233.

Les résultats du recensement sont également disponibles sous forme de disquettes, de CD-ROM et de tableaux non publiés.

GUATEMALA

1. Nom et adresse de l'organisme responsable du recensement:

Instituto Nacional de Estadística, 8a calle 9-55, Zona 1, Ciudad Guatemala, Guatemala 010001.

2. Recensements de population effectués depuis 1945 (années):

1950, 1964, 1973, 1981 et 1994. La présente description se réfère au recensement de population de 1994 (qui a eu lieu le 17 avril).

3. Champ du recensement:

a) Territoire couvert: Ensemble du pays.

b) Personnes couvertes: Ensemble de la population.

4. Période de référence:

La semaine précédant le recensement.

5. Principaux sujets:

a) Population totale, selon le sexe et l'âge:	oui
Population active par:	
b) Sexe et âge:	oui
c) Branche d'activité économique (industrie):	oui
d) Profession:	oui
e) Situation dans la profession:	oui
f) Niveau d'instruction le plus élevé:	oui
g) Durée du travail:	non
h) Autres caractéristiques:	non

Réf. a): L'âge est défini en termes d'années révolues à la date du dernier anniversaire et en termes d'année de naissance.

6. Concepts et définitions:

a) Population active: Elle comprend toutes les personnes âgées de 7 ans et plus qui, pendant la semaine de référence, étaient soit pourvues d'un emploi soit au chômage, conformément aux définitions données ci-dessous. La définition inclut les militaires de carrière mais exclut les conscrits (service militaire ou civil).

b) Emploi: Sont considérées comme «pourvues d'un emploi» les personnes qui, à la question «Qu'avez-vous fait la semaine précédant la date du recensement?», ont répondu qu'elles travaillaient ou qu'elles ne travaillaient pas mais avaient un emploi. Les catégories de réponses étaient: «a travaillé; n'a pas travaillé, mais avait un emploi; était à la recherche d'un emploi en ayant déjà travaillé auparavant; était à la recherche d'un premier emploi; vivait de ses rentes ou de sa retraite sans travailler; étudiait et ne travaillait pas; s'occupait des tâches ménagères au foyer et ne travaillait pas; autres.».

Il est indiqué que sont inclus dans cette définition:

i) les personnes travaillant sans rémunération dans une entreprise ou une affaire familiale;
ii) les personnes occupées, temporairement absentes de leur travail;
iii) les étudiants travaillant à temps partiel.

Toutes les catégories peuvent être identifiées séparément.

c) Chômage: Sont considérées comme «chômeurs» les personnes ayant répondu, à la question: «Qu'avez-vous fait pendant la semaine précédant la date du recensement?», qu'elles étaient à la recherche d'un premier emploi ou qu'elles étaient à la recherche d'un emploi en ayant déjà travaillé auparavant.

7. Classifications utilisées:

Aussi bien les personnes pourvues d'un emploi que les chômeurs (à l'exception des personnes à la recherche d'un premier emploi) sont classifiées par branche d'activité économique, par profession et d'après la situation dans la profession.

a) Branche d'activité économique (industrie): Pour déterminer la branche d'activité économique, on a demandé à l'intéressé quelle était l'activité exercée par l'usine, l'atelier, le bureau, l'exploitation agricole, l'établissement, etc., où il exerçait la profession qu'il avait indiquée. Des liens ont été établis avec la CITI-rév.3 au niveau des classes (4 chiffres).

b) Profession: Pour déterminer la profession, on a demandé quel était la profession, la fonction ou le type de travail exercé par la personne pendant la semaine de référence ou dans le cadre du dernier emploi qu'elle occupait. Des liens ont été établis avec la CITP-88 au niveau des groupes de base (4 chiffres).

c) *Situation dans la profession*: Pour déterminer cette caractéristique, on a demandé dans quelle catégorie se classait la personne dans sa profession principale. Le codage a été fait en six catégories: patron, travailleur pour son propre compte avec locaux, travailleur pour son propre compte sans locaux, employé du secteur public, employé du secteur privé, travailleur familial sans rémunération.

8. Principales différences par rapport au recensement précédent:
La seule chose qui ait changé est la limite d'âge, puisque lors du recensement de 1994 on a relevé les caractéristiques économiques des personnes âgées de 7 ans et plus (comparé à 10 ans et plus lors du recensement de 1981).

9. Publication des résultats du recensement:
Le titre exact de la publication dans laquelle sont présentés les résultats définitifs est «Características Generales de Habitación y Población», octobre 1995.

L'organisme responsable de cette publication est l'Institut national de statistique - INE - 8va. Calle 9-55 Zona 1.

Les résultats sont également disponibles sous forme de disquettes.

GUINEE EQUATORIALE

1. Nom et adresse de l'organisme responsable du recensement:
Direccion General de Estadística, Ministerio de Economia y Hacienda, Malabo.

2. Recensements de population effectués depuis 1945 (années):
1981 et 1994. La présente description se réfère au recensement de population de 1994 (qui a eu lieu le 11 septembre).

3. Champ du recensement:

a) Territoire couvert: Ensemble du pays.

b) Personnes couvertes: Ensemble de la population à l'exception des représentants diplomatiques résidant en Guinée équatoriale.

4. Période de référence:
La semaine précédant le recensement.

5. Principaux sujets:
a) Population totale, selon le sexe et l'âge: oui
Population active par:
b) Sexe et âge: oui
c) Branche d'activité économique (industrie): oui
d) Profession: oui
e) Situation dans la profession: non
f) Niveau d'instruction le plus élevé: ...
g) Durée du travail: non
h) Autres caractéristiques: non

Réf. a): L'âge est défini en termes d'année de naissance.

6. Concepts et définitions:

a) Population active: Elle comprend toutes les personnes âgées de 6 ans et plus qui, pendant la semaine de référence, étaient pourvues d'un emploi soit au chômage, conformément aux définitions données ci-dessous. Les questions relatives à l'activité économique ont été posées à un échantillon de 15,3 pour cent de la population. Les données concernant la population active et ses composantes (personnes pourvues d'un emploi et chômeurs) n'ont été compilées sous forme de tableaux que pour les personnes âgées de 6 à 64 ans. La définition exclut l'ensemble des forces armées, de même que les étudiants travaillant à temps partiel ou à la recherche d'un emploi.

b) Emploi: Sont considérées comme «pourvues d'un emploi» les personnes ayant travaillé pendant la semaine de référence. Pour déterminer si une personne doit être considérée comme pourvue d'un emploi, il a été demandé à l'intéressé ce qu'il avait fait la semaine précédant le recensement.

Il est indiqué que sont inclus dans cette définition:

i) les personnes occupées, temporairement absentes du travail;
ii) les travailleurs saisonniers ou occasionnels.

Aucune de ces deux catégories de peut être identifiée séparément.

c) *Chômage*: Sont considérées comme «chômeurs» les personnes qui, pendant la semaine de référence, ne travaillaient pas mais étaient à la recherche d'un emploi. Les questions utilisées pour déterminer si une personne peut être considérée comme «chômeur» sont: «Etes-vous à la recherche d'un emploi en ayant déjà travaillé auparavant?» et «Etes-vous à la recherche d'un premier emploi?».

7. Classifications utilisées:
Aussi bien les personnes pourvues d'un emploi que les chômeurs ayant déjà travaillé auparavant sont classifiés par branche d'activité économique et par profession.

a) Branche d'activité économique (industrie): Basée sur la question: «Quelle est l'activité de l'établissement commercial ou industriel dans lequel vous travaillez?». Pour coder la branche d'activité, on a utilisé la CITI-rév.3.

b) Profession: Les questions utilisées pour déterminer la profession sont: «Quelle est votre profession?» et «Quelle est votre catégorie de profession?». Pour coder le groupe de professions, on a utilisé 10 groupes de la classification nationale. Des liens ont été établis avec la CITP-88 au niveau des grands groupes (1 chiffre).

c) Situation dans la profession: Aucune classification n'a été faite d'après la situation dans la profession.

8. Principales différences par rapport au recensement précédent:
Pas de différence majeure.

9. Publication des résultats du recensement:
Les résultats définitifs ont été publiés en janvier 1995.

Le titre exact de la publication dans laquelle sont présentés les résultats est: «Características de la Población y de las Viviendas».

L'organisme responsable de cette publication est la Direction générale des statistiques, Ministère de l'économie et des finances, Malabo.

Les résultats du recensement sont également disponibles sur supports magnétiques.

GUYANE FRANCAISE

1. Nom et adresse de l'organisme responsable du recensement:
Institut national de la statistique et des études économiques (INSEE), Service régional de la Guyane, 1 rue Maillard Dumesle, B.P. 6017, 97306 Cayenne Cedex.

2. Recensements de population effectués depuis 1945 (années):
1954, 1961, 1967, 1974, 1982 et 1990. La présente description se réfère au recensement de 1990 (qui a eu lieu le 15 mars).

3. Champ du recensement:

a) Territoire couvert: Ensemble du territoire.

b) Personnes couvertes: Ensemble de la population.

4. Période de référence:
La semaine précédant le jour du recensement.

5. Principaux sujets:
a) Population totale, selon le sexe et l'âge: oui
Population active par:
b) Sexe et âge: oui
c) Branche d'activité économique (industrie): oui
d) Profession: oui
e) Situation dans la profession: oui
f) Niveau d'instruction le plus élevé: oui
g) Durée du travail: non
h) Autres caractéristiques: oui

Réf. a): L'âge est défini en termes d'année de naissance.

Réf. h): Le recensement a également rassemblé d'autres informations, telles que: le travail à temps complet et à temps partiel, l'activité principale, le nombre de salariés occupés par les personnes travaillant à leur propre compte, la durée de recherche d'un travail, etc.

6. Concepts et définitions:

a) Population active: Elle comprend toutes les personnes âgées de 14 ans et plus qui, pendant la semaine de référence étaient, soit pourvues d'un emploi, soit au chômage, conformément aux définitions données ci-dessous. La définition inclut les membres des forces armées (militaires de carrière et ceux du contingent). Les questions relatives à l'activité économique n'ont été posées qu'à un échantillon, dont étaient exclus les militaires logés en caserne et les détenus.

b) Emploi: Sont considérées comme «pourvues d'emploi» toutes les personnes qui, pendant la semaine de référence, ont exercé une profession, une fonction ou une activité économique, rémunérée ou non. Des questions spécifiques permettent de déterminer si une personne doit être considérée comme pourvue d'emploi, notamment: «Travaillez-vous (à temps complet ou à temps partiel)?»; «Etes-vous: salarié ou à votre compte (exploitant agricole, artisan, commerçant, industriel, profession libérale, aide familial non salarié, etc.)?», et «Si vous êtes à votre compte: combien de salariés employez-vous? (ne comptez ni les apprentis ni les gens de maison; dans l'agriculture, comptez seulement les salariés permanents)». La définition inclut aussi les personnes exerçant un travail d'utilité collective (TUC, etc.), celles placées par une agence d'intérim, celles sous contrat de travail à durée déterminée et celles sous contrat d'adaptation ou de qualification.

Il est indiqué que sont inclus dans cette définition:

i) les personnes travaillant sans rémunération dans une entreprise ou une exploitation familiale;
ii) les personnes engagées dans la production de produits de base destinés à l'autoconsommation;
iii) les personnes occupées, temporairement absentes du travail;
iv) les étudiants travaillant à temps partiel;
v) les travailleurs saisonniers ou occasionnels, pour autant qu'ils soient en activité à l'époque du recensement;
vi) les conscrits (service militaire ou civil);
vii) les apprentis (sous contrat) et les stagiaires (principalement en entreprise ou dans un centre de formation).

Seules les personnes appartenant aux catégories i), vi) et vii) peuvent être identifiées séparément.

c) Chômage: Sont considérées comme «chômeurs» toutes les personnes qui se sont déclarées spontanément en chômage et qui étaient à la recherche d'un travail. Les questions utilisées pour déterminer si une personne doit être considérée comme chômeur sont «Etes-vous chômeur (inscrit ou non à l'Agence nationale pour l'emploi)?», «Avez-vous déjà travaillé? (si oui, quelle était votre profession principale?», et «Cherchez-vous un emploi (depuis: moins de trois mois; trois mois à moins d'un an; un an à moins de deux ans; deux ans ou plus)?».

7. Classifications utilisées:
Aussi bien les personnes occupées que les chômeurs ayant précédemment travaillé de l'échantillon sont classifiés par profession. Seules les personnes occupées de l'échantillon sont classifiées par industrie et d'après la situation dans la profession.

a) Branche d'activité économique (industrie): Il a été demandé aux personnes interrogées d'indiquer l'adresse, le nom ou la raison sociale de l'établissement qui les emploie ou qu'elles dirigent, ainsi que l'activité exacte de cet établissement (par exemple: commerce de vin en gros, fabrication de charpentes métalliques, transport routier de voyageurs, etc.). Pour coder la branche d'activité, on a utilisé 100 groupes de la Nomenclature d'Activités et Produits (NAP). Il n'a pas été établi de liens avec la CITI.

b) Profession: Il a été demandé aux personnes interrogées d'indiquer la profession exercée actuellement ou en dernier, avec une identification aussi claire que possible de cette profession (par exemple: ouvrier électricien d'entretien, chauffeur de poids lourds, vendeur en électroménager, ingénieur chimiste, caissière de libre-service, etc.), en vue de déterminer le groupe de professions. Cependant, la question a été laissée ouverte, en ce sens que la personne interrogée était libre de formuler sa réponse. Le reclassement dans un groupe déterminé est fait lors du traitement informatique. Pour coder la profession, on a utilisé un système de codification directe en 42 groupes. Il n'a pas été établi de liens avec la CITP.

c) Situation dans la profession: Pour coder cette variable, on a utilisé les cinq catégories suivantes: indépendant à son compte; employeur; salarié; aide familial non rémunéré; autre.

8. Principales différences par rapport au recensement précédent:
La limite d'âge inférieure qui avait été retenue en 1982 pour l'inclusion des personnes dans la population active était de 15 ans.

De plus, lors du recensement de 1982, aussi bien les personnes occupées que les chômeurs ayant précédemment travaillé avaient été classifiés par industrie et d'après la situation dans la profession.

9. Publication des résultats du recensement:
Le titre de la publication contenant les résultats définitifs est: «Population, Emploi, Logements; Evolution 1975-1982-1990 (Série jaune)», 1992.

L'organisme responsable de cette publication est l'Institut national de la statistique et des études économiques (INSEE), 18 boulevard Adolphe-Pinard, 75675 Paris Cedex 14.

Les résultats du recensement de 1990 seront également disponibles sous forme de disquettes et de bandes magnétiques, ainsi que d'exploitations à la demande.

HONG-KONG

1. Nom et adresse de l'organisme responsable du recensement:
Census and Statistics Department, 21/F., Wanchai Tower I, 12 Harbour Road, Wanchai, Hong Kong.

2. Recensements de population effectués depuis 1945 (années):
Recensements complets: 1961, 1971, 1981 et 1991; recensements intermédiaires: 1966, 1976, et 1986. La présente description se réfère au recensement de 1991 (qui a eu lieu du 15 au 24 mars).

3. Champ du recensement:
a) Territoire couvert: Ensemble du pays.
b) Personnes couvertes: Ensemble de la population.

4. Période de référence:
Les sept jours précédant l'énumération. Toutefois, pour déterminer si une personne était en quête d'un emploi, on a utilisé une période de 30 jours antérieure à la date de référence du recensement.

5. Principaux sujets:

a) Population totale, selon le sexe et l'âge:	oui
Population active par:	
b) Sexe et âge:	oui
c) Branche d'activité économique (industrie):	oui
d) Profession:	oui
e) Situation dans la profession:	oui
f) Niveau d'instruction le plus élevé:	oui
g) Durée du travail:	non
h) Autres caractéristiques:	non

Réf. a): L'âge est défini en termes d'années révolues à la date du dernier anniversaire.

6. Concepts et définitions:

a) Population active: Elle comprend toutes les personnes âgées de 15 ans et plus qui, pendant les périodes de référence, étaient soit pourvues d'un emploi, soit au chômage, conformément aux définitions données ci-dessous. La définition inclut également les membres des forces armées. Les questions sur l'activité économique ont été posées à un septième de la population et aux seuls résidents présents à Hong Kong à la date de référence du recensement.

b) Emploi: Sont considérées comme «pourvues d'un emploi» toutes les personnes de l'échantillon qui ont répondu positivement à l'une ou l'autre des trois questions suivantes: «Avez-vous travaillé au cours des sept derniers jours moyennant une rémunération ou pour le profit, y compris en donnant des cours particuliers ou sur la base d'un tarif horaire?», «Aviez-vous un emploi au cours des sept derniers jours?» et «Avez-vous travaillé sans rémunération dans votre entreprise familiale au cours des sept derniers jours?».

Les personnes pourvues d'un emploi peuvent appartenir aux catégories suivantes:

i) les personnes travaillant sans rémunération dans une entreprise ou une affaire familiale;
ii) les personnes occupées, temporairement absentes de leur travail;
iii) les étudiants travaillant à temps partiel;
iv) les travailleurs saisonniers ou occasionnels;
v) les détenteurs de plusieurs emplois;
vi) les apprentis et les stagiaires.

Seules les personnes appartenant aux catégories i) et v) peuvent être identifiées séparément par des questions spécifiques. Par exemple: les personnes de la catégorie i) peuvent être identifiées par la question: «Avez-vous travaillé sans rémunération dans votre entreprise familiale au cours des sept derniers jours?»; celles de la catégorie v) peuvent être identifiées par la question: «Avez-vous exercé un emploi secondaire au cours des 30 derniers jours?».

c) *Chômage:* Sont considérées comme «chômeurs» toutes les personnes de l'échantillon qui ont répondu négativement aux trois questions posées sous 6 b). Elles ont été soumises à des questions supplémentaires: «Etiez-vous à la recherche d'un travail au cours des 30 derniers jours?», «Pourquoi n'étiez-vous pas en quête d'un travail?», «Etiez-vous disponible pour travailler au cours des sept derniers jours?» et «Pourquoi étiez-vous indisponible pour travailler?». Les réponses obtenues ont permis de classer les personnes interrogées soit comme «chômeurs», soit comme «inactifs».

7. Classifications utilisées:
Seules les personnes de l'échantillon qui sont pourvues d'un emploi sont classifiées par industrie, par profession et d'après la situation dans la profession.

a) *Branche d'activité économique (industrie):* On a posé aux personnes de l'échantillon pourvues d'un emploi deux types de questions. La question réservée aux salariés était: «Quel type d'industrie, d'affaires ou de services était pratiqué par votre employeur à l'endroit où vous travailliez?». La question réservée aux employeurs, aux travailleurs indépendants et aux travailleurs familiaux était: «Quel type d'industrie, d'affaires ou de services était pratiqué par vous-même ou votre famille?». Pour coder la branche d'activité, on a utilisé 87 codes de la classification nationale. Des liens ont été établis avec la CITI-Rév.3 au niveau des groupes (3 chiffres).

b) *Profession:* Basée sur les questions: «Quelle est votre profession?», «Quelles sont les principales tâches ou fonctions qui vous incombent dans votre profession?» et «Quelles sont la formation et les qualifications professionnelles exigées par cet emploi?». Pour coder la profession, on a utilisé 116 codes de la classification nationale des professions. Des liens ont été établis avec la CITP-88 au niveau des sous-groupes (3 chiffres).

c) *Situation dans la profession:* Basée sur la question: «Etiez-vous un employeur, un travailleur indépendant ou un salarié?». Les travailleurs familiaux non rémunérés, identifiés lors de la détermination des personnes pourvues d'un emploi, n'ont pas eu à répondre à cette question. Pour coder la situation dans la profession, on a utilisé les quatre groupes suivants: travailleur indépendant; employeur; salarié (y compris les travailleurs en extérieur); travailleurs familiaux non rémunérés.

8. Principales différences par rapport au recensement précédent:
Pas de différence majeure.

9. Publication des résultats du recensement:
Le titre de la publication contenant les résultats du recensement est «Hong Kong 1991 Population Census Summary Results», parue en octobre 1991 et qui constitue le premier rapport d'une série de publications récapitulatives.

L'organisme responsable de cette publication est le Département des statistiques et du recensement, Census Planning Section, Koway Court, 2/F, 111 Chai Wan Road.

Les résultats du recensement sont également disponibles sous forme de tableaux non publiés, de disquettes, de bandes magnétiques et de CD-ROM.

HONGRIE

1. Nom et adresse de l'organisme responsable du recensement:
Office Central de Statistique de Hongrie, Division des recensements (KSH-Népszámlálás), Budafoki út 59, H-1111 Budapest.

2. Recensements de population effectués depuis 1945 (années):
1949, 1960, 1970, 1980 et 1990. La présente description se réfère au recensement de 1990 (qui a eu lieu le 1er janvier).

3. Champ du recensement:
a) *Territoire couvert:* Ensemble du pays.

b) *Personnes couvertes:* Ensemble de la population excepté: les diplomates et employés étrangers des missions des pays étrangers; les militaires des contingents étrangers stationnés en Hongrie en vertu du Pacte de Varsovie et les membres de leurs familles; les touristes étrangers qui ne sont pas munis d'une carte de séjour.

4. Période de référence:
La période de référence retenue dans les questions posées est, en général, (c'est-à-dire pour les employés, les membres de coopératives, les travailleurs à leur propre compte et les personnes travaillant sans rémunération dans une affaire familiale non agricole) une courte période, à savoir la dernière semaine de 1989; pour les travailleurs familiaux non rémunérés dans l'agriculture, la période de référence retenue est une longue période, à savoir au minimum 90 jours ouvrables de travail de dix heures chacun au cours de l'année 1989.

5. Principaux sujets:
a) Population totale, selon le sexe et l'âge:	oui
Population active par:	
b) Sexe et âge:	oui
c) Branche d'activité économique (industrie):	oui
d) Profession:	oui
e) Situation dans la profession:	oui
f) Niveau d'instruction le plus élevé:	oui
g) Durée du travail:	non
h) Autres caractéristiques:	oui

Réf. a): L'âge est défini en termes d'année de naissance.

Réf. g): Cependant, dans le cadre du «programme représentatif» (touchant un échantillon de 20 pour cent de la population), une question a été posée pour savoir si la personne travaille à plein temps ou à temps partiel. Dans le cadre du même programme, le nombre d'heures effectuées a été demandé uniquement aux retraités qui avaient conservé une activité économique.

Réf. h): D'autres questions concernant l'activité de la personne ont été posées, notamment sur: le degré de qualification; le nom et l'adresse du lieu de travail; les moyens de transport utilisés et le temps nécessaire pour atteindre le lieu de travail et pour en revenir; la position dans l'effectif du travail; la date d'entrée dans la première occupation rémunérée; l'exercice éventuel d'une activité complémentaire et sa durée en 1989; etc. Une partie de ces questions a été posée à l'ensemble de la population active, tandis que d'autres questions n'ont été posées qu'aux personnes appartenant à l'échantillon de 20 pour cent.

6. Concepts et définitions:
a) *Population active:* Elle comprend toutes les personnes qui, pendant les périodes de référence, étaient soit pourvues d'un emploi, soit au chômage, conformément aux définitions données ci-dessous. La définition inclut également les membres des forces armées. Les étudiants travaillant à temps partiel, les étudiants à la recherche d'un emploi ainsi que les retraités pourvus d'emploi sont exclus de cette définition. Aucune limite d'âge minimum ou maximum n'a été retenue pour la collecte d'informations sur la population active et ses composantes; toutefois, la publication des résultats se limitera aux actifs âgés de 14 à 85 ans. Toutes les personnes devaient répondre à la question «Travaillez-vous, êtes-vous pourvu d'un emploi?». En cas de réponse négative, la personne devait préciser la raison de sa non-activité.

Dans le «programme de base» (appliqué à 80 pour cent de la population), aucune question relative à l'activité économique ne concernait les catégories suivantes: les retraités, rentiers et autres personnes dont le revenu ne provenait pas d'une activité du moment; les chômeurs à la recherche d'un emploi; les dépendants d'autrui. Par contre, bien que considérées comme «non économiquement actives», les personnes absentes de leur travail parce qu'elles bénéficiaient de l'allocation ou de la prime pour soins aux enfants devaient répondre à toutes les questions concernant leur situation antérieure à l'arrêt de travail.

Dans le «programme représentatif» (limité à un échantillon de 20 pour cent de l'ensemble de la population), les personnes pourvues d'un emploi devaient répondre à toutes les questions relatives à l'emploi et à la profession. Les retraités et personnes assimilées, de même que les chômeurs à la recherche d'un emploi, devaient répondre seulement aux questions concernant leur dernière activité économique, tandis que les retraités qui continuaient d'exercer une activité à plein temps ou à temps partiel devaient donner quelques précisions à ce sujet. Quant aux dépendants, ils devaient répondre aux questions posées sur les personnes dont ils étaient à charge.

b) Emploi: Sont considérées comme «pourvues d'emploi» toutes les personnes qui, pendant les périodes de référence, ont exercé une profession, une fonction ou une quelconque activité économique. La question posée pour déterminer si une personne doit être considérée comme pourvue d'emploi est la même que celle posée à toutes les personnes, comme indiqué sous 6 a) ci-dessus. En cas de réponse affirmative, la personne recensée devait fournir des précisions sur son activité, qu'elle se situe hors du foyer ou au foyer, avec ou sans rémunération.

Il est indiqué que sont inclus dans cette définition:

i) les personnes travaillant sans rémunération dans une entreprise ou une affaire familiale;

ii) les personnes engagées dans la production de produits destinés à l'autoconsommation;

iii) les personnes occupées, temporairement absentes de leur travail pour cause de congé (payé ou non) ou de participation à une formation en relation avec la profession;

iv) les conscrits (service militaire ou civil);

v) les travailleurs saisonniers ou occasionnels;

vi) les détenteurs de plusieurs emplois.

Les personnes appartenant aux catégories ci-dessus peuvent être identifiées séparément, soit d'après leur réponse à la question sur la situation dans la profession (employé; membre d'une coopérative; travailleur à son propre compte; personne exerçant une profession libérale; aide familial), soit d'après un code spécial. Les détenteurs de plusieurs emplois peuvent l'être dans le cadre du «programme représentatif», sur la base de la réponse à la question «En plus de votre occupation principale, avez-vous exercé une activité rémunérée complémentaire en 1989?».

c) Chômage: Sont considérées comme «chômeurs» toutes les personnes qui ont répondu «non» à la question posée sous 6 a) ci-dessus et qui ont déclaré qu'elles étaient à la recherche d'un travail ou d'un premier emploi. Les personnes qui ont invoqué d'autres raisons (telles que: bénéficient d'une subvention ou d'une allocation pour enfant; bénéficient d'une pension personnelle; bénéficient d'une rente d'invalidité ou de toute autre rente personnelle; bénéficient d'une pension ou d'une rente de veuf ou de veuve; fréquentent une crèche, un jardin d'enfants, une école primaire ou secondaire, une école supérieure ou une université), ainsi que les autres personnes dépendantes, sont exclues de la définition du chômage.

7. Classifications utilisées:
Aussi bien les personnes pourvues d'emploi que les chômeurs de l'échantillon ayant précédemment travaillé sont classifiés par industrie, par profession et d'après la situation dans la profession.

a) Branche d'activité économique (industrie): Les questions posées pour déterminer le groupe d'industrie concernent le nom de l'employeur et l'adresse du lieu de travail. La personne doit indiquer avec précision la nature du lieu de travail (par exemple: fabrique, siège d'une compagnie, magasin, école, institution sanitaire, etc.). Pour coder la branche d'activité, on a utilisé 38 groupes principaux, 104 branches et 294 branches individuelles (niveau de 4 chiffres) de la nomenclature hongroise.

Il n'a pas été établi de liens avec la CITI. Toutefois, un nouveau système national de classification des branches d'activité économique a été récemment établi; d'après ce nouveau système, adapté à la CITI-rév.3, un recodage d'au moins un échantillon représentatif des questionnaires permettra des comparaisons au plan international.

b) Profession: Les questions posées pour déterminer le groupe de professions se réfèrent à la nature de la profession de la personne recensée ainsi qu'à sa position hiérarchique dans l'effectif. Pour coder la profession, on a utilisé 16 groupes principaux, 144 groupes de professions et 808 professions individuelles (à 4 chiffres) de la nomenclature hongroise.

Il n'a pas été établi de liens avec la CITP. Toutefois, un nouveau système national de classification des professions sera élaboré; d'après ce nouveau système, adapté à la CITP-88 au niveau des 10 grands groupes et des sous-grands groupes, un recodage d'au moins un échantillon représentatif des questionnaires permettra des comparaisons au plan international.

c) Situation dans la profession: Des questions spécifiques ont été posées, aussi bien dans le cadre du «programme de base» que du «programme représentatif», pour déterminer la situation dans la profession. Pour coder cette variable, on a utilisé les huit groupes suivants: employé; membre de coopérative; travailleur à son propre compte d'occupation physique; travailleur à son propre compte d'occupation non physique; membre de famille travaillant sans rémunération pour un membre de coopérative agricole; membre de famille travaillant sans rémunération dans une exploitation agricole auxiliaire; membre de famille travaillant sans rémunération pour un travailleur à son propre compte agricole; membre de famille travaillant sans rémunération pour un travailleur à son propre compte non agricole.

8. Principales différences par rapport au recensement précédent:
Le principal changement qui caractérise le recensement de 1990 par rapport à celui 1980 concerne l'introduction du chômage comme nouvelle et importante composante de la population active.

Par ailleurs, le «programme représentatif» (appliqué à un échantillon de 20 pour cent de la population) comporte un certain nombre de questions nouvelles destinées à définir et à décrire la population active et ses composantes, et à mieux déterminer la situation dans la profession. D'autres questions permettent d'identifier l'occupation principale et les activités complémentaires, le travail à plein temps et le travail à temps partiel, le niveau d'éducation et de formation, le degré de qualification, etc.

9. Publication des résultats du recensement:
Les titres des publications contenant les résultats sont entre autres: «1. Preliminary data» août 1990, «Socio-occupational composition of active earners, households and families» 1992, «Place of work and place of residence of active earners» 1994, et «Detailed data of the 20% representative sample survey» 1995.

L'organisme responsable de ces publications est l'Office Central de Statistique de Hongrie, Division des Recensements (KSH-Népszámlálás), H-1111 Budapest.

Les résultats du recensement de 1990 sont également disponibles sous forme de disquettes, CD-ROM et système interactif (on-line).

ILE DE MAN

1. Nom et adresse de l'organisme responsable du recensement:
Economic Affairs Division, Isle of Man Government, Illiam Dhone House, 2 Circular Road, Douglas, Ile de Man IMI IPQ, Iles britanniques.

2. Recensements de population effectués depuis 1945 (années):
1951, 1961, 1966, 1971, 1976, 1981, 1986 et 1991. La présente description se réfère au recensement de population de 1991 (qui a eu lieu le 14 avril).

3. Champ du recensement:

a) Territoire couvert: Ensemble du pays.

b) Personnes couvertes: Ensemble de la population.

4. Période de référence:
La semaine précédant le jour du recensement, et cinq mois de l'année précédente (1er mai-30 septembre 1990) pour le travail saisonnier uniquement.

5. Principaux sujets:

a) Population totale, selon le sexe et l'âge:	oui
Population active par:	
b) Sexe et âge:	oui
c) Branche d'activité économique (industrie):	oui
d) Profession:	oui
e) Situation dans la profession:	oui
f) Niveau d'instruction le plus élevé:	non
g) Durée du travail:	oui
h) Autres caractéristiques:	oui

Réf. a): L'âge est défini en termes d'années révolues à la date du dernier anniversaire.

Réf. g): Les personnes pourvues d'un emploi sont invitées à indiquer leur durée de travail actuelle. Les travailleurs saisonniers doivent indiquer le nombre de semaines et le nombre d'heures par semaine pendant lesquelles ils ont travaillé au cours de la période de référence longue.

Réf. h): Le recensement a également permis de recouvrer des informations sur les permis de travail («Avez-vous un permis de travail?») et sur les moyens de transport utilisés pour se rendre sur le lieu de travail.

6. Concepts et définitions:

a) Population active: Elle comprend toutes les personnes âgées de 16 ans et plus qui, au cours de la période de référence, étaient soit pourvues d'un emploi soit au chômage, conformément aux définitions données ci-dessous. La définition exclut les étudiants qui travaillent à temps partiel et ceux qui sont à la recherche d'un emploi. Elle inclut toutefois l'ensemble des membres des forces armées. Il n'y a pas de conscription sur l'Ile de Man.

b) Emploi: Sont considérées comme «pourvues d'un emploi» toutes les personnes ayant déclaré avoir travaillé, pendant la semaine de référence, soit à plein temps (plus de 30 heures) soit à temps partiel (30 heures ou moins), que ce soit pour un employeur ou pour leur propre compte. Les enseignants travaillant 25 heures ou plus sont comptés comme travailleurs à temps complet.

Il est indiqué que sont inclus dans cette définition:

i) les personnes occupées, temporairement absentes du travail;
ii) les travailleurs saisonniers ou occasionnels;
iii) les détenteurs de plusieurs emplois;
iv) les apprentis et les stagiaires.

Seules les personnes appartenant aux catégories ii) et iii) peuvent être identifiées séparément.

c) Chômage: Sont considérées comme «chômeurs» toutes les personnes qui ont déclaré que pendant la semaine de référence elles étaient sans travail et à la recherche d'un emploi.

7. Classifications utilisées:

Seules les personnes pourvues d'un emploi ont été classifiées par branche d'activité économique, par profession et d'après la situation dans la profession.

a) Branche d'activité économique (industrie): Basée sur la question: «Dénomination de l'activité de l'employeur ou de l'activité indépendante? (par ex. service de nettoyage de bureaux; fabrication de nourriture pour animaux; installation de chauffage central; services juridiques professionnels)». Pour coder cette variable, on a utilisé 21 groupes de la classification nationale. Aucun lien n'a été établi avec la CITI.

b) Profession: Basée sur la question: «Quelle votre profession? Par ex. monteur gazier, employé comptable, superviseur bancaire, ou employé de bureau». Il était demandé aux personnes interrogées de donner une description du travail effectué, par ex. dactylographie sous dictée, gestion de comptes pour des clients privés, réparation de machines agricoles, livraison de marchandises aux clients. Pour coder la profession, on a utilisé 371 groupes de la Classification standard des emplois au Royaume-Uni (United Kingdom's Standard Occupational Classification, SOC). Des liens ont été établis avec la CITP-88 au niveau des sous-groupes (3 chiffres).

c) Situation dans la profession: Trois groupes ont été utilisés pour coder cette variable, à savoir: salarié; indépendant avec salariés; indépendant sans salariés.

8. Principales différences par rapport au recensement précédent:

Le recensement de 1986 n'avait pas collecté de données sur l'activité économique.

La limite d'âge inférieure était de 15 ans en 1981 (en 1981, l'âge de fin de scolarité obligatoire était de 15 ans. Il a été relevé à 16 ans avant 1991, ce qui explique le changement dans la couverture du recensement).

9. Publication des résultats du recensement:

Les résultats définitifs concernant la population active et ses diverses composantes ont été publiés dans une publication intitulée «Rapport sur le recensement de 1991, Ile de Man». Le volume I du Rapport est paru en mars 1991 et le volume II en février 1992. Des données complémentaires sont fournies dans «Statistiques 1995, Ile de Man».

L'organisme responsable de ces publications est la Division des affaires économiques, Illiam Dhone House, 2 Circular Road, Douglas, Ile de Man IMI IPQ, Iles britanniques.

Sous réserve du respect de la confidentialité, des informations complémentaires sont disponibles sous forme de tableaux non publiés ou de disquettes.

ILES CAIMANES

1. Nom et adresse de l'organisme responsable du recensement:

Statistics Office, Cayman Islands Government, Government Administration Building, George Town, Grand Cayman, B.W.I.

2. Recensements de population effectués depuis 1945 (années):

1960, 1970, 1979 et 1989. La présente description se réfère au recensement de population de 1989 (qui a eu lieu le 15 octobre).

3. Champ du recensement:

a) Territoire couvert: Ensemble du pays.

b) Personnes couvertes: Ensemble de la population.

4. Période de référence:

La semaine précédant le jour du recensement.

5. Principaux sujets:

a) Population totale, selon le sexe et l'âge: oui
Population active par:
b) Sexe et âge: oui
c) Branche d'activité économique (industrie):   oui
d) Profession: oui
e) Situation dans la profession: oui
f) Niveau d'instruction le plus élevé: oui
g) Durée du travail: oui
h) Autres caractéristiques: oui

Réf. a): L'âge est défini en termes d'années révolues à la date du dernier anniversaire.

Réf. g): On a demandé aux personnes pourvues d'un emploi de préciser la durée hebdomadaire normale du travail pour leur principal emploi.

Réf. h): Le recensement a aussi rassemblé des informations sur le revenu hebdomadaire tiré de l'emploi principal et sur les moyens de transport utilisés pour se rendre au travail.

6. Concepts et définitions:

a) Population active: Elle comprend toutes les personnes de 15 ans et plus qui, pendant la semaine de référence, étaient soit pourvues d'un emploi, soit au chômage, conformément aux définitions données ci-dessous. La définition inclut également tous les membres des forces armées.

b) Emploi: Sont considérées comme «pourvues d'un emploi» toutes les personnes qui, pendant la semaine de référence, ont travaillé au moins une heure. La question spécifique posée pour déterminer si une personne devait ou non être considérée comme pourvue d'un emploi était «La personne a-t-elle travaillé au cours de la semaine écoulée?».

Il est indiqué que sont inclus dans cette définition:

i) les personnes travaillant sans rémunération dans une entreprise ou une affaire familiale;
ii) les personnes occupées, temporairement absentes de leur travail;
iii) les étudiants travaillant à temps partiel;
iv) les travailleurs saisonniers ou occasionnels;
v) les détenteurs de plusieurs emplois;
vi) les apprentis et les stagiaires.

Seules les personnes appartenant aux catégories i), iii) et v) peuvent être identifiées séparément.

c) Chômage: Sont considérées comme «chômeurs» toutes les personnes qui, pendant la semaine de référence, étaient sans travail, disponibles et à la recherche d'un emploi.

7. Classifications utilisées:

Aussi bien les personnes pourvues d'un emploi que les chômeurs ayant précédemment travaillé sont classifiés par branche d'activité économique, par profession et d'après la situation dans la profession.

a) Branche d'activité économique (industrie): Basée sur la question: «Veuillez préciser le nom de votre principal employeur (ou le nom du dernier employeur pour lequel vous avez travaillé à plein temps) et décrivez avec précision la nature du travail exercé, par exemple finance, hôtellerie, vente au détail, construction, etc». Pour coder l'industrie, on a utilisé 65 groupes de la classification nationale. Des liens ont été établis avec la CITI-rév.3 au niveau des divisions (2 chiffres).

b) Profession: Basée sur la question: «Quelle est la profession de la personne (à savoir le travail auquel elle consacre le plus de temps ou le dernier emploi occupé à plein temps)?, par exemple juriste, banquier, fonctionnaire, électricien, plombier, etc.». Pour coder la profession, on a utilisé 94 groupes de la classification nationale. Des liens ont été établis avec la CITP-88 au niveau des sous-groupes (3 chiffres).

c) Situation dans la profession: Pour coder cette variable, quatre groupes ont été utilisés: travailleur indépendant sans salariés; travailleur indépendant avec salariés; employé à plein temps ou à temps partiel; travailleur non rémunéré dans une affaire familiale.

8. Principales différences par rapport au recensement précédent:
Pas de différence majeure.

9. Publication des résultats du recensement:
Les résultats définitifs du recensement ont été publiés en septembre 1990 dans une publication intitulée «Cayman Islands 1989 Census - Commentary and tabulations of results, volume I».

L'organisme responsable de la publication est le Bureau des sciences économiques et des statistiques, Government Administration Building, George Town, Grand Cayman, B.W.I.

Les résultats du recensement sont également disponibles sous forme de tableaux non publiés.

ILES COOK

1. Nom et adresse de l'organisme responsable du recensement:
Statistics Office, P.O. Box 125, Rarotonga.

2. Recensements de population effectués depuis 1945 (années):
1945, 1956, 1961, 1966, 1971, 1976, 1981, 1986 et 1991. La présente description se réfère au recensement de population de 1991 (qui a eu lieu le 1er décembre).

3. Champ du recensement:
a) Territoire couvert: Ensemble du pays.
b) Personnes couvertes: Ensemble de la population.

4. Période de référence:
Le mois précédant le recensement.

5. Principaux sujets:
a) Population totale, selon le sexe et l'âge: oui
Population active par:
b) Sexe et âge: oui
c) Branche d'activité économique (industrie): oui
d) Profession: oui
e) Situation dans la profession: oui
f) Niveau d'instruction le plus élevé: oui
g) Durée du travail: oui
h) Autres caractéristiques: non

Réf. a): L'âge est défini en termes d'années révolues à la date du dernier anniversaire.

Réf. g): La durée du travail se réfère à la durée normale du travail des personnes pourvues d'un emploi durant la semaine précédant le recensement (et, si ce chiffre n'est pas disponible, à la durée normale du travail pour une semaine classique).

6. Concepts et définitions:
a) Population active: Elle comprend toutes les personnes âgées de 15 ans et plus qui, pendant le mois de référence, étaient soit pourvues d'un emploi, soit au chômage, conformément aux définitions données ci-dessous. La définition inclut également les travailleurs temporaires d'origine ethnique différente. Les Iles Cook n'ont pas de forces armées.

b) Emploi: Sa détermination est basée sur la question suivante: «Position dans l'emploi: 1) employeur ayant sa propre entreprise ou sa propre plantation; 2) travailleur indépendant ou à son propre compte n'employant aucun salarié; 3) travailleur à plein temps percevant un traitement ou un salaire; 4) travailleur à temps partiel ou travailleur temporaire percevant une rémunération; 5) chômeur à la recherche d'un emploi; 6) travailleur familial non rémunéré travaillant sur une plantation, dans un

magasin ou autre, pour assurer sa consommation personnelle ou celle du ménage; 7) retraité; 8) étudiant à plein temps ne travaillant pas contre un traitement ou un salaire; 9) handicapé; 10) tâches ménagères». Les personnes qui se sont rangées dans les catégories 1, 2, 3, 4 et 6 ont été considérées comme «pourvues d'un emploi».

Il est indiqué que sont inclus dans cette définition:
i)   les personnes travaillant sans rémunération dans une entreprise ou une affaire familiale;
ii) les personnes engagées dans la production de produits de base destinés à l'autoconsommation;
iii) les personnes occupées, temporairement absentes de leur travail;
iv) les étudiants travaillant à temps partiel;
v)   les travailleurs saisonniers ou occasionnels;
vi) les apprentis et les stagiaires.

Seules les personnes appartenant aux catégories i) et ii) peuvent être identifiées séparément sur la base de leur position dans l'emploi.

c) Chômage: Sont considérées comme «chômeurs» toutes les personnes qui, pendant la période de référence, étaient sans emploi et à la recherche d'un travail. La définition inclut à la fois les chômeurs ayant précédemment travaillé et ceux n'ayant jamais travaillé.

7. Classifications utilisées:
Seules les personnes pourvues d'un emploi sont classifiées par branche d'activité économique, par profession et d'après la situation dans la profession.

a) Branche d'activité économique (industrie): Les questions spécifiques posées aux personnes pourvues d'un emploi afin de déterminer le groupe d'industrie, tant pour l'activité principale que pour l'activité secondaire, se réfèrent au nom de l'employeur, de l'entreprise, du gouvernement, du magasin ou de la personne les employant ainsi qu'au type d'affaires ou d'activités pratiquées (agriculture, pêche, commerce de détail, etc.) et au nombre d'heures effectuées la semaine précédente ou, si la personne recensée n'a pas travaillé cette semaine-là, à la durée normale du travail. Pour coder la branche d'activité économique, on a utilisé la CITI-rév.2 au niveau des groupes (4 chiffres), mais les données ne seront publiées qu'au niveau des branches (1 chiffre).

b) Profession: La question spécifique posée aux personnes pourvues d'un emploi, relativement à leur activité principale et secondaire, se réfère au travail effectué par la personne sur son lieu de travail pendant la période de référence, à savoir producteur d'agrumes, docker, comptable, etc.. Pour coder la profession, on a utilisé la CITP-88 au niveau des groupes de base (4 chiffres) mais les données ne seront publiées qu'au niveau des grands groupes (1 chiffre).

c) Situation dans la profession: La question posée était la même que celle indiquée sous 6 b). Pour coder la situation dans la profession, six groupes ont été utilisés: employeur ayant sa propre entreprise ou plantation; travailleur indépendant ayant sa propre entreprise mais n'employant aucun salarié; travailleur à plein temps percevant un traitement ou un salaire; travailleur à temps partiel ou travailleur occasionnel percevant une rémunération; travailleur familial travaillant sans rémunération dans une plantation, un magasin ou autre pour assurer sa consommation personnelle ou celle de son ménage («tâches ménagères» est utilisé au sens large afin d'englober la production issue de la pêche et de l'agriculture); autres.

8. Principales différences par rapport au recensement précédent:
Pas de différence majeure.

9. Publication des résultats du recensement:
Comme pour le recensement de 1986, de nombreux rapports contenant les résultats du recensement de 1991 ont été publiés entre 1992 et 1993 sous le titre général «Cook Islands Census of population and dwellings 1991». Ils sont disponibles auprès du Bureau des statistiques à Rarotonga.

L'organisme responsable de la publication des résultats du recensement est le Bureau des statistiques, P.O. Box 125, Rarotonga.

Les données du recensement ne sont disponibles que sous cette forme.

ILES MARIANNES DU NORD

1. Nom et adresse de l'organisme responsable du recensement:
Central Statistics Division, Capitol Hill, Saipan, MP 96950 en collaboration avec le Bureau du recensement des Etats-Unis.

2. Recensements de population effectués depuis 1945 (années):
1958, 1967, 1973, 1980 et 1990. La présente description se réfère au recensement de 1990 (qui a eu lieu le 1er avril).

3. Champ du recensement:
a) Territoire couvert: Ensemble du pays.

b) Personnes couvertes: Le recensement de 1990 comptabilise chaque occupant d'un «lieu de résidence habituel» défini comme l'endroit où une personne vit et dort la plupart du temps.

4. Période de référence:
La semaine avant le recensement et l'année précédant celle du recensement.

5. Principaux sujets:
a) Population totale, selon le sexe et l'âge: oui
Population active par:
b) Sexe et âge: oui
c) Branche d'activité économique (industrie): oui
d) Profession: oui
e) Situation dans la profession: oui
f) Niveau d'instruction le plus élevé: oui
g) Durée du travail: oui
h) Autres caractéristiques: oui

Réf. a): L'âge est défini à la fois en termes d'année de naissance et en termes d'années révolues à la date du dernier anniversaire.

Réf. g): On a demandé aux personnes pourvues d'un emploi de spécifier le nombre d'heures effectuées pendant la semaine de référence et, pour 1989, le nombre de semaines accomplies ainsi que la durée normale du travail.

Réf. h): Le recensement a aussi rassemblé des informations sur les moyens de transport utilisés et le temps nécessaire pour se rendre au travail aussi bien que sur le revenu total perçu en 1989.

6. Concepts et définitions:
a) Population active: Elle comprend toutes les personnes âgées de 15 ans et plus qui, pendant les périodes de référence, étaient soit pourvues d'un emploi, soit au chômage, conformément aux définitions données ci-dessous. Les membres des forces armées sont exclus de la définition.

b) Emploi: Sont considérées comme «pourvues d'un emploi» toutes les personnes qui, pendant la semaine de référence, ont travaillé: comme salarié pour le compte d'autrui; contre rémunération ou pour le profit dans leur propre entreprise; contre rémunération ou non dans une affaire ou une ferme à but lucratif dirigées par un membre de leur famille; à temps partiel (une heure ou deux). La question utilisée pour déterminer si une personne doit être considérée comme pourvue d'un emploi est: «Avez-vous travaillé, à plein temps ou à temps partiel, à un moment quelconque de la semaine écoulée?».

Il est indiqué que sont inclus dans cette définition:
i) les personnes travaillant sans rémunération dans une entreprise ou une affaire familiale;
ii) les personnes engagées dans la production de produits de base destinés à l'autoconsommation;
iii) les personnes occupées, temporairement absentes de leur travail;
iv) les étudiants travaillant à temps partiel;
v) les travailleurs saisonniers ou occasionnels;
vi) les apprentis et les stagiaires.

Toutes les catégories ci-dessus peuvent être identifiées séparément.

c) Chômage: Sont considérées comme «chômeurs» toutes les personnes ayant répondu positivement aux deux questions suivantes: «Etiez-vous à la recherche d'un travail rémunérateur au cours des quatre dernières semaines?» et «Auriez-vous pu accepter un travail la semaine passée si on vous en avait proposé un?».

7. Classifications utilisées:
Aussi bien les personnes pourvues d'un emploi que les chômeurs ayant précédemment travaillé sont classifiés par industrie, par profession et d'après la situation dans la profession.

a) Branche d'activité économique (industrie): Basée sur les questions: «Pour qui avez-vous travaillé?», «De quel type d'activité ou d'industrie s'agissait-il: hôpital, conserverie de poissons, boulangerie de détail, etc.?» et «S'agissait-il principalement de fabrication, de commerce en gros, de commerce au détail ou d'autre chose (agriculture, construction, services, fonction publique, etc.)?». Pour coder la branche d'activité économique, on a utilisé la classification industrielle type des Etats-Unis de 1987 (SIC). Aucun lien n'a été établi avec la CITI.

b) Profession: Basée sur les questions: «Quel type de travail faisiez-vous? (à savoir infirmière diplômée d'Etat, machinerie industrielle, mécanique, glaçage de gâteaux)» et «Quelles étaient vos principales activités ou fonctions? (à savoir soins aux malades, réparation de machines industrielles, glaçage de gâteaux, etc.)?». Pour coder la profession, on a utilisé le Manuel de classification type des professions des Etats-Unis (SOC). Le codage du recensement de 1990 a été effectué par le Bureau du recensement des Etats-Unis en utilisant le manuel SOC de 1980. Il n'a pas été établi de liens avec la CITP. Aucune adaptation n'a été faite pour la classification américaine des professions de 1990.

c) Situation dans la profession: Basée sur la question: «Etiez-vous: employé par une société ou une entreprise privées à but lucratif ou par un particulier moyennant un salaire, un traitement ou une commission; employé par une organisation privée, à but non lucratif, exemptée d'impôts ou caritative; fonctionnaire d'un gouvernement local ou territorial (région, commonwealth, etc.); fonctionnaire du gouvernement fédéral; travailleur indépendant travaillant dans sa propre entreprise, exploitation ou étude sans être inscrit au registre du commerce; travailleur indépendant travaillant dans sa propre société, exploitation ou étude et inscrit au registre du commerce; employé sans rémunération dans une entreprise ou une exploitation agricole familiale?». Pour coder la situation dans la profession, on a utilisé ces sept groupes.

8. Principales différences par rapport au recensement précédent:
Pas de différence majeure.

9. Publication des résultats du recensement:
Les résultats définitifs ont paru en mars 1992 dans une publication intitulée «1990 Census of Population and Housing: Social, Economic, and Housing Characteristics, Commonwealth of the Mariana Islands».

Les organismes responsables de cette publication sont soit le Département du Commerce des Etats-Unis, Bureau du recensement, Washington D.C. 20233, soit le Superintendant des documents, Bureau des publications du Gouvernement des Etats-Unis, Washington D.C. 20402.

Les résultats du recensement sont également disponibles sous forme de disquettes et de bandes magnétiques.

ILES VIERGES (AMERICAINES)

1. Nom et adresse de l'organisme responsable du recensement:
Eastern Caribbean Center, University of the Virgin Islands, St. Thomas Campus, St. Thomas, Iles vierges (américaines), 00802.

2. Recensements de population effectués depuis 1945 (années):
1950, 1960, 1970, 1980 et 1990. La présente description se réfère au recensement de 1990 (qui a eu lieu le 1er avril).

3. Champ du recensement:
a) Territoire couvert: Ensemble du pays.

b) Personnes couvertes: Ensemble de la population.

4. Période de référence:
La semaine précédant le jour du recensement et l'année précédant celle du recensement.

5. Principaux sujets:
a) Population totale, selon le sexe et l'âge: oui
Population active par:

b) Sexe et âge: oui
c) Branche d'activité économique (industrie): oui
d) Profession: oui
e) Situation dans la profession: oui
f) Niveau d'instruction le plus élevé: oui
g) Durée du travail: oui
h) Autres caractéristiques: oui

Réf. a): L'âge est défini en termes d'années révolues le jour du recensement.

Réf. g): Pour la période de référence courte: la durée du travail est définie à la fois comme la durée de travail habituelle des personnes pourvues d'un emploi et comme leur durée de travail effective, sur le lieu où ils exercent leur activité professionnelle. Pour la période de référence longue, il a été demandé aux personnes interrogées d'indiquer leur période de travail totale pendant toute l'année 1989, exprimée en mois, semaines, jours et heures.

Réf. h): Pour la période de référence courte, le recensement a permis de recouvrer des données sur les moyens de transport utilisés et le temps passé pour se rendre au travail. Pour la période de référence longue, il a été demandé aux personnes interrogées de donner des informations sur la source et le total de leurs revenus en 1989.

6. Concepts et définitions:

a) Population active: Elle comprend toutes les personnes âgées de 16 ans et plus qui, au cours de la période de référence, étaient soit pourvues d'un emploi soit au chômage, conformément aux définitions données ci-dessous. La définition inclut les membres des forces armées, mais elle exclut les étudiants travaillant à temps partiel et ceux en quête d'un emploi.

b) Emploi: La principale question utilisée pour déterminer si une personne peut être considérée comme occupée est la suivante: «X a-t-il travaillé à un moment ou à un autre la semaine dernière, soit à temps complet soit à temps partiel?».

Il est indiqué que sont inclus dans cette définition:

i) les personnes travaillant sans rémunération dans une entreprise ou une affaire familiale;
ii) les personnes occupées, temporairement absentes du travail;
iii) les travailleurs saisonniers ou occasionnels;
iv) les conscrits (service militaire ou civil);
v) les détenteurs de plusieurs emplois.

Toutes les catégories ci-dessus peuvent être identifiées séparément au moyen de questions spécifiques.

c) Chômage: Sont considérées comme «chômeurs» toutes les personnes qui, pendant la semaine de référence, étaient sans travail et à la recherche d'un emploi. Les questions utilisées pour déterminer si une personne doit être comptée comme chômeur sont les suivantes: «X était-il au chômage la semaine dernière?», «X a-t-il été à la recherche d'un emploi au cours des quatre dernières semaines?» et «X aurait-il pu prendre un emploi la semaine dernière si on lui en avait offert un?».

7. Classifications utilisées:

Aussi bien les personnes pourvues d'un emploi que les chômeurs ayant précédemment travaillé sont classifiés par branche d'activité économique, par profession et d'après la situation dans la profession. Les questions posées concernaient l'emploi occupé la semaine précédant le recensement (lorsqu'une personne était détentrice de plusieurs emplois, il lui était demandé de décrire celui qui lui demandait le plus d'heures de travail; lorsqu'une personne n'avait pas travaillé au cours de la semaine précédant le recensement, les questions se référaient à son activité ou à son emploi le plus récent depuis 1985).

a) Branche d'activité économique (industrie): Basée sur les questions: «Pour qui travaillait X, et de quel type ou branche d'activité économique s'agissait-il?» et «S'agit-il essentiellement: de production? de commerce de gros? de commerce de détail? d'une autre activité (agriculture, bâtiment, service, fonction publique, etc.)?». Pour coder la branche d'activité économique, huit groupes de la classification nationale ont été utilisés. Aucun lien n'a été établi avec la CITI.

b) Profession: Basée sur les questions: «Quel type de travail X effectuait-il?» et «Quelles étaient les activités ou les tâches les plus importantes de X?». Pour coder la profession, on a utilisé 39 groupes de la classification nationale. Aucun lien avec la CITP n'a été établi.

c) Situation dans la profession: Basée sur les questions: «X était-il employé par une ENTREPRISE A BUT LUCRATIF privée ou individuelle et rémunéré par un traitement, un salaire ou des commissions? Employé d'une organisation PRIVEE A BUT NON LUCRATIF, exemptée d'impôt ou caritative? Fonctionnaire d'une COLLECTIVITE LOCALE (territoriale ou autre)? Fonctionnaire du GOUVERNEMENT fédéral? TRAVAILLEUR INDEPENDANT NON CONSTITUE EN SOCIETE (commerce, profession libérale ou exploitation agricole)? TRAVAILLEUR INDEPENDANT CONSTITUE EN SOCIETE (commerce, profession libérale ou exploitation agricole)? TRAVAILLEUR SANS REMUNERATION dans une entreprise ou une exploitation agricole familiale?». Ce sont ces sept groupes qui ont été utilisés pour coder la situation dans la profession.

8. Principales différences par rapport au recensement précédent:
Pas de différence majeure.

9. Publication des résultats du recensement:
Les titres des documents contenant les résultats définitifs du recensement sont «STF-3 Résumé sur bande magnétique, Fichier 3» (disquette, bande magnétique et CD-ROM) et «CPH-5-55, Résumé des caractéristiques sociales, économiques et relatives au logement» (document imprimé), 1992.

L'organisme responsable de ces documents est le Bureau du recensement, Division des services aux utilisateurs de données, Service-clients, Washington, D.C. 20233.

Les résultats du recensement sont également disponibles sous forme de CD-ROM, bande magnétique, disquette et rapports écrits.

ILES VIERGES (BRITANNIQUES)

1. Nom et adresse de l'organisme responsable du recensement:
Development Planning Unit, B.V. Is. Government, Central Administration Complex, Road Town, Tortola.

2. Recensements de population effectués depuis 1945 (années):
1960, 1970, 1980 et 1991. La présente description se réfère au recensement de population de 1991 (qui a eu lieu le 12 mai).

3. Champ du recensement:
a) Territoire couvert: Ensemble du pays.

b) Personnes couvertes: Ensemble de la population.

4. Période de référence:
La semaine et l'année précédant le jour du recensement.

5. Principaux sujets:
a) Population totale, selon le sexe et l'âge: oui
Population active par:
b) Sexe et âge: oui
c) Branche d'activité économique (industrie): oui
d) Profession: oui
e) Situation dans la profession: oui
f) Niveau d'instruction le plus élevé: ...
g) Durée du travail: oui
h) Autres caractéristiques: oui

Réf. a): L'âge est défini à la fois en termes d'année de naissance et en termes d'années révolues à la date du dernier anniversaire.

Réf. g): On a demandé aux personnes pourvues d'un emploi de spécifier le nombre d'heures réellement effectuées pendant la semaine de référence ainsi que le nombre de mois travaillés au cours de l'année de référence.

Réf. h): Le recensement a également rassemblé des informations sur le paiement des salaires (hebdomadaire, mensuel, etc.), leur montant, sur le commerce ambulant (secteur informel) et sur les moyens de transport utilisés pour se rendre au travail.

6. Concepts et définitions:
a) Population active: Elle comprend toutes les personnes âgées de 15 ans et plus qui, pendant les périodes de référence, étaient soit pourvues d'un emploi, soit au chômage, conformément aux définitions données ci-dessous. La définition inclut également tous les membres des forces armées.

b) Emploi: Sont considérées comme «pourvues d'un emploi» toutes les personnes qui, pendant la période de référence, travaillaient ou avaient une activité professionnelle mais étaient absentes de leur travail. La question utilisée pour déterminer si une personne doit être considérée comme pourvue d'un emploi était: «Avez-vous travaillé pendant la période de référence ou exerciez-vous un travail duquel vous étiez absent?». La définition n'inclut pas les étudiants qui travaillent à temps partiel.

Il est indiqué que sont inclus dans cette définition:

i) les personnes travaillant sans rémunération dans une entreprise ou une affaire familiale;
ii) les personnes engagées dans la production de produits de base destinés à l'autoconsommation;
iii) les personnes occupées, temporairement absentes de leur travail;
iv) les travailleurs saisonniers ou occasionnels;
v) les apprentis et les stagiaires.

Aucune des catégories ci-dessus ne peut être identifiée séparément.

c) Chômage: Sont considérées comme «chômeurs» toutes les personnes qui, pendant la période de référence, ont précisé qu'elles avaient recherché du travail ou qu'elles souhaitaient travailler et étaient disponibles pour le faire.

7. Classifications utilisées:

Aussi bien les personnes pourvues d'un emploi que les chômeurs ayant précédemment travaillé sont classifiés par industrie, par profession et d'après la situation dans la profession.

a) Branche d'activité économique (industrie): Basée sur la question: «Quel type d'activité est exercé sur votre lieu de travail?». Pour coder la branche d'activité économique, on a utilisé la CITI-rév.3 au niveau des classes (4 chiffres).

b) Profession: Basée sur la question: «Quel type de travail exercez ou exerciez-vous dans votre activité professionnelle principale?». Pour coder la profession, on a utilisé la CITP-88 au niveau des groupes de base (4 chiffres).

c) Situation dans la profession: Basée sur la question: «Dirigiez-vous votre propre entreprise, travailliez-vous contre un salaire ou un traitement ou comme travailleur non rémunéré dans une entreprise familiale?». Pour coder la situation dans la profession on a utilisé cinq groupes: salarié du secteur public; salarié du secteur privé; travailleur non rémunéré; travailleur indépendant avec salariés (employeur); travailleur indépendant sans salariés (à son propre compte).

8. Principales différences par rapport au recensement précédent:

Pas de différence majeure.

9. Publication des résultats du recensement:

Les résultats définitifs du recensement sont parus en août 1994 dans une publication intitulée «British Virgin Islands, 1991 Population and Housing Census».

L'organisme responsable de la publication est l'Unité de planification du développement, Central Administration Complex, Road Town, Tortola.

Les résultats du recensement sont également disponibles sous forme de disquettes.

INDE

1. Nom et adresse de l'organisme responsable du recensement:

Office of the Registrar General and Census Commissioner, 2-A, Man Singh Road, New Delhi-110 011.

2. Recensements de population effectués depuis 1945 (années):

1951, 1961, 1971, 1981 et 1991. La présente description se réfère au recensement de la population de 1991 (qui a eu lieu le 1er mars).

3. Champ du recensement:

a) Territoire couvert: Ensemble du pays, à l'exception de Jammu et du Cachemire.

b) Personnes couvertes: Ensemble de la population, à l'exception des diplomates étrangers et de leurs familles et des ressortissants indiens résidant à l'étranger. Les membres du personnel diplomatique indien en poste à l'étranger, de même que leurs familles, ont été couverts par le recensement.

4. Période de référence:

L'année précédant le jour du recensement.

5. Principaux sujets:

a) Population totale, selon le sexe et l'âge:	oui
Population active par:	
b) Sexe et âge:	oui
c) Branche d'activité économique (industrie):	oui
d) Profession:	oui
e) Situation dans la profession:	oui
f) Niveau d'instruction le plus élevé:	oui
g) Durée du travail:	non
h) Autres caractéristiques:	non

Réf. a): L'âge est défini en termes d'années révolues à la date du dernier anniversaire.

6. Concepts et définitions:

a) Population active: Elle comprend toutes les personnes qui, au cours de l'année de référence, étaient habituellement soit pourvues d'un emploi soit au chômage, conformément aux définitions données ci-dessous. Aucun âge limite n'a été fixé pour l'inclusion dans la population active; toutefois, en ce qui concerne les personnes pourvues d'un emploi, les chiffres publiés incluent les personnes âgées de 5 ans et plus (à l'exception du premier extrait des résultats du recensement qui ne comportait aucune donnée relative à l'âge). La définition inclut les membres des forces armées.

Les données relatives à l'activité économique ont été traitées en deux phases. Dans une première phase, les tableaux ont été basés sur un échantillonnage de 10 pour cent de la population dans les Etats les plus importants comptant au moins 10 millions d'habitants, et sur un échantillonnage de 100 pour cent de la population dans les autres Etats plus petits et dans les territoires de l'Union. Dans une deuxième phase, les données relatives aux «travailleurs principaux» autres que les cultivateurs et les travailleurs agricoles, aux «travailleurs marginaux» et aux «non-travailleurs», à la recherche d'un emploi ou prêtes à en accepter un, ont été saisies dans l'ordinateur sur une base de 100 pour cent afin d'obtenir des tableaux plus détaillés et plus fiables pour les unités administratives de niveau inférieur.

b) Emploi: Les questions utilisées pour déterminer si une personne devait ou non être considérée comme pourvue d'un emploi étaient les suivantes: «Avez-vous travaillé à un moment ou à un autre l'année dernière?» et «Dans l'affirmative, avez-vous travaillé la majeure partie de l'année?».

Le travail peut être défini comme toute participation à une activité économiquement productive. Cette participation peut être de nature physique ou intellectuelle. Le travail ne comprend pas seulement l'activité effective mais aussi la supervision et la direction de l'activité.

Un travailleur principal est une personne qui a travaillé la majeure partie de l'année, c'est-à-dire pendant 183 jours ou plus, ou, en d'autres termes, pendant six mois ou plus. Un travailleur marginal est une personne qui a effectivement pu travailler à un moment ou à un autre l'année précédente, mais pas pendant la majeure partie de l'année. Des données sont également recouvrées sur l'éventuelle deuxième activité des travailleurs principaux.

Il est indiqué que sont inclus dans cette définition:

i) les personnes travaillant sans rémunération dans une entreprise ou une affaire familiale;
ii) les personnes pourvues d'un emploi, temporairement absentes du travail;
iii) les étudiants travaillant à temps partiel;
iv) les travailleurs saisonniers ou occasionnels;
v) les conscrits (service militaire ou civil);
vi) les apprentis et les stagiaires.

Les personnes travaillant sans rémunération dans une entreprise ou une affaire familiale peuvent être identifiées séparément à partir des tableaux du recensement relatifs aux travailleurs familiaux (à l'exception des personnes pratiquant la culture de la terre).

Les personnes pratiquant la culture de la terre pour leur propre consommation sont incluses dans la population active mais ne peuvent pas être identifiées séparément. Celles engagées dans la production d'autres produits destinés eux aussi à l'autoconsommation sont exclues de la population active. Aux fins du recensement, il faut entendre par culture de la terre la culture de céréales, de fibres légumineux, de colza et de canne à sucre mais ni la production de tubercules comestibles, de légumes, de fruits, de fourrage, ni l'horticulture, etc.

Les étudiants qui travaillent, et qui sont des travailleurs marginaux, peuvent être identifiés séparément au moyen de questions spécifiques. Cependant, le terme «travailleur marginal» utilisé pour le recensement n'a pas nécessairement la même signification que le terme «travailleur à temps partiel».

c) *Chômage*: Sont considérées comme «chômeurs» toutes les personnes qui n'ont pas travaillé du tout au cours de l'année de référence et qui ont donc été traitées comme «non-travailleurs». Il a été demandé à tous les «non-travailleurs» s'ils recherchaient un emploi ou s'ils étaient prêts à en accepter un.

Les étudiants à la recherche d'un premier emploi, et les personnes à la recherche d'un emploi ou prêtes à en accepter un et qui elles non plus n'avaient jamais travaillé auparavant, peuvent être identifiés séparément au moyen de questions spécifiques.

7. Classifications utilisées:
Seules les personnes pourvues d'un emploi, autres que les cultivateurs et les travailleurs agricoles, sont classifiées par branche d'activité, par profession et d'après la situation dans la profession.

a) *Branche d'activité économique (industrie)*: Afin de déterminer la branche d'activité économique, plusieurs questions ont été posées aux personnes interrogées quant à la nature de leur activité industrielle, commerciale ou de service. Pour coder la branche d'activité, on a utilisé 462 groupes de la Classification nationale des branches d'activité de 1987. Des liens ont été établis avec la CITI-Rév.3 au niveau des groupes (3 chiffres).

b) *Profession*: On a demandé aux personnes interrogées de décrire leur travail; cette question a été posée aussi bien aux «travailleurs principaux» qu'aux «travailleurs marginaux» afin de déterminer le groupe de profession. Pour coder la profession, on a utilisé 512 familles de professions de la Classification nationale des professions de 1968. Des liens ont été établis avec la CITP-68 au niveau des sous-groupes (2 chiffres).

c) *Situation dans la profession*: Pour déterminer la situation dans la profession, il a été demandé aux personnes interrogées de préciser à quelle catégorie de travailleurs elles appartenaient. Pour coder cette variable, on a utilisé trois groupes en cas d'activité familiale et quatre groupes pour les autres types d'activité, à savoir: employeur; salarié; travailleur isolé; travailleur familial. Par définition, il n'y a pas d'«employeur» en cas d'activité familiale.

8. Principales différences par rapport au recensement précédent:
En ce qui concerne le recouvrement des données, la seule différence est le fait que lors du recensement de 1991, la question relative à la recherche d'un emploi ou à la disponibilité par rapport à l'emploi n'a été posée qu'aux «non-travailleurs», alors qu'en 1981 elle avait été posée à la fois aux «non-travailleurs» et aux «travailleurs marginaux». S'agissant des personnes à la recherche d'un emploi ou prêtes à en accepter un, il leur a été demandé pour la première fois, en 1991, si elles avaient déjà travaillé auparavant, afin de mesurer les nouveaux entrants sur le marché du travail.

9. Publication des résultats du recensement:
Les tableaux du recensement de 1991 devaient être publiés en trois étapes: vers 1993, avant la fin de 1994 et avant la fin de 1995. Les chiffres totaux et définitifs concernant la population, obtenus par compilation manuelle, devaient être publiés avant la fin de 1992.

L'organisme responsable de la publication des résultats du recensement est l'Office de l'Officier général d'état civil et Commissaire au recensement de l'Inde, 2-A, Man Singh Road, New Delhi.

Les résultats définitifs sont également disponibles sous forme de disquettes, bandes magnétiques, etc. sous certaines conditions et selon certaines modalités.

INDONESIE

1. Nom et adresse de l'organisme responsable du recensement:
Central Bureau of Statistics, J1. Dr. Sutomo Nr. 8, P.O. Box 1003, Jakarta 10010.

2. Recensements de population effectués depuis 1945 (années):
1961, 1971, 1980 et 1990. La présente description se réfère au recensement de 1990 (qui a eu lieu le 31 octobre).

3. Champ du recensement:
a) *Territoire couvert*: Ensemble du pays.

b) *Personnes couvertes*: Ensemble de la population. Sont exclus du recensement les personnes vivant à l'extérieur de la zone de l'énumération, à savoir celles vivant dans la forêt (primitifs), les marins naviguant plus de six mois et les non résidents.

4. Période de référence:
La semaine précédant le jour du recensement. On a également demandé aux personnes de l'échantillon de spécifier si elles avaient ou non travaillé au cours de l'année écoulée.

5. Principaux sujets:
a) Population totale, selon le sexe et l'âge:	oui
Population active par:	
b) Sexe et âge:	oui
c) Branche d'activité économique (industrie):	oui
d) Profession:	oui
e) Situation dans la profession:	oui
f) Niveau d'instruction le plus élevé:	oui
g) Durée du travail:	oui
h) Autres caractéristiques:	oui

Réf. a): L'âge est défini en termes d'années révolues à la date du dernier anniversaire.

Réf. g): La durée du travail est définie à la fois comme la durée normale de travail effectué par toutes les personnes pourvues d'un emploi et comme la durée de travail effectif accompli par les personnes pourvues d'un emploi et présentes au travail.

Réf. h): Le recensement a aussi rassemblé des informations sur: le nombre total d'heures travaillées pour l'ensemble des emplois (travail principal et travail secondaire); le type d'industrie de l'emploi secondaire exercé pendant la semaine de référence; le type d'industrie pour l'année précédente; les raisons ayant entravé la recherche d'un emploi.

6. Concepts et définitions:
a) *Population active*: Elle comprend toutes les personnes de l'échantillon âgées de 10 ans et plus qui, pendant la semaine de référence, étaient soit pourvues d'un emploi, soit au chômage, conformément aux définitions données ci-dessous. Cependant, des questions concernant l'activité économique ont été posées à un échantillon de 5 pour cent obtenu par un sondage aléatoire à plusieurs degrés, avec comme unité de base les ménages. La définition inclut les membres des forces armées.

b) *Emploi*: Sont considérées comme «pourvues d'un emploi» toutes les personnes de l'échantillon qui, pendant la semaine de référence, ont effectué, pendant au moins une heure, à domicile ou à l'extérieur, un travail ayant une valeur économique. Les questions utilisées pour déterminer si une personne devait être considérée comme pourvue d'un emploi sont: «Activité principale la semaine précédente: 1) salarié; 2) étudiant; 3) tâches ménagères; 4) autre.» et: «Pour 2, 3 et 4, avez-vous également travaillé au moins une heure au cours de la semaine précédente?».

Il est indiqué que sont inclus dans cette définition:

i) les personnes travaillant sans rémunération dans une entreprise ou une affaire familiale;
ii) les personnes engagées dans la production de produits de base destinés à l'autoconsommation;
iii) les personnes occupées, temporairement absentes de leur travail;
iv) les étudiants travaillant à temps partiel;
v) les travailleurs saisonniers ou occasionnels;
vi) les conscrits (service militaire ou civil);
vii) les détenteurs de plusieurs emplois;
viii) les apprentis et les stagiaires.

Seules les personnes appartenant aux catégories i), iii) iv) et vii) peuvent être identifiées séparément.

c) *Chômage*: Sont considérées comme «chômeurs» toutes les personnes de l'échantillon qui, pendant la semaine de référence, étaient sans travail et à la recherche d'un emploi. Les questions posées aux personnes interrogées qui n'avaient pas travaillé au moins une heure la semaine précédente sont: «Avez-vous déjà travaillé?» et «Etiez-vous à la recherche d'un travail au cours de la semaine écoulée?».

7. Classifications utilisées:

Seules les personnes de l'échantillon qui sont pourvues d'un emploi sont classifiées par industrie, par profession et d'après la situation dans la profession.

a) Branche d'activité économique (industrie): Basée sur la question: «Veuillez spécifier le type d'industrie de la principale activité exercée au cours de la semaine écoulée». Pour coder la branche d'activité, on a utilisé 47 groupes de la classification nationale. Des liens avec la CITI-rév.2 ont été établis au niveau des divisions (2 chiffres).

b) Profession: Basée sur la question: «Veuillez spécifier votre profession principale au cours de la semaine écoulée». Pour coder la profession, on a utilisé 334 groupes de la classification nationale. Des liens avec la CITP-68 ont été établis au niveau des groupes de base (3 chiffres).

c) Situation dans la profession: Basée sur la question: «Veuillez spécifier votre situation dans la principale profession exercée au cours de la semaine écoulée». Pour coder la situation dans la profession, cinq groupes ont été utilisés: travailleur indépendant; travailleur indépendant assisté par un membre de sa famille ou un aide temporaire; employeur; salarié; travailleur familial non rémunéré.

8. Principales différences par rapport au recensement précédent:

Pas de différence majeure.

9. Publication des résultats du recensement:

Des résultats intermédiaires et provisoires ont été publiés en octobre 1991.

Le titre de la publication contenant les résultats définitifs du recensement est «The Results of the 1990 Population Census».

l'organisme responsable de cette publication est le Bureau central des statistiques, P.O. Box 1003, Jakarta 10010.

Les résultats bruts sont également disponibles sous forme de bandes magnétiques et de disquettes.

IRAN, REP. ISLAMIQUE D'

1. Nom et adresse de l'organisme responsable du recensement:

Statistical Centre of Iran, Dr. Fatemi Avenue, Tehran 14144.

2. Recensements de population effectués depuis 1945 (années):

1956, 1966, 1976, 1986 et 1991. La présente description se réfère au recensement de population de 1991 (qui a eu lieu le 11 septembre).

3. Champ du recensement:

a) Territoire couvert: Ensemble du pays.

b) Personnes couvertes: Ensemble de la population.

4. Période de référence:

Les sept jours précédant le jour du recensement.

5. Principaux sujets:

a) Population totale, selon le sexe et l'âge:	oui
Population active par:	
b) Sexe et âge:	oui
c) Branche d'activité économique (industrie):	oui
d) Profession:	oui
e) Situation dans la profession:	oui
f) Niveau d'instruction le plus élevé:	oui
g) Durée du travail:	non
h) Autres caractéristiques:	oui

Réf. a): L'âge est défini à la fois en termes d'année de naissance et en termes d'années révolues à la date du dernier anniversaire.

Réf. h): Le recensement a aussi rassemblé des informations sur la durée du chômage exprimée en mois.

6. Concepts et définitions:

a) Population active: Elle comprend toutes les personnes âgées de 10 ans et plus qui, pendant la période de référence, étaient soit pourvues d'un emploi, soit au chômage, conformément aux définitions données ci-dessous. Le recensement se double d'une étude sur les ménages basée sur un échantillon de 10 pour cent de la population; on a posé à toutes les personnes de l'échantillon âgées de 10 ans et plus des questions sur

leur activité économique. La définition inclut les membres des forces armées.

b) Emploi: Sont considérées comme «pourvues d'un emploi» toutes les personnes de l'échantillon qui, pendant la semaine de référence, ont effectué, à domicile ou à l'extérieur, un travail contre rémunération, pour le profit ou pour le compte d'un membre de la famille. Les personnes sans emploi permanent et ayant travaillé un minimum de deux jours pendant la période de référence, sont incluses dans la définition.

Il est indiqué que sont inclus dans cette définition:

i) les personnes travaillant sans rémunération dans une entreprise ou une affaire familiale;
ii) les personnes occupées, temporairement absentes du travail;
iii) les étudiants travaillant à temps partiel;
iv) les travailleurs saisonniers ou occasionnels s'ils n'étaient pas en quête d'un emploi;
v) les conscrits (service militaire ou civil);
vi) les apprentis et les stagiaires.

Les personnes appartenant aux catégories i) et iii) peuvent être identifiées séparément par des questions spécifiques sur leur emploi et leur niveau d'instruction.

c) Chômage: Sont considérées comme «chômeurs» toutes les personnes de l'échantillon qui, pendant la semaine de référence, étaient sans emploi et à la recherche d'un travail.

7. Classifications utilisées:

Seules les personnes de l'échantillon pourvues d'un emploi sont classifiées par industrie, par profession et d'après la situation dans la profession.

a) Branche d'activité économique (industrie): Pour déterminer le groupe d'industrie, on a demandé aux personnes pourvues d'un emploi d'indiquer l'endroit et les principales activités de leur lieu de travail. Pour coder cette variable, on a utilisé la CITI-rév.3 au niveau des classes (4 chiffres).

b) Profession: On a demandé aux personnes recensées d'indiquer précisément leur profession. Pour coder cette dernière, on a utilisé la CITP-68 au niveau des groupes de base (3 chiffres).

c) Situation dans la profession: Les personnes pourvues d'un emploi ont été classées dans une de ces cinq catégories: employeur; travailleur indépendant; salarié du secteur public (ouvrier ou employé); salarié du secteur privé (ouvrier ou employé); et travailleur familial non rémunéré.

8. Principales différences par rapport au recensement précédent:

Le recensement de 1986 était un recensement complet de tous les ménages pour lequel on avait posé à toutes les personnes âgées de 6 ans et plus les questions relatives à la population active et ses composantes. Le recensement de 1986 n'a rassemblé aucune information sur la durée du chômage.

9. Publication des résultats du recensement:

Les résultats définitifs du recensement de population sont parus en 1992 dans la publication intitulée «National Results of the 1991 Multi-Round Population Census».

L'organisme responsable de cette publication est le Centre des statistiques d'Iran, Dr. Fatemi Ave., Tehran 14144.

Les données sont disponibles sur papier mais également sous forme de disquettes et de bandes magnétiques.

IRLANDE

1. Nom et adresse de l'organisme responsable du recensement:

Central Statistics Office, Ardee Road, Rathmines, Dublin 6, Irlande.

2. Recensements de population effectués depuis 1945 (années):

1946, 1951, 1956, 1961, 1966, 1971, 1979, 1981, 1986 et 1991; le recensement de 1979 avait été effectué dans le but de réviser les délimitations des circonscriptions électorales. La présente description se réfère au recensement de population de 1991 (qui a eu lieu le 21 avril).

3. Champ du recensement:

a) Territoire couvert: Ensemble du pays.

b) Personnes couvertes: Ensemble de la population (population «de facto»).

4. Période de référence:

Le jour du recensement. Le statut principal de la personne au moment du recensement a été pris en compte sur la base du choix subjectif fait par la personne elle-même.

5. Principaux sujets:

a) Population totale, selon le sexe et l'âge:	oui
Population active par:	
b) Sexe et âge:	oui
c) Branche d'activité économique (industrie):	oui
d) Profession:	oui
e) Situation dans la profession:	oui
f) Niveau d'instruction le plus élevé:	oui
g) Durée du travail:	non
h) Autres caractéristiques:	non

Réf. a): La plupart des tableaux sont basés sur l'âge à la date du dernier anniversaire, mais certains tableaux sont basés sur l'année de naissance.

6. Concepts et définitions:

a) Population active: Elle comprend toutes les personnes âgées de 15 ans et plus qui, au moment du recensement, étaient soit pourvues d'un emploi soit au chômage, conformément aux définitions données ci-dessous. La définition inclut aussi les militaires de carrière.

b) Emploi: Sont considérées comme «pourvues d'un emploi» toutes les personnes qui, subjectivement, se considéraient comme telles le jour du recensement. Entrent aussi en principe dans cette définition toutes les personnes qui, à la date du recensement, effectuaient à domicile ou à l'extérieur, un travail ayant une valeur économique. Les étudiants qui travaillent à temps partiel sont exclus de la définition.

Il est indiqué que sont inclus dans cette définition:

i)   les personnes travaillant sans rémunération dans une entreprise ou une exploitation familiale;

ii) les personnes engagées dans la production de produits de base destinés à l'autoconsommation;

iii) les personnes occupées, temporairement absentes du travail;

iv) les travailleurs saisonniers ou occasionnels;

v)   les apprentis et les stagiaires.

Seules les personnes appartenant à la catégorie i) peuvent être identifiées séparément. L'incorporation des étudiants qui travaillent à temps partiel dépend de la façon dont ils décrivent leur statut actuel.

c) Chômage: Sont comptées comme «chômeurs» toutes les personnes qui, à la date du recensement, se considéraient subjectivement comme telles.

7. Classifications utilisées:

Aussi bien les personnes pourvues d'un emploi que les chômeurs ayant précédemment travaillé sont classifiés par branche d'activité économique, par profession et d'après la situation dans la profession.

a) Branche d'activité économique (industrie): Basée sur les questions:

«a) Employeur et activité de celui-ci (pour les personnes pourvues d'un emploi: si elles sont salariées, indiquer le nom de l'employeur et la nature de son activité; si elles travaillent à leur propre compte, indiquer la nature de l'activité); b) Adresse du lieu de travail (indiquer l'adresse complète et exacte à laquelle a effectivement lieu l'activité professionnelle: pour les personnes qui travaillent à partir d'un centre fixe ou d'un dépôt, en indiquer l'adresse; pour les personnes qui travaillent à domicile, par ex. les exploitants agricoles, les commerçants habitant sur leur lieu de travail, indiquer 'à domicile'. Pour les personnes qui n'ont pas de lieu de travail fixe, par ex. les voyageurs de commerce, indiquer 'aucun')».

Lorsque les informations relatives à l'employeur et au lieu de travail sont suffisantes, les données obtenues au moyen du recensement sont reliées à un registre des entreprises dont sont dérivés les codes d'activité et de lieu de travail.

Des liens avec la CITI (rév.2 et rév.3) ont été établis respectivement au niveau des catégories et des divisions (2 chiffres).

b) Profession: Basée sur les questions:

«Si vous travaillez, indiquez votre activité principale habituelle en en donnant une description complète»; «Si vous êtes chômeur ou retraité, décrivez la principale activité que vous exerciez auparavant»; «Les personnes décrites comme exploitants ou ouvriers agricoles doivent également indiquer quelles sont/étaient la ou les parcelles de terrain actuellement/précédemment exploitées».

Pour coder la profession, on a utilisé, afin de prendre en compte le titre exact, un système national de codification comportant 8.700 titres classés en 210 groupes de codes. Des liens avec la CITP (68 et 88) ont été établis, respectivement au niveau des sous-groupes et au niveau des groupes de base.

c) Situation dans la profession: Il a été demandé aux personnes interrogées d'indiquer leur situation (actuelle ou précédente) dans la profession. Pour coder cette variable, on a utilisé quatre groupes, à savoir: indépendant avec salariés; indépendant sans salariés; salarié; aide familial sans salaire ni traitement fixe).

8. Principales différences par rapport au recensement précédent:

Les principales différences de codification sont les suivantes:

– La «branche d'activité économique» est codée par liaison avec un registre des entreprises, en essayant de coder aussi le lieu de travail chaque fois que cela s'avère possible;

– La «profession» est codée à un niveau beaucoup plus détaillé qu'auparavant, ce qui permet de présenter les résultats en fonction de la classification SOC du Royaume-Uni et de la CITP-88, et en fonction, aussi, de la classification nationale en vigueur.

9. Publication des résultats du recensement:

Les données relatives à la population totale et à la population active sont parues en 1994 dans différentes publications, telles que par exemple «Rapports sur la population résidente (seconde série)», ainsi que dans les différents volumes contenant les résultats détaillés du recensement, présentés question par question.

L'organisme responsable de ces publications est l'Office central des statistiques, à Dublin.

Les résultats du recensement de 1991 sont également disponibles sous forme de tableaux circonstanciés (sur demande). Des statistiques concernant la population de telle ou telle petite région ou zone sont disponibles sous forme de documents écrits, de bandes magnétiques et de disquettes.

ITALIE

1. Nom et adresse de l'organisme responsable du recensement

Istituto Nazionale di Statistica (ISTAT), Via Adolfo Ravà 150, 00142 Rome.

2. Recensements de population effectués depuis 1945 (années):

1951, 1961, 1971, 1981 et 1991. La présente description se réfère au recensement de 1991 (qui a eu lieu le 20 octobre).

3. Champ du recensement:

a) Territoire couvert: Ensemble du pays.

b) Personnes couvertes: Ensemble de la population à l'exception des nationaux résidant à l'étranger, des étrangers munis d'un passeport diplomatique et des militaires de l'OTAN.

4. Période de référence:

La semaine précédant le jour du recensement.

5. Principaux sujets:

a) Population totale, selon le sexe et l'âge:	oui
Population active par:	
b) Sexe et âge:	oui
c) Branche d'activité économique (industrie):	oui
d) Profession:	oui
e) Situation dans la profession:	oui
f) Niveau d'instruction le plus élevé:	oui
g) Durée du travail:	oui
h) Autres caractéristiques:	oui

Réf. a): L'âge est défini en termes d'années révolues à la date du dernier anniversaire.

Réf. g): La durée du travail se réfère aux heures réellement effectuées par les personnes pourvues d'emploi, présentes au travail.

Réf. h): D'autres informations ont été collectées, notamment sur: la situation professionnelle ou non professionnelle, le lieu de travail ainsi que les moyens de transport utilisés et le temps consacré pour s'y rendre.

6. Concepts et définitions:

a) Population active: Elle comprend toutes les personnes âgées de 14 ans et plus qui, pendant la semaine de référence étaient, soit pourvues d'un emploi, soit au chômage, conformément aux définitions données ci-dessous. La définition inclut les militaires de carrière, mais elle exclut les personnes effectuant leur service militaire obligatoire; toutefois, ces dernières peuvent être identifiées séparément. Les étudiants travaillant à temps partiel et les étudiants en quête de travail sont exclus de la définition.

b) Emploi: Sont considérées comme «pourvues d'emploi» toutes les personnes qui, pendant la semaine de référence, ont exercé une profession, une fonction ou une activité économique, rémunérée ou sans rémunération.

Il est indiqué que sont inclus dans cette définition:

i) les personnes travaillant sans rémunération dans une entreprise ou une affaire familiale;
ii) les personnes occupées, temporairement absentes du travail;
iii) les travailleurs saisonniers ou occasionnels;
iv) les apprentis.

Seules les catégories i) et iv) ci-dessus peut être identifiées séparément. Les personnes effectuant leur service militaire obligatoire, bien que non incluses dans la population active, peuvent aussi être identifiées séparément.

c) Chômage: Sont considérées comme «chômeurs» toutes les personnes qui, pendant la semaine de référence, étaient sans emploi et à la recherche d'un emploi. Les personnes à la recherche de leur premier travail sont exclues de la définition.

7. Classifications utilisées:

Aussi bien les personnes pourvues d'emploi que les chômeurs ayant précédemment travaillé sont classifiés par industrie, par profession et d'après la situation dans la profession.

a) Branche d'activité économique (industrie): Les questions posées se réfèrent au lieu exact et à l'activité principale ou unique de l'établissement, de l'exploitation agricole, du commerce ou négoce, de l'entreprise etc., où la personne recensée travaille ou a travaillé en dernier lieu. Pour coder la branche d'activité, on a utilisé 60 divisions de la classification nationale des industries. Des liens avec la CITI-rév.3 ont été établis au niveau des divisions (2 chiffres).

b) Profession: Les deux questions posées se réfèrent, d'une part, au type de travail de la personne recensée (par exemple: enseignant du degré moyen, agriculteur, technicien électronicien, architecte, programmeur informaticien, secrétaire, électricien sur auto, etc.), en évitant des termes généraux tels qu'employé ou ouvrier; et, d'autre part, aux tâches principales accomplies par la personne dans le cadre de l'activité qu'elle exerce ou qu'elle a exercée en dernier lieu (par exemple: enseignement des mathématiques, culture de la vigne, contrôle de radar, élaboration de programmes, gestion de secrétariat, réparation des installations électriques des autos, etc.). Pour coder la profession, on a utilisé 35 groupes de la classification nationale des professions. Des liens avec la CITP-88 ont été établis au niveau des grands groupes (1 chiffre).

c) Situation dans la profession: La question spécifique se réfère au statut de la personne recensée vis-à-vis de son emploi. Pour coder cette variable, les 14 groupes suivants ont été utilisés: dirigeant; cadre dirigeant; employé; personnel des catégories spéciales (intermédiaire); chef d'équipe d'ouvriers, ouvrier (spécialisé, qualifié, manoeuvre); autre travailleur dépendant; apprenti; travailleur à domicile pour le compte d'une entreprise; gradé ou militaire de carrière des forces armées, ou assimilé; employeur; travailleur à son propre propre compte; profession libérale; membre d'une coopérative de producteurs et/ou de prestation de services; aide familial (par exemple: épouse aidant son mari commerçant, fils aidant son père agriculteur, etc.).

8. Principales différences par rapport au recensement précédent:

Lors du recensement de 1981, une seule question avait été po-

sée pour déterminer le groupe de professions, à savoir: «Indiquer la profession, l'art ou le métier exercés»; alors que lors du recensement de 1991, deux questions ont été utilisées à cette fin.

9. Publication des résultats du recensement:

Le titre définitif de la publication contenant les données sur la population active est «Popolazione e abitazioni» (95 fascicules provinciaux, 20 fascicules régionaux et un fascicule national). L'organisme responsable de la publication des résultats est l'Istituto Nazionale di Statistica (ISTAT), Rome.

Les résultats du recensement de 1991 sont également disponibles sous la forme de disquettes et de bandes magnétiques.

JAMAIQUE

1. Nom et adresse de l'organisme responsable du recensement:

Statistical Institute of Jamaica, 97B Church Street, Kingston.

2. Recensements de population effectués depuis 1945 (années):

1960, 1970, 1982 et 1991. La présente description se réfère au recensement de population de 1991 (qui a eu lieu le 8 avril).

3. Champ du recensement:

a) Territoire couvert: Ensemble du pays.

b) Personnes couvertes: Ensemble de la population.

4. Période de référence:

La semaine et l'année précédant le jour du recensement.

5. Principaux sujets:

a) Population totale, selon le sexe et l'âge:	oui
Population active par:	
b) Sexe et âge:	oui
c) Branche d'activité économique (industrie):	oui
d) Profession:	oui
e) Situation dans la profession:	oui
f) Niveau d'instruction le plus élevé:	oui
g) Durée du travail:	oui
h) Autres caractéristiques:	oui

Réf. a): L'âge est défini en termes d'années révolues à la date du dernier anniversaire.

Réf. g): La durée du travail des personnes pourvues d'un emploi se réfère au nombre d'heures effectuées pendant la période de référence courte et au nombre de mois travaillés pendant la période de référence longue.

Réf. h): On a demandé aux personnes pourvues d'un emploi de spécifier le montant de leur salaire.

6. Concepts et définitions:

a) Population active: Elle comprend toutes les personnes âgées de 14 ans et plus qui, pendant la semaine de référence étaient soit pourvues d'un emploi, soit au chômage, conformément aux définitions données ci-dessous. La définition inclut les membres des forces armées mais exclut les étudiants travaillant à temps partiel ou en quête d'un emploi.

b) Emploi: Sa détermination est basée sur la question suivante: «A quoi avez-vous occupé l'essentiel de votre temps au cours de la semaine précédant le jour du recensement?» par exemple: avez-vous travaillé, recherché un emploi, entretenu la maison ou autre». Les réponses possibles étaient: j'ai travaillé; j'avais un emploi mais j'étais absent de mon travail; j'étais à la recherche de mon premier emploi; autre, à la recherche d'un emploi; je n'étais pas à la recherche d'un emploi mais je souhaitais travailler et j'étais disponible; étudiant; tâches ménagères; retraité; handicapé, incapable de travailler; autre; sans réponse.

Il est indiqué que sont inclus dans cette définition:

i) les personnes travaillant sans rémunération dans une entreprise ou une affaire familiale;
ii) les personnes engagées dans la production de produits de base destinés à l'autoconsommation;
iii) les travailleurs saisonniers ou occasionnels;
iv) les conscrits (service militaire ou civil);
v) les apprentis et les stagiaires.

Seules les personnes appartenant à la première catégorie peuvent être identifiées séparément.

c) *Chômage*: La question posée pour déterminer le chômage était la même que celle indiquée sous 6 b). Sont considérées comme chômeurs les personnes qui, pendant la semaine de référence, étaient sans emploi, souhaitaient travailler et étaient disponibles pour le faire.

7. Classifications utilisées:
Aussi bien les personnes pourvues d'un emploi que les chômeurs ayant précédemment travaillé sont classifiés par industrie, par profession et d'après la situation dans la profession.

a) *Branche d'activité économique (industrie)*: Basée sur la question: «Quel type d'activité est ou était exercée sur votre lieu de travail?». Pour coder la branche d'activité économique, on a utilisé la classification nationale. Des liens ont été établis avec la CITI-rév.3 au niveau des divisions (2 chiffres).

b) *Profession*: Basée sur la question: «Quel type de travail effectuez-vous ou effectuiez-vous dans votre dernier emploi?». Pour coder la profession, on a utilisé la classification nationale. Des liens avec la CITP-88 ont été établis au niveau des sous-grands groupes (2 chiffres).

c) *Situation dans la profession*: Basée sur la question: «Travaillez-vous contre une rémunération, dirigez-vous votre propre entreprise ou autre?». Pour coder la situation dans la profession, on a utilisé 7 groupes, à savoir: salarié du secteur public; salarié du secteur privé; salarié en maison privée; travailleur non rémunéré; travailleur indépendant avec salariés; travailleur indépendant sans salariés; sans réponse.

8. Principales différences par rapport au recensement précédent:
Pas de différence majeure.

9. Publication des résultats du recensement:
Les résultats définitifs du recensement sont parus en 1995 dans diverses publications.

L'organisme responsable de la publication des résultats est l'Institut des statistiques de la Jamaïque, 97 B Church Street, Kingston.

Les résultats sont également disponibles sur disquettes, bandes magnétiques ou CD-ROM.

JAPON

1. Nom et adresse de l'organisme responsable du recensement:
Population Census Division, Statistics Bureau, Management and Coordination Agency, 19-1 Wakamatsu-cho, Shinjuku-ku, Tokyo 162.

2. Recensements de population effectués depuis 1945 (années):
1947, 1950, 1955, 1960, 1965, 1970, 1975, 1980, 1985 et 1990. La présente description se réfère au recensement de population de 1990 (qui a eu lieu le 1er octobre).

3. Champ du recensement:
a) *Territoire couvert*: Ensemble du pays, à l'exception des îles suivantes: 1) Habomai-gunto, Shikotan-to, Kunashiri-to et Etorofu-to; et 2) Takeshima à Goka-mura, Shimane-ken.

b) *Personnes couvertes*: Ensemble de la population, excepté: les membres du corps diplomatique étranger, leur suite et les personnes à leur charge; les militaires étrangers, y compris les civils qui les accompagnent et les personnes à leur charge; les nationaux résidant à l'étranger (parmi les Japonais résidant dans un autre pays, ceux susceptibles d'être absents de leur foyer pendant une période de 3 mois ou plus se situant autour de la date du recensement).

4. Période de référence:
La semaine précédant le jour du recensement (qui a eu lieu du 24 au 30 septembre 1990).

5. Principaux sujets:
a) Population totale, selon le sexe et l'âge: oui
Population active par:
b) Sexe et âge: oui
c) Branche d'activité économique (industrie): oui
d) Profession: oui
e) Situation dans la profession: oui
f) Niveau d'instruction le plus élevé: oui
g) Durée du travail: non
h) Autres caractéristiques: oui

Réf. a): L'âge est défini en termes d'années révolues à la date du dernier anniversaire.

Réf. h): Le recensement a aussi rassemblé des informations concernant la durée des trajets et les moyens de transport utilisés pour se rendre au travail.

6. Concepts et définitions:
a) *Population active*: Elle comprend toutes les personnes âgées de 15 ans et plus qui, pendant la semaine de référence, étaient soit pourvues d'un emploi, soit au chômage, conformément aux définitions données ci-dessous. La définition inclut les membres des forces armées qui sont considérés comme des fonctionnaires.

b) *Emploi*: La question utilisée pour déterminer si une personne doit être considérée comme pourvue d'un emploi est: «La personne a-t-elle travaillé au cours de la semaine allant du 24 au 30 septembre? 1) a surtout travaillé; 2) a travaillé tout en assumant les tâches ménagères; 3) a travaillé tout en poursuivant ses études; 4) détenteur d'un emploi mais temporairement absent du travail; 5) en quête d'un emploi; 6) tâches ménagères; 7) scolarisé; 8) autre». Les personnes qui se sont rangées dans les catégories 1, 2, 3 ou 4 ont été considérées comme «pourvues d'un emploi».

Il est indiqué que sont inclus dans cette définition:
i)   les personnes travaillant sans rémunération dans une entreprise ou une affaire familiale;
ii) les personnes occupées, temporairement absentes du travail;
iii) les étudiants travaillant à temps partiel;
iv) les travailleurs saisonniers ou occasionnels;
v)   les apprentis et les stagiaires: si la situation et le salaire ou le traitement de la personne sont garantis par l'entreprise pour laquelle elle travaille tout en poursuivant ses études, elle est considérée comme «pourvue d'un emploi» et incluse dans la population active.

Seules les personnes appartenant aux catégories ii) et iii) peuvent être identifiées séparément. Les étudiants qui travaillent à temps partiel peuvent être identifiés par le groupe «travaillent tout en poursuivant leurs études»; cependant, il n'est pas possible de distinguer entre travail à plein temps et travail à temps partiel pour les étudiants.

c) *Chômage*: Sont considérées comme «chômeurs» toutes les personnes qui, au cours de la période de référence, étaient sans emploi et à la recherche d'un emploi. La question utilisée pour déterminer si une personne doit être considérée comme étant au chômage est la même que celle indiquée sous 6 b) ci-dessus. Les étudiants en quête de travail sont exclus de la définition.

7. Classifications utilisées:
Seules les personnes pourvues d'un emploi ont été classifiées par branche d'activité économique, par profession et d'après la situation dans la profession.

a) *Branche d'activité économique (industrie)*: Des questions spécifiques ont été posées aux personnes pourvues d'un emploi concernant le nom de l'établissement et son type d'activité, ainsi que la nature des marchandises ou des biens produits. Pour coder la branche d'activité, on a utilisé 14 grands groupes, 75 groupes intermédiaires et 213 sous-groupes. Des liens ont été établis avec la CITI-rév.2 au niveau des grands groupes (3 chiffres).

b) *Profession*: Des questions spécifiques ont été posées aux personnes pourvues d'un emploi concernant leur profession et la nature de leur travail. Pour coder la profession, on a utilisé 10 grands groupes, 61 groupes intermédiaires et 294 sous-groupes. Des liens avec la CITP-68 ont été établis au niveau des grands groupes (1 chiffre).

c) *Situation dans la profession*: Des questions spécifiques ont été posées aux personnes pourvues d'un emploi pour déterminer leur situation dans la profession. Pour coder cette dernière, on a utilisé six groupes, à savoir: salarié (incluant les employés de bureau, les ouvriers, les fonctionnaires, les membres d'une corporation, les employés d'un magasin de détail privé, les employés de maison, les journaliers et les travailleurs temporaires, etc.); directeur d'une entreprise ou d'une société; travailleur indépendant avec salariés; travailleur indépendant sans salariés (les propriétaires d'une boutique ou d'une usine non enregistrée, agriculteurs, médecins, avocats, écrivains, aides familiaux à leur compte, colporteurs, etc. sont à classer soit dans la catégorie des «travailleurs indépendants avec salariés», soit dans celle des «travailleurs indépendants sans salariés» selon qu'ils ont ou non engagé des employés pour leur activité); travailleur familial; artisan à domicile.

8. Principales différences par rapport au recensement précédent:
Pas de différence majeure.

9. Publication des résultats du recensement:
Le titre de la publication contenant les résultats du recensement est: «1990 Population Census of Japan», 1994.

L'organisme responsable de cette publication est le Bureau des statistiques du Département sur le recensement de population, Management and Coordination Agency, 19-1 Wakamatsu-cho, Shinjuku-ku, Tokyo 162.

Les résultats du recensement sont également disponibles sous d'autres formes comme des tableaux non publiés et des bandes magnétiques.

KENYA

1. Nom et adresse de l'organisme responsable du recensement:
Central Bureau of Statistics in the Office of the Vice President and Ministry of Planning and National Development, P.O. Box 30266, Nairobi.

2. Recensements de population effectués depuis 1945 (années):
1948, 1962, 1969, 1979 et 1989. La présente description se réfère au recensement de population de 1989 (qui a eu lieu le 24 août).

3. Champ du recensement:
a) Territoire couvert: Ensemble du pays.

b) Personnes couvertes: Ensemble de la population.

4. Période de référence:
La semaine précédant le jour du recensement.

5. Principaux sujets:
a) Population totale, selon le sexe et l'âge: oui
Population active par:
b) Sexe et âge: oui
c) Branche d'activité économique (industrie):   non
d) Profession: oui
e) Situation dans la profession: oui
f) Niveau d'instruction le plus élevé: oui
g) Durée du travail: non
h) Autres caractéristiques: non

Réf. a): L'âge est défini en termes d'années révolues à la date du dernier anniversaire.

6. Concepts et définitions:
a) Population active: Elle comprend toutes les personnes âgées de 10 ans et plus qui, au cours de la semaine de référence, étaient soit pourvues d'un emploi soit au chômage, conformément aux définitions données ci-dessous. Les étudiants travaillant à temps partiel et les étudiants en quête d'emploi sont exclus de la définition.

b) Emploi: Sont considérées comme «pourvues d'un emploi» toutes les personnes qui, pendant la période de référence, travaillaient la plupart du temps moyennant traitement, salaire, commission, pourboires, forfait et paiement en nature. La question utilisée pour déterminer si une personne doit être considérée comme pourvue d'un emploi est: «A quoi avez-vous occupé l'essentiel de votre temps au cours des sept derniers jours précédant la nuit du recensement? 1) travail rémunéré ou lucratif; 2) congé/congé maladie; 3) travail dans une affaire familiale; 4) sans travail; 5) en quête d'emploi; 6) étudiant; 7) retraité; 8) handicapé; 9) ménagère; 10) autre».

Il est indiqué que sont inclus dans cette définition:
i)   les personnes travaillant sans rémunération dans une entreprise ou une affaire familiale;
ii)   les personnes engagées dans la production de produits de base destinés à l'autoconsommation;
iii)   les personnes occupées, temporairement absentes du travail;
iv)   les travailleurs saisonniers ou occasionnels;
v)   les apprentis et les stagiaires.

Seules les personnes appartenant à la catégorie iii) peuvent être identifiées séparément.

c) Chômage: Sont considérées comme «chômeurs» toutes les personnes qui, pendant la semaine de référence, étaient sans travail mais disponibles pour travailler et à la recherche d'un emploi. Les personnes qui ne recherchaient pas activement un travail étaient considérées comme chômeurs mais elles n'étaient pas classées dans la même catégorie que les précédentes.

7. Classifications utilisées:
Seules les personnes pourvues d'un emploi ont été classifiées par profession et d'après la situation dans la profession.

a) Branche d'activité économique (industrie): Aucune classification n'a été faite par branche d'activité économique.

b) Profession: Basée sur la question: «A quoi avez-vous passé l'essentiel de votre temps?», ex: employé de bureau, mécanicien automobile, instituteur, etc. Pour coder la profession, on a utilisé huit très grands groupes de la classification nationale. Des liens avec la CITP-88 ont été établis au niveau des grands groupes (1 chiffre).

c) Situation dans la profession: Basée sur la question: «Quel était votre emploi?». Pour coder la situation dans la profession, on a utilisé quatre groupes, à savoir: employeur; travailleur indépendant; salarié et travailleur familial.

8. Principales différences par rapport au recensement précédent:
Le recensement de 1989 était le premier recensement permettant de rassembler des informations sur la main-d'oeuvre.

9. Publication des résultats du recensement:
Les résultats définitifs du recensement de la population sont parus en juillet 1995 dans une publication intitulée «The Kenya Population Census 1989, Volume IX: The Labour Force».

L'organisme responsable de la publication des résultats est le Bureau central des statistiques, P.O. Box 30266, Nairobi.

LUXEMBOURG

1. Nom et adresse de l'organisme responsable du recensement:
Service central de la statistique et des études économiques (STATEC), B.P. 304, Luxembourg.

2. Recensements de population effectués depuis 1945 (années):
1947, 1960, 1966, 1970, 1981 et 1991. La présente description se réfère au recensement de population de 1991 (qui a eu lieu le 1er mars).

3. Champ du recensement:
a) Territoire couvert: Ensemble du pays.

b) Personnes couvertes: Ensemble de la population.

4. Période de référence:
Il n'a pas été établi de période de référence. Les questions posées se rapportent à la situation «actuelle» de la personne recensée.

5. Principaux sujets:
a) Population totale, selon le sexe et l'âge: oui
Population active par:
b) Sexe et âge: oui
c) Branche d'activité économique (industrie):   oui
d) Profession: oui
e) Situation dans la profession: oui
f) Niveau d'instruction le plus élevé: oui
g) Durée du travail: oui
h) Autres caractéristiques: oui

Réf. a): L'âge est défini en termes d'année de naissance, en termes d'années révolues à la date du dernier anniversaire et en termes d'âge exact à la date du recensement.

Réf. g): Il s'agit de la durée normale du travail des personnes pourvues d'un emploi.

Réf. h): Le recensement a aussi rassemblé des informations sur les moyens de transport utilisés pour se rendre au lieu du travail et pour en revenir, ainsi que sur le temps consacré à ces fins.

6. Concepts et définitions:
a) Population active: Elle comprend toutes les personnes qui, à la date du recensement étaient, soit pourvues d'un emploi, soit au chômage, conformément aux définitions données ci-dessous.

Il n'a pas été fixé de limites d'âge; toutefois, les données de population active, d'emploi et de chômage publiées se réfèrent uniquement aux personnes âgées de 15 ans et plus. Les membres des forces armées sont inclus dans la définition.

b) Emploi: Sont considérées comme «pourvues d'un emploi» toutes les personnes qui, à la question «Exercez-vous actuellement une profession?» posée lors du recensement, ont répondu par l'affirmative. Les personnes ayant répondu par la négative à cette question devaient préciser leur situation du moment à l'égard de la vie économique.

Il est indiqué que sont inclus dans cette définition:
i)   les personnes travaillant sans rémunération dans une entreprise ou une exploitation familiale;
ii) les personnes occupées, temporairement absentes du travail;
iii) les étudiants travaillant à temps partiel;
iv) les travailleurs saisonniers ou occasionnels;
v)   les apprentis et les stagiaires.

Seules les personnes appartenant aux catégories i) et v) ci-dessus peuvent être identifiées séparément par la question sur la situation dans la profession.

c) Chômage: Sont considérées comme «chômeurs» toutes les personnes qui, lors du recensement, ont répondu par la négative à la question «Exercez-vous actuellement une profession?» et étaient sans emploi et à la recherche d'un emploi pendant la période de référence. Les étudiants en quête de travail sont exclus de la définition.

7. Classifications utilisées:
Seules les personnes pourvues d'un emploi sont classifiées par industrie, par profession et d'après la situation dans la profession.

a) Branche d'activité économique (industrie): Des questions spécifiques sont posées aux personnes occupées, à savoir: le nom, l'adresse et la branche d'activité à laquelle se rattache l'entreprise, l'établissement ou l'administration qu'elles dirigent ou qui les emploie. Pour coder la branche d'activité, environ 500 groupes de la codification à quatre chiffres de la Nomenclature générale des activités économiques dans les Communautés européennes (NACE) ont été utilisés. Il n'a pas été établi de liens avec la CITI.

b) Profession: Une question spécifique est posée aux personnes occupées, à savoir: «Indiquez la profession ou le métier que vous exercez actuellement, même si vous n'êtes qu'apprenti ou si vous travaillez en aidant un membre de votre ménage dans sa profession». Pour coder la profession, on a utilisé la CITP-88 au niveau des groupes de base (4 chiffres).

c) Situation dans la profession: Basée sur la question: «Sous quel statut exercez-vous votre profession?». Pour coder cette variable, on a utilisé neuf catégories: exploitants agricoles, travailleurs intellectuels indépendants, autres indépendants, ouvriers, employés privés, fonctionnaires (employés publics), fonctionnaires internationaux, apprentis, aides familiaux non rémunérés.

8. Principales différences par rapport au recensement précédent:
Pas de différence majeure.

9. Publication des résultats du recensement:
Le titre de la publication contenant les résultats définitifs de ce recensement est: Série spéciale «Recensement de la Population» (1992/1993).

L'organisme responsable de cette publication est le Service central de la statistique et des études économiques (STATEC), B.P. 304, Luxembourg.

Les résultats du recensement de 1991 sont également disponibles sous forme de tableaux non publiés, de disquettes et de bandes magnétiques.

MACAO

1. Nom et adresse de l'organisme responsable du recensement:
The Census and Statistics Department of Macau, Rua Inacio Baptista no. 4-6 «D», Macau.

2. Recensements de population effectués depuis 1945 (années):
1960, 1981 et 1991. La présente description se réfère au recensement de 1991 (qui a eu lieu le 30 août).

3. Champ du recensement:
a) Territoire couvert: Ensemble du pays.
L'énumération a été totale sur l'Ile de Coloane, avec un échantillon de 20 pour cent sur la péninsule de Macao, et un échantillon de 40 pour cent sur l'Ile de Taipa.

b) Personnes couvertes: Ensemble de la population.

4. Période de référence:
Les sept jours précédant l'énumération. On a également utilisé une période de 30 jours avant la date du recensement comme période de référence pour déterminer si la personne interrogée était à la recherche d'un emploi.

5. Principaux sujets:
a) Population totale, selon le sexe et l'âge:	oui
Population active par:	
b) Sexe et âge:	oui
c) Branche d'activité économique (industrie):	oui
d) Profession:	oui
e) Situation dans la profession:	oui
f) Niveau d'instruction le plus élevé:	oui
g) Durée du travail:	non
h) Autres caractéristiques:	non

Réf. a): L'âge est défini en termes d'année de naissance et d'années révolues à la date du dernier anniversaire.

6. Concepts et définitions:
a) Population active: Elle comprend toutes les personnes âgées de 14 ans et plus qui, au cours des périodes de référence, étaient soit pourvues d'un emploi soit au chômage, conformément aux définitions données ci-dessous. La définition inclut les membres des forces armées.

b) Emploi: Sont considérées comme «pourvues d'un emploi» toutes les personnes qui, interrogées dans le cadre des différentes enquêtes respectives, ont répondu «pourvu d'un emploi» à la question «Quelle a été votre activité au cours des sept derniers jours? pourvu d'un emploi? chômeur? étudiant(e)? ménagère? autre?», ou qui ont répondu par l'affirmative aux questions suivantes: «Avez-vous eu une activité rémunérée au cours des sept derniers jours?» et «Avez-vous travaillé bénévolement ou en qualité de travailleur familial, par exemple en fabriquant des jouets ou des fleurs, en vous occupant d'enfants, en effectuant des travaux de couture ou en procédant à des investissements financiers?».

Il est indiqué que sont inclus dans cette définition:
i)   les personnes travaillant sans rémunération dans une entreprise ou une affaire familiale;
ii) les personnes pourvues d'un emploi, temporairement absentes du travail;
iii) les étudiants travaillant à temps partiel;
iv) les travailleurs saisonniers ou occasionnels;
v)   les conscrits (service militaire ou civil);
vi) les apprentis et les stagiaires.

Les personnes appartenant aux catégories ii) et iii) peuvent être identifiées séparément au moyen de leurs réponses à des questions spécifiques.

c) Chômage: Sont considérées comme «chômeurs» toutes les personnes qui, interrogées dans le cadre des enquêtes respectives, ont répondu «chômeur» à la question «Quelle a été votre activité au cours des sept derniers jours?» et ont répondu par l'affirmative aux questions suivantes: «Au cours des 30 derniers jours, avez-vous pris une quelconque initiative pour trouver un emploi?» et «Si un emploi convenable vous avait été offert au cours des sept derniers jours, l'auriez-vous accepté?».

7. Classifications utilisées:
Seules les personnes dont les enquêtes respectives ont permis de déterminer qu'elles étaient pourvues d'un emploi sont classifiées par branche d'activité économique et par profession. Aucune question n'a été posée aux personnes pourvues d'un emploi ou aux chômeurs en vue de déterminer leur situation dans la profession.

a) Branche d'activité économique (industrie): Basée sur la question: «Quel est le produit ou le service fabriqué ou fourni là où vous travaillez?». Pour coder la branche d'activité économique, on a utilisé 10 groupes de la classification nationale.

Des liens avec la CITI-Rév.3 ont été établis au niveau des catégories de classement (1 chiffre).

b) Profession: Basée sur les questions: «Quel est le titre de l'emploi que vous occupez? Si vous êtes directeur ou administrateur, quel est le nombre de personnes qui travaillent à votre cabinet?», «Quelles sont vos tâches principales et habituelles?» et «Utilisez-vous des instruments ou des outils dans votre travail? Dans l'affirmative, veuillez préciser lesquels». Pour coder la profession, on a utilisé 10 groupes de la classification nationale. Des liens ont été établis avec la CITP-88 au niveau des grands groupes (1 chiffre).

c) Situation dans la profession: Aucune classification n'a été faite.

8. Principales différences par rapport au recensement précédent:

En 1981, l'âge n'avait été défini qu'en termes d'année de naissance, la limite d'âge minimum pour la population active était de 10 ans et l'énumération était complète.

9. Publication des résultats du recensement:

Les chiffres du recensement sont parus en juin 1993 dans une publication intitulée «XIIIe Recensement de la population et IIIe Recensement des logements - Résultats généraux».

L'organisme responsable de cette publication est le Département du recensement et des statistiques de Macao, Rua Inacio Baptista No. 4-6 «D», Macao.

Les résultats du recensement sont également disponibles sous forme de tableaux non publiés et de disquettes.

MACEDOINE

1. Nom et adresse de l'organisme responsable du recensement:

Statistical Office of Macedonia, Dame Gruev 4, 91000 Skopje, Republic of Macedonia.

2. Recensements de population effectués depuis 1945 (années):

1948, 1953, 1961, 1971, 1981 et 1994. La présente description se réfère au recensement de 1994 (qui a eu lieu le 20 juin).

3. Champ du recensement:

a) Territoire couvert: Ensemble du pays.

b) Personnes couvertes: Ensemble de la population.

4. Période de référence:

Le jour du recensement.

5. Principaux sujets:

a) Population totale, selon le sexe et l'âge: oui
Population active par:
b) Sexe et âge: oui
c) Branche d'activité économique (industrie):   oui
d) Profession: oui
e) Situation dans la profession: oui
f) Niveau d'instruction le plus élevé: oui
g) Durée du travail: non
h) Autres caractéristiques: non

Réf. a): L'âge est défini en termes d'années révolues à la date du dernier anniversaire.

6. Concepts et définitions:

a) Population active: Elle comprend toutes les personnes âgées de 15 ans et plus qui, au moment du recensement, étaient soient pourvues d'un emploi, soit au chômage, conformément aux définitions données ci-dessous. Exceptionnellement les enfants âgés de 10 à 14 ans qui ne fréquentent plus l'école et exercent certaines activités agricoles comme berger, vacher et autres, sont inclus dans la définition. Les membres des forces armées sont également inclus dans la définition. Les étudiants travaillant à temps partiel et les étudiants en quête d'un emploi en sont exclus.

b) Emploi: Sont considérées comme «pourvues d'un emploi» toutes les personnes qui, au moment du recensement, exerçaient une profession en tant que salarié ou travailleur indépendant (sur un domaine agricole personnel ou familial, dans un atelier, etc.) dans l'optique de subvenir à leurs besoins.

Il est indiqué que sont inclus dans cette définition:

i) les personnes travaillant sans rémunération dans une entreprise ou une affaire familiale;

ii) les personnes engagées dans la production de produits de base destinés à l'autoconsommation;

iii) les personnes occupées, temporairement absentes de leur travail;

iv) les travailleurs saisonniers ou occasionnels;

v) les conscrits (service militaire ou civil).

Seules les personnes appartenant aux catégories i) et ii) peuvent être identifiées séparément.

c) Chômage: Sont considérées comme «chômeurs» toutes les personnes qui, au moment du recensement, étaient sans emploi et à la recherche d'un travail. Une distinction a été faite entre les personnes en quête d'un premier emploi et celles qui avaient déjà travaillé précédemment. Dans cette dernière catégorie, on a pu identifier séparément les victimes de banqueroute.

7. Classifications utilisées:

Aussi bien les personnes pourvues d'un emploi que les chômeurs ayant précédemment travaillé sont classifiés par profession. Seules les personnes pourvues d'un emploi sont classifiées par industrie et d'après la situation dans la profession. On a demandé aux chômeurs de préciser la branche d'activité économique et la situation dans l'emploi de leur soutien de famille.

a) Branche d'activité économique (industrie): On a demandé aux personnes interrogées d'indiquer leur lieu de travail (atelier, traiteur, etc.) ainsi que le nom de l'activité exercée (agriculture, artisanat en bois, etc.). Pour coder cette variable, on a utilisé 14 branches principales de la classification nationale. Chaque branche se divise en groupes puis en sous-groupes. Aucun lien n'a été établi avec la CITI mais on devrait y remédier à l'avenir.

b) Profession: On a demandé aux personnes recensées d'indiquer le titre de leur profession. Des instructions précisaient qu'il s'agissait de cerner avec précision le travail effectif accompli sur la période la plus longue. Pour coder cette variable, on a utilisé 10 grands groupes de la classification nationale. Chacun de ces grands groupes se divisait en groupes puis sous-groupes. Aucun lien n'a été établi avec la CITP mais on devrait y remédier à l'avenir.

c) Situation dans la profession: Pour coder cette variable, on a utilisé cinq groupes, à savoir: travailleur, propriétaire ou copropriétaire d'une entreprise, propriétaire ou copropriétaire d'un magasin privé avec des salariés; personne exerçant une activité indépendante ou avec l'aide de la famille; aide familial.

8. Principales différences par rapport au recensement précédent:

Les précédents recensements regroupaient sous le terme «population totale» toute personne ayant une résidence permanente dans la République de Macédoine sans prendre en compte son éventuelle absence ou la durée de son absence du territoire au moment du recensement.

Lors du recensement de 1994, conformément à la Loi sur le recensement, le terme de population totale regroupait:

i) les personnes ayant une résidence officielle (légale) dans la République de Macédoine, qu'elles séjournent au moment du recensement dans cette résidence ou ailleurs en Macédoine;

ii) les personnes détenant un permis de résidence dans la République de Macédoine et y habitant à titre temporaire depuis au moins une année mais possédant une résidence officielle (légale) en dehors de la Macédoine, exception faite des réfugiés et des personnes bénéficiant de soins humanitaires;

iii) les personnes qui ont une résidence officielle (légale) dans la République de Macédoine et les membres de leur famille qui, au moment du recensement, travaillaient temporairement à l'étranger pour une période maximale d'une année antérieure à la tenue du recensement;

iv) les personnes qui ont une résidence officielle (légale) dans la République de Macédoine et qui, au moment du recensement, travaillaient dans des corps diplomatiques ou consulaires de la République de Macédoine, aux Nations Unies ou dans ses organisations, dans des représentations de chambres de commerce à l'étranger, dans des sociétés implantées à l'étranger, au sein du personnel militaire de la République de Macédoine stationné à l'étranger, au titre de la coopération ou de l'enseignement international, technique et autres; les familles de ces catégories de personnel résidant temporairement à l'étranger sont incluses dans la définition.

9. Publication des résultats du recensement:
Les résultats définitifs seront publiés en 1996 dans une série de publications. Le titre de chaque publication dépend de la nature des données.

L'organisme responsable de ces publications est le Bureau des statistiques de Macédoine, Dame Gruev A, 91000 Skopje.

MADAGASCAR

1. Nom et adresse de l'organisme responsable du recensement:
Direction du Recensement Général de la Population et de l'Habitat, (DRGPH), B.P. 485, Antananarivo.

2. Recensements de population effectués depuis 1945 (années):
1975 et 1993. La présente description se réfère au recensement de population de 1993 (qui a eu lieu du 1er au 19 août).

3. Champ du recensement:

a) Territoire couvert: Ensemble du pays.

b) Personnes couvertes: Ensemble de la population non compris les nationaux résidant à l'étranger.

4. Période de référence:
La semaine précédant le jour de l'interview.

5. Principaux sujets:
a) Population totale, selon le sexe et l'âge: oui
Population active par:
b) Sexe et âge: oui
c) Branche d'activité économique (industrie): oui
d) Profession: oui
e) Situation dans la profession: oui
f) Niveau d'instruction le plus élevé: oui
g) Durée du travail: non
h) Autres caractéristiques: non

Réf. a): L'âge est défini en priorité en termes d'année de naissance, ou estimé en années quand la date de naissance n'est pas connue.

6. Concepts et définitions:

a) Population active: Elle comprend toutes les personnes âgées de 10 ans et plus qui, à la date du recensement étaient, soit pourvues d'un emploi, soit au chômage, conformément aux définitions données ci-dessous. Les membres des forces armées sont inclus dans la définition. Les étudiants qui travaillent à temps partiel ainsi que les étudiants en quête d'emploi sont exclus de la définition.

b) Emploi: Sont considérées comme «pourvues d'un emploi» toutes les personnes qui ont déclaré qu'elles étaient «occupées» pendant la semaine de référence, c'est-à-dire qui ont retiré, retireront ou espèrent retirer une rémunération en espèces ou en nature en échange d'une activité régulière à laquelle elles ont accordé la majeure partie de leur temps. La question utilisée pour déterminer si une personne devait être considérée comme pourvue d'un emploi était «Situation vis-à-vis de l'emploi: occupé; chômeur; en quête d'un premier emploi; ménagère; étudiant; retraité; incapacité de travail; autre».

Il est indiqué que sont inclus dans cette définition:
i) les personnes travaillant sans rémunération dans une entreprise ou une affaire familiale;
ii) les personnes engagées dans la production de produits de base destinés à l'autoconsommation;
iii) les personnes occupées, temporairement absentes du travail;
iv) les travailleurs saisonniers ou occasionnels;
v) les conscrits (service militaire ou civil);
vi) les apprentis et les stagiaires.

A l'exception de la catégorie ii), toutes les autres catégories peuvent être identifiées au moyen des questions concernant l'activité économique, la profession et la situation dans la profession.

c) Chômage: Sont considérées comme «chômeurs» toutes les personnes qui, suite à l'interruption d'un travail, restent sans emploi pendant un temps déterminé et dont l'activité principale pendant la semaine de référence est la recherche d'un nouvel emploi. Les personnes à la recherche de leur premier emploi n'entrent pas dans la définition, mais sont identifiées séparé-

ment. La question utilisée est la même que celle indiquée au paragraphe 6 b) ci-dessus.

7. Classifications utilisées:
Aussi bien les personnes pourvues d'un emploi que les chômeurs ayant précédemment travaillé sont classifiés par industrie, par profession et d'après la situation dans la profession.

a) Branche d'activité économique (industrie): Basée sur la question: «Quelle est (était) la nature de l'activité principale de l'établissement ou de l'employeur? ex: culture de riz, transport de marchandises, huilerie, enseignement...». Pour coder la branche d'activité, on a utilisé la CITI-rév.3 au niveau des groupes (3 chiffres).

b) Profession: Basée sur la question: «Durant la semaine précédant le ... 1993, quelle était la profession principale exercée par la personne occupée? pour les chômeurs, inscrire la dernière profession. Ex: commerçant de marchandises générales au détail ou en gros, chauffeur, cultivateur de riz, tailleur, pasteur». Si une personne exerce plusieurs professions, sa profession principale est celle qui lui procure le plus de revenus. Pour la profession, la CITP-88 a été utilisée au niveau des grands-groupes (1 chiffre).

c) Situation dans la profession: Basée sur la question: «Quelle est ou était votre situation vis-à-vis de votre profession?». Pour coder la situation dans la profession, on a utilisé sept catégories: indépendant; employeur; salarié permanent; salarié temporaire; apprenti; aide familiale; personne inclassable.

8. Principales différences par rapport au recensement précédent:
Le recensement de 1975 était divisé en trois parties (26-27 janvier: les grands centres urbains (sauf la capitale); 6-7 avril: la capitale et les autres centres urbains; 17-18 août: le milieu rural), alors que le recensement de 1993 a été exécuté simultanément sur tout le territoire national.

En 1975, on avait utilisé une longue période de référence (un mois).

Enfin, les nationaux résidant à l'étranger avaient été recensés en 1975 alors qu'ils ont été exclus en 1993.

9. Publication des résultats du recensement:
La publication des résultats définitifs était prévue en deux étapes: publication des tableaux statistiques (1 tome par Province) en avril 1996, et publication du volume sur l'analyse des données du recensement 1993 vers juin 1996.

L'organisme responsable de la publication est l'Institut National de la Statistique, B.P. 485, Antananarivo.

Les résultats seront également disponibles sous forme de disquettes.

MALAISIE

1. Nom et adresse de l'organisme responsable du recensement:
Department of Statistics, Malaysia, Jalan Cenderasari, 50514 Kuala Lumpur, Malaysia.

2. Recensements de population effectués depuis 1945 (années):
1947 et 1957 (Malaisie péninsulaire), 1960 (Sabah et Sarawak), 1970, 1980 et 1991 (ensemble de la Malaisie). La présente description se réfère au recensement de 1991 (qui a eu lieu le 14 août).

3. Champ du recensement:

a) Territoire couvert: Ensemble du pays.

b) Personnes couvertes: Ensemble de la population.

4. Période de référence:
La semaine précédant la date de l'énumération qui a eu lieu du 14 au 30 août 1991.

5. Principaux sujets:
a) Population totale, selon le sexe et l'âge: oui
Population active par:
b) Sexe et âge: oui
c) Branche d'activité économique (industrie): oui
d) Profession: oui
e) Situation dans la profession: oui
f) Niveau d'instruction le plus élevé: oui
g) Durée du travail: oui
h) Autres caractéristiques: non

Réf. a): L'âge est défini en termes d'année de naissance.

Réf. g): Il a été demandé aux personnes pourvues d'un emploi de spécifier le nombre d'heures effectuées au cours des sept jours précédant la date du recensement.

6. Concepts et définitions:

a) *Population active*: Elle comprend toutes les personnes âgées de 10 ans et plus qui, pendant la période de référence, étaient soit pourvues d'un emploi, soit au chômage, conformément aux définitions données ci-dessous. Cependant les résultats sur la profession et la branche d'activité économique concernent uniquement les personnes âgées de 15 à 64 ans, alors que ceux de la main-d'oeuvre concernent les personnes de 10 ans et plus. Les membres des forces armées sont inclus dans la définition.

b) *Emploi*: Sont considérées comme «pourvues d'un emploi» toutes les personnes qui, pendant la période de référence, ont travaillé au moins une heure. Les questions posées pour déterminer si une personne était occupée étaient les suivantes: «Avez-vous travaillé ces sept derniers jours?» et «Avez-vous travaillé au moins une heure ces sept derniers jours?». Pour les personnes pourvues d'un emploi mais absentes du travail, la question posée était: «Avez-vous un travail auquel vous pouvez retourner?».

Il est indiqué que sont inclus dans cette définition:

i) les personnes travaillant sans rémunération dans une entreprise ou une affaire familiale;
ii) les personnes occupées, temporairement absentes de leur travail;
iii) les étudiants travaillant à temps partiel;
iv) les travailleurs saisonniers ou occasionnels;
v) les conscrits (service militaire ou civil);
vi) les apprentis et les stagiaires.

Seules les personnes appartenant aux catégories i) et ii) peuvent être identifiées séparément. Les travailleurs saisonniers ou occasionnels ne sont inclus que s'ils travaillaient pendant la période de référence.

c) *Chômage*: Sont considérés comme «chômeurs» toutes les personnes qui, pendant la période de référence, étaient sans emploi et à la recherche d'un travail. Les questions posées pour déterminer si une personne doit être considérée comme étant au chômage étaient: «Etiez-vous à la recherche d'un travail ces sept derniers jours?» et «Pourquoi n'avez-vous pas cherché de travail? 1) j'estime qu'il n'existe pas de travail qui me convienne; 2) intempéries; 3) maladie/prison; 4) je dois démarrer prochainement un travail; 5) en attente de réponses à des demandes d'emploi ou a recherché un emploi antérieurement aux sept derniers jours; 6) non qualifié; 7) encore scolarisé; 8) homme ou femme au foyer; 9) je poursuis des études; 10) handicapé/infirme; 11) pas intéressé; 12) retraité/trop âgé; 13) trop jeune; 14) autres».

7. Classifications utilisées:

Seules les personnes pourvues d'un emploi sont classifiées par profession et d'après la situation dans l'emploi.

a) *Branche d'activité économique (industrie)*: Basée sur les questions: «Quelles sont les activités, les services ou les produits de votre lieu de travail?» et «Quels sont les nom et adresse de votre employeur?». Pour coder la branche d'activité économique, on a utilisé une classification à cinq chiffres basée sur la CITI-rév.2.

b) *Profession*: Basée sur les questions: «Quelle est votre profession?» et «Quelles sont vos fonctions ou la nature de votre travail?». Pour coder la profession, on a utilisé une classification à trois chiffres basée sur la CITP-68.

c) *Situation dans la profession*: Basée sur la question: «Quelle est votre situation dans la profession?». Pour coder la situation dans la profession on a utilisé quatre groupes, à savoir: i) employeur, ii) employé, iii) travailleur indépendant et iv) travailleur familial non rémunéré.

8. Principales différences par rapport au recensement précédent:

Le recensement de 1991 a classifié par industrie et par profession uniquement les personnes pourvues d'un emploi alors que celui de 1980 classifiait à la fois les personnes pourvues d'un emploi et les chômeurs ayant précédemment travaillé.

9. Publication des résultats du recensement:

Quatre rapports préliminaires couvrant diverses zones géographiques (Malaisie; Etat; districts administratifs, Mukins; zones sous autorité locale et zones urbaines et zones rurales) ont été publiés pendant la période 1991-1992. Un rapport intermédiaire était disponible mi-1993 de façon restrictive pour des agences gouvernementales sélectionnées. Il était prévu que les rapports définitifs soient publiés en 1995.

L'organisme responsable de la publication est le Département des statistiques de Kuala Lumpur.

Les résultats du recensement sont également disponibles sous forme de tableaux non publiés, de bandes magnétiques et de disques optiques.

MALDIVES

1. Nom et adresse de l'organisme responsable du recensement:

Ministry of Planning, Human ressources and Environment, Ghazee Building, Male'20 05.

2. Recensements de population effectués depuis 1945 (années):

1946, 1953, 1957, 1958, 1960, 1961, 1962, 1963, 1964, 1965, 1966, 1967, 1969, 1970, 1971, 1972, 1974, 1977, 1985 et 1990. La présente description se réfère au recensement de 1990 (qui a eu lieu le 25 mars).

3. Champ du recensement:

a) *Territoire couvert*: Ensemble du pays.

b) *Personnes couvertes*: Ensemble de la population.

4. Période de référence:

La semaine et les trois mois précédant le jour du recensement.

5. Principaux sujets:

a) Population totale, selon le sexe et l'âge:	oui
Population active par:	
b) Sexe et âge:	oui
c) Branche d'activité économique (industrie):	oui
d) Profession:	oui
e) Situation dans la profession:	oui
f) Niveau d'instruction le plus élevé:	oui
g) Durée du travail:	oui
h) Autres caractéristiques:	non

Réf. a): L'âge est défini en termes d'années révolues à la date du dernier anniversaire.

Réf. g): Pour les deux périodes de référence (courte et longue), il a été demandé aux personnes pourvues d'un emploi de spécifier la durée normale du travail ainsi que le nombre total d'heures effectuées.

6. Concepts et définitions:

a) *Population active*: Elle comprend toutes les personnes âgées de 12 ans et plus qui, pendant la période de référence courte étaient soit pourvues d'un emploi, soit au chômage, conformément aux définitions données ci-dessous. Elle exclut les membres des forces armées.

b) *Emploi*: Sont considérées comme «pourvues d'un emploi» toutes les personnes, y compris les travailleurs familiaux, qui travaillaient pendant la période de référence courte ou qui étaient pourvues d'un emploi duquel elles étaient temporairement absentes pour cause de maladie ou de blessure, de conflit de travail, de vacances et autres congés assimilés, d'absence sans autorisation, de mauvaise conjoncture économique due aux intempéries ou à des incidents mécaniques.

Il est indiqué que sont inclus dans cette définition:

i) les personnes travaillant sans rémunération dans une entreprise ou une affaire familiale;
ii) les personnes occupées, temporairement absentes du travail;
iii) les étudiants travaillant à temps partiel;
iv) les travailleurs saisonniers ou occasionnels;
v) les apprentis et les stagiaires.

Aucune des catégories ci-dessus ne peut être identifiée séparément.

c) *Chômage*: Sont considérées comme «chômeurs» toutes les personnes qui, pendant la période de référence courte, étaient sans emploi et à la recherche d'un travail rémunéré ou lucratif y compris celles qui n'avaient jamais travaillé précédemment. Les étudiants en quête de travail sont exclus de la définition.

7. Classifications utilisées:

Aussi bien les personnes pourvues d'un emploi que les chômeurs ayant précédemment travaillé sont classifiés par branche d'activité économique, par profession et d'après la situation dans la profession.

a) Branche d'activité économique (industrie): Basée sur la question: «Durant la période de référence (ou dans votre emploi actuel) pour quelle industrie avez-vous le plus travaillé?». Pour coder la branche d'activité économique, on a utilisé la CITI-rév.3 au niveau des classes (4 chiffres).

b) Profession: Basée sur la question: «Décrivez la nature spécifique ou la désignation de votre travail». Pour coder la profession, on a utilisé la CITP-88 au niveau des groupes (4 chiffres).

c) Situation dans la profession: Basée sur la question: «Quelle était la catégorie de votre emploi?». Pour coder cette variable, on a utilisé quatre groupes, à savoir: employeur, salarié, travailleur à son propre compte et travailleur familial (non rémunéré).

8. Principales différences par rapport au recensement précédent:
Pas de différence majeure.

9. Publication des résultats du recensement:
Les résultats définitifs du recensement sur la population active et ses composantes sont parus dans une publication intitulée: «Population and Housing Census of the Maldives 1990».

L'organisme responsable de cette publication est le Ministère de la planification, des ressources humaines et de l'environnement, Ghazee Building, Malé 20-05.

Les résultats du recensement sont également disponibles sous forme de disquettes, de tableaux non publiés et de CD-ROM.

MAROC

1. Nom et adresse de l'organisme responsable du recensement:
Direction de la Statistique, B.P. 178, Rabat.

2. Recensements de population effectués depuis 1945 (années):
1960, 1971, 1982 et 1994. La présente description se réfère au recensement de 1994 (qui a eu lieu du 2 au 20 septembre).

3. Champ du recensement:
a) Territoire couvert: Ensemble du pays.

b) Personnes couvertes: Ensemble de la population à l'exception des nationaux résidant à l'étranger.

4. Période de référence:
Le jour de l'interview.

5. Principaux sujets:
a) Population totale, selon le sexe et l'âge:	oui
Population active par:	
b) Sexe et âge:	oui
c) Branche d'activité économique (industrie):	oui
d) Profession:	oui
e) Situation dans la profession:	oui
f) Niveau d'instruction le plus élevé:	oui
g) Durée du travail:	non
h) Autres caractéristiques:	non

Réf. a): L'âge est défini en termes d'années révolues à la date du dernier anniversaire.

6. Concepts et définitions:
a) Population active: Elle comprend toutes les personnes âgées de 7 ans et plus pour les actifs occupés et de 15 ans et plus pour les chômeurs, qui, à la date du recensement, étaient soit pourvues d'un emploi, soit au chômage, conformément aux définitions ci-dessous. La définition inclut les membres des forces armées mais exclut les étudiants travaillant à temps partiel ou en quête de travail.

b) Emploi: Sont considérées comme «pourvues d'emploi» (actifs occupés) toutes les personnes âgées de 7 ans et plus qui, à la date du recensement, disposaient d'un «travail» ou exerçaient une quelconque activité économique. La question posée pour déterminer si une personne doit être considérée comme pourvue d'emploi est «Disposiez-vous d'un emploi à la date du recensement?».

Il est indiqué que sont inclus dans cette définition:

i)   les personnes travaillant sans rémunération dans une entreprise ou une affaire familiale;

ii)   les personnes engagées dans la production de produits de base destinés à l'autoconsommation;

iii)   les personnes occupées, temporairement absentes de leur travail;

iv)   les travailleurs saisonniers ou occasionnels, en particulier dans l'agriculture;

v)   les conscrits (service militaire ou civil);

vi)   les apprentis et les stagiaires.

Seules les catégories i), v) et vi) peuvent être identifiées séparément.

c) Chômage: Sont considérées comme «chômeurs» toutes les personnes âgées de 15 ans et plus qui, à la date du recensement, étaient sans travail et à la recherche d'un emploi. La définition couvre aussi bien les chômeurs ayant précédemment travaillé que les personnes à la recherche de leur premier emploi.

7. Classifications utilisées:
Aussi bien les personnes occupées que les chômeurs ayant précédemment travaillé sont classifiés par industrie, par profession et d'après la situation dans la profession.

a) Branche d'activité économique (industrie): La question posée concerne l'activité principale de l'entreprise ou du local dans lesquels les personnes travaillent ou ont travaillé en dernier lieu. Pour coder la branche d'activité, on a utilisé 215 groupes de la nomenclature nationale. Des liens avec la CITI-rév.3 ont été établis au niveau des classes (4 chiffres).

b) Profession: La question posée concerne la nature exacte de la profession que les personnes exercent ou ont exercée en dernier lieu. Pour coder la profession, on a utilisé plus de 65 sous grands-groupes de la nomenclature nationale. Des liens ont été établis avec la CITP-88.

c) Situation dans la profession: La question posée concerne la situation dans la profession principale exercée (ou exercée en dernier lieu). Pour coder la situation dans la profession, on a utilisé sept catégories, à savoir: employeur; indépendant avec local; indépendant à domicile; indépendant sans local; salarié; aide-familial; apprenti.

8. Principales différences par rapport au recensement précédent:
La principale différence consiste en l'actualisation des nomenclatures des professions et des activités économiques.

9. Publication des résultats du recensement:
Il était prévu que les résultats définitifs du recensement soient publiés à partir de 1995 dans les publications intitulées: «Population légale du Royaume» et «Caractéristiques socio-économiques (niveau national et niveau provincial de 65 provinces)».

L'organisme responsable de cette publication est la Direction de la Statistique, B.P. 178, Rabat.

Les résultats du recensement de 1994 seront également disponibles sous forme de tableaux non publiés, de disquettes et de bandes magnétiques.

MARTINIQUE

1. Nom et adresse de l'organisme responsable du recensement:
Institut national de la statistique et des études économiques (INSEE), Service régional de la Martinique, B.P. 7212, 97233 Schoelcher Cedex, Martinique.

2. Recensements de population effectués depuis 1945 (années):
1954, 1961, 1967, 1974, 1982 et 1990. La présente description se réfère au recensement de 1990 (qui a eu lieu le 15 mars).

3. Champ du recensement:
a) Territoire couvert: Ensemble du territoire.

b) Personnes couvertes: Ensemble de la population.

4. Période de référence:
La semaine précédant le jour du recensement.

5. Principaux sujets:
a) Population totale, selon le sexe et l'âge:	oui
Population active par:	
b) Sexe et âge:	oui
c) Branche d'activité économique (industrie):	oui
d) Profession:	oui

e) Situation dans la profession: oui
f) Niveau d'instruction le plus élevé: oui
g) Durée du travail: non
h) Autres caractéristiques: oui

Réf. a): L'âge est défini en termes d'année de naissance.

Réf. h): Le recensement a également rassemblé d'autres informations, telles que: le travail à temps complet et à temps partiel, l'activité principale, le nombre de salariés occupés par les personnes travaillant à leur propre compte, la durée de recherche d'un travail, etc.

6. Concepts et définitions:

a) Population active: Elle comprend toutes les personnes âgées de 14 ans et plus qui, pendant la semaine de référence, étaient soit pourvues d'un emploi, soit au chômage, conformément aux définitions données ci-dessous. La définition inclut aussi les membres des forces armées (militaires de carrière et ceux du contingent). Les questions relatives à l'activité économique n'ont été posées qu'à un échantillon, dont étaient exclus les militaires logés en caserne et les détenus.

b) Emploi: Sont considérées comme «pourvues d'emploi» toutes les personnes qui, pendant la semaine de référence, ont exercé une profession, une fonction ou une activité économique, rémunérée ou non. Des questions spécifiques permettent de déterminer si une personne doit être considérée comme pourvue d'emploi, notamment: «Travaillez-vous (à temps complet ou à temps partiel)?»; «Etes-vous: salarié ou à votre compte (exploitant agricole, artisan, commerçant, industriel, profession libérale, aide familial non salarié, etc.)?» et «Si vous êtes à votre compte: combien de salariés employez-vous? (ne comptez ni les apprentis ni les gens de maison; dans l'agriculture, comptez seulement les salariés permanents)». La définition inclut aussi les personnes exerçant un travail d'utilité collective (TUC, etc.), celles placées par une agence d'intérim, celles sous contrat de travail à durée déterminée et celles sous contrat d'adaptation ou de qualification.

Il est indiqué que sont inclus dans cette définition:

i) les personnes travaillant sans rémunération dans une entreprise ou une exploitation familiale;
ii) les personnes engagées dans la production de produits de base destinés à l'autoconsommation;
iii) les personnes occupées, temporairement absentes du travail;
iv) les étudiants travaillant à temps partiel;
v) les travailleurs saisonniers ou occasionnels, pour autant qu'ils soient en activité à l'époque du recensement;
vi) les conscrits (service militaire ou civil);
vii) les apprentis (sous contrat) et les stagiaires (principalement en entreprise ou dans un centre de formation).

Seules les personnes appartenant aux catégories i), vi) et vii) peuvent être identifiées séparément.

c) Chômage: Sont considérées comme «chômeurs» toutes les personnes qui se sont déclarées spontanément en chômage et qui étaient à la recherche d'un travail. Les questions utilisées pour déterminer si une personne doit être considérée comme chômeur sont «Etes-vous chômeur (inscrit ou non à l'Agence nationale pour l'emploi)?», «Avez-vous déjà travaillé? (si oui, quelle était votre profession principale?)» et «Cherchez-vous un emploi (depuis: moins de trois mois; trois mois à moins d'un an; un an à moins de deux ans; deux ans ou plus)?».

7. Classifications utilisées:

Aussi bien les personnes occupées que les chômeurs ayant précédemment travaillé de l'échantillon sont classifiés par profession. Seules les personnes occupées de l'échantillon sont classifiées par industrie et d'après la situation dans la profession.

a) Branche d'activité économique (industrie): Il a été demandé aux personnes interrogées d'indiquer l'adresse, le nom ou la raison sociale de l'établissement qui les emploie ou qu'elles dirigent, ainsi que l'activité exacte de cet établissement (par exemple: commerce de vin en gros, fabrication de charpentes métalliques, transport routier de voyageurs, etc.). Pour coder la branche d'activité, on a utilisé 100 groupes de la Nomenclature d'Activités et Produits (NAP). Il n'a pas établi de liens avec la CITI.

b) Profession: Il a été demandé aux personnes interrogées d'indiquer la profession exercée actuellement ou en dernier, avec une identification aussi claire que possible de cette profession (par exemple: ouvrier électricien d'entretien, chauffeur de poids lourds, vendeur en électroménager, ingénieur chimiste,

caissière de libre-service, etc.), en vue de déterminer le groupe de professions. Cependant, la question a été laissée ouverte, en ce sens que la personne interrogée était libre de formuler sa réponse. Le reclassement dans un groupe déterminé est fait lors du traitement informatique. Pour coder la profession, on a utilisé un système de codification directe en 42 groupes. Il n'a pas été établi de liens avec la CITP.

c) Situation dans la profession: Pour coder cette variable, on a utilisé les cinq catégories suivantes: indépendant à son compte; employeur; salarié; aide familial non rémunéré; autre.

8. Principales différences par rapport au recensement précédent:

La limite d'âge inférieure qui avait été retenue en 1982 pour l'inclusion des personnes dans la population active était de 15 ans.

De plus, lors du recensement de 1982, aussi bien les personnes occupées que les chômeurs ayant précédemment travaillé avaient été classifiés par industrie et d'après la situation dans la profession.

9. Publication des résultats du recensement:

Le titre de la publication contenant les résultats définitifs est: «Population, Emploi, Logements; Evolution 1975-1982-1990 (Série jaune)», 1992.

L'organisme responsable de cette publication est l'Institut national de la statistique et des études économiques (INSEE), 18 boulevard Adolphe-Pinard, 75675 Paris Cedex 14.

Les résultats du recensement de 1990 sont également disponibles sous forme de disquettes et de bandes magnétiques, ainsi que d'exploitations à la demande.

MAURICE

1. Nom et adresse de l'organisme responsable du recensement:

Central Statistical Office, Toorawa Centre, Sir S. Ramgoolam St., Port Louis.

2. Recensements de population effectués depuis 1945 (années):

1952, 1962, 1972, 1983 et 1990. La présente description se réfère au recensement de 1990 (qui a eu lieu le 1er juillet).

3. Champ du recensement:

a) Territoire couvert: Ensemble du pays.

b) Personnes couvertes: Ensemble de la population.

4. Période de référence:

La semaine précédant le jour du recensement pour l'activité actuelle et l'année précédente (1989) pour l'activité habituelle.

5. Principaux sujets:

a) Population totale, selon le sexe et l'âge: oui
Population active par:
b) Sexe et âge: oui
c) Branche d'activité économique (industrie):   oui
d) Profession: oui
e) Situation dans la profession: oui
f) Niveau d'instruction le plus élevé: oui
g) Durée du travail: oui
h) Autres caractéristiques: oui

Réf. a): L'âge est défini en termes d'années révolues à la date du dernier anniversaire.

Réf. g): Pour la période de référence courte, on a demandé aux personnes pourvues d'un emploi et présentes au travail de préciser les heures de travail réellement effectuées. Pour la période de référence longue, on leur a demandé de spécifier la période totale de travail effectué exprimée en nombre de semaines.

Réf. h): Le recensement a aussi rassemblé des informations sur: i) le type d'établissement; ii) le lieu du travail et iii) la durée de l'engagement auprès de l'actuel employeur ou du dernier employeur. De plus, on a demandé aux personnes qui déclaraient ne pas avoir été disponibles pour travailler la semaine précédente d'en donner le motif (obligations ménagères, études, maladie, blessure ou invalidité, retraité, autres).

6. Concepts et définitions:

a) Population active: Elle comprend toutes les personnes âgées de 12 ans et plus qui, pendant les périodes de référence, étaient généralement ou actuellement, pourvues d'un emploi ou au chômage, conformément aux définitions données ci-dessous. Les questions sur la population active n'ont pas été posées aux non-Mauritiens résidant généralement hors du pays. Il n'y a pas de conscription sur l'île Maurice.

b) Emploi: Sont considérées comme «pourvues d'un emploi» toutes les personnes qui, pendant la période de référence courte, ont effectué, à domicile ou à l'extérieur, un travail ayant une valeur économique. Les questions posées pour déterminer l'activité professionnelle actuelle d'une personne sont: «Combien d'heures avez-vous travaillé soit contre rémunération, soit pour le profit ou sans rémunération pour une affaire familiale durant la semaine allant du lundi 25 juin au dimanche 1er juillet 1990?» et «S'agissait-il d'un travail, d'une entreprise familiale, d'une propriété agricole ou d'une ferme où vous n'avez pas travaillé pour cause de maladie, de blessure, de vacances, de conflit de travail, d'inactivité saisonnière, de mauvaise conjoncture économique, etc.?». Une personne était considérée comme pourvue d'un emploi si la réponse à la première question était «une heure ou plus» ou si la réponse à la même question était négative mais positive à la seconde.

Il est indiqué que sont inclus dans cette définition:

i) les personnes travaillant sans rémunération dans une entreprise ou une affaire familiale;
ii) les personnes engagées dans la production de produits de base destinés à l'autoconsommation;
iii) les personnes occupées, temporairement absentes de leur travail;
iv) les étudiants travaillant à temps partiel;
v) les travailleurs saisonniers ou occasionnels;
vi) les apprentis et les stagiaires.

Seules les personnes appartenant aux catégories i), iii), iv) et vi) peuvent être identifiées séparément par des questions sur la position dans l'emploi et la situation dans la profession.

c) Chômage: Sont considérées comme «chômeurs» toutes les personnes qui, pendant les périodes de référence, étaient sans emploi et à la recherche d'un travail. Une personne était considérée comme «actuellement» au chômage si les réponses étaient respectivement «o heure» et «non» aux questions précédemment posées sous 6 b) et «oui» aux deux questions suivantes: «Avez-vous entrepris des recherches d'emploi à un moment quelconque au cours des huit dernières semaines?» et «Etiez-vous disponible pour démarrer un travail la semaine passée?» (voir aussi para. 5, Réf. h).

7. Classifications utilisées:

Aussi bien les personnes pourvues d'un emploi que les chômeurs ayant précédemment travaillé sont classifiés par branche d'activité économique, par profession et d'après la situation dans la profession.

a) Branche d'activité économique (industrie): Basée sur la question: «Décrivez avec précision l'activité de l'entreprise, de l'industrie ou du service où vous travaillez (travail actuel ou précédent). N'utilisez pas de termes vagues (comme agriculture, réparations, usine, école, magasin, etc.); utilisez des termes précis (comme culture de canne à sucre, réparation de voitures, fabrique de tricots, école primaire, ameublement, magasin d'électroménager, etc.). Si vous exercez plusieurs métiers, décrivez l'industrie, l'entreprise ou le service principal dans lequel vous avez travaillé». Pour coder l'industrie, on a utilisé 263 groupes de la classification nationale par industrie. Une correspondance univoque a été établie entre la classification nationale (3 chiffres) et la CITI-rév.2 au niveau des groupes (4 chiffres).

b) Profession: Basée sur la question: «Décrivez clairement la profession exercée par la personne (ou celle exercée en dernier). N'utilisez pas de termes vagues (comme employé de bureau, conducteur, ouvrier, enseignant, etc.; utilisez des termes précis (comme employé comptable, conducteur de bus, ébéniste, instituteur, etc.). Si la personne a un ou plusieurs emplois, décrivez celui dans lequel elle exerce depuis le plus longtemps». Pour coder la profession, on a utilisé la CITP-88 au niveau des groupes de base (4 chiffres).

c) Situation dans la profession: Pour coder cette variable, on a utilisé huit groupes, à savoir: travailleur indépendant avec des salariés; travailleur indépendant sans salariés; travailleur non rémunéré pour son conjoint ou un autre parent sur sa ferme ou son entreprise; apprenti rémunéré ou non; salarié payé au mois; salarié payé à la journée, à la semaine, à la quinzaine ou à la tâche; membre d'une coopérative de producteurs; autres.

8. Principales différences par rapport au recensement précédent:

Les principales différences sont les suivantes:

Le recensement de 1983 incluait seulement les personnes présentes la nuit du recensement, alors que celui de 1990 incluait aussi les membres habituels d'un ménage, absents à ce moment-là.

Lors du recensement de 1983, la période de référence était courte (une semaine).

Pour déterminer la position dans l'emploi d'une personne, (à savoir: pourvue d'un emploi, chômeur ou inactif) deux questions avaient été posées en 1983:

1) «La personne a-t-elle travaillé contre rémunération ou pour le profit (y compris les travailleurs indépendants et les travailleurs agricoles à leur compte); travaillé sans rémunération pour un membre de sa famille, dans sa ferme ou son entreprise, ou travaillé comme apprenti non rémunéré entre le lundi 27 juin et le samedi 2 juillet de cette année?. Si 'oui' spécifiez le nombre de jours travaillés y compris les congés payés». Si la réponse était positive, on considérait la personne comme pourvue d'un emploi.

2) «Si la réponse est négative, indiquez si la personne: a) avait un travail mais était malade ou en congé; b) était étudiant; c) était femme au foyer ou un parent assurant les tâches ménagères chez un proche, d) résident dans une institution; e) infirme; f) rentier; g) retraité; h) un enfant âgé de 12 à 15 ans, non scolarisé et ne cherchant pas d'emploi; i) sans travail mais recherchant activement un emploi; j) autres.» Une personne était considérée comme chômeur si la réponse à la question 1) était négative et celle à la question 2) «ne travaille pas mais recherche activement un emploi».

En 1983, les questions posées s'intéressaient au nombre de jours travaillés pendant la semaine de référence (y compris le nombre de jours de congés payés). Les membres de coopératives de producteurs n'apparaissaient pas comme un groupe distinct. La branche d'activité économique et la profession ont été demandées à toutes les personnes pourvues d'un emploi et aux chômeurs ayant précédemment travaillé puis codées respectivement au niveau 4 chiffres de la CITI-rév.2 et au niveau 3 chiffres de la CITP-68.

9. Publication des résultats du recensement:

Le titre de la publication contenant les résultats définitifs du recensement est: «1990 Housing and Population Census of Mauritius - Economic Characteristics, 1991».

L'organisme responsable de cette publication est le Bureau central des statistiques de Port Louis.

En outre certains tableaux sont disponibles sous forme de disquettes; des tableaux non publiés sont également disponibles sur demande.

MEXIQUE

1. Nom et adresse de l'organisme responsable du recensement:

Instituto Nacional de Estadística, Geografia e Informática (INEGI), Prolongación Héroe de Nacozari No2301 Sur, C.P. 20290, Aguascalientes, AGS., México, D.F.

2. Recensements de population effectués depuis 1945 (années):

1950, 1960, 1970, 1980 et 1990. La présente description se réfère au recensement de population de 1990 (qui a eu lieu du 12 au 16 mars).

3. Champ du recensement:

a) Territoire couvert: Ensemble du pays.

b) Personnes couvertes: Ensemble de la population.

4. Période de référence:

La semaine précédant le recensement, c'est-à-dire du 5 au 11 mars.

5. Principaux sujets:

a) Population totale, selon le sexe et l'âge: oui
Population active par:

b) Sexe et âge: oui
c) Branche d'activité économique (industrie):   oui
d) Profession: oui
e) Situation dans la profession: oui
f) Niveau d'instruction le plus élevé: ...
g) Durée du travail: oui
h) Autres caractéristiques: oui

Réf. a): L'âge est défini en termes d'années révolues à la date du dernier anniversaire.

Réf. g): La durée du travail se réfère au nombre d'heures effectivement travaillées par les personnes pourvues d'un emploi, qui travaillaient pendant la période de référence.

Réf. h): Ont été pris en compte les revenus du travail (hebdomadaires, mensuels, annuels).

6. Concepts et définitions:

a) *Population active*: Elle comprend toutes les personnes âgées de 12 ans et plus qui, pendant la semaine de référence, étaient soit pourvues d'un emploi soit au chômage, conformément aux définitions données ci-dessous. La définition inclut tous les membres des forces armées.

b) *Emploi*: Sont considérées comme «pourvues d'un emploi» les personnes âgées de 12 ans et plus ayant répondu par l'affirmative aux questions suivantes: «La semaine passée, l'intéressé a-t-il travaillé? S'il n'a pas travaillé, avait-il néanmoins un emploi?».

Il est indiqué que sont inclus dans cette définition:

i) les personnes travaillant sans rémunération dans une entreprise ou une affaire familiale;
ii) les personnes engagées dans la production de produits de base destinés à l'autoconsommation;
iii) les personnes occupées, temporairement absentes de leur travail;
iv) les étudiants travaillant à temps partiel;
v) les travailleurs saisonniers ou occasionnels;
vi) les conscrits (service militaire ou civil);
vii) les apprentis et les stagiaires.

Seules les personnes appartenant aux catégories i) et v) peuvent être identifiées séparément. L'identification de la catégorie i) est basée sur la question relative à la situation dans la profession, option: «travailleur sans rémunération dans une exploitation ou un commerce familial». S'agissant de la catégorie v), il n'y a pas de question spécifique pour l'identifier; on peut seulement obtenir une évaluation approximative de sa taille par la question concernant le «nombre d'heures travaillées la semaine passée».

c) *Chômage*: Sont considérées comme «chômeurs» les personnes ayant répondu par la négative aux questions utilisées pour la définition de l'emploi (voir ci-dessus), mais par l'affirmative à la question «Etes-vous à la recherche d'un emploi?».

7. Classifications utilisées:

Seules les personnes pourvues d'un emploi sont classifiées par branche d'activité économique, par profession et d'après la situation dans la profession.

a) *Branche d'activité économique (industrie)*: Pour déterminer la branche d'activité économique, les questions utilisées sont: «De quoi s'occupe l'établissement commercial, l'exploitation, l'entreprise, l'institution ou l'entité où vous travaillez?» et «Où travaillez-vous (par ex.: dans les champs, dans une usine, dans un atelier de mécanique)?». Pour coder cette variable, on a utilisé 14 secteurs, 57 sous-secteurs et 220 branches d'activité, comparables avec les branches et les catégories de la CITI-rév.2.

b) *Profession*: Pour déterminer la profession, les questions utilisées sont: «Quel est le métier, le poste ou la charge que vous exercez dans votre emploi principal?» et «Quelles sont vos tâches et fonctions dans votre emploi?». Pour coder cette variable, on a utilisé 18 groupes principaux, 129 sous-groupes, 508 groupes unitaires et 9600 professions individuelles, lesquels sont comparables à la CITP-88 au niveau des grands groupes, des sous-grands groupes, des sous-groupes et des groupes de base.

c) *Situation dans la profession*: Pour déterminer la situation dans la profession, on a demandé aux intéressés quel était celui des cinq groupes suivants auquel ils appartenaient dans leur emploi principal: employé ou ouvrier; journalier ou ouvrier agricole; travailleur indépendant; patron ou exploitant; travailleur sans rémunération dans une exploitation ou un commerce familial.

8. Principales différences par rapport au recensement précédent:

Dans le recensement de 1990, les données relatives au volume de la population active et celles concernant le nombre des économiquement inactifs ont été obtenues essentiellement sous la même forme que dans le recensement de 1980. Toutefois, étant donné que le fait d'utiliser comme période de référence la semaine précédant le recensement limite considérablement l'obtention des données concernant les personnes à la recherche d'un emploi, on a opté, lors du recensement de 1990, pour la solution consistant à ne plus distinguer ces personnes selon qu'elles avaient déjà travaillé auparavant ou étaient à la recherche d'un premier emploi, comme cela avait été le cas lors du recensement précédent.

En ce qui concerne la classification par type d'inactivité, le recensement ne comporte pas de rubrique particulière pour les rentiers, qui sont inclus dans la catégorie «autres inactifs».

A la différence du recensement précédent, celui de 1990 n'a retenu les caractéristiques économiques (branche d'activité, profession principale, situation dans la profession, heures de travail et revenus tirés de l'activité professionnelle) que pour les personnes pourvues d'un emploi, et non pour l'ensemble de la population active, ce qui a permis de simplifier la rédaction des questions posées sur ce sujet.

Pour déterminer l'activité économique, le recensement de 1990 comportait deux questions complémentaires, avec possibilité de réponse ouverte, contrairement au recensement précédent qui comportait la question fermée suivante: «Que cultive, fabrique, vend, transporte ou extrait l'établissement dans lequel vous exercez votre emploi principal (ou dans lequel vous avez exercé votre dernier emploi si vous êtes au chômage), ou quel service fournit-il?».

Pour déterminer la profession principale, le recensement de 1990 comportait deux questions ouvertes, au lieu d'une dans le recensement précédent: «La semaine passée, quelle était votre profession ou quelles étaient vos tâches dans votre emploi principal ou dans le dernier emploi que vous avez exercé si vous êtes au chômage?».

La question relative à la situation dans la profession n'est pas la même dans le recensement de 1990 que dans le recensement précédent. Elle s'en distingue de la façon suivante: i) elle ne comporte pas l'option: «membre d'une coopérative de production»; ii) l'option «travailleur rémunéré sous forme d'appointements, de salaire ou d'indemnité journalière, en espèces ou en nature», qui figurait dans le recensement précédent, a été divisée en deux options dans le recensement de 1990: «Employé ou ouvrier» et «Journalier ou ouvrier agricole»; iii) l'option «Travailleur non rémunéré sous forme d'appointements, de salaire, d'indemnités journalières ou autres, que ce soit en espèces ou en nature» a été restreinte, dans le recensement de 1990, aux travailleurs familiaux sans rémunération, et elle exclut donc les travailleurs non rémunérés autres que familiaux.

S'agissant de la variable «revenus», le recensement de 1980 prenait en compte le revenu total de l'ensemble des personnes âgées de 12 ans et plus, alors que celui de 1990 se limite aux revenus que les personnes pourvues d'un emploi tirent de l'exercice de leur activité professionnelle.

9. Publication des résultats du recensement:

Les résultats nationaux ont été publiés en mars 1992, de même que les résultats de chacune des 32 entités fédératives qui composent le pays.

Le titre exact de la publication dans laquelle sont présentés les résultats nationaux est «Estados Unidos Mexicanos; Resumen General; XI Censo General de Población y Vivienda, 1990».

L'organisme responsable de cette publication est l'Institut national de statistique, géographie et informatique (INEGI), Prolongacion Héroe de Nacozari No 2301 Sur, Aguascalientes, AGS.

Les résultats nationaux du recensement, de même que ceux correspondant aux entités fédératives, sont également disponibles sous forme de disquettes.

MONGOLIE

1. Nom et adresse de l'organisme responsable du recensement:

Bureau of Population Census, State Statistical Office, Ulaan Baatar.

2. Recensements de population effectués depuis 1945 (années):
1979 et 1989. La présente description se réfère au recensement de 1989 (qui a eu lieu le 5 janvier).

3. Champ du recensement:

a) Territoire couvert: Ensemble du pays.

b) Personnes couvertes: Ensemble de la population.

4. Période de référence:
Le jour du recensement.

5. Principaux sujets:
a) Population totale, selon le sexe et l'âge:　oui
Population active par:
b) Sexe et âge:　oui
c) Branche d'activité économique (industrie):　oui
d) Profession:　oui
e) Situation dans la profession:　oui
f) Niveau d'instruction le plus élevé:　oui
g) Durée du travail:　non
h) Autres caractéristiques:　non
Réf. a): L'âge est défini en termes d'années révolues à la date du dernier anniversaire.

6. Concepts et définitions:

a) Population active: Elle comprend toutes les personnes de 16 à 59 ans pour les hommes et de 16 à 54 ans pour les femmes qui étaient soit pourvues d'un emploi, soit au chômage, conformément aux définitions données ci-dessous. La définition exclut les membres des forces armées ainsi que les étudiants travaillant à temps partiel et les étudiants en quête d'un emploi.

b) Emploi: Sont considérées comme «pourvues d'un emploi» toutes les personnes âgées de 16 à 59 ans pour les hommes, et de 16 à 54 ans pour les femmes, figurant sur le registre de l'emploi d'une entreprise au moment du recensement.

Il est indiqué que sont inclus dans cette définition:

i) les personnes travaillant sans rémunération dans une entreprise ou une affaire familiale;
ii) les personnes engagées dans la production de produits de base destinés à l'autoconsommation;
iii) les personnes occupées, temporairement absentes de leur travail;
iv) les travailleurs saisonniers ou occasionnels;
v) les apprentis et les stagiaires.

Aucune des catégories ci-dessus ne peut être identifiée séparément.

c) Chômage: Sont considérées comme «chômeurs» toutes les personnes âgées de 16 à 59 ans pour les hommes, et de 16 à 54 ans pour les femmes, n'apparaissant sur le registre de l'emploi d'aucune entreprise au moment du recensement

7. Classifications utilisées:
Aussi bien les personnes pourvues d'un emploi que les chômeurs ayant précédemment travaillé sont classifiés par profession. Seules les personnes pourvues d'un emploi ont été classifiées par branche d'activité économique et d'après la situation dans la profession.

a) Branche d'activité économique (industrie): Pour déterminer cette variable, on a utilisé 12 groupes de la classification nationale: industrie; agriculture; construction; transports; communications; commerce; logement et services domestiques; sciences; santé publique, éducation physique; assurance; culture, éducation; art; autre. Aucun lien n'a été établi avec la CITI.

b) Profession: Pour coder cette variable, on a utilisé 982 groupes de la classification nationale. Aucun lien n'a été établi avec la CITP.

c) Situation dans la profession: Pour coder cette variable, on a utilisé cinq groupes, à savoir: gouvernement et services administratifs (ministères, commissions); services du secteur public; services administratifs de la province d'Aimag; services administratifs de districts; entreprises.

8. Principales différences par rapport au recensement précédent:
Pas de différence majeure.

9. Publication des résultats du recensement:
Les résultats définitifs du recensement concernant la population active et ses composantes sont parus en mars 1990 dans une publication intitulée «Population Census of Mongolia, 1989».

L'organisme responsable de cette publication est le Bureau national des statistiques à Ulaan Baatar.

Les résultats du recensement ne sont pas disponibles sous d'autres formes.

NAMIBIE

1. Nom et adresse de l'organisme responsable du recensement:
Central Statistics Office, National Planning Commission, Private Bag 13356, Windhoek.

2. Recensements de population effectués depuis 1945 (années):
1960, 1981 et 1991. La présente description se réfère au recensement de 1991 (qui a eu lieu le 20 octobre).

3. Champ du recensement:

a) Territoire couvert: Ensemble du pays.

b) Personnes couvertes: Ensemble de la population.

4. Période de référence:
La semaine précédent le recensement.

5. Principaux sujets:
a) Population totale, selon le sexe et l'âge:　oui
Population active par:
b) Sexe et âge:　oui
c) Branche d'activité économique (industrie):　oui
d) Profession:　oui
e) Situation dans la profession:　oui
f) Niveau d'instruction le plus élevé:　oui
g) Durée du travail:　non
h) Autres caractéristiques:　non
Réf. a): L'âge est défini en termes d'années révolues à la date du dernier anniversaire.

6. Concepts et définitions:

a) Population active: Elle comprend toutes les personnes âgées de 10 ans et plus qui, pendant la semaine de référence, étaient soit pourvues d'un emploi, soit au chômage conformément aux définitions données ci-dessous. Les membres des forces armées sont exclus de la définition.

b) Emploi: Sont considérées comme «pourvues d'un emploi» toutes les personnes qui, à la question «Au cours des sept jours précédant le recensement, avez-vous effectué un travail rémunéré, lucratif ou sans rémunération dans une affaire familiale?», ont répondu soit «oui» soit «non, mais j'avais un travail ou une entreprise».

Il est indiqué que sont inclus dans cette définition:

i) les personnes travaillant sans rémunération dans une entreprise ou une affaire familiale;
ii) les personnes engagées dans la production de produits de base destinés à l'autoconsommation;
iii) les personnes occupées, temporairement absentes de leur travail;
iv) les étudiants travaillant à temps partiel;
v) les travailleurs saisonniers ou occasionnels;
vi) les apprentis et les stagiaires.

Seules les personnes appartenant aux catégories i), iii) et iv) peuvent être identifiées séparément.

c) Chômage: Sont considérées comme «chômeurs» toutes les personnes qui, à la question indiquée sous 6 b), ont répondu soit «chômeur (travaillait antérieurement)», soit «chômeur (à la recherche d'un premier emploi)». Les étudiants en quête d'emploi sont exclus de la définition.

7. Classifications utilisées:
Aussi bien les personnes pourvues d'un emploi que les chômeurs ayant précédemment travaillé sont classifiés par branche d'activité économique, par profession et d'après la situation dans la profession.

a) Branche d'activité économique (industrie): Basée sur les questions: «Quel genre d'activités est mené sur votre lieu de travail?» et «Quels sont les principaux produits ou services délivrés sur votre lieu de travail?». Pour coder la branche d'activité, on a utilisé 307 groupes de la classification nationale. Des liens avec la CITI-rév.3 ont été établis au niveau des classes (4 chiffres).

b) *Profession*: Basée sur les questions: «Quelle sorte de travail effectuiez-vous?» et «Quelles sont les tâches essentielles inhérentes à votre travail?». Pour coder la profession, on a utilisé 396 groupes de la classification nationale. Des liens avec la CITP-88 ont été établis au niveau des groupes de base (4 chiffres).

c) *Situation dans la profession*: Basée sur la question: «Dans ce travail, étiez-vous: un employeur (avec salariés), un travailleur indépendant (sans salariés); un employé du gouvernement; un employé du secteur privé; un travailleur familial non rémunéré; un employé d'un gouvernement étranger, un employé d'une organisation internationale; autres?». Pour coder la situation dans la profession, on a utilisé les huit groupes prémentionnés.

8. Principales différences par rapport au recensement précédent:
Les limites d'âge utilisées dans le recensement de 1981 étaient de 16 à 65 ans pour les hommes et de 16 à 60 ans pour les femmes.

En 1981 la définition utilisée pour les «personnes en quête d'un travail» comprenait les personnes, dans les limites d'âge, qui n'avaient déclaré aucune activité économique, recherchaient activement un emploi et étaient disponibles pour démarrer un travail la semaine suivante.

9. Publication des résultats du recensement:
Les résultats définitifs sont parus en août 1993 dans la publication intitulée «Republic of Namibia, 1991 Population and Housing Census, Report A, Statistical tables (based on old districts)». Les données ont également été présentées dans des publications plus récentes telles que: «Republic of Namibia, 1991 Population and Housing Census, Report B, Volume I-III, Statistical tables (based on new regions)», avril 1994; «Republic of Namibia, 1991 Population and Housing Census, Report C, Statistics on enumeration areas», avril 1994; «Administrative and Methodological Report», août 1994 et «Republic of Namibia, 1991 Population and Housing Census, Basic analysis with highlights», 1995.

L'organisme responsable de ces publications est le Bureau central des statistiques, National Planning Commission, Private Bag 13356, Windhoek.

Les résultats définitifs sont également disponibles sous forme de disquettes.

NAURU

1. Nom et adresse de l'organisme responsable du recensement:
Department of Island Development and Industry ou Bureau of Statistics, Government Office, Yaren District, Rep. of Nauru.

2. Recensements de population effectués depuis 1945 (années):
1947, 1952, 1957, 1962, 1967, 1977, 1983 et 1992. La présente description se réfère au recensement de 1992 (qui a eu lieu le 17 avril).

3. Champ du recensement:
a) *Territoire couvert*: Ensemble du pays.

b) *Personnes couvertes*: Ensemble de la population.

4. Période de référence:
La semaine précédant le jour du recensement.

5. Principaux sujets:
a) Population totale, selon le sexe et l'âge:	oui

Population active par:
b) Sexe et âge:	oui
c) Branche d'activité économique (industrie):	oui
d) Profession:	oui
e) Situation dans la profession:	oui
f) Niveau d'instruction le plus élevé:	oui
g) Durée du travail:	oui
h) Autres caractéristiques:	oui

Réf. a): L'âge est défini en termes d'année de naissance.

Réf. g): On a demandé aux personnes pourvues d'un emploi de préciser la durée normale du travail et les heures réellement effectuées pendant la période de référence.

Réf. h): Le recensement a également rassemblé des informations sur l'emploi secondaire, le revenu principal et secondaire, le motif du chômage ainsi que sur le type et le nombre d'heures du travail traditionnel (pêche, plongée sous-marine, artisanat, etc.).

6. Concepts et définitions:
a) *Population active*: Elle comprend toutes les personnes qui, pendant la semaine de référence, étaient soit pourvues d'un emploi, soit au chômage, conformément aux définitions données ci-dessous. L'âge limite minimal retenu pour l'inclusion d'une personne dans la population active était de 10 ans. Cependant, dans les résultats publiés, il est fixé à 10 ans pour les tableaux généraux concernant le «Statut dans l'emploi» et le «Type d'employeur» et à 15 ans pour les tableaux spécifiques sur la «Classification des professions», etc. Il n'y a pas de forces armées à Nauru, exception faite de la police locale.

b) *Emploi*: Sont considérées comme «pourvues d'un emploi» toutes les personnes ayant travaillé un minimum d'une heure au cours de la semaine de référence.

Il est indiqué que sont inclus dans cette définition:
i) les personnes travaillant sans rémunération dans une entreprise ou une affaire familiale;
ii) les personnes engagées dans la production de produits de base destinés à l'autoconsommation;
iii) les personnes occupées, temporairement absentes de leur travail;
iv) les étudiants travaillant à temps partiel;
v) les détenteurs de plusieurs emplois;
vi) les apprentis et les stagiaires.

A l'exception des étudiants travaillant à temps partiel, toutes les catégories ci-dessus peuvent être identifiées séparément.

c) *Chômage*: Sont considérées comme «chômeurs» toutes les personnes qui, pendant la semaine de référence, étaient sans emploi, en droit de travailler mais incapables de trouver ne serait-ce qu'une heure de travail au cours des sept derniers jours. Les étudiants en quête d'emploi sont exclus de la définition.

7. Classifications utilisées:
Seules les personnes pourvues d'un emploi ont été classifiées par branche d'activité économique, par profession et d'après la situation dans la profession.

a) *Branche d'activité économique (industrie)*: Pour coder la branche d'activité économique, on a utilisé cinq «larges groupes d'industries» (subdivisés en «départements», «sections», «type d'activité», etc.), à savoir: gouvernement; administration locale; société des phosphates de Nauru; activités économiques; autre. Aucun lien n'a été établi avec la CITI.

b) *Profession*: On a demandé aux personnes pourvues d'un emploi de décrire leur profession en deux mots minimum. Pour coder cette variable, on a utilisé la classification nationale. Des liens avec la CITP-88 ont été établis au niveau des grands groupes (1 chiffre).

c) *Situation dans la profession*: Basée sur la question: «Pour qui travaillez-vous?». La situation dans la profession est déterminée par une combinaison entre le «lieu de travail» et la «profession». Pour coder cette variable, on a utilisé sept groupes, à savoir: fonctionnaire gouvernemental; fonctionnaire d'une administration locale; employé de la société des phosphates de Nauru (NPC); négociant, travailleur indépendant ou employeur; sociétaire d'une entreprise (employé ou employeur); membre d'une coopérative (employé ou employeur); autre.

8. Principales différences par rapport au recensement précédent:
Les données sur l'activité économique n'ont pas été collectées lors des recensements précédents.

9. Publication des résultats du recensement:
Les résultats définitifs du recensement concernant la population active et ses composantes ont été publiés en décembre 1993 dans une publication intitulée «1992 National Census of Nauru: Main Report». L'organisme responsable de la publication est le Bureau des statistiques, Services gouvernementaux, Yaren District. Les résultats du recensement sont également disponibles sous forme de tableaux non publiés après accord ministériel.

NEPAL

1. Nom et adresse de l'organisme responsable du recensement:

Central Bureau of Statistics, National Planning Commission Secretariat, Ramshah Path, Thapathali, Kathmandu.

2. Recensements de population effectués depuis 1945 (années):

1952/54, 1961, 1971, 1981 et 1991. La présente description se réfère au recensement de 1991 (qui a eu lieu le 22 juin).

3. Champ du recensement:

a) Territoire couvert: Ensemble du pays.

b) Personnes couvertes: Ensemble de la population.

4. Période de référence:

Les douze mois précédant le jour du recensement.

5. Principaux sujets:

a) Population totale, selon le sexe et l'âge:	oui
Population active par:	
b) Sexe et âge:	oui
c) Branche d'activité économique (industrie):	oui
d) Profession:	oui
e) Situation dans la profession:	oui
f) Niveau d'instruction le plus élevé:	oui
g) Durée du travail:	oui
h) Autres caractéristiques:	non

Réf. a): L'âge est défini en termes d'années révolues à la date du dernier anniversaire.

Réf. g): On a demandé aux personnes pourvues d'un emploi de spécifier le nombre total de mois travaillés au cours des douze derniers mois.

6. Concepts et définitions:

a) Population active: Le recensement n'a mesuré que l'emploi.

b) Emploi: Sont considérées comme «pourvues d'un emploi» toutes les personnes âgées de 10 ans et plus qui, pendant la période de référence, ont effectué, à domicile ou à l'extérieur, un travail ayant une valeur économique. La question utilisée pour déterminer si une personne doit être considérée comme pourvue d'un emploi est: «Quel travail avez-vous exercé au cours des 12 derniers mois? travail agricole, travail salarié ou rémunéré, travail dans une affaire familiale, aucun travail rémunéré». Les membres des forces armées sont inclus dans la définition.

Il est indiqué que sont inclus dans cette définition:

i)   les personnes travaillant sans rémunération dans une entreprise ou une affaire familiale;

ii) les personnes engagées dans la production de produits de base destinés à l'autoconsommation;

iii) les personnes occupées, temporairement absentes de leur travail;

iv) les étudiants travaillant à temps partiel;

v)   les travailleurs saisonniers ou occasionnels;

vi) les apprentis et les stagiaires.

Aucune des catégories ci-dessus ne peut être identifiée séparément.

c) Chômage: Ne s'applique pas.

7. Classifications utilisées:

Toutes les personnes pourvues d'un emploi ont été classées par branche d'activité économique, par profession et d'après la situation dans l'emploi.

a) Branche d'activité économique (industrie): Basée sur la question: «Où avez-vous travaillé au cours des 12 derniers mois?». Pour coder la branche d'activité, on a utilisé neuf groupes de la classification nationale. Des liens avec la CITI-rév.2 ont été établis au niveau des branches (1 chiffre).

b) Profession: Basée sur la question: «Quel travail avez-vous exercé au cours des 12 derniers mois?». Pour coder la profession, on a utilisé sept groupes de la classification nationale. Des liens avec la CITP-68 ont été établis au niveau des grands groupes (1 chiffre).

c) Situation dans la profession: Basée sur la question: «Quelle est votre situation dans la profession?». Les réponses se répartissaient entre quatre groupes, à savoir: salarié, employeur,

travailleur à son propre compte et travailleur familial non rémunéré.

8. Principales différences par rapport au recensement précédent:

Lors du recensement de 1981 on avait retenu une période courte (une semaine) et une période longue (un an). En 1991 on s'est limité à la période de référence longue (un an), mais on a ajouté des questions relatives à la durée du travail, etc..

9. Publication des résultats du recensement:

Les données définitives ont été publiées en novembre 1993 dans la publication intitulée «Population Census - 1991»: Vol. 1, Parties I à XV; Vol. II (Tableaux des ménages); Vol. III (Tableaux urbains) et Vol. IV (Tableaux géographiques).

L'organisme responsable de la publication est le Bureau central des statistiques, Thapathali, Kathmandu.

Les données sont également disponibles sur disquettes et bandes magnétiques.

NORVEGE

1. Nom et adresse de l'organisme responsable du recensement:

Statistik Sentralbyrä (Statistics Norway), Population Census Division, Postuttak, N.2201 Kongsvinger.

2. Recensements de population effectués depuis 1945 (années):

1946, 1950, 1960, 1970, 1980 et 1990. La présente description se réfère au recensement de 1990 (qui a eu lieu le 3 novembre).

3. Champ du recensement:

a) Territoire couvert: Ensemble du pays. Comme lors des précédents recensements, les habitants de Svalbard et Jan Mayen sont considérés comme résidents d'une municipalité sur le continent et non pas comptabilisés séparément dans les résultats du recensement. Il en est de même pour les nationaux étrangers.

b) Personnes couvertes: Ensemble de la population. Le recensement couvre l'ensemble des personnes qui résidaient en Norvège le 3 novembre 1990. Les questions concernant la population active ont été posées à l'ensemble des personnes pour les municipalités de moins de 6000 habitants et ailleurs sur la base d'un échantillon (20,0; 14,3; 10,0 ou 8,3 pour cent selon la taille de la population).

4. Période de référence:

La semaine précédant le jour du recensement (du 27 octobre au 2 novembre) et l'année débutant le 3 novembre 1989 et se terminant le 2 novembre 1990.

5. Principaux sujets:

a) Population totale, selon le sexe et l'âge:	oui
Population active par:	
b) Sexe et âge:	oui
c) Branche d'activité économique (industrie):	oui
d) Profession:	oui
e) Situation dans la profession:	oui
f) Niveau d'instruction le plus élevé:	oui
g) Durée du travail:	oui
h) Autres caractéristiques:	oui

Réf. a): L'âge est défini en termes d'année de naissance (définition générale). Il est aussi défini, lorsque c'est possible, en termes d'années révolues au 3 novembre 1990.

Réf. g): Lorsque la période de référence est courte, la durée du travail concerne aussi bien la durée normale du travail des personnes pourvues d'un emploi que les heures réellement effectuées pendant la semaine de référence. Pour la période de référence longue, la durée du travail concerne la période totale de travail effectuée par le salarié (exprimée en termes de mois de travail à temps complet ou à temps partiel).

Réf. h): Le recensement rassemble aussi des informations sur d'autres sujets en relation avec le travail comme: le lieu de travail, la fréquence et la durée des déplacements pour se rendre au travail (aller simple) et les moyens de transport utilisés à cet effet la semaine précédant le jour du recensement (à savoir la semaine du 27 octobre au 2 novembre).

Les variables extraites des registres étaient des informations démographiques (Registre central de la population), des informations sur le niveau d'éducation (Bureau central des statistiques), des informations sur le chômage (Agence pour l'emploi), des informations sur le revenu, etc. (registres fiscaux, de l'Administration nationale des assurances et autres).

6. Concepts et définitions:

a) Population active: Elle comprend toutes les personnes âgées de 16 ans et plus qui, pendant les périodes de référence, étaient soit pourvues d'un emploi, soit au chômage, conformément aux définitions données ci-dessous. Elle inclut les membres des forces armées.

b) Emploi: Les questions spécifiques utilisées pour déterminer si une personne devait être considérée comme «pourvue d'un emploi» étaient: «Avez-vous effectué un travail rémunérateur d'au moins 100 heures pendant l'année qui va du 3 novembre 1989 au 2 novembre 1990?» et «Avez-vous effectué un travail rémunérateur pendant la semaine du 27 octobre au 2 novembre 1990?».

Il est indiqué que sont inclus dans cette définition:

i)   les personnes travaillant sans rémunération dans une entreprise ou une affaire familiale;
ii) les personnes engagées dans la production de produits de base destinés à l'autoconsommation;
iii) les personnes occupées, temporairement absentes du travail;
iv) les étudiants travaillant à temps partiel;
v)   les travailleurs saisonniers ou occasionnels;
vi) les conscrits (service militaire ou civil);
vii) les apprentis et les stagiaires.

Seules les personnes appartenant aux catégories iii), iv) et vi) peuvent être identifiées séparément par des questions spécifiques. Ainsi les personnes de la catégorie iv) peuvent être identifiées par la question: «Pendant combien d'heures avez-vous effectué un travail rémunérateur au cours de la semaine du 27 octobre au 2 novembre 1990?» et par le registre de l'éducation. Les conscrits peuvent être identifiés sur la base des données fournies par les forces armées.

c) Chômage: Sont considérés comme «chômeurs» toutes les personnes enregistrées comme chômeurs le jour du recensement. Les étudiants en quête de travail sont exclus de la définition.

7. Classifications utilisées:

Seules les personnes de l'échantillon pourvues d'un emploi conformément à la définition ci-dessus sont classifiées par branche d'activité économique, par profession et d'après la situation dans la profession.

a) Branche d'activité économique (industrie): Basée sur les questions: «Donnez le nom et l'adresse du lieu de travail (entreprise) où vous avez effectué un travail rémunéré pendant la période la plus longue de l'année s'étendant du 3 novembre 1989 au 2 novembre 1990 (s'il n'y a pas de nom d'entreprise, précisez le nom du propriétaire ou de l'employeur; si vous travaillez dans votre propre entreprise sans nom précis, indiquer vos nom et adresse» et «Décrivez avec autant de précisions que possible l'activité de votre employeur (précisez par exemple: fabrique de meubles, vente de voitures, librairie, exploitation agricole, location de machines, architecture, etc.)». Pour 78 pour cent des personnes, la branche d'activité a été codée en établissant des liens avec le répertoire des entreprises (5 chiffres). Pour le codage manuel, on a utilisé 3 chiffres. Des liens avec la CITI-rév.2 ont été établis au niveau des groupes (4 chiffres). Plus tard des liens seront établis avec la CITI-rév.3.

b) Profession: Basée sur la question: «Quelle était votre profession (titre) sur votre lieu de travail? (N'utilisez pas de terme collectif comme travailleur industriel, conseiller, installateur, etc. mais un titre décrivant vos fonctions (soudeur, consultant publicitaire, installateur de téléphone, aide ménagère, plombier, coiffeur, infirmière, teinturier, cuisinier, tôlier, vendeur, instituteur de maternelle,...)?». Pour coder la profession, on a utilisé 84 groupes correspondant aux codes (3 chiffres) de la classification nordique type des professions. Des liens avec la CITP-68 ont été établis au niveau des grands groupes (1 chiffre).

c) Situation dans la profession: Les questions spécifiques posées aux personnes de l'échantillon pourvues d'un emploi pour déterminer leur situation dans la profession est en rapport avec le lieu de travail. Pour coder la situation dans la profession on a utilisé trois groupes, à savoir: emploi rémunéré permanent ou temporaire; travailleur indépendant (propriétaire si confirmé par le registre du commerce), membre de la famille employé sans salaire fixe dans une entreprise familiale.

8. Principales différences par rapport au recensement précédent:

En 1980, les questions sur la durée totale du travail pendant la période de référence longue concernaient le nombre d'heures, alors qu'en 1990 elles touchaient le nombre de mois (temps plein; temps partiel). De plus, lors du recensement de 1980, on n'avait posé aucune question sur la durée normale ou convenue du travail en ce qui concerne la période de référence courte.

La variable «inconnue» n'a pas été retenue comme valeur des données de 1990 (excepté pour l'emploi) puisque les données manquantes ont été remplacées par des estimations basées sur i) d'autres valeurs de variables données par la personne et ii) des réponses fournies par d'autres personnes («correspondantes»).

9. Publication des résultats du recensement:

Les résultats définitifs pour le pays tout entier (pour toutes les principales variables) sont disponibles sur bandes depuis février 1992 mais n'ont pas été publiés. Des chiffres provisoires basés sur la tabulation d'un échantillon de 10 000 réponses ont été publiés en avril 1991.

Le titre de la publication (en norvégien seulement) contenant les chiffres définitifs du recensement est «Folke-og Boligtelling 1990 Landssammendrag».

Une publication intitulée «Population and Housing Census, Main results» a été publiée en 1992 (en norvégien et en anglais).

L'organisme responsable de cette publication est le Bureau central des statistiques, Division du recensement de la population, Postuttak, N-2201, Kongsvinger.

Les résultats définitifs du recensement de 1990 sont également disponibles sous forme de tableaux non publiés, de disquettes, de bandes magnétiques, de base de données en ligne et de service à l'usager.

NOUVELLE-CALEDONIE

1. Nom et adresse de l'organisme responsable du recensement:

INSEE (Institut national de la statistique et des études économiques) 18, boulevard Adolphe Pinard, 75675 PARIS CEDEX 14.

2. Recensements de population effectués depuis 1945 (années):

1963, 1969, 1976, 1983 et 1989. La présente description se réfère au recensement de 1989 (qui a eu lieu le 4 avril).

3. Champ du recensement:

a) Territoire couvert: Ensemble du territoire.

b) Personnes couvertes: Ensemble de la population.

4. Période de référence:

La semaine précédant le jour du recensement.

5. Principaux sujets:

a) Population totale, selon le sexe et l'âge:	oui
Population active par:	
b) Sexe et âge:	oui
c) Branche d'activité économique (industrie):	oui
d) Profession:	oui
e) Situation dans la profession:	oui
f) Niveau d'instruction le plus élevé:	oui
g) Durée du travail:	oui
h) Autres caractéristiques:	oui

Réf. a): L'âge est défini en termes d'année de naissance.

Réf. g): La durée du travail se réfère à la durée normale du travail des personnes pourvues d'un emploi, et à la modalité d'exercice de la profession (de façon continue, saisonnière ou intermittente, ou exceptionnelle).

Réf. h): Le recensement a également rassemblé des informations détaillées sur la durée du chômage (moins de trois mois, trois mois à moins d'un an, un an à moins de deux ans; deux ans et plus).

6. Concepts et définitions:

a) Population active: Elle comprend toutes les personnes âgées de 14 ans et plus qui, pendant la période de référence étaient, soit pourvues d'un emploi, soit au chômage, conformément aux définitions données ci-dessous. La définition inclut les membres des forces armées (militaires de carrière et du contingent) mais exclut les étudiants travaillant à temps partiel ou en quête de travail.

b) Emploi: Sont considérées comme «pourvues d'emploi» toutes les personnes qui, pendant la période de référence, ont travaillé ou été absentes de leur travail pour raisons temporaires (congé, maladie, maternité).

Il est indiqué que sont inclus dans cette définition:

i) les personnes travaillant sans rémunération dans une entreprise ou une exploitation familiale;
ii) les personnes engagées dans la production de produits de base destinés à l'autoconsommation;
iii) les personnes occupées, temporairement absentes du travail;
iv) les travailleurs saisonniers ou occasionnels;
v) les conscrits (service militaire ou civil);
vi) les apprentis sous contrat et les stagiaires.

Les catégories ci-desssus peuvent être identifiées séparément.

c) Chômage: Sont considérées comme «chômeurs» toutes les personnes qui se sont déclarées spontanément en chômage pendant la période de référence.

7. Classifications utilisées:

Seules les personnes occupées ont été classifiées par industrie, par profession et d'après la situation dans la profession.

a) Branche d'activité économique (industrie): Des questions spécifiques ont été posées aux personnes occupées sur l'adresse, le nom ou la raison sociale et l'activité de l'établissement qui les emploie ou qu'elles dirigent. Pour coder la branche d'activité, on a utilisé 14 groupes de la classification nationale des industries. Il n'a pas été établi de liens avec la CITI.

b) Profession: On a demandé aux personnes occupées d'indiquer très précisément leur profession (par exemple: ouvrier électricien d'entretien, chauffeur de poids lourds, vendeur en électroménager, ingénieur chimiste, caissière de libre-service, etc.). Pour coder la profession, on a utilisé 33 groupes détaillés, regroupés par la suite en 6 grands groupes. Il n'a pas été établi de liens avec la CITP.

c) Situation dans la profession: Pour déterminer leur situation dans la profession, on a demandé aux personnes occupées quel était leur statut professionnel. On a utilisé neuf groupes: agriculteur et/ou éleveur, chasseur, pêcheur; aide familial; membre d'une profession libérale; artisan, commerçant, industriel; autre employeur ou travailleur indépendant; travailleur à domicile pour le compte d'une entreprise; apprenti sous contrat; salarié du secteur privé; salarié du secteur public.

8. Principales différences par rapport au recensement précédent:

En 1983, n'étaient considérées comme chômeurs que les personnes qui percevaient une indemnité de chômage.

9. Publication des résultats du recensement:

Les résultats définitifs du recensement ont été publiés en 1991.

Les titres des publications contenant les résultats définitifs sont:

– Images de la population de Nouvelle-Calédonie 1989 (INSEE).
– Recensement de la population de Nouvelle-Calédonie 1989: inventaire communal.
– L'activité en Nouvelle-Calédonie en 1989, 3 Tomes de tableaux. T1: Constructions logements; T2: Les ménages; T3: Activité individus.
– Inventaire tribal 1989, 3 Tomes: Province Iles Loyauté, Province Nord, Province Sud.

L'organisme responsable de cette publication est l'ITSEE (Institut territorial de la statistique et des études économiques, 5 rue du Général Galliéni, B.P. 823, Nouméa, Nouvelle-Calédonie.

Les résultats du recensement de 1989 sont également disponibles sous la forme de tableaux non publiés.

NOUVELLE-ZELANDE

1. Nom et adresse de l'organisme responsable du recensement:

Department of Statistics, 64 Kilmore Street, Christchurch 1.

2. Recensements de population effectués depuis 1945 (années):

1945, 1951, 1956, 1961, 1966, 1971, 1976, 1981, 1986 et 1991. La présente description se réfère au recensement de 1991 (qui a eu lieu le 5 mars).

3. Champ du recensement:

a) Territoire couvert: Ensemble du pays.

b) Personnes couvertes: Ensemble de la population.

4. Période de référence:

La période de référence retenue était le jour du recensement pour déterminer les personnes pourvues d'un emploi et les quatre semaines précédentes pour déterminer les chômeurs.

5. Principaux sujets:

a) Population totale, selon le sexe et l'âge:	oui
Population active par:	
b) Sexe et âge:	oui
c) Branche d'activité économique (industrie):	oui
d) Profession:	oui
e) Situation dans la profession:	oui
f) Niveau d'instruction le plus élevé:	oui
g) Durée du travail:	oui
h) Autres caractéristiques:	oui

Réf. a): L'âge est défini en termes d'années révolues à la date du dernier anniversaire.

Réf. g): La durée du travail se réfère aux heures réellement effectuées par les personnes pourvues d'un emploi, présentes au travail. Les personnes pourvues d'un emploi mais temporairement absentes de leur travail devaient indiquer la durée normale de leur travail.

Réf. h): On a également posé des questions sur les principaux moyens de transport utilisés pour se rendre au travail le jour du recensement et sur le revenu total perçu au cours de l'année se terminant le 31 mars 1991.

6. Concepts et définitions:

a) Population active: Elle comprend toutes les personnes âgées de 15 ans et plus qui, pendant les périodes de référence, étaient soit pourvues d'un emploi, soit au chômage, conformément aux définitions données ci-dessous. La définition exclut les visiteurs étrangers ne travaillant pas en Nouvelle-Zélande mais inclut les membres des forces armées.

b) Emploi: Sont considérées comme «pourvues d'un emploi» toutes les personnes qui, au moment du recensement, ont effectué, à domicile ou à l'extérieur, un travail ayant une valeur économique, moyennant salaire ou sans rémunération dans une entreprise familiale. La question utilisée pour déterminer si une personne doit être considérée comme pourvue d'un emploi était «Exerçez-vous une profession, une fonction ou tout autre activité économique?».

Il est indiqué que sont inclus dans cette définition:

i) les personnes travaillant sans rémunération dans une entreprise ou une affaire familiale;
ii) les personnes occupées, temporairement absentes du travail;
iii) les étudiants travaillant à temps partiel;
iv) les travailleurs saisonniers ou occasionnels;
v) les détenteurs de plusieurs emplois;
vi) les apprentis et les stagiaires.

Seules les personnes appartenant aux catégories i), iii) et v) peuvent être identifiées séparément par des questions spécifiques.

c) Chômage: Sont considérées comme «chômeurs» toutes les personnes qui, pendant les quatre semaines précédant le recensement, étaient disponibles pour travailler et activement à la recherche d'un emploi à temps plein ou partiel et qui n'exerçaient aucune profession, fonction ou autre activité économique le jour du recensement. Les questions utilisées pour déterminer si une personne devait être considérée comme chômeur, étaient «Etiez-vous à la recherche d'un travail rémunéré au cours des quatre dernières semaines?», «Quelles méthodes avez-vous utilisées pour chercher du travail?» et «Si un travail s'était présenté, auriez-vous pu le démarrer la semaine passée?».

7. Classifications utilisées:

Seules les personnes pourvues d'un emploi ont été classifiées par branche d'activité économique, par profession et d'après la situation dans la profession.

a) Branche d'activité économique (industrie): Basée sur les questions: «Pour qui travaillez-vous?», «Où travaillez-vous?» et «Quelle la principale activité exercée sur votre lieu de travail (élevage de moutons, maternité, transformation de la volaille, conseil en gestion d'entreprise, etc.)?». L'activité principale fait référence à l'affaire, l'industrie ou le service dominant offert par l'employeur. Pour coder la branche d'activité économique, on a utilisé la classification néo-zélandaise type par industrie (NZSIC) au niveau 5 chiffres. Des liens ont été établis avec la CITI-rév.2 au niveau des groupes (4 chiffres).

b) Profession: Basée sur les questions: «Quelle est votre profession?» et «Quelles sont les tâches ou les fonctions qui vous occupent le plus?». Pour coder la profession on a utilisé tous les groupes de la Classification néo-zélandaise type des professions (NZSCO). Des liens ont été établis avec la CITP-88 au niveau des groupes de base (4 chiffres).

c) Situation dans la profession: La question utilisée pour déterminer la situation dans la profession était: «Travaillez-vous comme: i) salarié (ouvrier ou employé); ii) travailleur indépendant sans salariés; iii) employeur; iv) travailleur non rémunéré dans une affaire familiale?». Pour coder la situation dans la profession, on a utilisé les quatre groupes précités.

8. Principales différences par rapport au recensement précédent:
Le recensement de 1991 incluait deux questions supplémentaires sur les méthodes employées pour rechercher du travail (voir 6 c) ci-dessus).

9. Publication des résultats du recensement:
Le titre de la publication contenant les résultats du recensement est: «National Population Summary», 1992.

L'organisme responsable de cette publication est le Département des statistiques, 64 Kilmore Street, Christchurch 1.

Les résultats du recensement sont également disponibles sous forme de tableaux non publiés, de disquettes, de bandes magnétiques et de CD-ROM.

OUGANDA

1. Nom et adresse de l'organisme responsable du recensement:
Ministry of Finance and Economic Planning, Department of Statistics, P.O. Box 13, Entebbe.

2. Recensements de population effectués depuis 1945 (années):
1948, 1959, 1969, 1980 et 1991. La présente description se réfère au recensement de 1991 (qui a eu lieu le 11 janvier).

3. Champ du recensement:
a) Territoire couvert: Ensemble du pays.

b) Personnes couvertes: Ensemble de la population.

4. Période de référence:
La semaine précédant le jour du recensement.

5. Principaux sujets:
a) Population totale, selon le sexe et l'âge:	oui
Population active par:	
b) Sexe et âge:	oui
c) Branche d'activité économique (industrie):	non
d) Profession:	oui
e) Situation dans la profession:	oui
f) Niveau d'instruction le plus élevé:	oui
g) Durée du travail:	non
h) Autres caractéristiques:	non

Réf. a): L'âge est défini en termes d'années révolues à la date du dernier anniversaire.

6. Concepts et définitions:
a) Population active: Elle comprend toutes les personnes âgées de 10 ans et plus qui, au cours de la période de référence, étaient soit pourvues d'un emploi, soit au chômage, conformément aux définitions données ci-dessous. Les questions relatives à la population active ont été posées à l'ensemble de la population urbaine et à 10 pour cent de la population rurale. Les membres des forces armées résidant dans des habitations privées sont inclus dans la définition.

b) Emploi: Sont considérées comme «pourvues d'un emploi» toutes les personnes qui, pendant la période de référence, ont effectué un travail. La question posée était: «Statut d'activité la semaine dernière: employé, travailleur indépendant, travailleur familial non rémunéré, étudiant, travailleur ménager, en quête d'emploi, handicapé, personne âgée, etc.».

Il est indiqué que sont inclus dans cette définition:

i) les personnes travaillant sans rémunération dans une entreprise ou une affaire familiale;
ii) les étudiants travaillant à temps partiel;
iii) les travailleurs saisonniers ou occasionnels;
iv) les conscrits (service militaire ou civil).

Seules les catégories i) et ii) peuvent être identifiées séparément.

c) Chômage: Sont considérées comme «chômeurs» toutes les personnes qui, pendant la semaine de référence, étaient sans emploi et à la recherche d'un travail. La question posée était la même que celle indiquée sous 6 b).

7. Classifications utilisées:
Seules les personnes «pourvues d'un emploi» sont classifiées par profession et d'après la situation dans la profession.

a) Branche d'activité économique (industrie): Aucune classification n'a été faite par branche d'activité économique.

b) Profession: Basée sur la question: «Profession la semaine dernière: quel genre de travail avez-vous effectué?». Pour coder la profession, on a utilisé 161 groupes de la classification nationale. On a élargi la CITP-88 (en utilisant les codes vides) pour inclure la classification nationale. Des liens ont été établis au niveau des sous-groupes (3 chiffres).

c) Situation dans la profession: La question posée pour déterminer la situation dans la profession était la même que celle indiquée sous 6 b). Pour coder la situation dans l'emploi, on a utilisé trois groupes, à savoir: employé, travailleur indépendant et travailleur familial non rémunéré.

8. Principales différences par rapport au recensement précédent:
Le recensement de 1969 ne comportait aucune information sur l'emploi.

9. Publication des résultats du recensement:
Les résultats définitifs du recensement sont parus dans les publications suivantes: «The 1991 Population and Housing Census Main Results (pre-Release)», octobre 1992, «The 1991 Population Housing Census National Summary», avril 1994 et «The 1991 Population and Housing Final Results (main Release)», janvier 1995.

L'organisme responsable de ces publications est le Département des statistiques, PO Box 13, Entebbe.

Des tableaux et des données non publiés sont également disponibles sous forme de disquettes.

PANAMA

1. Nom et adresse de l'organisme responsable du recensement:
Dirección de Estadística y Censo, Contraloría General de la República, Apartado 5213, Zona 5, Panamá, República de Panama.

2. Recensements de population effectués depuis 1945 (années):
1950, 1960, 1970, 1980 et 1990. La présente description se réfère au recensement de population de 1990 (qui a eu lieu le 13 mai).

3. Champ du recensement:
a) Territoire couvert: Ensemble du pays.

b) Personnes couvertes: Ensemble de la population, à l'exception des nationaux résidant à l'étranger et, du fait de l'intervention nord-américaine, des soldats qui se trouvaient dans le cadre de cette intervention à Panama au moment du recensement.

4. Période de référence:
La semaine précédant le recensement.

5. Principaux sujets:
a) Population totale, selon le sexe et l'âge:	oui
Population active par:	
b) Sexe et âge:	oui
c) Branche d'activité économique (industrie):	oui
d) Profession:	oui
e) Situation dans la profession:	oui
f) Niveau d'instruction le plus élevé:	oui
g) Durée du travail:	non
h) Autres caractéristiques:	oui

Réf. a): L'âge est défini en termes d'années révolues à la date du dernier anniversaire.

Réf. h): Des informations ont été recueillies sur les personnes employées de manière permanente et sur celles employées de manière occasionnelle, ainsi que sur le revenu total pendant le mois précédant la date du recensement.

6. Concepts et définitions:

a) Population active: Elle comprend toutes les personnes âgées de 10 ans et plus qui, pendant la semaine de référence, étaient soit pourvues d'un emploi soit au chômage, conformément aux définitions données ci-dessous. La définition inclut tous les membres des forces armées.

b) Emploi: Sont considérées comme «pourvues d'un emploi» les personnes ayant répondu par l'affirmative à la question suivante: «La semaine passée, avez-vous travaillé ou aviez-vous un travail dont vous étiez absent?».

Il est indiqué que sont inclus dans cette définition:

i)   les personnes travaillant sans rémunération dans une entreprise ou une affaire familiale;

ii) les personnes engagées dans la production de produits de base destinés à l'autoconsommation;

iii) les personnes occupées, temporairement absentes de leur travail;

iv) les étudiants travaillant à temps partiel;

v)   les travailleurs saisonniers ou occasionnels;

vi) les conscrits (service militaire ou civil);

vii) les apprentis et les stagiaires.

Seules les personnes appartenant aux catégories i) et v) peuvent être identifiées séparément au moyen de questions spécifiques.

c) Chômage: Sont considérées comme «chômeurs» les personnes qui, pendant la semaine de référence, n'avaient pas d'emploi ou de travail et qui, selon leurs déclarations, étaient à la recherche d'un emploi ou estimaient qu'il leur était impossible d'en trouver un.

7. Classifications utilisées:

Aussi bien les personnes pourvues d'un emploi que les chômeurs ayant déjà travaillé auparavant sont classifiés par branche d'activité économique, par profession et d'après la situation dans la profession.

a) Branche d'activité économique (industrie): Pour déterminer la branche d'activité économique, on a posé les questions suivantes: «Où travaillez-vous (où avez-vous travaillé la dernière fois)?» et «De quoi s'occupe le commerce, l'établissement, l'entreprise ou l'institution dans lequel vous travaillez (dans lequel vous avez travaillé)?».

b) Profession: Pour coder cette variable, on a utilisé 10 groupes de la classification nationale des professions. Ces groupes sont compatibles avec la CITP-68 au niveau des grands groupes (1 chiffre).

c) Situation dans la profession: Pour déterminer cette variable, on a demandé à la personne si dans son travail actuel ou antérieur, elle travaille ou avait travaillé en qualité de: salarié; travailleur indépendant ou travailleur pour son propre compte; travailleur familial sans rémunération; patron; membre ou associé d'une coopérative de production. Pour coder la situation dans la profession, on a utilisé les cinq groupes susmentionnés.

8. Principales différences par rapport au recensement précédent:

Pas de différence majeure.

9. Publication des résultats du recensement:

Le titre exact de la publication dans laquelle sont présentés les résultats définitifs du recensement est «Resultados finales básicos» (il y a trois publications - une par district: Panamá, Colón et San Miguelito - ainsi que des publications par provinces (février 1991)).

L'organisme responsable de ces publications est la Direction générale des statistiques et du recensement.

Les résultats du recensement sont également disponibles sous la forme de bandes magnétiques et de tableaux non publiés.

PAPOUASIE-NOUVELLE-GUINEE

1. Nom et adresse de l'organisme responsable du recensement:

National Statistical Office, P.O. Box 337, Waigani, NCD, Papua New Guinea.

2. Recensements de population effectués depuis 1945 (années):

1966, 1971, 1980 et 1990. La présente description se réfère au recensement de population de 1990 (qui a eu lieu du 9 au 13 juillet).

3. Champ du recensement:

a) Territoire couvert: L'Etat des Salomon au nord a été totalement exclu du recensement à cause d'une crise politique.

b) Personnes couvertes: Ensemble de la population, à l'exception du personnel diplomatique étranger et de leur famille.

4. Période de référence:

La semaine et les 12 mois précédant le recensement.

5. Principaux sujets:

a) Population totale, selon le sexe et l'âge:	oui
Population active par:	
b) Sexe et âge:	oui
c) Branche d'activité économique (industrie):	non
d) Profession:	oui
e) Situation dans la profession:	non
f) Niveau d'instruction le plus élevé:	oui
g) Durée du travail:	non
h) Autres caractéristiques:	non

Réf. a): L'âge est défini en termes d'années révolues à la date du dernier anniversaire.

6. Concepts et définitions:

a) Population active: Elle comprend toutes les personnes âgées de 10 ans et plus qui, pendant les périodes de référence, étaient soit pourvues d'un emploi, soit au chômage, conformément aux définitions données ci-dessous. On a utilisé une période de référence courte (une semaine) pour rassembler des informations sur l'activité du moment dans le secteur urbain et une période de référence longue (12 mois) pour collecter des informations sur l'activité habituelle dans le secteur rural. La définition inclut les membres des forces armées mais elle exclut les étudiants travaillant à temps partiel et les étudiants en quête d'un emploi.

b) Emploi: La question utilisée pour déterminer si une personne doit être considérée comme «pourvue d'un emploi» est: «A quoi avez-vous occupé l'essentiel de votre temps au cours des sept derniers jours? salarié; employeur avec salarié(s); travailleur indépendant y compris les aides non rémunérés; je cultivais la terre et je pêchais pour vendre les produits et subvenir à mes besoins; je cultivais la terre et je pêchais dans l'unique but de subvenir à mes besoins».

Il est indiqué que sont inclus dans cette définition:

i)   les personnes travaillant sans rémunération dans une entreprise ou une affaire familiale;

ii) les personnes engagées dans la production de produits de base destinés à l'autoconsommation;

iii) les personnes occupées, temporairement absentes de leur travail;

iv) les travailleurs saisonniers ou occasionnels;

v)   les conscrits (service militaire ou civil);

vi) les apprentis et les stagiaires.

Seules les personnes appartenant à la catégorie ii) peuvent être identifiées séparément.

c) Chômage: Sont considérées comme «chômeurs» toutes les personnes qui, pendant les périodes de référence, étaient sans travail et à la recherche d'une emploi ou disponibles pour travailler. La définition inclut les personnes restant à la maison sans aucune activité, pas même celle de rechercher un emploi parce qu'elles pensent que la chance d'en trouver un est nulle mais en reconnaissant parfois qu'elles accepteraient un emploi si on leur en proposait un.

7. Classifications utilisées:

Seules les personnes des zones urbaines pourvues d'un emploi sont classifiées par profession.

a) Branche d'activité économique (industrie): Aucune classification n'a été faite.

b) Profession: On a demandé aux personnes pourvues d'un emploi de décrire en deux mots minimum leur principale activité, à savoir l'activité économique qui occupe l'essentiel de leur temps: par exemple, vendeur, infirmier, chauffeur de taxi, etc. Pour coder la profession, on a utilisé neuf groupes de la classification nationale. Des liens avec la CITP-88 ont été établis au niveau des grands groupes (1 chiffre).

c) Situation dans la profession: Aucune classification n'a été faite.

8. Principales différences par rapport au recensement précédent:

En 1990 la définition du chômage a été élargie par l'inclusion des personnes disponibles pour travailler.

En 1990, on a utilisé une période de référence longue (12 mois) pour les questions sur l'activité économique dans les zones rurales alors qu'en 1980 on avait utilisé une période de référence courte (la semaine précédant le recensement) pour ces questions.

9. Publication des résultats du recensement:

Les résultats définitifs du recensement concernant la population active et ses composantes ont été publiés en août 1994 dans une publication intitulée «Report on the 1990 National Population and Housing Census in Papua New Guinea».

L'organisme responsable de cette publication est le Bureau national des statistiques (NSO), P.O. Box 337, Waigani, NCD.

Les résultats du recensement ne sont pas disponibles sous d'autres formes.

PARAGUAY

1. Nom et adresse de l'organisme responsable du recensement:

Dirección General de Estadística, Encuestas y Censos, Luis Alberto de Herrera 1010, c/Estados Unidos, Casilla de Correo No 1118, Asunción.

2. Recensements de population effectués depuis 1945 (années):

1950, 1962, 1972, 1982 et 1992. La présente description se réfère au recensement de population de 1992 (qui a eu lieu le 26 août).

3. Champ du recensement:

a) Territoire couvert: Ensemble du pays.

b) Personnes couvertes: Ensemble de la population.

4. Période de référence:

La semaine précédant le jour du recensement.

5. Principaux sujets:

a) Population totale, selon le sexe et l'âge:	oui
Population active par:	
b) Sexe et âge:	oui
c) Branche d'activité économique (industrie):	oui
d) Profession:	oui
e) Situation dans la profession:	oui
f) Niveau d'instruction le plus élevé:	oui
g) Durée du travail:	non
h) Autres caractéristiques:	non

Réf. a): L'âge est défini en termes d'années révolues à la date du dernier anniversaire.

6. Concepts et définitions:

a) Population active: Elle comprend toutes les personnes âgées de 10 ans et plus qui, pendant la semaine de référence, étaient soit pourvues d'un emploi soit au chômage, conformément aux définitions données ci-dessous. La définition inclut les conscrits mais exclut les militaires de carrière. Elle exclut également les étudiants travaillant à temps partiel ou à la recherche d'un emploi.

b) Emploi: Sont considérées comme «pourvues d'un emploi» les personnes ayant travaillé pendant la majeure partie de la semaine de référence. La question utilisée est: «Avez-vous travaillé pendant la majeure partie de la semaine passée? 1) A travaillé; 2) N'a pas travaillé, mais était pourvu d'un emploi; 3) Etait à la recherche d'un emploi et avait déjà travaillé auparavant; 4) Etait à la recherche d'un premier emploi; 5) Etait

occupé(e) aux tâches ménagères de son foyer; 6) Etait étudiant; 7) Vivait de ses rentes; 8) Etait retraité ou pensionné; 9) Faisait son service militaire obligatoire; 10) Autre situation».

Il est indiqué que sont inclus dans cette définition:

i) les personnes travaillant sans rémunération dans une entreprise ou une affaire familiale;

ii) les personnes occupées, temporairement absentes de leur travail.

Les personnes appartenant aux deux catégories ci-dessus peuvent être identifiées séparément.

c) Chômage: Sont considérées comme «chômeurs» les personnes qui, pendant la semaine de référence, étaient soit à la recherche d'un emploi en ayant déjà travaillé auparavant, soit à la recherche d'un premier emploi.

7. Classifications utilisées:

Aussi bien les personnes pourvues d'un emploi que les chômeurs sont classifiés par branche d'activité économique, par profession et d'après la situation dans la profession.

a) Branche d'activité économique (industrie): Basée sur la question: «De quoi s'occupe ou que produit l'entreprise, le commerce ou l'institution dans lequel vous travaillez (ou dans lequel vous travailliez)? Exemples: culture du coton, culture de légumes, construction de bâtiments, enseignement primaire, santé, confection de vêtements, commerce, etc». Pour coder la branche d'activité économique, on a utilisé 9 groupes de la classification nationale. Des liens ont été établis avec la CITI-rév.2 au niveau des branches (1 chiffre).

b) Profession: Basée sur la question: «Quelle est (était) votre profession principale dans l'emploi que vous occupez (occupiez)? Exemple: couturière, secrétaire, chauffeur, cordonnier, vendeur, agriculteur, maçon, électricien, médecin, etc.». Pour coder la profession, on a utilisé la CITP-88 au niveau des grands groupes (1 chiffre).

c) Situation dans la profession: Basée sur la question: «Dans cet emploi, êtes-vous (étiez-vous) employé, ouvrier ou journalier, patron ou employeur, travailleur pour son propre compte ou travailleur indépendant, travailleur familial sans rémunération, employé de maison?». Ce sont ces six groupes que l'on a utilisé pour coder cette variable.

8. Principales différences par rapport au recensement précédent:

Lors du recensement de 1992, la limite d'âge inférieur pour poser les questions relatives à l'activité économique avait été de 12 ans (10 ans pour le recensement de 1992).

9. Publication des résultats du recensement:

Les chiffres définitifs ont été publiés, pour Asunción, en août 1993, pour le Département central en octobre 1993 et pour le Département de Alto Paraná en mars 1994. Les résultats pour l'ensemble du pays ont été publiés en juillet 1994.

Le titre exact de la publication dans laquelle sont présentés les résultats définitifs est «Paraguay: Censo Nacional de Población y Viviendas».

L'organisme responsable de cette publication est la Direction générale des statistiques, des enquêtes et des recensements, Luis Alberto de Herrera 1010, c/ Estados Unidos, Casilla de Correo No 1118, Asuncion.

Les résultats du recensement sont également disponibles sous forme de disquettes et de tableaux non publiés.

PEROU

1. Nom et adresse de l'organisme responsable du recensement:

Instituto Nacional de Estadística y Informática, Av. 28 de Julio No 1056, Lima.

2. Recensements de population effectués depuis 1945 (années):

1961, 1972, 1981 et 1993. La présente description se réfère au recensement de population de 1993 (qui a eu lieu le 11 juillet).

3. Champ du recensement:

a) Territoire couvert: Ensemble du pays.

b) Personnes couvertes: Ensemble de la population.

4. Période de référence:

La semaine précédant le jour du recensement.

5. Principaux sujets:
a) Population totale, selon le sexe et l'âge: oui
Population active par:
b) Sexe et âge: oui
c) Branche d'activité économique (industrie):   oui
d) Profession: oui
e) Situation dans la profession: oui
f) Niveau d'instruction le plus élevé: oui
g) Durée du travail: non
h) Autres caractéristiques: non

Réf. a): L'âge est défini en termes d'années révolues à la date du dernier anniversaire pour les personnes de un an et plus (pour les mineurs de moins d'un an, l'âge retenu est le nombre de mois révolus).

6. Concepts et définitions:

a) Population active: Elle comprend toutes les personnes âgées de 6 ans et plus qui, pendant la semaine de référence, étaient soit pourvues d'un emploi soit au chômage, conformément aux définitions données ci-dessous. La définition inclut les militaires de carrière mais exclut les conscrits (service militaire ou civil).

b) Emploi: Sont considérées comme «pourvues d'un emploi» les personnes ayant travaillé pendant la semaine de référence. Pour déterminer si une personne est pourvue d'un emploi, les questions utilisées sont: «La semaine passée, travailliez-vous avec rémunération?», «Etiez-vous dans la situation où vous ne travailliez pas mais aviez un emploi?» et «Aidiez-vous un parent sans être rémunéré?».

Il est indiqué que sont inclus dans cette définition:

i)   les personnes travaillant sans rémunération dans une entreprise ou une affaire familiale;
ii) les personnes engagées dans la production de produits de base destinés à l'autoconsommation;
iii) les personnes occupées, temporairement absentes de leur travail;
iv) les étudiants travaillant à temps partiel;
v) les travailleurs saisonniers ou occasionnels.

Seules les personnes appartenant aux catégories i) et iii) peuvent être identifiées séparément au moyen de questions spécifiques. Pour la catégorie i), la question utilisée est: «Aidez-vous un parent sans être rémunéré?», et pour la catégorie iii), «Etiez-vous dans la situation où vous ne travailliez pas mais étiez pourvu d'un emploi?».

c) Chômage: Sont considérées comme «chômeurs» les personnes qui, pendant la semaine de référence, étaient à la recherche d'un emploi mais avaient déjà travaillé auparavant, ou qui étaient à la recherche d'un premier emploi.

7. Classifications utilisées:
Aussi bien les personnes pourvues d'un emploi que les chômeurs ayant déjà travaillé auparavant sont classifiés par branche d'activité économique, par profession et d'après la situation dans la profession.

a) Branche d'activité économique (industrie): Pour déterminer la branche d'activité économique, on a demandé aux intéressés de quoi s'occupe l'établissement commercial, l'organisme ou l'entreprise dans lequel ils travaillent (ou dans lequel ils travaillaient dans leur dernier emploi). Pour coder cette variable, on a utilisé la CITI-rév.3 au niveau des classes (4 chiffres).

b) Profession: Pour déterminer la profession, on a demandé quelle était la profession, la fonction ou le métier exercé principalement par l'intéressé pendant la semaine de référence ou la dernière fois qu'il a travaillé. Pour coder cette variable, on a utilisé la CITP-88 au niveau des sous-groupes (3 chiffres).

c) Situation dans la profession: Pour déterminer cette caractéristique, on a demandé quelle était la catégorie professionnelle dans laquelle se situait l'intéressé dans l'établissement commercial, l'organisme ou l'entreprise dans lequel il travaillait. Cette variable a été codée en six groupes (ouvrier, employé, travailleur familial sans rémunération, travailleur au foyer, travailleur indépendant ou à son propre compte, employeur ou patron).

8. Principales différences par rapport au recensement précédent:
Pas de différence majeure.

9. Publication des résultats du recensement:
Les résultats définitifs ont été publiés en novembre 1994.

Le titre de la publication dans laquelle ils sont présentés est «Resultados definitivos Perú Censos Nacionales 1993: IX de población y IV de Vivienda».

L'organisme responsable de cette publication est l'Institut national de statistiques et d'informatique, av. 28 de Julio, No1056, Lima, Pérou.

Les résultats du recensement sont également disponibles sous forme de disquettes.

PHILIPPINES

1. Nom et adresse de l'organisme responsable du recensement:
National Statistics Office, R. Magsaysay Boulevard, Sta Mesa, Manila.

2. Recensements de population effectués depuis 1945 (années):
1948, 1960, 1970, 1975, 1980 et 1990. La présente description se réfère au recensement de population de 1990 (qui a eu lieu le 1er mai).

3. Champ du recensement:

a) Territoire couvert: Ensemble du pays.

b) Personnes couvertes: Ensemble de la population, à l'exception: des ressortissants de pays étrangers qui comptent résider aux Philippines moins d'un an à compter de la date de leur arrivée; des ressortissants de pays étrangers affectés à une ambassade, un ministère, une légation, une chancellerie ou un consulat et résidant dans leur enceinte, quelle que soit la durée de leur séjour; du personnel militaire et civil étranger et de leur famille résidant sur la base militaire indépendamment de la durée de leur séjour; des ressortissants étrangers qui sont des responsables ou des fonctionnaires d'organisations internationales comme les Nations Unies, l'OIT ou l'USAID et qui peuvent être rappelés dans leur pays à la fin de leur mandat aux Philippines, ainsi que leur famille.

4. Période de référence:
La semaine précédant le jour du recensement. Cependant on a utilisé une longue période de référence (les douze derniers mois) pour l'activité ou la profession et la nature habituelles de l'activité ou de l'industrie.

5. Principaux sujets:
a) Population totale, selon le sexe et l'âge: oui
Population active par:
b) Sexe et âge: oui
c) Branche d'activité économique (industrie):   oui
d) Profession: oui
e) Situation dans la profession: non
f) Niveau d'instruction le plus élevé: oui
g) Durée du travail: non
h) Autres caractéristiques: oui

Réf. a): L'âge est défini en termes d'années révolues à la date du dernier anniversaire.

Réf. h): Le recensement a aussi rassemblé des informations sur la profession et le type d'affaires ou d'industrie habituellement menés par la personne interrogée au cours des douze derniers mois.

6. Concepts et définitions:

a) Population active: Elle comprend toutes les personnes âgées de 10 ans et plus qui, pendant la semaine de référence, étaient soit pourvues d'un emploi, soit au chômage, conformément aux définitions données ci-dessous. Les officiers militaires et les membres de leur famille âgés de 10 ans et plus résidant dans des habitations situées dans l'enceinte d'un camp militaire ou dans d'autres logements sont inclus dans la définition. Les soldats et autre personnel militaire résidant dans des casernes ou des camps militaires sans aucun membre de leur famille sont considérés comme population institutionnelle; dispensés à ce titre des questions sur l'activité économique, ils sont donc exclus de la définition.

Les questions relatives à l'activité économique ont été posées à 10 pour cent des personnes dans les municipalités comptant plus de 1 500 ménages, à 20 pour cent des personnes dans les municipalités comptant entre 500 et 1 500 ménages et à 100 pour cent des municipalités de moins de 500 ménages. La publication des données sur la population active ne se réfère qu'aux personnes âgées de 15 ans et plus.

b) Emploi: La question utilisée pour déterminer si une personne devait ou non être considérée comme pourvue d'un emploi était: «La personne a-t-elle exercé un travail ou une activité au cours des sept derniers jours?».

Il est indiqué que sont inclus dans cette définition:

i)   les personnes travaillant sans rémunération dans une entreprise ou une affaire familiale;
ii)   les personnes occupées, temporairement absentes du travail;
iii) les étudiants travaillant à temps partiel;
iv)   les travailleurs saisonniers ou occasionnels.

Aucune des catégories ci-dessus ne peut être identifiée séparément.

c) Chômage: Sont considérées comme «chômeurs» toutes les personnes qui, pendant la semaine de référence, étaient sans travail, disponibles et à la recherche d'un emploi. La question utilisée pour déterminer si une personne doit être considérée comme étant au chômage est la même que celle indiquée sous 6 b) ci-dessus. Dans le cas d'une réponse négative, on a posé les questions suivantes: «La personne était-elle disponible pour travailler au cours des sept derniers jours?», «La personne a-t-elle recherché un travail au cours des sept derniers jours?» et «Pourquoi n'a-t-elle pas recherché de travail?».

7. Classifications utilisées:

Seules les personnes de l'échantillon âgées de 15 ans et plus sont classifiées par industrie et par profession. Aucune classification n'a été faite d'après la situation dans la profession.

a) Branche d'activité économique (industrie): Basée sur la question: «Dans quel type d'affaires ou d'industrie a travaillé la personne au cours des sept derniers jours?». Pour coder la branche d'activité économique, on a utilisé, au niveau 3 chiffres, la classification philippine type par industrie de 1977, basée sur la CITI-rév.2.

b) Profession: Basée sur la question: «Quelle activité ou profession exerçait la personne au cours des sept derniers jours?». Pour coder la profession, on a utilisé, au niveau des groupes de base (4 chiffres), la classification philippine des professions de 1990 basée sur la CITP-88

c) Situation dans la profession: Aucune classification n'a été faite.

8. Principales différences par rapport au recensement précédent:

Lors du recensement de 1980, les questions relatives à l'activité économique ont été posées à un échantillon de 20 pour cent des personnes âgées de 15 ans et plus et aucune période de référence n'a été retenue dans le questionnaire du recensement.

Aucune question spécifique n'a été utilisée pour déterminer si une personne doit être considérée comme «pourvue d'un emploi» ou «chômeur».

Seules des questions intéressant la profession habituelle des personnes recensées et le type d'industrie dans laquelle elles exercent généralement leur activité ont été posées. Les questions utilisées étaient: «Quelle est la profession habituelle de la personne?» et «Dans quel type d'affaires ou d'industrie exerce-t-elle?».

La profession fait référence au travail spécifique ou au type d'emploi habituellement exercé par une personne travaillant l'essentiel de l'année ou, si la personne est au chômage au moment du recensement, à la nature du travail généralement effectué pendant la majeure partie de l'année. La branche d'activité économique fait référence au caractère et à la nature spécifiques de l'affaire ou de l'industrie ou du lieu dans lequel s'effectue le travail ou l'activité indiqué(e) par la personne recensée.

Lors du recensement de 1990, l'activité ou la profession habituelle se référait au type de travail ou d'activité exercé par la personne pendant la majeure partie des 12 mois précédant le recensement.

9. Publication des résultats du recensement:

Le titre de la publication contenant les résultats définitifs du recensement est «Report No. 3 - 1990 Census of Population and Housing», 1992.

L'organisme responsable de cette publication est le Bureau national des statistiques, R. Magsaysay Boulevard, Sta Mesa, Manila.

Les résultats du recensement sont également disponibles sous forme d'ouvrages imprimés classés par province et villes fortement urbanisées, de tableaux non publiés ainsi que de bandes magnétiques et de disquettes à usage public.

PORTO RICO

1. Nom et adresse de l'organisme responsable du recensement:

U.S. Census Bureau, Washington, DC, 20233. L'information méthodologique concernant le dernier recensement émane de: Planning Board Census Office of Puerto Rico, San Juan, P.R.

2. Recensements de population effectués depuis 1945 (années):

1950, 1960, 1970, 1980 et 1990. La présente description se réfère au recensement de 1990 (qui a eu lieu le 1er avril).

3. Champ du recensement:

a) Territoire couvert: Ensemble du pays.

b) Personnes couvertes: Ensemble de la population.

4. Période de référence:

La semaine précédant le jour du recensement pour les personnes pourvues d'un emploi, les quatre semaines précédant le jour du recensement pour les chômeurs et l'année précédente pour les autres cas.

5. Principaux sujets:

a) Population totale, selon le sexe et l'âge:	oui
Population active par:	
b) Sexe et âge:	oui
c) Branche d'activité économique (industrie):	oui
d) Profession:	oui
e) Situation dans la profession:	oui
f) Niveau d'instruction le plus élevé:	oui
g) Durée du travail:	oui
h) Autres caractéristiques:	oui

Réf. a): L'âge est défini en termes d'années révolues à la date du dernier anniversaire.

Réf. g): La durée du travail se réfère aussi bien à la durée normale du travail pendant la période de référence courte qu'à la période totale de travail effectué par les personnes pourvues d'un emploi au cours de l'année précédente (exprimée en nombre de semaines).

Réf. h): Le recensement a également rassemblé des informations sur d'autres sujets, à savoir: le revenu; la source de revenu; les moyens de transport utilisés et le temps nécessaire pour se rendre au travail; les mises à pied la semaine précédant le recensement; la dernière année travaillée et la formation professionnelle.

6. Concepts et définitions:

a) Population active: Elle comprend toutes les personnes âgées de 16 ans et plus qui, pendant les périodes de référence, étaient soit pourvues d'un emploi, soit au chômage, conformément aux définitions données ci-dessous. On a posé les questions relatives à l'activité économique à un échantillon de 17 pour cent des ménages (soit un sur six). La définition inclut les forces armées mais les données publiées ne concernent que la main d'oeuvre civile. Sont exclus de la définition: les étudiants travaillant à temps partiel, les étudiants à la recherche d'un emploi, les travailleurs saisonniers recensés hors-saison et qui n'étaient pas en quête d'un emploi et les personnes exerçant incidemment un travail familial non rémunéré.

b) Emploi: Les questions utilisées pour déterminer si une personne doit être considérée comme pourvue d'un emploi étaient: «La personne a-t-elle travaillé au cours de la semaine passée?» et «Combien d'heures a-t-elle effectuées au cours de la semaine passée?».

Il est indiqué que sont inclus dans cette définition:

i)   les personnes travaillant sans rémunération dans une entreprise ou une affaire familiale;
ii)   les personnes engagées dans la production de produits de base destinés à l'autoconsommation;
iii) les personnes occupées, temporairement absentes de leur travail;
iv)   les conscrits (service militaire ou civil);
v)   les apprentis et les stagiaires.

Seules les personnes appartenant à la catégorie iv) peuvent être identifiées séparément.

c) Chômage: Les questions utilisées pour déterminer si une personne devait être considérée comme chômeur étaient: «La personne était-elle à la recherche d'un emploi au cours des quatre dernières semaines?» et «La personne était-elle disponible pour accepter un travail la semaine dernière?».

7. Classifications utilisées:
Aussi bien les personnes pourvues d'un emploi que les chômeurs ayant précédemment travaillé sont classifiés par branche d'activité, par profession et d'après la situation dans la profession.

a) Branche d'activité économique (industrie): Basée sur les questions: «Pour qui travaillait cette personne?» et «De quel type d'activité ou d'industrie s'agissait-il? (s'agissait-il essentiellement de fabrication industrielle, de commerce de gros, de commerce de détail ou d'une autre activité?». Le système de classification par industrie comprend 231 catégories classées en 13 grands groupes d'industrie et se base sur le manuel de classification type par industrie (SIC) de 1972 et sur le supplément de 1977. Aucun lien n'a été établi avec la CITI mais on a procédé à une adaptation afin d'établir une comparaison internationale.

b) Profession: Basée sur les questions: «Quel type de travail effectuait cette personne?» et «Quelles étaient ses principales activités ou fonctions?». Le système de classification par profession comprend 503 catégories professionnelles spécifiques organisées en 6 groupes sommaires et 13 grands groupes. Ce système a été conçu de manière à être compatible avec le manuel de classification type des professions (SOC) de 1980. Aucun lien n'a été établi avec la CITP mais on a procédé à une adaptation afin d'établir une comparaison internationale.

c) Situation dans la profession: Basée sur la question: «La personne est-elle: un particulier sans activité lucrative; fonctionnaire municipal; fonctionnaire confédéré; fonctionnaire fédéral; travailleur indépendant dans son entreprise non enregistrée; travailleur indépendant dans son entreprise enregistrée; travailleur non rémunéré; autre?». Pour coder la situation dans la profession, on a utilisé les huit catégories précitées.

8. Principales différences par rapport au recensement précédent:
Pas de différence majeure.

9. Publication des résultats du recensement:
Le titre de la publication contenant les résultats définitifs du recensement de 1990 est: «Summary Social, Economic and Housing Characteristics», 1993.

L'organisme responsable de cette publication est le Bureau du recensement des E.U., Washington, DC, 20233.

Les résultats du recensement sont également disponibles sous forme de bandes magnétiques, de CD-ROM, de microfiches, de rapports imprimés et de disquette.

PORTUGAL

1. Nom et adresse de l'organisme responsable du recensement:
Instituto Nacional de Estatística, Ava. António José de Almeida, P-1078 Lisbonne Codex.

2. Recensements de population effectués depuis 1945 (années):
1950, 1960, 1970, 1981 et 1991. La présente description se réfère au recensement de 1991 (qui a eu lieu le 15 avril).

3. Champ du recensement:
a) Territoire couvert: Ensemble du pays.

b) Personnes couvertes: Ensemble de la population, à l'exception des nationaux résidant à l'étranger depuis un an ou plus.

4. Période de référence:
La semaine précédant le recensement (soit du 7 au 13 avril 1991).

Toutefois, en ce qui concerne le chômage, des intervalles différents ont été retenus (moins d'un mois, un mois à moins de quatre mois, quatre à sept mois, plus de sept mois).

5. Principaux sujets:
a) Population totale, selon le sexe et l'âge: oui
Population active par:

b) Sexe et âge: oui
c) Branche d'activité économique (industrie):   oui
d) Profession: oui
e) Situation dans la profession: oui
f) Niveau d'instruction le plus élevé: oui
g) Durée du travail: oui
h) Autres caractéristiques: oui

Réf. a): L'âge est défini en termes de date de naissance.

Réf. g): On a demandé aux personnes pourvues d'un emploi de spécifier le nombre d'heures travaillées dans la profession principale pendant la semaine de référence.

Réf. h): Le recensement a également rassemblé des informations sur d'autres sujets, notamment: le lieu de travail; la durée du trajet et les moyens de transport utilisés pour se rendre au lieu de travail et pour en revenir; la principale source de revenu au cours des 12 derniers mois; etc...

6. Concepts et définitions:
a) Population active: Elle comprend toutes les personnes âgées de 12 ans et plus qui, pendant la semaine de référence étaient, soit pourvues d'un emploi, soit au chômage, conformément aux définitions données ci-dessous. La définition inclut tous les membres des forces armées (militaires de carrière et ceux du contingent).

b) Emploi: Sont considérées comme «pourvues d'un emploi» toutes les personnes qui, pendant la semaine de référence, exerçaient une profession, une fonction ou une quelconque activité économique.

Il est indiqué que sont inclus dans cette définition:

i)   les personnes travaillant sans rémunération dans une entreprise ou une affaire familiale;
ii)   les personnes engagées dans la production de produits de base destinés à l'autoconsommation;
iii) les personnes occupées, temporairement absentes de leur travail;
iv) les étudiants travaillant à temps partiel;
v)   les travailleurs saisonniers ou occasionnels, pour autant qu'ils soient en activité à l'époque du recensement;
vi) les conscrits (service militaire ou civil); toutefois, seules les personnes astreintes au service militaire obligatoire sont identifiées séparément;
vii) les apprentis et les stagiaires.

Seules les catégories i), iii) et vi) ci-dessus peuvent être identifiées séparément.

c) Chômage: Sont considérées comme «chômeurs au sens élargi» toutes les personnes qui, pendant la semaine de référence, étaient sans travail et désireuses de travailler. Sont considérés comme «chômeurs au sens strict» toutes les personnes qui, pendant la semaine de référence, étaient sans travail et à la recherche d'un emploi et qui ont recherché du travail pendant les 30 derniers jours, ou qui étaient inscrites au centre de l'emploi. Les travailleurs saisonniers ou occasionnels qui étaient sans travail à l'époque du recensement sont également considérés comme chômeurs.

7. Classifications utilisées:
Aussi bien les personnes pourvues d'un emploi que les chômeurs ayant précédemment travaillé sont classifiés par industrie, par profession et d'après la situation dans la profession.

a) Branche d'activité économique (industrie): Basée sur la question: «Où exercez-vous (avez-vous exercé en dernier lieu) votre profession principale?». Pour coder la branche d'activité, on a utilisé la CITI-rév.3 au niveau des classes (4 chiffres).

b) Profession: La question posée concerne la profession principale exercée. Pour coder la profession, on a utilisé la CITP-88, mais avec des adaptations au niveau des groupes de base pour les amplifier.

c) Situation dans la profession: Une question a été posée aux personnes occupées et aux chômeurs ayant précédemment travaillé pour déterminer si elles exercent ou ont exercé leur activité principale en tant que: patrons; travailleurs à leur propre compte; travailleurs pour le compte d'autrui; travailleurs familiaux non rémunérés; membres actifs d'une coopérative de producteurs; conscrits (service militaire obligatoire); autres. Pour coder cette variable, on a utilisé les sept catégories ci-dessus.

8. Principales différences par rapport au recensement précédent:
Lors du recensement de 1991, deux nouvelles questions ont servi à identifier le type de chômage (au sens strict, au sens élargi et selon la durée), à savoir: i) «Avez-vous déjà

travaillé?» et, en cas de réponse affirmative, ii) «Voulez-vous travailler et vous avez recherché du travail au cours des 30 derniers jours, ou étiez-vous inscrit dans un centre d'emploi (depuis un mois et moins de quatre mois, depuis 4 mois et moins de sept mois, depuis 7 mois ou plus)?», iii) «Voulez-vous travailler et vous n'avez pas fait de recherches?» et iv) «Vous ne voulez pas travailler?».

Les personnes ayant déclaré vouloir travailler sont considérées comme chômeurs, même si elles n'ont pas recherché de travail. Par contre, celles qui ont déclaré qu'elles ne désirent pas travailler sont classées dans la population inactive.

La question relative aux principaux moyens d'existence n'a plus pris en compte les différents types de pensions, comme c'était le cas au recensement de 1981.

Les personnes effectuant leur service militaire obligatoire (militaires du contingent) ont fait l'objet d'une nouvelle catégorie dans la classification de la situation dans la profession.

9. Publication des résultats du recensement:
Les données définitives de la population active et de ses composantes devaient être publiées en 1993.

L'organisme responsable de la publication est l'Instituto Nacional de Estatística, Lisbonne.

Les résultats du recensement de 1991 sont également disponibles sous forme de tableaux non publiés, de disquettes et de bandes magnétiques.

REUNION

1. Nom et adresse de l'organisme responsable du recensement:
Service régional de l'INSEE à la Réunion, 15 rue de l'école, 97490 Ste Clotilde, La Réunion.

2. Recensements de population effectués depuis 1945 (années):
1954, 1961, 1967, 1974, 1982 et 1990. La présente description se réfère au recensement de 1990 (qui a eu lieu le 15 mars).

3. Champ du recensement:
a) Territoire couvert: Ensemble du territoire.

b) Personnes couvertes: Ensemble de la population.

4. Période de référence:
La semaine précédant le jour du recensement.

5. Principaux sujets:
a) Population totale, selon le sexe et l'âge: oui
Population active par:
b) Sexe et âge: oui
c) Branche d'activité économique (industrie):   oui
d) Profession: oui
e) Situation dans la profession: oui
f) Niveau d'instruction le plus élevé: oui
g) Durée du travail: non
h) Autres caractéristiques: oui

Réf. a): L'âge est défini en termes d'année de naissance.

Réf. h): Le recensement a également rassemblé d'autres informations, telles que: le travail à temps complet et à temps partiel, l'activité principale, le nombre de salariés occupés par les personnes travaillant à leur propre compte, la durée de recherche d'un travail, etc...

6. Concepts et définitions:
a) Population active: Elle comprend toutes les personnes âgées de 14 ans et plus qui, pendant la semaine de référence, étaient, soit pourvues d'un emploi, soit au chômage, conformément aux définitions données ci-dessous. La définition inclut aussi les membres des forces armées (militaires de carrière et ceux du contingent). Les questions relatives à l'activité économique n'ont été posées qu'à un échantillon, dont étaient exclus les militaires logés en caserne et les détenus.

b) Emploi: Sont considérées comme «pourvues d'un emploi» toutes les personnes qui, pendant la semaine de référence, ont exercé une profession, une fonction ou une activité économique, rémunérée ou non. Des questions spécifiques permettent de déterminer si une personne doit être considérée comme pourvue d'emploi, notamment: «Travaillez-vous (à temps complet ou à temps partiel)?»; «Etes-vous: salarié ou à votre compte (exploitant agricole, artisan, commerçant, industriel, profession libérale, aide familial non salarié, etc...)?» et «Si vous êtes à

votre compte: combien de salariés employez-vous? (ne comptez ni les apprentis ni les gens de maison; dans l'agriculture, comptez seulement les salariés permanents)». La définition inclut aussi les personnes exerçant un travail d'utilité collective (TUC, etc.), celles placées par une agence d'intérim, celles sous contrat de travail à durée déterminée et celles sous contrat d'adaptation ou de qualification.

Il est indiqué que sont inclus dans cette définition:
i) les personnes travaillant sans rémunération dans une entreprise ou une exploitation familiale;
ii) les personnes engagées dans la production de produits de base destinés à l'autoconsommation;
iii) les personnes occupées, temporairement absentes du travail;
iv) les étudiants travaillant à temps partiel;
v) les travailleurs saisonniers ou occasionnels, pour autant qu'ils soient en activité à l'époque du recensement;
vi) les conscrits (service militaire ou civil);
vii) les apprentis (sous contrat) et les stagiaires (principalement en entreprise ou dans un centre de formation).

Seules les personnes appartenant aux catégories i), vi) et vii) peuvent être identifiées séparément.

c) Chômage: Sont considérées comme «chômeurs» toutes les personnes qui se sont déclarées spontanément en chômage et qui étaient à la recherche d'un travail. Les questions utilisées pour déterminer si une personne doit être considérée comme chômeur sont «Etes-vous chômeur (inscrit ou non à l'Agence nationale pour l'emploi)?», «Avez-vous déjà travaillé? (si oui, quelle était votre profession principale?)» et «Cherchez-vous un emploi (depuis: moins de trois mois; trois mois à moins d'un an; un an à moins de deux ans; deux ans ou plus)?».

7. Classifications utilisées:
Aussi bien les personnes occupées que les chômeurs ayant précédemment travaillé de l'échantillon sont classifiés par profession. Seules les personnes occupées de l'échantillon sont classifiées par industrie et d'après la situation dans la profession.

a) Branche d'activité économique (industrie): Il a été demandé aux personnes interrogées d'indiquer l'adresse, le nom ou la raison sociale de l'établissement qui les emploie ou qu'elles dirigent, ainsi que l'activité exacte de cet établissement (par exemple: commerce de vin en gros, fabrication de charpentes métalliques, transport routier de voyageurs, etc.). Pour coder la branche d'activité, on a utilisé 100 groupes de la Nomenclature d'Activités et Produits (NAP). Il n'a pas établi de liens avec la CITI.

b) Profession: Il a été demandé aux personnes interrogées d'indiquer la profession exercée actuellement ou en dernier, avec une identification aussi claire que possible de cette profession (par exemple: ouvrier électricien d'entretien, chauffeur de poids lourds, vendeur en électronénager, ingénieur chimiste, caissière de libre-service, etc.), en vue de déterminer le groupe de professions. Cependant, la question a été laissée ouverte, en ce sens que la personne interrogée était libre de formuler sa réponse. Le reclassement dans un groupe déterminé est fait lors du traitement informatique. Pour coder la profession, on a utilisé un système de codification directe en 42 groupes. Il n'a pas été établi de liens avec la CITP.

c) Situation dans la profession: Pour coder cette variable, on a utilisé les cinq catégories suivantes: indépendant à son compte; employeur; salarié; aide familial non rémunéré; autre.

8. Principales différences par rapport au recensement précédent:
La limite d'âge inférieure qui avait été retenue en 1982 pour l'inclusion des personnes dans la population active était de 15 ans.

De plus, lors du recensement de 1982, aussi bien les personnes occupées que les chômeurs ayant précédemment travaillé avaient été classifiés par industrie et d'après la situation dans la profession.

9. Publication des résultats du recensement:
Le titre de la publication contenant les résultats définitifs est: «Population, Emploi, Logements; Evolution 1975-1982-1990 (Série jaune)», 1992.

L'organisme responsable de cette publication est l'Institut national de la statistique et des études économiques (INSEE), 18 boulevard Adolphe-Pinard, 75675 Paris Cedex 14.

Les résultats du recensement de 1990 sont également disponibles sous forme de disquettes et de bandes magnétiques, ainsi que d'exploitations à la demande.

ROUMANIE

1. Nom et adresse de l'organisme responsable du recensement:

Commission centrale pour le recensement de la population et des logements de 1992. Commission Nationale pour la Statistique, Bd. Libertatii 16, Sector 5, Bucarest 70542.

2. Recensements de population effectués depuis 1945 (années):

1948, 1956, 1966, 1977 et 1992. La présente description se réfère au recensement de 1992 (qui a eu lieu le 7 janvier).

3. Champ du recensement:

a) Territoire couvert: Ensemble du pays.

b) Personnes couvertes: Ensemble de la population ayant une résidence permanente dans le pays, non compris les personnes sans citoyenneté ou de citoyenneté étrangère (représentations diplomatiques, consulaires et commerciales, organisations internationales, entreprises étrangères, correspondants de presse).

4. Période de référence:

Une année (1991).

5. Principaux sujets:

a) Population totale, selon le sexe et l'âge:	oui
Population active par:	
b) Sexe et âge:	oui
c) Branche d'activité économique (industrie):	oui
d) Profession:	oui
e) Situation dans la profession:	oui
f) Niveau d'instruction le plus élevé:	oui
g) Durée du travail:	non
h) Autres caractéristiques:	non

Réf. a): L'âge est défini en termes d'année de naissance.

6. Concepts et définitions:

a) Population active: Elle comprend toutes les personnes âgées d'au moins 14 ans qui, durant la période de référence, constituaient la main-d'oeuvre disponible (utilisée ou non) pour la production de biens et de services dans l'économie nationale, conformément aux définitions données ci-dessous. Les membres des forces armées sont inclus dans la définition.

b) Emploi: Sont considérées comme «pourvues d'un emploi» toutes les personnes âgées de 14 à 80 ans, qui, durant la période de référence, ont exercé une activité économique moyennant un salaire ou un revenu, en espèces ou en nature, par contrat ou à leur propre compte.

Il est indiqué que sont inclus dans cette définition:

i)   les personnes travaillant sans rémunération dans une entreprise ou une exploitation familiale;

ii)   les personnes engagées dans la production de produits de base destinés à l'autoconsommation;

iii)   les personnes occupées, temporairement absentes du travail;

iv)   les étudiants travaillant à temps partiel;

v)   les travailleurs saisonniers ou occasionnels;

vi)   les conscrits (service militaire ou civil);

vii)   les apprentis et les stagiaires.

Seules les catégories i), ii) et vi) peuvent être identifiées séparément à partir des réponses aux questions sur la situation dans la profession.

Les personnes ayant déclaré qu'elles étaient à la retraite, ménagères, élèves-étudiants ou en quête d'emploi n'entrent pas dans la définition, même si elles ont travaillé de façon temporaire ou occasionnelle pendant la période de référence (spécialement dans l'agriculture).

c) Chômage: Sont considérées comme «chômeurs» toutes les personnes âgées de 14 à 64 ans pour les hommes, et de 14 à 59 ans pour les femmes qui, au moment du recensement, ont déclaré être sans emploi, même si elles avaient travaillé pendant la longue période de référence (1991), être disponibles pour travailler et à la recherche d'un emploi (ou de leur premier emploi). Les étudiants en quête de travail sont exclus de la définition.

7. Classifications utilisées:

Aussi bien les personnes pourvues d'emploi que les chômeurs (à l'exception des personnes à la recherche de leur premier emploi) sont classifiés par industrie, par profession et d'après la situation dans la profession.

a) Branche d'activité économique (industrie): Des questions spécifiques ont été posées aux personnes pourvues d'un emploi et aux chômeurs ayant déjà travaillé sur la nature de leur activité présente ou antérieure, ainsi que sur le type d'activité de l'entreprise ou de l'établissement pour lequel ils travaillent ou ont travaillé. Pour coder la branche d'activité, on a utilisé 99 groupes de la classification nationale. Des liens avec la CITI-rév.3, ont été établis au niveau des groupes (3 chiffres).

b) Profession: Des questions spécifiques ont été posées aux personnes pourvues d'un emploi et aux chômeurs ayant déjà travaillé pour déterminer le groupe de professions auxquel ils appartiennent ou ont appartenu. Il n'a pas été tenu compte des professions secondaires ou saisonnières, mais seulement de la profession principale, c'est-à-dire de celle qui a procuré la principale source de revenu de la personne recensée. Pour coder la profession, on a utilisé 437 groupes de base de la classification nationale. Des liens avec la CITP-88 ont été établis au niveau des sous-groupes (3 chiffres).

c) Situation dans la profession: Des questions spécifiques ont été posées aux personnes pourvues d'un emploi et aux chômeurs ayant déjà travaillé pour déterminer leur situation dans la profession exercée ou précédemment exercée. Les six groupes suivants ont été identifiés: employeur, personne travaillant à son propre compte, salarié, travailleur familial non rémunéré, membre d'une coopérative de producteurs, autres.

8. Principales différences par rapport au recensement précédent:

En 1992, une limite d'âge maximum a été retenue pour l'inclusion dans la population active et ses composantes; la période de référence retenue a été une longue période de référence (l'année 1991); la population active a été séparée en actifs occupés et en actifs non occupés (chômeurs); pour les classifications par industrie et par profession, des liens ont été établis respectivement avec la CITI-rév.3 et avec la CITP-88; aussi bien les personnes pourvues d'un emploi que les chômeurs ayant précédemment travaillé ont été classifiés d'après la situation dans la profession.

9. Publication des résultats du recensement:

Les résultats définitifs du recensement de 1992 ont été publiés en octobre 1993.

Les titres des publications contenant ces résultats sont: «Vol. I - Population - Structure démographique», «Vol. II - Population - Structure socio-économique» et «Vol. III - Etablissements, logements, ménages».

L'organisme responsable de ces publications est la Commission Nationale pour la Statistique, Bd. Libertatii 16, Sector 5, Bucarest 70542.

Les résultats sont également disponibles sous forme de disquettes et de bandes magnétiques.

ROYAUME-UNI

1. Nom et adresse de l'organisme responsable du recensement:

Pour l'Angleterre et le pays de Galles: Office of Population, Census Surveys, Room 816, St. Catherine's House, 10 Kingsway, London WC 2B 6JP.

Pour l'Ecosse: General Register Office (Scotland), Ladywell House, Ladywell Road, Edinburgh EH12 7TF.

Pour l'Irlande du Nord: Census Office, Castle Buildings, Stormont, Belfast BT4 8SJ.

2. Recensements de population effectués depuis 1945 (années):

1951, 1961, 1966, 1971, 1981 et 1991. La présente description se réfère au recensement de population de 1991 (qui a eu lieu le 21 avril). Elle concerne essentiellement l'Angleterre et le pays de Galles, mais les réponses s'appliquent aussi à l'Ecosse et à l'Irlande du Nord, de sorte que l'on peut considérer qu'elle représente la situation au Royaume-Uni.

3. Champ du recensement:

a) Territoire couvert: Ensemble du pays. (Voir aussi le para. 2 ci-dessus).

b) Personnes couvertes: Ensemble de la population.

4. Période de référence:
La semaine précédant le jour du recensement.

5. Principaux sujets:

a) Population totale, selon le sexe et l'âge: oui

Population active par:

b) Sexe et âge: oui
c) Branche d'activité économique (industrie):   oui
d) Profession: oui
e) Situation dans la profession: oui
f) Niveau d'instruction le plus élevé: oui
g) Durée du travail: oui
h) Autres caractéristiques: oui

Réf. a): L'âge est défini en termes d'année de naissance (date complète, avec jour, mois et année).

Réf. g): Les personnes pourvues d'un emploi devaient préciser la durée normale de leur travail.

Réf. h): Le recensement a aussi rassemblé des informations concernant le lieu de travail et les moyens de transport utilisés pour s'y rendre.

6. Concepts et définitions:

a) Population active: Elle comprend toutes les personnes âgées de 16 ans et plus qui, pendant la semaine de référence, étaient soit pourvues d'un emploi, soit au chômage, conformément aux définitions données ci-dessous. Comme lors du recensement de 1981, la situation économique et la situation dans la profession sont incluses dans les données recueillies sur l'ensemble de la population, alors que l'industrie, la profession et le lieu de travail ne sont étudiés que pour un échantillon de population de 10 pour cent. Les travailleurs saisonniers et les travailleurs occasionnels ne sont inclus dans la définition que s'ils travaillaient ou s'ils étaient en quête d'un emploi pendant la semaine de référence. La définition inclut également les militaires de carrière. Il n'y a pas de conscription au Royaume Uni.

b) Emploi: Sont considérées comme «pourvues d'un emploi» toutes les personnes qui, pendant la semaine de référence, travaillaient pour un employeur (à plein temps ou à temps partiel), pour leur propre compte, pour le compte du gouvernement ou qui étaient en stage de formation. La définition inclut les travailleurs temporaires et occasionnels et ceux qui tirent un salaire ou un profit de leur travail mais exclut les travailleurs non rémunérés (sauf ceux travaillant dans une affaire familiale). Elle inclut également les personnes ayant un emploi pendant la semaine de référence mais absentes du travail cette semaine-là pour cause de maladie, de vacances, de mise à pied temporaire ou de grève. Le travail à temps partiel est défini comme un travail dont la durée hebdomadaire ne dépasse pas 30 heures (sans compter les heures supplémentaires).

Il est indiqué que sont inclus dans cette définition:

i)   les personnes travaillant sans rémunération dans une entreprise ou une affaire familiale;
ii) les personnes occupées, temporairement absentes de leur travail;
iii) les étudiants travaillant à temps partiel;
iv) Les travailleurs saisonniers ou occasionnels (s'ils travaillaient pendant la semaine de référence);
v)   les apprentis et les stagiaires.

Seules les personnes appartenant à la catégorie iii) peuvent être identifiées séparément.

c) Chômage: Sont considérées comme «chômeurs» toutes les personnes qui, pendant la semaine de référence, attendaient de démarrer un travail qu'elles avaient déjà accepté ou qui étaient sans emploi et à la recherche d'un travail, y compris les personnes souhaitant travailler mais dans l'incapacité d'entreprendre des démarches en ce sens par suite de vacances ou de maladie temporaire.

7. Classifications utilisées:
Aussi bien les personnes pourvues d'un emploi que les chômeurs ayant précédemment travaillé sont classifiés par branche d'activité économique et par profession (par chômeurs on entend «les personnes ayant occupé un emploi au cours des dix dernières années»). Mais seules les personnes pourvues d'un emploi sont classées d'après la situation dans la profession (voir également para. 6 a) ci-dessus). Les personnes inactives

telles que les retraités devaient également donner des informations sur la durée de leur travail, la branche d'activité et la profession si elles avaient occupé un emploi au cours des dix dernières années.

a) Branche d'activité économique (industrie): Les personnes interrogées devaient donner le nom, l'adresse et l'activité de leur employeur (pour les travailleurs à leur propre compte: nom, adresse et nature de l'activité exercée par la personne). Pour coder la branche d'activité économique, on a utilisé 320 groupes basés sur la classification nationale des industries, mais le traitement des données s'est limité à un échantillon de 10 pour cent. Des liens (correspondances les plus approchantes) ont été établis avec la CITI-Rév.3 au niveau des divisions (2 chiffres).

b) Profession: On a demandé aux personnes interrogées de donner la désignation complète de leur travail actuel ou passé et de décrire les principales tâches qu'elles accomplissent ou accomplissaient dans ce travail. Les termes utilisés doivent être précis, par exemple: machiniste dans l'emballage; employé dans la transformation de la volaille; ajusteur d'outillage; responsable d'un pool de dactylos; comptable; plutôt que des termes génériques comme: ouvrier; employé dans une usine de transformation; responsable ou employé de bureau. Pour coder la profession, on a utilisé 371 groupes de la classification nationale des professions, mais le traitement des données s'est limité à un échantillon de 10 pour cent. Des liens avec la CITP-88 ont été établis au niveau des groupes mixtes.

c) Situation dans la profession: On a posé une question spécifique sur la situation économique. Pour coder cette variable, on a utilisé les cinq groupes suivants dans les tableaux employés pour le traitement de l'ensemble des données: salarié à plein temps; salarié à temps partiel; travailleur indépendant avec salariés; travailleur indépendant sans salariés; employé du gouvernement ou en formation.

8. Principales différences par rapport au recensement précédent:
Les principaux changements intervenus sont les suivants:
- utilisation d'une nouvelle classification des professions (Standard Occupational Classification - SOC);
- introduction d'une question sur la durée du travail;
- introduction d'une catégorie à part pour les personnes employées par le gouvernement ou en formation dans la question relative à la situation économique (qui inclut également la situation dans la profession de sorte que les apprentis et les stagiaires n'aient plus un statut séparé); et
- inclusion des étudiants qui travaillent dans la population active (en tant que salariés).

9. Publication des résultats du recensement:
Les premiers résultats nationaux sur la population active étaient disponibles en 1992. Des informations détaillées sur la branche d'activité économique, la profession, le lieu de travail, etc..., étaient disponibles en 1993.

De nombreux ouvrages ont été publiés. Les personnes souhaitant de plus amples informations doivent contacter Census Customer Services, OCPS, Segensworth Road, Titchfield, Hampshire PO15 5RR.

Les données du recensement ont également été diffusées dans de nombreux médias.

SAINT-VINCENT-ET-GRENADINES

1. Nom et adresse de l'organisme responsable du recensement:
Census Office, Statistical Office, Central Planning Division.

2. Recensements de population effectués depuis 1945 (années):
1960, 1970, 1980 et 1991. La présente description se réfère au recensement de population de 1991 (qui a eu lieu le 12 mai).

3. Champ du recensement:

a) Territoire couvert: Ensemble du pays.

b) Personnes couvertes: Ensemble de la population.

4. Période de référence:
La semaine et l'année précédant le jour du recensement.

5. Principaux sujets:

a) Population totale, selon le sexe et l'âge: oui
Population active par:
b) Sexe et âge: oui
c) Branche d'activité économique (industrie): oui
d) Profession: oui
e) Situation dans la profession: oui
f) Niveau d'instruction le plus élevé: oui
g) Durée du travail: oui
h) Autres caractéristiques: oui

Réf. a): L'âge est défini en termes d'années révolues à la date du dernier anniversaire.

Réf. g): Le recensement a permis de recueillir, auprès des personnes pourvues d'un emploi, des informations sur le nombre de mois pendant lesquels elles ont travaillé au cours de la période de référence d'un an, et sur le nombre d'heures travaillées au cours de la période de référence d'une semaine.

Réf. h): Le recensement a également permis de recouvrer des informations sur les revenus et les moyens de transports utilisés pour se rendre au travail.

6. Concepts et définitions:

a) Population active: Elle comprend toutes les personnes de 15 ans et plus qui, pendant la semaine de référence, étaient soit pourvues d'un emploi soit au chômage, conformément aux définitions données ci-dessous. Les militaires de carrière, les étudiants travaillant à temps partiel et les étudiants en quête d'un emploi sont exclus de la définition.

b) Emploi: Sont considérées comme «pourvues d'un emploi» toutes les personnes ayant déclaré qu'elle avaient passé l'essentiel de leur temps à travailler au cours de la période de référence courte. La question utilisée pour déterminer si une personne devait être comptée comme occupée était: «A quoi avez-vous consacré l'essentiel de votre temps au cours de la semaine passée? Par exemple: avez-vous travaillé, avez-vous recherché un emploi, êtes-vous resté à la maison ou avez-vous eu une autre activité?».

Il est indiqué que sont inclus dans cette définition:

i) les personnes travaillant sans rémunération dans une entreprise ou une affaire familiale;
ii) les personnes occupées, temporairement absentes du travail;
iii) les travailleurs saisonniers ou occasionnels;
iv) les apprentis et les stagiaires.

Seules les personnes appartenant aux catégories i) et ii) peuvent être identifiées séparément.

c) Chômage: Sont considérées comme «chômeurs» toutes les personnes qui, au cours de la semaine de référence, se trouvaient sans travail, étaient en quête d'un emploi ou désiraient travailler. La définition inclut aussi bien les personnes qui étaient activement engagées dans la recherche d'un emploi que celles qui ne faisaient rien pour trouver du travail parce qu'elles savaient qu'il n'y en avait pas.

7. Classifications utilisées:

Aussi bien les personnes pourvues d'un emploi que les chômeurs ayant précédemment travaillé sont classifiés par branche d'activité économique, par profession et d'après la situation dans la profession.

a) Branche d'activité économique (industrie): Basée sur la question: «Quel type d'activité est ou était exercé sur votre lieu de travail?». Pour coder cette branche d'activité économique, on a utilisé 17 groupes de la classification nationale. Des liens avec la CITI-Rév.3 ont été établis au niveau des catégories de classement (1 chiffre).

b) Profession: Basée sur la question: «Quel type de travail faites-vous ou faisiez-vous dans votre profession principale?». Pour coder la profession, on a utilisé 10 groupes de la classification nationale. Des liens avec la CITP-88 ont été établis au niveau des grands groupes (1 chiffre).

c) Situation dans la profession: Basée sur la question: «Etes-vous travailleur indépendant, percevez-vous un salaire ou un traitement, ou travaillez-vous sans rémunération dans une entreprise ou une affaire familiale?». Pour coder la situation dans la profession, six groupes ont été utilisés: salarié du gouvernement; salarié du secteur privé; travailleur non rémunéré; travailleur indépendant avec des employés rémunérés (employeur); travailleur indépendant sans employés rémunérés; ne sait pas/n'a rien indiqué.

8. Principales différences par rapport au recensement précédent:

Pas de différence majeure.

9. Publication des résultats du recensement:

Les chiffres définitifs concernant la population active ont été publiés sous le titre «1991 - Rapport sur le recensement de la population et des logements, volume 2».

L'organisme responsable de cette publication est l'Office statistique, Division de la planification centrale, Ministère des finances.

Les chiffres du recensement sont également disponibles sous forme de disquettes.

SAINTE-LUCIE

1. Nom et adresse de l'organisme responsable du recensement:

Statistics Department, Block A, 3rd floor, N.I.S. Building, The Waterfront, Castries, St. Lucia, West Indies.

2. Recensements de population effectués depuis 1945 (années):

1946, 1960, 1970, 1980 et 1991. La présente description se réfère au recensement de 1991 (qui a eu lieu le 12 mai).

3. Champ du recensement:

a) Territoire couvert: Ensemble de l'île.

b) Personnes couvertes: Ensemble de la population.

4. Période de référence:

La semaine et les 12 mois précédant le jour du recensement.

5. Principaux sujets:

a) Population totale, selon le sexe et l'âge: oui
Population active par:
b) Sexe et âge: oui
c) Branche d'activité économique (industrie): oui
d) Profession: oui
e) Situation dans la profession: oui
f) Niveau d'instruction le plus élevé: oui
g) Durée du travail: oui
h) Autres caractéristiques: oui

Réf. a): L'âge est défini en termes d'années révolues à la date du dernier anniversaire.

Réf. g): La durée du travail concerne le nombre d'heures réellement effectuées pendant la semaine de référence et la période totale de travail effectuée en nombre de mois pendant les 12 mois précédant le jour du recensement.

Réf. h): On a recueilli des informations sur le revenu et les moyens de transport utilisés pour se rendre au travail.

6. Concepts et définitions:

a) Population active: Elle comprend toutes les personnes âgées de 15 ans et plus qui, pendant les périodes de référence, étaient soit pourvues d'un emploi, soit au chômage conformément aux définitions données ci-dessous. Les étudiants travaillant à temps partiel et les étudiants en quête d'un emploi ont été exclus de la définition, tout comme les membres des forces armées.

b) Emploi: Sont considérées comme «pourvues d'un emploi» toutes les personnes qui ont surtout travaillé pendant les périodes de référence. Les questions posées pour déterminer si une personne doit être considérée comme «pourvue d'en emploi» sont: «A quoi avez-vous passé l'essentiel de votre temps au cours de ces 12 derniers mois?» et «A quoi avez-vous passé l'essentiel de votre temps la semaine dernière?». Les possibilités de réponses étaient: 1) J'ai travaillé; 2) J'ai un travail mais je n'ai pas travaillé; 3) j'ai recherché un emploi; 4) je souhaitais un travail et j'étais disponible; 5) j'ai effectué des tâches ménagères; 6) j'ai fréquenté l'école; 7) retraité; 8) invalide, incapable de travailler; 9) autres; 10) non précisé.

Il est indiqué que sont inclus de cette définition:

i) les personnes travaillant sans rémunération dans une entreprise ou une affaire familiale;
ii) les personnes occupées, temporairement absentes du travail.

Les personnes appartenant à ces deux catégories peuvent être identifiées séparément.

c) Chômage: Sont considérées comme «chômeurs» toutes les personnes qui, pendant les périodes de référence, étaient avant tout sans emploi, en attente d'emploi, disponibles et à la recherche d'un emploi.

7. Classifications utilisées:
Aussi bien les personnes pourvues d'un emploi que les chômeurs ayant précédemment travaillé sont classifiés par branche d'activité, par profession et d'après la situation dans la profession.

a) Branche d'activité économique (industrie): Basée sur la question: «Quel type d'activité est ou était effectué sur votre lieu de travail?». Les chômeurs devaient également répondre à la question suivante: «Quelle sorte de travail recherchez-vous ou souhaitez-vous?». Pour coder la branche d'activité, on a utilisé 17 groupes de la classification nationale. Des liens avec la CITI-rév.3 ont été établis au niveau des catégories de classement (1 chiffre).

b) Profession: Basée sur la question: «Quelle sorte de travail effectuez-vous ou effectuiez-vous dans votre occupation principale?». Pour coder la profession, on a utilisé neuf groupes de la classification nationale. Des liens avec la CITP-88 ont été établis au niveau des grands groupes (1 chiffre).

c) Situation dans la profession: Basée sur la question: «Avez-vous exécuté votre travail ou dirigé votre entreprise contre une rémunération, un salaire ou en tant que travailleur non rémunéré dans une affaire familiale?». Pour coder la situation dans la profession, on a utilisé six groupes, à savoir: salarié (organisme gouvernemental); salarié du secteur privé; travailleur non rémunéré; travailleur à son propre compte avec salariés (employeur); travailleur à son propre compte sans salariés et ne sais pas ou non précisé.

8. Principales différences par rapport au recensement précédent:
Le recensement de 1991 a rassemblé plus d'informations sur les chômeurs en quête d'emploi.

9. Publication des résultats du recensement:
Les résultats définitifs sont parus en 1995 dans la publication intitulée: «1991 Population & Housing Census Volumes 1-9».

L'organisme responsable de cette publication est le Département des statistiques, NIS Building, The Waterfront, Castries.

Des tableaux non publiés sont également disponibles auprès de cet organisme depuis mai 1992.

SAMOA

1. Nom et adresse de l'organisme responsable du recensement:
Department of Statistics, P.O. Box 1151, Apia, Western Samoa.

2. Recensements de population effectués depuis 1945 (années):
1951, 1956, 1961, 1966, 1971, 1976, 1981, 1986 et 1991. La présente description se réfère au recensement de 1991 (qui a eu lieu le 5 novembre).

3. Champ du recensement:
a) Territoire couvert: Ensemble du pays.

b) Personnes couvertes: Ensemble de la population.

4. Période de référence:
Une semaine (du 20 au 26 octobre 1991).

5. Principaux sujets:
a) Population totale, selon le sexe et l'âge: oui
Population active par:
b) Sexe et âge: oui
c) Branche d'activité économique (industrie):   oui
d) Profession: oui
e) Situation dans la profession: oui
f) Niveau d'instruction le plus élevé: non
g) Durée du travail: non
h) Autres caractéristiques: non

Réf. a): L'âge est défini à la fois en termes d'année de naissance et en termes d'années révolues à la date du dernier anniversaire.

6. Concepts et définitions:
a) Population active: Elle comprend toutes les personnes âgées de 10 ans et plus qui, pendant la semaine de référence, étaient soit pourvues d'un emploi, soit au chômage conformément aux définitions données ci-dessous. Cependant les données publiées concernent uniquement les personnes âgées de 15 ans et plus. La définition exclut les membres des forces armées.

b) Emploi: Sont considérées comme «pourvues d'un emploi» toutes les personnes qui, à la question concernant le type d'activité exercée, ont déclaré avoir travaillé pendant la semaine de référence.

Il est indiqué que sont inclus dans cette définition:
i)   les personnes travaillant sans rémunération dans une entreprise ou une affaire familiale;
ii)   les personnes engagées dans la production de produits de base destinés à l'autoconsommation;
iii) les personnes occupées, temporairement absentes de leur travail;
iv) les étudiants travaillant à temps partiel;
v)   les travailleurs saisonniers ou occasionnels;
vi) les apprentis et les stagiaires.

Aucune des catégories ci-dessus ne peut être identifiée séparément.

c) Chômage: Sont considérées comme «chômeurs» toutes les personnes qui, pendant la période de référence, étaient sans travail.

7. Classifications utilisées:
Seules les personnes pourvues d'un emploi ont été classifiées par branche d'activité économique, par profession et d'après la situation dans la profession.

a) Branche d'activité économique (industrie): Basée sur la question: «Type d'industrie, d'activité ou de services?». Pour coder l'industrie, on a utilisé la CITI-rév.2.

b) Profession: Basée sur la question: «Quelle est votre principale activité?». Pour coder la profession, on a utilisé la CITP-88 au niveau des sous-groupes (3 chiffres).

c) Situation dans la profession: Quatre groupes ont été utilisés pour coder cette variable, à savoir: employeur; salarié; travailleur indépendant; travailleur non rémunéré.

8. Principales différences par rapport au recensement précédent:
Lors du recensement de 1992, on a posé aux femmes se définissant comme ménagères une série de questions absentes des recensements précédents.

9. Publication des résultats du recensement:
Les données définitives du recensement sont parues en janvier 1993 dans une publication intitulée «Report of the Census of Population and Housing - 1991».

L'organisme responsable de la publication est le Département des statistiques, P.O. Box 1151, Apia, Western Samoa.

Les résultats du recensement ne sont pas disponibles sous d'autres formes.

SAMOA AMERICAINES

1. Nom et adresse de l'organisme responsable du recensement:
Economic Development and Planning Office, American Samoa Government, Pago Pago, A.S. 96799, conjointement avec le Bureau du recensement des Etats-Unis.

2. Recensements de population effectués depuis 1945 (années):
1945, 1950, 1956, 1960, 1970, 1974, 1980 et 1990. La présente description se réfère au recensement de 1990 (qui a eu lieu le 1er avril).

3. Champ du recensement:
a) Territoire couvert: Ensemble du pays.

b) Personnes couvertes: Le recensement de 1990 a pris en compte toute personne se trouvant à son «lieu de résidence habituel», défini comme le lieu où elle vit et dort la plupart du temps. Il a exclu: les personnes vivant habituellement ailleurs; les lycéens vivant ailleurs lorsqu'ils suivent leurs cours; les membres des forces armées vivant ailleurs et les personnes résidant ailleurs pendant la majeure partie de la semaine lorsqu'elles travaillent.

4. Période de référence:
La semaine avant le recensement et l'année précédant celle du recensement.

5. Principaux sujets:
a) Population totale, selon le sexe et l'âge: oui
Population active par:
b) Sexe et âge: oui
c) Branche d'activité économique (industrie):   oui
d) Profession: oui
e) Situation dans la profession: oui
f) Niveau d'instruction le plus élevé: oui
g) Durée du travail: oui
h) Autres caractéristiques: oui

Réf. a): L'âge est défini à la fois en termes d'année de naissance et en termes d'années révolues à la date du dernier anniversaire.

Réf. g): Pour les deux périodes de référence, la courte et la longue, les personnes pourvues d'un emploi étaient invitées à indiquer respectivement le nombre d'heures travaillées la dernière semaine précédant le recensement et la période de travail totale en 1989 (exprimée en nombre de semaines).

Réf. h): Le recensement a aussi rassemblé des informations sur le revenu total et sur les moyens de transport utilisés pour se rendre au travail.

6. Concepts et définitions:
a) Population active: Elle comprend toutes les personnes âgées de 16 ans et plus (à l'exception de celles engagées dans une production agricole de subsistance) qui, au cours de la période de référence, étaient soit pourvues d'un emploi soit au chômage, conformément aux définitions données ci-dessous. Elle inclut les membres des forces armées.

b) Emploi: Les questions utilisées pour déterminer si une personne devait être considérée comme pourvue d'un emploi étaient les suivantes: «X a-t-il travaillé à un moment ou à un autre la semaine dernière, soit à plein temps soit à temps partiel?» (y compris les travaux à temps partiel tels que la distribution de journaux, ou bien encore une activité non rémunérée dans une entreprise ou une affaire familiale; y compris également le service actif dans les forces armées; mais à l'exclusion du travail personnel à domicile, des devoirs scolaires ou des activités bénévoles) et «Pendant combien d'heures X a-t-il travaillé la semaine dernière, tous emplois confondus mais à l'exclusion de l'activité de subsistance?».

Il est indiqué que sont inclus dans cette définition:

i)   les personnes travaillant sans rémunération dans une entreprise ou une affaire familiale;
ii) les personnes pourvues d'un emploi, temporairement absentes du travail;
iii) les étudiants travaillant à temps partiel;
iv) les travailleurs saisonniers ou occasionnels;
v) les conscrits (service militaire ou civil);
vi) les apprentis et les stagiaires.

Aucune des catégories susmentionnées ne peut être identifiée séparément.

c) Chômage: Sont considérées comme «chômeurs» toutes les personnes qui, au cours de la période de référence, étaient sans emploi et à la recherche d'un emploi. Les questions utilisées pour déterminer si une personne devait ou non être considérée comme au chômage étaient les suivantes: «Etiez-vous temporairement absent du travail ou au chômage technique la semaine dernière?», «X a-t-il recherché un emploi rémunéré au cours des quatre dernières semaines?» et «X aurait-il été en mesure d'accepter un emploi la semaine dernière s'il lui en avait été offert un?».

7. Classifications utilisées:
Aussi bien les personnes pourvues d'un emploi que les chômeurs ayant précédemment travaillé sont classifiés par branche d'activité économique, par profession et d'après la situation dans la profession.

a) Branche d'activité économique (industrie): Basée sur les questions: «Pour qui travaillait X la dernière fois qu'il a exercé une activité professionnelle?», «De quel type ou branche d'activité économique s'agissait-il?» et «S'agissait-il essentiellement de fabrication industrielle, de commerce de gros, de commerce de détail ou d'une autre activité (agriculture, bâtiment, services, fonction publique, etc.)?». Pour coder la branche d'activité, on a

utilisé les 231 catégories - regroupées en 13 grands groupes d'activité économique - du Manuel de classification type des activités économiques. Des liens avec la CITI-Rév.2 ont été établis au niveau des Suppléments 1972 et 1977 des Etats-Unis.

b) Profession: Basée sur les questions: «Quel type de travail X effectuait-il (par exemple infirmière diplômée, mécanicien sur machine industrielle, pâtissier glacier?» et «Quelles étaient les activités ou les tâches les plus importantes de X (par exemple fourniture de soins à des patients, réparation de machines dans des usines, glaçage de gâteaux)?». Pour coder la profession, on a utilisé 13 grands groupes de professions du Manuel de classification type des professions (CTP). Aucun lien n'a été établi avec la CITP.

c) Situation dans la profession: Basée sur la question: «X était-il employé par une société ou une entreprise privée à but lucratif et rémunéré sous forme de salaire, d'honoraires ou de commissions; employé par une organisation privée à but non lucratif, exemptée d'impôts ou caritative; employé par des pouvoirs publics locaux ou territoriaux (région, commonwealth, etc.); fonctionnaire fédéral; travailleur indépendant, membre d'une profession libérale ou exploitant agricole non constitué en société; travailleur indépendant, membre d'une profession libérale ou exploitant agricole constitué en société; employé sans rémunération dans une entreprise ou une exploitation agricole familiale?». Pour coder la situation dans la profession, ce sont ces sept groupes que l'on a utilisés.

8. Principales différences par rapport au recensement précédent:
Pas de différence majeure.

9. Publication des résultats du recensement:
Le titre de la publication contenant les résultats définitifs du recensement est «1990 CPH-6-AS», paru en 1992.

Les organismes responsables de cette publication sont soit le Département du Commerce des Etats-Unis, Bureau du recensement, Washington D.C. 20233, soit le Superintendent des documents, Bureau des publications du Gouvernement des Etats-Unis, Washington D.C. 20402.

Les résultats du recensement sont également disponibles sous forme de fichiers STF 1 et 3, de disquettes et de bandes magnétiques.

SAO TOME-ET-PRINCIPE

1. Nom et adresse de l'organisme responsable du recensement:
Direcçao de Economia e Estatística, C.P. 256, Sao Tomé.

2. Recensements de population effectués depuis 1945 (années):
1950, 1960, 1970, 1981 et 1991. La présente description se réfère au recensement de 1991 (qui a eu lieu de 4 août).

3. Champ du recensement:
a) Territoire couvert: Ensemble du territoire.

b) Personnes couvertes: Ensemble de la population.

4. Période de référence:
La semaine précédant la date du recensement. Une courte période (la semaine antérieure au recensement) et une longue période de référence (les 12 mois précédant le recensement) sont utilisées dans les questions posées aux personnes pourvues d'un emploi sur leur temps de travail.

5. Principaux sujets:
a) Population totale, selon le sexe et l'âge: oui
Population active par:
b) Sexe et âge: oui
c) Branche d'activité économique (industrie):   oui
d) Profession: oui
e) Situation dans la profession: oui
f) Niveau d'instruction le plus élevé: oui
g) Durée du travail: oui
h) Autres caractéristiques: oui

Réf. a): L'âge est défini aussi bien en termes d'année de naissance qu'en termes d'années révolues à la date du dernier anniversaire.

Réf. g): La durée du travail se réfère aussi bien aux heures normales de travail des personnes pourvues d'un emploi et aux heures réellement effectuées par les personnes pourvues d'un emploi, présentes au travail, durant la semaine précédant le recensement qu'à la période totale de travail (en nombre de mois) pendant les 12 mois antérieurs au recensement.

Réf. h): Une question a également été posée aux personnes actives au sujet de leur revenu.

6. Concepts et définitions:

a) Population active: Elle comprend toutes les personnes âgées de 10 ans et plus qui, pendant la période de référence, étaient, soit pourvues d'un emploi, soit au chômage, conformément aux définitions données ci-dessous. La définition inclut les membres des forces armées.

b) Emploi: Sont considérées comme «pourvues d'emploi» toutes les personnes qui, interrogées sur leur «condition par rapport au travail» pendant la semaine de référence, ont déclaré qu'elles travaillaient.

Il est indiqué que sont inclus dans cette définition:

i)   les personnes travaillant sans rémunération dans une entreprise ou une affaire familiale;
ii)   les personnes engagées dans la production de produits de base destinés à l'autoconsommation;
iii) les personnes occupées, temporairement absentes du travail;
iv)   les étudiants travaillant à temps partiel;
v)   les travailleurs saisonniers ou occasionnels;
vi)   les conscrits (service militaire ou civil);
vii) les apprentis et les stagiaires.

Seules les personnes appartenant aux catégories i) et vii) ci-dessus peuvent être identifiées séparément au moyen de questions spécifiques.

c) Chômage: Sont considérées comme «chômeurs» toutes les personnes qui, interrogées sur leur «condition par rapport au travail» pendant la période de référence, ont déclaré qu'elles cherchaient soit un nouvel emploi soit un premier emploi. Les étudiants en quête de travail sont exclus de la définition.

7. Classifications utilisées:

Aussi bien les personnes pourvues d'un emploi que les chômeurs ayant précédemment travaillé sont classifiés par industrie, par profession et d'après la situation dans la profession.

a) Branche d'activité économique (industrie): La question posée pour déterminer le groupe d'industrie se réfère à la nature du lieu de travail (exploitation agricole, entreprise publique ou privée, etc.) ainsi qu'à la branche d'activité. Pour coder cette dernière, on a utilisé la CITI-rév.2 au niveau des branches (1 chiffre).

b) Profession: Les questions posées se réfèrent à la profession exercée pendant la semaine de référence (pour les chômeurs: à la profession exercée en dernier lieu). Pour coder la profession on a utilisé la CITP-88 jusqu'au niveau des sous-groupes (3 chiffres).

c) Situation dans la profession: Pour coder cette variable, les cinq catégories suivantes ont été utilisées: salarié; travailleur à son propre compte; employeur; travailleur familial non rémunéré; situation non déclarée.

8. Principales différences par rapport au recensement précédent:

Dans le recensement de 1981, aucune question n'avait été posée sur le temps total de travail ni sur le revenu des personnes pourvues d'un emploi.

9. Publication des résultats du recensement:

Le titre de la publication contenant les résultats définitifs est: «Principais Resultados do II. Recenseamento Geral da Populaçao e da Habitaçao».

L'organisme responsable de cette publication est la Direcçao de Economia e Estatistica, C.P. 256, Sao Tomé.

Les résultats du recensement de 1991 sont également disponibles sous d'autres formes, notamment sur disquettes.

SINGAPOUR

1. Nom et adresse de l'organisme responsable du recensement:

Department of Statistics, 8 Shenton Way, 10-01, Treasury Building, Singapore 0106.

2. Recensements de population effectués depuis 1945 (années):

1947, 1957, 1970, 1980 et 1990. La présente description se réfère au recensement de 1990 (qui a eu lieu le 30 juin).

3. Champ du recensement:

a) Territoire couvert: Ensemble du pays.

4. Période de référence:

La semaine précédant le recensement.

5. Principaux sujets:

a) Population totale, selon le sexe et l'âge: oui
Population active par:
b) Sexe et âge: oui
c) Branche d'activité économique (industrie):   oui
d) Profession: oui
e) Situation dans la profession: oui
f) Niveau d'instruction le plus élevé: oui
g) Durée du travail: non
h) Autres caractéristiques: oui

Réf. a): L'âge est défini en termes de date de naissance de la personne (l'âge a été calculé ainsi: date du recensement - date de naissance; le nombre de mois et de jours additionnels intervient comme une fraction d'année et s'exprime sous forme décimale).

Réf. h): Le recensement a également rassemblé des informations sur d'autres sujets, tels que: les salaires et les rémunérations, les primes, les revenus et les profits mensuels moyens (pour les travailleurs indépendants) et le mode de transport utilisé pour se rendre au travail.

6. Concepts et définitions:

a) Population active: Elle comprend toutes les personnes qui, pendant la semaine de référence, étaient soit pourvues d'un emploi, soit au chômage, conformément aux définitions données ci-dessous. Aucune limite d'âge n'a été fixée pour l'inclusion dans la population active, mais les données sur les caractéristiques économiques n'ont été exploitées que pour les personnes âgées de 15 ans et plus. La définition inclut les membres des forces armées, mais elle exclut les étudiants travaillant à temps partiel et les étudiants en quête d'un emploi.

b) Emploi: Sont considérées comme «pourvues d'un emploi» toutes les personnes qui i) travaillaient contre une rémunération ou pour le profit au cours des sept derniers jours, ou ii) qui travaillaient habituellement 15 heures minimales par semaine. Ces deux définitions ont été utilisées pour déterminer si une personne devait être considérée comme pourvue d'un emploi.

Il est indiqué que sont inclus dans cette définition:

i)   les personnes travaillant sans rémunération dans une entreprise ou une affaire familiale;
ii)   les personnes engagées dans la production de produits de base destinés à l'autoconsommation;
iii) les personnes occupées, temporairement absentes de leur travail;
iv)   les travailleurs saisonniers ou occasionnels;
v)   les conscrits (service militaire ou civil);
vi)   les apprentis et les stagiaires.

Seules les personnes appartenant aux catégories i) et v) peuvent être identifiées séparément. La question utilisée pour identifier les personnes de la catégorie i) était: «Avez-vous prêté main forte comme travailleur familial non rémunéré dans une affaire familiale?». Les données relatives aux militaires du contingent (catégorie v) ont été obtenues auprès du Ministère de la défense et préimprimées pour vérification et confirmation par les personnes concernées.

c) Chômage: Les questions utilisées pour déterminer si une personne devait être considérée comme «chômeur» étaient: «Etes-vous à la recherche d'un emploi?» et «Si oui, quelles mesures avez-vous prises en ce sens? i) inscription auprès d'une agence gouvernementale pour l'emploi; ii) réponses à des annonces ou candidature spontanée auprès d'entreprises; iii) sollicitation d'amis ou de connaissances; iv) autre; v) préparatifs en vue de monter votre propre affaire».

7. Classifications utilisées:

Seules les personnes pourvues d'un emploi ont été classifiées par branche d'activité économique, par profession et d'après la situation dans la profession.

a) Branche d'activité économique (industrie): Basée sur les questions: «Quel est le type d'activité mené par l'organisme ou l'entreprise où vous travaillez?» et «Quel est le principal type de produits fabriqué ou fourni?» ou «Quel type de services assure l'entreprise ou l'organisme où vous travaillez?». Pour coder l'industrie, on a utilisé 117 sous-groupes (3 chiffres), 317 groupes de base (4 chiffres) et 945 codes (5 chiffres) de la classification singapourienne type par industrie de 1990 (SSIC 90). Des liens ont été établis avec la CITI rév.3 au niveau des catégories de classement (1 chiffre).

b) Profession: Basée sur les questions: «Quelle est votre profession?» ou «Quel type de travail effectuez-vous?». Pour coder la profession on a utilisé 119 sous-groupes (3 chiffres), 314 groupes de base (4 chiffres) et 1 116 professions (5 chiffres) de la classification singapourienne type des professions (SSOC). Pour faciliter le codage des professions, des blancs ont été laissés dans le questionnaire du recensement afin que l'agent recenseur (ou la personne recensée, dans le cas d'un auto-recensement) puisse consigner la description des principales tâches et fonctions exécutées dans le travail. Des liens avec la CITP-88 ont été établis au niveau des grands groupes (1 chiffre).

c) Situation dans la profession: Basée sur la question: «Etes-vous: i) travailleur indépendant sans salarié; ii) travailleur indépendant avec salarié(s); iii) salarié (ouvrier ou employé); iv) conscrit; v) aide familial sans salaire fixe ou régulier?». Pour coder la situation dans la profession, on a utilisé les cinq catégories précitées.

8. Principales différences par rapport au recensement précédent:
Lors du recensement de 1980, la limite d'âge fixée pour l'inclusion dans la population active était de 10 ans et plus.

Lors du recensement de 1980, les militaires du contingent n'étaient pas identifiés séparément.

9. Publication des résultats du recensement:
Les résultats définitifs du recensement de 1990 sont parus en août 1993 dans une publication intitulée «Census of Population 1990 Statistical Release 4 - Economic Characteristics».

L'organisme responsable de cette publication est le Bureau du recensement de population, Department of Statistics, Singapore.

Les résultats du recensement ne sont pas disponibles sur disquettes ou bandes magnétiques.

SLOVAQUIE

1. Nom et adresse de l'organisme responsable du recensement:
Slovenského Statistického Urado, Mileticova 3, 824 67 Bratislava.

2. Recensements de population effectués depuis 1945 (années):
1950, 1961, 1970, 1980 et 1991. La présente description se réfère au recensement de la population de 1991 (qui a eu lieu à minuit entre le 2 et le 3 mars).

3. Champ du recensement:
a) Territoire couvert: Ensemble du pays.

b) Personnes couvertes: Ensemble des personnes résidant de manière permanente dans le pays, plus les nationaux résidant de manière permanente à l'étranger, mais à l'exclusion des membres du corps diplomatique ainsi que des membres des forces armées soviétiques et de leurs familles.

4. Période de référence:
A minuit entre le 2 et le 3 mars.

5. Principaux sujets:
a) Population totale, selon le sexe et l'âge:	oui
Population active par:	
b) Sexe et âge:	oui
c) Branche d'activité économique (industrie):	oui
d) Profession:	oui
e) Situation dans la profession:	oui
f) Niveau d'instruction le plus élevé:	...
g) Durée du travail:	non
h) Autres caractéristiques:	oui

Réf. a): L'âge est défini en termes d'année de naissance.

Réf. h): Le recensement a aussi rassemblé des informations sur le lieu de travail (adresse), la fréquence des déplacements entre le domicile et le lieu de travail (quotidiens, autres) et le temps nécessaire à ce trajet aller simple «de porte à porte» (en minutes).

6. Concepts et définitions:
a) Population active: L'activité économique est basée sur le concept de la population active du moment. La population active comprend donc toutes les personnes âgées de 15 ans et plus qui, au moment du recensement, étaient soient pourvues d'un emploi soit au chômage, conformément aux définitions données ci-dessous. Elle comprend également les membres des forces armées ainsi que les détenus, sur la base de l'équivalent civil de leur dernier travail ou de leur travail actuel.

b) Emploi: Sont considérées comme «pourvues d'un emploi» toutes les personnes ayant déclaré qu'elles étaient pourvues d'un emploi en qualité: d'employeur, de travailleur pour son propre compte, de salarié, de membre d'une coopérative agricole ou d'une coopérative de producteurs (y compris les retraités qui travaillent, les femmes en congé de maternité rémunéré et les travailleurs familiaux non rémunérés). Les étudiants qui travaillent à temps partiel sont exclus de la définition.

Il est indiqué que sont inclus dans cette définition:

i)   les personnes travaillant sans rémunération dans une entreprise ou une affaire familiale;
ii)   les personnes pourvues d'un emploi, temporairement absentes du travail;
iii) les travailleurs saisonniers ou occasionnels;
iv)   les conscrits (service militaire ou civil).

Seules les personnes appartenant à la catégorie i) peuvent être identifiées séparément. Les apprentis et les stagiaires, bien que non couverts par la définition de la population active, peuvent eux aussi être identifiés séparément.

c) Chômage: Sont considérées comme «chômeurs» toutes les personnes âgées de 15 à 59 ans (pour les hommes) et de 15 à 56 ans (pour les femmes) ayant déclaré être à la recherche d'un emploi au moment du recensement.

7. Classifications utilisées:
Aussi bien les personnes pourvues d'un emploi que les chômeurs ayant précédemment travaillé sont classifiés par branche d'activité économique, par profession et d'après la situation dans la profession.

a) Branche d'activité économique (industrie): Basée sur la question: «Indiquez le nom de l'établissement, de la coopérative, de l'administration, de l'organisation ou de l'école». Le codage des branches d'activité économique ou de la fréquentation scolaire a été effectué en fonction de listes spéciales d'organisations comportant des codes de branches basés sur les activités les plus fréquentes. Pour le traitement des résultats du recensement de 1991, on a utilisé une classification nationale comportant 47 groupes (c'est-à-dire les branches et les sous-branches de la classification nationale). La classification nationale des branches d'activité économique permet une comparaison complète avec la CITI-rév.3. Un tableau de conversion a été établi entre la classification nationale et la CITI-rév.3, au niveau des divisions (2 chiffres).

b) Profession: Il a été demandé aux personnes interrogées d'indiquer de façon aussi précise que possible quelles étaient leurs tâches et leurs fonctions. Les retraités qui ne travaillaient pas, les femmes en congé de maternité, les conscrits (service militaire), les détenus et les personnes à la recherche d'un emploi devaient indiquer quel avait été leur dernier emploi. Pour coder la profession, on a utilisé 91 groupes de la classification nationale. Des liens avec la CITP (CITP-68 et CITP-88) ont été établis au niveau des grands groupes (1 chiffre).

c) Situation dans la profession: Il a été demandé aux personnes interrogées d'indiquer la catégorie sociale à laquelle elles appartenaient, par ex. travailleur manuel, employé, membre d'une coopérative agricole, membre d'une coopérative de producteurs, employeur (avec un ou plusieurs salariés), exploitant agricole privé, commerçant à son propre compte, travailleur indépendant, travailleur familial non rémunéré, etc. Les travailleurs manuels et les employés devaient préciser le secteur de l'économie nationale (d'Etat, privé, coopératif, mixte). Pour coder la situation dans la profession, on a utilisé les neuf groupes suivants: travailleurs manuels et employés dans le secteur privé; autres travailleurs manuels et employés; membres de coopératives agricoles; membres d'autres coopératives; employeurs; exploitants agricoles privés; personnes travaillant pour leur propre compte; travailleurs indépendants; travailleurs familiaux non rémunérés.

8. Principales différences par rapport au recensement précédent:

En 1991, la définition de la population active a été élargie par l'inclusion des chômeurs à la recherche d'un emploi, mais aucune distinction n'a été faite en ce qui concerne les personnes à la recherche d'un premier emploi. Les retraités exerçant une activité professionnelle, ainsi que les bénéficiaires d'une pension de vieillesse ou d'invalidité percevant par ailleurs une rémunération, ont également été inclus dans la définition.

Lors des recensements de 1961, 1970 et 1980, les travailleurs familiaux non rémunérés avaient été comptés comme personnes à charge, c'est-à-dire comme inactifs, et les personnes qui s'étaient déclarées elles-mêmes comme chômeurs avaient été considérées comme pourvues d'emploi sur la base de leur dernier emploi.

Dans le recensement de 1991, la classification par situation dans la profession a été élargie par l'inclusion des employeurs, et les travailleurs familiaux non rémunérés ont été identifiés comme groupe spécial.

Enfin, la question relative au trajet domicile-travail a été élargie en 1991 par l'inclusion d'une question sur le temps nécessaire pour effectuer le trajet aller simple «de porte à porte».

9. Publication des résultats du recensement:

Le titre de la publication qui contient les chiffres définitifs du recensement est: «Recensement 1991 de la population et des logements». Cette publication est parue en 1992.

L'organisme responsable de cette publication est le Slovenského Statistického Urado, Mileticova 3, 824 67 Bratislava.

Les chiffres définitifs du recensement de 1991 sont également disponibles sous forme de disquettes et de bandes magnétiques.

SLOVENIE

1. Nom et adresse de l'organisme responsable du recensement:

Statistical Office of the Republic of Slovenia, Ljubljana, Vozarski pot 12.

2. Recensements de population effectués depuis 1945 (années):

1948, 1953, 1961, 1971, 1981, et 1991. La présente description se réfère au recensement de la population de 1991 (qui a eu lieu le 31 mars).

3. Champ du recensement:

a) Territoire couvert: Ensemble du pays.

b) Personnes couvertes: Ensemble de la population.

4. Période de référence:

Le jour et l'année précédant le jour du recensement.

5. Principaux sujets:

a) Population totale, selon le sexe et l'âge:	oui
Population active par:	
b) Sexe et âge:	oui
c) Branche d'activité économique (industrie):	oui
d) Profession:	oui
e) Situation dans la profession:	oui
f) Niveau d'instruction le plus élevé:	oui
g) Durée du travail:	non
h) Autres caractéristiques:	oui

Réf. a): L'âge est défini en termes d'année de naissance.

Réf. h): Le recensement a aussi rassemblé des informations sur les revenus réguliers des personnes interrogées, sur la fréquence, la durée (en minutes) et les moyens de transport utilisés pour se rendre au travail.

6. Concepts et définitions:

a) Population active: Elle comprend toutes les personnes âgées de 15 ans et plus qui, le jour du recensement, étaient soit pourvues d'un emploi, soit au chômage, conformément aux définitions données ci-dessous. Pour des catégories spécifiques de la population (femme au foyer, personnes travaillant principalement dans des fermes, retraités, travailleurs saisonniers travaillant occasionnellement), la période de référence utilisée pour déterminer leur activité était l'année précédant le jour du recensement. La définition inclut tous les membres des forces armées mais exclut les étudiants travaillant à temps partiel et les étudiants en quête d'emploi.

b) Emploi: Sont considérées comme «pourvues d'un emploi» toutes les personnes qui, à l'époque du recensement, exerçaient une profession contre rémunération ou des avantages en nature. Dans l'agriculture on inclut les membres de la famille participant à des activités ainsi que les agricultrices pourvu qu'ils soient principalement impliqués dans des travaux agricoles

Il est indiqué que sont inclus dans cette définition:

i) les personnes travaillant sans rémunération dans une entreprise ou une affaire familiale;

ii) les personnes engagées dans la production de produits de base destinés à l'autoconsommation;

iii) les personnes occupées, temporairement absentes du travail;

iv) les travailleurs saisonniers ou occasionnels;

v) les conscrits (service militaire ou civil);

vi) les apprentis et les stagiaires.

Seules les personnes appartenant à la catégorie i) peuvent être identifiées séparément.

c) Chômage: Sont considérées comme «chômeurs» toutes les personnes inscrites, au moment du recensement, dans des agences pour l'emploi comme demandeurs d'emploi à la recherche d'un premier ou d'un nouvel emploi.

7. Classifications utilisées:

Aussi bien les personnes pourvues d'un emploi que les chômeurs ayant précédemment travaillé sont classifiés par profession. Seules les personnes pourvues d'un emploi ont été classifiées par branche d'activité économique et d'après la situation dans la profession.

a) Branche d'activité économique (industrie): On a demandé aux personnes pourvues d'un emploi de spécifier l'industrie (branche d'activité économique) pour laquelle elles travaillaient ainsi que le nom et l'adresse de l'entreprise, de l'organisme ou de l'association les employant. Pour coder la branche d'activité économique on a utilisé 700 groupes de la classification des branches d'activité économique du Bureau central des statistiques de la République de Slovénie en vigueur au moment du recensement. La classification n'est pas directement comparable avec la CITI. Cependant, sur la base d'une combinaison entre les réponses et les estimations, des liens ont pu être établis avec la CITI, rév.2 au niveau des branches (1 chiffre).

b) Profession: On a demandé aux personnes de spécifier le type de travail accompli. Pour coder la profession, on a utilisé la classification des professions du Bureau central des statistiques de la République de Slovénie en vigueur à l'époque du recensement. Cette classification n'est pas directement comparable avec la CITP. Cependant sur la base de diverses données, des liens peuvent être établis avec la CITP-88 au niveau des grands groupes (1 chiffre).

c) Situation dans la profession: Pour coder cette variable, on a utilisé cinq groupes: salarié; propriétaire ou co-propriétaire (entreprise), propriétaire ou co-propriétaire (établissement de type artisanal), travailleur à son propre compte; travailleur familial non rémunéré.

8. Principales différences par rapport au recensement précédent:

Pas de différence majeure.

9. Publication des résultats du recensement:

Les résultats définitifs du recensement ont été publiés dans de nombreuses publications dont: «1991 Census of the population, Households, Housing and Agricultural Holdings in the Republic of Slovenia - Final data: Statistical information No.173 (July 1992)» et «No.189 (July 1992): population by activity and sex, Economically active population, by industry». La liste complète des publications est disponible dans: «Results of Surveys - Census of the population, households, housings and agricultural holdings in the Republic of Slovenia in 1991, No.617 (1994)».

L'organisme responsable de ces publications est le Bureau des statistiques de la République de Slovénie, Vozarski pot 12, Ljubljana.

Les résultats du recensement ne sont pas disponibles sous d'autres formes.

SOUDAN

1. Nom et adresse de l'organisme responsable du recensement:
Central Bureau of Statistics, P.O. Box 700, Khartoum.

2. Recensements de population effectués depuis 1945 (années):
1955-56, 1973, 1983 et 1993. La présente description se réfère au recensement de la population de 1993 (qui a eu lieu le 15 avril).

3. Champ du recensement:
a) Territoire couvert: Les trois régions du sud du pays, qui sont en état d'insurrection, n'ont pu être que partiellement couvertes par le recensement.

b) Personnes couvertes: Ensemble de la population.

4. Période de référence:
La semaine précédant le jour du recensement.

5. Principaux sujets:
a) Population totale, selon le sexe et l'âge: oui
Population active par:
b) Sexe et âge: oui
c) Branche d'activité économique (industrie): oui
d) Profession: oui
e) Situation dans la profession: oui
f) Niveau d'instruction le plus élevé: oui
g) Durée du travail: non
h) Autres caractéristiques: non

Réf. a): L'âge est défini en termes d'années révolues à la date du dernier anniversaire.

6. Concepts et définitions:
a) Population active: Elle comprend toutes les personnes âgées de 10 ans et plus qui, au cours de la semaine de référence, étaient soit pourvues d'un emploi soit au chômage, conformément aux définitions données ci-dessous. Les membres des forces armées sont exclus de cette définition, de même que les étudiants travaillant à temps partiel et les étudiants à la recherche d'un emploi.

b) Emploi: Sont considérées comme «pourvues d'un emploi» toutes les personnes qui, au cours de la semaine de référence, ont travaillé à leur domicile ou à l'extérieur, avec ou sans rémunération, pendant au moins deux jours. La définition inclut les personnes absentes du travail pour cause de maladie ou de congé.

Il est indiqué que sont inclus dans cette définition les personnes travaillant sans rémunération dans une entreprise ou une affaire familiale.

c) Chômage: Sont considérées comme «chômeurs» toutes les personnes qui, au cours de la semaine de référence, n'ont pas travaillé et étaient soit à la recherche d'un emploi soit prêtes à accepter un emploi si on leur en avait proposé un.

7. Classifications utilisées:
Aussi bien les personnes pourvues d'un emploi que les chômeurs ayant précédemment travaillé sont classifiés par branche d'activité économique, par profession et d'après la situation dans la profession. Ces questions ont été posées à tous les ménages ordinaires des zones urbaines et à un échantillon représentant 5% des ménages ordinaires des zones rurales.

a) Branche d'activité économique (industrie): Pour coder la branche d'activité, on a utilisé la CITI-Rév.2 au niveau des grands groupes (3 chiffres).

b) Profession: Pour coder la profession, on a utilisé la CITP-88 au niveau des groupes de base (4 chiffres).

c) Situation dans la profession: Pour coder cette variable, on a utilisé les cinq groupes suivants: salarié; employeur; travailleur pour son propre compte; travailleur familial non rémunéré; travailleur non rémunéré autre que familial.

8. Principales différences par rapport au recensement précédent:
Pas de différence majeure.

9. Publication des résultats du recensement:
Les résultats définitifs du recensement ont été publiés en juin 1995 dans un document intitulé «Quatrième recensement de la population du Soudan. Tableaux définitifs.».

L'organisme responsable de cette publication est le Bureau central des statistiques, B.P. 700, Khartoum.

Les résultats définitifs sont également disponibles sous forme de tableaux non publiés, de disquettes et de bandes magnétiques.

SUEDE

1. Nom et adresse de l'organisme responsable du recensement:
Statistics Sweden, I/BEF, S-701 89 Örebro.

2. Recensements de population effectués depuis 1945 (années):
1945, 1950, 1960, 1965, 1970, 1975, 1980, 1985 et 1990. La présente description se réfère au recensement de population de 1990 (qui a eu lieu le 1er novembre).

3. Champ du recensement:
a) Territoire couvert: Ensemble du pays.

b) Personnes couvertes: Ensemble de la population de tous âges excepté les membres du personnel diplomatique étranger et leurs familles installées dans le pays, les civils étrangers travaillant temporairement dans le pays comme saisonniers, les civils étrangers qui franchissent quotidiennement la frontière pour venir travailler en Suède, les civils étrangers résidant temporairement dans le pays autres que ceux mentionnés ci-dessus, les passagers en transit sur des navires mouillant dans les ports au moment du recensement.

4. Période de référence:
Un mois (octobre 1990).

5. Principaux sujets:
a) Population totale, selon le sexe et l'âge: oui
Population active par:
b) Sexe et âge: oui
c) Branche d'activité économique (industrie): oui
d) Profession: oui
e) Situation dans la profession: oui
f) Niveau d'instruction le plus élevé: oui
g) Durée du travail: oui
h) Autres caractéristiques: oui

Réf. a): L'âge est défini en termes d'année de naissance.

Réf. g): La durée du travail se réfère à la durée hebdomadaire normale du travail des personnes pourvues d'un emploi.

Réf. h): Le recensement a aussi rassemblé des informations sur les revenus (extraites des registres) et sur les moyens de transport utilisés.

6. Concepts et définitions:
a) Population active: Le recensement ne mesure que l'emploi.

b) Emploi: Sont considérées comme «pourvues d'un emploi» toutes les personnes âgées de 16 ans et plus qui, pendant le mois de référence, ont effectué à domicile ou à l'extérieur un travail ayant une valeur économique. Aucune question n'a été posée pour déterminer si une personne devait être considérée comme pourvue d'un emploi, mais on s'est basé sur le registre de l'emploi. Les critères utilisés étaient les suivants: un revenu minimal de 250 SEK en octobre 1990 ou, si la période n'est pas précisée, un minimum de 28 000 EK pour toute l'année.

Entrent dans cette définition les catégories suivantes pour autant que les critères de revenu soient respectés:
i) les personnes engagées dans la production de produits de base destinés à l'autoconsommation;
ii) les personnes occupées, temporairement absentes du travail;
iii) les étudiants travaillant à temps partiel;
iv) les travailleurs saisonniers ou occasionnels;
v) les conscrits (service militaire ou civil);
vi) les apprentis et les stagiaires.

Aucune des catégories susmentionnées ne peut être identifiée séparément.

c) Chômage: Ne s'applique pas.

7. Classifications utilisées:
Seules les personnes pourvues d'un emploi ont été classifiées par branche d'activité économique, par profession et d'après la situation dans la profession.

a) Branche d'activité économique (industrie): Les données sur l'industrie ont été obtenues du Registre central des entreprises du Bureau central des statistiques. Pour coder la branche d'activité économique, on a utilisé 340 groupes de la classification suédoise type, par industrie, de toutes les branches d'activité économique (SNI-1969). Des liens ont été établis avec la CITI-Rév.2 au niveau des groupes (4 chiffres).

b) Profession: Les questions spécifiques posées sont: i) pour une profession pré-indiquée (lors du recensement de 1985): «L'information pré-imprimée correspond-elle à votre profession ou à votre emploi actuel(le)?» et ii) dans le cas contraire: «Comment classifieriez-vous votre profession actuelle? Indiquez votre profession aussi précisément que possible afin de décrire au mieux vos tâches ou fonctions». Pour coder la profession, on a utilisé 321 groupes de la classification nordique des professions (NYK-1983). Des liens avec la CITP-68 ont été établis au niveau des grands groupes (1 chiffre).

c) Situation dans la profession: La situation dans la profession a été déterminée par les informations tirées du registre de l'emploi. Pour coder cette variable, on a utilisé quatre groupes: salarié; employeur; travailleur indépendant dans l'agriculture ou la sylviculture, marin.

8. Principales différences par rapport au recensement précédent:
Pas de différence majeure.

9. Publication des résultats du recensement:
Le laps de temps écoulé entre la date du recensement et la publication des résultats définitifs est de un an et demi à deux ans.

L'organisme responsable de cette publication est Statistics Sweden, I/BEF, S-701 89 Örebro, Sweden.

Les résultats définitifs du recensement sont également disponibles sous d'autres formes: «Computor tables» et «The Regional Statistical Database (RSDB) of Sweden», mars 1992.

SUISSE

1. Nom et adresse de l'organisme responsable du recensement:
Office fédéral de la statistique, Section de la structure de la population et des ménages, Hallwylstrasse 15, 3003 Berne.

2. Recensements de population effectués depuis 1945 (années):
1950, 1960, 1970, 1980 et 1990. La présente description se réfère au recensement de 1990 (qui a eu lieu le 4 décembre).

3. Champ du recensement:
a) Territoire couvert: Ensemble du pays.

b) Personnes couvertes: Ensemble de la population résidant habituellement dans le pays, à l'exception des diplomates étrangers et des membres de leur famille.

4. Période de référence:
Une courte période: la situation de la personne à fin novembre, au début de décembre ou le jour même du recensement.

5. Principaux sujets:
a) Population totale, selon le sexe et l'âge:	oui
Population active par:	
b) Sexe et âge:	oui
c) Branche d'activité économique (industrie):	oui
d) Profession:	oui
e) Situation dans la profession:	oui
f) Niveau d'instruction le plus élevé:	oui
g) Durée du travail:	oui
h) Autres caractéristiques:	oui

Réf. a): L'âge est défini en termes de date de naissance complète (jour, mois et année).

Réf. g): La durée du travail se réfère à la durée normale du travail des personnes pourvues d'un emploi.

Réf. h): D'autres informations ont également été rassemblées lors du recensement. Aux actifs, on a posé des questions sur la durée du trajet du domicile au lieu de travail ou à l'école («Combien de temps vous faut-il normalement pour vous rendre au travail ou à l'école?» et «Combien de fois par jour faites-vous ce trajet aller et retour?») ainsi que sur les moyens de transport utilisés à cette fin («Quel(s) moyen(s) de transport utilisez-vous normalement pour vous rendre au travail ou à

l'école? Si vous en utilisez plusieurs par jour, prière de les indiquer tous»). Aux personnes qui ne travaillent plus, c'est-à-dire aux personnes ayant cessé toute activité économique, on a demandé des indications sur la profession exercée avant la retraite et sur leur situation dans cette profession.

6. Concepts et définitions:
a) Population active: Elle comprend toutes les personnes âgées de 15 ans et plus qui, à la date du recensement, étaient, soit pourvues d'un emploi, soit au chômage, conformément aux définitions données ci-dessous. Les personnes travaillant moins d'une heure par semaine sont exclues de la définition. Celles effectuant leur service militaire obligatoire sont classées d'après leur activité dans la vie civile.

b) Emploi: Sont considérées comme «pourvues d'un emploi» toutes les personnes qui, à la date du recensement, ont exercé une profession, une fonction ou une activité lucrative, à plein temps ou à temps partiel. Les personnes occupées à temps partiel sont celles dont le nombre d'heures de travail atteint au maximum 80 pour cent de la durée habituelle du travail dans l'établissement ou la branche qui les emploie; toutefois, la durée hebdomadaire de leur travail doit atteindre au minimum une heure.

Il est indiqué que sont inclus dans cette définition:
i) les personnes travaillant sans rémunération dans une entreprise ou une affaire familiale;
ii) les personnes occupées, temporairement absentes du travail;
iii) les étudiants travaillant à temps partiel;
iv) les travailleurs saisonniers ou occasionnels, pour autant qu'ils soient en activité à l'époque du recensement;
v) les conscrits (service militaire ou civil), s'ils étaient actifs dans la vie civile;
vi) les détenteurs de plusieurs emplois;
vii) les apprentis et les stagiaires.

Seules les catégories iii) et vi), les travailleurs étrangers de la catégorie iv) et les apprentis liés par un contrat d'apprentissage, peuvent être identifiés séparément. Les travailleurs familiaux, rémunérés et non rémunérés, peuvent également être identifiés ensemble, mais pas séparément.

c) Chômage: Sont considérées comme «chômeurs» toutes les personnes qui, à l'époque du recensement, étaient sans emploi et à la recherche d'un emploi, ou qui possédaient une confirmation d'engagement ou un contrat pour un futur emploi. A noter que lors du recensement, le terme de «chômeurs» n'a pas été utilisé, mais qu'on a plutôt parlé de «personnes en quête d'un emploi», afin d'éviter toute confusion avec les «chômeurs» au sens de la statistique du marché du travail.

7. Classifications utilisées:
Seules les personnes pourvues d'un emploi sont classifiées par industrie. Aussi bien les personnes pourvues d'un emploi que les personnes en quête d'emploi et ayant précédemment travaillé sont classifiées par profession et d'après la situation dans la profession.

a) Branche d'activité économique (industrie): La question spécifique est «Où travaillez-vous?» et se réfère au lieu de travail et au nom de l'entreprise. A partir du nom de l'entreprise, on détermine la branche d'activité économique à l'aide du registre central des entreprises et établissements (REE) l'Office fédéral de la statistique. Pour coder la branche d'activité, on a utilisé 54 classes, 210 groupes et 703 genres de la Nomenclature générale des activités économiques de 1985.

L'attribution des codes pour les personnes travaillant dans des entreprises occupant une personne ou plus sera faite à l'aide d'un registre des entreprises et établissements.

Il existe une clé permettant l'accès de la nomenclature générale suisse des activités économiques à la CITI-rév.2 au niveau des catégories (2 chiffres).

b) Profession: Basée sur les questions: «Quelle activité professionnelle exercez-vous actuellement?» et «Quelle activité professionnelle avez-vous exercée en dernier?». Il a été demandé d'indiquer la profession avec la plus grande précision et, au besoin, d'en fournir une brève description; par exemple: «serrurier du bâtiment» et pas simplement «serrurier»; «vendeur» ou «employée de bureau» et non «employé(e)»; «ingénieur en machines» et non «ingénieur»; etc. Les personnes exerçant deux ou plusieurs professions ont été requises de n'indiquer que la plus importante. Pour coder la profession, on a utilisé 404 groupes. Le codage sera fait en même temps que ceux des professions apprises et du niveau de formation. Des liens ont été établis avec la CITP-88.

c) *Situation dans la profession*: Basée sur les questions: «Si vous avez présentement une activité professionnelle, veuillez indiquer votre situation professionnelle» et «Si vous cherchez un emploi ou si vous avez cessé votre activité professionnelle, veuillez indiquer votre dernière situation». Pour coder la situation dans la profession, on a utilisé sept catégories: indépendant(e) (par exemple: commerçant, entrepreneur, profession libérale, etc.); occupé(e) dans l'entreprise d'un membre de la famille; apprenti(e) avec contrat d'apprentissage ou de formation pratique accélérée; directeur/directrice, fondé(e) de pouvoir, fonctionnaire supérieur(e); cadre moyen ou inférieur (par exemple: chef de bureau, de service ou de groupe, gérant(e) de succursale, chef d'atelier, contremaître, chef d'équipe); employé(e), ouvrier/ouvrière, stagiaire; autre situation.

8. Principales différences par rapport au recensement précédent:
Le minimum d'heures hebdomadaires de travail requis pour être inclus dans la définition de l'emploi, qui était de six heures en 1980, a été ramené à une heure en 1990.

9. Publication des résultats du recensement:
L'organisme responsable de la publication des résultats définitifs du recensement est l'Office fédéral de la statistique, Hallwylstrasse 15, 3003 Berne.

Les résultats du recensement de 1990 sont également disponibles sous forme de tableaux non publiés, de disquettes et de bandes magnétiques.

REPUBLIQUE ARABE SYRIENNE

1. Nom et adresse de l'organisme responsable du recensement:
The Central Bureau of Statistics, Abou Rummaneh, Abdel Malek Ben Marwan Street, Damascus.

2. Recensements de population effectués depuis 1945 (années):
1960, 1970, 1976, 1981 et 1994. La présente description se réfère au recensement de population de 1994 (qui a eu lieu le 3 septembre).

3. Champ du recensement:
a) *Territoire couvert*: Ensemble du pays.

b) *Personnes couvertes*: Ensemble de la population.

4. Période de référence:
La semaine et l'année précédant la date du recensement.

5. Principaux sujets:
a) Population totale, selon le sexe et l'âge: oui
Population active par:
b) Sexe et âge: oui
c) Branche d'activité économique (industrie):   oui
d) Profession: oui
e) Situation dans la profession: oui
f) Niveau d'instruction le plus élevé: oui
g) Durée du travail: oui
h) Autres caractéristiques: non
Réf. a): L'âge est défini en termes d'année de naissance.
Réf. g): Pour la période de référence courte, on a demandé aux personnes pourvues d'un emploi de spécifier la durée normale de leur travail et les heures réellement effectuées. Pour la période de référence longue, on a demandé aux personnes pourvues d'un emploi de préciser la période totale travaillée exprimée en nombre de mois.

6. Concepts et définitions:
a) *Population active*: Elle comprend toutes les personnes âgées de 10 ans et plus qui, au moment du recensement, étaient soit pourvues d'un emploi, soit au chômage, conformément aux définitions données ci-dessous. Les questions relatives à l'activité économique ont été posées à un échantillon de 10% de la population. La définition inclut tous les membres des forces armées mais exclut les étudiants travaillant à temps partiel et les étudiants en quête d'emploi

b) *Emploi*: Sont considérées comme «pourvues d'un emploi» toutes les personnes qui ont effectué un travail ayant une valeur économique pendant une période minimale de 18 heures

au cours de la semaine se terminant avec la visite de l'agent recenseur.
Il est indiqué que sont inclus dans cette définition:
i)   les personnes travaillant sans rémunération dans une entreprise ou une affaire familiale;
ii)   les conscrits (service militaire ou civil);
iii)   les apprentis et les stagiaires.
Toutes les catégories ci-dessus peuvent être identifiées séparément.

c) *Chômage*: Sont considérées comme «chômeurs» toutes les personnes qui, pendant la semaine de référence, étaient à la recherche d'un emploi, désiraient travailler et étaient aptes à le faire mais ne trouvaient pas de travail.

7. Classifications utilisées:
Dans l'échantillon, aussi bien les personnes pourvues d'un emploi que les chômeurs ayant précédemment travaillé sont classifiés par branche d'activité économique, par profession et d'après la situation dans la profession.

a) *Branche d'activité économique (industrie)*: Pour coder la branche d'activité économique, on a utilisé la classification nationale au niveau 3 chiffres. Des liens ont été établis avec la CITI-Rév.3 au niveau des classes (4 chiffres).

b) *Profession*: Pour coder la profession, on a utilisé la classification nationale au niveau 3 chiffres. Des liens avec la CITP-88 ont été établis au niveau des sous-grands-groupes (2 chiffres).

c) *Situation dans la profession*: Pour coder cette variable, on a utilisé cinq groupes: employeur; travailleur indépendant; salarié, travailleur familial non rémunéré; apprenti non rémunéré.

8. Principales différences par rapport au recensement précédent:
En 1981, on avait uniquement utilisé une période de référence courte (la semaine précédant la date du recensement).

9. Publication des résultats du recensement:
Le laps de temps écoulé entre la date du recensement et la publication des résultats est approximativement d'un an et demi.
L'organisme responsable est le Bureau central des statistiques, Abou Roummaneh, Damascus.

TCHAD

1. Nom et adresse de l'organisme responsable du recensement:
Bureau central du Recensement (B.C.R.), B.P. 453, Ndjamena.

2. Recensements de population effectués depuis 1945 (années):
La présente description se réfère au recensement de 1993 (qui a eu lieu du 1er au 15 avril).

3. Champ du recensement:
a) *Territoire couvert*: Ensemble du pays, à l'exception de six cantons dans la préfecture du Logone oriental (Béboto, Bodo, Békan, Kaba Roangar, Goré rural et Yamodo) et de cinq villages du canton de Signar (préfecture de Ouaddoï): Andjaména, Ardéba, Fosso, Hiné Hésseina et Hille Koukon, de la bande d'Aouzou et de quelques îles du lac (pour cause d'insécurité).

b) *Personnes couvertes*: Ensemble de la population de tous âges, à l'exception des membres du corps diplomatique et consulaire.

4. Période de référence:
La semaine précédant le jour de l'interview, et pour les agriculteurs la dernière année (dernière saison des pluies).

5. Principaux sujets:
a) Population totale, selon le sexe et l'âge: oui
Population active par:
b) Sexe et âge: oui
c) Branche d'activité économique (industrie):   oui
d) Profession: oui
e) Situation dans la profession: oui
f) Niveau d'instruction le plus élevé: oui
g) Durée du travail: non
h) Autres caractéristiques: non
Réf. a): L'âge est défini en termes d'années révolues à la date du dernier anniversaire.

6. Concepts et définitions:

a) Population active: Elle comprend toutes les personnes âgées de 6 à 98 ans qui, pendant la période de référence étaient, soit pourvues d'un emploi, soit au chômage, conformément aux définitions ci-dessous. Les étudiants travaillant à temps partiel ainsi que les étudiants en quête de travail sont exclus de la définition, cependant que l'ensemble des forces armées fait partie de la définition.

b) Emploi: Sont considérées comme «pourvues d'emploi» toutes les personnes qui ont travaillé au cours de la semaine de référence, ou de la dernière saison s'il s'agit d'un agriculteur. Les femmes qui en plus des travaux ménagers s'occupent des travaux champêtres ou du commerce sont considérées comme occupées. La question utilisée est: «Situation professionnelle: 1) occupé; 2) chômeur; 3) en quête du premier travail; 4) ménagère; 5) rentier/retraité; 6) étudiant/élève; et 7) autre.»

Il est indiqué que sont inclus dans cette définition:

i) les personnes travaillant sans rémunération dans une entreprise ou une affaire familiale;

ii) les personnes engagées dans la production de produits de base destinés à l'autoconsommation;

iii) les personnes occupées, temporairement absentes du travail;

iv) les travailleurs saisonniers ou occasionnels;

v) les apprentis et les stagiaires.

Seules les personnes appartenant aux catégories i) et ii) ci-dessus peuvent être identifiées séparément.

c) Chômage: Sont considérées comme «chômeurs» toutes les personnes ayant déjà travaillé mais qui, pendant la période de référence, étaient sans travail et à la recherche d'un emploi. Les personnes à la recherche de leur premier emploi sont identifiées séparément.

7. Classifications utilisées:

Aussi bien les personnes occupées que les chômeurs ayant précédemment travaillé sont classifiés par industrie, par profession et d'après la situation dans la profession.

a) Branche d'activité économique (industrie): Basée sur la question: «Indiquez le caractère de l'activité de l'établissement ou de l'entreprise». A défaut, inscrivez le nom complet de l'établissement». Pour coder la branche d'activité, on a utilisé la CITI-rév.3 au niveau des 60 divisions (2 chiffres), avec quelques modifications, en particulier concernant les activités de récupération, qui occupent une importance considérable dans le secteur informel au Tchad.

b) Profession: Le type de profession se réfère à la profession exercée actuellement pour les personnes occupées, à la dernière profession exercée pour les chômeurs, et à la profession pour laquelle la personne passe le plus de temps pour les personnes qui exercent plusieurs professions. On a demandé des réponses le plus détaillées possibles, ex: planteur de coton, cultivatrice de mil, vendeur ambulant, vendeuse de (huile, poisson, légumes, arachides, riz…), vendeur sur table de (chaussures, sucre, thé, etc…). Pour coder la profession, on a utilisé la CITP-88 au niveau des sous-grands groupes (2 chiffres).

c) Situation dans la profession: Pour coder cette variable, on a utilisé les six catégories suivantes: salarié; indépendant; employeur; aide familial; apprenti (non rémunéré); et autre.

8. Principales différences par rapport au recensement précédent:

Ne s'applique pas.

9. Publication des résultats du recensement:

Les résultats définitifs sont parus en avril 1995 dans les publications suivantes: «Rapport de séminaire-atelier», «Rapport de synthèse» et «Rapport d'analyse de 10 thèmes».

L'organisme responsable de la publication est le Bureau central du recensement, B.P. 453, Ndjamena.

Les résultats du recensement de 1993 sont également disponibles sous forme de tableaux de données bruts. La base de données existe, mais pas sous forme de disquettes ni de bandes magnétiques.

REPUBLIQUE TCHEQUE

1. Nom et adresse de l'organisme responsable du recensement:

Statistical Office, Sokolovská 142, 18613 Prague 8 Karlin.

2. Recensements de population effectués depuis 1945 (années):

1950, 1961, 1970, 1980 et 1991. La présente description se réfère au recensement de la population de 1991 (qui a eu lieu à minuit entre le 2 et le 3 mars).

3. Champ du recensement:

a) Territoire couvert: Ensemble du pays.

b) Personnes couvertes: Ensemble de la population résidant en permanence dans le pays et les nationaux vivant en permanence à l'étranger; les membres des corps diplomatiques et les membres de l'armée soviétique ainsi que leurs proches sont exclus de la définition.

4. Période de référence:

A minuit entre le 2 et le 3 mars.

5. Principaux sujets:

a) Population totale, selon le sexe et l'âge:	oui
Population active par:	
b) Sexe et âge:	oui
c) Branche d'activité économique (industrie):	oui
d) Profession:	oui
e) Situation dans la profession:	oui
f) Niveau d'instruction le plus élevé:	oui
g) Durée du travail:	non
h) Autres caractéristiques:	oui

Réf. a): L'âge est défini en termes d'année de naissance.

Réf. h): Le recensement a aussi rassemblé des informations sur le lieu de travail (adresse), la fréquence des déplacements entre le domicile et le lieu de travail (quotidiens, autres) et le temps nécessaire à ce trajet aller simple «de porte à porte» (en minutes).

6. Concepts et définitions:

a) Population active: L'activité économique est basée sur le concept de la population active du moment. La population active comprend donc toutes les personnes âgées de 15 ans et plus qui, au moment du recensement, étaient soient pourvues d'un emploi soit au chômage, conformément aux définitions données ci-dessous. Elle comprend également les membres des forces armées ainsi que les détenus, sur la base de l'équivalent civil de leur dernier travail ou de leur travail actuel.

b) Emploi: Sont considérées comme «pourvues d'un emploi» toutes les personnes ayant déclaré qu'elles étaient pourvues d'un emploi en qualité: d'employeur, de travailleur pour son propre compte, de salarié, de membre d'une coopérative agricole ou d'une coopérative de producteurs (y compris les retraités qui travaillent, les femmes en congé de maternité rémunéré et les travailleurs familiaux non rémunérés). Les étudiants qui travaillent à temps partiel sont exclus de la définition.

Il est indiqué que sont inclus dans cette définition:

i) les personnes travaillant sans rémunération dans une entreprise ou une affaire familiale;

ii) les personnes occupées, temporairement absentes de leur travail;

iii) les travailleurs saisonniers ou occasionnels;

iv) les conscrits (service militaire ou civil).

Seules les personnes appartenant à la catégorie i) peuvent être identifiées séparément. Les apprentis et les stagiaires, bien que non couverts par la définition de la population active, peuvent eux aussi être identifiés séparément.

c) Chômage: Sont considérées comme «chômeurs» toutes les personnes âgées de 15 à 59 ans (pour les hommes) et de 15 à 56 ans (pour les femmes) ayant déclaré être à la recherche d'un emploi au moment du recensement.

7. Classifications utilisées:

Aussi bien les personnes pourvues d'un emploi que les chômeurs ayant précédemment travaillé sont classifiés par branche d'activité économique, par profession et d'après la situation dans la profession.

a) Branche d'activité économique (industrie): Basée sur la question: «Indiquez le nom de l'établissement, de la coopérative, de l'administration, de l'organisme ou de l'école». Le codage des branches d'activité économique ou de la fréquentation scolaire a été effectué en fonction de listes spéciales d'organisations comportant des codes de branches basés sur les activités les plus fréquentes. Pour le traitement des résultats du recensement de 1991, on a utilisé une classification nationale comportant 47 groupes (à savoir les branches et les sous-branches de la classification nationale). La classification nationale des branches d'activité économique permet une comparaison complète avec la CITI-rév.3. Un tableau de conversion a été établi entre la classification nationale et la CITI-rév.3 au niveau des divisions (2 chiffres).

b) Profession: On a demandé aux personnes interrogées d'indiquer avec une grande précision la nature de leurs tâches ou de leurs fonctions. Les retraités qui ne travaillaient pas, les femmes en congé de maternité, les conscrits (service militaire), les détenus et les personnes à la recherche d'un emploi devaient spécifier leur dernier emploi. Pour coder la profession, on a utilisé 91 groupes de la classification nationale. Des liens avec la CITP (CITP-68 et CITP-88) ont été établis au niveau des grands groupes (1 chiffre).

c) Situation dans la profession: On a demandé aux personnes interrogées d'indiquer la catégorie sociale à laquelle elles appartenaient, par ex. travailleur manuel, employé, membre d'une coopérative agricole, membre d'une coopérative de producteurs, employeur (avec un ou plusieurs salariés), exploitant agricole privé, commerçant à son propre compte, travailleur indépendant, travailleur familial non rémunéré, etc.. Les travailleurs manuels et les employés devaient préciser le secteur de l'économie nationale (public, privé, coopératif, mixte). Pour coder la situation dans la profession, on a utilisé les neuf groupes suivants: travailleurs manuels et salariés du secteur privé; autres travailleurs manuels et salariés; membres de coopératives agricoles; membres d'autres coopératives; employeurs; exploitants agricoles privés; personnes travaillant pour leur propre compte; travailleurs indépendants; travailleurs familiaux non rémunérés.

8. Principales différences par rapport au recensement précédent:

En 1991, la définition de la population active a été élargie par l'inclusion des chômeurs à la recherche d'un emploi, mais aucune distinction n'a été faite en ce qui concerne les personnes à la recherche d'un premier emploi. Les retraités exerçant une activité professionnelle, ainsi que les bénéficiaires d'une pension de vieillesse ou d'invalidité percevant par ailleurs une rémunération, ont également été inclus dans la définition.

Lors des recensements de 1961, 1970 et 1980, les travailleurs familiaux non rémunérés avaient été comptés comme personnes à charge, c'est-à-dire comme inactifs, et les personnes qui s'étaient déclarées elles-mêmes comme chômeurs avaient été considérées comme pourvues d'emploi sur la base de leur dernier emploi.

Dans le recensement de 1991, la classification par situation dans la profession a été élargie par l'inclusion des employeurs, et les travailleurs familiaux non rémunérés ont été identifiés comme groupe spécial.

Enfin, la question relative au trajet domicile-travail a été élargie en 1991 par l'inclusion d'une question sur le temps nécessaire pour effectuer le trajet aller simple «de porte à porte».

9. Publication des résultats du recensement:

Le titre de la publication qui contient les chiffres définitifs du recensement est: «Recensement 1991 de la population et des logements», 1992.

L'organisme responsable de cette publication est le Bureau des statistiques, Sokolovská 142, 18613 Prague 8 Karlin.

Les chiffres définitifs du recensement de 1991 sont également disponibles sous forme de disquettes et de bandes magnétiques.

THAILANDE

1. Nom et adresse de l'organisme responsable du recensement:

National Statistical Office, Larn Luang Road, Bangkok 10100.

2. Recensements de population effectués depuis 1945 (années):

1950, 1960, 1970, 1980 et 1990. La présente description se réfère au recensement de 1990 (qui a eu lieu le 1er avril)

3. Champ du recensement:

a) Territoire couvert: Ensemble du pays.

b) Personnes couvertes: Ensemble de la population à l'exception des tribus nomades, du personnel militaire et diplomatique étranger basé en Thaïlande et des membres de leur famille, des civils étrangers résidant en Thaïlande temporairement depuis moins de trois mois à la date du recensement et des immigrés vivant dans des camps mis à disposition par le gouvernement.

4. Période de référence:

On a demandé à un échantillon de 20 pour cent de la population la profession exercée la semaine précédant le recensement (à savoir du 25 au 31 mars) alors que le statut d'activité de l'année précédente (à savoir du 1er avril 1989 au 31 mars 1990) a concerné l'ensemble de la population.

5. Principaux sujets:

a) Population totale, selon le sexe et l'âge:	oui
Population active par:	
b) Sexe et âge:	oui
c) Branche d'activité économique (industrie):	oui
d) Profession:	oui
e) Situation dans la profession:	oui
f) Niveau d'instruction le plus élevé:	oui
g) Durée du travail:	non
h) Autres caractéristiques:	non

Réf. a): L'âge est défini à la fois en termes d'année de naissance et en termes d'années révolues à la date du dernier anniversaire.

6. Concepts et définitions:

a) Population active: Elle comprend toutes les personnes âgées de 13 ans et plus qui, pendant la semaine de référence, étaient soit pourvues d'un emploi, soit au chômage, conformément aux définitions données ci-dessous. La définition inclut l'ensemble des forces armées.

b) Emploi: Sont considérées comme «pourvues d'un emploi» toutes les personnes qui, un jour quelconque des périodes de référence, ont effectué un travail ayant une valeur économique, soit à domicile, soit à l'extérieur. Les questions utilisées pour déterminer si une personne doit être considérée comme pourvue d'un emploi étaient les suivantes: «Quel emploi a occupé l'essentiel de votre temps l'année dernière (du 1er avril 1989 au 31 mars 1990)?» et pour les personnes de l'échantillon: «Quel emploi a occupé l'essentiel de votre temps au cours de la semaine allant du 25 au 31 mars 1990?».

Il est indiqué que sont inclus dans cette définition:

i) les personnes travaillant sans rémunération dans une entreprise ou une affaire familiale;

ii) les personnes occupées, temporairement absentes de leur travail;

iii) les étudiants travaillant à temps partiel;

iv) les travailleurs saisonniers ou occasionnels;

v) les conscrits (service militaire ou civil).

Aucune des catégories ci-dessus ne peut être identifiée séparément.

c) Chômage: Sont considérées comme «chômeurs» les personnes sans travail qui étaient à la recherche d'un emploi n'importe quel jour de la semaine de référence. Les personnes de l'échantillon qui, à la seconde question citée au paragraphe 6 (b) ci-dessus, ont répondu: «Je n'ai pas travaillé», ont été considérées comme chômeurs. La définition inclut également les travailleurs saisonniers dans l'agriculture mais elle exclut les étudiants en quête d'emploi.

7. Classifications utilisées:

Aussi bien les personnes pourvues d'un emploi que les chômeurs ayant précédemment travaillé sont classifiés par branche d'activité économique et par profession. Mais seules les personnes pourvues d'un emploi sont classées d'après la situation dans la profession.

a) Branche d'activité économique (industrie): Basée sur la question: «L'année dernière, dans quel type d'industrie, d'activité ou de services étiez-vous engagé la plupart du temps? (décrivez les caractéristiques des biens ou du service; exemple: agriculture, usine d'eau gazeuse, école publique»). Pour coder la branche d'activité économique, on a utilisé 13 grands groupes de la classification nationale des industries. Des liens ont été établis avec la CITI-rév.2 au niveau des branches (1 chiffre).

b) Profession: Basée sur la question: «L'année dernière, quel type de travail effectuiez-vous la plupart du temps? (citez explicitement le travail effectué; exemple: riziculture, culture potagère, statistiques, comptabilité)». Pour coder la profession, on a utilisé la CITP-68 au niveau des sous-groupes (2 chiffres).

c) Situation dans la profession: Basée sur la question: «Quelle est votre situation dans la profession?». Pour coder cette variable, on a utilisé six groupes, à savoir: employeur; travailleur indépendant; fonctionnaire; salarié du secteur public; salarié du secteur privé; travailleur familial non rémunéré.

8. Principales différences par rapport au recensement précédent:
Lors du recensement de 1980, la limite d'âge minimale fixée pour l'inclusion dans la population active était de 11 ans.

9. Publication des résultats du recensement:
Le titre de la publication de 1993 contenant les résultats définitifs du recensement est «1990 Population and Housing Census».

L'organisme responsable de la publication des données du recensement est le Bureau national des statistiques, Social Statistics Division, Bangkok 10100.

Les résultats du recensement sont également disponibles sous forme de bandes magnétiques.

TRINITE-ET-TOBAGO

1. Nom et adresse de l'organisme responsable du recensement:
Central Statistical Office, P.O. Box 98, Port-of-Spain, Trinidad.

2. Recensements de population effectués depuis 1945 (années):
1946, 1960, 1970, 1980 et 1990. La présente description se réfère au recensement de 1990 (qui a eu lieu le 15 mai).

3. Champ du recensement:
a) Territoire couvert: Ensemble du pays.

b) Personnes couvertes: Ensemble de la population.

4. Période de référence:
La semaine et les 12 mois précédant la date du recensement pour le statut de l'activité principale.

5. Principaux sujets:
a) Population totale, selon le sexe et l'âge: oui
Population active par:
b) Sexe et âge: oui
c) Branche d'activité économique (industrie):   oui
d) Profession: oui
e) Situation dans la profession: oui
f) Niveau d'instruction le plus élevé: oui
g) Durée du travail: oui
h) Autres caractéristiques: oui

Réf. a): L'âge est défini en termes d'année de naissance.

Réf. g): La durée du travail se réfère à la durée normale du travail des personnes pourvues d'un emploi.

Réf. h): Le recensement a également rassemblé des informations sur d'autres sujets tels que la durée du travail la semaine précédente (y compris les heures supplémentaires), l'adresse du lieu de travail, le revenu brut perçu au cours de la dernière période de travail (semaine, quinzaine, mois, trimestre, autre).

6. Concepts et définitions:
a) Population active: Elle comprend toutes les personnes âgées de 15 ans et plus qui, pendant les périodes de référence, étaient soit pourvues d'un emploi, soit au chômage, conformément aux définitions données ci-dessous. La définition inclut également l'ensemble des forces armées.

b) Emploi: La question utilisée pour déterminer si une personne doit être considérée comme pourvue d'un emploi est: «Qu'avez-vous fait la semaine dernière? j'étais: a) détenteur d'un emploi et au travail; b) détenteur d'un emploi mais absent du travail; c) à la recherche de mon premier emploi; d) à la recherche d'un emploi; e) désireux de travailler et disponible les trois derniers mois; f) étudiant; g) occupé par les tâches ménagères; h) retraité; i) handicapé; j) personne âgée; k) je ne souhaitais pas travailler; l) autre; m) non précisé.» Les personnes qui se sont rangées dans les catégories a) ou b) ont été considérées comme «pourvues d'un emploi».

Il est indiqué que sont inclus dans cette définition:

i) les personnes travaillant sans rémunération dans une entreprise ou une affaire familiale;
ii) les personnes occupées, temporairement absentes de leur travail;
iii) les étudiants travaillant à temps partiel;
iv) les travailleurs saisonniers ou occasionnels;
v) les conscrits (service militaire ou civil);

vi) les apprentis et les stagiaires.

Seules les personnes appartenant aux catégories i), ii), v) et vi) peuvent être identifiées séparément par des questions spécifiques.

c) Chômage: Sont considérées comme «chômeurs» toutes les personnes qui, pendant la semaine de référence, étaient sans emploi et à la recherche d'un travail. La question utilisée pour déterminer si une personne doit être considérée comme étant au chômage est la même que celle indiquée sous 6 b), mais les réponses possibles étaient soit: c) à la recherche d'un premier emploi; soit d) à la recherche d'un emploi; et dans les deux cas: e) j'étais désireux de travailler et disponible les trois derniers mois. Les étudiants en quête d'emploi sont exclus de la définition.

7. Classifications utilisées:
Aussi bien les personnes pourvues d'un emploi que les chômeurs ayant précédemment travaillé sont classifiés par industrie, par profession et d'après la situation dans la profession.

a) Branche d'activité économique (industrie): Basée sur les questions: «Quel est le nom du ministère ou de l'établissement où X a travaillé ou avait un emploi? ex: ministère de la santé (Hôpital Ste Anne), agence de publicité Pete» et «Quel type d'activité y est exercé? ex: hôpital psychiatrique, conception ou publicité médiatique». Les enquêteurs devaient classifier les personnes à la recherche d'un premier emploi d'après la branche d'activité économique de la dernière demande d'emploi et les chômeurs ayant précédemment travaillé d'après la branche d'activité économique du dernier emploi occupé. Pour coder l'industrie, on a utilisé 9 grands groupes de la classification nationale des industries. Des liens ont été établis avec la CITI-rév.2 au niveau des branches (1 chiffre).

b) Profession: Basée sur les questions: «Quel type de travail effectuait X au cours de la semaine écoulée (emploi occupé)? ex: professeur du secondaire, comptable, mécanicien automobile» et «Quel était le titre de X (ex: enseignant échelon II, comptable échelon I, mécanicien automobile grade A)?». Les enquêteurs devaient classifier les personnes en quête d'un premier emploi d'après le type de travail pour lequel elles avaient postulé en dernier lieu, et les chômeurs ayant précédemment travaillé, d'après le dernier emploi occupé. Pour coder la profession, on a utilisé la CITP-88 au niveau des sous-groupes (3 chiffres).

c) Situation dans la profession: Basée sur la question: «Quel est le statut professionnel de X?». Pour coder la situation dans la profession, on a utilisé les neuf groupes suivants: gouvernement, service public; gouvernement, entreprise publique; secteur autre que le secteur public; travailleur non rémunéré; apprenti; travailleur indépendant sans salariés; travailleur indépendant avec salariés; n'a jamais travaillé; non précisé.

8. Principales différences par rapport au recensement précédent:
Pas de différence majeure.

9. Publication des résultats du recensement:
Le titre de la publication (parue en 1993) contenant les résultats du recensement est: «Population and Housing Census 1990», Volume III, Part 2: Economic activity.

L'organisme responsable de cette publication est le Bureau central des statistiques, Port of Spain, Trinidad.

Les résultats du recensement sont également disponibles sous d'autres formes comme des tableaux non publiés, des disquettes et des bandes magnétiques.

TURQUIE

1. Nom et adresse de l'organisme responsable du recensement:
State Institute of Statistics, Prime Ministry, Necatibey Caddesi No. 114, 06100 Ankara.

2. Recensements de population effectués depuis 1945 (années):
1945, 1950, 1955, 1960, 1965, 1970, 1975, 1980, 1985 et 1990. La présente description se réfère au recensement de 1990 (qui a eu lieu le 21 octobre).

3. Champ du recensement:

a) *Territoire couvert:* Ensemble du pays.

b) *Personnes couvertes:* Ensemble de la population à l'exception des nationaux résidant à l'étranger.

4. Période de référence:
La semaine précédant le jour du recensement.

5. Principaux sujets:

a) Population totale, selon le sexe et l'âge:	oui
Population active par:	
b) Sexe et âge:	oui
c) Branche d'activité économique (industrie):	oui
d) Profession:	oui
e) Situation dans la profession:	oui
f) Niveau d'instruction le plus élevé:	oui
g) Durée du travail:	non
h) Autres caractéristiques:	non

Réf. a): L'âge est défini en termes d'années révolues à la date du dernier anniversaire.

6. Concepts et définitions:

a) *Population active:* Elle comprend toutes les personnes âgées de 12 ans et plus qui, pendant la semaine de référence, étaient soit pourvues d'un emploi, soit au chômage, conformément aux définitions données ci-dessous. Les étudiants travaillant à temps partiel et les étudiants en quête d'un emploi sont exclus de la définition alors que les membres des forces armées en font partie.

b) *Emploi:* Sont considérées comme «pourvues d'un emploi» toutes les personnes ayant répondu positivement à la question: «Avez-vous effectué, la semaine dernière, un travail moyennant une rémunération ou un paiement en nature?; en cas de réponse négative: exercez-vous encore un métier?».

Il est indiqué que sont inclus dans cette définition:

i) les personnes travaillant sans rémunération dans une entreprise ou une affaire familiale;

ii) les personnes engagées dans la production de produits de base destinés à l'autoconsommation;

iii) les travailleurs saisonniers ou occasionnels;

iv) les conscrits (service militaire ou civil);

v) les apprentis et les stagiaires.

Aucune des catégories ci-dessus ne peut être identifiée séparément.

c) *Chômage:* Sont considérées comme «chômeurs» toutes les personnes qui, pendant la semaine de référence, étaient sans travail et ont répondu positivement à la question: «Etes-vous à la recherche d'un emploi?».

7. Classifications utilisées:
Seules les personnes pourvues d'un emploi ont été classifiées par branche d'activité économique et d'après la situation dans la profession. Aussi bien les personnes pourvues d'un emploi que les chômeurs ayant précédemment travaillé sont classifiés par profession.

a) *Branche d'activité économique (industrie):* Basée sur les questions: «Dans quel type d'endroit avez-vous travaillé la semaine dernière ou travaillez-vous encore actuellement? ex: champs, ministère de la justice, épicerie, coiffeur, etc.» et «Quel est le type d'activité exercée dans l'établissement où vous avez travaillé? ex: services publics, vente au détail, fabrique de réfrigérateurs, réparation de téléviseurs, etc...». Pour coder l'industrie, on a utilisé 10 groupes de la classification nationale. Des liens ont été établis avec la CITI-rév.2 au niveau des branches (1 chiffre).

b) *Profession:* Basée sur les questions suivantes: pour les personnes pourvues d'un emploi, «Type d'activité poursuivie la semaine passée ou de travail exercé encore actuellement: cultivateur, directeur de banque, dactylo, ouvrier de la construction, etc.»; et à la fois pour les personnes pourvues d'un emploi et les chômeurs ayant précédemment travaillé, «Quelle est votre activité principale?» (ex: charpentier, avocat, maçon, infirmière, etc.). Pour coder la profession, on a utilisé 7 groupes de la classification nationale. Des liens ont été établis avec la CITP-68 au niveau des grands groupes (1 chiffre).

c) *Situation dans la profession:* Basée sur la question: «Quelle était votre situation dans la profession exercée au cours de la semaine passée ou poursuivie encore actuellement?». Pour coder cette variable, on a utilisé quatre groupes, à savoir: salarié, employeur, travailleur indépendant et travailleur familial non rémunéré.

8. Principales différences par rapport au recensement précédent:
Lors du recensement de 1990, on n'avait pas identifié la branche d'activité économique (industrie) des chômeurs ayant précédemment travaillé.

9. Publication des résultats du recensement:
Les résultats définitifs ont été publiés fin 1993 dans une publication intitulée «1990 Census of Population-Social and Economic Characteristics of Population».

L'organisme responsable de cette publication est l'Institut national des statistiques, Bureau du premier ministre, Ankara.

Les données de la publication sont également disponibles sous forme de disquettes.

VANUATU

1. Nom et adresse de l'organisme responsable du recensement:
Statistics Office (NPSO), Private Mail Bag 19, Port-Vila.

2. Recensements de population effectués depuis 1945 (années):
1967, 1979 et 1989. Des recensements en zones urbaines ont aussi eu lieu en 1972 et 1986. La présente description se réfère au recensement de 1989 (qui a eu lieu le 16 mai).

3. Champ du recensement:

a) *Territoire couvert:* Ensemble du pays.

b) *Personnes couvertes:* Ensemble de la population, à l'exception des nationaux résidant à l'étranger au moment du recensement.

4. Période de référence:
La semaine précédant le jour du recensement.

5. Principaux sujets:

a) Population totale, selon le sexe et l'âge:	oui
Population active par:	
b) Sexe et âge:	oui
c) Branche d'activité économique (industrie):	oui
d) Profession:	oui
e) Situation dans la profession:	oui
f) Niveau d'instruction le plus élevé:	oui
g) Durée du travail:	non
h) Autres caractéristiques:	non

Réf. a): L'âge est défini en termes d'année de naissance.

6. Concepts et définitions:

a) *Population active:* Elle comprend toutes les personnes âgées de 10 ans et plus qui, à la date du recensement étaient, soit pourvues d'un emploi, soit au chômage, conformément aux définitions données ci-dessous. Les données effectivement publiées se réfèrent aux personnes âgées de 15 ans et plus car le groupe d'âge 10-14 ans contenait trop d'étudiants.

b) *Emploi:* Sont considérées comme «pourvues d'un emploi» toutes les personnes qui avaient travaillé au moins une heure au cours de la semaine précédente. Les étudiants qui travaillent à temps partiel sont exclus de la définition.

Il est indiqué que sont inclus dans cette définition:

i) les personnes travaillant sans rémunération dans une entreprise ou une affaire familiale;

ii) les personnes occupées, temporairement absentes de leur travail;

iii) les détenteurs de plusieurs emplois;

iv) les apprentis et les stagiaires.

Les personnes appartenant aux catégories i), ii) et iii) peuvent être identifiées séparément.

c) *Chômage:* Sont considérées comme «chômeurs» toutes les personnes sans travail mais activement lancées dans la recherche d'un emploi au cours de la semaine de référence. La question utilisée était: «Etiez-vous activement à la recherche d'un emploi au cours des sept derniers jours?».

7. Classifications utilisées:
Aussi bien les personnes pourvues d'un emploi que les chômeurs ayant précédemment travaillé sont classifiés par branche d'activité économique et par profession. Mais seules les personnes pourvues d'un emploi sont classées d'après la situation dans la profession.

a) Branche d'activité économique (industrie): Basée sur la question: «Dans quel type d'industrie travaille cette personne?». Pour coder la branche d'activité économique, on a utilisé la CITI-rév.2 au niveau d'1 chiffre, mais les codes ont été étendus jusqu'au niveau de 2 chiffres afin de répondre aux besoins locaux.

b) Profession: Basée sur la question: «Quel type de travail faisait cette personne?». Pour coder la profession, on a utilisé la CITP-68 au niveau des groupes de base (3 chiffres).

c) Situation dans la profession: Basée sur les questions: «Quel était le statut professionnel de cette personne?» et «Pour qui travaillait cette personne?». Pour coder la situation dans la profession, on a utilisé les quatre groupes suivants: travailleur indépendant; travailleur familial non rémunéré; salarié du secteur privé; salarié du secteur public.

8. Principales différences par rapport au recensement précédent:

Contrairement à celui de 1989, le recensement de 1979 demandait aux personnes interrogées de décrire leur activité au cours de l'année précédente.

9. Publication des résultats du recensement:

La publication de juillet 1991 contenant les résultats définitifs du recensement s'intitule: «Vanuatu National Population Census - May 1989 - Main Report».

L'organisme responsable de cette publication est le Bureau des statistiques, Private Mail Bag 19, Port Vila.

VENEZUELA

1. Nom et adresse de l'organisme responsable du recensement:

Oficina Central de Estadísticas e Informática, Presidencia de la República, Caracas, Venezuela.

2. Recensements de population effectués depuis 1945 (années):

1950, 1961, 1971, 1981 et 1990. La présente description se réfère au recensement de population de 1990 (qui a eu lieu le 21 octobre).

3. Champ du recensement:

a) Territoire couvert: Ensemble du pays.

b) Personnes couvertes: Ensemble de la population résidant habituellement dans le pays. Sont exclus cependant les Vénézuéliens résidant à l'étranger de manière permanente, les étrangers de passage dans le pays pour des vacances, pour des raisons commerciales ou pour un autre motif et qui ne restent pas plus de quatre mois au Vénézuela, ainsi que la population indigène vivant dans les forêts, qui fera l'objet d'une enquête en 1992.

4. Période de référence:

Le jour du recensement.

5. Principaux sujets:

a) Population totale, selon le sexe et l'âge:	oui
Population active par:	
b) Sexe et âge:	oui
c) Branche d'activité économique (industrie):	oui
d) Profession:	oui
e) Situation dans la profession:	oui
f) Niveau d'instruction le plus élevé:	oui
g) Durée du travail:	non
h) Autres caractéristiques:	oui

Réf. a): L'âge est défini en termes d'année de naissance et également en termes d'années révolues à la date du dernier anniversaire.

Réf. h): Des questions ont été posées sur la durée du chômage, le nombre de personnes travaillant dans l'entreprise, le revenu tiré de l'activité professionnelle, les autres types de revenus et l'activité dans le secteur non structuré.

6. Concepts et définitions:

a) Population active: Elle comprend toutes les personnes âgées de 12 ans et plus qui, le jour du recensement, étaient soit pourvues d'un emploi soit au chômage, conformément aux définitions données ci-dessous. La définition inclut toutes les personnes faisant leur service militaire.

b) Emploi: Sont considérées comme «pourvues d'un emploi» les personnes ayant répondu par l'affirmative à l'une des questions suivantes: «A travaillé?» ou «N'a pas travaillé mais est pourvu d'un emploi?».

Il est indiqué que sont inclus dans cette définition:

i)   les personnes travaillant sans rémunération dans une entreprise ou une affaire familiale;
ii) les personnes occupées, temporairement absentes de leur travail;
iii) les étudiants travaillant à temps partiel;
iv) les travailleurs saisonniers ou occasionnels;
v)   les conscrits (service militaire ou civil).

Seules les personnes appartenant aux catégories i) et ii) peuvent être identifiées séparément au moyen des questions suivantes, respectivement: i) «Votre travail consiste-t-il ou consistait-il à aider un membre de votre famille?» et ii) «Dans laquelle de ces situations vous trouvez-vous actuellement: ...; Ne travaille pas mais est pourvu d'un emploi?».

c) Chômage: Sont considérées comme «chômeurs» les personnes n'ayant pas de travail et ayant répondu par l'affirmative à l'une des questions suivantes: «Etes-vous à la recherche d'un emploi après avoir déjà travaillé auparavant?» ou «Etes-vous à la recherche d'un premier emploi?».

7. Classifications utilisées:

Dans les zones rurales, les personnes pourvues d'un emploi et les chômeurs ayant déjà travaillé auparavant, mais dans les zones urbaines, seulement un échantillon de ces personnes, sont classifiées par branche d'activité économique, par profession et d'après la situation dans la profession (l'échantillon utilisé pour les zones urbaines est estimé à 20 pour cent environ).

a) Branche d'activité économique (industrie): Basée sur la question: «De quoi s'occupe l'entreprise, l'organisme ou l'établissement commercial dans lequel vous travaillez (travailliez)? (exemple: transport de passagers, fabrique de meubles, plantation de café, enseignement, etc.)». Pour coder la branche d'activité économique, on a utilisé la CITI-rév.2 au niveau des branches (1 chiffre). Dans les publications, les résultats sont présentés au niveau de 1 chiffre, mais le codage lui-même a été effectué au niveau de 3 chiffres.

b) Profession: Basée sur la question: «Quelle est votre profession dans l'entreprise, l'organisme ou l'établissement commercial dans lequel vous travaillez (travailliez)? (par ex.: chauffeur, apprenti tourneur, agriculteur, institutrice, etc.)». Pour coder la profession, on a utilisé la CITP-68 au niveau des grands groupes (1 chiffre) pour les publications, mais le codage lui-même a été effectué au niveau de 3 chiffres.

c) Situation dans la profession: Basée sur la question: «Dans votre emploi, êtes-vous (étiez-vous): employé ou ouvrier du secteur public; employé ou ouvrier du secteur privé; employé de maison; membre d'une coopérative; employeur ou patron; travailleur indépendant (sans employés ni ouvriers); travailleur familial sans rémunération?». Ce sont ces sept groupes que l'on a utilisé pour coder la situation dans la profession.

8. Principales différences par rapport au recensement précédent:

En 1981, le recensement avait collecté des informations sur les caractéristiques économiques de toutes les personnes âgées de 12 ans ou plus. En 1990, on a cherché à connaître la situation, par rapport au travail et à l'emploi de toutes les personnes âgées de 12 ans ou plus, mais en ce qui concerne les autres caractéristiques économiques, les données n'ont été enregistrées que pour 20 pour cent de la population urbaine et pour l'ensemble de la population rurale.

En 1981, il avait été demandé aux intéressés quelles démarches ils avaient effectuées en vue d'obtenir un emploi. Cela n'a pas été le cas en 1990. On avait également cherché à connaître le nombre d'heures travaillées au cours de la semaine précédant le recensement. Cela n'a pas été fait en 1990.

S'agissant de la durée de l'inactivité, la question a été posée, tant aux hommes qu'aux femmes, aussi bien en 1981 qu'en 1990, mais les intervalles pris en considération n'ont pas été les mêmes (en 1981: jusqu'à 6 mois; plus de 6 mois mais moins de 12 mois; plus d'un an. En 1990: jusqu'à 6 mois; de 4 à 6 mois; de 7 à 12 mois; plus d'un an).

9. Publication des résultats du recensement:

Les résultats définitifs du recensement ont été publiés fin 1992. Les titres exacts des publications sont «El Censo 90 en Venezuela, XII Censo General de Población y Vivienda» et «El Censo 90 en ... (entité fédérale correspondante)».

L'organisme responsable de ces publications est l'Office central des statistiques et de l'informatique.

Les résultats du recensement sont également disponibles sous forme de tableaux non publiés, de cartes magnétiques, de disquettes, de micro-fiches et de vidéotextes. On peut aussi les obtenir sous une forme exploitable par de gros ordinateurs ou des micro-ordinateurs: pour les premiers, c'est le gestionnaire Informix qui est utilisé, et pour les seconds le gestionnaire Redatam.

VIET NAM

1. Nom et adresse de l'organisme responsable du recensement:
Département général de statistiques, Ministère du Travail, des Invalides de guerre et des affaires sociales, 2 - Hoang Van Thu, Hanoi.

2. Recensements de population effectués depuis 1945 (années):
1979, 1989 et 1994. La présente description se réfère au recensement de la population de 1994 (qui a eu lieu le 1er octobre).

3. Champ du recensement:
a) Territoire couvert: Ensemble des zones urbaines.

b) Personnes couvertes: Ensemble de la population.

4. Période de référence:
La semaine précédant le jour du recensement.

5. Principaux sujets:
a) Population totale, selon le sexe et l'âge:	oui
Population active par:	
b) Sexe et âge:	oui
c) Branche d'activité économique (industrie):	oui
d) Profession:	oui
e) Situation dans la profession:	oui
f) Niveau d'instruction le plus élevé:	...
g) Durée du travail:	oui
h) Autres caractéristiques:	non

Réf. a): L'âge est défini en termes d'année de naissance.

Réf. g): On a demandé aux personnes pourvues d'un emploi de préciser à la fois le nombre d'heures et le nombre de jours effectivement travaillés au cours de la semaine de référence.

6. Concepts et définitions:
a) Population active: Elle comprend toutes les personnes âgées de 15 à 55 ans pour les femmes, et de 15 à 60 ans pour les hommes, qui, pendant la période de référence, étaient soit pourvues d'un emploi, soit au chômage, conformément aux définitions données ci-dessous. Les questions relatives à l'activité économique n'ont été posées qu'à un échantillon de 2,5% de la population urbaine. Les membres des forces armées sont exclus de la définition.

b) Emploi: L'emploi est déterminé sur la base de la question suivante: «Au cours des sept derniers jours, aviez-vous un travail salarié ou non-salarié? Si oui, était-il semblable à celui du mois précédent?».

Il est indiqué que sont inclus dans cette définition:

i)   les personnes travaillant sans rémunération dans une entreprise ou une affaire familiale;
ii) les personnes engagées dans la production de produits de base destinés à l'autoconsommation;
iii) les personnes occupées, temporairement absentes du travail;
iv) les étudiants travaillant à temps partiel;
v)   les travailleurs saisonniers ou occasionnels;
vi) les apprentis et les stagiaires.

Aucune des catégories ci-dessus ne peut être identifiée séparément.

c) Chômage: Sont considérées comme «chômeurs» toutes les personnes qui se sont déclarées sans emploi au cours de la semaine de référence et qui ont répondu oui aux questions suivantes: «Auparavant, est-ce que vous aviez un travail? Est-il possible d'exercer ce travail pour le moment?» et «Avez-vous besoin de travailler?».

7. Classifications utilisées:
Aussi bien les personnes pourvues d'un emploi que les chômeurs ont été classifiés par industrie, par profession et d'après la situation dans la profession.

a) Branche d'activité économique (industrie): Basée sur la question: «Nom de votre agence/organisme? Nom de l'organisme de tutelle? Lieu de travail?». Pour coder la branche d'industrie, on a utilisé 20 groupes de la classification nationale. Il n'a pas été établi de liens avec la CITI.

b) Profession: Basée sur la question: «Quel a été votre travail principal au cours des sept derniers jours? Nom du travail, code». Pour coder la profession, on a utilisé 33 groupes de la classification nationale. Des liens ont été établis avec la CITP-68 au niveau des grands groupes (1 chiffre).

c) Situation dans la profession: Basée sur la question: «Avez-vous un travail salarié ou non salarié?». Pour coder cette variable, on a utilisé les deux groupes suivants: salarié, non salarié.

8. Principales différences par rapport au recensement précédent:
Pas de différence majeure.

9. Publication des résultats du recensement:
Information non disponible.

YEMEN

1. Nom et adresse de l'organisme responsable du recensement:
Central Statistical Organization, Ministry of Planning and Development, P.O. Box 13434, Sana'a.

2. Recensements de population effectués depuis 1945 (années):
Deux recensements ont été effectués dans chacun des deux pays avant leur unification, et un depuis l'unification.

1973 et 1988 dans les gouvernorats du sud et de l'est, c'est-à-dire dans l'ancienne République démocratique populaire du Yémen (RDPY).

1975 et 1986 dans les gouvernorats du nord et de l'ouest, c'est-à-dire dans l'ancienne République arabe du Yémen (RAY).

La présente description se réfère au recensement de population de 1994 (qui a eu lieu le 16 décembre), c'est-à-dire au premier recensement effectué pour le pays réunifié, la République du Yémen.

3. Champ du recensement:
a) Territoire couvert: Ensemble du pays.

b) Personnes couvertes: Ensemble de la population.

4. Période de référence:
La semaine précédant le jour du recensement.

5. Principaux sujets:
a) Population totale, selon le sexe et l'âge:	oui
Population active par:	
b) Sexe et âge:	oui
c) Branche d'activité économique (industrie):	oui
d) Profession:	oui
e) Situation dans la profession:	oui
f) Niveau d'instruction le plus élevé:	oui
g) Durée du travail:	non
h) Autres caractéristiques:	non

Réf. a): L'âge est défini en termes d'années révolues à la date du dernier anniversaire.

6. Concepts et définitions:
a) Population active: Elle comprend toutes les personnes âgées de 10 ans et plus qui, au cours de la semaine de référence, étaient soit pourvues d'un emploi soit au chômage, conformément aux définitions données ci-dessous. Les forces armées sont incluses dans la définition.

b) Emploi: L'emploi est déterminé sur la base de la question suivante: «Quel a été votre statut par rapport au marché du travail au cours de la semaine précédente?». Les réponses possibles étaient: pourvu(e) d'un emploi; ménagère et pourvue d'un emploi; étudiant et pourvu d'un emploi; au chômage mais ayant travaillé précédemment; au chômage mais n'ayant jamais travaillé; ménagère; étudiant; rentier; handicapé. Lorsqu'une personne déclarait qu'elle avait travaillé pendant deux jours ou plus, elle était comptée comme pourvue d'un emploi.

Il est indiqué que sont inclus dans cette définition:

i)   les personnes travaillant sans rémunération dans une entreprise ou une affaire familiale;

ii) les personnes engagées dans la production de produits de base destinés à l'autoconsommation;

iii) les personnes occupées, temporairement absentes du travail;

iv) les étudiants travaillant à temps partiel;

v) les travailleurs saisonniers ou occasionnels, pour autant qu'ils aient été occupés pendant la période de référence;

vi) les conscrits (service militaire ou civil);

vii) les détenteurs de plusieurs emplois;

viii) les apprentis et les stagiaires.

Les personnes appartenant aux catégories i),iv),vii) et viii) peuvent être identifiées séparément.

c) Chômage: Sont considérées comme «chômeurs» toutes les personnes qui ont travaillé moins de deux jours pendant la semaine de référence. La définition inclut à la fois les personnes en quête d'un premier emploi et les chômeurs ayant déjà travaillé précédemment, mais elle exclut les étudiants à la recherche d'un emploi.

7. Classifications utilisées:
Aussi bien les personnes pourvues d'un emploi que les chômeurs ayant précédemment travaillé sont classifiés par branche d'activité économique, par profession et d'après la situation dans la profession.

a) Branche d'activité économique (industrie): Basée sur les questions: «Quelle est votre principal emploi actuel?» et «Où travaillez-vous?». Pour coder cette variable, on a utilisé la CITI-Rév.3.

b) Profession: Basée sur la question: «Quelle est exactement votre profession?». Pour coder la profession, on a utilisé la CITP-88 au niveau des groupes de base (4 chiffres).

c) Situation dans la profession: Basée sur la question: «Quelle est votre situation dans la profession?». Pour coder cette variable, cinq groupes ont été utilisés, à savoir: salarié; travailleur indépendant; employeur; travailleur non rémunéré employé dans une entreprise ou une affaire familiale; et travailleur non rémunéré employé par d'autres tiers.

8. Principales différences par rapport au recensement précédent:
Pas de différence majeure.

9. Publication des résultats du recensement:
Les chiffres définitifs du recensement devaient paraître en 1996 dans une publication intitulée «Résultats du recensement de 1994 sur la population, le logement et les entreprises, Rapports No. 1 - 3».

L'organisme responsable de cette publication est l'Organisation centrale des statistiques, BP 13434, Sana'a.

Les résultats définitifs seront également disponibles sous forme de tableaux non publiés (imprimés sur demande). A titre exceptionnel et sur demande, ils pourront en outre être obtenus sur supports magnétiques.

ZAMBIE

1. Nom et adresse de l'organisme responsable du recensement:
Central Statistics Office, P.O. Box 31908, Lusaka.

2. Recensements de population effectués depuis 1945 (années):
1946, 1951, 1956, 1961, 1963, 1969, 1980 et 1990. La présente description se réfère au recensement de 1990 (qui a eu lieu le 20 août).

3. Champ du recensement:
a) Territoire couvert: Ensemble du pays.

b) Personnes couvertes: Ensemble de la population, à l'exception des nationaux résidant à l'étranger et des étrangers membres du corps diplomatique.

4. Période de référence:
La semaine et les 12 mois précédant le jour du recensement.

5. Principaux sujets:
a) Population totale, selon le sexe et l'âge:	oui
Population active par:	
b) Sexe et âge:	oui
c) Branche d'activité économique (industrie):	oui
d) Profession:	oui
e) Situation dans la profession:	oui

f) Niveau d'instruction le plus élevé:	oui
g) Durée du travail:	oui
h) Autres caractéristiques:	non

Réf. a): L'âge est défini en termes d'années révolues à la date du dernier anniversaire.

Réf. g): Seuls les détenteurs de plusieurs emplois ont été invités à indiquer leur période de travail totale au cours des 12 derniers mois (exprimée en nombre de mois).

6. Concepts et définitions:

a) Population active: Elle comprend toutes les personnes âgées de 12 ans et plus qui, au cours des périodes de référence, étaient soit pourvues d'un emploi soit au chômage, conformément aux définitions données ci-dessous. Les membres des forces armées sont inclus dans la définition.

b) Emploi: L'emploi est déterminé sur la base des questions suivantes: «Quelle a été la principale activité de X au cours des sept derniers jours?» (les réponses possibles étaient: activité professionnelle salariée ou indépendante; en congé; activité professionnelle non rémunérée ou travaux ménagers), et «Quelle a été l'activité principale de X depuis ... 1989?» (les réponses possibles étaient les mêmes que pour la première question).

Il est indiqué que sont inclus dans cette définition:

i) les personnes travaillant sans rémunération dans une entreprise ou une affaire familiale;

ii) les personnes engagées dans la production de produits de base destinés à l'autoconsommation;

iii) les personnes occupées, temporairement absentes du travail;

iv) les étudiants travaillant à temps partiel;

v) les travailleurs saisonniers ou occasionnels;

vi) les conscrits (service militaire ou civil);

vii) les détenteurs de plusieurs emplois.

Seules les personnes appartenant aux catégories i), ii) et iii peuvent être identifiées séparément au moyen de questions spécifiques et en fonction de leur situation dans la profession.

c) Chômage: Sont considérées comme «chômeurs» toutes les personnes qui, au cours des périodes de référence, étaient sans travail et à la recherche d'un emploi, ou ne cherchaient pas de travail mais désiraient travailler. Pour déterminer si une personne devait ou non être comptée comme chômeur, on a utilisé les mêmes questions que celles mentionnées au paragraphe 6 b) ci-dessus. Pour les chômeurs, les réponses spécifiques possibles étaient les suivantes: «Chômeur et à la recherche d'un emploi» et «Ne cherche pas d'emploi mais désireux de travailler». Les personnes qui répondaient «Homme ou femme au foyer», «Etudiant à temps complet» ou «Ne souhaite pas travailler pour d'autres raisons» étaient classées comme inactives.

7. Classifications utilisées:
Seules les personnes pourvues d'un emploi sont classifiées par branche d'activité économique, par profession et d'après la situation dans la profession.

a) Branche d'activité économique (industrie): Basée sur la question: «Quel type (principal) de produit ou de service est (était) produit là ou travaille (travaillait) X?». Pour coder la branche d'activité économique, on a utilisé la CITI-Rév.2 au niveau des branches (1 chiffre).

b) Profession: Basée sur la question: «Quel a été la principale profession de X depuis 1989?». Pour coder cette variable, on a utilisé 91 groupes de la classification nationale des professions. Des liens avec la CITP-68 ont été établis au niveau des grands groupes (1 chiffre).

c) Situation dans la profession: Basée sur la question: «Depuis 1989, X a-t-il été essentiellement: employeur; salarié; travailleur indépendant; travailleur sans rémunération dans une entreprise ou une affaire familiale?». Ce sont ces quatre catégories qui ont été utilisées pour coder la situation dans la profession.

8. Principales différences par rapport au recensement précédent:
En 1980, les questions relatives à l'activité économique des personnes interrogées n'avaient été posées qu'à un échantillon de population. Pour le recensement de 1990, elles ont été posées à toutes les personnes âgées de 12 ans et plus.

9. Publication des résultats du recensement:
Le titre de la publication, parue en août 1994, dans laquelle sont présentés les chiffres définitifs du recensement est: «Tableaux économiques et sociaux».

L'organisme responsable de cette publication est l'Office central des statistiques, BP 31908, Lusaka.

Les résultats du recensement sont également disponibles sous forme de tableaux non publiés et de disquettes.

ZIMBABWE

1. Nom et adresse de l'organisme responsable du recensement:
Central Statistical Office, Box CY342, Causeway.

2. Recensements de population effectués depuis 1945 (années):
1947, 1952, 1957, 1962, 1969, 1982 et 1992. La présente description se réfère au recensement de la population de 1992 (qui a eu lieu le 17 août).

3. Champ du recensement:
a) Territoire couvert: Ensemble du pays.

b) Personnes couvertes: Ensemble de la population présente au Zimbabwe le soir du recensement (population de facto), à l'exclusion des nationaux résidant à l'étranger.

4. Période de référence:
Les 12 mois précédant le jour du recensement.

5. Principaux sujets:
a) Population totale, selon le sexe et l'âge: oui
Population active par:
b) Sexe et âge: oui
c) Branche d'activité économique (industrie):   non
d) Profession: oui
e) Situation dans la profession: oui
f) Niveau d'instruction le plus élevé: oui
g) Durée du travail: non
h) Autres caractéristiques: non
Réf. a): L'âge est défini en termes d'années révolues à la date du dernier anniversaire.

6. Concepts et définitions:
a) Population active: Elle comprend toutes les personnes âgées de 10 ans et plus qui, pendant la période de référence, étaient soit pourvues d'un emploi soit au chômage, conformément aux définitions données ci-dessous. Toutefois, les résultats du recensement sont publiés avec un minimum de détails en ce qui concerne le groupe des 10-14 ans. La définition inclut l'ensemble des forces armées mais exclut les étudiants qui travaillent à temps partiel et les étudiants à la recherche d'un emploi.

b) Emploi: Sa détermination est basée sur la question suivante: «Quelle a été votre principale activité au cours des 12 derniers mois? salarié; employeur; travailleur indépendant; travailleur familial non rémunéré; demandeur d'emploi/chômeur; étudiant; ménagère; retraité/malade/trop âgé; autre».
Il est indiqué que sont inclus dans cette définition:
i) les personnes travaillant sans rémunération dans une entreprise ou une affaire familiale;
ii) les personnes engagées dans la production de produits de base destinés à l'autoconsommation;
iii) les personnes occupées, temporairement absentes du travail;
iv) les travailleurs saisonniers ou occasionnels;
v) les conscrits (service militaire et civil).
Seules les personnes appartenant aux catégories i) et ii) peuvent être identifiées séparément.

c) Chômage: Sont considérées comme «chômeurs» toutes les personnes qui, pendant la période de référence, étaient sans travail, recherchaient un emploi ou désiraient travailler.

7. Classifications utilisées:
Seules les personnes pourvues d'un emploi sont classifiées par profession, alors que toutes les personnes de 10 ans et plus sont classifiées d'après la situation dans la profession.

a) Branche d'activité économique (industrie): Aucune classification n'a été faite par branche d'activité économique.

b) Profession: Basée sur la question: «Quelle a été votre principale profession au cours des 12 derniers mois?». Pour coder la profession, on a utilisé 109 groupes de la classification nationale. Des liens avec la CITP-88 ont été établis au niveau des sous-groupes (3 chiffres).

c) Situation dans la profession: Basée sur la question: «Quelle a été votre principale activité au cours des 12 derniers mois?». Pour coder la situation dans la profession, quatre groupes ont été utilisés, à savoir: salarié; employeur; travailleur indépendant; et travailleur familial non rémunéré.

8. Principales différences par rapport au recensement précédent:
C'est une période de référence longue (12 mois) qui a été utilisée pour le recensement de 1992, alors qu'une période de référence courte (une semaine) avait été utilisée pour le recensement de 1982.

Dans le recensement de 1992, la question posée aux personnes pourvues d'un emploi afin de déterminer leur groupe de profession et leur situation dans la profession a été différente de celle du recensement de 1982.

9. Publication des résultats du recensement:
Les résultats définitifs ont paru en décembre 1994 dans une publication intitulée «Recensement de 1992: Profil national - Zimbabwe». Les chiffres définitifs concernant les provinces ont également tous été publiés.

L'organisme responsable de la publication de ces résultats est l'Office central des statistiques, BP CY342, Causeway.

Des tableaux non publiés et des données présentées sous d'autres formes sont également disponibles.

ANNEXE

Extrait de la
Résolution concernant les statistiques de la population active, de l'emploi, du chômage et du sous-emploi
Treizième Conférence internationale des statisticiens du travail
(Genève, 18-29 octobre 1982)

Concepts et définitions
La population active
5. La "population active" comprend toutes les personnes des deux sexes qui fournissent, durant une période de référence spécifiée, la main-d'oeuvre disponible pour la production de biens et services, comme définis par les systèmes de comptabilité et bilans nationaux des Nations Unies. Selon ces systèmes, la production de biens et services comprend toute la production et la transformation des produits primaires, que ceux-ci soient destinés au marché, au troc ou à l'autoconsommation, ainsi que la production pour le marché de tous les autres biens et services, et, dans le cas de ménages produisant de tels biens et services pour le marché, la production correspondante qui fait l'objet d'autoconsommation.
6. Deux mesures utiles de la population active sont la "population habituellement active" mesurée en fonction d'une longue période de référence telle que l'année et la "population active du moment", appelée encore "main-d'oeuvre", mesurée par rapport à une courte période de référence telle qu'une semaine ou un jour.

La population habituellement active
7. 1) La "population habituellement active" comprend toutes les personnes ayant dépassé un âge spécifié dont le statut principal vis-à-vis de l'activité, déterminé en termes de nombre de semaines ou de jours au cours d'une longue période spécifiée (telle que les douze mois précédents ou l'année civile précédente), était celui de "personnes pourvues d'un emploi" ou de "chômeurs", comme défini aux paragraphes 9 et 10.
2) Là où ce concept est considéré comme utile et applicable, la population habituellement active peut être subdivisée en personnes pourvues d'un emploi et en chômeurs suivant leur statut principal vis-à-vis de l'activité.

La main-d'oeuvre (la population active du moment)
8. La "main-d'oeuvre" ou "population active du moment" comprend toutes les personnes qui remplissent les conditions requises pour être incluses parmi les personnes pourvues d'un emploi ou les chômeurs, comme défini aux paragraphes 9 et 10 ci-dessous.

Emploi

9. 1) Les "personnes pourvues d'un emploi" comprennent toutes les personnes ayant dépassé un âge spécifié qui se trouvaient, durant une brève période de référence spécifiée telle qu'une semaine ou un jour, dans les catégories suivantes:

a) "emploi salarié":

a1) "personnes au travail": personnes qui, durant la période de référence, ont effectué un travail moyennant un salaire ou un traitement en espèces ou en nature;

a2) "personnes qui ont un emploi mais ne sont pas au travail": personnes qui, ayant déjà travaillé dans leur emploi actuel, en étaient absentes durant la période de référence et avaient un lien formel avec leur emploi. Ce lien formel avec l'emploi devrait être déterminé à la lumière des circonstances nationales, par référence à l'un ou plusieurs des critères suivants:

i) le service ininterrompu du salaire ou du traitement;

ii) une assurance de retour au travail à la fin de la situation d'exception ou un accord sur la date de retour;

iii) la durée de l'absence du travail qui, le cas échéant, peut être la durée pendant laquelle les travailleurs peuvent recevoir une indemnisation sans obligation d'accepter d'autres emplois qui leur seraient éventuellement proposés;

b) "emploi non salarié":

b1) "personnes au travail": personnes qui, durant la période de référence, ont effectué un travail en vue d'un bénéfice ou d'un gain familial, en espèces ou en nature;

b2) "personnes ayant une entreprise mais n'étant pas au travail": personnes qui, durant la période de référence, avaient une entreprise qui peut être une entreprise industrielle, un commerce, une exploitation agricole ou une entreprise de prestations de services, mais n'étaient temporairement pas au travail pour toute raison spécifique.

2) Dans la pratique, on peut interpréter la notion de "travail effectué au cours de la période de référence" comme étant un travail d'une durée d'une heure au moins.

3) Les personnes temporairement absentes de leur travail pour raison de maladie ou d'accident, de congé ou de vacances, de conflit du travail ou de grève, de congé-éducation ou formation, de congé-maternité ou parental, de mauvaise conjoncture économique ou de suspension temporaire du travail due à des causes telles que: conditions météorologiques défavorables, incidents mécaniques ou électriques, pénurie de matières premières ou de combustibles, ou toute autre cause d'absence temporaire avec ou sans autorisation, devraient être considérées comme pourvues d'un emploi salarié à condition qu'elles aient un lien formel avec leur emploi.

4) Les employeurs, les personnes travaillant à leur propre compte et les membres des coopératives de producteurs devraient être considérés comme travailleurs non salariés et classés comme "étant au travail" ou "n'étant pas au travail", selon les cas.

5) Les travailleurs familiaux non rémunérés devraient être considérés comme travailleurs non salariés indépendamment du nombre d'heures de travail effectué durant la période de référence. Les pays qui, pour des raisons particulières, préféreraient choisir comme critère une durée minimale de temps de travail pour inclure les travailleurs familiaux non rémunérés parmi les personnes pourvues d'un emploi devraient identifier et classer séparément les personnes de cette catégorie qui ont travaillé moins que le temps prescrit.

6) Les personnes engagées dans la production de biens et services pour leur propre consommation ou celle du ménage devraient être considérées comme travailleurs non salariés si une telle production apporte une importante contribution à la consommation totale du ménage.

7) Les apprentis qui ont reçu une rétribution en espèces ou en nature devraient être considérés comme personnes pourvues d'un emploi salarié et classés comme "étant au travail" ou "n'étant pas au travail" sur la même base que les autres catégories de personnes pourvues d'un emploi salarié.

8) Les étudiants, les personnes s'occupant du foyer et autres personnes principalement engagées dans des activités non économiques durant la période de référence et qui étaient en même temps pourvues d'un emploi salarié ou non salarié comme défini au sous-paragraphe 1) ci-dessus devraient être considérés comme ayant un emploi, sur la même base que les autres catégories de personnes ayant un emploi, et être identifiés séparément lorsque cela est possible.

9) Les membres des forces armées devraient être inclus parmi les personnes pourvues d'un emploi salarié. Les forces armées devraient comprendre aussi bien les membres permanents que les membres temporaires, comme spécifié dans la plus récente révision de la Classification internationale type des professions (CITP).

Chômage

10. 1) Les "chômeurs" comprennent toutes les personnes ayant dépassé un âge spécifié qui, au cours de la période de référence, étaient:

a) "sans travail", c'est-à-dire qui n'étaient pourvues ni d'un emploi salarié ni d'un emploi non salarié, comme défini au paragraphe 9;

b) "disponibles pour travailler" dans un emploi salarié ou non salarié durant la période de référence;

c) "à la recherche d'un travail", c'est-à-dire qui avaient pris des dispositions spécifiques au cours d'une période récente spécifiée pour chercher un emploi salarié ou un emploi non salarié. Ces dispositions spécifiques peuvent inclure: l'inscription à un bureau de placement public ou privé; la candidature auprès d'employeurs; les démarches sur les lieux de travail, dans les fermes ou à la porte des usines, sur les marchés ou dans les autres endroits où sont traditionnellement recrutés les travailleurs; l'insertion ou la réponse à des annonces dans les journaux; les recherches par relations personnelles; la recherche de terrain, d'immeubles, de machines ou d'équipement pour créer une entreprise personnelle; les démarches pour obtenir des ressources financières, des permis et licences, etc.

2) Dans les situations où les moyens conventionnels de recherche de travail sont peu appropriés, où le marché du travail est largement inorganisé ou d'une portée limitée, où l'absorption de l'offre de travail est, au moment considéré, insuffisante, où la proportion de main-d'oeuvre non salariée est importante, la définition standard du chômage donnée au sous-paragraphe 1) ci-dessus peut être appliquée en renonçant au critère de la recherche de travail.

3) Pour appliquer le critère de la disponibilité pour le travail, spécialement dans les situations couvertes par le sous-paragraphe 2) ci-dessus, des méthodes appropriées devraient être mises au point pour tenir compte des circonstances nationales. De telles méthodes pourraient être fondées sur des notions comme l'actuelle envie de travailler et le fait d'avoir déjà travaillé, la volonté de prendre un emploi salarié sur la base des conditions locales ou le désir d'entreprendre une activité indépendante si les ressources et les facilités nécessaires sont accordées.

4) En dépit du critère de recherche de travail incorporé dans la définition standard du chômage, les personnes sans travail et disponibles pour travailler, qui ont pris des dispositions pour prendre un emploi salarié ou pour entreprendre une activité indépendante à une date ultérieure à la période de référence, devraient être considérées comme chômeurs.

5) Les personnes temporairement absentes de leur travail sans lien formel avec leur emploi, qui étaient disponibles pour travailler et à la recherche d'un travail, devraient être considérées comme chômeurs conformément à la définition standard du chômage. Les pays peuvent, cependant, en fonction des situations et politiques nationales, préférer renoncer au critère de la recherche d'un travail dans le cas des personnes temporairement mises à pied. Dans de tels cas, les personnes temporairement mises à pied qui n'étaient pas à la recherche d'un travail mais qui étaient néanmoins classées comme chômeurs devraient être identifiées et former une sous-catégorie à part.

6) Les étudiants, les personnes s'occupant du foyer et les autres personnes principalement engagées dans des activités non économiques durant la période de référence et qui satisfont aux critères exposés aux sous-paragraphes 1) et 2) ci-dessus devraient être considérés comme chômeurs au même titre que les autres catégories de chômeurs et être identifiés séparément lorsque cela est possible.

INTRODUCCION

En este volumen de "Fuentes y Métodos: Estadísticas del trabajo" se presentan las descripciones metodológicas de censos de población realizados en el período 1989-1994. La publicación de estas descripciones tiene dos finalidades principales:

– proporcionar información básica sobre las prácticas seguidas por los países en la compilación de datos estadísticos acerca de la población total y la población económicamente activa, el empleo y el desempleo, recopilados en el marco de los censos de población; e

– ilustrar con ejemplos la comparabilidad de las estadísticas facilitadas por los países.

En un cuadro sinóptico se recogen las características esenciales de los censos a que se hace referencia.

Las descripciones que se presentan aquí abarcan 115 países. Se basan en la información que suministraron los organismos estadísticos nacionales encargados de establecer los censos. En algunos casos, la información se compiló a partir de publicaciones nacionales. Todas las descripciones se remitieron a los respectivos países, a fin de que éstos formularan sus comentarios al respecto; se tomaron debidamente en consideración todas las observaciones recibidas dentro del plazo determinado por el programa de publicación.

A fin de facilitar las comparaciones, la presentación de las descripciones se ordenó con arreglo a secciones y epígrafes comunes, como se muestra a continuación. Cada vez que ello fue posible, se indicaron las preguntas empleadas en cada censo para recabar la información correspondiente.

1. Nombre y dirección del organismo responsable del censo:
El nombre y la dirección del organismo responsable del censo se presentan en el idioma del país de que se trate o en el idioma de correspondencia oficial entre éste y la OIT.

2. Censos de población llevados a cabo desde 1945 (años):
Se indican los años en que se han establecido censos de población, a contar de 1945.

3. Alcance del censo:
a) Geográfico: Bajo este epígrafe se precisa si el censo abarcó todo un país o territorio, o , en casos de cobertura limitada, se señalan las zonas o comarcas que quedaron excluidas.

b) Personas comprendidas: Se indica la población englobada en el ámbito del censo, así como todo grupo que haya sido explícitamente excluido, como, por ejemplo, los extranjeros residentes o los nacionales que residen habitualmente en otro país o territorio.

4. Período de referencia:
Por período de referencia se entiende el lapso durante el cual se recopilaron los datos sobre las características económicas de la población. (Por ejemplo, un día, una semana o un año bien determinados).

5. Materias principales:
Se trata de los principales temas relativos a la actividad económica incluidos en el censo, organizados según la siguiente lista uniforme:
a) Población total, según sexo y edad: ...
Población económicamente activa por:
b) Sexo y grupo de edad: ...
c) Rama de actividad económica: ...
d) Ocupación: ...
e) Situación en el empleo: ...
f) Nivel más alto de educación: ...
g) Horas de trabajo: ...
h) Otras características: ...
Se señalan algunos pormenores relativos a los distintos temas, como, por ejemplo, el modo en que se determinó la edad, el concepto de tiempo de trabajo empleado (horas efectivamente trabajadas, horas normales de trabajo, etc.) o las diversas clases de información adicional acopiada en relación con la actividad económica de las personas censadas (ingresos, trabajo a tiempo completo, trabajo a tiempo parcial, etc.).

6. Conceptos y definiciones:
a) Población económicamente activa: Por lo que se refiere a la composición de la población económicamente activa, las definiciones nacionales usadas en los respectivos censos se han contrastado con respecto a la definición dada en la "Resolución sobre estadísticas de la población económicamente activa, del empleo, del desempleo y del subempleo", adoptada por la decimotercera Conferencia Internacional de Estadígrafos del Trabajo (octubre de 1982). La inclusión o exclusión de determinados grupos (jubilados, personas ocupadas en las labores del hogar, etc.) se señala en relación con la citada Resolución (los extractos pertinentes de la misma figuran en el Apéndice).

Bajo este epígrafe se mencionan los siguientes aspectos:

– los límites de edad que determinaron la inclusión (o la exclusión) de las personas censadas en la población económicamente activa;

– la inclusión o exclusión de los miembros de las fuerzas armadas.

b) Empleo: Se indica la definición nacional usada en el censo, además de las distintas categorías que ésta comprende y que, dado el caso, pueden identificarse por separado.

Las personas que tenían más de un empleo fueron mencionadas sólo cuando era posible identificarlas por separado.

c) Desempleo: Se indica la definición nacional empleada en el censo respectivo.

7. Clasificaciones utilizadas:
a) Rama de actividad económica: Cada vez que ello ha sido posible, se han indicado bajo este epígrafe las preguntas hechas para determinar el grupo de actividades económicas y el número de grupos usados para codificar los datos. También se ha indicado si la clasificación nacional está vinculada o no con la Clasificación Industrial Internacional Uniforme de todas las actividades económicas (CIIU), Revisión 2 (1968) o Revisión 3 (1990).

b) Ocupación: Cada vez que ello ha sido posible, se han indicado bajo este epígrafe las preguntas hechas para determinar el grupo de ocupaciones y el número de grupos usados para codificar los datos. También se ha indicado si la clasificación nacional está vinculada o no con la Clasificación Internacional Uniforme de Ocupaciones (CIUO-68 o CIUO-88).

c) Situación en el empleo:
Se ha indicado el número de grupos utilizado para codificar los datos y, cada vez que ello ha sido posible, los grupos mismos.

8. Diferencias principales con el censo anterior:
Se señalan bajo este epígrafe todos los cambios introducidos en el alcance del censo, los conceptos y las definiciones, etc., desde el censo anterior.

9. Publicación de los resultados del censo:
En esta sección se indican el título de la publicación ncaional en que aparecen los resultados definitivos del censo, el nombre del organismo responsable de dicha publicación y la eventual disponibilidad de los datos en soportes no impresos (disquetes, cintas magnéticas, CD-ROM, etc.).

ALBANIA

1. Nombre y dirección del organismo responsable del censo:
Commission du Plan d'Etat, Direction de la Statistique, Tirana.

2. Censos de población llevados a cabo desde 1945 (años):
1960, 1989. La presente descripción se refiere al censo de población de 1989 (realizado del 1 al 7 de abril de ese año).

3. Alcance del censo:
a) Geográfico: Todo el territorio.

b) Personas comprendidas: Toda la población.

4. Período de referencia:
No se fijó un período de referencia.

5. Materias principales:
a) Población total, según sexo y edad: sí
Población económicamente activa por:
b) Sexo y grupo de edad: sí
c) Rama de actividad económica: sí
d) Ocupación: sí

e) Situación en el empleo: sí
f) Nivel más alto de educación: sí
g) Horas de trabajo: no
h) Otras características: sí

Ref. a): La edad se determinó según el año y el mes de nacimiento.

Ref. h): También se recopilaron informaciones sobre los ingresos anuales percibidos durante el año anterior y sobre el número total de años trabajados por la persona censada al servicio del Estado o en una cooperativa. También se pidió a las personas empadronadas que indicasen en qué año iban a tomar su jubilación.

6. Conceptos y definiciones:

a) Población económicamente activa: Abarcó a todas las personas de 15 o más años de edad que tenían un empleo o estaban desempleadas, según las definiciones que se dan más adelante. La definición incluyó a los miembros de las fuerzas armadas.

b) Empleo: Para determinarlo se utilizó la pregunta siguiente: "¿Trabajó usted? 1) Sí; 2) No". A las personas que respondieron "No" se les preguntó si estaban o eran: 1) jubilado o de edad demasiado avanzada para trabajar; 2) jubilado inválido; 3) inactivo; 4) escolar o estudiante de niveles superiores; 5) en busca de empleo; 6) no busca empleo; 7) otra situación.

Se ha indicado que fueron incluidas las siguientes categorías:

i) personas que trabajan sin remuneración en una empresa o explotación familiar;
ii) personas que producen bienes primarios para el autoconsumo;
iii) personas ocupadas pero temporalmente ausentes de su trabajo;
iv) estudiantes que trabajan a tiempo parcial;
v) trabajadores estacionales u ocasionales;
vi) conscriptos del servicio militar o civil;
vii) aprendices y personas que siguen un curso de formación.

Ninguna de estas categorías puede identificarse por separado.

c) Desempleo: Se consideró "desempleada" a toda persona que dijo carecer de trabajo y estar buscando empleo. No quedaron incluidos en la definición los estudiantes que buscaban trabajo.

7. Clasificaciones utilizadas:

Sólo las personas ocupadas se clasificaron por rama de actividad económica, por ocupación y por situación en el empleo.

a) Rama de actividad económica: Para determinarla se hizo la siguiente pregunta: "¿En qué actividad económica trabaja usted?". Para codificar la rama de actividad económica se utilizó la clasificación nacional. No se establecieron enlaces con la CIIU.

b) Ocupación: Para determinarla se hizo la siguiente pregunta: "¿Qué profesión o cargo ejerce?". Para codificar la ocupación, se utilizó la clasificación nacional. No se establecieron enlaces con la CIUO.

c) Situación en el empleo: Para determinarla se hizo la siguiente pregunta: "¿Cuál es su situación laboral? 1) asalariado; 2) empleador; 3) miembro de una cooperativa". Para codificar esta variable se utilizaron los tres grupos enumerados.

8. Diferencias principales con el censo anterior:

No hubo diferencias significativas

9. Publicación de los resultados del censo:

Los resultados definitivos del censo se publicaron en 1991, en el volumen que lleva por título: "Recensement de la population et de l'habitat, 1989".

El organismo responsable de esta publicación es el Institut de la Statistique, Rr Lek Dukagjini n 5, Tirana.

No se dispone de los resultados en otros soportes.

ANGUILA

1. Nombre y dirección del organismo responsable del censo:

Government of Anguilla, Statistical Unit, Ministry of Finance, The Secretariat, Valley.

2. Censos de población llevados a cabo desde 1945 (años):

1960, 1974, 1984 y 1992. La presente descripción se refiere al censo de población de 1992 (realizado el 14 de abril de ese año).

3. Alcance del censo:

a) Geográfico: Todo el país.

b) Personas comprendidas: Toda la población.

4. Periodo de referencia:

El mes anterior al día del censo.

5. Materias principales:

a) Población total, según sexo y edad: sí
Población económicamente activa por:
b) Sexo y grupo de edad: sí
c) Rama de actividad económica: sí
d) Ocupación: sí
e) Situación en el empleo: sí
f) Nivel más alto de educación: sí
g) Horas de trabajo: no
h) Otras características: no

Ref. a): La edad se determinó según los años cumplidos en el último cumpleaños.

6. Conceptos y definiciones:

a) Población económicamente activa: Abarcó a todas las personas de 12 o más años de edad que, durante el período de referencia, estaban ocupadas o desempleadas, conforme a las definiciones que se dan más adelante. La definición incluye a los miembros de las fuerzas de policía.

b) Empleo: Para determinarlo se hicieron dos preguntas: "¿Cuál es la ocupación de la persona?", y "Si la persona no trabaja, ¿cuál es el motivo de su inactividad?".

Se ha indicado que fueron incluidas las siguientes categorías:

i) personas ocupadas pero temporalmente ausentes de su trabajo;
ii) estudiantes que trabajan a tiempo parcial;
iii) trabajadores estacionales u ocasionales;
iv) conscriptos del servicio militar o civil;
v) aprendices y personas que siguen un curso de formación.

Ninguna de estas categorías puede identificarse separadamente.

c) Desempleo: Se consideró "desempleada" a toda persona que se encontraba sin empleo y quería trabajar. La definición incluyó tanto a las personas que buscaban activamente un trabajo como a aquellas que no lo hacían porque sabían que no había empleos disponibles.

7. Clasificaciones utilizadas:

Sólo las personas ocupadas fueron clasificadas por rama de actividad económica, por ocupación y según la situación en el empleo.

a) Rama de actividad económica: Para determinarla se preguntó: "¿Para quién trabaja la persona?", y ¿Dónde trabaja?, por ejemplo, "en la empresa Cable and Wireless" o "en el Mariners Hotel". Para codificar la rama de actividad se utilizó la CIIU-Rev.3 a nivel de categorías de tabulación (clave de 1 dígito).

b) Ocupación: Para determinarla se preguntó: "¿Cuál es la ocupación de la persona?, por ejemplo, capataz de carpintería, mecánico de motores diésel, profesor de nivel primario". Para codificar la ocupación se utilizaron 39 grupos. Se establecieron enlaces con la CIUO-88 a nivel de grandes grupos (clave de 1 dígito).

c) Situación en el empleo: Para codificar esta variable se utilizaron tres grupos, a saber: trabajador del sector público; trabajador del sector privado; trabajador independiente.

8. Diferencias principales con el censo anterior:

No hubo diferencias significativas.

9. Publicación de los resultados del censo:

Los resultados definitivos del censo se publicaron en septiembre de 1992, en el volumen que lleva por título "Anguilla Census of Population".

El organismo responsable de la publicación es el Government of Anguilla, The Secretariat, Statistical Unit, Ministry of Finance, Valley.

Los datos recopilados por el censo se pueden obtener también en disquetes.

ANTIGUA Y BARBUDA

1. Nombre y dirección del organismo responsable del censo:
Census Office, Statistics Division, Upper Redcliffe Street, St. John's, Antigua.

2. Censos de población llevados a cabo desde 1945 (años):
1945, 1960, 1970 y 1991. La presente descripción se refiere al censo de población de 1991 (realizado el 28 de mayo de ese año).

3. Alcance del censo:
a) Geográfico: Todo el territorio.

b) Personas comprendidas: Toda la población.

4. Período de referencia:
La semana y el año anteriores al censo.

5. Materias principales:
a) Población total, según sexo y edad:	sí
Población económicamente activa por:	
b) Sexo y grupo de edad:	sí
c) Rama de actividad económica:	sí
d) Ocupación:	sí
e) Situación en el empleo:	sí
f) Nivel más alto de educación:	sí
g) Horas de trabajo:	sí
h) Otras características:	sí

Ref. a): La edad se determinó según los años cumplidos en el último cumpleaños.

Ref. g): El tiempo de trabajo se refiere a las horas efectivamente trabajadas durante la semana de referencia y al número de meses trabajados durante el año de referencia.

Ref. h): El censo también recolectó datos sobre: i) los medios de transporte utilizados para trasladarse al lugar de trabajo; ii) el trabajo efectuado en actividades del sector informal; iii) el último período en que se percibieron remuneraciones/ingresos; y iv) el salario bruto/los ingresos brutos percibidos durante dicho último período.

6. Conceptos y definiciones:
a) Población económicamente activa: Abarcó a todas las personas de 15 a 64 años de edad que, durante los períodos de referencia, estaban ocupadas o desempleadas, conforme a las definiciones que se dan más adelante. La definición no incluyó a los miembros de las fuerzas armadas.

b) Empleo: Para determinar si una persona debía contabilizarse o no como "ocupada" se preguntó "¿A qué se dedicó fundamentalmente durante los últimos 12 meses?", y "¿A qué se dedicó fundamentalmente la semana pasada?". Las respuestas posibles para ambas preguntas eran:" 1) Trabajé; 2) Tenía un empleo, pero no trabajé; 3) Busqué trabajo; 4) Quería trabajar y estaba disponible para hacerlo; 5) Trabajé en labores del hogar; 6) Asistí a clases; 7) Estaba ya jubilado; 8) Estaba inválido, incapacitado para trabajar; 9) Otra actividad; y 10) No respondió". Se contabilizó como "ocupadas" a las personas que indicaron las respuestas 1) o 2).

Se ha indicado que fueron incluidas las siguientes categorías:

i) personas que trabajan sin remuneración en una empresa o negocio familiar;

ii) personas que producen bienes primarios para el autoconsumo;

iii) personas ocupadas pero temporalmente ausentes de su trabajo;

iv) estudiantes que trabajan a tiempo parcial;

v) trabajadores estacionales u ocasionales.

Sólo las categorías i), iii) y iv) pueden identificarse por separado.

c) Desempleo: Para determinar si una persona debía contabilizarse como desempleada, además de las preguntas que figuran en el apartado b) de esta sección, se utilizaron las siguientes: "¿Tuvo algún tipo de trabajo durante los pasados doce meses, incluidas las tareas domésticas?" y "¿Ha trabajado o tenido un empleo alguna vez en su vida?".

7. Clasificaciones utilizadas:
Tanto las personas ocupadas como las desocupadas anteriormente ocupadas se clasificaron por rama de actividad económica, por ocupación y según la situación en el empleo.

a) Rama de actividad económica: Para determinarla se preguntó: "¿Qué clase de negocio o actividad se efectúa/se efectuaba en su lugar de trabajo?" y "¿Cuáles son el nombre y la dirección de su lugar de trabajo actual?".

Para codificar la rama de actividad se utilizaron 157 grupos de la clasificación nacional. Se establecieron enlaces con la CIIU-Rev.3 a nivel de grupos (clave de 3 dígitos).

b) Ocupación: Para determinarla se preguntó: "¿Qué tipo de trabajo desempeña o desempeñaba en su ocupación principal?". Para codificar la ocupación se utilizaron 136 grupos de la clasificación nacional. Se establecieron enlaces con la CIUO-88.

c) Situación en el empleo: Para determinarla se preguntó: "¿Se ocupó usted de su propia empresa o negocio, trabajó por un sueldo o un salario, o como trabajador no remunerado en una empresa familiar?". Para codificar esta variable se utilizaron seis grupos, a saber: 1) asalariado del sector público; 2) asalariado del sector privado; 3) trabajador no remunerado; 4) trabajador independiente con personal remunerado (empleador); 5) trabajador independiente sin personal remunerado (por cuenta propia); y 6) no sabía/no respondió.

8. Diferencias principales con el censo anterior:
No hubo diferencias significativas.

9. Publicación de los resultados del censo:
La publicación en que figuran los resultados del censo lleva por título: "1991 Population and Housing Census, Summary Report, Volume II, (Pard. 1)", y apareció en diciembre de 1994.

El organismo responsable de la publicación es la Statistics Division, Ministry of Finance & Social Security.

Los resultados del censo están disponibles también en cuadros inéditos y disquetes.

ANTILLAS NEERLANDESAS

1. Nombre y dirección del organismo responsable del censo:
Central Bureau of Statistics, Fort Amsterdam, Curaçao.

2. Censos de población llevados a cabo desde 1945 (años):
1960, 1972, 1981 y 1992. La presente descripción se refiere al censo de población de 1992 (realizado el 27 de enero de ese año).

3. Alcance del censo:
a) Geográfico: Todo el país.

b) Personas comprendidas: Toda la población.

4. Período de referencia:
La semana, el año y los cinco años anteriores al día del censo.

5. Materias principales:
a) Población total, según sexo y edad:	sí
Población económicamente activa por:	
b) Sexo y grupo de edad:	sí
c) Rama de actividad económica:	sí
d) Ocupación:	sí
e) Situación en el empleo:	sí
f) Nivel más alto de educación:	sí
g) Horas de trabajo:	sí
h) Otras características:	sí

Ref. a): La edad se determinó según el año de nacimiento y los años cumplidos en el último cumpleaños.

Ref. g): En lo que atañe a la semana y al año de referencia, se pidió indicar, respectivamente, las horas de trabajo habituales y el período total trabajado durante los últimos 12 meses (expresado en número de semanas). A las personas desempleadas se les pidió que indicaran cuánto tiempo habían trabajado a tiempo completo en los últimos cinco años.

Ref. h): El censo también recolectó datos sobre los medios de transporte utilizados para trasladarse al lugar de trabajo, la principal fuente de ingresos y el ingreso bruto total en el mes de enero de 1992. A los desempleados se les pidió que indicaran de qué manera habían buscado trabajo el mes anterior.

6. Conceptos y definiciones:

a) Población económicamente activa: Abarcó a todas las personas de 15 a 99 años de edad que durante la semana de referencia estaban ocupadas o desempleadas, conforme a las definiciones que se dan más adelante. La definición incluyó a los miembros de las fuerzas armadas.

b) Empleo: Se consideró "ocupada" a toda persona que durante la semana de referencia había trabajado o desempeñado un trabajo ocasional durante cuatro horas o más. La pregunta utilizada fue: "¿Trabajó la semana pasada, aun cuando fuese en forma ocasional durante cuatro o más horas?"

Se ha indicado que fueron incluidas las siguientes categorías:

i) personas que trabajan sin remuneración en una empresa o negocio familiar;
ii) personas ocupadas pero temporalmente ausentes de su trabajo;
iii) estudiantes que trabajan a tiempo parcial;
iv) trabajadores estacionales u ocasionales;
v) conscriptos del servicio militar o civil;
vi) aprendices y personas que siguen un curso de formación.

Sólo pueden identificarse por separado las categorías i), ii), iii), iv) y v).

c) Desempleo: Se consideró "desempleada" a toda persona que durante la semana de referencia estaba sin trabajo, buscaba uno o quería comenzar a trabajar por cuenta propia, y podía empezar a hacerlo en un plazo de dos semanas si encontraba trabajo.

7. Clasificaciones utilizadas:
Tanto las personas ocupadas como las desempleadas anteriormente empleadas se clasificaron por rama de actividad económica, por ocupación y por situación en el empleo.

a) Rama de actividad económica: Para determinarla se preguntó: "¿En qué empresa trabaja? (Nombre y dirección)" y "¿De qué clase de empresa se trata?". Para codificar la rama de actividad se utilizó la clasificación nacional, basada en la CIIU-Rev.3, que comprende 17 categorías.

b) Ocupación: Para determinarla se preguntó: "¿Cuál es su profesión? (nombre de la profesión y descripción precisa de la actividad)". Para codificar la ocupación se utilizó la clasificación nacional, basada en la CIUO-88, que comprende 10 grandes grupos.

c) Situación en el empleo: Para determinarla se preguntó: "¿Cuál es o era su situación económica?". Para codificar esta variable se utilizaron nueve grupos: empleador; trabajador parcialmente independiente (menos de 3 asalariados); empleado en servicio permanente; empleado en servicio temporal; servicio o trabajo ocasional; trabajador familiar (no remunerado); empleado con contrato de menos de seis meses; empleado con contrato de por lo menos seis meses; otras e indeterminado.

8. Diferencias principales con el censo anterior:
En 1981, la edad mínima era de 14 años. Además, la definición de empleo incluía al trabajador ocasional, el período de referencia abarcaba los dos últimos meses y se consideraba desempleado a quien estaba "buscando trabajo".

9. Publicación de los resultados del censo:
Los resultados definitivos del censo se publicaron en enero de 1993 con el título "Third Population and Housing Census, Netherlands Antilles 1992" (tres tomos).

La organización responsable de la publicación es el Central Bureau of Statistics, Fort Amsterdam, Curaçao.

Existen también cuadros inéditos de los resultados, a disposición de quienes los soliciten, y se ha previsto la edición de disquetes.

ARABIA SAUDITA

1. Nombre y dirección del organismo responsable del censo:
Central Department of Statistics, P.O. Box 3735, Riyad 11118.

2. Censos de población llevados a cabo desde 1945 (años):
1974 y 1992. La presente descripción se refiere al censo de población de 1992 (realizado el 27 de septiembre de ese año).

3. Alcance del censo:
a) Geográfico: Todo el país.
b) Personas comprendidas: Toda la población.

4. Período de referencia:
La semana anterior al día del censo.

5. Materias principales:
a) Población total, según sexo y edad: sí
Población económicamente activa por:
b) Sexo y grupo de edad: sí
c) Rama de actividad económica: sí
d) Ocupación: sí
e) Situación en el empleo: sí
f) Nivel más alto de educación: sí
g) Horas de trabajo: no
h) Otras características: no
Ref. a): La edad se determinó según los años cumplidos en el último cumpleaños.

6. Conceptos y definiciones:

a) Población económicamente activa: Abarcó a todas las personas de 12 o más años de edad que, durante el período de referencia, estaban sea ocupadas, sea desempleadas, conforme a las definiciones que se dan más adelante. No quedaron incluidos en la definición los estudiantes que trabajaban a tiempo parcial ni los que buscaban trabajo, pero sí lo fueron los miembros de las fuerzas armadas.

b) Empleo: Se consideró "ocupada" a toda persona que, durante el período de referencia, trabajó un mínimo de 15 horas en uno o más empleos, o estuvo ausente de dichos empleo o empleos por haberse encontrado enferma, en vacaciones, etc.

Se ha indicado que fueron incluidas las siguientes categorías:

i) personas que trabajan sin remuneración en una empresa o negocio familiar;
ii) personas que producen bienes primarios para el autoconsumo;
iii) personas ocupadas pero temporalmente ausentes de su trabajo;
iv) trabajadores estacionales u ocasionales;
v) conscriptos del servicio militar o civil;
vi) aprendices y personas que siguen un curso de formación.

Sólo las personas que trabajan sin remuneración en una empresa o negocio familiar pueden identificarse por separado.

c) Desempleo: Se consideró "desempleada" a toda persona que, durante el período de referencia, se encontraba sin trabajo, era capaz de trabajar, estaba dispuesta a hacerlo y estaba buscando una ocupación. Las personas desempleadas fueron clasificadas como "desempleado antes empleado" y "desempleado que nunca ha trabajado".

7. Clasificaciones utilizadas:
Sólo las personas ocupadas se clasificaron por rama de actividad económica y por situación en el empleo. Tanto las personas ocupadas como las desempleadas anteriormente empleadas se clasificaron por ocupación.

a) Rama de actividad económica: Para determinar el grupo de actividades económicas, se pidió a las personas ocupadas que indicaran cuál era la principal actividad económica de su respectivo empleador. Para codificar la rama de actividad se utilizó la CIIU-Rev.3 a nivel de divisiones (clave de 2 dígitos).

b) Ocupación: Para determinar el grupo de ocupaciones, se pidió a las personas ocupadas y a los desempleados previamente ocupados que precisaran cuál era su ocupación principal (el tipo de trabajo que la persona estaba o había estado desempeñando). Para codificar la ocupación, se utilizó la CIUO-68 a nivel de grupos primarios (clave de 3 dígitos).

c) Situación en el empleo: Para determinar esta variable, se pidió a las personas ocupadas que indicasen la posición que ocupaban en su trabajo. Para codificar la situación en el empleo se utilizaron cuatro grupos, a saber: empleador, trabajador independiente, trabajador asalariado y trabajador no remunerado.

8. Diferencias principales con el censo anterior:
No hubo diferencias significativas.

9. Publicación de los resultados del censo:
En marzo de 1995, se publicó un informe titulado "Preliminary Results of the General Population and Housing Census: 413 A.H." Se ha previsto publicar otros informes, pero aún no se han fijado las fechas de aparición.

El organismo responsable de estas publicaciones es el Central Department of Statistics, P.O. Box 3735, Riyad 11118.
No se dispone de los resultados en otros soportes.

ARGENTINA

1. Nombre y dirección del organismo responsable del censo:
Instituto Nacional de Estadística y Censos (INDEC), Diagonal Presidente Julio A. Roca 609, Código Postal 1067, Buenos Aires, Capital Federal.

2. Censos de población llevados a cabo desde 1945 (años):
1947, 1960, 1970, 1980 y 1991. La presente descripción se refiere al censo de población de 1991 (llevado a cabo el 15 de mayo).

3. Alcance del censo:
a) Geográfico: Todo el país, salvo las Islas Malvinas y las Islas del Atlántico Sur.

b) Personas comprendidas: Se pretendió abarcar a todos los grupos de poblaciones que se encontraban en territorio nacional en la fecha del censo, por lo tanto, se excluyeron los residentes argentinos en el extranjero y los extranjeros residentes en embajadas ubicadas en territorio argentino.

4. Periodo de referencia:
La semana anterior a la fecha del censo para definir el empleo y las últimas cuatro semanas para definir el desempleo.

5. Materias principales:
a) Población total, según sexo y edad: sí
Población económicamente activa por:
b) Sexo y grupo de edad: sí
c) Rama de actividad económica: sí
d) Ocupación: sí
e) Situación en el empleo: sí
f) Nivel más alto de educación: sí
g) Horas de trabajo: no
h) Otras características: no
Ref. a): Se definió la edad en términos de la edad al último cumpleaños.

6. Conceptos y definiciones:
a) Población económicamente activa: Incluye a todas las personas de 14 años y más, que durante los períodos de referencia se encontraban empleadas o desempleadas, tal y como se definen más adelante. Las preguntas de actividad económica se aplicaron a una muestra que varió entre el 10 por ciento en las localidades de 500 000 habitantes y más y el 20 por ciento en las de 100 000 a 499 999 habitantes. La definición incluye también todas las fuerzas armadas.

b) Empleo: Se consideran como "empleadas" a las personas que trabajaron en forma remunerada o no durante la semana de referencia. Las preguntas utilizadas para determinar si la persona estaba ocupada son "¿Durante la semana pasada, trabajó aunque sea por pocas horas?", "¿Hizo algo en su casa para afuera o ayudó a alguien en un negocio, chacra o trabajo?" y "¿Estuvo de licencia por enfermedad, vacaciones, etc.?".
Se ha indicado que quedan incluidas las siguientes categorías:
i) personas que trabajan sin remuneración en una empresa familiar;
ii) personas ocupadas pero temporalmente ausentes del trabajo por circunstancias transitorias como: enfermedad o accidente, conflicto de trabajo, vacaciones u otra clase de permiso, interrupción del trabajo a causa de condiciones climáticas o desperfectos en el equipo de producción;
iii) estudiantes que trabajan medio tiempo;
iv) trabajadores estacionales u ocasionales;
v) conscriptos del servicio militar o civil.
Las personas en las categorias i), ii), iii) y v) se pueden identificar separadamente, utilizando preguntas específicas.

c) Desempleo: Se consideran como "desempleadas" a las personas que buscaron trabajo durante las cuatro semanas de referencia, ya sea que hubieran trabajado antes, o que buscaron trabajo por primera vez. La pregunta utilizada para determinar si la persona estaba desempleada es "¿Durante las últimas cuatro semanas buscó trabajo?".

7. Clasificaciones utilizadas:
Sólo las personas ocupadas en las muestras se clasificaron por rama de actividad económica, por ocupación y según la situación en la ocupación.

a) Rama de actividad económica: La pregunta utilizada para establecer la rama de actividad económica es "¿A qué se dedica o qué produce el lugar o establecimiento donde trabaja?". Para codificar la rama de actividad económica se adoptó la CIIU-Rev.3 hasta el nivel de 3 (tres) dígitos.

b) Ocupación: La pregunta utilizada para determinar la ocupación es "¿Qué tareas hace en ese trabajo?". Para codificar la ocupación, se utilizaron 9 grupos de la clasificación nacional de 1980. Se estableció vínculos con la CIUO-88.

c) Situación en el empleo: La pregunta utilizada para determinar esta característica es "En el trabajo principal, en el que trabaja más horas, es: ¿Patrón?; ¿Obrero o empleado del sector privado?; ¿Obrero o empleado del sector público?; ¿Empleado en servicio doméstico?; ¿Trabajador por cuenta propia?; ¿Trabajador familiar sin remuneración fija?; ¿Ignorado?". Para codificar la situación en la ocupación se utilizaron los siete grupos precedentes.

8. Diferencias principales con el censo anterior:
Ciertas diferencias menores con el censo de 1980 conciernen esencialmente la formulación de las preguntas utilizadas para determinar:
– la rama de actividad: "El establecimiento o lugar en que trabaja, ¿es principalmente: agropecuario, industrial, comercial, de otro tipo?", "¿A qué se dedica o qué produce principalmente ese establecimiento?", y "El establecimiento en el que trabaja tiene ¿hasta 5 personas ocupadas?, ¿más de 5 personas ocupadas?".
– la ocupación: "¿Cuál es la ocupación, oficio o clase de trabajo que realiza?".
– la situación en la ocupación: "¿Qué posición tiene en el ejercicio de esa ocupación (empleado u obrero del sector público; empleado u obrero del sector privado; empleado doméstico; cuenta propia, no tiene empleados; patrón o socio, tiene empleados; trabajador familiar sin remuneración fija; ignorado)?".

9. Publicación de los resultados del censo:
Información no disponible.

ARUBA

1. Nombre y dirección del organismo responsable del censo:
Central Bureau of Statistics, L.G. Smith Boulevard no. 160.

2. Censos de población llevados a cabo desde 1945 (años):
1981 y 1991. La presente descripción se refiere al censo de población de 1991 (realizado el 6 de octubre de ese año).

3. Alcance del censo:
a) Geográfico: Todo el país.
b) Personas comprendidas: Toda la población.

4. Periodo de referencia:
La semana anterior al día del censo.

5. Materias principales:
a) Población total, según sexo y edad: sí
Población económicamente activa por:
b) Sexo y grupo de edad: sí
c) Rama de actividad económica: sí
d) Ocupación: sí
e) Situación en el empleo: sí
f) Nivel más alto de educación: ...
g) Horas de trabajo: sí
h) Otras características: sí
Ref. a): La edad se determinó según los años cumplidos en el último cumpleaños.
Ref. g): Se pidió a las personas ocupadas que precisaran cuál era su horario de trabajo habitual.
Ref. h): El censo también recopiló información sobre los medios de transporte utilizados para trasladarse al lugar de trabajo, la duración del empleo, los motivos por los que la persona censada está sin trabajo, cuántos meses trabajó la

persona desempleada en su última ocupación, los ingresos y las fuentes de ingreso.

6. Conceptos y definiciones:

a) Población económicamente activa: Incluye a todas las personas de 14 años y más, que durante la semana de referencia se encontraban empleadas o desempleadas, conforme a las definiciones que se dan más adelante. La definición incluyó a los miembros de las fuerzas armadas.

b) Empleo: Se consideró "ocupada" a toda persona que respondió afirmativamente a la pregunta: "¿Tiene usted una ocupación en la cual trabajó por lo menos 4 horas la semana pasada (o en la cual usted hubiese trabajado de no haberse encontrado en vacaciones, haciendo uso de una licencia de enfermedad o gravidez, o participando en una huelga, etc.)?".

Se ha indicado que fueron incluidas las siguientes categorías:

i) personas que trabajan sin remuneración en una empresa o negocio familiar;
ii) personas ocupadas pero temporalmente ausentes de su trabajo;
iii) estudiantes que trabajan a tiempo parcial;
iv) conscriptos del servicio militar o civil;
v) aprendices y personas que siguen un curso de formación.

Sólo las categorías i), iii) y iv) pueden identificarse por separado.

c) Desempleo: Se consideró "desempleada" a toda persona que, durante el período de referencia, no trabajó ni siquiera 4 horas, y que respondió afirmativamente a las siguientes preguntas: "¿Ha buscado usted empleo activamente en los últimos meses o se ocupó de preparativos para instalar una empresa o negocio propio?", y "¿Si encontrase empleo o instalara su propia empresa o negocio, podría usted comenzar a trabajar en un plazo de 2 semanas?". La definición no incluyó a los estudiantes que buscaban trabajo.

7. Clasificaciones utilizadas:

Tanto las personas ocupadas como las desempleadas se clasificaron por rama de actividad económica y por ocupación. Sólo se determinó la situación en el empleo de las personas ocupadas y de una muestra de la población activa desempleada.

a) Rama de actividad económica: Para determinarla se preguntó: "¿Dónde trabaja (trabajaba) usted? Sírvase indicar la dirección del lugar de trabajo, el nombre de la empresa/organismo empleador y el tipo de actividad desplegada por la empresa (o el empleador)". Para codificar la rama de actividad, se utilizó la CIIU-Rev.2, en el nivel de grupos (clave de 4 dígitos).

b) Ocupación: Para determinarla se preguntó: "¿Qué tipo de trabajo desempeña (desempeñaba) usted habitualmente? Sírvase indicar el nombre de su profesión, oficio o puesto de trabajo, y describa las características de éste". Para codificar la ocupación, se utilizó la CIUO-88 a nivel de grupos primarios (clave de 4 dígitos).

c) Situación en el empleo: Para codificar esta variable se utilizaron 6 grupos: empleador (con un personal mínimo de 3 empleados); pequeño empresario (hasta 3 empleados); trabajador asalariado, permanente o temporal; trabajador asalariado ocasional; trabajador no remunerado en una empresa o negocio familiar; otra ocupación (trabajador voluntario, miembro de cooperativa, etc.).

8. Diferencias principales con el censo anterior:

No hubo diferencias significativas.

9. Publicación de los resultados del censo:

Los resultados definitivos del censo se publicaron en octubre de 1992, en el volumen que lleva por título " Selected Tables - Third Population and Housing Census, Aruba - October 6, 1991".

El organismo responsable de esta publicación es el Central Bureau of Statistics, L.G. Smith Boulevard no. 160.

Los resultados del censo también se han editado en disquetes. Además, existen cuadros inéditos a disposición de quienes los soliciten.

AUSTRALIA

1. Nombre y dirección del organismo responsable del censo:

Australian Bureau of Statistics, P.O. Box 10, Belconnen ACT 2616.

2. Censos de población llevados a cabo desde 1945 (años):

1947, 1954, 1961, 1966, 1971, 1976, 1981, 1986 y 1991. La presente descripción se refiere al censo de 1991 (realizado el 6 de agosto de ese año).

3. Alcance del censo:

a) Geográfico: Todo el país.

b) Personas comprendidas: Toda la población, salvo los diplomáticos extranjeros y sus familias.

4. Período de referencia:

La semana anterior al censo en lo que atañe a los trabajadores a tiempo completo y a tiempo parcial, y las cuatro semanas anteriores al día del censo en el caso de quienes buscaban trabajo.

5. Materias principales:

a) Población total, según sexo y edad:	sí
Población económicamente activa por:	
b) Sexo y grupo de edad:	sí
c) Rama de actividad económica:	sí
d) Ocupación:	sí
e) Situación en el empleo:	sí
f) Nivel más alto de educación:	sí
g) Horas de trabajo:	sí
h) Otras características:	sí

Ref. a): La edad se determinó según los años cumplidos en el último cumpleaños.

Ref. g): Se pidió a la persona empleada que indicara las horas de trabajo efectivamente trabajadas en el empleo principal durante el período de referencia.

Ref. h): El censo también recolectó datos sobre el ingreso bruto y los medios de transporte utilizados para trasladarse al lugar de trabajo.

6. Conceptos y definiciones:

a) Población económicamente activa: Abarcó a todas las personas de 15 o más años de edad que durante el período de referencia estaban ocupadas o desempleadas, conforme a las definiciones que figuran más adelante. Quedaron excluidas todas las personas que no tenían un empleo o no habían buscado trabajo en las cuatro semanas anteriores al día del censo, a las que se consideró inactivas. La definición incluyó a los miembros de las fuerzas armadas.

b) Empleo: Se consideró "ocupada" a toda persona que durante el período de referencia desempeñaba un trabajo remunerado a tiempo completo o a tiempo parcial, o cualquier trabajo no remunerado en una empresa familiar. Se excluyeron las tareas domésticas, salvo si eran remuneradas por realizarse en otros hogares. Para determinar si una persona debía considerarse empleada, se utilizó la pregunta: "¿Tenía alguna clase de empleo a tiempo completo o a tiempo parcial la semana pasada?"

Se ha indicado que quedaron incluidas las categorías siguientes:

i) personas que trabajan sin remuneración en una empresa o negocio familiar;
ii) personas ocupadas pero temporalmente ausentes de su trabajo;
iii) estudiantes que trabajan a tiempo parcial;
iv) trabajadores estacionales u ocasionales;
v) aprendices y personas que siguen un curso de formación.

Sólo las categorías i) y ii) pueden identificarse por separado según la situación en el empleo y por una clasificación cruzada con datos sobre las horas trabajadas.

c) Desempleo: Se consideró "desempleada" a toda persona que no tenía trabajo ni buscaba uno. Para determinar si una persona debía considerarse desocupada, se preguntó: "¿Buscó trabajo activamente en algún momento de las cuatro últimas semanas?" Por "buscar trabajo activamente" se entendía estar inscrito en el Commonwealth Employment Service; escribir, llamar por teléfono o mantener entrevistas con empleadores eventuales; y publicar avisos para encontrar trabajo. De la definición se excluyó a los estudiantes que buscaban trabajo.

7. Clasificaciones utilizadas:
Tan solo las personas ocupadas se clasificaron por rama de actividad, por ocupación y por situación en el empleo.

a) Rama de actividad económica: Para determinarla se preguntó: "Respecto al trabajo principal desempeñado la semana pasada ¿cuál es el nombre comercial del empleador y la dirección del lugar de trabajo?", y "¿De qué rama de actividad, negocio o servicio se ocupa el empleador en esa dirección?" La información contenida en las respuestas permitió codificar las ramas de actividad. La clasificación de estas últimas se basó en la Australian Standard Industrial Classification (ASIC) y en el Industry and Destination Zone Index, en el que figura la lista de todos los establecimientos conocidos que llevan a cabo un actividad económica en Australia. Para codificar la rama de actividad se utilizaron 615 categorías; se establecieron enlaces con la CIIU-Rev.2 a nivel de grupos (4 dígitos).

b) Ocupación: Para determinarla se hicieron dos preguntas: "Respecto al trabajo principal desempeñado la semana pasada ¿cuál era su ocupación? (Indique el nombre completo del cargo, por ejemplo: auxiliar de contabilidad, diseñador de ingeniería civil, cocinero de platos rápidos, soldador, operador de máquina de extrusión; si es empleado público, indique la designación oficial del cargo y la ocupación, y si es miembro de las fuerzas armadas, el rango y la ocupación)"; y "¿Cuáles son las principales tareas o funciones que suele desempeñar en esa ocupación? (Dé una descripción lo más completa posible, por ejemplo: llevar los libros de contabilidad, preparar planos de construcción de represas, cocinar hamburguesas y papas fritas, cubrir suelos con revestimientos de corcho, manejar una máquina de extrusión de plástico)". La ocupación se clasificó conforme a la Australian Standard Classification of Occupations (ASCO) y fue codificada según el nivel de grupo primario de clasificación. Para codificarla se utilizaron 337 grupos codificados, incluidos 282 grupos primarios, 52 subgrupos, 8 grandes grupos y 3 códigos adicionales para procesar las respuestas con descripciones impropias. No se estableció enlace alguno con la CIUO (ni la CIUO-68 ni la CIUO-88).

c) Situación en el empleo: Para determinarla se pidió responder a la pregunta siguiente: "En el empleo principal desempeñado la semana anterior, ¿ganaba un salario, trabajaba por cuenta propia sin emplear a nadie, trabajaba por cuenta propia y empleaba a terceros; trabajaba como auxiliar sin remuneración?" Para codificarla se utilizaron las cuatro categorías siguientes: asalariado; trabajador independiente; empleador; auxiliar no remunerado.

8. Diferencias principales con el censo anterior:
No hubo diferencias significativas.

9. Publicación de los resultados del censo:
Los datos definitivos del censo sobre la población económicamente activa y los componentes de la misma (empleo y desempleo) se publicaron estado por estado, a partir de septiembre de 1992.

Los resultados provisionales del censo de 1991 se publicaron en la serie "First Counts for Statistical Local Areas" (Cat. no. 2701.1-8), también por estado, entre febrero y abril de 1992.

La ABS editó los resultados definitivos del censo, desglosados por estado, en la serie "Census Counts for Small Areas". El servicio de información de la ABS dispone de datos detallados que pueden obtenerse por pedido expreso.

Los resultados del censo de 1991 figuran también en informes temáticos, atlas sociales, matrices y mapas, así como en el Census Consultancy Service. Se utilizaron como soportes publicaciones impresas, disquetes, cintas magnéticas, microfichas, cartuchos de cinta magnética y CD-ROM. Para más información véase "1991 Census: A Guide to Products and Services" (Cat. No. 2910.0) o tómese contacto con Census Marketing, Australian Bureau of Statistics, P.O. Box 10, Belconnen ACT 2616, teléfono 61 6 252 7879, y telefax 61 6 253 1809.

AUSTRIA

1. Nombre y dirección del organismo responsable del censo:
Oesterreichisches Statistisches Zentralamt, Hintere Zollamtsstrasse 2B, A-1033 Vienna.

2. Censos de población llevados a cabo desde 1945 (años):
1951, 1961, 1971, 1981 y 1991. La presente descripción se refiere al censo de población de 1991 (realizado el 15 de mayo de ese año).

3. Alcance del censo:
a) Geográfico: Todo el país.

b) Personas comprendidas: Toda la población residente, de todas las edades, incluidos los extranjeros que viven permanentemente en Austria y los nacionales que trabajan temporalmente en el extranjero; quedaron excluidos las personas sujetas a jurisdicciones extraterritoriales y los nacionales que viven permanentemente en el extranjero.

4. Periodo de referencia:
Las últimas semanas anteriores al día del censo; en caso de duda, se tomó en consideración la situación de la persona el día del censo (15 de mayo).

5. Materias principales:
a) Población total, según sexo y edad:	sí
Población económicamente activa por:	
b) Sexo y grupo de edad:	sí
c) Rama de actividad económica:	sí
d) Ocupación:	sí
e) Situación en el empleo:	sí
f) Nivel más alto de educación:	sí
g) Horas de trabajo:	sí
h) Otras características:	sí

Ref. a): La edad de la persona censada se definió en función de su fecha de nacimiento exacta (es decir, día, mes y año).

Ref. g): Como horas de trabajo se consideraron las horas normales de trabajo tanto de las personas ocupadas a tiempo completo como de las ocupadas a tiempo parcial.

Ref. h): El censo también recogió informaciones sobre otros aspectos, tales como: frecuencia de los desplazamientos hasta el lugar de trabajo (diarios, no diarios); lugar de trabajo; tiempo utilizado cotidianamente para trasladarse al trabajo; medio de transporte habitual para cubrir la distancia más larga; clase de empleador (público o privado, doce categorías).

6. Conceptos y definiciones:
a) Población económicamente activa: Abarca a todas las personas de 15 o más años de edad que, durante el período de referencia, tenían un empleo o estaban desempleadas, según las definiciones que se dan más adelante. Esta definición incluye a los miembros de las fuerzas armadas.

b) Empleo: Se consideró "ocupada" a toda persona que tenía una actividad a tiempo completo (es decir, un mínimo de 33 horas de trabajo por semana) o a tiempo parcial (es decir, entre 12 y 32 horas por semana). Se incluyó a las mujeres con permiso por maternidad y a las personas con licencia parental no remunerada.

Se ha indicado que quedan incluidas las siguientes categorías:
i) personas que trabajan sin remuneración en una empresa o negocio familiar;
ii) personas que producen bienes primarios para el autoconsumo;
iii) personas ocupadas pero temporalmente ausentes de su trabajo;
iv) estudiantes que trabajan a tiempo parcial;
v) trabajadores estacionales u ocasionales;
vi) conscriptos del servicio militar o civil;
vii) aprendices y personas que siguen un curso de formación.

Sólo las categorías i), vi) y vii) pueden identificarse por separado. También se consideraron como "ocupados" a otros grupos de personas en curso de formación profesional (por ejemplo, las que estudian enfermería, las que siguen un curso de capacitación, o los voluntarios), pero éstos no pueden identificarse por separado.

c) Desempleo: Se consideró como "desempleada" a toda persona que carecía de trabajo y buscaba empleo. Quedan excluidos de esta definición los estudiantes en busca de trabajo.

7. Clasificaciones utilizadas:
Tanto las personas ocupadas como los desempleados anteriormente empleados han sido clasificados por rama de actividad económica, por ocupación y según la situación en el empleo.

a) Rama de actividad económica: Para determinarla se preguntó el nombre de la empresa o servicio (lugar de trabajo o empleador) y la rama de actividad económica correspondiente (por ejemplo, tejeduría, fábrica de ropa interior, comercio de telas al por mayor); a los independientes se les pidió que indicaran que tenían un negocio propio. Para codificar la rama de actividad económica, se utilizaron 117 grupos de la clasificación nacional de actividades económicas. Los enlaces con la clasificación CIIU-Rev.3 se han establecido a nivel de divisiones (clave de 2 dígitos).

b) Ocupación: Para determinarla se preguntó a las personas censadas la denominación exacta de la ocupación que tenían o que habían tenido, así como las funciones principales desempeñadas (por ejemplo, contador, vendedor de calzado, montador de aparatos de vídeo en una cadena de producción, asalariado a contrata en un servicio de bienestar social, carpintero o barredor de calles). Para codificar la ocupación, se utilizaron 175 grupos de la clasificación nacional de ocupaciones. Los enlaces con la clasificación CIUO-88 se han establecido a nivel de subgrupos principales (clave de 2 dígitos).

c) Situación en el empleo: Para determinar la situación que tenían o habían tenido, se pidió a las personas ocupadas y a los desempleados anteriormente empleados que indicasen si eran: independientes con empleados (empleador); independientes sin empleados (trabajadores por cuenta propia); trabajadores familiares no remunerados; asalariados/funcionarios públicos; obreros calificados; obreros semicalificados; obreros no calificados; o aprendices. Para codificar esta variable, se utilizaron los ocho grupos que se acaban de indicar.

8. Diferencias principales con el censo anterior:
Las principales diferencias se refieren a las clasificaciones utilizadas en 1991. En lo que atañe a las ramas de actividad económica, se introdujeron códigos adicionales con el fin de mejorar los enlaces con CIIU-89; en cuanto a la ocupación, se adoptó una serie de códigos resumida.

9. Publicación de los resultados del censo:
Los resultados del censo aparecieron en 1993, en diversas publicaciones de la serie "Beiträge zur österreichischen Statistik". El volumen en que figuran los datos del censo relativos a todo el país se titula "Hauptergebnisse II - Oesterreich", núm. de referencia 1030/20. La base de datos ISIS - Statistical Data Base contiene informaciones más pormenorizadas y clasificaciones de múltiples entradas adaptadas a las necesidades de los usuarios.

El organismo responsable de estas publicaciones es la Oesterreichisches Statistisches Zentralamt, de Viena.

Los resultados del censo también están a disposición de quienes lo soliciten en forma de folletos, documentos, disquetes y cintas magnéticas.

BAHAMAS

1. Nombre y dirección del organismo responsable del censo:
Department of Statistics, Ministry of Finance, P.O. Box N-3904, Nassau.

2. Censos de población llevados a cabo desde 1945 (años):
1953, 1963, 1970, 1980 y 1990. La presente descripción se refiere al censo de población de 1990 (realizado el 1o. de mayo de ese año).

3. Alcance del censo:
a) Geográfico: Todo el país.

b) Personas comprendidas: Toda la población, salvo los diplomáticos extranjeros residentes en Bahamas. También se estableció un registro, desglosado por sexo, de quienes estaban de visita en el país durante el período del censo, pero no se les entrevistó y, por ende, no fueron incluidos en el censo.

4. Período de referencia:
La semana que terminó el 28 de abril de 1990 y los 12 meses anteriores al censo.

5. Materias principales:
a) Población total, según sexo y edad:	sí
Población económicamente activa por:	
b) Sexo y grupo de edad:	sí
c) Rama de actividad económica:	sí

d) Ocupación:	sí
e) Situación en el empleo:	sí
f) Nivel más alto de educación:	sí
g) Horas de trabajo:	sí
h) Otras características:	sí

Ref. a): La edad se determinó según el año de nacimiento y los años cumplidos en el último cumpleaños.

Ref. g): Las horas de trabajo se refirieron al período total (en número de semanas) trabajado por las personas ocupadas durante el período de referencia largo.

Ref. h): El censo también recolectó información sobre el período en que la persona trabajó por última vez en un puesto fijo, al menos dos semanas, desde 1979 a la fecha del censo, y sobre el ingreso total de la persona durante los 12 meses anteriores a la fecha del censo.

6. Conceptos y definiciones:
a) Población económicamente activa: Abarcó a todas las personas de 15 o más años de edad que durante el período de referencia estaban ocupadas o desempleadas, conforme a las definiciones que figuran más adelante. La definición incluyó a los miembros de las fuerzas armadas.

b) Empleo:
Para determinar si una persona debía contabilizarse como "ocupada" se hicieron dos preguntas: "¿Cuál era su situación en el empleo principal durante la semana que terminó el 28 de abril de 1990?", y "¿cuál ha sido su situación en el empleo principal en los últimos 12 meses?" Se consideró "ocupada" a toda persona que respondió "ocupado" o "empleado pero sin trabajar".

Se ha indicado que fueron incluidas las siguientes categorías:
i)   personas que trabajan sin remuneración en una empresa o negocio familiar;
ii) personas que producen bienes primarios para el autoconsumo;
iii) personas ocupadas pero temporalmente ausentes de su trabajo;
iv) estudiantes que trabajan a tiempo parcial;
v)   trabajadores estacionales u ocasionales;
vi) conscriptos del servicio militar o civil;
vii) aprendices y personas que siguen un curso de formación.

Sólo las categorías i) y iii) pueden identificarse por separado con arreglo a sus respuestas a las preguntas sobre el empleo y la situación en el empleo.

c) Desempleo: Se consideró "desempleada" a toda persona que no tenía trabajo y buscaba uno. Se incluyó en esta categoría a quienes respondieron a las preguntas que figuran en el párrafo 6 b), indicando "en busca de un primer trabajo", "en busca de trabajo (cuando no sea el primero)" o "en busca de trabajo durante las últimas cuatro semanas".

7. Clasificaciones utilizadas:
Tanto las personas ocupadas como las desempleadas anteriormente empleadas se clasificaron por rama de actividad, por ocupación y por situación en el empleo.

a) Rama de actividad económica: Para determinarla se preguntó: "¿De qué rama de actividad o negocio se trata? (Indique, por ejemplo: comercio minorista, escuela primaria, bufete de abogados, banca, fábrica de cerveza, etc.)". Para codificarla se utilizaron nueve grupos. Se establecieron enlaces con la CIIU-Rev.2 a nivel de grandes divisiones (1 dígito).

b) Ocupación: Para determinarla se preguntó: "¿Qué clase de trabajo efectuó? (Describa su puesto con la mayor precisión posible, por ejemplo: auxiliar de venta, dactilógrafo, médico, mecánico de autos, ingeniero civil, conductor de taxi, ama de casa, etc.)". Para codificarla se utilizaron nueve grupos. Se establecieron enlaces con la CIUO-88 a nivel de grandes grupos (1 dígito).

c) Situación en el empleo: Para determinarla se preguntó: "¿Cuál era su situación en el empleo, la última vez que trabajó?". Para codificarla se utilizaron cinco grupos: empleado (sector privado); empleado (empresa estatal); trabajador familiar no remunerado; actividad independiente con auxiliares remunerados, actividad independiente sin auxiliares remunerados.

8. Diferencias principales con el censo anterior:
En el censo de 1980 se utilizó tan solo un período de referencia corto (la semana anterior al censo), pero se elaboraron tabulaciones únicamente sobre quienes habían trabajado durante algún tiempo en los 12 meses anteriores al censo.

Además, en la pregunta relativa al período de referencia corto (una semana) incluida en el censo de 1990 también se había pedido indicar si se había buscado trabajo en las últimas cuatro semanas (véase el párrafo 6 c)).

9. Publicación de los resultados del censo:
Los resultados definitivos del censo se editaron bajo el título "Commonwealth of the Bahamas - Report of the 1990 Census of Population: Economic Activity and Income", publicado en 1992.

La organización responsable de dicha publicación es el Department of Statistics, Ministry of Finance, P.O. Box N-3904, Nassau, Bahamas.

Los resultados del censo también están disponibles en cuadros inéditos y disquetes.

BAHREIN

1. Nombre y dirección del organismo responsable del censo:
Central Statistics Organization, Directorate of Statistics, Cabinet Affairs, P.O. Box 5835, Manama.

2. Censos de población llevados a cabo desde 1945 (años):
1950, 1959, 1965, 1971, 1981 y 1991. La presente descripción se refiere al censo de población de 1991 (realizado el 16 de noviembre de ese año).

3. Alcance del censo:
a) Geográfico: Todo el país.
b) Personas comprendidas: Toda la población.

4. Período de referencia:
La semana anterior al día del censo.

5. Materias principales:
a) Población total, según sexo y edad: sí
Población económicamente activa por:
b) Sexo y grupo de edad: sí
c) Rama de actividad económica: sí
d) Ocupación: sí
e) Situación en el empleo: sí
f) Nivel más alto de educación: sí
g) Horas de trabajo: no
h) Otras características: sí

Ref. a): La edad se determinó según los años cumplidos en el último cumpleaños.

Ref. h): El censo también acopió información acerca de la duración del desempleo.

6. Conceptos y definiciones:
a) Población económicamente activa: Incluye a todas las personas de 12 años y más que, durante la semana de referencia, se encontraban empleadas o desempleadas, conforme a las definiciones que se dan más adelante. La definición incluyó a los miembros de las fuerzas armadas.

b) Empleo: Se consideró "ocupada" a toda persona que, durante la semana de referencia, estaba desempeñando alguna actividad laboral remunerada fuera del hogar. Para determinar si una persona debía contabilizarse como "ocupada" se preguntó "¿Qué condición ocupa en su trabajo? 1) empleador; 2) trabajador independiente; 3) trabajador asalariado; 4) trabajador no remunerado; 5) desempleado anteriormente empleado; 6) desempleado que nunca ha trabajado; 7) estudiante; 8) ama de casa; 9) rentista; 10) incapacitado para trabajar; 11) no quiere trabajar; 12) no se aplica".

Se ha indicado que fueron incluidas las siguientes categorías:
i) personas que trabajan sin remuneración en una empresa o negocio familiar;
ii) personas que producen bienes primarios para el autoconsumo;
iii) personas ocupadas pero temporalmente ausentes de su trabajo;
iv) estudiantes que trabajan a tiempo parcial;
v) trabajadores estacionales u ocasionales;
vi) conscriptos del servicio militar o civil.

Sólo las personas que trabajan sin remuneración en una empresa o negocio familiar pueden identificarse por separado.

c) Desempleo: Se consideró "desempleada" a toda persona que, durante la semana de referencia, estaba sin empleo, pero era capaz y quería trabajar. Las personas desempleadas fueron clasificadas como "desempleado antes empleado" y "desempleado que nunca ha trabajado".

7. Clasificaciones utilizadas:
Sólo las personas ocupadas se clasificaron por rama de actividad económica y por situación en el empleo. Tanto las personas ocupadas como las desempleadas anteriormente empleadas se clasificaron por ocupación.

a) Rama de actividad económica: Para determinarla se preguntó: "¿Cuál es la principal actividad del establecimiento en que trabaja?". Para codificar la rama de actividad se utilizaron 17 grupos de la clasificación nacional. Se establecieron enlaces con la CIIU-Rev.3 a nivel de categorías de tabulación (clave de 1 dígito).

b) Ocupación: Para determinarla se preguntó: "¿Qué tipo de trabajo desempeñaba usted"? Para codificar la ocupación, se utilizó la Standard Arab Gulf Directory for Occupational Classification, en el nivel de 1 dígito. No se establecieron enlaces con la CIUO.

c) Situación en el empleo: Para determinarla se utilizó la misma pregunta que se aplicó al empleo, en 6 b). Para codificar la situación en el empleo se utilizaron los cuatro grupos siguientes: empleador; trabajador independiente; trabajador remunerado; trabajador no remunerado.

8. Diferencias principales con el censo anterior:
En el censo de 1981, la edad mínima para quedar incluido en la población económicamente activa era de 15 años.

9. Publicación de los resultados del censo:
Los resultados definitivos se publicaron en octubre de 1993, en los siguientes volúmenes: "The Population, Housing, Buildings and Establishments Census - 1991. I - Summary results. II - Demographic and social characteristics. III -Economic characteristics. IV - Characteristics of Housing, Buildings and Establishments".

El organismo responsable de esta publicación es el Directorate of Statistics, Central Statistics Organization, P.O. Box 5835, Manama.

Los resultados del censo se encuentran también disponibles en otras formas: cuadros inéditos, disquetes y cintas magnéticas.

BARBADOS

1. Nombre y dirección del organismo responsable del censo:
Barbados Statistical Service, 3rd Floor, National Insurance Building, Fairchild Street, Bridgetown.

2. Censos de población llevados a cabo desde 1945 (años):
1946, 1960, 1970, 1980 y 1990. La presente descripción se refiere al censo de población de 1990 (realizado el 1 de mayo de ese año).

3. Alcance del censo:
a) Geográfico: Todo el país.
b) Personas comprendidas: Toda la población.

4. Período de referencia:
La semana anterior a la fecha del censo y los doce meses anteriores al mismo.

5. Materias principales:
a) Población total, según sexo y edad: sí
Población económicamente activa por:
b) Sexo y grupo de edad: sí
c) Rama de actividad económica: sí
d) Ocupación: sí
e) Situación en el empleo: sí
f) Nivel más alto de educación: sí
g) Horas de trabajo: sí
h) Otras características: no

Ref. a): La edad se determinó según los años cumplidos en el último cumpleaños.

Ref. g): El tiempo de trabajo se refería al número total de horas de trabajo efectuadas durante la semana que terminó el 28 de abril, así como al número total de meses trabajados durante el período de doce meses que terminó el 30 de abril.

6. Conceptos y definiciones:

a) Población económicamente activa: Abarcó a todas las personas de 15 o más años de edad que, durante los períodos de referencia, estaban fundamentalmente ocupadas o fundamentalmente buscando trabajo, conforme a las definiciones que se dan más adelante. La definición incluyó a todos los miembros de las fuerzas armadas.

b) Empleo: Para determinar si una persona debía contabilizarse o no como "ocupada" se preguntó "¿Cuál fue su actividad principal durante los doce meses que terminaron el 30 de abril?" y "¿Cuál fue su actividad principal durante la semana que terminó el 28 de abril?". Las posibles respuestas eran: "1) trabajé; 2) tenía empleo pero no trabajé; 3) busqué trabajo; 4) trabajé en labores del hogar; 5) asistí a clases; 6) estaba ya jubilado; 7) estaba incapacitado para trabajar; 8) otra situación; y 9) no respondió".

Se ha indicado que fueron incluidas las siguientes categorías:

i)   personas que trabajan sin remuneración en una empresa o negocio familiar;
ii) personas ocupadas pero temporalmente ausentes de su trabajo;
iii) estudiantes que trabajan a tiempo parcial;
iv) trabajadores estacionales u ocasionales;
v)   conscriptos del servicio militar o civil;
vi) aprendices y personas que siguen un curso de formación.

Sólo las categorías i), ii)y iii) pueden identificarse por separado.

c) Desempleo: Es posible distinguir entre las personas de 15 o más años de edad una categoría integrada por aquellas personas que durante los períodos de referencia estuvieron fundamentalmente buscando trabajo.

7. Clasificaciones utilizadas:

Tanto las personas ocupadas como las desocupadas anteriormente ocupadas se clasificaron por rama de actividad económica, por ocupación y según la situación en la ocupación.

a) Rama de actividad económica: Para determinarla se preguntó: "¿En qué rama de actividad o tipo de empresa o negocio trabajó usted durante los pasados doce meses?". Para codificar la rama de actividad económica se utilizó la CIIU-Rev.3 a nivel de categorías de tabulación (clave de 1 dígito).

b) Ocupación: Para determinarla se preguntó: "¿Cuál fue el tipo de empleo o de ocupación principal que ejerció usted durante los pasados doce meses?". Para codificar la ocupación se utilizó la CIUO- 88, en el nivel de grandes grupos (clave de 1 dígito).

c) Situación en el empleo: Para determinarla se preguntó: "Durante los doce meses que terminaron el 30 de abril, ¿trabajó usted para un empleador o en calidad de independiente? ("trabajó para un empleador "incluye: el Estado; empresas privadas; domicilios particulares; en el medio familiar, no remunerado. En "calidad de independiente" incluye: por cuenta propia con personal remunerado y por cuenta propia sin personal remunerado)". Para codificar la situación en el empleo se utilizaron los seis grupos antes mencionados. También se utilizó un séptimo grupo ("no respondió").

8. Diferencias principales con el censo anterior:
No hubo diferencias significativas.

9. Publicación de los resultados del censo:
Los datos definitivos relativos a la población económicamente activa y sus componentes se publicaron en 1995, en un volumen que lleva por título "1990 Population Census of Barbados".

El organismo responsable de esta publicación es el Barbados Statistical Service, Fairchild Street, Bridgetown.

Los datos recopilados por el censo se pueden obtener también en disquetes y cintas magnéticas.

BELGICA

1. Nombre y dirección del organismo responsable del censo:
Institut national de Statistique (INS), 44 rue de Louvain, 1000 Bruselas.

2. Censos de población llevados a cabo desde 1945 (años):
1947, 1961, 1970, 1981 y 1991. La presente descripción se refiere al censo de población y viviendas de 1991 (realizado el 1 de marzo de ese año).

3. Alcance del censo:
a) Geográfico: Todo el territorio.

b) Personas comprendidas: Toda la población con residencia habitual en el país, es decir, incluidos los extranjeros residentes en Bélgica y los nacionales transitoriamente residentes en el extranjero, pero sin incluir a las personas de paso en Bélgica o a las personas sin autorización de instalación definitiva (con permiso de residencia provisional).

4. Periodo de referencia:
El día del censo, pero también se consideró la situación habitual de la persona censada.

5. Materias principales:
a) Población total, según sexo y edad:	sí
Población económicamente activa por:	
b) Sexo y grupo de edad:	sí
c) Rama de actividad económica:	sí
d) Ocupación:	sí
e) Situación en el empleo:	sí
f) Nivel más alto de educación:	sí
g) Horas de trabajo:	sí
h) Otras características:	sí

Ref. a): La edad se determinó según el año de nacimiento o los años cumplidos en el último cumpleaños; en la práctica, la mayor parte de los cuadros disponibles se establecieron de acuerdo con éste último criterio.

Ref. g): El tiempo de trabajo se refiere a la duración normal de la jornada laboral (en el caso de las personas ocupadas) y a las horas efectivamente trabajadas (en el caso de las personas ocupadas, presentes en el lugar de trabajo) durante el período de referencia.

Ref. h): También se recolectaron informaciones relativas a los medios de transporte utilizados y al tiempo necesario para trasladarse al lugar de trabajo y regresar al domicilio.

6. Conceptos y definiciones:
a) Población económicamente activa: Abarcó a todas las personas de 14 o más años de edad que, en la fecha del censo, estaban ocupadas o desempleadas, según las definiciones que se dan más adelante. Esta definición incluyó tanto a los militares de carrera como a los conscriptos (milicianos); estos últimos quedaron clasificados en la población económicamente activa desocupada.

b) Empleo: Se consideró "ocupada" a toda persona que respondió afirmativamente a la pregunta "¿Ejerce usted una profesión o un cargo o desempeña una actividad lucrativa? (responda afirmativamente también en el caso de que dicha profesión, cargo o actividad lucrativa sea de índole provisoria o no constituya su principal fuente de medios de subsistencia; también deben responder afirmativamente las personas que ayudan a un miembro del grupo familiar en su actividad económica; se debe responder afirmativamente incluso si la ocupación no se ejerce en el momento del censo por motivos de enfermedad, vacaciones, reducción de actividades, conflicto del trabajo, etc.)".

Se ha indicado que fueron incluidas las siguientes categorías:

i)   personas que trabajan sin remuneración en una empresa o negocio familiar;
ii)   personas que producen bienes primarios para el autoconsumo;
iii) estudiantes que trabajan a tiempo parcial;
iv)   trabajadores estacionales u ocasionales, a condición de que estuviesen ocupados en la fecha del censo;
v)   conscriptos del servicio militar o civil;
vi)   personas con más de un empleo;
vii) aprendices y personas que siguen un curso de formación.

Sólo las categorías i), iii), v), vi) y vii) pueden identificarse por separado, con arreglo a sus respuestas a determinadas preguntas. Los aprendices y las personas que seguían un curso de formacion pueden identificarse por separado, pero únicamente si su situación era objeto de un contrato.

c) Desempleo: Se consideró "desempleada" a toda persona que, en el momento del censo, estaba sin trabajo y buscaba uno, incluso si se trataba de un primer empleo. No quedaron incluidos en la definición los estudiantes que buscaban trabajo.

7. Clasificaciones utilizadas:
Tan sólo las personas ocupadas fueron clasificadas por rama de actividad económica, por ocupación y según la situación en el empleo.

a) Rama de actividad económica: Se pidió a las personas censadas que indicasen el nombre y la dirección del establecimiento, la institución o el servicio administrativo que dirigían o en el que estaban empleadas; también se les pidó que indicasen la naturaleza de las actividades de la empresa, institución o servicio (se dieron instrucciones especiales para no confundir estas actividades con la profesión de la persona censada).

Para codificar la rama de actividad se utilizaron 809 grupos que permitían establecer una correspondencia con la Nomenclatura General de Actividades Económicas de la Comunidad Europea (NACE, Rev.1). Se establecieron enlaces con la CIIU-Rev.2, en los niveles más detallados posibles. Se estudió la posibilidad de establecer enlaces con la CIIU-Rev.3.

b) Ocupación: Para determinarla se hicieron las siguientes preguntas: "Describa con precisión la profesión o el cargo que ejerce usted, a fin de poder deducir la índole del trabajo efectuado"; "Indique su grado de escalafón actual, describa sus funciones actuales o detalle las calificaciones profesionales requeridas que figuren en un decreto de nombramiento, un contrato de trabajo u otro documento equivalente"; "¿En qué sección del establecimiento, la institución o el servicio que le emplea trabaja usted? (recepción, informaciones; compras, aprovisionamiento; producción y explotación; ventas, despacho de pedidos; contabilidad y finanzas, etc.)".

Para codificar la ocupación se utilizaron alrededor de 1.700 grupos de la Clasificación Nacional de Ocupaciones. Se establecieron enlaces con la clasificación CIUO-88, a nivel de subgrupos (clave de 3 dígitos).

c) Situación en el empleo: Para determinarla se hizo la siguiente pregunta: "¿Ejerce usted su profesión en calidad de: trabajador independiente, jefe de un establecimiento o una empresa, no vinculado por un contrato de trabajo; jefe de un establecimiento o de una empresa, vinculado por un contrato de trabajo; trabajador auxiliar (de un independiente); empleado del sector público; obrero del sector público; empleado del sector privado; obrero del sector privado; aprendiz vinculado por un contrato de aprendizaje; trabajador doméstico o de servicio?". Para codificar la situación en el empleo se utilizaron los nueve grupos descritos. A los independientes y a los jefes de establecimiento o de empresa no vinculados por un contrato de trabajo se preguntó: "¿Emplea usted personal remunerado? Si la respuesta es afirmativa, ¿a cuántas personas emplea?". A las demás personas censadas se preguntó: "¿Dirige usted a personal subalterno? Si la respuesta es afirmativa, ¿a cuántas personas dirige usted?".

8. Diferencias principales con el censo anterior:

Sólo se modificó el procedimiento de acopio de datos. En efecto, en el curso de los censos precedentes, los empadronadores distribuyeron los cuestionarios y los recogieron durante una visita ulterior. En 1991, los boletines de censo, personalizados de acuerdo con las informaciones procedentes del Registro Nacional, se hicieron llegar por correo a las personas censadas. Los empadronadores que disponían de listados de los boletines remitidos, debían visitar todas las viviendas ubicadas en su respectiva circunscripción, y:

– recoger los formularios cumplimentados;
– distribuir, en caso necesario, boletines a las personas que no hubiesen recibido o hubieran extraviado los boletines personalizados, figurasen o no éstas en las listas de residentes en el sector.

La utilización de un sistema de lectura óptica permitió acelerar el examen de los boletines personalizados.

9. Publicación de los resultados del censo:

La publicación de las cifras definitivas referentes a la población activa lleva por título "Recensement général de la population du 1.3.1991 - Population active" (1994).

El organismo responsable de esta publicación es el Institut national de Statistique, de Bruselas.

Los resultados del censo de 1991 están disponibles también en cuadros, microfichas, disquetes, CD-ROM y cintas magnéticas.

BELICE

1. Nombre y dirección del organismo responsable del censo:

Central Statistical Office, Ministry of Finance, Belmopan.

2. Censos de población llevados a cabo desde 1945 (años):

1946, 1960, 1970, 1980 y 1991. La presente descripción se refiere al censo de población de 1991 (realizado el 12 de mayo de ese año).

3. Alcance del censo:

a) Geográfico: Todo el territorio.

b) Personas comprendidas: Toda la población.

4. Periodo de referencia:

La semana y el período de doce meses anteriores al día del censo.

5. Materias principales:

a) Población total, según sexo y edad:	sí
Población económicamente activa por:	
b) Sexo y grupo de edad:	sí
c) Rama de actividad económica:	sí
d) Ocupación:	sí
e) Situación en el empleo:	sí
f) Nivel más alto de educación:	sí
g) Horas de trabajo:	sí
h) Otras características:	sí

Ref. a): La edad se determinó según los años cumplidos en el último cumpleaños.

Ref. g): El censo recolectó información sobre el número de meses trabajados por las personas ocupadas durante el período de referencia largo, y sobre el número de horas trabajadas por estas mismas personas durante el período de referencia corto.

Ref. h): El censo recolectó información sobre los ingresos y sobre los medios de transporte utilizados para trasladarse al lugar de trabajo (a pie, bicicleta, automóvil u otro vehículo particular, transporte público, transporte de alquiler, etc.).

6. Conceptos y definiciones:

a) Población económicamente activa: Abarcó a todas las personas de 15 o más años de edad que, durante el período de referencia de doce meses, estaban ocupadas o desempleadas, conforme a las definiciones que se dan más adelante. La definición incluyó a los miembros de las fuerzas armadas que residían en domicilios particulares, pero no a los que habitaban en cuarteles y otros recintos militares.

b) Empleo: Se consideró "ocupada" a toda persona que, fundamentalmente, desempeñó alguna actividad laboral durante los períodos de referencia. Para determinar si una persona debía contabilizarse como ocupada se utilizaron las siguientes preguntas: "¿A qué se dedicó fundamentalmente durante los pasados doce meses?", y "¿A qué se dedicó fundamentalmente durante la semana pasada?". Las posibles respuestas eran: "1) trabajé; 2) tenía un empleo, pero no trabajé; 3) busqué trabajo; 4) quería trabajar y estaba disponible para hacerlo; 5) trabajé en labores del hogar; 6) asistí a clases; 7) estaba ya jubilado; 8) estaba inválido, incapacitado para trabajar; 9) otra actividad; y 10) no respondió".

Se ha indicado que fueron incluidas las siguientes categorías:

i) personas que trabajan sin remuneración en una empresa o negocio familiar;
ii) personas que producen bienes primarios para el autoconsumo;
iii) personas ocupadas pero temporalmente ausentes de su trabajo;
iv) estudiantes que trabajan a tiempo parcial, a condición de que su actividad laboral prime con respecto a sus estudios;
v) trabajadores estacionales u ocasionales;
vi) conscriptos del servicio militar o civil.

Las categorías i), iii), iv) y v) pueden identificarse por separado, con arreglo a sus respuestas a diversas preguntas.

c) Desempleo: Se consideró "desempleada" a toda persona que, durante los períodos de referencia, quería sobremanera trabajar, estaba disponible para hacerlo y estaba buscando empleo. La definición no incluyó a los estudiantes que buscaban empleo.

7. Clasificaciones utilizadas:

Tanto las personas ocupadas como las desempleadas anteriormente empleadas se clasificaron por rama de actividad económica y por ocupación. Tan sólo las personas ocupadas fueron clasificadas por situación en el empleo.

a) Rama de actividad económica: Para determinarla se preguntó: "¿Qué tipo de actividad se lleva o se llevaba a cabo en su lugar de trabajo?". Para codificar la rama de actividad se utilizó la clasificación nacional. Se establecieron enlaces con la CIIU-Rev.3 en el nivel de clases (clave de 4 dígitos).

b) Ocupación: Para determinarla se preguntó: "¿Qué tipo de trabajo desempeña o desempeñaba en su ocupación principal?". Para codificar la ocupación se utilizó la clasificación nacional. Se establecieron enlaces con la CIUO-88 a nivel de grupos primarios (clave de 4 dígitos).

c) Situación en el empleo: Para determinarla se preguntó: "¿Se ocupó usted de su propia empresa o negocio, trabajó por un sueldo o un salario, o como trabajador no remunerado en una empresa familiar?". Para codificar la situación en el empleo se utilizaron seis grupos, a saber: asalariado del sector público; asalariado del sector privado; trabajador no remunerado; trabajador independiente con personal remunerado (empleador); trabajador independiente sin personal remunerado (por cuenta propia); y no respondió.

8. Diferencias principales con el censo anterior:
En el censo de 1980 sólo se utilizó un período de referencia largo (doce meses).

9. Publicación de los resultados del censo:
Los resultados definitivos del censo se publicaron en 1992, en el volumen que lleva por título "Major Findings - 1991 Population and Housing Census".

El organismo responsable de la publicación es la Central Statistical Office in Belmopan, Ministry of Finance.

Los resultados también pueden obtenerse en cuadros inéditos y disquetes, cursando pedido a Central Statistical Office.

BENIN

1. Nombre y dirección del organismo responsable del censo:
Institut National de la Statistique et de l'Analyse Economique, Bureau central du recensement, B.P. 323, Cotonou.

2. Censos de población llevados a cabo desde 1945 (años):
1979 y 1992. La presente descripción se refiere al censo de 1992 (realizado del 15 al 29 de febrero de ese año).

3. Alcance del censo:

a) Geográfico: Todo el territorio.

b) Personas comprendidas: Toda la población, excepto los miembros del cuerpo diplomático y los nacionales residentes en el extranjero.

4. Período de referencia:
Los tres meses anteriores al día del censo.

5. Materias principales:

a) Población total, según sexo y edad:	sí
Población económicamente activa por:	
b) Sexo y grupo de edad:	sí
c) Rama de actividad económica:	sí
d) Ocupación:	sí
e) Situación en el empleo:	sí
f) Nivel más alto de educación:	sí
g) Horas de trabajo:	no
h) Otras características:	no

Ref. a): La edad se determinó según los años cumplidos en el último cumpleaños.

6. Conceptos y definiciones:

a) Población económicamente activa: Abarcó a todas las personas de 10 o más años de edad que, durante el período de referencia, estaban ocupadas o desempleadas, conforme a las definiciones que se dan más adelante. Sin embargo, los datos publicados relativos a la población económicamente activa, al empleo y al desempleo se refieren únicamente a las personas de 10 a 65 años de edad. Esta definición incluyó a todos los miembros de las fuerzas armadas. En cambio, no quedaron incluidos en ella los estudiantes con empleo a tiempo parcial ni los que buscaban trabajo.

b) Empleo: Se consideró "ocupada" a toda persona que había trabajado por lo menos una semana durante el período de referencia (los tres últimos meses). En particular, se consideró "ocupadas" a las mujeres que, además de ocuparse de las labores del hogar, habían trabajado por cuenta propia o por cuenta de la familia (vendedora, costurera, labriega, alfarera). A este respecto, se pidió precisar: "Ocupación: ocupado(a);

busca un primer empleo; desempleado(a); labores del hogar; escolar o estudiante de enseñanza media o superior; rentista".

Se ha indicado que fueron incluidas las siguientes categorías:

i) personas que trabajan sin remuneración en una empresa o negocio familiar;
ii) personas que producen bienes primarios para el autoconsumo;
iii) personas ocupadas pero temporalmente ausentes de su trabajo;
iv) trabajadores estacionales u ocasionales;
v) conscriptos del servicio militar o civil;
vi) aprendices y personas que siguen un curso de formación.

Sólo las categorías i) y vi) pueden identificarse por separado.

c) Desempleo: Se consideró "desempleada" a toda persona que ya hubiese trabajado, pero que, durante el período de referencia, estaba sin trabajo y buscaba empleo. Se clasificó por separado a las personas que buscaban un primer empleo.

7. Clasificaciones utilizadas:
Tanto las personas ocupadas como los desempleados anteriormente empleados fueron clasificados por rama de actividad, por ocupación y por situación en el empleo.

a) Rama de actividad económica: Para determinarla se hizo la siguiente pregunta: "¿Cuál es la actividad principal de la empresa o del empleador de la persona ocupada?". Por lo que se refiere a los desempleados, la rama de actividad se determinó en función de su último empleo. Para codificar la rama de actividad económica, se utilizaron nueve grupos. Se establecieron enlaces con la CIIU-Rev.2, a nivel de grandes divisiones (clave de 1 dígito).

b) Ocupación: Se pidió a los empadronadores que formularan la pregunta pertinente de conformidad con lo dispuesto en el manual de instrucciones, a fin de que se indicase la ocupación principal o la actividad que más había ocupado a la persona censada durante el período de referencia. Los desempleados debían señalar cuál había sido la última profesión ejercida durante el período de referencia. Se recomendó no usar términos genéricos, como: comerciante, funcionario, etc., sino indicar, por ejemplo: vendedora de ropas, vendedora de bollos, agente de policía, inspector de impuestos, etc. Para codificar la ocupación se utilizaron nueve grupos. Se establecieron enlaces con la clasificación CIUO-68, a nivel de grandes grupos (clave de 1 dígito).

c) Situación en el empleo: Para determinarla se hizo la siguiente pregunta: "¿En qué calidad ejerció la persona activa su profesión durante el período de referencia?". Para codificar esta variable se utilizaron las ocho categorías siguientes: trabajador independiente; empleador; asalariado de plantilla; asalariado ocupado temporalmente; miembro de cooperativa; aprendiz; trabajador familiar; otra situación.

8. Diferencias principales con el censo anterior:
En el censo de 1979 se había usado como período de referencia el mes anterior al día del censo.

9. Publicación de los resultados del censo:
Los resultados definitivos del censo aparecieron en diciembre de 1993 en la publicación que lleva por título: "Deuxième recensement général de la population et de l'habitation, février 1992. Volume I, résultats définitifs".

El organismo responsable de la publicación es el Institut National de la Statistique et de l'Analyse Economique, Bureau central du recensement (BCR), B.P. 323, Cotonou.

Los resultados del censo también están disponibles en cartuchos de Bernoulli.

BERMUDAS

1. Nombre y dirección del organismo responsable del censo:
Bermuda Government Statistical Department, P.O. Box HM 177, Hamilton HM AX.

2. Censos de población llevados a cabo desde 1945 (años):
1950, 1960, 1970, 1980 y 1991. La presente descripción se refiere al censo de 1991 (realizado el 20 de mayo de ese año).

3. Alcance del censo:

a) Geográfico: Todo el país.

b) Personas comprendidas: Toda la población.

4. Período de referencia:

La semana y el período de 12 meses anteriores al día del censo.

5. Materias principales:

a) Población total, según sexo y edad:	sí

Población económicamente activa por:

b) Sexo y grupo de edad:	sí
c) Rama de actividad económica:	sí
d) Ocupación:	sí
e) Situación en el empleo:	sí
f) Nivel más alto de educación:	sí
g) Horas de trabajo:	sí
h) Otras características:	sí

Ref. a): La edad se determinó según los años cumplidos al día del censo.

Ref. g): Se pidió a las personas de 16 y más años de edad que precisaran, cuando procediera, cuántos meses habían trabajado remunerados durante los últimos doce meses, sea para un empleador o en su propia empresa o negocio. Se preguntó a las personas ocupadas cuántas horas trabajaban normalmente en una semana cualquiera, incluidas las horas extraordinarias, fuesen éstas remuneradas o no.

Ref. h): El censo también recopiló información sobre los medios de transporte utilizados para trasladarse al lugar de trabajo, la hora de comienzo del trabajo y la escala de ingresos.

6. Conceptos y definiciones:

a) Población económicamente activa: Abarcó a todas las personas de 16 o más años de edad que, durante el período de referencia corto, estaban ocupadas o desempleadas, conforme a las definiciones que se dan más adelante. La definición incluyó a los miembros de las fuerzas armadas.

b) Empleo: Se consideró "ocupada" a toda persona que, durante la semana de referencia, desempeñó alguna actividad laboral remunerada, sea para un empleador sea en su propia empresa o negocio. Para determinar si una persona debía contabilizarse como ocupada se utilizó la siguiente pregunta: "La semana pasada, ¿cuál fue su ocupación principal, por ejemplo, estaba desempeñando un trabajo remunerado, buscaba otro empleo, asistía a clases, trabajaba en las labores del hogar o desplegaba otra actividad?". Las posibles respuestas eran: 1) tenía un trabajo remunerado; 2) tenía un empleo, pero no trabajé; 3) buscaba trabajo; 4) trabajé en tareas domésticas; 5) trabajé a título voluntario, sin remuneración; 6) era escolar o estudiante a tiempo completo; 7) estaba incapacitado para trabajar; 8) estaba ya jubilado; 9) otras actividades; y 10) no respondió.

Se ha indicado que fueron incluidas las siguientes categorías:

i) personas que trabajan sin remuneración en una empresa o negocio familiar;

ii) personas que producen bienes primarios para el autoconsumo;

iii) personas ocupadas pero temporalmente ausentes de su trabajo;

iv) estudiantes que trabajan a tiempo parcial;

v) trabajadores estacionales u ocasionales;

vi) conscriptos del servicio militar o civil;

vii) personas que tienen más de un empleo;

viii) aprendices y personas que siguen un curso de formación.

Sólo las categorías i), iii) y vii) pueden identificarse por separado.

c) Desempleo: Se consideró "desempleada" a toda persona que, durante la semana de referencia, no trabajó, sino que estuvo buscando un primer empleo o tratando de encontrar otro empleo, tras haber dejado una ocupación anterior por cualquier motivo.

7. Clasificaciones utilizadas:

Sólo las personas ocupadas fueron clasificadas por rama de actividad económica, por ocupación y según la situación en el empleo.

a) Rama de actividad económica: Para determinarla se preguntó: "¿Qué tipo de negocio o actividad se lleva a cabo fundamentalmente en su lugar de trabajo (principal)?, por ejemplo, banca, enseñanza primaria, servicios jurídicos, comercio detallista de confección, restauración, etc.". Para codificar la rama

de actividad se utilizaron 18 grupos de la clasificación nacional. Se establecieron enlaces con la CIIU-Rev.2, a nivel de grandes divisiones (clave de 1 dígito).

b) Ocupación: Para determinarla se preguntó: "¿Qué clase de trabajo efectúa en su empleo (principal)?, por ejemplo, vendedor, ingeniero civil, jefe de taller de imprenta, mecánico de automóviles, etc.". Para codificar la ocupación se utilizó la clasificación nacional. Se establecieron enlaces con la CIUO-68.

c) Situación en el empleo: Para determinarla se preguntó: "¿La semana pasada, trabajó (principalmente) en calidad de independiente o de asalariado?". Para codificar la situación en el empleo se utilizaron siete grupos, a saber: trabajador independiente con personal remunerado (empleador); trabajador independiente sin personal remunerado; trabajador al servicio de otra persona o entidad; empleado por el Gobierno de Bermudas; empleado por un gobierno extranjero; empleado por una empresa privada o por un particular; trabajador no remunerado en una empresa o una explotación agrícola familiar, y sin especificar.

8. Diferencias principales con el censo anterior:

Por lo general, los artículos incluidos en los cuestionarios se repiten de un censo al otro, con el fin de determinar si se han registrado cambios importantes. El cuestionario utilizado en Bermudas obedece a esta regla, pero también procura acopiar nuevos datos sobre algunos temas: a) el traslado al lugar de trabajo y la ubicación de éste; b) las condiciones físicas y mentales de la fuerza de trabajo, que inciden en las actividades cotidianas de algunas personas; y c) los ingresos de las personas.

9. Publicación de los resultados del censo:

Los resultados definitivos del censo se publicaron en los volúmenes que llevan por título "The 1991 Census of Population and Housing" (marzo de 1993) y "1991 Map Supplement" (noviembre de 1993).

El organismo responsable de estas publicaciones es el Bermuda Government Statistics Department, P.O. Box HM 177, Hamilton HM AX.

También se han preparado cuadros inéditos con los resultados del censo, los que pueden obtenerse cursando pedido a Bermuda Government Statistics Department.

BOLIVIA

1. Nombre y dirección del organismo responsable del censo:

Instituto Nacional de Estadística (INE), Plaza Mario Guzman Aspiazu No. 1, Casilla 6129, La Paz.

2. Censos de población llevados a cabo desde 1945 (años):

1950, 1976 y 1992. La presente descripción se refiere al censo de población de 1992 (realizado el 3 de junio).

3. Alcance del censo:

a) Geográfico: Todo el país.

b) Personas comprendidas: Toda la población excluidos a los nacionales que residen en el extranjero.

4. Período de referencia:

La semana anterior a la fecha del Censo.

5. Materias principales:

a) Población total, según sexo y edad:	sí

Población económicamente activa por:

b) Sexo y grupo de edad:	sí
c) Rama de actividad económica:	sí
d) Ocupación:	sí
e) Situación en el empleo:	sí
f) Nivel más alto de educación:	...
g) Horas de trabajo:	no
h) Otras características:	no

Ref. a): Se definió la edad por el último cumpleaños.

6. Conceptos y definiciones:

a) Población económicamente activa: Incluye a todas las personas de 7 años y más de edad, que durante la semana de referencia estaban empleadas o desempleadas, tal como se definen más adelante. La definición excluye a los conscriptos del servicio militar o civil pero incluye a los militares de carrera.

b) Empleo: Son consideradas "empleadas" las personas de 7 años y más, que declararon haber trabajado durante la semana de referencia.

Se ha indicado que quedan incluidas las siguientes categorías:

i)	personas trabajando sin paga en firma o negocio familiar;
ii)	personas en la producción de bienes primarios para autoconsumo;
iii)	personas empleadas y temporalmente ausentes del trabajo;
iv)	estudiantes que trabajan a tiempo parcial;
v)	trabajadores estacionales u ocasionales;
vi)	personas con más de un empleo;
vii)	aprendices y personas que siguen un curso de formación.

Las personas de las categorías i), iii) y vi) pueden identificarse por separado utilizando preguntas específicas.

c) Desempleo: Son consideradas como "desempleadas" las personas que durante la semana de referencia no trabajaron pero que buscaron trabajo. Las preguntas utilizadas para determinar si la persona estaba desempleada son "¿Buscó trabajo habiendo trabajado antes?" y "¿Buscó trabajo por primera vez?".

7. Clasificaciones utilizadas:
Sólo las personas ocupadas se clasifican por rama de actividad económica, por ocupación y según la situación en el empleo.

a) Rama de actividad económica: Según la pregunta: "¿Qué produce o a qué actividad se dedica el establecimiento donde trabaja (ó trabajó si es cesante)?". Para identificar la rama de actividad se preguntó a personas ocupadas por el nombre, dirección y sector de actividad económica de la empresa, establecimiento o administración que las empleaba o que dirigían. Para codificar la rama de actividad se utilizó la CIIU-Rev.3 a nivel de 4 dígitos.

b) Ocupación: Según la pregunta: "¿Durante la semana pasada (ó en su último empleo en caso de ser cesante), cuál fue su ocupación principal?". Para identificar el grupo de ocupaciones se solicitó a las personas ocupadas que indicaran con precisión la ocupación u oficio que ejercían en esos momentos. Para codificar el grupo de ocupaciones se utilizó la CIUO-88 a nivel de los subgrupos (3 dígitos).

c) Situación en el empleo: Para identificar la situación en la ocupación se utilizó los siete grupos siguientes: empleado, obrero, cuenta propia, patrón o empleador, miembro de cooperativa, profesional independiente, trabajador familiar.

8. Diferencias principales con el censo anterior:
No hubo diferencias significativas.

9. Publicación de los resultados del censo:
Los resultados finales se publicaron en mayo de 1993.

El título exacto de la publicación con los resultados finales es "Censo Nacional de Población y Vivienda 1992: Resultados finales".

La organización responsable de la publicación es el Instituto Nacional de Estadística, Plaza Mario Guzmán Aspiazu No. 1, Casilla 6129, La Paz.

Los resultados del censo se encuentran también disponibles en otras formas: archivos (documentos de trabajo); publicación de resultados en profundidad (Indicadores sociodemográficos de ciudades capitales de Departamento, según zonas censales, y de Provincias); y base de datos (discos magnéticos).

BOTSWANA

1. Nombre y dirección del organismo responsable del censo:
Central Statistics Office, Private Bag 0024, Gaborone.

2. Censos de población llevados a cabo desde 1945 (años):
1946, 1956, 1964, 1971, 1981 y 1991. La presente descripción se refiere al censo de población de 1991 (realizado del 14 al 28 de agosto de ese año).

3. Alcance del censo:
a) Geográfico: Todo el país.

b) Personas comprendidas: Toda la población.

4. Periodo de referencia:
El mes anterior al día de la entrevista.

5. Materias principales:
a) Población total, según sexo y edad: sí
Población económicamente activa por:
b) Sexo y grupo de edad: sí
c) Rama de actividad económica: sí
d) Ocupación: sí
e) Situación en el empleo: sí
f) Nivel más alto de educación: sí
g) Horas de trabajo: no
h) Otras características: no

Ref. a): La edad se determinó según los años cumplidos en el último cumpleaños.

6. Conceptos y definiciones:
a) Población económicamente activa: Abarcó a todas las personas de 12 o más años de edad que, durante el mes de referencia, estaban ocupadas o desempleadas, conforme a las definiciones que se dan más adelante. La definición incluyó a los miembros de las fuerzas armadas.

b) Empleo: Se consideró "ocupada" a toda persona que, durante el mes de referencia, desempeñó alguna actividad laboral remunerada con dinero, sea por cuenta propia o al servicio de un empleador. La definición incluyó también a las personas que trabajaban en explotaciones agrícolas familiares o cuidaban del ganado.

Se ha indicado que fueron incluidas las siguientes categorías:

i)	personas que trabajan sin remuneración en una empresa o negocio familiar;
ii)	personas que producen bienes primarios para el autoconsumo;
iii)	personas ocupadas pero temporalmente ausentes de su trabajo;
iv)	estudiantes que trabajan a tiempo parcial;
v)	trabajadores estacionales u ocasionales.

Sólo las categorías i) y ii) pueden identificarse por separado.

c) Desempleo: Se consideró "desempleada" a toda persona que, durante el mes de referencia, se encontraba sin trabajo y buscaba activamente empleo. La definición no incluyó a los estudiantes que buscaban trabajo.

7. Clasificaciones utilizadas:
Sólo las personas ocupadas fueron clasificadas por rama de actividad económica, por ocupación y según la situación en el empleo.

a) Rama de actividad económica: Para determinarla se preguntó: "¿Cuál es el principal producto fabricado, servicio prestado o actividad realizada en su lugar de trabajo?". Para codificar la rama de actividad se utilizaron nueve grupos de la clasificación nacional. Se establecieron enlaces con la CIIU-Rev.2, a nivel de grandes divisiones (clave de 1 dígito).

b) Ocupación: Para determinarla se preguntó: "¿Qué tipo de trabajo desempeñaba usted?". Para codificar la ocupación se utilizaron 10 grupos de la clasificación nacional. Se establecieron enlaces con la CIUO-88 a nivel de grandes grupos (clave de 1 dígito).

c) Situación en el empleo: Se pidió a las personas ocupadas que precisaran su situación en el empleo. Para codificar esta variable se utilizaron dos grupos: empleados (o sea, las personas que trabajaban para alguien a cambio de un sueldo o un salario, de honorarios, comisiones u otra forma de remuneración), y trabajadores independientes (es decir, las personas que desempeñaban una actividad por cuenta propia, por ejemplo: labriegos que cultivaban productos destinados a la venta, comerciantes, vendedores ambulantes, o zapateros remendones y peluqueros que trabajan en la calle, etc.).

8. Diferencias principales con el censo anterior:
El censo de 1991 acopió datos sobre la ocupación de las personas que indicaron trabajar en una empresa familiar y en explotaciones agrícolas y ganaderas.

9. Publicación de los resultados del censo:
Los datos definitivos se publicaron en 1994, en el volumen que lleva por título "1991 Population and Housing Census Administrative/Technical Report and National Statistical Tables".

El organismo responsable de esta publicación es la Central Statistics Office, Private Bag 0024, Gaborone.

Los resultados del censo están disponibles también en otros soportes, como disquetes y cuadros inéditos.

BRASIL

1. Nombre y dirección del organismo responsable del censo:
Instituto Brasileiro de Geografía e Estatística (IBGE/DPE/DEPOP), Rua Visconde de Niterói, 1246/Bloco B - 8o andar, Rio de Janeiro, RJ.

2. Censos de población llevados a cabo desde 1945 (años):
1950, 1960, 1970, 1980 y 1991. La presente descripción se refiere al censo de población de 1991 (realizado el 1 de septiembre).

3. Alcance del censo:
a) Geográfico: Todo el país.

b) Personas comprendidas: Toda la población (salvo los aborígenes).

4. Período de referencia:
Un año (del 1 de septiembre de 1990 al 31 de agosto de 1991).

5. Materias principales:
a) Población total, según sexo y edad:	sí
Población económicamente activa por:	
b) Sexo y grupo de edad:	sí
c) Rama de actividad económica:	sí
d) Ocupación:	sí
e) Situación en el empleo:	sí
f) Nivel más alto de educación:	sí
g) Horas de trabajo:	sí
h) Otras características:	sí

Ref. a): Se definió la edad en términos del mes y año de nacimiento; si no se conoce, se refiere a la edad supuesta.

Ref. g): Se refiere a las horas usualmente trabajadas por semana por las personas ocupadas, en la ocupación principal y en todas las ocupaciones ejercidas.

Ref. h): Se refiere a los ingresos de la ocupación principal y de otras ocupaciones ejercidas.

6. Conceptos y definiciones:
a) Población económicamente activa: Incluye a todas las personas de 10 años y más que, durante el año de referencia, se encontraban empleadas o desempleadas, conforme a las definiciones que se dan más adelante. La definición incluye también a todas las fuerzas armadas. Las preguntas de empleo y desempleo solo se refieren a una muestra del 20 por ciento de los hogares en los municipios con una población de 15 000 habitantes o menos, y del 10 por ciento en los municipios con una población de más de 15 000 habitantes.

b) Empleo: Se consideran "ocupadas" a las personas que, durante el año de referencia, trabajaron por dinero, ganancia o subsidios, etc., o que trabajaron sin remuneración por 15 horas o más semanales ayudando a un familiar con quien residen, y que contestaron afirmativamente a la pregunta "¿Trabajó todos o parte de los 12 últimos meses (del 1/9/1990 al 31/8/1991)?".

Se ha indicado que quedan incluidas las siguientes categorías:

i) personas que trabajan sin remuneración en una empresa familiar;
ii) personas ocupadas pero temporalmente ausentes de su trabajo;
iii) estudiantes que trabajan medio tiempo;
iv) trabajadores estacionales u ocasionales;
v) conscriptos del servicio militar o civil;
vi) personas con más de un empleo;
vii) aprendices y personas que siguen un curso de formación.

Solamente a las personas de las categorías i), iii) y vi) se pueden identificar separadamente a través de preguntas específicas.

c) Desempleo: Se consideran como "desempleadas" a las personas que nunca trabajaron pero buscaron trabajo durante el año de referencia, ya sea que hayan trabajado antes o no, y que contestaron negativamente a la pregunta utilizada para la definición del empleo.

7. Clasificaciones utilizadas:
Solo las personas ocupadas se clasificaron por rama de actividad económica, por ocupación y según la situación en el empleo.

a) Rama de actividad económica: Para establecer la rama de actividad económica se preguntó el nombre del negocio, de la organización, institución, etc., donde la persona ejerce su ocupación principal. Para codificar esta variable, se utilizaron 26 grupos de la clasificación nacional de actividades económicas, la cual es compatible con la CIIU-Rev.2 a nivel de grandes divisiones (1 dígito).

b) Ocupación: Para establecer la ocupación se preguntó por la profesión, cargo, función, etc., que ejerció usualmente la persona en el año de referencia. Si durante este período la persona cambió de trabajo en forma definitiva, se refiere al trabajo actual y no usual. Para codificar esta variable, se utilizaron 10 grandes grupos de la clasificación nacional de ocupaciones, la cual es comparable con la CIUO-68 a nivel de grandes grupos (1 dígito).

c) Situación en el empleo: Para determinar esta variable, se preguntó por la posición en el establecimiento, el negocio o la institución en la que trabajó la persona. Se codificó en 11 grupos (trabajador agrícola temporero; trabajador doméstico (empleado o cuenta propia); aparcero (empleado o cuenta propia); empleado del sector público (servicio público o empresa estatal); empleado del sector privado; trabajador por cuenta propia; empleador; sin remuneración).

8. Diferencias principales con el censo anterior:
En el censo de 1980 se utilizaron dos períodos de referencia, es decir, un período largo (de un año) para definir la población económicamente activa, el empleo y el desempleo, y un período corto (la semana anterior al censo) para medir las características de la población.

9. Publicación de los resultados del censo:
Los resultados definitivos del censo fueron publicados en 1993.

La organización responsable de la publicación de los resultados es el Instituto Brasileiro de Geografia e Estatistica, Av. Franklin Roosevelt 166, 10o. andar Centro, Rio de Janeiro, RJ.

Los resultados del censo están también disponibles en forma de cuadros no publicados, disquetes, cintas magnéticas y microfichas.

BRUNEI DARUSSALAM

1. Nombre y dirección del organismo responsable del censo:
Economic Planning Unit, Ministry of Finance, Bandar Seri Begawan 2012, Brunei Darussalam.

2. Censos de población llevados a cabo desde 1945 (años):
1971, 1981 y 1991. La presente descripción se refiere al censo de población de 1991 (realizado el 6 de agosto de ese año).

3. Alcance del censo:
a) Geográfico: Todo el país.

b) Personas comprendidas: Toda la población.

4. Período de referencia:
La semana anterior al empadronamiento.

5. Materias principales:
a) Población total, según sexo y edad:	sí
Población económicamente activa por:	
b) Sexo y grupo de edad:	sí
c) Rama de actividad económica:	sí
d) Ocupación:	sí
e) Situación en el empleo:	sí
f) Nivel más alto de educación:	sí
g) Horas de trabajo:	sí
h) Otras características:	sí

Ref. a): La edad se determinó según la fecha de nacimiento.

Ref. g): Se pidió a las personas ocupadas que indicaran las horas de trabajo efectivas durante el período de referencia.

Ref. h): El censo también recolectó información sobre el ingreso mensual bruto percibido en concepto de trabajo, así como sobre las primas recibidas en los últimos 12 meses.

6. Conceptos y definiciones:
a) Población económicamente activa: Abarcó a todas las personas de 15 o más años de edad que durante el período de referencia estaban ocupadas o desempleadas, conforme a las definiciones que figuran más adelante. La definición incluyó a los miembros de las fuerzas armadas, pero no a los estu-

diantes que trabajaban a tiempo parcial ni a los estudiantes que buscaban trabajo.

b) Empleo: Se consideró "ocupada" a toda persona que declaró haber trabajado durante el período de referencia. Para determinar si la persona debía contabilizarse como ocupada se utilizaron cuatro indicadores, a saber: "actividad económica; trabaja; busca trabajo; y otros".

Se ha indicado que fueron incluidas las siguientes categorías:

i) personas que trabajan sin remuneración en una empresa o negocio familiar;
ii) personas que producen bienes primarios para el autoconsumo;
iii) personas ocupadas pero temporalmente ausentes de su trabajo;
iv) trabajadores estacionales u ocasionales;
v) conscriptos del servicio militar o civil;
vi) aprendices y personas que siguen un curso de formación.

Ninguna categoría puede identificarse por separado.

c) Desempleo: Se consideró "desempleada" a toda persona que declaró haber estado buscando trabajo durante el período de referencia. Para determinar si la persona debía considerarse "desempleada" se utilizaron los mismos indicadores enumerados en el párrafo 6 b).

7. Clasificaciones utilizadas:

Sólo las personas ocupadas se clasificaron por rama de actividad, por ocupación y por situación en el empleo.

a) Rama de actividad económica: Se pidió a las personas ocupadas que indicaran el nombre y la dirección del empleador o la empresa, precisando la rama de actividad. Para codificar esta variable se utilizaron 10 grupos de la clasificación nacional. Se establecieron enlaces con la CIIU-Rev.3 a nivel de categorías de tabulación (1 dígito).

b) Ocupación: Se pidió a las personas ocupadas que detallaran su ocupación. Para codificarla se utilizaron 10 grupos de la clasificación nacional. Se establecieron enlaces con la CIOU-88 a nivel de grandes grupos (1 dígito).

c) Situación en el empleo: Se pidió a las personas ocupadas que describieran su situación en el empleo. Para codificar esta variable se utilizaron 4 grupos: empleador; empleado; trabajador por cuenta propia; y trabajador familiar.

8. Diferencias principales con el censo anterior:

No hubo diferencias significativas.

9. Publicación de los resultados del censo:

Los datos definitivos se editaron en 1993 en dos publicaciones, "Report on the 1991 Population Census - June 1993" y "Summary Tables of the 1991 Population Census - January 1993".

La organización responsable de estas publicaciones es la Economic Planning Unit, Ministry of Finance, B.S.B. 2012, Brunei Darussalam.

También están disponibles, para quienes los soliciten, otros cuadros del censo de 1991 no incluidos en estas publicaciones, únicamente en edición impresa.

BULGARIA

1. Nombre y dirección del organismo responsable del censo:

Institut national de statistique, Division "Recensement de la population" 2, rue P. Volov, Sofía.

2. Censos de población llevados a cabo desde 1945 (años):

1946, 1956, 1965, 1975, 1985 y 1992. La presente descripción se refiere al censo de población de 1992 (realizado el 4 de diciembre de ese año).

3. Alcance del censo:

a) Geográfico: Todo el territorio.

b) Personas comprendidas: Toda la población.

4. Periodo de referencia:

El día del censo.

5. Materias principales:

a) Población total, según sexo y edad: sí
Población económicamente activa por:

b) Sexo y grupo de edad: sí
c) Rama de actividad económica: sí
d) Ocupación: sí
e) Situación en el empleo: no
f) Nivel más alto de educación: sí
g) Horas de trabajo: no
h) Otras características: no

Ref. a): La edad se determinó según el año de nacimiento.

6. Conceptos y definiciones:

a) Población económicamente activa: Abarcó a todas las personas de 10 a 90 años de edad que, el día del censo, estaban ocupadas o desempleadas, según las definiciones que se dan más adelante. La definición incluyó a los miembros de las fuerzas armadas.

b) Empleo: Se consideró "ocupada" a toda persona que respondió afirmativamente a la pregunta "¿Trabaja usted hoy, 4.12.1992?".

Se ha indicado que fueron incluidas las siguientes categorías:

i) personas que trabajan sin remuneración en una empresa o negocio familiar;
ii) personas que producen bienes primarios para el autoconsumo;
iii) personas ocupadas pero temporalmente ausentes de su trabajo;
iv) estudiantes que trabajan a tiempo parcial;
v) trabajadores estacionales u ocasionales;
vi) conscriptos del servicio militar o civil;
vii) aprendices y personas que siguen un curso de formación.

Sólo pueden identificarse por separado las categorías ii) y iv).

c) Desempleo: Se consideró "desempleada" a toda persona que declaró que, en la fecha del censo, no trabajaba, estaba inscrita en el registro correspondiente y buscaba empleo. No quedaron incluidos en la definición los estudiantes que buscaban trabajo.

7. Clasificaciones utilizadas:

Todas las personas, a excepción de los desempleados, fueron clasificadas por rama de actividad económica. Tanto las personas ocupadas como las desempleadas anteriormente empleadas fueron clasificadas según la ocupación.

a) Rama de actividad económica: Para determinarla, se hizo una pregunta relativa al lugar de trabajo: concretamente, se pidió indicar el nombre, la actividad principal y la dirección de la empresa. Para codificar la rama de actividad se utilizaron 40 grupos y 184 subgrupos de la clasificación nacional. Se establecieron enlaces con la CIIU-Rev.3, a nivel de divisiones (clave de 2 dígitos).

b) Ocupación: Para determinarla se hizo la siguiente pregunta: "¿Qué profesión o cargo ejerce usted?". Para codificar la ocupación se utilizaron 46 grandes grupos y 642 subgrupos. Se establecieron enlaces con la clasificación CIUO-88, a nivel de subgrupos (clave de 3 dígitos).

c) Situación en el empleo: No se establecieron clasificaciones con arreglo a esta variable.

8. Diferencias principales con el censo anterior:

En el censo de 1992 se identificó por primera vez a los desempleados.

Además, en 1985, en las preguntas relativas a la actividad económica, se había utilizado un período de referencia corto, a saber, los tres meses anteriores a la fecha del censo; por otra parte, se aplicó un límite de edad mínima de 16 años para determinar la inclusión o exclusión de las personas censadas en la población económicamente activa.

9. Publicación de los resultados del censo:

Los resultados del censo se difundieron de 1993 a 1995, en un gran número de publicaciones, entre ellas "Demographic Characteristics (Volume I)" y "Socio-Economic Characteristics of the Population (Volume II)".

El organismo responsable de estas publicaciones es el Institut National de Statistique, Division "Recensement de la population", 2. rue P. Volov, Sofía.

También se dispone de los resultados del censo de 1992 en cuadros inéditos y disquetes.

BURUNDI

1. Nombre y dirección del organismo responsable del censo:
Département de la Population, Bureau Central de Recensement, Pavillon administratif No. 3, B.P. 174, Gitega.

2. Censos de población llevados a cabo desde 1945 (años):
1979 y 1990. La presente descripción se refiere al censo de 1990 (cuya fecha de referencia es la noche del 15 al 16 de agosto).

3. Alcance del censo:
a) Geográfico: Todo el territorio.

b) Personas comprendidas: Toda la población.

4. Período de referencia:
Los seis meses anteriores a la fecha del censo (o sea, del 15 de febrero al 15 de agosto de 1990). A las personas que no habían ejercido ninguna actividad económica durante este período se les preguntó si habían trabajado antes.

5. Materias principales:
a) Población total, según sexo y edad: sí
Población económicamente activa por:
b) Sexo y grupo de edad: sí
c) Rama de actividad económica: sí
d) Ocupación: sí
e) Situación en el empleo: sí
f) Nivel más alto de educación: sí
g) Horas de trabajo: no
h) Otras características: sí

Ref. a): La edad se determinó según los años cumplidos en el último cumpleaños.

Ref. h): También se acopiaron informaciones acerca del oficio aprendido por las personas ocupadas y por los desempleados.

6. Conceptos y definiciones:
a) Población económicamente activa: Abarcó a todas las personas de 10 o más años de edad que, durante el período de referencia, habían estado la mayor parte del tiempo ocupadas o desempleadas, según las definiciones que se dan más adelante. La definición incluyó también a los miembros de las fuerzas armadas que formaban parte de un hogar ordinario (por "hogar ordinario" se entendió, en general, todo grupo de personas, emparentadas o no, que habitaban un mismo domicilio y que, normalmente, contribuían en forma mancomunada a la satisfacción de sus necesidades alimentarias fundamentales, así como de otras necesidades vitales. Un hogar podía estar compuesto por una o más personas).

b) Empleo: Se consideró "ocupada" a toda persona que, durante el período de referencia, había ejercido la mayor parte del tiempo una profesión o un cargo o desempeñado una actividad económica. La definición abarcó también a los agricultores y los ganaderos, así como a las mujeres que se ocupaban regularmente, además de las labores del hogar, de labranza o de otros trabajos remunerados. La pregunta utilizada fue: "Durante los seis meses anteriores al 15 de agosto, la situación de X ha sido la mayor parte del tiempo: 1) ocupado(a); 2) desempleado(a); 3) estudiante; 4) ama de casa; 5) jubilado(a); 6) otra". La definición no incluyó a los estudiantes que trabajaban a tiempo parcial.

Se ha indicado que fueron incluidas las siguientes categorías:
i) personas que producen bienes primarios para el autoconsumo;
ii) personas ocupadas pero temporalmente ausentes de su trabajo;
iii) trabajadores estacionales u ocasionales;
iv) conscriptos del servicio militar o civil, miembros de hogares ordinarios;
v) aprendices y personas que siguen un curso de formación.

Sólo la categoría i) puede identificarse por separado. No obstante, también pueden identificarse por separado los estudiantes que trabajaban o que podían trabajar a tiempo parcial u ocasionalmente (por ejemplo, durante las vacaciones), así como las personas que trabajaban sin remuneracion en una empresa o negocio familiar, aun cuando estas categorías no están incluidas en la población económicamente activa.

c) Desempleo: Se consideró "desempleada" a toda persona que, durante el período de referencia, no tenía trabajo y se encontraba en busca sea de un primer empleo, sea de un nuevo empleo. La definición abarcó también a las personas que querían trabajar, pero que no estaban buscando activamente una ocupación por estimar que sus posibilidades de encontrar una eran nulas, y a las personas que debían comenzar a trabajar en los próximos 30 días en un empleo asalariado o a sueldo.

7. Clasificaciones utilizadas:
Sólo las personas ocupadas se clasificaron por rama de actividad económica, por ocupación y por situación en el empleo.

a) Rama de actividad económica: Para determinarla se preguntó: "¿En qué rama o ámbito de actividad económica trabaja el Sr. (o la Sra.) X?", y "¿Cuál es la actividad de la unidad de producción (moderna o tradicional) en que trabaja el Sr. (o la Sra.) X?" La rama de actividad corresponde al sector económico en que se ocupaba una persona que hubiese declarado haber ejercido una actividad principal durante el período de referencia. Para codificar la rama de actividad se utilizaron 10 grupos. Se establecieron enlaces con la CIIU-Rev.2 a nivel de grandes divisiones (clave de 1 dígito).

b) Ocupación: Para determinarla se hizo la siguiente pregunta: "¿Qué profesión ejerció X durante los seis meses anteriores al 15 de agosto de 1990?". Por "profesión" se entendió el tipo de trabajo desempeñado por una persona ocupada; no se debía considerar el rango, el grado o el cargo de la persona, como tampoco su oficio, sino únicamente la índole del trabajo efectuado durante el período de referencia. Para codificar la ocupación se utilizaron 10 grandes grupos. Los enlaces con la clasificación CIUO-88 se establecieron a nivel de grandes grupos (clave de 1 dígito).

c) Situación en el empleo: Para determinarla se hizo la siguiente pregunta: "¿El Sr. (o la Sra.) X ejerció su actividad en calidad de: empleador, asalariado, trabajador independiente, aprendiz, trabajador familiar o trabajador a destajo?". Para codificar la situación en el empleo, se utilizaron las seis categorías citadas. Además, se formularon preguntas "filtro", destinadas a determinar si la persona económicamente activa trabajaba sola, por cuenta propia o si tenía empleados.

8. Diferencias principales con el censo anterior:
En el censo de 1979:
a) el período de referencia considerado en las preguntas relativas a la población económicamente activa, al empleo y al desempleo fue la semana anterior al día del censo;
b) no figuraba la pregunta relativa a las calificaciones profesionales;
c) las preguntas acerca de la rama de actividad económica, la ocupación y la situación en el empleo se hicieron tanto a las personas ocupadas como a los desempleados.

9. Publicación de los resultados del censo:
La publicación de los resultados definitivos del censo estaba prevista para 1992.

El organismo responsable de la publicación de los resultados es el Département de la Population, Bureau Central de Recensement, B.P. 174, Gitega.

Los resultados del censo de 1990 están disponibles también en cuadros inéditos con los datos brutos y en disquetes.

CABO VERDE

1. Nombre y dirección del organismo responsable del censo:
Ministério do Plano e das Finanças, Direcçao Geral de Estatística, Divisao de Censos e Inquéritos, C.P. 116, Praia.

2. Censos de población llevados a cabo desde 1945 (años):
1960, 1970, 1980 y 1990. La presente descripción se refiere al censo de 1990 (realizado del 16 al 30 de junio de ese año).

3. Alcance del censo:
a) Geográfico: Todo el territorio.

b) Personas comprendidas: Toda la población, salvo los nacionales residentes en el extranjero.

4. Período de referencia:
La semana anterior a la fecha del empadronamiento.

5. Materias principales:
a) Población total, según sexo y edad: sí
Población económicamente activa por:
b) Sexo y grupo de edad: sí
c) Rama de actividad económica: sí
d) Ocupación: sí
e) Situación en el empleo: sí
f) Nivel más alto de educación: sí
g) Horas de trabajo: no
h) Otras características: sí

Ref. a): La edad se determinó según el año de nacimiento.

Ref. h): También se hicieron preguntas a las personas inactivas acerca de su principal medio de subsistencia.

6. Conceptos y definiciones:

a) Población económicamente activa: Abarcó a todas las personas de 10 o más años de edad que, durante la semana de referencia, estaban ocupadas o desempleadas, conforme a las definiciones que se dan más adelante. La definición incluyó a todos los miembros de las fuerzas armadas (militares de carrera y conscriptos).

b) Empleo: Se consideró "ocupada" a toda persona que, durante la semana de referencia, ejerció una profesión o un cargo, o desempeñó una actividad económica cualquiera, remunerada o no. A este respecto, se pidió indicar: "Situación laboral: 1) ocupado; 2) desempleado previamente empleado; 3) desempleado en busca de un primer empleo; 4) estudiante; 5) ama de casa; 6) jubilado o pensionado; 7) inválido o enfermo; y 8) otra".

Se ha indicado que fueron incluidas las siguientes categorías:

i)   personas que trabajan sin remuneración en una empresa o negocio familiar;
ii)   personas que producen bienes primarios para el autoconsumo;
iii)   personas ocupadas pero temporalmente ausentes de su trabajo;
iv)   estudiantes que trabajan a tiempo parcial;
v)   trabajadores estacionales u ocasionales;
vi)   conscriptos del servicio militar o civil;
vii)   aprendices y personas que siguen un curso de formación.

Sólo las categorías i), vi) y vii) pueden identificarse por separado, con arreglo a sus respuestas a determinadas preguntas.

c) Desempleo: Se consideró "desempleada" a toda persona que, durante la semana de referencia, no tenía trabajo, quería trabajar y se encontraba en busca sea de un primer empleo, sea de un nuevo empleo. La definición abarcó también a las personas que querían trabajar, pero que no estaban buscando activamente una ocupación por estimar que sus posibilidades de encontrar una eran nulas.

7. Clasificaciones utilizadas:
Tanto las personas ocupadas como las desempleadas anteriormente empleadas fueron clasificadas por rama de actividad económica, por ocupación y por situación en el empleo.

a) Rama de actividad económica: Para determinarla se hizo la siguiente pregunta: "Indique la actividad del establecimiento en que la persona censada trabaja o trabajó por última vez". Para codificar la ocupación, se utilizaron 10 grupos de la clasificación nacional. Se establecieron enlaces con la CIIU-Rev.2, a nivel de grandes divisiones (clave de 1 dígito).

b) Ocupación: Para determinarla se hizo la siguiente pregunta: "Describa la ocupación principal que desempeña o desempeñó en su último trabajo". Para codificar la ocupación se utilizaron nueve grupos de la clasificación nacional. Se establecieron enlaces con la clasificación CIUO-68 a nivel de grandes grupos (clave de 1 dígito).

c) Situación en el empleo: Para determinar su situación en el empleo que ocupaban, o en el último empleo que habían ocupado, tanto a las personas ocupadas como a las desempleadas anteriormente empleadas se hizo una pregunta específica. Para codificar la situación en el empleo se utilizaron siete categorías: trabajador independiente; empleador; funcionario o empleado; jornalero; aprendiz; miembro de cooperativa de producción; trabajador no remunerado.

8. Diferencias principales con el censo anterior:
En el censo de 1980, las preguntas de índole económica se hicieron a todas las personas de 7 o más años de edad; sin embargo, sólo se habían publicado los datos relativos a la población económicamente activa y sus componentes (empleo y

desempleo) correspondientes a las personas cuya edad era igual o superior a 14 años.

9. Publicación de los resultados del censo:
Los resultados del censo de 1990 aparecieron en la publicación que lleva por título: "IIo Recenseamento da Populaçao e Habitaçao - 1990", 1992.

El organismo responsable de esta publicación es la Direcçao Geral de Estatística, Ministério das Finanças e do Plano, Praia.

También se dispone de los resultados del censo de 1990 en cuadros inéditos, disquetes y cintas magnéticas.

CANADA

1. Nombre y dirección del organismo responsable del censo:
Statistics Canada, Jean-Talon Building, Section A-2, 5th floor, Tunney's Pasture, Ottawa.

2. Censos de población llevados a cabo desde 1945 (años):
1951, 1961, 1971, 1976, 1981, 1986 y 1991. La presente descripción se refiere al censo de población de 1991 (realizado el 4 de junio de ese año).

3. Alcance del censo:

a) Geográfico: Todo el país.

b) Personas comprendidas: Toda la población, salvo los extranjeros residentes. Las preguntas relativas a la fuerza de trabajo se hicieron a los residentes no institucionales de 15 o más años de edad.

4. Periodo de referencia:
La semana anterior al día del censo. Si la persona censada no había trabajado en dicha semana, debían registrarse la rama de actividad económica y la ocupación correspondientes al empleo de mayor duración ocupado desde el 1o. de enero de 1990.

5. Materias principales:
a) Población total, según sexo y edad: sí
Población económicamente activa por:
b) Sexo y grupo de edad: sí
c) Rama de actividad económica: sí
d) Ocupación: sí
e) Situación en el empleo: sí
f) Nivel más alto de educación: sí
g) Horas de trabajo: sí
h) Otras características: sí

Ref. a): La edad se determinó según el año de nacimiento o la fecha exacta de nacimiento (día, mes y año).

Ref. g): Por horas de trabajo se entendió el número de horas efectivas trabajadas en el empleo por las personas ocupadas.

Ref. h): El censo también recolectó datos sobre otros temas, a saber: la constitución o no en sociedad de las empresas de trabajadores independientes; el número de semanas trabajadas en el año calendario anterior, sea principalmente a tiempo completo, sea principalmente a tiempo parcial (no se incluyeron las labores domésticas ni el mantenimiento o las reparaciones efectuadas en el propio domicilio); y las fuentes de ingresos, incluido el empleo.

6. Conceptos y definiciones:

a) Población económicamente activa: Abarcó a todas las personas de 15 o más años de edad que, durante la semana de referencia, estaban ocupadas o desempleadas, conforme a las definiciones que se dan más adelante. Se formularon preguntas sobre la actividad económica a una muestra de 20 por ciento del universo. La definición incluyó a los miembros de las fuerzas armadas.

b) Empleo: Se consideró "ocupada" a toda persona incluida en la muestra que, durante la semana de referencia, tenía un empleo y estaba trabajando o temporalmente ausente del trabajo (es decir, separada temporalmente de su puesto, al que esperaba retornar, en vacaciones, en huelga, ausente por lockout, con licencia por enfermedad o ausente por otros motivos). Las preguntas utilizadas fueron las siguientes: "La semana pasada, ¿cuántas horas trabajó (sin contar el trabajo voluntario o las labores domésticas, de mantenimiento o de reparación del propio domicilio)?"; y "La semana pasada, ¿estaba ausente de su empleo o actividad?".

Se ha indicado que fueron incluidas las siguientes categorías:

i) personas que trabajan sin remuneración en una empresa o negocio familiar;

ii) algunas personas que producen bienes primarios para el autoconsumo;

iii) estudiantes que trabajan a tiempo parcial (únicamente los estudiantes de nivel post-secundario, a condición de que hubiesen estado disponibles para trabajar durante la semana de referencia);

iv) trabajadores estacionales u ocasionales;

v) conscriptos del servicio militar o civil;

vi) aprendices y personas que siguen un curso de formación.

Sólo pueden identificarse por separado, mediante preguntas específicas, las categorías i) y iii). La identificación de los estudiantes que trabajaban pudiera inducir a error, ya que se pidió a las personas censadas que dijeran si habían asistido a clases en los últimos nueve meses, es decir, a contar del último mes de septiembre; ello no implicaba necesariamente que aún estuvieran asistiendo a clases en la semana de referencia, o en el período en que habían trabajado en el empleo citado al indicar la rama de actividad económica y la ocupación (a tiempo parcial, o a tiempo completo, etc.).

c) Desempleo: Se consideró "desempleada" a toda persona incluida en la muestra que, la semana de referencia, se encontraba sin trabajo o temporalmente separada de su empleo, y esperaba retornar al trabajo. También se incluyó a las personas que habían concertado acuerdos definitivos para comenzar a trabajar en un plazo máximo de cuatro semanas. Las preguntas utilizadas fueron las siguientes: "La semana pasada, ¿estaba usted separado temporalmente de su empleo o ausente de su trabajo o actividad?"; "La semana pasada, ¿tenía un contrato definitivo para comenzar a trabajar en un nuevo empleo dentro de las próximas cuatro semanas?"; "¿Buscó usted trabajo durante las últimas cuatro semanas?" y "¿Hubiera podido comenzar a trabajar la semana pasada, si se le hubiese ofrecido un empleo?".

7. Clasificaciones utilizadas:

Tanto las personas ocupadas como las desempleadas anteriormente empleadas, incluidas en la muestra, se clasificaron por rama de actividad económica, por ocupación y por situación en el empleo. A estas personas se hicieron preguntas acerca de, respectivamente, su empleo u ocupación durante la semana de referencia y el empleo u ocupación de mayor duración que hubiesen tenido desde el 1o. de enero de 1990. A las personas que habían tenido varios empleos durante la semana de referencia se preguntó a cuál de éstos habían dedicado el mayor número de horas de trabajo.

a) Rama de actividad económica: Para determinarla se utilizaron las siguientes preguntas: "¿Para quién trabajó? (nombre de la compañía, organismo estatal, etc.; departamento, servicio, división, sección o establecimiento)"; "¿De qué tipo de empresa, industria o servicio se trata? (por ejemplo, finca dedicada al cultivo de trigo, caza mediante trampas, mantenimiento de carreteras, tienda de calzado, escuela secundaria, policía municipal)"; y "¿Cuál es la dirección del lugar de trabajo?". Para codificar la rama de actividad, se utilizaron 286 grupos primarios de la Clasificación Industrial Normalizada de 1970 y 296 grupos primarios de la Clasificación Industrial Normalizada de 1980. No se establecieron enlaces con la CIIU; sin embargo, se hicieron cálculos aproximados a fin de presentar datos, a la OIT y a otras instituciones de las Naciones Unidas, en el nivel de grandes divisiones del CIIU-Rev.2 (1 dígito).

b) Ocupación: Para determinarla se utilizaron las siguientes preguntas: "¿Qué tipo de trabajo desempeñaba? (por ejemplo, técnico laboratorista, empleado contable, director de departamento de ingeniería civil, profesor secundario, supervisor de unidad de tratamiento de datos, obrero de fábrica elaboradora de alimentos, guía pesquero; a los miembros de las fuerzas armadas sólo se les pidió que indicaran su rango)"; y "En este trabajo, ¿cuáles eran sus principales funciones o actividades? (por ejemplo, analizar muestras de sangre, comprobar facturas, coordinar proyectos de ingeniería civil, enseñar matemáticas, organizar programas de trabajo y controlar los sistemas de registro de datos, limpiar legumbres, o servir de guía a grupos de pescadores)". También se pidió indicar la dirección del lugar de trabajo habitual. Para codificar la ocupación, se utilizaron 496 grupos primarios de la Clasificación de Ocupaciones de 1971, 514 grupos primarios de la Clasificación Normalizada de Ocupaciones de 1980 y 505 grupos primarios de la nueva Clasificación Nacional de Ocupaciones. No se establecieron enlaces con la CIUO-88; sin embargo, se hicieron cálculos aproximados a fin de presentar datos, a la OIT y a otras instituciones de las

Naciones Unidas, en el nivel de grandes grupos del CIUO-68 (1 dígito).

c) Situación en el empleo: Para determinarla se utilizaron las siguientes preguntas: "En esta ocupación: ¿trabajaba usted principalmente mediando un sueldo, salario, propinas o comisiones; trabajaba sin remuneración para su cónyuge o para otro familiar en una explotación agrícola, empresa o negocio familiar; trabajaba en forma independiente sin personal remunerado (solo o en sociedad); trabajaba en forma independiente con personal remunerado (solo o en sociedad)?" A los trabajadores independientes se preguntó, además: "¿Está su finca o empresa constituida en sociedad?". Para codificar esta variable se utilizaron los cuatro grupos descritos.

8. Diferencias principales con el censo anterior:

En 1991 se amplió la cobertura del censo, agregándose los solicitantes de asilo, las personas con permiso de residencia de estudios o de trabajo, y personas con permisos expedidos por los ministerios.

9. Publicación de los resultados del censo:

Los resultados del censo se han publicado en la Nation Series, en los volúmenes: "Labour Force Activity" (número de catálogo 93-324); "Labour Force Activity of Women by Presence of Children" (número de catálogo 93-325); "Industry and Class of Worker" (número de catálogo 93-326); y "Occupation" (número de catálogo 93-327), aparecidos en 1993.

El organismo responsable de estas publicaciones es Statistics Canada, Ottawa.

Los resultados del censo están disponibles además en disquetes, cintas magnéticas y CD-ROM.

REP. CENTROAFRICANA

Se incluye en el presente volumen la descripción del censo realizado en la República Centroafricana en 1988, debido a que no estuvo preparada a tiempo para figurar en la primera edición.

1. Nombre y dirección del organismo responsable del censo:

Ministère de l'Economie, du Plan, des Statistiques et de la Coopération internationale, Bureau Central du Recensement (BCR), B.P. 696, Bangui.

2. Censos de población llevados a cabo desde 1945 (años):

1975 y 1988. La presente descripción se refiere al censo de 1988 (realizado del 8 al 22 de diciembre de ese año, y cuya fecha de referencia es el 15 de diciembre).

3. Alcance del censo:

a) Geográfico: Todo el territorio.

b) Personas comprendidas: Toda la población.

4. Periodo de referencia:

Los siete días anteriores al día del censo.

5. Materias principales:

a) Población total, según sexo y edad:	sí
Población económicamente activa por:	
b) Sexo y grupo de edad:	sí
c) Rama de actividad económica:	sí
d) Ocupación:	sí
e) Situación en el empleo:	sí
f) Nivel más alto de educación:	sí
g) Horas de trabajo:	no
h) Otras características:	no

Ref. a): La edad se determinó según los años cumplidos en el último cumpleaños, en el caso de las personas que indicaron el día, mes y año de nacimiento, y según el año de nacimiento para las demás.

6. Conceptos y definiciones:

a) Población económicamente activa: Abarcó a todas las personas de 6 o más años de edad que, durante el período de referencia, estaban ocupadas o desempleadas, conforme a las definiciones que se dan más adelante. La definición incluyó a los militares de carrera, pero no a las personas que cumplían su servicio militar obligatorio.

b) Empleo: Se consideró "ocupada" a toda persona que declaró haber ejercido, durante el período de referencia, una profesión, una función o una actividad económica cualquiera, remunerada o no, dentro o fuera de su domicilio. Así, también quedaron incluidas en la definición las mujeres que, además de las labores del hogar, se ocupan periódicamente de trabajos de labranza o de otras tareas. La definición no incluyó a los estudiantes que trabajaban a tiempo parcial.

Se ha indicado que fueron incluidas las siguientes categorías:

i) personas que trabajan sin remuneración en una empresa o negocio familiar (únicamente a tiempo completo);

ii) personas que producen bienes primarios para el autoconsumo;

iii) personas ocupadas pero temporalmente ausentes de su trabajo;

iv) trabajadores estacionales u ocasionales;

v) aprendices y personas que siguen un curso de formación.

Sólo las categorías i) y v) pueden identificarse por separado, con arreglo a sus respuestas a determinadas preguntas.

c) Desempleo: Se consideró "desempleada" a toda persona que declaró no haber tenido trabajo alguno durante el período de referencia. La definición incluyó tanto a los desempleados anteriormente empleados como a las personas en busca de un primer empleo.

Cabe hacer notar que el censo de 1988 subestimó el volumen de desempleo en cerca de 6 por ciento, a causa del período de referencia corto considerado (una semana) y de la falta de datos sobre el tiempo de trabajo. Asimismo, los trabajadores temporeros y las personas ocupadas en el sector informal proporcionaron datos muy exagerados acerca del número de personas ocupadas.

7. Clasificaciones utilizadas:

Tanto las personas ocupadas como los desempleados anteriormente empleados se clasificaron por rama de actividad, por ocupación y por situación en el empleo.

a) Rama de actividad económica: Para determinarla se preguntó cuál era la actividad del establecimiento en que trabajaba la persona censada (o en que había tenido su último empleo). Para codificar la rama de actividad económica se utilizó la clasificación CIIU-Rev.2, a nivel de grandes divisiones (clave de 1 dígito).

b) Ocupación: Tanto a las personas ocupadas como a los desempleados anteriormente empleados se hizo una pregunta destinada a determinar qué profesión ejercían o habían ejercido en su última actividad. Para codificar la ocupación se utilizó la CIUO-68, a nivel de grupos primarios (clave de 3 dígitos).

c) Situación en el empleo: Para determinar la situación en el empleo del momento o en el último empleo tanto de las personas ocupadas como de los desempleados anteriormente empleados se les hizo una pregunta concreta. Para codificar esta variable se utilizaron las 5 categorías siguientes: trabajador independiente, empleador, trabajador asalariado, trabajador familiar y aprendiz no remunerado.

8. Diferencias principales con el censo anterior:

Básicamente, en el censo de 1975 se habían utilizado las mismas preguntas y el mismo período de referencia a afectos de incluir o no a las personas censadas en la población económicamente activa y sus componentes (empleo y desempleo).

Como se indica en el párrafo 6 c), el uso de un período de referencia corto de una semana, por una parte, y los datos aportados por los trabajadores temporeros y los del sector informal, por otra, redundaron en la subestimación del volumen del desempleo y la sobrevaloración del número de personas ocupadas. En consecuencia, para el censo siguiente, que tendrá lugar en 1998, se ha previsto reformular las definiciones y el período de referencia.

9. Publicación de los resultados del censo:

Los resultados debían publicarse en 1992, en los volúmenes siguientes: "Tableaux statistiques", con los datos relativos a la población económicamente activa y sus componentes, y "Rapports d'analyse" (12 tomos de análisis temático).

El organismo responsable de estas publicaciones es el Bureau Central du Recensement (BCR), Division des Statistiques et des Etudes Economiques, con sede en Bangui.

Todos los datos relativos al censo de 1988 están registrados en discos duros, y también pueden obtenerse copias en disquetes.

COMORAS

1. Nombre y dirección del organismo responsable del censo:

Direction générale du Plan, Direction de la Statistique, B.P. 131, Moroni.

2. Censos de población llevados a cabo desde 1945 (años):

1958, 1966, 1980 y 1991. La presente descripción se refiere al censo de población y del hábitat de 1991 (realizado el 15 de septiembre de ese año).

3. Alcance del censo:

a) Geográfico: Todo el territorio, a excepción de la isla de Mayotte (bajo administración francesa).

b) Personas comprendidas: Toda la población, salvo los diplomáticos extranjeros y sus familias.

4. Período de referencia:

Un mes (agosto de 1991).

5. Materias principales:

a) Población total, según sexo y edad:	sí
Población económicamente activa por:	
b) Sexo y grupo de edad:	sí
c) Rama de actividad económica:	sí
d) Ocupación:	sí
e) Situación en el empleo:	sí
f) Nivel más alto de educación:	sí
g) Horas de trabajo:	no
h) Otras características:	sí

Ref. a): La edad se determinó según los años cumplidos en el último cumpleaños.

Ref. h): También se acopiaron datos sobre la remuneración mensual de los asalariados.

6. Conceptos y definiciones:

a) Población económicamente activa: Abarcó a todas las personas de 12 o más años de edad que estaban ocupadas o desempleadas durante el período de referencia, según las definiciones que se dan más adelante. Quedaron excluidos del ámbito de la definición los miembros de las fuerzas armadas.

b) Empleo: Para determinarlo se utilizó la pregunta siguiente: "¿Durante el mes de agosto, estaba o era X? asalariado permanente; asalariado temporal; desempleado; en busca de un primer empleo; ama de casa; escolar o estudiante de nivel superior; jubilado o rentista; inactivo u otra situación". Se consideró "con empleo permanente" a las personas ocupadas permanentemente en una actividad económica dada, que hubiesen trabajado por lo menos tres semanas durante el mes de referencia (salvo que hubieran estado enfermas o haciendo uso de una licencia o en vacaciones). La definición no incluyó a los estudiantes que trabajaban a tiempo parcial.

Se ha indicado que fueron incluidas las siguientes categorías:

i) personas que trabajan sin remuneración en una empresa o una explotación familiar;

ii) personas que producen bienes primarios para el autoconsumo;

iii) personas ocupadas pero temporalmente ausentes de su trabajo;

iv) trabajadores estacionales u ocasionales;

v) aprendices y personas que siguen un curso de formación.

Sólo pueden identificarse por separado las categorías i), iv) y v).

c) Desempleo: Se consideró "desempleada" a toda persona que, habiendo trabajado antes, se encontraba sin empleo durante la semana de referencia y buscaba una ocupación. Se identificó por separado a las personas en busca de un primer empleo.

7. Clasificaciones utilizadas:

Tanto las personas ocupadas como las desempleadas fueron clasificadas por rama de actividad. En cambio, tan sólo las personas ocupadas fueron clasificadas por ocupación y por situación en el empleo.

a) Rama de actividad económica: Para determinarla se hizo la siguiente pregunta: "¿Qué hace la empresa o el establecimiento en que trabaja X (o en que trabajó, si está desempleado(a)?". No se establecieron enlaces con la CIIU.

b) Ocupación: Para determinarla se hizo la siguiente pregunta: "¿Durante el mes de agosto de 1991, cuál fue la ocupación principal de X?". Para codificar la ocupación se utilizaron ocho grupos. No se establecieron enlaces con la CIUO.

c) Situación en el empleo: Para determinarla se hizo la siguiente pregunta: "¿X ejerce su actividad en calidad de empleador; trabajador independiente; asalariado del sector público; asalariado del sector privado; aprendiz no remunerado; trabajador a destajo; trabajador familiar?". Para codificar la situación en el empleo se utilizaron los siete grupos enumerados.

8. Diferencias principales con el censo anterior:
No hubo diferencias significativas

9. Publicación de los resultados del censo:
La publicación de los resultados definitivos del censo estaba prevista para el tercer trimestre de 1996, con el título: "Résultats du recensement général de la population et de l'habitat, 1991".

El organismo responsable de esta publicación es la Direction Nationale du recensement, B.P. 131, Moroni.

También se había previsto presentar los resultados en disquetes.

REPUBLICA DE COREA

1. Nombre y dirección del organismo responsable del censo:
National Statistical Office, Statistical Survey Bureau, Population Statistics Division, 90 Kyeongun-Dong, Jongro-Gu, Seúl 110-310.

2. Censos de población llevados a cabo desde 1945 (años):
1949, 1955, 1960, 1966, 1970, 1975, 1980, 1985 y 1990. La presente descripción se refiere al censo de población de 1990 (realizado el 1 de noviembre de ese año).

3. Alcance del censo:
a) Geográfico: Todo el país.

b) Personas comprendidas: Toda la población, salvo: los trabajadores y los estudiantes residentes en el extranjero; el personal diplomático y consular extranjero y sus familiares; el personal militar extranjero; el personal de gobiernos extranjeros y sus familiares.

4. Período de referencia:
Las preguntas relativas a la "ocupación remunerada" y "ocupación no remunerada" se remiten a un período de referencia largo, es decir, los doce meses entre el 1 de noviembre de 1989 y el 31 de octubre de 1990.

5. Materias principales:
a) Población total, según sexo y edad:	sí
Población económicamente activa por:	
b) Sexo y grupo de edad:	sí
c) Rama de actividad económica:	sí
d) Ocupación:	sí
e) Situación en el empleo:	sí
f) Nivel más alto de educación:	sí
g) Horas de trabajo:	no
h) Otras características:	no

Ref. a): La edad se determinó según los años cumplidos en el último cumpleaños.

6. Conceptos y definiciones:
a) Población económicamente activa: Se formularon preguntas sobre la actividad económica a una muestra de 10 por ciento de las personas de 15 o más años de edad. La definición no incluyó a los miembros de las fuerzas armadas residentes en cuarteles ni a las personas que cumplían el servicio militar.

b) Empleo: Se consideró que tenía una "ocupación remunerada" toda persona de 15 o más años de edad que, durante el período de referencia (es decir, entre el 1 de noviembre de 1989 y el 31 de octubre de 1990) desempeñó por más de 30 días un trabajo remunerado y tenía la intención de seguir trabajando por una remuneración, dentro o fuera de su domicilio. Para determinar si una persona debía o no ser contabilizada como ejerciendo una "ocupación remunerada" se preguntó: "En general, ¿ejerció la persona encuestada una actividad remunerada?". También había que considerar que tenía una "ocupación remunerada" toda persona que, sin completar 30 días, hubiera comenzado a trabajar poco antes del censo y tu-

viese la voluntad de seguir ejerciendo una actividad remunerada. En cambio, debían quedar excluidas de la definición las personas que, habiéndose jubilado antes del censo, no tuviesen la intención de proseguir una actividad remunerada.

Se ha indicado que fueron incluidas las siguientes categorías:
i) personas que trabajan sin remuneración en una empresa o negocio familiar;
ii) personas ocupadas pero temporalmente ausentes de su trabajo;
iii) estudiantes que trabajan a tiempo parcial;
iv) trabajadores estacionales u ocasionales;
v) aprendices y personas que siguen un curso de formación.

Sólo pueden identificarse por separado las personas incluidas en las categorías i), ii) y iii) que dieron respuestas como: "Trabajé además de ocuparme de labores del hogar", "Tenía un empleo pero estuve temporalmente ausente del trabajo", "Trabajé, además de asistir a clases", etc.

c) Desempleo: Las personas que "no tenían una ocupación remunerada" eran todas aquellas que, en la fecha del censo, "buscaban empleo", "se ocupaban de labores del hogar", "asistían a clases", "estaban ociosas", "eran ancianas" o "estaban enfermas"; no quedaron incluidos en esta categoría los estudiantes que buscaban trabajo. Para determinar si una persona debía ser o no contabilizada como sin ocupación remunerada, se utilizó la pregunta que figura en el párrafo 6 b), más arriba.

7. Clasificaciones utilizadas:
Sólo las personas que ejercían una ocupación remunerada incluidas en la muestra fueron clasificadas por rama de actividad económica, por ocupación y según la situación en el empleo.

a) Rama de actividad económica: Para determinarla se preguntó: "¿Cuál es el principal producto elaborado o la principal actividad desplegada en la empresa u oficina en que trabaja la persona censada?", y "Sírvase indicar el nombre de dicha empresa u oficina". Para codificar esta variable, se utilizaron 90 códigos basados en la Clasificación Industrial Normalizada de Corea, en el nivel de 3 dígitos, que permite enlaces con la CIIU-Rev.2.

b) Ocupación: Para determinarla se preguntó: "¿Qué tipo de trabajo desempeña la persona censada?", y "Sírvase indicar el puesto ocupado por ella en la empresa u oficina en que trabaja". Para codificar la ocupación se utilizaron 286 códigos basados en la Clasificación Normalizada de Ocupaciones de Corea. Se establecieron enlaces con la CIUO-68 a nivel de subgrupos (clave de 2 dígitos).

c) Situación en el empleo: Para determinarla se preguntó: "¿Cuáles son las condiciones de contratación de la persona que ejerce una ocupación remunerada?" Para codificar la situación en el empleo se utilizaron cuatro grupos: empleador, trabajador independiente, trabajador familiar no remunerado y trabajador asalariado.

8. Diferencias principales con el censo anterior:
Por lo que se refiere a las preguntas sobre la población económicamente activa, al empleo y al desempleo, en 1980 se utilizó un planteamiento basado en la "fuerza de trabajo" y se consideró un período de referencia corto (la semana anterior al día del censo); en cambio, en los censos de 1985 y 1990 se aplicó un enfoque basado en el concepto de "trabajador remunerado", y se consideró un período de referencia largo en la formulación de preguntas relativas, por ejemplo, al trabajo remunerado y al trabajo no remunerado, etc.

Además, la edad mínima utilizada en 1980 y 1985 para recopilar datos sobre la población económicamente activa y sus componentes fue de 14 años.

9. Publicación de los resultados del censo:
Los resultados definitivos del censo se publicaron en el volumen que lleva por título "1990 Population and Housing Census Report, Vol. 2, 10 Percent Sample, 3-1, Economic Activity".

El organismo responsable de esta publicación es la National Statistical Office, Statistical Survey Bureau, Population Statistics Division, 90 Kyeongun-Dong, Jongro-Gu, Seúl 110-310.

Los resultados del censo están también disponibles en cuadros inéditos y cintas magnéticas.

CHAD

1. Nombre y dirección del organismo responsable del censo:
Bureau central du Recensement (B.C.R.), B.P. 453, Ndjamena.

2. Censos de población llevados a cabo desde 1945 (años):
La presente descripción se refiere al censo de 1993 (realizado del 1 al 15 de abril de ese año).

3. Alcance del censo:
a) Geográfico: Todo el país, con excepción de seis cantones de la prefectura de Logone oriental (Béboto, Bodo, Bekan, Kaba Roangar, Goré rural y Yamodo), así como de cinco localidades del cantón de Signar (prefectura de Uadoi): Andjamena, Ardeba, Fosso, Hiné Hésseina e Hille Kukón, de la faja de Auzu y de algunas islas del lago Chad (por motivos de inseguridad).

b) Personas comprendidas: Toda la población, salvo los miembros del cuerpo diplomático y de los servicios consulares extranjeros.

4. Período de referencia:
La semana anterior al día del empadronamiento; en el caso de los agricultores, el año anterior (última estación de lluvias).

5. Materias principales:
a) Población total, según sexo y edad: sí
Población económicamente activa por:
b) Sexo y grupo de edad: sí
c) Rama de actividad económica: sí
d) Ocupación: sí
e) Situación en el empleo: sí
f) Nivel más alto de educación: sí
g) Horas de trabajo: no
h) Otras características: no

Ref. a): La edad se determinó según los años cumplidos en el último cumpleaños.

6. Conceptos y definiciones:
a) Población económicamente activa: Abarcó a todas las personas de 6 a 98 años de edad que, durante el período de referencia, estaban ocupadas o desempleadas, conforme a las definiciones que se dan más adelante. Quedaron excluidos del ámbito de la definición los estudiantes que trabajaban a tiempo parcial y los estudiantes que buscaban empleo; en cambio, fueron incluidos los miembros de las fuerzas armadas.

b) Empleo: Se consideró "ocupada" a toda persona que había trabajado durante la semana de referencia, o durante la última estación húmeda si se trataba de un agricultor. También se consideró "ocupadas" a las mujeres que, además de las labores domésticas, trabajaban en tareas de labranza o en el comercio. La pregunta utilizada a tal efecto fue: "¿Es su situación profesional: 1) ocupado; 2) desempleado(a); 3) en busca de un primer empleo; 4) ama de casa; rentista o jubilado; escolar o estudiante de niveles superiores; 7) otra situación?".

Se ha indicado que fueron incluidas las siguientes categorías:
i) personas que trabajan sin remuneración en una empresa o negocio familiar;
ii) personas que producen bienes primarios para el autoconsumo;
iii) personas ocupadas pero temporalmente ausentes de su trabajo;
iv) trabajadores estacionales u ocasionales;
v) aprendices y personas que siguen un curso de formación.

Sólo las categorías i) y ii) pueden identificarse por separado.

c) Desempleo: Se consideró "desempleada" a toda persona que hubiese trabajado antes, pero que, durante el período de referencia, estaba sin trabajo y buscaba empleo. Se identificó por separado a las personas en busca de un primer empleo.

7. Clasificaciones utilizadas:
Tanto las personas ocupadas como las desempleadas anteriormente empleadas se clasificaron por rama de actividad económica, por ocupación y por situación en el empleo.

a) Rama de actividad económica: Para determinarla se hizo la siguiente pregunta: "Indique la índole de la actividad que despliega el establecimiento o empresa para el que trabaja. Si no puede indicarla, anote el nombre completo del establecimiento o empresa". Para codificar la rama de actividad se utilizó la

CIIU-Rev.3, a nivel de divisiones (clave de 2 dígitos), con algunas modificaciones, relativas, en particular, a las actividades de recuperación de desechos, de gran importancia en el sector informal del Chad.

b) Ocupación: El tipo de ocupación se refiere a la que ejercían las personas ocupadas, a la última ocupación de los desempleados y a la actividad de mayor dedicación de las personas con varios empleos. Se pidió dar respuestas lo más completas posibles, por ejemplo: plantador de algodón, cultivador de mijo, vendedor ambulante, vendedora de (aceite, pescado, hortalizas, cacahuete, arroz, etc.), vendedor en mostrador (de calzado, azúcar, té, etc.). Para codificar la ocupación se utilizó la CIUO-88, en el nivel de subgrupos principales (clave de 2 dígitos).

c) Situación en el empleo: Para codificar esta variable se utilizaron las seis categorías siguientes: asalariado; trabajador independiente; empleador; trabajador familiar; aprendiz (no remunerado); otra categoría.

8. Diferencias principales con el censo anterior:
No se aplica.

9. Publicación de los resultados del censo:
Los resultados definitivos del censo aparecieron en abril de 1995, en las siguientes publicaciones: "Rapport de séminaire-atelier", "Rapport de synthèse" y "Rapport d'analyse de 10 thèmes".

El organismo responsable de estas publicaciones es el Bureau central du recensement, B.P. 453, Ndjamena.

Los resultados del censo de 1993 están disponibles también en cuadros con datos en bruto. Existe una base de datos informatizada, pero no se dispone de información presentada en disquetes o cintas magnéticas.

REPUBLICA CHECA

1. Nombre y dirección del organismo responsable del censo:
Statistical Office, Sokolovská 142, 18613 Praga 8 Karlin.

2. Censos de población llevados a cabo desde 1945 (años):
1950, 1961, 1970, 1980 y 1991. La presente descripción se refiere al censo de población de 1991 (realizado en la medianoche del 2 al 3 de marzo de año).

3. Alcance del censo:
a) Geográfico: Todo el país.

b) Personas comprendidas: Todas las personas con residencia permanente en el país y los nacionales checos con residencia permanente en el extranjero; quedaron excluidos los diplomáticos extranjeros, así como los miembros del ejército soviético y sus familiares.

4. Período de referencia:
La medianoche del 2 al 3 de marzo de 1991.

5. Materias principales:
a) Población total, según sexo y edad: sí
Población económicamente activa por:
b) Sexo y grupo de edad: sí
c) Rama de actividad económica: sí
d) Ocupación: sí
e) Situación en el empleo: sí
f) Nivel más alto de educación: sí
g) Horas de trabajo: no
h) Otras características: sí

Ref. a): La edad se determinó según el año de nacimiento.

Ref. h): El censo también recopiló datos sobre el lugar de trabajo (la dirección), la frecuencia de los desplazamientos a éste (todos los días, otras) y el tiempo necesario para ir desde el domicilio al lugar de trabajo (en minutos).

6. Conceptos y definiciones:
a) Población económicamente activa: La actividad económica se determinó con arreglo al concepto de actividad actual. Por consiguiente, en la población económicamente activa se incluyó a todas las personas de 15 o más años de edad que, en el momento del censo, estaban ocupadas o desempleadas, conforme a las definiciones que se dan más adelante. La definición abarcó también a los miembros de las fuerzas armadas y a la población penitenciaria, aplicándose en cada caso el equi-

valente civil del trabajo que dichas personas desempeñaban o habían desempeñado en su último empleo.

b) Empleo: Se consideró "ocupada" a toda persona que indicó estar desempeñando un trabajo en calidad de: empleador, trabajador por cuenta propia, trabajador asalariado o miembro de una cooperativa agrícola o de producción (fueron incluidas en la definición los pensionados que trabajaban, las mujeres que hacían uso de una licencia de maternidad y los trabajadores familiares no remunerados). La definición no incluyó a los estudiantes que trabajaban a tiempo parcial.

Se ha indicado que fueron incluidas las siguientes categorías:

i)   personas que trabajan sin remuneración en una empresa o negocio familiar;
ii)   personas ocupadas pero temporalmente ausentes de su trabajo;
iii) trabajadores estacionales u ocasionales;
iv)   conscriptos del servicio militar o civil.

Sólo puede identificarse por separado la categoría i). También puede identificarse por separado a los aprendices y las personas que siguen un curso de formación, aun cuando estas categorías no hayan quedado incluidos en el ámbito de la definición de población económicamente activa.

c) Desempleo: Se consideró "desempleado" a todo hombre de 15 a 59 años de edad y "desempleada" a toda mujer de 15 a 56 años de edad que indicaron haber estado buscando trabajo en el momento del censo.

7. Clasificaciones utilizadas:
Tanto las personas ocupadas como las desempleadas anteriormente empleadas fueron clasificadas por rama de actividad económica, por ocupación y según la situación en el empleo.

a) Rama de actividad económica: Para determinarla se preguntó: "Indique el nombre del establecimiento, la cooperativa, la oficina, el organismo o la escuela en que trabaja". La codificación de las ramas de actividad, así como de la enseñanza, se llevó a cabo con arreglo a listas especiales de organismos, y se utilizaron códigos por rama basados en las actividades principales. Para procesar los resultados del censo de 1991, se utilizó una clasificación nacional compuesta de 47 grupos (es decir, divisiones y subdivisiones de la clasificación nacional). La clasificación industrial nacional es enteramente comparable a la CIIU-Rev.3. Se elaboró una tabla de conversión entre la clasificación nacional y la CIIU-Rev.3 en el nivel de divisiones (clave de 2 dígitos).

b) Ocupación: Se pidió a las personas censadas que indicaran con la mayor precisión posible cuál era el trabajo o la función que desempeñaban. A los pensionados inactivos, a las mujeres con licencia de maternidad, a los conscriptos, a los presos y a las personas que buscaban empleo se pidió que indicaran cuál había sido su último empleo. Para codificar la ocupación se utilizaron 91 grupos de la clasificación nacional. Se establecieron enlaces con la CIUO (tanto CIUO-68 como CIUO-88) a nivel de grandes grupos (clave de 1 dígito).

c) Situación en el empleo: Se pidió a los encuestados que indicaran su grupo social, por ejemplo, obrero, empleado, miembro de cooperativa agrícola, miembro de cooperativa de producción, empleador (con uno o más empleados), agricultor independiente, comerciante independiente, trabajador independiente, trabajador familiar no remunerado, etc. A los obreros y a los empleados se pidió que precisaran en qué sector de la economía nacional trabajaban (estatal, privado, cooperativo, sector mixto). Para codificar la situación en el empleo se utilizaron los nueve grupos siguientes: obreros y empleados del sector privado; otras categorías de obreros y empleados; miembros de cooperativas agrícolas; miembros de otros tipos de cooperativas; empleadores; agricultores independientes; trabajadores por cuenta propia; trabajadores independientes; trabajadores familiares no remunerados.

8. Diferencias principales con el censo anterior:
En 1991, la definición de población económicamente activa se amplió con la inclusión de los desempleados en busca de una ocupación, pero no se distinguió entre ellos a quienes buscaban trabajo por primera vez. La definición abarcó también a los pensionados que trabajaban y a las personas que percibían pensiones de vejez o invalidez o jornales.

En los censos de 1961, 1970 y 1980, los trabajadores familiares no remunerados fueron clasificados como personas dependientes, es decir, económicamente inactivas, y las personas que se describieron a sí mismas como desempleadas quedaron clasificadas como ocupadas, basándose en su última ocupación.

En el censo de 1991, la clasificación según la situación en el empleo se amplió con la inclusión de los empleadores, y los trabajadores familiares no remunerados fueron identificados como grupo especial.

Por último, en el censo de 1991 se ha ampliado la cuestión del desplazamiento entre el domicilio y el lugar de trabajo, con la inclusión de una pregunta relativa al tiempo utilizado para ir del domicilio hasta el lugar de trabajo, o viceversa.

9. Publicación de los resultados del censo:
El volumen en que figuran los resultados definitivos del censo lleva por título: "1991 Population and Housing Census", y fue publicado en 1992.

El organismo responsable de esta publicación es la Statistical Office, Sokolovská 142, 18613 Praga 8 Karlin.

Los datos definitivos del censo de 1991 se encuentran también disponibles en disquetes y cintas magnéticas.

CHILE

1. Nombre y dirección del organismo responsable del censo:
Instituto Nacional de Estadísticas (INE), Avda. Bulnes 418, Santiago, Chile.

2. Censos de población llevados a cabo desde 1945 (años):
1952, 1960, 1970, 1982 y 1992. La presente descripción se refiere al censo de población de 1992 (realizado el 22 de abril).

3. Alcance del censo:
a) Geográfico: Todo el país.
b) Personas comprendidas: Toda la población.

4. Periodo de referencia:
La semana anterior al día del censo.

5. Materias principales:

a) Población total, según sexo y edad:	sí
Población económicamente activa por:	
b) Sexo y grupo de edad:	sí
c) Rama de actividad económica:	sí
d) Ocupación:	sí
e) Situación en el empleo:	sí
f) Nivel más alto de educación:	...
g) Horas de trabajo:	no
h) Otras características:	no

Ref. a): Se definió la edad según los años cumplidos.

6. Conceptos y definiciones:
a) Población económicamente activa: Incluye a todas las personas de 14 años y más, que durante la semana de referencia se encontraban empleadas o desempleadas, conforme a las definiciones que se dan más adelante. La definición incluye también a los militares de carrera pero excluye a los conscriptos en el servicio militar obligatorio.

b) Empleo: Se considera "empleadas" a las personas que durante la semana de referencia trabajaron en una ocupación que les dio dinero. La pregunta utilizada es "¿En cual de estas situaciones se encontraba la semana pasada? 1) Trabajando por ingreso; 2) Sin trabajar, pero tiene trabajo; 3) Trabajando para un familiar sin pago en dinero; 4) Buscando trabajo habiendo trabajado antes; 5) Buscando trabajo por primera vez; 6) En quehaceres de su hogar; 7) Estudiando sin trabajar; 8) Pensionado o jubilado sin trabajar; 9) Incapacitado permanente para trabajar; 10) Otra situación".

Se ha indicado que quedan incluidas las siguientes categorías:

i)   personas trabajando sin paga en firma o negocio familiar;
ii)   personas en la producción de bienes primarios para el autoconsumo;
iii) personas empleadas pero y temporalmente ausentes del trabajo;
iv)   estudiantes que trabajan a tiempo parcial;
v)   trabajadores estacionales u ocasionales, siempre y cuando en la semana de referencia se encontrasen ocupados;
vi)   aprendices y personas que siguen un curso de formación.

Solamente las personas de las categorías i) y iii) se pueden identificar separadamente.

c) Desempleo: Se consideran "desempleadas" las personas que no tenían trabajo la semana de referencia habiendo trabajado antes (cesantes), o que nunca antes habían trabajado y que en la semana de referencia estuvieron buscando empleo en forma activa (buscó trabajo por primera vez).

7. Clasificaciones utilizadas:
Tanto las personas ocupadas como las desocupadas con experiencia laboral se clasificaron por rama de actividad económica, por ocupación y según la situación en el empleo.

a) Rama de actividad económica: Para establecer la rama de actividad económica, la pregunta utilizada es "¿A qué se dedica principalmente el establecimiento, empresa, negocio, fábrica, etc., donde trabaja (o trabajaba, si está cesante)? Ejemplos: fábrica de camisas, hospital, ministerio, fundo ganadero, banco, supermercado, taller de radio y TV, tienda de géneros, etc". Esta variable se codificó utilizando la CIIU-Rev.3 a nivel de grupos (3 dígitos).

b) Ocupación: Para establecer la ocupación, la pregunta utilizada es "¿Indique la ocupación o tipo de trabajo que desempeña (o desempeñaba si está cesante)? Ejemplos: albañil, pediatria, sastre, mecánico de autos, operario de máquina téxtil, vendedor ambulante, etc.". Esta variable se codificó utilizando la CIUO-88, a nivel de los grupos primarios (4 dígitos).

c) Situación en el empleo: Para determinar esta característica, codificada en cinco grupos, la pregunta utilizada es "¿En este trabajo es (o era): patrón o empleador, trabajador por cuenta propia, trabajador para servicio doméstico del hogar, trabajador asalariado (empleado, obrero, jornalero), familiar no remunerado?".

8. Diferencias principales con el censo anterior:
No hubo diferencias significativas.

9. Publicación de los resultados del censo:
Los resultados finales se publicaron en septiembre de 1993.

El título exacto de la publicación con los resultados finales es "Resultados Generales - XVI Censo Nacional y V de Vivienda 1992".

La organización responsable de la publicación es el Instituto Nacional de Estadísticas, Avda. Bulnes 418, Santiago.

Los resultados del censo se presentan también en forma de disquetes.

CHINA

1. Nombre y dirección del organismo responsable del censo:
State Statistical Bureau, 38 Yuetan Nanjie, Sanlihe, Beijing 100826.

2. Censos de población llevados a cabo desde 1945 (años):
1953, 1964, 1982 y 1990. La presente descripción se refiere al censo de población de 1990 (realizado el 1 de julio de ese año).

3. Alcance del censo:
a) Geográfico: Todo el país.

b) Personas comprendidas: Toda la población.

4. Periodo de referencia:
Dos períodos: el día y el mes anteriores al día del censo.

5. Materias principales:
a) Población total, según sexo y edad:	sí

Población económicamente activa por:
b) Sexo y grupo de edad:	sí
c) Rama de actividad económica:	sí
d) Ocupación:	sí
e) Situación en el empleo:	no
f) Nivel más alto de educación:	sí
g) Horas de trabajo:	no
h) Otras características:	no

Ref. a): La edad se determinó según los años cumplidos en el último cumpleaños.

6. Conceptos y definiciones:
a) Población económicamente activa: Abarcó a todas las personas de 15 o más años de edad que, durante el mes de referencia, estaban ocupadas o desempleadas, conforme a las definiciones que se dan más adelante.

La definición incluyó a todos los miembros de las fuerzas armadas; en cambio, no quedaron incluidos los estudiantes que trabajaban a tiempo parcial ni los estudiantes que buscaban empleo.

b) Empleo: Se consideró "ocupada" a toda persona que percibía una remuneración por su trabajo, u otra forma de ingreso generado por una empresa o actividad. La definición abarcó a aquellas personas que tenían una ocupación regular en el período de referencia, y también a las que, si bien no tenían una ocupación regular, habían trabajado temporalmente el 30 de junio de 1990 y habían participado en los planes laborales organizados por los servicios sociales durante un período acumulado de al menos 16 días en junio.

Se ha indicado que fueron incluidas las siguientes categorías:

i) personas ocupadas pero temporalmente ausentes de su trabajo;
ii) trabajadores estacionales u ocasionales;
iii) personas que cumplen el servicio militar o civil;
iv) aprendices y personas que siguen un curso de formación.

Sólo pueden identificarse por separado las personas incluidas en la categoría iii).

c) Desempleo: Se consideró "desempleada" a toda persona en edad de trabajar (15 a 50 años para los varones y 15 a 45 años para las mujeres) que estaban en condiciones de hacerlo, buscaban trabajo en ese momento y se habían inscrito como "desempleados" en las oficinas estatales competentes de su localidad.

7. Clasificaciones utilizadas:
Sólo las personas ocupadas se clasificaron por rama de actividad económica y por ocupación. No se hizo ninguna clasificación según la situación en el empleo.

a) Rama de actividad económica: Para determinar los grupos de actividad económica, se pidió a las personas ocupadas que indicasen el nombre y la actividad propia al establecimiento en que trabajaban o en que habían trabajado por última vez. Además, debían indicar si se trataba de una unidad económica autónoma estatal, de una empresa colectiva o mixta, o de una empresa privada. En el caso de empresas de gran tamaño y complejidad (corporaciones industriales, grandes minas, otras plantas fabriles, etc.), debía señalarse con claridad el nombre de las unidades subordinadas. Por ejemplo, fundición de una empresa siderúrgica, sección de acondicionamiento de huevos, en una procesadora de productos avícolas, etc. Para codificar la rama de actividad se utilizaron 13 grupos de la clasificación nacional. Se establecieron enlaces con la CIIU-Rev.2, en el nivel de grandes divisiones (clave de 1 dígito).

b) Ocupación: Se hicieron preguntas a las personas ocupadas para determinar con precisión cuál era el trabajo que desempeñaban o para el cual se les había contratado. Por ejemplo, los trabajadores del sector industrial fueron registrados en categorías como ajustador, tipógrafo, conductor, etc. En cuanto al personal de oficina, éste se clasificó, por ejemplo, en categorías como planificador, estadígrafo, secretaria, etc. A las personas con más de un empleo se pidió que indicasen la ocupación a la que se dedicaban la mayor parte de su tiempo durante el año. Para codificar la ocupación se utilizaron 8 grupos de la clasificación nacional. Se establecieron enlaces con la CIUO-68, a nivel de grandes grupos (clave de 1 dígito).

c) Situación en el empleo: No se efectuó clasificación alguna según la situación en el empleo.

8. Diferencias principales con el censo anterior:
En el censo de 1990, se incluyó en la población económicamente activa a las personas que esperaban obtener un contrato de trabajo de un momento a otro; en cambio, en el censo de 1982 estas personas había sido clasificadas como económicamente inactivas.

Además, en 1990 se incluyó un rubro dedicado a la personas migrantes, en el que se pedía indicar, entre otras cosas, el lugar de residencia 5 años antes del censo.

9. Publicación de los resultados del censo:
Los resultados definitivos del censo de población se publicaron en agosto de 1993, en el volumen que lleva por título "Tabulation on the 1990 Population Census of the People's Republic of China".

El organismo responsable de esta publicación es el State Statistical Bureau, Sanlihe, Beijing.

CHIPRE

1. Nombre y dirección del organismo responsable del censo:
Department of Statistics and Research, 13 Lord Byron Avenue, P.C. 1444, Nicosia.

2. Censos de población llevados a cabo desde 1945 (años):
1946, 1960, 1973, 1976, 1982 y 1992. La presente descripción se refiere al censo de 1992 (realizado el 1 de octubre de ese año). El censo de 1976 fue el último celebrado antes del censo de 1992 en que se acopió información sobre la población económicamente activa.

3. Alcance del censo:
a) Geográfico: El censo abarcó únicamente el territorio controlado por el Gobierno chipriota.

b) Personas comprendidas: Toda la población.

4. Período de referencia:
La semana anterior al día de la entrevista.

5. Materias principales:
a) Población total, según sexo y edad:	sí
Población económicamente activa por:	
b) Sexo y grupo de edad:	sí
c) Rama de actividad económica:	sí
d) Ocupación:	sí
e) Situación en el empleo:	sí
f) Nivel más alto de educación:	sí
g) Horas de trabajo:	sí
h) Otras características:	sí

Ref. a): La edad se determinó según la fecha de nacimiento, es decir, el día, mes y año de nacimiento, y las personas se clasificaron con arreglo a su edad en el último cumpleaños.

Ref. g): Se pidió a las personas ocupadas que precisaran si trabajaban a tiempo completo (por lo menos 30 horas semanales) o a tiempo parcial (menos de 30 horas por semana).

Ref. h): Se acopió información sobre la duración del desempleo, medida en meses.

6. Conceptos y definiciones:
a) Población económicamente activa: Abarcó a todas las personas de 15 o más años de edad que, durante la semana de referencia, estaban ocupadas o desempleadas, conforme a las definiciones que se dan más adelante. La definición incluyó a los miembros de las fuerzas armadas.

b) Empleo: Se consideró "ocupada" a toda persona que respondió afirmativamente a las preguntas "¿Desempeña usted habitualmente una actividad laboral?" o "¿Trabajó usted la semana pasada, aunque sólo lo haya hecho por una hora?".

Se ha indicado que fueron incluidas las siguientes categorías:

i) personas que trabajan sin remuneración en una empresa o negocio familiar;
ii) personas ocupadas pero temporalmente ausentes de su trabajo;
iii) estudiantes que trabajan a tiempo parcial;
iv) trabajadores estacionales u ocasionales;
v) conscriptos del servicio militar o civil;
vi) aprendices y personas que siguen un curso de formación.

Los trabajadores estacionales u ocasionales quedaron incluidos en la definición únicamente si habían trabajado durante la semana de referencia. Sólo pueden identificarse por separado las categorías i), ii), v) y vi).

c) Desempleo: Se consideró "desempleada" a toda persona que respondió negativamente a las preguntas "¿Desempeña usted habitualmente una actividad laboral?" y "¿Trabajó usted la semana pasada, aunque sólo lo haya hecho por una hora?", y que indicó que estaba desempleada o buscando trabajo al precisar lo que había hecho durante la semana de referencia. La definición no incluyó a los estudiantes que buscaban trabajo.

7. Clasificaciones utilizadas:
Tanto las personas ocupadas como las desempleadas anteriormente empleadas fueron clasificadas por rama de actividad, por ocupación y por situación en el empleo.

a) Rama de actividad económica: Para determinarla se preguntó: "¿En qué tipo de empresa o de actividad trabaja/ha trabajado usted?". Para codificar la rama de actividad se utilizaron 61 grupos de la clasificación nacional. Se establecieron enlaces con la CIIU-Rev.3 a nivel de divisiones (clave de 2 dígitos).

b) Ocupación: Para determinarla se preguntó: "¿Qué tipo de trabajo desempeñó/hubiera desempeñado la semana pasada?". Para codificar la ocupación se utilizaron 30 grupos de la clasificación nacional. Se establecieron enlaces con la CIUO-88 a nivel de grandes grupos (clave de 1 dígito) y subgrupos principales (clave de 2 dígitos).

c) Situación en el empleo: Para determinarla se preguntó: "¿En su ocupación trabaja usted en calidad de: independiente (con empleados); independiente (sin empleados); trabajador asalariado; trabajador familiar no remunerado; aprendiz; otra situación?". La situación en el empleo se codificó conforme a estos seis grupos.

8. Diferencias principales con el censo anterior:
Por lo que se refiere al acopio de datos sobre la población económicamente activa, en el censo de 1992 se fijó una edad mínima de 15 años, mientras que en el censo de 1976 no se había establecido edad límite alguna.

En el censo de 1992 se clasificó según la rama de actividad, la ocupación y la situación en el empleo tanto a las personas ocupadas como a las desempleadas anteriormente empleadas, a diferencia del censo de 1976, en que se había clasificado por rama de actividad sólo a las personas ocupadas y por ocupación, a las personas ocupadas y a las desempleadas previamente empleadas, mientras que no se había establecido ninguna clasificación según la situación en el empleo.

9. Publicación de los resultados del censo:
Los datos definitivos sobre la población total y la población económicamente activa se publicaron en 1995, en los siguientes volúmenes:

Volume I: "General and Demographic Characteristics of the Population (June 1994)". Volume III: "Labour Force (1995)".

El organismo responsable de estas publicaciones es el Department of Statistics and Research, 13 Lord Byron Avenue, P.C. 162, Nicosia.

Algunos de los resultados del censo están disponibles también en cuadros inéditos y disquetes.

REPUBLICA DOMINICANA

1. Nombre y dirección del organismo responsable del censo:
Oficina Nacional de Estadística (ONE), Ave. México, Esquina Leopoldo Navarro, Edificio Gubernamental Juan Pablo Duarte (El Huacal) 9no. Piso, Santo Domingo.

2. Censos de población llevados a cabo desde 1945 (años):
1950, 1960, 1970, 1981 y 1993. La presente descripción se refiere al censo de población de 1993 (realizado el 24 y el 25 de Septiembre).

3. Alcance del censo:
a) Geográfico: Todo el país.

b) Personas comprendidas: Toda la población.

4. Período de referencia:
La semana anterior al día del censo.

5. Materias principales:
a) Población total, según sexo y edad:	sí
Población económicamente activa por:	
b) Sexo y grupo de edad:	sí
c) Rama de actividad económica:	sí
d) Ocupación:	sí
e) Situación en el empleo:	sí
f) Nivel más alto de educación:	no
g) Horas de trabajo:	no
h) Otras características:	no

Ref. a): Se definió la edad según los años cumplidos y el año de nacimiento.

6. Conceptos y definiciones:
a) Población económicamente activa: Incluye a todas las personas de 10 años y más, que durante la semana de referencia se encontraban empleadas o desempleadas, según las definiciones que se dan más adelante. Se incluyen a todos los miembros de las fuerzas armadas.

b) Empleo: Se consideran "empleadas" a las personas que informaron que en la semana de referencia hicieron algún trabajo o tenían empleo, recibieron paga por algún trabajo realizado esa semana o realizaron en su casa o en cualquier establecimiento o negocio de la familia algún trabajo no pagado. La pregunta utilizada para poder considerar una persona como ocupada es: "¿En cuál de estas situaciones se encontraba la semana pasada?

i) trabajo por ingreso;
ii) sin trabajar, pero tiene trabajo;
iii) trabajando para un familiar sin pago en dinero;
iv) buscando trabajo habiendo trabajado antes;
v) pensionado o jubilado sin trabajar;
vi) en quehaceres de su hogar;
vii) estudiando sin trabajar;
viii) buscando trabajo por primera vez;
ix) incapacitado permanente para trabajar;
x) no le interesa trabajar;
xi) no buscó trabajo, pero aceptaría si se le ofreciera;
xii) rentista."

Se ha indicado que quedan incluidas las siguientes categorías:

i) personas que trabajan sin remuneración en una empresa familiar;
ii) personas en la producción de bienes primarios para el autoconsumo;
iii) personas ocupadas pero temporalmente ausentes de su trabajo;
iv) estudiantes que trabajan a tiempo parcial;
v) conscriptos del servicio militar o civil.

Todas las categorías se pueden identificar separadamente.

c) Desempleo: Se consideran "desempleadas" a las personas que no trabajaron la semana de referencia, o que no habían trabajado antes, pero que estuvieron buscando trabajo. Se incluye a los trabajadores con experiencia laboral ("cesantes") y los que no habían trabajado antes ("trabajadores nuevos"). Se excluyen los estudiantes que buscaron trabajo.

7. Clasificaciones utilizadas:
Tanto las personas ocupadas como las desocupadas con experiencia laboral se clasificaron por rama de actividad económica, por ocupación y según la situación en el empleo.

a) Rama de actividad económica: Para establecer la rama de actividad económica se preguntó la actividad a la que se dedica el organismo, empresa, negocio u oficina en que trabaja o trabajó la persona la última vez. Para codificar esta variable, se utilizaron 10 grupos de la clasificación nacional. Los enlaces con la CIIU-Rev.2 se han establecido a nivel de grandes divisiones (1 dígito).

b) Ocupación: Para establecer la ocupación se preguntó por el oficio o empleo que desempeñó o desempeñaba en el lugar en que trabaja o trabajaba la persona. Para codificar esta variable, se utilizaron 10 grupos de la clasificación nacional. Los enlaces con la CIUO-68 se han establecido a nivel de los grandes grupos (1 dígito).

c) Situación en el empleo: Para determinar esta característica se preguntó si en el trabajo la persona se ubicaba en una de las siguientes cinco categorías: patrón o empleador, trabajador por cuenta propia, trabajador en servicio doméstico, trabajador asalariado (empleado, obrero, jornalero) y trabajador familiar no pagado.

8. Diferencias principales con el censo anterior:
En 1981, se levantó un censo de hecho y derecho, mientras que el censo levantado en 1993 fue solo de hecho.

En 1981, se utilizaron 14 preguntas para medir y caracterizar la situación laboral, lo que permitió profundizar más sobre las características económicas. Las preguntas que no se incluyeron en el censo más reciente fueron las siguientes:

"¿Si no trabajó, a que dedicó la mayor parte del tiempo la semana pasada?

¿Cuánto tiempo tiene sin trabajar?

¿Cuántas horas trabajó la semana pasada en todos sus empleos, o trabajos?

¿Para quién trabajó principalmente la semana pasada, o trabajaba en su último empleo o trabajo?".

El censo de 1981 midió el ingreso por concepto de salario en el empleo para un año o un mes. En cambio, el censo de 1993 midió el ingreso salarial durante una semana. En el censo de 1981 el parámetro para medir el tiempo era un año o un mes.

9. Publicación de los resultados del censo:
El título exacto de la publicación con los resultados finales es "Censo Nacional de Población y Vivienda 24 y 25 de septiembre de 1993; Resultados definitivos Region Sur-Oeste Vol.I, junio de 1996".

La organización responsable de la publicación es la Oficina nacional de estadística, ave. México, Esquina Leopoldo Navarro, edificio gubernamental Juan Pablo Duarte (El Huacal), 9no. Piso.

Los resultados del censo se encuentran también disponibles en forma de disquetes y de cuadros no publicados.

ECUADOR

1. Nombre y dirección del organismo responsable del censo:
Instituto Nacional de Estadísticas y Censos (INEC), Av. 10 de Agosto 229 y Pasaje Carlos Ibarra, Quito.

2. Censos de población llevados a cabo desde 1945 (años):
1950, 1962, 1974, 1982 y 1990. La presente descripción se refiere al censo de población de 1990 (que se efectuó el 25 de noviembre).

3. Alcance del censo:
a) Geográfico: Todo el país, excepto las áreas en conflicto momentáneo por problema indígena.

b) Personas comprendidas: Toda la población, excepto las personas que viven en las áreas indicadas más arriba.

4. Período de referencia:
La semana anterior al día del censo.

5. Materias principales:
a) Población total, según sexo y edad: sí
Población económicamente activa por:
b) Sexo y grupo de edad: sí
c) Rama de actividad económica: sí
d) Ocupación: sí
e) Situación en el empleo: sí
f) Nivel más alto de educación: ...
g) Horas de trabajo: sí
h) Otras características: sí

Ref. a): Se definió la edad según los años cumplidos.

Ref. g): Se refieren tanto al número de horas habitualmente trabajadas como al número de horas efectivamente trabajadas por las personas que trabajaron durante el período de referencia. La pregunta utilizada fue "¿Cuántas horas trabajó en la semana pasada en la ocupación indicada?".

6. Conceptos y definiciones:
a) Población económicamente activa: Incluye a todas las personas de 8 años y más de edad, que durante la semana de referencia estaban empleadas o desempleadas, según las definiciones que se dan más adelante. La definición incluye también a todos los miembros de las fuerzas armadas.

b) Empleo: Son consideradas "empleadas" todas las personas que trabajaron de forma independiente o dependiente durante la semana de referencia. Las preguntas utilizadas para poder considerar una persona como ocupada son "¿Qué hizo la semana pasada?" y "¿A lo mejor en la semana realizó o ayudó a realizar alguna actividad aunque sea sin remuneración?".

Se ha indicado que quedan incluidas las siguientes categorías:

i) personas que trabajan sin remuneración en una empresa o negocio familiar;
ii) personas ocupadas pero temporalmente ausentes de su trabajo;
iii) estudiantes que trabajan a tiempo parcial;
iv) trabajadores estacionales u ocasionales;
v) conscriptos del servicio militar o civil;
vi) aprendices y personas que siguen un curso de formación.

Ninguna de estas categorías puede identificarse separadamente.

c) Desempleo: Son consideradas como "desempleadas" las personas que contestaron negativamente las preguntas mencionadas en el apartado b) más arriba y que, durante la semana de referencia, buscaron trabajo habiendo trabajado anteriormente, o buscaron su primer empleo. Se excluyen los estudiantes que buscaron trabajo.

7. Clasificaciones utilizadas:

Tanto las personas ocupadas como las desocupadas que han trabajado anteriormente se clasificaron por rama de actividad económica, por ocupación y según la situación en el empleo.

a) Rama de actividad económica: Se determinó usando la pregunta: "¿A qué se dedica o qué produce principalmente el lugar, establecimiento o negocio donde desempeñó la ocupación que indica?". Se utilizó la CIIU-Rev.2 al nivel de tres dígitos para codificación y de un dígito para publicación de los datos.

b) Ocupación: Se determinó usando la pregunta: "¿Cuál fue la principal ocupación o trabajo que realizó durante la semana anterior o su último trabajo si estuvo cesante?". Se utilizó la CIUO-68 al nivel de los grandes grupos y de los grupos primarios.

c) Situación en el empleo: Se determinó usando la pregunta: "¿Cuál fue la posición o categoría en la ocupación que indica?". La situación en la ocupación se codificó en siete grupos: patrono o socio activo; cuenta propia; empleado o asalariado del: Municipio o Consejos Provinciales; Estado; Sector Privado; trabajador familiar sin remuneración; ignorado.

8. Diferencias principales con el censo anterior:

En 1982, el límite de edad inferior utilizado para identificar a la población económicamente activa y sus componentes (empleo y desempleo) fue de 12 años; en 1990, baja a 8 años.

La pregunta utilizada en 1982 para identificar las personas ocupadas fue "¿Qué hizo la mayor parte de los días comprendidos entre el 7 y el 13 de noviembre?"; en el censo de 1990 la pregunta fue "¿Qué hizo la semana pasada?".

El censo de 1990 incluye "¿A lo mejor en la semana pasada realizó o ayudó a realizar alguna actividad, aunque sin remuneración?" y "¿Cuántas horas trabajó la semana pasada en la ocupación indicada?".

En el censo de 1990, se incluye "impedido para trabajar" en las categorías de respuesta de actividad.

En 1990, se desglosó de la categoría de situación en el empleo "empleado o asalariado" los siguientes: del Municipio o Consejos Provinciales; del Estado; del Sector Privado.

Por último, en el censo de 1990 no se investigó sobre seguridad social.

9. Publicación de los resultados del censo:

El título exacto de la publicación en que se presentan los datos finales del censo es "V Censo de Población y IV de Vivienda 1990 - Resultados Definitivos, Resumen Nacional, Noviembre de 1991".

La organización responsable de la publicación es el Instituto Nacional de Estadísticas y Censos - INEC, Quito.

La información del censo de 1990 está también disponible en la forma como lo requiera el usuario.

EL SALVADOR

1. Nombre y dirección del organismo responsable del censo:

Dirección General de Estadística y Censos, 1a. Calle Poniente y 43 Avenida Norte, San Salvador, El Salvador.

2. Censos de población llevados a cabo desde 1945 (años):

1950, 1961, 1971 y 1992. La presente descripción se refiere al censo de población de 1992 (efectuado el 27 de septiembre).

3. Alcance del censo:

a) Geográfico: Todo el país.

b) Personas comprendidas: Toda la población.

4. Periodo de referencia:

La semana anterior a la fecha del censo.

5. Materias principales:

a) Población total, según sexo y edad:	sí
Población económicamente activa por:	
b) Sexo y grupo de edad:	sí
c) Rama de actividad económica:	sí
d) Ocupación:	sí
e) Situación en el empleo:	sí
f) Nivel más alto de educación:	sí
g) Horas de trabajo:	sí
h) Otras características:	no

Ref. a): Se definió la edad según los años cumplidos.

Ref. g): Se refiere a las horas habitualmente y efectivamente trabajadas por las personas ocupadas que trabajaron durante el período de referencia.

6. Conceptos y definiciones:

a) Población económicamente activa: Incluye a todas las personas de 10 años y más de edad, que durante la semana de referencia estaban empleadas o desempleadas, según las definiciones que se dan más adelante. La definición incluye a los miembros de las fuerzas armadas.

b) Empleo: Son consideradas "empleadas" las personas que trabajaron durante la semana de referencia. La pregunta utilizada es: "¿La semana anterior al inicio del censo usted: trabajó por pago en dinero o en especie; trabajó para otra persona sin remuneración; tenía empleo, empresa, finca propia, pero no trabajo; buscó trabajo y había trabajado antes; buscó trabajo por primera vez (nunca antes tuvo trabajo); no buscó trabajo por creer que no había; es ama de casa exclusivamente; estudió exclusivamente; es jubilado, pensionado o rentista; estaba recluido; está incapacitado permanentemente para trabajar; otro?".

Se ha indicado que quedan incluidas las siguientes categorías:

i) personas trabajando sin paga en firma o negocio familiar;
ii) personas empleadas y temporalmente ausentes del trabajo;
iii) estudiantes que trabajan a tiempo parcial;
iv) trabajadores estacionales u ocasionales;
v) aprendices y personas que siguen un curso de formación.

Las personas de las categorías i), ii), iii) y iv) pueden identificarse separadamente utilizando preguntas específicas.

c) Desempleo: Son consideradas "desempleadas" las personas que durante la semana de referencia no trabajaron pero que buscaron trabajo. Se incluyen las personas que ya habían efectuado arreglos para empezar a trabajar después de la semana de referencia, las que se encontraban temporal o indefinidamente suspendidas y sin remuneración, y las que creían que no había empleo disponible.

7. Clasificaciones utilizadas:

Tanto las personas ocupadas como las desocupadas se clasificaron por rama de actividad económica, por ocupación y según la situación en la ocupación.

a) Rama de actividad económica: Las preguntas utilizadas para identificar la rama de actividad son: "¿Dónde trabaja o trabajó (en el campo, en una fábrica, un taller mecánico, oficina privada o pública, en la calle, etc.)" y "¿A qué se dedica o qué produce usted o el establecimiento donde trabaja o trabajó por última vez?". Para codificar la rama de actividad se utilizó la CIIU-Rev.3 a nivel de 4 dígitos.

b) Ocupación: La pregunta utilizada para identificar el grupo de ocupaciones es "¿Cuál es la ocupación, empleo u oficio que desempeña o desempeñaba en el trabajo?". Para codificar la ocupación se utilizó la CIUO-88 a nivel de los grupos primarios.

c) Situación en el empleo: La pregunta utilizada para identificar la situación en el empleo es "¿En este trabajo usted es o era: empleado u obrero del sector público, empleado u obrero del sector privado, patrón o empleador, trabajador familiar sin sueldo, trabajador independiente (cuenta propia), empleado doméstico, trabajador en cooperativa productiva, ignorado?". Para codificar esta variable, se utilizaron los ocho grupos precedentes.

8. Diferencias principales con el censo anterior:

No hubo diferencias significativas.

9. Publicación de los resultados del censo:

Los resultados finales fueron publicados en diciembre de 1995.

El título exacto de la publicación con los resultados finales es "V Censos nacionales de población".

La organización responsable de la publicación es la Dirección General de Estadística y Censos, 1a. Calle Poniente y 43 Avenida Norte, San Salvador, El Salvador.

Los resultados del censo están también disponibles en forma de cuadros inéditos.

ESLOVAQUIA

1. Nombre y dirección del organismo responsable del censo:
Slovenského Statistického Urado, Mileticova 3, 824 67 Bratislava.

2. Censos de población llevados a cabo desde 1945 (años):
1950, 1961, 1970, 1980 y 1991. La presente descripción se refiere al censo de población de 1991 (realizado a partir de la medianoche del 2 al 3 de marzo de ese año).

3. Alcance del censo:
a) Geográfico: Todo el país.

b) Personas comprendidas: Toda la población con residencia permanente en el país y los nacionales que vivían en forma permanente en el extranjero; se excluyó a los miembros del cuerpo diplomático, los miembros del ejército soviético y a los familiares de ambas categorías.

4. Período de referencia:
Medianoche del 2 al 3 de marzo.

5. Materias principales:
a) Población total, según sexo y edad: sí
Población económicamente activa por:
b) Sexo y grupo de edad: sí
c) Rama de actividad económica: sí
d) Ocupación: sí
e) Situación en el empleo: sí
f) Nivel más alto de educación: ...
g) Horas de trabajo: no
h) Otras características: sí

Ref. a): La edad se determinó según la fecha de nacimiento.

Ref. h): El censo también recolectó información sobre el lugar de trabajo (la dirección), la frecuencia de traslado al trabajo (diaria u otras) y la duración del trayecto desde la casa al lugar de trabajo (en minutos).

6. Conceptos y definiciones:
a) Población económicamente activa: La actividad económica se basó en el concepto de actividad actual. Por ende, la población económicamente activa abarcó a todas las personas de 15 o más años de edad que durante el período de referencia estaban ocupadas o desempleadas, conforme a las definiciones que figuran más adelante. La definición incluyó a la población penitenciaria y a los miembros de las fuerzas armadas, según el equivalente civil del último trabajo desempeñado o del trabajo ocupado en el momento del censo (trabajo actual).

b) Empleo: Se consideró "ocupada" a toda persona que declaró tener una ocupación en cuanto: empleador; trabajador por cuenta propia; empleado o miembro de una cooperativa agrícola o de una cooperativa de producción (quedaron comprendidos los pensionistas que trabajaban, las mujeres en licencia por maternidad y los trabajadores familiares no remunerados). La definición no incluyó a los estudiantes que trabajaban a tiempo parcial.

Se ha indicado que fueron incluidas las siguientes categorías:
i) personas que trabajan sin remuneración en una empresa o negocio familiar;
ii) personas ocupadas pero temporalmente ausentes de su trabajo;
iii) trabajadores estacionales u ocasionales;
iv) conscriptos del servicio militar o civil.

Sólo la categoría i) puede identificarse por separado. Los aprendices y las personas que siguen un curso de formación, si bien no entraron en la definición de población económicamente activa, también pueden identificarse por separado.

c) Desempleo: Se consideró "desempleados" a los hombres de 15 a 59 años y las mujeres de 15 a 56 años que declararon estar buscando trabajo en el momento del censo.

7. Clasificaciones utilizadas:
Tanto las personas ocupadas como las personas desempleadas anteriormente empleadas fueron clasificadas por rama de actividad, por ocupación y por situación en el empleo.

a) Rama de actividad económica: Para determinarla se pidió a la persona censada que indicara el nombre del establecimiento, la cooperativa, la oficina, la organización o la institución do-

cente en la que trabajaba. Para codificar la rama de actividad o la asistencia a la institución docente se utilizó una lista especial de organizaciones con códigos establecidos en función de la actividad principal. Para ordenar los resultados del censo de 1991 se utilizó una clasificación nacional de 47 grupos (ramas y subramas de la clasificación nacional). Esta última es en todo comparable a la CIIU-Rev.3. Se estableció una tabla de conversión entre la clasificación nacional y la CIIU-Rev.3 a nivel de divisiones (2 dígitos).

b) Ocupación: Se pidió a la persona censada que indicara con la mayor precisión posible su trabajo o función. En el caso de los pensionistas que no trabajaban, las mujeres con licencia por maternidad, los conscriptos del servicio militar, los presos y quienes estaban buscando trabajo, se pidió que indicaran el último trabajo. Para codificar la ocupación se utilizaron 91 grupos de la clasificación nacional. Se establecieron enlaces con la CIUO-68 y la CIUO-88 a nivel de grandes grupos (1 dígito).

c) Situación en el empleo: Se pidió a la persona censada que indicara el grupo social al que pertenecía, por ejemplo: obrero, empleado, miembro de una cooperativa agrícola, miembro de una cooperativa de producción, empleador (con uno o más empleados), agricultor independiente, comerciante por cuenta propia, trabajador independiente, trabajador familiar no remunerado, etc. A los obreros y a los empleados se les pidió que indicaran el sector concreto de la economía nacional en que estaban ocupados (público, privado, cooperativo, mixto). Para codificar la situación en el empleo se utilizaron los 9 grupos enumerados a continuación: obrero o empleado del sector privado; obrero o empleado en otros sectores; miembro de cooperativa agrícola; miembro de otras cooperativas; empleador; agricultor independiente; trabajador por cuenta propia; trabajador independiente y trabajador familiar no remunerado.

8. Diferencias principales con el censo anterior:
En 1991, la definición de población económicamente activa se amplió, incluyéndose en ella a las personas desempleadas en busca de trabajo, sin diferenciar a quienes estaban en busca de un primer empleo. La definición abarcó igualmente a los pensionistas que trabajaban y a quienes recibían pensiones o prestaciones de vejez o de invalidez.

En los censos de 1961, 1970 y 1980, a los trabajadores familiares no remunerados se les había considerado personas a cargo, es decir, económicamente inactivas, y a quienes habían declarado estar desempleados se les había considerado ocupados, habida cuenta de su último trabajo.

En el censo de 1991, la situación en el empleo se amplió, incluyéndose a los empleadores y añadiéndose un grupo especial para los trabajadores familiares no remunerados.

Por último, en 1991 se amplió también la cuestión del traslado al trabajo, al añadirse una pregunta sobre el tiempo necesario para recorrer el trayecto de la casa al lugar de trabajo.

9. Publicación de los resultados del censo:
Los resultados definitivos del censo se publicaron en 1992, con el título "1991 Population and Housing Census".

La organización responsable de esta publicación es la Slovenského Statistického Urado, Mileticova 3, 824 67 Bratislava.

También se dispone de disquetes y cintas magnéticas con dichos resultados.

ESLOVENIA

1. Nombre y dirección del organismo responsable del censo:
Statistical Office of the Republic of Slovenia, Ljubljana, Vozarski pot 12.

2. Censos de población llevados a cabo desde 1945 (años):
1948, 1953, 1961, 1971, 1981 y 1991. La presente descripción se refiere al censo de población de 1991 (realizado el 31 de marzo de ese año).

3. Alcance del censo:
a) Geográfico: Todo el país.

b) Personas comprendidas: Toda la población.

4. Periodo de referencia:
El día del censo y el año anterior al día del censo.

5. Materias principales:
a) Población total, según sexo y edad: sí
Población económicamente activa por:
b) Sexo y grupo de edad: sí
c) Rama de actividad económica: sí
d) Ocupación: sí
e) Situación en el empleo: sí
f) Nivel más alto de educación: sí
g) Horas de trabajo: no
h) Otras características: sí

Ref. a): La edad se determinó según el año de nacimiento.

Ref. h): También se recopilaron informaciones sobre los ingresos regulares de las personas y sobre el desplazamiento hacia el lugar de trabajo (frecuencia, tiempo ocupado, en minutos, y medios de transporte utilizados).

6. Conceptos y definiciones:

a) Población económicamente activa: Abarcó a todas las personas de 15 o más años de edad que, el día del censo, estaban ocupadas o desempleadas, conforme a las definiciones que se dan más adelante. Para establecer la actividad de determinadas categorías de la población (amas de casa, personas ocupadas fundamentalmente en labores agrícolas, jubilados, trabajadores estacionales u ocasionales) se utilizó como período de referencia el año anterior o al día del censo. La definición incluyó a todos los miembros de las fuerzas armadas; en cambio, no quedaron incluidos los estudiantes que trabajaban a tiempo parcial ni los estudiantes que buscaban empleo.

b) Empleo: Se consideró "ocupada" a toda persona que, en el momento del censo, ejercía una profesión y percibía una remuneración en efectivo o en especie por su trabajo. Se incluyó en los hogares rurales a las esposas y los miembros del grupo familiar que se dedicaban fundamentalmente a ayudar en las tareas agropecuarias.

Se ha indicado que fueron incluidas las siguientes categorías:

i) personas que trabajan sin remuneración en una empresa o negocio familiar;
ii) personas que producen bienes primarios para el autoconsumo;
iii) personas ocupadas pero temporalmente ausentes de su trabajo;
iv) trabajadores estacionales u ocasionales;
v) conscriptos del servicio militar o civil;
vi) aprendices y personas que siguen un curso de formación.

Sólo la categoría i) puede identificarse por separado.

c) Desempleo: Se consideró "desempleada" a toda persona que, durante el período del censo, estaba inscrita en las agencias de colocación en calidad de solicitante de un primer empleo o de un nuevo empleo.

7. Clasificaciones utilizadas:
Tanto las personas ocupadas como las desempleadas anteriormente empleadas se clasificaron por ocupación. Sólo las personas ocupadas se clasificaron por rama de actividad económica y por situación en el empleo.

a) Rama de actividad económica: Para determinarla se pidió a las personas ocupadas que precisaran en qué industria (o rama de actividad económica) trabajaban, así como el nombre y la dirección de la empresa, el organismo o la asociación que las empleaba. Para codificar la rama de actividad económica se utilizaron 700 grupos de la clasificación de actividades establecida por la Oficina Central de Estadística de la República de Eslovenia, vigente en el momento del censo. Esta clasificación no es directamente comparable con la CIIU. Sin embargo, partiendo de la base de una combinación de preguntas y con arreglo a estimaciones, resulta posible establecer enlaces con la CIIU-Rev.2 a nivel de grandes divisiones (clave de 1 dígito).

b) Ocupación: Se pidió a las personas empadronadas que indicaran con precisión el tipo de trabajo que desempeñaban. Para codificar la ocupación, se utilizó la clasificación de ocupaciones establecida por la Oficina Central de Estadística de la República de Eslovenia, vigente en el momento del censo. Esta clasificación no es directamente comparable con la CIUO. Sin embargo, partiendo de la base de diversos datos, se puede establecer enlaces con la CIUO-88, a nivel de grandes grupos (clave de 1 dígito).

c) Situación en el empleo: Para codificar esta variable se utilizaron cinco grupos: trabajador asalariado; propietario/copropietario (empresa); propietario/copropietario (actividad artesanal); trabajador por cuenta propia; trabajador familiar no remunerado.

8. Diferencias principales con el censo anterior:
No hubo diferencias significativas.

9. Publicación de los resultados del censo:
Los resultados definitivos del censo se han difundido en diversas publicaciones, en particular: "1991 Census of the Population, Households, Housing and Agricultural Holdings in the Republic of Slovenia - Final data: Statistical information No. 173 (July 1992)" y "No. 189 (July 1992): population by activity and sex, Economically active population, by industry". La lista completa de las publicaciones figura en "Results of Surveys - Census of the population, households, housings and agricultural holdings in the Republic of Slovenia in 1991, No. 617 (1994)".

El organismo responsable de estas publicaciones es la Statistical Office of the Republic of Slovenia, Vozarski pot 12, Ljubljana.

No se dispone de otra forma de presentación de los resultados del censo de 1991.

ESPAÑA

1. Nombre y dirección del organismo responsable del censo:
Instituto Nacional de Estadística, Paseo de la Castellana, 183, 28046 Madrid.

2. Censos de población llevados a cabo desde 1945 (años):
1950, 1960, 1970, 1981 y 1991. La presente descripción se refiere al censo de población de 1991 (que se efectuó el 1 de marzo).

3. Alcance del censo:
a) Geográfico: Todo el país.

b) Personas comprendidas: Todas las personas residentes en el territorio nacional y las que se encontraban en el mismo en la fecha censal. Se excluyen las personas que no residen ni en viviendas familiares ni alojamientos y viviendas colectivas fijas (vagabundos, personas sin hogar, etc.).

4. Período de referencia:
La semana anterior al censo, es decir, del 22 al 28 de febrero de 1991.

5. Materias principales:
a) Población total, según sexo y edad: sí
Población económicamente activa por:
b) Sexo y grupo de edad: sí
c) Rama de actividad económica: sí
d) Ocupación: sí
e) Situación en el empleo: sí
f) Nivel más alto de educación: sí
g) Horas de trabajo: no
h) Otras características: sí

Ref. a): Se definió la edad en términos del año de nacimiento.

Ref. h): Algunas Comunidades Autónomas han recogido el lugar del trabajo y la forma de desplazamiento. Estas Comunidades son: Murcia, Andalucía, Canarias, Cataluña, Galicia, País Vasco y Navarra.

6. Conceptos y definiciones:

a) Población económicamente activa: Incluye a todas las personas de 16 años o más de edad que, durante la semana de referencia, se encontraban empleadas o desempleadas, tal y como se definen más adelante. Los datos sobre la población económicamente activa y sus componentes (empleo y desempleo) sólo se tabularon a partir de 16 años y más de edad. La definición incluye también a los militares de carrera pero excluye a los conscriptos en el servicio militar obligatorio.

b) Empleo: Se consideran como "empleadas" a todas las personas que han trabajado al menos una hora durante la semana de referencia. La definición incluye igualmente a las personas que, en dicha semana, estuvieron temporalmente ausentes de su trabajo por enfermedad, vacaciones, etc.

Se ha indicado que quedan incluidas las siguientes categorías:

i) personas trabajando sin remuneración en una empresa familiar;
ii) personas en la producción de bienes primarios para el autoconsumo;

iii) personas ocupadas pero temporalmente ausentes de su trabajo;

iv) estudiantes que trabajan a tiempo parcial;

v) trabajadores estacionales u ocasionales, que estaban ocupados en la semana de referencia;

vi) aprendices y personas que siguen un curso de formación, siempre que reciban algún tipo de remuneración.

Solamente las personas de las categorías i), iv) y v) arriba mencionadas pueden ser identificadas separadamente. Los trabajadores estacionales u ocasionales se consideran ocupados sólo si trabajaron al menos una hora durante la semana de referencia. Los conscriptos en el servicio militar o civil están excluidos de la población económicamente activa pero pueden ser identificados separadamente.

c) Desempleo: Parados o "desempleados" son todas las personas que, durante la semana de referencia, han estado simultáneamente: i) "sin trabajo", es decir, que no han tenido empleo por cuenta ajena o por cuenta propia; ii) "en busca de trabajo", es decir que han tomado medidas concretas para buscar un trabajo por cuenta ajena o hayan hecho gestiones para establecerse por su cuenta (por ejemplo: inscripciones en oficina de paro, gestiones en lugares de trabajo, respuesta a anuncios de periódico, etc.); iii) "disponibles para trabajar" en un empleo por cuenta propia o por cuenta ajena. Los parados se subdividen en parados que buscan primer empleo y parados que han trabajado anteriormente.

7. Clasificaciones utilizadas:

Tanto los ocupados como los desempleados con experiencia laboral se clasificaron por rama de actividad económica, ocupación y situación en el empleo. Estas variables se refieren a la ocupación principal de los ocupados y al último trabajo realizado para los desempleados.

a) Rama de actividad económica: Se determinó según la pregunta "¿Cuál es la actividad principal del establecimiento donde trabaja o trabajó (por ejemplo: producción agrícola; fabricación de juguetes; hotelería; etc.)?". Para codificar esta variable se utilizó la CIIU (Rev.2 y Rev.3) entre uno y dos dígitos.

b) Ocupación: Según la pregunta: "¿Cuál es la ocupación, profesión u oficio que desempeña o desempeñó (por ejemplo: dependiente de comercio; capataz de la construcción; etc.)?". Para codificar esta variable, se utilizó la CIUO (68 y 88) al nivel de subgrupos.

c) Situación en el empleo: Para determinar esta característica se preguntó por la situación en el trabajo ejercido. Esta variable se codificó en siete grupos: empresario, profesional o trabajador por cuenta propia que emplea personal; empresario, profesional o trabajador por cuenta propia que no emplea personal; miembro de cooperativa de trabajo asociado que trabaja en la misma; persona que trabaja sin remuneración reglamentada en la empresa o negocio de un familiar con el que convive; persona que trabaja con carácter fijo, a sueldo, comisión, jornal u otra clase de remuneración; persona que trabaja con carácter eventual o temporal a sueldo, comisión, jornal u otra clase de remuneración; otra situación.

8. Diferencias principales con el censo anterior:

La mayor innovación del censo de 1991 es que todas las preguntas serán codificadas y explotadas al 100 por cien, lo cual permitirá una mayor desagregación geográfica, aunque la ocupación y la actividad no podrán darse con el mismo grado de desagregación.

Por lo que se refiere a los criterios para clasificar la población en activa, ocupada, parada, etc., se han seguido los mismos criterios que en la Encuesta de Población Activa.

9. Publicación de los resultados del censo:

Los datos definitivos sobre la población económicamente activa y sus componentes (empleo y desempleo) se publicaron al final de 1993.

El título exacto de la publicación en que se presentan los datos finales del censo es "Censos de Población y Viviendas 1991".

La organización responsable de la publicación es el Instituto Nacional de Estadística, Madrid.

Los resultados del censo se encuentran también disponibles en la forma de disquetes, cintas magnéticas y CD-ROM.

ESTADOS UNIDOS

1. Nombre y dirección del organismo responsable del censo:

United States Bureau of the Census, Washington, DC 20233.

2. Censos de población llevados a cabo desde 1945 (años):

1950, 1960, 1970, 1980 y 1990. La presente descripción se refiere al censo de 1990 (realizado el 1o. de abril de ese año).

3. Alcance del censo:

a) Geográfico: Todo el país. Se realizaron censos separados en los territorios de ultramar, es decir, Samoa Americana, Guam, Islas Marianas del Norte, Palau, Puerto Rico e Islas Vírgenes.

b) Personas comprendidas: Toda la población, salvo los nacionales residentes en el extranjero.

La unidad muestral de base fue la vivienda, incluidos todos los ocupantes. En hogares colectivos, la unidad muestral fue la persona. La fracción muestral varió en función de los procedimientos de recolección de datos. Cuando se tuvieron en cuenta las razones muestrales de todo el país, resultó que aproximadamente una de cada seis unidades de vivienda figuraban en la muestra del censo.

4. Periodo de referencia:

La semana anterior a la entrevista, por lo que se refiere a la definición de la población activa actual, y el año 1989, en cuanto a la determinación de la situación de la fuerza de trabajo durante ese año.

La presente descripción se refiere a la población económicamente activa en el momento del censo.

5. Materias principales:

a) Población total, según sexo y edad:	sí
Población económicamente activa por:	
b) Sexo y grupo de edad:	sí
c) Rama de actividad económica:	sí
d) Ocupación:	sí
e) Situación en el empleo:	sí
f) Nivel más alto de educación:	sí
g) Horas de trabajo:	sí
h) Otras características:	sí

Ref. a): La edad se determinó según los años cumplidos en el último cumpleaños.

Ref. g): Las horas de trabajo se refirieron tanto a las efectivamente trabajadas por las personas ocupadas durante la semana de referencia, como a todo el período trabajado (en semanas) y a las horas habituales de trabajo en 1989.

Ref. h): El censo también recolectó información sobre: el lugar de trabajo; los medios de transporte para trasladarse al trabajo; la cantidad de pasajeros por vehículo privado; la duración del trayecto; la experiencia laboral en 1989; los ingresos y rentas percibidos en 1989; y la incapacidad para trabajar.

6. Conceptos y definiciones:

a) Población económicamente activa: Abarcó a todas las personas de 16 o más años de edad que durante el período de referencia estaban ocupadas o desempleadas, conforme a las definiciones que figuran más adelante. La definición incluyó a los miembros de las fuerzas armadas.

En lo que atañe a la actividad económica, se interrogó únicamente a una muestra de unidades y personas. A los miembros de las fuerzas armadas que vivían en cuarteles o estaban embarcados no se les interrogó respecto a la ausencia temporal del trabajo o de la empresa, a la búsqueda de trabajo o a la disponibilidad a aceptar uno nuevo.

b) Empleo: Las preguntas primordiales que se hicieron para determinar si una persona debía considerarse "ocupada" fueron: "¿Trabajó en algún momento de la semana pasada?" y "¿Cuántas horas trabajó la semana pasada en todos los empleos?". Otra de las preguntas fue: "¿Estuvo temporalmente ausente o despedido del trabajo o la empresa, la semana pasada?"

Se ha indicado que fueron incluidas las siguientes categorías:

i) personas que trabajan sin remuneración en una empresa, negocio o explotación agrícola familiar, a condición de que lo hayan hecho durante un mínimo de 15 horas en la semana de referencia;

ii) personas ocupadas pero temporalmente ausentes de su trabajo;

iii) estudiantes que trabajan a tiempo parcial;

iv) trabajadores estacionales u ocasionales (tan solo durante el período pertinente, ya que el trabajador ocasional no se consideró empleado durante el tiempo que estaba sin trabajo);

v) aprendices y personas que siguen un curso de formación.

Sólo las categorías i), iii) y iv) pueden identificarse por separado (mediante clasificaciones cruzadas de la población económicamente activa por situación en el empleo - clase de categoría del trabajador - y la situación en el empleo por las condiciones de contratación y las horas trabajadas la última semana). La situación en el empleo es un código global que utilizó información procedente de muchos rubros para determinar si la persona estaba ocupada, desempleada, no formaba parte de la fuerza de trabajo o pertenecía a las fuerzas armadas.

Los miembros de las fuerzas armadas de los Estados Unidos son "voluntarios"; aquéllos que residen en el país pueden identificarse por separado en el censo, utilizando la sección de situación en el empleo. En los EE.UU. no existe el servicio obligatorio, militares o civil.

c) Desempleo: Se consideró "desempleada" a toda persona que durante la semana de referencia estaba sin trabajo, buscaba uno (tanto en la semana de referencia como durante las tres semanas anteriores), o estaba dispuesta a trabajar. Se incluyó también a las personas suspendidas por motivos técnicos. Para determinar si una persona debía considerarse desempleada se hicieron las siguientes preguntas: "¿La semana pasada, estuvo temporalmente ausente o despedido del trabajo o la empresa?"; "¿Estuvo buscando trabajo durante las últimas cuatro semanas?"; y "¿La semana pasada, hubiera aceptado un empleo en el caso de que se lo hubieran ofrecido?"

7. Clasificaciones utilizadas:

Tanto las personas ocupadas como las desempleadas anteriormente empleadas de la muestra se clasificaron por rama de actividad, por ocupación y por situación en el empleo.

a) Rama de actividad económica: Para determinarla se preguntó: "¿Para quién trabaja la persona?"; "¿De qué clase de empresa o rama de actividad se trata?"; y "¿Cuál es la actividad principal: manufactura, comercio mayorista, comercio minorista, otras (agricultura, construcción, servicios, administración pública, etc.)?"

El sistema de clasificación se basó en la norma tipo de los EE.UU., de 1987, y fue elaborado para el censo de población. Para codificar las respuestas se utilizó el "Alphabetical Index of Industries and Occupations" y una lista de nombres de establecimientos extraídos de censos y encuestas económicas del país. En el censo de 1990 se utilizaron 236 categorías. Si bien no se establecieron enlaces con la CIIU, en aras de la comparación internacional se procedió a una adaptación de la clasificación por rama de actividad del United States 1970 Census al plano internacional (que en general sigue siendo válida para el sistema de los EE.UU. de 1990), lo más cercana posible al nivel de grandes divisiones (1 dígito).

b) Ocupación: Para determinarla se preguntó: "¿Qué clase de trabajo efectúa la persona?" y "¿Cuáles son la tareas y funciones más importantes que desempeña?"

El sistema de clasificación consta de 501 ocupaciones divididas en 6 secciones de síntesis y 13 grupos principales de ocupaciones. Dicha clasificación se elaboró de conformidad con el Standard Occupational Classification Manual de 1980 (SOC). No se establecieron enlaces con la CIUO, ni se hicieron adaptaciones de la clasificación por ocupación de los EE.UU., de 1990.

c) Situación en el empleo: Para determinarla se preguntó si la persona trabajaba para una empresa, para un negocio privado o para un particular, cuyas actividades tenían fines de lucro, mediando un salario o una comisión; si era empleada de una institución privada sin fines de lucro, exenta de impuestos o de beneficencia; si era empleado público de la administración local (ciudad, condado, etc.), de la administración de un estado o de la administración federal; si era independiente con una empresa, actividad profesional o explotación agrícola no constituida en sociedad; si era independiente con una empresa, actividad profesional o explotación agrícola constituida en sociedad; o si trabajaba en una empresa o explotación agrícola familiar sin recibir remuneración.

Se consideraron empleados a quienes pertenecían a todos los grupos, excepto el de los independientes con una empresa, actividad profesional o explotación agrícola no constituida en sociedad. Para codificar la situación en el empleo, se utilizaron los ocho grupos citados.

8. Diferencias principales con el censo anterior:

No hubo diferencias significativas.

9. Publicación de los resultados del censo:

Las principales publicaciones de los resultados definitivos del censo son: "1990 CPH-5: Summary Social, Economic and Housing Characteristics" y "1990 CP-2: Social and Economic Characteristics (Reports presenting sample data), January 1991-December 1993".

La organización responsable de dichas publicaciones es el US Bureau of the Census, Washington, DC, 20233.

También se dispone de los resultados del censo en cintas magnéticas, microfichas, sistemas informáticos de acceso en conexión directa, CD-ROM y disquetes para micrordenadores.

FILIPINAS

1. Nombre y dirección del organismo responsable del censo:

National Statistics Office, R. Magsaysay Boulevard, Sta Mesa, Manila.

2. Censos de población llevados a cabo desde 1945 (años):

1948, 1960, 1970, 1975, 1980 y 1990. La presente descripción se refiere al censo de población de 1990 (realizado el 1 de mayo de ese año).

3. Alcance del censo:

a) Geográfico: Todo el país.

b) Personas comprendidas: Toda la población, salvo: los ciudadanos extranjeros que pensaban residir en Filipinas menos de un año a contar de la fecha de ingreso al país; los ciudadanos extranjeros que trabajaban para una embajada, ministerio, legación, cancillería o consulado extranjero y que residían en los recintos de éstos, independientemente de la duración de su estancia en el país; el personal militar y civil de fuerzas armadas extranjeras, residente en sus bases, y sus familiares, independientemente de la duración de su estancia en el país; ciudadanos extranjeros dirigentes o funcionarios de organismos internacionales como las Naciones Unidas, la OIT o USAID, que regresan a su respectivo país una vez cumplida su misión en Filipinas, y sus familiares.

4. Período de referencia:

La semana anterior al día del censo. Sin embargo, por lo que atañe a la actividad u ocupación habituales y al negocio o sector de actividad habituales, se utilizó un período de referencia largo, a saber, los doce meses anteriores al día del censo.

5. Materias principales:

a) Población total, según sexo y edad:	sí
Población económicamente activa por:	
b) Sexo y grupo de edad:	sí
c) Rama de actividad económica:	sí
d) Ocupación:	sí
e) Situación en el empleo:	no
f) Nivel más alto de educación:	sí
g) Horas de trabajo:	no
h) Otras características:	sí

Ref. a): La edad se determinó según los años cumplidos en el último cumpleaños.

Ref. h): El censo también acopió datos sobre la ocupación habitual de las personas encuestadas y sobre el negocio o sector de actividad en que había trabajado durante los últimos 12 meses.

6. Conceptos y definiciones:

a) Población económicamente activa: Abarcó a todas las personas de 10 o más años de edad que, durante la semana de referencia, estaban sea ocupadas, sea desempleadas, conforme a las definiciones que se dan más adelante. Quedaron incluidos en la definición los oficiales de las fuerzas armadas y sus familiares de 10 o más años de edad que residían en viviendas ubicadas dentro de cuarteles o instalaciones militares. Los soldados y demás personal militar residentes en los cuarteles o bases militares sin sus familiares fueron contabilizados como "población institucional"; por lo tanto, no se les consultó sobre su actividad económica y quedaron excluidos de la definición.

Se hicieron preguntas acerca de la actividad económica al 10 por ciento de las personas residentes en municipios con más de 1 500 hogares, al 20 por ciento de las residentes en municipios con 500 a 1 500 hogares y al 100 por ciento de las residentes en municipios con menos de 500 hogares.

Los datos publicados relativos a la población económicamente activa sólo se refieren a las personas de 15 o más años de edad.

b) Empleo: Para determinar si una persona debía contabilizarse o no como ocupada se utilizó la siguiente pregunta: "¿Tuvo X un empleo, negocio o empresa durante los últimos siete días?".

Se ha indicado que fueron incluidas las siguientes categorías:

i) personas que trabajan sin remuneración en una empresa o negocio familiar;

ii) personas ocupadas pero temporalmente ausentes de su trabajo;

iii) estudiantes que trabajan a tiempo parcial;

iv) trabajadores estacionales u ocasionales.

Ninguna de estas categorías puede identificarse por separado.

c) Desempleo: Se consideró "desempleada" a toda persona que, durante la semana de referencia, no tenía trabajo, buscaba empleo y estaba disponible para trabajar. Para determinar si una persona debía contabilizarse o no como desempleada se usó la misma pregunta que figura en el apartado b) de esta misma sección. En caso de respuesta negativa, se pidió responder además a las preguntas: "¿Estuvo X disponible para trabajar durante los últimos 7 días?", "¿Buscó X trabajo durante los últimos siete días?" y, "¿Por qué no buscó X trabajo ?".

7. Clasificaciones utilizadas:

Las personas de 15 o más años de edad incluidas en las muestras fueron clasificadas por rama de actividad económica y por ocupación. No se hizo clasificación alguna según la situación en el empleo.

a) Rama de actividad económica: Para determinarla se preguntó: "¿En qué tipo de empresa o rama de actividad trabajó X durante los últimos 7 días?". Para codificar esta variable, se usó la Clasificación Industrial Normalizada de Filipinas de 1990, basada en la CIIU-Rev.2, en el nivel de 3 dígitos.

b) Ocupación: Para determinarla se preguntó: "¿Cuál fue la principal actividad u ocupación de X durante los últimos 7 días?" Para codificar la ocupación se utilizó la Clasificación de Ocupaciones de Filipinas, basada en la CIUO-88, en el nivel de grupos primarios (clave de 4 dígitos).

c) Situación en el empleo: No se efectuó clasificación alguna según esta variable.

8. Diferencias principales con el censo anterior:

En el censo de 1980, las preguntas relativas a la actividad económica se hicieron a una muestra de 20 por ciento de las personas de 15 o más años de edad, y en el cuestionario no se indicaron períodos de referencia.

Tampoco se hicieron preguntas para determinar si una persona debía contabilizarse como "ocupada" o "desempleada".

Sólo se incluyeron preguntas acerca de la ocupación habitual de la persona censada y de la rama de actividad en que ésta desplegaba habitualmente sus actividades. Las preguntas hechas fueron: "?Cuál es la ocupación habitual de X?" y "¿En qué tipo de empresa o sector de actividad trabajaba?".

Por "ocupación" se entendió el empleo u otra forma de actividad en la que la persona encuestada trabajaba habitualmente durante la mayor parte del año, o si ésta estaba desempleada en el momento del empadronamiento, el tipo de trabajo que había desempeñado antes durante la mayor parte del año. Por "sector de actividad económica" se entendió las características específicas y la naturaleza de la actividad comercial o industrial, o del lugar de trabajo en que se lleva a cabo la actividad económica relacionada con el empleo o la ocupación declarada por una persona dada.

En el censo de 1990, la actividad u ocupación habitual se refirió al tipo de empleo o actividad económica en que se ocupó la persona censada durante la mayor parte del período de 12 meses anteriores a la entrevista.

9. Publicación de los resultados del censo:

Los resultados definitivos del censo se publicaron en 1992, en el volumen que lleva por título: "Report No. 3 - 1990 Census of Population and Housing".

El organismo responsable de esta publicación es la National Statistics Office, R. Magsaysay Boulevard, Sta Mesa, Manila.

Los resultados del censo también están disponibles en volúmenes impresos correspondientes a las provincias y las grandes aglomeraciones urbanas, en cuadros inéditos y en cintas magnéticas y disquetes de acceso público.

FINLANDIA

1. Nombre y dirección del organismo responsable del censo:

Central Statistical Office of Finland (CSO), P.B. 504, 00101 Helsinki.

2. Censos de población llevados a cabo desde 1945 (años):

1950, 1960, 1970, 1975, 1980, 1985 y 1990. La presente descripción se refiere al censo de 1990 (realizado el 31 de diciembre de ese año).

De conformidad con una decisión tomada por Finlandia en 1979, el Censo de población y vivienda de 1980 fue el último que se realizó basándose directamente en datos recolectados mediante formularios. El Censo de población y vivienda de 1990 se llevó a cabo utilizando exclusivamente la información contenida en archivos y registros administrativos. Los preparativos para la celebración de censos basados en los registros administrativos comenzó, pues, en 1981; esta actividad supuso el establecimiento del Registro Nacional de Edificios y Viviendas, lo que se hizo sobre la base de los datos pertinentes recogidos en ocasión del Censo de población y vivienda de 1980.

En la medida en que la nueva modalidad de censo es la primera de alcance global que se basa enteramente en datos ya registrados y que no recurre en absoluto a cuestionarios, ha sido necesario llevar a cabo otro estudio, muestreal y suficientemente extenso, para analizar el período de ruptura de la serie cronológica, ocasionado por el cambio del método de acopio de datos. Para determinar la validez de los registros básicos que utilizará este nuevo tipo de censo, será preciso someterlos periódicamente (por ejemplo, cada cinco años) a estudios de control y de calidad independientes de los sistemas administrativos.

3. Alcance del censo:

a) Geográfico: Todo el país.

b) Personas comprendidas: Toda la población.

4. Período de referencia:

La semana del censo (25-31 de diciembre de 1990), por lo que se refería a la "actividad actual", y todo el año 1990 en el caso de la "actividad habitual".

5. Materias principales:

a) Población total, según sexo y edad:	sí
Población económicamente activa por:	
b) Sexo y grupo de edad:	sí
c) Rama de actividad económica:	sí
d) Ocupación:	sí
e) Situación en el empleo:	sí
f) Nivel más alto de educación:	sí
g) Horas de trabajo:	no
h) Otras características:	sí

Ref. a): La edad de la persona censada se definió en función de su fecha de nacimiento, que se obtuvo directamente del registro central de la población.

Ref. h): El censo también recolectó datos sobre: la ubicación del lugar de trabajo; la condición jurídica del empleador (empresa privada, Gobierno central, autoridades locales); la duración del empleo y del desempleo; los ingresos; la condición económica y social.

6. Conceptos y definiciones:

a) Población económicamente activa: Abarca a todas las personas de 15 a 74 años de edad que, en la semana del censo, tenían un empleo o estaban desempleadas, según las definiciones que se dan más adelante. La definición no incluye a las personas que cumplen el servicio militar ni a las poblaciones institucionales.

b) Empleo: Se consideró "ocupada" a toda persona que, de acuerdo con los Registros del Seguro de Jubilación, trabajó por lo menos un día durante la semana del censo (concepto de "actividad actual"), o seis meses durante el año de referencia (concepto de "actividad habitual"), dentro o fuera de su domicilio, y que, de acuerdo con los Registros Tributarios, tenían ingresos imponibles.

Se ha indicado que quedan incluidas las siguientes categorías:

i)   personas que trabajan sin remuneración en una empresa o negocio familiar: sólo se incluyó a una parte de este grupo, a saber, las personas que tenían un seguro de jubilación para empresarios (que no es obligatorio para los trabajadores familiares no remunerados);

ii) personas ocupadas pero temporalmente ausentes de su trabajo;

iii) estudiantes que trabajan a tiempo parcial;

iv) trabajadores estacionales u ocasionales;

v)   trabajadores con más de un empleo;

vi) aprendices y personas que siguen un curso de formación.

Sólo la categoría v) puede identificarse por separado, basándose en la información disponible en los Registros del Seguro de Jubilación.   Los datos relativos a las personas que cumplen el servicio militar o el servicio civil pueden obtenerse en registro especial del Ministerio de Defensa, aun cuando estas personas quedan excluidas de la definición de población económicamente activa.

c) Desempleo: Se consideró "desempleada" a toda persona que, de acuerdo con el Registro de personas desempleadas en busca de trabajo, del Ministerio de Trabajo, se encontraban desocupadas el 29 de diciembre de 1990, pero buscaban empleo y estaban disponibles para trabajar. Quedaron excluidos de esta definición los estudiantes que buscaban empleo.

7. Clasificaciones utilizadas:

Tanto las personas ocupadas como las personas desempleadas anteriormente empleadas han sido clasificadas por rama de actividad económica y por ocupación.   Sólo se ha clasificado según la situación en el empleo a las personas ocupadas.

a) Rama de actividad económica: Para determinarla (así como para obtener otras informaciones) se recurrió al Registro de Empresas y Establecimientos, de la Oficina Central de Estadística (CSO), que utiliza los mismos identificadores que los Registros Tributarios.   En el Registro de Empresas y Establecimientos figura el mismo código que puede utilizarse para transferir la información a las personas empleadas. El procedimiento varía un tanto, en función de si la empresa tiene uno o varios establecimientos.   Con respecto a algunos empresarios, la rama de actividad económica se deduce de los datos registrados en el Seguro de Jubilación, así como del tipo de ingresos.   Para codificar la rama de actividad económica, se utilizaron cerca de 460 grupos de la clasificación industrial uniforme establecida por la CSO.   Los enlaces con la clasificación CIIU (tanto CIIU-Rev.2 como CIIU-Rev.3) se han establecido a nivel de 4 dígitos.

b) Ocupación: La información utilizada para determinarla se obtiene de los Registros de Sueldos y Salarios, tanto del Gobierno central como de las autoridades locales, de los Registros Tributarios y del Registro de personas en busca de trabajo, del Ministerio de Trabajo. Las denominaciones de ocupaciones obtenidas en estos registros se codifican con el sistema automático creado por la CSO.   Para codificar la ocupación se utilizaron cerca de 400 grupos.   Los enlaces con la clasificación CIUO-68 se han establecido a nivel de grupos primarios (clave de 3 dígitos).   Se ha previsto establecer enlaces con la clasificación CIUO-88, pero ello no se ha hecho efectivo aún.

c) Situación en el empleo: La situación en el empleo de las personas se define utilizando informaciones sobre el tipo de seguro de empleo que tienen (jubilación de empleado o de empresario) y sobre sus fuentes de ingresos (sueldos, salarios o ganancias empresariales).   Para codificar la situación en el empleo, se utilizaron dos grupos principales: i) las personas que perciben sueldos y salarios, y ii) los empresarios (entre los que se incluye a los trabajadores por cuenta propia, los empleadores y los trabajadores familiares no remunerados).

8. Diferencias principales con el censo anterior:

El censo de 1990 se llevó a cabo basándose en datos que figuran en diversos registros; el método de acopio de datos fue totalmente distinto del que se empleó en el censo de 1985. Todos los datos utilizados para determinar la población económicamente activa se obtuvieron de registros administrativos, y no

se usaron cuestionarios. A pesar de las diferencias entre los métodos de recolección de datos, las definiciones relativas a la población económicamente activas y sus componentes no resultaron muy diferentes. La diferencia más importante en el contenido de los datos recogidos fue el hecho de que no se incluyeron datos sobre el trabajo a tiempo parcial.

Por regla general, en los registros figuran datos oficiales, es decir, datos que se refieren a la actividad laboral sujeta a tributación e incluida en el ámbito de los regímenes de seguros profesionales. Con el censo basado en los registros se pretende obtener fundamentalmente la misma información que se recoge con los censos mediante cuestionarios. Sin embargo, con el censo de 1990 no se pudo obtener datos sobre el tiempo de trabajo semanal ni sobre los medios usados para trasladarse a los lugares de trabajo.

Las ventajas de los censos establecidos a partir de registros se observan sobre todo en materia de datos sobre las personas. El censo de 1990 contiene, pues, información sobre el empleo de todos quienes tuvieron una ocupación durante ese año, y, en particular, sobre el número de empleos ocupados sucesivamente y sobre los empleos secundarios. Este censo permite, además, analizar la evolución de diversos grupos de la población, como, por ejemplo, las personas que dejan de ser estudiantes, desempleados o trabajadores familiares para incorporarse a la fuerza de trabajo, o aquéllas que, por el contrario, abandonan la fuerza de trabajo al jubilar, quedar desempleadas o dedicarse a las labores del hogar. En los registros también se consignan datos sobre el empleo de corta duración, lo que permitirá establecer las proporciones del empleo remunerado de los estudiantes, y, en particular, cuántos meses al año trabajan éstos.

9. Publicación de los resultados del censo:

Los datos definitivos del censo figuran en una publicación que lleva por título "Economic activity of the population", que apareció en 1993.

La organización responsable de esta publicación es la Central Statistical Office of Finland, P.B. 504, 00101 Helsinki.

Los resultados del censo de 1990 están disponibles también en cuadros inéditos, series de cuadros, disquetes y cintas magnéticas.

FRANCIA

1. Nombre y dirección del organismo responsable del censo:

Institut national de la statistique et des études économiques (INSEE), 18, boulevard Adolphe Pinard, Paris Cedex 14.

2. Censos de población llevados a cabo desde 1945 (años):

1954, 1962, 1968, 1975, 1982 y 1990. La presente descripción se refiere al censo de población de 1990 (realizado el 5 de marzo de ese año).

3. Alcance del censo:

a) Geográfico: Todo el país (Francia metropolitana).   En el mismo período se efectuó un censo aparte en los Departamentos de Ultramar, pero los datos recopilados se han procesado y utilizado independientemente de la información acopiada en la metrópoli.

b) Personas comprendidas: Todas las personas residentes en Francia durante un mínimo de seis meses, salvo los diplomáticos extranjeros y el personal extranjero de las embajadas que tuviesen por domicilio un edificio con estatuto de extraterritorialidad.

4. Período de referencia:

No se estableció período de referencia alguno.   Se pidió a las personas censadas que indicasen si estaban o no ejerciendo una actividad profesional en la fecha de referencia del censo, a saber, el 5 de marzo de 1990 a medianoche.

5. Materias principales:

a) Población total, según sexo y edad:	sí
Población económicamente activa por:	
b) Sexo y grupo de edad:	sí
c) Rama de actividad económica:	sí
d) Ocupación:	sí
e) Situación en el empleo:	sí
f) Nivel más alto de educación:	sí

g) Horas de trabajo: no
h) Otras características: sí

Ref. a): La edad se determinó por lo general según el año de nacimiento.

Ref. h): También se preguntó a las personas censadas si trabajaban a tiempo completo o a tiempo parcial.

6. Conceptos y definiciones:

a) Población económicamente activa: Abarcó a todas las personas de 15 o más años de edad que, en la fecha del censo, estaban ocupadas o desempleadas, según las definiciones que se dan más adelante. Las preguntas relativas a la actividad económica se formularon a todos los encuestados, pero sólo se han procesado y utilizado las respuestas de una muestra de una cuarta parte de ellos. Esta definición incluyó tanto a los militares de carrera como a las personas que cumplían su servicio militar.

b) Empleo: Se consideró "ocupada" a toda persona que, en la fecha del censo, tenía una actividad a tiempo completo o a tiempo parcial, sea por cuenta propia (agricultor, artesano, comerciante, industrial, miembro de una profesión liberal, etc.), sea como asalariado (obrero o empleado), o como trabajador familiar no remunerado (cónyuge, hijos u otros miembros de la familia de un agricultor, de un comerciante, etc.). Los trabajadores por cuenta propia debían indicar si tenían empleados asalariados y precisar su número (a excepción de los aprendices, el personal doméstico y, en la agricultura, de los asalariados no permanentes).

La definición incluyó también a las personas ocupadas en trabajos de utilidad pública (TUC, etc.), a las que tenían un contrato de readaptación profesional o de perfeccionamiento, así como a las que prestaban servicios por intermedio de agencias de colocación y a las que tenían un contrato de trabajo de duración limitada. Quedaron comprendidas, asimismo, las personas ocupadas que buscaban un nuevo empleo, los jubilados o las personas retiradas de sus negocios que habían reanudado una actividad económica, los agricultores retirados que habían conservado una pequeña explotación agrícola, y los miembros del clero.

Se ha indicado que fueron incluidas las siguientes categorías:

i)   personas que producen bienes primarios para el autoconsumo;
ii) personas ocupadas pero temporalmente ausentes de su trabajo;
iii) estudiantes que trabajan a tiempo parcial;
iv) conscriptos del servicio militar o civil;
v)   trabajadores estacionales u ocasionales, a condición de que estuviesen empleados el día del censo;
vi) personas en curso de formación remunerada, empleadas en una empresa.

Las categorías i) y vi) pueden identificarse por separado, en función de sus respuestas a las preguntas formuladas a tal efecto. También pueden identificarse por separado los conscriptos, que fueron incluidos por primera vez en el ámbito de la definición de población económicamente activa, como tercer componente de ésta, a continuación de los activos ocupados y de los desempleados.

c) Desempleo: Se consideró "desempleada" a toda persona censada que, en la fecha del censo, estaba sin trabajo y buscaba uno. Para determinar si una persona debía considerarse "desempleada", se preguntó "¿Está usted buscando empleo?" Si la respuesta era afirmativa, la persona debía precisar si buscaba empleo desde hacía "menos de tres meses", "tres meses a menos de un año", "un año a menos de dos años", o "dos o más años". Quedaron excluidos de esta definición los estudiantes que buscaban empleo.

7. Clasificaciones utilizadas:

Sólo las personas ocupadas incluidas en la muestra se clasificaron por rama de actividad, por ocupación y por situación en el empleo. Los desempleados anteriormente empleados fueron clasificados sólo según su última actividad.

a) Rama de actividad económica: Se pidió a las personas ocupadas de la muestra que respondieran a determinadas preguntas, indicando en particular la dirección, el nombre o la razón social y la actividad del establecimiento que las empleaba o que dirigían (por ejemplo: comercio mayorista de vinos, fabricación de estructuras metálicas, transporte de pasajeros por carretera, etc.), a fin de hacer posible su búsqueda en el fichero SIRENE (repertorio de empresas). Para codificar la rama de actividad económica se utilizaron 600 partidas de la Nomen-

clatura de Actividades y Productos (NAP). Se establecieron enlaces con la CIIU-Rev.2, a nivel de divisiones (clave de 2 dígitos).

b) Ocupación: Se hicieron preguntas específicas acerca de la profesión o el oficio ejercidos en el último lugar de trabajo (por ejemplo: obrero electricista de manutención, chófer de camión de carga, vendedor de electrodomésticos, ingeniero químico, cajera de tienda autoservicio, etc.). Para codificar la ocupación se utilizaron 455 partidas de la Nomenclatura de Profesiones y de Categorías Socioprofesionales (PCS). Se establecieron enlaces con la CIUO-68, a nivel de subgrupos (clave de 2 dígitos).

c) Situación en el empleo: Se preguntó a las personas no asalariadas si ejercían su profesión i) como empleadores o como trabajadores por cuenta propia, y, si la respuesta era afirmativa, si empleaban personas asalariadas (1 ó 2, de 3 a 9, o 10 ó más personas), o ii) como auxiliar de un miembro de la familia en la actividad de éste (empresa agrícola o artesanal, comercio, profesión liberal, etc.). A las personas asalariadas se preguntó si ejercían su profesión como tales (por lo que atañe a la agricultura, sólo se tuvo en cuenta a los asalariados con empleo permanente). Para codificar la situación en el empleo se utilizaron cuatro grandes grupos: trabajador asalariado, empleador, trabajador independiente sin empleados, trabajador familiar.

8. Diferencias principales con el censo anterior:

En el censo de 1990, la definición de población económicamente activa abarcó a los conscriptos, que hasta entonces habían quedado excluidos.

9. Publicación de los resultados del censo:

Los resultados definitivos del censo se publicaron en 1992.

La publicación en que figuran los resultados compendiados del censo lleva por título: Série "Logement-Population-Emploi"; la publicación en que figuran los resultados de la muestra (1/4 de las personas censadas) se titula: Série "Population-Activités-Ménages".

El organismo responsable de estas publicaciones es el Institut national de la statistique et des études économiques (INSEE), 18 boulevard Adolphe-Pinard, 75675 Paris Cedex 14.

También se dispone de los resultados del censo de 1990 en disquetes, cintas magnéticas y otras modalidades de presentación que se soliciten.

GABON

1. Nombre y dirección del organismo responsable del censo:

Bureau central du recensement, Direction générale de la statistique et des études économiques, B.P. 2119, Libreville.

2. Censos de población llevados a cabo desde 1945 (años):

1981 y 1993. La presente descripción se refiere al censo de 1993 (realizado el 31 de julio de ese año).

3. Alcance del censo:

a) Geográfico: Todo el territorio.

b) Personas comprendidas: Toda la población, a excepción de los diplomáticos y de los nacionales residentes en el extranjero.

4. Período de referencia:

La semana y los seis meses anteriores al día del censo.

5. Materias principales:

a) Población total, según sexo y edad: sí
Población económicamente activa por:
b) Sexo y grupo de edad: sí
c) Rama de actividad económica: sí
d) Ocupación: sí
e) Situación en el empleo: sí
f) Nivel más alto de educación: sí
g) Horas de trabajo: no
h) Otras características: no

Ref. a): La edad se determinó según los años cumplidos en el último cumpleaños.

6. Conceptos y definiciones:

a) Población económicamente activa: Abarcó a todas las personas de 10 o más años de edad que, durante el período de referencia largo, estaban ocupadas o desempleadas, según las definiciones que se dan más adelante. Esta definición incluyó a todos los miembros de las fuerzas armadas, pero no a los estudiantes que tenían un empleo a tiempo parcial o a los que buscaban trabajo.

b) Empleo: Se consideró "ocupada" a toda persona que declaró haber trabajado por lo menos una semana durante el período de referencia largo. Las preguntas utilizadas a este efecto fueron las siguientes: "¿Ha tenido usted una ocupación desde enero de 1993?", y, de ser así, "¿Durante cuanto tiempo?".

Se ha indicado que fueron incluidas las siguientes categorías:

i) personas que trabajan sin remuneración en una empresa o negocio familiar;
ii) personas que producen bienes primarios para el autoconsumo;
iii) personas ocupadas pero temporalmente ausentes de su trabajo;
iv) trabajadores estacionales u ocasionales;
v) conscriptos del servicio militar o civil;
vi) aprendices y personas que siguen un curso de formación.

Sólo las categorías I), III) y IV) pueden identificarse por separado.

c) Desempleo: Se consideró "desempleada" a toda persona que declaró haber trabajado sólo menos de una semana durante el período de referencia largo. Se utilizaron las mismas preguntas indicadas en el apartado b) de esta sección.

7. Clasificaciones utilizadas:
Tanto las personas ocupadas como las desempleadas anteriormente empleadas fueron clasificadas por rama de actividad económica, por ocupación y por situación en el empleo.

a) Rama de actividad económica: Para determinarla se hizo una pregunta relativa a la ocupación principal y al sector de actividad de la empresa en que trabajaba o había trabajado la persona empadronada. Para codificar la rama de actividad económica se utilizaron 40 grupos de la clasificación nacional. No se establecieron enlaces con la CIIU.

b) Ocupación: Para determinarla se hizo la siguiente pregunta: "¿Cuál es su ocupación?". Para codificar la ocupación se utilizaron 100 grupos de un dígito y 350 grupos de 4 dígitos. Se establecieron enlaces con la clasificación CIUO-88, a nivel de subgrupos (clave de 3 dígitos).

c) Situación en el empleo: Para determinarla se hizo la siguiente pregunta: "¿Trabaja usted por cuenta propia? a) si la respuesta es "Sí", ¿tiene empleados? Si la respuesta es "No", ¿percibe usted una remuneración por su trabajo? Si la respuesta a esta pregunta es "No", ¿trabaja usted para un familiar o está aprendiendo un oficio?". Para codificar esta variable se utilizaron seis grupos, a saber: trabajador independiente; asalariado; empleador; trabajador familiar; aprendiz; otra ocupación.

8. Diferencias principales con el censo anterior:
En 1993, se aplicó una edad mínima de 10 años, frente a 6 años en el censo de 1980.

En 1993, no se formularon preguntas destinadas a determinar la formación profesional, pero sí se hicieron preguntas relativas al sector de actividad económica y a las migraciones.

9. Publicación de los resultados del censo:
Se había previsto difundir los resultados del censo durante el segundo semestre de 1995, en las siguientes publicaciones: "Résultats bruts, Volume II" y "Analyse des résultats, Volume III".

El organismo responsable de estas publicaciones es el Bureau central du recensement, Direction générale de la statistique, B.P. 2119, Libreville.

Los resultados del censo de 1993 también están disponibles en disquetes.

GAMBIA

1. Nombre y dirección del organismo responsable del censo:
Central Statistics Department, Central Bank Building, Buckle Street, Banjul.

2. Censos de población llevados a cabo desde 1945 (años):
1963, 1973, 1983 y 1993. La presente descripción se refiere al censo de población de 1993 (realizado el 15 de abril de ese año).

3. Alcance del censo:
a) Geográfico: Todo el país.
b) Personas comprendidas: Toda la población.

4. Período de referencia:
El mes anterior al día del censo.

5. Materias principales:
a) Población total, según sexo y edad: sí
Población económicamente activa por:
b) Sexo y grupo de edad: sí
c) Rama de actividad económica: sí
d) Ocupación: sí
e) Situación en el empleo: sí
f) Nivel más alto de educación: sí
g) Horas de trabajo: sí
h) Otras características: no

Ref. a): La edad se determinó según los años cumplidos en el último cumpleaños.
Ref. g): El tiempo de trabajo se refiere al número de días trabajados por las personas ocupadas, en el lugar de trabajo, durante el período de referencia.

6. Conceptos y definiciones:
a) Población económicamente activa: Abarcó a todas las personas de 10 o más años de edad que, durante el mes de referencia, estaban sea ocupadas, sea desempleadas, conforme a las definiciones que se dan más adelante. La definición incluyó a los miembros de las fuerzas armadas, a excepción de los conscriptos. No quedaron incluidos en la definición los estudiantes con empleo a tiempo parcial ni los que buscaban trabajo.

b) Empleo: Para determinar si una persona debía contabilizarse o no como "ocupada" se preguntó "¿Cuál ha sido su actividad principal (durante los últimos treinta días)? 1) trabajé; 2) tenía un empleo, pero no trabajé; 3) no trabajé ni tenía un empleo; 4) trabajé en labores del hogar; 5) asistí a clases; 6) otra."; a las personas que indicaron las respuestas 4) o 6) se preguntó: "¿Ejerció usted una actividad remunerada con un salario o ganancias de otro orden? (comprendido el trabajo en una explotación agrícola o empresa familiar, e incluido el pago en especie)".

Se ha indicado que fueron incluidas las siguientes categorías:

i) personas que trabajan sin remuneración en una empresa o negocio familiar;
ii) personas que producen bienes primarios para el autoconsumo;
iii) personas ocupadas pero temporalmente ausentes de su trabajo;
iv) trabajadores estacionales u ocasionales;
v) aprendices y personas que siguen un curso de formación.

Solamente las personas de las categorías i) y iii) se pueden identificar separadamente.

c) Desempleo: Se consideró "desempleada" a toda persona que, durante el mes de referencia, se encontraba sin trabajo y buscaba empleo.

7. Clasificaciones utilizadas:
Tanto las personas ocupadas como las desocupadas anteriormente ocupadas se clasificaron por rama de actividad económica, por ocupación y según la situación en el empleo.

a) Rama de actividad económica: Para determinarla se preguntó: "¿Cómo se llama el establecimiento en que usted trabaja (si está desempleado: el último establecimiento en que trabajó)?", y "¿Cuál es el principal producto fabricado o el servicio prestado por este establecimiento?". Para codificar la rama de actividad se utilizaron 10 grupos de la clasificación nacional. Se establecieron enlaces con la CIIU-Rev.3 a nivel de categorías de tabulación (clave de 1 dígito).

b) Ocupación: Para determinarla se preguntó: "¿Cuál es su ocupación/trabajo principal (si está desempleado: cuál fue la naturaleza de su último trabajo)?". Para codificar la ocupación, se utilizó la CIUO-88 en el nivel de grandes grupos (clave de 1 dígito).

c) Situación en el empleo: Para determinarla se preguntó: "¿En qué calidad ejerce/ejerció su trabajo en el citado establecimiento?". Para codificar la situación en el empleo se utilizaron cinco grupos, a saber: trabajador remunerado con sueldo o salario; trabajador independiente, sin empleados; empleador; trabajador familiar no remunerado; otra situación.

8. Diferencias principales con el censo anterior:
No hubo diferencias significativas.

9. Publicación de los resultados del censo:
Se previó publicar los resultados definitivos del censo de población en diciembre de 1995, bajo el título "Population and Housing Census 1993, Economic Characteristics".

El organismo responsable de la publicación de los resultados es el Central Statistics Department, Central Bank Building, Buckle Street, Banjul.

Los resultados del censo están disponibles también en cuadros inéditos.

GIBRALTAR

1. Nombre y dirección del organismo responsable del censo:
Statistics Office, 6 Convent Place, Gibraltar.

2. Censos de población llevados a cabo desde 1945 (años):
1951, 1961, 1970, 1981, y 1991. La presente descripción se refiere al censo de población de 1991 (realizado el 14 de octubre de ese año).

3. Alcance del censo:

a) Geográfico: Todo el territorio.

b) Personas comprendidas: Toda la población. La definición no incluyó a los miembros de las fuerzas armadas destacadas en el territorio; en cambio quedaron incluidos los cónyuges del personal militar y los demás miembros del grupo familiar.

4. Periodo de referencia:
El día del censo.

5. Materias principales:
a) Población total, según sexo y edad: sí
Población económicamente activa por:
b) Sexo y grupo de edad: sí
c) Rama de actividad económica: sí
d) Ocupación: sí
e) Situación en el empleo: sí
f) Nivel más alto de educación: no
g) Horas de trabajo: no
h) Otras características: sí

Ref. a): La edad se determinó según los años cumplidos en el último cumpleaños.

Ref. h): El censo también recopiló información sobre los medios de transporte utilizados para trasladarse al lugar de trabajo (a pie, en bus, bicicleta, motocicleta o ciclomotor, automóvil o furgoneta).

6. Conceptos y definiciones:

a) Población económicamente activa: Abarcó a todas las personas de 15 o más años de edad que, el día del censo, estaban sea ocupadas, sea desempleadas, conforme a las definiciones que se dan más adelante. No quedaron incluidos en la definición los miembros de las fuerzas armadas, los estudiantes con empleo a tiempo parcial ni los estudiantes que buscaban trabajo.

b) Empleo: Se consideró "ocupada" a toda persona que, el día del censo, tenía un trabajo a tiempo completo o a tiempo parcial. Se pidió a las personas ocupadas que indicaran la ocupación que tenían en ese momento, precisando si se trataba de trabajo a tiempo completo o a tiempo parcial. Quedaron incluidas en la definición las personas que se preparaban a entrar en funciones en un empleo que ya habían aceptado, y las mujeres empleadas a tiempo completo o a tiempo parcial.

Se ha indicado que fueron incluidas las siguientes categorías:

i) personas que trabajan sin remuneración en una empresa o negocio familiar;

ii) personas ocupadas pero temporalmente ausentes de su trabajo.

Ninguna de estas categorías puede identificarse separadamente.

c) Desempleo: Se consideró "desempleada" a toda persona que, el día del censo, estaba sin trabajo y buscaba empleo.

7. Clasificaciones utilizadas:
Sólo las personas ocupadas fueron clasificadas por rama de actividad económica, por ocupación y según la situación en el empleo.

a) Rama de actividad económica: Para determinar los grupos de actividad, se formuló una sola pregunta a las personas ocupadas. Esta fue: "Si usted trabaja para una empresa privada, o si es independiente, indique su actividad o la del empleador (por ejemplo, comercio de detalle, imprenta, hotelería, banca, peluquería, etc.). Si trabaja para el Estado, indique el Ministerio y el Servicio". También se pidió señalar el nombre y la dirección del empleador o del lugar de trabajo. Para codificar la rama de actividad, se utilizaron 23 grupos de la clasificación nacional. Se establecieron enlaces con la CIIU-Rev.3, en el nivel de categorías de tabulación (clave de 1 dígito).

b) Ocupación: Para determinar el grupo de ocupaciones, se pidió a las personas ocupadas que indicaran su ocupación, utilizando para ello la terminología más precisa posible (por ejemplo, mecánico de automóviles, técnico en radio, ingeniero civil, contador colegiado, economista, etc., y, por lo que atañe a los trabajadores de la administración pública, jefe de departamento, funcionario ejecutivo, funcionario o auxiliar administrativo, secretaria de dirección o mecanógrafa). Para codificar la ocupación, se utilizaron 125 grupos de la clasificación nacional. No se establecieron enlaces con la CIUO.

c) Situación en el empleo: Para determinar esta variable, se pidió a las personas ocupadas que indicaran si eran asalariados, trabajadores independientes o empleadores. Los trabajadores familiares fueron incluidos en la categoría "asalariados".

8. Diferencias principales con el censo anterior:
En el censo de 1981 se aplicó un período de referencia de una semana. Además, tanto las personas ocupadas como las desempleadas anteriormente empleadas fueron clasificadas por rama de actividad económica, por ocupación y por situación en el empleo.

9. Publicación de los resultados del censo:
Los resultados definitivos del censo se publicaron en noviembre de 1992, en el volumen que lleva por título "Census of Gibraltar 1991".

El organismo responsable de esta publicación es la Statistics Office de Gibraltar.

Se pueden solicitar ejemplares de esta publicación a Government Publications Office, 6 Convent Place, Gibraltar. Los datos no se han editado ni en disquetes, ni en cintas magnéticas.

GRANADA

1. Nombre y dirección del organismo responsable del censo:
Central Statistical Office, Ministry of Finance, Financial Complex, The Carenage, Saint George's, Granada.

2. Censos de población llevados a cabo desde 1945 (años):
1960, 1970 y 1991. La presente descripción se refiere al censo de población de 1991 (realizado el 12 de mayo de ese año).

3. Alcance del censo:

a) Geográfico: Todo el país.

b) Personas comprendidas: Toda la población.

4. Periodo de referencia:
La semana anterior al día del censo.

5. Materias principales:
a) Población total, según sexo y edad: sí
Población económicamente activa por:
b) Sexo y grupo de edad: sí
c) Rama de actividad económica: sí
d) Ocupación: sí
e) Situación en el empleo: sí
f) Nivel más alto de educación: sí
g) Horas de trabajo: sí
h) Otras características: sí

Ref. a): La edad se determinó según los años cumplidos en el último cumpleaños.

Ref. g): El tiempo de trabajo se refiere al número de horas efectivamente trabajadas por las personas ocupadas.

Ref. h): El censo también recolectó información sobre los medios de transporte utilizados para trasladarse al lugar de trabajo.

6. Conceptos y definiciones:

a) Población económicamente activa: Abarcó a todas las personas de 15 o más años de edad que, durante la semana de referencia, estaban ocupadas o desempleadas, conforme a las definiciones que se dan más adelante. La definición incluyó a los miembros de las fuerzas armadas.

b) Empleo: Para determinarlo, se hicieron las siguientes preguntas: "¿A qué se dedicó usted fundamentalmente la semana pasada? Por ejemplo, trabajó, buscó empleo, se ocupó de labores del hogar o tuvo otra actividad?", y "¿Tuvo algún trabajo la semana pasada, cualquiera haya sido su duración, incluyendo ocupaciones como la asistencia prestada en una empresa o negocio familiar, el comercio callejero o el trabajo a domicilio?".

Se ha indicado que fueron incluidas las siguientes categorías:

i) personas que trabajan sin remuneración en una empresa, negocio o explotación agrícola familiar;

ii) personas ocupadas pero temporalmente ausentes de su trabajo;

iii) estudiantes que trabajan a tiempo parcial.

Todas estas categorías pueden identificarse por separado.

c) Desempleo: Para determinar esta variable, se utilizaron las mismas preguntas que figuran en el párrafo 6 b). Se consideró "desempleada" a toda persona que, durante la semana de referencia, no tenía trabajo y estaba buscando empleo.

7. Clasificaciones utilizadas:

Tanto las personas ocupadas como las desempleadas anteriormente empleadas se clasificaron por rama de actividad económica y por ocupación. Sólo las personas ocupadas fueron clasificadas por situación en el empleo.

a) Rama de actividad económica: Para determinarla se preguntó: "¿Qué tipo de actividad se efectúa/se efectuaba en su lugar de trabajo?" y "¿Cuáles son el nombre y la dirección de su lugar de trabajo actual?". Para codificar la rama de actividad se utilizó la CIIU-Rev.3.

b) Ocupación: Para determinarla se preguntó: "¿Qué tipo de trabajo desempeña o desempeñaba en su ocupación principal?". Para codificar la ocupación se utilizó la CIUO-88, en el nivel de grupos primarios (clave de 4 dígitos).

c) Situación en el empleo: Para determinarla se preguntó: "¿Trabajó usted como asalariado, dirigiendo su propia empresa o negocio, o como trabajador no remunerado?". Para codificar la situación en el empleo se utilizaron 6 grupos: trabajador en una empresa o negocio familiar; trabajador asalariado del sector público; trabajador asalariado del sector privado; trabajador no remunerado; empresario con personal remunerado (empleador); empresario sin personal remunerado (trabajador por cuenta propia).

8. Diferencias principales con el censo anterior:

No hubo diferencias significativas.

9. Publicación de los resultados del censo:

Se ha previsto publicar los resultados definitivos del censo en diciembre de 1996.

El organismo responsable de la publicación de los resultados del censo es la Central Statistical Office, Financial Complex, The Carenage, Saint George's.

Los resultados se podrán obtener también en disquetes y cuadros inéditos.

GRECIA

1. Nombre y dirección del organismo responsable del censo:

Office national de statistique de Grèce (ONSG), Direction des Recensements, 43-45, rue Agissilaou, 10166 Atenas.

2. Censos de población llevados a cabo desde 1945 (años):

1951, 1961, 1971, 1981 y 1991. La presente descripción se refiere al censo de 1991 (realizado el 17 de marzo de ese año).

3. Alcance del censo:

a) Geográfico: Todo el territorio.

b) Personas comprendidas: Toda la población.

4. Período de referencia:

La semana anterior a la fecha del censo y los doce meses anteriores a censo (marzo de 1990-febrero de 1991).

5. Materias principales:

a) Población total, según sexo y edad:	sí
Población económicamente activa por:	
b) Sexo y grupo de edad:	sí
c) Rama de actividad económica:	sí
d) Ocupación:	sí
e) Situación en el empleo:	sí
f) Nivel más alto de educación:	sí
g) Horas de trabajo:	sí
h) Otras características:	sí

Ref. a): La edad se determinó según el año de nacimiento.

Ref. g): Por tiempo de trabajo se entendió el número de horas afectivamente trabajadas por las personas ocupadas, en el lugar de trabajo, durante el período de referencia corto.

El censo también recolectó información sobre los medios de transporte utilizados y sobre el tiempo necesario para trasladarse al lugar de trabajo.

6. Conceptos y definiciones:

a) Población económicamente activa: Abarcó a todas las personas de 10 o más años de edad que, durante los períodos de referencia, estaban habitualmente ocupadas o desempleadas, conforme a las definiciones que se dan más adelante. No fueron incluidas las personas que cumplían su servicio militar obligatorio.

b) Empleo: Se consideró "ocupada" a toda persona que, durante los períodos de referencia, ejerció una profesión o un cargo o desempeñó una actividad económica cualquiera. Para determinar si una persona debía considerarse o no "ocupada" se preguntó "¿Ha trabajado X en el período de marzo de 1990 a febrero de 1991?" y "¿Qué empleo tuvo X durante la semana anterior al censo (10 a 16 de marzo de 1991)?".

Se ha indicado que fueron incluidas las siguientes categorías:

i) personas que trabajan sin remuneración en una empresa o negocio familiar;

ii) personas que producen bienes primarios para el autoconsumo;

iii) personas ocupadas pero temporalmente ausentes de su trabajo;

iv) estudiantes que trabajan a tiempo parcial;

v) trabajadores estacionales u ocasionales, a condición de que estuviesen activos en el momento del censo;

vi) aprendices y personas que siguen un curso de formación.

Sólo la categoría i) puede identificarse por separado, con arreglo a las respuestas a la pregunta sobre la situación en el empleo.

c) Desempleo: Se consideró "desempleada" a toda persona que, durante la semana de referencia, estaba sin trabajo, buscaba empleo y estaba disponible para empezar a trabajar de inmediato. La definición abarcó también a los jóvenes y demás personas en busca de un primer empleo. Por el contrario, no incluyó a las personas ocupadas que buscaban otro empleo, que quedaron clasificadas como "ocupadas".

7. Clasificaciones utilizadas:

Tanto las personas ocupadas como las desempleadas anteriormente empleadas fueron clasificadas por rama de actividad económica, por ocupación y por situación en el empleo.

a) Rama de actividad económica: La pregunta formulada recababa información sobre el tipo de actividad de la empresa, la explotación, el establecimiento o el servicio en que la persona censada trabajaba o había trabajado por última vez. Para codificar la rama de actividad se utilizó el nivel de grupos de la CIIU-Rev.3 (clave de 3 dígitos).

b) Ocupación: Para determinarla, se pidió indicar la naturaleza exacta de la profesión que la persona censada sea ejercía, sea había ejercido en su último trabajo. Para codificar la ocupación se utilizó la CIUO-68, a nivel de grupos primarios (clave de 3 dígitos).

c) Situación en el empleo: Para determinarla se hizo la siguiente pregunta: "¿En qué calidad ejerce (ejerció) X la ocupación indicada?". Para codificar la situación en el empleo se utilizaron cuatro categorías, a saber: empleador (con uno o más asalariados); trabajador independiente; asalariado, contratado por mes o por día; trabajador familiar (en la empresa o la explotación agrícola familiar).

8. Diferencias principales con el censo anterior:
Las diferencias registradas en el censo de 1991 son las siguientes:
- El carácter exhaustivo del procesamiento de los datos.
- Además de un período de referencia corto (la semana anterior al día del censo), se usó un período de referencia largo (el año anterior al censo).
- Las personas que habían trabajado por lo menos una hora durante el período de referencia corto fueron consideradas "ocupadas", y quedaron, pues, incluidas en el ámbito de la definición de "empleo".
- Por primera vez se acopiaron datos sobre los medios de transporte y el tiempo utilizados para trasladarse al trabajo.

9. Publicación de los resultados del censo:
Los resultados de este censo aparecieron en la publicación que lleva por título "Résultats du recensement de la population et des habitations effectué le 17 mars 1991".

El organismo responsable de esta publicación es la Office National de Statistique de Grèce, Direction de l'Information Statistique et des Publications, 14-16 rue Lycourgou, 10166 Atenas.

Los resultados del censo de 1991 están disponibles también en cuadros inéditos, disquetes y cintas magnéticas.

GUADALUPE

1. Nombre y dirección del organismo responsable del censo:
Institut national de la statistique et des études économiques (IN-SEE), Service régional de la Guadeloupe, Avenue Paul Lacave, B.P. 96, 97102 Basse-Terre, Guadalupe.

2. Censos de población llevados a cabo desde 1945 (años):
1954, 1961, 1967, 1974, 1982 y 1990. La presente descripción se refiere al censo de 1990 (realizado el 15 de marzo de ese año).

3. Alcance del censo:
a) Geográfico: Todo el territorio.
b) Personas comprendidas: Toda la población.

4. Período de referencia:
La semana anterior al día del censo.

5. Materias principales:
a) Población total, según sexo y edad: sí
Población económicamente activa por:
b) Sexo y grupo de edad: sí
c) Rama de actividad económica: sí
d) Ocupación: sí
e) Situación en el empleo: sí
f) Nivel más alto de educación: sí
g) Horas de trabajo: no
h) Otras características: sí

Ref. a): La edad se determinó según el año de nacimiento.

Ref. h): El censo también recolectó datos sobre otros temas, a saber: el trabajo a tiempo completo y el trabajo a tiempo parcial, la actividad principal, el número de asalariados empleados por las personas que trabajaban por cuenta propia, la duración del período de búsqueda de trabajo, etc.

6. Conceptos y definiciones:
a) Población económicamente activa: Abarcó a todas las personas de 14 o más años de edad que, durante la semana de referencia, estaban ocupadas o desempleadas, conforme a las definiciones que se dan más adelante. Esta definición incluyó también a los miembros de las fuerzas armadas (tanto los militares de carrera como las personas que cumplían su servicio militar). En lo que atañe a la actividad económica, se interrogó únicamente a una muestra de personas, en la que no quedaron incluidos los militares residentes en los cuarteles y las personas detenidas en establecimientos penitenciarios.

b) Empleo: Se consideró "ocupada" a toda persona que, durante la semana de referencia, ejerció una profesión o un cargo o desempeñó una actividad económica cualquiera, remunerada o no. Para determinar si una persona debía considerarse "ocupada" se hicieron preguntas específicas, en particular:

"¿Trabaja usted (a tiempo completo o a tiempo parcial)?"; "¿Es usted: asalariado o trabajador por cuenta propia (agricultor, artesano, comerciante, industrial, miembro de profesión liberal, trabajador familiar no remunerado, etc.)?", y "Si usted trabaja por cuenta propia: ¿cuántas personas asalariadas emplea? (no incluya a los aprendices o al personal doméstico; si es agricultor, incluya únicamente a los asalariados permanentes)". La definición abarcó también a las personas que desempeñaban un trabajo de utilidad pública (TUC, etc.), a las ocupadas por una agencia de colocación, a las empleadas según un contrato de duración limitada y a las empleadas según un contrato de readaptación o perfeccionamiento profesional.

Se ha indicado que fueron incluidas las siguientes categorías:
i) personas que trabajan sin remuneración en una empresa o explotación familiar;
ii) personas que producen bienes primarios para el autoconsumo;
iii) personas ocupadas pero temporalmente ausentes de su trabajo;
iv) estudiantes que trabajan a tiempo parcial;
v) trabajadores estacionales u ocasionales, a condición de que estuviesen activos en el momento del censo;
vi) conscriptos del servicio militar o civil;
vii) aprendices (bajo contrato) y personas que siguen un curso de formación (principalmente en una empresa o un centro de formación).

Sólo pueden identificarse por separado las categorías i), vi) y vii).

c) Desempleo: Se consideró "desempleada" a toda persona que indicó espontáneamente que esa era su situación y que buscaba empleo. Para determinar si una persona debía considerarse "desempleada" se preguntó "¿Está usted desempleado(a) (inscrito(a) o no en la Agencia Nacional del Empleo)?", "¿Ha trabajado ya? (si este es el caso, ¿cuál fue su ocupación principal?)", y "¿Busca usted empleo (desde hace: menos de tres meses; más de tres meses y menos de un año; más de un año pero menos de dos años; dos o más años)?".

7. Clasificaciones utilizadas:
Tanto las personas ocupadas como las desempleadas anteriormente empleadas fueron clasificadas por ocupación. Sólo las personas ocupadas incluidas en la muestra fueron clasificadas por rama de actividad y por situación en el empleo.

a) Rama de actividad económica: Se pidió a las personas censadas que indicasen la dirección, el nombre o la razón social del establecimiento que las empleaba o que dirigían, así como la actividad exacta de dicho establecimiento (por ejemplo: comercio mayorista de vinos, fabricación de estructuras metálicas, transporte terrestre de pasajeros, etc.). Para codificar la rama de actividad económica se utilizaron 100 grupos de la Nomenclatura de Actividades y Productos (NAP). No se establecieron enlaces con la CIIU.

b) Ocupación: Se pidió a las personas censadas que indicasen la ocupación que ejercían o que habían ejercido la última vez que habían trabajado, procurando definirla de la manera más precisa posible (por ejemplo: obrero electricista de manutención, chófer de camión de carga, vendedor de electrodomésticos, ingeniero químico, cajera de almacén de autoservicio, etc.), a efectos de determinar el grupo de ocupaciones. Sin embargo, se dejó la posibilidad de que la persona encuestada formulase su propia respuesta. La clasificación en un grupo determinado se efectuó durante el tratamiento informatizado de los datos. Para codificar la ocupación se utilizó un sistema de codificación directa en 42 grupos. No se establecieron enlaces con la CIUO.

c) Situación en el empleo: Para codificar esta variable se utilizaron cinco categorías, a saber: independiente por cuenta propia; empleador; asalariado; trabajador familiar no remunerado; otra situación.

8. Diferencias principales con el censo anterior:
En 1982, para incluir a una persona en la población económicamente activa se había aplicado un límite de edad mínima de 15 años.

Además, en el censo de 1982 se había clasificado por rama de actividad y por situación en el empleo tanto a las personas ocupadas como a los desempleados anteriormente empleados.

9. Publicación de los resultados del censo:
La publicación en que figuran los resultados definitivos del censo lleva por título: "Population, Emploi, Logements; Evolution 1975-1982-1990 (Série jaune)", 1992.

El organismo responsable de esta publicación es el Institut national de la statistique et des études économiques (INSEE), 18 boulevard Adolphe-Pinard, 75675 París Cedex 14.

También se dispone de los resultados del censo de 1990 en disquetes, cintas magnéticas y otras modalidades de presentación que se soliciten.

GUAM

1. Nombre y dirección del organismo responsable del censo:
Guam Department of Commerce, Suite 601, ITC Bldg, 590 S. Marine Drive, Tamuning 96911.

2. Censos de población llevados a cabo desde 1945 (años):
1950, 1960, 1970, 1980 y 1990. La presente descripción se refiere al censo de población de 1990 (realizado el 1 de abril de ese año).

3. Alcance del censo:
a) Geográfico: Todo el territorio.

b) Personas comprendidas: Toda la población.

4. Período de referencia:
La semana anterior a la fecha del censo y el año anterior al año del mismo.

5. Materias principales:
a) Población total, según sexo y edad: sí
Población económicamente activa por:
b) Sexo y grupo de edad: sí
c) Rama de actividad económica: sí
d) Ocupación: sí
e) Situación en el empleo: sí
f) Nivel más alto de educación: sí
g) Horas de trabajo: sí
h) Otras características: sí

Ref. a): La edad se determinó tanto según el año de nacimiento como de los años cumplidos en el último cumpleaños.

Ref. g): El tiempo de trabajo se refiere a la vez a las horas efectivamente pasadas en el lugar de trabajo por las personas ocupadas durante la semana de referencia y al período total (expresado en horas o en semanas) trabajado por estas personas durante 1989.

Ref. h): El censo también recolectó datos sobre: la ubicación del lugar de trabajo; el tipo de transporte usado para trasladarse al lugar de trabajo; el número de pasajeros transportados por cada vehículo (sólo en lo que atañe a los vehículos particulares); el tiempo necesario para cubrir el trayecto hasta el lugar de trabajo; los ingresos en concepto de sueldos, salarios, propinas y comisiones; los ingresos derivados de la explotación así como de la propiedad individual o en asociación de explotaciones agrícolas o de empresas y negocios no agrícolas.

6. Conceptos y definiciones:
a) Población económicamente activa: Abarcó a todas las personas de 15 o más años de edad que, durante los períodos de referencia, estaban sea ocupadas, sea desempleadas, conforme a las definiciones que se dan más adelante. No obstante, sólo se previó la publicación de los datos relativos a las personas de 16 o más años de edad. La definición incluyó a los miembros de las fuerzas armadas.

b) Empleo: Para determinar si una persona debía contabilizarse o no como "ocupada" se preguntó "¿Trabajó usted en algún momento la semana pasada, ya sea a tiempo completo o a tiempo parcial?" y "¿Trabajó usted el año pasado (1989), aunque haya sido sólo por unos días, en un empleo remunerado, o en una empresa, negocio o explotación agrícola propia, sin contar las actividades de subsistencia?".

Se ha indicado que fueron incluidas las siguientes categorías:
i)	personas que trabajan sin remuneración en una empresa o negocio familiar;
ii)	personas que producen bienes primarios para el autoconsumo;
iii)	personas ocupadas pero temporalmente ausentes de su trabajo;
iv)	estudiantes que trabajan a tiempo parcial;
v)	trabajadores estacionales u ocasionales;
vi)	aprendices y personas que siguen un curso de formación.

Sólo las categorías i) y ii) pueden identificarse por separado, según las respuestas dadas a determinadas preguntas.

c) Desempleo: Se consideró "desempleada" a toda persona que, durante la semana de referencia, estaba sin trabajo pero buscaba empleo. Para determinar si una persona debía contabilizarse como desempleada se utilizaron las siguientes preguntas: "La semana pasada, ¿estaba separada temporalmente de su empleo o ausente de su trabajo o actividad?"; "¿Ha buscado un trabajo remunerado con dinero durante las últimas cuatro semanas?"; "¿Estaba en condiciones de trabajar la semana pasada, si se le hubiera ofrecido un empleo?"; "¿Cuándo trabajó por última vez en un empleo, empresa, negocio o explotación agrícola, aunque sólo haya sido por pocos días?".

7. Clasificaciones utilizadas:
Tanto las personas ocupadas como las desempleadas que hubiesen trabajado un período cualquiera durante el año anterior al año del censo (1989) fueron clasificadas por rama de actividad económica, por ocupación y por situación en el empleo.

a) Rama de actividad económica: Para determinarla se preguntó: "¿Para quién trabajó usted?"; "¿En qué tipo de empresa o de rama de actividad?"; "¿Se trata fundamentalmente de industria manufacturera, comercio mayorista, comercio al detalle, construcción, otra actividad?". Para codificar la rama de actividad económica, se utilizaron 13 grandes grupos y 231 categorías de la Clasificación Industrial Normalizada de los Estados Unidos (US-SIC 1972 y suplemento de 1977). No se establecieron enlaces con la CIIU.

b) Ocupación: Para determinarla se preguntó: "¿Qué tipo de trabajo desempeñó?" y "¿Cuáles fueron sus actividades o funciones más importantes?". Para codificar la ocupación se utilizaron 13 grandes grupos y 503 categorías de la Clasificación Industrial Normalizada de los Estados Unidos. No se establecieron enlaces con la CIUO.

c) Situación en el empleo: Para determinarla se preguntó: "¿Trabajaba usted en calidad de: 1) empleado de una compañía o empresa privada, o de una persona, remunerado con un sueldo, un salario o comisiones; 2) empleado de un organismo privado sin fines lucrativos, exento de impuestos o caritativo; 3) empleado del Gobierno local o territorial (del territorio, de la mancomunidad, etc.); 4) empleado del Gobierno federal; 5) trabajador independiente en empresa propia, práctica de profesion liberal o explotación agrícola no constituida en sociedad; 6) trabajador independiente en empresa propia, práctica de profesión liberal o explotación agrícola constituida en sociedad; 7) trabajador no remunerado en empresa, negocio o explotación agrícola familiar". Para codificar la situación en el empleo se utilizaron los siete grupos mencionados.

8. Diferencias principales con el censo anterior:
La única diferencia entre los censos de 1980 y 1990 fue la inclusión en este último del personal de las fuerzas armadas en las preguntas relativas al sector de actividad económica, la ocupación y la situación en el empleo.

9. Publicación de los resultados del censo:
En agosto de 1991, se divulgaron diversos cuadros con datos resumidos del censo de 1990. El documento completo se publicó en 1992.

El organismo responsable de la publicación de estos materiales es el servicio Puerto Rico and Outlying Areas Branch, Decennial Planning Division, U.S. Bureau of the Census, Washington, D.C. 20233.

Los resultados del censo están disponibles también en disquetes, CD-ROM y cuadros inéditos.

GUATEMALA

1. Nombre y dirección del organismo responsable del censo:
Instituto Nacional de Estadística, 8a calle 9-55, Zona 1, Ciudad Guatemala, Guatemala 010001.

2. Censos de población llevados a cabo desde 1945 (años):
1950, 1964, 1973, 1981 y 1994. La presente descripción se refiere al censo de población de 1994 (efectuado el 17 de abril).

212

3. Alcance del censo:

a) Geográfico: Todo el país.

b) Personas comprendidas: Toda la población.

4. Periodo de referencia:
La semana anterior a la fecha del censo.

5. Materias principales:

a) Población total, según sexo y edad:	sí

Población económicamente activa por:

b) Sexo y grupo de edad:	sí
c) Rama de actividad económica:	sí
d) Ocupación:	sí
e) Situación en el empleo:	sí
f) Nivel más alto de educación:	sí
g) Horas de trabajo:	no
h) Otras características:	no

Ref. a): Se definió la edad según los años cumplidos y según el año de nacimiento.

6. Conceptos y definiciones:

a) Población económicamente activa: Incluye a todas las personas de 7 años y más, que durante la semana de referencia se encontraban empleadas o desempleadas, tal y como se definen más adelante. La definición incluye a los militares de carrera pero excluye a los conscriptos en el servicio militar o civil.

b) Empleo: Se consideran "empleadas" a las personas que contestaron que trabajaron o que no trabajaron pero tenían trabajo, a la pregunta: "¿Qué hizo la semana anterior a la fecha del censo?" Las categorías de respuesta eran: Trabajó; No trabajó, pero tenía trabajo; Buscó trabajo pero trabajaba antes; Buscó trabajo por primera vez; Vivió de su renta o jubilación y no trabajó; Estudió y no trabajó; Quehaceres del hogar y no trabajó; Otros.

Se ha indicado que quedan incluidas las siguientes categorías:

i) personas que trabajan sin remuneración en una empresa familiar;

ii) personas ocupadas pero temporalmente ausentes de su trabajo;

iii) estudiantes que trabajan a tiempo parcial.

Todas las categorías pueden identificarse separadamente.

c) Desempleo: Son consideradas como "desempleadas" las personas que contestaron que buscaron trabajo por primera vez o que buscaron trabajo pero trabajaron antes a la pregunta "¿Qué hizo la semana anterior a la fecha del censo?".

7. Clasificaciones utilizadas:
Tanto las personas ocupadas como las desocupadas (a excepción de las personas que buscan trabajo por primera vez) se clasificaron por rama de actividad económica, por ocupación y según la situación en el empleo.

a) Rama de actividad económica: Para determinar esta variable se preguntó la actividad a la que se dedicaba la fábrica, taller, oficina, finca, establecimiento, etc, en donde llevó a cabo la ocupación que indicó. Los enlaces con la CIIU-Rev.3 se han establecido a nivel de 4 dígitos.

b) Ocupación: Para establecer la ocupación se preguntó por la ocupación, el tipo de trabajo u oficio que realizó la persona durante la semana de referencia, o el último trabajo que tuvo. Los enlaces con la CIUO-88 se han establecido a nivel de grupos primarios (4 dígitos).

c) Situación en el empleo: Para determinar esta característica se preguntó por la categoría que tenía en la ocupación principal, codificada en 6 categorías (patrono, cuenta propia con local, cuenta propia sin local, empleado público, empleado privado, familiar no remunerado).

8. Diferencias principales con el censo anterior:
Lo único que cambió fue el límite de edad, ya que para el censo de 1994 se investigó las características económicas a partir de 7 años y más de edad (10 años en el censo de 1981).

9. Publicación de los resultados del censo:
El título exacto de la publicación con los resultados finales es "Características Generales de Habitación y Población", octubre de 1995.

La organización responsable de la publicación es el Instituto Nacional de Estadística - INE - 8va. Calle 9-55 Zona 1.

Los resultados están también disponibles en disquetes.

GUAYANA FRANCESA

1. Nombre y dirección del organismo responsable del censo:
Institut national de la statistique et des études économiques (IN-SEE), Service régional de la Guyane, 1 rue Maillard Dumesle, B.P. 6017, 97306 Cayena Cedex.

2. Censos de población llevados a cabo desde 1945 (años):
1954, 1961, 1967, 1974, 1982 y 1990. La presente descripción se refiere al censo de 1990 (realizado el 15 de marzo de ese año).

3. Alcance del censo:

a) Geográfico: Todo el territorio.

b) Personas comprendidas: Toda la población.

4. Periodo de referencia:
La semana anterior al día del censo.

5. Materias principales:

a) Población total, según sexo y edad:	sí

Población económicamente activa por:

b) Sexo y grupo de edad:	sí
c) Rama de actividad económica:	sí
d) Ocupación:	sí
e) Situación en el empleo:	sí
f) Nivel más alto de educación:	sí
g) Horas de trabajo:	no
h) Otras características:	sí

Ref. a): La edad se determinó según el año de nacimiento.

Ref. h): El censo también recolectó datos sobre otros temas, a saber: el trabajo a tiempo completo y el trabajo a tiempo parcial, la actividad principal, el número de asalariados empleados por las personas que trabajaban por cuenta propia, la duración del período de búsqueda de trabajo, etc.

6. Conceptos y definiciones:

a) Población económicamente activa: Abarcó a todas las personas de 14 o más años de edad que, durante la semana de referencia, estaban ocupadas o desempleadas, conforme a las definiciones que se dan más adelante. Esta definición incluyó también a los miembros de las fuerzas armadas (tanto los militares de carrera como las personas que cumplían su servicio militar). En lo que atañe a la actividad económica, se interrogó únicamente a una muestra de personas, en la que no quedaron incluidos los militares residentes en los cuarteles y las personas detenidas en establecimientos penitenciarios.

b) Empleo: Se consideró "ocupada" a toda persona que, durante la semana de referencia, ejerció una profesión o un cargo o desempeñó una actividad económica cualquiera, remunerada o no. Para determinar si una persona debía considerarse "ocupada" se hicieron preguntas específicas, en particular: "¿Trabaja usted (a tiempo completo o a tiempo parcial)?"; "¿Es usted: asalariado o trabajador por cuenta propia (agricultor, artesano, comerciante, industrial, miembro de profesión liberal, trabajador familiar no remunerado, etc.)?", y "Si usted trabaja por cuenta propia: ¿cuántas personas asalariadas emplea? (no incluya a los aprendices o al personal doméstico; si es agricultor, incluya únicamente a los asalariados permanentes)". La definición abarcó también a las personas que desempeñaban un trabajo de utilidad pública (TUC, etc.), a las ocupadas por una agencia de colocación, a las empleadas según un contrato de duración limitada y a las empleadas según un contrato de readaptación o de perfeccionamiento profesional.

Se ha indicado que fueron incluidas las siguientes categorías:

i) personas que trabajan sin remuneración en una empresa o explotación familiar;

ii) personas que producen bienes primarios para el autoconsumo;

iii) personas ocupadas pero temporalmente ausentes de su trabajo;

iv) estudiantes que trabajan a tiempo parcial;

v) trabajadores estacionales u ocasionales, a condición de que estuviesen ocupados en el momento del censo;

vi) conscriptos del servicio militar o civil;

vii) aprendices (bajo contrato) y personas que siguen un curso de formación (principalmente en una empresa o un centro de formación).

Sólo pueden identificarse por separado las categorías i), vi) y vii).

c) Desempleo: Se consideró "desempleada" a toda persona que indicó espontáneamente que esa era su situación y que buscaba empleo. Para determinar si una persona debía considerarse "desempleada" se preguntó "¿Está usted desempleado(a) (inscrito(a) o no en la Agencia Nacional del Empleo)?", "¿Ha trabajado ya? (si este es el caso, ¿cuál fue su ocupación principal?)", y "¿Busca usted empleo (desde hace: menos de tres meses; más de tres meses pero menos de un año; más de un año pero menos de dos años; dos o más años)?".

7. Clasificaciones utilizadas:
Tanto las personas ocupadas como las desempleadas anteriormente empleadas incluidas en la muestra fueron clasificadas por ocupación. Sólo las personas ocupadas incluidas en la muestra fueron clasificadas por rama de actividad y por situación en el empleo.

a) Rama de actividad económica: Se pidió a las personas censadas que indicasen la dirección, el nombre o la razón social del establecimiento que las empleaba o que dirigían, así como la actividad exacta de dicho establecimiento (por ejemplo: comercio mayorista de vinos, fabricación de estructuras metálicas, transporte terrestre de pasajeros, etc.). Para codificar la rama de actividad económica se utilizaron 100 grupos de la Nomenclatura de Actividades y Productos (NAP). No se establecieron enlaces con la CIIU.

b) Ocupación: Se pidió a las personas censadas que indicasen la ocupación que ejercían o que habían ejercido la última vez que habían trabajado, procurando definirla de la manera más precisa posible (por ejemplo: obrero electricista de manutención, chófer de camión de carga, vendedor de electrodomésticos, ingeniero químico, cajera de almacén de autoservicio, etc.), a efectos de determinar el grupo de ocupaciones. Sin embargo, se dejó la posibilidad de que la persona encuestada formulase su propia respuesta. La clasificación en un grupo determinado se efectuó durante el tratamiento informatizado de los datos. Para codificar la ocupación se utilizó un sistema de codificación directa en 42 grupos. No se establecieron enlaces con la CIUO.

c) Situación en el empleo: Para codificar esta variable se utilizaron cinco categorías, a saber: independiente por cuenta propia; empleador; asalariado; trabajador familiar no remunerado; otra situación.

8. Diferencias principales con el censo anterior:
En 1982, para incluir a una persona en la población económicamente activa se había aplicado un límite de edad mínima de 15 años.

Además, en el censo de 1982 se había clasificado por rama de actividad y por situación en el empleo tanto a las personas ocupadas como a los desempleados anteriormente empleados.

9. Publicación de los resultados del censo:
La publicación en que figuran los resultados definitivos del censo lleva por título: "Population, Emploi, Logements; Evolution 1975-1982-1990 (Série jaune)", 1992.

El organismo responsable de esta publicación es el Institut national de la statistique et des études économiques (INSEE), 18 boulevard Adolphe-Pinard, 75675 París Cedex 14.

También se dispone de los resultados del censo de 1990 en disquetes, cintas magnéticas y otras modalidades de presentación que se soliciten.

GUINEA ECUATORIAL

1. Nombre y dirección del organismo responsable del censo:
Dirección General de Estadística, Ministerio de Economía y Hacienda, Malabo.

2. Censos de población llevados a cabo desde 1945 (años):
1981 y 1994. La presente descripción se refiere al censo de población de 1994 (efectuado el 11 de septiembre).

3. Alcance del censo:

a) Geográfico: Todo el país.

b) Personas comprendidas: Toda la población, excluidos los representantes diplomáticos residentes en Guinea Ecuatorial.

4. Periodo de referencia:
La semana anterior a la fecha del censo.

5. Materias principales:
a) Población total, según sexo y edad: sí
Población económicamente activa por:
b) Sexo y grupo de edad: sí
c) Rama de actividad económica: sí
d) Ocupación: sí
e) Situación en el empleo: no
f) Nivel más alto de educación: ...
g) Horas de trabajo: ...
h) Otras características: no
Ref. a): Se definió la edad en términos del año de nacimiento.

6. Conceptos y definiciones:

a) Población económicamente activa: Incluye a todas las personas de 6 años y más de edad, que durante la semana de referencia estaban empleadas o desempleadas, según las definiciones que se dan más adelante. Se plantearon preguntas sobre actividad económica a una muestra de 15,3 por ciento de la población. Los datos sobre la población económicamente activa y sus componentes (empleo y desempleo) sólo se tabularon entre 6 y 64 años. La definición excluye todas las fuerzas armadas. Se excluyen también a los estudiantes que trabajan a tiempo parcial o que buscan trabajo.

b) Empleo: Son consideradas "empleadas" las personas que trabajaron durante la semana de referencia. Para considerar una persona como ocupada se preguntó qué hizo en la semana anterior al día del censo.

Se ha indicado que quedan incluidas las categorías siguientes:
i) personas empleadas y temporalmente ausentes del trabajo;
ii) trabajadores estacionales u ocasionales.

Ninguna de estas categorías puede identificarse separadamente.

c) Desempleo: Son consideradas "desempleadas" las personas que durante la semana de referencia no trabajaron pero que buscaron trabajo. Las preguntas utilizadas para determinar si la persona estaba desempleada son "¿Buscó trabajo habiendo trabajado antes?" y "¿Buscó trabajo por primera vez?".

7. Clasificaciones utilizadas:
Tanto las personas ocupadas como las desempleadas que han trabajado anteriormente se clasificaron por rama de actividad económica y por ocupación.

a) Rama de actividad económica: Establecida sobre la base de la pregunta: "¿A qué actividad se dedica la empresa, negocio en la que usted trabajó?". Para codificar la rama de actividad se utilizó la CIIU-Rev.3.

b) Ocupación: Para establecer la ocupación, las preguntas utilizadas son "¿Cuál es su ocupación?" y "¿Cuál es su categoría de ocupación?". Para codificar el grupo de ocupaciones se utilizaron diez grupos de la clasificación nacional. Los enlaces con la CIUO-88 se han establecido al nivel de los grandes grupos (1 dígito).

c) Situación en el empleo: No se hizo ninguna clasificación según la situación en el empleo.

8. Diferencias principales con el censo anterior:
No hubo diferencias significativas.

9. Publicación de los resultados del censo:
Los resultados finales se publicaron en enero de 1995, en el volumen titulado "Características de la Población y de las Viviendas".

La organización responsable de la publicación es la Dirección General de Estadística, Ministerio de Economía y Hacienda, Malabo.

Los resultados del censo se encuentran también disponibles en soportes magnéticos.

HONG KONG

1. Nombre y dirección del organismo responsable del censo:
Census and Statistics Department, 21/F., Wanchai Tower I, 12 Harbour Road, Wanchai, Hong Kong.

2. Censos de población llevados a cabo desde 1945 (años):

Censos completos: 1961, 1971, 1981 y 1991; censos intermedios por muestreo: 1966, 1976 y 1986. La presente descripción se refiere al censo de 1991 (realizado del 15 al 24 de marzo de ese año).

3. Alcance del censo:

a) Geográfico: Todo el territorio.

b) Personas comprendidas: Toda la población.

4. Periodo de referencia:

Los 7 días anteriores al empadronamiento. No obstante, para determinar si los encuestados habían estado buscando trabajo, se usó un período de 30 días anteriores a la fecha de referencia del censo.

5. Materias principales:

a) Población total, según sexo y edad:	sí
Población económicamente activa por:	
b) Sexo y grupo de edad:	sí
c) Rama de actividad económica:	sí
d) Ocupación:	sí
e) Situación en el empleo:	sí
f) Nivel más alto de educación:	sí
g) Horas de trabajo:	no
h) Otras características:	no

Ref. a): La edad se determinó según los años cumplidos en el último cumpleaños.

6. Conceptos y definiciones:

a) Población económicamente activa: Abarcó a todas las personas de 15 o más años de edad incluidas en la muestra que, durante los períodos de referencia, estaban sea ocupadas, sea desempleadas, conforme a las definiciones que se dan más adelante. La definición incluyó a los miembros de las fuerzas armadas. Se hicieron preguntas sobre la actividad económica a una muestra de 1/7; sólo se consultó a los residentes presentes en Hong Kong durante las fechas de referencia del censo.

b) Empleo: Se consideró "ocupada" a toda persona incluida en la muestra que respondió afirmativamente a una de las siguientes preguntas: "¿Ejerció usted una actividad remunerada, mediante salario o ganancias, durante los últimos 7 días, incluidas la prestación de cursos privados y trabajos pagados por hora?", "¿Tuvo un empleo en los últimos 7 días?" y "¿Trabajó sin remuneración en una empresa o negocio de su familia durante los últimos siete días?".

Se ha indicado que fueron incluidas las siguientes categorías de personas ocupadas:

i) personas que trabajan sin remuneración en una empresa o negocio familiar;

ii) personas ocupadas pero temporalmente ausentes de su trabajo;

iii) estudiantes que trabajan a tiempo parcial;

iv) trabajadores estacionales u ocasionales;

v) trabajadores con más de un empleo;

vi) aprendices y personas que siguen un curso de formación.

Sólo pueden identificarse por separado las categorías i) y v), en función de sus respuestas a determinadas preguntas. Por ejemplo: las personas que han de incluirse en la categoría i) pueden identificarse según sus respuestas a la pregunta "¿Trabajó sin remuneración en una empresa o negocio de su familia durante los últimos siete días?"; las de la categoría v) pueden identificarse según sus respuestas a la pregunta "¿Tuvo usted un empleo secundario durante los últimos 30 días?".

c) Desempleo: Se consideró "desempleada" a toda persona incluida en la muestra que respondió negativamente a las tres preguntas que figuran en el párrafo 6 b). Además, a esta categoría de personas se pidió que respondieran a las siguientes preguntas: "¿Estuvo usted buscando trabajo durante los últimos 30 días?", "En caso de no haberlo hecho, ¿cuál fue el motivo?", "¿Estaba usted disponible para trabajar durante los últimos 7 días?" y "Si éste no fue el caso, ¿por qué no estaba disponible para trabajar?". Sobre la base de sus respuestas, las personas fueron clasificadas como "desempleados" o "económicamente inactivos".

7. Clasificaciones utilizadas:

Sólo las personas ocupadas incluidas en la muestra fueron clasificadas por rama de actividad económica, por ocupación y según la situación en el empleo.

a) Rama de actividad económica: A las personas ocupadas incluidas en la muestra se hicieron dos tipos de preguntas. La pregunta hecha a los asalariados fue: "¿Qué tipo de actividad, negocio o servicio se llevaba a cabo en el lugar de trabajo del establecimiento para el que usted trabajaba?". A los empleadores, trabajadores independientes y trabajadores familiares se preguntó: "¿Qué tipo de actividad, negocio o servicio llevaba a cabo usted/llevaba a cabo su familia?". Para codificar la rama de actividad se utilizaron 87 códigos de la clasificación nacional. Se establecieron enlaces con la CIIU-Rev.3 a nivel de grupos (clave de 3 dígitos).

b) Ocupación: Para determinarla se preguntó: "¿Cuál era su ocupación?", "¿Cuáles eran las principales tareas o funciones que usted tenía que desempeñar en esa ocupación?" y "¿Qué formación académica o calificaciones profesionales se requerían para desempeñar ese trabajo?". Para codificar la ocupación se utilizaron 116 códigos de la clasificación nacional de ocupaciones. Se establecieron enlaces con la CIUO-88 a nivel de subgrupos (clave de 3 dígitos).

c) Situación en el empleo: Para determinarla se preguntó: "¿Era usted empleador, trabajador independiente o trabajador asalariado?". Esta pregunta no se aplicó a los trabajadores familiares no remunerados, en la medida en que quedaron identificados al determinarse la categoría de "personas ocupadas". Para codificar la situación en el empleo se utilizaron los 4 grupos siguientes: trabajadores independientes; empleadores; trabajadores asalariados (incluidos los trabajadores a domicilio); trabajadores familiares no remunerados.

8. Diferencias principales con el censo anterior:

No hubo diferencias significativas.

9. Publicación de los resultados del censo:

Los resultados del censo se publicaron en octubre de 1991, con el título de "Hong Kong 1991 Population Census Summary Results", volumen que constituyó la primera entrega de la serie de publicaciones resumidas.

El organismo responsable de esta publicación es la Census Planning Section, Census and Statistics Department, Koway Court, 2/F, 111 Chai Wan Road.

Los resultados del censo están también disponibles en cuadros inéditos, disquetes, cintas magnéticas y discos CD-ROM.

HUNGRIA

1. Nombre y dirección del organismo responsable del censo:

Office Central de Statistique de Hongrie, Division des recensements (KSH-Népszámlálás), Budafoki út 59, H-1111 Budapest.

2. Censos de población llevados a cabo desde 1945 (años):

1949, 1960, 1970, 1980 y 1990. La presente descripción se refiere al censo de 1990 (realizado el 1 de enero de ese año).

3. Alcance del censo:

a) Geográfico: Todo el territorio.

b) Personas comprendidas: Toda la población, con excepción de: los diplomáticos y el personal extranjero de las misiones diplomáticas extranjeras; los militares de contingentes extranjeros destacados en Hungría en virtud del Pacto de Varsovia, así como los miembros de sus familias; los turistas extranjeros que no estaban en posesión de un permiso de residencia.

4. Periodo de referencia:

En las preguntas hechas se consideró, en general (es decir, para los asalariados, los miembros de cooperativas, los trabajadores por cuenta propia y las personas ocupadas sin remuneración en una empresa familiar no agrícola), un período de referencia corto, a saber, la última semana de 1989; en lo que atañe a los trabajadores familiares no remunerados ocupados en la agricultura, se consideró un período de referencia largo, a saber, un mínimo de 90 jornadas laborables de 10 horas cada una durante 1989.

5. Materias principales:

a) Población total, según sexo y edad:	sí
Población económicamente activa por:	
b) Sexo y grupo de edad:	sí
c) Rama de actividad económica:	sí
d) Ocupación:	sí

e) Situación en el empleo: sí
f) Nivel más alto de educación: sí
g) Horas de trabajo: no
h) Otras características: sí

Ref. a): La edad se determinó según el año de nacimiento.

Ref. g): Sin embargo, en el marco de un "programa representativo" (relativo a una muestra de 20 por ciento de la población), figuraba una pregunta destinada a determinar si la persona censada trabajaba a tiempo completo o a tiempo parcial. En este mismo programa se pidió a los jubilados que habían conservado una actividad económica (y únicamente a ellos) que indicasen el número de horas trabajadas.

Ref. h): Asimismo, se formularon otras preguntas relativas a la actividad de la persona censada, en particular sobre: su nivel de calificación profesional; el nombre y la dirección de su lugar de trabajo; los medios de transporte y el tiempo necesario para trasladarse a dicho lugar de trabajo y regresar a su domicilio; su posición jerárquica en el personal; la fecha de ingreso a su primera ocupación remunerada; el ejercicio eventual de una actividad complementaria durante 1989 y su duración; etc. Parte de estas preguntas se hicieron a toda la población económicamente activa, mientras que otras preguntas se formularon sólo a las personas incluidas en la muestra de 20 por ciento, antes citada.

6. Conceptos y definiciones:

a) Población económicamente activa: Abarcó a todas las personas que, durante los períodos de referencia, estaban ocupadas o desempleadas, conforme a las definiciones que se dan más adelante. La definición incluyó a los miembros de las fuerzas armadas. No quedaron incluidos en ella los estudiantes con empleo a tiempo parcial, los estudiantes que buscaban trabajo ni los jubilados que tenían una actividad económica. No se aplicó ningún límite de edad mínima o máxima a los efectos de recolectar información sobre la población económicamente activa y sus componentes; no obstante, se publicarán sólo los resultados referentes a las personas activas de 14 a 85 años de edad. Se pidió a todas las personas censadas que respondiesen a la pregunta "¿Trabaja usted, tiene un empleo?". A quienes respondieran negativamente, se pidió indicar con precisión los motivos de su inactividad económica.

En el "programa de base" (que se aplicó al 80 por ciento de la población), no se formuló pregunta alguna acerca de la actividad económica de las siguientes categorías: los jubilados, pensionados y otras personas cuyos ingresos no provenían de una actividad que efectuasen en ese momento; los desempleados en busca de empleo; las personas a cargo de terceros. En cambio, aunque fueron consideradas "no económicamente activas", las personas ausentes de su trabajo en virtud de una licencia para cuidar de los hijos debían responder todas las preguntas aplicables a su situación anterior a la suspensión del trabajo.

En el "programa representativo" (que abarcó una muestra de 20 por ciento de la población), las personas ocupadas debían responder a todas las preguntas relativas al empleo y la ocupación. Los jubilados y afines, así como los desempleados en busca de trabajo, debían responder únicamente a las preguntas relativas a su última actividad económica, mientras que los jubilados que seguían ejerciendo una actividad económica, sea a tiempo completo, sea a tiempo parcial, debían aportar algunas precisiones al respecto. Las personas a cargo debían responder a las preguntas que se les hicieron en relación con las personas de las que dependían.

b) Empleo: Se consideró "ocupada" a toda persona que, durante los períodos de referencia, ejerció una profesión o una función o desempeñó alguna actividad económica. Para determinar si una persona debía considerarse "ocupada" se utilizó la misma pregunta formulada a todas las personas a que se refiere el apartado a) de esta misma sección. En caso de respuesta afirmativa, la persona censada debía aportar indicaciones precisas acerca de su actividad, tuviese ésta lugar dentro o fuera del domicilio y fuese o no remunerada.

Se ha indicado que fueron incluidas las siguientes categorías:

i) personas que trabajan sin remuneración en una empresa o negocio familiar;

ii) personas que producen bienes primarios para el autoconsumo;

iii) personas ocupadas pero temporalmente ausentes de su trabajo debido a que se encontraban haciendo uso de una licencia (pagada o no) o recibían una formación relacionada con su ocupación;

iv) conscriptos del servicio militar o civil;

v) trabajadores estacionales u ocasionales;

vi) trabajadores con más de un empleo.

Todas estas categorías pueden identificarse por separado, con arreglo a sus respuestas a la pregunta sobre la situación en el empleo (asalariado; miembro de una cooperativa; trabajador por cuenta propia; miembro de una profesión liberal; trabajador familiar), o según un código especial. Las personas que tenían más de un empleo pueden identificarse por separado en el marco del "programa representativo", basándose en las respuestas a la pregunta "Además de su ocupación principal, ¿ha ejercido usted una actividad remunerada complementaria durante 1989?".

c) Desempleo: Se consideró "desempleada" a toda persona que respondió "no" a la pregunta citada en el párrafo a) de la presente sección y que indicó estar buscando un nuevo trabajo o un primer empleo. Quedaron excluidas de la definición de "desempleo" las personas a cargo y todas las personas cuya inactividad económica se explicó por otros motivos (como: percibe un subsidio o una asignación familiar a menor de edad; percibe una pensión personal; percibe una pensión de invalidez u otra forma de renta personal; percibe una pensión de viudez; asiste a una guardería infantil, un establecimiento preescolar, una escuela primaria o secundaria, un establecimiento de estudios superiores o una universidad).

7. Clasificaciones utilizadas:

Tanto las personas ocupadas como las desempleadas anteriormente empleadas, incluidas en la muestra, se clasificaron por rama de actividad económica, por ocupación y por situación en el empleo.

a) Rama de actividad económica: Para determinar el grupo de actividad económica se preguntó el nombre del empleador y la dirección del lugar de trabajo. Se pidió indicar con precisión la índole del lugar de trabajo (por ejemplo: fábrica, casa central de la empresa, almacén, escuela, establecimiento sanitario, etc.). Para codificar la rama de actividad económica se utilizaron 38 grupos principales, 104 grandes divisiones y 294 divisiones individuales (nivel de 4 dígitos) de la nomenclatura húngara.

No se establecieron enlaces con la CIIU. No obstante, recientemente se ha establecido un nuevo sistema nacional de clasificación de las ramas de actividad económica; conforme con este nuevo sistema, adaptado a la CIIU-Rev.3, será posible codificar nuevamente por lo menos una muestra representativa de los cuestionarios cumplimentados, a fin de obtener resultados comparables a nivel internacional.

b) Ocupación: Para determinar el grupo de profesiones se hicieron preguntas relativas a la naturaleza de la ocupación de la persona censada, así como a su posición jerárquica en el personal de la empresa. Para codificar la ocupación se utilizaron 16 grupos principales, 144 grupos de profesiones y 808 profesiones por separado (nivel de 4 dígitos) de la nomenclatura húngara.

No se establecieron enlaces con la CIUO. Empero, está prevista la preparación de un nuevo sistema nacional de clasificación de ocupaciones; de conformidad con este nuevo sistema, adaptado a la CIUO-88 en los niveles de 10 grandes grupos y de subgrupos principales, será posible codificar nuevamente una muestra representativa de los cuestionarios cumplimentados, al objeto de obtener resultados comparables a nivel internacional.

c) Situación en el empleo: Para determinar la situación en el empleo se hicieron preguntas concretas, tanto en el marco del "programa de base" como del "programa representativo". Para codificar esta variable se utilizaron los ocho grupos siguientes: asalariado; miembro de una cooperativa; trabajador por cuenta propia en actividades manuales; trabajador por cuenta propia en actividades no manuales; familiar que trabaja sin remuneración para miembro de cooperativa agrícola; familiar que trabaja sin remuneración en explotación agrícola complementaria; familiar ocupado sin remuneración por trabajador agrícola por cuenta propia; familiar ocupado sin remuneración por trabajador por cuenta propia en actividades no agrícolas.

8. Diferencias principales con el censo anterior:

El principal cambio introducido en el censo de 1990 con respecto al de 1980 se refiere a la incorporación del desempleo como nueva e importante componente del concepto de población económicamente activa.

Además, el "programa representativo" (aplicado a una muestra de 20 por ciento de la población) contiene un cierto número de nuevas preguntas destinadas a definir y describir la población económicamente activa y sus componentes, así como a determinar mejor la situación en el empleo. Otras preguntas sirven para identificar la ocupación principal y las actividades complementarias, el trabajo a tiempo completo y el trabajo a tiempo parcial, los niveles de escolaridad y de formación, el nivel de calificaciones profesionales, etc.

9. Publicación de los resultados del censo:
Las principales publicaciones de los resultados del censo son: "1. Preliminary data" agosto de 1990, "Socio-occupational composition of active earners, households and families" 1992, "Place of work and place of residence of active earners" 1994, y "Detailed data of the 20% representative sample survey" 1995.

El organismo responsable de estas publicaciones es la Office Central de Statistique de Hongrie, Division des Recensements (KSH-Népszámlálás), H-1111 Budapest.

Los resultados del censo también están disponibles en disquetes, CD-ROM y en consulta informática en tiempo real.

INDIA

1. Nombre y dirección del organismo responsable del censo:
Office of the Registrar General and Census Commissioner, 2-A, Man Singh Road, New Delhi-110 011.

2. Censos de población llevados a cabo desde 1945 (años):
1951, 1961, 1971, 1981 y 1991. La presente descripción se refiere al censo de población de 1991 (realizado el 1o. de marzo de ese año).

3. Alcance del censo:
a) Geográfico: Todo el país, salvo Jammu y Cachemira.

b) Personas comprendidas: Toda la población, excepto los diplomáticos extranjeros y sus familias, y los nacionales residentes en el extranjero. El personal de las misiones de la India en el extranjero y sus familias entraron en el censo.

4. Periodo de referencia:
El año anterior al día del censo.

5. Materias principales:
a) Población total, según sexo y edad:	sí
Población económicamente activa por:	
b) Sexo y grupo de edad:	sí
c) Rama de actividad económica:	sí
d) Ocupación:	sí
e) Situación en el empleo:	sí
f) Nivel más alto de educación:	sí
g) Horas de trabajo:	no
h) Otras características:	no

Ref. a): La edad se determinó según los años cumplidos en el último cumpleaños.

6. Conceptos y definiciones:
a) Población económicamente activa: Abarcó a todas las personas que durante el período de referencia estaban ocupadas o desempleadas, conforme a las definiciones que figuran más adelante. No se fijó limite de edad alguno; ahora bien, en el caso de las personas ocupadas, los resultados publicados se refieren a las personas de 5 o más años de edad (salvo los del resumen provisional del censo, que no contiene datos sobre la edad). La definición incluyó a los miembros de las fuerzas armadas.

Los datos relativos a la actividad económica se procesaron en dos etapas. En la primera, los cuadros se basaron en un muestreo del 10 por ciento de las personas de los estados más grandes de la India (con una población de diez millones o más habitantes); en los estados más pequeños y los territorios federados se tomó como base el 100 por ciento de los datos. En la segunda, se procesó el 100 por ciento de los datos relativos a los "trabajadores principales" - exceptuando a los cultivadores y los obreros agrícolas -, a los "trabajadores marginales" y a los "trabajadores desocupados" en busca de trabajo o dispuestos a trabajar, a efectos de obtener tabulaciones más detalladas y fiables por lo que se refería a las unidades administrativas menores.

b) Empleo:
Para determinarlo se preguntó: "¿Trabajó en algún momento del año pasado?" y "De ser así ¿lo hizo la mayor parte del año pasado?".

El trabajo puede definirse en términos de participación en cualquier actividad económicamente productiva. Dicha participación puede ser tanto física como intelectual. Las tareas de supervisión y dirección del trabajo también se consideraron trabajo.

Trabajador "principal" es quien trabajó la mayor parte del año, es decir, 183 días como mínimo o, si se prefiere, 6 o más meses. "Trabajador marginal" es quien trabajó durante algún tiempo el año anterior, pero no la mayor parte del año. También se recolectaron datos sobre el empleo secundario del trabajador principal.

Se ha indicado que fueron incluidas las siguientes categorías:

i) personas que trabajan sin remuneración en una empresa o negocio familiar;

ii) personas ocupadas pero temporalmente ausentes de su trabajo;

iii) estudiantes que trabajan a tiempo parcial;

iv) trabajadores estacionales u ocasionales;

v) conscriptos del servicio militar o civil;

vi) aprendices y personas que siguen un curso de formación.

Las personas que trabajaron en una empresa familiar sin recibir remuneración pueden identificarse por separado, utilizando la tabulación del censo sobre trabajadores familiares (exceptuando a los cultivadores).

Quienes cultivaban la tierra para consumo propio se incluyeron en la población económicamente activa pero no se pueden identificar por separado. Quienes se dedicaban a otras actividades de producción para consumo propio quedaron excluidos de la población económicamente activa. En el censo, se consideró cultivador a quien plantaba cereales, leguminosas, plantas textiles, oleaginosas y caña de azúcar, pero no a quien se dedicaba al cultivo de raíces comestibles, verduras, frutas, cultivos forrajeros, horticultura, etc.

Los estudiantes que trabajaban, considerados trabajadores marginales, pueden identificarse por separado mediante preguntas concretas. El término "trabajador marginal" utilizado en el censo no coincide forzosamente con el de trabajador a tiempo parcial.

c) Desempleo: Se consideró "desempleada" a toda persona que durante el año de referencia no trabajó en absoluto y que, por consiguiente, se consideró desocupada. A todas las personas desocupadas se les preguntó si estaban buscando trabajo o dispuestas a trabajar.

Los estudiantes en busca de trabajo y las demás personas aptas para trabajar que buscaban trabajo y que nunca habían trabajado antes se pueden identificar por separado mediante preguntas concretas.

7. Clasificaciones utilizadas:
Sólo las personas ocupadas se clasificaron por rama de actividad, por ocupación y por situación en el empleo, exceptuando a los cultivadores y los obreros agrícolas.

a) Rama de actividad económica: Para determinarla, se pidió a la persona censada que indicara la índole de la rama de actividad, oficio o servicio donde trabajaba. Para codificarla se utilizaron 462 grupos de la National Industrial Classification de 1987. Se establecieron enlaces con la CIIU-Rev.3 a nivel de grupos (3 dígitos).

b) Ocupación: Para determinarla, se pidió a la persona censada que describiera su trabajo; tanto a los trabajadores principales como a los trabajadores marginales se les pidió responder a esta pregunta para determinar el grupo de ocupación. Para codificar la ocupación, se utilizaron 512 familias de ocupación de la National Classificacion of Occupations de 1968. Se establecieron enlaces con la CIUO-68 a nivel de subgrupos (2 dígitos).

c) Situación en el empleo: Para determinarla, se pidió a la persona censada que indicara la clase de trabajadores en que se ubicaba. Para codificar esta variable se utilizaron tres grupos en el caso de la empresa familiar y cuatro en el resto, a saber: empleador, empleado, trabajador individual y trabajador familiar. Según la definición, en la empresa familiar no hay "empleador".

8. Diferencias principales con el censo anterior:
La única diferencia en la recolección de datos fue que en el censo de 1991 la pregunta sobre la búsqueda de trabajo y la

aptitud para trabajar se hizo tan solo al "trabajador desocupado"; en el censo de 1981 se había hecho también a los trabajadores marginales. En el caso de las personas aptas para trabajar que buscaban trabajo, en 1991 se les preguntó por primera vez si ya habían trabajado, a efectos de determinar quienes ingresaban en la fuerza de trabajo.

9. Publicación de los resultados del censo:
La publicación de los cuadros relativos al censo de 1991 estaba prevista en tres etapas, alrededor de 1993, a fines de 1994 y a fines de 1995. Los totales definitivos sobre la población, basados en una compilación manual, debían editarse hacia fines de 1992.

La organización responsable de la publicación de los resultados del censo es la Office of the Registrar General and Census Commissioner, 2-A, Man Singh Road, New Delhi-110 011.

Los resultados finales están disponibles también en disquetes, cintas magnéticas, etc., y pueden solicitarse con arreglo a ciertas condiciones.

INDONESIA

1. Nombre y dirección del organismo responsable del censo:
Central Bureau of Statistics, J1. Dr. Sutomo Nr. 8, P.O. Box 1003, Yakarta 10010.

2. Censos de población llevados a cabo desde 1945 (años):
1961, 1971, 1980 y 1990. La presente descripción se refiere al censo de población de 1990 (realizado el 31 de octubre de ese año).

3. Alcance del censo:
a) Geográfico: Todo el país.

b) Personas comprendidas: Toda la población. Quedaron excluidos de este censo por muestreo todas las personas domiciliadas fuera de la zona de empadronamiento, es decir, los habitantes de la selva (primitivos), los marinos embarcados por más de 6 meses y los no residentes.

4. Periodo de referencia:
La semana anterior al día del censo. A las personas incluidas en la muestra se pidió también que precisaran si habían trabajado o no en el curso del año anterior.

5. Materias principales:
a) Población total, según sexo y edad:	sí
Población económicamente activa por:	
b) Sexo y grupo de edad:	sí
c) Rama de actividad económica:	sí
d) Ocupación:	sí
e) Situación en el empleo:	sí
f) Nivel más alto de educación:	sí
g) Horas de trabajo:	sí
h) Otras características:	sí

Ref. a): La edad se determinó según los años cumplidos en el último cumpleaños.

Ref. g): El tiempo de trabajo se refiere tanto a la jornada laboral habitual de todas las personas ocupadas como a las horas efectivamente trabajadas por éstas en el lugar de trabajo.

Ref. h): El censo también recolectó datos sobre: el número total de horas trabajadas en todos los empleos (es decir, el empleo principal y los adicionales); el tipo de actividad económica realizada en el segundo empleo ocupado durante la semana de referencia; el tipo de actividad económica en la que el encuestado trabajó durante el año anterior; el motivo invocado para no buscar trabajo.

6. Conceptos y definiciones:
a) Población económicamente activa: Abarcó a todas las personas de 10 o más años de edad incluidas en la muestra que, durante la semana de referencia, estaban sea ocupadas, sea desempleadas, conforme a las definiciones que se dan más adelante. No obstante, las preguntas relativas a la actividad económica se hicieron sólo a una muestra de 5 por ciento; se aplicó un método de muestreo aleatorio de niveles múltiples y se usó el hogar como unidad máxima de muestreo. La definición incluyó a los miembros de las fuerzas armadas.

b) Empleo: Se consideró "ocupada" a toda persona incluida en la muestra que, durante la semana de referencia, había desempeñado una actividad laboral remunerada cualquiera, dentro o fuera del hogar, por lo menos durante una hora. Para determinar si una persona debía contabilizarse como ocupada se utilizaron las preguntas "¿Cuál fue su actividad fundamental durante la semana pasada: 1) trabajé; 2) asistí a clases; 3) me ocupé de labores del hogar; 4) otra?", y "Además de las opciones 2), 3) o 4), ¿tuvo una actividad laboral de por lo menos una hora durante la semana pasada?".

Se ha indicado que fueron incluidas las siguientes categorías:

i) personas que trabajan sin remuneración en una empresa o negocio familiar;

ii) personas que producen bienes primarios para el autoconsumo;

iii) personas ocupadas pero temporalmente ausentes de su trabajo;

iv) estudiantes que trabajan a tiempo parcial;

v) trabajadores estacionales u ocasionales;

vi) conscriptos del servicio militar o civil;

vii) personas con más de un empleo;

viii) aprendices y personas que siguen un curso de formación.

Sólo las categorías i), iii), iv) y vii) pueden identificarse por separado.

c) Desempleo: Se consideró "desempleada" a toda persona incluida en la muestra que, durante la semana de referencia, se encontraba sin trabajo y buscaba empleo. A las personas censadas que indicaron no haber trabajado por lo menos una hora se hicieron las preguntas "¿Ha ejercido alguna actividad laboral en su vida?" y "¿Buscó usted trabajo durante la semana pasada?".

7. Clasificaciones utilizadas:
Sólo las personas ocupadas incluidas en la muestra fueron clasificadas por rama de actividad económica, por ocupación y según la situación en el empleo.

a) Rama de actividad económica: Para determinarla se dió la siguiente instrucción: "Sírvase precisar el tipo de producción o de servicios inherentes a la actividad fundamental en que trabajó la semana pasada". Para codificar la rama de actividad se utilizaron 47 grupos de la clasificación nacional. Se establecieron enlaces con la CIIU-Rev.2 a nivel de divisiones (clave de 2 dígitos).

b) Ocupación: Para determinarla se pidió: "Sírvase precisar su ocupación en la actividad fundamental en que trabajó la semana pasada". Para codificar la ocupación se utilizaron 334 grupos de la clasificación nacional. Se establecieron enlaces con la CIUO-68 a nivel de grupos primarios (clave de 3 dígitos).

c) Situación en el empleo: Para determinarla se pidió: "Sírvase precisar cuál fue su situación laboral en la actividad fundamental en que trabajó la semana pasada". Para codificar la situación en el empleo se utilizaron 5 grupos: trabajador independiente; trabajador independiente asistido por miembros de su familia o por mano de obra temporal; empleador; trabajador asalariado; trabajador familiar no remunerado.

8. Diferencias principales con el censo anterior:
No hubo diferencias significativas.

9. Publicación de los resultados del censo:
En octubre de 1991 se publicaron resultados preliminares o provisorios.

Los resultados definitivos del censo se publicaron en 1990, en el volumen que lleva por título "The Results of the 1990 Population Census".

El organismo responsable de esta publicación es el Central Bureau of Statistics, P.O. Box 1003, Yakarta 10010.

Los datos brutos del censo están disponibles también en cintas magnéticas y disquetes.

IRAN, REP. ISLAMICA DEL

1. Nombre y dirección del organismo responsable del censo:
Statistical Centre of Iran, Dr. Fatemi Avenue, Teherán 14144.

2. Censos de población llevados a cabo desde 1945 (años):
1956, 1966, 1976, 1986 y 1991. La presente descripción se re-

fiere al censo de población de 1991 (realizado el 11 de septiembre de ese año).

3. Alcance del censo:

a) Geográfico: Todo el país.

b) Personas comprendidas: Toda la población.

4. Periodo de referencia:
Los siete días anteriores al día del censo.

5. Materias principales:

a) Población total, según sexo y edad: sí

Población económicamente activa por:

b) Sexo y grupo de edad: sí
c) Rama de actividad económica: sí
d) Ocupación: sí
e) Situación en el empleo: sí
f) Nivel más alto de educación: sí
g) Horas de trabajo: no
h) Otras características: sí

Ref. a): La edad se determinó según el año de nacimiento y los años cumplidos en el último cumpleaños.

Ref. h): El censo también acopió información acerca de la duración del desempleo, medida en meses.

6. Conceptos y definiciones:

a) Población económicamente activa: Abarcó a todas las personas de 10 o más años de edad que, durante el período de referencia, estaban sea ocupadas, sea desempleadas, conforme a las definiciones que se dan más adelante. El censo se combinó con una encuesta de hogares hecha sobre una muestra de 10 por ciento; se formularon preguntas acerca de la actividad económica a todas las personas de 10 o más años de edad incluidas en la muestra. La definición incluyó a los miembros de las fuerzas armadas.

b) Empleo: Se consideró "ocupada" a toda persona incluida en la muestra que, durante la semana de referencia, estaba desempeñando alguna actividad laboral remunerada mediante salario, beneficios o ganancias para el grupo familiar, dentro o fuera del hogar. También se incluyó en la definición a las personas que, sin tener un empleo permanente, habían trabajado por lo menos dos días durante el período de referencia.

Se ha indicado que fueron incluidas las siguientes categorías:

i) personas que trabajan sin remuneración en una empresa o negocio familiar;
ii) personas ocupadas pero temporalmente ausentes de su trabajo;
iii) estudiantes que trabajan a tiempo parcial;
iv) trabajadores estacionales u ocasionales, a condición de no estuviesen buscando empleo;
v) reclutas del servicio militar o civil;
vi) aprendices y personas que siguen un curso de formación.

Las categorías i) y iii) pueden identificarse por separado, en función de sus respuestas a determinadas preguntas relativas al empleo y al nivel de formación escolar.

c) Desempleo: Se consideró "desempleada" a toda persona incluida en la muestra que, durante la semana de referencia, no tenía trabajo y estaba buscando empleo.

7. Clasificaciones utilizadas:
Sólo las personas ocupadas incluidas en la muestra fueron clasificadas por rama de actividad económica, por ocupación y según la situación en el empleo.

a) Rama de actividad económica: Para determinar los grupos de actividad económica, se pidió a las personas ocupadas que indicaran la ubicación del lugar de trabajo y la actividad principal realizada allí. Para codificar la rama de actividad se utilizó la CIIU-Rev.3 a nivel de clases (clave de 4 dígitos).

b) Ocupación: Para determinarla, se pidió a las personas censadas que indicaran con precisión el nombre de su ocupación. Para codificar la ocupación, se utilizó la CIUO-68 a nivel de grupos primarios (clave de 3 dígitos).

c) Situación en el empleo: Las personas ocupadas fueron clasificadas con arreglo a las siguientes categorías: empleador; trabajador por cuenta propia; trabajador asalariado del sector público); trabajador asalariado del sector privado; y trabajador familiar no remunerado.

8. Diferencias principales con el censo anterior:
El de 1986 fue un censo completo, de todos los hogares, en el que las preguntas relativas a la población económicamente activa y sus componentes se hicieron a todas las personas de 6 o

más años de edad. En dicho censo no figuraban preguntas sobre la duración del desempleo.

9. Publicación de los resultados del censo:
Los resultados definitivos del censo de población de 1991 se publicaron en 1992, en el volumen que lleva por título "National Results of the 1991 Multi-Round Population Census".

El organismo responsable de esta publicación es el Statistical Centre of Iran, Dr. Fatemi Ave., Teherán 14144.

Además de la versión impresa, los datos pueden obtenerse en disquetes y cintas magnéticas.

IRLANDA

1. Nombre y dirección del organismo responsable del censo:
Central Statistics Office, Ardee Road, Rathmines, Dublin 6, Irlanda.

2. Censos de población llevados a cabo desde 1945 (años):
1946, 1951, 1956, 1961, 1966, 1971, 1979, 1981, 1986 y 1991. El censo de 1979 tuvo por objetivo revisar la delimitación de las circunscripciones electorales. La presente descripción se refiere al censo de 1991 (realizado el 21 de abril de ese año).

3. Alcance del censo:

a) Geográfico: Todo el país.

b) Personas comprendidas: Toda la población (sobre la base de la situación "de facto").

4. Periodo de referencia:
El día del censo. Se tuvo en cuenta la situación en el empleo en el momento del censo, indicada por la propia persona censada.

5. Materias principales:

a) Población total, según sexo y edad: sí

Población económicamente activa por:

b) Sexo y grupo de edad: sí
c) Rama de actividad económica: sí
d) Ocupación: sí
e) Situación en el empleo: sí
f) Nivel más alto de educación: sí
g) Horas de trabajo: no
h) Otras características: no

Ref. a): La mayor parte de los cuadros se basaron en la edad que la persona censada tenía en su último cumpleaños, pero también se prepararon algunos cuadros basándose en el año de nacimiento.

6. Conceptos y definiciones:

a) Población económicamente activa: Abarca a todas las personas de 15 o más años de edad que, en la fecha del censo, tenían un empleo o estaban desempleadas, según las definiciones que se dan más adelante. Esta definición incluye a los militares de carrera.

b) Empleo: Se consideró "ocupada" a toda persona que, a su juicio, lo estaba el día del censo. Se incluyó, en principio, a todas las personas que, en la fecha del censo, efectuaban cualquier trabajo con valor económico dentro o fuera del hogar. La definición no incluyó a los estudiantes que trabajaban a tiempo parcial.

Se ha indicado que quedan incluidas las siguientes categorías:

i) personas que trabajan sin remuneración en una empresa o negocio familiar;
ii) personas que producen bienes primarios para el autoconsumo;
iii) personas ocupadas pero temporalmente ausentes de su trabajo;
iv) trabajadores estacionales u ocasionales;
v) aprendices y personas que siguen un curso de formación.

Sólo la categoría i) puede identificarse por separado. La inclusión de los estudiantes que trabajaban a tiempo parcial dependió de la manera en qué describieron la situación que tenían en la ocupación en el momento del censo.

c) Desempleo: Se consideró "desempleada" a toda persona que, a su juicio, estaba desocupada el día del censo.

7. Clasificaciones utilizadas:

Tanto las personas ocupadas como las personas desempleadas anteriormente empleadas han sido clasificadas por rama de actividad económica, por ocupación y según la situación en el empleo.

a) Rama de actividad económica: Para determinarla se preguntó: "a) el nombre y la actividad del empleador (por lo que se refiere a las personas ocupadas, se les pidió que indicaran el nombre del empleador y la naturaleza de su actividad, si eran asalariadas, o la naturaleza de su negocio, si eran independientes. En cuanto a los desempleados, se les pidió que indicaran el nombre y la naturaleza de la actividad del último empleador); b) la dirección del lugar de trabajo (se pidió la dirección completa y exacta del lugar de trabajo efectivo: a quienes trabajaban en un centro o depósito fijo, la dirección de éste; a quienes trabajaban a domicilio, como, por ejemplo, los agricultores o los tenderos con domicilio en las propias instalaciones, se les pidió responder 'En casa'. Las personas sin lugar de trabajo fijo, por ejemplo, los viajantes de comercio, debían responder 'Sin dirección')".

Cada vez que los datos sobre el empleador y la dirección del lugar de trabajo han resultado suficientes, se han establecido enlaces entre las inscripciones del censo y el registro comercial del que proceden los códigos sobre la actividad y el lugar de trabajo. En los otros casos, la actividad y el lugar de trabajo se han codificado directamente, sin tener en cuenta el registro comercial.

Los enlaces con la clasificación CIIU (tanto CIIU-Rev.2 como CIIU-Rev.3) se han establecido a nivel de divisiones (clave de 2 dígitos).

b) Ocupación: Para determinarla se pidió a las personas que trabajaban que indicasen su principal ocupación habitual y la describiesen en detalle; a los desempleados o jubilados se les pidió describir la principal ocupación que habían tenido antes; a las personas designadas como agricultores o trabajadores agrícolas se les pidió que señalasen la superficie del terreno que trabajaban entonces o que habían trabajado anteriormente.

Para codificar la ocupación, se utilizó un sistema nacional de codificación que comprende 8.700 títulos repartidos en 210 grupos de códigos y que determina con exactitud la denominación de los trabajos. Los enlaces con las clasificaciones CIUO-68 y CIUO-88 se han establecido a nivel de subgrupos y de grupos primarios, respectivamente.

c) Situación en el empleo: Se pidió a las personas censadas que precisaran cuál era su situación en el empleo en el momento del censo o antes de éste. Para codificar la situación en el empleo, se utilizaron cuatro grupos, a saber: independiente, con empleados remunerados; independientes sin empleados remunerados; asalariados; familiares que prestan ayuda (sin percibir un salario o remuneración fijos).

8. Diferencias principales con el censo anterior:

Las principales diferencias de codificación son:
- "la rama de actividad económica" se ha codificado estableciendo enlaces con un registro comercial, y cuando ello ha sido posible se ha codificado también el lugar de trabajo;
- "la ocupación" se ha codificado en un nivel más detallado que en censos anteriores, lo que ha permitido presentar los resultados según la clasificación SOC del Reino Unido y de conformidad con CIUO-88, así como con las clasificaciones nacionales vigentes.

9. Publicación de los resultados del censo:

Los datos sobre la población total y económicamente activa aparecieron en 1994 en diversas publicaciones, tales como "Local Population Reports (second series)", y en volúmenes detallados y organizados por materia.

La organización responsable de estas publicaciones es la Central Statistics Office, de Dublín.

Los resultados del censo de 1991 se presentan también en cuadros especiales, los que están a disposición de quienes lo soliciten. Las estadísticas de población correspondientes a subdivisiones territoriales están disponibles en ediciones impresas, cintas magnéticas y disquetes.

ISLA DE MAN

1. Nombre y dirección del organismo responsable del censo:

Economic Affairs Division, Isle of Man Government, Illiam Dhone House, 2 Circular Road, Douglas, Isle of Man IMI 1PQ, British Isles.

2. Censos de población llevados a cabo desde 1945 (años):

1951, 1961, 1966, 1971, 1976, 1981, 1986 y 1991. La presente descripción se refiere al censo de población de 1991 (realizado el 14 de abril de ese año).

3. Alcance del censo:

a) Geográfico: Todo el país.

b) Personas comprendidas: Toda la población, de todas las edades.

4. Período de referencia:

La semana anterior al día del censo, y cinco meses del año anterior (1 de mayo al 30 de septiembre de 1990) únicamente en lo que atañe al trabajo estacional.

5. Materias principales:

a) Población total, según sexo y edad:	sí
Población económicamente activa por:	
b) Sexo y grupo de edad:	sí
c) Rama de actividad económica:	sí
d) Ocupación:	sí
e) Situación en el empleo:	sí
f) Nivel más alto de educación:	no
g) Horas de trabajo:	sí
h) Otras características:	sí

Ref. a): La edad de la persona censada se definió en función de su último cumpleaños.

Ref. g): A las personas ocupadas se les pidió que indicaran las horas efectivamente trabajadas; a los trabajadores estacionales, el número de semanas y el número de horas semanales trabajadas durante el período de referencia largo.

Ref. h): También se recolectó información sobre los permisos de trabajo ("¿Tienen estas personas un permiso de trabajo vigente?") y sobre los medios de transporte utilizados para trasladarse al trabajo.

6. Conceptos y definiciones:

a) Población económicamente activa: Abarca a todas las personas de 16 o más años de edad que, durante el período de referencia, tenían un empleo o estaban desempleadas, según las definiciones que se dan más adelante. Esta definición no incluye a los estudiantes que trabajaban a tiempo parcial ni a los que buscaban trabajo. En cambio, en ella se incluye a todos los miembros de las fuerzas armadas; no hay conscriptos en la Isla de Man.

b) Empleo: Se consideró como "ocupadas" a todas las personas que indicaron que durante la semana de referencia trabajaban sea a tiempo completo (más de 30 horas), sea a tiempo parcial (30 horas o menos), para un empleador o en forma independiente. Se consideró como ocupados a tiempo completo a los maestros y profesores que dijeron trabajar 25 horas o más.

Se ha indicado que quedan incluidas las siguientes categorías:

i) personas ocupadas pero temporalmente ausentes de su trabajo;
ii) trabajadores estacionales u ocasionales;
iii) trabajadores con más de un empleo;
iv) aprendices y personas que siguen un curso de formación.

Sólo las categorías ii) y iii) pueden identificarse por separado.

c) Desempleo: Se consideró "desempleada" a toda persona que indicó haber estado sin trabajo y buscando uno durante la semana de referencia.

7. Clasificaciones utilizadas:

Sólo las personas ocupadas han sido clasificadas por rama de actividad económica, por ocupación y según la situación en el empleo.

a) Rama de actividad económica: Para determinarla se preguntó el nombre y la actividad del empleador o la actividad del trabajador independiente, por ejemplo, "presta servicios de aseo de oficinas", "fabrica alimento para animales", "instala sistemas de calefacción central", o "presta servicios jurídicos especializados" Para codificar la rama de actividad económica, se utilizaron 21 grupos de la clasificación nacional. No se han establecido enlaces con la clasificación CIIU.

b) Ocupación: Para determinarla se preguntó cuál era la ocupación de la persona censada, por ejemplo, gasista, empleado de contabilidad, supervisor bancario o empleado de oficina. Se pidió a las personas censadas que describieran el trabajo ejecutado, por ejemplo, mecanografía a partir de dictado en cinta, gestión de cuentas de clientes particulares, reparación de maquinaria agrícola, o reparto de mercancías a los clientes. Para codificar la ocupación, se utilizaron 371 grupos de la clasificación SOC (Clasificación Normalizada de Ocupaciones del Reino Unido). Los enlaces con la clasificación CIUO-88 se han establecido a nivel de subgrupos (clave de 3 dígitos).

c) Situación en el empleo: Para codificar esta variable se utilizaron tres grupos, a saber: asalariado; independiente con empleados; independiente sin empleados.

8. Diferencias principales con el censo anterior:
En el censo de 1986 no se recolectaron datos sobre la actividad económica.

En 1981, el límite de edad mínimo era de 15 años (en 1981, la edad mínima para dejar la enseñanza escolar era de 15 años. En 1991, la edad mínima se elevó a 16 años, lo que explica la modificación del alcance del censo).

9. Publicación de los resultados del censo:
Los datos definitivos del censo en lo que atañe a la población económicamente activa y a las partes que la componen figuraron en una publicación titulada "Isle of Man Census Report 1991". El volumen I de este informe se publicó en marzo de 1991, y el volumen II, en febrero de 1992. Otros datos se incluyeron en "Isle of Man Labour Statistics 1995".

La organización responsable de esta publicación es la Economic Affairs Division, Illiam Dhone House, 2 Circular Road, Douglas, Isle of Man IMI IPQ, British Isles.

Los resultados del censo también están disponibles en cuadros no publicados y disquetes, que se suministran a reserva de confidencialidad.

ISLAS CAIMAN

1. Nombre y dirección del organismo responsable del censo:
Statistics Office, Cayman Islands Government, Government Administration Building, George Town, Grand Cayman, B.W.I.

2. Censos de población llevados a cabo desde 1945 (años):
1960, 1970, 1979 y 1989. La presente descripción se refiere al censo de población de 1989 (realizado el 15 de octubre de ese año).

3. Alcance del censo:
a) Geográfico: Todo el país.

b) Personas comprendidas: Toda la población.

4. Periodo de referencia:
La semana anterior al día del censo.

5. Materias principales:
a) Población total, según sexo y edad: sí
Población económicamente activa por:
b) Sexo y grupo de edad: sí
c) Rama de actividad económica: sí
d) Ocupación: sí
e) Situación en el empleo: sí
f) Nivel más alto de educación: sí
g) Horas de trabajo: sí
h) Otras características: sí

Ref. a): La edad se determinó según los años cumplidos en el último cumpleaños.

Ref. g): Se pidió a las personas ocupadas que precisaran el número de horas que trabajaban habitualmente en su empleo principal.

Ref. h): El censo también recopiló información sobre el ingreso semanal obtenido en el empleo principal y sobre los medios de transporte utilizados para trasladarse al lugar de trabajo.

6. Conceptos y definiciones:
a) Población económicamente activa: Abarcó a todas las personas de 15 o más años de edad que, durante la semana de referencia, estaban ocupadas o desempleadas, conforme a las definiciones que se dan más adelante. La definición incluyó a todos los miembros de las fuerzas armadas.

b) Empleo: Se consideró "ocupada" a toda persona que, durante el período de referencia, trabajó por lo menos una hora. Para determinar si una persona debía ser contabilizada como "ocupada" se usó la pregunta "¿Tuvo la persona encuestada un empleo durante toda o parte de la semana pasada?".

Se ha indicado que fueron incluidas las siguientes categorías:
i)   personas que trabajan sin remuneración en una empresa o negocio familiar;
ii)   personas ocupadas pero temporalmente ausentes de su trabajo;
iii)   estudiantes que trabajan a tiempo parcial;
iv)   trabajadores estacionales u ocasionales;
v)   trabajadores con más de un empleo;
vi)   aprendices y personas que siguen un curso de formación.

Sólo las categorías i), iii) y v) pueden identificarse por separado.

c) Desempleo: Se consideró "desempleada" a toda persona que, durante la semana de referencia, no tenía trabajo, buscaba empleo y estaba disponible para trabajar.

7. Clasificaciones utilizadas:
Tanto las personas ocupadas como las desocupadas anteriormente ocupadas se clasificaron por rama de actividad económica, por ocupación y según la situación en la ocupación.

a) Rama de actividad económica: Para determinarla se preguntó: "Sírvase indicar el principal empleador de la persona encuestada (o del último empleador a tiempo completo) y describa claramente qué servicios presta o qué productos fabrica el empleador, por ejemplo, finanzas, hoteles, comercio de detalle, construcción, etc." Para codificar la rama de actividad, se utilizaron 65 grupos de la clasificación nacional. Se establecieron enlaces con la CIIU-Rev.3 a nivel de divisiones (clave de 2 dígitos).

b) Ocupación: Para determinarla se preguntó: "¿Cuál es la ocupación de la persona encuestada (es decir, aquella a la que dedica la mayor parte de su tiempo, o el último empleo a tiempo completo)?, por ejemplo, abogado, empleado bancario, empleado público, electricista, fontanero, etc." Para codificar la ocupación se utilizaron 94 grupos de la clasificación nacional. Se establecieron enlaces con la CIUO-88 a nivel de subgrupos (clave de 3 dígitos).

c) Situación en el empleo: Para codificar esta variable se utilizaron cuatro grupos: trabajador independiente, sin empleados; trabajador independiente con empleados; asalariado a tiempo completo o a tiempo parcial; trabajador no remunerado en una empresa o negocio familiar.

8. Diferencias principales con el censo anterior:
No hubo diferencias significativas.

9. Publicación de los resultados del censo:
Los datos definitivos del censo aparecieron en septiembre de 1990, en la publicación que lleva por título "Cayman Islands 1989 Census - Commentary and tabulations of results, volume I".

El organismo responsable de esta publicación es la Economics and Statistics Office, Government Administration Building, George Town, Grand Cayman, B.W.I.

Los resultados del censo están disponibles también en cuadros inéditos.

ISLAS COOK

1. Nombre y dirección del organismo responsable del censo:
Statistics Office, P.O. Box 125, Rarotonga.

2. Censos de población llevados a cabo desde 1945 (años):
1945, 1956, 1961, 1966, 1971, 1976, 1981, 1986 y 1991. La presente descripción se refiere al censo de población de 1991 (realizado el 1 de diciembre de ese año).

3. Alcance del censo:

a) Geográfico: Todo el territorio.

b) Personas comprendidas: Toda la población.

4. Período de referencia:
El mes anterior al censo.

5. Materias principales:

a) Población total, según sexo y edad:	sí
Población económicamente activa por:	
b) Sexo y grupo de edad:	sí
c) Rama de actividad económica:	sí
d) Ocupación:	sí
e) Situación en el empleo:	sí
f) Nivel más alto de educación:	sí
g) Horas de trabajo:	sí
h) Otras características:	no

Ref. a): La edad se determinó según los años cumplidos en el último cumpleaños.

Ref. g): El tiempo de trabajo se refiere al número total de horas efectivamente trabajadas por las personas ocupadas durante la semana anterior al censo (si este dato no era conocido, al número de horas habitualmente trabajadas por semana).

6. Conceptos y definiciones:

a) Población económicamente activa: Abarcó a todas las personas de 15 o más años de edad que, durante el mes de referencia, estaban ocupadas o desempleadas, conforme a las definiciones que se dan más adelante. La definición incluyó también a los trabajadores temporeros a contrata, de distinto origen étnico. Las Islas Cook no tienen fuerzas armadas.

b) Empleo: Para determinarlo se hizo la siguiente pregunta: "Indique su actividad profesional: 1) empleador, dueño de empresa o plantación; 2) actividad por cuenta propia/independiente sin empleados; 3) trabajador asalariado a tiempo completo; 4) trabajador asalariado, a tiempo parcial u ocasional; 5) desempleado en busca de trabajo; 6) trabajador familiar no remunerado, ocupado en una plantación, almacén u otra empresa o negocio, cuya producción está destinada al propio consumo o al de su hogar; 7) jubilado; 8) estudiante a tiempo completo que no ejerce una actividad remunerada; 9) incapacitado para trabajar; 10) labores del hogar". Se contabilizó como "ocupadas" a las personas que indicaron las respuestas 1), 2), 3), 4) o 6).

Se ha indicado que fueron incluidas las siguientes categorías:

i) personas que trabajan sin remuneración en una empresa o negocio familiar;
ii) personas que producen bienes primarios para el autoconsumo;
iii) personas ocupadas pero temporalmente ausentes de su trabajo;
iv) estudiantes que trabajan a tiempo parcial;
v) trabajadores estacionales u ocasionales;
vi) aprendices y personas que siguen un curso de formación.

Sólo las categorías i) y ii) pueden identificarse por separado con arreglo a su actividad profesional.

c) Desempleo: Se consideró "desempleada" a toda persona que, durante el período de referencia, se encontraba sin trabajo y buscaba empleo. La definición incluyó tanto a las personas desempleadas que habían trabajado anteriormente como a aquellas sin experiencia laboral.

7. Clasificaciones utilizadas:
Sólo las personas ocupadas fueron clasificadas por rama de actividad económica, por ocupación y según la situación en el empleo.

a) Rama de actividad económica: Para determinar el grupo de actividades económicas, se pidió a las personas ocupadas que, tanto en relación a su ocupación principal como a su ocupación secundaria, indicasen el nombre del empleador, la empresa, el servicio estatal, el establecimiento comercial o la persona para la que trabajaban, el tipo de empresa o actividad en la que estaban ocupadas, por ejemplo, agricultura, pesca, comercio de detalle, etc., y el número de horas trabajadas en la semana anterior, o, en caso de no haber trabajado, el número de horas semanales que trabajaban habitualmente. Para codificar la rama de actividad económica, se utilizó la CIIU-Rev.2 a nivel de grupos (clave de 4 dígitos); no obstante, sólo se previó la publicación de los datos en el nivel de grandes divisiones (1 dígito).

b) Ocupación: Para determinarla, se pidió a las personas ocupadas que, tanto en relación a su ocupación principal como a su ocupación secundaria, indicasen cuál era su función respec-

tiva en el lugar de trabajo durante el período de referencia, por ejemplo, cultivador de cítricos, mano de obra en desembarcadero, empleado contable, etc. Para codificar la ocupación se utilizó la CIUO-88 en el nivel de grupos primarios (clave de 4 dígitos), pero sólo se previó la publicación de los datos en el nivel de grandes grupos (1 dígito).

c) Situación en el empleo: Para determinarla, se utilizó la misma pregunta a que se refiere el párrafo 6 b). Para codificar la situación en el empleo se utilizaron seis grupos: empleador, dueño de empresa o de plantación; trabajador en actividad por cuenta propia o independiente, sin empleados; trabajador asalariado a tiempo completo; trabajador asalariado, a tiempo parcial u ocasional; trabajador familiar no remunerado, ocupado en una plantación, almacén u otra empresa o negocio, cuya producción está destinada al propio consumo o al de su hogar (las "labores domésticas" abarcan la pesca y la agricultura de autoconsumo); otra actividad.

8. Diferencias principales con el censo anterior:
No hubo diferencias significativas.

9. Publicación de los resultados del censo:
Al igual que el censo de 1986, los resultados del censo de 1991 se divulgaron en una serie de publicaciones aparecidas entre 1992 y 1993 bajo el título genérico de "Cook Islands Census of population and dwellings 1991". Los interesados en obtenerlas pueden cursar pedido a la Statistics Office de Rarotonga.

El organismo responsable de la publicación de los resultados del censo es el Statistics Office, P.O. Box 125, Rarotonga.

No se dispone de los resultados en otros soportes.

ISLAS MARIANAS DEL NORTE

1. Nombre y dirección del organismo responsable del censo:
Central Statistics Division, Capitol Hill, Saipan, MP 96950, junto con el US Bureau of the Census.

2. Censos de población llevados a cabo desde 1945 (años):
1958, 1967, 1973, 1980 y 1990. La presente descripción se refiere al censo de población de 1990 (realizado el 1 de abril de ese año).

3. Alcance del censo:

a) Geográfico: Todo el territorio.

b) Personas comprendidas: En el censo de 1990, el empadronamiento se hizo en el "lugar de residencia habitual" de los encuestados, es decir, en el lugar en que estos vivían y pernoctaban la mayor parte del tiempo.

4. Período de referencia:
Dos períodos: la semana anterior al censo y el año anterior al año del mismo.

5. Materias principales:

a) Población total, según sexo y edad:	sí
Población económicamente activa por:	
b) Sexo y grupo de edad:	sí
c) Rama de actividad económica:	sí
d) Ocupación:	sí
e) Situación en el empleo:	sí
f) Nivel más alto de educación:	sí
g) Horas de trabajo:	sí
h) Otras características:	sí

Ref. a): La edad se determinó tanto en función del año de nacimiento como de los años cumplidos en el último cumpleaños.

Ref. g): Se pidió a las personas ocupadas que precisaran el número de horas trabajadas durante la semana de referencia, así como, por lo que se refería a 1989, el número de semanas trabajadas y el horario de trabajo habitual.

Ref. h): El censo también recopiló información sobre los medios de transporte utilizados para trasladarse al lugar de trabajo y el tiempo necesario para hacerlo, así como sobre los ingresos totales percibidos en 1989.

6. Conceptos y definiciones:

a) Población económicamente activa: Abarcó a todas las personas de 15 o más años de edad que, durante los períodos de referencia, estaban sea ocupadas, sea desempleadas, conforme a las definiciones que se dan más adelante. La definición no incluyó a los miembros de las fuerzas armadas.

b) Empleo: Se consideró ocupada a toda persona que, durante la semana de referencia, desempeñó alguna actividad remunerada, sea como asalariada, sea en su propia empresa o negocio; que trabajó, remunerada o no, en una empresa o explotación agrícola comercial de un familiar o pariente, o que trabajó a tiempo parcial (por ejemplo, una o dos horas). Para determinar si una persona debía ser contabilizada o no como "ocupada" se preguntó: "¿Trabajó usted durante toda o parte de la semana pasada, sea a tiempo completo, sea a tiempo parcial?".

Se ha indicado que fueron incluidas las siguientes categorías:

i) personas que trabajan sin remuneración en una empresa o negocio familiar;

ii) personas que producen bienes primarios para el autoconsumo;

iii) personas empleadas y temporalmente ausentes del trabajo;

iv) estudiantes que trabajan a tiempo parcial;

v) trabajadores estacionales u ocasionales;

vi) aprendices y personas que siguen un curso de formación.

Todas estas categorías pueden identificarse por separado.

c) Desempleo: Se consideró "desempleada" a toda persona que respondió afirmativamente a las dos preguntas siguientes: "¿Ha buscado usted trabajo remunerado durante las pasadas 4 semanas?", y "¿Hubiera podido usted aceptar un empleo la semana pasada, de habérsele ofrecido uno?".

7. Clasificaciones utilizadas:

Tanto las personas ocupadas como las desocupadas anteriormente ocupadas se clasificaron por rama de actividad económica, por ocupación y según la situación en la ocupación.

a) Rama de actividad económica: Para determinarla se preguntó: "¿Para quén trabajó usted?", "¿En qué tipo de empresa, industria o establecimiento trabajó, por ejemplo, hospital, envasadora de pescado, panadería artesanal, etc.?", y "¿Se trata principalmente de manufactura, comercio al por mayor, comercio de detalle o de otro sector (agricultura, construcción, servicios, sector estatal, etc.)?". Para codificar la rama de actividad se utilizó la Clasificación Normalizada de Actividades Económicas (SIC) de los Estados Unidos, de 1987. No se establecieron enlaces con la CIIU.

b) Ocupación: Para determinarla se preguntó: "¿Qué tipo de trabajo desempeñaba usted (por ejemplo, enfermería de nivel de diploma, manutención de máquinaria industrial, mecánica, repostería, etc.)" y "¿Cuáles eran sus actividades o tareas más importantes (por ejemplo, cuidado de pacientes, reparación de máquinas en una fábrica, decoración de tartas y pasteles, etc.)?". Para codificar la ocupación se utilizó el Manual de Clasificación Normalizada de Ocupaciones (SOC) de los Estados Unidos. La codificación de los datos acopiados en el censo de 1990 estuvo a cargo del Bureau of Census de los Estados Unidos, que utilizó a tal efecto el SOC de 1980. No se establecieron enlaces con la CIUO. Los datos no se adaptaron a la clasificación de ocupaciones de 1990.

c) Situación en el empleo: Para determinarla se preguntó: "¿Trabajaba usted en calidad de: empleado de una compañía o empresa privada, o de una persona, remunerado con un sueldo, un salario o comisiones; empleado de un organismo privado sin fines lucrativos, exento de impuestos o caritativo; empleado del Gobierno local o territorial (del territorio, de la mancomunidad, etc.); empleado del Gobierno federal; trabajador independiente en empresa propia, en el ejercicio de una profesión liberal o en una explotación agrícola no constituidas en sociedad; trabajador independiente en empresa propia, en el ejercicio de una profesión liberal o en una explotación agrícola constituidas en sociedad; trabajador no remunerado en empresa, negocio o explotación agrícola familiar?". Para codificar la situación en el empleo se utilizaron los 7 grupos indicados.

8. Diferencias principales con el censo anterior:

No hubo diferencias significativas.

9. Publicación de los resultados del censo:

Los resultados definitivos del censo se publicaron en marzo de 1992, en el volumen que lleva por título "1990 Census of Population and Housing: Social, Economic, and Housing Characteristics, Commonwealth of the Mariana Islands".

Los organismos responsables de esta publicación son: el Department of Commerce de los Estados Unidos, el Bureau of the Census, Washington, D.C. 20233, y el Superintendent of Documents, U.S. Government Printing Office, Washington, D.C. 20402.

Los resultados del censo están disponibles también en disquetes y cintas magnéticas.

ISLAS VIRGENES BRITANICAS

1. Nombre y dirección del organismo responsable del censo:

Development Planning Unit, B.V.Is. Government, Central Administration Complex, Road Town, Tortola.

2. Censos de población llevados a cabo desde 1945 (años):

1960, 1970, 1980 y 1991. La presente descripción se refiere al censo de población de 1991 (realizado el 12 de mayo de ese año).

3. Alcance del censo:

a) Geográfico: Todo el país.

b) Personas comprendidas: Toda la población.

4. Periodo de referencia:

Dos períodos: la semana y el año anteriores al día del censo.

5. Materias principales:

a) Población total, según sexo y edad:	sí
Población económicamente activa por:	
b) Sexo y grupo de edad:	sí
c) Rama de actividad económica:	sí
d) Ocupación:	sí
e) Situación en el empleo:	sí
f) Nivel más alto de educación:	...
g) Horas de trabajo:	sí
h) Otras características:	sí

Ref. a): La edad se determinó según el año de nacimiento y los años cumplidos en el último cumpleaños.

Ref. g): Se pidió a las personas ocupadas que indicaran el número de horas efectivamente trabajadas durante la semana de referencia y el número de meses trabajados durante el año de referencia.

Ref. h): El censo también recopiló información sobre la periodicidad de las remuneraciones (semanal, mensual, etc.), sobre los ingresos percibidos por período, sobre las actividades ambulantes (comercio en el sector informal) y sobre los medios de transporte utilizados para trasladarse al lugar de trabajo.

6. Conceptos y definiciones:

a) Población económicamente activa: Abarcó a todas las personas de 15 o más años de edad que, durante los períodos de referencia, estaban sea ocupadas, sea desempleadas, conforme a las definiciones que se dan más adelante. La definición incluyó a todos los miembros de las fuerzas armadas.

b) Empleo: Se consideró "ocupada" a toda persona que, durante los períodos de referencia, sea trabajó, sea tenía un empleo pero no trabajó. Para determinar si una persona debía ser contabilizada o no como "ocupada" se preguntó: "¿Trabajó usted durante el período de referencia o, aunque tenía un empleo, no trabajó?". La definición no incluyó a los estudiantes que trabajaban a tiempo parcial.

Se ha indicado que fueron incluidas las siguientes categorías:

i) personas que trabajan sin remuneración en una empresa o negocio familiar;

ii) personas que producen bienes primarios para el autoconsumo;

iii) personas ocupadas pero temporalmente ausentes de su trabajo;

iv) trabajadores estacionales u ocasionales;

v) aprendices y personas que siguen un curso de formación.

Ninguna de estas categorías puede identificarse por separado.

c) Desempleo: Se consideró "desempleada" a toda persona que indicó que había buscado trabajo durante los períodos de referencia, o que quería trabajar y estaba disponible para hacerlo.

7. Clasificaciones utilizadas:

Tanto las personas ocupadas como las desocupadas anteriormente ocupadas se clasificaron por rama de actividad económica, por ocupación y según la situación en la ocupación.

a) **Rama de actividad económica:** Para determinarla se preguntó: "¿Qué tipo de actividad se lleva o se llevaba a cabo en su lugar de trabajo?". Para codificar la rama de actividad se utilizó la CIIU-Rev.3 a nivel de clases (clave de 4 dígitos).

b) **Ocupación:** Para determinarla se preguntó: "¿Qué tipo de trabajo desempeña o desempeñaba en su ocupación principal?". Para codificar la ocupación se utilizó la CIUO-88, en el nivel de grupos primarios (clave de 4 dígitos).

c) **Situación en el empleo:** Para determinarla se preguntó: "¿Se ocupó usted de su propia empresa o negocio, como trabajador asalariado o como trabajador familiar no remunerado?". Para codificar la situación en el empleo se utilizaron 5 grupos: trabajador remunerado del sector estatal; trabajador remunerado del sector privado; trabajador no remunerado; empresario con personal remunerado (empleador); empresario sin personal remunerado (trabajador por cuenta propia).

8. Diferencias principales con el censo anterior:
No hubo diferencias significativas.

9. Publicación de los resultados del censo:
Los resultados definitivos del censo se publicaron en 1992, en el volumen que lleva por título "British Virgin Islands, 1991 Population and Housing Census".

El organismo responsable de esta publicación es la Development Planning Unit, Central Administration Complex, Road Town, Tortola.

Los resultados están también disponibles en disquetes.

ISLAS VIRGENES (EE.UU)

1. Nombre y dirección del organismo responsable del censo:
Eastern Caribbean Center, University of the Virgin Islands, St. Thomas Campus, St. Thomas, U.S. Virgin Islands 00802.

2. Censos de población llevados a cabo desde 1945 (años):
1950, 1960, 1970, 1980 y 1990. La presente descripción se refiere al censo de 1990 (realizado el 1 de abril de ese año).

3. Alcance del censo:
a) **Geográfico:** Toda la zona.
b) **Personas comprendidas:** Toda la población, de todas las edades.

4. Período de referencia:
La semana anterior al día del censo y el año anterior al año del censo.

5. Materias principales:
a) Población total, según sexo y edad:	sí
Población económicamente activa por:	
b) Sexo y grupo de edad:	sí
c) Rama de actividad económica:	sí
d) Ocupación:	sí
e) Situación en el empleo:	sí
f) Nivel más alto de educación:	sí
g) Horas de trabajo:	sí
h) Otras características:	sí

Ref. a): La clasificación según la edad se basó en los años cumplidos por la persona censada a la fecha del censo.

Ref. g): Al considerarse el período de referencia corto, las horas de trabajo se referían tanto a las horas habitualmente trabajadas por las personas ocupadas como a las horas que trabajaron efectivamente. Al considerarse el período de referencia largo, se pidió a las personas ocupadas que precisaran el período total trabajado durante todo el año 1989, expresado en meses, semanas, días y horas.

Ref. h): Al considerarse el período de referencia corto, el censo recogió datos sobre los medios de transporte y el tiempo utilizados para trasladarse al trabajo. Al considerarse el período de referencia largo, se recabó información sobre el ingreso total de las personas y sus fuentes de ingresos durante 1989.

6. Conceptos y definiciones:
a) **Población económicamente activa:** Abarca a todas las personas de 16 o más años de edad que, durante la semana de referencia, tenían un empleo o estaban desempleadas, según las definiciones que se dan más adelante. Esta definición incluye a los miembros de las fuerzas armadas. En cambio, que-

dan excluidos de la definición los estudiantes que tenían un empleo a tiempo parcial o los que buscaban trabajo.

b) **Empleo:** Para determinar si cabía considerar a una persona como "ocupada" se preguntó sobre todo si había trabajado en algún momento de la semana anterior al censo, sea a tiempo completo, sea a tiempo parcial.

Se ha indicado que quedan incluidas las siguientes categorías:
i) personas que trabajan sin remuneración en una empresa o negocio familiar;
ii) personas ocupadas pero temporalmente ausentes de su trabajo;
iii) trabajadores estacionales u ocasionales;
iv) conscriptos del servicio militar o civil;
v) trabajadores con más de un empleo.

Todas las categorías que se acaban de indicar pueden identificarse por separado en función de preguntas específicas.

c) **Desempleo:** Se consideró como "desempleada" a toda persona que, durante la semana de referencia, carecía de trabajo y buscaba empleo. Para determinar si cabía considerar a una persona como desempleada, se preguntó también si se encontraba inactiva la semana anterior al censo, por cesación de su empleo o de su negocio; si había estado buscando trabajo durante las últimas cuatro semanas; y si hubiera podido emplearse la semana anterior, de haber tenido una oferta.

7. Clasificaciones utilizadas:
Tanto las personas ocupadas como los desempleados anteriormente empleados han sido clasificados por rama de actividad económica, por ocupación y según la situación en el empleo. Las preguntas hechas se relacionaban con el trabajo ocupado la semana anterior al censo (a las personas que tenían más de un empleo se les pidió que describieran aquél al que dedicaban el mayor número de horas de trabajo; las que no habían trabajado en dicha semana debían referirse al trabajo o el negocio más reciente que habían tenido desde 1985).

a) **Rama de actividad económica:** Para determinarla se preguntó para quién y en qué tipo de empresa o rama económica había trabajado la persona censada, y si se trataba principalmente de una industria manufacturera, de comercio al por mayor, de comercio de detalle, o de otra actividad (agricultura, construcción, servicios, empresa estatal, etc.). Para codificar la rama de actividad económica, se utilizaron siete grupos de la clasificación nacional. No se han establecido enlaces con la clasificación CIIU.

b) **Ocupación:** Para determinarla se preguntó qué clase de trabajo efectuaba la persona censada y cuáles eran sus actividades o funciones más importantes. Para codificar la ocupación, se utilizaron 39 grupos de la clasificación nacional. No se han establecido enlaces con la clasificación CIUO.

c) **Situación en el empleo:** Para determinarla se preguntó si la persona censada trabajaba para una empresa o negocio privado o para un particular cuyas actividades tenían fines de lucro, mediando un salario o una comisión; si estaba empleada por una organización privada de beneficencia o sin fines lucrativos, exenta de impuestos; si era empleado público local (del territorio, etc.) o empleado público federal; si era independiente, con un negocio, actividad profesional o explotación agrícola no constituidos en sociedad; si era independiente, con un negocio, actividad profesional o explotación agrícola constituidos en sociedad; o si trabajaba sin remuneración en un negocio o explotación agrícola familiar. Para codificar la situación en el empleo, se utilizaron los siete grupos que se acaban de indicar.

8. Diferencias principales con el censo anterior:
No hubo diferencias significativas.

9. Publicación de los resultados del censo:
Los documentos en que figuran los resultados definitivos del censo se titulan "STF-3 Summary Tape, File 3" (disponible en disquetes, cinta magnética y CD-ROM) y "CPH-5-55, Summary Social, Economic and Housing Characteristics" (impreso), 1992.

La organización responsable de estos documentos es el Bureau of the Census, Data User Services Division, Customer Services, Washington, D.C. 20233.

Los resultados del censo también están disponibles en CD-ROM, cinta magnética, disquetes y documentos impresos.

ITALIA

1. Nombre y dirección del organismo responsable del censo:
Istituto Nazionale di Statistica (ISTAT), Via Adolfo Ravà 150, 00142 Roma.

2. Censos de población llevados a cabo desde 1945 (años):
1951, 1961, 1971, 1981 y 1991. La presente descripción se refiere al censo de 1991 (realizado el 20 de octubre de ese año).

3. Alcance del censo:
a) Geográfico: Todo el territorio.

b) Personas comprendidas: Toda la población, con la excepción de los nacionales residentes en el extranjero, de los extranjeros con pasaporte diplomático y del personal militar de la OTAN.

4. Periodo de referencia:
La semana anterior al día del censo.

5. Materias principales:
a) Población total, según sexo y edad: sí
Población económicamente activa por:
b) Sexo y grupo de edad: sí
c) Rama de actividad económica: sí
d) Ocupación: sí
e) Situación en el empleo: sí
f) Nivel más alto de educación: sí
g) Horas de trabajo: sí
h) Otras características: sí

Ref. a): La edad se determinó según los años cumplidos en el último cumpleaños.

Ref. g): Por horas de trabajo se entendió el número de horas efectivamente trabajadas en el empleo por las personas ocupadas.

Ref. h): Se recolectaron otras informaciones, en particular sobre: la situación profesional o no profesional, el lugar de trabajo, los medios de transporte utilizados para trasladarse al lugar de trabajo y el tiempo necesario para hacerlo.

6. Conceptos y definiciones:
a) Población económicamente activa: Abarcó a todas las personas de 14 o más años de edad que, durante la semana de referencia, estaban ocupadas o desempleadas, conforme a las definiciones que se dan más adelante. La definición incluyó a los militares de carrera, pero no a las personas que cumplían su servicio militar obligatorio; no obstante, éstas pueden identificarse por separado. Quedaron excluidos del ámbito de la definición los estudiantes que trabajaban a tiempo parcial y los estudiantes que buscaban trabajo.

b) Empleo: Se consideró "ocupada" a toda persona que, durante la semana de referencia, había ejercido una profesión o un cargo o desempeñado alguna actividad económica, ya fuese remunerada o sin remuneración.

Se ha indicado que fueron incluidas las siguientes categorías:
i) personas que trabajan sin remuneración en una empresa o negocio familiar;
ii) personas ocupadas pero temporalmente ausentes de su trabajo;
iii) trabajadores estacionales u ocasionales;
iv) aprendices.

Sólo las categorías i) y iv) pueden identificarse por separado. Las personas que cumplían su servicio militar obligatorio también pueden identificarse por separado, aun cuando no hayan sido incluidas en la población económicamente activa.

c) Desempleo: Se consideró "desempleada" a toda persona que, durante la semana de referencia, se encontraba sin empleo y buscaba uno. La definición no abarcó a las personas en busca de un primer empleo.

7. Clasificaciones utilizadas:
Tanto las personas ocupadas como las desempleadas anteriormente empleadas se clasificaron por rama de actividad económica, por ocupación y por situación en el empleo.

a) Rama de actividad económica: Se formularon preguntas encaminadas a precisar el lugar de trabajo de la persona censada y la actividad principal o única del establecimiento, la explotación agrícola, el comercio, negocio o empresa, etc., en que ésta trabajaba o había tenido su último trabajo. Para codificar la rama de actividad se utilizaron 60 divisiones de la clasificación nacional de industrias. Se establecieron enlaces con la CIIU-Rev.3 a nivel de divisiones (clave de 2 dígitos).

b) Ocupación: Se hicieron dos preguntas, relativas, respectivamente, al tipo de trabajo desempeñado por la persona censada (por ejemplo: profesor de enseñanza media, agricultor, técnico en electrónica, arquitecto, programador informático, secretaria, electricista de automóviles, etc.), evitándose el uso de términos genéricos, como "empleado" u "obrero"; y a las principales tareas que le incumbían en el marco de la actividad que ejercía o había ejercido en su último empleo (por ejemplo: enseñanza de matemáticas, cultivo de viñas, control de radar, elaboración de programas, gestión de secretaría, reparación de circuitos eléctricos de automóviles, etc.). Para codificar la ocupación, se utilizaron 35 grupos de la clasificación nacional de ocupaciones. Los enlaces con la clasificación CIUO-88 se establecieron a nivel de grandes grupos (clave de 1 dígito).

c) Situación en el empleo: Se hizo una pregunta encaminada a determinar la condición de la persona censada en su empleo. Para codificar esta variable se utilizaron los siguientes 14 grupos: jefe de empresa; miembro del personal directivo; asalariado; miembro de categorías especiales del personal (nivel intermedio); jefe de cuadrilla de obreros, obrero (especializado, calificado, peón); otras categorías de trabajador independiente; aprendiz; trabajador a domicilio, por cuenta de una empresa; suboficial o militar de carrera, o afines; empleador; trabajador por cuenta propia; miembro de profesión liberal; miembro de cooperativa de producción y/o de prestación de servicios; trabajador familiar (por ejemplo: esposa que ayuda a su marido comerciante, hijo que ayuda a su padre agricultor, etc.).

8. Diferencias principales con el censo anterior:
En el censo de 1981 se hizo sólo una pregunta para determinar el grupo de ocupaciones, a saber: "Indique la profesión, el arte o el oficio que ejerce"; mientras que en el censo de 1991, se formularon dos preguntas con tal fin.

9. Publicación de los resultados del censo:
El título definitivo de la publicación en que figuran los datos sobre la población económicamente activa es "Popolazione e abitazioni" (95 fascículos provinciales, 20 fascículos regionales y un fascículo nacional).

El organismo responsable de la publicación de los resultados del censo es el Istituto Nazionale di Statistica (ISTAT), de Roma.

Los resultados del censo de 1991 están disponibles también en disquetes y cintas magnéticas.

JAMAICA

1. Nombre y dirección del organismo responsable del censo:
Statistical Institute of Jamaica, 97B Church Street, Kingston.

2. Censos de población llevados a cabo desde 1945 (años):
1960, 1970, 1982 y 1991. La presente descripción se refiere al censo de población de 1991 (realizado el 8 de abril de ese año).

3. Alcance del censo:
a) Geográfico: Todo el país.

b) Personas comprendidas: Toda la población.

4. Periodo de referencia:
Dos períodos: la semana y el año anteriores al día del censo.

5. Materias principales:
a) Población total, según sexo y edad: sí
Población económicamente activa por:
b) Sexo y grupo de edad: sí
c) Rama de actividad económica: sí
d) Ocupación: sí
e) Situación en el empleo: sí
f) Nivel más alto de educación: sí
g) Horas de trabajo: sí
h) Otras características: sí

Ref. a): La edad se determinó según los años cumplidos en el último cumpleaños.

Ref. g): El tiempo de trabajo se refería al número total de horas de trabajo efectuadas por las personas ocupadas durante el período de referencia corto, así como al número total de meses trabajados durante el período de referencia largo.

Ref. h): Se pidió a las personas ocupadas que indicasen el monto de los ingresos percibidos por su trabajo.

6. Conceptos y definiciones:

a) Población económicamente activa: Abarcó a todas las personas de 14 o más años de edad que, durante la semana de referencia, estaban sea ocupadas, sea desempleadas, conforme a las definiciones que se dan más adelante. La definición incluyó a los miembros de las fuerzas armadas. En cambio, de ella quedaron excluidos los estudiantes ocupados a tiempo parcial y los que buscaban empleo.

b) Empleo: Para determinarlo se hizo la siguiente pregunta: "¿A qué se dedicó usted principalmente durante la semana anterior al día del censo? Por ejemplo, trabajó, buscó empleo o se ocupó de labores del hogar, etc?". Las posibles respuestas eran: trabajé; tenía empleo pero no trabajé; busqué trabajo por primera vez; otras actividades, al tiempo que buscaba empleo; no busqué empleo, pero quería trabajar y estaba disponible para hacerlo; asistí a clases; me ocupé de labores del hogar; estaba ya jubilado; estaba inválido, incapacitado para trabajar; otras actividades; no respondió.

Se ha indicado que fueron incluidas las siguientes categorías:

i) personas que trabajan sin remuneración en una empresa o negocio familiar;

ii) personas que producen bienes primarios para el autoconsumo;

iii) trabajadores estacionales u ocasionales;

iv) conscriptos del servicio militar o civil;

v) aprendices y personas que siguen un curso de formación.

Sólo pueden identificarse por separado las personas que quedaron incluidas en la primera categoría.

c) Desempleo: Para determinar esta variable se utilizó la misma pregunta que figura en el párrafo 6 b). Se consideró "desempleada" a toda persona que, durante la semana de referencia, se encontraba sin trabajo, quería trabajar y estaba disponible para hacerlo.

7. Clasificaciones utilizadas:

Tanto las personas ocupadas como las desempleadas anteriormente ocupadas se clasificaron por rama de actividad económica, por ocupación y según la situación en el empleo.

a) Rama de actividad económica: Para determinarla se preguntó: "¿Qué tipo de actividad se lleva o se llevaba a cabo en su lugar de trabajo?". Para codificar la rama de actividad se utilizó la clasificación nacional. Se establecieron enlaces con la CIIU-Rev.3 a nivel de divisiones (clave de 2 dígitos).

b) Ocupación: Para determinarla se preguntó: "¿Qué tipo de trabajo desempeña usted actualmente o desempeñaba en su última ocupación?". Para codificar la ocupación se utilizó la clasificación nacional. Se establecieron enlaces con la CIUO-88 a nivel de subgrupos principales (clave de 2 dígitos).

c) Situación en el empleo: Para determinarla se preguntó: "¿Trabaja usted en calidad de asalariado , en su propia empresa o negocio o en otra condición?". Para codificar la situación en el empleo se utilizaron siete grupos, a saber: asalariado del sector público; asalariado en empresa privada; asalariado en servicio doméstico; trabajador no remunerado; independiente con personal remunerado; independiente sin personal remunerado; no respondió.

8. Diferencias principales con el censo anterior:

No hubo diferencias significativas.

9. Publicación de los resultados del censo:

Los resultados definitivos del censo de población se divulgaron en 1995, en diversas publicaciones.

El organismo responsable de la publicación de los resultados es el Statistical Institute of Jamaica, 97 B Church Street, Kingston.

Los resultados están disponibles también en disquetes, cintas magnéticas y discos compactos.

JAPON

1. Nombre y dirección del organismo responsable del censo:

Population Census Division, Statistics Bureau, Management and Coordination Agency, 19-1 Wakamatsu-cho, Shinjuku-ku, Tokio 162.

2. Censos de población llevados a cabo desde 1945 (años):

1947, 1950, 1955, 1960, 1965, 1970, 1975, 1980, 1985 y 1990. La presente descripción se refiere al censo de población de 1990 (realizado el 1 de octubre de ese año).

3. Alcance del censo:

a) Geográfico: Todo el país, con excepción de las siguientes islas: 1) Habomai-gunto, Shikotan-to, Kunashiri-to y Etorofu-to; y 2) Takeshima en Goka-mura, y Shimane-ken.

b) Personas comprendidas: Toda la población, salvo: los diplomáticos extranjeros, su personal y sus familiares; el personal militar extranjero, sean soldados propiamente dichos o civiles, y sus familiares; los nacionales residentes en el extranjero (más precisamente, aquellos que, en el momento del censo, se preveía que permanecerían por lo menos 3 meses en el extranjero).

4. Período de referencia:

La semana anterior al día del censo (o sea, del 24 al 30 de septiembre de 1990).

5. Materias principales:

a) Población total, según sexo y edad:	sí
Población económicamente activa por:	
b) Sexo y grupo de edad:	sí
c) Rama de actividad económica:	sí
d) Ocupación:	sí
e) Situación en el empleo:	sí
f) Nivel más alto de educación:	sí
g) Horas de trabajo:	no
h) Otras características:	sí

Ref. a): La edad se determinó según los años cumplidos en el último cumpleaños.

Ref. h): El censo también recopiló información sobre los medios de transporte utilizados para trasladarse al lugar de trabajo y sobre el tiempo necesario para tal fin.

6. Conceptos y definiciones:

a) Población económicamente activa: Abarcó a todas las personas de 15 o más años de edad que, durante la semana de referencia, estaban sea ocupadas, sea desempleadas, conforme a las definiciones que se dan más adelante. La definición incluyó también las fuerzas de la defensa nacional, clasificadas como empleados estatales.

b) Empleo: Para determinar si una persona debía ser contabilizada como "ocupada" se usó la pregunta "¿Ejerció la persona encuestada alguna actividad laboral durante toda o parte de la semana del 24 al 30 de septiembre? Las respuestas posibles eran: 1) fundamentalmente trabajé; 2) trabajé, además de atender las labores de hogar; 3) trabajé, además de asistir a clases; 4) tenía un empleo, pero estuve temporalmente ausente del trabajo; 5) estuve buscando empleo; 6) me ocupé de labores del hogar; 7) asistí a clases". Se contabilizó como "ocupadas" a las personas que indicaron las respuestas 1), 2), 3) o 4).

Se ha indicado que fueron incluidas las siguientes categorías:

i) personas que trabajan sin remuneración en una empresa o negocio familiar;

ii) personas ocupadas pero temporalmente ausentes de su trabajo;

iii) estudiantes que trabajan a tiempo parcial;

iv) trabajadores estacionales u ocasionales;

v) aprendices y personas que siguen un curso de formación: a las personas cuya situación en el empleo y cuyas remuneraciones son garantizadas por el empleador mientras se encuentren siguiendo alguna formación se las consideró "ocupadas", y quedaron incluidas en la población económicamente activa.

Sólo pueden identificarse por separado las personas incluidas en las categorías ii) y iii). Los estudiantes que trabajaban a tiempo parcial pueden identificarse dentro de la categoría que respondió "trabajé, además de asistir a clases"; sin embargo, por lo que se refiere al empleo de los estudiantes, no es posible distinguir entre quienes tenían una ocupación a tiempo parcial y quienes trabajaban a tiempo completo.

c) Desempleo: Se consideró "desempleada" a toda persona que, durante el período de referencia, se encontraba sin trabajo y buscaba empleo. Para determinar si una persona debía contabilizarse como desempleada, se utilizó la misma pregunta que figura en el apartado b) de esta sección. La definición no incluyó a los estudiantes que buscaban trabajo.

7. Clasificaciones utilizadas:
Sólo las personas ocupadas fueron clasificadas por rama de actividad económica, por ocupación y según la situación en el empleo.

a) Rama de actividad económica: A las personas ocupadas se pidió concretamente que indicasen el nombre del establecimiento para el que trabajaban, el tipo de actividad allí realizada y la clase de productos o mercancías fabricados. Para codificar la rama de actividad se usaron 14 grupos principales, 75 grupos intermedios y 213 subgrupos. Se establecieron enlaces con la CIIU-Rev.2 a nivel de agrupaciones (clave de 3 dígitos).

b) Ocupación: A las personas ocupadas se pidió que respondieran a determinadas preguntas relativas a la ocupación y al tipo de trabajo desempeñado. Para codificar esta variable, se utilizaron 10 grandes grupos, 61 grupos intermedios y 294 subgrupos. Se establecieron enlaces con la CIUO-68 a nivel de grandes grupos (clave de 1 dígito).

c) Situación en el empleo: Se hicieron preguntas específicas a las personas ocupadas para determinar su situación en el empleo. Para codificar esta variable se utilizaron seis grupos, a saber: trabajador asalariado (incluidos los empleados de oficina, los obreros fabriles, los funcionarios públicos, el personal directivo del sector privado, el personal de las empresas de comercio de detalle, el personal doméstico, los jornaleros, los trabajadores temporeros, etc.); directores de empresas o corporaciones; trabajador independiente, con personal remunerado; trabajador independiente, sin personal remunerado (los propietarios individuales de tiendas o fábricas, agricultores, médicos de consulta privada, abogados, escritores, prestadores de servicios domésticos que trabajan por cuenta propia, vendedores ambulantes, etc., debían clasificarse en "trabajador independiente con personal remunerado" o "trabajador independiente sin personal remunerado"); trabajador familiar; artesano que trabaja a domicilio.

8. Diferencias principales con el censo anterior:
No hubo diferencias significativas.

9. Publicación de los resultados del censo:
La publicación en que figuran los resultados del censo lleva por título "1990 Population Census of Japan", aparecida en 1994.

El organismo responsable de esta publicación es la Population Census Division, Statistics Bureau, Management and Coordination Agency, 19-1 Wakamatsu-cho, Shinjuku-ku, Tokio 162.

Los resultados del censo están también disponibles en cuadros inéditos y cintas magnéticas.

KENYA

1. Nombre y dirección del organismo responsable del censo:
Central Bureau of Statistics in the Office of the Vice-President and Ministry of Planning and National Development, P.O. Box 30266, Nairobi.

2. Censos de población llevados a cabo desde 1945 (años):
1948, 1962, 1969, 1979 y 1989. La presente descripción se refiere al censo de población de 1989 (realizado el 24 de agosto de ese año).

3. Alcance del censo:
a) Geográfico: Todo el país.
b) Personas comprendidas: Toda la población.

4. Periodo de referencia:
La semana anterior al día del censo.

5. Materias principales:
a) Población total, según sexo y edad:	sí
Población económicamente activa por:	
b) Sexo y grupo de edad:	sí
c) Rama de actividad económica:	no
d) Ocupación:	sí
e) Situación en el empleo:	sí
f) Nivel más alto de educación:	sí

g) Horas de trabajo:	no
h) Otras características:	no

Ref. a): La edad se determinó según los años cumplidos en el último cumpleaños.

6. Conceptos y definiciones:

a) Población económicamente activa: Abarcó a todas las personas de 10 o más años de edad que, durante la semana de referencia, estaban ocupadas o desempleadas, conforme a las definiciones que se dan más adelante. No quedaron incluidos en la definición los estudiantes con empleo a tiempo parcial ni los que buscaban trabajo.

b) Empleo: Se consideró "ocupada" a toda persona que, durante el período de referencia, dedicó la mayor parte de su tiempo de trabajo a una actividad remunerada mediante un sueldo, un salario, comisiones, propinas u otra forma de remuneración contractual, así como en especie. Para determinar si una persona debía considerarse o no "ocupada" se preguntó "¿Cuál fue la actividad principal de X durante los siete días anteriores a la noche del censo? 1) trabajó por un salario u otros ingresos; 2) estuvo en vacaciones o con licencia de enfermedad; 3) trabajó en una empresa o negocio familiar; 4) no trabajó ; 5) estuvo buscando trabajo; 6) asistió a la escuela; 7) estaba ya jubilado; 8) estaba incapacitado para trabajar; 9) trabajó en labores del hogar; 10) otra actividad".

Se ha indicado que fueron incluidas las siguientes categorías:
i) personas que trabajan sin remuneración en una empresa o negocio familiar;
ii) personas que producen bienes primarios para el autoconsumo;
iii) personas ocupadas pero temporalmente ausentes de su trabajo;
iv) trabajadores estacionales u ocasionales;
v) aprendices y personas que siguen un curso de formación.

Tan sólo la categoría iii) puede identificarse por separado.

c) Desempleo: Se consideró "desempleada" a toda persona que, durante la semana de referencia, no tenía trabajo, quería trabajar y se encontraba en busca de un empleo. Las personas que no estaban buscando activamente una ocupación fueron consideradas "desempleadas", pero quedaron clasificadas en una categoría distinta de los desempleados que buscaban trabajo activamente.

7. Clasificaciones utilizadas:
Sólo las personas ocupadas fueron clasificadas por rama de actividad económica y por situación en el empleo.

a) Rama de actividad económica: No se efectuó clasificación alguna por rama de actividad.

b) Ocupación: Para determinarla se preguntó: "¿Cuál fue la ocupación principal de X?, por ejemplo, empleado de oficina, mecánico de motores, profesor de enseñanza primaria, etc.". Para codificar la ocupación se utilizaron ocho grupos generales de la clasificación nacional. Se establecieron enlaces con la CIUO-88 a nivel de grandes grupos (clave de 1 dígito).

c) Situación en el empleo: Para determinarla se preguntó: "¿En qué condición estaba trabajando X?" Para codificar la situación en el empleo se utilizaron cuatro grupos, a saber: empleador; trabajador independiente; trabajador asalariado; trabajador familiar.

8. Diferencias principales con el censo anterior:
El censo de 1989 fue el primero concebido para recopilar información sobre la fuerza de trabajo.

9. Publicación de los resultados del censo:
Los resultados definitivos del censo de población se publicaron en julio de 1995, en un volumen titulado "The Kenya Population Census 1989, Volume IX: The Labour Force".

El organismo responsable de la publicación de los resultados es el Central Bureau of Statistics, P.O. Box 30266, Nairobi.

LUXEMBURGO

1. Nombre y dirección del organismo responsable del censo:
Service central de la statistique et des études économiques (STATEC), B.P. 304, Luxemburgo.

2. Censos de población llevados a cabo desde 1945 (años):
1947, 1960, 1966, 1970, 1981 y 1991. La presente descripción se refiere al censo de población de 1991 (realizado el 1 de marzo de ese año).

3. Alcance del censo:
a) Geográfico: Todo el territorio.

b) Personas comprendidas: Toda la población.

4. Período de referencia:
No se fijó un período de referencia. Las preguntas formuladas se referían a la situación "actual" de las personas censadas.

5. Materias principales:
a) Población total, según sexo y edad: sí
Población económicamente activa por:
b) Sexo y grupo de edad: sí
c) Rama de actividad económica: sí
d) Ocupación: sí
e) Situación en el empleo: sí
f) Nivel más alto de educación: sí
g) Horas de trabajo: sí
h) Otras características: sí

Ref. a): La edad se determinó según el año de nacimiento, la edad cumplida en el último cumpleaños y la edad exacta en la fecha del censo.

Ref. g): Se trata del tiempo de trabajo normal de las personas ocupadas.

Ref. h): El censo permitió también recopilar información sobre los medios de transporte utilizados para trasladarse al lugar de trabajo y regresar al domicilio, así como sobre el tiempo dedicado a tales fines.

6. Conceptos y definiciones:
a) Población económicamente activa: Abarcó a todas las personas que, en la fecha del censo, estaban ocupadas o desempleadas, conforme a las definiciones que se dan más adelante. No se fijaron límites de edad; empero, los datos sobre la población económicamente activa, el empleo y el desempleo se refieren únicamente a las personas de 15 o más años de edad. La definición incluyó a los miembros de las fuerzas armadas.

b) Empleo: Se consideró "ocupada" a toda persona censada que respondió afirmativamente a la pregunta "¿Ejerce usted actualmente una profesión?". Las personas que dieron una respuesta negativa debían precisar cuál era en ese momento su situación en la vida económica.

Se ha indicado que fueron incluidas las siguientes categorías:

i) personas que trabajan sin remuneración en una empresa o negocio familiar;
ii) personas ocupadas pero temporalmente ausentes de su trabajo;
iii) estudiantes que trabajan a tiempo parcial;
iv) trabajadores estacionales u ocasionales;
v) aprendices y personas que siguen un curso de formación.

Sólo las categorías i) y v) pueden identificarse por separado, con arreglo a las respuestas a la pregunta sobre la situación en el empleo.

c) Desempleo: Se consideró "desempleada" a toda persona censada que respondió negativamente a la pregunta "¿Ejerce usted actualmente una profesión?", que no tenía trabajo y estaba buscando empleo durante el período de referencia. No quedaron incluidos en el ámbito de la definición los estudiantes que buscaban trabajo.

7. Clasificaciones utilizadas:
Sólo las personas ocupadas se clasificaron por rama de actividad económica, por ocupación y por situación en el empleo.

a) Rama de actividad económica: Para determinarla, se pidió a las personas ocupadas que respondiesen a preguntas específicas, a saber: el nombre, la dirección y la rama de actividad de la empresa, el establecimiento o el servicio administrativo que dirigían o en el que estaban empleados. Para codificar la rama de actividad, se utilizaron alrededor de 500 grupos de la codificación de cuatro dígitos empleada por la Nomenclatura General de Actividades Económicas de la Comunidad Europea (NACE). No se establecieron enlaces con la CIIU.

b) Ocupación: Para determinarla, se pidió concretamente a las personas ocupadas: "Indique la profesión o el oficio que usted ejerce actualmente, incluso si sólo es aprendiz o si trabaja como auxiliar en la actividad económica de un miembro de su grupo familiar". Para codificar la ocupación se utilizó el nivel de grupos primarios de la CIUO-88 (clave de 4 dígitos).

c) Situación en el empleo: Para determinarla se hizo la siguiente pregunta: "¿En qué calidad ejerce usted su profesión?". Para codificar esta variable se utilizaron nueve categorías: agricultor, trabajador intelectual independiente, otros trabajadores independientes, obrero, empleado sector privado, funcionario (empleado público), funcionario internacional, aprendiz, trabajador familiar no remunerado.

8. Diferencias principales con el censo anterior:
No hubo diferencias significativas

9. Publicación de los resultados del censo:
Los resultados definitivos del censo figuran en la publicación que lleva por título: Série spéciale "Recensement de la Population" (1992/1993).

El organismo responsable de esta publicación es el Service central de la statistique et des études économiques (STATEC), B.P. 304, Luxemburgo.

Los resultados del censo de 1991 están disponibles también en cuadros inéditos, disquetes y cintas magnéticas.

MACAO

1. Nombre y dirección del organismo responsable del censo:
The Census and Statistic Department of Macau, Rua Inácio Baptista No. 4-6 "D", Macao.

2. Censos de población llevados a cabo desde 1945 (años):
1960, 1981 y 1991. La presente descripción se refiere al censo de 1991 (realizado el 30 de agosto de ese año).

3. Alcance del censo:
a) Geográfico: Todo el territorio.

El empadronamiento se llevó a cabo en forma completa en la isla de Coloane, y sobre muestras de 20 por ciento en la península de Macao y de 40 por ciento en la isla Taipa.

b) Personas comprendidas: Toda la población.

4. Período de referencia:
Los siete días anteriores al empadronamiento. También se utilizó un período de referencia de 30 días antes de la fecha del censo para determinar si una persona estaba buscando trabajo.

5. Materias principales:
a) Población total, según sexo y edad: sí
Población económicamente activa por:
b) Sexo y grupo de edad: sí
c) Rama de actividad económica: sí
d) Ocupación: sí
e) Situación en el empleo: sí
f) Nivel más alto de educación: sí
g) Horas de trabajo: no
h) Otras características: no

Ref. a): La edad se determinó según el año de nacimiento y los años cumplidos en el último cumpleaños.

6. Conceptos y definiciones:
a) Población económicamente activa: Abarcó a todas las personas de 14 y más años de edad que durante el período de referencia estaban ocupadas o desempleadas, conforme a las definiciones que figuran más adelante. La definición incluyó a los miembros de las fuerzas armadas.

b) Empleo: Se consideró "ocupada" a toda persona censada que indicó "tengo trabajo" al responder a la pregunta ¿Qué ha hecho en los últimos siete días: "tengo trabajo; estoy desempleado; soy estudiante; soy independiente en empresa familiar; otros?", o que contestó afirmativamente a las preguntas siguientes: "¿En los últimos 7 días, trabajó por dinero? e ¿Hizo algún trabajo remunerado en especies o se ocupó como trabajador familiar, por ejemplo, en la fabricación de juguetes o de flores artificiales, el cuidado de niños, la costura, o en inversiones financieras?"

Se ha indicado que fueron incluidas las siguientes categorías:
i) personas que trabajan sin remuneración en una empresa o negocio familiar;
ii) personas ocupadas pero temporalmente ausentes de su trabajo;

iii) estudiantes que trabajan a tiempo parcial;
iv) trabajadores estacionales u ocasionales;
v) conscriptos del servicio militar o civil;
vi) aprendices y personas que siguen un curso de formación.

Las categorías ii) y iii) pueden identificarse por separado mediante las respuestas a preguntas concretas.

c) *Desempleo*: Se consideró "desempleada" a toda persona censada que respondió "desempleado" a la pregunta: "Durante los últimos siete días ¿cuál fue su actividad?", y dio una respuesta afirmativa a las preguntas: "Durante los últimos 30 días ¿hizo algún esfuerzo por encontrar trabajo?" y "Si durante los últimos siete días le hubieran ofrecido un empleo apropiado ¿lo hubiera aceptado?"

7. Clasificaciones utilizadas:
Sólo las personas ocupadas fueron clasificadas por rama de actividad y por ocupación. No se hicieron preguntas para determinar la situación en el empleo, ni a las personas ocupadas ni a las desempleadas.

a) *Rama de actividad económica*: Para determinarla se preguntó: "¿Cuál es el producto fabricado o el servicio prestado en el lugar donde trabaja?" Para codificar la rama de actividad se utilizaron 10 grupos de la clasificación nacional. Se establecieron enlaces con la CIIU-Rev.3 a nivel de categorías de tabulación (1 dígito).

b) *Ocupación*: Para determinarla se preguntó: "¿Cuál es el nombre del cargo que ocupa? Si es gerente o administrador ¿cuántos empleados de oficina tiene?"; "¿Cuáles son las tareas principales de las que suele ocuparse?"; y "¿Utiliza alguna herramienta en su trabajo? De ser así, indique lo que corresponda." Para codificar la ocupación se utilizaron 10 grupos de la clasificación nacional. Se establecieron enlaces con la CIUO-88 a nivel de grandes grupos (1 dígito).

c) *Situación en el empleo*: No se hizo clasificación alguna.

8. Diferencias principales con el censo anterior:
En 1981, la edad se definió según el año de nacimiento, la edad mínima para la población económicamente activa fue 10 años y el empadronamiento fue completo.

9. Publicación de los resultados del censo:
Los resultados se publicaron en junio de 1993, con el título "XIII Population Census & III Housing Census - Global Results".

La organización responsable de esta publicación es The Census and Statistics Department of Macau, Rua Inácio Baptista No. 4-6 "D", Macao.

También se dispone de los resultados del censo en cuadros inéditos y disquetes.

MACEDONIA

1. Nombre y dirección del organismo responsable del censo:
Statistical Office of Macedonia, Dame Gruev 4, 91000 Skopje, República de Macedonia.

2. Censos de población llevados a cabo desde 1945 (años):
1948, 1953, 1961, 1971, 1981 y 1994. La presente descripción se refiere al censo de población de 1994 (fecha de referencia: 20 de junio de ese año).

3. Alcance del censo:
a) *Geográfico*: Todo el país.

b) *Personas comprendidas*: Toda la población.

4. Periodo de referencia:
El día del censo.

5. Materias principales:
a) Población total, según sexo y edad:	sí
Población económicamente activa por:	
b) Sexo y grupo de edad:	sí
c) Rama de actividad económica:	sí
d) Ocupación:	sí
e) Situación en el empleo:	sí
f) Nivel más alto de educación:	sí
g) Horas de trabajo:	no
h) Otras características:	no

Ref. a): La edad se determinó según los años cumplidos en el último cumpleaños.

6. Conceptos y definiciones:
a) *Población económicamente activa*: Abarcó a todas las personas de 15 o más años de edad que, en el momento del censo, estaban ocupadas o desempleadas, conforme a las definiciones que se dan más adelante. Excepcionalmente, se incluyó a los niños de 10 a 14 años de edad que no asistían a la escuela y que estaban ocupados en algunas actividades agropecuarias, como pastor de ovinos, de bovinos u oficios afines. La definición incluyó a los miembros de las fuerzas armadas. No quedaron incluidos en la definición los estudiantes con empleo a tiempo parcial ni los que buscaban trabajo.

b) *Empleo*: Se consideró "ocupada" a toda persona que, en el momento del censo, estaba desempeñando alguna actividad laboral, como empleado o como trabajador independiente (sea en una explotación agrícola propia o familiar, sea en un taller, o en otra forma de empresa) con el fin de obtener medios de subsistencia.

Se ha indicado que fueron incluidas las siguientes categorías:

i) personas que trabajan sin remuneración en una empresa o negocio familiar;
ii) personas que producen bienes primarios para el autoconsumo;
iii) personas ocupadas pero temporalmente ausentes de su trabajo;
iv) trabajadores estacionales u ocasionales;
v) conscriptos del servicio militar o civil.

Sólo las categorías i) y ii) pueden identificarse por separado.

c) *Desempleo*: Se consideró "desempleada" a toda persona que, en el momento del censo, se encontraba sin trabajo y buscaba empleo. Se distinguió a las personas en busca de un primer empleo de las que ya habían trabajado antes. Entre estas últimas, pueden identificarse por separado aquellas cuyas empresas se fueron a la quiebra.

7. Clasificaciones utilizadas:
Tanto las personas ocupadas como las desempleadas anteriormente empleadas se clasificaron por ocupación. Sólo las personas ocupadas se clasificaron por rama de actividad económica y por situación en el empleo. A las personas desempleadas se les pidió que indicaran la rama de actividad y la situación en el empleo de la persona de quien dependían.

a) *Rama de actividad económica*: Se pidió a la persona censada que indicara el lugar en que estaba trabajando (taller, servicio de alimentación u otro tipo de establecimiento comercial) y la denominación de la actividad en que se ocupaban (agricultura, producción de artesanía en madera, etc.). Para codificar esta variable se utilizaron 14 ramas de la clasificación nacional. Cada rama se divide en grupos, y éstos, en subgrupos. Se previó establecer ulteriormente los enlaces con la CIIU.

b) *Ocupación*: Para determinarla se pidió a las personas censadas que anotaran el nombre de su ocupación. En las instrucciones se insistió en que se trataba de indicar el trabajo efectivo al que se había dedicado más tiempo. Para codificar la ocupación se utilizaron 10 grupos principales de la clasificación nacional. Cada grupo principal se divide en tipos, y éstos, en subtipos. Se previó establecer ulteriormente los enlaces con la CIUO.

c) *Situación en el empleo*: Para codificar esta variable se utilizaron cinco grupos: trabajador; propietario o copropietario de una empresa; propietario o copropietario de un negocio privado, que contrata personal; persona dedicada a una actividad independiente, sola o con la ayuda de familiares; trabajador familiar auxiliar.

8. Diferencias principales con el censo anterior:
En censos anteriores, por "población total" se había entendido a todas las personas que tenían residencia permanente en la República de Macedonia, independientemente de que hubiesen estado ausentes o no en el momento del censo y del tiempo que durase su permanencia en el extranjero.

En el censo de 1994, de conformidad con la Ley de Censos, la población total abarcó a:

i) las personas con residencia oficial (legal) en la República de Macedonia, estuviesen o no en el momento del censo presentes en su lugar de residencia oficial (legal) o en otro lugar de Macedonia;
ii) las personas en posesión de un permiso de residencia en la República de Macedonia y que hubiesen permanecido provisionalmente en el país durante al menos un año, pero que tuviesen residencia oficial (legal) en el extranjero,

salvo los refugiados y las personas bajo protección por motivos humanitarios;

iii) las personas que tenían residencia oficial (legal) en la República de Macedonia, así como sus familiares, y que en el momento del censo y por un período máximo de un año antes de éste hubiesen estado trabajando temporalmente en el extranjero;

iv) las personas que tenían residencia oficial (legal) en la República de Macedonia y que, en el momento del censo, estuviesen trabajando en las oficinas diplomáticas y las representaciones consulares de la República de Macedonia, en las Naciones Unidas o sus instituciones, en oficinas de representación de la Cámara de Comercio en el extranjero y en oficinas comerciales instaladas en el extranjero, así como el personal militar de la República de Macedonia en el extranjero y los ciudadanos que tomasen parte en actividades internacionales de cooperación, educativas o de otra índole, y las personas temporalmente residentes en el extranjero por estar incorporadas al grupo familiar de las personas antedichas.

9. Publicación de los resultados del censo:
Los resultados definitivos del censo se editarán en 1996, en una serie de publicaciones cuyos títulos corresponderán al contenido de cada entrega.

La organización responsable de la publicación es la Statistical Office of Macedonia, Dame Gruev 4, 91000 Skopje.

MADAGASCAR

1. Nombre y dirección del organismo responsable del censo:
Direction du Recensement Général de la Population et de l'Habitat, (DRGPH), B.P. 485, Antananarivo.

2. Censos de población llevados a cabo desde 1945 (años):
1975 y 1993. La presente descripción se refiere al censo de población de 1993 (realizado del 1 al 19 de agosto de ese año).

3. Alcance del censo:
a) Geográfico: Todo el territorio.

b) Personas comprendidas: Toda la población, salvo los nacionales residentes en el extranjero.

4. Período de referencia:
La semana anterior a la fecha del empadronamiento.

5. Materias principales:
a) Población total, según sexo y edad:	sí
Población económicamente activa por:	
b) Sexo y grupo de edad:	sí
c) Rama de actividad económica:	sí
d) Ocupación:	sí
e) Situación en el empleo:	sí
f) Nivel más alto de educación:	sí
g) Horas de trabajo:	no
h) Otras características:	no

Ref. a): La edad se determinó primordialmente según el año de nacimiento, pero también se estimó en años en aquellos casos en se desconocía la fecha de nacimiento.

6. Conceptos y definiciones:
a) Población económicamente activa: Abarcó a todas las personas de 10 o más años de edad que estaban ocupadas o desempleadas en la fecha del censo, según las definiciones que se dan más adelante. La definición incluyó a los miembros de las fuerzas armadas. No quedaron incluidos en la definición los estudiantes con empleo a tiempo parcial ni los que buscaban trabajo.

b) Empleo: Se consideró "ocupada" a toda persona que indicó que esa había sido su situación durante la semana de referencia, es decir, que había obtenido, iba a obtener o esperaba obtener una remuneración en efectivo o en especie a cambio de una actividad laboral regular a la que había dedicado la mayor parte de su tiempo. Para determinar si una persona debía considerarse "ocupada", se utilizó la pregunta "Indique su situación laboral: ocupado(a); desempleado(a); en busca de un primer empleo; ama de casa; estudiante; jubilado(a); incapaz de trabajar; otra".

Se ha indicado que fueron incluidas las siguientes categorías:

i) personas que trabajan sin remuneración en una empresa o negocio familiar;

ii) personas que producen bienes primarios para el autoconsumo;

iii) personas ocupadas pero temporalmente ausentes de su trabajo;

iv) trabajadores estacionales u ocasionales;

v) conscriptos del servicio militar o civil;

vi) aprendices y personas que siguen un curso de formación.

Con la excepción de la categoría ii), todas las demás categorías pueden identificarse con arreglo a sus respuestas a las preguntas sobre la actividad económica, la ocupación y la situación en el empleo.

c) Desempleo: Se consideró "desempleada" a toda persona que, a raíz de una interrupción de su actividad laboral, había quedado sin empleo durante un tiempo determinado y cuya actividad principal durante la semana de referencia había sido la búsqueda de una nueva ocupación. Las personas que buscaban un primer empleo no fueron incluidas en la definición, pero fueron identificadas por separado. A tal efecto, se usó la misma pregunta indicada en el párrafo b) de esta sección.

7. Clasificaciones utilizadas:
Tanto las personas ocupadas como los desempleados anteriormente empleados se clasificaron por rama de actividad, por ocupación y por situación en el empleo.

a) Rama de actividad económica: Para determinarla se hizo la siguiente pregunta: "¿Cuál es (era) la índole de la actividad principal del establecimiento o el empleador para el que trabajaba?, por ejemplo: cultivo de arroz, transporte de mercancías, fabricación de aceite, enseñanza". Para codificar la rama de actividad se utilizó la CIIU-Rev.3 a nivel de grupos (clave de 3 dígitos).

b) Ocupación: Para determinarla se hizo la siguiente pregunta: "¿Durante la semana anterior a _ de 1993, cuál fue la actividad principal ejercida por la persona ocupada? (se ruega a los desempleados que indiquen su última ocupación). Por ejemplo: comerciante de artículos generales detallista o mayorista, chófer, cultivador de arroz, sastre, pastor". En el caso de las personas con varias ocupaciones, se consideró ocupación principal aquella que era fuente de los ingresos más importantes. Para codificar la ocupación se utilizó la CIUO-88, en el nivel de grandes grupos (clave de 1 dígito).

c) Situación en el empleo: Para determinarla se hizo la siguiente pregunta: "¿Cuál es o era su situación en su ocupación?". Para codificar la situación en el empleo se utilizaron siete categorías: trabajador independiente; empleador; asalariado permanente; asalariado temporal; aprendiz; trabajador familiar; situación inclasificable.

8. Diferencias principales con el censo anterior:
El censo de 1975 se dividió en tres partes (26-27 de enero: grandes centros urbanos (excepto la capital); 6-7 de abril: capital y demás centros urbanos; 17-18 de agosto: regiones rurales), mientras que el censo de 1993 se efectuó simultáneamente en todo el territorio nacional.

En 1975 se había utilizado un período de referencia largo (un mes).

Por último, el censo de 1975 había abarcado a los nacionales residentes en el extranjero, que fueron excluidos del censo de 1993.

9. Publicación de los resultados del censo:
Se había previsto publicar los resultados definitivos del censo de 1993 en dos etapas: primeramente, los cuadros estadísticos (1 volumen por provincia) en abril de 1996, y luego, un volumen analítico, en junio de 1996.

El organismo responsable de la publicación es el Institut National de la Statistique, B.P. 485, Antananarivo.

Los resultados estarán también disponibles en disquetes.

MALASIA

1. Nombre y dirección del organismo responsable del censo:
Department of Statistics, Malaysia, Jalan Cenderasari, 50514 Kuala Lumpur, Malasia.

2. Censos de población llevados a cabo desde 1945 (años):

1947 y 1957 (en la península de Malasia), 1960 (en Sabah y Sarawak), 1970, 1980 y 1991 (en toda Malasia). La presente descripción se refiere al censo de población de 1991 (realizado el 14 de agosto de ese año).

3. Alcance del censo:

a) Geográfico: Todo el país.

b) Personas comprendidas: Toda la población.

4. Periodo de referencia:

La semana anterior a la fecha del empadronamiento. Este se llevó a cabo del 14 al 30 de agosto de 1991.

5. Materias principales:

a) Población total, según sexo y edad:	sí
Población económicamente activa por:	
b) Sexo y grupo de edad:	sí
c) Rama de actividad económica:	sí
d) Ocupación:	sí
e) Situación en el empleo:	sí
f) Nivel más alto de educación:	sí
g) Horas de trabajo:	sí
h) Otras características:	no

Ref. a): La edad se determinó según el año de nacimiento.

Ref. g): Se pidió a las personas ocupadas que indicaran cuántas horas habían trabajado durante los siete días anteriores a la fecha de la entrevista.

6. Conceptos y definiciones:

a) Población económicamente activa: Abarcó a todas las personas de 10 o más años de edad que, durante el período de referencia, estaban ocupadas o desempleadas, conforme a las definiciones que se dan más adelante. Sin embargo, los resultados publicados acerca de la ocupación y la actividad económica sólo se refieren a las personas entre 15 y 64 años de edad; en cambio, los resultados relativos a la población activa se remiten a la población de 10 o más años de edad. La definición incluyó a los miembros de las fuerzas armadas.

b) Empleo: Se consideró "ocupada" a toda persona que, durante el período de referencia, trabajó por lo menos una hora. Para determinar si una persona estaba ocupada se utilizaron las siguientes preguntas: "¿Trabajó durante los últimos siete días?"; y "¿Trabajó por lo menos una hora durante los últimos siete días?". A las personas empleadas que no habían trabajado se preguntó: "¿Va a retomar su trabajo?".

Se ha indicado que fueron incluidas las siguientes categorías:

i) personas que trabajan sin remuneración en una empresa o negocio familiar;

ii) personas ocupadas pero temporalmente ausentes de su trabajo;

iii) estudiantes que trabajan a tiempo parcial;

iv) trabajadores estacionales u ocasionales;

v) conscriptos del servicio militar o civil;

vi) aprendices y personas que siguen un curso de formación.

Las categorías i) y ii) pueden identificarse por separado. Los trabajadores estacionales u ocasionales quedan incluidos únicamente si estaban trabajando durante el período de referencia.

c) Desempleo: Se consideró "desempleada" a toda persona que, durante el período de referencia, se encontraba sin trabajo y buscaba empleo. Para determinar si una persona debía considerarse "desempleada" se utilizaron las siguientes preguntas: "¿Buscó trabajo durante los pasados siete días?"; y "¿Cuál fue el principal motivo por el que no buscó trabajo?: 1) consideró que no encontraría un empleo apropiado; 2) se lo impidió el mal tiempo; 3) estaba enfermo o en reposo obligatorio; 4) tenía ya un trabajo que comenzará pronto; 5) esperaba la respuesta a candidaturas presentadas o había estado buscando trabajo anteriormente a los últimos siete días; 6) no estaba debidamente calificado; 7) no había terminado su escolaridad; 8) era ama de casa; 9) tenía previsto continuar sus estudios; 10) era inválido o discapacitado; 11) no le interesaba; 12) estaba jubilado o era demasiado anciano; 13) era demasiado joven; y 14) otros motivos".

7. Clasificaciones utilizadas:

Sólo las personas ocupadas se clasificaron por rama de actividad económica, por ocupación y por situación en el empleo.

a) Rama de actividad económica: Para determinarla se utilizaron las siguientes preguntas: "¿Cuáles son las actividades, servicios o productos que se despliegan, prestan o elaboran en su lugar de trabajo?"; y "Señale el nombre y la dirección de su empleador". Para codificar la rama de actividad se utilizó una clasificación de 5 dígitos, basada en la CIIU-Rev.2.

b) Ocupación: Para determinarla se utilizaron las siguientes preguntas: "¿Cuál es su ocupación?"; y "¿Cuáles son sus funciones o cuál es la índole de su trabajo?". Para codificar la ocupación se utilizó una clasificación de 3 dígitos, basada en la CIUO-68.

c) Situación en el empleo: Para determinarla se preguntó: "¿Cuál es su situación laboral?". Para codificar esta variable se utilizaron cuatro grupos, a saber: empleador; empleado; trabajador independiente; y trabajador familiar no remunerado.

8. Diferencias principales con el censo anterior:

En el censo de 1991, sólo las personas ocupadas fueron clasificadas por rama de actividad y por ocupación, mientras que en el censo de 1980 lo habían sido tanto las personas ocupadas como las desempleadas anteriormente empleadas.

9. Publicación de los resultados del censo:

En el período 1991-1992 se publicaron cuatro informes preliminares que abarcaban diversas regiones (por ejemplo, Malasia, Estado y distritos administrativos; Mukins; y las regiones bajo administración local, así como las zonas urbano/rurales). A mediados de 1993, se puso a disposición de los organismos estatales un informe intermedio de circulación restringida. Se preveía que los informes definitivos fuesen publicados en 1995.

La organización responsable de la publicación es el Department of Statistics, Kuala Lumpur.

Los datos del censo existen también en cuadros inéditos, cuadros de muestras y CD-ROM.

MALDIVAS

1. Nombre y dirección del organismo responsable del censo:

Ministry of Planning, Human Resources and Environment, Ghazee Building, Malé 20-05.

2. Censos de población llevados a cabo desde 1945 (años):

1946, 1953, 1957, 1958, 1960, 1961, 1962, 1963, 1964, 1965, 1966, 1967, 1969, 1970, 1971, 1972, 1974, 1977, 1985 y 1990. La presente descripción se refiere al censo de población de 1990 (realizado el 25 de marzo de ese año).

3. Alcance del censo:

a) Geográfico: Todo el país.

b) Personas comprendidas: Toda la población.

4. Periodo de referencia:

La semana y los tres meses anteriores al día del censo.

5. Materias principales:

a) Población total, según sexo y edad:	sí
Población económicamente activa por:	
b) Sexo y grupo de edad:	sí
c) Rama de actividad económica:	sí
d) Ocupación:	sí
e) Situación en el empleo:	sí
f) Nivel más alto de educación:	sí
g) Horas de trabajo:	sí
h) Otras características:	no

Ref. a): La edad se determinó según los años cumplidos en el último cumpleaños.

Ref. g): Por lo que atañe al período de referencia corto y al período de referencia largo, se pidió a las personas ocupadas que indicaran, respectivamente, las horas de trabajo habituales y el número total de horas trabajadas.

6. Conceptos y definiciones:

a) Población económicamente activa: Abarcó a todas las personas de 12 o más años de edad que, durante el período de referencia corto, estaban ocupadas o desempleadas, conforme a las definiciones que se dan más adelante. La definición no incluyó a los miembros de las fuerzas armadas.

b) Empleo: Se consideró "ocupada" a toda persona, incluidos los trabajadores familiares, que trabajó durante el período de referencia corto, o que tenía un empleo en el que ya había trabajado pero del cual estaba temporalmente ausente por causa de enfermedad o accidente, conflicto laboral, vacaciones o alguna forma de excedencia, o ausente sin permiso o debido a una desorganización provisional del trabajo por motivos de fuerza mayor, como fenómenos metereológicos o fallas mecánicas.

Se ha indicado que fueron incluidas las siguientes categorías:

i) personas que trabajan sin remuneración en una empresa o negocio familiar;
ii) personas ocupadas pero temporalmente ausentes de su trabajo;
iii) estudiantes que trabajan a tiempo parcial;
iv) trabajadores estacionales u ocasionales;
v) aprendices y personas que siguen un curso de formación.

Ninguna de estas categorías puede identificarse por separado.

c) Desempleo: Se consideró "desempleada" a toda persona que, durante el período de referencia corto, se encontraba sin trabajo y buscaba un empleo o una actividad remunerada, incluidas las personas que nunca habían trabajado antes. La definición no incluyó a los estudiantes que buscaban trabajo.

7. Clasificaciones utilizadas:
Tanto las personas ocupadas como las desempleadas anteriormente empleadas se clasificaron por rama de actividad económica, por ocupación y por situación en el empleo.

a) Rama de actividad económica: Para determinarla se preguntó: "Durante la semana de referencia (o en su empleo actual), ¿en qué empresa trabajó la mayor parte del tiempo?" Para codificar la rama de actividad se utilizó la CIIU-Rev.3 en el nivel de clases (4 dígitos).

b) Ocupación: Para determinarla se preguntó: "Describa el tipo de trabajo específico realizado en su ocupación o indique su designación exacta". Para codificar la ocupación se utilizó la CIUO-88, en el nivel de grupos primarios (4 dígitos).

c) Situación en el empleo: Para determinarla se preguntó: "¿Cuál era la categoría de su empleo?" Para codificar esta variable se utilizaron cuatro grupos: empleador; empleado; trabajador independiente; y trabajador familiar (no remunerado).

8. Diferencias principales con el censo anterior:
No hubo diferencias significativas.

9. Publicación de los resultados del censo:
El título de la publicación con los resultados finales es "Population and Housing Census of the Maldives 1990".

La organización responsable de la publicación es el Ministry of Planning, Human Resources and Environment, Ghazee Building, Malé 20-05.

Los resultados del censo existen también en cuadros inéditos, disquetes y CD-ROM.

MARRUECOS

1. Nombre y dirección del organismo responsable del censo:
Direction de la Statistique, B.P. 178, Rabat.

2. Censos de población llevados a cabo desde 1945 (años):
1960, 1971, 1982 y 1994. La presente descripción se refiere al censo de 1994 (realizado del 2 al 20 de septiembre de ese año).

3. Alcance del censo:

a) Geográfico: Todo el territorio.

b) Personas comprendidas: Toda la población, salvo los nacionales residentes en el extranjero.

4. Período de referencia:
El día del empadronamiento.

5. Materias principales:
a) Población total, según sexo y edad: sí
Población económicamente activa por:
b) Sexo y grupo de edad: sí
c) Rama de actividad económica: sí
d) Ocupación: sí
e) Situación en el empleo: sí
f) Nivel más alto de educación: sí
g) Horas de trabajo: no
h) Otras características: no

Ref. a): La edad se determinó según los años cumplidos en el último cumpleaños.

6. Conceptos y definiciones:

a) Población económicamente activa: Abarcó a todas las personas de 7 o más años de edad y de 15 o más años de edad que, en la fecha del censo, estaban, respectivamente, ocupadas o desempleadas, según las definiciones que se dan más adelante. La definición incluyó a los miembros de las fuerzas armadas, pero no a los estudiantes que trabajaban a tiempo parcial ni a los estudiantes que buscaban trabajo.

b) Empleo: Se consideró "ocupada" ("activa ocupada") a toda persona de 7 o más años de edad que, en la fecha del censo, tenían un "trabajo" o ejercían una actividad económica cualquiera. Para determinar si una persona debía considerarse "ocupada" se preguntó "¿Tenía usted un empleo en la fecha del censo?".

Se ha indicado que fueron incluidas las siguientes categorías:

i) personas que trabajan sin remuneración en una empresa o negocio familiar;
ii) personas que producen bienes primarios para el autoconsumo;
iii) personas ocupadas pero temporalmente ausentes de su trabajo;
iv) trabajadores estacionales u ocasionales, en particular en la agricultura;
v) conscriptos del servicio militar o civil;
vi) aprendices y personas que siguen un curso de formación.

Sólo pueden identificarse por separado las categorías i), v) y vi).

c) Desempleo: Se consideró "desempleada" a toda persona de 15 o más años de edad que, en la fecha del censo, estaban sin trabajo y en busca de un empleo. La definición incluyó tanto a los desempleados anteriormente empleados como a las personas en busca de un primer empleo.

7. Clasificaciones utilizadas:
Tanto las personas ocupadas como las desempleadas anteriormente empleadas fueron clasificadas por rama de actividad económica, por ocupación y por situación en el empleo.

a) Rama de actividad económica: Para determinarla se preguntó cuál era la actividad principal de la empresa o el establecimiento en que trabajaba o había trabajado por última vez la persona censada. Para codificar la rama de actividad económica se utilizaron 215 grupos de la nomenclatura nacional. Se establecieron enlaces con la CIIU-Rev.3 en el nivel de clases (clave de 4 dígitos).

b) Ocupación: Para determinarla, se pidió indicar la naturaleza exacta de la profesión que la persona censada sea ejercía, sea había ejercido en su último trabajo. Para codificar la ocupación, se utilizaron más de 65 grandes subgrupos de la nomenclatura nacional. Se establecieron enlaces con la CIUO-88.

c) Situación en el empleo: La pregunta formulada se refería a la situación en el empleo principal que la persona censada tenía (o había tenido cuando trabajó por última vez). Para codificar la situación en el empleo se utilizaron siete categorías, a saber: empleador; trabajador independiente con local; trabajador independiente a domicilio; trabajador independiente sin local; asalariado; trabajador familiar; aprendiz.

8. Diferencias principales con el censo anterior:
La principal diferencia es la actualización de las nomenclaturas de las ocupaciones y de las actividades económicas.

9. Publicación de los resultados del censo:
Se había previsto la difusión de los resultados definitivos del censo a partir de 1995, en dos publicaciones: "Population légale du Royaume" y "Caractéristiques socio-économiques (niveau national et niveau provincial de 65 provinces)".

El organismo responsable de estas publicaciones es la Direction de la Statistique, B.P. 178, Rabat.

Se previó que los resultados del censo de 1994 estarían disponibles también en cuadros inéditos, disquetes y cintas magnéticas.

MARTINICA

1. Nombre y dirección del organismo responsable del censo:
Institut national de la statistique et des études économiques (IN-

SEE), Service régional de la Martinique, B.P. 7212, 97233 Schoelcher Cedex, Martinica.

2. Censos de población llevados a cabo desde 1945 (años):

1954, 1961, 1967, 1974, 1982 y 1990. La presente descripción se refiere al censo de 1990 (realizado el 15 de marzo de ese año).

3. Alcance del censo:

a) *Geográfico*: Todo el territorio.

b) *Personas comprendidas*: Toda la población.

4. Período de referencia:

La semana anterior al día del censo.

5. Materias principales:

a) Población total, según sexo y edad: sí
Población económicamente activa por:
b) Sexo y grupo de edad: sí
c) Rama de actividad económica: sí
d) Ocupación: sí
e) Situación en el empleo: sí
f) Nivel más alto de educación: sí
g) Horas de trabajo: no
h) Otras características: sí

Ref. a): La edad se determinó según el año de nacimiento.

Ref. h): El censo también recolectó datos sobre otros temas, a saber: el trabajo a tiempo completo y el trabajo a tiempo parcial, la actividad principal, el número de asalariados empleados por las personas que trabajaban por cuenta propia, la duración del período de búsqueda de trabajo, etc.

6. Conceptos y definiciones:

a) *Población económicamente activa*: Abarcó a todas las personas de 14 o más años de edad que, durante la semana de referencia, estaban ocupadas o desempleadas, conforme a las definiciones que se dan más adelante. Esta definición incluyó también a los miembros de las fuerzas armadas (tanto los militares de carrera como las personas que cumplían su servicio militar). En lo que atañe a la actividad económica, se interrogó únicamente a una muestra de personas, en la que no quedaron incluidos los militares residentes en los cuarteles y las personas detenidas en establecimientos penitenciarios.

b) *Empleo*: Se consideró "ocupada" a toda persona que, durante la semana de referencia, ejerció una profesión o un cargo o desempeñó una actividad económica cualquiera, remunerada o no. Para determinar si una persona debía considerarse "ocupada" se hicieron preguntas específicas, en particular: "¿Trabaja usted (a tiempo completo o a tiempo parcial)?"; "¿Es usted: asalariado o trabajador por cuenta propia (agricultor, artesano, comerciante, industrial, miembro de profesión liberal, trabajador familiar no remunerado, etc.)?", y "Si usted trabaja por cuenta propia: ¿cuántas personas asalariadas emplea? (no incluya a los aprendices o al personal doméstico; si es agricultor, incluya únicamente a los asalariados permanentes)". La definición abarcó también a las personas que desempeñaban un trabajo de utilidad pública (TUC, etc.), a las ocupadas por una agencia de colocación, a las empleadas según un contrato de duración limitada y a las empleadas según un contrato de readaptación o perfeccionamiento profesional.

Se ha indicado que fueron incluidas las siguientes categorías:

i)   personas que trabajan sin remuneración en una empresa o explotación familiar;

ii)   personas que producen bienes primarios para el autoconsumo;

iii)   personas ocupadas pero temporalmente ausentes de su trabajo;

iv)   estudiantes que trabajan a tiempo parcial;

v)   trabajadores estacionales u ocasionales, a condición de que estuviesen activos en el momento del censo;

vi)   conscriptos del servicio militar o civil;

vii)   aprendices (bajo contrato) y personas que siguen un curso de formación (principalmente en una empresa o un centro de formación).

Sólo pueden identificarse por separado las categorías i), vi) y vii).

c) *Desempleo*: Se consideró "desempleada" a toda persona que indicó espontáneamente que esa era su situación y que buscaba empleo. Para determinar si una persona debía considerarse "desempleada" se preguntó "¿Está usted desempleado(a) (inscrito(a) o no en la Agencia Nacional del Empleo)?", "¿Ha trabajado ya? (si este es el caso, ¿cuál fue su

ocupación principal?)", y "¿Busca usted empleo (desde hace: menos de tres meses; más de tres meses y menos de un año; más de un año pero menos de dos años; dos o más años)?".

7. Clasificaciones utilizadas:

Tanto las personas ocupadas como las desempleadas anteriormente empleadas fueron clasificadas por ocupación. Sólo las personas ocupadas incluidas en la muestra fueron clasificadas por rama de actividad y por situación en el empleo.

a) *Rama de actividad económica*: Se pidió a las personas censadas que indicasen la dirección, el nombre o la razón social del establecimiento que las empleaba o que dirigían, así como la actividad exacta de dicho establecimiento (por ejemplo: comercio mayorista de vinos, fabricación de estructuras metálicas, transporte terrestre de pasajeros, etc.). Para codificar la rama de actividad económica se utilizaron 100 grupos de la Nomenclatura de Actividades y Productos (NAP). No se establecieron enlaces con la CIIU.

b) *Ocupación*: Se pidió a las personas censadas que indicasen la ocupación que ejercían o que habían ejercido la última vez que habían trabajado, procurando definirla de la manera más precisa posible (por ejemplo: obrero electricista de manutención, chófer de camión de carga, vendedor de electrodomésticos, ingeniero químico, cajera de almacén de autoservicio, etc.), a efectos de determinar el grupo de ocupaciones. Sin embargo, se dejó la posibilidad de que la persona encuestada formulase su propia respuesta. La clasificación en un grupo determinado se efectuó durante el tratamiento informatizado de los datos. Para codificar la ocupación se utilizó un sistema de codificación directa en 42 grupos. No se establecieron enlaces con la CIUO.

c) *Situación en el empleo*: Para codificar esta variable se utilizaron cinco categorías, a saber: independiente por cuenta propia; empleador; asalariado; trabajador familiar no remunerado; otra situación.

8. Diferencias principales con el censo anterior:

En 1982, para incluir a una persona en la población económicamente activa se había aplicado un límite de edad mínima de 15 años.

Además, en el censo de 1982 se había clasificado por rama de actividad y por situación en el empleo tanto a las personas ocupadas como a los desempleados anteriormente empleados.

9. Publicación de los resultados del censo:

La publicación en que figuran los resultados definitivos del censo lleva por título: "Population, Emploi, Logements; Evolution 1975-1982-1990 (Série jaune)", 1992.

El organismo responsable de esta publicación es el Institut national de la statistique et des études économiques (INSEE), 18 boulevard Adolphe-Pinard, 75675 París Cedex 14.

También se dispone de los resultados del censo de 1990 en disquetes, cintas magnéticas y otras modalidades de presentación que se soliciten.

MAURICIO

1. Nombre y dirección del organismo responsable del censo:

Central Statistical Office, Toorawa Centre, Sir S. Ramgoolam St., Port Louis.

2. Censos de población llevados a cabo desde 1945 (años):

1952, 1962, 1972, 1983 y 1990. La presente descripción se refiere al censo de población de 1990 (realizado el 1o. de julio de ese año).

3. Alcance del censo:

a) *Geográfico*: Todo el país.

b) *Personas comprendidas*: Toda la población.

4. Período de referencia:

La semana anterior al día del censo, en cuanto a la actividad actual, y el año anterior (es decir, 1989) en cuanto a la actividad habitual.

5. Materias principales:

a) Población total, según sexo y edad: sí
Población económicamente activa por:
b) Sexo y grupo de edad: sí
c) Rama de actividad económica: sí

d) Ocupación: sí
e) Situación en el empleo: sí
f) Nivel más alto de educación: sí
g) Horas de trabajo: sí
h) Otras características: sí

Ref. a): La edad se determinó según los años cumplidos en el último cumpleaños.

Ref. g): En lo que atañe al período de referencia corto, se pidió a las personas ocupadas que indicaran sus horas de trabajo efectivas en el empleo. En cuanto al período de referencia largo, se pidió a las personas ocupadas que indicaran el período total trabajado, expresado en cantidad de semanas.

Ref. h): El censo también recolectó datos sobre: el tipo de establecimiento; el lugar de trabajo; y la duración de la relación de trabajo con el empleador del momento o el empleador más reciente. Además, a las personas que dijeron no haber estado disponibles para trabajar durante la semana anterior al censo se les pidió que indicaran los motivos de tal situación (cumplimiento de obligaciones familiares, estudios, enfermedad, accidente o invalidez, jubilación completa, otros motivos).

6. Conceptos y definiciones:

a) Población económicamente activa: Abarcó a todas las personas de 12 o más años de edad que, durante los períodos de referencia, estaban ocupadas o desempleadas, ya sea en forma permanente o habitual, conforme a las definiciones que se dan más adelante. No se hicieron preguntas sobre la actividad económica a los extranjeros que se encontraban en Mauricio en los períodos de referencia, pero que habitualmente residían fuera de su territorio. En Mauricio no existe servicio militar obligatorio.

b) Empleo: Se consideró "ocupada" a toda persona que, durante el período de referencia corto, estaba desempeñando alguna actividad laboral remunerada, dentro y fuera del hogar. Para determinar la actividad "actual" de la persona se utilizaron las preguntas siguientes: "¿Cuántas horas en total trabajó por una remuneración, en calidad de asalariado, independiente o trabajador familiar, durante la semana del lunes 25 de junio al domingo 1o. de julio de 1990?"; y "Señale si estaba ocupado en un empleo, negocio propio, empresa familiar o explotación agrícola en el que no pudo trabajar por motivo de enfermedad, accidente, feriado, conflicto laboral, receso estacional, desorganización provisional, etc.". Se consideró "actualmente ocupada" a toda persona que respondió "Una hora o más" a la primera pregunta, o si respondió "0 horas" a la primera pregunta y "Sí" a la segunda.

Se ha indicado que fueron incluidas las siguientes categorías:

i)   personas que trabajan sin remuneración en una empresa o negocio familiar;
ii)   personas que producen bienes primarios para el autoconsumo;
iii) personas ocupadas pero temporalmente ausentes de su trabajo;
iv)   estudiantes que trabajan a tiempo parcial;
v)   trabajadores estacionales u ocasionales;
vi)   aprendices y personas que siguen un curso de formación.

Sólo las categorías i), iii), iv) y vi) pueden identificarse por separado, mediante preguntas específicas relativas a la categoría de empleo y a la situación en el empleo.

c) Desempleo: Se consideró "desempleada" a toda persona que, durante los períodos de referencia, se encontraba sin trabajo y buscaba empleo. Se consideró "actualmente desempleada" a toda persona que respondió "0 horas" y "No", respectivamente, a las preguntas que figuran en el párrafo 6 b), y "Sí" a las dos preguntas siguientes: "¿Inició alguna gestión para buscar trabajo en algún momento durante las pasadas ocho semanas?"; y "¿Estaba disponible para trabajar durante la semana pasada?". (Véase también el párrafo 5, ref. h).

7. Clasificaciones utilizadas:

Tanto las personas ocupadas como las desempleadas anteriormente empleadas se clasificaron por rama de actividad económica, por ocupación y por situación en el empleo.

a) Rama de actividad económica: Para determinarla se preguntó: "Describa en forma completa las actividades industriales, comerciales o de servicios que se despliegan en su lugar de trabajo (actual o último). No emplee términos genéricos (como agricultura, reparaciones, fábrica, escuela, tienda, etc.), sino designaciones precisas (como cultivo de caña de azúcar, reparación de automóviles, confección de prendas de punto, escuela primaria, fabricación de mobiliario casero, tienda

de electrodomésticos, etc.). En caso de haber trabajado en más de una actividad, describa aquélla en que desempeñó el trabajo principal." Para codificar la rama de actividad se utilizaron 263 grupos de la clasificación nacional de actividades. Se estableció una correspondencia unívoca entre la clasificación nacional de 3 dígitos y la CIIU-Rev.2 en el nivel de grupos (4 dígitos).

b) Ocupación: Para determinarla se preguntó: "Describa claramente el trabajo que desempeñaba (o que desempeñó) en su último trabajo. No emplee términos genéricos (como oficinista, chófer, obrero fabril, profesor, etc.), sino designaciones precisas (como auxiliar de contabilidad, conductor de autobús, obrero ebanista, maestro primario, etc.). En caso de haber trabajado en más de una ocupación, describa aquélla a la que dedicó más tiempo." Para codificar la ocupación se utilizó la CIUO-88, en el nivel de grupos primarios (4 dígitos).

c) Situación en el empleo: Para codificar esta variable se utilizaron ocho grupos: trabajador independiente, con personal; trabajador independiente, sin personal; trabajador no remunerado al servicio del cónyuge o de otro familiar en una explotación agrícola; aprendiz, remunerado o no; empleado remunerado mensualmente; empleado remunerado a jornal, a la semana, cada dos semanas o por tarea; miembro de cooperativa de producción; otras.

8. Diferencias principales con el censo anterior:

Cabe mencionar las siguientes diferencias:

El censo de 1983 abarcó únicamente a las personas presentes en la noche del censo, mientras que el de 1990 incluyó también a los miembros del grupo familiar que estaban ausentes aquella noche.

En el censo de 1983 se usó sólo un período de referencia corto, de una semana.

Para determinar la situación en la actividad (es decir, empleado, desempleado o inactivo), en 1983 se hicieron dos preguntas:

i)   "¿Trabajó mediando una remuneración o ganancia (incluidos el empleo independiente y el trabajo en una explotación agrícola propia), ayudó sin remuneración a un miembro de su grupo familiar en la finca, empresa o negocio familiar, o trabajó como aprendiz no remunerado algún día entre el lunes 27 de junio y el sábado 2 de julio del año en curso? Si la respuesta es 'Sí', indique la cantidad de días trabajados, incluidos los días en que tomó vacaciones pagadas". Si la respuesta era afirmativa, se consideró que la persona estaba empleada.

ii)   "Si la respuesta a la pregunta anterior es 'No', indique si la persona: a) tenía un empleo pero estaba enferma o en vacaciones; o si se trataba de: b) un estudiante; c) una ama de casa o un familiar que ayuda en el trabajo doméstico; d) una persona internada en una institución; e) una persona con discapacidad permanente; f) un rentista; g) un jubilado; h) un niño mayor de 12 años pero menor de 15, que no asiste a la escuela y no está buscando trabajo; i) una persona sin trabajo y buscando activamente uno; j) otra categoría". Se consideró desempleada a toda persona que respondiese "No" a la primera pregunta, y "sin trabajo y buscando activamente uno" a la segunda.

En 1983, se preguntó por la cantidad de días trabajados durante la semana de referencia (incluidos los días de vacaciones pagadas). Los miembros de las cooperativas de productores no figuraron como grupo aparte. Se preguntó la rama de actividad y la ocupación a todas las personas ocupadas y a las desempleadas anteriormente empleadas, datos que se codificaron, respectivamente, en los niveles de 4 dígitos de la CIIU-Rev.2 y de 3 dígitos de la CIUO-68.

9. Publicación de los resultados del censo:

Los resultados definitivos del censo se publicaron bajo el título "1990 Housing and Population Census of Mauritius - Economic Characteristics", en 1991.

La organización responsable de la publicación es la Central Statistical Office, Port Louis.

Algunos cuadros existen también en disquetes; los cuadros inéditos están a disposición de quienes los soliciten.

234

MEXICO

1. Nombre y dirección del organismo responsable del censo:

Instituto Nacional de Estadística, Geografía e Informática (INEGI), Prolongación Héroe de Nacozari No. 2301 Sur, C.P. 20290, Aguascalientes, AGS., México, D.F.

2. Censos de población llevados a cabo desde 1945 (años):

1950, 1960, 1970, 1980 y 1990. La presente descripción se refiere al censo de población de 1990 (realizado del 12 al 16 de marzo).

3. Alcance del censo:

a) *Geográfico*: Todo el país.

b) *Personas comprendidas*: Toda la población.

4. Periodo de referencia:

La semana anterior al levantamiento, es decir, del 5 al 11 de Marzo.

5. Materias principales:

a) Población total, según sexo y edad:	sí
Población económicamente activa por:	
b) Sexo y grupo de edad:	sí
c) Rama de actividad económica:	sí
d) Ocupación:	sí
e) Situación en el empleo:	sí
f) Nivel más alto de educación:	...
g) Horas de trabajo:	sí
h) Otras características:	sí

Ref. a): Se definió la edad en términos al último cumpleaños.

Ref. g): Se refiere a las horas efectivamente trabajadas por las personas ocupadas que trabajaron durante el periodo de referencia.

Ref. h): Se estudiaron los ingresos por trabajo (a la semana, a la quincena, al mes, al año).

6. Conceptos y definiciones:

a) *Población económicamente activa*: Incluye a todas las personas de 12 años y más que, durante la semana de referencia, se encontraban empleadas o desempleadas, tal y como se definen más adelante. La definición incluye a todos los miembros de las fuerzas armadas.

b) *Empleo*: Se consideran "empleadas" a las personas de 12 años y más, que respondieron afirmativamente a las preguntas "La semana pasada, esta persona: ¿trabajó?; ¿tenía trabajo, pero no trabajó?".

Se ha indicado que quedan incluidas las siguientes categorías:

i) personas que trabajan sin remuneración en una empresa familiar;

ii) personas en la producción de bienes primarios para el autoconsumo;

iii) personas ocupadas pero temporalmente ausentes de su trabajo;

iv) estudiantes que trabajan medio tiempo;

v) trabajadores estacionales u ocasionales;

vi) conscriptos del servicio militar o civil;

vii) aprendices y personas que siguen un curso de formación.

Solamente a las personas de las categorías i) y v) se pueden identificar separadamente. Para la categoría i), su identificación se logra por la pregunta sobre la situación en el trabajo, en la opción "Trabajador sin pago en el negocio o predio familiar". Para la categoría v), no hay una pregunta con el propósito explícito de identificarla; sólo se puede obtener una aproximación de su volumen por la pregunta "Horas trabajadas la semana pasada".

c) *Desempleo*: Se consideran como "desempleadas" a las personas que respondieron negativamente a las preguntas utilizadas para la definición del empleo más alto, pero afirmativamente a la pregunta "¿buscó trabajo?".

7. Clasificaciones utilizadas:

Solamente las personas ocupadas se clasificaron por rama de actividad económica, por ocupación y según la situación en el empleo.

a) *Rama de actividad económica*: Para establecer la rama de actividad económica, las preguntas utilizadas son "¿A qué se dedica el negocio, predio, empresa, institución o lugar donde trabajó?" y "¿En dónde trabaja (por ejemplo: en el campo, en una fábrica, en un taller mecánico)?". Se utilizaron 14 sectores, 57 subsectores y 220 ramas de actividad para codificar esta variable, comparables con las grandes divisiones y las divisiones de la CIIU-Rev.2.

b) *Ocupación*: Para establecer la ocupación, las preguntas utilizadas son "¿Cuál es el oficio, puesto o cargo que tiene en su trabajo principal?" y "¿Cuáles son las tareas o funciones que hace en su trabajo?". Se utilizaron 18 grupos principales, 129 subgrupos, 508 grupos unitarios y 9600 ocupaciones individuales para codificar esta variable, los cuales son comparables con la CIUO-88 a nivel de grandes grupos, subgrupos principales, subgrupos y grupos primarios.

c) *Situación en el empleo*: Para determinar esta característica, se preguntó por la categoría que tenía en su empleo principal, codificada en cinco grupos (empleado u obrero; jornalero o peón; trabajador por su cuenta; patrón o empresario; trabajador sin pago en el negocio o predio familiar).

8. Diferencias principales con el censo anterior:

Respecto al censo de 1980, los volúmenes de la población económicamente activa y de la población económicamente inactiva se captaron esencialmente de la misma forma; sin embargo, dado que la semana anterior al levantamiento limita considerablemente la captación de los buscadores de trabajo, en el censo de 1990 se optó por no distinguirlos según si tienen experiencia laboral o buscan trabajo por primera vez, como se hizo en el censo anterior.

Respecto de la clasificación del tipo de inactividad, el censo no consideró un rubro exclusivo para ubicar a los rentistas, que quedaron incluidos en la categoría de "otros inactivos".

A diferencia del censo anterior, el de 1990 sólo captó las características económicas (rama de actividad, ocupación principal, situación en la ocupación, horas de trabajo e ingresos por trabajo) de la población ocupada, en lugar de hacerlo para la población económicamente activa, lo que permitió simplificar la redacción de las preguntas del tema.

Para captar la actividad económica, el censo de 1990 incluyó dos preguntas complementarias con opción de respuesta abierta, a diferencia del censo anterior que incluyó la siguiente pregunta cerrada: "¿Qué cultiva, fabrica, vende, transporta, extrae o qué servicio da el establecimiento donde tuvo su empleo principal, o el último que tuvo, si estaba desempleado?".

Para captar la ocupación principal, el censo de 1990 incluyó dos preguntas abiertas; el censo anterior solo preguntó una: "La semana pasada, ¿cuál fué su ocupación u oficio en su empleo principal, o en el último que tuvo si estaba desempleado?".

La pregunta sobre la situación en la ocupación del censo de 1990 se distingue de la del censo anterior en lo siguiente: i) Se eliminó la opción "Miembro de cooperativa de producción"; ii) La opción "Trabajador por un sueldo, salario o jornal en dinero o en especie" del censo pasado se dividió en dos opciones: "Empleado u obrero" y "Jornalero o peón"; iii) La alternativa "Trabajador sin recibir sueldo, salario, jornal u otra forma de pago en dinero o especie" del censo pasado se restringió a trabajadores familiares sin pago, excluyendo a los trabajadores no familiares no remunerados.

Respecto de la variable "ingreso", el censo de 1980 captó el ingreso total de la población de 12 años y más; en cambio el censo de 1990 se limitó a captar los ingresos que la población ocupada recibe por su trabajo.

9. Publicación de los resultados del censo:

Los resultados nacionales se publicaron en marzo de 1992, así como los resultados de cada una de las 32 entidades federativas del país.

El título exacto de la publicación con los resultados nacionales es "Estados Unidos Mexicanos; Resumen General; XI Censo General de Población y Vivienda, 1990".

La organización responsable de la publicación es el Instituto Nacional de Estadística, Geografía e Informática (INEGI), Prolongación Héroe de Nacozari No. 2301 Sur, Aguascalientes, AGS.

Los resultados nacionales del censo, así como los correspondientes a las entidades federativas, se presentan también en disquetes.

MONGOLIA

1. Nombre y dirección del organismo responsable del censo:
Bureau of Population Census, State Statistical Office, Ulan Bator.

2. Censos de población llevados a cabo desde 1945 (años):
1979 y 1989. La presente descripción se refiere al censo de población de 1989 (realizado el 5 de enero de ese año).

3. Alcance del censo:
a) *Geográfico*: Todo el país.

b) *Personas comprendidas*: Toda la población.

4. Periodo de referencia:
El día del censo.

5. Materias principales:
a) Población total, según sexo y edad: sí

Población económicamente activa por:

b) Sexo y grupo de edad: sí

c) Rama de actividad económica: sí

d) Ocupación: sí

e) Situación en el empleo: sí

f) Nivel más alto de educación: sí

g) Horas de trabajo: no

h) Otras características: no

Ref. a): La edad se determinó según los años cumplidos en el último cumpleaños.

6. Conceptos y definiciones:
a) *Población económicamente activa*: Abarcó a los varones de 16 a 59 años de edad y a las mujeres de 16 a 54 años que estaban ocupados o desempleados, conforme con las definiciones que se dan más adelante. La definición no incluyó a los miembros de las fuerzas armadas. Tampoco quedaron incluidos los estudiantes con empleo a tiempo parcial ni los que buscaban trabajo.

b) *Empleo*: Se consideró "ocupado" a todo varón de 16 a 59 años de edad y a toda mujer de 16 a 54 años que figuraban en la lista de trabajadores de cualquier empresa en el momento del censo.

Se ha indicado que fueron incluidas las siguientes categorías:

i) personas que trabajan sin remuneración en una empresa o negocio familiar;

ii) personas que producen bienes primarios para el autoconsumo;

iii) personas ocupadas pero temporalmente ausentes de su trabajo;

iv) trabajadores estacionales u ocasionales;

v) aprendices y personas que siguen un curso de formación.

Ninguna de estas categorías puede identificarse separadamente.

c) *Desempleo*: Se consideró "desempleado" a todo varón de 16 a 59 años de edad y "desempleada" a toda mujer de 16 a 54 años que no figuraban en la lista de trabajadores de ninguna empresa en el momento del censo.

7. Clasificaciones utilizadas:
Tanto las personas ocupadas como las desempleadas anteriormente empleadas se clasificaron por ocupación. Sólo las personas ocupadas se clasificaron por rama de actividad económica y por situación en el empleo.

a) *Rama de actividad económica*: Para determinarla, se utilizaron 12 grupos de la clasificación nacional: industria; agricultura; construcción; transporte; comunicaciones; comercio; vivienda y servicios públicos; ciencia; salud pública y cultura física; seguros; cultura, educación y arte; y otras actividades. No se establecieron enlaces con la CIUO.

b) *Ocupación*: Para codificar esta variable, se utilizaron 982 grupos de la clasificación nacional. No se establecieron enlaces con la CIUO.

c) *Situación en el empleo*: Para codificar esta variable, se utilizaron cinco grupos: organismos estatales y de la administración (ministerios, servicios, etc.); empresas del sector público; organismos administrativos provinciales; organismos administrativos de distrito; empresas.

8. Diferencias principales con el censo anterior:
No hubo diferencias significativas.

9. Publicación de los resultados del censo:
Los datos definitivos relativos a la población económicamente activa y sus componentes se publicaron en marzo de 1990, en el volumen que lleva por título "Population Census of Mongolia, 1989".

El organismo responsable de esta publicación es la State Statistical Office, Ulan Bator.

No se dispone de los resultados en otros soportes.

NAMIBIA

1. Nombre y dirección del organismo responsable del censo:
Central Statistics Office, National Planning Commission, Private Bag 13356, Windhoek.

2. Censos de población llevados a cabo desde 1945 (años):
1960, 1981 y 1991. La presente descripción se refiere al censo de población de 1991 (realizado el 20 de octubre de ese año).

3. Alcance del censo:
a) *Geográfico*: Todo el país.

b) *Personas comprendidas*: Toda la población.

4. Periodo de referencia:
La semana anterior al día del censo.

5. Materias principales:
a) Población total, según sexo y edad: sí

Población económicamente activa por:

b) Sexo y grupo de edad: sí

c) Rama de actividad económica: sí

d) Ocupación: sí

e) Situación en el empleo: sí

f) Nivel más alto de educación: sí

g) Horas de trabajo: no

h) Otras características: no

Ref. a): La edad se determinó según los años cumplidos en el último cumpleaños.

6. Conceptos y definiciones:
a) *Población económicamente activa*: Abarcó a todas las personas de 10 o más años de edad que, durante la semana de referencia, estaban ocupadas o desempleadas, conforme a las definiciones que se dan más adelante. La definición no incluyó a los miembros de las fuerzas armadas.

b) *Empleo*: Se consideró "ocupada" a toda persona que, a la pregunta "Durante los siete días anteriores al día del censo, ¿trabajó por una remuneración en calidad de asalariado, independiente o trabajador familiar?", respondió "Sí" o "No, pero tenía un empleo o una empresa".

Se ha indicado que fueron incluidas las siguientes categorías:

i) personas que trabajan sin remuneración en una empresa o negocio familiar;

ii) personas que producen bienes primarios para el autoconsumo;

iii) personas ocupadas pero temporalmente ausentes de su trabajo;

iv) estudiantes que trabajan a tiempo parcial;

v) trabajadores estacionales u ocasionales;

vi) aprendices y personas que siguen un curso de formación.

Sólo las categorías i), iii) y iv) pueden identificarse por separado.

c) *Desempleo*: Se consideró "desempleada" a toda persona que, a la pregunta formulada en el párrafo 6 b), respondió sea "Desempleado (anteriormente ocupado)", sea "Desempleado (en busca de un primer empleo)". La definición no incluyó a los estudiantes que buscaban trabajo.

7. Clasificaciones utilizadas:
Tanto las personas ocupadas como las desempleadas anteriormente empleadas se clasificaron por rama de actividad económica, por ocupación y por situación en el empleo.

a) *Rama de actividad económica*: Para determinarla se preguntó: "¿Qué tipo de actividad se lleva a cabo en su lugar de trabajo?"; y "¿Cuáles son los principales productos o servicios que se fabrican o se prestan en su lugar de trabajo?". Para codificar la rama de actividad se utilizaron 307 grupos de la clasificación nacional. Los enlaces con la CIIU-Rev.3 se establecieron en el nivel de clases (4 dígitos).

b) Ocupación: Para determinarla se preguntó: "¿Qué tipo de trabajo desempeñaba usted?"; y "¿Cuáles eran sus principales funciones en este empleo?". Para codificar la ocupación se utilizaron 396 grupos de la clasificación nacional. Se establecieron enlaces con la CIUO-88 a nivel de grupos primarios (4 dígitos).

c) Situación en el empleo: Para determinarla se preguntó: "En este empleo, ¿trabajaba como: empleador (con personal remunerado); trabajador por cuenta propia (sin personal remunerado); empleado estatal; empleado particular; trabajador familiar no remunerado; empleado de un gobierno extranjero; empleado de una organización internacional; otro puesto?". Para codificar esta variable se utilizaron los ocho grupos indicados.

8. Diferencias principales con el censo anterior:
En el censo de 1981 se aplicaron edades límite, de 16 a 65 años para los hombres y de 16 a 60 años para las mujeres.

En 1981, se había definido como "persona en busca de trabajo" a toda persona dentro de los límites de edad que declarase no tener una actividad económica, estar buscando activamente empleo y ser capaz de comenzar a trabajar en el plazo de una semana de encontrar una ocupación.

9. Publicación de los resultados del censo:
Los resultados definitivos se publicaron en agosto de 1993, bajo el título "Republic of Namibia, 1991 Population and Housing Census, Report A, Statistical tables (based on old districts)". Los datos se han presentado también en publicaciones más recientes, como: "Republic of Namibia, 1991 Population and Housing Census, Report B, Volumes I-III, Statistical tables (based on new regions)", en abril de 1994; "Republic of Namibia, 1991 Population and Housing Census, Report C, Statistics on enumeration areas", en abril de 1994; "Administrative and Methodological Report", en agosto de 1994; y "Republic of Namibia, 1991 Population and Housing Census, Basic analysis with Highlights", en 1995.

La organización responsable de estas publicaciones es el Central Statistics Office, National Planning Commission, Private Bag 13356, Windhoek.

Los resultados definitivos están disponibles en disquetes.

NAURU

1. Nombre y dirección del organismo responsable del censo:
Department of Island Development and Industry, o también el Bureau of Statistics, Government Office, Distrito de Yaren, República de Nauru.

2. Censos de población llevados a cabo desde 1945 (años):
1947, 1952, 1957, 1962, 1967, 1977, 1983 y 1992. La presente descripción se refiere al censo de población de 1992 (realizado el 17 de abril de ese año).

3. Alcance del censo:
a) Geográfico: Todo el país.
b) Personas comprendidas: Toda la población.

4. Periodo de referencia:
La semana anterior al día del censo.

5. Materias principales:
a) Población total, según sexo y edad:	sí

Población económicamente activa por:
b) Sexo y grupo de edad:	sí
c) Rama de actividad económica:	sí
d) Ocupación:	sí
e) Situación en el empleo:	sí
f) Nivel más alto de educación:	sí
g) Horas de trabajo:	sí
h) Otras características:	sí

Ref. a): La edad se determinó según el año de nacimiento.

Ref. g): Se pidió a las personas ocupadas que precisaran cuál era su horario de trabajo habitual y cuántas horas habían trabajado efectivamente durante el período de referencia.

Ref. h): El censo también recopiló información sobre el empleo secundario, sobre los ingresos principales y los ingresos secundarios, sobre las causas del desempleo, sobre el tipo de actividades laborales tradicionales (pesca, buceo, productos artesanales, etc.) y sobre el tiempo dedicado a éstas.

6. Conceptos y definiciones:
a) Población económicamente activa: Abarcó a todas las personas que, durante la semana de referencia, estaban sea ocupadas, sea desempleadas, conforme a las definiciones que se dan más adelante. La edad mínima para quedar incluido en la población económicamente activa fue de 10 años. Ahora bien, en lo que atañe a la publicación de los resultados, los cuadros generales sobre "situación en el empleo" y "tipo de empleador" se establecieron teniendo en cuenta la edad mínima de 10 años, pero los cuadros sobre cuestiones precisas como "clasificación profesional" y otras se establecieron aplicando una edad mínima de 15 años. Nauru no tiene otras fuerzas armadas que las de policía local.

b) Empleo: Se consideró "ocupadas" a todas las personas que habían trabajado al menos una hora durante la semana de referencia.

Se ha indicado que fueron incluidas las siguientes categorías:
i) personas que trabajan sin remuneración en una empresa o negocio familiar;
ii) personas que producen bienes primarios para el autoconsumo;
iii) personas ocupadas pero temporalmente ausentes de su trabajo;
iv) estudiantes que trabajan a tiempo parcial;
v) personas con más de un empleo;
vi) aprendices y personas que siguen un curso de formación.

Exceptuando la categoría iv), todas las demás pueden identificarse por separado.

c) Desempleo: Se consideró "desempleada" a toda persona que, durante la semana de referencia no tenía empleo aun cuando estaba en condiciones de trabajar, pero no había podido encontrar ni siquiera una hora de trabajo en los últimos 7 días. La definición no incluyó a los estudiantes que buscaban trabajo.

7. Clasificaciones utilizadas:
Sólo las personas ocupadas fueron clasificadas por rama de actividad económica, por ocupación y según la situación en el empleo.

a) Rama de actividad económica: Para codificar esta variable, se utilizaron 5 "grupos generales de actividad" (divididos en "departamentos", "secciones", "tipo de actividad", etc.): sector estatal; administración local; Nauru Phosphate Corporation; otras empresas privadas; otras actividades. No se establecieron enlaces con la CIIU.

b) Ocupación: Se pidió a las personas ocupadas que describieran su ocupación, utilizando por lo menos dos palabras. Para codificar la ocupación se utilizó la clasificación nacional. Se establecieron enlaces con la CIUO-88 en el nivel de grandes grupos (clave de 1 dígito).

c) Situación en el empleo: Para determinarla se preguntó: "¿Para quién trabajó usted?". La situación en el empleo quedó determinada en función del "lugar de trabajo" y de la "ocupación". Para codificar esta variable se utilizaron 7 grupos: empleado del Estado; empleado de la administración local; empleado de la Nauru Phosphate Corporation (NPC); comerciante, trabajador por cuenta propia o empleador; colaborador o socio de una empresa (empleado o empleador); colaborador o miembro de una cooperativa (empleado o empleador); otra actividad.

8. Diferencias principales con el censo anterior:
En los censos anteriores no se recopilaron datos sobre la actividad económica.

9. Publicación de los resultados del censo:
Los resultados definitivos que se refieren a la población económicamente activa y sus componentes se publicaron en diciembre de 1993, en un volumen que lleva por título "1992 National Census of Nauru: Main Report".

El organismo responsable de esta publicación es el Bureau of Statistics, Government Offices, Distrito de Yaren.

Los resultados del censo existen también en cuadros inéditos, pero su divulgación está sujeta a una autorización ministerial.

NEPAL

1. Nombre y dirección del organismo responsable del censo:
Central Bureau of Statistics, National Planning Commission Secretariat, Ramshah Path, Thapathali, Kathmandu.

2. Censos de población llevados a cabo desde 1945 (años):
1952/54, 1961, 1971, 1981 y 1991. La presente descripción se refiere al censo de población de 1991 (realizado el 22 de junio de ese año).

3. Alcance del censo:
a) Geográfico: Todo el país.

b) Personas comprendidas: Toda la población.

4. Período de referencia:
El período de 12 meses anterior al día del censo.

5. Materias principales:
a) Población total, según sexo y edad:	sí
Población económicamente activa por:	
b) Sexo y grupo de edad:	sí
c) Rama de actividad económica:	sí
d) Ocupación:	sí
e) Situación en el empleo:	sí
f) Nivel más alto de educación:	sí
g) Horas de trabajo:	sí
h) Otras características:	no

Ref. a): La edad se determinó según los años cumplidos en el último cumpleaños.

Ref. g): Se pidió a las personas ocupadas que indicaran el total de meses trabajados durante los últimos 12 meses.

6. Conceptos y definiciones:
a) Población económicamente activa: El censo mide sólo el empleo.

b) Empleo: Abarcó a todas las personas de 10 o más años de edad que, durante el período de referencia, desempeñaban alguna actividad con valor económico, dentro o fuera del hogar. Para determinar si una persona estaba ocupada se preguntó: "Indique en qué trabajó durante los pasados 12 meses: agricultura, trabajo asalariado, empresa familiar propia, no tuvo trabajo remunerado". La definición incluyó a los miembros de las fuerzas armadas.

Se ha indicado que fueron incluidas las siguientes categorías:

i) personas que trabajan sin remuneración en una empresa o negocio familiar;

ii) personas que producen bienes primarios para el autoconsumo;

iii) personas ocupadas pero temporalmente ausentes de su trabajo;

iv) estudiantes que trabajan a tiempo parcial;

v) trabajadores estacionales u ocasionales;

vi) aprendices y personas que siguen un curso de formación.

Ninguna de estas categorías puede identificarse por separado.

c) Desempleo: No se aplica.

7. Clasificaciones utilizadas:
Todas las personas ocupadas se clasificaron por rama de actividad económica, por ocupación y por situación en el empleo.

a) Rama de actividad económica: Para determinarla se preguntó: "¿Dónde trabajó en los últimos 12 meses?". Para codificar la rama de actividad se utilizaron nueve grupos de la clasificación nacional. Se establecieron enlaces con la CIIU-Rev.2, a nivel de grandes divisiones (1 dígito).

b) Ocupación: Para determinarla se preguntó: "¿En qué trabajó durante los últimos 12 meses?". Para codificar la ocupación se utilizaron siete grupos de la clasificación nacional. Se establecieron enlaces con la CIUO-68, a nivel de grandes grupos (1 dígito).

c) Situación en el empleo: Para determinarla se preguntó: "¿Cuál era su situación en el trabajo?" Las respuestas se registraron en uno de cuatro grupos, a saber: empleador; empleado; trabajador por cuenta propia; y trabajador familiar no remunerado.

8. Diferencias principales con el censo anterior:
En el censo de 1981 se utilizaron un período de referencia corto (una semana) y uno largo (un año). En 1991, sólo se utilizó un período de referencia de un año, y se añadieron preguntas relativas, por ejemplo, a la duración del trabajo, etc.

9. Publicación de los resultados del censo:
Los resultados definitivos del censo se publicaron en noviembre de 1993, bajo el título "Population Census - 1991": Vol. I, Part I to XV; Vol. II (Household Tables); Vol. III (Urban Tables); and Vol. IV (Geographical Tables).

La organización responsable de la publicación es el Central Bureau of Statistics, Thapathali, Kathmandu.

Los datos del censo existen también en disquetes y cintas magnéticas.

NORUEGA

1. Nombre y dirección del organismo responsable del censo:
Statistik Sentralbyrä (Estadísticas de Noruega), Population Census Division, Postuttak, N-2201 Kongsvinger.

2. Censos de población llevados a cabo desde 1945 (años):
1946, 1950, 1960, 1970, 1980 y 1990. La presente descripción se refiere al censo de población de 1990 (realizado el 3 de noviembre de ese año).

3. Alcance del censo:
a) Geográfico: Todo el país. Al igual que en censos anteriores, los noruegos residentes en Svalbard y Jan Mayen fueron registrados como residentes de un municipio del territorio continental y, por ende, no figuran por separado en los resultados del censo. Tampoco figuran en éste los extranjeros residentes en Svalbard y Jan Mayen.

b) Personas comprendidas: Toda la población. El censo abarcó a todas las personas inscritas como residentes en Noruega el 3 de noviembre de 1990. Las preguntas relativas a la actividad económica se formularon con arreglo a dos criterios: empadronamiento completo en los municipios con menos de 6.000 habitantes, y muestreo en los municipios con una población de 6.000 o más habitantes (muestras de 20,0, 14,3, 10,0 u 8,3 por ciento, según el número de habitantes).

4. Período de referencia:
Una semana antes del día del censo (es decir, el período del 27 de octubre al 2 de noviembre) y un año antes del mismo (el período del 3 de noviembre de 1989 al 2 de noviembre de 1990).

5. Materias principales:
a) Población total, según sexo y edad:	sí
Población económicamente activa por:	
b) Sexo y grupo de edad:	sí
c) Rama de actividad económica:	sí
d) Ocupación:	sí
e) Situación en el empleo:	sí
f) Nivel más alto de educación:	sí
g) Horas de trabajo:	sí
h) Otras características:	sí

Ref. a): La edad se determinó según el año de nacimiento (definición principal). También se determinó, en la medida de lo posible, según la edad de la persona censada al 3 de noviembre de 1990.

Ref. g): En lo que atañe al período de referencia corto, por horas de trabajo se entendió a la vez el horario habitual, en el empleo, de las personas ocupadas y las horas efectivas trabajadas, en el empleo, durante la semana. En cuanto al período de referencia largo, las horas de trabajo se remitieron al período total trabajado por las personas ocupadas (expresado en meses de empleo a tiempo completo o a tiempo parcial).

Ref. h): El censo también recolectó datos sobre otros temas relacionados con el trabajo, tales como: lugar de trabajo; frecuencia y duración del traslado al lugar de trabajo (trayecto de ida); y medios de transporte usados a tal efecto durante la semana de referencia.

De diversos registros se recabaron las siguientes variables: datos demográficos (del Registro Central de Población); datos sobre educación (del registro de la CBS relativo a la escolaridad cursada); datos sobre el desempleo declarado (de la Dirección de Trabajo); datos sobre los ingresos, etc. (de los registros tributarios, la Administración Nacional de Seguros y otras entidades).

6. Conceptos y definiciones:

a) Población económicamente activa: Abarcó a todas las personas de 16 o más años de edad incluidas en la muestra que, durante los períodos de referencia, estaban ocupadas o desempleadas, conforme a las definiciones que se dan más adelante. La definición incluyó a los miembros de las fuerzas armadas.

b) Empleo: Para determinar si una persona debía contabilizarse o no como ocupada se utilizaron las siguientes preguntas: "¿Ejerció una actividad remunerada por lo menos durante 100 horas en el año transcurrido del 3 de noviembre de 1989 al 2 de noviembre de 1990?"; y "¿Ejerció una actividad remunerada durante la semana del 27 de octubre al 2 de noviembre de 1990?".

Se ha indicado que fueron incluidas las siguientes categorías:

i) personas que trabajan sin remuneración en una empresa o negocio familiar;

ii) personas que producen bienes primarios para el autoconsumo;

iii) personas ocupadas pero temporalmente ausentes de su trabajo;

iv) estudiantes que trabajan a tiempo parcial;

v) trabajadores estacionales u ocasionales;

vi) conscriptos del servicio militar o civil;

vii) aprendices y personas que siguen un curso de formación.

Sólo pueden identificarse por separado, mediante preguntas específicas, las categorías iii), iv) y vi). Por ejemplo, se puede identificar a las personas en la categoría iv) haciendo la pregunta "¿Cuántas horas trabajó remunerado en la semana del 27 de octubre al 2 de noviembre de 1990?", y consultando el registro de estudiantes. Los conscriptos pueden identificarse recabando datos de las fuerzas armadas.

c) Desempleo: Se consideró "desempleada" a toda persona que el día del censo estaba inscrita como tal. No quedaron incluidos en la definición los estudiantes que buscaban trabajo.

7. Clasificaciones utilizadas:

Tan solo las personas ocupadas incluidas en la muestra con arreglo a la definición de empleo que antecede fueron clasificadas por rama de actividad, por ocupación y por situación en el empleo.

a) Rama de actividad económica: Para determinarla se preguntó: "Indique el nombre y la dirección del lugar de trabajo (empresa o negocio) en el que desempeñó una actividad remunerada durante la mayor parte del año transcurrido entre el 3 de noviembre de 1989 y el 2 de noviembre de 1990 (si no puede indicar la razón social de la empresa, anote el nombre del propietario o del empleador; si trabaja como independiente, sin razón social, indique su propio nombre y dirección)"; y "Describa de la manera más precisa posible la actividad desplegada por el empleador (por ejemplo: fabricación de muebles, venta de automóviles, comercio de libros, agricultura, alquiler-venta (leasing) de maquinaria, arquitectura, etc.)". Por lo que se refiere al 78 por ciento de las personas censadas, la rama de actividad se codificó estableciendo enlaces con el Registro de Empresas, que les asigna 5 dígitos. A efectos de la compilación manual, se utilizaron 3 dígitos. Se establecieron enlaces con la CIIU-Rev.2 a nivel de grupos (4 dígitos). Se previó establecer ulteriormente los enlaces con la CIIU-Rev.3.

b) Ocupación: Para determinarla se hizo la siguiente pregunta: "¿Cuál era su ocupación (cargo) en este lugar de trabajo? (no use nombres genéricos, como, por ejemplo, obrero fabril, asesor o técnico, sino denominaciones más explícitas, como soldador, consultor en publicidad, reparador de teléfonos, auxiliar doméstico, fontanero, peluquero, enfermera, limpiador, cocinero, laminador de metales, vendedor, docente de enfermería, etc.)" Para codificar la ocupación, se utilizaron 84 grupos correspondientes al nivel de 3 dígitos de la Clasificación Normalizada de Ocupaciones en los Países Nórdicos. Se establecieron enlaces con la CIUO-68, a nivel de grandes grupos (1 dígito).

c) Situación en el empleo: Para determinarla, se pidió a las personas empleadas que respondieran a preguntas relativas al puesto de trabajo. Para codificarla, se utilizaron tres grupos, a saber: empleado remunerado permanente o temporal; trabajador independiente (propietario de empresa, en el caso de que ésta estuviese debidamente registrada); trabajador familiar sin remuneración fija, empleado en empresa familiar.

8. Diferencias principales con el censo anterior:

En el censo de 1980, las preguntas sobre el total de horas trabajadas en el período de referencia largo se referían precisamente al número de horas, mientras que en el censo de 1990 se referían al número de meses (trabajados sea a tiempo completo, sea a tiempo parcial). Además, en el censo de 1980 no se hicieron preguntas sobre los horarios normales o convenidos, en relación con el período de referencia corto. La respuesta "desconocido" no figura como valor de variable en los datos de 1990 (salvo en el caso de los municipios, por lo que se refiere al empleo), puesto que los datos que faltaban fueron sustituidos por estimaciones basadas en otros valores de variable dados por la persona censada y por respuestas de otras personas con "características afines".

9. Publicación de los resultados del censo:

Los resultados definitivos del censo relativos a todo el país (variables principales) existen en cintas magnéticas desde febrero de 1992, pero no se han publicado. En abril de 1991 se publicaron cifras provisorias basadas en la tabulación de una muestra de 10.000 formularios de respuesta.

La publicación con los resultados definitivos del censo (sólo en noruego) lleva por título "Folke-og Boligtelling 1990 Landssammendrag".

Los principales resultados se publicaron en 1992, bajo el título "Population and Housing Census. Main Results" (ediciones en noruego y en inglés).

La organización responsable de la publicación es el Central Bureau of Statistics, Population Census Division, Postuttak, N-2201 Kongsvinger.

Los resultados definitivos del censo de 1990 existen también en forma de cuadros inéditos, disquetes, cintas magnéticas y bases de dato de acceso en conexión directa; también se pueden solicitar al servicio de atención al público (pagadero).

NUEVA CALEDONIA

1. Nombre y dirección del organismo responsable del censo:

INSEE (Institut national de la statistique et des études économiques) 18, boulevard Adolphe Pinard, 75675 PARIS CEDEX 14.

2. Censos de población llevados a cabo desde 1945 (años):

1963, 1969, 1976, 1983 y 1989. La presente descripción se refiere al censo de 1989 (realizado el 4 de abril de ese año).

3. Alcance del censo:

a) Geográfico: Todo el territorio.

b) Personas comprendidas: Toda la población.

4. Período de referencia:

La semana anterior al día del censo.

5. Materias principales:

a) Población total, según sexo y edad:	sí
Población económicamente activa por:	
b) Sexo y grupo de edad:	sí
c) Rama de actividad económica:	sí
d) Ocupación:	sí
e) Situación en el empleo:	sí
f) Nivel más alto de educación:	sí
g) Horas de trabajo:	sí
h) Otras características:	sí

Ref. a): La edad se determinó según el año de nacimiento.

Ref. g): El "tiempo de trabajo" se refirió a la vez al horario normal de trabajo de las personas ocupadas y a las modalidades de ejercicio de la ocupación (en forma continua, estacional o intermitente, o excepcional).

Ref. h): El censo también recolectó datos pormenorizados sobre la duración del desempleo (menos de tres meses, de tres meses a un año, de un año a menos de dos años, dos o más años).

6. Conceptos y definiciones:

a) Población económicamente activa: Abarcó a todas las personas de 14 o más años de edad que, durante el período de referencia, estaban ocupadas o desempleadas, según las definiciones que se dan más adelante. La definición incluyó a los miembros de las fuerzas armadas (tanto los militares de carrera como los conscriptos), pero no a los estudiantes que trabajaban a tiempo parcial ni a los estudiantes que buscaban trabajo.

b) Empleo: Se consideró "ocupada" a toda persona que, durante el período de referencia, había trabajado o estado ausente de su trabajo por causas transitorias (vacaciones, enfermedad, maternidad).

Se ha indicado que fueron incluidas las siguientes categorías:

i) personas que trabajan sin remuneración en una empresa o negocio familiar;

ii) personas que producen bienes primarios para el autoconsumo;

iii) personas ocupadas pero temporalmente ausentes de su trabajo;

iv) trabajadores estacionales u ocasionales;

v) conscriptos del servicio militar o civil;

vi) aprendices bajo contrato y personas que siguen un curso de formación.

Todas las categorías antes citadas pueden identificarse por separado.

c) Desempleo: Se consideró "desempleada" a toda persona que indicó espontáneamente que esa era su situación durante el período de referencia.

7. Clasificaciones utilizadas:

Tan sólo las personas ocupadas se clasificaron por rama de actividad económica, por ocupación y según la situación en el empleo.

a) Rama de actividad económica: Se pidió a las personas ocupadas que respondieran a preguntas específicas, indicando en particular la dirección, el nombre o la razón social y la actividad del establecimiento que las empleaba o que dirigían. Para codificar la rama de actividad económica se utilizaron 14 grupos de la clasificación nacional industrial. No se establecieron enlaces con la CIIU.

b) Ocupación: Se pidió a las personas ocupadas que indicasen con un máximo de exactitud su profesión (por ejemplo: obrero electricista de manutención, chófer de camión de carga, vendedor de electrodomésticos, ingeniero químico, cajera de almacén de autoservicio, etc.). Para codificar la ocupación se utilizaron 33 grupos detallados, los que luego se agruparon en 6 grandes grupos. No se ha previsto establecer enlaces con la CIUO.

c) Situación en el empleo: Para determinar su situación en el empleo, se pidió a las personas ocupadas que indicasen cuál era su situación profesional. Se utilizaron nueve grupos: agricultor o ganadero, cazador o pescador; auxiliar familiar; miembro de una profesión liberal; artesano, comerciante o industrial; otra categoría de empleador o de trabajador independiente; trabajador a domicilio por cuenta de una empresa; aprendiz bajo contrato; asalariado del sector privado; asalariado del sector público.

8. Diferencias principales con el censo anterior:

En 1983, no se consideró "desempleadas" a las personas que percibían un subsidio de desempleo.

9. Publicación de los resultados del censo:

Los resultados definitivos del censo se publicaron en 1991.

Los títulos de las publicaciones en que figuran los resultados definitivos son:

− Images de la population de Nouvelle-Calédonie 1989 (INSEE).

− Recensement de la population de Nouvelle-Calédonie 1989: inventaire communal.

− L'activité en Nouvelle-Calédonie en 1989, 3 tomos de cuadros. T1: Constructions logements; T2: Les ménages; T3: Activité individus.

− Inventaire tribal 1989, 3 Tomes: Province Iles Loyauté, Province Nord, Province Sud.

El organismo responsable de esta publicación es el ITSEE (Institut territorial de la statistique et des études économiques, 5 rue du Général Galliéni, B.P. 823, Nouméa, Nouvelle-Calédonie.

También se dispone de los resultados del censo de 1989 en cuadros inéditos.

NUEVA ZELANDIA

1. Nombre y dirección del organismo responsable del censo:

Department of Statistics, 64 Kilmore Street, Christchurch 1.

2. Censos de población llevados a cabo desde 1945 (años):

1945, 1951, 1956, 1961, 1966, 1971, 1976, 1981, 1986 y 1991. La presente descripción se refiere al censo de 1991 (realizado el 5 de marzo de ese año).

3. Alcance del censo:

a) Geográfico: Todo el país.

b) Personas comprendidas: Toda la población.

4. Período de referencia:

Se utilizaron dos períodos de referencia, el día del censo, para determinar las personas ocupadas, y las cuatro semanas anteriores al mismo, para determinar las personas desempleadas.

5. Materias principales:

a) Población total, según sexo y edad:	sí
Población económicamente activa por:	
b) Sexo y grupo de edad:	sí
c) Rama de actividad económica:	sí
d) Ocupación:	sí
e) Situación en el empleo:	sí
f) Nivel más alto de educación:	sí
g) Horas de trabajo:	sí
h) Otras características:	sí

Ref. a): La edad se determinó según los años cumplidos en el último cumpleaños.

Ref. g): El tiempo de trabajo se refiere al número de horas efectivamente trabajadas por las personas ocupadas en su lugar de trabajo. Se pidió a las personas ocupadas temporalmente ausentes de su empleo que indicaran su tiempo de trabajo habitual.

Ref. h): También se hicieron preguntas sobre los principales medios de transporte usados para trasladarse al trabajo el día del censo y sobre el ingreso total en el año que concluyó el 31 de marzo de 1991.

6. Conceptos y definiciones:

a) Población económicamente activa: Abarcó a todas las personas de 15 o más años de edad que, durante los períodos de referencia, estaban sea ocupadas, sea desempleadas, conforme a las definiciones que se dan más adelante. No quedaron incluidos los visitantes extranjeros que no trabajaban en Nueva Zelandia. En cambio, la definición incluyó a los miembros de las fuerzas armadas.

b) Empleo: Se consideró "ocupada" a toda persona que, en el momento del censo, estaba desempeñando una actividad laboral de valor económico, remunerada o no, dentro o fuera del hogar. Para determinar si una persona debía contabilizarse o no como ocupada se preguntó: "¿Tiene usted un empleo, un negocio o empresa, una explotación agrícola o ejerce una profesión liberal?".

Se ha indicado que fueron incluidas las siguientes categorías:

i) personas que trabajan sin remuneración en una empresa o negocio familiar;

ii) personas ocupadas pero temporalmente ausentes de su trabajo;

iii) estudiantes que trabajan a tiempo parcial;

iv) trabajadores estacionales u ocasionales;

v) trabajadores con más de un empleo;

vi) aprendices y personas que siguen un curso de formación.

Sólo pueden identificarse por separado las personas incluidas en las categorías i), iii) y v), en función de sus respuestas a determinadas preguntas.

c) Desempleo: Se consideró "desempleada" a toda persona que, durante las cuatro semanas anteriores al censo, había buscado trabajo activamente y estaba disponible para trabajar a tiempo completo o a tiempo parcial, y que el día del censo no estaba ocupada en un empleo, empresa o explotación agrícola ni ejerciendo una profesión liberal. Para determinar si una persona debía contabilizarse o no como desempleada, se utilizaron las preguntas: "¿Buscó usted un trabajo remunerado durante las pasadas cuatro semanas?", "¿Qué medios usó para buscar un trabajo remunerado?" y "¿Si se le hubiera ofrecido un empleo, hubiese podido comenzar a trabajar la semana pasada?".

7. Clasificaciones utilizadas:
Sólo las personas ocupadas fueron clasificadas por rama de actividad económica, por ocupación y según la situación en el empleo.

a) Rama de actividad económica: Para determinarla se preguntó: "¿Para quién trabaja usted?", "¿Dónde trabaja usted?" y "¿Cuál es la principal actividad que se lleva a cabo en su lugar de trabajo (crianza de ovinos, hospital de maternidad, matadero de aves, consultoría de gestión empresarial, etc.)?". Por actividad principal se entendió el negocio, empresa, industria o actividad de servicios primordial del empleador. Las ramas de actividad se codificaron según el nivel de 5 dígitos de la Clasificación Industrial Normalizada de Nueva Zelandia (NZSIC). Se establecieron enlaces con la CIIU-Rev.2 a nivel de grupos (clave de 4 dígitos).

b) Ocupación: Para determinarla se preguntó: "¿Qué ocupación tiene usted?" y "¿A qué tareas o funciones dedica la mayor parte de su tiempo?". Para codificar la ocupación se utilizaron todos los grupos de la Clasificación Industrial Normalizada de Nueva Zelandia (NZSCO). Se establecieron enlaces con la CIUO-88 a nivel de grupos primarios (clave de 4 dígitos).

c) Situación en el empleo: Para determinar esta variable se preguntó "¿En su actividad laboral es usted: i) trabajador asalariado; ii) trabajador independiente sin personal; iii) empleador, con empresa o negocio propio; iv) trabajador familiar no remunerado?". Para codificar la situación en el empleo se utilizaron los cuatro grupos citados.

8. Diferencias principales con el censo anterior:
En el censo de 1991 se agregaron dos preguntas relativas a los métodos de búsqueda de trabajo (véase el párrafo 6 c), más arriba).

9. Publicación de los resultados del censo:
La publicación en que figuran los resultados del censo lleva por título "National Population Summary", 1992.

El organismo responsable de esta publicación es el Department of Statistics, 64 Kilmore Street, Christchurch 1.

Los resultados del censo están también disponibles en cuadros inéditos, disquetes, cintas magnéticas y discos compactos.

PANAMA

1. Nombre y dirección del organismo responsable del censo:
Dirección de Estadística y Censo, Contraloría General de la República, Apartado 5213, Zona 5, Panamá, República de Panamá.

2. Censos de población llevados a cabo desde 1945 (años):
1950, 1960, 1970, 1980 y 1990. La presente descripción se refiere al censo de población de 1990 (realizado el 13 de mayo).

3. Alcance del censo:
a) Geográfico: Todo el país.

b) Personas comprendidas: Toda la población, salvo los nacionales residentes en el extranjero y, por efecto de la intervención norteamericana, los soldados que se encontraban con este fin en Panamá al momento del censo.

4. Período de referencia:
La semana anterior a la fecha del censo.

5. Materias principales:
a) Población total, según sexo y edad:	sí
Población económicamente activa por:	
b) Sexo y grupo de edad:	sí
c) Rama de actividad económica:	sí
d) Ocupación:	sí
e) Situación en el empleo:	sí
f) Nivel más alto de educación:	sí
g) Horas de trabajo:	no
h) Otras características:	sí

Ref. a): Se definió la edad según los años cumplidos.

Ref. h): Se recogieron informaciones sobre los empleados permanentes y los eventuales y sobre el ingreso total durante el mes anterior a la fecha del censo.

6. Conceptos y definiciones:
a) Población económicamente activa: Incluye a todas las personas de 10 años y más que, durante la semana de referencia, se encontraban empleadas o desempleadas, según las definiciones que se dan más adelante. La definición incluye también todas las fuerzas armadas.

b) Empleo: Se consideran "empleadas" las personas que respondieron afirmativamente a la pregunta siguiente: "¿Trabajó la semana pasada o tiene algún empleo del cual estuvo ausente la semana pasada?".

Se ha indicado que quedan incluidas las siguientes categorías:

i) personas que trabajan sin remuneración en una empresa familiar;
ii) personas en la producción de bienes primarios para el autoconsumo;
iii) personas ocupadas pero temporalmente ausentes de su trabajo;
iv) estudiantes trabajando medio tiempo;
v) trabajadores estacionales u ocasionales;
vi) conscriptos en el servicio militar o civil;
vii) aprendices y personas que siguen un curso de formación.

Solamente las personas de las categorías i) y v) se pueden identificar separadamente a través de preguntas específicas

c) Desempleo: Se consideran "desempleadas" las personas que, durante la semana de referencia, no tenían ocupación o trabajo y declararon que estaban buscando empleo o que era imposible encontrar trabajo.

7. Clasificaciones utilizadas:
Tanto las personas ocupadas como las desocupadas anteriormente ocupadas se clasificaron por rama de actividad económica, por ocupación y según la situación en el empleo.

a) Rama de actividad económica: Para establecer la rama de actividad económica se utilizaron las preguntas siguientes: "¿Donde trabaja o trabajó la última vez?" y "¿A qué se dedica ese negocio, establecimiento, empresa o institución, donde trabaja o trabajó?". Se utilizaron 18 grupos de la clasificación nacional de actividades económicas para codificar esta variable. Estos grupos son compatibles con todos los grupos de la CIIU-Rev.3.

b) Ocupación: Para establecer la ocupación se preguntó lo siguiente: "¿Qué ocupación, oficio o trabajo realizó la semana pasada o la última vez que trabajó?". Se utilizaron 10 grupos de la clasificación nacional de ocupaciones. Estos grupos son compatibles con la CIUO-68 al nivel de los grandes grupos (1 dígito).

c) Situación en el empleo: Para determinar esta variable se preguntó si la persona en su trabajo actual o anterior trabaja o trabajó como: empleado asalariado; independiente o cuenta propia; trabajador familiar sin sueldo; patrono; miembro de una cooperativa de producción o asentamiento. Para codificar la situación en la ocupación se utilizaron los cinco grupos arriba mencionados.

8. Diferencias principales con el censo anterior:
No hubo diferencias significativas.

9. Publicación de los resultados del censo:
El título exacto de la publicación en que se presentarán los datos finales del censo será "Resultados finales básicos" (se harán tres publicaciones por distrito: Panamá, Colón y San Miguelito, y las publicaciones provinciales (febrero de 1991)).

La organización responsable de las publicaciones es la Dirección de Estadística y Censo.

Los resultados del censo están también disponibles en la forma de cintas magnéticas y de cuadros no publicados.

PAPUA NUEVA GUINEA

1. Nombre y dirección del organismo responsable del censo:
National Statistical Office, P.O. Box 337, Waigani, NCD, Papua Nueva Guinea.

2. Censos de población llevados a cabo desde 1945 (años):
1966, 1971, 1980 y 1990. La presente descripción se refiere al censo de población de 1990 (realizado del 9 al 13 de julio de ese año).

3. Alcance del censo:

a) Geográfico: La provincia de Salomón del Norte quedó completamente excluida del censo, debido a los problemas planteados por una crisis política.

b) Personas comprendidas: Toda la población, salvo el personal diplomático extranjero y sus familiares.

4. Período de referencia:
La semana y el período de 12 meses anteriores al censo.

5. Materias principales:
a) Población total, según sexo y edad:	sí
Población económicamente activa por:	
b) Sexo y grupo de edad:	sí
c) Rama de actividad económica:	no
d) Ocupación:	sí
e) Situación en el empleo:	no
f) Nivel más alto de educación:	sí
g) Horas de trabajo:	no
h) Otras características:	no

Ref. a): La edad se determinó según los años cumplidos en el último cumpleaños.

6. Conceptos y definiciones:

a) Población económicamente activa: Abarcó a todas las personas de 10 o más años de edad que, durante los períodos de referencia, estaban sea ocupadas, sea desempleadas, conforme a las definiciones que se dan más adelante. El período de referencia corto (una semana) se utilizó para acopiar datos sobre la actividad actual en el sector urbano, mientras que el período de referencia largo (12 meses) se usó para acopiar datos sobre la actividad habitual en el sector rural. La definición incluyó a los miembros de las fuerzas armadas. En cambio, no quedaron incluidos en ella los estudiantes con empleo a tiempo parcial ni los que buscaban trabajo.

b) Empleo: Para determinar si una persona debía considerarse o no "ocupada" se preguntó "¿Cuál ha sido la actividad principal de usted durante los últimos siete días: tuvo un trabajo asalariado; atendió de su empresa o negocio, ocupando personal remunerado; trabajó como independiente, empleando mano de obra auxiliar no remunerada; practicó la agricultura o la pesca, de subsistencia o comercial; practicó la agricultura o la pesca, únicamente de subsistencia?".

Se ha indicado que fueron incluidas las siguientes categorías:

i) personas que trabajan sin remuneración en una empresa o negocio familiar;

ii) personas que producen bienes primarios para el autoconsumo;

iii) personas ocupadas pero temporalmente ausentes de su trabajo;

iv) trabajadores estacionales u ocasionales;

v) conscriptos del servicio militar o civil;

vi) aprendices y personas que siguen un curso de formación.

Sólo pueden identificarse por separado las personas incluidas en la categoría ii).

c) Desempleo: Se consideró "desempleada" a toda persona que, durante los períodos de referencia (véase el párrafo 6 a)) no tenía trabajo y estaba buscando una ocupación o estaba disponible para trabajar. Quedaron comprendidas en el concepto las personas que permanecían en su domicilio inactivas, sin siquiera buscar empleo, por considerar que no tenían ninguna posibilidad de encontrar uno, pero que manifestaron su voluntad de aceptar cualquier puesto de trabajo en caso de que se les ofreciera la oportunidad.

7. Clasificaciones utilizadas:
Sólo fueron clasificadas por ocupación las personas ocupadas en las zonas urbanas.

a) Rama de actividad económica: No se efectuó clasificación alguna por rama de actividad.

b) Ocupación: Se pidió a las personas ocupadas que describiesen su actividad principal, es decir, aquella actividad económica en que ocupaban la mayor parte de su tiempo: por ejemplo, dependiente auxiliar de comercio, enfermera, conductor de taxi, etc., empleando por lo menos dos palabras. Para codificar la ocupación se utilizaron nueve grupos de la clasificación nacional. Se establecieron enlaces con la CIUO-88 a nivel de grandes grupos (clave de 1 dígito).

c) Situación en el empleo: No se efectuó clasificación alguna según la situación en el empleo.

8. Diferencias principales con el censo anterior:
En 1990, la definición de "desempleo" se amplió, abarcando a las personas que estaban disponibles para trabajar.

En lo que atañe a las preguntas sobre la actividad económica en las zonas rurales, en 1990 se aplicó un período de referencia largo (12 meses), mientras que en 1980 se usó un período corto (una semana).

9. Publicación de los resultados del censo:
Los resultados definitivos del censo relativos a la población económicamente activa y sus componentes se publicaron en agosto de 1994, en un volumen que lleva por título "Report on the 1990 National Population and Housing Census in Papua New Guinea".

El organismo responsable de esta publicación es la National Statistics Office (NSO), P.O. Box 337, Waigani, NCD.

No se dispone de los resultados del censo en otros soportes.

PARAGUAY

1. Nombre y dirección del organismo responsable del censo:
Dirección General de Estadística, Encuestas y Censos, Luis Aberto de Herrera 1010, c/ Estados Unidos, Casilla de Correo No. 1118, Asunción.

2. Censos de población llevados a cabo desde 1945 (años):
1950, 1962, 1972, 1982 y 1992. La presente descripción se refiere al censo de población de 1992 (realizado el 26 de agosto).

3. Alcance del censo:
a) Geográfico: Todo el país.

b) Personas comprendidas: Toda la población.

4. Período de referencia:
La semana anterior al día del censo.

5. Materias principales:
a) Población total, según sexo y edad:	sí
Población económicamente activa por:	
b) Sexo y grupo de edad:	sí
c) Rama de actividad económica:	sí
d) Ocupación:	sí
e) Situación en el empleo:	sí
f) Nivel más alto de educación:	sí
g) Horas de trabajo:	no
h) Otras características:	no

Ref. a): Se definió la edad en términos de la edad al último cumpleaños.

6. Conceptos y definiciones:

a) Población económicamente activa: Incluye a todas las personas de 10 años y más, que durante la semana de referencia estaban empleadas o desempleadas, tal y como se definen más adelante. La definición excluye a los conscriptos pero incluye a los militares de carrera. Se excluyen también a los estudiantes que trabajan a tiempo parcial o que buscan trabajo.

b) Empleo: Son consideradas "empleadas" las personas que trabajaron durante la mayor parte de la semana de referencia. La pregunta utilizada es: "¿Trabajó la mayor parte de la semana pasada? 1) Trabajó; 2) No trabajó, pero tiene trabajo; 3) Buscó trabajo habiendo trabajado antes; 4) Buscó su primer trabajo; 5) Realizó quehaceres del hogar; 6) Es estudiante; 7) Vivió de su renta; 8) Es jubilado o pensionado; 9) Servicio militar obligatorio; 10) Otra situación".

Se ha indicado que quedan incluidas las siguientes categorías:

i) personas trabajando sin paga en firma o negocio familiar;

ii) personas empleadas y temporalmente ausentes del trabajo.

Las dos categorías arriba mencionadas se pueden identificar separadamente.

c) Desempleo: Son consideradas "desempleadas" las personas que buscaron trabajo habiendo trabajado anteriormente, o buscaron su primer empleo, durante la semana de referencia.

7. Clasificaciones utilizadas:
Tanto las personas ocupadas como las desocupadas están clasificadas por rama de actividad económica, por ocupación y según la situación en el empleo.

a) Rama de actividad económica: Se determinó mediante la pregunta: "¿A qué se dedica o qué produce la empresa, negocio o institución donde trabaja (o trabajaba)? Ejemplos: cultivo de algodón, cultivo de hortalizas, construcción de edificios, enseñanza primaria, salud, confección de ropa, comercio, etc." Para codificar la rama de actividad económica se utilizaron 9 grupos de la Clasificación nacional. Se han establecido vínculos con la CIIU-Rev.2 a nivel de las grandes divisiones (1 dígito).

b) Ocupación: Se determinó mediante la pregunta: "¿Cuál es (o fue) su ocupación principal en el trabajo? Ejemplos: modista, secretaria, chofer, zapatero, vendedor, agricultor, albañil, electricista, médico, etc.". Para codificar la ocupación se utilizó la CIUO-88 al nivel de los grandes grupos (1 dígito).

c) Situación en el empleo: Se determinó mediante la pregunta: "¿En ese trabajo es (o era)? empleado, obrero o jornalero, patrón o empleador, cuenta propia o trabajador independiente, trabajador familiar no remunerado, empleado doméstico". Para codificar esta variable se utilizaron los seis grupos precedentes.

8. Diferencias principales con el censo anterior:
En el censo de 1982, el límite inferior de edad era 12 años para plantear las preguntas sobre la actividad económica (10 años en el censo de 1992).

9. Publicación de los resultados del censo:
Las cifras definitivas se publicaron para Asunción en agosto de 1993, para el Departamento Central en octubre de 1993, y para el Departamento Alto Paraná en marzo de 1994. Los resultados a nivel de todo el país se publicaron en julio de 1994.

El título exacto de la publicación con los resultados finales es "Paraguay: Censo Nacional de Población y Viviendas".

La organización responsable de la publication es la Dirección General de Estadística, Encuestas y Censos, Luis Alberto de Herrera 1010, c/ Estados Unidos, Casilla de Correo No. 1118, Asunción.

Los resultados del censo se presentan también en forma de disquetes y de cuadros no publicados.

PERU

1. Nombre y dirección del organismo responsable del censo:
Instituto Nacional de Estadística e Informática, Av. 28 de Julio No. 1056, Lima.

2. Censos de población llevados a cabo desde 1945 (años):
1961, 1972, 1981 y 1993. La presente descripción se refiere al censo de población de 1993 (realizado el 11 de julio).

3. Alcance del censo:
a) Geográfico: Todo el país.
b) Personas comprendidas: Toda la población.

4. Periodo de referencia:
La semana anterior al día del censo.

5. Materias principales:

a) Población total, según sexo y edad:	sí
Población económicamente activa por:	
b) Sexo y grupo de edad:	sí
c) Rama de actividad económica:	sí
d) Ocupación:	sí
e) Situación en el empleo:	sí
f) Nivel más alto de educación:	sí
g) Horas de trabajo:	no
h) Otras características:	no

Ref. a): Se definió la edad en términos de la edad al último cumpleaños para las personas de un año y más (para menores de un año, la edad será el número de meses cumplidos).

6. Conceptos y definiciones:
a) Población económicamente activa: Incluye a todas las personas de 6 años y más, que durante la semana de referencia se encontraban empleadas o desempleadas, tal y como se definen más adelante. La definición incluye a los militares de carrera pero excluye a los conscriptos en el servicio militar o civil.

b) Empleo: Se consideran "empleadas" a las personas que trabajaron durante la semana de referencia. Las preguntas utilizadas para determinar si la persona estaba empleada son "La semana pasada se encontraba: ¿Trabajando por algún ingreso?, ¿No trabajó pero tenía trabajó? y ¿Ayudando a un familiar sin pago alguno?".

Se ha indicado que quedan incluidas las siguientes categorías:
i) personas trabajando sin paga en firma o negocio familiar;
ii) personas en la producción de bienes primarios para autoconsumo;
iii) personas empleadas y temporalmente ausentes del trabajo;
iv) estudiantes trabajando medio tiempo;
v) trabajadores estacionales u ocasionales.

Solamente las personas de las categorías i) y iii) se pueden indentificar separadamente a través de preguntas específicas. Para la categoría i), la pregunta utilizada es: "¿Ayudando a un familiar sin pago alguno?" y para la categoría iii), la pregunta utilizada es: "¿No trabajó pero tenía trabajó?".

c) Desempleo: Se consideran "desempleadas" a las personas que durante la semana de referencia buscaron trabajo pero habían trabajado antes, o que buscaron trabajo por primera vez.

7. Clasificaciones utilizadas:
Tanto las personas ocupadas como las desocupadas con experiencia laboral se clasificaron por rama de actividad económica, por ocupación y según la situación en el empleo.

a) Rama de actividad económica: Para establecer la rama de actividad económica se preguntó la actividad a la que se dedica el negocio, organismo o empresa donde trabaja la persona o donde trabajaba en su último empleo. Para codificar esta variable se utilizó la CIIU-Rev.3 al nivel de clases (4 dígitos).

b) Ocupación: Para establecer la ocupación se preguntó por la ocupación, oficio o profesión desempeñada principalmente por la persona en la semana de referencia o la última vez que trabajó. Para codificar esta variable, se utilizó la CIUO-88, a nivel de subgrupos (3 dígitos).

c) Situación en el empleo: Para determinar esta característica se preguntó por la categoría ocupacional en el negocio, organismo o empresa en la que trabajó la persona. Se codificó en seis grupos (obrero, empleado, trabajador familiar no remunerado, trabajador del hogar, trabajador independiente o por cuenta propia, empleador o patrono).

8. Diferencias principales con el censo anterior:
No hubo diferencias significativas.

9. Publicación de los resultados del censo:
Los resultados finales se publicaron en noviembre de 1994.

El título de la publicación es "Resultados definitivos Perú Censos Nacionales 1993: IX de Poblacion y IV de Vivienda".

La organización responsable de la publicación es el Instituto Nacional de Estadística e Informática, av. 28 de Julio, No. 1056, Lima, Perú.

Los resultados del censo se presentan también en forma de disquetes.

PORTUGAL

1. Nombre y dirección del organismo responsable del censo:
Instituto Nacional de Estatística, Ava. António José de Almeida, P-1078 Lisboa Codex.

2. Censos de población llevados a cabo desde 1945 (años):
1950, 1960, 1970, 1981 y 1991. La presente descripción se refiere al censo de 1991 (realizado el 15 de abril de ese año).

3. Alcance del censo:
a) Geográfico: Todo el territorio.

b) Personas comprendidas: Toda la población, con la excepción de los nacionales residentes en el extranjero desde hacía por lo menos un año.

4. Periodo de referencia:
La semana anterior al censo (es decir, del 7 al 13 de abril de 1991).

Sin embargo, por lo que se refiere al desempleo, se consideraron distintos intervalos (menos de un mes, de un mes a menos de cuatro meses, de cuatro a siete meses, más de siete meses).

5. Materias principales:

a) Población total, según sexo y edad: sí

Población económicamente activa por:

b) Sexo y grupo de edad: sí
c) Rama de actividad económica: sí
d) Ocupación: sí
e) Situación en el empleo: sí
f) Nivel más alto de educación: sí
g) Horas de trabajo: sí
h) Otras características: sí

Ref. a): La edad se determinó según la fecha de nacimiento.

Ref. g): Se pidió a las personas ocupadas que indicaran el número de horas trabajadas en su ocupación principal durante la semana de referencia.

Ref. h): El censo también recolectó datos sobre otros temas, a saber: el lugar de trabajo; los medios de transporte utilizados para trasladarse al lugar de trabajo y regresar al domicilio, así como la duración de dichos trayectos; la principal fuente de ingresos durante los últimos 12 meses; etc.

6. Conceptos y definiciones:

a) Población económicamente activa: Abarcó a todas las personas de 12 o más años de edad que, durante la semana de referencia, estaban ocupadas o desempleadas, conforme a las definiciones que se dan más adelante. La definición incluyó a todos los miembros de las fuerzas armadas (militares de carrera y conscriptos).

b) Empleo: Se consideró "ocupada" a toda persona que, durante la semana de referencia, había ejercido una profesión o un cargo, o desempeñado alguna actividad económica.

Se ha indicado que fueron incluidas las siguientes categorías:

i) personas que trabajan sin remuneración en una empresa o negocio familiar;
ii) personas que producen bienes primarios para el autoconsumo;
iii) personas ocupadas pero temporalmente ausentes de su trabajo;
iv) estudiantes que trabajan a tiempo parcial;
v) trabajadores estacionales u ocasionales, a condición de que estuviesen activos en el momento del censo;
vi) conscriptos del servicio militar o civil; sin embargo, sólo se identificaron por separado las personas que cumplían el servicio militar obligatorio;
vii) aprendices y personas que siguen un curso de formación.

Sólo las categorías i), iii) y vi) pueden identificarse por separado.

c) Desempleo: Se consideró "desempleada en un sentido amplio" a toda persona que, durante la semana de referencia, se encontraba sin empleo y quería trabajar. Se consideró "desempleada en un sentido estricto" a toda persona que, durante la semana de referencia, se encontraba sin trabajo y buscaba empleo, había buscado empleo durante los últimos 30 días o estaba inscrita en el servicio del empleo. También se consideró "desempleados" a los trabajadores estacionales u ocasionales que se encontraban sin trabajo en el momento del censo.

7. Clasificaciones utilizadas:

Tanto las personas ocupadas como las desempleadas anteriormente empleadas, incluidas en la muestra, se clasificaron por rama de actividad económica, por ocupación y por situación en el empleo.

a) Rama de actividad económica: Para determinarla se hizo la siguiente pregunta: "¿Dónde ejerce usted (o ejerció por última vez) su ocupación principal?" Para codificar la rama de actividad se utilizó la CIIU-Rev.3 a nivel de clases (clave de 4 dígitos).

b) Ocupación: La pregunta formulada se refería a la ocupación principal ejercida. Para codificar la ocupación, se utilizó la clasificación CIUO-88, pero adaptándola a nivel de los grupos básicos, a fin de ampliarlos.

c) Situación en el empleo: Tanto a las personas ocupadas como a los desempleados anteriormente empleados se hizo una pregunta destinada a determinar si ejercían o habían ejercido su actividad principal en calidad de: empleador; trabajador por cuenta propia; trabajador por cuenta de terceros; trabajador familiar no remunerado; miembro activo de cooperativa de producción; conscripto (servicio militar obligatorio); otras.

Para codificar esta variable se utilizaron las siete categorías enumeradas.

8. Diferencias principales con el censo anterior:

En el censo de 1991, se incluyeron dos nuevas preguntas para determinar el tipo de desempleo (en sentido estricto, en sentido amplio y en función de su duración), a saber: i) "¿Ha trabajado usted?" y, en caso de respuesta afirmativa, ii) "¿Quiere trabajar y ha buscado trabajo durante los últimos 30 días, o ha estado inscrito(a) en un servicio de empleo (desde hace un mes y hace menos de cuatro meses, desde hace cuatro meses y menos de siete meses, desde hace siete o más meses)?", iii) "¿Quiere usted trabajar pero no ha buscado empleo?" y iv) "¿No quiere usted trabajar?".

Las personas que dijeron querer trabajar se consideraron "desempleadas" aunque no hubiesen buscado empleo. Por el contrario, las que indicaron que no querían trabajar quedaron incluidas en la población inactiva.

La pregunta relativa a los principales medios de subsistencia dejó de tener en cuenta las diferentes clases de pensiones, a diferencia de lo hecho en el censo de 1981.

Las personas que cumplían su servicio militar obligatorio (conscriptos) fueron incluidas en una nueva categoría de situación en el empleo.

9. Publicación de los resultados del censo:

Los resultados definitivos relativos a la población económicamente activa y sus componentes debían publicarse en 1993.

El organismo responsable de la publicación de los resultados del censo es el Instituto Nacional de Estatística, Lisboa.

Los resultados del censo de 1991 están disponibles también en cuadros inéditos, disquetes y cintas magnéticas.

PUERTO RICO

1. Nombre y dirección del organismo responsable del censo:

U.S. Census Bureau, Washington, DC, 20233. La información metodológica relativa al último censo fue suministrada por la Oficina de la Comisión de Planificación del Censo de Puerto Rico, San Juan, Puerto Rico.

2. Censos de población llevados a cabo desde 1945 (años):

1950, 1960, 1970, 1980 y 1990. La presente descripción se refiere al censo de 1990 (realizado el 1 de abril de ese año).

3. Alcance del censo:

a) Geográfico: Todo el país.

b) Personas comprendidas: Toda la población.

4. Período de referencia:

La semana anterior al día del censo, en lo que atañe a las personas ocupadas, las 4 semanas anteriores anteriores al día del censo, por lo que se refiere a las personas desempleadas, y el último año, en lo relativo a otros factores económicos.

5. Materias principales:

a) Población total, según sexo y edad: sí

Población económicamente activa por:

b) Sexo y grupo de edad: sí
c) Rama de actividad económica: sí
d) Ocupación: sí
e) Situación en el empleo: sí
f) Nivel más alto de educación: sí
g) Horas de trabajo: sí
h) Otras características: sí

Ref. a): La edad se determinó según los años cumplidos en el último cumpleaños.

Ref. g): El tiempo de trabajo se refiere a la vez a las horas habituales de trabajo efectuadas durante el período de referencia corto, y al período total trabajado por las personas ocupadas durante el último año (expresado en semanas).

Ref. h): El censo también recolectó datos sobre otros aspectos, a saber: ingresos; tipo de ingresos; medios de transporte usados para trasladarse al lugar de trabajo y tiempo necesario para hacerlo; despidos registrados la última semana; último año en que trabajó la persona censada; formación profesional adquirida.

6. Conceptos y definiciones:

a) Población económicamente activa: Abarcó a todas las personas de 16 o más años de edad que, durante los períodos de referencia, estaban sea ocupadas, sea desempleadas, conforme a las definiciones que se dan más adelante. Se hicieron preguntas sobre la actividad económica a una muestra de 17 por ciento de todas las viviendas (uno de cada seis hogares). La definición incluyó a las fuerzas armadas, pero los datos publicados se refieren sólo a la fuerza de trabajo civil. Quedaron excluidos de la definición: los estudiantes con empleo a tiempo parcial, los estudiantes que buscaban empleo, los trabajadores estacionales empadronados fuera de temporada, que no estuviesen buscando trabajo, y los trabajadores familiares no remunerados que trabajaban esporádicamente.

b) Empleo: Para determinar si una persona debía ser contabilizada o no como "ocupada" se usaron las preguntas "¿Trabajó X durante toda o parte de la semana pasada?", y "¿Cuántas horas dedicó X a su trabajo la semana pasada?".

Se ha indicado que fueron incluidas las siguientes categorías:

i)   personas que trabajan sin remuneración en una empresa o negocio familiar;

ii) personas que producen bienes primarios para el autoconsumo;

iii) personas ocupadas pero temporalmente ausentes de su trabajo;

iv) conscriptos del servicio militar o civil;

v)   aprendices y personas que siguen un curso de formación.

Sólo pueden identificarse por separado las personas incluidas en la categoría iv).

c) Desempleo: Para determinar si una persona debía contabilizarse o no como desempleada se preguntó: "¿Ha buscado trabajo X durante las pasadas 4 semanas?" y "¿Hubiera podido X comenzar a trabajar la semana pasada?".

7. Clasificaciones utilizadas:

Tanto las personas ocupadas como las desempleadas anteriormente empleadas incluidas en la muestra, se clasificaron por rama de actividad económica, por ocupación y por situación en el empleo.

a) Rama de actividad económica: Para determinarla se preguntó: "¿Para quién trabajó X?" y "¿En qué tipo de empresa o actividad trabajó (por ejemplo, se trata principalmente de una industria manufacturera, de un establecimiento comercial mayorista, de un establecimiento minorista, etc.)?". El sistema de clasificación por rama de actividad económica consistió de 231 categorías repartidas en 13 grupos de actividad principales. Este sistema se basó en el Manual de Clasificación Normalizada de las Actividades Económicas (SIC), de 1972, y en el suplemento de 1977 de dicho Manual. No se establecieron enlaces con la CIIU, pero se preparó una adaptación comparable a nivel internacional.

b) Ocupación: Para determinarla se preguntó: "¿Qué tipo de trabajo desempeñó X?" y "¿Cuáles fueron sus actividades o funciones más importantes?". El sistema de clasificación de ocupaciones comprendió 503 categorías profesionales ordenadas en 6 grupos resumidos y 13 grupos principales. Esta clasificación era compatible con el Manual de Clasificación Normalizada de Ocupaciones (SOC), de 1980. No se establecieron enlaces con la CIUO, pero se preparó una adaptación comparable a nivel internacional.

c) Situación en el empleo: Para determinarla se preguntó: "¿Tenía X una actividad privada no lucrativa; o trabajaba para la administración municipal; para la administración del territorio asociado de Puerto Rico; para el Gobierno federal; era trabajador independiente, dueño de empresa no constituida en sociedad; o independiente dueño de empresa constituida en sociedad; era trabajador no remunerado; tenía otra actividad?". Para codificar esta variable se utilizaron las ocho categorías indicadas.

8. Diferencias principales con el censo anterior:
No hubo diferencias significativas.

9. Publicación de los resultados del censo:
Los resultados del censo de 1990 se publicaron en 1993, en el volumen que lleva por título "Summary Social, Economic and Housing Characteristics".

El organismo responsable de esta publicación es el U.S. Census Bureau, Washington, DC, 20233.

Los resultados del censo están también disponibles en cintas magnéticas, discos CD-ROM y microfichas, informes impresos y disquetes.

REINO UNIDO

1. Nombre y dirección del organismo responsable del censo:
Por lo que se refiere a Inglaterra y Gales: Office of Population, Census Surveys, Room 816, St. Catherine's House, 10 Kingsway, Londres WC 2B 6JP.

Por lo que se refiere a Escocia: General Register Office (Scotland), Ladywell House, Ladywell Road, Edinburgo EH12 7TF.

Por lo que se refiere a Irlanda del Norte: Census Office, Castle Buildings, Stormont, Belfast BT4 8SJ.

2. Censos de población llevados a cabo desde 1945 (años):
1951, 1961, 1966, 1971, 1981 y 1991. La presente descripción se refiere al censo de población de 1991 (realizado el 21 de abril de ese año). Los datos corresponden fundamentalmente a Inglaterra y Gales, pero las respuestas se refieren también a Escocia e Irlanda del Norte, y pueden considerarse, por ende, representativas de la situación en todo el Reino Unido.

3. Alcance del censo:
a) Geográfico: Todo el país. (Véase también el párrafo 2, más arriba).

b) Personas comprendidas: Toda la población.

4. Período de referencia:
La semana anterior al día del censo.

5. Materias principales:

a) Población total, según sexo y edad:	sí
Población económicamente activa por:	
b) Sexo y grupo de edad:	sí
c) Rama de actividad económica:	sí
d) Ocupación:	sí
e) Situación en el empleo:	sí
f) Nivel más alto de educación:	sí
g) Horas de trabajo:	sí
h) Otras características:	sí

Ref. a): La edad se determinó según el año de nacimiento (fecha completa, es decir, día, mes y año).

Ref. g): Se pidió a las personas ocupadas que precisaran cuál era su horario de trabajo habitual.

Ref. h): El censo también recolectó información acerca del lugar de trabajo y de los medios de transporte utilizados para trasladarse a éste.

6. Conceptos y definiciones:

a) Población económicamente activa: Incluyó a todas las personas de 16 o más años de edad que, durante la semana de referencia, se encontraban sea ocupadas, sea desempleadas, conforme a las definiciones que se dan más adelante. En lo que atañe al censo de 1981, se recopilaron datos sobre la situación económica y la situación en el empleo en todo el universo del censo, mientras que la información sobre la rama de actividad económica, la ocupación y el lugar de trabajo se acopió en una muestra de 10 por ciento. En cuanto a los trabajadores estacionales y ocasionales, la definición abarcó sólo a aquellos que estaban ocupados o buscando trabajo durante la semana de referencia. La definición incluyó también al cuadro profesional de las fuerzas armadas. No hay conscriptos en el Reino Unido.

b) Empleo: Se consideró "ocupada" a toda persona que, durante la semana de referencia, estaba trabajando para un empleador (a tiempo completo o a tiempo parcial), tenía una actividad independiente, era empleado público o tomaba parte en un programa estatal de capacitación. La definición abarcó las diversas formas del trabajo asalariado o retribuido con alguna forma de ganancia, incluidos el trabajo ocasional y el trabajo temporal, pero no incluyó el trabajo no remunerado (salvo el desempeñado en una empresa familiar). Fueron incluidas también las personas que habían tenido un trabajo durante la semana de referencia, pero habían estado ausentes por motivos de enfermedad, vacaciones, reducción de personal o huelga. Se entendió por trabajo a tiempo parcial toda actividad laboral desempeñada durante un máximo de 30 horas por semana (excluidas las horas extraordinarias).

Se ha indicado que fueron incluidas las siguientes categorías:

i) personas que trabajan sin remuneración en una empresa o negocio familiar;

ii) personas ocupadas pero temporalmente ausentes de su trabajo;

iii) estudiantes que trabajan a tiempo parcial;

iv) trabajadores estacionales u ocasionales (a condición de que hubiesen trabajado durante la semana de referencia);

v) aprendices y personas que siguen un curso de formación.

Tan sólo la categoría iii) puede identificarse por separado.

c) Desempleo: Se consideró "desempleadas" a todas las personas que, durante la semana de referencia, se aprestaban a comenzar a trabajar, habían aceptado una oferta de trabajo o estaban desocupadas pero en busca de empleo, incluidas aquellas que querían trabajar pero no podían buscar uno por motivo de vacaciones o de enfermedad pasajera.

7. Clasificaciones utilizadas:

Tanto las personas ocupadas como las desempleadas anteriormente empleadas incluidas en la muestra fueron clasificadas según el sector de actividad económica y la ocupación (el criterio para incluir a los desempleados fue "que hubiesen tenido un empleo en los últimos 10 años"). Sólo las personas ocupadas fueron clasificadas según la situación en el empleo (véase también el párrafo 6 a), más arriba). A las personas económicamente inactivas, por ejemplo, los jubilados, que hubiesen tenido un empleo en los últimos 10 años se pidió también que indicaran el tiempo de trabajo, la rama de actividad económica y la ocupación correspondientes.

a) Rama de actividad económica: Se pidió a los encuestados que indicasen el nombre, la dirección y la actividad económica del empleador (en el caso de los trabajadores independientes: el nombre, la dirección del lugar de trabajo y la índole de su actividad económica). Aunque para codificar la rama de actividad económica se utilizaron 320 grupos basados en la clasificación nacional de industrias, sólo se procesaron los datos relativos a una muestra de 10 por ciento. Se establecieron enlaces (los más adecuados) con la CIIU-Rev.3 a nivel de divisiones (clave de 2 dígitos).

b) Ocupación: Se pidió a las personas censadas que indicasen la denominación completa del trabajo que ejercían o que habían ejercido en su último empleo, y que describiesen las principales funciones del mismo. Debía usarse una terminología precisa, como, por ejemplo, maquinista de empacadora, obrero en matadero de pollos, reparador de herramientas y de instrumentos de calibración, mecanógrafo jefe, o empleado contable, en vez de denominaciones genéricas como maquinista, obrero en planta procesadora, supervisor o empleado. Para codificar la ocupación se utilizaron 371 grupos de la clasificación nacional de ocupaciones, pero sólo se procesaron los datos relativos a la muestra de 10 por ciento. Se establecieron enlaces con la CIUO-88 a nivel de grupos mixtos.

c) Situación en el empleo: El censo incluyó una pregunta destinada específicamente a establecer la situación económica de los encuestados. Para codificar la situación en el empleo, en los cuadros basados en todo el universo se utilizaron los siguientes cinco grupos: trabaja para un empleador, a tiempo completo; trabaja para un empleador, a tiempo parcial; trabaja en forma independiente y emplea a otras personas; trabaja en forma independiente, sin empleados; trabaja para un organismo estatal o participa en un programa estatal de capacitación.

8. Diferencias principales con el censo anterior:

Las principales modificaciones fueron:

– el empleo de una nueva clasificación de ocupaciones (la Clasificación Normalizada de Ocupaciones - SOC);

– se incluyó una pregunta acerca del tiempo de trabajo;

– en la pregunta relativa a la situación económica se introdujo una categoría aparte para las personas empleadas por el Estado o que participaban en programas de capacitación organizados por éste (la pregunta incluyó también una escala de categorías de empleo, según la cual dejó de distinguirse entre aprendices y personas que seguían cursos de formación); y

– la inclusión de los estudiantes que trabajan en la población económicamente activa, en calidad de "ocupados".

9. Publicación de los resultados del censo:

Los primeros resultados nacionales acerca de la población económicamente activa estuvieron disponibles en 1992. La información pormenorizada sobre las ramas de actividad económica, la ocupación, el lugar de trabajo, etc., estuvo disponible en 1993.

Los resultados aparecieron en diversas publicaciones. Las personas interesadas en disponer de mayores informaciones al respecto pueden dirigirse a Census Customer Services, OPCS, Segensworth Road, Titchfield, Hampshire PO15 5RR.

Los datos relativos al censo se han difundido por diversos medios y soportes.

REUNION

1. Nombre y dirección del organismo responsable del censo:

Service régional de l'INSEE à la Réunion, 15 rue de l'école, 97490 Ste Clotilde, La Réunión.

2. Censos de población llevados a cabo desde 1945 (años):

1954, 1961, 1967, 1974, 1982 y 1990. La presente descripción se refiere al censo de 1990 (realizado el 15 de marzo de ese año).

3. Alcance del censo:

a) Geográfico: Todo el territorio.

b) Personas comprendidas: Toda la población.

4. Periodo de referencia:

La semana anterior al día del censo.

5. Materias principales:

a) Población total, según sexo y edad:	sí
Población económicamente activa por:	
b) Sexo y grupo de edad:	sí
c) Rama de actividad económica:	sí
d) Ocupación:	sí
e) Situación en el empleo:	sí
f) Nivel más alto de educación:	sí
g) Horas de trabajo:	no
h) Otras características:	sí

Ref. a): La edad se determinó según el año de nacimiento.

Ref. h): El censo también recolectó datos sobre otros temas, a saber: el trabajo a tiempo completo y el trabajo a tiempo parcial, la actividad principal, el número de asalariados empleados por las personas que trabajan por cuenta propia, el tiempo pasado en busca de trabajo, etc.

6. Conceptos y definiciones:

a) Población económicamente activa: Abarcó a todas las personas de 14 o más años de edad que, durante la semana de referencia, estaban ocupadas o desempleadas, conforme a las definiciones que se dan más adelante. La definición incluyó a los miembros de las fuerzas armadas (militares de carrera y conscriptos). En lo que atañe a la actividad económica, se interrogó únicamente a una muestra de personas, de la que quedaron excluidos los militares residentes en los cuarteles y las personas detenidas en establecimientos penitenciarios.

b) Empleo: Se consideró "ocupada" a toda persona que, durante la semana de referencia, había ejercido una profesión o un cargo o desempeñado alguna actividad económica, ya fuese remunerada o sin remuneración. Para determinar si una persona debía contabilizarse como ocupada se utilizaron diversas preguntas, y en particular: "¿Trabaja usted (a tiempo completo o a tiempo parcial)?"; "¿Es usted: asalariado o trabajador por cuenta propia (agricultor, artesano, comerciante, industrial, miembro de profesión liberal, trabajador familiar no remunerado, etc.)?", y "En caso de que usted trabaje por cuenta propia: ¿a cuántos asalariados emplea? (no tenga cuenta de los aprendices ni del personal doméstico; si es agricultor, contabilice únicamente a los asalariados permanentes)". En el ámbito de la definición quedaron incluidas las personas que desempeñaban un trabajo de utilidad pública (TUC, etc.), las ocupadas por una agencia de colocación, las empleadas según un contrato de duración limitada y las empleadas según un contrato de readaptación o de perfeccionamiento profesional.

Se ha indicado que fueron incluidas las siguientes categorías:

i) personas que trabajan sin remuneración en una empresa o una explotación familiar;

ii) personas que producen bienes primarios para el autoconsumo;

iii) personas ocupadas pero temporalmente ausentes de su trabajo;

iv) estudiantes que trabajan a tiempo parcial;
v) trabajadores estacionales u ocasionales, a condición de que estuviesen activos en el momento del censo;
vi) conscriptos del servicio militar o civil;
vii) aprendices (bajo contrato) y personas que siguen un curso de formación (principalmente en una empresa o un centro de formación).

Sólo las categorías i), vi) y vii) pueden identificarse por separado.

c) *Desempleo*: Se consideró "desempleada" a toda persona que indicó espontáneamente que esa era su situación y que buscaba empleo. Para determinar si una persona debía considerarse "desempleada" se preguntó "¿Está usted desempleado(a) (inscrito(a) o no en la Agencia Nacional del Empleo)?", "¿Ha trabajado ya? (si este es el caso, ¿cuál fue su ocupación principal)?", y "¿Busca usted empleo (desde hace: menos de tres meses; más de tres meses pero menos de un año; más de un año pero menos de dos años; dos o más años)?".

7. Clasificaciones utilizadas:
Tanto las personas ocupadas como las desempleadas anteriormente empleadas fueron clasificadas por ocupación. Sólo las personas ocupadas incluidas en la muestra fueron clasificadas por rama de actividad y por situación en el empleo.

a) *Rama de actividad económica*: Se pidió a las personas censadas que indicasen la dirección, el nombre o la razón social del establecimiento que las empleaba o que dirigían, así como la actividad exacta de dicho establecimiento (por ejemplo: comercio mayorista de vinos, fabricación de estructuras metálicas, transporte terrestre de pasajeros, etc.). Para codificar la rama de actividad económica se utilizaron 100 grupos de la Nomenclatura de Actividades y Productos (NAP). No se establecieron enlaces con la CIIU.

b) *Ocupación*: Se pidió a las personas censadas que indicaran la ocupación que ejercían o que habían ejercido en su último trabajo, precisándola de la manera más clara posible (por ejemplo: obrero electricista de manutención, chófer de camión de carga, vendedor de electrodomésticos, ingeniero químico, cajera de tienda autoservicio, etc.), a fin de determinar el grupo de ocupaciones. Sin embargo, también se permitió que la persona censada formulase libremente su respuesta. La clasificación en un grupo determinado se llevó a cabo durante el procesamiento informatizado de los datos. Para codificar la ocupación se utilizó un sistema de codificación directa en 42 grupos. No se establecieron enlaces con la CIUO.

c) *Situación en el empleo*: Para codificar esta variable se utilizaron las cinco categorías siguientes: trabajador independiente por cuenta propia; empleador; asalariado; trabajador familiar no remunerado; otra categoría.

8. Diferencias principales con el censo anterior:
La edad mínima aplicada en el censo de 1982 para determinar la inclusión de las personas en la población económicamente activa fue de 15 años.

Además, en el censo de 1982 se clasificaron por rama de actividad económica y por situación en el empleo tanto las personas ocupadas como las desempleadas anteriormente empleadas.

9. Publicación de los resultados del censo:
La publicación en que figuran los resultados definitivos del censo lleva por título: "Population, Emploi, Logements; Evolution 1975-1982-1990 (Série jaune)", 1992.

El organismo responsable de esta publicación es el Institut national de la statistique et des études économiques (INSEE), 18 boulevard Adolphe-Pinard, 75675 París Cedex 14.

También se dispone de los resultados del censo de 1990 en disquetes, cintas magnéticas y otras modalidades de presentación que se soliciten.

RUMANIA

1. Nombre y dirección del organismo responsable del censo:
Commission centrale pour le recensement de la population et des logements de 1992. Commission Nationale pour la Statistique, Bd. Libertatii 16, Sector 5, Bucarest 70542.

2. Censos de población llevados a cabo desde 1945 (años):
1948, 1956, 1966, 1977 y 1992. La presente descripción se refiere al censo de 1992 (realizado el 7 de enero de ese año).

3. Alcance del censo:
a) *Geográfico*: Todo el territorio.

b) *Personas comprendidas*: Toda la población con residencia permanente en el país, salvo las personas sin ciudadanía o con ciudadanía extranjera (representantes diplomáticos, consulares o comerciales, personal de organizaciones internacionales, de empresas extranjeras y corresponsales de prensa).

4. Período de referencia:
Un año (1991).

5. Materias principales:

a) Población total, según sexo y edad:	
Población económicamente activa por:	
b) Sexo y grupo de edad:	sí
c) Rama de actividad económica:	sí
d) Ocupación:	sí
e) Situación en el empleo:	sí
f) Nivel más alto de educación:	sí
g) Horas de trabajo:	no
h) Otras características:	no

Ref. a): La edad se determinó según el año de nacimiento.

6. Conceptos y definiciones:
a) *Población económicamente activa*: Abarcó a todas las personas de 14 o más años de edad que, durante el período de referencia, constituían la fuerza de trabajo disponible (estuviera o no utilizada) para la producción de bienes y servicios en la economía nacional, según las definiciones que se dan más adelante. La definición incluyó a los miembros de las fuerzas armadas.

b) *Empleo*: Se consideró "ocupada" a toda persona de 14 a 80 años de edad que, durante el período de referencia, ejercía una actividad económica remunerada por un salario o un ingreso, sea en metálico o en especie, y bajo contrato o por cuenta propia.

Se ha indicado que fueron incluidas las siguientes categorías:
i) personas que trabajan sin remuneración en una empresa o negocio familiar;
ii) personas que producen bienes primarios para el autoconsumo;
iii) personas ocupadas pero temporalmente ausentes de su trabajo;
iv) estudiantes que trabajan a tiempo parcial;
v) trabajadores estacionales u ocasionales;
vi) conscriptos del servicio militar o civil;
vii) aprendices y personas que siguen un curso de formación.

Sólo pueden identificarse por separado las categorías i), ii) y vi) con arreglo a sus respuestas a las preguntas sobre la situación en el empleo.

Quedaron excluidas del ámbito de la definición las personas que indicaron ser jubiladas, escolares o estudiantes, ocuparse de labores del hogar o estar en busca de empleo, incluso si hubiesen trabajado temporalmente o en forma ocasional durante el período de referencia (especialmente en la agricultura).

c) *Desempleo*: Se consideró "desempleado" a todo varón de 14 a 64 años de edad y "desempleada" a toda mujer de 14 a 59 años de edad que, por lo que se refiere al momento del censo, indicó haberse encontrado sin trabajo, incluso si hubiese trabajado durante el período de referencia largo (1991), y haber estado disponible para trabajar y buscando un empleo (o de un primer empleo). Quedaron excluidos de esta definición los estudiantes que buscaban empleo.

7. Clasificaciones utilizadas:
Tanto las personas ocupadas como las desempleadas (salvo las personas en busca de un primer empleo) se clasificaron por rama de actividad, por ocupación y por situación en el empleo.

a) *Rama de actividad económica*: Para determinarla, se hicieron preguntas específicas a las personas ocupadas y a los desempleados anteriormente empleados acerca de la naturaleza de sus actividades del momento o anteriores, así como sobre el tipo de actividad de la empresa o establecimiento para el que trabajaban o habían trabajado. Para codificar la rama de actividad económica se utilizaron 99 grupos de la clasificación nacional. Se establecieron enlaces con la CIIU-Rev.3, a nivel de grupos (clave de 3 dígitos).

b) Ocupación: Para determinar el grupo de ocupaciones en el que trabajaban o habían trabajado, se formularon preguntas específicas tanto a las personas ocupadas como a las desempleados anteriormente empleados. No se tuvieron en cuenta las ocupaciones secundarias o estacionales, sino únicamente la ocupación principal, o sea, la que constituía la principal fuente de ingresos de la persona censada. Para codificar la ocupación se utilizaron 437 grupos básicos de la clasificación nacional. Se establecieron enlaces con la clasificación CIUO-88, a nivel de subgrupos (clave de 3 dígitos).

c) Situación en el empleo: Se formularon preguntas específicas a las personas ocupadas y a los desempleados anteriormente empleados a fin de determinar su situación en el empleo que ocupaban o habían ocupado. Se identificaron los siguientes seis grupos: empleador, trabajador por cuenta propia, trabajador asalariado, trabajador familiar no remunerado, miembro de cooperativa de producción, otras.

8. Diferencias principales con el censo anterior:
Se aplicó un límite de edad máxima para determinar la inclusión o exclusión de las personas censadas en la población económicamente activa y sus componentes; se utilizó un período de referencia largo (el año 1991); la población económicamente activa se desglosó en población activa ocupada y población activa desempleada (desempleados); en lo que atañe a las clasificaciones por sector de actividad y por ocupación, se establecieron enlaces, respectivamente, con la CIIU-Rev.3 y la CIUO-88; tanto las personas ocupadas como los desempleados anteriormente empleados se clasificaron según la situación en el empleo.

9. Publicación de los resultados del censo:
Los resultados definitivos del censo de 1992 se publicaron en octubre de 1993.

Los títulos de las publicaciones en que figuran los resultados definitivos son: "Vol. I - Population - Structure démographique", "Vol. II - Population - Structure socio-économique" y "Vol. III - Etablissements, logements, ménages".

El organismo responsable de estas publicaciones es la Comission Nationale pour la Statistique, Bd. Libertatii 16, Sector 5, Bucarest 70542.

También se dispone de los resultados definitivos en disquetes y cintas magnéticas.

SAMOA

1. Nombre y dirección del organismo responsable del censo:
Department of Statistics, P.O. Box 1151, Apia, Western Samoa.

2. Censos de población llevados a cabo desde 1945 (años):
1951, 1956, 1961, 1966, 1971, 1976, 1981, 1986 y 1991. La presente descripción se refiere al censo de población de 1991 (realizado el 5 de noviembre de ese año).

3. Alcance del censo:
a) Geográfico: Todo el país.
b) Personas comprendidas: Toda la población.

4. Periodo de referencia:
La semana del 20 al 26 de octubre de 1991.

5. Materias principales:
a) Población total, según sexo y edad:	sí
Población económicamente activa por:	
b) Sexo y grupo de edad:	sí
c) Rama de actividad económica:	sí
d) Ocupación:	sí
e) Situación en el empleo:	sí
f) Nivel más alto de educación:	no
g) Horas de trabajo:	no
h) Otras características:	no

Ref. a): La edad se determinó según el año de nacimiento y los años cumplidos en el último cumpleaños.

6. Conceptos y definiciones:
a) Población económicamente activa: Abarcó a todas las personas de 10 o más años de edad que, durante la semana de referencia, estaban sea ocupadas, sea desempleadas, conforme a las definiciones que se dan más adelante. No obstante, sólo se publicaron los datos relativos a las personas de 15 años de edad o mayores. La definición no incluyó a los miembros de las fuerzas armadas.

b) Empleo: Se consideró "ocupadas" a todas las personas que, al preguntárseles en qué clase de actividad se ocupaban, indicaron que habían trabajado durante la semana de referencia.

Se ha indicado que fueron incluidas las siguientes categorías:
i) personas que trabajan sin remuneración en una empresa o negocio familiar;
ii) personas que producen bienes primarios para el autoconsumo;
iii) personas ocupadas pero temporalmente ausentes de su trabajo;
iv) estudiantes que trabajan a tiempo parcial;
v) trabajadores estacionales u ocasionales;
vi) aprendices y personas que siguen un curso de formación.

Ninguna de estas categorías puede identificarse por separado.

c) Desempleo: Se consideró "desempleada" a toda persona que, durante el período de referencia, se encontraba sin trabajo.

7. Clasificaciones utilizadas:
Sólo las personas ocupadas fueron clasificadas por rama de actividad económica, por ocupación y según la situación en el empleo.

a) Rama de actividad económica: Para determinarla se preguntó: "¿En qué clase de actividad industrial, comercial o de servicios trabaja usted?". Para codificar la rama de actividad se utilizó la CIIU-Rev.2.

b) Ocupación: Para determinarla se preguntó: "¿Cuál es su principal ocupación?". Para codificar la ocupación se utilizó la CIUO-88, en el nivel de subgrupos (clave de 3 dígitos).

c) Situación en el empleo: Para codificar esta variable se utilizaron 4 grupos: empleador; trabajador asalariado; trabajador independiente; trabajador no remunerado.

8. Diferencias principales con el censo anterior:
En el censo de 1992 se incluyó por primera vez una serie de preguntas destinadas especialmente a las mujeres que se designaran a sí mismas como amas de casa.

9. Publicación de los resultados del censo:
Los resultados definitivos del censo se publicaron en enero de 1993, en el volumen que lleva por título "Report of the Census of Population and Housing - 1991".

El organismo responsable de esta publicación es el Department of Statistics, P.O. Box 1151, Apia, Western Samoa.

No se dispone de los resultados en otros soportes.

SAMOA AMERICANA

1. Nombre y dirección del organismo responsable del censo:
Economic Development and Planning Office, American Samoa Government, Pago Pago, A.S. 96799, junto con US Bureau of the Census.

2. Censos de población llevados a cabo desde 1945 (años):
1945, 1950, 1956, 1960, 1970, 1974, 1980 y 1990. La presente descripción se refiere al censo de población de 1990 (realizado el 1o. de abril de ese año).

3. Alcance del censo:
a) Geográfico: Toda la zona.

b) Personas comprendidas: Toda persona en su "residencia habitual", es decir, el lugar donde suele vivir y dormir. Del censo se excluyó a: las personas que suelen vivir en otra parte; los estudiantes universitarios que viven en otra parte mientras asisten a la facultad; los miembros de las fuerzas armadas que viven en otra parte y las personas que por razones de trabajo, residen casi toda la semana en otra parte.

4. Periodo de referencia:
La semana anterior al censo y el año anterior al año del censo.

5. Materias principales:
a) Población total, según sexo y edad:	sí
Población económicamente activa por:	
b) Sexo y grupo de edad:	sí
c) Rama de actividad económica:	sí

d) Ocupación: sí
e) Situación en el empleo: sí
f) Nivel más alto de educación: sí
g) Horas de trabajo: sí
h) Otras características: sí

Ref. a): La edad se determinó según el año de nacimiento y los años cumplidos en el último cumpleaños.

Ref. g): Tanto para el período de referencia corto como para el largo se pidió a las personas ocupadas que indicaran, respectivamente, el número de horas trabajadas la semana anterior y el período total de trabajo en 1989 (en número de semanas).

Ref. h): El censo también recolectó información sobre el ingreso total y los medios de transporte para trasladarse al lugar de trabajo.

6. Conceptos y definiciones:

a) Población económicamente activa: Abarcó a todas las personas de 16 o más años de edad que durante el período de referencia estaban ocupadas (salvo quienes practicaban la agricultura de subsistencia) o desempleadas, conforme a las definiciones que figuran más adelante. La definición incluyó a los miembros de las fuerzas armadas.

b) Empleo: Para determinar si una persona debía considerarse ocupada se preguntó: "¿Trabajó en algún momento de la semana pasada, ya sea a tiempo completo o a tiempo parcial?" (El término "trabajo" incluye labores a tiempo parcial como, por ejemplo, la distribución de documentos o la ayuda no remunerada en una empresa o explotación agrícola familiar, y el servicio activo en las fuerzas armadas; no se incluyen el propio trabajo doméstico, los estudios o el trabajo voluntario); y "¿Cuántas horas trabajó la semana pasada en todos los empleos, exceptuando las actividades de subsistencia?"

Se ha indicado que fueron incluidas las siguientes categorías:

i) personas que trabajan sin remuneración en una empresa o negocio familiar;
ii) personas ocupadas pero temporalmente ausentes de su trabajo;
iii) estudiantes que trabajan a tiempo parcial;
iv) trabajadores estacionales u ocasionales;
v) conscriptos del servicio militar o civil;
vi) aprendices y personas que siguen un curso de formación.

Ninguna de estas categorías puede identificarse por separado.

c) Desempleo: Se consideró "desempleada" a toda persona que durante el período de referencia estaba sin trabajo o buscaba uno. Para determinar si una persona debía considerarse desempleada, se preguntó: "¿Estuvo temporalmente ausente o despedido de su empleo o empresa la semana pasada?"; "¿Ha buscado trabajo para ganar dinero durante las últimas 4 semanas?"; y "¿Hubiera podido aceptar un empleo la semana pasada, si se le hubiera ofrecido?"

7. Clasificaciones utilizadas:

Tanto las personas ocupadas como las desempleadas anteriormente empleadas se clasificaron por rama de actividad, por ocupación y por situación en el empleo.

a) Rama de actividad económica: Para determinarla se preguntó: "¿Quién fue su último empleador?"; "¿De qué clase de empresa o rama de actividad se trataba?"; y "¿Cuál es la actividad principal: manufactura, comercio mayorista, comercio minorista, otros (agricultura, construcción, servicios, administración pública, etc.)"? Para codificar la rama de actividad se utilizaron 231 categorías, clasificadas en 13 grandes grupos del Standard Industrial Classification Manual (SIC). Se establecieron enlaces con los suplementos especiales sobre los Estados Unidos, de 1972 y 1977, de la CIIU-Rev.2.

b) Ocupación: Para determinarla se preguntó: "¿Qué clase de trabajo estaba haciendo (por ejemplo, enfermera diplomada, mécanico de maquinaria industrial, repostero)?" y "¿Cuáles eran sus actividades o funciones más importantes? (por ejemplo, asistencia a pacientes, reparación de la maquinaria industrial de la fábrica, glasear las tortas)". Para codificar la ocupación se utilizaron 13 grupos principales del Standard Occupational Classification Manual (SOC). No se establecieron enlaces con la CIUO.

c) Situación en el empleo: Para determinarla se preguntó si la persona trabajaba para una empresa o negocio privado o para un particular, cuyas actividades tenían fines de lucro, mediando un salario o una comisión; si era empleada de una institución privada sin fines de lucro, exenta de impuestos o de beneficencia; si era empleada pública de la administración local

(territorial, commonwealth, etc.), o de la administración federal; si era independiente con una empresa, actividad profesional o explotación agrícola no constituida en sociedad; si era independiente con una empresa, actividad profesional o explotación agrícola constituida en sociedad; o si trabajaba en una empresa o explotación agrícola familiar sin recibir remuneración. Para codificar la situación en el empleo, se utilizaron los siete grupos citados.

8. Diferencias principales con el censo anterior:
No hubo diferencias significativas.

9. Publicación de los resultados del censo:
Los resultados definitivos del censo se publicaron en 1992 con el título "1990 CPH-6-AS".

Las organizaciones responsables de dicha publicación son el U.S. Department of Commerce, U.S. Bureau of the Census, Washington, D.C. 20233 y el Superintendent of Documents, U.S. Government Printing Office, Washington, D.C. 20402.

También se dispone de los resultados en ficheros STF 1 y 3, disquetes y cintas magnéticas.

SAN VICENTE Y LAS GRANADINAS

1. Nombre y dirección del organismo responsable del censo:
Census Office, Statistical Office, Central Planning Division.

2. Censos de población llevados a cabo desde 1945 (años):
1960, 1970, 1980 y 1991. La presente descripción se refiere al censo de población de 1991 (realizado el 12 de mayo de ese año).

3. Alcance del censo:
a) Geográfico: Todo el país.

b) Personas comprendidas: Toda la población.

4. Período de referencia:
La semana y el año anteriores al día del censo.

5. Materias principales:
a) Población total, según sexo y edad: sí
Población económicamente activa por:
b) Sexo y grupo de edad: sí
c) Rama de actividad económica: sí
d) Ocupación: sí
e) Situación en el empleo: sí
f) Nivel más alto de educación: sí
g) Horas de trabajo: sí
h) Otras características: sí

Ref. a): La edad de la persona censada se definió en función de su último cumpleaños.

Ref. g): El censo recabó datos de las personas ocupadas sobre el número de meses trabajados durante el año de referencia y el número de horas trabajadas durante la semana de referencia.

Ref. h): El censo también recolectó información sobre los ingresos y los medios de transporte utilizados para trasladarse al trabajo.

6. Conceptos y definiciones:

a) Población económicamente activa: Abarca a todas las personas de 15 o más años de edad que, durante la semana de referencia, tenían un empleo o estaban desempleadas, según las definiciones que se dan más adelante. De esta definición quedan excluidos los militares de carrera, los estudiantes que trabajaban a tiempo parcial y los estudiantes que buscaban trabajo.

b) Empleo: Se consideró "ocupada" a toda persona que dijo haber trabajado durante la mayor parte del período de referencia corto. Para determinar si la persona censada debía considerarse como "ocupada" se preguntó qué había hecho principalmente durante la semana anterior al censo, por ejemplo, si había trabajado, buscado empleo, efectuado tareas domésticas u otra actividad.

Se ha indicado que quedan incluidas las siguientes categorías:

i) personas que trabajan sin remuneración en una empresa o negocio familiar;

ii) personas ocupadas pero temporalmente ausentes de su trabajo;

iii) trabajadores estacionales u ocasionales;

iv) aprendices y personas que siguen un curso de formación.

Sólo las categorías i) y ii) pueden identificarse por separado.

c) Desempleo: Se consideró "desempleada" a toda persona que durante la semana de referencia carecía de trabajo, deseaba trabajar y estaba disponible para hacerlo. La definición incluye a aquellas personas que buscaban activamente un empleo, y también a aquellas que no hacían nada por encontrar un trabajo porque sabían que no había puestos vacantes.

7. Clasificaciones utilizadas:

Las personas ocupadas y los desempleados anteriormente empleados han sido clasificados por rama de actividad económica, por ocupación y según la situación en el empleo.

a) Rama de actividad económica: Para determinarla se preguntó a la persona censada qué tipo de actividad se llevaba a cabo en el lugar donde trabajaba o había trabajado antes. Para codificar la rama de actividad económica, se utilizaron 17 grupos de la clasificación nacional. Los enlaces con la clasificación CIIU-Rev.3 se han establecido a nivel de categorías (clave de 1 dígito).

b) Ocupación: Para determinarla se preguntó qué tipo de trabajo desempeñaba la persona censada en su ocupación principal. Para codificar la ocupación, se utilizaron 10 grupos de la clasificación nacional. Los enlaces con la clasificación CIUO-88 se han establecido a nivel de grandes grupos (clave de 1 dígito).

c) Situación en el empleo: Para determinarla se preguntó a la persona censada si tenía un negocio propio, era asalariada o se ocupaba como trabajador familiar no remunerado. Para codificar la situación en el empleo, se utilizaron seis grupos: asalariado del sector estatal; asalariado del sector privado; trabajador no remunerado; propietario de negocio con asalariados a cargo (empleador); propietario de negocio sin asalariados (trabajador por cuenta propia); no sabe/no responde.

8. Diferencias principales con el censo anterior:

No hubo diferencias significativas.

9. Publicación de los resultados del censo:

Los datos definitivos del censo sobre la población económicamente activa y sus componentes han aparecido en la publicación titulada "1991 - Population and Housing Census Report, Volume 2"

La organización responsable de dicha publicación es la Statistical Office, Central Planning Division, Ministry of Finance.

Los datos del censo también están disponibles en disquetes.

SANTA LUCIA

1. Nombre y dirección del organismo responsable del censo:

Statistics Department, Block A, 3rd floor, N.I.S. Building, The Waterfront, Castries, St. Lucia, West Indies.

2. Censos de población llevados a cabo desde 1945 (años):

1946, 1960, 1970, 1980 y 1991. La presente descripción se refiere al censo de población de 1991 (realizado el 12 de mayo de ese año).

3. Alcance del censo:

a) Geográfico: Toda la isla.

b) Personas comprendidas: Toda la población.

4. Periodo de referencia:

La semana y el período de 12 meses anteriores al día del censo.

5. Materias principales:

a) Población total, según sexo y edad:	sí

Población económicamente activa por:

b) Sexo y grupo de edad:	sí
c) Rama de actividad económica:	sí
d) Ocupación:	sí
e) Situación en el empleo:	sí
f) Nivel más alto de educación:	sí
g) Horas de trabajo:	sí
h) Otras características:	sí

Ref. a): La edad se determinó según los años cumplidos en el último cumpleaños.

Ref. g): Por horas de trabajo se entendió el número de horas de trabajo efectivas durante la semana de referencia, y por período total trabajado, el número de meses trabajados durante los 12 meses anteriores al día del censo.

Ref. h): Se acopió información acerca de los ingresos y los medios de transporte hasta el lugar de trabajo.

6. Conceptos y definiciones:

a) Población económicamente activa: Abarcó a todas las personas de 15 o más años de edad que, durante los períodos de referencia, estaban fundamentalmente ocupadas o desempleadas, conforme a las definiciones que se dan más adelante. La definición no incluyó a los estudiantes con empleo a tiempo parcial, a los que buscaban trabajo y a los miembros de las fuerzas armadas.

b) Empleo: Se consideró "ocupada" a toda persona que, fundamentalmente, desempeñó alguna actividad laboral durante los períodos de referencia. Para determinar si una persona debía contabilizarse como ocupada se utilizaron las siguientes preguntas: "¿Cuál fue su actividad principal en los pasados 12 meses?"; y "¿Cuál fue su actividad principal la semana pasada?". Las posibles respuestas eran: "1) Trabajé; 2) Tenía un empleo, pero no trabajé; 3) Busqué trabajo; 4) Quería trabajar y estaba disponible para hacerlo; 5) Trabajé en labores del hogar; 6) Asistí a la escuela; 7) Estaba ya jubilado; 8) Estaba ya retirado por invalidez; 9) Otras; y 10) No respondió".

Se ha indicado que fueron incluidas las siguientes categorías:

i) personas que trabajan sin remuneración en una empresa o negocio familiar;

ii) personas ocupadas pero temporalmente ausentes de su trabajo.

Ambas categorías pueden identificarse por separado.

c) Desempleo: Se consideró "desempleada" a toda persona que, durante la semana de referencia, se encontraba fundamentalmente sin trabajo, quería trabajar, estaba disponible para trabajar o estaba buscando trabajo.

7. Clasificaciones utilizadas:

Tanto las personas ocupadas como las desempleadas anteriormente empleadas se clasificaron por rama de actividad económica, por ocupación y por situación en el empleo.

a) Rama de actividad económica: Para determinarla se preguntó: "¿Qué tipo de actividad se lleva o se llevaba a cabo en su lugar de trabajo?". A las personas desempleadas se preguntó también: "¿Qué tipo de trabajo buscaba o esperaba encontrar?". Para codificar la rama de actividad se utilizaron 17 grupos de la clasificación nacional. Se establecieron enlaces con la CIIU-Rev.3 a nivel de categorías de tabulación (1 dígito).

b) Ocupación: Para determinarla se preguntó: "¿Qué tipo de trabajo desempeña o desempeñaba en su ocupación principal?". Para codificar la ocupación se utilizaron nueve grupos de la clasificación nacional. Se establecieron enlaces con la CIUO-88 a nivel de grandes grupos (1 dígito).

c) Situación en el empleo: Para determinarla se preguntó: "¿Tenía usted su propia empresa, trabajaba mediando un sueldo o salario o era trabajador familiar no remunerado?" Para codificar esta variable se utilizaron seis grupos, a saber: empleado público; empleado particular; trabajador no remunerado; empresario con personal remunerado (empleador); empresario sin personal remunerado (trabajador por cuenta propia); no sabe/no responde.

8. Diferencias principales con el censo anterior:

En el censo de 1991, se procuró obtener más datos sobre las personas desempleadas en busca de empleo.

9. Publicación de los resultados del censo:

Los resultados definitivos del censo se publicaron en 1995, bajo el título "1991 Population & Housing Census Volumes 1- 9.".

La organización responsable de la publicación es el Statistics Department, NIS Building, The Waterfront, Castries.

Los datos del censo existen también en cuadros inéditos, disponibles en el Departamento de Estadística desde mayo de 1992.

SANTO TOME Y PRINCIPE

1. Nombre y dirección del organismo responsable del censo:
Direcçao de Economia e Estatística, C.P. 256, Santo Tomé.

2. Censos de población llevados a cabo desde 1945 (años):
1950, 1960, 1970, 1981 y 1991. La presente descripción se refiere al censo de 1991 (realizado el 4 de agosto de ese año).

3. Alcance del censo:
a) Geográfico: Todo el territorio.

b) Personas comprendidas: Toda la población.

4. Periodo de referencia:
La semana anterior a la fecha censo. En las preguntas formuladas a las personas ocupadas en relación con su tiempo de trabajo se utilizaron un período de referencia corto (la semana anterior al censo) y un período de referencia largo (los 12 meses anteriores).

5. Materias principales:
a) Población total, según sexo y edad:	sí
Población económicamente activa por:	
b) Sexo y grupo de edad:	sí
c) Rama de actividad económica:	sí
d) Ocupación:	sí
e) Situación en el empleo:	sí
f) Nivel más alto de educación:	sí
g) Horas de trabajo:	sí
h) Otras características:	sí

Ref. a): La edad se determinó según el año de nacimiento y también según los años cumplidos en el último cumpleaños.

Ref. g): El tiempo de trabajo se refiere tanto al horario normal de trabajo de las personas ocupadas y a las horas efectivamente trabajadas por las personas ocupadas, presentes en el lugar de trabajo durante la semana anterior al censo, como al período total de trabajo (en meses) durante los 12 meses anteriores al censo.

Ref. h): También se hizo una pregunta sobre el ingreso de las personas activas.

6. Conceptos y definiciones:
a) Población económicamente activa: Abarcó a todas las personas de 10 o más años de edad que, durante el período de referencia, estaban ocupadas o desempleadas, según las definiciones que se dan más adelante. La definición incluyó a los miembros de las fuerzas armadas.

b) Empleo: Se consideró "ocupada" a toda persona que, al referirse a su "condición en relación al trabajo" durante la semana de referencia, señaló que trabajaba.

Se ha indicado que fueron incluidas las siguientes categorías:
i) personas que trabajan sin remuneración en una empresa o negocio familiar;
ii) personas que producen bienes primarios para el autoconsumo;
iii) personas ocupadas pero temporalmente ausentes de su trabajo;
iv) estudiantes que trabajan a tiempo parcial;
v) trabajadores estacionales u ocasionales;
vi) conscriptos del servicio militar o civil;
vii) aprendices y personas que siguen un curso de formación.

Sólo las categorías i) y vii) pueden identificarse por separado, con arreglo a sus respuestas a determinadas preguntas.

c) Desempleo: Se consideró "desempleada" a toda persona que, al preguntársele cuál era su "condición en relación al trabajo" durante el período de referencia, declaró que estaba en busca sea de un nuevo empleo sea de un primer empleo. No quedaron incluidos en la definición los estudiantes que buscaban trabajo.

7. Clasificaciones utilizadas:
Tanto las personas ocupadas como los desempleados anteriormente empleados se clasificaron por rama de actividad, por ocupación y por situación en el empleo.

a) Rama de actividad económica: Para determinar la rama de actividad se hizo una pregunta destinada a precisar el lugar de trabajo (explotación agrícola, empresa pública o privada, etc.) así como la rama de actividad económica misma. Para codificar la rama de actividad económica se utilizó la clasificación CIIU-Rev.2, a nivel de grandes divisiones (clave de 1 dígito).

b) Ocupación: Las preguntas hechas estaban destinadas a determinar la ocupación ejercida durante la semana de referencia (en el caso de los desempleados: la última ocupación ejercida). Para codificar la ocupación se utilizó la CIUO-88, a nivel de subgrupos (clave de 3 dígitos).

c) Situación en el empleo: Para codificar esta variable se utilizaron las siguientes cinco categorías: asalariado; trabajador por cuenta propia; empleador; trabajador familiar no remunerado; situación no declarada.

8. Diferencias principales con el censo anterior:
En el censo de 1981 no se formuló ninguna pregunta relativa al tiempo total de trabajo ni al ingreso de las personas ocupadas.

9. Publicación de los resultados del censo:
La publicación en que figuran los resultados definitivos del censo lleva por título: "Principais Resultados do II. Recenseamento Geral da Populaçao e da Habitaçao".

El organismo responsable de esta publicación es la Direcçao de Economia e Estatistica, C.P. 256, Sao Tomé.

Los resultados del censo de 1991 están disponibles también en otros soportes, en particular, en disquetes.

SINGAPUR

1. Nombre y dirección del organismo responsable del censo:
Department of Statistics, 8 Shenton Way, 10-01, Treasury Building, Singapur 0106.

2. Censos de población llevados a cabo desde 1945 (años):
1947, 1957, 1970, 1980 y 1990. La presente descripción se refiere al censo de 1990 (realizado el 30 de junio de ese año).

3. Alcance del censo:
a) Geográfico: Todo el país.

4. Periodo de referencia:
La semana anterior al día de la entrevista.

5. Materias principales:
a) Población total, según sexo y edad:	sí
Población económicamente activa por:	
b) Sexo y grupo de edad:	sí
c) Rama de actividad económica:	sí
d) Ocupación:	sí
e) Situación en el empleo:	sí
f) Nivel más alto de educación:	sí
g) Horas de trabajo:	no
h) Otras características:	sí

Ref. a): La edad de la persona censada se determinó según su fecha de nacimiento (el cálculo fue el siguiente: fecha del censo menos fecha de nacimiento; los meses y días adicionales se expresaron como fracción decimal del año).

Ref. h): El censo también recolectó datos sobre otros aspectos, como: sueldos y salarios, bonificaciones, ingresos o ganancias mensuales (en el caso de las personas independientes) y medios de transporte usados para trasladarse al lugar de trabajo.

6. Conceptos y definiciones:
a) Población económicamente activa: Abarcó a todas las personas que, la semana de referencia, estaban sea ocupadas, sea desempleadas, conforme a las definiciones que se dan más adelante. No se fijaron límites de edad para incluir o no a los encuestados en la población económicamente activa, pero sólo se tabularon datos económicos relativos a personas de 15 o más años de edad. La definición incluyó a los miembros de las fuerzas armadas. En cambio, no quedaron incluidos en ella los estudiantes que trabajaban a tiempo parcial ni los que buscaban empleo.

b) Empleo: Se consideró "ocupada" a toda persona que: i) ejerció un trabajo remunerado con un salario o con ganancias durante los últimos 7 días, o ii) trabajaba habitualmente por lo menos 15 horas por semana. Estas dos definiciones se usaron para determinar si una persona debía contabilizarse como ocupada.

Se ha indicado que fueron incluidas las siguientes categorías:

i) personas que trabajan sin remuneración en una empresa o negocio familiar;
ii) personas que producen bienes primarios para el autoconsumo;
iii) personas ocupadas pero temporalmente ausentes de su trabajo;
iv) trabajadores estacionales u ocasionales;
v) conscriptos del servicio militar o civil;
vi) aprendices y personas que siguen un curso de formación.

Sólo las personas incluidas en las categorías i) y v) pueden identificarse por separado. Para establecer qué personas se incluían en la categoría i) se preguntó: "¿Ha prestado usted su colaboración en cualquier empresa o negocio familiar en calidad de trabajador familiar no remunerado?". Los datos relativos a las personas que cumplían el servicio militar (categoría v)) se obtuvieron del Ministerio de Defensa, y se imprimieron a fin de presentarlos por adelantado a los interesados, para su verificación y confirmación.

c) Desempleo: Para determinar si una persona debía contabilizarse o no como "desempleada" se utilizaron las preguntas: "¿Está usted buscando trabajo?" y "Si su respuesta a la pregunta anterior es afirmativa, ¿en qué ha consistido su búsqueda de trabajo: i) se ha inscrito en el Servicio Público de Empleo; ii) ha respondido a anuncios o enviado ofertas de servicio directas; iii) ha solicitado la ayuda de amigos o parientes; iv) otras iniciativas; v) ha iniciado preparativos para instalar su propia empresa o negocio?".

7. Clasificaciones utilizadas:
Sólo las personas ocupadas fueron clasificadas por rama de actividad económica, por ocupación y según la situación en el empleo.

a) Rama de actividad económica: Para determinarla se preguntó: "¿Qué tipo de actividad efectúa la empresa u organismo para el que trabaja?" y "¿Cuál es el principal tipo de producto elaborado o procesado allí?", o "¿Qué tipo de servicios presta la empresa u organismo para el que trabaja?". Para codificar la rama de actividad, se utilizaron 117 subgrupos (clave de 3 dígitos), 317 grupos primarios (4 dígitos) y 945 epígrafes (5 dígitos) de la Clasificación Industrial Normalizada de Singapur, de 1990 (SSIC 90). Se establecieron enlaces con la CIIU-Rev.3 a nivel de categorías de tabulación (clave de 1 dígito).

b) Ocupación: Para determinarla se preguntó: "¿Cuál es su ocupación?" o "¿Qué tipo de trabajo desempeña usted?". Para codificar la ocupación, se utilizaron 119 subgrupos (clave de 3 dígitos), 314 grupos primarios (4 dígitos) y 1 116 ocupaciones (5 dígitos) de la Clasificación Normalizada de Ocupaciones de Singapur (SSOC). Para facilitar la codificación de esta variable, se previó el espacio necesario en el formulario de empadronamiento para que el agente censador (o la persona censada, si ésta cumplimentaba el formulario) anotara la descripción de las principales funciones/tareas cumplidas en el marco de la ocupación. Se establecieron enlaces con la CIUO-88 a nivel de grandes grupos (clave de 1 dígito).

c) Situación en el empleo: Para determinarla se preguntó: "¿Es usted: i) trabajador independiente sin personal remunerado; ii) trabajador independiente con personal remunerado?; iii) trabajador asalariado; iv) empleado del Servicio Nacional; v) trabajador familiar auxiliar, sin remuneración fija o regular?". Para codificar la situación en el empleo se utilizaron los 5 grupos mencionados.

8. Diferencias principales con el censo anterior:
En el censo de 1980, la edad mínima para quedar incluido en la población económicamente activa era de 10 años.

En ese mismo censo, no se clasificó por separado a las personas que cumplían el servicio militar.

9. Publicación de los resultados del censo:
Los resultados definitivos del censo de 1990 se publicaron en agosto de 1993, en el volumen que lleva por título "Census of Population 1990 Statistical Release 4 - Economic Characteristics".

El organismo responsable de esta publicación es el Census of Population Office, Department of Statistics, Singapur.

Los resultados del censo no están disponibles ni en disquetes, ni en cinta magnética.

REPUBLICA ARABE SIRIA

1. Nombre y dirección del organismo responsable del censo:
The Central Bureau of Statistics, Abou Rummaneh, Abdel Malek Ben Marwan Street, Damasco.

2. Censos de población llevados a cabo desde 1945 (años):
1960, 1970, 1976, 1981 y 1994. La presente descripción se refiere al censo de población de 1994 (realizado el 3 de septiembre de ese año).

3. Alcance del censo:
a) Geográfico: Todo el país.
b) Personas comprendidas: Toda la población.

4. Periodo de referencia:
La semana y el año anteriores a la fecha del empadronamiento.

5. Materias principales:
a) Población total, según sexo y edad: sí
Población económicamente activa por:
b) Sexo y grupo de edad: sí
c) Rama de actividad económica: sí
d) Ocupación: sí
e) Situación en el empleo: sí
f) Nivel más alto de educación: sí
g) Horas de trabajo: sí
h) Otras características: no

Ref. a): La edad se determinó según el año de nacimiento.
Ref. g): En lo que atañe al período de referencia corto, se pidió a las personas ocupadas que indicaran sus horas de trabajo habituales y las horas efectivamente trabajadas. En cuanto al período de referencia largo, se pidió a las personas ocupadas que indicaran el período total trabajado, expresado en número de meses.

6. Conceptos y definiciones:
a) Población económicamente activa: Abarcó a todas las personas de 10 o más años de edad que, en el momento del censo, estaban ocupadas o desempleadas, conforme a las definiciones que se dan más adelante. Se formularon preguntas sobre la actividad económica a una muestra de 10 por ciento del universo. La definición incluyó a todos los miembros de las fuerzas armadas. En cambio, no quedaron incluidos en ella los estudiantes que trabajaban a tiempo parcial ni los que buscaban trabajo.

b) Empleo: Se consideró "ocupada" a toda persona que efectuó cualquier trabajo con valor económico al menos durante 18 horas en el curso de la semana que concluyó el día de la visita del empadronador.

Se ha indicado que fueron incluidas las siguientes categorías:
i) personas que trabajan sin remuneración en una empresa o negocio familiar;
ii) conscriptos del servicio militar o civil;
iii) aprendices y personas que siguen un curso de formación.

Todas las categorías pueden identificarse separadamente.

c) Desempleo: Se consideró "desempleada" a toda persona que, durante la semana de referencia, estaba buscando empleo, quería trabajar y estaba en condiciones de hacerlo, pero no había encontrado una ocupación.

7. Clasificaciones utilizadas:
En lo que atañe a la muestra, tanto las personas ocupadas como las desempleadas anteriormente empleadas fueron clasificadas por rama de actividad económica, por ocupación y según la situación en el empleo.

a) Rama de actividad económica: Para codificar esta variable se utilizó la clasificación nacional, a nivel de 3 dígitos. Se establecieron enlaces con la CIIU-Rev.3 a nivel de clases (clave de 4 dígitos).

b) Ocupación: Para codificar la ocupación se utilizó la clasificación nacional en el nivel de 3 dígitos. Se establecieron enlaces con la CIUO-88 a nivel de subgrupos principales (clave de 2 dígitos).

c) Situación en el empleo: Para codificar esta variable se utilizaron cinco grupos: empleador; trabajador independiente; trabajador remunerado; trabajador familiar no remunerado; aprendiz no remunerado.

8. Diferencias principales con el censo anterior:
En el censo de 1981 se usó sólo un período de referencia corto (la semana anterior a la fecha del censo).

9. Publicación de los resultados del censo:
Los resultados definitivos del censo debían publicarse un año y medio después de la fecha de su realización.

El organismo responsable de la publicación es la Central Bureau of Statistics, Abou Roummaneh, Damascus.

SUDAFRICA

1. Nombre y dirección del organismo responsable del censo:
Central Statistical Service, Private Bag x 44, Steyn's Arcade, 274 Schoeman Street, Pretoria 0001.

2. Censos de población llevados a cabo desde 1945 (años):
1946, 1951, 1960, 1970, 1980, 1985 y 1991. La presente descripción se refiere al censo de población de 1991 (realizado el 7 de marzo de ese año).

3. Alcance del censo:
a) Geográfico: La República de Sudáfrica (quedaron excluidos los territorios de Transkei, Bophuthatswana, Venda y Ciskei).

b) Personas comprendidas: Toda la población.

4. Período de referencia:
El día del censo.

5. Materias principales:

a) Población total, según sexo y edad:	sí
Población económicamente activa por:	
b) Sexo y grupo de edad:	sí
c) Rama de actividad económica:	sí
d) Ocupación:	sí
e) Situación en el empleo:	sí
f) Nivel más alto de educación:	sí
g) Horas de trabajo:	no
h) Otras características:	sí

Ref. a): La edad se determinó según el año de nacimiento y los años cumplidos en el último cumpleaños.

Ref. h): El censo también acopió información acerca de los ingresos anuales.

6. Conceptos y definiciones:
a) Población económicamente activa: Abarcó a todas las personas que, el día del censo, estaban ocupadas o desempleadas, conforme a las definiciones que se dan más adelante. No se fijaron límites de edad para la inclusión en los diferentes componentes de la población económicamente activa. No obstante, los datos publicados se refieren a las personas de 15 o más años de edad. La definición no incluyó a los extranjeros residentes empleados por gobiernos extranjeros, a las personas residentes por períodos inferiores a tres meses, a los estudiantes que trabajaban a tiempo parcial y a los que buscaran empleo; en cambio, incluyó a los miembros de las fuerzas armadas.

b) Empleo: Se consideró "ocupada" a toda persona que describió su situación en el empleo en el día del censo como "empleador/trabajador independiente" u "ocupado".

Se ha indicado que fueron incluidas las siguientes categorías:

i) personas que trabajan sin remuneración en una empresa o negocio familiar;
ii) personas que producen bienes primarios para el autoconsumo;
iii) personas ocupadas pero temporalmente ausentes de su trabajo;
iv) trabajadores estacionales u ocasionales;
v) conscriptos del servicio militar o civil;
vi) aprendices y personas que siguen un curso de formación.

Sólo los aprendices y las personas que siguen un curso de formación en artesanía pueden identificarse por separado.

c) Desempleo: Se consideró "desempleada" a toda persona que describió su situación en el empleo en el día del censo como "desempleado (en busca de trabajo)". Las personas que no trabajaban y no se encontraban buscando empleo no se consideraron desempleadas, y fueron catalogadas por separado.

7. Clasificaciones utilizadas:
Sólo las personas ocupadas fueron clasificadas por rama de actividad. Tanto las personas ocupadas como las desempleadas anteriormente empleadas se clasificaron por ocupación y por situación en el empleo.

a) Rama de actividad económica: Para determinar los grupos de actividad económica, se pidió a las personas empleadas y a los trabajadores independientes que indicaran el nombre y la rama económica del empleador o del trabajador independiente (por ejemplo, fábrica de vidrio, mina de oro, construcción de puentes, corredores de bolsa, administración de campamentos para turistas, salón de belleza, etc.). Para codificar la rama de actividad se utilizaron 40 grupos de la clasificación nacional. Se establecieron enlaces con la CIIU-Rev.2 a nivel de divisiones (2 dígitos).

b) Ocupación: Para determinar los grupos de ocupaciones, se pidió a las personas ocupadas y a las desempleadas anteriormente empleadas que indicaran su ocupación principal o su última ocupación, precisando la índole del trabajo desempeñado (por ejemplo, albañil, mecanógrafo, trabajador doméstico, etc.). A los funcionarios públicos se pidió que señalaran su grado o categoría profesional (por ejemplo, subdirector, brigadier, etc.). Para codificar la ocupación se utilizaron 165 grupos de la clasificación nacional. Se establecieron enlaces con la CIUO-68, pero no siempre en el mismo nivel.

c) Situación en el empleo: Para determinarla, se pidió tanto a las personas ocupadas como a las desempleadas anteriormente empleadas que indicaran la situación de su empleo, para lo que se utilizaron dos grupos de codificación, a saber: empleador o trabajador independiente (incluidos los trabajadores por cuenta propia y los trabajadores familiares); y empleado.

8. Diferencias principales con el censo anterior:
Por lo que se refiere a los procedimientos de recolección de datos, el empadronamiento de cerca del 20 por ciento de la población en 88 zonas se hizo por muestreo. Para cada una de estas zonas se preparó una muestra probabilística representativa, que sirvió para enumerar a las personas que pernoctaban habitualmente en chozas y otros locales. La muestra se estableció mediante técnicas de fotografía aérea, durante febrero de 1991, poco antes del día del censo. Anteriormente se habían tomado fotografías desde el aire de algunas zonas escogidas para perfeccionar el diseño de la muestra. Estas zonas se fotografiaron de nuevo en febrero de 1991.

9. Publicación de los resultados del censo:
Los resultados finales brutos se publicaron en marzo de 1992, y los resultados definitivos ajustados para compensar el recuento incompleto, en diciembre de 1992. Existen también otras publicaciones con los resultados del censo.

La organización responsable de estas publicaciones es el Central Statistical Service, Private Bag x44, Pretoria 0001.

En el Central Statistical Service se pueden obtener también cuadros inéditos, informes publicados en cinta magnética y los datos completos del censo en cinta magnética. Se puede solicitar también la compilación de tabulaciones especiales, servicio pagadero a efectos de sufragar el costo de la prestación.

SUDAN

1. Nombre y dirección del organismo responsable del censo:
Central Bureau of Statistics, P.O. Box 700, Khartoum.

2. Censos de población llevados a cabo desde 1945 (años):
1955-56, 1973, 1983 y 1993. La presente descripción se refiere al censo de población de 1993 (realizado el 15 de abril de ese año).

3. Alcance del censo:

a) Geográfico: El censo se llevó a cabo sólo parcialmente en las tres regiones meridionales del país, debido a la insurrección que tiene lugar allí.

b) Personas comprendidas: Toda la población.

4. Periodo de referencia:
La semana anterior al día del censo.

5. Materias principales:

a) Población total, según sexo y edad:	sí

Población económicamente activa por:

b) Sexo y grupo de edad:	sí
c) Rama de actividad económica:	sí
d) Ocupación:	sí
e) Situación en el empleo:	sí
f) Nivel más alto de educación:	sí
g) Horas de trabajo:	no
h) Otras características:	no

Ref. a): La edad se determinó según los años cumplidos en el último cumpleaños.

6. Conceptos y definiciones:

a) Población económicamente activa: Abarcó a todas las personas de 10 y más años de edad que durante el período de referencia estaban ocupadas o desempleadas, conforme a las definiciones que figuran más adelante. La definición excluyó a los miembros de las fuerzas armadas, a los estudiantes que trabajaban a tiempo parcial y a los estudiantes que buscaban trabajo.

b) Empleo: Se consideró "ocupada" a toda persona que durante la semana de referencia había trabajado dos días como mínimo, dentro o fuera de su domicilio, y remunerada o no.

Se ha indicado que las personas que trabajan sin remuneración en una empresa o negocio familiar son incluidas en la definición.

c) Desempleo: Se consideró "desempleada" a toda persona que durante la semana de referencia estaba sin trabajo y buscaba uno, o hubiera aceptado un empleo si se le hubiera ofrecido.

7. Clasificaciones utilizadas:
Tanto las personas ocupadas como las desempleadas previamente empleadas se clasificaron por rama de actividad, por ocupación y por situación en el empleo. Las preguntas al respecto se hicieron en todos los hogares de las zonas urbanas y en una muestra de 5 por ciento de hogares de las zonas rurales.

a) Rama de actividad económica: Para codificarla se utilizó el nivel de agrupaciones de la CIIU-Rev.2 (3 dígitos).

b) Ocupación: Para codificarla se utilizó el nivel de grupos primarios de la CIUO-88 (4 dígitos).

c) Situación en el empleo: Para codificar esta variable se utilizaron cinco grupos, a saber: empleado, empleador, trabajador por cuenta propia, trabajador familiar no remunerado, trabajador no remunerado al servicio de terceros.

8. Diferencias principales con el censo anterior:
No hubo diferencias significativas

9. Publicación de los resultados del censo:
Los datos definitivos figuran en la publicación "Fourth Population Census of Sudan. Final Tabulation", de junio de 1995.

La organización responsable de esta publicación es el Central Bureau of Statistics, P.O. Box 700, Khartoum.

También se dispone de los resultados definitivos en cuadros inéditos, disquetes y cintas magnéticas.

SUECIA

1. Nombre y dirección del organismo responsable del censo:
Statistics Sweden, I/BEF, S-701 89 Örebro.

2. Censos de población llevados a cabo desde 1945 (años):
1945, 1950, 1960, 1965, 1970, 1975, 1980, 1985 y 1990. La presente descripción se refiere al censo de población de 1990 (realizado el 1 de noviembre de ese año).

3. Alcance del censo:

a) Geográfico: Todo el país.

b) Personas comprendidas: Toda la población, salvo: los diplomáticos extranjeros y sus familias residentes en el país; los civiles extranjeros que residen transitoriamente en el país en calidad de trabajadores estacionales; los civiles extranjeros fronterizos que cruzan todos los días la frontera para trabajar en el país; otros civiles extranjeros, temporalmente residentes en el país; los viajeros a bordo de navíos amarrados a puerto en el momento del censo.

4. Periodo de referencia:
Un mes (octubre de 1990).

5. Materias principales:

a) Población total, según sexo y edad:	sí

Población económicamente activa por:

b) Sexo y grupo de edad:	sí
c) Rama de actividad económica:	sí
d) Ocupación:	sí
e) Situación en el empleo:	sí
f) Nivel más alto de educación:	sí
g) Horas de trabajo:	sí
h) Otras características:	sí

Ref. a): La edad se determinó según el año de nacimiento.

Ref. g): El tiempo de trabajo se refiere al número de horas normalmente trabajadas a la semana por las personas ocupadas.

Ref. h): El censo también recolectó información acerca de los ingresos (datos obtenidos de registros), así como sobre los medios de transporte utilizados.

6. Conceptos y definiciones:

a) Población económicamente activa: El censo mide sólo el empleo.

b) Empleo: Se consideró "ocupada" a toda persona no menor de 16 años que, durante el mes de referencia, estaba desempeñando alguna actividad laboral de valor económico cuantificable, dentro o fuera del hogar. No se hicieron preguntas para determinar si la persona empadronada debía contabilizarse como "ocupada", sino que se utilizaron los datos que figuraban en un registro de empleo. Los criterios aplicados fueron los siguientes: se consideró "ocupado" a quien había percibido ingresos iguales o superiores a 250 coronas durante octubre de 1990, o a 28 000 coronas anuales, en caso de desconocerse los datos del período de referencia.

Se ha indicado que fueron incluidas las siguientes categorías, a condición de que se cumpliesen los criterios relativos a los ingresos:

i) personas que producen bienes primarios para el autoconsumo;
ii) personas ocupadas pero temporalmente ausentes de su trabajo;
iii) estudiantes que trabajan a tiempo parcial;
iv) trabajadores estacionales u ocasionales;
v) conscriptos del servicio militar o civil;
vi) aprendices y personas que siguen un curso de formación.

Ninguna de estas categorías puede identificarse por separado.

c) Desempleo: No se aplica.

7. Clasificaciones utilizadas:
Las personas ocupadas se clasificaron por rama de actividad económica, por ocupación y según la situación en el empleo.

a) Rama de actividad económica: Los datos acerca de la rama de actividad económica se sacaron del registro SCB Central Register of Enterprises. Para codificar esta variable, se utilizaron 340 grupos de la Swedish Standard Industrial Classification of all Economic Activities (SNI-1969). Se establecieron enlaces con la CIIU-Rev.2 a nivel de grupos (clave de 4 dígitos).

b) Ocupación: Para determinarla, se pidió responder a preguntas i) referidas a una lista preestablecida de ocupaciones (del censo de 1985), "¿Corresponde su actual ocupación o cargo a alguna de las actividades incluidas en la lista?", o ii) sin relación con la lista preestablecida, "¿Cómo clasifica usted su ocupación? Indique su ocupación de la manera más esmerada posible, a fin de que describa adecuadamente sus tareas o responsabilidades". Para codificar la ocupación se utilizaron 321 grupos de la Nordic Classification of Occupations (NYK-1983). Se establecieron enlaces con la CIUO-68 a nivel de grandes grupos (clave de 1 dígito).

c) Situación en el empleo: Para determinar esta variable se utilizaron los datos sacados del registro citado mas arriba. Para codificar esta variable se utilizaron cuatro grupos: trabajador asalariado; empleador; trabajador independiente en la agricultura o la silvicultura; marino.

8. Diferencias principales con el censo anterior:
No hubo diferencias significativas.

9. Publicación de los resultados del censo:
Los resultados definitivos de los censos suelen publicarse después de un año y medio o dos años de la fecha de su realización.

El organismo responsable de la publicación de los resultados definitivos es Statistics Sweden, I/BEF, S-701 89 Örebro, Suecia.

También se dispone de los resultados del censo de 1990 en otros soportes, concretamente en "Computor tables" y "The Regional Statistical Database (RSDB) of Sweden", disponibles desde marzo de 1992.

SUIZA

1. Nombre y dirección del organismo responsable del censo:
Office fédéral de la statistique, Section de la structure de la population et des ménages, Hallwylstrasse 15, 3003 Berna.

2. Censos de población llevados a cabo desde 1945 (años):
1950, 1960, 1970, 1980 y 1990. La presente descripción se refiere al censo de 1990 (realizado el 4 de diciembre de ese año).

3. Alcance del censo:

a) Geográfico: Todo el territorio.

b) Personas comprendidas: Toda la población habitualmente residente en el país, salvo los diplomáticos extranjeros y sus familias.

4. Período de referencia:
Un período corto: la situación de la persona censada a fines de noviembre, a principios de diciembre o el mismo día del censo.

5. Materias principales:
a) Población total, según sexo y edad: sí
Población económicamente activa por:
b) Sexo y grupo de edad: sí
c) Rama de actividad económica: sí
d) Ocupación: sí
e) Situación en el empleo: sí
f) Nivel más alto de educación: sí
g) Horas de trabajo: sí
h) Otras características: sí

Ref. a): La edad se determinó según la fecha de nacimiento exacta (es decir, día, mes y año).

Ref. g): El tiempo de trabajo se refiere a las horas normales de trabajo de las personas ocupadas.

Ref. h): Durante el censo también se acopiaron otras informaciones. A las personas económicamente activas se formularon preguntas relativas al tiempo necesario para cubrir el trayecto entre el domicilio y el lugar de trabajo o la escuela ("¿Cuánto tiempo demora normalmente para llegar a su trabajo o a la escuela?", y "¿Cuántas veces al día recorre este trayecto ida y vuelta?"), así como sobre los medios de transporte usados a tal efecto ("¿Qué medio(s) de transporte usa habitualmente para ir a su trabajo o a la escuela? Si emplea varios al día, sírvase indicarlos todos"). A las personas que no trabajaban, es decir a las que habían cesado toda actividad económica, se pidieron datos sobre la profesión ejercida antes de jubilar y acerca de su situación en esa ocupación.

6. Conceptos y definiciones:

a) Población económicamente activa: Abarcó a todas las personas de 15 o más años de edad que, en la fecha del censo, estaban ocupadas o desempleadas, según las definiciones que se dan más adelante. Las personas que trabajaban menos de una hora por semana quedaron excluidas del ámbito de la definición. Las que cumplían con su servicio militar obligatorio fueron clasificadas con arreglo a la actividad que tenían en la vida civil.

b) Empleo: Se consideró "ocupada" a toda persona que, en la fecha del censo, ejercía una profesión, una función o una actividad lucrativa a tiempo completo o a tiempo parcial. Se consideró "ocupadas a tiempo parcial" a aquellas personas cuyo tiempo de trabajo era a lo más igual al 80 por ciento del horario de trabajo habitual en el establecimiento o la rama de actividad en que trabajaban; con todo, la duración semanal de su tiempo de trabajo debía ser de por lo menos una hora.

Se ha indicado que fueron incluidas las siguientes categorías:

i) personas que trabajan sin remuneración en una empresa o negocio familiar;

ii) personas ocupadas pero temporalmente ausentes de su trabajo;

iii) estudiantes que trabajan a tiempo parcial;

iv) trabajadores estacionales u ocasionales, a condición de que estuviesen activos en el momento del censo;

v) conscriptos (servicio militar o servicio civil), a condición de que estuviesen económicamente activos en la vida civil;

vi) poseedores de varios trabajos;

vii) aprendices y personas que siguen un curso de formación.

Sólo pueden identificarse por separado las categorías iii) y vi), los trabajadores extranjeros de la categoría iv) y los aprendices con un contrato de aprendizaje. Los trabajadores familiares también pueden identificarse agrupados, pero no por separado.

c) Desempleo: Se consideró "desempleada" a toda persona que, en el momento del censo, estaba sin trabajo y buscaba uno, o tenía una confirmación de contratación para un empleo futuro. Cabe hacer notar que durante el censo no se utilizó el término "desempleado", sino que se habló más bien de "persona en busca de empleo", a fin de evitar posibles confusiones con los "desempleados", en el sentido que se da a esta denominación en las estadísticas sobre el mercado de trabajo.

7. Clasificaciones utilizadas:
Tan sólo las personas ocupadas se clasificaron por rama de actividad. Tanto las personas ocupadas como las personas en busca de empleo previamente empleadas se clasificaron por ocupación y por situación en el empleo.

a) Rama de actividad económica: Concretamente, se preguntó "¿Dónde trabaja usted?", entendiéndose por "dónde" el lugar de trabajo y el nombre de la empresa. Conocido éste último, se determinó la rama de actividad económica basándose en el Registro Central de Empresas y Establecimientos (REE), de la Oficina Federal de Estadística. Para codificar la rama de actividad se utilizaron 54 clases, 210 grupos y 703 géneros de la Nomenclatura General de Actividades Económicas de 1985.

La asignación de códigos a las personas que trabajan en empresas que emplean a una o más personas se hará sirviéndose de un registro de empresas y establecimientos.

Existe una clave que permite la conversión entre la nomenclatura general suiza de actividades económicas y la CIIU-Rev.2 a nivel de divisiones (clave de 2 dígitos).

b) Ocupación: Para determinarla se preguntó: "¿Qué actividad profesional ejerce usted actualmente?" y "¿Qué actividad profesional ejerció en su último trabajo?" Se pidió a las personas censadas que indicaran su ocupación con la mayor exactitud posible y, de ser necesario, que la describieran brevemente; por ejemplo: "cerrajero en la construcción", y no simplemente "cerrajero"; "vendedor" o "empleado de oficina" y no "empleado(a)"; "técnico maquinista" y no "técnico"; etc. A las personas que tenían dos o más ocupaciones se pidió que indicaran sólo la más importante. Para codificar la ocupación se utilizaron 404 grupos. La codificación se hará al mismo tiempo que la de las profesiones aprendidas y del nivel de formación. Se establecieron enlaces con la CIUO-88.

c) Situación en el empleo: Para determinarla se preguntó: "Si usted ejerce actualmente una actividad profesional, sírvase indicar cuál es su situación en el empleo" y "Si usted busca un empleo o si ha cesado su actividad profesional, sírvase indicar cuál fue su última ocupación". Para codificar la situación en el empleo se utilizaron siete categorías: trabajador independiente (por ejemplo: comerciante, empresario, profesión liberal, etc.); empleado(a) en la empresa de un miembro de la familia; aprendiz con contrato de aprendizaje o de formación práctica acelerada; director(a), apoderado(a), funcionario(a) superior; directivo de nivel medio o inferior (por ejemplo: jefe(a) de oficina, de servicio o de sección, gerente(a) de sucursal, jefe(a) de taller, capataz, jefe(a) de equipo); empleado(a), obrero(a), persona en curso de formación; otra situación.

8. Diferencias principales con el censo anterior:
La cantidad mínima de horas de trabajo semanales exigidas para ser incluida en la categoría del empleo, que era de seis en 1980, se redujo a una hora en el censo de 1990.

9. Publicación de los resultados del censo:
El organismo responsable de la publicación de los resultados definitivos del censo es la Office fédéral de la statistique, Hallwylstrasse 15, 3003 Berne.

También se dispone de los resultados del censo de 1990 en cuadros inéditos, disquetes y cintas magnéticas.

TAILANDIA

1. Nombre y dirección del organismo responsable del censo:
National Statistical Office, Larn Luang Road, Bangkok 10100.

2. Censos de población llevados a cabo desde 1945 (años):
1950, 1960, 1970, 1980 y 1990. La presente descripción se refiere al censo de 1990 (realizado el 1 de abril de ese año).

3. Alcance del censo:

a) Geográfico: Todo el país.

b) Personas comprendidas: Toda la población, salvo: las tribus nómades montañesas; el personal militar y diplomático extranjero y sus familiares residentes en el país; las personas civiles nacionales de otros países con residencia temporal en Tailandia, que hubieran estado en el país desde hacía por lo menos tres meses antes de la fecha del censo; y los inmigrantes instalados en campamentos creados por el Gobierno.

4. Período de referencia:
Por lo que se refiere a la ocupación, respecto de la cual se hicieron preguntas a una muestra de 20 por ciento, se consideró la semana anterior al censo (25 a 31 de marzo); en cuanto a la situación en la actividad, sobre la que se consultó a todas las personas censadas, se tomó el año anterior al censo (1 de abril de 1989 al 31 de marzo de 1990).

5. Materias principales:

a) Población total, según sexo y edad:	sí
Población económicamente activa por:	
b) Sexo y grupo de edad:	sí
c) Rama de actividad económica:	sí
d) Ocupación:	sí
e) Situación en el empleo:	sí
f) Nivel más alto de educación:	sí
g) Horas de trabajo:	no
h) Otras características:	no

Ref. a): La edad se determinó tanto según el año de nacimiento como de los años cumplidos en el último cumpleaños.

6. Conceptos y definiciones:

a) Población económicamente activa: Abarcó a todas las personas de 13 o más años de edad que, durante la semana de referencia, se encontraban sea ocupadas, sea desempleadas, conforme a las definiciones que se dan más adelante. La definición incluyó a los miembros de las fuerzas armadas.

b) Empleo: Se consideró "ocupada" a toda persona que, durante los períodos de referencia indicados, estaba desempeñando, un día cualquiera, alguna actividad laboral con valor económico, dentro o fuera del hogar. Para determinar si una persona debía contabilizarse o no como ocupada se utilizaron las siguientes preguntas: "¿A qué empleo dedicó X la mayor parte de su tiempo el año pasado (1.04.1989-31.03.1990)?" y, en lo que atañe a la muestra de 20 por ciento, "¿A qué empleo dedicó X la mayor parte de su tiempo durante la semana del 25 al 31 de marzo de 1990?".

Se ha indicado que fueron incluidas las siguientes categorías:

i) personas que trabajan sin remuneración en una empresa o negocio familiar;
ii) personas ocupadas pero temporalmente ausentes de su trabajo;
iii) estudiantes que trabajan a tiempo parcial;
iv) trabajadores estacionales u ocasionales;
v) personas que cumplen el servicio militar o civil.

Ninguna de estas categorías puede identificarse por separado.

c) Desempleo: Se consideró "desempleada" a toda persona que estaba sin trabajo, pero que había buscado empleo por lo menos durante un día de la semana de referencia. También se consideró "desempleadas" a las personas incluidas en la muestra de 20 por ciento que respondieron "No trabajé" a la segunda pregunta que figura en el párrafo 6 b). La definición abarcó asimismo a las personas que esperaban trabajar en una temporada agrícola ulterior. La definición no incluyó a los estudiantes que buscaban trabajo.

7. Clasificaciones utilizadas:
Tanto las personas ocupadas como las desempleadas que habían trabajado antes fueron clasificadas por rama de actividad económica y por ocupación. Tan sólo las personas ocupadas fueron clasificadas por situación en el empleo.

a) Rama de actividad económica: Para determinarla se preguntó: "¿En qué actividad, empresa o servicio trabajó usted la mayor parte del tiempo el año pasado (indique las características de los bienes producidos o los servicios prestados, por ejemplo: agricultura, planta purificadora de agua, establecimiento escolar estatal)". Para codificar la rama de actividad se utilizaron 13 grandes grupos de la Clasificación Nacional de Actividades Económicas. Se establecieron enlaces con la CIIU-Rev.2, a nivel de grandes divisiones (clave de 1 dígito).

b) Ocupación: Para determinarla se preguntó: "¿A qué tipo de empleo dedicó usted la mayor parte de su tiempo de trabajo el año pasado? (sírvase indicar con precisión la actividad desplegada, por ejemplo: cultivo de arroz, cultivo de hortalizas, estadística, contabilidad)". Para codificar la ocupación se utilizó la CIUO-68, en el nivel de subgrupos (clave de 2 dígitos).

c) Situación en el empleo: Para determinarla se preguntó: "¿Cuál es su situación en el empleo?". Para codificar esta variable, se utilizaron 6 grupos: empleador; trabajador por cuenta propia; empleado estatal; empleado de empresa del sector estatal; empleado del sector privado; trabajador familiar no remunerado.

8. Diferencias principales con el censo anterior:
En el censo de 1980, la edad mínima para quedar incluido en la población económicamente activa fue de 11 años.

9. Publicación de los resultados del censo:
Los resultados definitivos del censo se publicaron en 1993, en el volumen que lleva por título "1990 Population and Housing Census".

El organismo responsable de esta publicación es el National Statistical Office, Social Statistics Division, Bangkok 10100.

Los resultados del censo están disponibles también en cintas magnéticas.

TRINIDAD Y TABAGO

1. Nombre y dirección del organismo responsable del censo:
Central Statistical Office, P.O. Box 98, Port-of-Spain, Trinidad.

2. Censos de población llevados a cabo desde 1945 (años):
1946, 1960, 1970, 1980 y 1990. La presente descripción se refiere al censo de población de 1990 (realizado el 15 de mayo de ese año).

3. Alcance del censo:

a) Geográfico: Todo el país.

b) Personas comprendidas: Toda la población.

4. Período de referencia:
Dos períodos: la semana, y los 12 meses anteriores a la fecha del empadronamiento por lo que se refiere a la situación en la actividad principal.

5. Materias principales:

a) Población total, según sexo y edad:	sí
Población económicamente activa por:	
b) Sexo y grupo de edad:	sí
c) Rama de actividad económica:	sí
d) Ocupación:	sí
e) Situación en el empleo:	sí
f) Nivel más alto de educación:	sí
g) Horas de trabajo:	sí
h) Otras características:	sí

Ref. a): La edad se determinó según el año de nacimiento.

Ref. g): El tiempo de trabajo se refiere a las horas habitualmente trabajadas por las personas ocupadas.

Ref. h): El censo también recopiló datos sobre otros temas, como el número de horas trabajadas durante la semana anterior (incluidas las horas extraordinarias), la dirección del lugar de trabajo, los ingresos brutos durante el último período de pago (la semana, dos semanas, el mes, el trimestre, otro).

6. Conceptos y definiciones:

a) Población económicamente activa: Abarcó a todas las personas de 15 o más años de edad que, durante los períodos de referencia, estaban sea ocupadas, sea desempleadas, conforme a las definiciones que se dan más adelante. Además, la definición incluyó a los miembros de las fuerzas armadas.

b) Empleo: Para determinar si una persona debía contabilizarse o no como "ocupada" se preguntó: "¿Qué hizo la semana pasada a) tenía un empleo y trabajó; b) tenía un empleo, pero no trabajó; c) estuvo en busca de un primer empleo; d) buscó trabajo; e) quería trabajar y estaba disponible para hacerlo por más de tres meses; f) asistió a clases; g) se ocupó de las labores del hogar; h) estaba jubilado; i) estaba inválido; j) estaba pensionado por edad avanzada; k) no quería trabajar; l) otra actividad; m) no respondió". Se contabilizó como "ocupadas" a las personas que indicaron las respuestas a) o b).

Se ha indicado que fueron incluidas las siguientes categorías:

i) personas que trabajan sin remuneración en una empresa o negocio familiar;
ii) personas ocupadas pero temporalmente ausentes de su trabajo;
iii) estudiantes que trabajan a tiempo parcial;
iv) trabajadores estacionales u ocasionales;
v) conscriptos del servicio militar o civil;
vi) aprendices y personas que siguen un curso de formación.

Sólo pueden identificarse por separado, en función de sus respuestas a determinadas preguntas, las personas en las categorías i), ii), v) y vi).

c) Desempleo: Se consideró "desempleada" a toda persona que, durante la semana de referencia, estaba sin trabajo pero buscaba empleo. Para determinar si una persona debía contabilizarse o no como desempleada se utilizó la misma pregunta que figura en el párrafo 6 b); las opciones de respuesta eran c) estuvo en busca de un primer empleo; d) buscó trabajo; y e) quería trabajar y estaba disponible para hacerlo por más de tres meses. La definición no incluyó a los estudiantes que buscaban trabajo.

7. Clasificaciones utilizadas:

Tanto las personas ocupadas como las desocupadas anteriormente ocupadas se clasificaron por rama de actividad económica, por ocupación y según la situación en el empleo.

a) Rama de actividad económica: Para determinarla se preguntó: "¿Cómo se denomina el departamento estatal o establecimiento en que X trabajaba/estaba empleado (por ejemplo, Ministerio de Salud (Hospital Santa Ana), Pete's Advertising Agency, etc.)?", y "¿Qué tipo de actividades tenían lugar allí (por ejemplo, servicios de psiquiatría hospitalaria, diseño y materiales publicitarios para medios de comunicación, etc.)?". Se pidió a los empadronadores que clasificaran a las personas en busca de un primer empleo según la rama de actividad a la que habían presentado su última oferta de servicios, y a las personas desempleadas previamente empleadas según la rama de actividad en que se incluía su último lugar de trabajo. Para codificar la rama de actividad se utilizaron 9 grandes grupos de la clasificación nacional de actividades. Se establecieron enlaces con la CIIU-Rev.2, en el nivel de grandes divisiones (clave de 1 dígito).

b) Ocupación: Para determinarla se preguntó: "¿Qué clase de trabajo desempeñó (qué empleo tuvo) X durante la semana pasada (por ejemplo, profesor de enseñanza secundaria, auxiliar contable, mecánico de automóviles)?", y "¿Cuál era la denominación del puesto de trabajo de X (por ejemplo, profesor de escalón II, auxiliar contable de escalón I, mecánico de automóviles grado A)?". Se pidió a los empadronadores que clasificaran a las personas en busca de un primer empleo según el tipo de trabajo al que habían postulado en su última oferta de servicios, y a las personas desempleadas previamente empleadas según el último empleo ocupado. Para codificar la ocupación, se utilizó la CIUO-88, en el nivel de subgrupos (clave de 3 dígitos).

c) Situación en el empleo: Para determinarla se preguntó: "¿Qué tipo de categoría de trabajador se aplica a X?". Para codificar la situación en el empleo se utilizaron los nueve grupos siguientes: empleado estatal de servicio público; empleado de empresa del sector público; empleado del sector privado; trabajador no remunerado; aprendiz; trabajador por cuenta propia sin personal remunerado; trabajador por cuenta propia con personal remunerado; no ha trabajado nunca; no respondió.

8. Diferencias principales con el censo anterior:

No hubo diferencias significativas.

9. Publicación de los resultados del censo:

Los resultados definitivos del censo se publicaron en 1993, en el volumen que lleva por título "Population and Housing Census 1990, Volume III, Part 2: Economic activity".

El organismo responsable de esta publicación es la Central Statistical Office, Port of Spain, Trinidad.

Los resultados del censo están también disponibles en otros soportes, como cuadros inéditos, disquetes y cintas magnéticas.

TURQUIA

1. Nombre y dirección del organismo responsable del censo:

State Institute of Statistics, Prime Ministry, Necatibey Caddesi No. 114, 06100 Ankara.

2. Censos de población llevados a cabo desde 1945 (años):

1945, 1950, 1955, 1960, 1965, 1970, 1975, 1980, 1985 y 1990. La presente descripción se refiere al censo de población de 1990 (realizado el 21 de octubre de ese año).

3. Alcance del censo:

a) Geográfico: Todo el país.

b) Personas comprendidas: Toda la población, salvo los nacionales residentes en el extranjero.

4. Período de referencia:

La semana anterior al día del censo.

5. Materias principales:

a) Población total, según sexo y edad:	sí
Población económicamente activa por:	
b) Sexo y grupo de edad:	sí
c) Rama de actividad económica:	sí
d) Ocupación:	sí
e) Situación en el empleo:	sí
f) Nivel más alto de educación:	sí
g) Horas de trabajo:	no
h) Otras características:	no

Ref. a): La edad se determinó según los años cumplidos en el último cumpleaños.

6. Conceptos y definiciones:

a) Población económicamente activa: Abarcó a todas las personas de 12 o más años de edad que, durante la semana de referencia, estaban sea ocupadas, sea desempleadas, conforme a las definiciones que se dan más adelante. La definición no incluyó a los estudiantes con empleo a tiempo parcial ni a los que buscaban trabajo; en cambio, quedaron incluidos los miembros de las fuerzas armadas.

b) Empleo: Se consideró "ocupada" a toda persona que respondió afirmativamente a las preguntas siguientes: "¿Tuvo usted un trabajo la semana pasada, remunerado en efectivo o en especie?" y "Si tal no fue el caso, ¿tiene usted un empleo en la actualidad?".

Se ha indicado que fueron incluidas las siguientes categorías:

i) personas que trabajan sin remuneración en una empresa o negocio familiar;
ii) personas que producen bienes primarios para el autoconsumo;
iii) trabajadores estacionales u ocasionales;
iv) conscriptos del servicio militar o civil;
v) aprendices y personas que siguen un curso de formación.

Ninguna de estas categorías puede identificarse por separado.

c) Desempleo: Se consideró "desempleada" a toda persona que, durante la semana de referencia, estaba sin trabajo, y que respondió afirmativamente a la pregunta "¿Está usted buscando empleo?".

7. Clasificaciones utilizadas:

Sólo las personas ocupadas se clasificaron por rama de actividad económica y por situación en el empleo. Tanto las personas ocupadas como las desempleadas anteriormente empleadas se clasificaron por ocupación.

a) Rama de actividad económica: Para determinarla se preguntó: "¿En qué clase de lugar de trabajo tuvo lugar su actividad laboral la semana pasada, o se desarrolla ésta actualmente (por ejemplo, el campo, el Ministerio de Justicia, una tienda de comestibles, una peluquería, etc.)?", y "¿Cuál es la naturaleza del trabajo efectuado en el lugar donde usted está empleado (por ejemplo, servicios públicos, comercio de detalle, fabricación de refrigeradores, reparación de televisores, etc.)?". Para codificar la rama de actividad se utilizaron 10 grupos de la clasificación nacional. Se establecieron enlaces con la CIIU-Rev.2, en el nivel de grandes divisiones (clave de 1 dígito).

b) Ocupación: Para determinarla se preguntó a las personas ocupadas: "¿Qué clase de trabajo desempeñó usted la semana pasada, o desempeña en la actualidad (por ejemplo, agricultor, gerente de banco, mecanógrafo, obrero de la construcción, etc.)?"; a las personas ocupadas y a las desempleadas anteriormente empleadas se les preguntó: "¿Cuál es su ocupación principal (por ejemplo, carpintero, abogado, albañil, enfermera, etc.)?". Para codificar la ocupación se utilizaron 7 grupos de la clasificación nacional. Se establecieron enlaces con la CIUO-68, en el nivel de grandes grupos (clave de 1 dígito).

c) Situación en el empleo: Para determinarla se preguntó: "¿Cuál era su situación en el empleo que tuvo la semana pasada o en su empleo actual?". Para codificar esta variable se utilizaron cuatro grupos: trabajador asalariado, empleador, trabajador independiente y trabajador familiar no remunerado.

8. Diferencias principales con el censo anterior:

En el censo de 1990 no se determinó cuál era la rama de actividad económica (sector) de las personas desempleadas anteriormente empleadas.

9. Publicación de los resultados del censo:

Los resultados definitivos se publicaron a fines de 1993 en el volumen que lleva por título "1990 Census of Population - Social and Economic Characteristics of Population".

El organismo responsable de la publicación es el State Institute of Statistics, Prime Ministry, Ankara.

Los datos incluidos en la citada publicación están disponibles también en disquetes.

UGANDA

1. Nombre y dirección del organismo responsable del censo:

Ministry of Finance and Economic Planning, Department of Statistics, P.O. Box 13, Entebbe.

2. Censos de población llevados a cabo desde 1945 (años):

1948, 1959, 1969, 1980 y 1991. La presente descripción se refiere al censo de población de 1991 (realizado el 11 de enero de ese año).

3. Alcance del censo:

a) Geográfico: Todo el país.

b) Personas comprendidas: Toda la población.

4. Periodo de referencia:

La semana anterior al día del censo.

5. Materias principales:

a) Población total, según sexo y edad:	sí
Población económicamente activa por:	
b) Sexo y grupo de edad:	sí
c) Rama de actividad económica:	no
d) Ocupación:	sí
e) Situación en el empleo:	sí
f) Nivel más alto de educación:	sí
g) Horas de trabajo:	no
h) Otras características:	no

Ref. a): La edad se determinó según los años cumplidos en el último cumpleaños.

6. Conceptos y definiciones:

a) Población económicamente activa: Abarcó a todas las personas de 10 o más años de edad que, durante el período de referencia, estaban ocupadas o desempleadas, conforme a las definiciones que se dan más adelante. Se hicieron preguntas sobre la actividad económica a toda la población urbana y al 10 por ciento de la población rural. La definición incluyó a los miembros de las fuerzas armadas que residían en domicilios privados.

b) Empleo: Se consideró "ocupada" a toda persona que desempeñó alguna actividad laboral durante el período de referencia. La pregunta utilizada fue: "Indique la situación laboral que tenía la semana pasada: empleado, trabajador independiente, trabajador familiar no remunerado, estudiante, ocupado en labores domésticas, buscaba trabajo, retirado por invalidez, de edad demasiado avanzada para trabajar, etc."

Se ha indicado que fueron incluidas las siguientes categorías:

i) personas que trabajan sin remuneración en una empresa o negocio familiar;
ii) estudiantes que trabajan a tiempo parcial;
iii) trabajadores estacionales u ocasionales;
iv) conscriptos del servicio militar o civil.

Sólo las categorías i) y ii) pueden identificarse por separado.

c) Desempleo: Se consideró "desempleada" a toda persona que, durante el semana de referencia, se encontraba sin trabajo y buscaba empleo. Se utilizó la misma pregunta que figura en el párrafo 6 b).

7. Clasificaciones utilizadas:

Tan solo las personas ocupadas fueron clasificadas por ocupación y por situación en el empleo.

a) Rama de actividad económica: No se efectuó clasificación alguna por rama de actividad.

b) Ocupación: Para determinarla se preguntó: "¿Qué clase de trabajo efectuó en la ocupación que tenía la semana pasada?". Para codificar la ocupación se utilizaron 161 grupos de la clasificación nacional. Se amplió la CIUO-88 (usando códigos vacíos) a fin de incorporar la clasificación Ocupaciones Nacionales Corrientes. Se establecieron enlaces a nivel de subgrupos (3 dígitos).

c) Situación en el empleo: Para determinarla se hizo la misma pregunta que figura en el párrafo 6 b). Para codificar esta variable se utilizaron tres grupos: empleado, trabajador independiente y trabajador familiar no remunerado.

8. Diferencias principales con el censo anterior:

En el censo de población de 1969 no se recolectaron datos sobre el empleo.

9. Publicación de los resultados del censo:

Los resultados definitivos del censo de población aparecieron en las siguientes publicaciones: "The 1991 Population and Housing Census Main Results (edición preliminar)", en octubre de 1992; "The 1991 Population and Housing Census National Summary", en abril de 1994; y "The 1991 Population and Housing Final Results (edición principal)", en enero de 1995.

La organización responsable de la publicación es el Department of Statistics, P.O. Box 13, Entebbe.

Los resultados del censo existen también en forma de cuadros inéditos y disquetes.

VANUATU

1. Nombre y dirección del organismo responsable del censo:

Statistics Office (NPSO), Private Mail Bag 19, Port-Vila.

2. Censos de población llevados a cabo desde 1945 (años):

1967, 1979 y 1989. Además, en 1972 y 1986 se llevaron a cabo censos en las zonas urbanas. La presente descripción se refiere al censo de 1989 (realizado el 16 de mayo de ese año).

3. Alcance del censo:

a) Geográfico: Todo el país.

b) Personas comprendidas: Toda la población, salvo los nacionales de Vanuatu residentes en el extranjero en el momento del censo.

4. Periodo de referencia:
La semana anterior al día del censo.

5. Materias principales:
a) Población total, según sexo y edad: sí
Población económicamente activa por:
b) Sexo y grupo de edad: sí
c) Rama de actividad económica: sí
d) Ocupación: sí
e) Situación en el empleo: sí
f) Nivel más alto de educación: sí
g) Horas de trabajo: no
h) Otras características: no
Ref. a): La edad se determinó según el año de nacimiento.

6. Conceptos y definiciones:

a) Población económicamente activa: Abarcó a todas las personas de 10 o más años de edad que, en el momento del censo, estaban sea ocupadas, sea desempleadas, conforme a las definiciones que se dan más adelante. Sin embargo, habida cuenta de que el grupo de edad de 10-14 años estaba compuesto en gran medida por escolares, sólo se publicaron los datos relativos a las personas de 15 años de edad o mayores.

b) Empleo: Se consideró "ocupada" a toda persona que había trabajado al menos una hora durante la semana de referencia. La definición no incluyó a los estudiantes que trabajaban a tiempo parcial.

Se ha indicado que fueron incluidas las siguientes categorías:

i) personas que trabajan sin remuneración en una empresa o negocio familiar;
ii) personas ocupadas pero temporalmente ausentes de su trabajo;
iii) personas con más de un empleo;
iv) aprendices y personas que siguen un curso de formación.

Sólo las personas incluidas en las categorías i), ii) y iii) pueden identificarse por separado.

c) Desempleo: Se consideró "desempleada" a toda persona que, durante la semana de referencia, se encontraba sin trabajo pero buscaba activamente empleo. A este respecto se preguntó: "¿Estuvo la persona encuestada buscando activamente trabajo en los últimos 7 días?".

7. Clasificaciones utilizadas:
Tanto las personas ocupadas como las desempleadas anteriormente empleadas se clasificaron por rama de actividad económica y por ocupación. Sólo se clasificó según la situación en el empleo a las personas ocupadas.

a) Rama de actividad económica: Para determinarla se preguntó: "¿En qué clase de actividad económica está ocupada la persona encuestada?". Para codificar la rama de actividad económica, se utilizó la CIIU-Rev.2 en el nivel de 1 dígito, pero los códigos se ampliaron a 2 dígitos para adecuar la clasificación a las necesidades locales.

b) Ocupación: Para determinarla se preguntó: "¿Qué tipo de trabajo desempeñaba la persona encuestada?". Para codificar la ocupación se utilizó la CIUO-68, en el nivel de grupos primarios (clave de 3 dígitos).

c) Situación en el empleo: Para determinarla se preguntó: "¿Cuál era la situación de la persona encuestada en su empleo?", o "¿Para quién trabajaba?". Para codificar la situación en el empleo se utilizaron los 4 grupos siguientes: trabajador independiente; trabajador en empresa familiar (no remunerado); trabajador asalariado en el sector privado; trabajador asalariado del sector estatal.

8. Diferencias principales con el censo anterior:
A diferencia del censo de 1989, en 1979 se pidió a las personas empadronadas que describiesen la ocupación que habían tenido el año anterior.

9. Publicación de los resultados del censo:
Los resultados definitivos del censo se publicaron en julio de 1991, en el volumen que lleva por título "Vanuatu National Population Census - May 1989 - Main Report".

El organismo responsable de esta publicación es la Statistics Office, Private Mail Bag 19, Port Vila.

VENEZUELA

1. Nombre y dirección del organismo responsable del censo:
Oficina Central de Estadística e Informática, Presidencia de la República, Caracas, Venezuela.

2. Censos de población llevados a cabo desde 1945 (años):
1950, 1961, 1971, 1981 y 1990. La presente descripción se refiere al censo de población de 1990 (efectuado el 21 de Octubre).

3. Alcance del censo:

a) Geográfico: Todo el país.

b) Personas comprendidas: Toda la población con residencia habitual en el país. Se excluyeron los venezolanos residenciados en el extranjero en forma permanente, el extranjero que se encuentra de paso en el país por vacaciones, negocio u otro motivo con menos de cuatro meses en el país, y la población indígena selvática que será objeto de investigación en el año 1992.

4. Periodo de referencia:
El día del censo.

5. Materias principales:
a) Población total, según sexo y edad: sí
Población económicamente activa por:
b) Sexo y grupo de edad: sí
c) Rama de actividad económica: sí
d) Ocupación: sí
e) Situación en el empleo: sí
f) Nivel más alto de educación: sí
g) Horas de trabajo: no
h) Otras características: sí
Ref. a): Definen la edad el año de nacimiento y también la edad al último cumpleaños.
Ref. h): Se preguntó por la duración del desempleo, el número de personas que trabajan en la empresa, el ingreso proveniente del trabajo y los otros tipos de ingresos, y el sector informal.

6. Conceptos y definiciones:

a) Población económicamente activa: Incluye a todas las personas de 12 años y más que se encontraban empleadas o desempleadas el día del censo, tal y como se definen más adelante. La definición incluye a todas las personas que cumplen servicio en las fuerzas armadas.

b) Empleo: Se consideran "empleadas" a las personas que respondieron afirmativamente a una de las preguntas siguientes: "?Trabajando?" o "?Sin trabajar pero tiene trabajo?".

Se ha indicado que quedan incluidas las siguientes categorías:

i) personas que trabajan sin remuneración en una empresa familiar;
ii) personas ocupadas pero temporalmente ausentes del trabajo;
iii) estudiantes que trabajan medio tiempo;
iv) trabajadores estacionales u ocasionales;
v) conscriptos del servicio militar o civil.

Solamente las personas de las categorías i) y ii) se pueden identificar separadamente a través de las preguntas siguientes, respectivamente: i) "¿En este trabajo, es o era ayudante familiar?" y ii) "¿En cual de estas situaciones se encuentra actualmente: ...; Sin trabajar pero tiene trabajo?".

c) Desempleo: Se consideran "desempleadas" a las personas que estaban sin trabajo y respondieron afirmativamente a una de las preguntas siguientes: "¿Buscando trabajo, habiendo trabajado antes?" o "?Buscando trabajo por primera vez?".

7. Clasificaciones utilizadas:
Todas las personas ocupadas como las desocupadas con experiencia laboral en las áreas rurales, pero solamente una muestra de tales personas en las áreas urbanas, se clasificaron por rama de actividad económica, por ocupación y según la situación en el empleo (el procedimiento es estimado a una muestra de 20 por ciento en las áreas urbanas).

a) Rama de actividad económica: Para determinarla se preguntó: "¿A qué se dedica la empresa, organismo o negocio donde trabaja (o trabajaba)? (Ej: transporte de pasajeros, fábrica de muebles, cultivo de café, educación, etc.)". Para codificar la rama de actividad se utilizó la CIIU-Rev.2 al nivel de grandes divisiones (1 dígito). Las publiciones se presentaron a nivel de 1 dígito, pero el proceso de codificación se realizó a 3 dígitos.

b) Ocupación: Para determinarla se preguntó: "¿Cual es su ocupación en la empresa, organismo o negocio donde trabaja (o trabajaba)? (Ej: chofer, aprendiz de tornero, agricultor, maestra, etc.)". Para codificar la ocupación, se utilizó la CIUO-68 al nivel de los grandes grupos (1 dígito) para las publiciones, pero el proceso de codificación se realizó a 3 dígitos.

c) Situación en el empleo: Para determinarla se preguntó: "¿En este trabajo es (o era): empleado u obrero del sector público; empleado u obrero del sector privado; servicio doméstico; miembro de cooperativa; empleador o patrono; trabajador por cuenta propia (que no tiene empleados ni obreros); ayudante familiar no remunerado?". Se codificó en los siete grupos arriba indicados.

8. Diferencias principales con el censo anterior:
En 1981, las características económicas se le investigaron a toda la población de 12 años y más. En 1990, si bien a toda la población de 12 años y más se le investigó su situación en la fuerza de trabajo, solo a un 20 per ciento de la población urbana y a toda la población rural se le registraron las restantes características económicas.

En 1981, se investigaron las diligencias para conseguir trabajo, mientras que en 1990 no. También se investigaron las horas trabajadas la semana anterior al censo, mientras que en 1990 no.

En relación a la duración de la cesantía, si bien se investigó con respecto a ambos sexos en 1981 y en 1990, los intervalos de tiempo considerados fueron diferentes (En 1981: hasta 6 meses; más de 6 meses hasta 12 meses; más de un año. En 1990: hasta 3 meses; de 4 a 6 meses; de 7 a 12 meses; más de un año).

9. Publicación de los resultados del censo:
Los resultados finales se publicaron al final de 1992. El título exacto de la publicación es "El Censo 90 en Venezuela, XII Censo General de Población y Vivienda" y "El Censo 90 en (entidad federal que corresponda)".

La organización responsable de la publicación es la Oficina Central de Estadística e Informática.

Los resultados del censo están también disponibles en la forma de cuadros no publicados, cintas magneticas, disquetes, microfichas y video textos. También se presentaran para sistemas Mainframix y Micros: para el primero se utiliza el manejador Informix, y para el segundo se utiliza el Redatam.

VIET NAM

1. Nombre y dirección del organismo responsable del censo:
Département général de statistiques, Ministère du Travail, des Invalides de guerre et des affaires sociales, 2 - Hoang Van Thu, Hanoi.

2. Censos de población llevados a cabo desde 1945 (años):
1979, 1989 y 1994. La presente descripción se refiere al censo de población de 1994 (realizado el 1 de octubre de ese año).

3. Alcance del censo:
a) Geográfico: Todas las zonas urbanas.
b) Personas comprendidas: Toda la población.

4. Periodo de referencia:
La semana anterior al día del censo.

5. Materias principales:
a) Población total, según sexo y edad: sí
Población económicamente activa por:
b) Sexo y grupo de edad: sí
c) Rama de actividad económica: sí
d) Ocupación: sí
e) Situación en el empleo: sí
f) Nivel más alto de educación: ...
g) Horas de trabajo: sí
h) Otras características: no

Ref. a): La edad se determinó según el año de nacimiento.

Ref. g): Se pidió a las personas ocupadas que indicaran a la vez el número de horas y el número de días efectivamente trabajados durante la semana de referencia.

6. Conceptos y definiciones:
a) Población económicamente activa: Abarcó a todas las mujeres de 15 a 55 años de edad y a los varones de 15 a 60 años que, durante el período de referencia, estaban ocupado(a)s o desempleado(a)s, según las definiciones que se dan más adelante. En lo que atañe a la actividad económica, se interrogó únicamente a una muestra de 2,5 por ciento de la población urbana. La definición no incluyó a los miembros de las fuerzas armadas.

b) Empleo: Para determinarlo se utilizó la pregunta siguiente: "Durante los pasados siete días, ¿ha tenido usted un trabajo, sea asalariado o no asalariado? Si la respuesta es "Sí", ¿fue este trabajo similar al que tuvo el mes anterior?".
Se ha indicado que fueron incluidas las siguientes categorías:
i) personas que trabajan sin remuneración en una empresa o negocio familiar;
ii) personas que producen bienes primarios para el autoconsumo;
iii) personas ocupadas pero temporalmente ausentes de su trabajo;
iv) estudiantes que trabajan a tiempo parcial;
v) trabajadores estacionales u ocasionales;
vi) aprendices y personas que siguen un curso de formación.
Ninguna de estas categorías puede identificarse por separado.

c) Desempleo: Se consideró "desempleada" a toda persona que dijo no haber tenido empleo durante la semana de referencia y que respondió afirmativamente a las siguientes preguntas: "¿Tuvo un trabajo antes?", "¿Puede ejercer ese trabajo en la actualidad?" y "¿Tiene usted necesidad de trabajar?".

7. Clasificaciones utilizadas:
Tanto las personas ocupadas como los desempleados anteriormente empleados se clasificaron por rama de actividad, por ocupación y por situación en el empleo.

a) Rama de actividad económica: Para determinarla se hizo la siguiente pregunta: "¿Cuál es el nombre del servicio u organismo en que trabaja, del organismo superior, o del lugar de trabajo?". Para codificar la rama de actividad económica se utilizaron 20 grupos de la clasificación nacional. No se establecieron enlaces con la CIIU.

b) Ocupación: Para determinarla se hizo la siguiente pregunta: "¿Cuál ha sido su trabajo principal durante los últimos siete días? Indique el nombre o el código del trabajo". Para codificar la ocupación, se utilizaron 33 grupos de la clasificación nacional. Se establecieron enlaces con la CIUO-68, a nivel de grandes grupos (clave de 1 dígito).

c) Situación en el empleo: Para determinarla se hizo la siguiente pregunta: "¿Tiene usted un trabajo asalariado o no asalariado?". Para codificar esta variable se utilizaron los dos grupos siguientes: asalariado; no asalariado.

8. Diferencias principales con el censo anterior:
No hubo diferencias significativas

9. Publicación de los resultados del censo:
No se dispone de información al respecto.

YEMEN

1. Nombre y dirección del organismo responsable del censo:
Central Statistical Organization, Ministry of Planning and Development, P.O. Box 13434, Sana'a.

2. Censos de población llevados a cabo desde 1945 (años):
Se realizaron dos censos en cada uno de los países antes de su unificación, y se ha llevado a cabo uno desde la unificación.
1973 y 1988 en las gobernaciones del sur y del este, es decir, en la ex República Popular Democrática del Yemen.
1975 y 1986 en las gobernaciones del norte y del oeste, es decir, en la ex República Arabe del Yemen.
La presente descripción se refiere al censo de población de 1994 (que tuvo lugar el 16 de diciembre de ese año), el primero realizado en la República del Yemen unificada.

3. Alcance del censo:

a) Geográfico: Todo el país.

b) Personas comprendidas: Toda la población, de todas las edades.

4. Período de referencia:
La semana anterior al día del censo.

5. Materias principales:

a) Población total, según sexo y edad: sí
Población económicamente activa por:
b) Sexo y grupo de edad: sí
c) Rama de actividad económica: sí
d) Ocupación: sí
e) Situación en el empleo: sí
f) Nivel más alto de educación: sí
g) Horas de trabajo: no
h) Otras características: no

Ref. a): La edad de la persona censada se definió en función de su último cumpleaños.

6. Conceptos y definiciones:

a) Población económicamente activa: Abarca a todas las personas de 10 o más años de edad que, durante la semana de referencia, tenían un empleo o estaban desempleadas, según las definiciones que se dan más adelante. Esta definición incluye a los miembros de las fuerzas armadas.

b) Empleo: Para determinar el empleo se preguntó cuáles habían sido los vínculos de la persona censada con la fuerza de trabajo durante la semana de referencia. Las respuestas posibles eran: trabajador; ama de casa y trabajadora; estudiante y trabajador; desempleado anteriormente ocupado; desempleado que nunca ha trabajado; ama de casa; estudiante; productor autosuficiente; y persona incapacitada. Se consideró "ocupada" a toda persona que declaró haber trabajado por lo menos dos días durante la semana de referencia.

Se ha indicado que quedan incluidas las siguientes categorías:

i)   personas que trabajan sin remuneración en una empresa o negocio familiar;
ii) personas que producen bienes primarios para el autoconsumo;
iii) personas ocupadas pero temporalmente ausentes de su trabajo;
iv) estudiantes que trabajan a tiempo parcial;
v)   trabajadores estacionales u ocasionales (a condición de que estuviesen ocupados durante el período de referencia);
vi) conscriptos del servicio militar o civil;
vii) trabajadores con más de un empleo;
viii) aprendices y personas que siguen un curso de formación.

Las categorías i), iv), vii) y viii) pueden identificarse por separado.

c) Desempleo: Se consideró "desempleada" a toda persona que había trabajado menos de dos días durante la semana de referencia. La definición incluye también a las personas que buscaban un primer empleo y a los desempleados anteriormente empleados. En cambio, no incluye a los estudiantes que buscaban trabajo.

7. Clasificaciones utilizadas:
Tanto las personas ocupadas como los desempleados anteriormente empleados han sido clasificados por rama de actividad económica, por ocupación y según la situación en el empleo.

a) Rama de actividad económica: Para determinarla se preguntó cuál era la principal ocupación de la persona censada, y dónde trabajaba. Para codificar la rama de actividad económica, se utilizó la clasificación CIIU-Rev.3.

b) Ocupación: Para determinarla se preguntó cuál era exactamente la ocupación de la persona censada. Para codificar la ocupación, se utilizó la clasificación CIUO-88 a nivel de grupos primarios (clave de 4 dígitos).

c) Situación en el empleo: Para determinarla se preguntó a la persona censada cuál era su situación en el empleo. Para codificarla, se utilizaron cinco grupos, a saber: trabajador asalariado; trabajador independiente; empleador; trabajador familiar no remunerado; trabajador no remunerado al servicio de terceros.

8. Diferencias principales con el censo anterior:
No hubo diferencias significativas.

9. Publicación de los resultados del censo:
La publicación de los datos definitivos está prevista para 1996, en un volumen que llevará por título "The Results of the 1994 Population Housing and Establishments Census, Reports no 1-3".

La organización responsable de esta publicación es la Central Statistical Organization (CSO), P.O. Box 13434, Sana'a.

Los resultados definitivos también estarán disponibles en cuadros no publicados (cuya versión impresa se suministrará a quienes lo soliciten). Excepcionalmente, se podrán solicitar copias en soporte magnético.

ZAMBIA

1. Nombre y dirección del organismo responsable del censo:
Central Statistics Office, P.O. Box 31908, Lusaka.

2. Censos de población llevados a cabo desde 1945 (años):
1946, 1951, 1956, 1961, 1963, 1969, 1980 y 1990. La presente descripción se refiere al censo de 1990 (realizado el 20 de agosto de ese año).

3. Alcance del censo:

a) Geográfico: Todo el país.

b) Personas comprendidas: Toda la población. Se excluyó a los nacionales que vivían en el extranjero y a los diplomáticos extranjeros.

4. Período de referencia:
La semana y los doce meses anteriores al día del censo.

5. Materias principales:

a) Población total, según sexo y edad: sí
Población económicamente activa por:
b) Sexo y grupo de edad: sí
c) Rama de actividad económica: sí
d) Ocupación: sí
e) Situación en el empleo: sí
f) Nivel más alto de educación: sí
g) Horas de trabajo: sí
h) Otras características: no

Ref. a): La edad de la persona censada se definió en función de su último cumpleaños.

Ref. g): Sólo a las personas con más de un empleo se pidió que indicaran el tiempo total trabajado en los últimos doce meses (expresado en número de meses).

6. Conceptos y definiciones:

a) Población económicamente activa: Abarca a todas las personas de 12 o más años de edad que, durante los períodos de referencia, tenían un empleo o estaban desempleadas, según las definiciones que se dan más adelante. Esta definición incluye a los miembros de las fuerzas armadas.

b) Empleo: Para determinar el empleo se preguntó en qué se había ocupado principalmente la persona censada durante los últimos siete días (las respuestas posibles eran: trabajó por una remuneración o un beneficio; estaba con licencia; trabajó sin remuneración en una empresa o negocio familiar), y en qué se había ocupado principalmente desde 1989 (se proponían las mismas respuestas que para la primera pregunta).

Se ha indicado que quedan incluidas las siguientes categorías:

i)   personas que trabajan sin remuneración en una empresa o negocio familiar;
ii) personas que producen bienes primarios para el autoconsumo;
iii) personas ocupadas pero temporalmente ausentes de su trabajo;
iv) estudiantes que trabajan a tiempo parcial;
v)   trabajadores estacionales u ocasionales;
vi) conscriptos del servicio militar o civil;
vii) trabajadores con más de un empleo.

Sólo las categorías i), ii) y iii) pueden identificarse por separado en función de preguntas específicas y de su situación en el empleo.

c) Desempleo: Se consideró "desempleada" a toda persona que, durante los períodos de referencia, carecía de trabajo y buscaba empleo o no estaba en busca de empleo pero sí disponible para trabajar. Para determinar si una persona debía considerarse o no como desempleada, se usaron también las preguntas indicadas antes en 6 b). Para las personas desempleadas, las respuestas específicas posibles eran: "sin trabajo y en busca de empleo" y "no busca empleo pero sí está disponible para trabajar". Las personas que indicaron como respuestas "madre de familia/ama de casa a tiempo completo", "estudiante a tiempo completo" o "no está disponible para trabajar por otros motivos" quedaron clasificadas entre la población económicamente inactiva.

7. Clasificaciones utilizadas:
Sólo las personas ocupadas han sido clasificadas por rama de actividad económica, por ocupación y según la situación en el empleo.

a) Rama de actividad económica: Para determinarla se preguntó qué se producía o qué servicios se prestaban principalmente en el lugar donde trabajaba o había trabajado la persona censada. Para codificar la rama de actividad económica, se utilizó la clasificación CIIU-Rev.2 a nivel de grandes divisiones (clave de 1 dígito).

b) Ocupación: Para determinarla se preguntó cuál había sido la ocupación principal de la persona censada desde 1989. Para codificar la ocupación, se utilizaron 91 grupos de la clasificación nacional de ocupaciones. Los enlaces con la clasificación CIUO-68 se han establecido a nivel de grandes grupos (clave de 1 dígito).

c) Situación en el empleo: Para determinarla se preguntó en qué calidad había trabajado principalmente la persona censada desde 1989, a saber, como empleador, como asalariado, como independiente o como trabajador familiar no remunerado. Para codificar la situación en el empleo, se utilizaron las cuatro categorías que se acaban de indicar.

8. Diferencias principales con el censo anterior:
Mientras que en 1980 las preguntas relativas a la actividad económica de las personas se aplicaron a una muestra, en el censo de 1990 estas preguntas se hicieron a todas las personas de 12 o más años de edad.

9. Publicación de los resultados del censo:
Los resultados definitivos del censo figuran en "Economic and Social Tables", obra publicada en agosto de 1994.

La organización responsable de esta publicación es la Central Statistics Office, P.O. Box 31908, Lusaka.

Los resultados del censo también están disponibles en cuadros no publicados y disquetes.

ZIMBABWE

1. Nombre y dirección del organismo responsable del censo:
Central Statistical Office, Box CY342, Causeway.

2. Censos de población llevados a cabo desde 1945 (años):
1947, 1952, 1957, 1962, 1969, 1982 y 1992. La presente descripción se refiere al censo de población de 1992 (realizado el 17 de agosto de ese año).

3. Alcance del censo:
a) Geográfico: Todo el país.

b) Personas comprendidas: Todas las personas, de todas las edades, que se encontraban en Zimbabwe en la noche del censo (la población "de facto"). No se incluyó a los nacionales que estaban en el extranjero.

4. Periodo de referencia:
Los doce meses anteriores al día del censo.

5. Materias principales:

a) Población total, según sexo y edad:	sí
Población económicamente activa por:	
b) Sexo y grupo de edad:	sí
c) Rama de actividad económica:	no
d) Ocupación:	sí
e) Situación en el empleo:	sí
f) Nivel más alto de educación:	sí
g) Horas de trabajo:	no
h) Otras características:	no

Ref. a): La edad de la persona censada se definió en función de su último cumpleaños.

6. Conceptos y definiciones:
a) Población económicamente activa: Abarca a todas las personas de 10 o más años de edad que, durante el período de referencia, tenían un empleo o estaban desempleadas, según las definiciones que se dan más adelante. Sin embargo, en los resultados publicados del censo sólo se incluyen datos mínimos sobre el grupo de edad de 10-14 años. Esta definición incluye a todos los miembros de las fuerzas armadas. En cambio, no incluye a los estudiantes que tenían un empleo a tiempo parcial o a los que buscaban trabajo.

b) Empleo: Para determinar el empleo se preguntó cuál había sido la actividad principal de la persona censada en los últimos doce meses. Las respuestas posibles eran: trabajador asalariado; empleador; trabajador por cuenta propia; trabajador familiar no remunerado; en busca de trabajo/desempleado; estudiante; ama de casa; jubilado/enfermo/demasiado anciano para trabajar; otras.

Se ha indicado que quedan incluidas las siguientes categorías:
i) personas que trabajan sin remuneración en una empresa o negocio familiar;
ii) personas que producen bienes primarios para el autoconsumo;
iii) personas ocupadas pero temporalmente ausentes de su trabajo;
iv) trabajadores estacionales u ocasionales;
v) conscriptos del servicio militar o civil.

Sólo las categorías i) y ii) pueden identificarse por separado.

c) Desempleo: Se consideró como "desempleada" a toda persona que, durante el período de referencia, no había trabajado, se encontraba en busca de empleo, o estaba disponible para trabajar.

7. Clasificaciones utilizadas:
Sólo las personas ocupadas han sido clasificadas por rama de actividad económica, mientras que todas las personas de 10 o más años de edad se han clasificado según la situación en el empleo.

a) Rama de actividad económica: No se estableció clasificación alguna según la rama de actividad económica.

b) Ocupación: Para determinarla se preguntó cuál había sido la ocupación principal de la persona censada durante los últimos doce meses. Para codificar la ocupación, se utilizaron 109 grupos de la clasificación nacional. Los enlaces con la clasificación CIUO-88 se han establecido a nivel de subgrupos (clave de 3 dígitos).

c) Situación en el empleo: Para determinarla se preguntó cuál había sido la actividad principal de la persona censada durante los últimos doce meses. Para codificar la situación en el empleo, se utilizaron cuatro grupos, a saber: trabajador asalariado; empleador; trabajador por cuenta propia; y trabajador familiar no remunerado.

8. Diferencias principales con el censo anterior:
En el censo de 1992 se utilizó un período de referencia largo (doce meses), mientras que en el censo de 1982 se había usado un período corto (una semana).

La pregunta que se hizo en el censo de 1992 a las personas ocupadas para determinar sus grupos de ocupación y su situación en el empleo fue diferente de la que se había hecho en el censo de 1982.

9. Publicación de los resultados del censo:
Los resultados definitivos del censo aparecieron en diciembre de 1994 en una publicación titulada "Census 1992: National Profile - Zimbabwe". También se han publicado todos los resultados definitivos provinciales.

La organización responsable de esta publicación es la Central Statistical Office, Box CY342, Causeway.

Los resultados también están disponibles en cuadros no publicados y en otros soportes.

APENDICE

Extracto de la
Resolución sobre estadísticas de la población económicamente activa, del empleo, del desempleo y del subempleo
Decimotercera Conferencia Internacional de Estadísticos del Trabajo
(Ginebra, 18-29 de octubre de 1982)

Conceptos y definiciones
Población económicamente activa

5. La "población económicamente activa" abarca todas las personas de uno u otro sexo que aportan su trabajo para producir bienes y servicios económicos, definidos según y como lo hacen los sistemas de cuentas nacionales y de balances de las Naciones Unidas, durante un período de referencia especificado. De acuerdo con estos sistemas, la producción de bienes y servicios económicos incluye toda la producción y tratamiento de productos primarios - se destinen éstos al mercado, al trueque o al autoconsumo -, la producción de todos los otros artículos y servicios para el mercado y, en el caso de los hogares que produzcan artículos y servicios para el mercado, la parte de esta producción destinada a su propio consumo.

6. Dos mediciones útiles de la población económicamente activa son la "población habitualmente activa", medida en relación a un largo período de referencia, tal como un año, y la "población actualmente activa" o fuerza de trabajo, medida en relación con un corto período de referencia, tal como una semana o un día.

Población habitualmente activa

7. 1) La "población habitualmente activa" comprende a todas las personas que tengan más de cierta edad especificada, cuya situación principal en la actividad, determinada en función del número de semanas o días, durante un período largo dado (tal como los doce meses o el año civil precedentes), era la de "persona con empleo" o "persona desempleada", según definiciones en los párrafos 9 y 10.

2) Cuando este concepto se considere útil y aplicable, la población habitualmente activa puede dividirse en "personas con empleo" y "personas desempleadas", de acuerdo con su situación principal en la actividad.

La fuerza de trabajo (población actualmente activa)

8. La "fuerza de trabajo" o "población actualmente activa" comprende todas las personas que reúnan los requisitos necesarios para ser incluidas en las categorías de personas con empleo o personas desempleadas, tal como se las define en los párrafos 9 y 10 más adelante.

Empleo

9. 1) Se considerará como "personas con empleo" a todas las personas que tengan más de cierta edad especificada y que durante un breve período de referencia, tal como una semana o un día, estuvieran en cualquiera de las siguientes categorías:

a) Con "empleo asalariado":

a1) "trabajando": personas que durante el período de referencia hayan realizado algún trabajo por un sueldo o salario en metálico o en especie;

a2) "con empleo pero sin trabajar": personas que, habiendo trabajado en su empleo actual, no estaban trabajando temporalmente durante el período de referencia y mantenían un vínculo formal con su empleo. Este vínculo formal al empleo debería determinarse en función de las circunstancias nacionales, de acuerdo con uno o más de los siguientes criterios:

i) pago ininterrumpido de sueldos o salarios;

ii) garantía de reintegración en el empleo al término de la contingencia o un acuerdo respecto de la fecha de reintegración;

iii) duración de la ausencia del trabajo, la cual, cuando sea el caso, puede ser aquélla por la que los trabajadores pueden percibir una compensación social sin obligación de aceptar otros trabajos.

b) Con "empleo independiente":

b1) "trabajando": las personas que durante el período de referencia hayan realizado algún trabajo para obtener beneficios o ganancia familiar, en metálico o en especie;

b2) "con una empresa pero sin trabajar": las personas que, teniendo una empresa - sea industrial, comercial, de explotación agrícola o de prestación de servicios -, estaban temporalmente

ausentes del trabajo durante el período de referencia por cualquier razón específica.

2) Por razones prácticas, la noción "algún trabajo" puede interpretarse como una hora de trabajo por lo menos.

3) Las personas ausentes de su trabajo temporalmente por causa de enfermedad o accidente, días festivos o vacaciones, huelga, paro de empleadores, licencia de estudios o de formación profesional, licencia de maternidad o paternidad, coyuntura económica difícil, desorganización o suspensión temporal del trabajo por razones tales como mal tiempo, averías mecánicas o eléctricas, escasez de materias primas o combustibles, u otras ausencias temporales con o sin licencia, deberían considerarse como personas con empleo asalariado, siempre que mantuvieran un vínculo formal con su empleo.

4) Debería considerarse como personas con empleo independiente a los empleadores, trabajadores por cuenta propia y miembros de cooperativas de producción, y clasificarse "trabajando" o "con empleo pero sin trabajar", según sea el caso.

5) Debería considerarse como personas con empleo independiente a los trabajadores familiares no remunerados que estén trabajando, sin consideración al número de horas trabajadas durante el período de referencia. Los países que, por razones particulares, prefieren introducir un criterio de tiempo mínimo de trabajo como condición para incluir a los trabajadores familiares no remunerados entre las personas con empleo, deberían identificar y clasificar aparte a los que trabajan menos del tiempo prescrito.

6) Las personas ocupadas en la producción de bienes y servicios económicos, para consumo propio o del hogar, deberían considerarse como personas con empleo independiente, si dicha producción constituye una aportación importante al consumo total del hogar.

7) Los aprendices que hayan recibido una retribución en metálico o en especie deberían considerarse como personas con empleo asalariado y clasificarse como "trabajando" o "con empleo pero sin trabajar", sobre las mismas bases que las demás personas con empleo asalariado.

8) Los estudiantes, trabajadores del hogar y otras dedicadas principalmente a actividades no económicas durante el período de referencia, y que al mismo tiempo tenían un empleo asalariado o un empleo independiente, según definiciones en el subpárrafo 1) anterior, deberían considerarse como personas con empleo, sobre las mismas bases que las otras categorías de personas con empleo, y, si fuese posible, clasificarse aparte.

9) Los miembros de las fuerzas armadas deberían figurar entre las personas con empleo asalariado. Las fuerzas armadas incluirían los miembros permanentes y temporales, como se ha especificado en la última edición revisada de la Clasificación Internacional Uniforme de Ocupaciones (CIUO).

Desempleo

10. 1) "Personas desempleadas" son todas aquellas personas que tengan más de cierta edad especificada y que durante el período de referencia se hallen:

a) "sin empleo", es decir, que no tengan un empleo asalariado o un empleo independiente, tal como se las define en el párrafo 9;

b) "actualmente disponibles para trabajar", es decir, disponibles para trabajar en empleo asalariado o en empleo independiente durante el período de referencia; y

c) "en busca de empleo", es decir, que habían tomado medidas concretas para buscar un empleo asalariado o un empleo independiente en un período reciente especificado. Las medidas concretas pueden incluir el registro en oficinas de colocación públicas o privadas, solicitudes directas a los empleadores, diligencias en los lugares de trabajo, explotaciones agrícolas, fábricas, mercados u otros lugares de concurrencia, avisos en los periódicos o respuestas a las ofertas que aparecen en ellos, solicitud de ayuda a amigos y familiares, búsqueda de terrenos, edificios, maquinaria o equipos para establecer su propia empresa, gestiones para conseguir recursos financieros, solicitudes para obtener permisos y licencias, etc.

2) En situaciones en que los medios convencionales de búsqueda de empleo son insuficientes, en que el mercado laboral está bastante desorganizado o es de alcance limitado, en que la absorción de la mano de obra es, en el momento considerado, inadecuada, o en que la fuerza de trabajo está compuesta principalmente por personas con empleo independiente, la definición estándar de desempleo dada en el subpárrafo 1) anterior puede aplicarse suprimiendo el criterio de búsqueda de empleo.

3) Al aplicar el criterio de disponibilidad actual para trabajar, especialmente en las situaciones descritas en el subpárrafo 2) anterior, deberían encontrarse métodos apropiados, a fin de tener en cuenta las circunstancias nacionales. Estos métodos podrían basarse en nociones tales como el deseo actual de trabajar y que haya trabajado ya, la voluntad de aceptar un empleo remunerado con sueldo o salario en las condiciones prevalecientes en la localidad, y la disposición para emprender una actividad independiente, de contar con los recursos financieros y las facilidades indispensables.

4) Aunque la definición estándar de desempleo implica el criterio de búsqueda de trabajo, las personas sin empleo y actualmente disponibles para trabajar, que hayan tomado medidas para empezar a trabajar en un empleo asalariado o en un empleo independiente, en una fecha subsiguiente al período de referencia, deberían ser consideradas como desempleadas.

5) Se debería considerar como desempleadas a las personas ausentes temporalmente de su trabajo, y sin un vínculo formal a su empleo, que se hallaban actualmente disponibles para trabajar y buscando empleo, de conformidad con la definición estándar de desempleo. Sin embargo, y dependiendo de las circunstancias y políticas nacionales, los países podrían preferir suprimir el criterio de búsqueda de empleo en el caso de personas suspendidas de su trabajo. En tales casos, las personas suspendidas de su trabajo que no estaban en busca de empleo, pero que se incluyen en la categoría de desempleadas, deberían ser identificadas como una subcategoría aparte.

6) Los estudiantes, trabajadores del hogar y otras personas dedicadas principalmente a actividades no económicas durante el período de referencia, que satisfagan los criterios establecidos en los subpárrafos 1) y 2) anteriores, deberían considerarse como personas desempleadas, sobre las mismas bases de las otras categorías de personas desempleadas, y, si fuese posible, clasificarse aparte.

STATISTICS ON OCCUPATIONAL WAGES AND HOURS OF WORK AND ON FOOD PRICES

OCTOBER INQUIRY RESULTS, 1994 AND 1995

STATISTIQUES DES SALAIRES ET DE LA DURÉE DU TRAVAIL PAR PROFESSION ET DES PRIX DES PRODUITS ALIMENTAIRES

RÉSULTATS DE L'ENQUÊTE D'OCTOBRE, 1994 ET 1995

ESTADISTICAS SOBRE SALARIOS Y HORAS DE TRABAJO POR OCUPACION Y PRECIOS DE ARTICULOS ALIMENTICIOS

RESULTADOS DE LA ENCUESTA DE OCTUBRE, 1994 Y 1995

1996

Special supplement to the
Bulletin of Labour Statistics
Supplément spécial au
Bulletin des statistiques du travail
Suplemento especial al
Boletín de Estadísticas del Trabajo

ISSN 1020-0134
ISBN 92-2-007351-X

Price: 35 Swiss francs
Prix: 35 francs suisses
Precio: 35 francos suizos

Just published

Household Income and Expenditure Statistics

No. 4   1979-1991

This fourth edition of *Household Income and Expenditure Statistics* provides information on the level and distribution of household income and expenditure obtained from household surveys. It contains the results of household income and expenditure surveys carried out in 82 countries, areas and territories from 1979 onwards.

XXXVIII + 391 pp.   ISBN 92-2-007344-7

Vient de paraître

Statistiques des revenus et des dépenses des ménages

Nº 4   1979-1991

Cette quatrième édition des *Statistiques des revenus et des dépenses des ménages* fournit des indications, recueillies dans le cadre d'enquêtes auprès des ménages, sur le montant et la ventilation des revenus et des dépenses des ménages. Elle présente les résultats d'enquêtes effectuées dans 82 pays, zones et territoires depuis 1979.

XXXVIII + 391 pp.   ISBN 92-2-007344-7

Acaba de aparecer

Estadísticas de ingresos y gastos de los hogares

Núm. 4   1979-1991

Esta cuarta edición de *Estadísticas de ingresos y gastos de los hogares* proporciona información sobre el nivel y la distribución de los ingresos y los gastos de los hogares procedente de diversos estudios sobre el tema. Contiene los resultados de las encuestas sobre ingresos y gastos de los hogares llevadas a cabo en 82 países, zonas y territorios a partir de 1979.

XXXVIII + 391 pp.   ISBN 92-2-007344-7

Publications of the International Labour Office

ISCO-88 INTERNATIONAL STANDARD CLASSIFICATION OF OCCUPATIONS

ISCO-88 is an indispensable tool for obtaining comparable occupational data on a cross-country, regional or worldwide basis. In addition, it represents a standard classification system which can serve as a model for developing or revising a national occupational classification. ISCO-88 has a hierarchical, four-layer structure built on the basis of the type of job and on the similarity of the skill level and specialization.

ISBN 92-2-106438-7   65 Swiss francs

Available from booksellers, ILO offices in many countries or direct from ILO Publications, International Labour Office, CH-1211 Geneva 22, Switzerland.

Publications du Bureau international du Travail

CITP-88 CLASSIFICATION INTERNATIONALE TYPE DES PROFESSIONS

La CITP-88 est un outil de travail indispensable pour l'obtention de données sur les professions comparables au niveau national, régional ou mondial. De plus, elle représente un système de classification type pouvant servir de modèle pour élaborer ou réviser une classification nationale des professions. La CITP-88 a une structure hiérarchique fondée sur la nature du travail effectué et sur la similitude des niveaux de qualification et de spécialisation.

ISBN 92-2-206438-0   65 francs suisses

Les commandes peuvent être passées par l'intermédiaire des principales librairies ou des bureaux locaux du BIT, ou adressées directement à Publications du BIT, Bureau international du Travail, CH-1211 Genève 22, Suisse.

Publicaciones de la Oficina Internacional del Trabajo

CIUO-88 CLASIFICACION INTERNACIONAL UNIFORME DE OCUPACIONES

La CIUO-88 es un instrumento indispensable para obtener datos comparables a nivel nacional, regional o mundial. Además, es un sistema de clasificación estándar que puede servir como modelo para desarrollar o revisar una clasificación nacional de ocupaciones. La CIUO-88 tiene una estructura jerárquica en cuatro niveles construida de acuerdo al tipo de empleo y a la semejanza en el grado y la especialización de las calificaciones.

ISBN 92-2-306438-4   65 francos suizos

Las publicaciones de la OIT pueden obtenerse en las librerías importantes o dirigiéndose a: Publicaciones de la OIT, Oficina Internacional del Trabajo, CH-1211 Ginebra 22, Suiza.